DATE DUE

			PRINTED IN U.S.A.

Literature Criticism from 1400 to 1800

Guide to Gale Literary Criticism Series

For criticism on	Consult these Gale series
Authors now living or who died after December 31, 1959	*CONTEMPORARY LITERARY CRITICISM (CLC)*
Authors who died between 1900 and 1959	*TWENTIETH-CENTURY LITERARY CRITICISM (TCLC)*
Authors who died between 1800 and 1899	*NINETEENTH-CENTURY LITERATURE CRITICISM (NCLC)*
Authors who died between 1400 and 1799	*LITERATURE CRITICISM FROM 1400 TO 1800 (LC)* *SHAKESPEAREAN CRITICISM (SC)*
Authors who died before 1400	*CLASSICAL AND MEDIEVAL LITERATURE CRITICISM (CMLC)*
Black writers of the past two hundred years	*BLACK LITERATURE CRITICISM (BLC)*
Authors of books for children and young adults	*CHILDREN'S LITERATURE REVIEW (CLR)*
Dramatists	*DRAMA CRITICISM (DC)*
Hispanic writers of the late nineteenth and twentieth centuries	*HISPANIC LITERATURE CRITICISM (HLC)*
Native North American writers and orators of the eighteenth, nineteenth, and twentieth centuries	*NATIVE NORTH AMERICAN LITERATURE (NNAL)*
Poets	*POETRY CRITICISM (PC)*
Short story writers	*SHORT STORY CRITICISM (SSC)*
Major authors from the Renaissance to the present	*WORLD LITERATURE CRITICISM, 1500 TO THE PRESENT (WLC)*

ISSN 0740-2880

Volume 29

Literature Criticism from 1400 to 1800

Criticism of the Works of
Fifteenth, Sixteenth, Seventeenth, and
Eighteenth-Century Novelists, Poets, Playwrights,
Philosophers, and Other Creative Writers, from
the First Published Critical Appraisals
to Current Evaluations

Jennifer Allison Brostrom, Editor

Dana Ramel Barnes
Jelena O. Krstovic´
Mary Onorato
James E. Person, Jr.
Associate Editors

Gale Research Inc.

An International Thomson Publishing Company

ITP
Changing the Way the World Learns

NEW YORK • LONDON • BONN • BOSTON • DETROIT • MADRID
MELBOURNE • MEXICO CITY • PARIS • SINGAPORE • TOKYO
TORONTO • WASHINGTON • ALBANY NY • BELMONT CA • CINCINNATI OH

STAFF

Jennifer Allison Brostrom, *Editor*

Dana Ramel Barnes, Jelena O. Krstović, Michael Magoulias, Mary L. Onorato, James E. Person, Jr., *Associate Editors*

Matthew C. Altman, Gerald R. Barterian, Ondine Le Blanc, *Assistant Editors*

Susan M. Trosky, *Managing Editor*

Marlene S. Hurst, *Permissions Manager*
Margaret A. Chamberlain, Linda M. Pugliese, *Permissions Specialists*
Susan Brohman, Diane Cooper, Maria Franklin, Arlene Johnson, Josephine M. Keene,
Michele Lonoconus, Maureen Puhl, Shalice Shah,
Kimberly F. Smilay, Barbara A. Wallace, *Permissions Associates*
Edna Hedblad, Tyra Y. Phillips, Lori Schoenenberger, *Permissions Assistants*

Victoria B. Cariappa, *Research Manager*
Eva M. Felts, Mary Beth McElmeel, *Research Associates*
Shirley Gates, Amy Beth Wieczorek, *Research Assistants*

Mary Beth Trimper, *Production Director*
Deborah Milliken, *Production Assistant*

Cynthia Baldwin, *Product Design Manager*
Sherrell Hobbs, *Macintosh Artist*
Willie Mathis, *Camera Operator*

∞™ This book is printed on acid-free paper that meets the minimum requirements of American National Standard for Information Sciences—Permanence Paper for Printed Library Materials, ANSI Z39.48-1984.

Library of Congress Catalog Card Number 94-29718
ISBN 0-8103-8945-2
ISSN 0740-2880
Printed in the United States of America
Published simultaneously in the United Kingdom
by Gale Research International Limited
(An affiliated company of Gale Research Inc.)

I(T)P™   Gale Research Inc., an International Thomson Publishing Company.
ITP logo is a trademark under license.

10 9 8 7 6 5 4 3 2 1

Contents

Preface   vii

Acknowledgments   xi

Preface

*L*iterature Criticism from 1400 to 1800 (LC) presents criticism of world authors of the fifteenth through eighteenth centuries. The literature of this period reflects a turbulent time of radical change that saw the rise of modern European drama, the birth of the novel and personal essay forms, the emergence of newspapers and periodicals, and major achievements in poetry and philosophy. Many of these historical forces continue to influence modern art and society. *LC,* therefore, provides valuable insight into the art, life, thought, and cultural transformations that took place during these centuries.

Scope of the Series

LC provides an introduction to the great poets, dramatists, novelists, essayists, and philosophers of the fifteenth through eighteenth centuries; and to the most significant interpretations of these authors' works. Because criticism of this literature spans nearly six hundred years, an overwhelming amount of scholarship confronts the student. *LC* therefore organizes this material into volumes addressing specific historical and cultural topics, for example, "Literature of the Spanish Golden Age," or "Literature and the New World." Every attempt is made to reprint the most noteworthy, relevant, and educationally valuable essays available.

Readers should note that there is a separate Gale reference series devoted exclusively to Shakespearean studies. Although belonging properly to the period covered in *LC,* William Shakespeare has inspired such a tremendous and ever-growing corpus of secondary material that the editors have deemed it best to give his works extensive coverage in a separate series, *Shakespearean Criticism*.

Each author entry in *LC* presents a survey of critical response to an author's oeuvre. Early criticism is offered to indicate initial responses, later selections document any rise or decline in literary reputations, and retrospective analyses provide students with modern views. The size of each author entry is a relative reflection of the scope of criticism available in English. Every attempt has been made to identify and include the seminal essays on each author's work and to include recent commentary providing modern perspectives.

The need for *LC* among students and teachers of literature and history was suggested by the proven usefulness of Gale's *Contemporary Literary Criticism (CLC), Twentieth-Century Literary Criticism (TCLC),* and *Nineteenth-Century Literature Criticism (NCLC),* which excerpt criticism of works by nineteenth- and twentieth-century authors. There is no duplication of critical material in any of these literary criticism series. Major authors may appear more than once in one or more of the series because of the great quantity of critical material available, and his or her relevance to a variety of thematic topics.

Thematic Approach

Beginning with Volume 12, all the authors in each volume of *LC* are organized around such themes as specific literary or philosophical movements, writings surrounding important political and historical events, the philosophy and art associated with eras of cultural transformation, and the literature of specific social or ethnic groups. Each volume contains a topic entry providing a historical and literary overview, and several author entries, which examine major representatives of the featured period.

Organization of the Book

Each entry consists of the following elements: author or thematic heading, introduction, list of principal works, annotated works of criticism (each preceded by a bibliographical citation), and a bibliography of further reading. Also, most author entries contain author portraits and other illustrations.

- The **Author Heading** consists of the author's full name, followed by birth and death dates. (If an author wrote consistently under a pseudonym, the pseudonym is used in the author heading, with the real name given in parentheses on the first line of the biographical and critical introduction.) Also located here are any name variations under which an author wrote, including transliterated forms for authors whose native languages use nonroman alphabets. Uncertain birth or death dates are indicated by question marks. Topic entries are preceded by a **Thematic Heading,** which simply states the subject of the entry.

- The **Introduction** to each entry provides social and historical background important to understanding the criticism, and an overview of the biography and career of the featured author.

- Most *LC* author entries include **Portraits** of the author. Many entries also contain illustrations of materials pertinent to an author's career, including author holographs, title pages, letters, or representations of important people, places, and events in an author's life.

- The **List of Principal Works** is ordered chronologically, by date of first book publication, identifying the genre of each work. In the case of foreign authors whose works have been translated into English, the title and date of the first English-language edition are given in brackets beneath the foreign-language listing. Unless otherwise indicated, dramas are dated by first performance, not first publication.

- **Criticism** is arranged chronologically in each author entry to provide a useful perspective on changes in critical evaluation over time. For the purpose of easy identification, the critic's name and the date of first composition or publication of the critical work are given at the beginning of each piece of criticism. Unsigned criticism is preceded by the title of the source in which it appeared. All titles by the author featured in the critical entry are printed in boldface type. Publication information (such as publisher names and book prices) and some parenthetical numerical references (such as footnotes or page and line references to specific editions of works) have been occasionally deleted to provide smoother reading of the text.

- Critical essays are prefaced by **Annotations** as an additional aid to students using *LC*. These explanatory notes may provide several types of useful information, including: the reputation of a critic, the importance of a work of criticism, the commentator's individual approach to literary criticism, the intent of the criticism, and the growth of critical controversy or changes in critical trends regarding an author's work. In some cases, these notes cross-reference the work of critics within the entry who agree or disagree with each other.

- A complete **Bibliographical Citation** of the original essay or book follows each piece of criticism.

- An annotated bibliography of **Further Reading** appears at the end of each entry and suggests resources for additional study. In some cases, significant essays for which the editors could not obtain reprint rights are included here.

Cumulative Indexes

Each volume of *LC* includes a cumulative **Author Index** listing all the authors that have appeared in the following sources published by Gale: *Contemporary Literary Criticism, Twentieth-Century Literary Criticism, Nineteenth-Century Literature Criticism, Literature Criticism from 1400 to 1800, and Classical and Medieval Literature Criticism,* along with cross-references to the Gale series *Short Story Criticism, Poetry Criticism, Children's Literature Review, Authors in the News, Contemporary Authors, Contemporary Authors Autobiography Series, Contemporary Authors Bibliographical Series, Dictionary of Literary Biography, Concise Dictionary of Literary Biography, Something about the Author, Something about the Author Autobiography Series, and Yesterday's Authors of Books for Children.* Readers will welcome this cumulative author index as a useful tool for locating an author within the various series. The index, which includes authors' birth and death dates, is particularly valuable for those authors who are identified with a certain period but whose death dates cause them to be placed in another, or for those authors whose careers span two periods. For example, F. Scott Fitzgerald is found in *TCLC,* yet a writer often associated with him, Ernest Hemingway, is found in *CLC.*

Beginning with Volume 12, *LC* includes a cumulative **Topic Index** that lists all literary themes and topics treated in *LC, NCLC, TCLC,* and the *CLC* Yearbook. Each volume of *LC* also includes a cumulative **Nationality Index** in which authors' names are arranged alphabetically under their respective nationalities and followed by the numbers of the volumes in which they appear.

Each volume of *LC* also includes a cumulative **Title Index,** an alphabetical listing of all literary works discussed in the series. Each title listing includes the corresponding volume and page numbers where criticism may be located. Foreign-language titles that have been translated followed by the tiles of the translation—for example, *El ingenioso hidalgo Don Quixote de la Mancha (Don Quixote).* Page numbers following these translated titles refers to all pages on which any form of the titles, either foreign-language or translated, appear. Title of novels, dramas, nonfiction books, and poetry, short story, or essays collections are printed in italics, while individual poems, short stories, and essays are printed in roman type within quotation marks.

A Note to the Reader

When writing papers, students who quote directly from any volume in the Literary Criticism Series may use the following general forms to footnote reprinted criticism. The first example pertains to material drawn from periodicals, the second to material reprinted from books.

T. S. Eliot, "John Donne," *The Nation and the Athenaeum,* 33 (9 June 1923), 321-32; excerpted and reprinted in *Literature Criticism from 1400 to 1800,* Vol. 10, ed. James E. Person, Jr. (Detroit: Gale Research, 1989), pp. 28-9.

Clara G. Stillman, *Samuel Butler: A Mid-Victorian Modern* (Viking Press, 1932); excerpted and reprinted in *Twentieth-Century Literary Criticism,* Vol. 33, ed. Paula Kepos (Detroit: Gale Research, 1989), pp. 43-5.

Suggestions Are Welcome

Since the series began, features have been added to *LC* in response to various suggestions, including a nationality index, a Literary Criticism Series topic index, and thematic organization of entries.

Readers who wish to suggest new features, themes or authors to appear in future volumes, or who have other suggestions, are cordially invited to write to the editor.

Acknowledgments

The editors wish to thank the copyright holders of the excerpted criticism included in this volume, the permissions managers of many book and magazine publishing companies for assisting us in securing reprint rights. We are also grateful to the staffs of the Detroit Public Library, the Library of Congress, the University of Detroit Mercy Library, Wayne State University Purdy/Kresge Library Complex, and the University of Michigan Libraries for making their resources available to us. Following is a list of the copyright holders who have granted us permission to reprint material in this volume of *LC-29*. Every effort has been made to trace copyright, but if omissions have been made, please let us know.

COPYRIGHTED EXCERPTS IN *LC,* VOLUME 29, WERE REPRINTED FROM THE FOLLOWING PERIODICALS:

COPYRIGHTED EXCERPTS IN *LC,* VOLUME 29, WERE REPRINTED FROM THE FOLLOWING BOOKS:

Development of a Form. The Johns Hopkins Press, 1969. Copyright © 1969 by John Chalker. Reprinted by permission of the publisher. —Cohen, Ralph. From *The Unfolding of "The Seasons".* The Johns Hopkins Press, 1970. Copyright © 1970 by Ralph Cohen. Reprinted by permission of the publisher.—Colgan, Maurice. From "Ossian: Success or Failure for the Scottish Enlightenment?" in *Aberdeen and the Enlightenment.* Edited by Jennifer J. Carter and Joan H. Pittock. © The Contributors 1987. All rights reserved.— Crawford, Thomas. From *Society and Lyric: A Study of the Song Culture of Eighteenth-Century Scotland.* Scottish Academic Press, 1979. © 1979 Thomas Crawford. All rights reserved. Reprinted by permission of the publisher and the author.—Daiches, David. From *Robert Fergusson.* Scottish Academic Press, 1982. © 1982 David Daiches. All rights reserved. Reprinted by permission of the publisher.—Ericson-Roos, Catarina. From *The Songs of Robert Burns: A Study of the Unity of Poetry and Music.* Uppsala, 1977. © Catarina Ericson-Roos. Reprinted by permission of the author.—Fitzhugh, Robert T. From *Robert Burns: The Man and the Poet; A Round, Unvarnished Account.* Houghton Mifflin, 1970. Copyright © 1970 by Robert T. Fitzhugh. All rights reserved. Reprinted by permission of Houghton Mifflin Company.—Freeman, F. W. From "Robert Fergusson: Pastoral and Politics at Mid Century," in *The History Scottish Literature: 1660-1800, Vol. 2.* Edited by Andrew Hook. Aberdeen University Press, 1987. © The Contributors 1987. All rights reserved. Reprinted by permission of the publisher.— Freeman, F. W. From *Robert Fergusson and the Scots Humanist Comprise.* Edinburgh University Press, 1984. © 1984 Edinburgh University Press. Reprinted by permission of the publisher.—Golden, Morris. From *The Self Observed: Swift, Johnson, Wordsworth.* Johns Hopkins Press, 1972. Copyright © 1972 by The Johns Hopkins Press. All rights reserved. Reprinted by permission of the publisher.—Greene, Donald. From "From Accidie to Neurosis: 'The Castle of Indolence Revisited'," in *English Literature in the Age of Disguise.* Edited by Maximillan E. Novak. University of California Press, 1977. Copyright © 1977 by The Regents of the University of Califonria. Reprinted by permission of the publisher.—Heywood, Ian. From *The Making of History: A Study of the Literary Forgeries of James Macpherson and Thomas Chatterton in Relation to Eighteenth-Century Ideas of History and Fiction.* Fairleigh Dickinson University Press, 1986. © 1986 by Associated University Presses, Inc. Reprinted by permission of the publisher.—Highet, Gilbert. From *The Powers of Poetry.* Oxford University Press, 1960. © 1960, renewed 1988 by Gilbert Highet. Reprinted by permission of Curtis Brown Ltd.—Freeman, F. W. From "Robert Fergusson: Pastoral and Politics at Mid Century," in *The History Scottish Literature: 1660-1800, Vol. 2.* Edited by Andrew Hook. Aberdeen University Press, 1987. © The Contributors 1987. All rights reserved. Reprinted by permission of the publisher.—Kinghorn, Alexander Manson. From an introduction to *Poems by Allan Ramsay and Robert Fergusson.* Edited by Alexander Manson Kinghorn and Alexander Law. Scottish Academic Press, 1974. Introduction, Textual Notes and Glossary © 1974 A. M. Kinghorn and A. Law. All rights reserved. Reprinted by permission of the publisher.—Kinghorn, Alexander M. "Biographical and Critical Introduction: The Gentle Shepherd," in *The Works of Allan Ramsay, Vol. IV.* edited by Alexander M. Kinghorn and Alexander Law. William Blackwood & Sons Ltd., 1970. © The Scottish Text Society 1970. Reprinted by permission of the publisher.—Kinghorn, Alexander M. From "Biographical and Critical Introduction: Ramsay as Translator," in *The Works of Allan Ramsay, Vol. IV.* Edited by Alexander M. Kinghorn and Alexander Law. William Blackwood & Sons Ltd., 1970. © The Scottish Text Society 1970. Reprinted by permission of the publisher.—Leneman, Leah. From "The Effects of Ossian in Lowland Scotland," in *Aberdeen and the Enlightment: Proceedings of a Conference Held at the University of Aberdeen.* Edited by Jennifer J. Carter and Joan H. Pittock. Aberdeen University Press, 1987. © The Contributors 1987. All rights reserved.—Low, Donald A. From "Robert Burns (1759-96)," in *A Handbook to English Romanticism.* Edited by Jean Raimond and J. R. Watson. St. Martin's Press, 1992. Each article © contributor (see contents) 1992. All rights reserved. Reprinted with permission of St. Martin's Press, Incorporated.—MacLaine, Allan H. From *Allan Ramsay.* Twayne, 1985. Copyright © 1985 by G. K. Hall & Company. All rights reserved. Reprinted with the permission of Twayne Publishers, Inc., an imprint of Simon & Schuster Macmillan Publishing Company.—MacLaine, Allan H. From *Robert Fergusson.* Twayne, 1965. Copyright © 1965, by Twayne Publishers, Inc. All rights reserved. Reprinted with the permission of Twayne Publishers, Inc., an imprint of Simon & Schuster Macmillan Publishing Company.—McGuirk, Carol. From *Robert Burns and the Sentimental Era.* University of Georgia Press, 1985. © 1985 by the University of Georgia Press. All rights reserved. Reprinted by permission of the author.—McKillop, Alan Dugald. From "A Poem Sacred to the Memory of Sir Issac Newton: Introduction" and "Britannia: Introduction," in *The Castle of Indolence and Other Poems.* By James Thomson, edited by Alan Dugald McKillop. University of Kansas Press, 1961. © copyright 1961

Robert Burns

1759-1796

(Born Robert Burnes) Scottish poet and lyricist.

The following entry provides critical essays on Burns, published from 1960 through 1992. For further information, see *LC*, Volume 3.

INTRODUCTION

Called the national poet of Scotland, Burns has attained an almost mythical stature not only in his native land but around the world. He is revered as the poet of "the common man," the "heaven-taught ploughman" who expressed the soul of a nation and sang of universal humanity. His work made acceptable for the first time the use of the Scots dialect in elevated poetry, and his depiction of rural Scottish life and manners marked a radical departure from the stately and decorous subjects typical of eighteenth-century poetry. Burns is admired for his naturalness, compassion, humor, and fervent championship of the innate freedom and dignity of humanity.

Biographical Information

Burns was born in Alloway, Ayrshire to an impoverished tenant farmer and his wife. Although he received little formal schooling, his father, William Burnes (whose famous son later altered the spelling of the family name), was an intelligent man who sought to provide his sons with as much education as possible. He managed to employ a tutor for young Robert and his brother Gilbert, and this, together with Burns's extensive reading, furnished the poet with an adequate knowledge of English literature; it was only later that he discovered and studied the Scottish poetry of his heritage. Burns's family moved from one rented farm to another during his childhood, at each place enduring hard work and financial difficulties. While a young man, Burns acquired a reputation for charm and wit, and began to indulge in numerous love affairs. In 1786, he pledged to marry Jean Armour, who had become pregnant. Her parents forbade the match, but demanded financial restitution from Burns. Angry at this rejection by the Armours, and hurt by what he deemed the too-ready capitulation of their daughter to their demands, Burns resolved to sail to Jamaica to start a new life. The plan never materialized, however, for that year his *Poems, Chiefly in the Scottish Dialect* was published in Kilmarnock. The volume catapulted Burns to sudden, remarkable, but short-lived, fame; upon its success he went to Edinburgh, where for a season he was feted and much admired by the literati, though he remained in relative obscurity for the rest of his life. In the meantime, he was still involved with Jean Armour, who again became pregnant, and whom he was finally able to marry in 1788. Burns carried on his dual professions of poet and tenant farmer until the next year when he obtained a post in the

excise service. It was not an office for which he was particularly well suited, nor one which he enjoyed, but it freed him from the labor of farming. Most of Burns's major poems, with the notable exception of "Tam o' Shanter," had been written by this point in his life; the latter part of his creative career was devoted to collecting and revising the vast body of existing Scottish folk songs. In 1796, at the age of 37, Burns died from rheumatic heart disease, apparently caused by excessive physical exertion and frequent undernourishment as a child.

Major Works

While the theme of freedom—political, religious, personal, and sexual—dominates Burns's poetry and songs, the themes of love and fellowship also recur. The poem beginning "Is there, for honest poverty," generally referred to by its refrain, "A man's a man for a' that," is an implicitly political assertion of Burns's beliefs in equality and freedom. His outrage over what he considered the false and restricting doctrine of the Scottish church is clear in such satirical poems as "Holy Willie's Prayer" and "The Holy Fair." The first of these concerns a self-professed member of the elect, who through his own narration inadvertently exposes his hypocrisy and ethical deficiencies.

"The Holy Fair," a lively, highly descriptive account of a religious gathering, contrasts the dour, threatening view of life espoused by the Calvinist preachers with the reality of life as it is actually lived. The simple celebrants, after dutifully and respectfully attending to the sermons, continue their pleasurable everyday pursuits—the enjoyment of conviviality, drink, and romance, which are ever present in Burns's work. "Scotch Drink," a rousing drinking song, celebrates the joys of love and friendship. The title of "The Jolly Beggars" indicates Burns's attitude toward the main characters of this cantata. Poor and disreputable as these jolly beggars are, they have found their personal freedom and happiness in living outside the mainstream of society. Burns's innumerable love poems and songs are acknowledged as touching expressions of the human experience of love in all its phases: the sexual love of "The Fornicator"; the more mature love of "My Luve is Like a Red, Red Rose"; the happiness of a couple grown old together in "John Anderson, My Jo." Another frequently cited aspect of Burns's poetry is its vitality. Whatever his subject, critics find in his verses a riotous celebration of life, an irrepressible joy in living; Bonamy Dobrée has said that Burns "sang of life because he possessed so unusual, so shining a quantity of it." This vitality is often expressed through humor, which is prevalent in Burns's work, from the bawdy humor of "The Jolly Beggars" and the broad farce of "Tam o Shanter," to the irreverent mockery of "The Twa Dogs" and the sharp satire of "Holy Willie's Prayer." Burns's subjects and characters are invariably humble, their stories told against the background of the Scottish rural countryside. Although natural surroundings figure prominently in his work, Burns differed from succeeding Romantic poets in that he had little interest in nature itself, which in his poetry serves but to set the scene for human activity and emotion.

Critical Reception

Although the initial publication of Burns's poems in 1786 was attended by immense popular approbation, eighteenth-century critics responded with more reserve. Sentimental poems such as "The Cottar's [or 'Cotter's'] Saturday Night" and "To a Mountain Daisy" received the most favorable attention; Burns's earthier pieces, when not actually repressed, were tactfully ignored: "The Jolly Beggars," now considered one of his best poems, was rejected for years on the ground that it was coarse and contained low subject matter. Although these assessments held sway until well into the nineteenth century, more recent critics have taken an opposing view. "The Cottar's Saturday Night," an idealized portrait of a poor but happy family, is today regarded as affectedly emotional and tritely moralizing. "To a Mountain Daisy," ostensibly occasioned by the poet's inadvertent destruction of a daisy with his plow, is now considered one of Burns's weakest poems. Like "The Cottar's Saturday Night," it is sentimental and contains language and images which contemporary critics find bathetic and false. "To a Mountain Daisy" is often compared to "To a Mouse," as the situations described in the poems are similar; the latter is the poet's address to a mouse he has disturbed with his plow. Most critics today believe that "To a Mouse" expresses a genuine emotion

that the other poem lacks, and does so in more engaging language. Interestingly, "To a Mountain Daisy" was written primarily in standard English, while "To a Mouse" is predominantly in Scots; critical reaction to these two poems neatly encapsulates the debate over whether Burns's best work is in English or Scots. It has long been asserted as a general tenet that for Burns, English was the language of thought and Scots the language of emotion. Most modern critics have found this assessment of Burns's poetic bilingualism too simplistic, pointing out that few of Burns's poems are written entirely in English or in Scots. The pieces most commentators acknowledge as his best are those in which he judiciously mingled the two languages.

PRINCIPAL WORKS

Poems, Chiefly in the Scottish Dialect (poetry) 1786
"Tam o'Shanter" (poetry) 1791; published in *The Antiquities of Scotland*
Poems Ascribed to Robert Burns, the Ayrshire Bard (poetry) 1801
Reliques of Robert Burns, Consisting Chiefly of Original Letters, Poems, and Critical Observations on Scottish Songs (letters, poetry, criticism) 1808
The Poetry of Robert Burns. 4 vols. (poetry, songs) 1896-97
The Letters of Robert Burns. 2 vols. (letters) 1931

CRITICISM

Thomas Crawford (essay date 1960)

SOURCE: "Poet of the Parish," in *Burns: A Study of the Poems and Songs,* Oliver and Boyd, 1960, pp. 111-46.

[*In the following essay, Crawford analyzes Burns's attempt at treating local themes in a universal manner in his poetry.*]

Many poems of Burns's first period embody the experience of a rural community in a way that has rarely been equalled in English. Ever since neolithic times, the settled village has been, next to the family, the most fundamental unit of society; it has survived war and pestilence, flood and famine, the fall of empires and the decline of civilisations. An art which successfully reflects the way of life of such a community will tend to have a universality broader and more general, though not necessarily deeper, than that of any other sort; it will tend to mirror, not what the best or the cleverest men have seen and felt, but what the overwhelming majority of our species have met with during, let us say, the last five thousand years. There is nothing more international than nationality, nothing more all-embracing than locality.

Nevertheless, a writer like Burns is faced with certain pitfalls; in his rendering of the life of the parish, he will often be tempted to be too narrowly particular, too minutely realistic, too restricted to the vernacular, too faithful to the customs and idiosyncrasies of his district. If he wishes to reach a larger audience than the men of his own place and time, he must concentrate on those aspects of the village which have the largest relevance; he must paint the streaks of the tulip without destroying the general form and shape of the flower. The moon that rises over Cumnock hills must still be recognisably the moon that shines over Fujiyama or the Urals.

Burns's development as a poet was from his immediate surroundings outwards the nation and finally to all mankind, but this movement was never simple and gradual; it never followed a straight line. One might have expected him to reproduce universal emotions in those poems, early or late, where his aim was to "transcribe the various feelings, the loves, the griefs, the hopes, the fears, in his own breast." All too often, in poems of this sort, the result comes perilously close to mawkishness and bathos. Conversely, one might have expected his descriptions of the "sentiments and manners" of his "rustic compeers" to be of documentary interest only; instead of that, they often transcend parochial mediocrity and acquire a solidity that seems independent of time and place. But on other occasions Burns is unable to make the necessary leap from the particular to the general.

In the course of a letter to Mrs Dunlop dated 21 Aug. 1788, Burns calls to mind a fragment of one of his "manners-painting" poems which is of extraordinary importance to the critic because it presents in concentrated form the raw material of the whole *genre*. In Aug. 1785 Robert had been in love with Betsy Miller, one of the Mauchline belles; her brother had recently married a sister of "Sandy Bell, who made a Jamaica fortune," and the "braw" Betsy began to put on airs because of her new sister-in-law's wealth—£500. The result was a comic burlesque, entitled **"A Mauchline Wedding"**:

> When Eighty-five was seven months auld,
>   And wearing thro' the aught,
> When rotting rains and Boreas bauld
>   Gied farmer-folks a faught;
> Ae morning quondam Mason Will,
>   Now Merchant Master Miller,
> Gaed down to meet wi' Nansie Bell
>   And her Jamaica siller,
>   To wed, that day.

In the second verse there occurs a detail that seems even more narrowly confined than the mention of Cumnock, which John Ruskin [in "Fiction, Fair and Foul," in *On the Old Road,* 1899] thought so limiting; it is a hill with the name of Blacksideen:

> The rising sun o'er Blacksideen
>   Was just appearing fairly,
> When Nell and Bess get up to dress
>   Seven lang half-hours o'er early!
> Now presses clink, and drawers jink,
>   For linens and for laces:
> But modest Muses only *think*

> What ladies' underdress is,
>   On sic a day!

By now we have moved away from Blacksideen to a region common to Burns and the author of *The Rape of the Lock:* the target is female affectation and pride in dress. As befits the humbler sphere that Burns is describing, the texture of his verse is coarser than Pope's, and the scene is freed from any suggestion of prurience by the presence of a typically Burnsian delight in human character:

> But we'll suppose the stays are lac'd,
>   And bonie bosom steekit;
> Tho', thro' the lawn—but guess the rest!
>   An angel scarce durst keek it.
> Then stockins fine, o' silken twine,
>   Wi' cannie care are drawn up;
> An' garten'd tight, whare mortal wight—

> —As I never wrote it down, my recollection does not entirely serve me.

The fourth stanza is surely as good as many of those in his published poems:

> But now the gown wi' rustling sound
>   Its silken pomp displays;
> Sure there's no sin in being vain
>   O' siccan bonie claes!
> Sae jimp the waist, the tail sae vast—
>   Trouth, they were bonie birdies!
> O Mither Eve, ye wad been grave
>   To see their ample hurdies
>   Sae large that day!

In the first couplet Burns expresses the movement of silk as surely as ever Herrick conveyed the liquefaction of Julia's clothes, while in the second the point of view of the two girls is ironically assumed in order the more fully to display their naïve delight in their new finery; it is, of course, Burns's favourite trick when he writes satire. Like most Scots girls, Nell and Bess have been brought up to distrust the vanity of dress, so that in reproducing their very turn of expression the couplet mirrors also a conflict at the very centre of their minds. By the equation of "burd," a girl, with "bird," a flying feathered creature (the conflict of homonyms had probably long existed in Scotland), the stanza ends with the comedy of the bird-hizzies strutting like Papagenas across the Mauchline scene, and scandalising the common mother of us all with the shameless violation of Eve's state of nature provided by their enormous behinds.

The fragment ends in a flurry of colour and movement as Nell, Bessy and their father enter the post-chaise that will take them to the ceremony:

> Then Sandy, wi's red jacket braw,
>   Comes whip-jee-woa! about,
> And in he gets the bonie twa—
>   Lord, send them safely out!
> And auld John Trot wi' sober phiz,

As braid and braw's a Bailie,
His shouthers and his Sunday's giz
　　Wi' powther and wi' ulzie
　　　　Weel smear'd that day. . . .

Burns explains that the poem was never finished because his quarrel with Bess ended before he had time to write another line; if it had been completed, it might have become as lively a rendering of a lower-class marriage as Suckling's "Ballad upon a Wedding." This fragment was never intended for publication but was probably meant to be recited before a small number of Mauchline lads who knew the Miller family; and though Burns was certainly rhyming "for fun" here, he still had the taste of a particular group in view. As soon as he puts pen to paper he moves away from Mason Will and Blacksideen to the *universale in re,* the "concrete universal" that is to say, to those characteristics that Nell and Bess have in common with all clothes-conscious young women, and John Trot with all pompous fathers; despite the quarrel with Bess which set him writing, he produced a distanced but not unsympathetic presentation of the people concerned. If this is satire, it has a far more tolerant appreciation of the essential humanity of its victims than Swift's, Dryden's, or even Pope's, and it lacks the element of condescension to one's class-inferiors which mars Suckling's poem.

"The Court of Equity" may have been written for the same audience as that for which **"A Mauchline Wedding"** was intended: the "ram-stam billies" Smith ("the slee'st, pawkie thief"), Richmond and Hunter. Together with "Poet Burns" they were the *élite* of Mauchline's "fornicator loons," chosen by the rank and file to form a Court of Equity:

To take beneath our strict protection,
The stays-unlacing quondam maiden,
With GROWING life and anguish laden,
Who by the Scoundrel is deny'd
Who led her thoughtless steps aside.

Clockie Brown the watchmaker and Sandy Dow the Coachman are indicted because they have been so dishonourable as to

　　　　　　　refuse assistance
To those whom [they have] given existence,

and are summoned to appear before the Court in the Whitefoord Arms on the fourth of June next. If Brown does not then acknowledge his crime and face up to his responsibilities he will be tied naked to the village pump while the girl he has ruined does what she likes with him for at least three hours. The poem ends with a parody of legal language; but in spite of this, and the euphemisms for certain actions and parts of the body derived from the watchmaker's trade, the verse does not attain the distinction of the fragment on William Miller's wedding. **"The Court of Equity"** is local bawdry and nothing more; it does not rise beyond the level of moderately competent light verse.

"The Auld Farmer's New-Year Morning Salutation to his Auld Mare, Maggie, on giving her the accustomed Ripp of Corn to Hansel in the New-Year," provides yet another example of Burns's manners-painting strain. It has often been considered as a poem of essentially the same sort as **"To a Mouse,"** important primarily as exhibiting Robert's sympathy with the lower animals; and its language has been widely praised. Miss [Christina] Keith, for instance, says [in *The Russet Coat,* 1956] that it "shares with '**Halloween**' . . . the honour of having the finest Lallans Burns ever wrote," and that no poem "has more verbs to the square inch—and all of them verbs of motion." It seems to me, however, that the Scots of **"The Auld Farmer's Salutation"** is often a matter of the individual word, so that in spite of the sound and movement of lines like

How thou wad prance, an' snore, an' skriegh,
　　An' tak the road!

or

Thou never lap, an' sten't, an' breastit,
　　Then stood to blaw,

the vernacular is not so creatively employed as in **"Death and Doctor Hornbook,"** where Scottishness is more consistently bound up with phrasing and idiom.

It is not Burns who speaks in **"The Auld Farmer's Salutation,"** but a character whom he has projected, and the poem is primarily a naturalistic sketch whose source is a gently humorous and pathetic appreciation of personality and mood. The life of man and beast has been a shared struggle on the road and in the fields, from which the main values to emerge are independence, companionship and sheer survival against odds:

Monie a sair darg we twa hae wrought,
An' wi' the weary warl' fought!
An' monie an anxious day I thought
　　We wad be beat!
Yet here to crazy age we're brought,
　　Wi' something yet.

The horse, man's comrade in the life-long battle against nature, is perhaps intended as a symbol of friendship; if so, I cannot feel that the symbolism is as vivid, or as moving, as it might have been.

In **"The Auld Farmer's Salutation"** the poet gets so completely inside his subject's brain at a unique moment of time that his very success constitutes an artistic limitation—largely because the farmer does not see the full meaning of his life. Although his situation obviously implies a criticism of society, the old man only hints at his sufferings: "monie a sair darg" and "monie an anxious day." Like most Scots (and many Englishmen and Americans) he is shy of giving expression to his deepest emotions; but his understatement is so extreme as to form a real barrier to the non-Scottish reader. One feels that the farmer does not want to understand *why* his life has been such a hard one; all he can do is to endure. **"The Auld Farmer's Salutation"** is photography, not painting; it is documentary, not art of the most highly creative or imaginative kind. At the level of dramatic empathy which does not go beyond the limits of a single occasion it is a fine poem; but—in my view at least—it does not rise above the local and the particular as the greatest of Burns's works certainly do. From the standpoint of literary history, however, the poem's novelty resides mainly in its particularity. In the Great Britain of 1786, to report a humble person's mind as completely as Burns does here was in itself an act with tremendous possibilities for the future, pointing forward to Wordsworth and the Lyrical Ballads.

"The Auld Farmer's Salutation" is generally ascribed to January 1786. Almost exactly a year before that date, Burns had written the best of all his purely local poems—**"Death and Doctor Hornbook: A True Story."** Even in Scotland, where education has long been idolised, teachers have never been well paid; and the Tarbolton schoolmaster's pittance was so meagre that he had been forced to open a little grocer's shop in order to make ends meet. Gilbert Burns tells us that "having accidentally fallen in with some medical books, and become most hobby-horsically attached to the study of medicine, he had added the sale of a few medicines to his little trade. He had got a shop-bill printed, at the bottom of which, overlooking his own incapacity, he had advertised that 'Advice would be given in common disorders at the shop gratis'." Robert used this situation as the occasion for a work which converts the ridicule of self-importance and pretence into pure comedy of the most fantastic and unrealistic sort. His humour consists in inflating his victim to superhuman proportions in order simultaneously to deflate him; Hornbook is larger than the real dominie, John Wilson, just as Holy Willie is larger than the real William Fisher. Such exaggeration is, of course, found elsewhere in Scottish poems and novels; but that it is a specifically Scottish characteristic may well be doubted, for it occurs in most of the great comic creations of European literature. One finds it, with individual modifications, in writers as different from each other as Rabelais, Shakespeare, Ben Jonson, Molière, Dickens and Joyce.

As Miss Christina Keith has pointed out, **"Death and Doctor Hornbook"** looks forward to **"Tam o' Shanter,"** both in landscape and in narrative skill. In the very first verse the point of view of the poem is established as a datum from which the work can proceed; it is in fact a poetic construct, a selection from the attitudes of the real Burns which becomes a framework around which he organises his piece. Some books, says Burns, are lies from beginning to end, some lies have never been written down, and

> Ev'n ministers, they hae been kend,
>   In holy rapture,
> A rousing whid at times to vend,
>   And nail't wi' Scripture.

Unlike these, the story we are going to hear

Is just as true's the Deil's in hell
  Or Dublin city.

This statement superficially resembles the well-known device by which writers like Defoe or Swift palm off their own inventions as the relations of actual voyagers or as the memoirs of somebody who actually lived through the Great Plague, but in reality it is more complex than that; there is an underlying audacity which implies that the Deil is *not* in Hell, or even in Dublin—but that he is just as much a fabrication as the story whose truth Burns vouches for so loudly. The stanza is a triumph of ambiguity in some Empsonian sense.

Miss Keith rightly praises the rhythmic effects of the third stanza, with its precise reflection of the staggering, erratic gait of a drunken man on his way home:

> I stacher'd whyles, but yet took tent ay
>   To free the ditches;
> An' hillocks, stanes, an' bushes, kend ay
>   Frae ghaists an' witches.

But the effect is as much the result of diction as of sound-values: it is the amount he "kens" that is important, his tipsy confidence in his ability to distinguish between the natural and supernatural worlds.

Inebriation is the ideal preliminary for an encounter with the unseen; and sure enough, as he is approaching Tarbolton Mill, three hundred yards or so to the east of the village, he meets with *"Something"*—a supernatural figure called "Death," although in actual fact it incorporates some of the traditional attributes of Time, such as the beard and the scythe:

> Its stature seem'd lang Scotch ells twa;
> The queerest shape that e'er I saw,
> For fient a wame it had ava;
>   And then its shanks,
> They were as thin, as sharp an' sma'
>   As cheeks o' branks.

Death is seen through friendly eyes, as is Satan in the **"Address to the Deil."** He is as concrete as Coila in **"The Vision."** The effect is that everything is localised, and the whole universe, including Death, has shrunk to kailyard dimensions—this in spite of the tallness of Burns's allegorical personage. The poet and Death sit down to "have a crack"; and Death is full of complaints about Doctor Hornbook, who peddles certain infallible specifics with strange Latin names, like *"sal-marinum* o' the seas," the *"farina* of beans an' pease," *"aqua-fontis"* [sic], *"urinus spiritus* of capons":

> 'Or mite-horn shavings, filings, scrapings,
>   Distill'd *per se;*
> *Sal-alkali* o' midge-tail clippings,
>   And monie mae.'

When the poet comments that this will ruin the local gravedigger, Death groans out an "eldritch laugh" at such *naïveté.* The trouble is that for every person that Hornbook saves from natural death, he kills a score with his physic, thus cheating Death of his lawful prey. Just as Death is about to tell Burns of a scheme he has to get his own back on Hornbook, the church clock strikes "some wee short hour ayont the twal," and the two have to part:

> I took the way that pleas'd mysel,
>   And sae did Death.

In **"Death and Doctor Hornbook"** Burns succeeded in converting an apparent limitation into a source of positive strength. The comedy arises from the grotesque belittling of universals like death and human folly, which transmutes satire into fantasy; in order to make Death (or Death-Time) into a comic figure, Burns had to parochialise him through the intermediary of the raciest and most intimate conversation that it was possible for him to create. Dialogue here is not primarily a matter of choosing individual words, as it tends to be in **"The Auld Farmer's New Year Morning Salutation"**; it is rather an affair of idiom. Perhaps nowhere else in Burns do we get so close to the actual give-and-take of village conversation. To the seven examples noted by Miss Keith one might add another seven—or a score, for the whole poem is a synthesis of colloquial, racy and semi-proverbial expressions:

> At length, says I: 'Friend, whare ye gaun?
>   Will ye go back?'

> 'Come, gie's your hand, an' say we're gree't. . . .'

> 'Sax thousand years are near-hand fled
> Sin' I was to the butching bred. . . .'

> 'Fient haet o't wad hae pierc'd the heart
>   Of a kail-runt.'

> 'Just shit in a kail-blade an' send it,
>   As soon 's he smells't,
> Baith their disease and what will mend it,
>   At once he tells't.'

> 'Waes me for Johnie Ged's Hole now. . . .
> Nae doubt they'll rive it wi' the plew:
>   They'll ruin Johnie!'

The extraordinary skill with which Burns fits the dialogue into his metre is something new—not only in Burns, but in Scots poetry. Here he has achieved complete fusion between a traditional stanzaic form and living conversation. Of English poets, only Swift, Pope, Prior, Byron, and T. S. Eliot have achieved a comparable excellence, though there are foreshadowings amongst the poets of the Restoration period. Unlike these English conversational poets, who are concerned primarily with the speech of the upper classes, Burns weds his form to a selection of the language of the people themselves, and in doing so shows unique skill.

I cannot agree with Dr [David] Daiches [*Robert Burns*, 1952] that the main interest of **"Death and Doctor Horn-book"** lies in its technical perfection, that its satire can be dismissed as "rather crude," or that it is "an amusing squib at best." On the contrary, here are both poetry and comedy of a high order, as well a highly creative use of all the resources of spoken Scots.

One of the last of Burns's purely parochial poems is **"Tam Samson's Elegy,"** written in the interval between the publication of the Kilmarnock volume and his departure for Edinburgh. Samson was a noted sportsman, especially fond of curling and shooting; and the poem is a linguistic *tour-de-force* in which the technical terms of these occupations are pressed into the service of the mock-elegy in order to describe the old man's imagined death. In the sixth and seventh stanzas, the traditional elegiac theme of "all Nature mourns" is transformed into its exact opposite:

> Now safe the stately sawmont sail,
> And trouts bedropp'd wi' crimson hail,
> And eels, weel-kend for souple tail,
>   And geds for greed,
> Since, dark in Death's fish-creel, we wail
>   Tam Samson dead!

> Rejoice, ye birring paitricks a';
> Ye cootie moorcocks, crousely craw;
> Ye maukins, cock your fud fu' braw
>   Withouten dread;
> Your mortal fae is now awa:
>   Tam Samson's dead!

There are lines as good as any Burns wrote—

> The Brethren o' the mystic level
> May hing their head in woefu' bevel. . . .

> Or up the rink like Jehu roar. . . .

> 'Lord, five!' he cry'd, an' owre did stagger. . . .

—and there emerges a clear impression of yet another of the "social, honest men" whom Robert loved. Tam Samson is completely alive—an unforgettable member of the gallery of Burnsian characters. He is worthy simply because he exists, a congeries of minute particulars; yet at the same time he is the Universal Sportsman. To find his like we have to go to Scott's Dandie Dinmont, or the novels of Surtees, or Sassoon's *Diary of a Foxhunting Man,* or the idyllic figure of "Uncle" in Tolstoy's *War and Peace.*

There is nothing obscurely parochial about the "sentiments and manners" underlying **The Auld Farmer's Salutation,"** however bare and restrained they may appear in the telling; nor does one need to know the exact meaning of such technicalities in the vocabulary of curling as "wick a bore" in order to appreciate the warmth and simple honesty of Tam Samson. It is quite otherwise with **"Halloween."** The customs and habits in which it centres were so unfamiliar to at any rate the more sophisticated of his fellow-countrymen that Burns had himself to append a series of explanatory notes—an itemised account of the superstitions of the natives—in order that the poem should be understood by contemporary readers.

Most Scottish and American critics share the view of critics like W. E. Henley ["Essay on Burns," in *The Poetry of Robert Burns,* 1896-7, edited by W. E. Henley and T. F. Henderson] and John Speirs [*The Scots Literary Tradition,* 1940] that Burns is the last and finest flower of an old vernacular tradition before it withered into inevitable decay. If they are right, then **"Halloween"** should be among the very best things Burns ever did. Its language is pure vernacular Scots, its subject a series of rustic *genre* pictures: homely, vigorous and concrete, full of a pulsating, joyous movement, and free from any taint of the abstract or the rhetorical. And yet, considered as a whole, the poem fails to please. Burns is always at his best when he connects local themes and personalities with the abiding interests of the nation and the universal preoccupations of mankind. Here, for once, he fails: and he fails because, for all its movement and activity, the poem does not *develop*. It revolves upon a single spot; and, furthermore, it seems to narrow in smaller and smaller gyrations. It is true that in the second stanza there is an attempt to unite a local scene with the heroes and symbols of nationhood:

> Amang the bonie winding banks,
> > Where Doon rins, wimplin, clear;
> Where Bruce ance ruled the martial ranks,
> > An' shook his Carrick spear. . . .

Bruce was at one and the same time an Ayrshire man and a leader of national resistance, and the mention of his name is surely intended to remind us that the "merry, friendly, country-folks" of the poem belong to a nation as well as to a parish. But the placing of the stanza is unfortunate; it comes so early that we soon forget it in our contemplation of the rustic highjinks that follow. Though there is none of Jonson's intellectual wit, the comedy of **"Halloween"** is Jonsonian rather than Shakespearian. The characters are both objectified and framed, and their frantic animal gaiety seems to explode in miniature, as if seen through the wrong end of a telescope. Take the eighth stanza, in which a young girl puts two nuts in the fire to foretell the outcome of her courtship:

> Jean slips in twa, wi' tentie e'e;
> > Wha 'twas, she wadna tell;
> But this is *Jock,* an' this is *me,*
> > She says in to hersel:
> He bleez'd owre her, an' she owre him,
> > As they wad never mair part;
> Till fuff! he started up the lum,
> > And Jean had e'en a sair heart
> > > To see't that night.

This is one of the vividest stanzas in the poem: but the distorted accentuation of "máir part" and "sáir heart," forced on Burns by his metre, serves to dehumanise the emotions and subordinate them to the rhythm of an unending Bacchanalian dance. It is instructive to compare Burns's treatment of Jean in this stanza with his attitude in the seventh and eighth stanzas of the later dramatic lyric **"Tam Glen."**

In **"Tam Glen,"** Burns's sole concern is to transmute into poetry the loving and delighted recognition of character; in **"Halloween,"** there are elements of superciliousness, of conscious superiority, and even of thinly disguised cruelty. Peasant and small-town humour is often of the sort which rejoices in the misfortunes and discomfiture of others, but the admission does not thereby turn **"Halloween"** into a great comic poem. In **"Halloween"** there is altogether too much whimsical rusticity disporting itself for the amusement of such educated readers as have the patience to look up the glossary. Here, for example, is fighting Jamie Fleck, who sows hemp-seed, drags a dung-fork behind him as a harrow, and calls out the traditional charm:

> . . . 'Hemp-seed I saw thee,
> > An' her that is to be my lass
> Come after me, an' draw thee
> > > As fast this night.'

In spite of his boast that he does not believe in such old wives' tales:

> He whistl'd up *Lord Lenox' March,*
> > To keep his courage cheery;
> Altho' his hair began to arch,
> > He was sae fley'd an' eerie;
> Till presently he hears a squeak,
> > An' then a grane an' gruntle;
> He by his shouther gae a keek,
> > An' tumbl'd wi' a wintle
> > > Out-owre that night.

> He roar'd a horrid murder-shout,
> > In dreadfu' desperation!
> An' young an' auld come rinnin out,
> > An' hear the sad narration:
> He swoor 'twas hilchin Jean M'Craw,
> > Or crouchie Merran Humphie—
> Till stop! she trotted thro' them a';
> > An' wha was it but grumphie
> > > Asteer that night?

The commotion of all this is superb, and the passage reads like a rehearsal for the sixth, seventh and eighth stanzas of the **"Address to the Deil";** but in spite of these undoubted merits it is marred by its tone. However much he may try, the modern reader cannot altogether share in mean guffaws at the physical defects of the helpless and the deformed; he is unable to appreciate these lines to the full, just as he feels considerable embarrassment when reading a more fantastic exercise in the comedy of cruel flyting, the lyric **"Willie Wastle":**

> She's bow-hough'd, she's hem-shin'd,
> > Ae limpin leg a hand-breed shorter;
> She's twisted right, she's twisted left,
> > To balance fair in ilka quarter;

She has a hump upon her breast,
    The twin o' that upon her shouther:
Sic a wife as Willie had,
    I wad na gie a button for her.

The worst stanzas of **"Halloween"** are the fifteenth and sixteenth, containing the grandmother's reminiscences, where it almost seems as if we are expected to laugh at senility; and the best are the twenty-fourth, twenty-fifth and twenty-sixth, which describe the amorous and sensual widow:

A wanton widow Leezie was,
    As cantie as a kittlin;
But och! that night, amang the shaws,
    She gat a fearfu' settlin!
She thro' the whins, an' by the cairn,
    An' owre the hill gaed scrievin;
Whare three lairds' lands met at a burn,
    To dip her left sark-sleeve in
                Was bent that night.

Whyles owre a linn the burnie plays,
    As thro' the glen it wimpl't;
Whyles round a rocky scaur it strays,
    Whyles in a wiel it dimpl't;
Whyles glitter'd to the nightly rays,
    Wi' bickerin, dancin dazzle;
Whyles cookit underneath the braes,
    Below the spreading hazel
                Unseen that night.

Amang the brachens, on the brae,
    Between her an' the moon,
The Deil, or else an outler quey,
    Gat up an' gae a croon:
Poor Leezie's heart maist lap the hool;
    Near lav'rock-height she jumpit,
But mist a fit, an' in the pool
    Out-owre the lugs she plumpit,
            Wi' a plunge that night.

And they owe their brilliance almost entirely to their onomatopoeic quality, so all-pervasive as to evoke—not sounds merely, as in

  But och! that night amang the shaws,

which reflects the very "sough" of the wind in the trees—but sights, moods, and—above all—human *character*.

The reader, if he has been responding actively to the poem, creates for himself a picture of the widow's whole personality and appearance: small, dark, vivacious, playful and exquisitely silly. His heart jumps with hers, and he can almost feel the bitter chill of the water as it fills her ears. He laughs; but there is no malice or cruelty in his reaction, because the ducking does not endanger life or limb or even beauty. It is the middle stanza of the three just quoted that lifts the whole incident to the level of poetry, gaining an extra dimension from the reader's recollection of the opening stanza of the whole poem:

Upon that night, when fairies light
    On Cassilis Downans dance,
Or owre the lays, in splendid blaze,
    On sprightly coursers prance;
Or for Colean the rout is taen,
    Beneath the moon's pale beams;
There, up the Cove, to stray and rove,
    Amang the rocks and streams
            To sport that night:

The stream which the widow seeks is white, cool and dazzling like the fairies, and dances as lightly as they; it is as "cantie"—and even as treacherous, despite its apparent placidity, as Leezie herself. Then, as so often with Burns, the poem ends suddenly and abruptly, like some country dances, in a rather perfunctory description of "social glee." It is all over, Burns's longest flight in relatively uncontaminated vernacular Scots; and it is nearly as unsatisfactory as such purely "English" poems of his as those addressed to Robert Graham of Fintry. True, Burns here secures effects that are more impressive than anything in either of the poems to Graham: a breathless, never-ending motion reminiscent of "Christ's Kirk on the Green," Dunbar's "Dance of the Sevin Deidly Synnis," or that anonymous folk-ballad which is known to all Scotsmen and many Englishmen and Americans—"The Ball of Kirriemuir." But the very merits of **"Halloween"** are also its defects. It is all particulars, and lacks that saving infusion of the general, uniting and giving significance to details and minutiae, which is essential if a poem, or a scholarly treatise, or a scholarly treatise, or a scientific dissertation, is to achieve the highest excellence. **"Halloween,"** it is true, is not entirely without a tincture of philosophy. In its Rousseauistic preference for the natural and in its criticism of "art" (*i.e.,* civilisation), the poem is in intention similar to **"The Cotter's Saturday Night,"** but the reader would never guess this for himself if it were not for the epigraph:

Yes! let the rich deride, the proud disdain,
The simple pleasures of the lowly train:
To me more dear, congenial to my heart,
One native charm, than all the gloss of art.
                         GOLDSMITH.

If it was part of Burns's purpose to illustrate this sentiment, his actual achievement was quite different. There is a detachment, a withdrawnness about the humour which would seem to make **"Halloween"** the perfect *exemplum* of W. P. Ker's judgment on the poet [in *On Modern Literature,* edited by T. S. Spencer and J. Sutherland, 1955]:

But one must note that he does not 'render' or interpret the life of rural Scotland simply as one of the people. He stands apart. His is not the voice of the people, but the voice of a judge to whom the people are more or less indifferent, who is far above them, and who sees them as small creatures moved by slight and trivial motives.

This is borne out by Burns's own lofty comment in his preface to the poem:

The passion of prying into futurity makes a striking part of the history of human nature in its rude state, in all ages and nations; and it may be some entertainment to a philosophic mind, if any such should honour the author with a perusal, to see the remains of it among the more unenlightened in our own.

Precisely because in **"Halloween"** Burns has applied the tones and attitudes of a certain type of satire to ordinary everyday life, he is less universal, more embarrassingly parochial, and less truly national than in any other of his longer poems. The consequence is that **"Halloween"** is today read almost exclusively by Burns scholars. while, despite the sneers of professional critics, **"The Cotter's Saturday Night"** finds a welcome among quite ordinary readers throughout the world.

Like everything else that Burns wrote, **"The Jolly Beggars, A Cantata,"** was influenced by literary tradition— by the burlesque cantatas so popular in the eighteenth century, where the trick consists in using recitatives to link songs set to popular tunes; by Gay's *Beggar's Opera;* and by innumerable stall-ballads and chapbooks celebrating the happy lives of beggars and tinkers and vagabonds of all sorts. Typical of this whole class of popular literature is the English song, "A Beggar, a Beggar, a Beggar I'll be" (1660), with its amusing use of the thieves' slang of the time:

A Craver my Father, a Maunder my Mother,
A Filer my Sister, a Filcher my Brother . . .
In White wheaten Straw when their Bellies were
  full,
There was I begot between Tinker and Trull.
    And therefore a Beggar, a Beggar I'll be,
    For none leads a Life more jocund than he.

The beginnings of this convention have been traced (at least in English) to the sixteenth century, but (as Miss Keith points out) its sources go much further back, to Old French and the medieval Latin lyrics. The first vernacular examples in Scotland were "The Gaberlunzie Man" and "The Jolly Beggar," two songs traditionally attributed to King James V (*regn.* 1513-42). Now the sixteenth century was an age of agrarian crisis and of "study rogues and vagabonds," displaced peasants and monks, many of whom were forced into a wandering life in town or country. Their very existence-was a denial of the values and conventions of village communities and corporate towns; they were, surely, lower-class picaroons, the popular counterparts of those upper-class adventurers who were the originals of the heroes of the sixteenth-century Spanish novel. As Dr [A.] Kettle has pointed out [in *An Introduction to the English Novel*, 1951], in another connexion:

The best illustration in English literature of the social phenomenon which gave rise to the picaresque novel is the Falstaff section of *Henry IV.* (Poins would have made an admirable picaresque hero with his vitality and resource and lack of morals.) Falstaff and his cronies are of varying social origin; but they are all the rejects of feudalism, and they belong to the

Elizabethan rather than to the fifteenth-century world. In another sense they do not 'belong' to any society at all. They are without roots. They have no fixed abode. They live on their wits. They have no morals except the good new rule of each for himself and the devil take the hindmost. And they mock every sanctity of the feudal world—chivalry, honour, filial piety, allegiance, even kingship.

In the country districts and the slum areas of towns like London and Bristol there were ragged equivalents of Pistol and Poins—the innumerable "rufflers, whipjacks, hookers, priggers of prancers, palliards, walking morts" and "kinchin coves" of Elizabethan rogue literature. It seems hardly accidental that the two great periods of agrarian change in British history, when society appears to have produced more than its usual quota of lawless vagabonds, footpads and prostitutes, were also ages in which the lower orders brought into being a large number of ballads and songs celebrating the prowess of the delinquent and the maladjusted. This is perhaps the place to recollect Dr Daiches's remark that **"The Jolly Beggars"** appeals "to humanity's 'unofficial self' (to employ the useful phrase coined by George Orwell) to a degree extremely rare in literature": a comment which applies not only to Burns's cantata, but holds good, to a lesser extent, of all the beggar songs of the eighteenth century. Labourers and small farmers struggling to remain in the state into which it had pleased the Lord to call them inevitably dreamed their dreams of irresponsible freedom, in which beggary and crime seemed preferable to the eternal struggle to make ends meet. "Acclaimed in chaps and broadsides for his love of liberty and his disdain of the proprieties," the Jovial Beggar had become, even before Burns got hold of him, something of a "popular Ideal"; and it is as such an archetype that he appears in **"The Merry Beggars,"** one of the immediate precursors of Robert's work:

Whoe'er would be merry and free,
    Let him list and from us he may learn;
In palaces who shall you see
    Half so happy as we in a barn?

Burns took this wish-fulfilment fantasy of the masses, corresponding almost exactly to the educated profligate's obsession with the symbolic figure of Macheath, and made it into a great lyrical dramatic poem.

Nae mair then, we'll care then,
    Nae farther can we fa',

he had written in the **"Epistle to Davie"** when contemplating the possibility of destitution; **"The Jolly Beggars"** extracts the last ounce of meaning from such a situation, using it to frame a root-and-branch criticism of organised community life and morality from a point of view as extreme in its own way as those sometimes found in Byron and Shelley. The world of **"The Jolly Beggars"** is in opposition not simply to the aristocracy or the citizen class or the "unco guid," but to every kind of social stability and institutional cohesion; yet, paradoxically enough, it is at the same time a grotesque parody of the real world of catch-as-catch-can, and even to a certain extent of the very special individualism which, as we have seen, is expressed in the **"Second Epistle to Lapraik."** It is also Burns's version of the Superman and his noblest tribute to instinct and libido. Over twenty years ago, Christopher Caudwell [in his *Illusion and Reality*, 1937 and *Studies in a Dying Culture*, 1938] characterised as the supreme illusion of modern times the idea that man is most free when he is liberated from social restraint, when he is allowed to live according to some inner primeval urge, or secret prompting of the blood; and he traced the development of this concept from Marlowe through Rousseau to Freud and D. H. Lawrence. Burns in this cantata gives vent to his own special variant of primitivism, and it is one which—in spite of Matthew Arnold—*does* constitute a genuine "criticism of life."

I do not think that Miss Keith is altogether right when she compares **"The Jolly Beggars"** with the literary world of the *Vie de Bohème*: "To Burns' beggars, as to Mürger, life is but that—noise and song and Bohemia." The beggars' circle is more anarchistic than even the life of declassed students in a nineteenth-century Paris garret; and the poem is much more corrosive of accepted values than, say, the paintings of Toulouse-Lautrec. "Nothing," says Miss Keith, "—neither drink nor lust—can unite this pack," thereby putting her finger on one of the main qualities of the work. Though the beggars are a group, they have no abiding mutual loyalty, since their coming-together is altogether fortuitous. But because they burn with the flame of vitality, because the Life Force works in them still, they are the embodiment of a positive value. The competition of merchants and lairds is pettifogging and therefore evil, but the rivalry of wolves and tigers is good; are they not vigorous, earthy, and free from hypocrisy, and are not these qualities to be commended above the deceptions of civilised life? No doubt this is Burns's own special version of pastoral, and no doubt it is possible to see the concept of the Noble Savage behind it all; but the really important thing, the essential point of difference from other expressions of the Rousseauistic myth, is that Burns neither arcadianises nor sentimentalises his ragged crew. They are that they are; in **"The Jolly Beggars,"** existence and essence are one. . . .

"The Jolly Beggars" pushes parochialism to the level of the utmost universality. Beginning with the actual observation of a scene in a village inn (so Burns's friend Richmond assures us), it concentrates in dramatic form the essence of "ram-stam," of all that is best in the early epistles. It takes its origin from that world of "Scotch drink" and "Scotch manners" which Matthew Arnold thought so unlovely; how then was Arnold compelled to call it a "puissant and splendid production"? "In the world of **'The Jolly Beggars'**," he says [in "The Study of Poetry," in *Essays in Criticism*, second series, 1954], "there is more than hideousness and squalor, there is bestiality; yet the piece is a superb poetic success. It has a breadth, truth, and power which make the famous scene in Auerbach's Cellar, of Goethe's *Faust,* seem artificial and tame beside it, and which are only matched by Shakespeare and Aristophanes." The reason, I think, lies in this: the parochial unloveliness of **"The Jolly Beggars"** is made to mirror a general European squalor and a general European energy of which Rousseau and Blake, each in his own way, were also aware—and at the same time to express the quintessence of a popular dream with a very long history behind it. **"The Jolly Beggars"** is the other side of the medal to "Man was made to Mourn." It is the poetry of lasting human values as they appear in times of agrarian revolution, and the flower of all the beggar literature of both Scotland and England.

Gilbert Highet (essay date 1960)

SOURCE: "Burns: A Mouse and a Louse," in *The Powers of Poetry,* Oxford University Press, Inc., 1960, pp. 74-81.

[*A Scottish-born writer and critic, Highet was a classical scholar and distinguished educator. His important studies* Juvenal the Satirist *(1954) and* The Anatomy of Satire *(1962) were scholarly works that received wide recognition in the literary community. Below, Highet examines Burns's use of Scottish dialect and meter in his odes "To a Mouse" and "To a Louse."*]

Two of the most sympathetic poems in our language are about vermin. One is about a mouse; the other is about a louse. They are in the same pattern of meter, run to approximately the same size, and were written by the same author. In their own tiny way they are masterpieces of wit and charm. I think the poem about the little mouse might just conceivably have been composed by several other poets, but I do not believe that anybody else in the world at that time could have produced an address to a louse and filled it, in spite of its repulsive subject, so full of grace and sympathy.

The poet was Robert Burns. The pieces are his ode **'To a Mouse,'** which he published when he was twenty-six, and his ode **'To a Louse,'** produced in the following year. Not many of us know the complete poems nowadays, because they are written in southern Scottish dialect, and in old-fashioned dialect which is now opaque even to the Scots themselves. (I remember how terribly puzzled I was at school, when I first read the mouse lyric, by hearing Burns say, 'A daimen icker in a thrave 's a sma' request.' It means 'An odd ear of corn in a whole sheaf is a small request' from a mouse to a farmer; but it contains three obsolete words.) Still, everyone who is not illiterate knows something of these poems: the two famous quotations— 'The best laid schemes o' mice and men / Gang aft agley' (meaning 'go often awry') and 'O wad some Pow'r the giftie gie us / To see oursels as others see us!' To take subjects so unpromising as a mouse and a louse, and to build them into poems containing wisdom so memorably expressed as these two sentences, was the work of a true genius.

True genius; but misunderstood, and despised. Burns was writing in 1785, during the proud and pompous eighteenth century, when a man scarcely dared to appear in decent society without silver buckles on his shoes, and when only lofty subjects and elevated language were thought worthy of notice either in conversation or in poetry. There is a ridiculous story in Boswell's *Life of Samuel Johnson* about a hack poet of that age who determined to compose an improving poem in the manner of the great Roman Vergil. In his *Georgics* Vergil had demonstrated that it was possible, with skill and taste, to write fine poetry about a subject so simple and prosaic, and even squalid, as farming. The eighteenth-century hack determined to rival Vergil in English, and chose a subject which he thought was both novel and important: the sugar industry of Jamaica and the other British West Indian islands. He was successful enough, no doubt, when he described the graceful rows of waving sugar canes, the rich earth, the warm, glorious sun. But then he had to deal with the various enemies of sugar cane, and give directions for combating them. One of the worst of these enemies is naturally vermin. The poet felt bound to discuss this un-amiable subject, and began a new paragraph:

> Now, Muse, let's sing of rats.

When he read it to his friends, they could not keep from laughing: he altered it; and in the final version the rats are thus eloquently periphrased:

> Nor with less waste the whiskered vermin race,
> A countless clan, despoil the lowland cane.

Surely, he thought, that would be noble enough to make the rats poetical.

Burns was not a conventional hack. Revolution bubbled in his soul, and occasionally boiled over. He therefore chose subjects which were, as the critics of his time put it, 'low.' If he had written of princes leading their armies into battle on mettlesome steeds, or described the grandeur of a regal stag hunt, with dukes and duchesses galloping through mighty forests after the noblest of game, he would surely have been much respected in his own day. Since he wrote about mice and lice, he was admired by only a few, and snubbed by others.

To make things worse, he did not write in the 'pure' language of southeastern England, but in the southern Scottish dialect—and this at a time when even English itself was sometimes thought to be rather vulgar, and anyone who wished to be cultured larded his own language with phrases of French from time to time. Society preferred to speak and read southeastern English, and a poet who wrote in Scottish dialect was—almost by definition—not a poet. (This particular type of snobbery has persisted down to the present time. Many living Scotsmen and Scotswomen can remember that they were forbidden, at school, to use Scottish words and phrases, not because they belonged to a dialectal pattern different from southeastern English, but on the ground that they were 'wrong' and 'common'—as it *is* genuinely wrong and common in English to say 'the ryne in Spyne' rather than 'the rain in Spain.')

Burns had a further handicap. He did not usually write in the accepted English meters, the neat couplets of Mr. Dryden and Mr. Pope (which were ultimately derived from Greek and Latin via Italian and French). He liked to use Scottish measures, cheerful little lilts which did not sound like a rococo chamber orchestra performing a measured gavotte, but like a village fiddler batting out a jolly strathspey and reel. Many of his finest poems were set to the rhythm and music of old Scots folk songs, which meant that—although they were often cleaner and wittier than the original folk-song words—they still reeked of the soil. They wore not satin and buckled shoes, but hodden gray and muddy boots. They had the sweaty hair of a farmer, instead of the powdered wig of a gentleman. They were not Polite. They were Coarse. Some traces of that feeling still linger. It is still a little shocking to think of a poet writing about a piece of body vermin. Our ancestors had far more body vermin than we have; but they prided themselves far more upon their delicate spiritual feelings. That sensitivity made them look askance on Burns for his coarseness, even while they were admiring his poems for the fiery genius that glowed through every one of them. Though his contemporaries made him into a celebrity in Edinburgh, they did not accept him. Without putting the feeling into words, they knew that he was a revolutionary poet.

The poems that Burns wrote about the mouse and the louse are revolutionary poems. They do not preach the forcible overthrow of an established political order and the violent eradication of all those attached to it; but they are utterances which were, in the time of Burns, quietly new, gently shocking, and ultimately destructive of long-accepted aesthetic and social standards.

The poem on the louse is, I suppose, technically an ode: it is all addressed to the little insect, and it is in a lyric meter. But in fact it is a dramatic monologue, and should be imagined as a Breughel picture put into motion. Its title is:

'To a Louse, on seeing one on a lady's bonnet, at church.'

The old Scottish words sometimes sound puzzling, but they give it energy, while the general meaning of the poem is entirely clear. Burns is sitting at service in the little kirk of Mauchline. He is behind, and very close to, the prettiest girl in the neighborhood. Naturally. As he gazes at her, a louse slowly emerges from her dress at her neckline, walks up her hair, and climbs up her hat to the very top, where it sits, surveying the congregation, and inspiring Rabbie with one of his finest lyric poems.

> Ha! whare ye gaun, ye crowlin ferlie [*monster*]?
> Your impudence protects you sairly;
> I canna say but ye strunt [*swagger*] rarely
>   Owre gauze and lace;
> Tho' faith, I fear, ye dine but sparely
>   On sic a place.
>
> Ye ugly, creepin', blastit wonner [*oddity*],
> Detested, shunned, by saunt an' sinner,

How daur [*dare*] ye set your fit [*foot*] upon her,
  Sae fine a Lady?
Gae somewhere else, and seek your dinner
  On some poor body.

Swith [*Get away*], in some beggar's haffet
  squattle [*Temple; crouch*];
There ye may creep, and sprawl, and sprattle
Wi' ither kindred, jumping cattle,
  In shoals and nations;
Whare horn nor bane [*comb of horn or bone*]
  ne'er daur unsettle
  Your thick plantations.

Now haud you [*hold on*] there, ye're our of
  sight,
Below the fatt'rils [*ribbons*], snug an' tight;
Na, faith ye yetl Ye'll no be right
  Till ye've got on it,
The vera tapmost, towering height
  O' Miss's bonnet.

My sooth! right bauld [*bold*] ye set your nose
  out
As plump and grey as onie grozet [*any
  gooseberry*];
O for some rank, mercurial rozet [*rosin*],
  Or fell, red smeddum [*powder*],
I'd gie you sic a hearty dose o't,
  Wad dress your droddum [*fix your wagon*]!

I wad na been surprised to spy
You on an auld wife's flainen toy [*flannel cap*];
Or aiblins [*perhaps*] some bit duddie boy,
  On's wyliecoat [*ragged vest*];
But Miss's fine Lunardi [*bonnet*], fye!
  How daur ye do 't?

O Jenny, dinna toss your head,
An' set your beauties a' abroad [*all abroad*]!
Ye little ken what cursed speed
  The blastie's [*dwarf*] makin'!
Thae [*those*] winks and finger-ends, I dread,
  Are notice takin'!

O wad some Pow'r the giftie [*little gift*] gie us
To see oursels as others see us!
It wad frae monie a blunder free us
  And foolish notion:
What airs in dress an' gait wad lea'e [*leave*] us,
  And ev'n Devotion!

It is a clever and charming poem. It particular, it is delightful to see how Burns, in stanza after stanza, traces the steady, relentless movement of the louse from the first moment when it emerges from the poor girl's dress and begins to make its way up to the pinnacle of its Everest. It was a surprise to Burns, and we hear his surprise echoed in his opening words: 'Ha! whare ye gaun, ye crowlin ferlie?' I suppose he would have been still more astounded if the louse had looked around and explained that it was going to climb to the very tip top of the young lady's hat. Why? *Because it was there!* Nevertheless, it is irresistibly comic to watch the horrid little beast making its pedestrian, pediculous way through the complicated ribbons and lace and gauze of a fantastically fashionable Italian creation, until it achieves the supreme pinnacle, high above the pretty girl's head, where others in the congregation can see it, while we must sit and watch it in civil, reverent silence. It would be against religion to interrupt the church service by speaking to a neighbor; and it would be frankly impossible to say, 'Excuse me, Miss Jenny, but you have a louse on your hat.' (She might reply, 'You have a bee in your bonnet.')

But there is satire in the poem as well as outright comedy. Burns addresses the louse, and explains to it that, on a well-dressed girl with some social aspirations, it is quite out of place. On a dirty, verminous beggar, it would be at home; or on a self-neglecting old woman, or on a badly reared child; but *not* on a member of good society. This is the same Rabbie Burns who wrote 'A man's a man for a' that.' He said, and he believed, that rank was but the stamp on the coin; what mattered was the metal, false or true gold, of which the coin was made. And the famous final stanza:

O wad some Pow'r the giftie gie us
To see oursels as others see us!
It wad frae monie a blunder free us
  And foolish notion:
What airs in dress an' gait wad lea'e us,
  And ev'n Devotion!

—that stanza reminds us that Burns wrote many of his most telling poems against the misuses of religion. He knew perfectly well that Miss Jenny, when she dressed for church that Sabbath morning, was thinking less about the psalms she would sing and the doctrinal content of the sermon she would hear than about the effect of her fine new hat on all the men and all the other women. In eight short stanzas, less than fifty lines, Burns has given us a brilliantly comic little drama, a gentle assertion of social equality, and a nipping satire on religious hypocrisy.

The other poem is as pathetic as the louse poem is comic. Burns was plowing on the farm which he and his brother Gilbert had rented. The soil was not good, the weather was wretched; the whole Burns family, poor already, could well be destitute in a year. As Rab drove the plowshare through the sour, wet earth one bleak November day, it smashed through the nest of a little field mouse. The homeless creature ran away in panic and despair. It was gone in a moment, soon to die of cold and wet; but it lingered in Burns's mind. In his poem he speaks to it from a heart full of love and sorrow and genuine sympathy. The conclusion is world-famous:

But, Mousie, thou art no thy lane [*art not alone*]
In proving foresight may be vain;
The best laid schemes o' mice and men
  Gang aft agley [*go often awry*];
And lea'e us nought but grief and pain
  For promised joy.

Burns ends by saying that the tiny creature, miserable and terrified, is still less unhappy than he himself, with nothing but dreary memories and a grimly threatening future. Only a few months later, he was so desperate that he resolved to leave his home forever, and emigrate to Jamaica. In order to raise the nine pounds he required for the fare, he published a collection of his poems. Quite unexpectedly, it was successful, and brought him some money, and some temporary distinction. But it was not to last. In a few years, too few years, he died as pitifully as a mouse in a flooded ditch.

It is a true poem, Burns's address to a mouse; but it was also, in his time, a new poem. Very few other poets would have thought of writing a serious piece on such a trivial subject; and of all the hundreds of millions of men who have plowed the soil and disturbed small vermin, very few have ever felt much sympathy for them, none have expressed it as warmly as Robert Burns. The country tenant-farmer with the big heart and the eloquent voice—he belonged to a new age altogether, the age which was coming and which he did not live to see. I wish he had escaped from Britain, and crossed the Atlantic, not to Jamaica but to the newly independent United States of America. He would have had a longer and happier life, even if he had written no more poetry. And he might have done greater things than he did. The plowman with his head full of immortal eloquence, hating hypocrisy and loving liberty, was an elder brother of our seventh President, Andrew Jackson, and of a still greater man with a still nobler heart, who was born in a log cabin and went to his grave from the White House.

Allan H. MacLaine (essay date 1965)

SOURCE: "The *Christis Kirk* Tradition: Its Evolution in Scots Poetry to Burns, Part IV," in *Studies in Scottish Literature,* Vol. II, No. 4, April, 1965, pp. 234-50.

[*In the following excerpt, MacLaine analyzes Burns's use of the* Christis Kirk *genre, which he describes as a "distinctively Scottish genre . . . [which] well demonstrates [Burns's] ability to make distinguished poetry out of the most ordinary stuff of life."*]

It would seem almost inevitable that Burns, ardent student of Scots poetry that he was, would sooner or later try his hand at the *Christis Kirk* genre. As a matter of fact, he produced six substantial poems more or less closely related to the genre, a group of poems which, taken together, represent the last brilliant flowering and culmination of the *Christis Kirk* tradition. These poems were all composed in the years 1785 and 1786, the period of Burns's greatest creativity, as follows: **"A Mauchline Wedding"** (August, 1785), **"Hallowe'en"** (November, 1785), **"The Jolly Beggars"** (ca. November, 1785), **"The Ordination"** (ca. November, 1785), **"The Holy Fair"** (autumn, 1785), and **"A Dream"** (June, 1786). Three of these, **"A Mauchline Wedding," "The Ordination,"** and **"A Dream,"** may be treated

briefly.

"Mauchline Wedding" seems to have been Burns's earliest experiment in the *Christis Kirk* genre. He enclosed the manuscript of this fragment in a letter to Mrs. Dunlop of August 21, 1788, but the piece was almost certainly composed in August of 1785, at the time of the actual wedding which it portrays. Slight though it is, **"A Mauchline Wedding"** is of considerable interest as a very early example of Burns's developing satiric style which was shortly to flower in masterpieces like **"Holy Willie's Prayer."** The poem is a burlesque description, mildly bawdy and high-spirited, of a local wedding in Burns's own country town of Mauchline. Written in the traditional stanza form, **"A Mauchline Wedding"** strikes the reader as a hastily written occasional piece, not intended for publication, but nevertheless marked by Burns's characteristic skill and vitality. Both in subject matter and form it obviously belongs to the *Christis Kirk* genre, and is even more closely tied into the tradition by the fact that Burns echoes passages in all three of the *Christis Kirk* poems of Fergusson. The opening lines of Burns's first two stanzas, for example, read as follows:

> When Eighty-five was seven months auld,
> And wearing thro' the aught [*eighth*],
> When rotting rains & Boreas bauld [*bold*]
> Gied farmer-folks a faught [*struggle, fight*] . . .
> The rising sun o'er Blacksideen [*name of a local hill*]
> Was just appearing fairly,
> When Nell & Bess get up to dress
> Seven lang half hours o'er early!

These lines are clearly similar in conception to the corresponding lines in the first two stanzas of Fergusson's *Hallow-fair:*

> At *Hallowmas,* when nights grow lang,
> And *starnies* [*stars*] shine fu' clear,
> Whan fock [*folk*], the nippin cald to bang,
> [*defeat*],
> Their winter *hap-warms* [*mantles*] wear . . .
> Upo' the tap o' ilka lum [*chimney*]
> The sun began to keek [*peep*],
> And bad the trig [*spruce*] made maidens come
> A sightly joe [*sweetheart*] to seek . . .

A picture of girls rising earlier than usual on a festive day also appears in stanza six of *Leith Races.* Much more conclusive than these passages, however, are the final lines of **"A Mauchline Wedding,"** depicting the emergence of the bride's father:

> And auld John Trot wi' sober phiz [*face*]
> As braid & bra's [*portly and finely dressed*] a Bailie,
> His shouthers [*shoulders*] & his Sunday's giz [*wig*]
> Wi' powther [*powder*] & wi' ulzie [*oil*]
> Weel smear'd that day.

Here Burns is unmistakably recalling the sparkling second stanza of Fergusson's *The Election:*

> Haste, EPPS, quo' John, an bring my gez [*wig*],
>   Take tent [*heed*] ye dinna't spulzie [*spoil*].
> Last night the barber ga't a friz [*curl*]
>   An' straikit [*stroked*] it wi' ulzie [*oil*].
> Hae done your PARITCH [*porridge*] lassie Liz,
>   Gi'e me my sark [*shirt*] an' gravat [*tie*];
> I'se be as braw's the Deacon is
>   Whan he taks AFFIDAVIT
>   O' FAITH the day.

There can be no doubt about these verbal parallels, which clearly show that Burns, in this first casual attempt, was writing not only within the general limits of the tradition but also in direct imitation of Fergusson's masterpieces in this genre.

"The Ordination" is a daring satire on Ayrshire church politics. In general, it is concerned with the struggle within the Kirk between the rigidly orthodox Calvinists or "Auld Lichts" and the Moderates or "New Lichts," Burns, of course, favoring the latter. More specifically, the poem was occasioned by the presentation of James Mackinlay, a staunch "Auld Licht," to the Laigh Kirk in Kilmarnock, where he succeeds a series of Moderates and where he will be counted on by the orthodox, including Russell (a fellow minister in Kilmarnock), to extirpate the former heresies and restore the pure faith. Burns's method of attack in **"The Ordination"** is to write an ironic celebration of this victory of orthodoxy. He portrays, with mock approbation, the vulgar, gloating triumph of the "Auld Lichts" in such a way as to make them appear as repulsive and ridiculous as possible. He makes his poem read like a wild, bacchanalian celebration, and uses the swinging folksy rhythm of the *Christis Kirk* stanza, with conscious irony, to depict this theological victory over "common sense."

> Gurst Common-sense, that imp o' hell,
>   Cam in wi' *Maggie Lauder*:
> But Oliphant aft made her yell,
>   An' Russell sair misca'd her:
> This day Mackinlay taks the flail,
>   An' he's the boy will blaud [*slap*] her!
> He'll clap a shangan [*cleft stick*] on her tail,
>   An' set the bairns to daud [*pelt*] her
>   Wi' dirt this day.

"The Ordination" lacks the kind of universal significance which has made **"Holy Willie's Prayer"** (also written on a local and ephemeral issue) one of the classic satires of all time. The poem is not great, but is very effective as far as it goes; and it remains quite readable today. Burns's satiric method here is a brilliant conception in itself, the product of a shrewd and powerful intellect, and serves the author's purpose admirably. One could scarcely think of a better way of ridiculing the "Auld Lichts" on this occasion. Burns here uses Ramsay's form of the *Christis Kirk* stanza, but he manipulates it deftly to suit the special effects he intends, using feminine rimes in the trimeter lines throughout to reinforce the tone of witty

mockery. The execution of the poem as a whole is, in fact, masterly and highly original. This hard-hitting satire represents, indeed, a bold new departure in the *Christis Kirk* tradition, which is here for the first time adapted as a vehicle for an attack on local church politics, an extension of the genre which was probably suggested to Burns by Fergusson's success with *The Election*, a political satire.

"A Dream," the other political piece which Burns composed in the *Christis Kirk* stanza, is less successful than **"The Ordination"** and deserves only cursory comment. Apart from meter, **"A Dream"** bears little resemblance to the *Christis Kirk* type. It is really a monologue in which the poet addresses in a dream King George III and other members of the royal family at the birthday levee of June, 1786. The poet's remarks are not in the best taste, combining some rather forced expressions of respect and good wishes with condescending advice and unpleasantly familiar comments on the King's family. Stanza 5, in an admonishing vein, will illustrate the general tone:

> Far be't frae me that I aspire
>   To blame your legislation,
> Or say, ye wisdom want, or fire
>   To rule this mighty nation:
> But faith! I muckle [*greatly*] doubt, my sire,
>   Ye've trusted ministration
> To chaps wha in a barn or byre [*cow-shed*]
>   Wad [*would have*] better fill'd their station,
>   Than courts you day.

Burns, of course, handles the *Christis Kirk* meter here with his usual skill and vigor (note the feminine rimes as in **"The Ordination"**); but the poem as a whole fails to ring true.

"Hallowe'en," Burns's second poem in the *Christis Kirk* genre, was written about November, 1785. This is a very ambitious piece, Burns's longest work in the *Christis Kirk* stanza, and was, as might be expected in an early attempt, strongly affected by the work of both Ramsay and Fergusson, though the immediate suggestion came from Mayne's *Hallowe'en*. Fergusson's influence shows up in Burns's use of four rimes in the octave, a modification of the traditional stanza which, as we have seen, was introduced by the Edinburgh poet. There are, moreover, one or two verbal echoes of Fergusson in the poem. But although Fergusson was undoubtedly the model for the skillful technique of the poem, Ramsay's influence on its content was decisive and unfortunate. We have noticed in Ramsay's sequels to *Christis Kirk on the Green* the antiquarian emphasis and the introduction of old-fashioned marriage customs, such as the "bedding" of the bride, the "creeling" of the groom, and "riding the stang." In **"Hallowe'en"** Burns builds his entire poem around the Ayrshire folk customs connected with this festival. As a result, **"Hallowe'en"** is a paradise for the folklorist, but rather a bore for the lover of poetry. Burns crams his twenty-eight stanzas with Hallowe'en superstitions recorded one after another. This self-conscious antiquarianism makes his description of a merry gathering of country folk on this night seem unnatural and forced; the characters are inadequately sketched and are made to go through a long series of superstitious rites. They do virtually nothing else in the poem. Burns simply puts them through their Hallowe'en paces, failing to render a really convincing impression of what such a celebration must have been like. Many of the customs he describes, moreover, are very much of a kind and become monotonous. That Burns was fully aware of the studied antiquarianism of his poem is clear from his own foreword: "The passion of prying into Futurity makes a striking part of the history of Human Nature in its rude state, in all ages and nations; and it may be some entertainment to the philosophical mind, if any such should honour the Author with a perusal, to see the remains of it, among the more enlightened in our own." Since the poet had this objective in mind, it is no wonder that **"Hallowe'en"** gives the impression not so much of an actual party at which Burns had been present, but rather of an artificial conglomeration of all the Hallowe'en rites he had ever observed or heard about. And many of the customs he describes are of so specialized and local a nature that they are apt to be entirely lost on the general reader. Take, for example, stanza 4:

> Then, first an' foremost, thro' the kail,
>   Their stocks maun a' be sought ance;
> They steek [*shut*] their een [*eyes*], an' grape
>   [*grope*] an' wale [*choose*]
>   For muckle [*big*] anes, an' straught [*straight*]
>   anes.
> Poor hav'rel [*foolish*] Will fell aff the drift [*lost
>   the way*],
>   An' wandered thro' the bow-kail [*cabbage*],
> An' pow't [*pulled*], for want o' better shift
>   [*choice*],
>   A runt [*stalk*], was like a sow-tail,
>   Sae bow't [*bent*] that night.

Burns apparently realized that such a stanza would be utterly unintelligible to many readers, and he was therefore obliged to prepare an elaborate set of notes to explain his poem to the uninitiated. His explanatory note on the stanza cited above, for instance, is much longer than the stanza itself.

It is unfortunate that Burns insisted on packing this poem with folklore, for in many respects **"Hallowe'en"** is an excellent piece of work. It is, of course, strictly within the *Christis Kirk* tradition, embodying most of the characteristics of the genre. We have here the typical peasant celebration as the subject, the use of dialogue, the frequent transitions, the satire of cowardice, the lighting up of individual characters and incidents, the broadly humorous treatment, and the point of view of the amused spectator. Notwithstanding the touches of genial satire, Burns's attitude toward the superstitious country folk in the poem is, of course, wholly sympathetic.

"Hallowe'en" is of further interest for its experimental technique. Burns takes the hint from Fergusson not only in his use of Fergusson's four-time octave, but also in his attempt at internal rime. We have noted that Fergusson

introduced internal rimes sparingly and judiciously, once in *Hallow-fair* (stanza 2) and once in *Leith Races* (stanza 8). Burns in **"Hallowe'en"** tries this technique on a more ambitious scale, working internal rimes into the tetrameter lines throughout stanza 1, and in the first quatrains of stanzas 3 and 6. After stanza 6, he wisely gives up the attempt. In these passages Burns seems to be exercising his technical virtuosity for its own sake, without a sound artistic reason. Consequently, the internal riming in stanzas 1 and 3 appears heavy and forced. In stanza 6, however, where the internal rimes do not interfere with the natural development of the thought, he achieves a pleasing effect:

> The lasses staw [*stole*] frae 'mang them a',
>   To pou [*pull*] their stalks o' corn;
> But Rab slips out, an' jinks [*dodges*] about,
>   Behint the muckle thorn.

Despite this largely unsuccessful experiment with internal rime, **"Hallowe'en"** is, on the whole, brilliantly executed. The rhythm and movement of the poem are brisk and spirited; Burns handles the complex verse form with accomplished skill. As Ramsay and Fergusson had done before him, Burns frequently changes the pace of his stanzas by using feminine endings in the trimeter lines of a whole stanza or the second quatrain of a stanza. This device tends to vary the tempo and is often quite effective. In view of this fine craftsmanship, **"Hallowe'en"** might have been a first-rate poem had Burns been less self-conscious in the handling of his folk materials.

We come finally to two of Burns's greatest masterpieces, **"The Jolly Beggars"** and **"The Holy Fair."** In the immense variety of its materials, the multiplicity of its sources, and in its dazzling synthesis of distinct poetic styles, **"The Jolly Beggars"** is certainly the richest and most complex of all Burns's works. This unique poem (there has never been anything quite like it before or since) has had its sources traced, its main features clarified, and its extraordinary appeal analyzed by a host of commentators, including [William E.] Henley and [T. F.] Henderson [in *The Poetry of Robert Burns,* 1896-97], who, in a now famous sentence, epitomized it perfectly as an "irresistible presentation of humanity caught in the act and summarized for ever in the terms of art." It is not my purpose here to launch into a full discussion of this many-sided "cantata," but only to demonstrate its connection with the *Christis Kirk* tradition. Surprisingly enough, this connection has been neglected in the numerous critiques of **"The Jolly Beggars,"** except that the bare fact that three of the stanzas are in the *Christis Kirk* form is usually mentioned. But the relationship to the genre is much closer, as I will try to show.

Let us look first at the verse forms of **"The Jolly Beggars."** Burns, in this piece, employs a great variety of meters, including the pure *Christis Kirk* meter in the three stanzas mentioned above which comprise the seventh *Recitativo.* Here Burns uses Ramsay's two-rime octave, but replaces the "that day" refrain with "that night" in the bob line as he had done in **"Hallowe'en."** The influence of the *Christis Kirk* meter, however, extends beyond this single passage. In addition, there are three other stanzas in the *Recitativo* sections which are in the *Christis Kirk* form without the final tag line: the single stanza of the second *Recitativo* (Ramsay's two-rime octave), and the two stanzas of the sixth *Recitativo* (Fergusson's four-rime octave). Taking all six stanzas together, we find that nearly half of the total lines of the *Recitativo* sections are in the *Christis Kirk* stanza or in a modified form thereof. Finally, the caird's song is also in this stanza, without the bob but with the internal rimes in the tetrameter lines which Burns had experimented with in "Hallowe'en." Altogether, some sixty-seven lines of "The Jolly Beggars" are in the pure or modified *Christis Kirk* stanza, a total which makes it by far the most important verse form in the poem, the *Cherrie and the Slae* stanza being second with forty-two lines. The full significance of this metrical influence from the *Christis Kirk* tradition upon "The Jolly Beggars" has never been recognized.

Secondly, I am convinced that Burns's careful study of the *Christis Kirk* poems had much to do with the original conception of "The Jolly Beggars" and with the handling of the materials in the poem. The obvious and immediate sources of the poem are, of course, well known. First of all, there was the beggar theme, which came to Burns from his keen observation of real beggars about the Ayrshire countryside and also, undoubtedly, from his reading of parts of the vast literature about beggars, a literature which had its roots deep in the medieval past. Burns certainly knew several specimens of this beggar-poetry, including *The Gaberlunzie-Man* and *The Jolly Beggar,* ascribed to King James V of Scotland; *The Merry Beggars* and *The Happy Beggars* in Ramsay's *Tea-Table Miscellany;* and Gay's *Beggar's Opera.* As for his "cantata" form, Burns clearly got the idea for this from *The Merry Beggars* (which, incidentally, he echoes in several phrases of his poem), and from Ramsay's worthless effort, *A Scots Cantata,* with probably additional suggestions from Gay and from Ramsay's *Gentle Shepherd.* But in putting his beggar theme and cantata form together, Burns had another large body of poetry to draw upon—the *Christis Kirk* tradition. Burns had in the *Christis Kirk* poems, which he knew intimately and had already followed in "A Mauchline Wedding" and "Hallowe'en," a wealth of precedent for an ambitious and artistic poem of social description. In these poems he had observed descriptions of boisterous lower class celebrations, presented within a narrative framework and interspersed with dialogue. In "The Jolly Beggars" the cantata scheme required formal songs, which take the place of dialogue; but, except for dialogue, most of the ingredients of the *Christis Kirk* formula are there. We have the usual opening stanza, setting the season and the scene, and then move swiftly into the first brilliant little vignette, that of the "sodger" and his "tozie drab." In "The Jolly Beggars" as in all of the *Christis Kirk* poems, the technique is to light up an individual character (or group of characters) picked out from the general confusion of the celebration, show him in action, and then go on quickly to the next and the next. Through this highlighting of specific details, a vivid impression of the whole is achieved. A study of the *Recitativo* sections of "The Jolly Beggars" reveals that Burns here uses precisely the same kind of brief characterization, rapid transition, rollicking tempo, and broad humor which we have observed as typical of the *Christis Kirk* genre. The drunkenness, the horseplay, the tolerant satire are here, too, and the point of view of the superior and detached spectator. (It should be noted, though, that Burns's detachment is not complete: he seems at times to be putting his own sentiments into the beggars' mouths.)

Although there is no evidence that Burns had any particular *Christis Kirk* poem in mind when he wrote "The Jolly Beggars," the general influence of the *Christis Kirk* genre that he knew so well is, I think, undeniable. It is true that Burns found suggestions for his theme, his cantata form, and for specific details elsewhere; and it is equally obvious that there are many elements in this rich and complex poem that have nothing to do with the *Christis Kirk* tradition. Nevertheless, in view of the broad general resemblances noted above, it seems clear that in his overall conception of "The Jolly Beggars" and in his handling of the *Recitativo* sections Burns had his favorite *Christis Kirk* poems in mind and followed their traditional pattern as far as his cantata form would allow. The fact that he uses the *Christis Kirk* stanza more than any other verse form in the poem supports this position. In short, the *Christis Kirk* tradition is an important part of the background of "The Jolly Beggars;" and "The Jolly Beggars," uniquely different though it is, may legitimately be considered as part of the *Christis Kirk* tradition.

Apart from the trivial "Dream" (June, 1786), "The Holy Fair" was Burns's final effort in the *Christis Kirk* genre; and this magnificent poem makes a fitting culmination of the ancient tradition. "The Holy Fair" is a socio-religious satire, happily combining the familiar type of satiric social description with the new kind of anti-clerical religious satire on local themes that Burns had already tried in "The Ordination" and other works. The poem falls strictly within the *Christis Kirk* pattern, being in the traditional stanza, dealing with a rural celebration, and having all the other distinctive features of the genre. It describes a "Holy Fair" in Burns's village of Mauchline, an important religious occasion on which congregations from several parishes gathered together to hear their various ministers preach in turn. That most of the folk who came to this religious festival also took advantage of the opportunity for some hearty socializing is made delightfully clear in the poem.

In writing "The Holy Fair" Burns leaned heavily on earlier *Christis Kirk* poems, especially on Fergusson's *Hallow-fair* and *Leith Races,* though there are also a few verbal echoes from elsewhere. But the vital stimulating influence behind "The Holy Fair" was unquestionably Fergusson. Burns here uses the four-rime octave of *Hallow-fair* and *Leith Races* once again, and, significantly, parallels Fergusson's opening references to the season:

Hallow-fair:
At *Hallowmass,* when nights grow lang,

And *starnies* shine fu' clear . . .

Leith Races:
In July month, ae bonny morn,
    Whan Nature's rokelay [*cloak*] green . . .

Holy Fair:
Upon a simmer Sunday morn,
    When Nature's face is fair . . .

Hallow-fair provided Burns with several other scattered suggestions, including his opening description of sunrise ("The rising sun, owre Galston Muirs, / Wi' glorious light was glintin"), which follows Fergusson's ("Upo' the tap o' ilka lum / The sun began to keek"). Similarly, Burns's portrait of country farmers coming into the fair ("Here farmers gash, in ridin graith") parallels *Hallow-fair* ("Here country John in bannet blue"), while his reference to Sunday clothes ("'I'll get my Sunday's sark on'") echoes the same poem ("And eke his Sunday's claise on"). But more important than these incidental suggestions from *Hallow-fair* was Burns's imitation of the entire opening section of *Leith Races*. Burns takes over Fergusson's introductory machinery, transforming his "Mirth" into "Fun" and adding two extra mythological figures, "Superstition" and "Hyprocrisy." The two poems parallel each other with extraordinary closeness in these opening stanzas. Burns's "Fun" performs precisely the same function in the poem as her counterpart in *Leith Races:* she is a fresh and jolly girl who offers to accompany the poet to the fair for the fun of observing and laughing at the sights to be seen there, especially the antics of Superstition and Hypocrisy:

"I'm gaun to Mauchline Holy Fair,
    To spend an hour in daffin [*fooling*]:
Gin ye'll go there, you runkl'd [*wrinkled*] pair,
    We will get famous laughin
        At them this day."

Moreover, as in *Leith Races* Burns's "Fun" sets the tone of light-hearted observation and tolerant satire which prevails throughout the poem. It should be noted further that, in addition to incorporating Fergusson's introductory method, Burns also follows in a general way the structure of *Leith Races:* after the mythological introduction, Burns portrays the various folk on their way to the fair, then the activities at the fair itself, and finally the aftermath. Burns's final stanza, incidentally, resembles in content the last stanza of *Leith Races* and, more closely, the ending of Ramsay's *Christis Kirk*, Canto II. These extensive borrowings from Fergusson and others in **"The Holy Fair"** are significant in showing that in this poem Burns was fully aware of the tradition in which he was writing and was consciously modeling his work on earlier masterpieces in the *Christis Kirk* genre.

Yet in spite of the fact that Burns here followed the traditional pattern in a general way, that he borrowed machinery and other suggestions from Fergusson and elsewhere, **"The Holy Fair"** remains inimitably Burns's own—a fresh, daring, and original piece of work. In **"The Holy Fair"** Burns recreates the age-old *Christis Kirk* tra-

dition in terms of his own experience and special purposes; and he does so with superb artistry. Perhaps the most important feature of the poem, which sets it apart and makes it a different experience, is its mixture of religious and secular satire, its delightful emphasis on the paradoxes and incongruities emerging from the intensely human scene at the fair.

Here some are thinkin on their sins,
    An' some upo' their claes [*clothes*];
Ane curses feet that fyl'd [*soiled*] his shins,
    Anither sighs an' prays:
On this hand sits a chosen swatch [*sample*]
    Wi' screw'd-up, grace-proud faces;
On that a set o' chaps, at watch,
    Thrang [*busy*] winkin on the lasses
        To chairs that day.

Notice the gay mockery of the Calvinist doctrine of Election implicit in the phrase "a chosen swatch." The whole poem is, in fact, brilliantly organized to show this glaring contrast between the ostensible religious purpose of the fair and the boisterous and throughly irreverent activities which go on there. Burns focuses attention in one stanza on the pulpit where the preachers are thundering out hellfire sermons, and in the next stanza on the crowd of country folk round about, many of whom are thoroughly enjoying themselves, eating, drinking, gossiping, napping, and making love, utterly uninhibited by the sound of the preacher's voice bringing "tidings o' damnation." The poem flashes back and forth, illuminating the religious and social aspects of the fair in turn, as Burns makes hilarious fun of the different preachers and lights up humorous scenes in the crowd with breathtaking verve and rapidity. The final stanza, where the poet comments on secular love-making and drinking in terms of the theological jargon of the preachers, brilliantly sums up the point of the whole poem:

How monie hearts this day converts
    O' sinners and o' lasses!
Their hearts o' stane, gin night [*by nightfall*], are gane
    As saft as onie flesh is:
There's some are fou o' love divine;
    There's some are fou o' brandy;
An' monie jobs that day begin,
    May end in houghmagandie [*fornication*]
        Some ither day.

The fact that **"The Holy Fair"** is based on this two-fold satiric theme and skillfully arranged to illustrate a single, fundamental contrast gives it firmer structure, more clear-cut direction, sharper emphasis, and more profound significance than either *Hallow-fair* or *Leith Races*, or, for that matter, any other of its predecessors in the pure *Christis Kirk* tradition. And the execution of the poem is equally brilliant. Burns had learned much from his study of the fine craftsmanship of Fergusson, and here he surpasses the Edinburgh poet in the incisive force and incomparable expressiveness of his style. **"The Holy Fair"** is an almost faultless poem, bursting with vitality, rich in its texture, delightful in its humor—every stanza a work of art. Take, for example, Burns's uproariously comic portrait of the preacher Moodie:

> Now a' the congregation o'er
>   Is silent expectation;
> For Moodie speels [*climbs*] the holy door,
>   Wi' tidings o' damnation:
> Should Hornie [*the Devil*], as in ancient days,
>   'Mang sons o' God present him;
> The vera sight o' Moodie's face
>   To's ain het [*hot*] hame had sent him
>   Wi' fright that day.
>
> Hear how he clears the points o' Faith
>   Wi' rattlin and thumpin!
> Now meekly calm, now wild in wrath,
>   He's stampin, an' he's jumpin!
> His lengthen'd chin, his turn'd-up snout,
>   His eldritch [*unearthly*] squeel an' gestures,
> O how they fire the heart devout—
>   Like cantharidian plaisters
>   On sic a day!

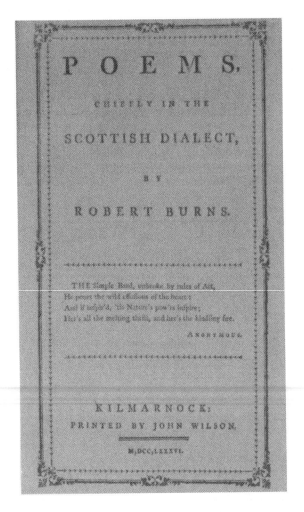

Title page of Poems, Chiefly in the Scottish Dialect.

"The Holy Fair" is certainly one of Burns's very greatest performances, and it is also, in my opinion, the most perfect single poem in the long history of the *Christis Kirk* tradition.

It should be clear from what has been said above that Burns, in his *Christis Kirk* poems, followed the lead of Fergusson in making the genre a vehicle for social criticism, for the treatment of local and contemporary issues. But Burns went farther than Fergusson in this direction, treating political questions (**"A Dream"**), for example, even more specifically than Fergusson had done, and extending the subject matter of the genre in **"The Ordination"** and **"The Holy Fair"** to include religious satire. Additionally, in **"The Jolly Beggars"** he used the genre to expound revolutionary social ideas. Only in **"Hallowe'en"** does he hark back to a kind of Ramsayesque antiquarianism. Before Burns, all of the *Christis Kirk* poems (even Fergusson's) had been intended almost exclusively as entertainment; most of them were seasoned with good-natured social satire, it is true; but by and large they were meant only to delight and amuse the educated classes. Burns was the only poet to employ this ancient poetic tradition to attack what might be called "burning questions" of the day. His treatment is always, of course, comic in mood; but its implications are serious and pointed to an extent unapproached by any of the earlier practitioners in the genre with the possible exception of Fergusson in *The Election*. We find, then, a new kind of emphasis which gives Burns's poems added significance and power, a kind of undertone of vitality and passionate interest. Burns gives us something more than robust humor and whimsical observation. And in doing this as brilliantly as he has—at least in his three best poems in the genre, **"The Ordination" "The Jolly Beggars,"** and **"The Holy Fair"**—Burns added a new dimension to the whole *Christis Kirk* tradition. . . .

Frederick L. Beaty (essay date 1968)

SOURCE: "Burns's Comedy of Romantic Love," in *PMLA*, Vol. 83, No. 2, May, 1968, pp. 429-38.

[*In the essay below, Beaty assesses the humorous aspects of Burns's love poetry.*]

The eighteenth-century adaptation of sentiment to comedy, as well as the Scottish vernacular tradition, afforded Robert Burns ample precedent for his humorous love poetry. He was obviously interested in examining the comic spirit, as random comments in his letters indicate; yet he apparently elaborated no critical manifesto of his own to explain his practice. Perhaps because he was often regarded as an inspired but untaught genius who succeeded without conscious artistry, influential critics of the early nineteenth century usually looked not to him for illustrations of their comic theories but rather to Jean Paul Richter, who had obligingly translated his own precepts into creative examples. Not until after many of the speculations about humor had crystallized into definite concepts could Burns's achievement be fully analyzed. Just as his poetry had unwittingly sanctioned in advance many of the tenets enunciated in Wordsworth's preface to *Lyrical Ballads* (1800), so too his portrayals of comic love anticipated theories of subsequent analysts and, consequently, have become increasingly meaningful in the light of critical doctrines articulated after his practice.

As Romantic critics saw it, the dichotomy between humor and wit inherited from the eighteenth century constituted one of the basic cleavages between neoclassicism and their own aesthetic of natural sensibility. In his introduction to *Lectures on the English Comic Writers,* [William] Hazlitt made the distinction explicit: "Humour is the describing the ludicrous as it is in itself; wit is the exposing it, by comparing or contrasting it with something else. Humour is, as it were, the growth of nature and accident; wit is the product of art and fancy." Thus wit, being contrived, aggressive, and generally derisive, was considered the province of the mind; whereas humor, being natural, emotional, and empathically understanding, belonged essentially to the heart. Similarly [Thomas] De Quincey, when he attempted to popularize Richter's philosophical theories on the comic, carefully emphasized the distinction between wit as "a purely intellectual thing" and humor as a phenomenon that brought into play "the *moral* nature" involving the will, affections, disposition, and temperament. Humor in Richter's creative works, according to De Quincey, was interwoven with pathos, his gentle satire characterized by smiles rather than by scornful laughter. Subsequently [Thomas] Carlyle, who had assimilated much of the comic psychology in Richter's *Vorschule der Aesthetik* (1804), demeaned the irony and caricature of neoclassical satirists to a position conspicuously lower than that of humor. "True humour," Carlyle explained in his second essay on Richter ["Jean Paul Friedrich Richter," 1827, *The Works of Thomas Carlyle,* edited by H. D. Traill, 1896-99], "springs not more from the head than from the heart; it is not contempt, its essence is love; it issues not in laughter, but in still smiles, which lie far deeper." Through a kinship with sensibility, therefore, the ultimate justification of humor resembled that for human love: it helped unite man with mankind.

Despite objections from purists who preferred their emotions and their genres unalloyed, the analogy of love and humor was generally endorsed by Romantic critics as a valid precept for life, as well as art. Even the delicate question of whether the heart was capable of sympathetic laughter had an apologist in [Charles] Lamb, who differentiated between "the petrifying sneer of a demon which excludes and kills Love" and "the cordial laughter of a man which implies and cherishes it." By laughing *with* rather than *at* humanity, one might enjoy himself while heightening his benevolent proclivities. And if humor was produced by what was universally comic, laughter, especially from a man sufficiently perceptive to associate the ludicrous with traits in himself, could prove highly edifying. [John] Keats, in the letter that evolves his principle of imaginative identification, selfless sympathy, and suspended judgment known as "negative capability," significantly progressed toward this doctrine from a statement praising the superiority of humor over wit. As Keats realized, humor enabled an imaginative understanding whereby one was made to *feel* rather than (as in wit) to *start.* Furthermore, the artistic advantages of humor were seen to rest on valid psychological grounds. As both De Quincey and Carlyle pointed out in their respective analyses of Richter, humor prevented sensibility from deteriorating into a lachrymose or maudlin sentimentality. However serious the emotion of love might be, a touch of the comic—what Bergson in his essay *Laughter* defined as "a momentary anesthesia of the heart"—contributed to a healthful perspective. The conjunction of active and passive, far from annihilating one another, restored a sane equilibrium appropriate to the Romantic goal of unified sensibilities. By its very nature life was seen to be full of inconsistencies, incongruities, paradoxes, and frustrations imposed by mundane limitations. Yet if the dominant principle of life was (like that of its creator) love, then the force striving for unity with the infinite tended to transcend finite limitations. Hence the juxtaposition of finite and infinite, which Richter postulated as the true source of humor, contributed to the desired totality of existence.

The soundness of Romantic insight, striving for the union of reason, sentiment, intellectual intuition, and imagination, was later confirmed by professional psychologists. Sigmund Freud, who endorsed many of the Romantic theories on the comic derived from Richter, further demonstrated that joking, however pleasurable, was also a serious matter. He analyzed humor in the following manner, according to the circumstances of its origin:

> The forms in which humour is manifested are, moreover, determined by two peculiarities which are connected with the conditions under which it is generated. Humour may, in the first place, appear merged with a joke or some other species of the comic; in that case its task is to get rid of a possibility implicit in the situation that an affect may be generated which would interfere with the pleasurable outcome. In the second place, it may stop this generating of an affect entirely or only partially; this last is actually the commoner case since it is easier to bring about, and it produces the various forms of "broken" humour—the humour that smiles through tears.

Subsequent psychologists have likewise explained the compatibility of love and humor in their own terms without seriously disrupting Romantic concepts. While love is customarily associated now with the integrative or self-transcending tendency and the comic spirit with the self-assertive, human emotions are usually mixed. Love, in all except its hypothetically pure instances, is sufficiently ambivalent to include some of the self-assertive. Sexual love, particularly from the masculine point of view, contains enough of the aggressive to invite forms of the comic that are indeed far less sympathetic than humor. Nor does laughter provoked by such instances undermine the essential seriousness, for the emotions meet on common ground.

Yet exactly how much of prevalent theory on comic love Burns was consciously aware of is difficult to ascertain. It seems likely, however, that he may have been acquainted with one of the longest treatises on the comic spirit, that by the Scottish philosopher-poet James Beattie, whose poems and essays Burns greatly admired. Continuing the traditions first popularized by Addison and Steele (and later by Sterne), Beattie, in his "Essay on Laughter and Ludicrous Composition" (1776), claimed that laughter arising from innocent mirth was not only therapeutically desirable but also indicative of a benevolent, rather than a spiteful, nature. Moreover, he predicted a kind of literature of which Burns was to become the chief poetical exponent. "As romantic love in its natural regular procedure is now become so copious a source of joy and sorrow, hope and fear, triumph and disappointment," Beattie asserted, "we might reasonably conclude, that in its more whimsical forms and vagaries it could scarce fail to supply materials for laughter." His views on the *vis comica* were essentially standard, even though his terminology differed somewhat from that of other aestheticians and his specific definitions perhaps did not indicate rigid classification. *Wit* he described as the "unexpected discovery of resemblance between ideas supposed dissimilar"—a kind of *discordia concors* such as Dr. Johnson saw in metaphysical analogies. *Humor* Beattie identified with the "comic exhibition of singular characters, sentiments, and imagery." Yet he certainly divided the comic spirit into two categories according to the responses it evoked: the *ridiculous* arousing contempt or disapproval, and the *ludicrous* producing a simple, undefinable, risible emotion. This latter reaction was brought about by the pleasant awareness of inconsistencies—often in an unusual mixture of similarity and contrariety. As the "Essay" further analyzed it, innocent laughter could be purely "animal" if occasioned by tickling or sudden gladness and "sentimental" when it proceeded from feeling or sentiment. Since theories such as these were already formulated, Burns, who was especially sensitive to the incongruities of certain character traits in particular situations, had only to put the sentimental comic into practice.

Before fully understanding Burns's treatment of "romantic love," however, one must recognize that to him sexual attraction was the most natural and inspiring justification for existence. Complete gratification in love became virtually synonymous with the pursuit of happiness; and from this basic premise, which colored all he had to say about love, stemmed the related attitudes expressed throughout his poetry. Associated from the beginning with poetic inspiration, this "delicious Passion," as he explained to Dr. John Moore, was held "to be the first of human joys, our dearest pleasure here below." His most celebrated affirmation of loyalty to the eternal feminine, **"Green Grow the Rashes, O,"** divides humanity into those with hearts and those without. Though the "war'ly race" may seek and often find riches, Burns declares that true enjoyment, a fulfillment of the heart, will never be theirs. As spokesman for the other race, he vows his preference for the simple, unassuming joys of making love, one of the few inalienable rights of the poor. In an uncertain, anxiety-filled world the lasses alone make life bearable and meaningful. Nor does the poet assume that a man's love ought to be confined to one girl. In opposition to grave Calvinistic strictures condemning earthly joys, he cites

scriptural (and therefore irrefutable) authority that Solomon, traditionally the wisest of men and devotee of infinite variety, "dearly lov'd the lasses." Carrying matters a step further in the poems he contributed to *The Merry Muses of Caledonia,* Burns is often very explicit, sometimes by means of clever metaphors, about the unsurpassed pleasures women afford sexually. Obversely, he characterizes the loss of physical love as tantamount to death in life. A good example occurs in lines from **"Epistle to James Smith,"** which express fears that the worst blight of senility will be deprivation of that greatest joy— "dear, deluding Woman." The same poem also affirms the basic cleavage between those men, including Burns, who can appreciate the pleasures of a full life and that other segment—the "douce folk that live by rule"—whose stagnant lives lack affection, sentiment, and happiness even in their prime. Similarly, the poem **"To Major Logan"** distinguishes between the "purse-proud race" obsessed with respectability and those who respond to the gadflies of feeling. Declaring his lot with the latter, Burns defies priests who condemn women for the fall of mankind, adding sincerely: "I like them dearly . . . / God bless them a'!"

Quite logically, a belief so devoutly affirmed had to be translated into practice, and many of Burns's poems celebrate the following of natural inclination—a precept he advocated most convincingly from the masculine viewpoint. Despite some admissions, as in the **"Epistle to a Young Friend,"** that illicit affection hardened the heart and petrified the feelings, he usually assumed that the most ardent flames of love ought to be kindled immediately because they were too often of short duration. Hence he advised his brother William: ". . . try for intimacy as soon as you feel the first symptoms of the passion." Somewhat like his bard in **"The Jolly Beggars,"** Burns usually regarded it a mortal sin to thwart a divinely implanted instinct. Being a man entailed fulfilling the obligations of manhood, and whoever shirked them was not entitled to the name. In an attempt to refine a coarse original of his song **"The Tailor,"** Burns implies this argument as explanation for the central character's behavior. Whereas in the earlier version the tailor sadistically had taken advantage of a sleeping maiden, in Burns's humorous redaction he attains his goal because he is charming and ingratiating. (This alteration itself indicates how the poet frequently softened the harsh original without radically changing its import.) The profession of Burns's tailor provides him with nothing more than an entrée; his real vocation is that of a lover who "kend the way to woo." In one choice line the poet laconically sums up all that is indelicate in the earlier account, adds what is needed to conclude the anecdote, and comments on the action: "The Tailor prov'd a man, O!"

A much richer psychological treatment of this theme appears in the song **"Had I the Wyte."** A man obviously disturbed by his recent excursion into adultery tries to allay his conscience by repeated questioning whether he ought to be blamed for his actions. Part of the humor no doubt stems from the transposition of the customary roles in love—of an aggressive Lady Booby plotting the seduction of a relatively passive Joseph Andrews. But the crowning achievement in the lyric is the speaker's unwitting revelation of his own naïveté and his unwillingness to admit that the married woman had actually manipulated him. Knowing that he would not wish his valor impugned, she had shrewdly called him "a coward loon" for his reluctance to enter her house. Then perceiving his vanity and susceptibility to pity, she complained of how cruelly her absent husband treated her and thereby threw all the blame for her own actions upon a tyrannical spouse. What indeed could a sympathetic young man do but comfort and console her? In retrospect he protests:

> Could I for shame refus'd her?
> And wadna manhood been to blame
> Had I unkindly used her?

After performing his duty, he reveals some uncertainty about true manly behavior by recounting that on the following morning he tried to drown his compunction in brandy, though he continues to solicit our comforting assurance that he was not the one to blame.

A somewhat different aspect of the problem is reflected in many of Burns's autobiographical poems that poignantly describe the suffering inflicted by conventional morality on natural deeds of love. The concept of vice as a virtue carried to excess was difficult for him to comprehend when the virtue was love and when others of his acquaintance seemingly enjoyed the pleasures without concomitant pains. Nevertheless, his overall attitude was remarkably consistent in that he not only fulfilled his obligations of manhood but also assumed all the parental responsibilities that his encompassing affections and limited financial means could provide. The pathos tinged with humor in poems concerning his own difficulties with unplanned parenthood no doubt reveals his mixed reactions. Probably the best illustration occurs in **"A Poet's Welcome to His Love-Begotten Daughter,"** which expresses his great delight upon first becoming an illegitimate father. Assuring his child by Elizabeth Paton that she is just as welcome as though she had been invited, he addresses her as

> Sweet fruit o' monie a merry dint,
> My funny toil is no a' tint:
> Tho' thou cam to the warl' asklent,
>   Which fools may scoff at,
> In my last plack thy part's be in't
>   The better half o't.

Not even the pains attendant on illegitimacy could diminish the swaggering bravado he assumes in a few of his poems celebrating propagation of bastards. One reason for such boasting on his part was undoubtedly the private masculine audience to whom such poems were initially addressed. Furthermore, his defiance of ecclesiastical authorities, who in some cases had been no better than he, for the penance and fine they imposed upon him could best be expressed with mocking raillery. Though in **"A Poet's Welcome to His Love-Begotten Daughter"** he merely disclaims any objection to being called "fornicator," he boldly asserts his right to that distinction in **"The**

Fornicator" of *The Merry Muses*. That Burns sincerely believed he had been made to suffer excessively is clear from his repeated comparison of himself to Biblical "men of God," who achieved ultimate salvation despite rather cavalier attitudes toward the seventh commandment. King David and King Solomon, both famous as poets and adulterers, provided him with choice illustrations of sexual energy as the true manifestation of vitality. In **"Reply to a Trimming Epistle Received from a Tailor,"** a devil-may-care poem regarding Burns's own ill repute, the poet argues that even though he may give women's "wames a random pouse," the manly sport of fornication should not call down great abuse from men who admire King David as one of the "lang-syne saunts." Burns then concludes with a fanciful tale, the true index of his indignation, about how he made fools of the Kirk Session that assessed punishment for his transgression. According to this account, the defendant candidly admitted he would never be any better unless he were gelded; and the minister, perhaps on the analogy that an offending eye ought to be plucked out, immediately endorsed amputation of whatever proved to be his "sp'ritual foe." But instead Burns facetiously recommended putting the offending part under the guidance of the lass—a suggestion that pleased the Session "warst of a'" and ended the interview.

The autobiographical poem that even the most devoted followers of Burns sometimes find difficult to justify is the **"Epistle to John Rankine,"** with its elaborate metaphor of game-poaching. First must be remembered, however, the character of the individual for whose enjoyment it was originally intended. The opening lines of the **"Epistle"** characterize its recipient as "rough, rude, ready-witted Rankine," a man apparently well known for his rowdy festivities, stories, sprees, and exposés of hypocritical clergymen. Hence the principal anecdote was especially appropriate. Then too, the tradition of witty comparisons was so well established in Scottish vernacular poetry that Burns's analogy of poaching and promiscuous lovemaking would not have appeared so derogatory to the woman as it may seem today. As Burns put it,

> 'Twas ae night lately, in my fun,
> I gaed a rovin wi' the gun,
> An' brought a paitrick to the grun'—
>   A bonie hen;
> And, as the twilight was begun,
>   Thought nane wad ken.

Indeed many of Burns's poems employ metaphors, such as ploughing, threshing, playing the fiddle, filling the bowl, and shooting wild birds, that were common in the Scottish tradition long before he used them. In **"The Bonie Moor-Hen,"** to cite another example, he tells of a fair game bird that had long eluded hunters until she was finally taken by a young man with a brass firelock that dazzled her eyes. Thus in the poem addressed to Rankine the implied comparison of his affair with Elizabeth Paton, the servant girl who bore his first child, to shooting down a partridge that did not rightfully belong to him and consequently having to pay a guinea's fine in the Poacher-Court (Kirk Session) ought to be regarded as a clever and natural treatment of the subject. If it reveals a sportive flippancy toward the begetting of bastards, it is nevertheless distinct from mere locker-room braggadocio. By connecting two of the most primitive survival drives in man—hunting for food and gratifying the sexual impulse—it atavistically reveals a basic masculine desire to make a sportive pleasure of necessity.

Nevertheless, Burns's depiction of young girls who have unwisely yielded to the rapture of love shows highly sympathetic insight, sometimes mixed with restrained masculine humor, into their various plights. Portraying them without reproach, ridicule, or sentimentality, he accepts their condition as an unfortunate though natural consequence of love. The "sleepy bit lassie" in **"The Tailor Fell Thro' the Bed"** naïvely thought the tailor could do her no harm, and indeed he gave her such satisfaction that now she longs for his return. Slightly graver complications have ensued for the girl in **"Jumpin John."** Despite her parents' warning, she yielded only to discover her folly; yet the second stanza implies that because of her excellent dowry and "bonie black e'e" the lad who beguiled her may yet decide to marry her. Less bright are the hopes of the girl in **"To the Weaver's Gin Ye Go,"** who laments the loss of her happiness for granting more than her heart to a weaver lad. Though reluctant to tell what occurred, she now fears that information will soon become increasingly obvious to everyone. In a similar plight is the unfortunate lass in **"Robin Shure in Hairst,"** who has discovered how false her Robin's promises were—he has not provided for her even during pregnancy. But the subtlest and perhaps most appealing characterization of such a girl appears in the first set of lyrics entitled **"Duncan Gray."** Whereas her friends can still enjoy themselves, she now has the cares of unintentional motherhood, which she with half-hearted jocularity blames on the bad girthing. While she and Duncan were riding a horse on Lammas night, she recalls, the girthing broke, and one fall followed another. Now she wistfully hopes that Duncan will keep his oath so that all (including the bad girthing) may be rectified. Also from the feminine point of view, **"The Rantin Dog, the Daddie o't"** expresses the anxieties of an unwed, expectant mother who seeks assurance that Rob, the rollicking father of her child, will assume his paternal obligations. Quite understandably she finds it difficult to joke about her very serious plight, and adding to the embarrassment is her realization that she has taken in earnest what had only been poked in fun.

Burns's songs about courtship are also rich in portraits of charming young girls who, tempering good humor with common sense, know what they want and cleverly overcome obstacles to their goals. An outstanding example is the lass in **"O, Whistle an' I'll Come to Ye, My Lad."** Since there seems to be parental objection to her lover, she gives him explicit instructions on how to reach her without letting anyone else know. And though she wants him to ignore her publicly, she nevertheless insists that he is not to court another, even in jest, for fear he may accidentally be enticed away. In **"Last May a Braw Wooer"** a girl not so completely in control of the situation

pretends to be virtually inaccessible and, to her dismay, almost loses the young man to a rival. With cunning, however, she proceeds to win him back and reveals her dissembling nature even in her public reasons for marrying him—not for her own sake but, ironically, just "to preserve the poor body in life." Another song, **"O, for Ane-and-Twenty, Tam,"** expresses the view of a minor heiress who has decided on her husband but is obliged temporarily to wait. Her inheritance seems to depend upon her family's consent to the marriage; yet she is determined to have both Tam, whom they do not endorse, and the inheritance if he will just wait three years until she comes of age. Especially winsome is the maiden in **"I'm O'er Young to Marry Yet,"** who pleads with her suitor that at her tender age and as her mother's only child she is psychologically unprepared for marriage. But unwilling to reject his proposal completely, she suggests that should he come again next summer she will be older and perhaps ready to reconsider.

Timidity in men, on the other hand, is a topic rarely mentioned by Burns. Significantly, in his gallery of lovers the traditionally humorous bashful young men are almost nonexistent. He did, however, compose to the tune of "The Bashful Lover" lyrics entitled **"On a Bank of Flowers,"** portraying a lad who is shy only at first. Having chanced upon lightly clad Nelly asleep among summer flowers, Willie begins by merely gazing, wishing, then fearing, and blushing. When Nelly awakes and sees him, she flees in terror; yet Willie, presumably having overcome his initial hesitancy, overtakes her in the woods.

The most despicable variety of courtship in Burns's view was that which hypocritically aimed at marriage for money, and he was particularly scornful of men offering themselves as marketable commodities. **"There's a Youth in This City"** pokes fun at a handsome, elegantly attired young man in search of a wealthy girl to marry. Several prospects with commendable fortunes are eager to have him, but actually he loves none of them so much as himself. A thoroughly cynical attitude toward the transience of feminine beauty is satirized in the song **"A Lass wi' a Tocher,"** in which a man extols woman's wealth as her only enduring attraction. Without denying the witchcraft of youthful beauty, he brazenly expresses his preference for a lass with "acres o' charms." The girl in **"My Tocher's the Jewel"** sees through the pretended love of just such a man. Though he has praised her beauty and her family, she shrewdly understands that her greatest appeal for him is her dowry and therefore bids him try his fortune elsewhere. Of course, shallow-hearted girls may also prefer silver to love. Meg o' the Mill, in the second set of lyrics by that title, foolishly jilts a desirable miller for a repulsive but rich laird. In all these instances, as in Burns's poems of social protest, wealth is seen to be a corrupting influence.

Comedy of a more playful sort is produced by refining the natural instinct of courtship into sophisticated skill—such as the fine art of seduction. In **"Extempore to Gavin Hamilton,"** a poem that strips the ornamental tinsel from many seemingly important matters and shows them for what they are—"naething"—Burns relates how he applied the same technique to a female Whig. Her initial refusal to have faith in a poet, as well as his exalted reference to "Her Whigship," arouses our antipathy toward a pretentious woman who deserves to be not only corrected but leveled. The poet's adroitness in the game of "love for love's sake" is so great that, despite her inevitable objections while they "grew lovingly big," he taught her "her terrors were—naething." Burns concludes:

> Her Whigship was wonderful pleased,
>   But charmingly tickled wi' ae thing;
> Her fingers I lovingly squeezed,
>   And kissed her, and promised her—naething.

Whatever the consequences, seduction might be regarded as a challenging sport in which each of the two individuals, while abiding by the rules of the game, fulfills his prescribed part.

By transposing the customary roles of male and female, as Thurber has often done in our day, Burns provided another rich source of the comic, well exemplified in **"Wha Is That at My Bower Door."** In the original song the woman is blatantly aggressive whereas the man is meekly compliant. In Burns's version, the woman, though less conniving, is still manipulator of the action and puts up only token resistance to letting her lover, Findlay, in. He, on the other hand, understands his obligations: he must argue until she deludes herself into thinking that, against her better judgment, his rhetoric has overwhelmed her. These pretenses are clear from the dialogue; the girl introduces in conditional clauses exactly what she ought to fear while Findlay counters with his assurance that each condition will be fulfilled. When he promises to abide by her last stipulation—never to tell what may transpire in her bower—there is no longer any need for him to remain outside. By superficially maintaining her pretenses, however, the girl preserves her self-respect—at least in her own opinion.

Burns was also interested in burlesquing artificial conventions of courtship in his second set of lyrics entitled **"Duncan Gray."** When he sent the words of this song to George Thomson, he observed that the melody "precludes sentiment" and that "the ludicrous is its ruling feature." Both Meg, with the proud disdain of a courtly lady, and Duncan, with his lachrymose despair verging on suicide, so overplay their roles that they achieve the comedy of exaggeration. Excessive sentimentality in Duncan, however, produces its own reaction, for he banishes affectation by realizing the absurdity of dying for "a haughty hizzie." As he recovers his health, Meg, discovering how much his love had meant to her, grows ill pining for him. The fact that Duncan is "a lad o' grace," as well as a shrewd psychologist trained in Scottish common sense philosophy, permits all to turn out well. Pitying Meg, who suffers as he himself once languished, he demonstrates his true worth by magnanimously refusing to cause her death. The guarded manner in which he accepts her indicates he has learned a very practical lesson in amatory psychology: nothing is quite so attractive as casual indifference.

In other instances Burns used the playful treatment of love to shatter some of mankind's treasured illusions. **"I Murder Hate by Field or Flood"** mocks exalted, unrealistic notions of heroic death for noble causes. Instead of endorsing the usual demands of military heroism, whereby a soldier kills his fellow man, the poet would much rather spend his blood in "Life-giving wars of Venus," rather "make one more / Than be the death of twenty." Somewhat more seriously, he maintains the same idea in a poem entitled **"Nature's Law"**:

> Let other heroes boast their scars,
>   The marks o' sturt and strife,
> But other poets sing of wars,
>   The plagues o' human life!
> Shame fa' the fun: wi' sword and gun
>   To slap mankind like lumber!
> I sing his name and nobler fame
>   Wha multiplies our number.

Perhaps because of its limited range of possibilities, Burns rarely approached the comical aspects of married love with the geniality and compassion required of true humor. In writing of domestic situations, he easily turned from humor to satire, and it should not be surprising that the preponderance of marriage poems are, by their very nature, sharp, succinct, and often epigrammatic. This antipathy toward the marital state, revealed with varying degrees of aggressiveness in the majority of his poems treating comic love, is exactly what one should expect. According to Freud's analysis, no institution in our society has been more carefully guarded by accepted morality or more vulnerable to attack than the connubial relationship. The prevalence of cynical jokes deriding wedlock as bedlock illustrates the unconscious antagonism which men in particular feel toward rigid suppression of sexual liberty. Since this hostility can be temporarily freed from the unconscious by means of some clever witticism—a "pleasure premium," that enables us to laugh at what we revere—tendentious wit aimed at marriage momentarily overcomes whatever inhibitive power exists and permits us to enjoy a release of aggression, often quite contrary to what our sober thoughts might recommend. Burns's practice would indeed tend to support Freud's theory. Regarding marriage as a mixed blessing, he was not able, as he admits in **"Yestreen I Had a Pint o' Wine,"** to resign himself wholeheartedly to its restraints. Yet his ability to identify imaginatively with either opponent in marital warfare not only relieved him of acerbity but permitted him, usually with the verbal economy of an excellent raconteur, to turn even the worst situation into a good joke.

One group of his poems about marriage emphasizes the change which a husband feels has occurred in his wife since their wedding. Stanza vi of **"Extempore to Gavin Hamilton"** cogently points out how during courtship the lover sparkles and glows when "Approaching his bonie bit gay thing," but after the irrevocable ceremony he learns he has acquired a dressed-up "naething." Sometimes a disenchanted husband, as in **"The Weary Pund o' Tow,"** becomes so embittered with a lazy, tippling wife that, after her death, he vows to hang himself rather than marry again. The unfortunate man in **"O, Ay My Wife She Dang Me"** may have suffered even more; yet there is something admirably winning about his resignation to fate. Though the peace and rest he anticipated in marriage were never realized, at least he has the consolation of knowing that, after suffering "pains o' hell" on earth, he is assured of bliss above. The husband in the justly admired **"Whistle o'er the Lave o't"** has also had his hopes shattered, but through an amazing humor born of suffering he seems to be chuckling while cataloguing his woes. All that he had associated with Maggie before the wedding has now changed to its antithesis, and but for fear Maggie would find out, he would even name the one he wishes were in her grave. Implying far more than he expresses, he refrains from elaborating on each unpleasantness and turns it into jest by whistling about what cannot be altered. No doubt the evasive and suggestive quality that makes him a fascinating conversationalist also renders him a most exasperating husband to a shrew. All these cited poems, as well as others, demonstrate how painfully husbands learn that married love is subject to mutability.

A considerable number of marriage poems are concerned primarily with exposing and ridiculing an intolerable wife. In so doing, they also reveal the curious relationship between the shortcomings of one spouse and the weaknesses of the other. For example, in **"The Tyrant Wife,"** which was published also under the title of **"The Henpecked Husband,"** Burns expresses the belief that a shrew is partially the fault of a spineless, fearful husband who deserves reproach rather than pity. The anomalous situation would never occur if the husband of such a woman wisely subdued her by breaking either her spirit or her heart. The efficacy of such action is demonstrated in **"She Play'd the Loon or She Was Married,"** in which the man expresses doubt concerning his wanton wife's ability to behave unless she is controlled as a child ought to be ruled—namely, by the rod. Perhaps the only suffering husband who genuinely elicits our pity, however, is the one in **"Kellyburn Braes."** There the unfortunate man yields his termagant wife to the devil, who in turn discovers her to be more than a match for him and his demons. Upon returning the shrew to her husband, the devil admits that he had never been truly in hell until he acquired a wife.

Among several poems that disparage the husband without particularly ennobling the wife, some make light of the essentially serious affliction of impotence in advanced age. The young woman in **"What Can a Young Lassie"** temporarily evokes our sympathy with complaints about her peevish, jealous old husband until she reveals her plan to torment him to death and then use his "auld brass" to buy herself a "new pan." The subject receives an almost poignant treatment in **"The Deuk's Dang o'er My Daddie,"** where acrid hostility between the lusty wife and her incapable spouse is mixed with remembrance of happier bygone days and nights. Two of Burns's songs deal with an equally old marital jest, cuckoldry, but they do so in a manner characteristic of his humor. The women of **"O, An Ye Were Dead, Guidman"** and **"The Cooper o' Cuddy"** are openly and defiantly committing adultery with their lovers while their husbands do nothing but resign themselves to their proverbial horns. Though some compassion is naturally directed toward the poor, helpless cuckolds, the comic pleasure derived from these two lyrics stems less from a debasement of the husbands than from our fascination with the brazen, resolute determination of the hussies to satisfy their desires.

Burns could hardly write of love without relating it humorously to another of his chief delights, John Barleycorn, which he recognized as a true, though unscrupulous, liberator of man's psychic energy. In some instances alcohol could demean its imbiber to such a ludicrous state that he became excellent material for mordantly satirical, aggressive comedy. Especially when associated with Calvinistic moral attitudes, as in **"Holy Willie's Prayer,"** tippling served to accentuate what Burns considered the irreconcilability of canon law with man's instinctive nature. Willie's anthropomorphic concept of God—capriciously unjust, vindictive, and incapable of love—reveals the speaker himself. Since his sexual drive is wholly identified with proscribed pleasure, what Burns would have called human love can never be anything but lust in Willie Fisher, who ironically justifies his own promiscuity by pleading drunkenness. Also in **"The Holy Fair"** a perversion of what ought to be the celebration of divine love in a communion service is allied with alcohol and lechery. Superstition and hypocrisy in the preaching tent combined with careless fun in an adjacent tavern justify the poet's attack on the Scottish Kirk—a corruption of faith that ideally should be characterized by good deeds, sincerity, and love. Hence he comments ironically on the man who, by letting his hand wander over the bosom of his lass during a sermon, makes a mockery of both religion and human love. And as the scene moves to the tavern, he portrays a predominant mood of lechery whereby liquor alters Venus Uranus into a lusty pandemic lass. Thus what began with a hardhearted religion leads, through the stimulation of drink, to a parody of love—"houghmagandie."

With less satire and far greater humor, Burns treats the bibulous freeing of emotion more sympathetically in **"Tam o' Shanter."** Just as good Scotch drink presumably released Burns's thoughts and feelings for poetical composition, so too it heightens Tam's amiability toward both Souter Johnie and the landlady, causing him to postpone his return to a hostile, sullen wife. Unfortunately it later contributes to his admiration for an attractive witch dancing lustily in a sark so short that it barely covers, and as a result Tam is momentarily deprived of rational control. Quite unconsciously he roars out the ingenuous praise that almost undoes him. With mock-serious didacticism, Burns in the conclusion warns that the path leading from alcohol to lecherous contemplation often culminates in disaster. The negative moral lesson is, of course, a variant of the admonition in a classic naughty story pertinent to mice and ardent men. Because Tam loses his head to drink and a "cutty sark," his mare is bereft of her tail.

An entirely different attitude toward the combination of love and alcohol is found in **"The Jolly Beggars,"** which in some manuscripts bore the title **"Love and Liberty."** The beggars, who have a simple, intuitively acute perception of man's nature, possess no inhibitions whatever and accept the basic instincts without any concern for what is ordinarily called ethical standards. What might in polite society be condemned as obscene is from their point of view perfectly normal. Indeed the comedy of this cantata, which is universally considered Burns's masterpiece, verges on what Freud analyzed as the naïvely comical—the effect often produced in adult listeners by the spontaneous, forthright comments of children. The poet's sympathy with (and at times even undisguised envy of) a segment of humanity usually thought beneath contempt is just as sincere as the beggars' childlike, irrepressible, and irresistibly appealing candor. Had these uninhibited outcasts been deliberately attacking institutions of the society which they rejected, then some of their satirical jibes might be considered tendentious wit: the reader would have to assume that through enticement of comic pleasure they were trying to elicit his hostility against principles which he had been conditioned to respect unquestioningly, despite an unconscious dislike. And there are indeed occasional touches of such wit in their oblique comments on marriage, respectability, legality, and religion, particularly in the Merry Andrew's song and the final chorus:

A fig for those by law protected!
  Liberty's a glorious feast,
Courts for cowards were erected,
  Churches built to please the priest!

Yet these bits of aggression are casually tossed off at inhabitants of a world having little contact with theirs. The supremely winning quality of the beggars is their belief in both love and liberty not in the negative sense of revolt against restraint but rather as positive virtues. The old soldier and his doxy, both of whom enjoy their present indulgence in love and drink rather than the exploits of their former military careers; the professional Merry Andrew who, unlike the hypocritical fool, calls himself what he is; the female pickpocket whose Highland lover died on the gallows for defiance of Lowland laws; the small fiddler who proposes cohabitation with the pickpocket but has only brief enjoyment of her; the bold tinker who offers himself to the same "unblushing fair"; the bard who, resigning himself to the loss of one mistress because he has two others left, sings in praise of free love and freely flowing drink—all reveal in an unsophisticated way their refusal to be duped by the sham, hypocritical cant of society.

There is something wonderfully refreshing, as Burns himself acknowledged in his commonplace book, about associating with such people. Though their actual deeds may be no better than those of many ostensibly respectable friends, the beggars' mental attitude is more appealing because of its honesty, sincerity, and total lack of pretension. They spontaneously express by both precept and example what all of us know intuitively but have been taught to renounce. The occasional intrusion of artificial

diction on their unaffected vernacular, to which many critics have objected, subtly reminds us of conventional society's futile attempt to overlay and encroach upon their natures; yet the beggars remain essentially loyal to all that is natural in humanity. They have indeed achieved the "happy state" described in one of Burns's favorite quotations: ". . . when souls each other draw, / When love is liberty, and nature law" (Pope's "Eloïsa to Abelard," ll. 91-92). Especially when we compare the beggars' adherence to their own code of behavior with the contrasting failure of society to abide by its ethical standards, we realize the supreme humor with which the poet conceived his work.

There were inevitably nineteenth-century critics who let Burns's personal frailties and artistic improprieties prejudice their estimates of his achievement. Yet among the most objectively perceptive, his extraordinary ability to fuse the seemingly heterogeneous elements of love and comedy by means of uniquely incisive humor did not go wholly unnoticed. Lamb, who was quick to recognize in Burns some qualities he himself possessed, observed "a jocular pathos, which makes one feel in laughter." After reading a collection of Burns's unpublished letters, Byron remarked: "What an antithetical mind!—tenderness, roughness—delicacy, coarseness—sentiment, sensuality—soaring and grovelling, dirt and deity—all mixed up in that one compound of inspired clay!" Carlyle, equally aware of these paradoxes, especially stressed "the tenderness, the playful pathos" and shrewdly perceived that the principle of love which characterized Burns's poetry "occasionally manifests itself in the shape of Humour." Aside from the drollery associated with caricature, Carlyle claimed for Burns "in his sunny moods, a full buoyant flood of mirth" related to his ability to be a "brother and often playmate to all Nature." To emphasize this extraordinary ability Carlyle especially cited those poems expressing a fellow feeling with animals, presumably because mice, mares, and sheep would seem the most difficult creatures with whom a love poet could imaginatively identify himself. And while some genteel critics regarded his subject matter as crudely unpoetical, Matthew Arnold thought Burns had provided a genuine criticism of life, ironic though it was. Despite a revulsion from "Scotch drink, Scotch religion, and Scotch manners," Arnold stressed the "overwhelming sense of the pathos of things" and singled out for illustration of particular merit those works treating love humorously. If such poems lacked the requisite high seriousness that excluded their author from the Victorian Valhalla of poetical heroism, it was because Burns (like Chaucer, with whom Arnold repeatedly compared him) believed that many serious observations on life could be uttered more effectively in jest than in grave solemnity.

Richard Wilbur (essay date 1968)

SOURCE: "Explaining the Obvious," in *Responses: Prose Pieces, 1953-1976*, Harcourt & Company, 1976, pp. 139-45.

[*Wilbur is an American poet respected for the craftsman-*

Daiches praises Burns's satires and verse letters:

Burns's greatest poetic achievement is his satires. These show a command of a greater variety of poetic skills, a subtler and more complex use of the medium of poetry, than any other kind of poetry he wrote. . . . Another important group are his verse letters. This is not a kind of poetry that has ever been popular in England. But in Scotland it had been a tradition since the beginning of the eighteenth century, and Burns learned of the tradition from Ramsay. It represented a handling of language peculiarly suited to his genius, counterpointing the formal and the colloquial, moving out from the carefully localised picture of the poet in a specific time and place to his reflexions as they arise naturally from the given situation to a progressively widening circle of comment that culminates in a series of clinching epigrams before the poet returns to himself and his correspondent to sign off in an adroitly turned conclusion. These verse letters show remarkable skill in combining a colloquial ease with a formal pattern in such a way that each brings out new significance in the other.

David Daiches, in More Literary Essays, *University of Chicago Press, 1968.*

ship and elegance of his verse. He employs formal poetic structures and smoothly flowing language as a response to disorder and chaos in modern life. In the following essay, first published in The New York Times Book Review *in 1968, Wilbur examines the structure and tone of Burns's poem, "A Red, Red Rose."*]

O My Luve's like a red, red rose,
    That's newly sprung in June;
O My Luve's like the melodie
    That's sweetly played in tune.

As fair art thou, my bonnie lass,
    So deep in luve am I;
And I will luve thee still, my dear,
    Till a' the seas gang dry.

Till a' the seas gang dry, my dear,
    And the rocks melt wi' the sun:
O I will luve thee still, my dear,
    While the sands o' life shall run.

And fare thee weel, my only luve,
    And fare thee weel awhile!
And I will come again, my luve,
    Though it were ten thousand mile.

Some months ago a professor friend, who was putting together a textbook on explication, invited me to take a poem of my own choosing and attempt a model commentary on it. I began, of course, by trying to think of something knotty about which to be clever, but the lines from Burns which I have quoted, and which are often in my mind, kept proposing themselves. I am fond of **"A Red, Red Rose,"** and what we like, we like to talk about. Was

there, however, anything much to be said about a poem so admirably simple? My curiosity obliged me to write what follows.

The first four lines of Burns's poem are often quoted as examples of simile, and the remaining quatrains could reasonably be searched, in a beginners' English class, for such other rhetorical devices as hyperbole. Except for these illustrative uses, however, the poem does not seem to invite analysis. What is being asserted is very plain; a man is declaring his deep and lasting love for a woman; and one would not listen straight-faced to any interpretation which sought, for example, to discover religious allegory in the poem's "rose symbolism" or "end-of-the-world motif."

The individual words of the poem present no difficulties or ambiguities, and there is no actual need of footnotes to tell us that "gang" and "weel" are Scots dialect words for "go" and "well." I suppose that some reader might waver between two understandings of lines 5 and 6—do they mean "My love is proportional to your beauty" or "You are as fair, and I as enamored, as the foregoing would suggest"?—but the uncertainty would not derail his reading of the whole.

There is really no end to what need not be said about this poem, and, of course, it is one mark of the good critic that he abstains from busywork. If we encountered the phrase "all Hell broke loose" in a poem by T. S. Eliot, we would be well advised to trace it back as far as "Paradise Lost," with a view to applying Milton's adjacent lines and general thought to the Eliot passage. But if we found the same phrase in a doggerel poem by Robert W. Service, we would presumably have the sense to forget about Milton, and to remember that the expression in question is well established in offhand, everyday speech.

A similar discrimination is called for in deciding how much to make of the supposed echoes and borrowings in this little Burns poem. The words "Till a' the seas gang dry" might legitimately put us in mind of Isaiah's Jehovah, who thunders, "Behold, at my rebuke I dry up the sea," or of this sort of thing from Revelation: "And I saw a new heaven and a new earth: for the first heaven and the first earth are passed away; and the sea is no more."

But the good likelihood that such passages underlie Burns's line need not be dwelt upon. The poem has precious little to do with Isaiah or John, and it would be foolishly pedantic to leave the amorous preserve of Burns's little song for the domain of prophecy. The most we should say of "Till a' the seas gang dry" is that, in a Bible-quoting age and a Calvinist culture, it was a ready and vivid way of saying "Indefinitely," and that in any age it is intelligible without recourse to Scripture.

Burns's editors tell us that **"A Red, Red Rose"** also contains borrowings, of a more provable kind, from Scottish folk songs. This is not surprising, since at the time of the poem's composition Burns was engaged in gathering and editing the traditional songs of his countrymen. Do we need to know the folk sources on which Burns drew? Probably not. It might somewhat improve our feeling for the convention in which Burns was writing if we saw a few of his words in their original settings; but those settings, those contexts, would be unlikely to add anything specific to our understanding of his straightforward utterance here. Self-evidently, **"A Red, Red Rose"** is an autonomous work, the articulate gesture of one imagination, and its echoes enforce no excursions.

Or that is how it strikes me and most people. But supposing there were some reader unable to prove the unity of the poem on his pulses, someone who saw it instead as a loose sheaf or anthology of pretty lines—could one hope to change his mind for him? The attempt would best begin, I should think, with an apparent concession: the implicit dramatic situation of the poem *can* seem inconsistent or uncertain. In the first four lines, Burns's lover is praising his love in the third person, and to nobody in particular; she does not seem in any sense to be "there." In the second and third quatrains, however, repeated assurances of fidelity are directed to the beloved, who now turns up in the second person. Should one imagine her as present, or merely as present to mind? Is she being addressed, or evoked? The question can be difficult to decide, and the "fare thee weel" of the last stanza can leave one still in doubts. If this is a good-bye poem, spoken to a woman, is not the fact of parting unconscionably delayed? Or if the poem is not to be read as arising from an implicit "scene," may one not condemn the thirteenth line as abrupt and opportunistic, a way of getting a little more hyperbolic mileage out of the material?

Such questions and charges cannot be answered with that air of scientific demonstration to which explication so often aspires; but a reasonable argument for the poem's coherent shape can be made on two grounds, the rhetorical and the psychological. George Gascoigne once said that when praising a lady the poet should "neither praise her chrystal eye nor her cherry lip, etc.," these notions being trite and obvious; he should, rather, find some means whereby his pen might "walk in the superlative degree." Burns's first quatrain consists of comparisons that are essentially stale poetic compliments, *trita et obvia,* but which are freshened and rendered "sincere" by colloquial simplicity and the implications of dialect. The effect is of a pastoral eloquence, and this eloquence, warming to itself, proceeds in the remainder to speak of love not in roses and melodies but in brave hyperboles which stop just short of eternity and infinity. The peak of excitement comes in lines 8 and 9, where the poet's first bold figure is raptly or vauntingly repeated, with one stanza sailing on into the next; lines 12 and 16 then continue and exhaust the hyperbolic attack. What we seem to have, then, is a poem that moves from one rhetoric to another, a flight of words that begins on the ground of conventional simile and soars into excessive affirmations which, though not without literary precedent, here seem spontaneous. The shape of the poem can be described as the escape of a fervent imagination into its own language, and anyone may prove this in a moment by reading the poem aloud, *con amore.*

There is also another and congruent development in the poems as I read it, and that is the movement of the thought away from the nominal subject. Burns's first stanza may be conventional compliment, but it has to do with the young lady, and argues a concentration of the poet's thought upon the definition of her beauty. From line 6 onward, however, that subject has been left behind; "my dear" becomes almost perfunctory, and in the most striking and exultant passages of the poem what the poet celebrates is the stamina of his own feeling. All of the magnitudes of the poem belong, not to the lady, but to the lover's devotion. It may be argued that love-songs, if they are to be fresh, cannot forever be dealing foursquare with the addressee, but must come at her with some inventive obliquity. But whereas such a song as Byron's "There Be None of Beauty's Daughters" (which I recommend for general comparison) withdraws from its lady into the elaboration of a simile, and then converts all into praise of her at the close, Burns's poem forsakes the lady to glory in Love itself, and does not really return. We are dealing, in other words, with romantic love, in which the beloved is a means to high emotion, and physical separation can serve as a stimulant to ideal passion. Once this is recognized, once we see that the emotion of the poem is self-enchanted and entails a spiritual remove, the presence or absence of the lady becomes unimportant, and the idea of parting seems less the occasion of feeling than an expression of it.

It is oddly difficult to write about romantic love without inclining to denounce or ridicule it; we have our reservations about that emotional economy even in the present age, when a version of romantic of love is celebrated by all media, high or low, and the speeches of Friar Laurence are impatiently cut in every production of *Romeo.* We still understand when La Rochefoucauld says, "There are some people so full of themselves, that when they are in love, they find means to be occupied with their passion, without being so with the person they love." Molière's Alceste still amuses us by telling Célimène that he could wish her wretched, friendless, and obscure, so that he then might raise her from the dust and

> proudly prove
> The purity and vastness of my love.

We join Célimène in laughing at a lover who can so separate "his love" from its presumptive object as to imagine exalting the one at the cost of the other's suffering. We can also be persuaded by W. H. Auden's criticism of romantic love in his poem "As I Walked Out One Evening." The "I" of Auden's poem overhears a lover making large promises which are surely reminiscent of Burns:

> I'll love you, dear, I'll love you
>   Till China and Africa meet,
> And the river jumps over the mountain
>   And the salmon sing in the street.
>
> I'll love you till the ocean
>   Is folded and hung up to dry,

And the seven stars go squawking
  Like geese about the sky . . .

The poem then proceeds to rebut these lines, saying that the human heart is too selfish and perverse to make such promises in good faith, and that the one real hope lies in striving, despite all weakness, to

          love your crooked neighbor
With your crooked heart.

How far does Burns's poem expose itself to that kind of correction? Not at all. His poem is not a play, within which the consequences of romantic feeling can be tested in action; it is an effusion *in vacuo*. Nor is Burns's poem an argument or meditation, as Auden's essentially is. It is a song. Like all true songs, it is simple and relaxed in its language, allowing only so much point or verbal brilliance per line; it is full of repetitions of word and idea; its grammatical divisions coincide with the line endings; it is perfectly suited to being set and sung, and though beautiful in itself could profit by the complement; finally, it has one thought or mood, which is developed to full intensity. While some poems—the Auden poem just cited, for one—make artful use of song techniques for the projection of complex and contradictory matter, the song in pure form is an unqualified cry. A cry does not argue with itself or with us; nor we with it. We do not question the resentment of the still-charmed lover in Campion's "When Thou Must Home," or the right of D'Urfey's "Roaring Boy" to roar; **"A Red, Red Rose"** is one state of soul handsomely vented, and that is all we ask. The emotions of song are privileged.

Robert T. Fitzhugh (essay date 1970)

SOURCE: "Poet: Kilmarnock Edition," in *Robert Burns: The Man and the Poet; A Round, Unvarnished Account,* Houghton Mifflin Co., 1970, pp. 107-23.

[*In this excerpt, Fitzhugh discusses several poems included in Burns's 1786 collection,* Poems Chiefly in the Scottish Dialect.]

Poems Chiefly in the Scottish Dialect, by Robert Burns, Kilmarnock, 1786, was a well-printed paper-bound volume of 240 pages, priced at three shillings. Burns and his friends had gathered over 300 subscriptions, enough to defray expenses, before printing began. In his original proposal to his subscribers, Burns had offered only Scotch poems, but he finally included half a dozen melancholy and moralizing English pieces apparently to increase the volume's appeal. And, it should be noted, although the subscribers and the presumed audience were to be almost entirely local, or at least Scottish, Burns added a liberal glossary of his Scots vocabulary. The 612 copies brought in £90, of which the printer's bill took £34/3/—; but Burns says that he cleared only £20. Perhaps the difference is accounted for partly by the £9 passage money for Jamaica which he paid down, and may have lost. His settlement with Betty Paton took a substantial amount, and he must

have given some to the family at Mossgiel. Burns cannot have had much in his pocket when he set out for Edinburgh.

The Kilmarnock volume made Burns famous at once. Review notices appeared promptly in Edinburgh and London. But Burns withheld from his book, or wrote within three months of its appearance, enough poems and songs to make another volume of the same size and quality. Some of this poetry, and a few songs, he added to his Edinburgh edition of April, 1787, but most of the poetry he never published at all. Later he sent the bulk of the songs to James Johnson and George Thomson for their collections. Of the unpublished poetry, some was too personal to appear publicly (**"A Poet's Welcome"**), or too likely to provoke recrimination (the epistle to John M'Math), or too broad (**"The Court of Equity"**), or even downright bawdy (**"The Fornicator"**).

Of the poems written by November, 1786, . . . there are five of limited interest—three moralizing and melancholy pieces (**"Despondency"**, **"Lament,"** and **"To Ruin"**), and two parochial poems that require heavy annotation (**"Hallowe'en"** and **"The Ordination"**). The opening stanzas of **"Hallowe'en"** are promising, but the poem progresses to a detailed account of Ayrshire folk customs, and fails to transcend its particularities. **"The Ordination"** concerns a Kilmarnock parish quarrel over patronage.

A song, and two minor poems, of serious social comment, are readable enough, and contain memorable passages. The song, **"Man Was Made to Mourn,"** is a vigorous recital of human suffering and injustice, and the inequality of human reward, with the famous lines,

    Man's inhumanity to man
      Makes countless thousands mourn.

This song concludes, in the words of the aged protagonist,

    The poor, oppressèd, honest man
      Had never, sure, been born,
    Had there not been some recompense
      To comfort those that mourn!

    O Death! the poor man's dearest friend,
      The kindest and the best!
    Welcome the hour my agèd limbs
      Are laid with thee, at rest!
    The great, the wealthy fear thy blow,
      From pomp and pleasure torn;
    But, oh! a blest relief to those
      That weary-laden mourn!

Of the two minor poems, one is bitterly ironic, with a cumbersome explanatory heading:

  "Address of Beelzebub": To the Right Honorable the Earl of Breadalbane, President of the Right Honorable the Highland Society, which met on the 23rd of May last, at the *Shakespeare,* Covent Garden, to concert ways and means to frustrate the desires of five hundred Highlanders who, as the Society were informed by Mr. M'Kenzie of Applecross, were so audacious as to attempt an escape from their lawful lords and masters whose property they were, by emigrating from the lands of Mr. Macdonald of Glengary to the wilds of Canada, in search of that fantastic thing—Liberty.

In this Address, the Devil, writing from Hell, urges the lords and masters to "lay aside a' tender mercies," and not merely to distrain and rob such ungrateful and troublesome tenants,

> But smash them! crush them a' to spails [*chips*]
> An' rot the dyvors [*bankrupts*] i' the jails!
> The young dogs, swinge [*whip*] them to the labour:
> Let wark an' hunger make them sober!
> The hizzies [*girls*], if they're aughtlins fawsont [*at all good looking*]
> Let them in Drury Lane be lesson'd! [*as prostitutes*]
>
> An' if the wives an' dirty brats
> Come thiggin [*begging*] at your doors an' yetts [*gates*],
> Flaffin wi' duds [*flapping with vermin*] an' grey wi' beas' [*fleas*],
> Frightin awa your deuks an' geese,
> Get out a horsewhip or a jowler [*bulldog*],
> The langest thong, the fiercest growler,
> An' gar [*make*] the tattered gypsies pack [*beat it*]
> Wi' a' their bastards on their back!

The other poem, **"A Dedication to Gavin Hamilton, Esq."** like the Author's Preface to *Tristram Shandy* appears in the middle of the volume. It opens with some banter, and then proceeds to ironic sympathy. Hamilton, although he is "the poor man's friend in need, / The gentleman in word and deed," does not satisfy his orthodox neighbors because he is generous and kind merely from "carnal inclination" and not because he subscribes to proper Calvinist doctrine. Burns continues,

> Morality, thou deadly bane,
> Thy tens o' thousands thou hast slain!
> Vain is his hope, whase stay an' trust is
> In moral mercy, truth, and justice!
>
> No—stretch a point to catch a plack [*make money*].
> Abuse a brother to his back;
> Steal thro' the winnock [*window*] frae a whore,
> But point the rake that taks the door;
> Be to the poor like onie whunstane,
> And haud their noses to the grunstane;
> Ply ev'ry art o' legal thieving;
> No matter—stick to sound believing.

He adds a good deal more in the same mordant vein.

There are also ten light-hearted and felicitous poems, laced and graced with pungent observations, but all essentially *jeux d'esprit.* These poems give an idea of the vivacity and salty readiness which so delighted those who heard Burns speak. **"Scotch Drink"** celebrates whiskey and Scotland, and parodies Fergusson's "Caller [Fresh] Water," **"To a Haggis"** was written to amuse a gathering of Ayrshire friends, **"Adam Armour's Prayer"** is good-natured ridicule of his brother-in-law to be, **"Poor Mailie's Elegy"** pays further tribute to that immortal sheep, **"The Inventory"** presents a versified report to a tax gatherer, **"Epistle to a Young Friend"** gives "good advice" to Robert Aiken's (the tax gatherer's) son, **"Tam Samson's Elegy"** is rough joking on a good friend, **"The Brigs of Ayr"** has fun with municipal improvements pushed by Burns' friend John Ballantine, **"Lines on Meeting with Lord Daer"** is a bread and butter note celebrating a dinner, and **"Nature's Law"** bursts into joy on the birth of Jean's twins. . . .

It remains to comment on a few major poems so far unnoticed but written by November 1786. First, **"The Twa Dogs,"** which Burns used to open the Kilmarnock volume. Here, after a famous description of the two *dogs,* not merely speakers in the guise of dogs, Burns has them discuss their masters, and the rich and the poor, and the gentles and the cotters, all with admirable good sense and humor, and then lets them part without coming to conclusions, although simple life obviously comes off the better, and the gentles are shown up for the hollow-hearted wastrels they too often are. In the central speech, dog Luath, the ploughman's collie, answers dog Caesar, the aristocratic democrat who would just as soon make love to a mongrel, and who has remarked that "surely poor-folk maun [must] be wretches!" . . .

"The Auld Farmer's New-Year Morning Salutation to his Auld Mare, Maggie," shows Burns being kindly and warm without the sentimentality to which he was prone. He catches the old man's feeling for his work partner of many years, and he creates sure and clean the quality and tone of a farmer's life. Much of the old man's affection for Maggie, for example, comes from her having done good work on the farm, and from her having given him healthy colts to sell. Here, as in **"The Twa Dogs,"** the language, the feeling, the purpose, the illustrations are finely at one.

This is not true of **"The Cotter's Saturday Night,"** in which the style and the statement are often at odds, and the commentary seems intrusive and self-conscious rather than a natural out-growth of the narrative. What Burns says in **"The Cotter"** he says in Epistles and elsewhere—the simple and natural life is better than the artificial, love and friendship are life's richest rewards, the lower classes are the strength of the country, and Scotland for Aye. The poem, a projection of Burns' father and his household, idealizes the life of poverty, family affection, and honest work, and poor is he who denies the virtues it celebrates. The father's homecoming and the family gathering, the supper, and the Bible reading, are generally touching and right, but such lines as these jar the effect of stanza five:

The parents partial eye their hopeful years;
Anticipation forward points the view.

Stanzas nine and ten begin the self-conscious intrusions. And after stanza twelve, only the satiric seventeen is more than competent; and not a few stanzas seem contrived. Burns no doubt hoped to elevate the poem by introducing the manner of his admired English models, but the result is unfortunate.

And yet the poem is still widely admired, and properly so, for a reason neatly stated by Henley and Henderson. "Burns's verse falls naturally into two main divisions. One, and that the larger, appeals with persistency and force, on the strength of some broadly human qualities, to the world in general: for the reason that the world in general is rich in sentiment but lacks the literary sense. The other, being a notable and lasting contribution to literature, is the concern of comparatively few." Yet for the few, also, **"The Cotter"** certainly leaves its mark and makes its point, even while they are conscious of its defects.

Three of Burn's most famous poems help further to illustrate the remark quoted above, and all follow a similar pattern—a series of narrative-descriptive stanzas which lead up to a sententious conclusion. **"To a Louse"** is artistically by far the best, and by far the least popular. **"To a Mountain Daisy"** is generally agreed to be the weakest. But **"To a Mouse"** has always enjoyed high popularity, and critical esteem as well. The distress of the "wee, sleekit, cowrin, tim'rous beastie" is vivid and touching; and "the best laid schemes o' mice an' men gang aft agley," surely; but what of a mouse as a symbol for brotherhood? The general experience of man is otherwise. Who feels "social union" with a mouse? In this central symbolism the poem is artificial and contrived, and sentimental. And the self-pity of its conclusion is not appealing. But for the great majority who are "rich in sentiment but lack the literary sense," these remarks are beside the point. The poem moves them, and Burns was not writing for academic critics.

Professor Sir Walter Raleigh makes a shrewd comment to this same effect. "The Scottish people feel a hearty, instinctive, and just dislike for biographers of Burns. The life of Burns, full as it was of joy and generous impulse, full also of error, disappointment, and failure, makes a perfectly devised trap for the superior person. Almost everyone is superior to Robert Burns in some one point or other—in conjugal fidelity, in worldly prudence, or in social standing. Let him be careful to forget his advantages before he approaches this graveside, or his name will be added to the roll of the failures." True, and fair enough. But it could be wished that Sir Walter had added: The story of Burns is the more moving the more fully told, and the wonder of the man and his work the more deeply felt, the more completely it is understood. Romanticizing admirers no less than "superior persons" have too often made a monstrous caricature of Burns.

"To a Louse" seems a perfect poem. It opens briskly, it

sets a memorable scene, it tells a lively story, it maintains its tone of genial irony with a rich association of incident and image, and it moves quickly and surely to its conclusion, probably the most famous stanza Burns ever wrote. It may be remarked that one's feeling about a louse, and about the occasion, are entirely appropriate to the satiric purpose of the poem, in which not one figure or image is inept, not one line weak. And the theme is quintessential Burns—the absurdity of pretence, especially religious pretence. . . .

A stanza from the epistle to William Simpson makes an apt comment on **"The Vision."**

The Muse, nae poet ever fand [*found*] her,
Till by himsel he learn'd to wander,
Adown some trottin' burn's [*brook's*] meander
          An' no think lang;
O, sweet to stray, an' pensive ponder
          A heart-felt sang!

In **"The Vision"** written over a period of time, and revised, Burns "thinks lang," for forty-six stanzas, and the poem is mainly a versified record of his thoughts about Scotland, and poetry, and his place as a "rustic bard." (He makes it clear that he feels he is one of the "humbler ranks.") Here is Burns' *apologia,* his **"Defence of Poesie,"** his view of his calling as an honorable one and significant to his country and his people. The poem opens with stanzas describing the poet weary after a day of threshing. Stanza four continues:

All in this mottie [*dusty*], misty clime,
I backward mus'd on wasted time:
How I had spent my youthfu' prime,
          An' done naething,
But stringing blethers up in rhyme,
          For fools to sing.

Had I to guid advice but harkit,
I might, by this, hae led a market,
Or strutted in a bank and clarkit
          My cash-account:
While here, half-mad, half-fed,
          half-sarkit [*-shirted*],
          Is a' th' amount.

Suddenly there appears the figure of Coila, in the trim shape of Jean Armour.

A "hair-brain'd, sentimental trace,"
Was strongly markèd in her face;
A wildly-witty, rustic grace
          Shone full upon her;
Her eye, ev'n turn'd on empty space,
          Beam'd keen with honor.

The lassie wears a mantle bearing a map of Ayrshire, with pictures on it of distinguished figures, historical and contemporary. She is the spirit of the district (Kyle), and a member of a "light aerial band" which Burns invents to inspire Scotland and Kyle. Coila speaks of patriots, soldiers, poets, improving landlords, judges, professors, rustic bards, artisans, wooers—all important in the general society; she says she has had Burns in her care since his birth, and points to what he has done under her influence:

> When youthful Love, warm-blushing, strong,
> Keen-shivering, shot thy nerves along,
> Those accents grateful to thy tongue,
>   Th' adorèd *Name*,
> I taught thee how to pour in song
>   To soothe thy flame.
>
> I saw thy pulse's maddening play,
> Wild-send thee Pleasure's devious way,
> Misled by Fancy's meteor-ray,
>   By passion driven;
> But yet the light that led astray
>   Was light from Heaven.
>
> I taught thy manners-painting strains
> The loves, the ways of simple swains,
> Till now, o'er all my wide domains
>   Thy fame extends;
> And some, the pride of Coila's plains,
>   Become thy friends.

Finally she encourages him,

> Then never murmur nor repine;
> Strive in thy humble sphere to shine;
> And trust me, not Potosi's mine [*of gold, silver,
>   and copper*],
>   Nor king's regard,
> Can give a bliss o'ermatching thine,
>   A rustic Bard.
>
> To give my counsels all in one:
> Thy tuneful flame still careful fan;
> Preserve the dignity of Man,
>   With soul erect;
> And trust the Universal Plan
>   Will all protect.

Then she places a holly wreath on his head, and "like a passing thought" fades away. It should be noted that Coila encourages her Scots poet in purest English, as a serious-minded and thoughtful Scot should. This elaborate poem is smoothly versified, and of biographical interest, but after the opening stanzas it does not have the full force and grace of Burns at his best.

As we have seen, Burns took his position as poet seriously, and he enjoyed his success, but he recognized that it helped him little in what he called "the sober science of life." In June, 1786, he had written David Brice that his Kilmarnock edition was to be his "last foolish action," after which he intended to "turn a wise man as fast as possible." All during the exciting months which followed in Edinburgh, he was worried about his problem of a livelihood, made even greater by his more prominent position. He felt he could not live on his poetry, and fame paid no bills. His essential position was much the same

after both his publications as before. . . .

Raymond Bentman (essay date 1972)

SOURCE: "Robert Burns's Declining Fame," in *Studies in Romanticism*, Vol. 11, No. 3, Summer, 1972, pp. 207-24.

[*In the following essay, Bentman contends that Burns's poetry is a significant part of British literary history, despite his declining popularity in recent decades.*]

Robert Burns's poetry is all but ignored in current scholarship of British literature. During the past twenty-five years, critics and scholars have often acted as if his poetry did not exist or have treated him as if he were a poet worth scant attention. This recent indifference to Burns's poetry has not been effected, as is usual in such instances of declining fame, by a critical downgrading of his work. It seems, rather, to result from an assumption that Burns is not in a British tradition. He is ignored because he is considered either to be in a purely Scottish tradition or to be one of those rare poets who are in no tradition at all.

I submit that Burns figures in the major tradition of British poetry and is indeed significant in the transition from the style of poetry written in the early eighteenth century to the style of poetry written in the early nineteenth century. Burns considered himself a follower of the important British poets who preceded him. The important poets who followed Burns considered him an important predecessor of their own theories and practices. His language, while presenting certain problems peculiar to dialect literature, does not separate him from poetry in standard English. On the contrary, it demonstrates some aspects of the development of British poetic diction. And he demonstrates, in thought and technique, part of the actual process of change that occurred during the latter half of the eighteenth century, the change that allowed Romantic poetry to grow out of the poetry of the Augustan Age.

Yet wherever one looks in the scholarship and criticism of the past twenty-five years, Burns is given little or no attention. Works which discuss the eighteenth century generally, works which concentrate on the poetry of "sensibility" in the eighteenth century, and works which concentrate on the transition from eighteenth-century to early nineteenth-century ideas and styles mention Burns either incidentally or not at all. Studies of the influence of the eighteenth-century writers who might well have influenced Burns, such as Thomson, may discuss Thomson's influence on Cowper, Crabbe, or Blake, but not on Burns. Works which trace the origins of the nineteenth-century Romantic movement into the eighteenth century, discussing Cowper, Crabbe, Blake, treat Burns as if he had no significant influence. Even an essay devoted to demonstrating Burns's anticipation of nineteenth-century comic theories [Frederick L. Beaty, "Burns' Comedy of Romantic Love," *PMLA*, 83, 1968] makes Burns "unwitting" and almost irrelevant to the Romantic poets: "His poetry had unwittingly sanctioned in advance many of the tenets enunciated in Wordsworth's preface to *Lyrical Ballads*." Why not: "Burns influenced Wordsworth"? The author of **"The Holy Fair," "The Jolly Beggars," "Address to the Deil," "Holy Willie's Prayer," "To a Louse," "Epistle to J. Lapraik," "Epistle to Davie,"** would seem to be one of the most important satirists between Pope and Byron, yet histories of English satire, even of the satire of the late eighteenth century, make, at the most, a passing reference to Burns as a satirist. Anthologies have begun to exclude him. H. E. Pagliaro excludes him from an anthology of eighteenth-century literature [*Major English Writers of the Eighteenth Century*, 1969], without explanation. Donald Davie excludes him from an anthology of poetry of the late eighteenth century [*The Late Augustans*, 1958]. *The Penguin Book of Satirical Verse* [edited by Edward Lucie-Smith, 1967] ignores him. And anthologies of Romantic poetry, even those with sections on eighteenth-century Romantic poetry, frequently exclude him. The few studies which run counter to this trend, and which attempt to document Burns's position in the British tradition, fall on barren ground. No one refutes them and no one accepts them.

Yet it has not always been so. Historians of the late nineteenth and early twentieth centuries saw Burns as a major predecessor of Romantic poetry. Hugh Walker [*English Satire and Satirists*, 1925] devoted an entire chapter to Burns and Byron in his history of English satire. Alan Dugald McKillop [*English Literature from Dryden to Burns*, 1948] saw him as the terminal figure in the period beginning with Dryden, and George Sherburne [in *A Literary History of England*, edited by Albert C. Baugh, 1948] considered him and Cowper the major predecessors of Wordsworth. The change in attitude has mostly taken place in the past twenty or thirty years.

Two assumptions seem to have effected this change. One argument, which is often explicitly stated, but not usually given in general works as a reason for omitting Burns, is that Burns is a Scottish, not a British poet. He did write some "English" poems, the theory goes, but they were always bad and unimportant. The second argument is not explicitly stated but seems to run through much of the thinking about Burns. It is consistent with the general shift in taste that has taken place in the past twenty or thirty years, which has resulted in **"The Jolly Beggars"** being preferred to **"The Cotter's Saturday Night."** This argument postulates a good Burns and a bad Burns. The bad Burns is primarily English in diction and sentimental in tone, the Burns of **"The Cotter's Saturday Night," "Man Was Made to Mourn," "The Lament," "Despondency,"** etc. He is influenced by bad poetry of the eighteenth century and has some influence on the bad poetry of the nineteenth century—including bad poetry by good poets. This is the Burns who admired English poetry, was admired by nineteenth-century poets, and to whom the older historians referred when they considered Burns a poet in the British tradition. This Burns deserves little critical attention because he is part of a tiresome, insignificant trend. The good Burns, the Burns of **"To a Mouse," "To a Louse," "Epistle to J. Lapraik," "Holy Willie's Prayer," "The Jolly Beggars," "Tam**

O'Shanter," many of the songs, is considered a rare example of a British poet who does not participate in the British tradition. Since he is an original and is without significant influence, he has no place in general studies of the period.

These theories have distorted our reading of British literary history and have resulted in a misreading of Burns's poetry. They have obscured significant relationships between Augustan and Romantic poetry, in particular those similarities which demonstrate that Romantic poetry in some ways evolved out of Augustan poetry. And they have, worse, contributed to the failure to recognize a body of poetry that, in partaking of the actual groping for new expression, has particular relevance now.

Burns considered himself a part of a British tradition and showed little awareness that a purely Scottish tradition even existed. He did admire Ramsay and Fergusson and expressed a desire to "kindle at their flame" (Preface to the Kilmarnock Edition). But he also referred to Goldsmith as his "favorite poet" and to Cowper as "the best Poet out of sight since Thomson." *The Task* was "a glorious Poem." Thomson was the one poet whom he repeatedly mentioned and praised, starting with his list of favorite authors "of the sentimental kind" in 1783 and continuing to **"Address to the Shade of Thomson"** in 1791. Thomson was one of the great joys in life, an "important addition" to his early reading (the autobiographical letter), a criterion of excellence, and a poet who has "looked into Nature for himself: you meet with no copied description." He named Pope as the paragon of poets who have "raised the laugh" and he wished for Pope's "satire's darts" (**"To the Rev. John M'Math"**). He quoted most frequently (after the Bible) Shakespeare, Thomson, Pope, Young, Milton, Addison, Blair, Gray, Shenstone, and Goldsmith, in that order. He apparently had an easy familiarity with a number of British poets of his own century, and looked to British poets for guidance.

There is, of course, no question of the Scottish influence on Burns, of Fergusson on his early poems and of Ramsay on his songs, of both poets on his verse forms, his language, his subject matter, and of the Scottish songs on his songs. One need spend only a few days in Scotland to see how Scottish Burns was, how typical of his countrymen he was in his assured manliness, his musicality, his easy democracy, his capacity for friendship, his passionate temperament, his marvelous love of life. And the Scottish elements in his poetry have been frequently pointed out most convincingly. Yet there is a negative side. Burns rarely quoted Ramsay or Fergusson. Ramsay is the only poet about whom Burns found occasion to make unfavorable remarks. Burns never mentioned Dunbar, Henryson, Lindsay, or Ramsay's *The Evergreen*, Negative evidence is, I grant, always suspect. But it is surely difficult to argue a strong influence from authors who are never so much as referred to. His pro-Scottish, anti-English remarks tend more to deal with history and politics—e.g. the Scottish struggle for freedom—than literary heritage. When he looks for literary training, he turns to English literature. For example, when he talks about giving himself a "preparatory course . . . of Men and Books" he begins with Shakespeare.

Burns's general popularity in England in the later eighteenth century is unmistakable. Lucylle Werkmeister ["Robert Burns and the London Daily Press," *MP*, 63, 1966] has pointed out Burns's popularity in London newspapers between 1787 and 1797. The magazines are full of imitations, reviews of book-length imitations, commemorations, even parodies. He seemed to be very much part of the literary scene in early nineteenth-century London. The interest, as I have pointed out elsewhere, was shared by most of the important poets of the early nineteenth century, especially Wordsworth and Keats.

Since Burns knew and admired the best eighteenth-century British poetry, and since his poetry was known and admired by the best nineteenth-century British poets, it seems to me that any notable similarities that Burns's poetry has with British poetry before and after him would describe a trend. To deny that such similarities are a part of the development of British poetry is surely a distortion of historical method and forces the facts to fit the theory.

Burns's language is always at the fore of any discussion of his place in British poetry. Certain poems, customarily called his "English" poems—e.g. **"Man Was Made to Mourn," "Despondency"**—are regarded as evidence that Burns could not write well in English, from which it is deduced that he is not connected with English literature. I agree that these poems are bad. Their badness, however, does not result from Burns's inability to use English well but from his inability to write good sentimental poetry. He uses Scottish, as I have pointed out elsewhere [in "Robert Burns's use of Scottish Diction," *From Sensibility to Romanticism: Essays in Honor of Frederick Pottle,* edited by Frederick Hilles and Harold Bloom, 1965], in a way that anticipates and probably influences Wordsworth's and Coleridge's theories of poetic diction. And he uses English words as competently as he uses Scottish words.

"Despondency," for example, deals with the same theme as **"To a Mouse,"** that life for all living beings is painful and uncertain. But in **"Despondency"** Burns neither clarifies nor makes concrete the vague and abstract subject. The principal metaphor is that of a man walking down the road of life, carrying and galled by a huge burden. "Grief" and "care," which describe the burden, repeat each other, unlike "grief an' pain" of **"To a Mouse."** When we are told that the road of life is "rough" and "weary" and that the load is "galling," we know no more about the trouble the poet is experiencing than we did in the first line. Yet Burns uses "gall" effectively in **"Address to the Deil"** to describe Job's state: "While scabs an' botches did him gall." The trite metaphor of "sick'ning scenes" contrasts with the more direct diction of "prospects drear" of **"To a Mouse,"** which is further developed by the sensuous imagery: "the winter's sleety dribble / An' cranreuch cauld!" In **"Despondency"** the failure of "pierce" ("What sorrows yet may pierce me thro'") is due more to the lack of supporting imagery in the poem than Burns's inability to use the word effectively (cf. "His piercin words, like

Highlan' swords, / Divide the joints an' marrow"—**"The Holy Fair"**). "Too justly I may fear" contrasts with the "guess an' fear" of **"To a Mouse."** In the latter phrase, uncertainty makes the fear worse. That the second line of **"Despondency"** is an impossible cliché, that "set" becomes unfortunately entangled with "burden," that "life" is apparently both the road and the burden, that the meter, used effectively in **"Epistle to Davie,"** is ridiculously inappropriate to this subject, are all aspects of the general ineptness of the poem. Obviously lines like "How blest the Solitary's lot . . . Within his humble cell" display more than bad diction.

Mr. Thomas Crawford is the only critic I know of in this century who states his admiration for the sentimental poems and the only critic who takes the trouble actually to read the poems rather than repeat the clichés about them. But his defense of them is based on their ideas or on rather generalized poetic techniques. In his discussion of **"Man Was Made to Mourn,"** for example, he argues that the poem "gains rather than loses from the repetition of certain key words, such as 'pleasure' (three times), 'youthful' (four times), 'poor' (four times), 'weary' (four times), 'age' or 'aged' (three times). . . . Much of our delight in reading it comes from these recurring, and partially varied, sounds and concepts." Mr. Crawford does not explain how the poem "gains" or how we achieve this "delight." To my mind a repetition is effective when a word is developed to acquire richer meaning as it is repeated. "Aged" and "youthful" are accompanied either by no images or by trite ones, "aged step," "aged limbs," "youthful breast," or by words that do not develop the meaning, "youthful prime" (two times). "Weary" is accompanied by "worn with care" or "life"; "poor" by such images as "weeping wife" and "helpless offspring." "Pleasure" has only one image, "On Pleasure's lap carest," which suggests either inversion or infantilism. Mr. Crawford ignores other problems of the poem, for example that it is spoken by an old man who spends all his time standing at the "banks of Ayr" giving gratuitous sermons on the wastefulness of everyone but himself, "Oh Man! . . . How Prodigal of time." That the old man contradicts himself in stanzas five, seven, eight, and ten, that he leaves points unfinished in stanzas four and six, and that the person addressed understandably disappears in the course of the sermon are, again, indications that something is wrong with the entire conception of the poem.

The badness does not result from Burns's weakness in using English words but from his weakness in writing poetry of abstraction. His best poems express intense feeling derived from experience and conveyed by sensuous detail. Their themes are closely interrelated with the imagery and often appear to grow out of it. The sentimental poems fail because Burns is apparently so uneasy in a tradition which does not call for sensuous detail that he does not control metrics, imagery, or diction. In the sentimental poems Burns uses English because he follows an eighteenth-century tradition but he would have failed in any language when writing abstract poetry.

Sir James A. H. Murray demonstrated [in "Historical Introduction," *The Dialect of the Southern Counties of Scotland,* 1873], a long time ago, that Burns did not write in vernacular Scottish but in a mixture of Scottish and English, and William Allen Neilson [in "Burns in English," *Anniversary Papers by Colleagues and Pupils of George Lyman Kittredge,* 1913] demonstrated that many of Burns's best works, especially his songs, are almost entirely in English. Burns's language obviously presents special problems, as do other aspects of his regionalism, but it does not in itself exclude him from the British tradition.

Burns's poetry seems to me to participate in and even inaugurate a great many shifts in ideas and style in the transition from Augustanism to Romanticism. I wish to discuss here two of them as examples of Burns's contribution to British literary history: the statiric identification of sexual desire with religious enthusiasm and the lyrical image of man wandering through nature.

The association of sexual desire with religious fervor is, of course, ancient in Western thinking and Western literature. In England the baroque poets, like their counterparts on the continent, used the association as a metaphor which expresses a particular human experience. That the physical sensations of intense religious feeling and sexual impulse are similar seemed to Donne and Crashaw to exalt both. The Augustans, in their reaction against Enthusiasm, took over the image which combines religion with sexuality as they took over so many metaphysical conceits, turned it upside down, and made it satirical. By the middle of the eighteenth century the idea became commonplace. The lesser satirists imitated and exaggerated the satirical image as they so frequently imitated and exaggerated Butler's, Dryden's, Swift's, and Pope's ideas and styles. But they tended, now, with the movement of Dissenters toward a more restrained style of worship, to apply the image to the Methodists. In Christopher Anstey's *New Bath Guide,* for example, a silly young virgin is unable to distinguish between Visionary Election and rape. In Even Lloyd's *The Methodist,* the whole Methodist movement, or at least White-field's branch of it, is a scheme of the devil's for mass seduction. The satirist may, with this image, be attacking the Methodist movement or the whole of mankind, but in either case he sees the combination as an example of depravity. This tradition, by the time it reached Burns, would seem to have been taken as far as it could go.

But Burns, characteristically, transforms the satiric conceit, freshens it, alters its statement. He does not satirize from the standpoint of a less enthusiastic religion, as his satiric predecessors did, but from the Enlightenment's standpoint of no organized religion. The alternative to the Holy Fair, for example, is not the Church of England or the New Lights of the Church of Scotland, but a kind of general common sense. He alters the older satiric attitude toward the participants from one of condemnation to one of amused acceptance. The men attending the Holy Fair are not cynically using the similarity of sensation between sexual desire and religious enthusiasm as an opportunity for seduction. Neither the men nor the women are hypo-

critically using the antinomian implications of Calvinism (as Dissenters and Methodists often do in Augustan satire and as Holy Willie does in one of Burns's less innovative satires) as an excuse to seek sexual opportunities. Nor do they go to the Fair naively expecting religious inspiration but allowing themselves to be easily diverted. Rather, no one seems very clear which of the two experiences he comes to the Fair for in the first place, The transformation from love of God to love of sexual intercourse is portrayed as a consequence of human nature. The satire is directed against those who expect otherwise rather than against those who are subject to what Burns suggests is inevitable and not reprehensible.

Burns uses the satiric techniques of Augustan satire, particularly of his favorite satirist, Pope, but changes them to serve his varied tones. For example, he uses ironic quotation. The young men and women leave the Holy Fair, in the evening:

> Wi' faith an' hope, an' love an' drink,
> They're a' in famous tune.

The "drink" reflects back onto the first three nouns, making them ambiguous. These nouns can, indeed, refer to Christian virtues. But the first two can imply the men's faith and hope that the women will prove compliant, the "love" can mean sexual desire or sexual love. When Pope uses Biblical quotations the distinction is precise:

> Yet, to be just to these poor men of pelf,
> Each does but hate his Neighbour as himself.
> 　　　　　　　　　　　(*Epistle to Bathurst,* 109-10)

Pope sees the Biblical admonition as clear. He also says that some people depart from it completely. Burns says that Biblical admonitions are ambiguous (he may even be satirizing Protestant dependence on Bible-reading) and most people neither quite obey them nor quite disregard them. Pope expresses the polarities of love and hate. He may grant that most people behave somewhere in between, but he unambiguously advocates the Christian ideal. Burns expects less from mankind and is satisfied with less. That "love" can mean many things to many men does not in Burns, as in Donne, lend a mystical elevation to all the meanings, but neither does it denigrate them.

Burns's puns contrast with Pope's similarly, in this same passage from **"The Holy Fair"**:

> There's some are fou o' love divine;
> There's some are fou o' brandy . . .

> Or her, whose life the Church and Scandal share,
> For ever in a Passion, or a Pray'r.
> 　　　　　　　　　　(**"Epistle to a Lady,"** 105-106)

Pope's "passion" can refer either to sexual desire or to the suffering of a martyr. The hypocrite he describes can alternate her feelings but she cannot have them both as the same feeling. Burns's "love divine" is partly love of God, partly wonderful drunken desire simultaneously.

Burns uses this combination in **"The Jolly Beggars,"** a work that, in being a mock-cantata, descends from the Augustan mock-poem and, in describing low life with a musical form generally reserved for more exalted subjects, derives from *The Beggar's Opera*. In the **"Concluding Hymn"** Burns uses music ironically, making the words and music wittily inappropriate to each other, much in the way that Gay uses music throughout *The Beggar's Opera*. Yet this hymn that toasts "callets" and asks "Does the sober bed of marriage / Witness brighter scenes of love?" is not a violent parody of religion in the manner of Medmenham Abbey but an affirmation of a way of life. The beggars allow to the "sober bed of marriage" as much love as to their own, illicit, sexual encounters. But they refuse to allow it more. The justification of sexual license within the form of a hymn, then, like the conclusion of **"The Holy Fair,"** asserts that religion and sexual pleasure often cannot be separated and the insistence that they always can be is self-delusion and hypocrisy. Sexual license is not, for all people, depravity, and can, for people in certain styles of life, become part of a true religion.

Donne's treatment of the identification of lust with faith says that every aspect of man can be exalted. Pope's treatment says that every aspect of man can be depraved. Burns's treatment says that we can praise man without exalting him, we can observe man's shortcomings without condemning him, and we can accept man as an imperfect being without trying to change him.

Burns prefigures certain attitudes which Byron expresses about Christianity and sexual desire, that some people use the similarity as an excuse for illusory self-exaltation, as Donna Julia rationalizes her sexual attraction to Juan:

> And then there are such things as Love divine,
>
> . . . . .
>
> Thus Julia said—and thought so, to be sure;
> And so I'd have her think, were *I* the man
> On whom her reveries celestial ran. (*Don Juan*)

Byron, like Burns, says that few take Christianity's sexual restrictions seriously: "ladies . . . break the—Which commandment is't they break? / (I have forgot the number . . .)" (*Don Juan*). Byron follows Burns in arguing that the belief in Christian sexual denial is a symptom of man's pride. Both exclude orthodox Christianity as a satiric alternative and substitute the satiric alternative that man accept his limitations rather than aspire to ideals of which he is incapable.

The doctrine that we should accept man's limitations can lead away from satire to lyricism. Byron occasionally follows this lead, but more frequently moves toward a different form of satire, ironically driving to its logical conclusion the very acceptance Burns advocates. In **"The Jolly Beggars"** the party stops at its high point. In *Don Juan* we go on to the next morning, facing the hangover, the bills, and the moral complications.

Burns, however, in turning from satires to songs, develops the lyrical implications of his satiric ideas:

> The Kirk an' State may join, and tell
>   To do sic things I maunna:
> The Kirk an' State may gae to Hell,
>   And I'll gae to my Anna.
>   **("Yestreen I Had A Pint o' Wine")**

In his songs he does not often discuss the identification of religious feelings with sexual desire, but concentrates on its implications. He develops, from the Augustan satiric conceit, an almost religious belief in man's sensations, emotions, and senses:

> Ghaist nor bogle shalt thou fear—
> Thou'rt to Love and Heav'n sae dear
> Nocht of ill may come thee near,
>   My bonie dearie.
>   **("Ca' the Yowes to the Knowes")**

> As fair art thou, my bonie lass,
>   So deep in luve am I,
> And I will luve thee still, my dear,
>   Till a' the seas gang dry.
>   **("A Red, Red Rose")**

His treatment of a different theme, that of wandering in nature, demonstrates how this belief emerges in Romantic poetry.

The theme of wandering is another ancient poetic subject which changes form in the Augustan period. The tragic theme of wandering as a curse, the romantic theme of wandering in search of Adventure, and the comic theme of bewildered wandering in search of something not clearly defined are among the several older variations. Augustan satire employs the old satiric themes of the naif wandering in search of absolutes (*Rasselas*) or the observer of the human scene wandering through the city in search of satiric material (*Trivia*). Burns does follow these satiric variations, with his characteristic changes in tone, in such works as **"Address to the Deil"** and **"Tam O'Shanter."** But more significant, I think, is his inheritance of a variation that is probably original with Augustan poetry and occurs mostly among the Descriptive School of poets, the theme of deliberately wandering footloose, usually in a rustic scene, not in search of anything specific but aware of the natural world and responsive to it. The theme as such occurs, to greater and lesser degrees, in such poems as Denham's "Cooper's Hill," Waller's "On St. James's Park," Anne Finch's "A Nocturnal Reverie," Pope's "Windsor Forest," Dyer's "Grongar Hill," Goldsmith's "The Traveller," and so forth. But most significantly, it appears in Burns's two favorite poets, Thomson and Cowper.

Thomson and Cowper both structure their major works, *The Seasons* and *The Task,* around the theme of wandering. Thomson started his earliest section, *Winter,* with "Pleas'd have I wander'd through your rough domain" (l. 10) and carried the theme through the sections written later, at times applying it to the actions of natural phenomena: clouds are "wanderers of heaven" (*Winter,* l. 80), the Nile "wanders wild o'er solitary tracts" (*Summer,* l.

817). He combines his own wanderings with that of nature: "Here wandering oft, fired with restless thirst / Of thy applause, I solitary court / Th' inspiring breeze" (*Autumn*, ll. 668-670). He also employs variations on this theme, particularly emphasizing the profusion and freedom of nature, "Oft let me wander o'er the dewy fields / Where freshness breathes . . . Where the raptured eye / Hurries from joy to joy" (*Spring*, ll. 103-111).

Cowper, like Thomson, structures his entire poem about the idea of wandering, both physically and mentally, and like Thomson, seems to note things as they happen to appear, to think thoughts as they happen to occur. *The Task* becomes interesting, of course, when he starts his "ramble." His muse is "wand'ring," and he frequently employs synonomous words and phrases, "Roving as I rove, / Where shall I find an end, or how proceed," "There early stray'd / My fancy, ere liberty of choice / Had found me." The opportunity to wander is, in Cowper, somehow intrinsic to the superiority of the rural life: "God made the country, and man made the town. . . . Our groves were planted to console at noon / The pensive wand'rer in their shades."

Both Thomson and Cowper do, at times, impose some theory on their rambling observations. Thomson imposes the Noble Savage theory (*Autumn*) for example, and Cowper sees nature as a demonstration of Calvinistic Christianity. Yet they both seem, almost unawares, to accept certain philosophic and poetic assumptions. As Burns says of *The Task:*

> Is not the Task a glorious Poem? The Religion
> of
> The Task, bating a few scraps of Calvinistic
> Divinity,
> is the Religion of God & Nature; the Religion
> that
> exalts, that ennobles man.

Thomson and Cowper do not, however, develop this idea beyond occasional observations. It remains for Burns to develop the implications of their unexplored assumptions and techniques. If one can make some sense out of nature by simply wandering through it and allowing one's senses to respond, and if one can report these responses in poetry, then one can create poetry which is based on a "Religion of God & Nature," and which, in allowing man to apprehend this religion solely through his senses, "exalts . . . ennobles man." Burns does create such poetry. He develops the image of wandering through nature, combining it with more complex poetic devices than Cowper or Thomson used, to express, as do the Romantic poets after him, a new vision of God, nature, and ennobled man.

To Burns, learning to wander through nature and joining in the rhythm of nature's wandering is essential to the writing of poetry:

> The Muse, nae poet ever fand her,
> Till by himsel he learn'd to wander,
> Adown some trottin burn's meander,

> An' no think lang:
> O, sweet to stray, an' pensive ponder
> A heart-felt sang!
> **("To William Simpson of Ochiltree")**

In his satiric poetry, the opportunity to wander in and enjoy nature is a satiric alternative. The way to deal with the evils of the world is not to correct them but to ignore them, using the freedom of nature as an opportunity which social injustice, human cruelty, economic inequality, even the hardness of natural phenomena, simply cannot touch:

> What tho', like commoners of air,
> We wander out, we know not where,
> But either house of hal'?
> Yet Nature's charms, the hills and woods,
> The sweeping vales, and foaming floods,
> Are free alike to all.
> **("Epistle to Davie")**

Then, as in his treatment of so many other ideas, that which in the satires and epistles is explicit, a bit didactic, becomes implicit in the songs and seems to grow out of the imagery.

Burns will often place the song in a natural setting that has no logical association with the action. But he will make the speaker and the natural phenomena move in similar ways so that the emotions of the speaker become reflected in nature:

> The crystal waters round us fa',
> The merry birds are lovers a',
> The scented breezes round us blaw,
> A wandering wi' my Davie.
> **("Now Rosy May")**

He often explicitly compares wandering humans to wandering streams, drawing the poetic implications that humans achieve a degree of freshness, freedom, the capacity for uncluttered feeling, by being like things in nature:

> There, dearest Chloris, wilt thou rove
> By wimpling burn and leafy shaw,
> And hear my vows o' truth and love,
> And say thou lo'es me best of a'?
> **("Sae Flaxen Were Her Ringlets")**

In **"Sweet Afton"** Burns plays on the similar sounds of "winding," and "wander," the alliteration with "wild," "woodland," "wanton," "water," "wave," and the related but varied kinds of nature's motions described by "glides," "blow," "rises," and "wave," and entwines all these techniques with the speaker's gentle feeling for nature and his love. The interlocking of emotion and poetic techniques, the combination of feelings for both nature and humans, and the breadth of emotion expressed by "lofty," "clear," "sweet," "pleasant," "wild," "lonely," and "wanton," unite human emotions with nature as successfully, barring a few lapses in diction, as does any poem in British literature:

> How lofty, sweet Afton, thy neighboring hills,

Far mark'd with the courses of clear, winding
    rills!
There daily I wander, as noon rises high,
My flocks and my Mary's sweet cot in my eye.
How pleasant thy banks and green vallies below,
Where wild in the woodlands the primroses blow . . .

Thy crystal stream, Afton, how lovely it glides,
And winds by the cot where my Mary resides!
How wanton thy waters her snowy feet lave,
As, gathering sweet flowerets, she stems thy
    clear wave!

Burns uses the image of wandering, in the songs, mostly to express happy love. But he goes beyond those limits, using similar movements and similar sounds to imply that the emotions of man and the motions of nature are one, that loving people can see this unity simply by giving themselves over to their own feelings and to the nature comprehended by their senses.

This idea, expressed by this image of wandering, is taken over by Wordsworth to a great extent and by Coleridge, Byron, and Keats to a lesser extent. Coleridge employs the theme occasionally ("This Lime-tree Bower My Prison" and "Frost at Midnight"). Byron satirizes the theme (*Don Juan*). Keats theorizes on the device in a way similar to Burns ("Fancy" and "I Stood Tip-Toe") and employs it in some of his earlier poetry, characteristically inverting it so that nature seems to take meaning from man. The River Alpheus speaks: "I will delight thee all my winding course. . . . 'Mid exuberant green, / I roam in pleasant darkness" (*Endymion*). And Wordsworth uses it most frequently. Much of his early work seems strongly influenced by Burns, whose work he knew and admired from the time he was seventeen.

> . . . and should the chosen guide
> Be nothing better than a wandering cloud,
> I cannot miss my way. . . .
>   . . . . .
>   . . . whither shall I turn,
> By road or pathway, or through trackless field,
> Up hill or down, or shall some floating thing
> Upon the river point me out my course?
>   (*The Prelude*)

Like Burns he sees this capacity to wander in nature as a symbol of personal freedom:

> For I, bred up 'mid Nature's luxuries,
> Was a spoiled child, and rambling like the wind,
> As I had done in daily intercourse
> With those crystalline rivers, solemn heights,
> And mountains, ranging like a fowl of the air,
> I was ill-tutored for captivity.
>   (*The Prelude*)

In some of his shorter poems, such as "To the Cuckoo" and "I Wandered Lonely as a Cloud," he uses the wandering theme as the image around which to construct the poem. In the latter poem, for example, his own wander-

ings are paralleled by similarly free actions in nature, all described in human terms, but with a gradually increasing purposefulness that gives meaning to his walk and to his recollected thoughts, without denying him the freedom granted natural phenomena. As Mr. Frederick Pottle points out [in "The Eye and the Object in the Poetry of Wordsworth," *YR*, 40, Autumn 1950], the flowers are "fluttering," that is, being moved; then "dancing," that is, self-moving; then "tossing their heads in sprightly dance," self-moved with emotion. In the third stanza "glee," "gay," and "jocund" tell the reader how to take the emotions, the same emotions ascribed to the flowers. Without any direct statement, and with only faintly apparent artistry, he brings the wandering of the speaker and the fluttering of the flowers together in a manner strikingly similar to Burns.

In "Tintern Abbey" Wordsworth seems to go beyond Burns, in ascribing an order within nature, so that when he does join nature's wanderings, it guides him beyond freedom to a deeper understanding. He parallels the action and the mood of his own wanderings with the boundings "like a roe" of childhood, with the "sportive woods run wild," with the "Wye! thou wanderer thro' the woods," and with the "presence" which is a "motion and a spirit" that "rolls through all things" and which becomes, when order is restored, "The guide, the guardian of my heart, and soul / Of all my moral being." Wordsworth remains a "lover of the meadows and the woods" but can feel a "sense sublime"

> Whose dwelling is the light of setting suns,
> And the round ocean and the living air,
> And the blue sky, and in the mind of man.

Burns creates a religion of man and nature, developing the themes of Thomson and Cowper, but does not realize all the philosophic implications that are part of Wordsworth's nature mysticism.

Burns shows the transition from Augustan to Romantic modes in a number of other ways. He creates, in his description of animals—not as talking parodies of humans nor as allegories of human traits but as real creatures with no more attributes than animals normally have—symbols of the universality of beauty and sympathy which anticipate the animal poems of Wordsworth, Coleridge, and Shelley. He uses Pope's satiric technique of the shifting persona, changing the naif to a wide-eyed country bumpkin. But this bumpkin seems to improve in intelligence until he is the clear voice of Romantic simplicity, symbolizing the universality of human understanding. He takes the Standard Habbie verse form from Fergusson and introduces, under the influence of Pope, ironic rhyme, parallel and contrast within the line. He uses the short fourth and sixth lines for further variation to give some of the rhythms of ordinary conversation in a way that anticipates both Byron's conversational ottava rima and Wordsworth's attempt at conversational diction.

Burns seems to have achieved the fearless honesty of Byron, the perfect simplicity of Wordsworth, the sensuous passivity of Keats. Yet he achieved all this Romantic feeling without losing the common-sensical social awareness of Pope. He sought a way to deal with what he called a "vile warl'" but he sought this way in self-expression, in personal freedom, and in reliance on his emotions. He often combined in one passage an awareness of the every-day world and all its difficulties, a faith in the guidance of art, and a belief in nature not just as a symbol of order but as a guide and comforter and part of ourselves at once:

> Alas! what bitter toil an' straining—
> But truce with peevish, poor complaining!
> Is Fortune's fickle *Luna* waning?
>   E'en let her gang!
> Beneath what light she has remaining,
>   Let's sing our sang.
>   **("Epistle to James Smith")**

The current trend, which insists that Burns is not a transition poet, denies him his rightful position as one of the great innovators in British poetry and excludes an important dimension from his poetry. There are, I believe, many of us who do not share the Augustan belief that the old political and religious schemes will make the world better and who cannot feel a sense sublime nor see into the life of things. For those of us who believe that the perceptions of each man are enormously important, that man's feelings do provide a basis from which he can attempt to give the world some meaning, but who do not believe that man can or indeed should ascend to visionary insight in order to understand the world, Burns provides a poetry that is marvelously human.

Gertrude M. White (essay date 1973)

SOURCE: "Don't Look Back: Something Might Be Gaining on You," in *The Sewanee Review,* Vol. LXXXI, No. 4, Autumn, 1973, pp. 870-74.

[*Here, White examines Burns's struggle to reconcile "the English literary tradition with which alone his formal education was concerned, and the Scottish literary tradition as he encountered it."*]

"There are gains for all our losses; /There is balm for every pain." So a now largely unremembered poet of the previous century assures us. We need the assurance. For if we are led, by any unusual stimulation of the mind and the imagination, to see our world reflected in the mirror of another time, we incline to think the poet's assurance in vain. Too often we find ourselves lamenting the losses, not celebrating the gains, and feeling the pain rather than the balm. . . .

Burns is commonly thought by the uninstructed to be—in the phrase applied by Milton to Shakespeare—"Fancy's child", ignorant and spontaneous, warbling his "native wood notes wild". This impression is mistaken, at best an oversimplification, at worst a gross error. Burns was heir not of one but of two different and sharply opposed tra-

ditions: the English literary tradition with which alone his formal education was concerned, and the Scottish literary tradition as he encountered it. Mr. [David] Daiches [in his *Robert Burns and His World,* 1972] briefly but cogently sketches the historical development of both traditions, their relationship to each other, and the effect of both on Burns's work.

On the one hand, Burns was faced with the demand of the Scottish Enlightenment that he write in pure standard English; for these men regarded their native tongue as corrupt and despised the verse written in Scots dialect by Burns's predecessors, Robert Fergusson and Allan Ramsay. But, says Mr. Daiches, "poetry demands that the whole man speak and therefore requires a language which, however different from the spoken vernacular, is not deliberately cut off from it." So, although Burns had already written several poems in the neo-classic idiom preferred by the Edinburgh arbiters of taste, if he had written consistently in this style "he would have been remembered, if at all, as a very minor eighteenth-century English versifier."

On the other hand, Burns was no untutored peasant, ignorant of the long and rich tradition of English poetry—a pose he sometimes liked to adopt. He had learned much of that tradition, for from the beginning he was a poetic craftsman whose letters reveal the most precise concern with wording and rhythm. If he rejected the canons of the *literati,* this does not mean that he produced vernacular poetry based entirely on the spoken Scots of Ayrshire. Rather, he learned from Fergusson to produce his own combination of Scots and English, of the colloquial and the literary. He steered a canny course between the Charybdis of a learned sterility and the Scylla of a primitive and "natural" vernacular.

This analysis of the historical and literary situation of Burns's time and place does more than characterize his problem and his achievement: it suggests also questions and even perhaps answers of interest to everyone concerned with literature and with education today. First of all, notice that this Ayrshire peasant, his father a bankrupt tenant farmer, so poor in youth that he suffered permanent damage to his health from hardship and malnutrition, nevertheless had been taught to read and write from the best models of English prose and poetry then available: from the Bible, Shakespeare, and Milton, from Dryden, Pope, and Thomson, from Gray, Shenstone, and Addison. Consider his tutor's account of his methods of instruction and his aims in teaching:

> The books most commonly used in the school were, the *Spelling Book,* the *New Testament,* the *Bible,* Mason's [actually Masson's] *Collection of Prose and Verse,* and Fisher's *English Grammar.* . . . As soon as they were capable of it, I taught them to turn verse into its natural prose order; sometimes to substitute synonimous expressions for poetical words, and to supply all the ellipses. These, you know, are the means of knowing that the pupil understands his author. These are excellent helps to the arrangement of words in sentences, as well as to a variety of expressions.

Compare these materials and this training with the texts and methods now in use in American public schools, especially in the earlier grades, and it is at once apparent that few products of our public school system have had anything like the grounding in the fundamental disciplines of reading, writing, and thinking that Burns enjoyed.

To say this is not to suggest that we can or should wish to return to the conditions of eighteenth-century Scotland; nor to deny that the problems facing educators today are vastly different from and more formidable than any Burns's tutor could have envisioned; nor to assert that the average pupil is a Burns. We might well, however, immersed though we are and must be in the modern world, ponder what values, what goals, what achievements have been jettisoned along the way, and ask whether it was necessary and inevitable that so much be lost. What would Burns, I wonder, have said if anyone in his day had—conceivably!—raised the caw of "elitism"? We know what he thought of a preposterous and intolerant religious elite: we have **"Holy Willie's Prayer"** to tell us. But what might so gifted a satirist have written about the "Dick and Jane" series, or the content of a fashionable course in Modern Literature at any contemporary university? What would he have said to those who mouth such phrases as "verbal manipulation" to characterize the great intellectual disciplines based on language; those who claim that the university today must concern itself rather with areas of learning hitherto regarded as the province of private and individual experience? The *bon vivant* who customarily wrote two versions of his folk songs, one for publication, the other for the amusement of the Tarbolton Bachelor's Club, certainly knew—as we are so often told today—that there are other ways of learning besides "verbal manipulation" and other objects for manipulation than words. He might have marvelled, all the same, at a Department of English Language and Literature that granted academic credit for courses exploring such non-verbal modes of learning. . . .

Again, consider Burns's plight as a man of genius, acknowledged and accepted as such but patronized insufferably by the educated members of a snobbish, class-bound society. Burns's social and intellectual life was cut off from his domestic and emotional circumstances, causing him bitter pain and loss, thwarting his virtues, encouraging his vices. Far from a model of bourgeois virtue though he may have been, Burns was not the rake nor irresponsible Bohemian he has often been made out. But his world as he knew it offered no satisfaction nor fulfillment to his whole nature; rather, its elements were set at variance with one another. How much support or real acceptance does our seemingly more tolerant and less hierarchal society offer such a man? Are the lives or the deaths of our poets, on the whole, more edifying? Our acceptance, our tolerance, is for the most part one of the surface only, our artists and intellectuals as lonely and as alone as was Burns.

One clear advantage that Burns enjoyed over any modern stands out in this vivid picture of a poet and his world. Burns knew nature intimately and at first hand, with a casual, matter-of-fact familiarity no longer possible, at least in America. We can ski, go camping or sailing, interest ourselves in ecology, or retire to a cottage on Cape Cod or a cabin in the Tetons. But we use nature as a recreation, or a refuge, or a cause. We cannot know it as Burns did or write of it with the ease, the realism, the unstudied naturalness that give his verse such freshness and spontaneity. Perhaps the same is true of our knowledge of that part of nature called human, and especially of the experience of love. For Burns is a great love poet, concerned above all with the realized moment of experience; his poetry of love is simple, sensuous, and passionate, as a great poet said poetry should be. And this special sense of the reality of emotional or sensuous experience was for him a gift and a grace, not a creed. His love poems are an example and a reproach to young poets of the Now generation, so often either assertive and rhetorical or lost in the tenuous mazes of abstraction. . . .

Kenneth Rexroth (essay date 1973)

SOURCE: "Robert Burns," in *The Elastic Retort: Essays in Literature and Ideas,* The Seabury, 1973, pp. 72-6.

[*Rexroth was one of the leading pioneers in the revival of jazz and poetry in the San Francisco area during the 1940s and 1950s. His early poetry was greatly influenced by the surrealism of André Breton, but his later verse became more traditional in style and content, though by no means less complex. However, it was as a critic and translator that Rexroth gained prominence in American letters. As a critic, his acute intelligence and wide sympathy allowed him to examine such varied subjects as jazz, Greek mythology, and the Kabbalah. As a translator, Rexroth was largely responsible for introducing the West to both Chinese and Japanese classics. Below, Rexroth describes Burns as a rebel, attributing his frustration to the "conflict between his situation [as a working man] and his potential [as a well-educated man]."*]

Robert Burns is a special case in the literature of the British Isles. He is one of the few writers prior to the twentieth century who was a working man. True, he was not a member of the proletariat, but a farmer. He has often been called a peasant poet. In fact his father was a yeoman who went bankrupt trying to establish himself as a moderately large-scale independent farmer. This is a very different background from that of the traditional highland Scottish shepherd or peasant songster. Nonetheless Robert Burns worked hard with his hands most of his life. He was one of the few writers at the end of the eighteenth century to hold fast to the principles of the French Revolution. Liberty, equality and fraternity are warp and woof of the fabric from which all his poems were cut. He was incapable of thinking in any other terms. The reason of course is that in Scotland the small independent proprietor was a decisive influence on the form of the culture and was also, in the tremendous changes at the dawn of the Industrial Revolution, being subject to a process of internal colonization both by the English and by the Scots aristocracy. Burns' father's long struggle and final bankruptcy were not isolated phenomena, but part of a social movement. Far more than the English, the Scottish farmers caught in this historical process were rebellious. They were rebellious because many of them were comparatively well educated.

Burns was taught by a country schoolmaster and learned even the elements of Latin and a smattering of French. Since the mid-eighteenth century was the low point of English secondary and higher education, he was probably a little better educated than the average member of the upper class to the south. It is this conflict between his situation and his potential that made him, like thousands of other Scots, an incorrigible rebel. In France itself the Revolution was not productive of a literature of its own—at least of a very high quality. It has been said that Robert Burns is the only major Jacobin poet. "Jacobin" is easily confused with "Jacobite" and with reason. Scotland is a separate country with its own traditions, and at least back before James the First of England and Sixth of Scotland, its own great literature in its own language. After the final extinction of hopes for a Stuart Restoration, or an autonomous Scotland, in 1745, with the failure of the romantic Bonnie Prince Charlie, and the enforced total union with England, there was a great upsurge of Scottish cultural nationalism. For centuries Scottish writers had thought in one language and written in another. Burns, to preserve his integrity—a vague word, better say the efficient functioning of his sensibility and intelligence—was forced back into the arms of the common people from whom he came. His verse in English is mediocre and sometimes silly. It was so obviously written for the provincial belles of Scottish salons, young ladies who prided themselves on their southern accents and their familiarity with sentimental English novels. For all his efforts to captivate, however, when it came to decision, Burns' love affairs were with women of his own class or classes, daughters of farmers and declassé intellectuals.

Their Scottish language should not mislead one in understanding Burns' longer poems, the great satires, **"The Holy Fair," "Holy Willie's Prayer,"** and his one comic narrative, **"Tam o' Shanter."** They are not folkloristic but like so much Jacobin poetry, Roman in inspiration. But they differ decidedly from eighteenth-century satirical verse in England or France. Like their Roman models, the English and French wrote about "the Town." Samuel Johnson's satires are scarcely altered translations from the Roman poet Juvenal. Burns satirized the middle class of people, whether farmers, craftsmen, or small merchants. In France the Revolution was struggling to capture power for the middle class. Scotland had evolved a well-organized middle class society almost unnoticed. Its social upheavals had come from outside, from struggle with England. With the exception of Thomas Dekker, who greatly resembles Burns, the English city comedies of the early seventeenth century are written from outside by declassed intellectuals whose sympathies were with the *ancien régime*. Burns, like Dickens, wrote of the commonality from inside and so his satire had an authenticity and an accuracy which makes it still appropriate.

The long poems are not much read today—few long poems by anybody are. It is for his songs that Burns is famous throughout the world. More than any other one factor they have sustained the cultural consciousness of Scotland. The literary mind is a dangerous thing to turn loose on folklore. The educated editor and adaptor usually spoils whatever he touches. Walter Scott's improvements of the ballads of the Scottish Border, with only one or two exceptions, lessen their sources and rob them of their peculiar wonder. William Morris' adaptations of folklore, ballads and sagas can be read today only with the grimmest effort. Except Burns, only the Finn Elias Lönnrot was able to gather the fragmentary songs and legends of his people and transmute them into something both more wonderful and more socially powerful than the originals. Lönnrot's *Kalevala* is a different thing than its sources, a haunting, dreamlike, fragmentary epic, really meaningful only to modern Finns. Their ancestors, could they read it, would be vastly puzzled. Burns did something different. He wrote songs in his youth, some of them adaptations of folk songs. In his later years, at the height of his poetic powers, he gathered, edited, altered, expanded, combined hundreds of folk songs. Where he changed, he not only changed for the better, but he changed entirely within the folkloristic context, and intensified the specific glamour and wonder of his sources. Sometimes the song is completely rewritten. **"John Anderson, My Jo"** is changed from a bawdy song to one of long, enduring married love. **"Ca' the Yowes tae the Knowes"** is subtly altered line for line—literally glamorized—but always within the context. This is the same context that produced the scalp tingling lines of balladry, "About the mid houre of the nicht she heard the bridles ring," "Half ower Half ower tae Aberdower tis fiftie fathoms deep." Lines like these give the great ballads their stunning impact and their haunting permanence.

Burns is the only literary poet working on folk material who could do anything like this. He did it hundreds of times, so that his poems are not just the only Scottish folksong most people know, even in Scotland, but they establish a sensibility which remains characteristic of the best Scottish poetry to this day. "Yestreen, when tae the tremblin string / The dance gaed thro' the lighted ha'," "While waters wimple tae the sea; / While day blinks in the lift sae hie," "Aft hae I roved by bonnie Doon, / To see the woodbine twine; / And ilka bird sang o' its luve, / And sae did I o' mine," "Had we never loved sae kindly, / Had we never loved sae blindly, / Never met—or never parted, / We had ne'er been broken-hearted." . . . these lines are not only bathed in the uncanny light of folk song at its best, but they establish the specific tradition we think of as Scottish. The poetry of Hugh MacDiarmid (Scotland's greatest poet since Burns, and now with the passing of all the heroic generation of Modernist poetry in America and Great Britain, one of the two greatest living poets, I was going to say in Britain or America, but actually I suppose in any country) owes everything to this exact glamour, this vein of phosphorescent precious metal first opened up by Burns.

And finally MacDiarmid, the revolutionary nationalist,

raises one last point. Burns took the folk songs of Scottish nationalism, of Stuart legitimism, and subtly altered them into something quite different. Jacobite becomes Jacobin "Had Bonnie Prince Charlie won, a regime of barbarism, superstition, and incurable civil war, dominated by a mindless and decayed aristocracy, would have been fastened on Scotland." Nobody believes that today, largely due to the myth established by Burns' subtle rewriting of Jacobite folk-songs. The Stuarts certainly did not believe in freedom of any kind. The songs of their partisans, filtered through the mind of Burns, become battle songs of freedom, hymns to the integrity and independence of the individual—the individual, middle kind of man who is educated, cultivated and yet works for a living—for example, the Scottish engineers who built bridges and railroads and factories, and spread the Industrial Revolution across the world, and who relaxed over a bottle of uisquebaugh in the evening, singing **"Scots Wha Hae Wi' Wallace Bled."**

Alexander Scott (essay date 1975)

SOURCE: "The Satires: Underground Poetry," in *Critical Essays on Robert Burns,* edited by Donald A. Law, Routledge & Kegan Paul, 1975, pp. 90-105.

[*In the following essay, Scott details what were considered the scandalous aspects of Burns's satires.*]

The unanimity of praise for the satires among modern Scottish critics of Burns is remarkable in a literary scene where controversy is more usual than consent. To David Daiches [in his *Robert Burns,* 1950], **'The Holy Tulzie'** is 'brilliant' and 'extraordinarily effective'; **'Holy Willie's Prayer'** possesses 'cosmic irony' and 'perfect dramatic appropriateness'; **'The Holy Fair'** is at once 'the finest of those [poems] in the Kilmarnock volume which show the full stature of Burns as a poet working in the Scots literary tradition' and a creation with 'revolutionary implications'; **'The Twa Dogs'** is 'brisk, sharp-toned . . . with wit and point'; **'Address to the Deil'** is 'effective' in that it 'blows up' the doctrine of original sin; **'The Ordination'** is (again) 'effective', this time in 'the contrast between the form and the ostensible theme'; and **'Address of Beelzebub'** is 'bitter and biting'. To Thomas Crawford [in his *Burns,* 1960], **'The Holy Tulzie'** shows 'developing still further the technique used in . . . the **"Epistle to John Rankine"**—the apparent assumption of the standards, beliefs and language of the opposite party'; **'Holy Willie's Prayer'** is 'one of the finest satires of all time'; **'The Holy Fair'** shows 'complete mastery of traditional poetic skills'; **'The Twa Dogs'** has 'a pleasing manner'; **'The Ordination'** is 'one of the finest and freshest things Burns ever did'; and **'Address of Beelzebub'** is 'the most savage of all Burns's satires'. To David Craig [in his *Scottish Literature and the Scottish People 1680-1830,* 1961], despite his distrust of 'reductive criticism' and 'the reductive idiom and the poor man's defensive pose' in much eighteenth-century Scots satirical writing, 'Burns was in a wonderfully original and rich vein in the poems that may be called his satires'.

All these works had been written before the publication in July 1786 of the Kilmarnock edition which created for Burns the national—and international—reputation he has enjoyed ever since. Yet references to the satires in the contemporary reviews are few and far between. The *Edinburgh Magazine* of October 1786, noting that 'some of his subjects are serious, but those of the humorous kind are the best', illustrates the point by quoting **'Address to the Deil'** and excerpts from **'The Holy Fair'**, but none of the other satirical pieces is so much as mentioned by name; the *Monthly Review* (London) of December 1786 expresses the opinion that 'our author seems to be most in his element when in the sportive humorous strain', but neither discusses nor illustrates the work which would exemplify that remark—perhaps because of a view that 'the poems of this cast . . . so much abound with provincial phrases and allusions to local circumstances, that no extracts from them would be sufficiently intelligible to our English readers'; the *Lounger* (Edinburgh) of December 1786, where the reviewer was the novelist Henry Mackenzie, mentions the 'Dialogue of the Dogs' [*sic*] among other 'lighter and more humorous poems' which demonstrate 'with what uncommon penetration and sagacity this heaven-taught ploughman, from his humble unlettered station, has looked upon men and manners', but in defending Burns against the charge of 'irreligion' by remarking that 'we shall not look upon his lighter muse as the enemy of religion (of which in several places he expresses the justest sentiments) though she has been somewhat unguarded in her ridicule of hypocrisy', Mackenzie leaves the religious satires unrecorded by either title or quotation; and the *English Review* (London) of February 1787, while adducing **'Address to the Deil'** and **'The Holy Fair'** to exemplify its view that 'the finest poems . . . are of the humorous and satirical kind, and in these our author appears to be most at home', devotes most of its space to the discussion of poems from which humour and satire are entirely absent.

The temptation to berate those early critics of Burns for obtuseness, however strong it may be, and however apparently justified in the eyes of readers of his collected poems, does not survive reference to the Kilmarnock edition. For of all the satires mentioned in the first paragraph above, only three, **'The Holy Fair'**, **'The Twa Dogs'** and **'Address to the Deil'**, find a place in its pages. The others have been suppressed, either by the poet himself, or by the poet following the views of his adviser, the lawyer Robert Aiken, **'Dear Patron of my Virgin Muse'**. When Burns made his first bow to the public, he chose to do so with his strong right arm tied behind his back.

If at first sight this seems to be extraordinary behaviour for a novice, who might be expected to wish to make the maximum impact upon his readers, the appearance is deceptive. Burns and his adviser had sufficient reasons for deciding against the inclusion in the Kilmarnock edition of those satires which are now among the most highly praised of all his works. Most of them were certainly libellous—and, in the eyes of some of those local readers in the west of Scotland for whom the Kilmarnock edition was printed by subscription, they might have appeared blasphemous at worst, and at best in extremely poor taste.

The clue to the situation lies in Burns's famous autobiographical letter to Dr Moore [in *The Letters of Robert Burns*, edited by J. De Lancey Ferguson, 1931] where, discussing the earliest of his satires, **'The Holy Tulzie'**, he writes:

> The first of my poetic offspring that saw the light was a burlesque lamentation on a quarrel between two reverend Calvinists, both of them dramatis person in my Holy Fair.—I had an idea myself that the piece had some merit; but to prevent the worst, I gave a copy of it to a friend who was very fond of these things, and told him I could not guess who was the Author of it, but that I thought it pretty clever.—With a certain side of both clergy and laity it met with a roar of applause.

But there are always two sides (at least) to any Scottish reaction to works of art of a controversial kind, and how others among 'both clergy and laity' must have reacted to **'The Holy Fair'** is indicated by their reception of its immediate successor, **'Holy Willie's Prayer'**—'It alarmed the kirk-session so much that they held three successive meetings to look over their holy artillery, if any of it was pointed against profane Rhymers'.

Both **'The Holy Tulzie'** and **'Holy Willie's Prayer'** were attacks on *local* personalities in the church—hence the caution, 'to prevent the worst', which led Burns to pretend ignorance of the authorship of the former when passing it out in manuscript. Rural Ayrshire in the late eighteenth century was still under a clerical discipline—or Calvinist dictatorship—whose restrictive power was all the greater for its basis in a public opinion which Henry Mackenzie, reflecting 'moderate' Edinburgh views, described [in the *Lounger,* December 1786] as 'the ignorance and fanaticism of the lower class of the people in the country where these poems were written, a fanaticism of that pernicious sort which sets faith in opposition to good works'. Moreover, at the time **'The Holy Tulzie'** and **'Holy Willie's Prayer'** were composed, early in 1785, Burns had placed himself in a highly vulnerable position *vis-à-vis* the kirk: 'Unluckily for me, my idle wanderings led me, on another side, point-blank within the reach of their heaviest metal'. Less metaphorically, he was responsible for the pregnancy of Elizabeth Paton, the Burns family's domestic servant, who bore him a daughter on 22 May 1785, and consequently he would be required to appear on the church's stool of repentance, 'arrayed . . . in the black sackcloth gown of fornication', for three successive Sundays. After that penance he would be regarded as having made his peace with the kirk, provided there were no other scandals appertaining to his person. But if his authorship of **'The Holy Tulzie'** and **'Holy Willie's Prayer'** had been avowed, or even acknowledged, the clerical authorities would have had every reason (in their own view) to continue to hold him under the ban of their baleful displeasure.

A year later, in the spring of 1786, when Burns was selecting poems for the Kilmarnock edition, he would have been in even worse trouble had all the facts of his sexual irregularities come to light, for at that time he had made himself a bigamist by contracting two irregular marriages, firstly with Jean Armour—who bore him twins on 3 September—and secondly (and secretly) with Mary Campbell. From the consequences of those follies he was rescued, through no merit of his own, by the sudden death of **'Highland Mary'** in the autumn of that year. By then, however, the Kilmarnock edition had already been published, with most of the anti-clerical satires omitted.

Yet, ironically enough, the same system of clerical dictatorship which compelled Burns to deny the dignity of print to some of his liveliest poems would appear to have been responsible for their original composition. While the poet's Commonplace Book makes it plain that he had reached a 'moderate' view in religion, opposed to the narrow fundamentalist ('Auld Licht') principles of his local kirk-session, at least as early as 1784, it was not until 'the thorns were in his own flesh' and he found himself in peril of the kirk's censure as a result of his affair with Elizabeth Paton that he was stimulated into writing about the Calvinists of his own district in terms of the kind of attack which has traditionally been regarded as the best means of defence.

A notorious dispute about parish boundaries between two 'Auld Licht' ministers, 'hitherto sworn friends and associates', who 'lost all command of temper' when the matter was discussed at the Presbytery of Ayr, and 'abused each other . . . with a fiery violence of invective', presented the poet with a golden opportunity for satire. The whole of **'The Holy Tulzie'** is an extended metaphor, the nature of which is succinctly indicated by the poem's alternative title **'The Twa Herds',** but the very orthodoxy of the time-hallowed images of the minister as shepherd and the congregation as his flock gives a keener edge to the mockery of the treatment, and the poet's adoption of the persona of an Auld Licht sympathizer, professing horror and dismay at the 'bitter, black outcast' between the two guardians of sanctity, sharpens the irony to a more penetrating point. Again, the presentation of the two pastors as actual—as well as metaphorical—Scottish shepherds, their business to protect the sheep 'frae the fox / Or worrying tykes', their practice to trap 'the Fulmart, Wil-cat, Brock and Tod' and 'sell their skin', deprives them of dignity and makes their blowing of 'gospel horns' and swinging of 'the Gospel-club' all the more ludicrous by the brilliantly daring association of the scriptural with the mundane—while the presentation of their flocks as real sheep ('the Brutes') puts beyond argument the propriety of patronage in the presentation of parish ministers, since it would appear that the only alternative is to 'get the Brutes the pouer themsels / To chuse their Herds'. Technically, too, the poet's command of the Habbie Simson stanza is already consummate, although this is only the third occasion he has employed it.

Despite those various virtues, however, the poem falls short of being a masterpiece. As Hilton Brown remarks [in his *There Was a Lad,* 1949], '[Burns] was always lazy

. . . even in his best days many of his most promising openings peter out for lack of just that finish and pulling together which an extra ounce of effort would have supplied', and he gives **'The Holy Tulzie'** as an example of this fault. The poem ends too abruptly, as if the writer had suddenly run out of steam. But even before that point is reached, readers from other airts than eighteenth-century Ayrshire find themselves in difficulty and compelled to start grubbing in editorial notes. During the first fifty-four lines, no such grubbing is necessary, for even although we know nothing about the two protagonists, 'Moodie man and wordy Russell' as Burns punningly names them, their natures and their functions emerge so clearly from the verse that they quickly establish themselves in our minds as recognizable clerical types, as true to life now as then. But in the next thirty lines the poet lets loose an avalanche of ministers' names, all of them familiar enough to his original local audience, but now unknown to fame except for their appearance here and elsewhere in Burns's work, and none of them sufficiently delineated to achieve a living reality in the verse. From being a local poem which yet contains implications of wider significance, **'The Holy Tulzie'** here becomes parochial, concerned with personalities of interest only to a limited circle of readers. Those very elements which gave the poem much of its notoriety among Burns's Ayrshire contemporaries decrease its appeal to the present day.

Some stanzas of **'Holy Willie's Prayer'** suffer from the same disability. To say as much is not to deny a jot of the brilliance of Burns's parody of the style of 'the Scottish Presbyterian eloquence' with its incongruous combination of the Biblical and the broad, or the satirical skill of the presentation of his protagonist, the arch-hypocrite of Calvinist fanaticism, disguising yet revealing his lust and greed under 'a veil that is rent', a tattered screen of sanctified self-interest, and betraying himself out of his own all too awfully eloquent mouth. For the first sixty-six of the poem's one hundred and two lines, Holy Willie is a prototype as well as a local personality, and given the slightest acquaintanceship on the reader's part with the doctrines of original sin and predestination, the theme of Christianity unchristianized is of universal—and ageless—relevance. Even the introduction, by name, of Willie's most hated 'enemy', Gavin Hamilton, requires no external explanation, for he too is not only individual but representative, a personality who enjoys the pleasures frowned upon by the kirk ('He drinks, and swears, and plays at cartes') while possessing such charm that he commits the even greater 'crime' of winning more regard than the community's religious leader ('Frae G—d's ain priest the people's hearts / He steals awa').

But then occur two stanzas in which Willie demands that the Lord should 'hear my earnest cry and prayer / Against that Presbytery of Ayr!' and describes 'that glib-tongu'd Aiken' who created such terror among the godly that even 'Auld wi' hingin lip gaed sneaking'. These lines are a good deal less than self-explanatory to readers unaware of what occurred when Gavin Hamilton appealed to the 'moderate' Presbytery of Ayr, against the adverse judgment on his alleged absence from public worship passed

by the 'Auld Licht' kirk in the parish of Mauchline, and won his case thanks to the successful pleading of his lawyer and friend Robert Aiken. To 'the rustic inmates of the hamlet who constituted Burns's first audience, the affair was so recent, and the gossip concerning it so rife, that detailed description would have been otiose, but what was daylight to them is darkness to us unless we are given editorial assistance, for the parochial nature of the subject-matter defeats unaided comprehension.

Both **'The Holy Tulzie'** and **'Holy Willie's Prayer'** are concerned with specific local religious scandals, so notorious in the west country that, had the poems been printed, the characters who feature in them could not have failed to be recognized, even if their names had been omitted and replaced by asterisks. The risk of a libel action, or of clerical condemnation, or of both, was too great for that unconfessed bigamist among 'rakish rooks', Robert Burns, to include them in the Kilmarnock edition—even although there can be little doubt, human nature being what it is, that those subjects of scandal and concern had created much of that local interest in the author which led to his first publication being so heavily subscribed by his neighbours. **'The Holy Tulzie'** remained unpublished during the poet's lifetime, the first to appear in print being **'Holy Willie's Prayer'**, in an anonymous pamphlet of 1789, when it was accompanied—appropriately—by 'quotations from the Presbyterian eloquence'.

This linking of Burns's late-eighteenth-century poem with a work published in 1694 as a result of the religious strife in seventeenth-century Scotland is significant, for although Professor James Kinsley [in his *The Poems and Songs of Robert Burns,* 1968, Vol. III] indicates a more recent model for **'Holy Willie's Prayer'** ('Burns may have taken a hint from Ramsay's "Last Speech of a Wretched Miser to his hoard"'), it has much in common with Drummond of Hawthornden's late near-vernacular poem, 'A Character of the Anti-Covenanter, or Malignant', first published among the posthumous poems in the 1711 edition of Drummond's works. Here Drummond, himself an 'anti-Covenanter, or Malignant' (or Cavalier), adopts the persona of a Covenanter in order to 'attack' the Cavalier view, in exact anticipation of the way in which Burns, himself a moderate (with the same dislike of Presbyterian extremism as the Cavaliers had possessed before him), adopts the persona of an Auld Licht in order to 'attack' the moderate standpoint, and in each poem the Calvinist fanatic who is the protagonist brings down the reader's condemnation upon himself while seeking to destroy the opposition.

'A Character of the Anti-Covenanter', 106 lines long—only four lines longer than **'Holy Willie's Prayer'**—is written in octosyllabic couplets instead of the 'standard Habbie' of Burns, but its jaunty, irregular rhythms, its at least equally irregular rhymes, its brutal jocularity, its plain blunt energy—at the opposite pole of style from the stately and mellifluous decorum of Drummond's earlier verse, published during his lifetime—give it a force no less devastating, and no less remarkable for its counterpointing of the profound and the profane, than the later work.

There is, however, one major difference between the two poems, for the speaker in Drummond is not identified by any nickname; he represents all extreme Calvinists rather than, like Holy Willie, a particular spokesman speaking for all. In the same way, the targets at which the earlier extremist fires his musket are not specific opponents like Gavin Hamilton and Robert Aiken, but each and every member of the 'malignant' party. It may be argued that Burns's particularity of characterization gives **'Holy Willie's Prayer'** more point (although in fact Hamilton is as much a type as an individual, and Aiken is scarcely particularized at all, except as 'glib-tongu'd'), or it may be held that this very particularization narrows the range of Burns's attack, compared with Drummond's; but it is beyond dispute that the present-day reader of Drummond does not require to acquaint himself with seventeenth-century Scottish biography in order to gain full appreciation of his poem, as must be done with regard to the following century in respect of **'Holy Willie's Prayer'**.

Unlike that dramatic lyric, Burns's next religious satire, **'The Holy Fair',** which followed in the autumn of the same year, was considered 'safe' enough for inclusion in the Kilmarnock edition—although that safety was ensured only by a liberal substitution of asterisks for proper names whose owners would have regarded their appearance in print in such a context as being highly improper. A further measure of safety arises from the fact that **'The Holy Fair'** is less personal than public, less concerned with the follies committed by particular individuals than with the festivities enjoyed by a whole community, for the poem belongs to a Scots tradition of 'come-to-the-fair' verse-comedy traceable to the medieval celebration of village life in 'Christ's Kirk on the Green' (which had been brought up to date earlier in the eighteenth century by Allan Ramsay, with the addition of extra cantos of his own).

Again, **'The Holy Fair'** is not concerned with one specific, easily recognizable occurrence—an undignified row between two Calvinist ministers, or a legal battle between fundamentalist priest and liberal parishioner—but might derive from observation of any and every public communion held in the open air in the west of Scotland. The scene is in fact set in Burns's local parish of Mauchline, as we now know (from the manuscript), but the asterisks in the Kilmarnock edition give no clue to this, and there are no merely parochial descriptive details (except perhaps the mention of 'Racer Jess', the half-witted daughter of 'Poosie Nansie' Gibson, who kept a local tavern) which might give the game—and the name—away to readers not already in the know. Moreover, the references to the various preachers who waste the sweetness (or sourness) of their eloquence on the desert air—while 'the godly . . . gie the jars an' barrels / A lift that day' and 'the lads an' lasses . . . are cozie i' the neuk'—are of such a generalized kind that their actual identities, indicated in the printed text only by asterisks, matter little or nothing.

> Now a' the congregation o'er,
>   Is silent expectation;
> For ****** speels the holy door,

> Wi' tidings o's-lv-t————n:
> Should *Hornie,* as in ancient days,
>   'Mang sons o' G————present him,
> The vera sight o' ******'s face,
>   To's ain *het hame* had sent him
>   Wi' fright that day.

Who cares, or needs to care, that scholarly research has revealed the minister there as 'Sawnie', otherwise Alexander Moodie (of **'The Holy Tulzie'**), 'educated at Glasgow, ordained to Culross in 1759, and minister of Riccarton from 1762'? What difference does it make to the reader's enjoyment to know that the asterisks in '***** opens out his cauld harangues' represent that grand old Caledonian cognomen, Smith? Yet Burns himself, publishing his volume while he poised precariously on the razor's edge dividing acknowledged fornication from unadmitted bigamy, was compelled to care, and the difference between asterisks and actuality was vital. He might risk revealing the truth in **'The Holy Fair',** but not the whole truth. The real identities of his preaching protagonists remained 'underground'.

Of all the many poems in the 'Christ's Kirk' tradition, **'The Holy Fair'** is the most masterly, in its command of verse technique, the idiomatic cut and thrust of its style, the combination of comedy and criticism in its action and characterization, and the cunning of its transitions between panoramic views of general activities and close-ups of individuals and particularities. Yet Hilton Brown, while finding the poem 'excellent as a descriptive piece', dismisses it as 'surely too crude for successful satire', a view which seems eccentric—unless the critic is using 'crude' in the sexual sense, expressing disapproval of such scenes as the lover taking advantage of everyone else's eyes being fixed on the preacher, and engaging meantime in intimate caresses of his 'ain dear lass'. But this is surely to have overlooked the central theme of the poem, the triumphant survival of life-creating sexuality even under the dreary domination of the most repressive puritanism.

The satire on Calvinism in **'Address to the Deil'** (written in the winter of 1785-6) is so indirect, and so devoid of specific local references, that it was included in the Kilmarnock edition almost as written. Almost, but not quite. In lines 61-6 the demands of decorum have led to the toning down of the tragic tale of how devilish witchcraft deprives the new bridegroom of his virility at the most vital of all moments; and in lines 85-90 'my bonie Jean, / My dearest part' is removed from the poem. The first of these departures from the manuscript is significant in showing how Burns, despite his contempt for convention, was the kind of rebel poet who is not above deciding, on occasion, that discretion is the better part of valour where the interests of publication are concerned—and even then he was not discreet enough for some, since the Rev. Hugh Blair advised that even the revised stanza 'had better be left out, as indecent' from the Edinburgh edition of 1787.

Of the revision of lines 85-90 Kinsley takes the view that it was 'probably made just before going to press, to remove the allusion to Jean Armour, from whom he was estranged', but this does much less than justice to the difficulty and danger of Burns's situation in June 1786, when he was secretly married not only to a pregnant Jean Armour but also to Mary Campbell (whose reputation was far from being impregnable). 'Estranged' from Jean Armour, Burns undoubtedly was, when her parents compelled her to acquiesce in the defacement of the 'marriage certificate' which the poet had given her and then packed her off to Paisley in the hope that she might contrive a more suitable match; but he did not languish after her for long. On the contrary, the speed with which he was off with the old love and on with the new, and his recklessness in giving the second girl the same kind of documentary evidence of his 'honourable intentions' as he had already presented to the first, put him in a position of vulnerability to the law—if his secrets were discovered—that would have weakened even the steeliest nerves. For Burns to have published a declaration of his regard for Jean ('A dancin, sweet, young, handsome queen / Wi' guileless heart') at a time when he was risking a charge of bigamy—against which he could have defended himself only by swearing that she had no claim upon him whatsoever—would have been an act of self-destruction too apparent for even the most impractical poet to ignore. As far as his published work was concerned, it was imperative that Jean be kept 'underground', consigned to oblivion, become a non-person. And so it happened, Burns replacing her person with 'the Soul of Love', an unconscious irony which was lost upon those of his original readers who had not already encountered the poem in manuscript. Even in its altered state, the 'Address' remains one of his most attractive works, a humorous mock-attack on the Great Enemy which reduces more orthodox assaults upon him to the status of superstitious nonsense, but the excised stanzas have a bite and a particularity lacking from their published counterparts.

The last of the religious satires composed before the Kilmarnock edition made Burns famous, **'The Ordination'** (written early in 1786) was as parochial in origin as **'The Holy Tulzie'** and **'Holy Willie's Prayer'**, and it suffered the same fate, exclusion. For all the asterisks with which the text is bespattered fail to conceal from even the most cursory reader that the scene is Kilmarnock and the occasion the presentation to the ministry of the Laigh Kirk there of a fundamentalist minister, the Rev. James Mackinlay, who owned his preferment to the favour of the patron, the Earl of Glencairn. Written to console the moderate party in their defeat, the poem uses the pastoral imagery of **'The Holy Tulzie'** to present a ludicrously grotesque picture of Kilmarnock's Auld Licht congregation in the shape of a ram which has had only 'scanty' feeding while the Moderates held the field but which can now revel in rich repasts of *'gospel kail'* and *'runts o' grace'* provided by the fundamentalist Mackinlay. The work's daring juxtapositions of the sacred and the profane must have seemed blasphemous to contemporary readers of the evangelical persuasion, and the concluding episode, when Orthodoxy flogs Learning, Common Sense and Morality through the town as if they were rogues and vagabonds, possesses a brutal jocularity, equating 'righteousness' with sadistic revenge, which lays it open to the

same change. This is the only one of Burns's pre-Kilmarnock satires occasioned by a Moderate defeat rather than by an Evangelical upset, and the sharper bitterness of its tone may well reflect the rage felt by the poet's party, and by the author himself, at their discomfiture on a battleground where they had begun to believe that they were on the winning side.

But Burns did not leave **'The Ordination'** unacknowledged and underground for very long. Although he omitted it from the Kilmarnock, he found it a place in the Edinburgh edition of 1787, and one can only speculate on the reasons which led him on that occasion to accept a risk which he had refused to take a year earlier, and which he still refused on behalf of **'The Holy Tulzie'** and **'Holy Willie's Prayer'**. Perhaps he had realized that irony remains unnoticed by persons without a sense of humour, and that a poem written in the style of a victory-song for the fundamentalists might well be interpreted as such by them and hence escape their strictures? Whatever the explanation, there is no doubt that Burns experienced some difficulty in finding sufficient previously unpublished poems for the Edinburgh edition to justify it in the eyes of readers who had already bought the earlier book—this accounts for his inclusion in the Edinburgh collection of **'Death and Dr Hornbook'**, a *jeu d'esprit* which has been greatly admired for its witty command of dialogue but which the poet himself had considered 'too trifling and prolix' to publish in the Kilmarnock volume. He may have felt that, having 'got away' with **'The Holy Fair'** in the Kilmarnock, where it had even been praised and quoted in the reviews, he might now take a chance on the publication of another religious satire, and chose **'The Ordination'** as being less of a pointed personal attack on individuals than **'The Holy Tulzie'** and **'Holy Willie's Prayer'**. The question must remain in doubt, but—given the necessity of finding some 'new poems' for the Edinburgh volume—the hypothesis seems not unreasonable.

In his religious satires, Burns is the artist-intellectual in rebellion against the obscurantism of local public opinion, and his allies are the men of education who favoured patronage (exercised by land-owning heritors) in the establishment of parish ministers, rather than election by the elders of individual kirks, as the uneducated majority preferred. In his social satires, however, Burns becomes the lower-class radical hostile to the gentry, and his allies are the same peasant masses—the crofters and small farmers—for whose fundamentalist religious opinions he had the highest contempt. **'The Twa Dogs'** (early 1786), an eclogue consisting of canine comparisons between the virtues and vices of the rich and the poor, much to the latter's advantage, eschews all discussion of religion, and its implicit Biblical moral, that 'Satan still finds work for idle hands to do', in contrasting the idle aristocracy with the hard-working peasantry, avoids any scriptural association. This is perhaps 'natural' enough, in the sense that the dialogue is conducted between a pair of brute beasts to whom the spiritual aspects of existence might be expected to remain unknown, but in view of Burns's own religious alignment, the omission is also highly significant.

Radical as 'The Twa Dogs' is in its attack on the privileged, its inclusion in the Kilmarnock volume placed its unprivileged author in no danger of any kind of prosecution or persecution by authority. When social criticism emerges from the mouths—or muzzles—of dogs, it is bound to create the effect that their bark is worse than their bite. Moreover, Burns takes care to make exceptions to his general strictures on the gentry—'there's some exceptions, man an' woman'—and thereby provides the opportunity for any reader belonging to the upper classes to include himself among the exceptional few to whom the satire does not apply. Again, the introductory descriptions of the two canine characters have such charm as to make it well-nigh impossible to take offence at anything they say. Their dialogue is both racy and pointed, and Burns's success in giving his octosyllabic couplets the cadence of Scots vernacular speech is so remarkable as to be quite unremarked in the reading. Yet, at the same time, one can appreciate the doubt in Hilton Brown's mind when he commented that 'to talk of . . . **"The Twa Dogs"** . . . as "poetry" seems to strain a little the accepted meaning of words' and preferred to consider the work's medium as being verse; for in capturing the tone of conversation Burns frequently strays so far from the poetical that passage after passage is no more than rhythmical rhyming prose, entirely devoid of imagery.

Different in every way, except its octosyllabic couplets, is **'Address of Beelzebub'**, also written in 1786, but never published in Burns's lifetime. Dated from 'Hell 1st June Anno Mundi 5790', and signed by Beelzebub, the poem is only too particular in the point of its attack, being directed to

> the Rt Honble JOHN, EARL OF BREADALBANE, President of the Rt Honble the HIGHLAND SOCIETY, which met, on the 23d of May last, at the Shakespeare, Covent garden, to concert ways and means to frustrate the designs of FIVE HUNDRED HIGHLANDERS who, as the Society were informed by Mr McKenzie of Applecross, were so audacious as to attempt to escape from theire lawful lords and masters whose property they are by emigrating from the lands of Mr McDonald of Glengary to the wilds of CANADA, in search of that fantastic thing—LIBERTY.

The savage sarcasm of the poem's sixty-two lines makes it one of the most fiercely effective of Burns's works, a furious condemnation of aristocratic arrogance, which lashes authority with as stinging a whip as his lordship is pictured as using on 'the tatter'd gipseys' who are wives to those 'Poor, dunghill sons of dirt an' mire', his Highland tenants. For attempting to interfere with their freedom of choice, Breadalbane is not only doomed but also pre-eminently damned, fated to a special place in hell, 'The benmost newk, aside the ingle / At my right hand', and the brutality of the punishment to be inflicted by him upon the lower orders ('smash them! crush them a' to spails!') is evoked by Burns in a passage of such ferocious energy as to make eternal hell-fire seem no outrageous sentence when compared with the crime.

Yet the power in the land which permitted Breadalbane

and his associates among the Scottish gentry to curtail the liberties of their tenants was also too great for a mere tenant-farmer such as Burns to risk defying it by publication, however violently he might denounce that power in manuscript. In a Scotland where political—and judicial—authority was concentrated in the 'happy few' who constituted the landed interest, and where that authority was well-nigh absolute (as Burns and other radicals were to discover to their cost when they dared to favour the French Revolution a few years later), the public defiance of a belted earl by an untitled nobody from the hilts of a plough might well have exposed the latter to a legal system for which the social hierarchy was still sacrosanct, and would certainly have placed him beyond the pale so far as any prospect of public employment was concerned. It is even a matter of doubt whether he could have continued as a tenant-farmer, for as a 'marked man', a radical who had published an attack on one of the greatest landlords in the country, he would have found most other landlords refusing to rent him a farm. Such were the perils daunting enough to force the freest spirit in eighteenth-century Scotland to confine **'Address of Beelzebub'** to an underground existence.

Ironically, it seems to have been safer to satirize the monarch in far-off London than a mere magnate with a Scottish estate. When King George III's birthday was celebrated on 4 June 1786 with a Pindaric ode by the poet-laureate, Burns immediately retorted with **'A Dream'**, and inserted it into the copy for the Kilmarnock edition just before it went to press. Although his aristocratic acquaintance Mrs Dunlop informed him that the work was disliked by 'numbers at London' and suggested that he amend it for the Edinburgh edition, Burns rejected her advice on the grounds that 'I set as little by kings, lords, clergy, critics etc. as all these respectable Gentry do by my bardship'. This appears to be very bold, but in fact it is little more than bravado. For while some readers of **'A Dream'** might take offence at its tone of impudent familiarity, addressing the king and his family as if they were near neighbours, the poem is innocent of any attack on the institution of monarchy. On the contrary, it protests the author's 'loyal, true affection' alongside its waggish depreciation of the flattery of courtiers and the pecadilloes of the royal princes. Its publication might be regarded as being in doubtful taste, but it could scarcely be denounced for advocating revolutionary principles of equality, since its democratic attitude remains implicit, as a matter of manner, and is never explicitly stated, and even stressed, as in the overt onslaught upon aristocracy in **'Address of Beelzebub'**.

After the publication of the Kilmarnock edition in July 1786 and Burns's consequent departure from his native heath to become consecutively a literary lion in Edinburgh, a farmer in Dumfries-shire, and an exciseman in Dumfries, there was a marked decline in his satirical production, both in quantity and in quality. For this there would appear to have been two reasons—rootlessness and respectability. Burns the famous poet, elevated out of the ranks of the tenantry and commissioned as an officer in the Excise, and domiciled in a district different from that in which he had shared the trials and tribulations of the labouring life, was inevitably distanced from the people and the places, the pulpits and the politics, which had provided his radical attacks on religious orthodoxy and aristocratic privilege. Occasionally he attempted to hark back to his parochial past in Ayrshire, but **'A New Psalm for the Chapel of Kilmarnock'** (25 April 1789), written in the mock-scriptural style of **'Holy Willie's Prayer'**, was innocuous enough—in its avoidance of personalities—for immediate publication in the London *Morning Star,* while **'The Kirk of Scotland's Garland'** (autumn 1789), published as an anonymous broadsheet, is a repetitive catalogue of individual insults rather than a rounded poem. Well might the author ask himself, 'Poet Burns, Poet Burns, wi' your priest-skelping turns, / Why desert ye your auld native shire?' The short answer, financial necessity (''tis luxury in comparison of all my preceding life'), had been expressed more poignantly by the poet a twelvemonth earlier, in his **'Extemporaneous Effusion on being appointed to the Excise'**—

> Searching auld wives' barrels,
> Ochon, the day!
> That clarty barm should stain my laurels;
> But—what'll ye say?

Nemerov lauds Burns's distinction as a poet:

What I've come to care for most in Burns is the marvelous freshness and friendliness of his voice. Much as he may have admired—to the point of emulation—Milton's figure of Satan, he doesn't sound that way at all, though he has his own dignity there is not much that's awesome about it. He sounds like a friend if you want him to be, a trait he shares with such great writers as Socrates, Montaigne, and Freud.

Also his musicality—in the songs, yes, but not there alone, the musicality of the verse itself is fine, especially in his handling of measure and the rime of that favorite traditional stanza—the triple rime cut off by a bob and then an added fourth and a bob again—for instance:

> Ah Nick! Ah Nick! it is na fair,
> First showing us the tempting ware,
> Bright wines and bonnie lasses rare,
> To put us daft;
> Syne weave, unseen, thy spider snare
> O'Hell's damned waft.

Making that sound easy, colloquial, conversational and idiomatic as it does is something that demands the greatest skill, a virtuoso's mastery of the instrument of speech—the line, the rime, the weaving of the sentence so as to fit just right with the stanza . . . our impression of its simplicity comes from his hardest work.

Howard Nemerov, in a speech delivered to the Burns Society in 1979, reprinted in New and Selected Essays, *Southern Illinois University Press, 1985.*

> These muvin' things ca'd wives and weans
> Wad muve the very hearts o' stanes!

With the solitary exception of **'Tam o' Shanter'**—his only excursion into narrative—the rest of the best of Burns is not satire but song.

Catarina Ericson-Roos (essay date 1977)

SOURCE: "Love and the Lassies," in *The Songs of Robert Burns: A Study of the Unity of Poetry and Music,* Uppsala, 1977, pp. 31-53.

[*In this essay, Ericson-Roos analyzes the women of Burns's love poetry, asserting that "Burns shows an extraordinary psychological insight into the feminine mind."*]

The majority of Burns's songs deal with love, love seen from the poet's point of view or love seen through the eyes of one of the lovers. There are conventional pieces, droll and humorous scenes, young love, mature love, and erotic love. There are love-songs where the emphasis lies on sentiment, others where it lies on character or on action. Among all these songs we find Burns's most interesting and exciting characters. These are his young girls in love and particularly those who speak for themselves in the songs. Here Burns shows an extraordinary psychological insight into the feminine mind and as Christina Keith points out [in her *The Russet Coat: A Critical Study of Burns' Poetry and of Its Background,* 1956], at the time he wrote them he had "had great experience of girls, at any rate of the particular girl he had chosen as his type". These girls display a considerable amount of independence, of self-confidence, of self-knowledge, and of knowledge of the world. Their world is love, and love exclusively, but into this world they grow and through love they grow, from the first stage of girlhood and innocence into womanhood and experience. They come into conflict with convention and the code of female behaviour and with their parents' opinions, but in all situations they show strength of mind and individuality. A passive woman who lets herself be subdued cannot be found among these young women. Furthermore, as Christina Keith has shown [in *The Russet Coat*], Burns carried on the tradition of the Scottish folk-songs and ballads in which free love had managed to survive in spite of the Reformation and John Knox's attack on women. The Kirk had an iron grip on the people and on women, who had a very low status. Love flourished, however, where the Kirk could not reach it, in the Borders and in the Highlands, and with it the free and independent woman. In these songs we find the women of the old Scotland, women who "were captivating, free and elegant, without the remotest shadow of subjection".

The youngest and most innocent of these girls is to be found in **"Tam Glen"**, a song which gives a portrait of a highly infatuated girl who is totally engrossed in the thoughts of her lover. Excitedly, she chatters away without stop about her dear Tam Glen, naively she believes in superstitious omens, and with growing self-confidence she reacts against her parents' opinions. The situation is common enough: the mother warns her against flattering men and the father wants her to marry for money. She listens to neither for the only advice she wants to hear is to marry Tam Glen. With the impatience of a very young girl in love, she begs and bribes her sister:

> Come counsel, dear Tittie, don't tarry;
>   I'll gie you my bonie black hen,
> Gif ye will advise me to Marry
>   The lad I lo'e dearly, Tam Glen.—

Her character, her girlishness and her state of mind with its agitation and restlessness is conveyed through words and music. The quick flight of her thoughts and the intensity of her chatter lie embodied in the quick tempo of the tune (the 9/8-time is suggestive of this) and in the syllabic setting for the undotted notes, which makes one pronounce each word quickly and vigorously and with equal force. Kinsley notes the preoccupation with the name and also how the "girl's persistent chatter" is sustained by the melody. She speaks uninterruptedly, her heart seems to beat quickly, and she has hardly time to take a breath before she starts talking again. The shortness of the tune (it is only four bars long), the monotonous melody and the even rhythm captures this very well. Only at the end of the second and fourth bars does the tune come to a rest on a crotchet and on these cadences the repeated name of Tam Glen and its rhymes fall.

At one point in each stanza there is an intensification of the girl's emotions. This happens in the last bar, where the melody emphatically rises. There is a large and unexpected upward skip to the highest note of the tune-followed by a gradual descent to the tonic. This feature of the tune reinforces the climax of the fourth lines of each stanza and, as the mode is minor, it lends them a sense of despair and exasperation. But there is also irritation and impatience in the expression and the high note brings out the important question words "what", "when" and "wha". These lines are also the keys to the girl's state of mind. Young as she seems and new as the sensation is to her, she is full of wonder, questions and impatience: "*what will I do*", "*wha can think sae*" and "*wha will I get*".

Another young, inexperienced but less impatient girl appears in **"I'm o'er young to Marry Yet"**, a more uncomplicated song with humorous implications. This girl is being courted by a man somewhat older than herself, but she rejects him, claiming that she is too young to marry. Yet she is intelligent—and witty—enough to see that it will not be long before she is ready to say yes. She measures time by the seasons, and half a year, from winter to summer, is what she believes she needs to be old enough to marry. The song is spun around the contrasts between winter and summer, young and old, mother's child and man's woman, innocence and experience, the present and the future. The girl is now her mother's "ae bairn" (*only child*), she is "o'er young", and "o'er young" is repeated

four times in the chorus, it is "winter" and "frosty" and both words are emphasized through the rise in the melody. But what will come is implied strongly enough in the last stanza of the song:

> Fu' loud and shill the frosty wind
>   Blaws thro' the leafless timmer [*trees*], Sir;
> But if ye come this gate again,
>   I'll aulder be gin simmer [*towards*], Sir.

The light note of the song is struck already in the old chorus from which Burns took his start [*Notes on Scottish Song by Robert Burns: Written in an Interleaved Copy of the Scots Musical Museum with Additions by Robert Riddell and Others,* 1908, edited by James C. Dick; hereafter referred to as *Notes*] and the skittish, cheerful and innocent character of the young girl is suggested in the light-tripping reel-tune, the even rhythm, the quick tempo, the high register, the rising phrases, and the major mode. [In his *Burns: A Study of the Poems and Songs,* 1960, Thomas] Crawford acknowledges the importance of the tune and says that "the words and music combine to give us a girl's mood shortly after puberty—shy, blushing, yet full of the knowledge of what she is and what she must become".

In the first line of the song ("I am my mammy's ae bairn") the significance and implications of the word "ae" are emphasized in the musical context. It emphatically falls on a rising melodic line as well as on two notes in the otherwise syllabic setting of the song. The fact that the girl is her mother's only child is one of the reasons she gives to the man for not marrying him, and therefore "'twad be a sin / To tak me frae my mammy yet". The other reason for her denial of the man is that she shudders at the thought of creeping into bed with him: "And lying in a *man's* bed, / I'm fley'd it make me irie, Sir" (*afraid; frightened*). In this example (from stanza 1) "man's" falls on two notes, emphasizing an implied antithesis—to lie in a man's bed and not in one's own—and in stanza 2 ("And you an' I in *ae* bed, / In trowth, I dare na venture, Sir") the word "ae" is accented. A man and one bed, that is a collocation which is quite beyond her field of experience.

The "Sir" at the end of every second line has several functions. It makes the song more personal (the girl addresses one particular man) at the same time as it shows the girl's respect for the older man, but the word is also needed for technical reasons. Without it the cadence would end rather heavily on "winter", "timmer" etc. [In his *Robert Burns,* 1966, David] Daiches notes this and says that "the diction flows with a happy directness and a fine dramatic feeling, while the monosyllable 'Sir' provides just what the poem needs to bring the rhythms of the reel into the diction and fit the piece perfectly to its tune".

A girl who ventures into bed with a man with less hesitation is "the sleepy bit lassie" in **"The Taylor fell thro' the bed, & c."** "She thought that a Taylor could do her nae ill" and once she has been initiated she joyfully sings out her longing and her passion. The song has a wide register and, as [James] Kinsley points out [as editor of

The Poems and Songs of Robert Burns, 1968], it moves "from comedy through passion to longing, and a last touch of comedy". Only the second and fourth stanzas are Burns's own (*Notes*), but, as Kinsley notes, these, and the change in the third stanza from the traditional "The night it is short and the day it is lang, / It's a dear-won tipence to lie wi' a man" to "The day it is short and the night it is land, / The dearest siller that ever I wan" completely change the character of the song and the girl. Her frank and spontaneous passion now successfully corresponds to the free swing of the tune. It is major and has a dotted 6/8 rhythm which, along with the upward leap of an octave in the first and third bars, both enlivens the comical note in the song and expresses the girl's uninhibited joy in love-making.

Very free and independent for her eighteen years, mature and full of opposition against her parents is the girl of **"O, for ane and twenty Tam"**. She will not be oppressed by them any longer, nor will she marry a fool for his money. She knows her worth and as soon as she comes of age ("ane and twenty") she will marry the boy she loves. Her maturity and strength is expressed through both text and tune. The melancholy high part with its stronger minor quality, its small intervals and intensifying upward direction enhances the girl's bitter feelings against her parents, expressed in the first stanza: "They snool me sair, and haud me down, / And gar me look like bluntie, Tam" (snool *snub*; sair *sore*; haud *hold*; gar *make*; bluntie *fool*). It also makes her opposition, expressed in the more relaxed chorus, psychologically logical. This girl has none of the worries of the girl in **"Tam Glen"**, she is not dependent on anybody, and in the last stanza she gives her hand in pledge to the boy: "But hearst thou, laddie, there's my loof, / I'm thine at ane and twenty, Tam!" (*hand given in pledge*). The girl in **"Tam Glen"** is on her way to self-confidence and independence, but she still feels that "to anger them a' is a pity" (meaning her parents) and she needs her sister's support. The tune of **"O for ane"** is slow and much less excited than that of **"Tam Glen"**. The emphatic high starts of the upbeats in the chorus ("*An O*", "*An* hey") give the girl's words a sense of conviction. She takes her time and rests on the cadences with the repeated "twenty Tam", and there is also a refrain-line in each stanza and a chorus to give the song a more balanced expression. Burns conceived of this song as fairly slow and he was not pleased with the setting in *SMM* [*The Scots Musical Museum Originally Published by James bunson with Illustrations of the Lyric Poetry and Music of Scotland by William Stenhouse,* vol. I, 1853; facsimile edition, 1960] (where it is marked as "canty" *lively*). In a letter to Thomson [printed in *The Letters of Robert Burns,* edited by J. De Lancey Ferguson, 1931] he writes: "but if you will get any of our ancienter Scots Fiddler to play you, *in Strathspey time* (my italics), 'The Moudiewort,' (that is the name of the air) I think it will delight you". The younger girl in **"Tam Glen"** is restlessly babbling on with no sense of pause anywhere: "She keeps on at it too—as they do—dinning the name at you in verse after verse", as Christina Keith puts it. Her conversation with her sister is intimate, worried, secret and whispering, whereas the girl in **"O for ane"** is critical,

extrovert, straightforward and free.

She shares her strength of character with the girl in **"Country Lassie"** Just like her this girl is not prepared to listen to the materialistic and moral advice of her elders or let them decide for her, and she knows that "the tender heart o' leesome loove, / The gowd and siller canna buy" (*dear love*). The poem is set to a beautiful, slightly melancholy tune, but the length and complexity of the poem, along with its dialogue form, make the ties between text and tune seem weaker in this song and allow less insight into character.

"The gallant Weaver" also has the theme of the conflict between love and money but is less dramatic than the songs discussed above. Its major tune is gently undulating, its tempo is slow, and the rhythm alternates smoothly between crotchets and quavers. The opening scene is all pleasantness, the "Cart rins rowin to the sea, / By mony a flower and spreading tree" (*rolling*), and with conviction and confidence the girl calmly sings:

> My daddie sign'd my tocher-band [*marriage-settlement*]
> To gie the lad that has the land,
> But to my heart I'll add my hand
>   And give it to the Weaver.—

Because of the musical pattern there is no sense of opposition or excitement in the third line of the quoted stanza. The air flows on at the same unvaried pace, having almost the same melodic curve here as for the first line. Emotional peaks are levelled out, and the impression is conveyed that this girl knows what she wants and that a parental decision cannot upset her or make her change her mind. This optimism is reinforced by the last stanza which lies on the high part of the tune, has a repetitional pattern and positive words like "rejoice" and "delight".

Another girl who is confronted with a materialistic love is the girl in **"My Tochers the Jewel"**. The conflict in this song does not lie between the girl and her parents, but within the girl herself, for she has seen through her lover: "My laddie's sae meikle in love wi' the siller, / He canna hae luve to spare for me" (*much*). She presents this situation in the first half-stanza with a striking antithesis between "O meikle thinks my Luve o' my beauty" and the bitter truth of "But little thinks my Luve, I ken brawlie, / My tocher's the jewel has charms for him" (*know well; dowry*). This last line is intensified through the lift in the tune followed by a descent. There is melancholy and sadness in the girl's voice, an expression which is conveyed entirely by the slow, minor tune. In the second stanza she shows that she has insight and strength, and she despises the money-seeking lover: "But an ye be crafty, I am cunnin, / Sae ye wi' anither your fortune maun try" (an *if*; maun *must*). As Kinsley points out the song is not quite homogeneous as the last half stanza is old and not made an organic part of the song.

"When she can ben she bobbed" is not a song about or by a lassie as much as to a lassie. The singer (probably a man) wants to implant in the girl's mind just those values which we have seen are held high by the young girls in the other songs:

> O never look down, my lassie at a',
> O never look down, my lassie at a';
> Thy lips are as sweet and thy figure compleat,
>   As the finest dame in castle or ha'.—

As noted by Kinsley, Burns took his start (lines 1-6) from a traditional song which presents a flirtatious laird who spites his wife for the collier lassie and "the lass in the stable". Burns changes the character of this man and makes him the true lover who chooses the collier lassie for love, instead of the wealthy "dochter of a lord" for her money. the girl, who is presented as shy and submissive in the first, traditional stanza ("O when she cam ben she bobbed fu' law" *indoors; curtseyed very low*), is then told to keep her head high and be proud, for her worth lies not in her economic status. The tune is light and lilting (6/8-time and major) but also emphatic with its snaps and upward skips and runs. This gives weight to the man's words, yet keeps the song at a light-hearted level. The lift of an octave in the second two-bar phrase should be noticed, for it gives a new intensification to the repetition in the second line of each stanza which passes unnoticed if the song is read.

A young girl's wishes might not only conflict with the expectations of the parents, as in many of the songs above, but also with society's claims for virtue, innocence and honour. In **"Wha is that at my bower door?"** the girl makes strong attempts to resist the man, as it is expected of her, but the song shows her slowly yielding to him, only a little anxious that anybody will know. The idea of the dialogue-form of the song is very old and Burns had an immediate model in a broadside. As pointed out by Kinsley, this has the same structure, with questions and answers, as Burns's own song, but lacks the humour and insight into character:

> Who's that at my chamber door?
>   And who but I? quoth Finlay.
> Lown carle [*rascal fellow*], come no further.
>   Indeed not I, quoth Finlay.

From this old broadside stanza and in the tradition of the night-visiting songs Burns develops the theme in his own way, creating, with a strong sense of humour, a "carle" who is self-assured, masculine and straightforward in his attempts to be let in by the girl:

> Wha is that at my bower-door?
>   O wha is it but Findlay;
> Then gae your gate [*go your way*], ye'se nae be here!
>   Indeed maun [*must*] I, quo' [*said*] Findlay.—

Findlay's character remains constant throughout the song. His lines are only slightly varied with a touch of humour, as he teasingly takes up the preceding words of the girl:

"In my bower *if ye should stay, / Let me stay, quo'* Findlay" or "Here this night *if ye remain, / I'll remain,* quo' Findlay". He sets out with one intention—to make the girl let him in—and he makes no attempts to conceal this. He is certain that her hesitation is only a conventional attitude and that his honest, but slightly provoking manner will force her into a quicker decision. She, in turn, shows that she knows perfectly well what it is all about. She is on her guard and puts Findlay on trial by being seemingly resistant. "Before the morn ye'll work mischief", she says and goes on:

> Gif I rise and let you in,
>   Let me in, quo' Findlay;
> Ye'll keep me waukin wi' your din;
>   Indeed will I, quo' Findlay.—

Crawford describes the situation this way: "From the very start, despite all appearances to the contrary, she has wanted to let Findlay into the bower, and she ends as absolute mistress of the situation. Findlay has made a binding promise to her (to be secret)—that is, he has yielded to her femininity; and the joke is that he thinks that *he* has conquered her!"

The tune suits the poem perfectly. It has a simplicity which allows the oppositions to be exposed, the oppositions between the questions and answers, between the apparent change in the girl's attitude and the constancy in Findlay's, and between her worries and his self-confidence. It is short, consisting of only eight bars, where one bar in the music corresponds to one line in the lyric. Significantly the girl's words are sung to arched or descending phrases, whereas Findlay's lie on the arched or more aggressive ascending ones. Especially the second and sixth bars (corresponding to the second line of each stanza) are very emphatic in their assertive upward direction. This becomes the climax of each stanza and helps to express the joy Findlay takes in challenging the girl's female code of coyness. It is also the point where he teases her by repeating her words. A sense of strength and assurance is also embodied in the dotted four-beat rhythm of the tune and in the lack of an upbeat. The potency of the "direct attack" on "*Wha* is that", "*What* mak ye", "*Gif* I rise" brings out a tone of irritation in the attitude of the girl. This points to a strong attempt to cover up the desire to let him in, but it is also a sign of her independence. The girl is, as has been pointed out, not completely in Findlay's power.

Even more illustrative of this double-standard of morality is the **"Scotish Ballad"**. In this song it is very obvious how the girl tries to cover up her real feelings by keeping up a pretence of irritation and haughtiness. Yet she knows her feminine influence and when she risks the loss of her lover she is quick to act. Passivity is not a feature of Burns's heroines. [In *The Tuneful Flame: Songs of Robert Burns as He Sang Them*, editor Robert D., 1957] Thornton asserts that "never was there a girl more confident of her charm or more able to turn her lover inside out by teasing". The song has a very human humour and touch of subtle irony, and it is set to a tune of splendid momentum and liveliness. With gentleness Burns takes the ardent lover and the proud girl through a development where, as Kinsley puts it, "she begins in the pretences of the conventionally indifferent mistress, and ends by accepting her suitor—though with the humorous understatement characteristic of the Scots", and where "he begins with the traditional protestations of the sophisticated lover, falls back on appeals to greed and ambition, and in the end betrays a natural, comically desperate passion".

The irony in the handling of the characters and the pathetic overstatement in the love-effusions of the boy is to a great extent embodied in the way the words are set to the music. The middle-cadence in the second two-bar phrase is an ascending line ending on a long dotted crotchet. The words falling on this note are subsequently prolonged, and dimensions and implications are brought out which cannot be heard in a read version. There is irritation in the girl's first lines: "Last May a braw wooer cam down the lang glen, / And sair wi' his love he did *deave me*" (*handsome; deafen*), and mocking despise in her rendering of the boy's pathetic words: "He spak o' the darts in my bonie black een, / And vow'd for my love he was *dying*". Her incisive answers to the boy fall on the emphatic rise in the third two-bar phrase, and the rise-fall followed by a dotted upward leap from the fifth to the tonic expresses the energy which the girl needs to convince herself and him of her indifference. She protests, "I said, there was *naething* I hated like men", and her "naething" is saucily spat out on this upward leap. However, already in the second stanza it is clear that she is desperately trying to keep up pretences ("I said, he might die when he liked for JEAN—/ The Lord forgie me for lying, for lying") and in the third stanza she reveals that she has some feelings for the boy ("I never loot on that I kend it, or car'd" *showed; was aware of*).

In these three opening stanzas the first two phrases (a + b) of the tune are devoted to the boy and the last three (c + d + e) to the girl. The contrast between the two, thus reinforced by the music, is also emphasized by her resolute "I *said*" and "I *never*", falling on the rise up to the dotted tonic, which prolongs and accents the verbs. The irony lies in the opposition between what she says and what she actually feels, and the implications are obvious: she says one thing, but means and feels another. As the story proceeds it is the lover's turn to pretend, and being close (as she believes) to losing him, the girl has to act. She gives him a wink and "My wooer he caper'd as he'd been in drink, / And vow'd I was his dear lassie, dear lassie". Here the leap in the first bar of c makes the verb "caper'd" illustrative of the physical demonstration of the lover's joy. Crawford speaks in terms of "character, motive and mask" about this song, and if the mask was indifference with the girl at the beginning, it has now developed into irony and humour. In the last stanza the boy is back to the passion of the first part of the song, but the girl's answer this time expresses compassionate understatement:

> He begged, for Gudesake! I wad be his wife,
>   Or else I wad kill him wi' sorrow:

So e'en [*simply*] to preserve the poor body in life,
>   I think I maun [*must*] wed him tomorrow, tomorrow,
>   I think I maun wed him tomorrow.—

The songs discussed so far have been songs of courtship. They have caught the young girls in the act of choosing (or refusing) a lover or a husband, and they have thrown light on the conflicts which might then arise. There has been a stress on personal strength, self-confidence and independence more than on the actual feelings of love. Some of the songs have been light-hearted, suggesting young girls, others have been humorous and most of them have been set to brisk, extrovert tunes. In another group of songs the themes are spun around longing and affectionate love, the relationships are more definitely established and the tunes are of a reflective character. In his essay on different types of folk-songs [*Folk-song in Buchan and Folk-song of the North-East* 1963] Gavin Greig makes a distinction between "apostrophic", introspective love-songs, and biographic, narrative ones, a distinction which applies very well to the songs in the following. To the latter group belong **"My Harry was a Gallant gay"** and **"Wae is my heart"** in which the girls speak about their love and their longing rather than addressing themselves straight to the beloved. The apostrophic songs, on the other hand, represent "the higher kind of lyric where the lover utters his own feelings in direct appeal to the object of his adoration". Songs of this type are the musical and lyrical translation of a central feeling and as Greig puts it, they give "unlimited scope for intensity of feeling and expression".

Such a song is **"For the sake o' Somebody"** in which a most generous and tender love is expressed, a love which is not seeking its own ends but is directed to the beloved person. There is a continuous return to the word "somebody" and a preoccupation of thought around this person. The lyric is beautifully suited to the structure, rhythm and melody of the tune, and the emotional dimensions of the song cannot be understood if text and tune are not considered together as one unity.

The tune consists of two almost identical sections, ab + a¹b, where a¹ lacks the upbeats and also has a heavier rhythm with longer first and third beats. In a and a¹ the phrases have an upward direction and the same melody is repeated twice, but the second time one fifth higher. This lift is strongly intensifying, and with his instinctive perception of the inherent expression of the tune Burns makes the lyrical meaning in both stanzas correspond to it:

> My heart is sair [*sad*], I dare na tell,
>   My heart is sair for Somebody;
>   . . . . .
> Ye Powers that smile on virtuous love,
>   O, sweetly smile on Somebody!

Whereas the first line is tentative, the second is more definite and more passionate: "My heart is sair" not for anybody, but for "Somebody", and "Ye Powers that smile" on all lovers, smile especially on "Somebody". In both stanzas one word is repeated in both lines to hold them more firmly together ("sair" and "smile"). On the descent in b the girl gives proof of her love: she could "wake a winter-night" for her lover (stanza 1) and she bids the heavenly powers to keep him from danger (stanza 2).

For the second half of the tune there is a refrain with the change of the rhythm in a¹. As the rhythmical swing in the music is stronger here, the first and third beats being heavier, these lines seem more extrovert, and more overflowing with the joy of love. But the four-beat lilt and the arched melodic contour is also very expressive of sighing and yearning, and the intensity of the long close *o* of "*O*hon" (often an expression of lament) and "*O*hey" gives added emphasis to these feelings. The refrain-lines lead up to the protestation in the last couplet of each stanza, "I could range the warld round" and "I wad do—what wad I not", and this "For the sake o' Somebody". The fusion of the two arts, poetry and music, is most perfect in this song. The generous love and the passionate longing is embodied in both text and tune, and the simplicity and sensitivity with which the one is coupled to the other makes the song an organic whole, where each part is dependent on and enhanced by the other.

Another apostrophic song is **"Ay waukin O"**, the lyrical and musical expression of a young girl lying awake at night, unable to sleep for thoughts of her dearie. Her longing, her unrest, her infatuation, her sadness, and her weariness, all this lies embodied in the short lyric and in its tune. The structure, the diction and the tonal language are extremely simple and nothing seems superfluous in this song. Through very small means it captures the desolate situation like a Japanese lyric, and the song itself is like a weary sigh.

The chorus expresses the girl's longing, her melancholy and her sighing. On two long notes (minims) the "Ay" and the "Oh" fall, being the utterance of her love-sick heart. The minor melody drops here, enhancing that sadness, but it rises in the second bar (taking line 2) as if to express her impatience and her unrest. In the third bar it monotonously repeats the same note four times before it falls again (line 3). It finally reaches its peak in the rise of the last bar, reinforcing the intensity of the girl's feelings. The stanzas contain the thoughts occupying the girl's mind and keeping her awake. The second (see below) is only a variation of the chorus and the other two are impressionistic lines, capturing the tired thoughts passing through her mind:

> When I sleep I dream,
>> When I wauk I'm irie [*melancholy*];
> Sleep I can get nane,
>> For thinking on my Dearie.—

The music lies higher here, it has more dotted notes and seems to embody her unrest and excitement. But each poetical line is sung to a falling melodic phrase, each one starting anew as if it is an effort for the girl to express her thoughts, tired and sad as she is.

A narrative variant of the same theme is **"How lang and dreary is the night"** of which the first version (without the chorus) appeared in *SMM*. The second version, with a chorus and set to another tune, was sent to Thomson. This song, however, lacks the simplicity and concentrated emotional impact of **"Ay waukin O"**. Its tune is more active with melodic rises, a large upward skip in the first bar and a dotted rhythm. As it is decidedly major it also fails to convey the sadness expressed in the lyric. The song is not a naked direct expression of a longing heart as **"Ay waukin O"** is, but the lyrical expansion about this feeling.

In the narrative **"My Harry was a Gallant gay"** the theme of longing and sadness is opposed to that of strength and vengeance. There are tensions within the girl of her tender feelings towards Highland Harry and of her bitter feelings toward those who saw to his banishment, and these tensions are embodied both in the tune and in the poetical interpretation of the tune. The predominant thought in the girl's mind is that of Highland Harry's return home, and in the refrain it is kept alive throughout the whole song. The form of the tune is abcb¹, where ab takes the stanzas and cb¹ the chorus. Burns has followed the musical structure with the repeated b-phrase and connected his own stanzas with the theme of the old chorus (Notes) by letting each last line take up the refrain of the latter:

a	My Harry was a gallant gay,
	Fu' stately strade he on the plain;
b	But now he's banish'd far awa,
	I'll never see him *back again,*
c	O for him back again,
	O for him back again,
b¹	I wad gie a' Knockhaspie's land
	For Highland Harry *back again.*

In the chorus the girl's emotions intensify and get unbounded sway. At this point the tune changes register (it lifts by an octave) and the long first beat for "O" (n.b. the expressive lack of the upbeat) embodies all her unfulfilled longing.

With its interplay of dotted notes and snaps, its limited tonal material (the scale is pentatonic and bars 1 and 5 are built up on the tonic) and its assertive authentic range the tune is very powerful. All this is particularly effective in the first lines of the first and last stanzas, where the snaps accent the alliterations and make the words sound forceful and fierce. There is pride in the girl's voice when she sings, "My Harry was a gallant gay, / Fu' stately strade he on the plain", and for "stately" the tune makes a large upward leap, emphasizing that word. The alliteration in "*st*ately *st*rade" also adds to the sense of power as it helps to accent the beat. But the girl's happy reverie comes to a sudden end in line 3, where she bursts out, "*But now* he's banish'd far awa". Dramatically the tune now lifts and rises to the top note, before it descends into the refrain.

In the second stanza the girl's sadness is expressed. The

descent of the tune in bar 2 here becomes finely expressive of the despondency in "I wander dowie up the glen" (*sad*), as if she slowly drops her head. The stanza is a good example of the expressive flexibility of a tune. From having been powerful in the first stanza it now responds to the more lyrical expression of the words. In the last stanza the girl gathers up strength and its first half expresses suppressed anger and threat. On the melodic ascent in b, however, she cheers up at the thought of seeing her lover again: "Then I might see the joyfu' sight, / My Highland Harry back again".

"Jamie come try me" also expresses the longing of a girl, but is more purely a song of the senses and a song of the passions. It is an interpretation of emotions only and says nothing about the circumstances around these emotions. It "calls up a picture of someone 'just waiting to be asked'—breathless with desire, and almost beseeching Jamie to take the first step", as Crawford puts it. The contents, language and structure of the lyric in combination with the character of the tune also suggest a slightly older girl than the ones in the songs discussed above.

The impact of the song is largely dependent on the tune, and the emotional connotations of the words can only be fully understood if the song is sung. The lyric has a very tightly knit structure which is moulded on that of the tune. At five places the two-bar phrases end on a minim and a crotchet, an ending which carries the repeated "try me" and its rhymes. The three remaining phrases have, melodically and rhythmically, a less final character. They take the repeated "love", and as these musical phrases more definitely lead on to the next, the poetical lines are correspondingly subordinate clauses leading onto the following main clause. The chorus introduces the theme round which the two stanzas are spun:

a	Jamie come try me,
a	Jamie come try me,
b	If thou would win my love
a	Jamie come try me.

b	If thou should ask my love,
a	Could I deny thee?
b	If thou would win my love,
a	Jamie come try me.

The first "Jamie come try me" is sung on an assertively ascending melodic line going from the tonic to its octave. It lacks the upbeat which makes the invitation more direct and straightforward. After this first attempt the girl becomes sensuous and alluring and her words are sung in a low register and with less directness (the melodic curve is now arched). Then there is a sudden tone of despair in her tune. It leaps up one octave and on this high note the word "if" falls. It jumps down again, but ascends from there and comes back to the last "Jamie come try me". This time it lies very high and therefore has a stronger intensity.

The stanzas, set to the second half of the tune, are spun round the if-questions and the tune in this section remains in the high register, giving more emphasis to these questions. For "Could I deny thee?" and "Wha could espy thee?" the melody rises, after which there is a return to the refrain of the song which is now sung to a passively descending melodic line: it is the last appeal, it is the least forceful, yet the snaps give it a certain urgency.

On the printed page this simple poem reveals very little of its emotional overtones. The sensuality, the urgent and alluring appeal, the intensity of the questions, the underlying despair, the wide emotional range of the song; all this lies embodied in the tune with its slow tempo, its great range, its melodic contour and the gentle lilt of the triple rhythm. One would never read the song as slowly as one can sing it, and one would not rest so pleadingly on "try", "deny" and "espy". A reading of the lyric becomes tediously regular, particularly because of the repetitions.

Another song which is even more lifeless and stereotype in print is **"Stay, my Charmer, can you leave me?"** Sung to its tune, however, it has an emotional dimension which the words alone are not capable of conveying. The song is about the cruelty of love:

> Stay, my Charmer, can you leave me;
> Cruel, cruel to deceive me!
> Well you know how much you grieve me:
>   Cruel Charmer, can you go!
>   Cruel Charmer, can you go!

The first two lines sound trite and conventional without their beautiful melodic lines, but when delivered in music they display the conflicting emotions within the woman. The melodic contour is for the first line passively descending and the plea to stay is filled with a feeling of resignation and hopelessness. But in the second line the despised woman gets excited at the thought of the deceiver: the melody changes direction and now emphatically rises. It is the cruelty of the committed "crime" which is the overwhelming feeling and the word "cruel" is repeated twice, the second time more incisively on the top note of the rising line. The word comes back, in lines 4 and 5, but are then connected with "Charmer". Line 4 is set to a descending phrase, it is passive, accepting facts, whereas line 5 is a sudden outburst of pain making the end of the song highly dramatic. There is an abrupt change of register of an octave and a fourth and a rise at the end of the phrase which changes the mechanical repetition of "Cruel Charmer, can you go!" into a kind of haunting thought in the lover's mind. The impact of the second stanza is weaker because of its stilted language and repeated "by". But the music levels out the grossest effects of this and lends different colours to each line. What was said about the repeated "cruel" in lines 4 and 5 applies equally to "do not" in lines 9 and 10.

"Wae is my heart" is also a song about the pains of love, although presented with more pretentiousness than the songs above. The grief felt by the girl is heightened by the slow tune with its falling contour and dramatic upward leap in the first half, and the higher and livelier second half, which makes the lyrical expression there more intense and more urgent. The fact that bars 1 and 3 lack upbeats gives added emphasis to the important words "wae" and "lang" in stanza 1, to the repeated "love" in stanza 2, and to the longing "O" in stanza 3. But the song is not one of Burns's best. Its somewhat rhetorical style ("Love, thou hast pleasures, and deep hae I loved; / Love thou hast sorrows, and sair hae I proved") and the name "Phillis" give it a tinge of eighteenth-century English poetry, which is not quite in unison with the unpretentiousness of the Scottish tune.

A love-song of a more uncomplicated and happy kind is **"Young Jockey was the blythest lad"**. Through the frequent use of repetitions and words with pleasant associations Burns gives this lyric an extrovert character which finely responds to the cheerful expression of the tune. He also takes advantage of the contrast between the two sections of the tune to convey the emotions behind the girl's words. The first four lines of stanza 1 describe the lad in an objective way: "Fu' blythe" the lad whistles and "Fu' lightly" he dances, and as if to imprint this on the listener the word "blythe" is used twice. With the lift in the second half of the tune, its shift from minor to major and its less jerky rhythm, the lyric now speaks of the girl's feelings for the boy, and her face seems to light up at the thought of her own relations to him:

> He roos'd [*praised*] my een sae bonie blue,
>   He roos'd my waist sae genty sma
>   [*gracefully slender*];
> And ay my heart came to my mou,
>   When ne'er a body heard or saw.

In the second stanza the minor first part of the tune with its energetic, snapped rhythm becomes aptly descriptive of the scene—young Jockey "toils" on the plain through "wind and weet" (*rain*) and through "frost and snaw". In the last half-stanza the lad comes home, he takes the girl in his arms, and the gaiety of the situation is enhanced by the switch to the high register and the major quality of the tune, and the tension of the hard work is released through the smoother rhythm.

One group of Burns's females grow from girlhood to womanhood through the experience of motherhood. A common feature of Scottish life in the eighteenth century which is reflected in the folk-songs, is the young girl who has been seduced and deserted by her lover. Burns picked up this traditional theme and to tunes of both light-hearted and reflective characters he wrote lyrics which mirror different aspects of such situations. He shows deep understanding and sympathy for these girls, and his fine psychological insight into the female mind reveals itself particularly in these songs.

A young and very inexperienced girl is depicted in **"To the Weaver's gin ye go"** in which the girl's encounter with the erotic side of love comes very abruptly. Her "heart was ance as blythe and free / As simmer days were lang", but innocence met with bitter experience and her singing changed to sighing. There is a foreshadowing of

the disastrous event already at the beginning ("But a bonie, westlin weaver lad / Has gart me change my sang" *made*), and although there are elements of delight and joy and excitement in the song there is also a sense of doom hovering over it. The shame and fear of the girl is the underlying sentiment of the song and it is expressed in the last stanza:

> But what was said, or what was done,
>   Shame fa' [*befall*] me gin [*if*] I tell;
> But Oh! I fear the kintra [*country people*] soon
>   Will ken [*know*] as weel's mysel!

Her words are sung to the low, monotonous part of the tune, which is centered round one note (F-sharp) and has a descending melodic contour.

Although it is lively, the tune also strikes a tone of regret and hopelessness through the incessant drumming character of the reiterated F-sharp. This also calls to mind the regular thump of the loom, which accompanies the girl's sighing and sobbing (notice the monotonous effect of the repetition and alliteration in "But the *w*eary, *w*eary *w*arpin o't", *w*eaving).

But, as Kinsley points out, the "blend of delight and regret" is also palpable in the chorus because of its "melancholy final phrase". This chorus, which is traditional (*Notes*), is a jocular, yet serious comment on the girl's words in the stanzas. What happens if a girl goes to the weaver at night is said only by implication, and the chorus is meant as a warning to other young girls:

> To the weaver's gin [*if*] ye go, fair maids,
>   To the weaver's gin ye go,
> I rede [*warn*] you right, gang ne'er at night,
>   To the weaver's gin ye go.

As it is not the girl who speaks in it, it becomes the comment of a detached observer and recalls the function of the chorus in a Greek drama. The tune has an assertively rising melodic line in major, before it falls into minor in the last bar, which gives it that curiously sad twist at the end. Alexander Keith [in his *Burns and Folk-Song,* 1922] aptly describes the significance of this minor end thus: "Sprightly enough through three-quarters of its length, it [the chorus] drops to the minor in the concluding bar, with an odd simulation of warning, a sort of admonitory, cautious finger wagged before the face of the lassie to enforce the prophecy of the dire consequences, 'to the weaver's gin ye go.'"

The girl of **"Here's his health in water"** is in the same predicament. She is pregnant, deserted, and has to stand "the kintra clatter" (*the country people's gossip*), but she has a less worried and more cheerful attitude than the weaver-lassie. She curses the "wanton sides" and the flattering tongue of the boy, yet with a shrug of the shoulders she gives him the toast:

> Although my back be at the wa',
>   And though he be the fautor [*wrong-doer*],

Although my back be at the wa',
Yet here's his health in water.—

There is no sadness or regret in this song. The tune is gay and extrovert, and in the first half its melodic lines are mainly falling, except at the end where it emphatically rises one octave and the girl can be imagined lifting her hand for the toast: "Yet here's his health in water". In the second half there is emphasis on "O wae gae by" (*may evil befall*), "Sae brawly's he" (*admirably*) and "Till for his sake" because of the lifts in the tune. This is where the girl reveals that she is angry with the boy, but she quickly resumes her attitude of "never mind" and forgives him.

"The rantin dog the Daddie o't" is also a song in which a young mother tries to grasp her situation with humour. It presents a young girl who enjoys life, love and sex and lets nothing depress her. She has a remedy for all the difficulties she might meet as an unmarried mother, and this is "the rantin dog the daddie o't" (*merry-making*). Her tune is cheerful and her attitude optimistic. She knows much more about life than the girl in **"To the Weaver's gin ye go"**, and she also knows how to meet it with both its hardships and its joys. The young weaver-lassie is filled with fear and shame after her introduction to sex, but this lassie thoroughly enjoys it, in spite of the fact that it puts her on the "creepie-chair" (tree-legged stool, used as a stool of repentance in church). In a very female way she asks for protection ("O Wha my babie-clouts will buy" *babie-linen*) and attention ("O Wha will tent me when I cry" *care for*), and in a frank and open manner she sings out her passion ("Wha will mak me fidgin fain; / Wha will kiss me o'er again" *make me excited*).

The tune of the song consists of two sections (taking one stanza each) which are melodically built up in the same way. The first two-bar phrase of each section, corresponding to one line in the lyric, lies within the F-major triad, the second within the E-flat major, the third again within the F-major, and the fourth, which is exactly the same in both sections, leads on to the end-cadence, which is in F-major. For this air Burns has created a song with a very fine sense of structure and unity. The material he used was partly traditional, partly Ramsay's, and partly his own. A song in David Herd's collection [*The Ancient and Modern Scots Songs, heroic ballads, &c. now first collected into one body*, second edition, 1776] probably gave him the idea of the repeated question-word:

O wha will shoe thy bonny feet?
Or wha will glove thy hand?
Or wha will lace thy middle-jimp?

whereas he owed the metre, the binding-rhyme (aaab/cccb/dddb etc.) and the thematic material to "The Cordial", Ramsay's song set to the same tune in *SMM*:

What if I shou'd waking *ly*
When the Hoboys are gawn *by*,
Will ye tent me when I *cry*,
     My Dear, I'm faint and iry?

To the aaab-stanza Burns added the form of the triple question from Herd, so that the three lines are not only united at the end by the same rhyme, but also at the beginning by the same word. Each line is thought-contained, just like the two-bar phrase is self-contained in the triad. Finally, he made the last line a refrain and an answer to the questions, which was an original idea, not suggested by any known material:

O Wha my babie-clouts will buy,
O Wha will tent me when I cry;
Wha will kiss me where I lie,
The rantin dog the daddie o't.

This corresponds to the musical pattern where the last phrase, common to both sections of the tune, carries the refrain, and the three triad-phrases the questions. Kinsley notes this and points out how well the air "sustains the triple question and the energetic answer of Burns's stanza". This is a beautiful example of the unity of poetry and music which by far excels that of Ramsay's song. The repetitions suggest an urgency in the girl's questions and the nuances in her voice are brought about by the variations provided by the tonal shifts between F and E-flat major and by the change of register between the two halves of the tune.

Just as optimistic in a similar situation is the girl in **"Duncan Gray"**, based on a traditional bawdy song. Although the sexual references of the old song are subtilized, Burns has kept the style and the droll situation. It is particularly because of the laughing refrain (taken from the old song and very expressive on two long emphatic notes) in the first half-stanzas that the song refuses to be serious, and this in spite of the fact that the girl shows indignation with Duncan Gray:

Weary fa' you [*a curse on you*], Duncan Gray,
     Ha, ha the girdin [*girthing, copulating*] o't,
Wae gae by you [*may evil befall*], Duncan Gray,
     Ha, ha the girdin o't;
When a' the lave [*the rest*] gae to their play,
Then I maun [*must*] sit the lee-lang day [*all day*],
And jeeg [*rock*] the cradel wi' my tae
     And a' for the bad girdin o't.—

The song has a very gay tune. It is brisk and energetic and has an undotted four-beat rhythm which finely sustains the vigorous language. Because of this cheerful musical dimension and because of the prospect of marriage in the last stanza, there is no tragedy about this song.

A more reflective song is **"Bonie Dundee"**. It has a wider emotional range as it expresses affectionate love towards both lover and child, and it is also the one which is most centred round the theme of mother and child. It expresses an almost holy stillness, yet also the shivering of passionate love. It is the most romantic of the songs in this group, and lyric and tune in conjunction sensitively convey the tenderness of the girl's feelings. The song is partly tradi-

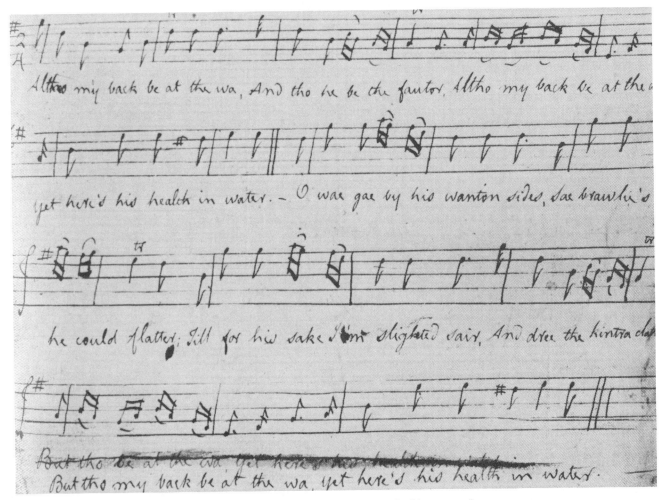

Burns's musical manuscript of "Here's his health in water."

tional, but the second stanza is definitely by Burns. There are many versions of the old song, but Kinsley points out that "Burns's fragment is the only one that expresses the feelings of the seduced girl". The first half of the tune (AA) lies low, whereas the second (BC) is intenser in the higher register. It starts high, leaps down an octave but rises again in a very expressive way. On the whole the intervals are dramatically wider in B than in A, which is more evenly undulating. The triple rhythm has a lullaby-quality which finely sustains the tenderness of the lyric and creates an image of the young mother rocking the child in her lap.

The first, traditional, stanza perceptively responds to the difference of expression between the two halves of the tune. The first half-stanza (for the low part of the tune) is an objective presentation of the situation. It introduces the theme of the girl who has been made pregnant by "a young brisk Sodger Laddie", whereas the second half-stanza takes us straight into the emotional life of this girl:

> O gin [*that*] I saw the laddie that gae me't!
>   Aft has he doudl'd [*dandled*] me upon his
>   knee;

> May Heaven protect my bonie Scots laddie,
>   And send him safe hame to his babie and
>   me.

With the intensive lifts in the tune her thoughts seem to wander away to the laddie she is in love with and they merely touch upon the child. On the return to the low part of the tune in the first four lines of the second stanza all her attention now turns to the baby, the music being illustrative of an action almost—from having wistfully looked away, she now looks down at the baby in her lap. To the rocking tune she gives him her blessings: "My blessins upon thy sweet, wee lippie! / My blessins upon thy bonie e'e brie!" (*eye-brow*). The music gives variation to the repeated blessings as the second lies a fifth higher than the first. From "my blessins" she moves to "Thy smiles are sae like my blyth Sodger laddie", which prepares for the switch of attention in the last four lines (for the high part of the tune). Here Burns makes the girl react in the same way as she did in the first stanza: she turns away from the baby again, her thoughts are still centred round it, but they are now also circling round the "dadie dear". They are the proud but affectionate thoughts of a mother, who has great dreams for her son. Best of all he will be like his father and remind her of him. The transition from the low part of the tune to the more dramatic and intense second half is marked in the text by the word "but":

> But I'll big [*build*] a bow'r on yon bonie banks,
>   Whare Tay rins wimplin [*runs meandering*]
> by sae clear;
> And I'll cleed [*clothe*] thee in the tartan sae fine,
>   And mak thee a man like thy dadie dear.

Common in sentiment is **"I look to the North"**, which is also about a dreaming girl who wistfully hopes for her lover's return. She also has been left alone with her baby, but her thoughts are less centred round the child. The rocking is more of an accompaniment to her thoughts of her lover. In the first stanza she looks to the north, she looks to the south and she looks to the east. Her thoughts span wide over the "far foreign land" and the "wide rolling sea", but nowhere does she find her lover. The tune lies low, it is undotted and not very exciting. In the second half of the song, however, it lifts an octave, it urgently repeats itself on a rising fifth, and most important, the rhythm changes from equal to dotted quavers. Her eyes now turn towards the west, and "West" is mentioned twice, and her dreams become happier: "For far in the West lives he I lo'e best, / The Man that is dear to my babie and me".

As we have seen the girls in the group of songs discussed in this chapter are full-fledged characters, capable of deep emotions and intelligent thinking. They are caught in various life-situations, acting and feeling, something which makes them and their emotions seem very real. There is a wide range of brisk and extrovert tunes as well as of more reflective ones, and a happy wedding of text and tune brings out the characters of the girls and enhances their emotions. Their language is conversational, the poetic diction limpid and the musical idiom simple. The majority of the girls also come alive through the fact that they speak for themselves in the songs—life is viewed through their eyes and described in their own words. . . .

Mary Ellen Brown (essay date 1981)

SOURCE: "'That Bards are Second-Sighted is Nae Joke': The Orality of Burns's World and Work," in *Studies in Scottish Literature,* Vol. XVI, 1981, pp. 208-16.

[*In the following essay, Brown examines the influence of the folkloric milieu on Burns's poetry.*]

Robert Burns is remembered as much for his personality and character as for his poetry and songs. It is a bit ironic that as an individual his roots in a peasant class are extolled, even emphasized; however, as a creative artist his debt to written, elite precedents are principally cited. Both are probably somewhat extreme positions: as an individual Burns both represented and transcended his class and station of birth; as a poet and songwright he followed the example of earlier writers while being influenced simultaneously by the oral literary forms which flourished in

the milieu of his birth.

The stress on Burns's literary sources is a natural and explicable one: those who study Burns as literary historians and critics see him and his work through the dimension of time and often in comparison with other written work—the tangible records of the artistic endeavors of the past; and he does seem to have been the culmination of the Scottish literary tradition and to have profited greatly from exposure to English literature. Burns himself lauded various of his predecessors and tried, in so much as was possible, to read the best of past artistry and to keep abreast of current efforts. But the primary matrix in which he lived was not so totally a literate one, for much of the artistic communication he experienced with his contemporaries was oral and aural: the ballads and folk-songs he imbided from multiple hearings and the legends and other narratives which punctuated convivial conversation, reflecting a grassroots view of the past, deep belief, or perhaps comic description, were a more pervasive and typical—if, unfortunately, ephemeral—part of the everyday world in which he lived than the poetry of Robert Fergusson or Thomas Gray. The oral artistic creations, cumulatively built and recreated, passed on from generation to generation, stable in general form but varied in individual particularization were his birth-right and a natural and universal part of the general society in which he lived—where traditional custom, belief, and practice dominated and overt creativity and innovation were not sought. This traditionally oriented way of life and the oral artistic communications it supported and sustained played a far more significant role in shaping and determining the directions of Burns's artistry than has been recognized.

It is perhaps instructive to divide Burns's work into two parts—that which came before Edinburgh and that after. Before Edinburgh Burns was in many senses a local poet, communicating to a local audience about aspects of their shared traditional life. Thus the poetry of this period deals primarily with folk life, with description of the rural existence, resulting sometimes in frankly occasional pieces; and Burns makes his larger comments about life against this backdrop, which was his milieu and naturally became an important part of his creative view. The example of Robert Fergusson no doubt was influential. The publication of the Kilmarnock edition in 1786 was the culmination of this very local poetry which drew its inspiration from the region of the poet's birth. Edinburgh marked a transition to a far more aware and conscious artistry. Burns was cognizant of some of the overt reasons for his recognition in the capital city—his humble origins which, nonetheless, did not limit his literate communications but which made him stand out, even then, as a representative example of what a rural "peasant" might become. By extension, a nation of Burnses might arise and aid in Scotland's own identity crisis, acute in the 18th century, following the Union of the Crowns in 1603 and more importantly the Union of the Parliaments in 1707. And it was in Edinburgh, away from his usual environment, that Burns achieved the proper perspective to discern consciously the breadth and depth of the oral artistry of his milieu, as traditional artistry which flowed from the people and was transmitted from generation to generation by word of mouth. In his own way, he saw this as an important part of Scotland's past which should be saved as one way perhaps of reaffirming Scotland. Nationalism contributed both to his fame in Edinburgh and to his own subsequent artistic and creative endeavors. In Edinburgh he was brought into contact with the force of nationalism and through his collaboration with James Johnson in *The Scots Musical Museum* sought to make himself the anonymous bard of Scotland by celebrating the oral and traditional artistry, long passed on. He wrote the Earl of Eglinton that "there is scarcely anything to which I am so feelingly alive as the honor and welfare of old Scotia; and as a Poet I have no higher enjoyment than singing her sons & daughters." After Edinburgh the oral or verbal traditional inheritance became his primary preoccupation as he collected, edited, and imitated songs for the *Museum,* for his own manuscript collection later called the **Merry Muses of Caledonia,** and his work towards the end of his life for George Thomson's *Select Collection.* **"Tam o' Shanter"** too reflects this involvement with and interest in oral art, built as it was out of current legendary traditions and written to accompany a drawing of Alloway Krik published by the antiquary Francis Grose in *The Antiquities of Scotland.* Burns's own deepened interest in antiquities led him to acquire familiarity with virtually all extant books of Scottish music—texts and tunes—and strengthened his communication with Robert Riddell, an amateur antiquary, and such Edinburgh enthusiasts as William Tytler of Woodhouselee and later his son Alexander Tytler.

Like all writers or creative artists, Burns was not an isolate, nor can he be realistically divorced from the milieu in which he lived. He was a product of what had gone before and what was and his artistry often lay in uniquely blending, juxtaposing, or representing this. He was a part of a long tradition. When T. S. Eliot reminds us in "Tradition and the Individual Talent" [in *The Sacred Wood,* 1950] that all artists are a part of a tradition and are representatives of it, he is referring essentially to literary and elite aesthetic traditions. I must also add—any artist is, as well, a product of a cultural tradition. And it is Burns's cultural tradition which has been slighted and frequently overlooked in most serious studies of him and his work.

The rural Ayrshire into which Burns was born might be described as a modified peasant society: it was rurally based and dominated by near subsistence level agriculture; its people were essentially homogeneous and thus shared a body of knowledge, mostly oral. In other words, it was a society in most aspects characterized by a preference for the old ways, for what had always been, the "tried and true." This society often provided the background and informing principle for Burns's writing; and the oral artistry found in such a society shaped both the form, content, style, and process of much of his work. These traditional manifestations of culture—folk-ways or folk life and oral literature—might be broadly called *folklore.*

In a multiplicity of ways, Burns's art was affected by

folklore: the traditional life and art available to him. The content of his poems and songs overtly drew upon the repeated themes, made reference to known locale as well as to facets of the shared oral art; utilized phrases, lines, and stanzas extant in the tradition; described custom, practice, belief, and milieu; and repeatedly used the structures and forms of the traditional oral artistry circulating in his milieu. Not only was the content and often the structure of his work drawn from the folkloric milieu, but his very medium of communicating—the Scots vernacular—and stylistic devices such as repetition and frequent use of refrain assert his cultural heritage. And in several works he replicates the traditional matrix for artistic communication. Scottish traditional life and especially its oral and artistic forms dominated Burns's own aesthetic perspective and formed, frequently, the very basis for his creativity.

Burns was not the only local person writing poetry and songs; in fact he is undoubtedly related to a local poet tradition which sprang up in the eighteenth century. A more literate tradition, based in large measure initially on the once oral poetic and song tradition justly celebrated in the works of such persons as David Herd, Walter Scott, William Motherwell and later in the nineteenth century Francis James Child, the local poet tradition grew organically from the earlier oral form of artistry which produced such tauted anthology pieces as "Sir Patrick Spens" and "Lord Randal, My Son." As literate art replaced aspects of the oral and pride in authorship replaced anonymity, the printed word gained prestige as media of communication over the ephemeral, though exceedingly artistic, oral performance. The local poet replaced the oral bard, assuming his subjects, his forms and structures, his metrical patterns and rhyme schemes. But his literacy enabled him to draw as well from earlier and contemporary written art, and thus the local poet tradition may well provide the important bridge between the great Scottish oral artistry and the literate vernacular tradition with roots going back to Makars. In its developing stages, the local poet tradition, which persists today, shows clearly its affinity with the earlier oral art and its artistic milieu.

Burns then was not an oddity in writing poems and songs. He knew others who shared his predilection for rhyme and exchanged verse epistles with several—notably John Lapraik. And his audience was conceived of originally as a local one, interested both in a confined geographical area and in current events and issues—thus most of his early poetry. Additionally, his audience was known to him; it included his friends and his neighbors; and as often as not he read or recited his productions aloud to them or circulated them in handwritten manuscript. The audience he addressed—their politics, ethos—no doubt affected what lines he added or cut, aptly illustrated in his lengthy correspondence with Mrs. Dunlop and the manuscript versions he frequently sent her. This reflects an attitude more akin to oral communication than to the impersonality of the written literary world where the reading public is only generally known and where literary text is fixed and unchanging. Burns's audience always retained a specific quality for him, even when he was no longer a local, but more nearly a national, poet. The principal edition of his work, the 1786 Kilmarnock edition, was essentially aimed at a relatively local audience, though his Preface looked beyond it. This concern with the conception of audience is characteristic of oral communication; it reflects a need for immediate response, for give and take. Like the folksongs and narratives which were passed on in small, local, mostly homogeneous groups, Burns's poetry and songs sought that same milieu either with a more contemporary subject or in his songs an analogous—sometimes similar—subject, tune, or form.

If his audience was local and shared his world, that matrix of necessity found its way into his creative work as an essential ingredient in facilitating communication. He began with the shared world, the familiar which he knew and to which he—as are all outstanding writers—was extraordinarily sensitive. This in no way should imply that he was but a describer, an ethnographer, for he selected and focused on aspects of the shared world as a base from which to draw broader conclusions and generalizations about the human condition. And in transferring reality to creative work, whether destined for oral or written transmission, his own unique personality and background—albeit shaped by the common tradition—contributed to an equally individual perception of the world. Nonetheless his depiction of the world held in common with his audience lay within the recognizable parameters of general experience and formed the essential understood grounding which often effectively drew the readers or hearers of his work into the poem or song and provided them with a basis for the response all artistic endeavors strive for if they are indeed media of communication. Burns wrote about what he knew using familiar forms and familiar language as well as familiar content. From a specific account of aspects of religious controversy rampant in Burns's day in **"The Ordination"** and in **"The Kirk of Scotland's Garland—a new Song"** to a depiction of a gathering of three friends, including himself, in **"Willie brew'd a pack o' maut"**, Burns drew on his own environment for surface content. The obvious and identifiable are especially blatant in his frankly occasional and extemporary poems and songs, which, like **"At Roslin Inn"**, remark on the obvious and record an impression; they remain not as a great testimony to his poetic power, but as testimony to his spur-of-the-moment poetic ability.

The celebration of the immediate, often a shared experience, links Burns with both the earlier ballad and song and the later poet-laureate traditions. Many of his occasional poems are said to have been off-the-cuff extemporaneous productions. Some were composed in writing and remain today incised in windows of various inns he frequented. Other works he created mentally, in memory, and later, after a long journey on horseback perhaps, put in writing. The oral sound rather than the written text may well have controlled his composition. His use of proverbs and sayings from oral tradition, phrases from traditional songs, not to mention the whole stanzas and refrains which provided the basic creating materials for many of his songs indicates a form of composition at least akin to oral formulaic composition. Multiple ver-

sions of some of his works may also reflect a concept of artistic product which does not insist on fixity of text; such disregard for a definitive text is another element linking Burns to the world of traditional oral composition. But it would be inaccurate to deny him the literacy that was his and the reflection that must have been a part of his creative production. For Burns, in many ways, is a kind of transition figure—an individual who straddled both the literate and the non-literate worlds and his own method of composition reflected compositional approaches from both worlds—the oral and the written.

He composed and wrote, of course, as all artists do—at least in part—in order to communicate, perhaps to influence. But he created as well to provide solace for himself:

> However as I hope my poor, country Muse, who, all rustic, akward, and unpolished as she is, has more charms for me than any other of the pleasures of life beside—as I hope she will not then desert me, I may, even then, learn to be, if not happy, at least easy, and south a sang to sooth my misery.—

And he created to relieve tension—as entertainment—as part of life. Creating, composing was for Burns as for oral poets past and present organically a part of life he led:

> Leeze me on rhyme! it's ay a treasure,
> My chief, amaist my only pleasure,
> At hame, a-fiel, at wark or leisure,
>   The Muses, poor hizzie!
> Tho' rough an' raploch be her measure,
>   She's seldom lazy.
>
> Haud tae the Muse, my dainty Davie:
> The warl' may play you [monie] a shavie;
> But for the Muse, she'll never leave ye,
>   Tho' e'er sae puir,
> Na, even tho' limpan wi' the spavie
>   Frae door tae door.
>
>   (ll. 37-48)

And poetic and song form, set off as distinct from daily discourse, allowed Burns to use the form and its rules to write of love for women whom he could not ordinarily address in that manner and to write of subjects, especially bawdry, he might not so widely discuss in polite conversation. The functions of his art were many.

Burns's focus in his early work on local topics, his frequent use of traditional material, his acceptance of the fluidity of texts, his stress on audience and the oral socialization of his own works, and his articulated views on the function of composition—all suggest Burns's strong ties to the traditional and largely oral matrix of late eighteenth-century Ayrshire. This is not meant to diminish his relationship with the literary world with which his contact was not primarily through social interaction but rather through print. He read; he felt a debt to Allan Ramsay, to Robert Fergusson and others—both Scottish and English. And it was through the creative medium—writing and related print—he shared with them that his work lives today. But the literary and literate world was superimposed on the traditional and oral world which formed the very basis of his being. It provided him with forms and structures, the content and contexts on which to build. Scottish tradition and Scottish oral artistry were his birthright.

Robert P. Wells (essay date 1982)

SOURCE: "Burns and Narrative," in *The Art of Robert Burns,* edited by R.D.S. Jack and Andrew Noble, Vision and Barnes & Noble, 1982, pp. 59-75.

[*In the following essay, Wells explores the narrative structure and didactic content of several of Burns's poems.*]

Almost everyone, if asked to categorize Burns's work, would describe him as a lyric poet; indeed, the popular image is that of incomparable master of love-songs. Burns, in keeping with his lyrical inclinations, is very much an occasional poet; his canon, in fact, contains well over one hundred poems of a more expository or dramatic nature: verse epistles, addresses, laments and elegies, a cantata, dramatic prologues and fragments, descriptions, epigrams, dialogues, and dramatic monologues.

No one, I believe, would place Burns among the narrative poets. Including **'Tam o' Shanter'**, there are barely a handful of poems Burns himself thought of as 'a true story' or 'a tale'. My present purpose is not to challenge the established view. Yet Burns's 'occasional' poems do make use of a variety of narrative techniques; and in this essay I intend to examine some of these poems in terms of narrative kind and structure.

The first task in such an undertaking is to establish a definition of narrative, momentarily omitting from the general description considerations of genre and tone. I am concerned here only with fictitious narratives. Fictitious narratives may be divided into two basic kinds: stories, and story-like narratives which I shall call mimetic transcripts.

Story (or *Tale*): in prose or verse, a narrative which is a sequence of connected mimetic events or episodes, the sum of which comprises a complete whole (i.e. represents an action) with a definite beginning, middle, and end; further, it has unity in that the transposition or removal of any of its connected incidents will disjoin and dislocate the whole. A story must be concerned with human or anthropomorphic agents. A story must have the element of *peripeteia,* depicting a change of some kind in the agent or agents (e.g. misery to happiness, or vice versa), an unexpected change which, though unforeseen, is a necessary or probable outcome of the agents' actions. This *peripeteia* frequently but not invariably involves *anagnorisis,* recognition in the agents of this change and their own part in effecting it. Most often recognition means movement from illusion or opinion to fact or reality, a shift from ignorance to knowledge. A story must also have a sense of being addressed directly to a real or imagined audience (as opposed to lyric forms, which do not necessarily presuppose an external audience). A story may be brief, a single complete episode, such as an anecdote; or developed, a story of several or many episodes. Stories may be simple or interwoven. By simple, I mean a single unified tale usually but not necessarily unfolding sequentially (events may be removed from chronological sequence, as in a flashback); by interwoven, two or more tales joined together to form a whole. Stories may be told from the point of view of the first or third person, or in combination. These qualities are equally applicable to tragic or to comic tales.

There are many varieties of stories, often based on non-fictional narrative modes: mimetic autobiographies, biographies, epistles, journals, reports of experience, allegories, and fantasies (e.g. faerie tales, 'science fiction'). In these latter two unrealistic modes especially sequential events are often impossible or highly improbable in nature and so neither necessary nor probable outcomes of antecedent episodes, although such stories usually follow an internal logic. These separate categories may also appear in combination with one another; thus we may find allegory joined with fantasy (e.g. Aesop's *Fables*), and so on.

Mimetic Transcript: in prose or verse, a fictional narrative which may have many or all save one of the essential qualities of a proper story, that one element being the lack of a distinct *peripeteia*. Without *peripeteia,* the 'story' must be considered a mimetic transcript. A mimetic transcript may have many or all of the recognizable appurtenances of a story, such as fictional characters or real characters in fictional situations, dialogue, a sequence of connected mimetic incidents, or even contain a tale or tales within the whole work, yet not of itself comprise a story as previously defined. Mimetic transcripts sometimes lack unity as well as *peripeteia* in that episodes may not relate the chronicle of an agent or agents but that of a distinct group of people; or in that episodes may be transposed or deleted without seriously disrupting the whole work.

There are several varieties of mimetic transcripts, corresponding largely with the different varieties of story: biography, allegory, diary, fantasy, and so forth. This is to be expected of story-like narratives. One major kind of mimetic transcript, equivalent to the anecdote among stories, is the situational mimetic transcript. A situational mimetic transcript is one in which meaning is not dependent upon 'story' but upon a particular context; it involves narrative elements at only a rudimentary level. It tends to be brief, a whole but usually single episode; and it does not in itself comprise an action, although it may involve descriptions of activity. In verse it is often cast in a lyric form, and may take the shape of a mimetic complaint, lament, argument, dialogue or dramatic monologue reported by or tacitly assumed to be reported by another witnessing it. 'Situational' does not mean static—i.e. purely descriptive—but a single scene that raises the impression of mimetic action by providing details of an agent's life and thought even though no action takes place and so no change occurs in the characters' circumstances and emotional states.

The basic difference between stories and mimetic transcripts, reflected in their structures, is one of purpose. It is a division that arises from different patterns of emphasis. Stories can often appear to have no ulterior aim other than self-fulfilment; mimetic transcripts almost invariably appear to have been written as a means of conveying a particular idea or set of ideas. A story concerns itself with, and closely directs itself toward, the expression of plot. A story may have an underlying theme, but theme is usually subordinate to the plot, made manifest through plot. A mimetic transcript conversely tends to place much greater emphasis on theme. The expression of theme takes precedence over the vehicle conveying it. That is, dominated by thematic considerations, mimetic transcripts often appear as 'dramatic' expressions of observation (e.g. fictional travel books, addresses, catalogues), discourse (e.g. philosophy, monologue, debate, dream-vision, parable), and satire, a mode necessarily governed by theme. Divided by differences of design rather than subject matter, both forms have an equal potential for aesthetic excellence.

What may seem complex in the abstract will become clearer as this theory is applied in practical terms. To that end, I shall begin with a comparison of **'Tam o' Shanter'** and **'Death and Doctor Hornbook'** as narratives, and then proceed to discussions of various other narrative poems. I do not intend to examine more than a few examples representative of Burns's narrative art—for instance, **'Holy Willie's Prayer'** (a dramatic monologue), **'The Cotter's Saturday Night'** (observation of scene), and **'The Holy Fair'** (a peasant festival), among others. But I believe the exploration of only a few of the available kinds of stories and mimetic transcripts will enable us to draw some general conclusions about Burns and narrative verse.

I begin with **'Tam o' Shanter'** and **'Death and Doctor Hornbook'** because, according to their subtitles, both poems are tales in Burns's own estimation. **'Tam o' Shanter'** is a comic tale of the supernatural, the account of Tam o' Shanter's drunken confrontation with the Devil and several of his devotees; it is told by an ironical 'I'-narrator outside the action described. Tam's adventure is simple and, if fantastic, straightforward. Despite the poem's elaborate introduction, the narrator's frequent digressive intrusions, and the mocking *moralitas* which summarizes the import of the night's events, it may be demonstrated that the poem fits the criteria of a story as defined above. It has unity, in that a complete action is portrayed in a sequence of episodes that lead logically but not inevitably from one to the next: Tam, drunk on market-day, leaves a tavern for home at midnight in a terrible storm; on the way he spies the haunted kirk of Alloway ablaze with light, and, riding up to investigate, he is amazed to see a witches' dance at which the Devil himself provides the music; struck by the charms of the scantily clad young witch Nanny, Tam forgets himself and cries 'Weel done, Cutty-sark!'; instantly the witches give chase, and Tam narrowly escapes over the Brig o' Doon

and home, his gray mare Meg sacrificing her tail to Nanny during her frantic dash for safety. The loss of any component episodes or the disruption of their sequence would seriously affect the story as a whole.

The story has a probable but unforeseen outcome. The reversal of fortune is an unexpected movement from joy ('O'er a' the ills o' life victorious') to terror at the threat of destruction ('In hell they'll roast thee like a herrin'). This *peripeteia* occurs when Tam unwittingly calls attention to himself by shouting his encouragement to Nanny. We may say that his drink-induced mistake is accompanied by *anagnorisis,* for he immediately recognizes his error and its consequences. The dénouement and resolution of the action swiftly follow, a comic anticlimax in which the threat of death is absurdly reduced to the loss of a horse's tail.

Even the lengthy introduction and deliberately inappropriate concluding 'lesson', although strictly speaking not part of the action, are essential components in the narrative's comic structure. The opening stanzas establish the scene, set the comic tone in discussing wifely wisdom, and provide a foreshadowing of events. This foreshadowing turns out to be ironical, in that what almost happens to Tam coincides with the far-fetched, nagging warnings of his wife Kate:

> She prophesied that late or soon,
> [Tam] would be found deep drown'd in Doon;
> Or catched wi' warlocks in the mirk
> By Alloway's auld haunted kirk.

Except that this is an outsider's account (and apart from the comic eroticism of Nanny's dance), Tam's adventures sound suspiciously like an excuse concocted by a drink-fuddled husband to turn aside his wife's wrath. We can almost visualize her grudging acceptance of it, as the tale obligingly confirms her dire predictions. This quality of private joke further increases the ridiculousness of the tale.

The narrator, however, calls the story's veracity into question himself by referring ironically to 'this tale o' truth'. The tongue-in-cheek *moralitas* that follows is an example of comic misdirection, humorously confounding the reader's expectations by providing absurdly inappropriate commentary. The sabotaged 'lesson' rounds off the ironic strategy of the poem: by drawing our attention to the sufferings of Meg (an innocent creature) and away from Tam (a sinner who escapes physically unscathed), the narrator completely deflates the seriousness of the final admonition. In effect he winks at Tam's follies, and mocks those who give the story credence.

The narrator is omnipresent although he does not seem to be fully omniscient; he could be considered a secondary character. He hovers close to the action, shaping our perceptions of and guiding our responses to events. Seventy lines, a third of the poem in fact, are taken up with the narrator's commentary. 'Atmospheric' catalogues comprise a further twenty lines, lists of the horrible places that Tam passes on the road and of the grisly sights displayed as a kind of macabre stage-dressing to the witches' sabbath. The narrator, placing himself among the neighbourly tavern-frequenters, introduces the scene in his own *persona*. A little later, when the tale is barely begun, he steps back from the immediate scene to offer philosophical reflections on the transitory nature of pleasure, and—with mock-heroic delight—on the follies of courage induced by drink. He further interrupts with a comic apostrophe on the appearance of the witches, with a brief use of the traditional humility *topos*; and with a warning addressed directly to Tam in full flight. Still in character, he finally offers his ironical *moralitas*.

The narrator seems to adopt different 'voices' for his various discursive intrusions. For example, he briefly elevates his diction to a rather Latinate, formal English in order to achieve a philosophical tone; or he mimics the shrewish quality of Kate's 'advice' to Tam, scolding advice that sounds like a medieval flyting: 'thou was a skellum, / A blethering, blustering, drunken blellum', et cetera. These dramatically effective postures represent basic shifts in perspective, in tone, but equally different levels of the narrator's involvement in the action—now a drinking companion, now musing aloud outside and above the scene, now at Tam's side advising him. The teller and the tale are inextricably linked, and our appreciation of the story depends as much on our knowledge of the narrator's personality and sympathies as on our awareness of the slowly unfolding action.

'Death and Doctor Hornbook' bears a certain broad similarity to **'Tam o' Shanter'**. Both deal humorously with supernatural encounters, and both are told by genial 'I'-narrators who purport to be inebriated. **'Death and Doctor Hornbook'**, however, is a fantastic mimetic transcript of a dialogue between a narrator-character and the personification of Death; the poem is intended to satirize a pretentious but otherwise unqualified local apothecary, John Wilson. The poem, constructed with some of the constituent components of narrative, projects a story-like appearance. It has an ironical introduction; it animates two fictional agents in a particular locale who meet one night and carry on a dialogue; and it is a single, unified episode (although incomplete in that their dialogue is interrupted before Death makes a final revelation of his planned vengeance against the usurper Hornbook). But the narrative lacks a necessary *peripeteia*. There is no action other than discussion. While engaged in conversation neither Death nor the narrator takes actions or makes choices that result in any kind of reversal for themselves or others. They do not even alter in condition, physical or emotional: when they take their separate roads the narrator is no less drunk and Death no less ineffective than before their meeting. Nothing is different; nothing has *happened*, apart from an exchange of information. Without *peripeteia*, it follows that there is no *anagnorisis*, no recognition of a self-wrought reversal. The narrative could be considered the account of a situation, their meeting; but it could not be described as a story.

We learn a great deal about Hornbook, who is exaggerated into a larger-than-life figure in order to sharpen the comic contrast with his lowly reality. But his malignant activities are reported to us, not presented dramatically. The reason for this is simple: the focus of the poem, as is common among mimetic transcripts, is on theme rather than on plot. The impossible dialogue becomes a convenient and memorable vehicle for ridiculing Burns's victim, Wilson; it provides a solid foundation upon which to build his ideas, offering a maximum of satirical effectiveness and a minimum of personal risk.

The poem's basic premise rests on the incongruity of Death being made redundant due to the ministrations of Hornbook, who deals out life and death in the form of absurdly named medicines. Through the device of Death's self-pitying complaints, the poem is structured in such a way as to turn Hornbook into an inhuman object. Rather than a self-animated character with complex wants, needs, abilities, and choices, Hornbook is depicted as the mechanical, impersonal, ubiquitous force that death is traditionally thought to be. Death, in contrast, has a variety of human personality traits, and decided limitations. Because Hornbook is transformed into an object, sympathy for him is put out of reach, enhancing his ridiculousness. Ironically, we are instead invited to sympathize with Death, unable to earn his bread for the first time 'Sin [he] was to the butching bred', and piqued at the inequity of Hornbook slaying a score with malpractice for every one Death used to take off naturally. The use of this theme, which has its roots in Classical literature, is a potent, and well-executed, satiric strategy. Further, the narrator saves himself from the accusation of slander by carefully establishing his context: first, he claims his account 'Is just as true as the Deil's in h-ll, / Or Dublin city', superstitious nonsense; and second, he claims to be drunk, predicating unreliability. He is able to make wild, insulting, and damaging charges against 'Hornbook' while at the same time ironically disclaiming them as lies.

Initially, this may seem a dry method of approaching two vibrant, joyously comic poems; but an understanding of narrative structure is an essential first step toward appreciating the poet's purposes, his thematic emphases. The eighteenth century, known foremost as an age of satire, continued to value the ancient justification for imaginative literature, to teach and delight (*utile et dulce*). In narrative art, mimetic transcripts are particularly well suited to didactic productions of all kinds—to debate, satire, discourse, propaganda, parable. Stories may be didactic as well. But where an imbalance exists between the two functions, stories tend to be weighted more heavily toward delight; mimetic transcripts tend to be orientated toward education. Mimetic transcripts seem to be driven primarily by thematic considerations: that is, we can imagine Burns first deciding he wanted to ridicule Wilson, then casting about for the best method of achieving his purpose; we cannot imagine the reverse of that process. However, with **'Tam o' Shanter'**, we can envisage Burns holding the initial desire to tell a good story. For this reason mimetic transcripts often appear to be set pieces, stationary single episodes raising and resolving a limited theme. While this is by no means an inflexible rule, the majority of Burns's mimetic transcripts follow this pattern. Burns is not generally considered a didactic poet. Yet given the predilections of the age, no one should be surprised to find that a high percentage of Burns's narrative poems—not to mention various addresses and epistles—are fundamentally exemplary in nature, even if only mockingly so as in **'Tam o' Shanter'**.

Satire is particularly favoured as an educational device, able to expose the ridiculous and discourage the emulation of folly in a delightful way, bringing credit to the satirist. And nowhere is satire more effectively employed than in Burns's dramatic monologue, **'Holy Willie's Prayer'**, the situational mimetic transcript of a hypocrite's confession and supplication to the Lord. As a satire it achieves the desirable state of serving both topical and universal interests.

'Holy Willie's Prayer', brilliantly conceived, compact and energetic, is not a story. Through the device of over-hearing his devotions we learn everything essential about Willie's nature; but although he reveals the secrets of his heart Willie does not experience any kind of reversal while confiding in his image of God. He does not change one jot from first to last; in fact, the poem would be destroyed if he did, if he realized even for a moment what he was truly saying. He is, and must be, fixed in his ways, comically inflexible and thus, by implication, past redemption. Dispensing with a wry or mocking narrator, Burns gets inside Willie's mind, causing him to damn himself, unconsciously and so ironically. Willie remains serenely unaware of his many transgressions and of his uncharitable—not to say unchristian—attitudes. Or, if he does acknowledge a fault—for instance, confessing to several forays into the gratification of 'fleshly lust'—he displaces the blame, compounding the sin through a failure to recognize his responsibilities.

Out of Willie's mouth drop blind admissions of all of the traditional Seven Deadly Sins. He confesses to *lust*, which he sees as visited on him to try his spirit (lest he 'O'er proud and high should turn'); and he uses *gluttony* in the guise of drunkenness to excuse himself ('that Friday I was fou / When I cam near her'). He is *envious* of his foe Gavin Hamilton, not of Hamilton's venial slips ('He drinks, and swears, and plays at cartes'), which are tame compared to Willie's own malefactions, but of the 'mony taking arts' that enable him to steal 'frae God's ain priest the people's hearts'. Proof of Hamilton's success lies in his ability to raise the congregation's laughter at the accusations of the auld-licht faction against him. Willie has been publicly humiliated by Hamilton and the lawyer Aitken, and his revenge takes the shape of self-righteous *wrath*. He maliciously—and, of course, impotently—calls down the Lord's terrible 'curse' and 'vengeance' upon them and upon all those of 'that Presbytry of Ayr', unwitting comic blasphemy. Then, having distributed the Lord's punishments to suit himself, his *avarice* manifests itself as a request for enlarged

> mercies *temporal* and divine!
> That I for grace *and gear* may shine,

> Excell'd by nane!

> (my italics)

He had earlier described his salvation in terms of 'gifts and grace', seeming to equate showy, material prosperity with the singular blessings of Providence, temporal bounty with spiritual grace. With this request his prayer has returned to its place of beginning, having explored the idea of sin and salvation. This gives the poem a circular structure.

From the phrase 'excell'd by nane' it is apparent that *pride* is Willie's chief sin. He conceives of himself as 'a chosen sample . . . a pillar . . . a guide, a ruler and example / To a' thy flock', like so much of his prayer absurd presumption. He is indeed an example, but not, ironically, in the way he thinks: he is a ridiculous, negative model to be eschewed by all true Christians. Spiritual *sloth* is born out of this pride in that, though he admits he is mere 'dust / Defil'd wi' sin', he regards himself as one of the elect, predestined for salvation, and so has no fear of damnation, whatever he does. His belief that he is a righteous man is of course comical to any outside observer. But worse, even if it were true, moral behaviour is quite pointless. It does no good to serve the people as an example if salvation is denied them in any event, if damnation exclusively depends on God's whims and 'no for ony gude or ill' committed in this life. **'Holy Willie's Prayer'**, masterfully exposing a creed in a sharply defined dramatic setting, does not merely condemn an odious and adept practitioner of religious double-think but the whole system of extreme Calvinist belief which necessarily produces such creatures.

Almost all of Burns's satires and burlesques—for example, **'The Holy Tulzie'**, **'The Mauchline Wedding'**, the **'Address to the Deil'**, or the mock-heroic testament **'Death and Dying of Poor Mailie'**—are mimetic transcripts. Most are intended to edify as well as poke fun at persons, ideas, or literary genres. But Burns's efforts to be movingly informative are not invariably satiric or comic. **'The Cotter's Saturday Night'**, to cite a well-known instance, employs the structure of a mimetic transcript in order to depict the life of the average farm family and to discourse seriously on the felicities of such an existence.

The poem's narrative elements are arranged to explore a series of scenes, not to relate the tale of an individual's actions and their results. Narrated by an omniscient 'Patriot-bard', the poem traces the activities and especially the attitudes of one cottage family from dusk through the reading of the Bible before retiring to bed one Saturday in November. The time-scale is narrow, but the implications of the scene are universal. The account is purely descriptive, interspersed with commentary by the narrator. We follow in detail the family's home-gathering after toil, supper, the arrival of Jenny's young man, and their homely worship services. There is no dialogue. Only a few moral imperatives or prayers are quoted; and, in the same unrealistically elevated diction, the poet is once moved to declare his emotional experience of love. The few characters who are distinguished as individuals, the

Father, Mother, Jenny and her beau, are representative stereotypes. Real personalities are better fitted for stories, where circumstance, motive and choice precipitate the plot. These characters are not real personalities but highly idealized figures. Indeed, the entire portrait is intended to represent the ideal, despite the realistic touches by the way. Each scene, each character, becomes a subject for extended philosophical discussion by the poet, who weaves together the several related themes of the good life, order, obedience, simplicity of heart, patriotism, and the manifestations of love, which descend as grace and bounty from the Creator and encompass even the smallest child. The scenes, insignificant in themselves, build into a pattern of moral consequence. In fact, the narrative's structure and materials (the scene, the characters, the narrator's rhapsodic or reverent tone) are wholly governed by didactic demands. Like **'The Auld Farmer's New-Year-morning Salutation'**, it is a narrative of distilled emotion. The list of soberly didactic mimetic transcripts, including **'The Vision'**, **'Man Was Made to Mourn'**, **'To a Mouse'**, and even the allegorical **'John Barleycorn'**, is somewhat shorter than the list of humorous didactic narratives, but it is nonetheless substantial.

Though I have pointed out that didacticism is a neglected aspect of Burns's art, I do not mean to imply that his narratives are solely or necessarily intended to offer serious moral instruction or even to be comically edifying. Most do have a moral point to make, and are designed to satisfy powerful thematic motives as well as aesthetic pleasure. Some, however, seem to be born primarily out of a spirit of fun: for example, **'The Holy Fair'** and **'Love and Liberty'**, more popularly known as **'The Jolly Beggars'**. Both poems, to be sure, are comical mimetic transcripts; but both are more celebratory than informative. They are lively, exuberant, and roguishly attractive.

The personification of Fun, in fact, is the narrator's guide in **'The Holy Fair'**. Superstition and Hypocrisy are also in attendance, assuring a satirical flavour as well. This poem is identical in prosody, and similar in episodic development, tone and intention, to **'The Ordination'** and **'Halloween'**. It may therefore serve as a representative of the group.

'The Holy Fair' chronicles the activities of a gathering of Christians during a typical summer religious festival in Mauchline; it is a portrait of social *mores* and not a tale. Narrative components—episodic development, a heterogeneous congregation of characters pursuing a variety of activities and interests, dialogue, the visible spectrum of emotions—are set in motion for the purpose of painting a comedy of manners. The narrator, aloof from the scenes he describes, roves among the throng like a good-humoured camera, focusing, as it were, at random. Stanzas regularly begin or change direction with 'Here' or 'Now', signals pointing to each fresh set of observations, observations which act as implicit social criticisms. The foibles of both sexes and of all professions are much in evidence, but no one is scrutinized for very long, nor earnestly ridiculed. Few characters are even named; most are character types, representative figures, or indistinguishable in

their various groups. They have recognizable traits, but are not full-blooded personalities.

A tableau effect is built up piecemeal. The events follow a rough chronology, growing ever more boisterous, but no other pattern; scenes seem to be haphazardly arranged, to appear less well-knit than in the sequential unfolding of a story. Unity is not fully apparent, a feature of some mimetic transcripts: scenes could be rearranged or even deleted without seriously damaging the structure of the whole poem. But the narrator's quick leap from one small, deftly sketched cameo to the next helps to ensure the rollicking pace and lively tone of humane delight. It is a narrative of comic behaviour, concerned with atmosphere, motive and faithful observation rather than action. Its air of jollity sharpens the incongruity of juxtaposing carnal and divine love throughout, the secular and spiritual aspects of charity, both generously lubricated with strong drink. The narrative's quick metre, indulgent comic tone, and episodic structure act in concert to preclude any suggestion of seriousness or indecorous disapproval. Because his levity is not diminished, the narrator's implicit superior judgements of his neighbours' ethics and beliefs do not give offence by striking a holier-than-thou attitude. Involvement in the revels, personal remarks, would destroy his neutral vantage. As it is, he can poke fun in all directions without behaving as a spoilsport or colouring his observations by partaking in the action.

'Love and Liberty' is concerned wholly with secular matters; however, the same riotous, bacchanalian spirit of **'The Holy Fair'** still prevails. As the title suggests, freedom and love—of the most basic kind—are the twin themes that bind the various songs together. The poem is a celebration of freedom from social responsibilities and moral obligations, expressed by a varied cast of vivacious low-life characters, outcasts who harbour no higher desires than enjoying the fleeting pleasures of warmth, sex, and alcohol in an atmosphere of convivial fellowship. They have nothing to lose, and consequently nothing to fear, scorning the values and flouting the conventions that pertain to social stations above their own.

The poem, a cantata, is a collection of 'character'-songs linked by the bridging recitative passages of an omniscient narrator. Burns no doubt identified himself with the Bard who closes the poem. But the Bard is distinct from the narrator, who simply observes, and does not comment on, the festive scene. The narrative contains at least one story, the rivalry of the Fiddler and the Tinker for the 'raucle Carlin's' affections. The Fiddler attempts to charm her with a carefree song; the bullying Tinker threatens the Fiddler, and sings to the doxie an aggressive song of self-advertisement; 'o'ercome' with passion—and liquor—'th'unblushing fair' surrenders to the Tinker's blandishments, resulting in felicity for him and short-lived grief for the Fiddler, who soon finds comfort elsewhere. However, the presence of one or more stories in a text is not enough to transform a narrative into a story: 'Love and Liberty' is the mimetic transcript of a beggars' revel, an interweaving of separate character-revealing songs and tales into a complex, thematically unified new whole.

The songs, as exemplified by the Fiddler-Tinker rivalry, are appropriate to their assigned speakers. The crippled Soldier sings a swaggering, patriotic air; his trull, with an agreeable comic self-awareness, expresses her preferences for the camp follower's life; the pickpocketing Highland widow laments the political forces that turned her into an outlaw; and, after the Tinker's quarrel, the Bard rounds off the foregoing with a toast to love and women. Asked for an encore, the Bard provides a general climax to the libertines' feast which tightly knits together the different thematic threads: his song rejoices in sensual pleasure, freedom from care, love in its many forms, and scorn for the laws of society as represented by the church and court. Although the previous songs are more amoral than openly rebellious in nature, we are to understand that he functions as spokesman, his attitudes epitomizing the spirit of the group at large. It is a vibrant song conducted with the characteristic *brio* of Burns at his rakish best. The patriotism of the Soldier aside, the various views expressed throughout are anti-Establishment in the extreme, and the poem can hardly be described as exemplary or edifying.

Certain songs could be reordered, but there is a general pattern discernible in their presentation. The Soldier loves his country, the doxie loves the soldiers; the Tinker and Fiddler campaign for the attentions of the unattached widow, the strong prevailing but without violence or genuine loss of amicability; and the Bard voices an all-embracing salutation to earthy, unsentimental love. The structure is that of theme-and-variations, the unity of idea, rising to a crescendo climax in the final song. In fact, most of the mimetic transcripts that I have examined or mentioned are organized on the principle of theme-and-variations.

It should be evident by now that Burns rarely attempts to animate or explore complex personalities in his narratives. The characters in his mimetic transcripts are usually personifications (Death, Fun) or stereotypes. They are figures of convenience, presented entire and not developed. Occasionally, as with Holy Willie, we see deep into the core of an individual. Yet even Willie symbolizes a code of belief (extreme Calvinism) as well as the Seven Deadly Sins. Most often, as in **'Love and Liberty'**, with its characters drawn from low-ranked occupations, the agents are limited to fixed qualities associated with a trade, a trait, a belief, a narrow aspect of behaviour. They function in a proscribed way; and they are usually used to illustrate a point or promote an idea, as do the rich and poor dogs or the new and old bridges in the slightly comic but essentially philosophical dialogues of **'The Twa Dogs'** or **'The Brigs of Ayr'**. Burns's use of character types and spokesmen reflects the fundamental aim of mimetic transcripts aptly to express ideas.

Burns wrote only a few verse stories, and those rather late in his career. Most of his efforts in narrative modes come in the form of mimetic transcripts—monologues, dialogues and dramatic scene-paintings harnessed in the service of satire, comical and sentimental observation, and philosophical discourse. The majority of these mimetic transcripts were written prior to his first trip to Edinburgh, near the beginning of his professional career. Many of his verse addresses and epistles also appeared at this time, so he was then obviously interested in philosophical issues, questioning behaviour in individuals and in society at large, and exploring concepts. He had always written lyrics. But later, as the work of song-collecting and song-writing increasingly demanded his attention, Burns virtually abandoned theme-orientated verse in favour of more purely emotive expressions. Despite his numerous efforts in narrative genres and the lasting popularity of **'Holy Willie's Prayer'** and **'Tam o' Shanter'**, Burns is remembered as a lyric poet. This bias has nothing to do with the quantity of lyric as opposed to narrative verse produced over his lifetime. The reason for this lies instead in the natures of lyrical and occasional verse. A number of his songs have a timeless, universal quality which has helped to assure them a lasting place in people's hearts. Lyrical emotions have not changed, whereas interest in the topical issues and social concepts of his philosophical verse has largely faded from the world.

Limited by considerations of space, I have had to slight significant features of Burns's narrative art: for example, his use of traditional genres, rooted in Classical and especially medieval and folk literature; or matters of craft— prosody, patterns of imagery, techniques of creating tone, all of which contribute to the final experience of the poem in the reader's mind. I have instead concentrated on aspects of kind and structure—narrative perspective, the use of character types, the arrangement of scenes—especially as they relate to thematic purpose. First it has been necessary to establish the existence of a body of verse which may be properly described as narrative. In considering narrative function and effect, I think it should be evident by now that, early on, Burns was strongly concerned with didacticism, and that most of his narratives are of a kind designed to express ideas in an agreeable form.

Carol McGuirk (essay date 1985)

SOURCE: "'Tam o' Shanter': The Truth of the Tale," in *Robert Burns and the Sentimental Era*, The University of Georgia Press, 1985, pp. 149-61.

[Below, McGuirk analyzes Burns's use of irony in "Tam o' Shanter."]

"Tam o' Shanter" tells the story of a drunken farmer who encounters a witches' dance on his way home from a market day carousal in Ayr. The poem offers an adult's retrospective view of horror stories; there is an overtone of indulgent irony in the sections of the poem that describe the witches' dance and its gruesome concomitants. Thomas Carlyle [*On Heroes, Hero Worship and the Heroic in History*, 1966], writing of the poem, objects to its evident detachment:

> **"Tam o' Shanter"** itself, which enjoys so high a favour, does not appear to us, at all decisively, to come under this last category [of Burns's melodious, aerial,

poetical poems]. It is not so much a poem, as a piece of sparkling rhetoric; the heart and body of the story still lies hard and dead. He has not gone back, much less carried us back, into that dark, earnest, wondering age . . . he does not attempt, by any new-modelling of his supernatural ware, to strike anew that deep mysterious chord of human nature, which once responded to such things.

Carlyle's objection to Burns's "cold" treatment of supernatural themes is essentially that of a Romantic throwing off the traces of eighteenth-century skepticism and restraint to which Burns does hold in **"Tam o' Shanter."** It was not the grotesque activities of witches and Satan that piqued Burns's imagination as he wrote; it was the behavior of his protagonist, ordinary Tam, when confronted by those weird phenomena. Like Burns's songs, **"Tam o' Shanter"** adapts folk sources to emphasize a central character's independence and vitality; and like them it shares John Aikin's view [in *Essays on Song-Writing, with a Collection of such English Songs as are most Eminent for poetical Merit, to which are Added, Some Original pieces,* n.d.] that local tales should be integrated within an emotional perspective by the bard who works with them.

Perhaps no other poem by Burns illustrates so well the false conclusions to which false assumptions about the poet inevitably lead. The notion that Burns is always autobiographical, for instance, has led several critics to miss the irony of Burns's masterpiece. Thomas Crawford, whose discussion of **"Tam o' Shanter"** [in his *Burns: A Study of the Poems and Songs,* 1960] provided my own interpretation's point of departure ("pleasure" and "community" as key words in the poem, and the alternation between several narrative "voices"), nonetheless illustrates the shortcomings of an autobiographical approach in several of his generalizations:

> The strain of realism that runs through the work derives, at the level of the superficial and the merely obvious, from Burns's own quizzical recognition that he, too—emancipated man of the eighteenth century though he was—could, in the appropriate circumstances, feel some of the terrors that afflict the superstitious and the simple-minded. . . . [**"Tam o' Shanter"**] is typical not only of Burns, but of the Scottish mind; for it is—next to **"The Vision"**—the most genuinely *national* of all his poems.

What Crawford praises as the "strain of realism" in **"Tam o' Shanter"** is its descriptive, autobiographical component. Burns was a riding officer for the Excise; in his later life, he spent most of his free time at taverns such as the Globe Inn at Dumfries. As a child, he had been spellbound by tales of local atrocities and supernatural visitations spun by a relative, Betty Davidson; many of her stories had focused on weird happenings at Alloway's nearby ruined kirk. Since **"Tam o' Shanter"** begins at a tavern, describes a wild, drunken ride, and features a witches' dance at Alloway kirk, it is clear that autobiographical material is an important factor. It is not all-important, however, because it fails to provide a means of

analyzing the complex tone of the poem—the implied attitude toward the things described. Crawford's praise of a descriptive "strain of realism" had led him in the passage quoted above to see superstitious terror as part of the emotional message in **"Tam o' Shanter."** For all his reservations about **"Tam o' Shanter,"** Carlyle is actually closer to the truth when he speaks of its sparkling "rhetoric," which distances readers from any naive immersion in horror. Burns's presentation of the supernatural material is mock-heroic (as was Pope's presentation of Belinda in one of Burns's favorite poems, *The Rape of the Lock*); in any mock-heroic work, the challenge to critics is determining where the irony stops.

It is a challenge that critics working from the current assumptions about Burns fail even to perceive, let alone to meet. Critics whose thesis has been Burns's inability to master English diction become trapped when they turn to **"Tam o' Shanter"** in discussion of whether the epic digressions in the poem (brilliant examples of bravura English) disprove their position. (Kurt Wittig [in his *The Scottish Tradition in Literature,* 1958], wanting to praise the poem but disliking any English influence, concludes that these passages are "near English.") Critics wedded to the notion of an earthy, "peasant" Burns usually prefer Burns's other, less obviously artful, masterwork, **"Love and Liberty."** Those who approach Burns from eighteenth-century perspectives usually do appreciate the elegance and irony of **"Tam o' Shanter,"** yet seldom consider the relationship of tone to the folkloric subject. Others, such as Carlyle, are drawn to its subject but baffled by its tone. Indeed, while illustrating the partial truth of all the labels that have been applied to Burns—the poet of the people, the national bard, the Romantic in love with excess, the Augustan in love with form—**"Tam o' Shanter"** also illustrates their only partial adequacy by seeming to transcend them all.

Before coming to the particulars of the poem, I should make one point about Burns's ironic treatment of supernatural forces. The story of Tam's ride as Burns received it from local sources itself existed on different levels. The prose summary that Burns supplied to Captain Grose along with his poem relates the history of a nameless Carrick farmer who, while riding home from Ayr one night, discovers a witches' dance in progress at Alloway kirk (as mentioned above, a source for local ghost stories; incidentally, this was also the burial place of Burns's father). A humorous variant, however, was also current in Burns's day. Douglas Graham, an acquaintance of Burns and tenant of the farm "Shanter" in Carrick, once had told his superstitious wife a similar tale of interrupting a witches' dance—to account for his late return from a market-day journey to Ayr. The joke was that shrewish Helen Graham had actually believed her husband's story. In short, the original for "Tam" himself used folk material ironically, to deceive a real-life "Kate." It is fitting, then, that Burns's poem demonstrates a dual perspective on its own truth, as it alternates narrative between an artful narrator and a drunken protagonist.

The first twelve lines of **"Tam o' Shanter"** provide, as

usual in Burns, a context stanza for the poem to follow. Neither the poet-narrator nor Tam is yet in evidence. This stanza speaks of "we," meaning by that a convivial male fellowship of farmers and local tradesmen, drawn together temporarily at the close of the Ayr market day by a common disinclination to leave their tavern and return home to their wives:

> When chapman billies leave the street,
> And drouthy neebors, neebors meet,
> As market-days are wearing late,
> An' folk begin to take the gate;
> While we sit bousing at the nappy,
> And getting fou and unco happy,
> We think na on the lang Scots miles,
> The mosses, waters, slaps, and styles,
> That lie between us and our hame,
> Whare sits our sulky sullen dame,
> Gathering her brows like gathering storm,
> Nursing her wrath to keep it warm.

From within this fellowship, Tam is then presented: "This truth fand honest *Tam o' Shanter*, / As he frae Ayr ae night did canter. . . ."

The poem has already begun to complicate its relationship to a local source. "Honest" Tam is drawn from real life liar Douglas Graham; and Graham's lie about witches is the "truth" that Tam will soon find (or that will soon find Tam—the phrasing is ambiguous). The poem then modulates to ironic praise of the percipience of Tam's "ain wife Kate," who has warned him about the danger of riding by the haunted kirk after midnight:

> O *Tam!* hadst thou but been sae wise,
> As ta'en thy ain wife *Kate's* advice!
> She tauld thee weel thou was a skellum,
> A blethering, blustering, drunken blellum;
> That frae November till October,
> Ae market-day thou was nae sober;
> That ilka melder, wi' the miller,
> Thou sat as lang as thou had siller;
> That every naig was ca'd a shoe on,
> The smith and thee gat roaring fou on;
> That at the L———d's house, even on Sunday,
> Thou drank wi' Kirkton Jean till Monday.
> She prophesied that late or soon,
> Thou would be found deep drown'd in Doon;
> Or catch'd wi' warlocks in the mirk,
> By *Alloway's* auld haunted kirk.

Our first extended view of Tam is provided by a hostile witness, his wife. Even in this first glimpse of our "hero's" character, ironic distance prevails.

This is increased when Burns's narrator (until this point silent except for a passing couplet in praise of Ayr) emerges to underscore Kate's ill temper by appearing to regret Tam's disregard of her "sweet counsels":

> Ah, gentle dames! it gars me greet,
> To think how mony counsels sweet,

> How mony lengthen'd sage advices,
> The husband frae the wife despises!

Kate's invective has stressed Tam's extremes of misconduct, but the narrator returns us to Tam as a norm: all husbands neglect the "sage" advice of their wives. This changing perspective on Tam is so far the most dynamic feature of the poem. There is no amassing of tension about Tam's imminent encounter with a witches' dance. The supernatural theme is actually deflated by the context in which it is first mentioned: the lurid and spiteful prophecy of Kate.

Then the tale itself properly begins. Lines 37 to 78 constitute the first segment of the poem after the introduction. Tam is described as "planted unco right" by the fireside, the best seat in the tavern. He is enjoying his drink ("reaming swats that drank divinely"), the "queerest stories" of his crony Souter (cobbler) Johnny, and even the "secret" favors of the landlady. All these pleasurable activities work as Burns undoubtedly intended: to create an atmosphere of total gratification for Tam. This tavern is a perfect place:

> Care, mad to see a man sae happy,
> E'en drown'd himsel amang the nappy:
> As bees flee hame wi' lades o' treasure,
> The minutes wing'd their way wi' pleasure:
> Kings may be blest, but *Tam* was glorious,
> O'er a' the ills o' life victorious!

Here the narrator has taken over the poem to meditate on the implications of Tam's simple pleasures, and in the next fifteen lines, he warms to his meditative theme:

> But pleasures are like poppies spread,
> You seize the flower, its bloom is shed;
> Or like the snow falls in the river,
> A moment white—then melts for ever;
> Or like the borealis race,
> That flit ere you can point their place;
> Or like the rainbow's lovely form
> Evanishing amid the storm.—
> Nae man can tether time nor tide;
> The hour approaches *Tam* maun ride;
> That hour, o' night's black arch the key-stane,
> That dreary hour he mounts his beast in;
> And sic a night he taks the road in,
> As ne'er poor sinner was abroad in.

. . . Passages such as the last two quoted from **"Tam o' Shanter"** show an unusually condensed integration of local and literary influences. Critics have mentioned literary sources for these epic digressions in **"Tam o' Shanter"** from writings as diverse as *The Rape of the Lock,* Thomson's *The Seasons* (the rainbow image), Ovid, Dr. Johnson, and, from the vernacular poets, Allan Ramsay and Hamilton of Gilbertfield. And in telling the tale of Douglas Graham, Burns also suggests a number of autobiographical themes. His point of departure is Ayr—close to his birthplace at Alloway—and behind his description of tavern life at Ayr is his own adult experience of its pleasures at Dumfries.

Burns's letters often distinguish between his life and his art, asserting his values in two modes—"as a man and as a poet." In **"Tam o' Shanter,"** especially in these early lines on the pleasures of sociable carousing and the reluctance with which working men leave them for home and renewed responsibility, Burns views the tavern culture both descriptively (as a man) and evocatively (as a poet). Tam is his "man" and the narrator is his "poet," and the narrative alternates between their two levels of appreciation.

In the ensuing section—lines 74 to 104—Burns seems to remember he had promised Captain Grose a horror story, and he describes the violent storm into which Tam reluctantly emerges from the shelter and good fellowship of the tavern. It is worth mentioning, as do most commentators on this poem, that Burns rode through many night storms in the course of his work. As usual, when Burns is moved to describe natural forces in order to explicate his human theme, his description is authoritative and precise:

> The wind blew as 'twad blawn its last;
> The rattling showers rose on the blast;
> The speedy gleams the darkness swallow'd;
> Loud, deep, and lang, the thunder bellow'd:
> That night, a child might understand,
> The Deil had business on his hand.

Like line 13, in which Tam either finds or is himself found out by "truth," lines 77 and 78 are fundamentally equivocal. A "child might understand" that the bad weather signified Satan's presence in the countryside: how might an adult react? The narrator seems daunted, but feckless Tam mounts his old mare Meg, "despising wind, and rain and fire." The difference between Tam and the narrator is drink. Tam is just sober enough for a gesture of prudence, "glowring around . . . / Lest bogles catch him unawares". Tam proceeds without incident until he reaches the ruined kirk, the very place mentioned in Kate's "prophecy." Before description of the witches' dance Tam discovers there, the narrator describes some grim local landmarks: the boulder where "Charlie" had broken his neck in a drunken fall, the well at which "Mungo's mither" had committed suicide, the cairn of a murdered infant. This is local color directed to Captain Grose, a collector of such stories.

Tam's ride brings him to Alloway, where he hears in the distance, through the noise of the storm, unholy sounds of "mirth and dancing." Yet the narrator interrupts, with another digression, any focusing of tension that may have been created by the description of Tam's stormy progress:

> Inspiring bold *John Barleycorn!*
> What dangers thou canst make us scorn!
> Wi' tipenny, we fear nae evil;
> Wi' usquabae, we'll face the devil!—
> *The swats sae reamed in Tammie's* noddle,
> Fair play, he car'd na deils a boddle.

Such passages, in which an external voice ironically discusses "Tammie," seem to disprove the notion of James Kinsley [*Robert Burns and the peasantry,* 1974] and Ian Campbell ["Burns's Poems and Their Audience," in *Critical Essays on Robert Burns,* edited by Donald Low, 1975] that this poem is a "dramatic monologue." The digressions seem intentionally to distance us from any immediate identification with Tam; at least, his simplicity is deliberately contrasted with the more intricate consciousness of the narrator.

What Tam sees at Alloway follows his wife Kate's prediction. It is a satanic festival, with "Auld Nick" himself playing the pipes for a community of witches. In contrast to the male fellowship at Ayr, the witches' dance at Alloway is largely female. The sole woman of the prologue, a tavern landlady, is here paralleled by the "proprietor" at the dance, musician Satan. (Warlocks are mentioned, but not described.) And Kate's admonitory presence in the opening section of the poem is paralleled by Tam's appreciative presence at the witches' dance. After more scene setting (swords, scimitars, tomahawks, a knife, the enshrouded dead holding candles, the chained corpse of a hanged murderer, two more dead infants), Burns proceeds to his central interest: Tam's response to all this. Drunken Tam, "amaz'd and curious," watches the dance, while the narrator again interposes himself—he has aesthetic objections to Tam's involvement:

> Now *Tam!* O *Tam!* had thae been queans,
> A' plump and strapping in their teens,
> Their sarks, instead o' creeshie flannen,
> Been snaw-white seventeen hunder linnen!
> Thir breeks o' mine, my only pair,
> That ance were plush, o' gude blue hair,
> I wad hae gi'en off my hurdies,
> For ae blink o' the bonic burdies!
>
> But wither'd beldams, auld and droll,
> Rigwoodie hags wad spean a foal,
> Lowping and flinging on a crummock,
> I wonder didna turn thy stomach.

Tam's taste is vindicated, however; there is one young recruit at the dance. In yet another of the poem's symmetrical oppositions, the narrator's offer of his worn-out breeches is quickly followed by description of the young witch Nannie largely in terms of her scanty shift—a present received in childhood from her grandmother which she has now outgrown:

> But *Tam* kend what was what fu' brawlie,
> There was ae winsome wench and wawlie,
> That night enlisted in the core,
> (Lang after kend on *Carrick* shore;
> For mony a beast to dead she shot,
> And perish'd mony a bony boat,
> And shook baith meickle corn and bear,
> And kept the country-side in fear:)
> Her cutty sark, o' Paisley harn,
> That while a lassie she had worn,
> In longitude tho' sorely scanty,

It was her best, and she was vauntie.—

The poem perceives the witches' dance much as it has perceived the drunkenness of market-day tradesmen in Ayr: not as something to be censured so much as something that is a feature of local life. Incidentally, the folkloric content of the narrative has at this point become explicitly parenthetical.

The next section begins with the narrator's confession of the inadequacy of his Muse to "sing" of Nannie's dance in suitably epic terms. For the only moment in the poem, Tam takes initiative away from the narrator when, losing his "reason a' thigither," he cries out, "Weel-done, Cutty-sark!" in response to an especially bold leap of Nannie's. My earlier discussion of sentimental fiction stressed its voyeuristic overtones, and Tam's presence at the witches' dance has created some tension related to voyeurism. Will Tam just look on, or will he assert himself as a responsive presence and deal with the consequences? Made heroic by drink, pot-valiant Tam does "roar out" a reaction to what he sees. His outcry stops the dance, and the "hellish legion" "sallies" out against him.

In an earlier section of the poem, Tam's precious hours of respite at the tavern were compared to the homeward journey of bees. Here, the angry sortie of the witch community is evoked with the same simile:

> As bees bizz out wi' angry fyke,
> When plundering herds assail their byke;
> As open pussie's mortal foes,
> When, pop! she starts before their nose;
> As eager runs the market-crowd,
> When "Catch the thief!" resounds aloud;
> So Maggie runs, the witches follow,
> Wi' mony an eldritch skreech and hollow.

This poem began with a description of market-day crowds. Its transition to a conclusion is marked by another reference to them; in this case, to the market outcry against a petty thief. The earlier allusion stressed the common inclination of the community to relax after work; this instance stresses their common organization against an intruder.

Burns's earlier long poem, the cantata **"Love and Liberty,"** offered a mirror image of Calvinism. The narrative in **"Tam o' Shanter"** also presents a series of opposing reflections on central themes. Indeed, **"Tam o' Shanter"** is structured by the opposition of the hedonistic community of men-drinkers at the beginning of the poem and the hedonistic community of women-dancers at its climax. The distance between the two societies is bridged in literary terms by the narrator because he applies similarly epic descriptions to both. The two cultures are bridged emotionally by Tam, with his instinctive shout of approval for Nannie. Kate stood opposed to the tavern culture in the prologue, but Tam, though an outsider, reacts to Nannie with an instinctive shout of "weel done" in the gesture that earns him the "heroic" status the narrator has applied ironically to him from the beginning. This response changes him from outsider to intruder, and another bridge becomes central to the poem: Tam must reach the keystone of the bridge of Doon to elude the witches' pursuit.

The concluding twenty-five lines, in which Tam's old mare Meg saves her master's life but loses her tail to a vindictive Nannie, account for Tam's fate after his exclamation. By now, a reader is sure that Tam is heroic enough to deserve survival, if only to prove Kate's "prophecy" ultimately false. He is not found drowned at Doon, but Meg and Tam do not come off entirely unscathed. There is a warning implicit in Maggie's lost tail:

> Now, wha this tale o' truth shall read,
> Ilk man and mother's son, take heed:
> Whene'er to drink you are inclin'd,
> Or cutty-sarks run in your mind,
> Think, ye may buy the joys o'er dear,
> Remember Tam o' Shanter's mare.

It is characteristic of the symmetrically inclined narrator that he concludes his "tale" with Maggie's loss of hers (or its homonymic counterpart). However, this warning is no strong deterrent: like all the narrator's warnings throughout the poem, it seems designed to be disregarded.

What is the truth of the tale, then? It is not to be found in the narrator's parodic moral. The tale, in fact, suggests exactly its opposite: don't think, don't remember. **"Tam o' Shanter"** celebrates the tendency of people—for good or ill—to refuse to reckon the price of their pleasures. The drinking at the tavern goes on each evening despite the disapproval of the farmers' wives. (The purpose of the prologue is to emphasize Tam's habitual, not just occasional, drunkenness.) The dancing in the kirkyard goes on with similar regularity, despite societal and even divine sanctions. Indeed, the witches are a perfect symbol for the tendency Burns saw in human nature to prefer self-assertion to prudent abstention. Witches give up a hope for a feeling, a concept of redemption for a sensation of present pleasure. The narrator does not stint his description of the gruesome trappings of the witches' dance, but it is basically hedonism, not evil, that he perceives in their conduct. Tam himself acts from a motive similar to Nannie's when his "roar" of approval indicates the victory of his instinct for pleasurable response over his less powerful one for self-protection and caution.

If this notion of the inexorably instinctive basis for human behavior were the whole "truth" of **"Tam o' Shanter,"** however, the poem would not sound so different from **"Love and Liberty,"** which shares that central theme. The difference is that in **"Tam o' Shanter"** the view that imprudence is a prerequisite to heroism is stated ironically: the reader is left to puzzle out views on instinct and repression that Burns presented unequivocally in **"Love and Liberty."** No character in **"Tam o' Shanter"** is unequivocally perceived. (Even Kate, spokeswoman for prudence, demonstrates in her diatribe a quality of reckless energy that is not exactly circumspect.) And in **"Tam o' Shanter,"** Burns complicates the tone by his artist-in-residence narrator, whose high-flown digressions actually keep the poem going until Tam reaches the witches' dance. The cautious narrator's application of literary allusion to Tam's simple pleasures and temptations shows that Burns uses art itself as a kind of "prudence" in the poem: he uses it to anticipate consequences, to order and control things, and to counter Tam's policy of playing life by ear.

The poem shifts perspective between Tam and the narrator, the man and the poet—between life and literature. In a way, the truth of the tale is this very sense that human instinct and creative synthesis follow parallel if not always contiguous paths and that an affectionate irony in presenting both can be the "bridge" between them. In **"Tam o' Shanter"** it is a double consciousness, expressed as irony, that brings both life and art, energy and order, into the world of the poem. The tendency of the narrator to enlarge and reflect on the events in the poem is as necessary to **"Tam o' Shanter"** as the tendency of its "hero" to pursue immediate gratification. A special feature of the irony in Burns's poem is that, though certainly not tragic, it is not exclusively comic. In the ironic distance between Tam's and the narrator's perspectives we can see Burns's assertion of a mediating consciousness somewhere between the facts of life and the seductive lies of fancy. "Honest Tam's" heroism may be qualified by drunkenness and some other defects of character, but he is still much more than the butt of a poet's joke, as was Cowper's John Gilpin, for instance. Cowper's "diverting tale" also features the misadventures of a working man on horseback, but Cowper's mockery is directed against incompetent Gilpin, who cannot get his horse to stop. Burns's ironic view of Tam stops short of imposing haplessness on him. Tam is a good rider and his one speaking line, "Weel done," establishes him as an aggressive presence. The irony in **"Tam o' Shanter"** is a sympathetic and integrating force, like the stress on mutual affection that underlies Burns's love songs. In **"Tam o' Shanter,"** an affectionate irony brings together an artful narrator and artless Tam in a world where both can operate freely. Like so much of Burns's best work, **"Tam o' Shanter"** chooses to perceive its world optimistically.

In "Night the Second" of *The Four Zoas* (1795-1804), William Blake introduces to his epic some of the same themes that engaged Burns in his mock-epic:

> What is the price of Experience? do men buy it
>   for a song?
> Or Wisdom for a dance in the street? No, it is
>   bought with the price
> Of all that a man hath, his house, his wife, his
>   children.
> Wisdom is sold in the desolate market where
>   none come to buy,
> And in the wither'd field where the farmer
>   plows for bread in vain.
>
> *(Complete Writings)*

It is either Burns's shortcoming or his distinction—I think chiefly the latter—that perceiving as Blake did a central disjunction between joyous human instincts and the generally downhill course of life, Burns still addressed himself to issues like Blake's largely in an affirmative spirit. For Burns in his later years, whatever his personal disappointments, a song—a Scottish song—became exactly the "price of Experience." In **"Tam o' Shanter"** the market is far from "desolate"; and the beauty of a song—or the "wisdom" of a witches' dance—happens to be truth enough.

Christopher MacLachlan (essay date 1986)

SOURCE: "Point of View in Some Poems of Burns," in *Scottish Literary Journal,* Vol. 13, No. 1, May, 1986, pp. 5-20.

[*In this essay, MacLachlan examines Burns's varying role as narrator in the context of his literary-historical position.*]

A recent volume of essays on Burns [*The Art of Robert Burns,* edited by R. D. S. Jack and Andrew Noble, 1982] has placed new emphasis on the poet's adoption of roles. 'Burns's use and arguable abuse of a poetic *persona,*' the editors write in their introduction, 'the distinction discernible between the creativity present in his best, mainly early, poetry and songs and the much more questionable "self-creativity" displayed in his letters is . . . a theme of considerable interest' for many of the contributors to their volume. This interest centres upon Burns's letters, where they remark upon 'the plasticity Burns felt he had to adopt in order either to fashion a tone suitable to his correspondent or to achieve the social role or position he desired'.

Sampson outlines Burns's role in the revival of poetry in the Scots dialect:

[Burns's use of Scots was] initially regarded as an unfortunate result of his origins. After his death, however, commentators began to suggest that his version of the vernacular 'hardly ever transgressed the propriety of English grammar'. This apologetic tone gradually became more assertive. James Currie, Burns's first editor, pointed out that the language of the poetry had not prevented its general circulation in England. Indeed there were over a hundred separate printings of Burns's poetry in England between 1787 and 1835. Scots vernacular came to be regarded as an aspect of Burns's authenticity, and dislike of it was designated 'accidental, not natural'. Finally, Jeffrey was able to enlist Burns, without reservation, in the cause of Scottish nationalism: 'We may perhaps be allowed to say, that the Scotch is, in reality, a highly poetical language; and that it is an ignorant, as well as an illiberal prejudice, which would seek to confound it with the barbarous dialects of Yorkshire or Devon.' It was perhaps partly because of this change in Burns's reputation that the use of dialect became more common generally in the nineteenth century; even 'the barbarous dialects of Yorkshire or Devon' became respectable.

David Sampson, in the Modern Language Review, *Vol. 80, No. 1, January, 1985.*

The result is an enigma, the problem of deciding 'not only the degree of sincerity present towards the person addressed, but also the degree of sincerity in the writer towards himself at the moment of composition'. Consideration of where Burns seems to stand in relation to what he is writing can, I think, be usefully extended from the letters to the poetry. It must, however, be accompanied by an awareness of Burns's complex literary-historical position, especially his combination of Scottish and English influences and trends, in short, the classic insight of twentieth-century Burns criticism, given classic statement by [David] Daiches [*Robert Burns,* 1952] and [Thomas] Crawford [*Burns: A Study of the Poems and Songs,* 1960].

The starting point for such a consideration of Burns must be that fascinating poem, **"The Cotter's Saturday Night."** Here we have one of Burns's most obvious attempts to straddle his two cultures. On the English side are the allusions to Gray, Goldsmith and others, the quotations from Pope and the use of the Spenserian stanza. This last was adopted by Burns as a signal to his readers of the kind of poem he was writing—rustic, moralising, perhaps slightly archaic, certainly nostalgic. Its affinities are with Shenstone and Beattie. The stanza form, then, along with the allusions and literary echoes, appeals to a developed literary taste. Yet in contrast the subject of the poem is a Scottish working-class household, observed with often minute accuracy. Where in Gray's *Elegy* the ploughman merely 'homeward plods his weary way', Burns, in a stanza which is surely an elaboration of Gray's opening one, carefully lists the cotter's tools, 'his spades, his mattocks and his hoes' (line 16), with an assured familiarity Gray cannot match. Repeatedly **"The Cotter's Saturday Night"**, shows such first-hand acquaintance with its subject, as, of course, we would expect. So Burns, even more obviously than Fergusson in 'The Farmer's Ingle', brings together English influences, mainly literary, and his own Scottish experience.

What is curious about the poem, and perhaps the reason for its ultimate failure, is the position of the poet himself. He seems somehow outside the poem, for all his intimate understanding of its subject. As Daiches says, 'Burns's attempt both to *be* his subject and to stand outside it and show it off to a genteel audience spoils the poem'. He appears able to describe the cotter and his family at first hand, but also seems detached from these scenes, seeing them from a different point of view from the cotter's, because of his awareness of a broader culture, implied in the form and allusions of the poem. The way the poem is written conflicts with what it wishes to say; and yet Burns's effusive patriotism at the end and his explicit rejection of some aspects of a grander culture than the cottar's ('luxury's contagion', he calls it in stanza 20) work against a simple identification of Burns with the literary culture he is exploiting. The poet comes to occupy an uncomfortable isolation, being neither a cotter nor, by his own assertion, a man of easy refinement, though his affinities with each contribute to his estrangement from its opposite.

Given the awkwardness of Burns's point of view in **"The Cotter's Saturday Night,"** the reader should approach the central purpose of the poem with care. The climax of the poem is the scene of religious worship in stanzas 12 to 17. The view of religion presented is both selective and not a little tendentious. It is noteworthy that Burns describes family worship, without a clergyman or ritual, and without a sermon. It consists of prayer, hymn-singing and Bible reading: in other words, a churchless religion, without institutions or intellectual discussion. It is very much an emotional occasion, one of 'heartfelt raptures' (stanza 13). The Bible passages mentioned in stanza 14 concern 'how the *royal Bard* did groaning lye', 'Job's pathetic plaint' and 'rapt *Isaiah's* wild, seraphic fire'; the hymns and prayers similarly have emotional effects on the worshippers. Metters of doctrine and church government are absent. Instead, the attention is upon 'the language of the *Soul*', which proceeds, not from method or art, but from the heart (stanza 17). Here, surely, is a view of religion which is sentimental, in the Sternian sense, and Burns seems genuinely to admire this form of Christianity, perhaps because of its limitations. It is curious, though, that it should have met with favour elsewhere, even among the orthodox, because its corollary, an antipathy to formal religion, is obvious from stanza 17.

Burns's antipathy to formal religion is, of course, made even more obvious in his religious satires. What he attacks in them are the opposites of what he approves of in **"The Cotter's Saturday Night."** In the greatest of the satires, **"Holy Willie's Prayer,"** Burns completely adopts a role, for satiric purposes. He disappears, leaving the victim to condemn himself in his own words. Like Swift, Burns shows complete mastery of his victim's language—or languages, for many of the satirical touches come from the switches in language in the poem. Willie's self-satisfied rhetoric at the prayer's beginning fractures into something less controlled when he blurts out his own misdemeanours with Meg and Leezie's lass or remembers his humiliation by Gavin Hamilton. But the unctuous rhetoric is intrinsically satirical. As Daiches explains, while Willie maintains a tone of religious solemnity and often sounds conventionally pious, his meaning is outrageous and morally absurd. He glorifies a God who condemns ten out of eleven to hell without regard for their actions, good or bad; he affects humility at having been chosen by this God six thousand years ago; and he contrives to excuse his sexual incontinence as a penance he has to bear. In all this Willie is quite orthodox. Burns does not travesty Willie's Calvinism; he merely lets it speak for itself, and, as Daiches says, 'there is certainly nothing left of his creed by the time the poem comes to an end . . . a character damns himself and his doctrine before the reader's eyes'. The poem is much more than a personal lampoon. It goes beyond that, beyond satirising Willie Fisher, to attack through him the more rigid traditions of the Scottish Kirk, perhaps even of Christianity itself.

The question I want to ask is where Burns himself stands in all this. Daiches writes of his 'apparent indifference' to the way Holy Willie's beliefs are progressively self-destroyed, and of course such detachment is tactically necessary to allow the victim enough rope to hang himself.

But aloof though he may be, Burns in not entirely absent from the poem and we can discern his position fairly well. Three points can be made. First, Burns clearly sees the forms of religion as a natural hiding place for hypocricy. Willie s language is a screen for his real thoughts, by Burns's genius here made transparent for us, but not, one supposes, always so penetrable to the view; indeed, Willie himself seems unaware of his real meaning. Traditional language, and perhaps even traditional religion, appear empty conventions, apt to be filled with human selfishness and corruption. Second, Burns finds the very outward forms of this religion repugnant: the ferocity and lack of mercy of the Calvinist God; his inexorable logic of election and damnation; his readiness for vengeance and openness to Willie Fisher's kind of specious wheedling. Burns hates the very face of Willie's creed, quite apart from the hypocrisy behind it. Third, in opposition to this rejected religion Burns places human pleasure and satisfaction, including the sexual. We know Willie is a hypocrite because he admits he is 'fash'd wi' fleshly lust' and his objection to Gavin Hamilton is that 'he drinks, and swears, and plays at cartes', that is, he enjoys some of the ordinary freedoms of human society. Over against the image of man Holy Willie presents (and hides behind) is another image, the Burnsian one, based on a contempt for logic-chopping, a hatred of hell-and-damnation preachers and their God, a conviction of their hypocrisy in maintaining a part which human nature cannot sustain and a belief in the essential innocence and worthiness of happiness, both social and sexual, provided it is free from cant and bigotry.

There are clear connections between the positive view of human nature discernible in **"Holy Willie's Prayer"** and the view of religion in **"The Cotter's Saturday Night."** The cotter and his family avoid the hypocrisy of Holy Willie by frankness of emotion and innocence of intellect and demonstrate in their simple pleasures, sketched in the earlier part of the poem, the natural joys of humanity, including sexual love. Yet the idyll is never quite convincing. It is too selective. There is, for instance, an aspect of rural life hardly mentioned in the poem which is closely related to the religious. This is the supernatural. Burns's attitude to this is complex and revealing, as can be seen in another poem, **"Halloween."**

Neither Daiches nor Crawford warms to **"Halloween"**: the first calls it 'tedious', the second finds it parochial and quotes W.P. Ker on Burns's aloofness in the poem: 'his is not the voice of the people, but the voice of a judge to whom the people are more or less indifferent, who is far above them, and who sees them as small creatures moved by slight and trivial motives'. Once again, Burns's point of view in relation to his poem seems to be the issue. One can begin by noting the poem's place in the eighteenth century's growing if sometimes uncomprehending interest in both the supernatural and in folklore. In turning to this subject, Burns shows himself once again in touch with his times. Yet although there was growing fascination with the emotional effects of horror and the irrational, as well as a widespread feeling that the genius of the untutored claimed attention, there was considerable

diffidence about both. Frequently they had to be justified on antiquarian or anthropological grounds. This is the pose struck by Burns in the headnote to the poem. The first sentence mentions 'the manners and traditions of the country', as though it were not *his* own rural environment. Burns talks of the importance of these to 'the Peasantry in the West of Scotland', which sufficiently distances him from them and gives the poem an anthropological purpose. In the next sentence he elevates this into philosophy: 'the passion of prying into Futurity makes a striking part of the history of Human Nature, in its rude state, in all ages and nations . . . ' He goes on to refer to the 'philosophic mind' of the potential reader, as opposed to the 'more unenlightened' subjects of the poem itself.

All this sounds nervous or apologetic, as though Burns cannot present the poem as it is but must justify it as a serious study. Yet it is hardly to be doubted that Burns himself had participated in many of the superstitious rituals he presents in this cold, quasi-scientific manner. As with **"The Cotter's Saturday Night,"** Burns seems split between an intimate acquaintance with his subject and a detached manner of presenting it. He takes both the supernatural and the common people seriously enough to write a poem of over two hundred and fifty lines about them and yet is careful to reassure the reader of his own possession of 'a philosophic mind'. The awkwardness of this position is, I suspect, related to his own religious views. Against the harsh logic of Calvinism Burns sets the heart and its affections, what he calls 'the language of the *Soul*'. But too strong a reaction against reason would tilt over into the irrational. To prefer the cotter's simple religion before 'Religion's pride' and Holy Willie's hypocrisy is fine, so long as it does not run to an acceptance of superstition. As **"Halloween"** shows, such superstition is part of the outlook of the cotter's class, even if it is carefully excluded from **"The Cotter's Saturday Night."** Burns has to perform a balancing act whose strain shows in both poems. Folk-superstition also threatens his view of human nature. He is against hell-fire and damnation and for a more humane set of values; he must be similarly suspicious of the supernatural, as it appears in folk-customs. He rejects the Calvinist doctrines of a vengeful God and man's depravity as bogeymen; and hence must reject bogeymen too. But superstitions are less easy to combat than theology, partly because they are not presented as propositions you can debate and partly because they are acquired in a manner which renders them tenacious, as Burns himself noted in his autobiographical letter to Dr Moore of 2 August 1787. After mentioning the old woman who filled his boyish mind with stories of the supernatural, he goes on to say that they 'had so strong an effect on my imagination that to this hour, in my nocturnal rambles, I sometimes keep a sharp look-out in suspicious places; and though nobody can be more sceptical than I am in such matters, yet it often takes an effort of philosophy to shake off these idle terrors'. This ambivalence, between the strong effect on the imagination of these dark wonders and the effort of reason which attempts to dismiss them as old wives' tales, is clear in this passage, and so too, in the jocular tone, is the escape from the dilemma. Burns resolves his embarrassment by treating the superstitious humorously.

"Halloween" therefore describes the various folk customs faithfully enough, but almost every one is undercut by a comic outcome. In stanza IV, Will gets lost in the dark and pulls a cabbage stalk instead of a kail stalk; in stanza XII Merran gets such a fright when her blue thread is caught in the kiln that she fails to stay the question; and in stanza XXII Meg is frightened by a rat in the barn and runs through the midden to escape. The broadest humour is contained in the incident of Jamie Fleck and the hemp seed (stanzas XVII to XX): he sows the seed, glances back and sees a terrible apparition, which turns out to be, not his future beloved, but Grumphie the sow. Here Burns provides a common-sense resolution of the mystery (rather like Ann Radcliffe's practice in her Gothic novels); there is a vision, but it is not supernatural. Similarly, in stanza XXVI, Leezie is so frightened by a noise in the dark that she jumps in the pool; the sound might have come from the devil, but Burns also adds the possibility that it came from a cow. In short, **"Halloween"** shows the same lack of involvement noticeable in **"The Cotter's Saturday Night."** The detail is true and faithful, but it is observed from outside, and Burns, both in and out of the poem, seems detached and aloof. The power and mystery of the supernatural are neutralised by the philosophical pose and by humour.

This seems to bring us close to Carlyle's judgment on **"Tam o'Shanter"**:

> He has not gone back, much less carried us back, into that dark, earnest, wondering age, when the tradition was believed, and when it took its rise; he does not attempt, by any new-modelling of his supernatural ware, to strike anew that deep mysterious chord of human nature, which once responded to such things; and which lives in us too, and will for ever live . . .

This certainly applies to **"Halloween,"** although it is central to my argument that Burns, far from wishing to go back into 'that dark, earnest, wondering age' of superstition, was fearful of doing so and adopted certain devices to exorcise the supernatural. At least one of these devices, the philosophical headnote to the poem, derives from an Anglified literary culture which also confuses Burns's standpoint in **"The Cotter's Saturday Night."**

Carlyle's remarks, however, apply not to **"Halloween"** or **"The Cotter's Saturday Night"** but to **"Tam o'Shanter"** and as such seem quite beside the point. He seems, as Crawford says, 'Quite out of touch with the hostility of the Enlightenment towards the supernatural'. Yet, if anything, the poem is remarkable for *not* treating the supernatural with disdain. Indeed, **"Tam o'Shanter"** can be best described as a poem which combines Enlightened attitudes with traditional material and finds the literary means, in various modifications of English literary forms, to make this synthesis not merely convincing but a creative whole. As in **"The Cotter's Saturday Night"** the essentially unsophisticated subject is surrounded by evidence of sophisticated literary taste; and as in **"Hallow-**

een" the supernatural is undercut by humour. But the difference in **"Tam o'Shanter"** is that the literary form adopted is an ironic one, so that neither the sophisticated culture nor the sceptical humour is unequivocal and what might have been a conflict of values becomes instead a range of ambiguities, among which the unsophisticated and the supernatural may, just, survive.

The literary form of **"Tam o'Shanter,"** as Mabel I. Mackenzie ["A New Dimension for 'Tam o'Shanter'", in *Studies in Scottish Literature,* I, 1963-64] and, apparently independently, John MacQueen [*The Enlightenment and Scottish Literature Volume I: Progress and Poetry,* 1982] make clear, is mock-heroic. Burns takes over a form much used in Augustan English literature and employs it, with wit and skill, as the medium for a Scottish folk narrative. Both aspects of the work gain from the association, and the final effect is nicely balanced between literary sophistication and earthy humour, all darkened with horrible imaginings. The close amalgam of the neo-classical and the local is evident is the very epigraph to the poem:

> Of Brownys and of Bogillis full is this boke.

This comes, as Professor MacQueen notes, from Gavin Douglas's invocation to the sixth book of the *Aeneid,* the book in which Aeneas descends into the underworld. 'Like Aeneas in Virgil's Book VI' says MacQueen **"Tam o'Shanter"** pays a visit to the Otherworld' (Dr Mackenzie is more racy: 'Tam does not descend to the underworld; it comes up to him'). Along with epic echoes in the fable of the poem, there are stylistic parallels. Both critics note the use of epic similes: 'the bees which appear in Homer, Virgil, Spenser and Milton are not missing from Burns's poem. They appear twice . . . '. Their second appearance, at line 193, is as an intrusion between the outrush of the witches after Tam and the result of their pursuit. Not for the first time the impatient reader damns the narrator's love of his own eloquence. His moralising interjections are similar. Appropriate though they may be to a would be heroic poem, there are too many to be taken seriously. Lines 33 to 36 are a brief sample:

> Ah, gentle dames! it gars me greet,
> To think how mony counsels sweet,
> How mony lengthen'd sage advices
> The husband frae the wife despises!

The penultimate line here rhetorically elaborates on the 'counsels sweet' of its predecessor, thus delaying the conclusion of the sentence. The speaker dwells oratorically on his words and makes them seem more decorative than functional. This is part of the irony, along with the implications of the word 'lengthen'd' and the suggestion that all this moves the narrator to tears. A similar ironic posturing surely affects the oft-disputed lines 59 to 66:

> But pleasures are like poppies spread,
> You seize the flow'r, its bloom is shed;
> Or like the snow falls in the river,
> A moment white—then melts for ever;

> Or like the borealis race,
> That flit ere you can point their place;
> Or like the rainbow's lovely form
> Evanishing amid the storm.

Here Burns, as Dr Mackenzie says, 'piles up similes in carefully stated, neo-classical language', what Daiches calls 'a deliberately "fancy" English . . . as though to draw attention to the literary quality of the utterance'. The difficulties the passage has caused seem to me to come exactly from the problem Jack and Noble define, 'to decide not only the degree of sincerity present towards the person addressed, but also the degree of sincerity in the writer towards himself at the moment of composition'. In a mock-heroic poem, however, such ambiguity is not merely permitted, but a peculiar grace.

Another mock-heroic feature of **"Tam o'Shanter,"** is its use of prophecy to anticipate the action. Just as Pope introduces the Baron's prayer in Canto 2 of *The Rape of the Lock,* amid several other prophetic touches, so Burns introduces Tam's wife:

> She prophesied that late or soon
> Thou would be found deep drown'd in Doon;
> Or catch'd wi' warlocks in the mirk,
> By Alloway's auld haunted kirk.
>
> (ll. 29-32)

And like the Baron's, only half this wish is granted, or nearly (a point made by Dr Mackenzie). The prophetic elements, however, shade into the Gothic ones, another literary influence on the poem, in Tam's night ride:

> By this time he was cross the ford,
> Whare, in the snaw, the chapman smoor'd;
> And past the birks and meikle stane,
> Whare drunken Charlie brak's neck-bane;
> And thro' the whins, and by the cairn,
> Whare hunters fand the murder'd bairn;
> And near the thorn, aboon the well,
> Whare Mungo's mither hang'd hersel.
>
> (ll. 89-96)

This is an accumulation of ominous portents of disaster, comic in its exaggeration, but also an exploitation of the grim and ghastly, something pursued into the kirkyard itself, especially in the list of things Tam sees on the table:

> Five tomahawks, wi' blude red-rusted;
> Five scymitars, wi' murder crusted;
> A garter, which a babe had strangled;
> A knife, a father's throat had mangled . . .
>
> (ll. 135-138)

Ironically, these lines are perfectly neo-classical in their balanced organisation, yet what is described is far removed from neo-classical taste. Another, and less lurid, departure from neo-classicism is the low-life setting, which, although it is part of the mock-heroic effect, is not treated ironically. The opening of the poem describes a common-place scene and the joviality in the tavern, too, is described straightforwardly; there may be a moral point, serious or otherwise, here but we are not being asked to make a social judgment, or to judge the characters for anything other than their excess.

It is this *genre* quality of the poem, however, which gives it body, filling out the mock-heroic literary scheme with solid fare. **"Tam o' Shanter"**'s exact topography and its use of local superstitions and folk-lore balance its literary sophistication. Some of these allusions are slight, as in the reference to 'snaw-white seventeen hunder linnen' in line 154, or the later four lines on the cutty sark itself:

> Ah! little kend thy reverend grannie,
> That sark she coft for her wee Nannie,
> Wi' twa pund Scots, ('twas a' her riches),
> Wad ever grac'd a dance o' witches!
>
> (ll. 175-178)

By means of such allusions, **"Tam o' Shanter"** is connected in a multitude of ways, great and small, with a real society, economy and culture. Burns takes once again the role of recorder of local life which he plays in **"The Cotter's Saturday Night"** and **"Halloween"**. The Gothic incidents of Tam's journey, for instance, have a folk-lore quality—each landmark has a traditional story attached to it—and the poem is full of asides which link it to a context of superstition and legend; for example, there is Nannie's career as a witch:

> For mony a beast to dead she shot,
> And perish'd mony a bony boat,
> And shook baith meikle corn and bear,
> And kept the country-side in a fear . . .
>
> (ll. 166-169)

Killing cattle, wrecking boats, blighting crops—these are the traditional accusations made against witches. The supernatural and uncanny element of the poem gains much from these circumstantial details and references to real superstitions. We cannot dismiss as a literary joke a poem so obstinately rooted in popular conviction, in what a recognisable community of real people believed to be true. At the same time, Burns's use of a very Augustan mode of writing shows his detachment from the subject matter. He has preserved his distance once again, so that it is not immediately obvious whether he believes in Tam's witches or not, or whether he believes in the devil here at all. All this is to the good. The supernatural element in the poem is the better for remaining ambiguous, neither easily dismissed nor quite free from common-sense scepticism; and, like the great mock-heroic poems of Dryden and Pope, **"Tam o' Shanter"** uses the form to unsettle the reader and his sense of values in a satiric way.

A major unsettling factor is the shifting standpoint of Burns himself, acting as narrator of the poem. It is tempting, indeed, to separate the two and talk of the poem as an exercise in the use of a poetic mask or persona (like **"Holy Willie's Prayer"**) Earlier, the ironic nature of one of the narrator's intrusions (lines 33 to 36) was described. The very first paragraph puts him in an equivocal position: he says that '*we* sit bousing at the nappy' and that '*we* think na on the lang Scots miles . . . That lie between *us* and *our* hame' (lines, 5, 7 and 9), which makes him a crony of Tam's and hence no fit judge of him. The implicit association between Tam and the narrator contributes to the curious effect of lines 59 to 66, which, as noted above, present a series of beautiful sentiments, aptly expressed, but perhaps a little too self-advertisingly poetical. The narrator seems to call attention to his superior refinement and cultured outlook. In contrast, in lines 151 to 162 he reveals a lustful quality. Tam is staring at the witches dancing in their underclothes. The narrator rebukes him, but not, as we might expect, for his interest in the sight of underdressed females, but rather because the females in question are not worth looking at. And the narrator makes his point by saying that, if they had been young girls, he would have given his own breeches for a sight of them, an obvious sexual quibble. This almost makes the narrator a hypocrite, one whose moral rectitude is a pose and who really shares the immoral desires of those he admonishes. The narrator formally comments and moralises, but his meaning subverts convention. He is a device of irony and humour, sometimes, indeed, a device of intensification, as in lines 201 to 204, where he prophesies a false ending to the tale:

Ah Tam! Ah Tam! thou'll get thy fairin!
In Hell they'll roast thee like a herrin!
In vain thy Kate awaits thy comin!
Kate soon will be a woefu' woman!

The lack of moral consistency in the narrator prepares us for the tongue-in-cheek moral at the end.

What, then, is the real moral of **"Tam o' Shanter"**? Here it helps to draw upon the conclusions already reached in considering other poems by Burns. In **"Holy Willie's Prayer"** Burns counters the Calvinist view of man with another, in which human pleasure, including sexual pleasure, has a positive value. **"Tam o' Shanter"** is about this pleasure, but the description of it comes with a warning about its transience and the retribution that falls, or may fall, upon indulgers. Tam's boozing is clearly an indulgence in pleasure. It is excessive, perhaps, but otherwise Burns hardly condemns it. The mock-heroic style, with its ironic presentation of heroic values, allows Burns to slip out of a conventional moral judgment without being forced into an aggressive unorthodoxy. The tavern scene, then, is one of gaiety and abundance, associated with positive qualities: note the prominence of the word 'divinely' in the description of Tam, sitting

Fast, by an ingle, bleezing finely,
Wi' reaming swats, that drank divinely;
And at his elbow, Souter Johnny,
His ancient, trusty, drouthy crony;
Tam lo'ed him like a vera brither. . . .

(ll. 39-43)

Brotherly love is not the only kind in evidence:

The landlady and Tam grew gracious,
Wi' favours, secret, sweet, and precious:

(ll. 47-48)

As Crawford says, 'the drink, the warmth, the talk, the landlady's "secret favours"—*these* are the Pleasures that are "like poppies spread"' and for these Tam has to pay, with the hardships of his night journey through storm (although admittedly the alcohol at least fortifies him somewhat). The importance of this cycle of pleasure and retribution is clear when it is noticed that it occurs three times in the poem. First, in the first paragraph, where it is described in general terms; the boozers in the pub eventually have to face the journey home:

Whare sits our sulky sullen dame,
Gathering her brows like gathering storm,
Nursing her wrath to keep it warm.

(ll. 10-12)

This of course is Tam's particular case, a point made by Daiches, at the very least, he has to pay for his pleasure by a soaking in the storm and a tongue-lashing from Kate, of which we are given a sample. But the second half of the poem transposes the theme into an eldritch key; now the pleasure/retribution cycle becomes weird, and perhaps symbolic. Tam's erotic pleasure in Nannie's dancing is punished by the pursuit of the witches, leading to the loss of his mare's tail—a fairly obvious sexual innuendo. As MacQueen says, 'the poem ends with a castration symbol', but in writing that 'Tam has escaped, but he has finally lost the virility which he almost recovered at the Kirk' MacQueen seems to me to confuse the symbol with reality. MacQueen's view is that Nannie the witch is 'Kate's opposite'. It seems more coherent to take Nannie as the supernatural equivalent of the vengeful wife, the third manifestation of what MacQueen himself calls 'an unnamed archetype, brooding like a storm outside the inn' in the first paragraph of the poem. The agents of retribution in the poem, then, are female: 'our sulky sullen dame', Kate the wife and Nannie the witch. The moral, on the other hand, is directed towards the other sex, 'ilk man and mother's son'. There is, of course, a class of females in sympathy with Tam in the poem. It is represented by Kirkton Jean, who provides drink on Sundays (lines 27 to 28), the landlady who flirts with Tam and lastly Tam's faithful grey mare, Meg, who both suffers symbolically for him at the end and also symbolically lifts a leg for him (line 80). This class of female is allied with Tam and his male friends in a world of pleasure. Opposed to them are wives and witches, who significantly meet in a church and are engaged in a parody of a religious service led by a figure in black.

As W. Montgomerie writes [in his *New Judgments: Robert Burns,* 1947], 'Auld Nick's place in the poem is significantly in the Kirk', though why, given Burns's views on the Kirk's hypocrisy and moral depravity, he should add that the devil is 'in opposition to it' is not easy to follow. Montgomerie goes on to call Auld Nick 'a creature of the historical past, like his warlocks and witches,

A manuscript page of "Tam o' Shanter," in Burns's handwriting.

like the dead'; as such, rather than being 'part of the human personality suppressed by Calvinism', as Montgomerie would have it, he is in fact an apt representation of rigid Calvinism itself. Of course, what his congregation do looks, at first sight, much like a drunken orgy and this is how Tam sees it; but he is swiftly disabused. Just as Holy Willie has little difficulty persuading himself of the theological justification for his own sins of the flesh and yet attacks Gavin Hamilton for lesser indulgences, each witch, happy enough to go 'at it in her sark' (line 150), turns in self-righteous anger upon the man who, like the boy in the fable, has the temerity to remark on the exiguity of dress. The spell breaks, and the witches' fury is roused, when Tam shouts out the truth; just as one supposes the kind of celebration described in **"The Holy Fair,"** could not long survive that poem's revelation of its connection, despite high pretensions, with drink and houghmagandie. In **"The Holy Fair"** as in **"Holy Willie's Prayer,"** Burns cuts through the disguise of cant and self-delusion and shows us the human reality. In so doing he attracted the opprobrium of the orthodox. It is this pattern of events that occurs in **"Tam o'Shanter,"** although in that Gothic fantasy Burns attacks conventional religion much more severely than he does elsewhere, by placing the devil himself at its centre, and depriving him of any hypocritical disguise.

Despite its vividness and humour **"Tam o' Shanter"** is fundamentally a pessimistic poem. Victory, however hollow, goes to the forces of convention and the pleasures of life are shown to be transient and penalised. This accounts for a degree of pathos in the poem, which centres upon Tam o' Shanter himself. As MacQueen points out, only two adjectives are applied directly to Tam. In line 129 he is termed 'heroic', appropriately enough, but with some irony, given the poem's mock-heroic nature. The other adjective occurs when the character is first mentioned; in line 13 he is 'honest Tam o' Shanter'. What 'honest' means here is not clear, but it becomes more so after the aside about Ayr:

> Auld Ayr, wham ne'er a town surpasses,
> For honest men and bonny lasses.
>
> (ll. 15-16)

The conjunction with that sort of female suggests that honest men are those of a convivial and fun-loving disposition, which is a paradox given the usual meaning of 'honest'. This is part of the poem's subversion of conventional morality, of conventional honesty. Tam, then, is the representative of the Burnsian attitude to life, in opposition to the pious and the douce. But the most interesting description of Tam is more extended and occurs at the height of the pub scene, when our hero is in his element:

> Kings may be blest, but Tam was glorious,
> O'er a' the ills o' life victorious!
>
> (ll. 57-58)

Again, there is irony here, as well as pathos. Tam is glorious—for the moment; he is victorious over life's ills—an enviable position, while it lasts. Immediately after this couplet come the similes on the transience of pleasure, culminating in the bleak proverb, 'Nae man can tether time or tide' (line 67). In lines 57 and 58, then, are concentrated the poem's central meaning: the power of pleasure and its transience, the conflict between Tam's euphoria and the ills of life which have assailed and will again assail him. Perhaps that is why virtually every critic of the poem draws attention to these lines. None, however, has noted an evident allusion, perhaps because it is so obvious, to a well-known song (in Britain, at least) which requests a blessing on a king (or queen) and wishes he (or she) may be victorious, happy and glorious. At a key point in the poem, then, Burns expresses himself in an allusive way. With his hero getting fou in an Ayrshire pub, he lifts his diction with a reference to a poem with quite other associations. The effect, of course, is mock-heroic, though not entirely so. At this point in the poem Tam indeed is a king, or rather, as Mackenzie says, he 'has attributes a king might envy'. The poem balances between mocking Tam and glorifying him, and it does so by successfully combining Scots and English in a way which is typical of Burns's genius and nowhere more evident than in **"Tam o' Shanter"**. But the balancing, too, is typical of Burns, leaving the reader in teasing doubt of his exact position, so that reading the poem requires a constant alertness to the play of meanings and values around the text and to the shifting point of view of the poet.

Stephen R. McKenna (essay date 1987)

SOURCE: "Spontaneity and the Strategy of Transcendence in Burns's Kilmarnock Verse-Epistles," in *Studies in Scottish Literature, Vol. XXIV,* 1987, pp. 78-90.

[In the following essay, McKenna offers a thematic and structural analysis of Burns's verse-epistles.]

As a group, Robert Burns's verse-epistles have been consistently ignored by commentators, or at best have received only passing attention by those who expend their energies in analyzing his better known (and in many cases better) poems and songs. Two notable exceptions to this rule are the essays by John C. Weston ["Burns's Use of The Scots Verse-Epistle Form," *Philological Quarterly,* 49 (April 1970)] and G. Scott Wilson ["Robert Burns: The Image and the Verse-epistles," in *The Art of Robert Burns,* edited by R.D.S. Jack and Andrew Noble, 1982]. Weston views the epistles of Ramsay and Hamilton, Fergusson, and Burns in terms of a distinct sub-genre—the Scots verse-epistle—whose conventions Burns inherited and utilized for the purposes of creating a self-portrait. Wilson, more narrowly, views Burns's epistles strictly in terms of the financial and psychological motives behind the poet's image-making. In addition to these studies, I offer a thematic and structural analysis of Burns's first published epistles in the hope that it will shed additional light on his artistic purposes, achievements and shortcomings in this special and problematic poetic genre.

The epistle-as-poem creates certain structural and stylistic problems. Because Burns's early epistles were written as private communications before becoming public poetic matter, transitions from the particular to the universal within the epistles had to occur if they were to be of more than arcane historical or scholarly interest to the wider universal audience that the poet undoubtedly envisioned. Indeed, for an epistle to be a great poem in its own right it must speak to a wider audience than the person or persons to whom it was nominally written. The problem inherent in this poetic genre (though certainly not limited to epistles alone) is that if the poet strives to create universally applicable themes in the epistle, then the epistle runs the risk of evolving into a poem with a salutation and a conclusion awkwardly appended. At worst, the universal sentiments may be clumsily inserted so that the movement from the particular to the universal and vice versa will appear abrupt and unnatural. The perfect resolution of these tensions would be to have the particular epistolary message itself be a universal statement—and this is no mean feat. With varying degrees of success, Burns's Kilmarnock verse-epistles illustrate the poet's struggles with and attempts to overcome just such problems of integration and balance. Furthermore, in the order they are arranged, the epistles display Burns's growing self-confidence as a poet not only in relationship to his art, but to his place within the social order as well. The epistle to James Smith, though not Burns's first attempt at the epistle from, is the first epistle to appear in the Kilmarnock edition. This

epistle opens with a three-stanza epistolary introduction wherein Burns intimately and with good humor greets and flatters Smith. Burns then easily launches forth into seven stanzas of self-referential poetic theorizing. The transition from Burns's particular communication with Smith in the introduction to the more universal poetic concerns is facilitated by what I call Burns's "spontaneity formula":

> Just now I've taen the fit o' rhyme,
> My barmie noddle's working prime,
> My fancy yerket up sublime
>   Wi' hasty summon:
> Hae ye a leisure-moment's time
>   To hear what's comin?

(*ll.* 19-24)

Burns here, and elsewhere, uses the spontaneity formula in an attempt to give the illusion that the epistle is an effortless and unpremeditated outpouring of thought and feeling neatly arranged in the intricacies of the Habbie Stanza form. The spontaneity formula is in fact an illusion of art. Burns no doubt worked for hours over these seemingly spontaneous stanzas.

Weston, it should be noted, sees this sort of spontaneity in terms of the Scots epistolary conventions:

> Since all Scots epistles before him discuss the poetic productions of the correspondents, he includes quite naturally theories of poetic composition in keeping with his view of himself: the true poet is always untaught and only composes carelessly for the pleasure and as a spontaneous emotional release of feeling, generally for women and nature, thus awakening those feelings in others.

This is true on the thematic level. However, Burns's use of spontaneity is quite a bit more utilitarian than Weston indicates here. For Burns, spontaneity formulas become structurally significant as transitional devices whereby Burns moves from the epistolary particulars, relevant solely to the addressee, to poetic universals, as will be seen especially in regard to the epistles to William Simson, the first and second epistles to Lapraik, **"To a Young Friend,"** and to David Sillar. In addition, a spontaneity formula is sometimes used to conclude the epistles as well—as in the epistles to John Rankine, Sillar, the first epistle to Lapraik, and to Smith.

In the self-referential section of the epistle to james Smith, Burns views himself from two perspectives: the poet in relation to other people and, more importantly, the poet in relation to an external power principle. (This principle assumes various forms in the different epistles, but essentially it is made manifest by "Fortune" and the "Muse.") For Burns, this principle is intimately connected with the second function of the spontaneity formula—the introduction of self-referential artistic themes. The basis of this professedly spontaneous outpouring of verse is, of course, his "Muse" in her various disguises:

The star that rules my luckless lot,
Has fated me the russet coat,
An' damn'd my fortune to the groat;
   But, in requit,
Has blest me with a *random-shot*
    O' countra wit.

(ll. 31-6)

Though Burns makes clearer the interconnectedness of the Muse, fortune, and his own spontaneity in other epistles, he here illustrates a central epistolary theme. Burns sees himself as the passive recipient and observer of the workings of the external power principle. Verbs such as "rules," "has fated," "damn'd," and "has blest" all indicate that he is at the mercy of powers far larger than himself. Indeed, Burns vows to "wander on with tentless heed / . . . Till fate shall snap the brittle thread" (ll. 55, 57). Though these sentiments were poetic commonplaces long before his day, Burns uses them to lay the groundwork for the more general and more universal philosophical interlude on life, death and fate (ll. 61-120). By means of the epistle's general concern with fortune's (or more specifically, misfortune's) application to existence, Burns's own struggles become representative of every person's philosophical struggles with life's meaning. He transcends the potentially bleak vision of existence with the optimism of defiance:

And others, like your humble servan',
Poor wights! nae rules nor roads observin;
To right or left, eternal swervin,
   They zig-zag on;
Till curst with Age, obscure an' starvin,
   They aften groan.

Alas! what bitter toil an' straining—
But truce with peevish, poor complaining!
Is Fortune's fickle *Luna* waning?
   E'en let her gang!
Beneath what light she has remaining.
   Let's sing our Sang.

(ll. 109-20)

This brings Burns back to an intense preoccupation with his own creative powers, centering on a defiant affirmation of poetry's transcendent value and on his growing self-confidence as a poet. Fortune may indeed be unfair, and life may indeed be a struggle, but Burns claims he will be content with a "rowth o' rhymes" (l. 126) and "sterling Wit" (l. 137). This poetic gift and the exploitation of it to the utmost represent his more general key to transcendence, as will be seen in regard to the other epistles.

Regrettably, the power and force of Burns's proclamation of poetic confidence loses its climactic vitality in the clumsy, overt address to the wider audience that he uses to terminate the epistle. Here is Burns's attempt to relate didactically and blatantly the particular personal application of the epistle to the universal human condition of the wider audience he envisions for himself. Yet, bombast aside, the last stanza, by means of another spontaneity

formula, abruptly breaks the address to the universal audience and returns to Smith for a fond farewell:

Whilst I—but I shall haud me there—
Wi' you I'll scarce gang *ony where*—
Then *Jamie,* I shall say nae mair,
   But quat my sang,
Content *with* You to make a *pair,*
   Whare'er I gang.

(ll. 169-74)

And quit he does. This seemingly chatty epistle has no real conclusion. It merely stops, as though it were in fact composed on the spot in a single draft. If it were composed on the spot, as the spontaneity formula would have us believe, this would account for the abrupt termination. But since in all likelihood it was not composed as a one-shot finished product, this problem of ending an epistle thus becomes a function of the poet having to strike a balance between the particular and the universal, by having in effect two vastly different audiences simultaneously.

Nowhere is this problem of the conclusion more evident than in the **"Epistle to Davie."** The lapse into Shenstonian sentiment at the epistle's end has been noted by numerous commentators, so I will not rehearse their arguments here. Yet this epistle also demonstrates a remarkable degree of internal coherence and universal application. As [James] Kinsley notes in his commentary [*The Poems and Songs of Robert Burns,* 1968], this epistle in all likelihood was composed as a poem before Burns made an epistle of it, and in essence it still remains a poem of social commentary with an epistolary conclusion appended to it.

However, a striking feature of this epistle, in contrast to so many others, is the ease and fluidity with which it moves to its universal theme. Burns dispenses with the traditional epistolary introduction. By the end of the first stanza he gives us a traditional Scottish poetic introduction involving the gloomy winter exterior contrasted to the warm and snug interior of his home. By means of a spontaneity formula (ll. 4-6) he makes a passing reference to himself, and then he plunges into the heart of his matter—his social commentary on the benefits of simple poverty, which is a theme common to many of Burns's epistles as well as to much of his poetry. This epistle's thematic core comes in stanza five, concluding that neither titles, money, learning, nor any of the superficial social rewards are of transcendent value because "The *heart* ay's the part ay, / That makes us right or wrang" (ll. 69-70). We can witness this theme actually operating in many of his satires.

Throughout the social commentary in the **"Epistle to Davie"** we find a consistent focus on the role of fortune in controlling people's lives. Fortune makes Burns, as well as the "Great-folk," who and what they are; it gives them their respective gifts. Again, fortune is the active agent, the power principle, and people are the passive beneficiaries or victims. Yet one of the key elements of the social commentary here is Burns's insistence on the vast difference in attitude toward fortune between himself and the "Great-folk." They are "careless, and fearless, / Of either Heaven or Hell" (ll. 81), whereas Burns recognizes his own helplessness in the face of the external forces. Burns resolves this theme, as he does in most of the other epistles, by passively and graciously accepting his lot and by using the gifts of fortune (and the Muse) to fullest advantage, thereby asserting a measure of creative free will. Though he focusses on the predominance of fortune in life, Burns in his epistles is not a strict determinist by any means. As we can see in the spontaneity formulas, the muse inspires him, but he will ultimately determine the direction his creation will take.

Unfortunately, when the focus of **"The Epistle to Davie"** turns to the addressee the insight and force drown in the saccharine sentimentality of English neoclassical poetics. Stanza eight provides the flimsiest of transitions from the probing insight of his social consciousness to the transparent superficialities of the Shenstonian hymn to love. As if sensing this, Burns excuses himself and provides a conclusion for the epistle—again by using a spontaneity formula:

> O, how that *name* inspires my style!
> The words come skelpan, rank and file,
>   Amaist before I ken!
> The ready measure rins as fine,
> As *Phoebus* and the famous *Nine*
>   Were glowran owre my pen.
>
> (*ll.* 141-6)

The next epistle that appears in the Kilmarnock edition is the **"Epistle to a Young Friend."** Structurally, this one bears many similarities to the **"Epistle to Davie."** Both epistles have only brief introductions and then plunge into the central thematic issue by way of a transitional spontaneity formula:

> But how the subject theme may gang,
>   Let time and chance determine;
> Perhaps it may turn out a Sang;
>   Perhaps, turn out a Sermon.
>
> (*ll.* 5-8)

Of course, the **"Epistle to a Young Friend"** turns out to be a sermon of a type unusual in Burns's canon. Like that to David Sillar, the **"Epistle to a Young Friend"** concerns the interplay of fortune and life. More so than the **"Epistle to Davie,"** the one to Burns's young friend Andrew Aiken functions structurally and thematically as a genuine epistle, as opposed to being a poem with a salutation and conclusion added. Burns skillfully moves from the salutation to the beginning of his meditation on life by keeping Andrew's presence before us (and before Andrew himself) through the first two stanzas, by which time the poet eases us into the subject matter of the epistle—the paternal advice to Andrew (and by extension, to all innocent, idealistic youth) on how to get along in a less than ideal world. The apparent tone of Burns's sermon in the **"Epistle to a Young Friend"** is unlike that in

any of the other Kilmarnock epistles in that he takes a dim view of life at the capricious hands of fortune, yet he does so without the overt, optimistic corrective that characterizes the epistle to James Smith. He preaches not merely acceptance but placation of the external power principles as the means by which to overcome life's seemingly inescapable potential for unpleasantness.

As advice on how to get on in the world, we can take Burns's epistle at face value, believing in the momentary sincerity of ". . . may ye better reck the *rede,* / Than ever did th' *Adviser*!" (ll. 87-8). Indeed, the dark view expressed in this epistle fits well thematically with the poems immediately preceding it in the Kilmarnock edition: **"Despondency, an Ode," "Man was made to Mourn," "Winter, a Dirge," "A Prayer, in the Prospect of Death," "To a Mountain Daisy,"** and **"To Ruin."** Burns uses the epistle to his young friend in a seemingly deliberate attempt to point out his own weaknesses, thereby lending force and sincerity to the last line. Yet, the epistle preaches the benefit of a divided self, of a self insulated and isolated from the necessary joys and shocks of life that form the experiences by which everyone, especially the young and innocent, must learn and grow. Since the import of this epistle is so out of character given what we know about the poet (and presumably what Burns's immediate audience knew as well), an interpretation of this epistle as being at least partially ironic is too tempting to be resisted.

The two epistles to Lapraik included in the Kilmarnock edition best illustrate the strengths and weaknesses of the epistle genre and of Burns's skill in employing it. The **"Epistle to J. L*****k, An Old Scotch Bard"** opens with a poetic setting reminiscent of the **"Epistle to Davie."** Yet, whereas the epistle to Sillar begins in a serious tone and remains so, Burns in the first stanza of the epistle to Lapraik undercuts the serious call to the Muse by having the sources of his inspiration be "briers an' woodbines . . . Paitricks . . . And morning Poosie whiddan seen" (ll. 1-3). Hardly the stuff of which epic invocations are made. Burns carries this light, comic tone throughout the epistle by means of self-deprecating humor and by the satire on schooling.

As a poetic letter to the addressee, the first epistle to Lapraik fulfills its nominal function—namely introducing Burns's personality and character (or the image of these) to a man who has never met him. For this reason, Lapraik would have no doubt taken a great interest in Burns's six-stanza homage to his (Lapraik's) talent as a song writer. Yet this homage also illustrates the chronic problem of self-referential material in the epistle-as-poem. We can admire the poetic skill employed in writing the epistle, but in the final analysis Burns's intimate communication to Lapraik forms a closed world to which we are afforded little access. However, the epistle to Lapraik, in typical Burns fashion, does move from the closed world of particulars to the more universal concerns of the relationship of art and the artist to society—a favorite theme in these Kilmarnock epistles. Burns skillfully maneuvers away from his immediate relation to Lapraik and, while still keeping himself in the foreground, moves to the discussion of himself as poet in relation to the social forces around him. The result is not only poetic theorizing, but pointed social satire as well. This satire, similar to the themes of the other epistles, centers on the role of fortune in human affairs. Burns portrays himself as "just a *Rhymer* like by chance" (l. 50), and he links his poetic abilities to the Muse by way of another, albeit oblique, spontaneity formula: "Whene'er my Muse does on me glance, / I jingle at her" (ll. 53-4). This formula leads Burns to the heart of his universal theme wherein he illustrates the relative merits of inspiration versus formal learning. This culminates in stanza twelve:

> A set o' dull, conceited Hashes,
> Confuse their brains in *Colledge-classes*!
> They *gang in* Stirks, and *come out* Asses,
>   Plain truth to speak;
> An' syne they think to climb Parnassus
>   By dint O' Greek!
>
> <div align="right">(<i>ll.</i> 67-72)</div>

The remainder of this epistle addresses itself primarily to Lapraik and does not carry the satiric edge of the central section. In striving for a conclusion Burns verges on lapsing into sentimentality similar to that found at the end of the **"Epistle to Davie,"** though fortunately Burns holds his climactic sentiment in check by again relying on a spontaneity formula in the last stanza: "But to conclude my lang epistle, / As my auld pen's worn to the grissle . . ." (ll. 127-8). This epistle is one of the more successful in accomplishing its nominal task—namely to introduce Burns to a man whose poetic talent he admires but whom he does not know. Yet, the elevation of particulars to universals in the epistle-as-poem is less effective here than in other epistles.

The second epistle to Lapraik, however, is a masterpiece of the epistle genre. Here Burns adroitly moves from the particular to the universal and back again with supreme craftsmanship and rhetorical power of a kind only partially realized in the other epistles. The particular message of the personal communication is itself a universal vision of the glorification of simple, poetic poverty. This epistle no doubt was inspired as a response to and commentary on Lapraik's financial misfortunes in the years before Burns made his acquaintance as well as on Burns's own precarious financial state. Burns elevates the topic of poverty to a matter of fate and utilizes this to make a scathing statement on the nature of the materialist versus that of the artist. Burns's ringing conclusion boasts of the poet's transcendent nature.

Initially, the epistle opens with the traditional epistolary acknowledgement of the addressee's previous letter. It then moves to a self-referential comic discussion of the Muse-as-wench, echoing Fergusson's similar treatment of the Muse in his "King's Birth-Day in Edinburgh." However, unlike Burns's treatment of the Muse in his other epistles, here he boastfully attempts to control her. The feeling produced by this epistle is that, in relation to his poetic powers, he controls this "ramfeezl'd hizzie" as much as she controls him. The ultimate effect of the extended introduction is, of course, a highly comic boast about Burns's own creative powers. This characterization of the Muse-as-wench culminates in Burns's longest and most complex spontaneity formula:

> Sae I gat paper in a blink,
> An' down gaed *stumpie* in the ink:
> Quoth I, 'Before I sleep a wink,
>   'I vow I'll close it;
> 'An' if ye [the Muse] winna mak it clink,
>   'By Jove I'll prose it!'
>
> Sae I've begun to scrawl, but whether
> In rhyme, or prose, or baith thegither,
> Or some hotch-potch that's rightly neither,
>   Let time mak proof;
> But I shall scribble down some blether
>   Just clean aff-loof.
>
> <div align="right">(<i>ll.</i> 31-42)</div>

These lines create the impression of present time by means of the shifting tenses of the verbs from past to future in each of the stanzas. Burns is seemingly poised between the past moment of inspiration and the future act of actually writing what turns out to be the well-integrated content of the epistle.

Burns's boastful, defiant address to the Muse in the introduction is later echoed in his view of fortune; he begins the philosophizing on fortune and Lapraik's poverty in equally defiant terms:

> My worthy friend, ne'er grudge an' carp,
> Tho' Fortune use you hard an' sharp;
> Come, kittle up your *moorlan harp*
>   Wi' gleesome touch!
> Ne'er mind how Fortune *waft* an' *warp;*
>   She's but a b-tch.
>
> <div align="right">(<i>ll.</i> 43-8)</div>

And just as Burns triumphs over the lethargic Muse, he similarly triumphs over fortune's eternal torment: "I, Rob, am here" (l. 60). The only thing he desires from this external power is that it "'Gie me o' wit an' sense a lift . . .'" (l. 74). Burns skillfully interweaves the themes of fortune and poetic ability with the class consciousness of rich versus poor. And unlike most of the other epistles, the second epistle to Lapraik does not falter or lose its focus at the end. Burns here needs no spontaneity formula by which to conclude because he effectively unites the temporal and universal thematic strands into a rhetorically powerful and universally applicable coda in the last stanzas:

> O *Mandate*, glorious and divine!
> The followers O' the ragged Nine,
> Poor, thoughtless devils! yet may shine
>   In glorious light,
> While sordid sons o' Mammon's line
>   Are dark as night!
>
> Tho' here they scrape, an' squeeze, an' growl,
> Their worthless nievfu' of a soul,

May in some *future carcase* howl,
    The forest's fright;
Or in some day-detesting *owl*
    May shun the light.

Then may L*****k and B***** arise,
To reach their native, kindred skies,
And *sing* their pleasures, hopes an' joys,
    In some mild sphere,
Still closer knit in friendship's ties
    Each passing year!

                  (*ll.* 91-108)

Thus, he resolves the issue of fortune's negative social effects on the artist by means of the artist's own transcendent power, though he couches this power in the passivity of reincarnation.

"To W. S***n, Ochiltree"** lacks the unity and cohesiveness of the second epistle to Lapraik. The epistle to Simson begins with two traditionally epistolary stanzas followed by three self-referential stanzas apparently following up on the theme of Simson's previous letter to Burns. Then quite abruptly in stanza six Burns begins his panegyric to Scotland, which occupies eleven stanzas. This praise of Scotland's glorious past offers a development on the theme of the poet's transcendent nature as it culminated in the second epistle to Lapraik. The poet not only transcends, but like a god he can also bestow transcendence.

The epistle to Simson serves not only as a boast of Scotland's one-time (and future) glory; it simultaneously praises the native, vernacular poetic traditions that in large part have helped create for Burns this glorious past and will poetically elevate Scotland's rivers to the universal stature of the Tiber, Thames, and the Seine. Burns is indeed speaking from his own experience of reading Blind Hary's *Wallace* when he (Burns) writes:

At Wallace' name, what Scottish blood,
But boils up in a spring-tide flood!
Oft have our fearless fathers strode
    By Wallace' side,
Still pressing onward, red-wat-shod,
    Or glorious dy'd!

                  (*ll.* 61-6)

Through nature—particularly Scottish nature—the poet will find his Muse, whereby he will fulfill the great role of singing the praises of Scotland and transcend the mean, base existence of the worldly folk:

The warly race may drudge an' drive,
Hog-shouther, jundie, stretch an' strive
Let me fair Nature's face descrive,
    And I, wi' pleasure,
Shall let the busy, grumbling hive
    Bum owre their treasure.

                  (*ll.* 91-6)

Thomas Crawford sees this stanza as being the real conclusion of the epistle [in his *Burns: A Study of the Poems and Songs*, 1960]. This is true only if we wish to view the panegyric as stating the central thematic purpose of the epistle and to view the postscript as merely an addition, an afterthought. Indeed, Burns would have us believe that this is the case. He employs yet another spontaneity formula to create the impression that his charming little lunar allegory was not the idea closest to his heart at the time of composing the epistle; and, as Crawford affirms, the introduction to the postscript serves to heighten the epistle's informality:

My memory's no worth a preen;
I had amaist forgotten clean,
Ye bad me write you what they mean
    By this *new-light.* . . .

                  (*ll.* 109-12)

Again Burns utilizes the spontaneity formula as a transitional device to get to his central concern. In this epistle, however, there are two messages, two themes, that Burns wants to convey. One is the universal—the nature of the poet's role in creating a national myth. The other is more particular—the Auld Licht / New Licht argument—though through the use of allegory even this narrow historic subject becomes comically emblematic for all the dogmatic conflicts between old truths and the new ones that challenge them.

Though these two thematic purposes appear divergent given the epistle's structure, they are not unrelated to Burns's larger poetic philosophy as expressed in the epistles. There is in fact thematic unity to the epistle to Simson. Both the hymn to Scotland and the allegory of the moon conclude with Burns proclaiming the poet's ability and need to transcend the myopic values and parochial concerns of the un-poetic people.

The epistle to Rankine is Burns's earliest epistle, though the last to appear in the Kilmarnock edition. In many ways it is quite unremarkable when placed in comparison with the other, more philosophical epistles. However, beyond the biographical element there are several characteristics that are worthy of note. There exists the chronic problem of transition from the particular epistolary intimacy to the more universal allegory of the partridge. Here Burns has no transition. The epistle moves abruptly into its comic core. Yet this little story does echo (and in reality prefigures) the defiant attitudes found in many of the other epistles. Burns, through particularly bawdy humor, undercuts the seriousness with which the Kirk views fornication and its punishment. And in keeping with many of the other epistles, Burns relies on a spontaneity formula to conclude his epistle to Rankine: "It pits me ay as mad's a hare; / So I can rhyme nor write nae mair" (ll. 73-4). The speaker gets in trouble, but he has the last laugh at the restricting social value system whose rules and parochialism he adroitly satirizes.

This theme of transcendence characterizes, to a greater or lesser degree, all of the Kilmarnock epistles. Burns capitalizes on the fact that most people, regardless of rank or circumstance, believe at one time or another in some sort of external force that controls life—the Muse, fortune, God, or whatever—and to which all people are answerable. Indeed, most people at one time or another feel, as Burns does, that they have been blessed with gifts or cursed by forces beyond human control, that there is no choice but to be thankful for the good and strive as hard as possible to overcome the bad.

Additionally, Burns's epistles grapple with the problems and philosophies of life within the social organizations. He raises the fundamental and eternal considerations of the relationships between art, the artist, and society. In Weston's words.

> He keeps the formula of an elite group in confict with the majority by dramatizing his idea that poets, lovers, and sentimentalists are at basic odds with the materialists of this world.

In this sense, the Kilmarnock epistles serve as a poetic manifesto, a defense of poetry in the classic sense, whereby Burns provides his audience the context and criteria by which to view the other works in his first volume and by which the wider audience can also view itself.

John Ashmead and John Davison (essay date 1991)

SOURCE: "Words, Music, and Emotion in the Love Songs of Robert Burns," in *Eighteenth-Century Life,* Vol. 15, Nos. 1 & 2, February & May, 1991, pp. 225-42.

[*Here, Ashmead and Davison explore several features of Burns's love songs, noting the connection he establishes between music and emotion.*]

Robert Burns' greatest songs rank with the finest in Europe, such as the best German *lieder.* Perhaps a fifth of Burns' 350 songs, including some of his best, were love songs written about particular women. Considering that so many of his songs originated in affairs of the heart, it is not surprising that in August 1783 Burns wrote in his commonplace book: 'There is certainly some connection between Love, and Music & Poetry'. This essay will analyse five love songs in order to sample the artistry of Burns and gain insight into his remarkable fusion of words, music and personal emotion.

Our first love song shows how the double tonic of the music reinforces the verbal dialogue of the words. Our second selection has a relatively simple text, almost never anthologised; yet, in combination with the music, it becomes one of the finest of Burns' love songs. The third song shows the use of alliterative phonesthemes that combine with the music to create an almost physical sense of love in a river landscape. The fourth song exemplifies Burns' gift for adapting dance tunes, in this case that specially Scottish dance, the strathspey, with its characteristic Scotch snap. Our final love song is one of Burns' most moving combinations of words and music.

Burns grew up on a Scottish farm, and many of his love songs concern rural courtship. A few of them, mindful of the cold rainy nights in Scotland, are about those comfort-loving lads who go to a young woman's house at midnight, asking for admission. For one such song, **'O let me in this ae night',** we have discovered a forgotten but superior verbal text, not reprinted since its original appearance in 1792.

'O let me in this ae night' belongs to the sub-genre of midnight dialogue, which Burns knew well. The plot of the tame version, still in print in Burns anthologies [*The Poems and Songs of Robert Burns,* edited by James Kinsley, 1968; *The Songs of Robert Burns: Now First Printed with the Melodies for Which They Were written; A study in Tone-Poetry* edited by James Chalmers Dick, 1903, reprinted in 1973] is simple enough. The young woman tells her lover she won't let him in even once, for the wildest wind is nothing compared to what a woman suffers from a faithless lover. The original bawdy version, however, was made of the stronger stuff that one expects of folklife songs; it concluded with a raucous stanza in which the passionate pair make love so strenuously that the bottom falls out of the bed, and the lassie's mother discovers them:

> But ere a' was done, and a' was said,
> Out fell the bottom of the bed;
> The lassie lost her maidenhead,
>   And her mither heard the din, jo.

From 1793 to 1795 Burns had trouble over this song with the second of his two editors, George Thomson. We may guess that the sticking point was, as Burns phrased it in September 1794, 'would you have the denouement to be successful or otherwise? Should she "let him in," or not?' Burns himself had no objection to bawdy songs, as shown by his own collection, **The Merry Muses of Caledonia.** But as he states several times, it was not the custom to sing such songs before the ladies in late eighteenth-century Scotland. To attract a more general audience, Burns had to write the bland words now usually printed for this song.

In the version we rediscovered, and much prefer, the woman finally does let her lover into her chamber, though just this once, and on condition that 'ye mauna do't again, jo'! At the end, the man has a final joyful chorus after his successful admission—a kind of musical afterglow.

> TITLE: **'O let me in this ae night'**
> FIRST LINE: O Lassie are ye sleepin yet,
> TUNE: 'Will ye lend me your loom Lass'
>
> [MAN'S CHORUS]
>
> O let me in this ae night, this ae, ae night;
> O let me in this ae night, and I'll no come back
>   again, jo.
>
> O Lassie are ye sleepin yet,
> Or are ye waukin [*waking*] I wad [*would*] wit,

For love has bound me hand and fitt [*foot*],
   And I wad fain be in, jo.

[MAN'S CHORUS]

The morn it is the term-day [*a rent collection
   day*],
I maun [*must*] awa, I canna stay
O pity me before I gae [*go*],
   And rise and let me in, jo.

[MAN'S CHORUS]

The night it is baith [*both*] cauld [*cold*] and weet
   [*wet*];
The morn it will be snow and sleet,
My shoon are frozen to my fett
In standing here my lane [*alone*], jo.

[MAN'S CHORUS]

I am the laird o' Windy-wa's [*lord of boasters*].
I cam na [*not*] here without a cause,
And I hae gotten mony [*many*] fa's
   In comin' thro' the plain, jo.

[MAN'S CHORUS]

My father's walking in the street,
My mither the chamber keys does keep,
My chamber-door does chirp & cheep,
   I daur [*dare*] na let you in, jo.

[WOMAN'S CHORUS]

O gae your ways this ae night, this ae, ae night,
O gae your ways this ae night, for I daur na let
   you in, jo.

But I'll come stealing softly in,
And cannily [*skilfully*] mak little din;
My fittstep-tre [*footstep tread*] there's nane can
   ken
For the sughin [*rushing*] wind and raing, jo.

[MAN'S CHORUS]

Cast up the door unto the weet,
Cast off your shoon frae off your feet,
Syne [*next*] to my chamber ye may creep,
   But ye mauna [*must not*] do't again, jo.

O leeze me [*I'm pleased by*] on this ae night,
   this ae, ae night!
The joys we've had this ae night, your chamber
   wa's within, jo!

At this point it may be helpful to provide a digression on the modal scales and the Scottish double tonic, which marked a major difference from the high art music of Burns' day. As in many Scots tunes, the modality in **'O let me in this ae night'** is ambiguous: the six-note scale can be thought of as Phrygian/Aeolian (lacking the second degree) ending on the tonic, or as Aeolian/Dorian (lacking the sixth degree) ending on the dominant. . . .

[It] is unclear which of two different notes is to be felt as the tonic, or note of greatest repose and finality. This ambiguity may be called the principle of the 'double tonic'. The term 'double tonic' is already in use to describe situations in which the two implied tonics are a whole tone apart. We are extending its definition to include the numerous cases where the two tonics are a minor third or . . . a perfect fourth apart.

Modal scales . . . are common in British folk music, in church chants and in Medieval and Renaissance music. Composers such as Haydn and Mozart, however, used only the major scale and a mixture of the two forms of minor known as the melodic and harmonic minor. . . .

The use of other scales seemed archaic, rustic or eccentric to most eighteenth-century composers. In the arrangements of the modal tunes of Burns' repertory published in James Johnson's *Scots Musical Museum* and George Thomson's *Select Collection of Original Scottish Airs,* and in subsequent volumes throughout the nineteenth century, attempts were made to minimise the very modal twists that are now considered most interesting.

Burns chose tunes that used an amazing variety of scales: major, harmonic and melodic minor, Aeolian (natural minor), Mixolydian, Dorian and several so-called 'gapped' (six-tone or hexatonic, and five-tone or pentatonic) scales. It has often been observed that these gapped scales are common in the Scottish repertory. Even the tunes in seven-note scales often deemphasise one or two of the notes, using them only rarely, or as a kind of cosmetic adornment of a basically pentatonic or hexatonic substructure that shows through clearly. Many of the tunes are therefore full of leaps (intervals larger than a second), and some are not easy to sing, a difficulty frequently compounded by a wide vocal range of an octave plus a fifth or sixth.

Furthermore, a common characteristic of the Scots tune repertory is the delight in ambiguity of the key centre or tonic, described above as the 'double tonic'. The penchant for the double tonic leads to the frequent occurrence of endings that, compared to the norm in Western European folk and art song, seem oddly inconclusive. To the educated ear, the tune of **'O let me in this ae night'** will appear to end on a note that may be heard as either the fifth degree of one scale or the first degree (tonic) of another.

The resulting ambiguity, the double-tonic effect, seems unusually appropriate for the back-and-forth dialogue of this song, especially in the more dramatic version that we have rediscovered. In the repertory of Burns songs, this suspenseful ambiguity of the tonic has a quality of wild independence; it is one of the special delights of such Scottish songs. . . .

Our second love song, **'Jamie come try me'**, demonstrates Burns' unusual gift for characterising, and drama-tising, the women of his songs. If one does no more than read the text, this song will not seem like much; no doubt that is why it is not included in the standard Burns anthol-ogies. Once sung, however, it is transformed into an impressive work of art. An emotional ballad, it suppress-es the narrative action that may have led to its passionate climax and concentrates on pure feeling.

Here the issue of structure is relevant. The form of almost all Burns' songs and dance tunes is strict: two (rarely three) balanced strains of four or eight measures each. The symmetrical tunes go well both with the orderly, balanced figures of British-Isles folk dance and with the common quatrain or octave (essentially two quatrains) of much European poetry. When danced, each musical strain repeats 'A A B B'. When sung, however, each strain is heard only once, 'A B', though with verbal lyrics of many stanzas the musical 'A B' will of course repeat as a unit. Because almost all Burns' songs use the music more than once through, they are categorised as 'strophic'.

When it comes to joining tunes and words, Burns' short type of metrically regular melody goes with the common folk verbal stanza, usually in tetrameter quatrain, often riming (verbally) 'a b c b' and fitting closely the musical 'A B' structure above. Countless hymns, ballads and oth-er folklife songs are the prototypes for this basic word-music relationship. This poetic quatrain, some critics ar-gue, is at the basis of all verbal or non-musical poetry. It is no accident, then, that Burns in his sung poetry, never, so far as we know, uses his favourite verbal poetic form, the habbie stanza, a non-quatrain form.

In **'Jamie come try me'**, the young woman narrator re-veals her deepest longings, for one meaning of 'try' was to have sexual intercourse before marriage. Though [Thomas] Crawford sees her as 'just waiting to be asked' [in his *Burns: A Study of The Poems and Songs,* 1960], she is not really persuading her Jamie to 'try her'. Instead, she is expressing her inner longing for Jamie to take the action that she cannot. And much of the power of the song comes about as she both expresses and suppresses her desire.

The song is deeply emotional. In the introductory chorus the woman singer three times stresses the phrase 'try me' with a long half note on 'try' and a quarter note on 'me', concluding with the highest of the two dozen notes. The word 'me' is from the high end of the vowel frequency scale, so that the musical and verbal settings both rein-force the tension of the chorus. The number of accents in each line is unusually short—two or at most three—giv-ing the song a breathless quality. And the song's wide range and wide musical leaps, even beyond the octave in the second line of the chorus, suggest a strong inner monologue, which proceeds not in a rational line but rather by rushes of emotion.

In the verses proper (the first stanza following the intro-ductory chorus), the woman singer continues to the high-est part of the song, rising from 'If thou should ask my love' to the higher note, here given to the 'de' of the

word 'deny' in the phrase 'Could I deny thee?' The song is marked 'Very Slow' in Johnson's *Scots Musical Muse-um,* where the 'de' in 'deny' gets two eighth notes, and the second syllable in the word gets a half note. In fact, if sung in the full eighteenth-century style, it gets a strongly accented appoggiatura with its accompanying trill. Such a powerful concentration on a single word is hardly possi-ble in a verbal reading, but it is remarkably moving when sung slowly and emotionally.

After a repeat of the chorus, the final stanza begins: 'If thou should kiss me, love, / Wha could espy thee?' The secretive word 'espy', like 'deny' in the parallel stanza, divides its syllables, again with a strong accent on its second syllable and a singing time that is far longer than anything possible in a verbal recitation. This song gives outer melodic expression to emotions usually reserved for the inner voice alone. As often in the finer songs of Burns, there is an ironic ambiguity, a hint that the emotion ex-pressed here may find its ultimate expression only in song—except as the audience hears and becomes involved with this passionate melody.

> TITLE: **'Jamie come try me'**
> FIRST LINE: If thou should ask my love
> TUNE: 'Jamie come try me'
>
> [CHORUS]
>
> Jamie come try me,
>   Jamie come try me,
> If thou would win my love
>   Jamie come try me.
>
> If thou should ask my love,
>   Could I deny thee?
> If thou would win my love
>   Jamie come try me.
>
> [CHORUS]
>
> If thou should kiss me, love,
>   Wha [*who*] could espy thee?
> If thou wad [*would*] be my love,
>   Jamie come try me.

What about Burns himself in love? Our third selection, **'Flow gently sweet Afton'**, is a well-known Burns song, strikingly effective in its association of words, music and subject. Folk tradition associates this song with Mary Campbell (1763-86), and Gilbert Burns, the poet's broth-er, thought **'Afton Water'** was about her. It is known that by May 1786 Burns was in love with Mary Campbell— the 'Highland Mary' of many Burns legends. She was a tall, fair-haired, blue-eyed dairy maid. According to Burns' own note: 'My Highland lassie was a warm-hearted, charming young creature as ever blessed a man with gen-erous love.'

Perhaps because Burns was contemplating going to Ja-maica, these two lovers exchanged Bibles, and possibly also vows, at the banks of the Ayr on 14 May 1786 (the

Bible Burns received from Mary still exists). Mary then went to the West Highlands, perhaps to prepare for their coming life together. After returning in October, however, she caught a malignant fever and died at Greenock on 20 October 1786. When her grave was opened in 1920, it contained the board of an infant's coffin. The hagiographers attribute this child to Burns and Mary Campbell, though that attribution seems debatable.

By early February 1789 Burns was expressing his pleasure in Scots songs that included 'the names and landskip-features of rivers, lakes or woodlands.' But Burns was not in the habit of writing songs just about landscape; and so Mary dominates this country pastoral. Attempts to cast Highland Mary, in this and other songs, in the role of Beatrice to Burns' Dante have problems with the story that, even when going with Burns, Mary had an affair with one Montgomery. Burns perhaps knew that her morals were questionable but could not resist her. Whatever her character, he seems never to have recovered completely from this love affair; all his life he kept her in passionate memory. Writing to his confidante Mrs Dunlop on 13 December 1789, Burns said of the world to come, which he wished for but did not firmly believe in: 'There should I, with speechless agony of rapture, again recognise my lost, my ever dear MARY, whose bosom was fraught with Truth, Honor, Constancy, & Love.'

It is just possible that the melody of **'Flow gently sweet Afton'** is Burns' own, for he contributed it to Johnson's *Scots Musical Museum,* and it has no source in a previous manuscript or publication. It is a good tune, and its replacement with the later, more familiar, but less interesting tune (composed by Alexander Hume) seems unwarranted. The original tune, with its shifting, almost floating modality, gives the song a strange, hypnotic quality. There is a brilliant stress on the phonestheme *fl,* associated in many English words with bird flight and with flying and floating motions generally. Although we must caution ourselves against familiar but perhaps overworked associations of music with streams (or on the other hand, with mountains!), here the verbal sounds strongly corroborate such an association. And the gentle rise and fall of the melody, less angular than many of the Scots tunes, goes well with so riverine a song.

Like the classical Arethusa, who changed into a fountain, Mary seems almost at one with the river in which she walks, or by which she sleeps. For in this song there is a shimmering union of musical modalities, of floating and chiming sounds, of the Afton river landscape and, above all, of Burns' haunting memory of his lost but forever beloved Mary.

TITLE: **'Flow gently sweet Afton'**
FIRST LINE: Flow gently sweet Afton among
   thy green braes
TUNE: 'Afton Water'

Flow gently sweet Afton, among thy green braes
   [*hills by a river*],
Flow gently, I'll sing thee a song in thy praise;

My Mary's asleep by thy murmuring stream,
Flow gently, sweet Afton, disturb not her dream.

Thou stock dove whose echo resounds thro' the
   glen,
Ye wild whistling blackbirds in yon thorny den,
Thou green crested lapwing thy screaming
   forbear,
I charge you disturb not my slumbering Fair.

How lofty, sweet Afton, thy neighbouring hills,
Far mark'd with the courses of clear, winding
   rills;
There daily I wander as noon rises high,
My flocks and my Mary's sweet Cot [*cottage*] in
   my eye.

How pleasant thy banks and green vallies below,
Where wild in the woodlands the primroses blow
   [*blossom*];
There oft as mild ev'ning weeps over the lea
   [*untilled fallow ground*],
The sweet scented birk [*birch*] shades my Mary
   and me.

Thy crystal stream, Afton, how lovely it glides,
And winds by the cot where my Mary resides;
How wanton thy waters her snowy feet lave,
As gathering sweet flowerets she stems thy clear
   wave!

Flow gently, sweet Afton, among thy green
   braes,
Flow gently, sweet River, the theme of my lays;
My Mary's asleep by thy murmuring stream,
Flow gently, sweet Afton, disturb not her dream!

Our fourth love song is Burns' honeymoon strathspey, **'I love my Jean'**. The story of Burns' involvement with, and eventual marriage to, Jean Armour (1767-1834) is too complex for more than a brief mention here. In 1785 he first met and fell in love with this woman, whom he later described as 'a certain clean-limb'd, handsome bewitching young Hussy.' Her father fainted upon hearing about their relationship. In April 1786, when Burns sent his proposals for his first book of poems to the printer, Jean Armour was pregnant. Though Jean and Robert therefore agreed to marry, in writing and by declaration, in a way that was legal in Scottish common law, Jean's father had their names cut out of the document and refused to accept Burns as a son-in-law. Feeling that Jean had deserted him, Burns soon turned to Highland Mary, with whom he exchanged vows.

In June 1786 the printer's copy of Burns' *Poems* was ready. Burns was carousing and even planning relocation in Jamaica. On 25 June 1786 he acknowledged to the kirk session his share in the affair with Jean Armour in order to obtain a certificate that he was single. On 9 July he had to appear in church to do a penance (the first of three) for fornication. He was spared the creepie chair, in which the sinner sat facing the congregation during a whole service.

In **'Robert Burns' Answer'** the unrepentant poet wrote of being publicly castigated, using the habbie stanza he favoured for his satires:

> A furnicator lown [*rogue*] he call'd me,
> An' said my fau't [*fault*] frae bliss expell'd me;
> I own'd the tale was true he tell'd me,
>   'But what the matter,'
> Quo' I, 'I fear unless ye geld me,
>   'I'll ne'er be better.'

Sometime in the summer of 1787, between tours of Scotland, Burns, now based in Edinburgh, visited Jean Armour and got her pregnant again. When her family found out that she had not made Burns marry her, they forced her to leave their home. Jean was in desperate straits, but her time was soon to come. For Burns, meanwhile, it was a year of love, music and poetry. From the fall of 1787, Burns' connection with James Johnson's *Scots Musical Museum* came increasingly to dominate his poetical production. The first volume (1787)—perhaps partly edited by Burns, but with only two songs by him—had no special Scots flavour. But the second through the fifth volumes (1788-96) were in fact under the control of Burns and reflected his passion for Scottish songs.

On 4 December Burns met—by her arrangement—Mrs Agnes Craig M'Lehose (1759-1841), whom he called 'Clarinda'. From here on the stories of Clarinda and Jean necessarily intertwine. Clarinda had a fine figure and some education. An ingenious law agent, James M'Lehose, had tricked her into marriage at age seventeen, and she had quickly produced four children for him. His cruelty made her leave him, and after the death of her surgeon father she took a small flat in Edinburgh. Burns' usual tactic in a love affair, as his rather timid brother Gilbert later noted, was to press on, in a frank and ultimately physical approach. Even while this courtship was going on, Burns heard in December of Jean Armour's misfortunes and asked Willie Muir (of Tarbolton) to house her.

In the new year, however, Clarinda, who now called Burns 'Sylvander', was writing of their meeting on 12 January 1788: 'But though our enjoyment did not lead beyond the limits of virtue, yet to-day's reflections have not been altogether unmixed with regret'. She seems to have yielded somewhat more on their meeting of 23 January, for she wrote of it: 'My heart reproaches me of last night. If you wish Clarinda to regain her peace, determine against everything but what the strictest delicacy warrants'. And after their meeting on 26 January she wrote: 'Though I disapprove, I have not been unhappy about it.'

Perhaps because of the strain of coping with teasing Clarinda, Burns had an affair about this time with one Jenny Clow, a serving maid who gave him a son. While this episode was going on, his problems with Clarinda continued. In February 1788 one of Clarinda's closest associates, probably her uncle Lord Craig, wrote to Burns objecting to the damage he was doing to her reputation. Burns apologised. Shortly after, on 18 February, he left Edinburgh, and on 23 February he saw Jean again at Willie's Mill. That same day he wrote to Clarinda of poor Jean: 'Here was tasteless insipidity, vulgarity of soul, and mercenary fawning; there [with Clarinda], polished good sense, heaven-born genius, and the most generous, the most delicate, the most tender Passion.—I have done with her, and she with me.'

In late February 1788 Burns visited Ellisland (Dumfries) to see a farm offered to him for rent by Patrick Millar of Dalswinton. Once in the countryside, far from being done with Jean, Burns was seeing her again. On 3 March Jean bore Burns a second set of twins. On that day he wrote to Robert Ainslie about Jean:

> I have reconciled her to her fate . . . I have reconciled her to her mother. I have taken her a room. I have taken her to my arms. I have given her a mahogany bed. I have given her a guinea, and I have f———d her till she rejoiced with joy unspeakable and full of glory. But—as I always am on every occasion—I have been prudent and cautious to an astonishing degree; I swore her privately and solemnly never to attempt any claim on me as a husband, even though anybody should persuade her she had such a claim (which she has not) neither during my life, nor after my death.

Then he wrote that he had taken her to bed on some dry horse litter. Burns then returned briefly to Edinburgh and to Clarinda, still not linked definitely to Jean. Finally, he went back to settle at Ellisland, and in April he at last publicly married Jean. A year later, Clarinda, in a lost letter, called Burns a villain, but he refused to acquiesce in that name. His own analysis of his two kinds of love affairs, in a letter to George Thomson of November 1794, was phrased in terms of poetry:

> Conjugal-love is a Passion which I deeply feel, & highly venerate; but some-how it does not make such a figure in Poesy as that other species of the Passion—

> "Where Love is liberty & Nature law.—"
>   [Pope, *Eloisa to Abelard*, l. 92]

> Musically speaking, the first is an instrument of which the gamut is scanty & confined, but the tones inexpressibly sweet; while the last, has powers equal to all the intellectual Modulation of the Human Soul.— Still, I am a very Poet in my enthusiasm of the Passion.

There is perhaps one difference between Burns' love for Jean and his love for Clarinda that has not been previously regarded by biographers as having some weight in this decision. Jean had a splendid repertory of Scots folksongs and was a fine singer. Burns wrote of her to Peter Hill on 2 March 1790: 'My Good-wife too, has a charming "woodnote wild".' We have no such record of Clarinda, whose own poetry is a weak imitation of the worst in eighteenth-century English style.

The honeymoon strathspey Burns wrote for Jean shows his special genius for adapting instrumental dance tunes and remaking them into song tunes. Among his favourites were reel and jig dance tunes as well as the dance tune type peculiar to eighteenth-century Scotland (and perhaps invented then and there), the strathspey. It features the rhythmic pattern sometimes called the 'Scotch snap', which is almost an emblem of Scots music. This pattern . . . fits the rhythm not only of many Gaelic words but also of certain English words, such as 'little', where the stressed syllable is short and the unstressed syllable may be somewhat prolonged.

For Burns, the strathspey had a special nationalist charm, perhaps because as a youth he had been to a Scottish dancing school. In September 1794 he wrote to George Thomson: 'Many of our Strathspeys, ancient & modern, give me most exquisite enjoyment, where you & other judges would probably be shewing signs of disgust'. Crawford calls **'I love my Jean'** 'the best of all the songs inspired by Jean Armour.' In it Jean is associated with flowers and all the bonny birds that sing. It lacks the tension of a number of Burns' love songs, and that fact may explain why in the end Jean Armour always won out over his other loves.

As so often in a Burns song of love, the major rhymes (in this instance in the second half of both octaves) cluster around the name of the beloved. Burns uses the long octave stanza and an even longer tune (by William Marshall, butler to the duke of Gordon) that accommodates sixteen lines. The tune then covers both stanzas of the song, when sung only once through. The tune has an 'A B C B' structure (each letter representing a quarter of the tune), and the parallel endings of its two halves correspond to the verbal endings of both Burns' stanzas, which rhyme the name of his beloved Jean.

Burns' words and music share a sense that the most effective locus for placement of the climax lies between half and three-quarters of the way through a stanza or tune. To be precise, the musical climax will lie in the third unit of a four-unit structure, or in the fifth or sixth unit of an eight-unit structure. The crucial verbal communication of a stanza will also occur most often at those points.

Musically, the most common expression of a climax will be a decisive rise to a higher register, often including the highest pitch of the tune. Verbally, especially in the rhyme words, there may sometimes be a preference for high frequency vowels. A higher musical pitch, along with higher frequency vowels, will make for greater effort in voice production, and therefore more tension and excitement in performance. **'I love my Jean'** is an example of this climax placement within the octave structure.

The 'C' part of the tune (the third quarter) is, somewhat unusually, lower in pitch than the beginning of the 'A' part, perhaps in correspondence with the text. For in the higher first octave, large landscape features appear, and in the lower second octave, there are small intimate features of nature—flowers and birdsongs. At the end, however, the surging climax of the 'B' part comes again as the poet rhapsodises over his Jean.

'It was during the honeymoon', wrote Burns. Was this dance perhaps a favourite of Jean and Robbie Burns? At any rate, in the song the Scotch snap of its swaying strathspey rhythm suggests the lover in 1788, walking or riding over the irregular, picturesque Scots landscape towards his distant love. After some two hundred years, the song still conveys something of his calm exuberance at that rite of passage. Jean, a fine singer, must have taken pleasure in this musical tribute from her often errant husband, who she once said should have had two wives.

TITLE: **'I love my Jean'**
FIRST LINE: Of a' the airts the wind can blaw
TUNE: 'Miss Admiral Gordon's Strathspey'

Of a' the airts [*directions*] the wind can blaw,
 I dearly like the west,
For there the bony lassie lives,
 The lassie I lo'e best:
There's wild-woods grow, and rivers row [*roll*],
 And mony [*many*] a hill between,
But day and night my fancy's flight
 Is ever wi' my Jean.

I see her in the dewy flowers,
 I see her sweet and fair;
I hear her in the tunefu' birds,
 I hear her charm the air:
There's not a bonie flower that springs
 By fountain, shaw [*Small wood in a hollow place*], or green,
There's not a bony bird that sings,
 But minds [*reminds*] me o' my Jean.

Our final selection, **'Ae fond kiss'**, is a song as great in technique as in emotion. How Burns came to write this love song for Clarinda while married to Jean is a matter of some interest. In may 1788 Burns settled in Ellisland, where Jean joined him in December. Upon gaining a commission as an exciseman on 14 July 1788, he moved closer to his goal of relocating in Dumfries. His assignment to active duty with the excise did not come until 10 October 1789, however, and his actual move to Dumfries did not occur until November 1791. Throughout this period, Burns, now remarried for the third time, was far from inactive in his combination of love, music and poetry.

On 22 March 1791 Anne Park bore Burns' daughter Elizabeth at Dumfries. Anne Park was the niece of Mrs Hyslop, who managed the Globe Tavern, which still stands in Dumfries and still preserves the chair in which Robert Burns sat. Except for **'Yestreen I had a pint o' wine,'** which sings of 'The gowden locks of Anna', we know little about her. With her usual tolerance, Jean took the illegitimate baby Elizabeth into the Burns household. On 31 March Jean herself gave birth to William Nicol (1791-1872), who later served as a colonel in India.

Clarinda and Sylvander somehow reconciled in the autumn of 1791. Clarinda knew about Jenny Clow, by whom Burns had a child while he was suitor to Clarinda and starting to think of Jean again. Perhaps that infidelity of late 1788 now brought them together, for in November

1791 Clarinda wrote Burns that Jenny Clow was dying and needed help: 'In circumstances so distressing, to whom can she so naturally look for aid as to the father of her child'. Somehow Clarinda and Sylvander arranged a meeting on 6 December 1791. We can only guess at the passion of this final reunion. On the 27th, then back in Dumfries, Burns sent Clarinda one of his greatest love songs, **'Ae fond kiss'**, written after their final meeting.

Here is an example of an apparently cheerful tune in a major, almost hexatonic mode (Ionian/Mixolydian) being used for a song of deep sadness. As Mozart and others knew, melodies in a major key, if performed slowly and in the right manner, may convey sorrow, as this song does. The many upward and downward leaps create a kind of keening or sobbing effect, and their large intervals express the sorrow of this final farewell.

Repeated measure-long or half-measure-long bits of melody give the tune an insistent, almost wailing monotony. . . . Running through the poem are two nucleus rhymes with similar emotional repetition: 'ae' (ae, nae, naething, sae—eight rhymes) and 'ever' (sever, for ever, never—nine rhymes). Figures and rhymes reinforce and play on and against each other.

Writing in her journal on 6 December 1831, the fortieth anniversary of her last farewell with Burns, Clarinda wrote: 'This day I can never forget. Parted with Burns, in the year 1791, never more to meet in this world. Oh, may we meet in Heaven!' She died ten years later at the age of eighty-three. Of Clarinda there remain a few tantalising letters, some inconsequential poems and an astonishingly beautiful silhouette portrait, cut in her youth by John Miers. For a time Burns wore this 'shade', as he called it, in a breast pin next to his heart. Walter Scott felt this song contained 'the essence of a thousand love tales'. The refrain—'Ae fond kiss, and then we sever! / Ae fareweel, Alas, forever!'—remains a tribute to the power and the passing of love.

> TITLE: **'Ae fond kiss'**
> FIRST LINE: Ae fond kiss, and then we sever
> TUNE: 'Rory Dall's Port'
>
> Ae [*one*] fond kiss, and then we sever;
> Ae farewell, and then forever!
> Deep in heart-wrung tears I'll pledge thee,
> Warring sighs and groans I'l wage thee.
> Who shall say that Fortune grieves him
> While the star of hope she leaves him?
> Me, nae [*no*] cheerfu' twinkle lights me;
> Dark despair around benights me.
>
> I'll ne'er blame my partial fancy,
> Naething could resist my Nancy:
> But to see her was to love her;
> Love but her, and love for ever.
> Had we never lov'd sae [*so*] kindly,
> Had we never lov'd sae blindly,
> Never met—or never parted,
> We had ne'er been broken-hearted.

> Fare thee weel, thou first and fairest!
> Fare thee weel, thou best and dearest!
> Thine be ilka [*every*] joy and treasure,
> Peace, Enjoyment, Love and Pleasure!
> Ae fond kiss, and then we sever;
> Ae fareweel, Alas, forever!
> Deep in heart-wrung tears I'll pledge thee,
> Warring sighs and groans I'l wage thee.

In making a final comparison of the songs of Burns to the great German *lieder,* we can say that the practice of Burns, in matching his words to traditional music, was in general the opposite of the masters of *lieder* Whereas they usually composed music for the poetry of others, Burns took his folklife music as given, repeatedly sang and memorised it and gradually fitted his words to that music. Burns' songs, therefore, constitute a unique hybrid between folk song and art song, with many of the best features of both.

Though our five examples do not include the whole range of Burns' achievement in song, they do illustrate many of the most striking and significant features. Among them are the use of double tonic to reinforce a text; the transformation of apparently inconspicuous words through music; the conjunction of high frequency notes and high frequency vowel sounds to convey emotion; the reinforcement of key words by musical ornamentation; the linkage of musical leaps and verbal excitement; the utilisation of phonesthemes and music together to depict a pastoral landscape; the adaptation to song of an instrumental dance tune peculiar to Scotland (the strathspey); and, in our final song, an incandescent fusion of words and music.

These predominantly modal songs of Burns continually demonstrate a complex texture of irony and even melancholy, as in our second and fifth examples. They are far from the lighthearted folk songs from which they often derive. In the first Kilmarnock edition of 1786, Burns had included only four songs. At the end of his life, however, he revealed in a letter to George Thomson of 18 May 1796 that he had in mind a collection of all the songs he had written for both Johnson and Thomson: 'When your Publication is finished, I intend publishing a Collection, on a cheap plan, of all the songs I have written for you, the Museum, &c.—at least of all the songs of which I wish to be called the Author.—I do not propose this so much in the way of emolument, as to do justice to my Muse.' This passage suggests that late in life Burns believed that his muse involved both words and music. Our analysis of five love songs indicates that, as far as possible, criticism of the songs of Burns should always include both music and words. Furthermore, it should be recognised that the songs of Burns are at least as important as his verbal poetry as a means of obtaining insight into his darkly complex genius.

Alan Bold (essay date 1991)

SOURCE: "Dialect and Diction in Burns," in *A Burns Companion,* Macmillan Academic and Professional Ltd., 1991, pp. 79-88.

[In this essay, Bold contends that Burns's poems written in the Scots dialect are superior to those he wrote in English.]

In a book generally dismissive of Scots as a literary language, Edwin Muir suggested that when he 'wished to express his real judgement [Burns] turned to English' (Edwin Muir, *Scott and Scotland,* 1936). Muir's supposition that, for Burns, Scots was 'a language for sentiment but not for thought' simply ignores the evidence of Burns's poetry in pursuit of the argument that, since the sixteenth and early seventeenth centuries, the Scottish people had felt in Scots and thought in English. Muir's patronising remarks about Burns's Scots verse are as crass as those the poet had to put up with in his lifetime, as an anecdote illustrates.

On 1 February 1787 the 11th Earl of Buchan, David Erskine, wrote to Burns about the Kilmarnock Edition, praising 'These little doric pieces of yours in our provincial dialect'. As usual, Burns was not above 'kissing the arse of a peer' (as he accused the Douglas brothers of doing in his **'Ballad Second: The Election'**), and replied in the humble role he had assumed: 'I must return to my rustic station, and, in my wonted way, woo my rustic Muse at the Ploughtail'. In August 1791 Lord Buchan again wrote to Burns, inviting him to travel to Ednam (seventy-five miles from Ellisland), the birthplace of James Thomson, to attend 'the coronation of the bust of Thomson, on Ednam Hill, on the 22d of September; for which day perhaps [Mr Burns's] muse may inspire an ode suited to the occasion'.

In his reply (29 August 1791), Burns declined the invitation, on account of the harvest, but thanked 'your Lordship for the honour, the very great honour, you have done me, in inviting me to the coronation of the bust of Thomson'. As for an ode, Burns declared himself unequal to the task of emulating Collins's 'Ode Occasioned by the Death of Mr Thomson' but he enclosed an **'Address to the Shade of Thomson, on Crowning his Bust at Ednam, Roxburghshire, with Bays'**. Collins's ode begins:

> In yonder grave a Druid lies,
>   Where slowly winds the stealing wave!
> The year's best sweets shall duteous rise
>   To deck its poet's sylvan grave!

Burns's address ends:

> So long, sweet Poet of the year!
>   Shall bloom that wreath thou well has won;
> While Scotia, with exulting tear,
>   Proclaims that Thomson is her son.

There is not much to choose qualitatively between the two quatrains, Burns simply going through the metrical motions in honour of a poet he genuinely admired.

Burns need not have bothered with his occasional ode for the ceremonial occasion was a farce. As the bust of Thomson had been broken—'in a midnight frolic during

[September] race week'—Lord Buchan laid a laurel wreath on a copy of Thomson's *The Seasons*. Burns commented on this in his quatrains **'On Some Commemorations of Thomson'**. This time he broke into Scots, after the first line, and gave his honest opinion of the likes of Lord Buchan:

> Dost thou not rise, indignant Shade,
>   And smile wi spurning scorn,
> When they wha wad hae starved thy life
>   Thy senseless turf adorn?

> They wha about thee mak sic fuss
>   Now thou art but a name,
> Wad seen thee damn'd ere they had spar'd
>   Ae plack to fill thy wame.

That, reminiscent of his attack on the Edinburgh gentry who wasted money on cards while Fergusson starved (**'Epistle to William Simson'**), represents Burns's honest opinion of poets and aristocratic patrons. And when he was most honest as a poet, he was most Scottish.

Writing to George Thomson on 19 October 1794, Burns confessed:

> These English Songs gravel me to death.—I have not that command of the language that I have of my native tongue.—In fact, I think that my ideas are more barren in English than in Scottish.

By that time Burns had seen three editions of his poems published and must have reflected, on reading them, that his English efforts were pastiches of favourites like Pope, Thomson, Shenstone and Gray whereas his poems 'chiefly in the Scottish dialect' were masterful. He had no longer any need for the diffidence he showed in January 1787 when writing to Dr John Moore:

> For my part, my first ambition was, and still my strongest wish is, to please my Compeers, the rustic Inmates of the Hamlet . . . I know very well, the novelty of my character has by far the greatest share in the learned and polite notice I have lately got; and in a language where Pope and Churchill have raised the laugh, and Shenstone and Gray drawn the tear; where Thomson and Beattie have painted the landskip, and Littleton and Collins described the heart; I am not vain enough to hope for distinguished Poetic fame.

Using the language of Pope, Shenstone and Gray, he was destined to come off second best.

Quoting some lines from Burns's **'On the Death of Lord President Dundas'**, Matthew Arnold ('The Study of Poetry', *Essays in Criticism,* Second Series, 1888) remarked 'By his English poetry Burns in general belongs to the eighteenth century, and has little importance for us. Evidently [**'On the Death of Lord President Dundas'**] is not the real Burns, or his name and fame would have disappeared long ago.' This judgement of one poet by another is just. Burns became internationally celebrated through his Scots poems, not his English pastiches. Remarkably, Burns achieved such recognition by casting his finest work in a national language in a state of atrophy though his linguistic efforts were not always appreciated by his contemporaries. Several of his admirers, including Dr John Moore, urged the poet to write in English rather than Scots. On 23 May 1787 Moore gave the poet some gratuitous advice: 'you already possess a great variety of expression and command of the English language; you ought, therefore, to deal more sparingly, for the future, in the provincial dialect'.

Similarly, various early reviewers regretted the language of his verse. James Anderson, discussing the Kilmarnock Edition in the *Monthly Review* of December 1786, felt that Burns was badly limited by his language:

> We much regret that these poems are written in some measure in an unknown tongue, which must deprive most of our Readers of the pleasure they would otherwise naturally create; being composed in the Scottish dialect, which contains many words that are altogether unknown to an English reader . . .

John Logan, writing in the *English Review*, February 1787, regretted that 'his provincial dialect confines his beauties to one half of the island'. An unsigned notice in the *General Magazine and Impartial Review* (1787), worried over the linguistic resources of Burns:

> It is greatly to be lamented that these poems are 'chiefly in the Scottish dialect', as it must necessarily confine their beauties to a small circle of readers, and as the author has given good specimens of his skill in the English . . .

All the collections of Burns's verse published in the poet's lifetime—the Kilmarnock Edition of 1786 and the Edinburgh editions of 1787 and 1793—are entitled *Poems, Chiefly in the Scottish Dialect*. In the Preface to the Kilmarnock Edition, Burns introduces himself as a poetic primitive who 'sings the sentiments and manners, he felt and saw in himself and his rustic compeers around him, in his and their native language'. Two stanzas from separate verse-epistles in the Kilmarnock Edition reinforce this proclamation of faith in the natural, though not naive, use of a native language:

> Gie me ae spark o Nature's fire,
> That's a' the learning I desire;
> Then, tho' I drudge thro dub an mire
>   At pleugh or cart,
> My Muse, tho hamely in attire,
>   May touch the heart.

> In days when mankind were but callans
> At grammar, logic, an sic talents,
> They took nae pains their speech to balance,
>   Or rules to gie;
> But spak their thoughts in plain, braid Lallans,
>   Like you or me.

The implication is obvious: Burns's muse is to make an

emotional appeal through the use of the familiar language of Lallans (Lowland Scots); what he also (in **'The Brigs of Ayr'**) called 'braid Scots' (broad Scots). Linguistically, the situation was not so simple as Burns suggests.

Scots, like English a dialect of Anglo-Saxon, had developed as an indigenous and eloquently expressive language in Scotland and, by the first half of the sixteenth century, had acquired 'it's full status as a national speech adequate for all the demands laid on it, for poetry, for literary and official prose, public records and the ordinary business transactions of life' (David Murison, *The Guid Scots Tongue*, 1977). However, Scots began to be undermined by the triumph of the Protestant Reformation in 1560. In the absence of a Scots translation of the Bible, the Reformers adopted a translation completed in 1560 by English refugees in Geneva. This had profound linguistic implications. The word of God, the sacred logos, was given in English. Scots began to be perceived as an inferior language, suitable for everyday conversation and comic verse but lacking the scriptural authority of English.

In 1603 the Scottish and English crowns were both conferred on James VI and I and with the Union of Crowns the Scottish court followed the king to London. The king himself began to write poetry in English and other Scottish poets followed the royal example. Consecrated by the Geneva Bible and commended by the court, the king's English was twice-blessed. With the parliamentary Act of Union, 1 May 1707, English became the official language of Scotland (North Britain) as well as England.

Born into a nation reduced to provincial status, Burns looked back in anger and indignation at the 'parcel of rogues' (the thirty-one Scottish commissioners) who sold Scotland 'for English gold'. The first stanza of his patriotic lament **'Such a Parcel of Rogues in a Nation'** (1792) conveys his feelings, ironically enough, in a Scots-accented English.

> Fareweel to a' our Scottish fame,
>   Fareweel our ancient glory!
> Fareweel ev'n to the Scottish name,
>   Sae famed in martial story!
> Now Sark rins o'er the Solways sands,
>   An Tweed rins to the ocean,
> To mark where England's province stands—
>   Such a parcel of rogues in a nation!

'England's province' set about accomodating the English in style. Scottish expressions—'Scotticisms'—became, for the intellectuals, synonymous with vulgarisms. David Hume used Scottish words in convivial conversation but scrupulously avoided them in his philosophical writing. In 1761 Edinburgh's Select Society, of which Hume was a founder-member, employed an actor (ironically, an Irishman, Thomas Sheridan, father of Richard Brinsley Sheridan) to coach its members in the southern pronunciation of English. In 1779 James Beattie, a man Burns admired both as poet and (Common Sense) philosopher, published his *Scotticisms, Arranged in Alphabetical Order, Designed to Correct Improprieties of Speech and Writing.* According to Dugald Stewart, Burns avoided Scots expressions in conversation:

> Nothing, perhaps, was more remarkable among his various attainments, than the fluency, and precision, and originality of his language, when he spoke in company; more particularly as he aimed at purity in his turn of expression, and avoided more successfully than most Scotchmen the peculiarities of Scottish phraseology.

Burns, however, would have been anxious to impress a university philosopher like Stewart with his command of the English language. In other circumstances he may well have used a Scots as rich as that in his letter of 1 June 1787 to William Nicol. . . .

It was not only Burns's rural upbringing in Ayr that gave him a more creative attitude to Scots than his urban contemporaries. If he spoke Scots at home, he also knew that Scots had an artistic dimension beyond everyday conversation for, as a child, he heard songs and ballads of the oral tradition from his mother and his mother's friend Betty Davidson. Though he was educated as 'an excellent English scholar' these songs and ballads (some of which he adapted, like 'John Barleycorn', some of which he preserved, like 'Tam Lin') became an inescapable part of his poetic inheritance. Still, it took a decidedly literary movement to give him poetic motion and the confidence to generate his own artistic energy.

If Scots was deplored as a conversational medium in polite urban society, Scottish poets were not willing to abandon the rich literary resources of Scots. Initiating a revival in the 1720s Allan Ramsay used Scots in his most successful poems and, following this precedent, Robert Fergusson found his own voice in Scots, writing vigorously vernacular poems about the urban vitality of his native Edinburgh. Burns studied Ramsay's work and, in 1782, bought a copy of the Second Edition of Fergusson's *Poems*. It was, as Burns repeatedly acknowledged, the Scots revivalist verse of Ramsay and Fergusson that prompted him to apply himself to the art of poetry. In the Preface to the Kilmarnock Edition, he confessed himself unequal to 'the genius of a Ramsay, or the glorious dawnings of the poor, unfortunate Fergusson'; in the **'Epistle to J. Lapraik'** he hoped for 'a spunk o Allan's glee / Or Fergusson's, the bauld an slee'. In his Inscription for Fergusson's headstone (erected at his expense) he directed Scotland to 'the Poet's Dust'; in his **'Apostrophe to Fergusson'** (1787) he lamented 'my elder brother in misfortune, / By far my elder brother in the Muse'; in **'Lines on Fergusson, the Poet'** he acclaimed the 'Heaven-taught Fergusson'; and in his Autobiographical Letter to Dr John Moore he said he had abandoned rhyme 'but meeting with Fergusson's Scotch poems [in 1782], I strung anew my wildly-sounding, rustic lyre with emulating vigour'.

As the Kilmarnock and First Edinburgh Editions demonstrated, Burns used Scots not only for emotional outbursts and descriptive 'manners-painting' (**'The Vision'**) but for

ecclesiastical satire (**'The Holy Fair'**, for example), social comment (**'The Twa Dogs'**), political evaluation (**'A Dream'**), philosophical reflection (**'To a Mouse'**), graveyard humour (**'Death and Doctor Hornbook'**) and matters of morality (**'Address to the Unco Guid'**). For all his role-playing as a poetic ploughman, Burns took his Scots work extremely seriously, denying that the use of dialect alone automatically produced poetry. Writing to Mrs Dunlop in 1789 he complained 'my success has encouraged such a shoal of ill-spawned monsters to crawl into public notice under the title of Scots Poets, that the very term, Scots Poetry, borders on the burlesque'. The Scots-writing Scottish poet had to use the language poetically and not rest passively on the linguistic laurels of the past.

Burns was enough of a product of his period to assume English affectations: his professed admiration for Shenstone, his elegant epistolary style, his ability to hold his own as a conversationalist in polite company (Scott, who heard Burns speak, thought his conversation 'expressed perfect self-confidence, without the slightest presumption'). As a poet, however, he transcended his period by renewing the Scots tradition in a startling way, applying his art to a bewildering variety of subjects. Writing in Scots he managed, by great artistry, to stimulate a conversational tone that sounded anything but artificial. Not so in English. All poetic language is, by definition, artificial but, for Burns, English was excruciatingly artificial—indeed alien—as a poetic medium.

Burns's poems in English are, by general consent, his weakest artistic efforts. The Kilmarnock Edition has poems that alternate Augustan English with Scots, most effectively in **'The Cotter's Saturday Night'** where the first English stanza is in deliberate contrast to the Scots stanzas that follow. In **'Epistle to Davie'**, however, the use of English in the ninth and tenth stanzas vitiates the overall impact of the verse, as Burns awkwardly imitates the insipid English diction of favourite poets like Shenstone. Ending 'A Solemn Meditation' Shenstone writes:

> O life! how soon of ev'ry bliss forlorn!
>   We start false joys, and urge the devious race:
> A tender prey, that cheers our youthful morn,
>   Then sinks untimely, and defrauds the chase.

Beginning **'The Lament'** Burns similarly expresses world-weariness in an inflated English full of affectation:

> O Thou pale Orb, that silent shines,
>   While care-untroubled mortals sleep!
> Thou seest a *wretch,* who inly pines,
>   And wanders here to wail and weep!

A poet had to achieve other effects than pining and wandering and wailing and weeping in English.

Shortly after he arrived in Edinburgh, Burns composed an **'Address to Edinburgh'** which duly appeared in the First Edinburgh Edition. Here Burns might have risen racily to the occasion. After all, he was wordly enough to observe what went on in the capital with 'bucks strutting, ladies flaring, blackguards sculking, whores leering' and he knew 'Auld Reikie' by his favourite Scots poet, Fergusson:

> Auld Reikie, wale o ilka town
> That Scotland kens beneath the moon;
> Where couthy chiels at e'ening meet
> Their bizzing craigs and mous to weet;
> And blythly gar auld care gae bye
> Wi blinkit and wi bleering eye . . .

Alas, Burns was unable to emulate Fergusson on this occasion, beginning his poem by apostrophising 'Edina! Scotia's darling seat!'

Whereas his Scots poems had vividly explored the landscape of Ayrshire in unforgettably energetic language, this English poem praises the capital through a catalogue of unconvincing personifications:

> Here Wealth still swells the golden tide,
>   As busy Trade his labour plies;
> There Architecture's noble pride
>   Bids elegance and splendour rise:
> Here Justice, from her native skies,
>   High wields her balance and her rod;
> There Learning, with his eagle eyes,
>   Seeks Science in her coy abode.

The poem is constructed around clichés—'noble pride', 'native skies', 'eagle eyes'—and comprises a sustained cliché which makes it typical of Burns's English poems.

Burns's poems in Scots were inspirational, his poems in English were occasional. The English Pindaric ode that appears, framed by Scots, in **'A Winter Night'** was occasional in that the occasion was a set-piece, an exercise in a particular form and little more than that: 'my first attempt in that irregular kind of measure in which many of our finest Odes are wrote'. To please the likes of Robert Riddell Burns wrote occasional poems for particular places. **'Verses in Friars' Carse Hermitage'**—with clichés such as 'russet weed', 'silken stole', 'idle dream'—may have gratified one man but never reached out to an international audience the way the great Scots poems did, and do.

The most celebrated English passage in Burns is that in **'Tam o Shanter'** beginning 'But pleasures are like poppies spread' which has some of the delicacy of the Milton of 'L'Allegro' ('There on beds of violet blue, / And fresh-blown roses washt in dew') and is an advance on **'Address to Edinburgh'**. It does not, however, support Muir's argument, in *Scott and Scotland,* about the intellectual superiority of English to Scots . . . and it functions poetically because its languid diction interrupts the narrative and allows Burns to put an urgent stress on the Scots dialect that immediately follows it: 'Nae man can tether time or tide, / The hour approaches Tam maun ride'. Had the succeeding lines been in Burns's best Augustan English, it is a safe bet to say the poem would have plodded along, not galloped along the way it does.

English poetic diction was alien to Burns's artistic talent and temperament. He could imitate English poets as witness his **'From Esopus to Maria'** which is a parody of Pope's 'Eliosa to Abelard': 'In these deep solitudes and awful cells, / Where heavenly pensive contemplation dwells' (Pope); 'From these drear solitudes and frowsy cells / Where Infamy with sad Repentance dwells' (Burns). He could echo Shenstone and Thomson and Gray. Such derivative pieces, though, make no advance on the originals and are remarkable only as a contrast with Burns's Scots poems. For when he was not imitating Pope and others, Burns was emulating Fergusson—and surpassing him because he imaginatively raised the Scots dialect to an international poetic language.

Not all Burns's poems in an English diction are atrocious, of course; some snatches of song, some epitaphs and epigrams, and the English passage in **'Tam o Shanter'** show he was not always insipid when writing in English, but these are brief bursts, odd exceptions to the rule. Similarly, not all Burns's poems 'chiefly in the Scottish dialect' are masterpieces but enough of them are to show that for Burns (as for few other poets) Scots was a poetic language capable of expressing any feeling—or thought— that excited him.

Donald A. Low (essay date 1992)

SOURCE: "Robert Burns (1759-96)," in *A Handbook to English Romanticism,* edited by Jean Raimond and J.R. Watson, St. Martin's Press, 1992, pp. 42-44.

[*Low has edited two well-regarded books on Burns,* Robert Burns: The Critical Heritage *(1974) and* Critical Essays on Robert Burns *(1975). In the following essay, he provides a brief overview of Burns's career as a poet.*]

Robert Burns, the eldest son of a tenant farmer in Ayrshire, Scotland, grew up to a life of hard physical work, poverty, and acute awareness of social disadvantage. It was to find 'some kind of counterpoise' to this harsh set of circumstances, and to amuse himself by transcribing 'the various feelings, the loves, the griefs, the hopes, the fears, in his own breast', that he began to write poetry. By his mid-twenties he displayed exceptional mastery of both satire and lyric in Lowland Scots. In the summer of 1786, when he was on the point of abandoning farming in Scotland and emigrating to the West Indies, he published his first collection of poems, in an edition of 612 copies printed in the country town of Kilmarnock. *Poems, Chiefly in the Scottish Dialect* met with such success that he changed all his plans, and journeyed to Edinburgh, where he was enthusiastically welcomed by a number of leading literary figures, partly because the quality of his work appeared to confirm current primitivist theories of genius. Among them was Henry Mackenzie, whose sentimental novel *The Man of Feeling* Burns had long admired and claimed to prize 'next to the Bible'. In an influential essay in his periodical *The Lounger,* Mackenzie praised the 'power of genius' of 'this Heaven-taught ploughman', and he helped Burns arrange publication of an expanded edition of his *Poems* in the spring of 1788.

With the money he earned from publication, Burns toured the Scottish Borders and Highlands, and spent a second winter in Edinburgh. Eventually he returned, somewhat reluctantly, to tenant farming in south-west Scotland. He combined excise work with farming for a time, then became a full-time excise officer in Dumfries. His most famous poem, **'Tam o' Shanter'**, was written in 1790, but for the most part he devoted the leisure hours of his later years to the writing and collecting of Scottish songs, in which he was passionately interested. From 1788 until his death he was the principal contributor to and virtual editor of the greatest of all Scottish song collections, James Johnson's *Scots Musical Museum* (6 vols, 1787-1803). He also supplied the words of many songs for George Thomson's *Select Collection of Original Scottish Airs* (5 vols, 1793-1818), which boasted among its musical contributors Haydn and Beethoven. In all, he wrote some 200 songs.

Burns admired the poetry of Gray, Goldsmith and Shenstone, as well as the sentimental prose of his fellow countrymen Henry Mackenzie and James Macpherson. His reading in the literature of sentiment profoundly influenced him. Its effects can be seen in such poems as **'To a Mountain Daisy'** and **'The Cotter's Saturday Night'**, both of which greatly appealed to his contemporaries; in many of his songs; and in his rather stilted letters. He was at his best, however, in satires such as **'The Holy Fair'** and **'Address to the Deil'**, or when the expression of sentimental ideas was controlled and balanced by his fund of common sense and down-to-earth humour, as for instance in his Scots verse epistles and mock elegies. 'What an antithetical mind!' exclaimed Byron, 'tenderness, roughness—delicacy, coarseness—sentiment, sensuality—soaring and grovelling, dirt and deity—all mixed up in that one compound of inspired clay!'

Burns was indebted both to 'polite' literature in English and to a vernacular oral tradition which is often homely and as often racy. What makes him exceptionally interesting is that, like all major writers, he makes up his own rules and defies facile categorising. Thus in one mood he harks back to the robust values and belief in clarity of Pope, his greatest eighteenth-century predecessor in poetic satire; in another he writes sentimentally, almost as if cast in the role of Harley, Mackenzie's Man of Feeling; and every so often—arguably while obeying his deepest artistic instinct—he anticipates the energy and cutting edge of full-blown Romantic protest. It is, above all, in song that his combination of simplicity, real personal feeling and memorable phrasing places him with the Romantics. **'A Man's a Man for A' That'**, for example, bears the stamp of his mind no less clearly than *The Marriage of Heaven and Hell* has that of Blake. Like nearly all his songs, it was given to the world casually and anonymously; but its powerfully direct assertion of Burns's vision of shared humanity and anticipated social and political change has carried it round the world, along with love songs such as **'Ae Fond Kiss'** and the now traditional song of parting, **'Auld Lang Syne'**.

Wordsworth more than once acknowledged a debt to Burns, writing in one poem of the particular sadness he felt when the Scottish poet died at the age of thirty-seven:

> I mourned with thousands, but as one
> More deeply grieved, for He was gone
> Whose light I hailed when first it shone,
> And showed my youth
> How Verse may build a princely throne
> On humble truth.
>
> ('At the Grave of Burns', ll. 31-6)

FURTHER READING

Brown, Mary Ellen. *Burns and Tradition*. London: Macmillan Press, 1984, 176 p.

 Explores Burns's use of traditional content, form, and style in his works, stating that he "became and continues to be a figure in the Scottish legendary and customary tradition."

Daiches, David. "Calvinism and the Poetic Imagination: From Burns to Hogg, Problems of Antinomianism." In his *God and the Poets: The Gifford Lectures, 1983*, pp. 133-52. London: Oxford University Press, 1984.

 Outlines the effect of eighteenth-century religious beliefs on Burns's poetry.

Damrosch, Leopold, Jr. "Burns, Blake, and the Recovery of Lyric." *Studies in Romanticism* 21, No. 4 (Winter 1982): 637-60.

 Traces the history of the lyric and its use by several poets, particularly Burns and William Blake.

Davison, Edward. "Robert Burns." *The Literary Review* 13, No. 4 (Summer 1970): 475-79.

 Assesses Burns's popularity.

Donaldson, William. "The Glencairn Connection: Robert Burns and Scottish Politics, 1786-1796." In *Studies in Scottish Literature*, Vol. XVI, edited by G. Ross Roy, pp. 61-79. Columbia: University of South Carolina Press, 1981.

 Studies the effect of Scottish politics on Burns's poetry.

Jack, R. D. S. and Noble, Andrew, eds. *The Art of Robert Burns*. London: Vision Press, 1982, 240 p.

 Includes several essays focusing on "the distinct literary modes and poetic forms employed by Burns."

Kinsley, James. "Burns and the *Merry Muses*." In *Renaissance and Modern Studies* IX (1965): 5-21.

 Appraises Burns's 1800 collection of poetry, *Merry Muses of Caledonia*.

Kramer, Aaron. "Robert Burns and Langston Hughes." *Freedomways* 8, No. 2 (Spring 1968): 159-66.

 Suggests that Burns and Langston Hughes are both "people's" poets.

Low, Donald A., ed. *Critical Essays on Robert Burns.* London: Routledge & Kegan Paul, 1975, 191 p.

Collection of essays on Burns, including criticism by Thomas Crawford, James Kinsley, and David Daiches.

Schneider, Mary W. "The Real Burns and 'The Study of Poetry.'" *Victorian Poetry* 26, Nos. 1-2 (Spring/Summer 1988): 135-40.

Centers on the debate between Matthew Arnold and John Campbell Shairp about the real Burns.

Simpson, Kenneth. "Burns and Scottish Society." *Eighteenth-Century Life* 15, Nos. 1-2 (February/May 1991): 210-24.

Contends that the relationship between Burns and his social environment was a source of the many and sometimes contradictory voices in his writings.

Weston, John C. "Robert Burns's Use of the Scots Verse-Epistle Form." *Philological Quarterly* XLIX, No. 2 (April 1970): 188-210.

Explores the origin and use of the Scottish verse-epistle genre, stating that Burns "found in the Scots epistle a perfect medium for the expression of an important part of his personality with its corresponding vision."

Additional coverage of Burns's life and career is contained in the following sources published by Gale Research: *Concise Dictionary of British Literary Biography,* 1789-1832; *Dictionary of Literary Biography,* Vol. 109; *DISCovering Authors*; *Literature Criticism from 1400-1800,* Vol. 3; *Poetry Criticism,* Vol. 6; and *World Literature Criticism.*

Eighteenth-Century Scottish Poetry

INTRODUCTION

Often considered the golden age of Scottish poetry, eighteenth-century Scotland witnessed a struggle to reconcile its traditional language and cultural heritage with extreme political and social change. With the Scottish Reformation and the formal establishment of Presbyterianism in 1690, Scotland forged a new alliance with England, which had a lasting effect on the cultural significance of the Scots language. The Presbyterian church banned secular literature, thus suppressing the vernacular Scots songs that had been flourishing. Furthermore, no Scots Bible existed; the English Bible became the standard. The infusion of English culture and politics into Scotland culminated in 1707 with an official Parliamentary Union that made Scotland a part of the British Empire.

Scotland's literati generally reacted either by embracing the English literary tradition or by rebelling against England's cultural domination and reviving the Scots vernacular. Recognizing the distinguished history of English letters, a group of poets known as the Scottish Augustans began to write primarily in English. James Thomson (1700-1748), for example, combined proper English language with idiosyncratic, Latinate diction in such works as *The Seasons* (1730), a blank-verse meditation on nature. Heavily Miltonic, the poem was praised by figures such as William Hazlitt, and some critics have cited *The Seasons* as a precursor to British Romanticism. Scottish Augustan poetry also includes Robert Blair's *The Grave* (1743), William Falconer's *The Shipwreck* (1762), and James Beattie's *The Minstrel* (1771, 1774). Other Scottish writers, however, feared the loss of their native character and responded to English influence with a surge of nationalism—a flowering of Scots vernacular poetry and the rise of the native novel. Compilations such as James Watson's *Choice Collection of Comic and Serious Scots Poems both Ancient and Modern* (1706-1711) brought traditional poems into wide circulation, thus helping to restore the popularity of Scots verse. The chief promoter of vernacular poetry was Allan Ramsay (1686-1758), a patriotic Jacobite who wrote in Scots, English, and Anglo-Scots, and whose work as an editor and poet strongly influenced such later figures as Robert Fergusson and Robert Burns. For the collections *The Ever Green* (1724) and *The Tea-Table Miscellany* (1724-37), Ramsay drew heavily upon the Bannatyne manuscript, a collection of fifteenth- and sixteenth-century Scottish ballads and songs, and poetry by Scottish poets Robert Henryson, Alexander Scott, and William Dunbar. Ramsay's own Scots compositions in works such as *The Gentle Shepherd* (1725) revived several traditional meters, and his exploration of traditional genres

including the comic elegy, mock testament, and pastoral; together with his creation of the Scots verse epistle; elevated Scots from what was commonly regarded as the language of bawdy and comic songs to a vehicle for serious poetry. Several influential collections followed Ramsay's example, including David Herd's *Ancient and Modern Scottish Poems* (1769), Thomas Percy's *Reliques of Ancient English Poetry* (1765), John Pinkerton's *Select Scottish Ballads* (1781-1783), and Walter Scott's *Minstrelsy of the Scottish Border* (1802-3). Most famous (or infamous) of the anthologies that appeared during this time were James Macpherson's "translations" of ancient Gaelic manuscripts—*Fragments of Ancient Poetry, Collected in the Highlands of Scotland* (1760), *Fingal* (1762), *Temora* (1763), and *The Poems of Ossian* (1765)—which are now widely considered forgeries. The most important link between Ramsay and Burns, however, was Robert Fergusson (1750-1774), whose *Poems* (1773) drew upon both the English poetic tradition and the Scots genres popularized by Ramsay. Fergusson was highly regarded for his realistic depictions of Edinburgh and the surrounding countryside. His poems "Leith Races," "Plainstanes and Causey," and "Farmer's Ingle" were emulated by Burns in "The Holy Fair," "The Twa Brigs," and "The Cotter's Saturday Night."

The last and greatest of the poets of the Scots vernacular revival, Robert Burns (1759-1796) is considered the national poet of Scotland. Burns was influenced by "the excellent Ramsay, and the still more excellent Ferguson [*sic*]," although his *Poems, Chiefly in the Scottish Dialect* (1786) and his contributions to James Johnson's *Scots Musical Museum* (1787-1803) and George Thomson's *Select Collection of Original Scotish Airs for the Voice* (1793-1818), reveal a more fluent use of the Scots dialect. Scots, as a vernacular language, lent itself to Burns' depiction of Scottish rural life, and Burns also expanded its use by addressing more serious topics such as Scottish nationalism and the importance of freedom. Burns resuscitated traditional poetic forms, imbuing them with contemporary issues and a mastery of traditional Scots. With the death of Burns, Scottish poetry (especially Scots vernacular poetry) generally declined. The progression of the Industrial Revolution irreversibly modernized Scotland, further alienating the society from its traditions. London increasingly became the literary capital of Britain, while emigration in the early nineteenth century largely emptied Scotland of its native talents. Furthermore, some critics contend that Burns exhausted the poetic potential of Scots, with vernacular poets who followed unable to improve on his work due to the limitations of the language itself. Although some twentieth-century versifiers have experimented with the Scots vernacular, critics generally agree that Scotland's literati have never surpassed the age of Ramsay, Fergusson, and Burns.

REPRESENTATIVE WORKS

James Beattie
  *The Minstrel; or, The Progress of Genius. A
    Poem.* 2 vols.   1771, 1774
Robert Blair
  The Grave 1743
Robert Burns
  Poems, Chiefly in the Scottish Dialect 1786
  The Poetry of Robert Burns. 4 vols. 1896-97
William Falconer
  The Shipwreck 1762
Robert Fergusson
  Poems by Robert Fergusson 1773
  The Poetry of Robert Fergusson. 2 vols. 1954-56
David Herd
  (Editor) *Ancient and Modern Scottish Poems* 1769
James Johnson
  (Editor) *The Scots Musical Museum* 1787-1803
James Macpherson
  *Fragments of Ancient Poetry, Collected in the
    Highlands of Scotland, and Translated from the
    Galic or Erse Language* 1760
  Fingal, an Ancient Poem in Six Books 1762
  Temora, an Ancient Epic Poem, in Eight Books
    1763
  The Poems of Ossian 1765
Thomas Percy
  (Editor) *Reliques of Ancient English Poetry* 1765
John Pinkerton
  (Editor) *Select Scottish Ballads.* 2 vols. 1781-83
Allan Ramsay
  (Editor) *The Ever Green* 1724
  The Gentle Shepherd 1725
  (Editor) *Tea-Table Miscellany.* 4 vols. 1724-37
Walter Scott
  (Editor) *Minstrelsy of the Scottish Border* 1802-3
George Thomson
  (Editor) *Select Collection of Original Scotish Airs
    for the Voice* 1793-1818
James Thomson
  The Seasons. A Poem 1730
  *The Castle of Indolence: an Allegorical Poem.
    Written in Imitation of Spenser* 1748
James Watson
  (Editor) *Choice Collection of Comic and Serious
    Scots Poems both Ancient and Modern* 1706-11

OVERVIEWS

J. H. Millar

SOURCE: "Eighteenth-Century Poetry: Burns," in *A Literary History of Scotland*, T. Fisher Unwin, 1903, pp. 370-429.

[*In the following excerpt, Millar surveys the development of Scottish poetry during the eighteenth century, examining the role of the classical English-language tradition and the revival of local vernacular verse, which culminat-* ed with the poetry of Robert Burns.]

Poetry is an art more provocative of imitation than prose; and it is not surprising that, when to excel in the use of English and to eschew the Scots dialect became the mark of an enlightened mind and a cultivated taste, a considerable number of Scottish writers should have betaken themselves to verse as their form of literary expression. In too many of these it is impossible, even for partiality, to ignore "the vain stiffness of a lettered Scot." But they must all be supposed to have served some purpose, and it is proposed to take a brief survey of their performances before passing on to the vernacular poetry, in which we shall find a great deal more that is worth dwelling on.

By far the greatest poet and most accomplished artist of the Scots versifiers who wrote in English during the eighteenth century was James Thomson (1700-48), a native of Ednam in Roxburghshire, and a son of the manse. *The Seasons* (1726-30) and *The Castle of Indolence* (1746) are poems which well repay minute examination and detailed criticism, though the lyric, *Rule Britannia* (1740), is better remembered by the general. But they belong essentially to English literature, on which the former exerted no little influence, and of which both are justly esteemed among the most pleasing ornaments of the second class. To treat Thomson as a characteristically Scottish poet would be as absurd as to devote time and space to Dr. John Arbuthnot (1667-1735), whose proper place is with the London wits of the age of Anne and of the first two Georges. Similar considerations recommend an equally summary treatment of Dr. John Armstrong, whose *Economy of Love* (1736), doubtless for excellent reasons, does not appear . . . in any edition of his works that I have been fortunate enough to fall in with; whose *Art of Preserving Health* (1744) is better than its title might lead one to expect; and whose *Taste: An Epistle to a young Critic* (1753) is a satire of the familiar type in rhymed heroics. His brother in medicine, Dr. Smollett, was a greater favourite of the muses. *The Tears of Scotland* (1746) is a piece very creditable to his good feeling; the *Ode to Leven Water,* which appeared in *Humphry Clinker* (1771), is more excellent still; and if the *Ode to Independence* (1773) had fulfilled the promise of its opening lines, we had been blessed in him with a writer of odes superior to most of his rivals in that sort of composition, and perhaps not so very far beneath the level of Gray himself.

Robert Blair (1699-1746) was not one of those who followed the road to London; and he died, as he had lived for fifteen years, minister of Athelstaneford, in East Lothian, in which cure he was the predecessor of John Home. His poem, *The Grave* (1743), enjoyed unbounded popularity both in its own day, and at a much later period. Suggested, it may be, by Young's *Night Thoughts,* the first instalment of which had appeared in the preceding year, it has, at all events, the merit of comparative brevity, and it works, with considerable skill, the vein of gloom which that long-winded exercise in blank verse opened, and which found such favour with the public of the eighteenth century. In the structure and cadence of his measures, however, Blair owes very little to Young; but rather . . . stands debtor to the Elizabethan dramatists. Certainly there is no echo of Thomson, or of any other writer of blank verse later than the Elizabethans, in the concluding passage of a poem, in which good single lines are not infrequent, but which contains nothing else of such refreshing and unexpected beauty:—

> Thus at the shut of even the weary bird
> Leaves the wide air, and, in some lonely brake,
> Cowers down and dozes till the dawn of day,
> Then claps his well-fledged wings and bears
>   away.

David Hume was always willing to give to any of his friends the "hand" which "every fellow likes." He indulged in extravagant eulogy of John Home's *Douglas;* and another poet whom he went out of his way to praise at considerable length was William Wilkie (1721-72), the minister of Ratho, and Professor of Natural Philosophy at St. Andrews. Wilkie was a man of real erudition, though of the most eccentric manners; and in 1757 he published a classical epic, entitled the *Epigoniad,* in nine books and about six thousand lines. This masterpiece was thought, perhaps by Wilkie, and certainly by Wilkie's friends, to afford a striking proof of the vast strides which Scotland had made along the road which leads from barbarism and ignorance to refinement and learning. Nevertheless, the *Critical Review,* then under the editorship of Smollett, had spoken disrespectfully of the great work on its first appearance, and had called attention to certain mistakes in expression and prosody by which it was disfigured. To repair this injustice, Hume addressed a long letter to "the authors" of that periodical in 1759, in which, after premising that "no literary journal was ever carried on in this country with equal spirit and impartiality," he goes on to extenuate the faults complained of on the ground that they proceeded "entirely from the author's being a Scotchman, who had never been out of his own country," and then engages in a defence of the book, pointing out its merits, and illustrating them by quotations. A more curious piece of fatuity was never perpetrated by a genius of the first order than this critical essay of Hume's. So at least it is apt to strike a generation whose standards of taste are very different from his. No amount of special pleading will make the *Epigoniad* a great poem. It is well enough in its way, and is preferable to Glover's *Leonidas* or *Athenaid.* The episode of the Cyclops, for example, in book iv., might be worse, though even there Wilkie never comes up to the not very exacting measure of Pope's, or Broome's, *Odyssey.* The whole thing is "as dead as mutton"; it is the offspring of convention and rule, not of passion, or sensibility, or vision. Wilkie's *Fables* (1768) are very much better, though far from being in the front rank of such trifles, with the possible exception of *The Hare and the Partan,* which is in the vernacular of the Lothians.

Nor is it possible to be at all enthusiastic over *The Shipwreck* (1762) of William Falconer (1732-69), a piece of frigid classicism, memorable chiefly as affording, in an occasional cadence or turn of phrase, some anticipation of Crabbe's manner. It is difficult even to counterfeit

interest in the fortunes of Palemon, and Albert, and Anna; and if the reading of the poem once begun is not soon desisted from, it is because of the peculiar fascination which arises from the mingling of two such incongruous elements as the poetical diction of the eighteenth century and the terms of the seaman's art. The result is so quaint that a specimen may be pardoned:—

> A lowering squall obscures the southern sky,
> Before whose sweeping breath the waters fly;
> Its weight the topsails can no more sustain—
> Reef topsails, reef! the master calls again.
>
> The halyards and top bow-lines soon are gone,
> To clue lines and reef tackles next they run:
> The shivering sails descend; the yards are
>   square;
> Then quick aloft the ready crew repair:
> The weather earings and the lee they past,
> The reefs enrolled and every point made fast.
>
>   . . . . .
>
> Deep on her side the reeling vessel lies:
> Brail up the mizen quick! the master cries,
> Man the clue-garnets! let the main-sheet fly!
> It rends in thousand shivering shreds on high!

The contrast between this stilted and lumbering stuff and the rapid and masterly handling of technicalities displayed, say, in *M'Andrew's Hymn* is striking and suggestive.

James Beattie (1735-1803) may not have been an acute metaphysician (and he signally failed to demolish Hume), or a cool-headed critic (for he fell a willing victim to the famous Macpherson imposture [i.e., the publication of *Fragments of Ancient Poetry collected in the Highlands* (1760), *Fingal* (1762), and *Temora* (1763), which James Macpherson (1736-96) claimed to have translated from ancient Gaelic manuscripts but which many historians now consider to be forgeries]), or yet a great poet (for he never seems quite to know what he would be at). But at least he deserves our thanks for the effort he made to escape from the common groove, and to provide the public with a commodity bearing a stronger superficial resemblance to poetry than the *Epgoniads* and *Shipwrecks* could boast of. He did not, indeed, altogether abandon the rhymed heroic couplet, and his lines *On the proposed monument to Churchill* (1765) are a typical specimen of the conventional satire: not without vigour and point, but immeasurably below satire as it comes from the hands of a true master, like Pope. In the *Hermit* he employs with laudable freedom and ease a galloping sort of measure, in considerable request for bacchanalian lyrics, to which class that poem does not belong; and in his *chef d'œuvre, The Minstrel* (1770-74), he betakes himself to the Spenserian stanza, to write in which was a favourite exercise of almost all the poets and poetasters of the age from Thomson (or indeed from Prior and Pope) down to William Julius Mickle (1734-88), the translator of the *Lusiad,* the reputed author of at least one spirited and popular song in his national dialect, and the undoubted author of the ballad of *Cumnor Hall,* which fascinated the youthful ear of Scott. Beattie seems to share with many of his fellow versifiers the suspicion that there is something inherently and incurably ridiculous in the Spenserian stanza. He, like them, appears never to get rid of the feeling that he is writing a parody. And accordingly, every now and then, he gives to his verse a ludicrous turn, of which, it must in fairness be owned, the metre of Spenser when wedded to commonplace and degrading ideas is readily susceptible, owing to the lofty and ennobling associations with which that poet invested it. Hence a want of steady aim, an infirmity of artistic purpose, is very noticeable in the *Minstrel,* which is disjointed in structure and confused in arrangement. Yet Beattie, one may venture to think, had some true feeling for what we call nature, and was not insensible to the charm of the "melodies of morn," or the "sheep-fold's simple bell," or "the full choir that wakes the universal grove," or any of the other phenomena which he notes and records, in a vocabulary that was, unfortunately, not yet emancipated from the thraldom of "poetic" convention. The following stanzas, though the first is more in his jocose than in his serious vein, may serve to give a tolerably accurate idea of his versification:—

> The dream is fled. Proud harbinger of day,
> Who scar'dst the vision with thy clarion shrill,
> Fell chanticleer! who oft hath reft away
> My fancied good, and wrought substantial ill!
> O to thy cursed scream, discordant still,
> Let harmony aye shut her gentle ear:
> Thy boastful mirth let jealous rivals spill,
> Insult thy crest, and glossy pinions tear,
> And ever in thy dreams the ruthless fox appear!

> Forbear, my muse. Let love attune thy line.
> Revoke the spell. Thine Edwin frets not so.
> For how should he at wicked chance repine
> Who feels from every change amusement flow?
> Even now his eyes with smiles of rapture glow,
> As on he wanders through the scenes of morn,
> Where the fresh flowers in living lustre blow,
> Where thousand pearls the dewy lawns adorn,
> A thousand notes of joy in every breeze are
>   born.

The names of Michael Bruce (1746-67) and John Logan (1748-88) recall a rather squalid, but at the same time characteristic, controversy. On the death of the former, the latter obtained Bruce's manuscripts and papers from his father, with a view to their publication, and in 1770 brought out a volume purporting to contain Bruce's poems, together with some pieces by other hands. Bruce's relations, according to the story, were astonished to find that the youth's "Gospel Sonnets" were not included in this collection, and the suspicion of unfair dealing on the part of Logan became to their minds a certainty when in 1781 Logan published a volume of his own poems in which were to be found certain sacred verses alleged to be Bruce's, and an amended version of an *Ode to the Cuckoo,* which had formed part of the 1770 publication. On the one hand, then, it is said that Logan deliberately turned Bruce's manuscripts to his own account, and false-

ly claimed to be the author of poems which he had never written: on the other hand, this accusation is indignantly denied, and, though it is admitted that Logan's conduct and behaviour were not always such as becomes a minister of the gospel, his authorship of the *Ode* and of sundry other pieces in dispute is strenuously maintained. The evidence in support of either contention is extremely unsatisfactory. There is a vast amount of hearsay, and a great deal about manuscripts which A said that B told him that C had seen. Local patriotism has, of course, stepped in to supply deficiencies in solid fact, and, the village of Kinnesswod being inferior in population and importance to the port of Leith, the clamour of the Bruce faction has naturally been shriller and more insistent than that of Logan's partisans. Moreover, Logan's is not so picturesque a figure as that of the youthful poet, nor has he the moral support of an aged parent. Also, it may be questioned whether the participators in this wretched squabble have always taken pains to forget that Bruce was a Seceder, whereas Logan belonged to the Establishment, and was a Moderate.

The one thing certain is that, apart from the grave aspersions cast upon Logan's personal character, the matter is not worth fighting about. The *Ode to the Cuckoo,* round which the battle has raged most hotly, is a poor enough affair in all conscience. It contains two really good lines, and only two:—

> Thou hast no sorrow in thy song,
>   No winter in thy year.

The rest or it is essentially commonplace, and in parts indisputably pedestrian. No man need be ambitious to be reckoned the author of such a quatrain as this:—

> O could I fly, I'd fly with thee:
>   We'd make with social wing
> Our annual visit o'er the globe,
>   Companions of the Spring.

In the 1770 version, there is one line which positively declines to scan. This was corrected in the later edition, and indeed all the changes made by Logan are for the better. As for Bruce's acknowledged work, it may be wonderful for his age, and considering the circumstances of his upbringing; but it will not suffer the application of any reasonably high standard. That his imitative faculty was strong is manifest. Not only does he follow the "classical" convention with abject fidelity, calling his friend Mr. Arnot, for instance, in *Lochleven,* by the name of Agricola, but he makes no scruple of appropriating earmarked words and phrases from his models. *The Elegy to Spring* is neither more nor less than a palpable imitation of Gray. It is perhaps a misfortune for the memory of this hapless young man that his champions should persist in attributing to his praiseworthy efforts, not merely comparative, but, absolute merit. Were it not for their misdirected zeal, it would be superfluous to subject them to any serious examination.

In addition to the volume of poems already referred to

Logan was responsible for a tragedy, entitled *Runnamede,* which, like Home's *Douglas,* gave great offence to the "wild" party in the Church. But it is not as a dramatist, or an original poet, that he deserves to be held in remembrance. His claim upon the regard of posterity is founded on the *Translations and Paraphrases in verse of several passages of Sacred Scripture* (1781), collected and prepared by a Committee of the General Assembly of the Church of Scotland in order to be sung in churches. Of this anthology, which consists of sixty-seven "paraphrases" and five "hymns," Logan was to all intents and purposes the editor. Addison, Watts, Doddridge, and other less eminent writers were drawn upon; and in the case of almost all, save Addison, considerable alterations were made upon the original text. The practice of emendation in such circumstances is, as a rule, highly reprehensible. But in this case it was abundantly justified by success. Scarce one of the modifications which we owe to Logan but is a self-evident improvement; scarce one but vouches for his true ear, sound judgment, and correct taste. The *Paraphrases* form incomparably the best collection of sacred lyrics (or "Gospel sonnets"), for its size, which has ever been made in the English language. Devout, dignified, and reticent, they afford a truly admirable medium for expressing the religious feelings and aspirations of an intelligent, educated, and self-respecting people. Their genuine piety is untainted by extravagance, their grave severity unruffled by hysteria. They that seek for glitter, and banality, and noise, must turn to the more comprehensive volumes of a later date, whence they will not be sent empty away. It is one of the most significant symptoms of the degeneration which, as some believe, is overtaking the Scottish character, that this excellent little collection is falling into something like desuetude in public worship.

The "classical" tradition was sufficiently prolific. It produced some one's *Albania* (1737) in blank verse and the *Clyde* (1764) of John Wilson (1720-89) in rhymed heroics, both typical specimens of their kinds. It may also be said to have been an unconscionable time in dying, and its extinction by no means coincides with the close of the eighteenth century. A particularly favourable specimen of what it could produce is to be found in the *Scenes of Infancy* (1803) of John Leyden, who will have to be adverted to in another connection.

> The waning harvest moon shone cold and bright;
> The warder's horn was heard at dead of night;
> And as the massy portals wide were flung,
> With stamping hoofs the rocky pavement rung.

Such lines are at all events much preferable to the performances of the amiable James Grahame (1765-1811), advocate, and clerk in holy orders of the Church of England. Blank verse was the metre of Grahame's choice, and the excellence of his intention will scarce atone for the futility of his execution. *The Rural Calendar, The Birds of Scotland,* and *The Sabbath* (1803), his *chef d'œuvre,* are conventional, ineffective, and tedious. But he deserves a niche in the Caledonian Temple of fame for the following exquisite example of the genuine "poetic diction," culled from his versified ornithology:—

> Within the fabric rude
> Or e'er the new moon waxes to the full
> The assiduous dam eight spotted spheroids sees.

Few poets have surpassed this elegant periphrasis for eggs. The last of the "classical" Anglo-Scottish poets who need be mentioned is Robert Pollok (1798-1827), a native of Renfrewshire, who become a Seceder Minister. The *Course of Time* (1827) enjoyed great renown in its day. John Wilson greeted it with loud applause; and the moral lessons it inculcates were justly thought to be beyond exception. But all its choice passages—even the once celebrated screed on Byron—are of no significance for the present generation; and Pollok, for us, is merely one of the not insignificant band of his countrymen who with indomitable perseverance have confronted the obstacles presented by narrow means and humble circumstances, only to perish in the very moment when victory has been achieved.

In the Scottish vernacular verse of the eighteenth century we possess one of the happiest illustrations of what is called a "school" of poetry, culminating in the supreme achievement of an acknowledged and unsurpassed master. The members of the school were numerous, and were drawn from every class of the community and almost every part of the country. But there is a certain unity of tone and feeling, as well as of method and craftsmanship, in the work of all of them. None of them attempted to be "original" in the hackneyed sense of the word. Each tried to accommodate his effort to some old and well-proved convention. The new wine was put into old bottles, so to say; but the old bottles stood the strain. And from many men whom it would be affectation to class as great poets there emanated lyrics which only a practised and delicate sense or discrimination can distinguish from the writing of men whose pre-eminence it were no less affectation to dispute. The rhythms, the metres, the manner which had been established as the invariable concomitants of Scots poetry upwards or two centuries before, were once more summoned to the poet's aid; and "emulation" (an almost technical term with Burns in discussing his art) accomplished what less judicious and well-regulated ambition had probably failed to perform.

By the beginning of the eighteenth century the religious or, rather, ecclesiastical gloom in which the Scots had been involved for a hundred years and more began to be dissipated. The nation had time to take breath, and to recall the "makaris" and singers in whom generations less sophisticated with theological subtleties had taken unaffected delight, and whose memory had never become wholly obliterated. The *Choice Collection of Comic and Serious Scots poems both ancient and modern* (1706-11) put forth by James Watson (d. 1722) doubtless met some public demand, and being, as its preface tells us, "the first of its nature which has been published in our own native Scots dialect," it marks the beginning of a vigorous revival of interest in the poetry of the vernacular. The contents of the work are extremely varied. They embrace many English pieces, like Montrose's verse, Sir George Mack-

enzie's *Caelia's Country-house and Closet,* and Colonel
Cleland's *Halloo my Fancie, whither wilt thou go?;* macaronics like Drummond's *Polemo-Middinia;* and Scots
poems like Montgomerie's *The Cherry and the Slae,* and
Christis Kirk on the Green. The most valuable and interesting ingredients of the miscellany, however, are Sempill's *Piper of Kilbarchan* and *Sanny Brigs;* Hamilton of
Gilbertfield's *Bonny Heck;* the octosyllabics on the old
theme of the fashionable extravagances of the age, entitled *The Speech of a Fife Laird;* and, above all, the *Blythsome Bridal,* a jingle of rare spirit and gusto. The following catalogue of typical Scots "vivers" might well be set
for translation and paraphrase in schools where such exercises are indulged in:—

> There will be Tartan, Dragen, and Brachen,
>   And fouth of good gappocks of Skate;
> Pow-sowdie and Drammock and Crowdie,
>   And callour Nowt-feet in a plate;
> And there will be Partans and Buckies,
>   Speldens and Haddocks anew;
> And sing'd Sheepsheads and a Haggize,
>   And Scadlips to sup till ye're fow.
>
> There will be good lappered-milk Kebucks,
>   And Sowens, and Farles, and Baps,
> And Swats and scraped Paunches,
>   And Brandie in stoups and in caps.
> And there will be Meal Kail and Castocks,
>   And Skink to sup till you rive,
> And Rosts to rost on a brander,
>   Of Flouks that was taken alive.

Of this lyric, as of *The Barring of the Door, Leader Haughs
and Yarrow, Maggie Lauder, Maggie's Tocher, My Jo
Janet, Toddlin' Hame,* and a host of other pieces, the
origin and date are unknown, or, at best, uncertain. As in
the case of the ballads, already discussed, we may be
pretty sure that they did not spring automatically from a
common artistic consciousness, or unconsciousness, but
that some one man was originally responsible for bringing them into the world. As they flew *viva per ora virum,*
they became modified according to the intelligence and
taste of the transmitter. Sometimes they were improved,
sometimes they suffered, in the process. But of none
perhaps can we positively say that we possess the text in
the state in which it left the author's hands, and, in point
of fact, many have been touched up deliberately and not
by accident. It was the Scots tradition to seize upon some
snatch of ancient song and write a new poem up to and
about it. The method had its advantages and its drawbacks. Some of those who practised it (not very many, be
it said) were tasteless botchers. The greatest of all the
vampers was a genius, whose touch transformed the poorest dross into gold. If we consider the fate of *Auld Lang
Syne* we see the best and the worst of the system. In
Watson's *Collection* we find an Anglicised version, possibly by Sir Robert Ayton, which is respectable but not
much more:—

> Should old acquaintance be forgot,
>   And never thought upon,

> The flames of love extinguished,
>   And freely past and gone?
> Is thy kind heart now grown so cold
>   In that loving breast of thine,
> That thou canst never once reflect
>   On Old-long-syne?
>
>   . . . . .
>
> But since that nothing can prevail,
>   And all hope is in vain,
> From these rejected eyes of mine
>   Still showers of tears shall rain:
> And though thou hast me now forgot,
>   Yet I'll continue thine,
> And ne'er forget for to reflect
>   On Old-long-syne.

Allan Ramsay caught the hint, and turned out something
even more frigid and uninspiring:—

> Should auld acquaintance be forgot,
>   Tho' they return with scars?
> These are the noble hero's lot,
>   Obtained in glorious wars:
> Welcome, my Varo, to my breast,
>   Thy arms about me twine,
> And make me once again as blest
>   As I was lang syne.

Finally came "the immortal exciseman," and what he made
of it, even an Englishman may be supposed to know. So
that, on the whole, when the drawbacks and the advantages of the tradition are weighed against one another, it is
by no means clear that we have not come off a good deal
better than we should have done had the primitive texts
descended to us in all their purity, and the Scots poets
betaken themselves to the discovery of new modes of
expression.

Watson was excellent, so far as he went. But the collections which did for the songs of Scotland what Tom Durfey
had done for those of England, and a great deal more,
were the work of Allan Ramsay (1686-1758), a native of
Leadhills, in Lanarkshire, who became first a barber and
periwig-maker and afterwards a bookseller in Edinburgh.
The contents of his *Evergreen* (1724) are chiefly derived
from the Bannatyne MS. (*supra* p. 207), and consist of
old poems like *Christis Kirk on the Green, The Thistle
and the Rose, Robeno and Makyne,* and so forth. The
Tea-table Miscellany (1724-40), on the other hand, exhibits the lyrical side of Scots poetry, and with all its
faults is a most meritorious anthology. "Our Scots tunes,"
as Ramsay not unjustly says, "have an agreeable gaiety
and natural sweetness that make them acceptable wherever they are known, not only among ourselves, but in other
countries." Accordingly he set himself, with the assistance of certain "ingenious young gentlemen," to provide
sets of verses, modelled more or less closely upon those
handed down by tradition, which should be not unworthy
of the airs with which they were to be conjoined. The
"ingenuity" of the editor and his subordinates may some-

times have been misplaced, and their zeal may have out-run discretion; but it cannot be doubted that Ramsay has preserved much for us that might otherwise have been irrevocably lost. And what is particularly noticeable in him is his fearless and confident assertion of the claims of the national muse. Foreign decorations and accessories are to be avoided. "The morning rises as she does in the Scottish horizon. We are not carried to Greece or Italy for a shade, a stream, or a breeze. The groves rise in our valleys, the rivers flow from our own fountains, and the winds blow upon our own hills." This is the very spirit of Burns.

Ramsay himself was the chief contributor to his *Miscellany,* and many of the specimens of his work—not perhaps, always the best—won great popularity. In merit, they vary considerably. Now and then he "tunes his lyre" to a purely English strain; but it is difficult to be enthusiastic over

> Ye powers! was Damon then so blest
> To fall to charming Delia's share?

Some of the most acceptable have been those which hit off a mean between poetical English and broad Scots. But he is in his most characteristic and felicitous lyrical vein when writing in the Doric. The success of *Bessy Bell and Mary Gray* (with which it is interesting to compare *Genty Tibby and Sonsy Nelly*—a different treatment of the same theme), of *This is no my ain house,* of *The Lass of Patie's Mill,* and of *For the sake of somebody* is not surprising or undeserved. As a favourable illustration of his capabilities, I submit three stanzas of *The Young Laird and Edinburgh Katy,* merely premising that here, as in the rest of Ramsay's lyrical triumphs, it is impossible to state precisely how much is his and how much the work of some *vates ignotus.*

> Now wat ye wha I met yestreen,
>> Coming down the street, my jo?
> My mistress, in her tartan screen,
>> Fou' bonny, braw, and sweet, my jo.
> My dear (quoth I) thanks to the night,
>> That never wished a lover ill,
> Since ye're out of your mother's sight,
>> Let's tak' a walk up to the hill.
>
> O Katy! Wiltu gang wi' me,
>> And leave the dinsome town a while?
> The blossom's sprouting frae the tree,
>> And a' the simmer's gaun to smile;
> The mavis, nightingale, and lark,
>> The bleating lambs and whistling hind,
> In ilka dale, green, shaw, and park,
>> Will nourish health and glad ye'r mind.
>
> Soon as the clear goodman of day
>> Does bend his morning draught of dew,
> We'll gae to some burnside and play
>> And gather flowers to busk ye'r brow;
> We'll pu' the daisies on the green,
>> The luckan gowans frae the bog;

> Between hands now and then we'll lean,
>> And sport upo' the velvet fog.

There is here true, if not very profound, feeling; and we are conscious of the presence of that simple, yet resolute, determination to extract from life every drop of pleasure it can afford which is so persistent a note in Scottish poetry, and which Ramsay himself so frankly inculcates in the following lines:—

> Be sure ye dinna quit the grip
>> Of ilka joy, when ye are young;
> Before auld age your vitals nip,
>> And lay ye twa fold o'er a rung.

It is the philosophy of Burns, except in his hours of remorse.

The volume of Allan Ramsay's original poetry, apart from song-writing, is considerable, and we may say of him, as he says of John Cowper, that

> He was right nacky in his way,
> And eydent baith be night and day.

His English poems, which include a number of so-called odes and elegies, are of little interest and significance, when they are not positively bad. *Health* and *The Morning Interview,* both in rhymed heroics, are the result of injudicious "emulation" of Pope, and little instruction or amusement can be derived from *Tartana; or the Plaid,* in which he implores the Caledonian beauties "who have long been both the muse and subject of [his] song," to assist their bard,

> who, in harmonious lays
> Designs the glory of your plaid to raise.

Much better are his *Fables* (1722-30), in Scots octosyllabics, though he never attains the freedom and lightness of touch that distinguish the

> Dear lad, wha linkan o'er the lee,
> Sang Blowsalind and Bowzybee.

In the "familiar epistles" which passed between him and Hamilton of Gilbertfield in the *Habbie Simson* metre he not only gives his talents fairer play, but provides a model of which Burns was not slow to avail himself to admirable purpose. Two poems of heavier calibre and more ambitious design would of themselves have marked out Ramsay from the general run of Scottish "bards." The brace of cantos which he added to *Christis Kirk on the Green* (1716) are characteristic of one aspect of the age and of the race—grimy, squalid, and coarse; full of what is known as "realism," but lacking that touch of genius which a Burns might have supplied, and in whose absence the spirit of gaiety has evaporated, and mirth has sunk into gross and unredeemed buffoonery. *The Gentle Shepherd* (1725), which has generally been regarded as Ramsay's masterpiece, is much pleasanter reading than the *Christis Kirk* cantos, though it is difficult to classify.

The work is, in truth, a curious blend of the mock-pastoral of Gay with the realistic-pastoral, if we may call it so, of Crabbe. Anomalous though the species be, the experiment is in the main successful. The mild burlesque of the conventional idyll with its Damons and Phyllises that runs through the poem mingles very happily with the pictures of Scottish peasant life, which, if some of its harsher features have been eliminated from the representation, is depicted with faithfulness and sympathy.

But to many judges it must always seem that the very cream of Ramsay's work is to be found in his vernacular pieces, on some topic of purely local or personal interest, which the genius of the author has so handled as to raise it out of the parochial and particular into the region of the artistic and universal. When treating such themes Ramsay's metre is that of *Habbie Simson,* except in the cases in which he employs that of *The Cherry and the Sale.* But he handles both with equal firmness and dexterity. Here are a couple of stanzas from *The Poet's Wish,* in which stands revealed a "gausie" shopkeeping Scots Horace, but a Horace, notwithstanding:—

> Whaever by his canny fate
> Is master of a good estate,
>   That can ilk thing afford,
> Let him enjoy't withouten care,
> And with the wale of curious fare
>   Cover his ample board.
> Much dawted by the gods is he
>   Wha to the Indian plain
> Successfu' ploughs the wally sea,
>   And safe returns again,
>   With riches, that hitches
>   Him high aboon the rest
>   Of sma' fowk, and a' fowk,
>   That are with poortith prest.
>
> For me, I can be well content
> To eat my bannock on the bent,
>   And kitchen't wi' fresh air;
> Of lang-kail I can make a feast,
> And cantily haud up my crest,
>   And laugh at dishes rare.
> Nought frae Apollo I demand,
>   But through a lengthened life,
> My outer fabric firm may stand,
>   And saul clear without strife.
>   May he then, but gie then,
>   Those blessings for my skair;
>   I'll fairly and squarely
>   Quit a' and seek nae mair.

In the same measure are the humorous *Address to the Town Council of Edinburgh,* praying them to suppress the piracy of the author's works by the street ballad-vendors, and *The Vision,* a poem in a loftier strain, which he in vain endeavoured to palm off as a genuine antique in the *Evergreen.*

In the less complicated and shorter stanza to which I have referred we have a quartette of *Elegies;* on *Maggy Johntoun,* who kept an alehouse at Bruntsfield links, on *Lucky Wood,* who kept a tavern in the Canongate, on *Patie Birnie,* "the famous fiddler of Kinghorn," and on *John Cowper,* the Kirk-Treasurer's man (as who should say, the Proctor's bulldog), to whom were entrusted the duties of *agent de moeurs* in Edinburgh. All of these, in their way, are little masterpieces, and nothing could surpass in their own department the glimpses of "low life" which they afford, or the mordant and sardonic flavouring which is so skillfully thrown in from time to time, and in which *John Cowper* pre-eminently excels. Unfortunately, quotation from that particular elegy is practically impossible, and we must content ourselves with a fragment from *Maggy Johnstoun:*—

> When we were wearied at the gowff
> Then Maggy Johnstoun's was our howff;
> Now a' our gamesters may sit dowff,
>   Wi' hearts like lead;
> Death wi' his rung rax'd her a yowff,
>   And sae she died.
>
> Maun we be forced thy skill to tine,
> For which we will right sair repine?
> Or hast thou left to bairns of thine
>   The pawky knack
> Of brewing ale almaist like wine,
>   That gar'd us crack?
>
> Sae brawly did a pease-scon toast
> Biz i' the queff, and flie the frost;
> There we got fou wi' little cost,
>   And muckle speed:
> Now, wae worth death! our sport's a' lost,
>   Since Maggy's dead.

In the *Last Speech of a Wretched Miser* the grimness of tone is strongly marked, though the piece cannot be ranked along with such a triumph of art as the scene of the elder Dumbiedykes' death in the *Heart of Midlothian.* The following verses, however, show power of no ordinary kind:—

> O gear! I held ye lang thegither;
> For you I starved my guid auld mither,
> And to Virginia sauld my brither,
>   And crush'd my wife;
> But now I'm gawn, I kenna whither,
>   To leave my life!
>
> My life! my god! my spirit yearns,
> Not on my kindred, wife, or bairns,—
> Sic are but very laigh concerns
>   Compar'd with thee;
> When now this mortal rottle warns
>   Me I maun die.
>
> It to my heart gaes like a gun,
> To see my kin, and graceless son,
> Like rooks, already are begun
>   To thumb my gear,
> And cash that hasna seen the sun

This fifty year.

These must suffice, for we shall have to be satisfied with the mere mention of *Lucky Spence's Last Advice,* which marks the high-tide of Allan Ramsay's genius. The old Scots world of license, which the Church so zealously sought to crush, and in reality helped to sustain, by its too rigorous discipline, is nowhere mirrored with so punctual a fidelity to fact as in this sordid and gloomy, but wonderful, essay in dramatic satire.

Ramsay's attitude to life is essentially that of the prosperous Scots merchant with a strong taste for letters. His love of good fare and good drink does not quench his liking for the pleasures of the mind, and, though for the most part he leaves delicacy and refinement of feeling to others, his sense of humour is strong, he is no foolish optimist, and his view of what he sees around him is essentially that of a sane and healthy man. In his hostility to the puritanical faction in the Church—an hostility always implicit, and at times surprisingly frank in expression—he never varies, and, as in his deviations from the straight and narrow path of conduct he wandered less far than Burns, the less his need to indulge in short-lived paroxysms of repentance. We may regard him in his character as a type of the pleasure-loving Scot, who knows how to keep within bounds, and in his art as a poet who reached a high level of eminence himself, and served the literature of his country even better by preparing the waste places for the approaching arrival of a master.

The anti-ecclesiastical bias, of which Ramsay had no monopoly, comes out strongly in a *Collection of Scots Poems,* bearing to be by "the late Mr. Alexander Pennecuik and others." Of Pennecuik we know little more than that he was a contemporary and rival of Ramsay's, and that he died in 1730. *Rome's Legacy to the Church of Scotland,* an avowed "satyr" on the stool of repentance in rhymed heroics, is intensely bitter in feeling, though it must yield in merit to the dialogue in the eternal *Habbie Simson* measure between the Kirk-treasurer and Meg. In the same metre we have a spirited *Elegy on Robert Forbes,* another John Cowper, two stanzas from which will show how closely the author clung to the established convention:—

> Limmers and lairds he'll nae mair chase,
> Nae mair we'll see his pawky face
> Keek thro' close-heads, to catch a brace
>   Of waping morts,
> Play bogle-bo, a bonny chase
>   About the ports.

> . . . . .

> We lov'd to see his Judas face
> Repeating preachings, saying grace,
> Unto the tune of Chevy Chase
>   Shaking his head;
> Wha will he get to fill his place?
>   For now he's dead.

Pennecuik has also a tolerable sketch of a domestic interior on a winter's night, which describes how—

> My lucky dad, an honest Whig,
> Was telling tales of Bothwell Brig;
> He could not miss to mind th' attempt
> For he was sitting peeling hemp;
> My aunt, wha none dare say has no grace,
> Was reading on the *Pilgrim's Progress;*
> The meikle tasker, Davie Dallas,
> Was telling blads of William Wallace;
> My mother bade her second son say
> What he'd by heart of *Davie Lindsay;*

and so forth: a passage not without interest as indicating the attachment of the Scottish lower orders, even when imbued with the covenanting tradition, to the literature of their country. But if *The Merry Wives of Musselburgh's Welcome to Meg Dickson* be really Pennecuik's, all that can be said is that for once his lips were touched by the genuine flame. As a specimen of the kind which we may call the burlesque-supernatural it has no equal in Scots verse between Dunbar's *Dance* and *Tam o' Shanter,* with the precise tone and spirit of which its own are identical. Burns's masterpiece has the great advantage of being written in a more rapid and flowing measure, and the execution of the two pieces cannot for one moment be compared. But the *Merry Wives* has caught the right note of boisterous mirth tempered with terror, and we can imagine that—

> At night when souters leave their lingles,
> And bairns come laden hame with singles,
> And auld wives kindle up their ingles
>   To last till ten—

the poem was assured of an attentive and delighted audience. As for the poems of the other Alexander Pennecuik, of New Hall and Romanno (1652-1722), they are of no great merit, and therefore by us are negligeable.

We must glance rapidly at the minor vernacular poets of the century before passing on to Fergusson and Burns. Some of them were among the "ingenious young gentlemen" who assisted Allan Ramsay, and not the least notable of these, though he had ceased to be "young," was William Hamilton of Gilbertfield (1665?-1751), the author of *Willie was a Wanton Wag,* and of *The last dying words of Bonnie Heck,* which appeared originally in Watson, and was loudly applauded at a later date for its fluency and finish by Ramsay. I forbear to trouble the reader, who has already had a good deal of the *Habbie Simson* stanza and will shortly have more, with any extract from a poem which is of no great intrinsic excellence, but derives its chief importance from being a link in the order of succession in Scots poetry. Hamilton also deserved well of his country by publishing in 1722 an edition (though far from a good one) of Blind Harry's *Wallace.* His namesake, William Hamilton of Bangour (1704-54) is best remembered, not by his *Contemplation, or the triumph of love,* but by his exquisite *Busk ye, busk ye, my bonny bonny bride.* Robert Crawford (d. 1733) contributed to the *Tea-Table Miscellany* a well-known, but somewhat tame, lyric, *The Bush aboon Traquair,* and George Halket (d. 1756), the schoolmaster of Rathen in Aberdeenshire, is alleged by some to have been the author of the plaintive *Logie o' Buchan.* Another north-countryman, Alexander Geddes (1737-1802), who was a Roman Catholic priest with a marked tendency to scepticism, produced the Jacobite lyric of *Lewie Gordon,* and (probably) that monument of Aberdonian facetiousness, *The Wee Wifeikie,* besides reviving the tradition of macaronic verse. Like most Jacobite poetry, *Lewie Gordon* was composed when the hopes of the Pretender's party had been extinguished by the failure of the enterprise of '45. Practically the only piece of real value which is contemporary with that attempt is *Hey, Johnnie Cope,* a spirited song in the broadside manner by Adam Skirving (1719-1803), an East Lothian farmer. Here, as in other instances, it is fair to own that the words derive substantial assistance from an inimitable tune.

Of somewhat greater importance than most of those just mentioned was Alexander Ross (1699-1784), a native of Aberdeenshire, who for many years was parish schoolmaster of Lochlee, in the adjacent county of Forfar. It was predicted by one of Ross's admirers that—

> ilka Mearns and Angus bairn
> Thy tales and songs by heart shall learn,

and the prophecy was fulfilled—at least as regards *Helenore, or the Fortunate Shepherdess* (1778). For many years this pastoral, the debt of which to Allan Ramsay is palpable enough, was a prime favourite in every cottage in the braes of Angus, under the name of "Lindy and Nory." In so far, however, as Ross's fame is national rather than provincial, it rests upon two or three of his songs, which have immense spirit and vigour. We subjoin a specimen from *The Rock and the Wee Pickle Tow,* and from the better known *Woo'd an' Married an' A'.*

> For now when I mind me I met Maggy Grim,
> This morning just at the beginning o't,
> She was never ca'd chancy, but canny and slim,
> And sae it has fared of my spinning o't.
> But if my new rock was anes cutted and dry
> I'll all Maggie's cann and her cantrips defy,
> And, but any sussie, the spinning I'll try,
> And ye shall all hear of the spinning o't.

> O, no' Tibby, her dother, tak' tent fat ye say,
> The never a rag we'll be seeking o't,
> Gin ye anes begin, ye'll tarveal's night and day
> Sae 'tis vain ony mair to be speaking o't.
> Since lammas I'm now gaing thirty and twa
> And never a dud sark had I yet great or sma';
> And what waur am I? I'm as warm and as braw
> As thrummy-tailed Meg that's a spinner o't.

> The girse had na freedom of growing
> As lang as she wasna awa',
> Nor in the town could there be stowing
> For wooers that wanted to ca'.

> For drinking and dancing and brulyies,
> And boxing and shaking of fa's,
> The town was for ever in tulyies;
> But now the lassie's awa.

> But had they but ken'd her as I did,
> Their errand it wad hae been sma';
> She neither kent spinning nor carding,
> Nor brewing nor baking ava'.
> But wooers ran a' mad upon her,
> Because she was bonny and braw,
> And sae I dread will be seen on her,
> When she's by hand and awa'.

The 1804 edition of Ross's poems also contains a poem by Francis Douglas, named *Rural Love,* in octosyllabic metre, and *The Farmer's Ha',* by Dr. Charles Keith, an excellent transcript of one aspect of rural life, as the vivid picture of John the hired-man's return from the smithy testifies:—

> Of John's return spak ilka nook,
> They aft gaed to the door to look,
> For they were on the tenter-hook
> For Smithy chat;
> And now, I trow, like printed book
> He gies them that.

But scarce any of the minor versifiers had the race and "smeddum" of John Skinner (1721-1807), a clergyman in orders of the Scottish Episcopal Church, who wrote an *Ecclesiastical History of Scotland* (1788) in prose, and enlivened his family and neighbours by numerous productions in a lighter vein. His *Ewie wi' the Crookit Horn* has always enjoyed a high reputation, and as for *Tullochgorum,* of which a couple of verses are here given, has not Burns pronounced it to be "the best Scotch song Scotland ever saw"?

> O, Tullochgorum's my delight,
> It gars us a' in ane unite,
> And any sumph that keeps up spite,
> In conscience I abhor him.
> For blythe and cheery we's be a',
> Blythe and cheery, blythe and cheery,
> Blythe and cheery we's be a'
> And mak' a happy quorum.
> For blythe and cheery we's be a',
> As lang as we hae breath to draw,
> And dance till we be like to fa'
> The reel of Tullochgorum.

> There needs na' be sae great a phrase,
> Wi dringing dull Italian lays,
> I wadna gie our ain strathspeys
> For half a hundred score o' 'em.
> They're dowff and dowie at the best,
> Dowff and dowie, dowff and dowie,
> They're dowff and dowie at the best,
> Wi a' their variorum.
> They're dowff and dowie at the best,
> Their allegros and all the rest,

They canna please a Scottish taste,
   Compar'd wi' Tullochgorum.

Poetical composition, it should be added, was by no means
confined to the male sex, and many women, from Earls'
daughters to alehouse keepers, it is said, engaged in the
pastime. [Lady Wardlaw is by] far the most distinguished
of our Scottish Sapphos of the eighteenth century. . . .
Her senior by twelve years, Lady Grizel Baillie (1665-
1746), by birth a Hume of Marchmont, was responsible
for the pathetic lyric, *Werena my heart licht I wad dee;*
Jane Elliot (1727-1805), a daughter of Sir Gilbert Elliot,
afterwards Lord Minto, produced one version of *The Flowers of the Forest* in 1756, and Mrs. Cockburn (1712?-94),
Sir Walter Scott's kinswoman and friend, another, nine
years later; while in the *Auld Robin Gray* of Lady Anne
Barnard (1750-1825), a daughter of the Earl of Balcarres,
we have what is probably the most popular (Burns's work
apart) of the sentimental ditties with which Scots poetry
abounds. Joanna Baillie (1762-1851), who has been already mentioned in another connection, contributed to the
common stock *The Weary Pund of Tow, Tam o' the Lin,*
and *Saw ye Johnny Comin',* all excellent, and distinguished
by a strong sense of humour. Lastly, though we depart a
little from strict chronological order, it may be convenient here to mention Carolina Oliphant, Lady Nairne
(1766-1845), one of the most prolific and successful of
Scottish songstresses. To her we owe *The Land o' the
Leal,* the precise locality of which territory has been the
occasion of so much innocent and ludicrous misunderstanding to the Southron. She, too, claims the *Laird of
Cockpen,* an essay in a very different strain, which it is
almost impossible to overpraise, as well as *Caller Herrin',* an extremely nimble and tripping piece of versification, the tune of which has suggested many hideous variations to composers who make such undertakings their
business. To Lady Nairne, also, belong *The Auld House,
John Tod,* besides *Wha'll be King but Charlie?, Will ye
no come back again?,* and many other lyrics in which
belated loyalty to the house of Stuart found not unworthy
or unpleasing, though at times unconvincing enough,
expression. A verse or two from the last-named song may
fitly conclude what we have to say on the lesser Scots
poets of the age which extends, roughly speaking, from
the manhood of Allan Ramsay to the death of Burns.

   Bonnie Charlie's now awa'
      Safely owre the friendly main;
   Mony a heart will break in twa,
      Should he ne'er come back again.

      Will ye no come back again?
      Will ye no come back again?
      Better lo'ed ye canna be,
      Will ye no come back again?

   English bribes were a' in vain,
      An' e'en tho' puirer we may be,
   Siller canna buy the heart
      That aye beats for thine and thee.

         Will ye no, &c.

   Sweet's the laverock's note and lang,
      Lilting wildly up the glen;
   But aye to me he sings ae sang—
      Will ye no come back again?

         Will ye no, &c.

The bards of Caledonia, to do them justice, have never
been slow to discuss the origins of their art, or to acknowledge the extent of their obligations to their predecessors. Not one of the fraternity was more candid in this
respect than Burns, who indicates his poetical models in
the poem addressed *To William Simpson of Ochiltree*
(1785). After naming Ramsay and Gilbertfield he mentions "Fergusson, the writer chiel, a deathless name," and
then devotes the following verse to the memory of that
unfortunate victim of ill-health and hard living:—

   O Fergusson! Thy glorious parts
   Ill suited law's dry, musty arts!
   My curse upon your whunstane hearts,
      Ye En'brugh gentry!
   The tythe of what ye waste at cartes
      Wad stow'd his pantry.

Robert Fergusson (1750-54), in truth, stands in the direct
line of succession between Ramsay and Burns. Had he
lived longer, it seems not extravagant to suppose that he
might have accomplished something inferior only to the
very best of what Burns has left us, and, short though his
career was, we can at least say of him that he helped with
Ramsay to furbish up and re-fashion the instrument with
which Burns was to achieve such astonishing effects.

Fergusson's English verse, it need scarce be said, is poor
and unimportant. In the vernacular his *métier* was the
descriptive satire as practised by Ramsay, and if Fergusson's workmanship be a shade smoother and more finished than Allan's, they approach their themes in much
the same spirit and from much the same point of view.
We have the boisterous gaiety, from which true mirth
seems sometimes to be absent, the sardonic laugh, the
biting irony; and though Fergusson made shipwreck of
his life and Ramsay did not, it cannot be maintained
without undue refinement that the habitual mood of the
younger man as expressed in his work, is much, if at all,
more reckless than that of the elder. In the case of one
poem, however, our proposition must be qualified. *Braid
Claith,* of which the theme may be summarised as "to
him that hath," displays a temper to which the more cautious and prosperous Ramsay rarely if ever gives expression. Nor can we fail to notice that Fergusson nourishes
a violent animosity against those representatives of law
and order, the City Guard, a feeling in which Ramsay
does not appear to have participated.

The *Ode to the Gowdspink* is fresh and sincere: qualities
none too common in an age when even in the vernacular
the poet was apt to think himself bound to sing the praises of nature by rule and measure. But the *Gowdspink* and
the *Farmer's Ingle* notwithstanding, Fergusson is essentially the poet of the town, and that town is Edinburgh.

Leith Races, Caller Water, Hallowfair, The Daft Days, the *Address to the Tron-Kirk Bell, The Mutual complaint of the Plainstanes and Causeway,* and *Auld Reikie* are fundamentally urban. They waft to our nostrils a whiff from the wynds and closes, a blast from the taverns and merry meetings, of an old, unsavoury, and battered but fascinating capital. Its whole life is described with some of Swift's ease and fluency (and some also of Swift's particularity in matters where detail is best avoided) in his *Auld Reikie,* of which the following lines may serve as a sample:—

> Now Morn, wi' bonny purple smiles,
> Kisses the air-cock o' St. Giles;
> Rakin their een, the servant lasses
> Early begin their lies and clashes.
> Ilk tells her friend o' saddest distress,
> That still she bruiks frae scoulin' mistress;
> And wi' her Jo in turnpike stair,
> She'd rather snuff the stinkin' air,
> As be subjected to her tongue,
> Whan justly censured in the wrong.

> . . . . .

> Now stairhead critics, senseless fools!
> Censure their aim and pride their rules,
> In Luckenbooths, wi' glowrin' eye,
> Their neebours' sma'est faults descry.
> If ony loun shou'd dander there,
> O' awkward gait and foreign air,
> They trace his steps till they can tell
> His pedigree as weel's himsel'.
> When Phoebus blinks wi' warmer ray
> And schools at noonday get the play,
> Then bus'ness, weighty bus'ness comes;
> The trader glow'rs; he doubts, he hums;
> The lawyers eke to cross repair,
> Their wigs to shaw, and toss an air;
> While busy agent closely plies,
> And a' his kittle cases tries.

It would possibly be rash to predicate of any of Fergusson's poems that they might be mistaken for the work of Burns. Here and there are to be discovered flaws in the technique, otiose epithets, harsh inversions, tame expressions, from which Burns at his best is wholly free. But if any pieces of Fergusson's could pass for Burns's, they would be, perhaps, *Caller Water,* which was plainly the model of *Scotch Drink,* and *Hallowfair,* to which also the indebtedness of the younger poet is considerable. Here are three spirited stanzas from what, upon the whole, is Fergusson's most successful performance:—

> "Here chapmen billies tak' their stand,
>   An' shaw their bonny wallies;
> Wow! but they lie fu' gleg aff hand
>   To trick the silly fallows:

> Heh, sirs! what cairds and tinklers come,
>   And ne'er-do-weel horse-coupers,
> And spae-wives, fenzying to be dumb,

> Wi' a' siclike landloupers,
>   To thrive that day!

> Here Sawney cries, frae Aberdeen,
>   'Come ye to me fa need;
> The brawest shanks that e'er were seen
>   I'll sell ye cheap an' guid;
> I wyt they are as protty hose
>   As come frae weyr or leem:
> Here, tak a rug an' shaw's your pose;
>   Forseeth, my ain's but teem
>   And light this day.'

> Ye wives, as ye gang through the fair,
>   O mak your bargains hooly!
> O' a' thir wylie loons beware,
>   Or fegs! they will ye spiulzie.
> For, fairn-year, Meg Thomson got,
>   Frae thir mischievous villains,
> A scaw'd bit o' a penny note,
>   That lost a score o' shillins
>   To her that day.

But it is time to clear the decks for action, and to lay ourselves alongside of perhaps the most interesting and certainly the most perilous of all the topics which Scottish literature suggests—the poetry of Burns.

Burns marks the close, not the beginning, of a dynasty of poets. He was, not the founder of a school, but, its most finished and its final product. In him the vernacular poetry of Scotland reached its highest consummation. . . .

-J. H. Millar

Robert Burns was born in 1759, at Alloway, near Ayr, to William Burns, or Burness, a man of Kincardineshire origin, who was never rich in this world's gear, but was distinguished by an unusual measure of the uprightness and intelligence which have always been regarded as the most precious inheritance of the Scots peasantry. Originally a gardener by occupation, William Burness took the small farm of Mount Oliphant in 1766, whence he moved to Lochlie, in the parish of Tarbolton, in 1777. There he died in 1784, after a life of arduous and unremitting toil. Robert's education, as may be supposed, was punctually attended to, and his father was not slow to make those sacrifices on behalf of his family, the willingness to undergo which is the best proof of the value in which education is really held among any people. Robert supplemented the labours of his instructor by devouring every book he came across; and it seems by no means extravagant to conjecture that when he reached the period of adolescence he was a great deal better read (the ancient classics, perhaps, apart) and a great deal better educated generally than Lord Byron at the same time of life.

He had naturally been bred to the plough, and an abortive attempt to set up as a flax-dresser at Irvine, in 1781, did not long withdraw him from the stilts. After his father's death, he entered with his brother Gilbert upon the tenancy of the farm of Mossgiel, in the parish of Mauchline. But the enterprise did not prosper greatly, and, moreover, in the course of a couple of years, Burns had, as the saying goes, made the countryside too hot to hold him by a series of notorious amours which we may be dispensed from even attempting to enumerate. He was on the point of sailing to the West Indies in 1786, when his steps were suddenly diverted from the quay at Greenock to the Scottish capital. At the end of July in that year there had issued from the press at Kilmarnock a small volume of *Poems, chiefly in the Scottish Dialect,* which had been received by the public, not only in the South-west of Scotland but also in Edinburgh, with enthusiastic approbation. Blind Dr. Blacklock had written of the work to Dr. Lawrie, the minister of Loudoun, in a strain of high commendation and encouragement. The sight of this letter at once altered the new poet's resolution, which, perhaps, had never been very staunch, and made Edinburgh his destination instead of Jamaica. He reached it on the 28th of November, 1786.

The story of Burns's season in the capital, of how he was welcomed by all that was most distinguished in rank, or literature, or fashion, of how Scott met him at Adam Ferguson's, of how he held high revel, not alas! with his peers, but with Crochallan Fencibles and the St. Andrew's Lodge of Freemasons—has been too often told to need repetition here. That Burns sustained the trying process of being "lionised" with much greater coolness and composure than most men in his circumstances would have been able to do, is a truism. He carried himself in the best company which Edinburgh had to afford with a manly independence, and a natural good breeding, which none has ever ventured to impugn, and which was only qualified by the tendency unduly to assert his own dignity when he conceived himself in any way slighted. But he had none of the devouring self-consciousness which was apt to betray Hogg into inexcusable familiarities, and even in the moments when his better self was practically effaced he would have been incapable of such an outrage as the pages in which the Shepherd sought to defame his departed friend and patron, Scott. From the Duchess of Gordon, from Robertson, from Blair, from Mackenzie, Burns received nothing but kindness. What demoralised him was, not their attention, but, the flattery of the fifth-rate people who were glad to bask in the countenance of "Caledonia's bard," and to get drunk in his company. In literature as on the turf, and indeed in most other walks of life, it is the hangers-on who are hateful, and who do the mischief; and the type of man who gave Burns an irresistible impetus down the primrose way is excellently represented by a ruffian like William Nicol. Close association with creatures of this description, and "superfluous banquetings" in their society, might well ruin a character less easy-going and less "formed for pleasure" than that of Burns. Meanwhile, he had furnished himself with a more or less handsome supply of money by means of a new edition of his poems, published in Edinburgh, by

Creech, in 1787, with considerable additions. This edition was reproduced in London in the same year, and a still further enlarged edition was issued by Creech in 1793.

Of the Sylvander and Clarinda episode, which began upon Burns's return to Edinburgh, in December, 1787, the less said the better. The flirtation is one of the silliest and most affected in the whole record of such affairs, and, as Scott remarks with his plain good sense, the name of Sylvander is "sufficient of itself to damn a whole file of love-letters." In the following spring Burns performed the most sensible act attributed to him in his dealings with women; that is to say, he married Jean Armour, who had already borne him several children, and who made him an excellent and loyal wife. In the same year (1788) he took the farm of Ellisland, in Dumfriesshire, and in 1789 his means of livelihood were increased by his appointment to the post of an exciseman. The farming speculation had to be abandoned in 1791, and the poet then moved with his wife and family into the town of Dumfries. His muse had not been idle since he left Edinburgh. He contributed largely to Johnson's *Musical Museum,* which began to appear in 1787, and indeed he became almost the editor of that collection. He also assisted George Thomson in compiling his *Original Scottish Airs* (1793-1818), declining absolutely to accept of any pecuniary gratification for his labours. Almost all his most characteristic lyrical work appeared in one or other of these publications. But his impaired constitution was unable long to withstand the trials to which life in Dumfries, with all that life involved, subjected it. Death put a final period to his sufferings and struggles in 1796.

Burns's personality was so masterful and striking that we cannot be surprised when we find that criticism of his life and criticism of his works have been intermingled in an unusually pernicious degree. Professed admirers of his compositions have thought it necessary to tone down incontrovertible facts, and even to play upon the greediness of the public for a soul-satisfying myth, in order that the bard may be represented as a model member of the community. On the other hand, those who resent his attitude to the Calvinistic section of the Church, against which he waged bitter war, are disposed to ignore his very best performances, and, with minds fixed on *Thou lingering Star,* or *The Cottar's Saturday Night,* to breathe the pious wish, *O si sic omnia!* National partiality, moreover, has been a complicating element in Burns criticism to an extent incredible to those who are unacquainted with the collective vanity which animates the more impulsive section of the nation. There is reason to believe that much information about the poet, amassed by an indefatigable, though by no means discriminating, inquirer in a past generation, was withheld by him from the world for fear of incurring popular obloquy. It is a mere fact that Mr. Stevenson's *Essay* on Burns was rejected by the cautious editor of the *Encyclopædia Britannica* because it ran counter to Scottish tradition, and the circumstance that the epithet which instinctively occurs to a commentator as applicable to that admirable sketch is "courageous," shows how deep a hold prejudice is believed to have taken of the critical sense of the public. Lastly, so long as Burns Clubs continue to

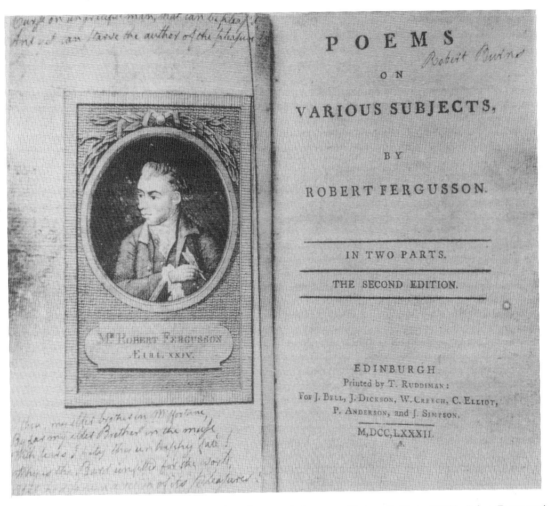

Frontispiece and title page of Robert Burns's copy of Robert Fergusson's Poems on Various Subjects *(1779). Below Fergusson's portrait, Burns wrote, "O though, my elder brother in Misfortune, / By far my elder Brother in the Muse."*

exist for the purpose of mingling oratorical flourishes with what is politely called "conviviality," so long will there never be wanting a yearly supply of assiduous if unconscious efforts to darken counsel and to obscure the truth. Inasmuch as these highly popular institutions as yet exhibit no symptoms of decay, it seems incumbent upon the critic to endeavour as far as possible to divest himself of all prepossessions, national or otherwise, and to approach the consideration of the poet's character and works with an open mind.

First, then, and that briefly, of Burns's character. No man of sense, who realises that the life of all men must needs be a more or less faithful illustration of the confession, *Video melior a proboque, deteriora sequor,* will be disposed to judge him with a rigorous severity. It is only the pedant, or the prig, or the sentimentalist, who will desiderate in Burns that uniform consistency of thought or feeling to which no human being was ever privileged to attain, or who will attempt to draw out a reasoned and systematised scheme of his theological and ethical views. Like the vast majority of his fellow creatures, he was a being of impulse and of moods; and none save the veriest

greenhorn will be astonished to think that the *Epistle to John Rankine* proceeded from the same pen as the *Epistle to a Young Friend,* or will trouble to inquire whether the bard of the *Reply to a Trimming Epistle* or the bard of *Highland Mary* is "the true Burns." Both bards are the true Burns. That he possessed many generous and engaging qualities is as certain as that their virtue was seriously impaired by not a few obvious defects. It may be doubted, however, whether the legacy of his example has, upon the whole, been beneficial to the mass of his countrymen. A pessimist might be forgiven for holding that he has confirmed them in some of their darling vices. Too often have his shortcomings been pleaded, expressly or by implication, as a justification for those of men who were never exposed to one tenth part of his temptations!

But the cardinal flaw in his character was unquestionably his want of chivalrous feeling where women are concerned. To impute this to his being a peasant is to give an explanation neither flattering to the Scottish commonalty, nor, I venture to think, altogether satisfactory. That he could, in the exercise of his art, assume the tone and spirit of chivalry and romance to perfection, we have ample demonstration in such incomparable pieces as *Bonnie Lesley, Go fetch to me a pint o' wine,* and *It was a' for our Rightfu' King.* Yet in his letters he reveals a state of mind with regard to the relations of the sexes which to call ungentlemanly were, indeed, grotesque as well as inept, but for which the epithet "inhuman" would not be much too severe. He was, indeed, fated to supply in his own person a signal instance of that petrifaction of feeling which, himself has assured us, is the result of "tempting th'illicit rove." In other matters he is sincere, genuine, *bon enfant;* here he is a consistent and incurable *poseur.* We waive a certain intolerable and unquotable letter to Ainslie. We rest the proposition upon many passages in his correspondence in which the language is well within the bounds of decorum, but whose total effect is the very opposite of pleasant. Something, no doubt, must be allowed for the vicious taste of his age—the age of the dawning of romance—to which "sensibility" was all in all. The trail of Rousseau smeared many a page even in the country of David Hume. Nevertheless, Burns took up the fashion of the day with much too great a gusto to permit us to absolve him from complicity in its offence. He is almost hateful when he begins to talk in his knowing and jocose way about "a certain delicious passion" in which he had been "initiated" at the age of fifteen; and when his gallantry begins to find expression in doubtful French, he is unendurable. No; the spectacle of the "old hawk" "on the pounce," of the veteran "battering himself into a warm affection" for some luckless or worthless girl, is the reverse of agreeable; and referring the reader on this head to Mr. Stevenson's *Essay,* we gladly turn from the discussion of Burns's character to the discussion of his work.

The first and most essential point to bear in mind is one which has been mentioned already, but which can scarce be too strongly emphasised. It is, that Burns marks the close, not the beginning, of a dynasty of poets. He was, not the founder of a school, but, its most finished and its final product. In him the vernacular poetry of Scotland reached its highest consummation; through his instrumentality it ceased to be merely the poetry of a small and remote nation, and was elevated for a short space to the level of the great poetry of the world; and with his death (certain symptoms of posthumous vitality notwithstanding) it died. Burns himself, as has been remarked, was under no delusion as to the debt he owed to his literary ancestors, for Burns was never a "common Burnsite." While disclaiming "servile imitation" he admits, in the preface to the Kilmarnock edition, that he has "often had his eye" on Ramsay and Fergusson, "with a view to kindle at their flame." It is hardly an exaggeration to assert that of almost every one of his poetical pieces the form and mode of treatment can be directly traced, not merely to the general tone and convention of Scots poetry, but to a specific exemplar from the pen of some named or nameless predecessor. That the same is emphatically true of his lyrics has been ascertained beyond all dubiety. . . .

A model then, of some sort, Burns behoved to have; but all models were not equally propitious to the play of his genius. Of English models, except those of the broadside

or the bacchanalian variety, he could make little or nothing, and this is especially true of English eighteenth-century models which exercised a peculiarly sinister influence on his muse. He handled the rhymed heroic, for example, with less freedom and success even than Ramsay, as the *Brigs of Ayr* and the *Epistle to Robert Graham of Fintry, Esq.,* testify. *The Cottar's Saturday Night* (designed, apparently, to show what Robert Aiken, Esq., "in a cottage would have been") never quite throws off the bondage of Shenstone, though in one or two passages the fetters are strained to bursting, and the piece bids fair to be first rate. Of the ostensibly English poems and songs, such as *Thou ling'ring Star,* or *Clarinda, Mistress of my Soul,* we can say no more than that the world might have dispensed with them only less easily than with such a stilted English lyric, masquerading in Scots of a sort, as *Scots wha ha'e.* Mr. Henley is probably not far out when he pronounces his most successful English performance to be *The gloomy night is gathering fast.* On the other hand, in *The Whistle* and more especially in portions of *The Jolly Beggars,* the poet displays a command of the rapid, uproarious, anapaestic measure, so popular in England, for which a dismal failure like *No Churchman am I* had scarcely prepared us.

The models which best served Burns's turn for poetry other than what is lyrical, were the old favourites of the Scots vernacular muse with their distinctive cadences and measures. We have the octave with three rhymes in *Mary Morison* and *The Lament,* though in the latter the vocabulary and idiom are English, or, at all events, not Scots, and the total effect is consequently something artificial. The easier octave with four rhymes is well exemplified in the *Address to the Unco Guid* and the *Epistle to a Young Friend.* We have the elaborate, ambitious, and spirited metre of *The Cherry and the Slae* in *The Epistle to Davie,* which is inferior to Ramsay's *Vision,* and (employed to infinitely better purpose) in some portions of the *recitativo* in *The Jolly Beggars.* We have the modernised form of the *Christis Kirk* stanza, with its characteristic "bobwheel," in such admirable descriptive pieces as *The Holy Fair, The Ordination,* and *Hallowe'en.* We have fresh, fluent, and eminently vigorous octosyllabics in *The Twa Dogs, The Death and Dying Words of poor Mailie,* and *Tam o' Shanter.* And, lastly, we have the six-line stave with two rhymes, associated with *Habbie Simson,* which was unquestionably Burns's favourite measure. In this are composed most of his *Epistles* to and elegies upon various personages—the *Address to the Deil, The Auld Farmer's New Year morning Salutation to his Auld Mare Maggie, To a Louse, Death and Dr. Hornbook,* the *Address to a Haggis, On the late Captain Grose's peregrinations through Scotland, Holy Willie's Prayer*—in short all the pieces, apart from the lyrics, *Tam o' Shanter,* and *The Jolly Beggars,* which would probably be selected by nine persons out of ten as most patently typical of Burns's achievement in poetry. As for the lyrics, their range and variety of rhythm and measure are limited only by those of the airs to which they had to be accommodated.

There is scarce an emotion adapted for expression in lyrical poetry which is not represented somewhere or other among the songs of Burns. He showered his compositions as the fancy took him upon his correspondents—upon Mrs. Dunlop, upon Johnson, upon Thomson, as the case might be—with all the unconsciousness of their comparative merits which sometimes characterises prolific genius. Now, his contribution would be some frigid poem in the classical vein, without a hint of the "lyrical cry;" now it would be some exquisite and flawless gem, compact in the crucible of his brain from the fragments of some half-forgotten, and not over-decent, traditional stave. Thus it is that, even if we lay aside so much of his work as may be set down for best and second-best, contenting ourselves with the *very* best only, the volume of his lyrical production is as remarkable in bulk as it is extensive in scope. If we attempt a rough classification of the moods which here find utterance, we shall find that there are the two Burnses: Burns *qui pleure,* and Burns *qui rit,* though perhaps the one is never far apart from the other. The unaffected, yet artful, tenderness of lyrics like *Ye Banks and Braes,* and *My Luve is like a red, red rose,* can never fail to captivate; the noble melancholy of *Go fetch to me a pint of wine,* or *It was a' for our rightfu' King;* must needs ever "echo in the heart and be present in the memory."

> Now a' is done that men can do,
>   And a' is done in vain,
> My Love and Native Land fareweel
>   For I maun cross the main,
>   My dear—
>   For I maun cross the main.
>
> He turned him right and round about
>   Upon the Irish shore,
> And gae his bridle-reins a shake,
>   With adieu for evermore,
>   My dear—
>   Adieu for evermore.

What "amatory lay" was ever more graceful and melodious than *Mary Morison*—so manifestly the superior of her Highland namesake whether in earth or heaven?

> Yestreen, when to the trembling string
>   The dance gaed thro' the lighted ha',
> To thee my fancy took its wing,
>   I sat, but neither heard or saw;
>   Tho' this was fair and that was braw,
> An' yon the toast of a' the town,
>   I sigh'd and said amang them a':—
> Ye are na Mary Morison!

Of what is deservedly the most famous of Burns's lyrics there is little to be said.

> Had we never lov'd sae kindly,
> Had we never lov'd sae blindly,
> Never met—or never parted—
> We had ne'er been broken-hearted.

The world of those competent to form an opinion has long been unanimous in ranking this "superb groan" of despair with the choicest work of Catullus. Yet it may be allowable to refer to it, *par parenthèse,* as a complete refutation of the idea that the success of a poet's exertions depends in any way upon the degree in which he himself at the moment of composition experiences the emotions to which he gives voice. If ever any snatch of song was informed with "sincerity," in the technical sense of the word, it is *Ae fond kiss and then we sever.* If ever any love affair bore all the marks of insincerity and affectation on both sides, it is Burns's flirtation with Mrs. M'Lehose, the close of which inspired those verses as surely as its inception inspired the sixteen lines of ineptitude which we know as *Clarinda, mistress of my soul.* Truly, the wind of genius bloweth where it listeth, and whether, to use a phrase of Burns's, the "bosom" of the bard is "strongly interested" or not in what he writes about, appears to make uncommonly little difference in the ultimate result.

It is not, however, one may trust, presumptuous to indicate a preference for the Burns *qui rit* before his more gloomy brother, or to find an even higher intensity of genius in the lyrics in which life is viewed in a more cheerful and less despondent aspect. William Nicol was, as we have said, a detestable fellow, but assuredly *Willie brewed a peck of maut* is the prince of all drinking songs of its type.

> It is the moon, I ken her horn,
>   That's blinking in the lift sae hie:
> She shines sae bright to wyle us hame,
>   But, by my sooth, she'll wait a wee!
>
> *Chorus:*
>
> We are na fou, we're nae that fou,
>   But just a drappie in our e'e!
> The cock may craw, the day may daw,
>   And aye we'll taste the barley-bree!

The frame of mind in which a man may justly be said to be—

>   glorious,
> O'er all the ills of life victorious,

has never been depicted with such inimitable precision and spirit. Many and beautiful, if sometimes a little artificial and exotic, are the songs which the collapse of the Jacobite movement called into being; but not one is there more manly, more redolent of the Borders, than *Kenmure's on and awa'.*

> Here's him that's far awa', Willie,
>   Here's him that's far awa'!
> And here's the flower that I lo'e best—
>   The rose that's like the snaw!

Yet it is, perhaps, when we approach what he might have called a more tender theme that the bard excels himself; nor should we quarrel with any one who chose to maintain that his most glorious triumphs in the field of lyric verse are—not *My Nanie, O* (infinitely superior as it is to

Ramsay's version with its abominable "bagnio"), nor yet *Bonnie Lesley,* which it is difficult to praise too highly, but—*Corn Rigs* and (in a somewhat different vein) *Green grow the rashes, O.* Here is the whole of the latter, "faked" from Heaven alone knows what fragments of ancient sculduddery:—

Chorus:

> Green grow the rashes, O;
> Green grow the rashes, O;
> The sweetest hours that e'er I spend,
> Are spent among the lasses, O.

I.

> There's nought but care on ev'ry han',
> In every hour that passes, O:
> What signifies the life o' man,
> An' 'twere na for the lasses, O?

II.

> The war'ly race may riches chase,
> An' riches still may fly them, O:
> An' tho' at last they catch them fast,
> Their hearts can ne'er enjoy them, O.

III.

> But gie me a cannie hour at e'en,
> My arms about my dearie, O,
> An' war'ly cares an' war'ly men
> May a' gae tapsalteerie, O.

IV.

> For you sae douce ye sneer at this;
> Ye're nought but senseless asses, O;
> The wisest man the warl' e'er saw,
> He dearly lov'd the lasses, O.

V.

> Auld nature swears, the lovely dears
> Her noblest work she classes, O;
> Her 'prentice han' she try'd on man,
> An' then she made the lasses, O.

And here is the last stanza of *Corn Rigs:*—

> I hae been blythe with comrades dear;
> I hae been merry drinking;
> I hae been joyfu' gath'rin gear;
> I hae been happy thinking.
> But a' the pleasures e'er I saw
> Tho' three times doubl'd fairly—
> That happy night was worth them a',
> Amang the rigs o' barley.

> Corn rigs, an' barley rigs,
> An' corn rigs are bonnic;

> I'll ne'er forget that happy night
> Amang the rigs wi' Annie.

In both these songs—and both, it must be remembered, were the work of years prior to the visit to Edinburgh and the *Musical Museum*—we have Burns, the Scots peasant, and Burns, the inspired song-writer, in their most characteristic moments: humour, playfulness, high spirits in the one, passion *plus* the infinite capacity for pleasure in the other, and consummate art in both, combining to produce a whole, the precise equivalent of which no other country in the world can show.

For vivid narrative, for graphic description, for insight into character, for the power of judging men at a glance, for wide sympathy and deep penetration, the intense concentration of the lyric affords little or no scope. For these and the like excellences we must turn to Burns's other poems, nor shall we turn in vain. Occasionally, no doubt, he displays a weakness for what may be called petty pathos—the *Mouse* and the *Daisy* are two instances of the failing, and they have, of course, entranced the hearts of that less intelligent section of Burns *amateurs,* who would be much shocked to hear that neither of these exercises can for one moment compare with the *Louse.* But the true test for the *Mouse* and the *Daisy* is some piece like the *Death of Poor Mailie;* or the *Elegy* on that most celebrated of ewes; or, perhaps best of all, the *Auld Farmer to his Auld Mare.* Every one of these three pieces is wholly delightful: instinct with humour, with kindliness, with humanity. But the *Mouse* and the *Daisy* in comparison are instinct with nothing save a feeble and even sickly sentimentality. The *Salutation* expresses what thousands of men must have felt in a vague way on such an occasion as that postulated, but what they could never have given articulate expression to even in the most shambling prose. It is a striking example of the particular raised to the universal—of familiar things made new. But neither the *Mouse* nor the *Daisy* expresses what any ploughman ever felt, nor even what Burns ever felt. All that *they* express is what a ploughman might have desired to feel, if, living in the last quarter of the eighteenth century, he had aspired to live up to the character of a poet. And consequently they need trouble us no longer, having served their turn as convenient foils for setting off the beauties of better poems than themselves.

> My poor toop-lamb, my son an' heir,
> O, bid him breed him up wi' care!
> An' if he live to be a beast,
> To pit some havins in his breast!
> An' warn him—what I winna name—
> To stay content wi' yowes at hame;
> An' no to rin an' wear his cloots,
> Like other menseless, graceless brutes.

> An' niest my yowie, silly thing;
> Gude keep thee frae a tether string!
> O, may thou ne'er forgather up,
> Wi' ony blastit, moorland toop;
> But ay keep mind to moop an' mell
> Wi' sheep o' credit like thysel!

An' now, my bairns, wi' my last breath,
I lea'e a blessin' wi you baith:
An' when you think upo' your mither,
Mind to be kind to ane anither.

I wat she was a sheep o' sense,
An' could behave hersel' wi' mense:
I'll say't, she never brak a fence
    Thro' thievish greed.
Our Bardie, lanely, keeps the spence,
    Sin Mailie's dead.

Or, if he wanders up the howe,
Her livin' image in her yowe
Comes bleatin' till him, owre the knowe,
    For bits o' bread;
An' down the briny pearlies rowe
    For Mailie dead.

She was nae get o' moorlan tips,
Wi' tawted ket, an' hairy hips;
For her forbears were brought in ships
    Frae 'yont the Tweed;
A bonnier fleesh ne'er crossed the clips
    Than Mailie's dead.

Wae worth the man wha first did shape
That vile, wanchancie thing—a rape!
It makes guid fellows girn an' gape,
    Wi chokin dread;
An' Robin's bonnet wave wi' crape
    For Mailie dead.

In the epigram Burns is almost invariably trivial and ineffective. In satire, on the other hand, when he "lets himself go," he is terrible and overwhelming. His quarrel with the Kirk was a bitter one; but there is something more than ordinarily pungent and envenomed in *Holy Willie's Prayer.* Never, in all probability, has so tremendous an invective against Calvinism, or rather anti-nomianism, been launched by an enemy of that scheme of thought. Here are a few stanzas:—

I bless and praise Thy matchless might,
When thousands Thou hast left in night,
That I am here before Thy sight,
    For gifts an' grace
A burning and a shining light
    To a' this place.

What was I, or my generation,
That I should get sic exaltation.
I, wha deserv'd most just damnation
    For broken laws
Sax thousand years ere my creation
    Thro' Adam's cause!

When from my mither's womb I fell,
Thou might hae plunged me deep in hell,
To gnash my gooms, and weep, and wail,
    In burning lakes,
Whare damnèd devils roar and yell,

Chained to their stakes.

Yet I am here, a chosen sample,
To show Thy grace is great and ample;
I'm here a pillar o' Thy temple,
    Strong as a rock,
A guide, a buckler, an example
    To a' thy flock!

Here is the teaching of David Hume brought down from the closet "into the street" with a vengeance! Yet perhaps Burns's animus against the ecclesiastical tyranny which still prevailed in the West of Scotland, is not less felicitous in expression when it finds vent in the species of sardonic raillery of which, in common with Ramsay and Fergusson, he possessed a fine gift. Descriptive satire is unquestionably a *genre* in which he excelled, as *The Holy Fair* and *The Ordination* bear witness, and the revolt against the theology of the high-flyers is no less thorough-going when it finds expression in the pleasant jocosity of the *Address to the Deil,* than when it appears stripped of all disguise in the panoply of war. When the perturbing theological element is eliminated, his delineations of manners and his judgments on men are equally remarkable. *Death and Dr. Hornbook,* which is at bottom nothing but a fragment of parochial satire, is so transfigured by his genius that it has delighted thousands who neither knew nor cared that its victim was a certain John Wilson, school-master of Tarbolton. *Hallowe'en* is a consummate picture of a state of society and of modes of thought and feeling which the "march of progress" has, it may be, rather smothered than destroyed; but probably Burns's wisest, as it is his most kindly, pronouncement on the life of the community around him is *The Twa Dogs.* In what excellent keeping is this sketch of the rural festivities incident to the New Year!—

That merry day the year begins,
They bar the door on frosty win's;
The nappy reeks wi' mantling ream,
An' sheds a heart-inspiring steam;
The luntin' pipe, and sneeshin' mill,
Are handed round wi' right guid will;
The cantie auld folks crackin crouse,
The young anes rantin' through the house,
My heart has been sae fain to see them,
That I for joy hae barkit wi' them

Place alongside of this the wonderfully accurate picture of the Scottish landed gentry of the time:—

O would they stay aback frae courts,
An' please themsels wi' countra sports,
It wad for every ane be better,
The laird, the tenant, an' the cotter!
For they frank, rantin', ramblin' billies,
Fient haet o' them's ill-hearted fellows:
Except for breakin o' their timmer,
Or speakin' lightly o' their limmer,
Or shootin' of a hare or moor-cock,
The ne'er-a-bit they're ill to poor folk.

Such a passage is worth a hundred of the full-dress denunciations of Luxury (with a capital L) in which Burns occasionally thought it his duty to indulge, or of those vehement assertions of the equality of the peasant and the laird, to which the progress of the French Revolution held out so tempting an inducement.

It remains to speak of what will probably be admitted to be Burns's two masterpieces, and in dealing with acknowledged masterpieces the critic's best policy is to be brief. *Tam o' Shanter* is perhaps the most popular of all the poet's writings, apart from those in the sentimental vein, and the preference awarded to it is not surprising. Even a very dull man can hardly escape taking some of its good points, and though we may question whether an Englishman is ever able to extract the very last drop of enjoyment from this, or from any other, piece in the Scots vernacular, its spirit and hilarity are so contagious that no one will surely refuse to be made merry. Subject it to the trying ordeal of being "spouted" by the common village reciter (in whose repertory it always finds a prominent place), and it will emerge triumphant: unspoilt even by *his* resolute efforts to vulgarise and to mar. The drinking at the tavern, the ride home, the orgy in the church, the wild pursuit, the ultimate escape—each scene, each episode, is described with inexpressible vividness and enthusiasm; and each is so well proportioned and adjusted that the artist's supreme success lies in the piece as a whole as much as in any one of its constituent parts. For this reason it has been thought well to offer here no excerpt, not even the lines which lead up to Tam's imprudent exclamation of applause. Truly Francis Grose never did a better day's work than when he engaged Burns to write this "pretty tale," as he calls it, for his *Antiquities of Scotland* (1789-91).

The inherent force and overpowering spirit of *The Folly Beggars* are perhaps sufficient to account for the inferior popularity of that "cantata" as compared with *Tam o' Shanter*. Had Burns swerved for one moment from the path of true craftsmanship, had he relaxed the severity of the artist and emitted the smallest whine of sentiment, had he dowered any one of his marvellous gallery of mendicants and mumpers with those virtues which draw the tear to the eye and the snuffle to the nose, *The Folly Beggars* might have stood first in the hearts of its author's countrymen as securely as it does in the estimation of those best qualified to form an opinion. But Burns was loyal to his artistic instincts, and consequently the rank and file of his adorers, while paying the usual quota of lip-service, are puzzled, and do not quite know what to make of a piece which Scott pronounced to be, "for humorous description and nice discrimination of character," "inferior to no poem of the same length in the whole range of English poetry." The collection of lyrics, each assigned to an appropriate personage, is declared by the same high authority to be unparalleled in the English language. To expand or amplify such eulogy were impertinent. Yet we may call attention to the extraordinary *crescendo* movement of the little drama as one of its most striking characteristics. From a splendid start, it goes on

getting better and better, and wilder and wilder, until at length it culminates in that astonishing finale which fairly takes the reader's breath away. Here, after all, it is impossible to help feeling, is the mood which Burns expresses more adequately, more completely than any other—the spirit of rebellion against "law, order, discipline," the reckless self-assertion of the natural man who would fain, if he could, be a law unto himself, that violent revolt against the trammels and conventions of society, which may indeed win a temporary success, but is sure in the long run to be extinguished by the indomitable fact that man is a "social" animal. It is this mood that underlies the spirited piece of inverted snobbery, known as *A man's a man for a' that*; it is this mood that animates *M'Pherson's Farewell*, with its glorious refrain—

> Sae rantingly, sae wantonly,
>   Sae dauntingly gaed he,
> He play'd a spring, and danc'd it round
>   Beneath the gallows-tree;

It is this mood that breaks out with a cry of fierce defiance in that marvellous glorification of illicit love:—

> O, wha my babie-clouts will buy?
> O, wha will tent me when I cry?
> Wha will kiss me where I lie?—
>   The rantin dog, the daddie o't!
>
> O, wha will own he did the faut?
> O, wha will buy the groanin maut?
> O, wha will tell me how to ca't?
>   The rantin dog, the daddie o't!

Finally, it is this mood that finds its crowning and eternal triumph of expression in the conclusion of *The Folly Beggars*:—

> So sung the Bard, and Nansie's wa's
> Shook with a thunder of applause,
>   Re-echoed from each mouth!
> They toom'd their pocks, they pawn'd their
>   duds,
> They scarcely left to coor their fuds,
>   To quench their lowin drouth.
> Then owre again the jovial thrang
>   The Poet did request
> To lowse his pack, an' wale a sang,
>   A ballad o' the best:
> He rising, rejoicing
>   Between his twa Deborahs,
> Looks round him, an' found them
>   Impatient for the chorus—

> *Air.*

> I.

> See the smoking bowl before us!
>   Mark our jovial, ragged ring!
> Round and round take up the chorus,
>   And in raptures let us sing:

Chorus.

A fig for those by law protected!
    Liberty's a glorious feast,
Courts for cowards were erected,
    Churches built to please the priest!

II.

What is title, what is treasure,
    What is reputation's care?
If we lead a life of pleasure,
    'Tis no matter how or where.

III.

With the ready trick and fable
    Round we wander all the day.
And at night in barn or stable
    Hug our doxies on the hay.

IV.

Does the train-attended carriage
    Thro' the country lighter rove?
Does the sober bed of marriage
    Witness brighter scenes of love?

V.

Life is all a variorum,
    We regard not how it goes;
Let them prate about decorum
    Who have character to lose.

VI.

Here's to budgets, bags, and wallets!
    Here's to all the wandering train!
Here's our ragged brats and callets!
    One and all, cry out, Amen!

Chorus.

A fig for those by law protected!
    Liberty's a glorious feast,
Courts for cowards were erected,
    Churches built to please the priest!

Such, then, is the work of Burns, after whose death, as has been already remarked, the vernacular muse of Scotland may also be said to have fallen into a decline. Robert Tannahill (1774-1810), it is true, whose local reputation has always outrun his deserts, wrote some tolerable songs, like *Fessie the Flower of Dunblane*; Scott turned out a few poetical pieces of rare merit in the Scots tongue; Hogg . . . had his periods of inspiration; and one or two writers, of whom Bozzy's son, the ill-fated Sir Alexander Boswell (1775-1822) may serve for an example, occasionally worked the traditional humorous vein of Scottish song with happy results. But though vigorous attempts have been made to galvanise the muse into the semblance

of life, it is plain to all with an eye to see or an ear to hear that she is as dead as dead can be; and it seems a tolerably safe prophecy to predict that no fruit worth the trouble of picking and preserving will now ever be yielded by the fertile and long-lived national tradition of poetry which was summed up and perfected in Robert Burns.

THE SCOTTISH AUGUSTANS

A. M. Oliver

SOURCE: "The Scottish Augustans," in *Scottish Poetry: A Critical Survey,* edited by James Kinsley, Cassell and Company Ltd., 1955, pp. 119-49.

[*In the following essay, Oliver discusses eighteenth-century Scottish poetry written in English, faulting its didacticism and conventionality, and praising its original treatment of supernatural themes.*]

The eighteenth-century Scots who wrote English verse, but little or no verse in Scots, are described conveniently by the title of this [essay]—conveniently, but inaccurately. In the sense in which Horace or Pope was Augustan, in poise, clear self-knowledge and serene self-esteem, in mastery of technique and consummate propriety of expression, in a word, in classical perfection, there are no Scottish Augustans. Nor are there many English. The eighteenth-century critics were the first to note the unsatisfactory character of eighteenth-century poetry:

But not to one in this benighted age
    Is that diviner inspiration giv'n,
That burns in Shakespeare's or in Milton's page,
    The pomp and prodigality of heav'n.
        [Thomas Gray, "Stanzas to Mr. Bentley"]

Johnson voices Gray's lament more temperately, but no less decisively [in *The Life of Samuel Johnson* (1904)]: 'There was no poetry, nothing that towered above the common mark.' The nineteenth century, reacting violently, disliked its predecessor without much discrimination. The more dispassionate and painstaking studies of our own time modify the familiar picture, here and there, in detail, but leave it essentially unchanged. One emerges from an open-minded reading of [*The Works of English Poets* (1810), edited by Alexander Chalmers,] with a confirmed impression of immense copiousness and limited inspiration—'Though few can write, yet fewer can refrain'. Trivial themes were handled without urgency. Turning a copy of verses was a social accomplishment, and if the verses had a recognizable origin in Latin poetry, so much the better. Classical authority sanctioned the 'kinds'—epic, didactic, pastoral—which were cultivated side by side with the more congenial and adaptable satire and epistle. The authority of the classics was supported by the immense weight and prestige of Pope. Beside his splendid achievement the efforts of the 'rebels'—Lady Winchilsea, Akenside, even Collins—are slight and fragmentary. Devitalized and mechanical classicism, abortive and spurious romanticism—to how much verse of the period do these discouraging terms apply! They apply to verse by both Scots and English; but the Scots had, in addition, disadvantages peculiar to themselves.

Augustan poetry is central and metropolitan. The Scottish writers of the eighteenth century, drawn along that 'noblest prospect' by the centripetal force of London, were drawn too late; they had spent their formative and impressionable years far from the circumference of wit. Their origins lay in another country, and this marks their verse both for good and bad.

Geography, common sense and expediency triumphed, in the Union of 1707, over history and sentiment. Sentiment had been more accurately reflected in the Act of Security and the Alien Act, passed, by Scotland and by England respectively, not three years before they became, in law but not in love, a United Kingdom. Swift greeted the Act of Union with contempt:

Blest revolution! which creates
Divided hearts, united states!
See how the double nation lies;
Like a rich coat with skirts of frize.

Poverty was indeed the chief Scottish motive for union, and Thomson, in so frequently celebrating British wealth and commerce, is sensibly enjoying the mess of pottage for which a birthright had been paid. The Scots had little else with which to pay. Their blend of poverty with pride had long been disliked by the English, but Skelton, in attacking it, had the advantage of detesting an enemy. The eighteenth-century Englishman, beholding it on nearer view, was not less repelled. Poverty had prevented travel and intercourse in the early, impressionable years. It had not, as would have been the case in England, prevented formal education. Had it done so, the Scots might have stayed at home, or filtered quietly south to fulfil humble and unassuming rôles in the rigidly stratified society of eighteenth-century England. In fact, the Scots who crossed the Border tended to be able men of sound education and narrow culture and experience, whose blend of pride and poverty, self-assurance and self-distrust, was unfamiliar and disconcerting. They were regarded as foreigners, and, in their mutual support and admiration, their haunting of the 'Breetish' coffeehouse, as foreigners they acted. The London Scottish displayed a team spirit which was natural but tactless. Their speech was not English, but it was close enough to it to irritate rather than to endear.

They felt their identity, and unluckily they showed it. The feeling of separateness was intensified by regret. Arbuthnot's *A Sermon preach'd to the people at the Mercat-Cross of Edinburgh; on the subject of the Union* is cool and rational. It explains succinctly to the Scots what solid advantages they will reap, what illusory shadows they sacrifice. Arbuthnot himself is consistently pleased. His family history, his success and popularity, his happy and adaptable nature ensured this. But throughout the century there is audible an undertone of sadness. It is more than an undertone in John Ramsay's final words on Dundas of Arniston. 'He left it to younger men to bow to the Dagon of English taste. Though Scotland had lost its rank among the nations, he could say, as the Trojan did of his country after the fall, "Fuimus Troes, fuit Ilium et ingens gloria Teucrorum."' The least sentimental were moved, at times, to mourn the end of an auld sang. Smollett refers unemotionally in his prose to North Britain, but, when *facit indignatio versum*, he names his verse *The Tears of Scotland*. 'Butcher' Cumberland on the one hand, Bute and his placemen on the other, helped to increase the strain of which Churchill's satire and Johnson's *obiter dicta* are merely the most amusing and celebrated evidences. Of course, there were personal friendships; no one was more charming to individual Scots than Johnson was. But one can love a sinner while not ceasing to hate the sin. Before Walter Scott made of the national marriage of convenience a friendly, tolerant and civilized companionship, a century of uneasy adjustment and hearty dislike was to elapse.

This was an unfavourable atmosphere for poetry, especially for Augustan poetry, which is so largely a social growth, depending on and addressed to an audience of equals. The Scot, writing in this atmosphere, was further handicapped by writing in a language which was not his mother-tongue. To say so is easy; fully to realize the fact, and its implications, is not so easy. To the educated Scot of the early and mid-century, who used the dialect in all his familiar relationships, who lectured in and listened to Latin on formal occasions, English was not even a second but actually a third language. It was deliberately learned, chiefly by study of the *Tatler,* the *Spectator* and the *Guardian.* 'Those admirable papers prepared the minds of our countrymen for the study of the best English authors, without a competent knowledge of which no man was accounted a polite scholar'. Ramsay goes on to say [in *Scotland and Scotsmen in the Eighteenth Century* (1888)] that to render the dialect 'polished and correct would have been a Herculean labour, not likely to procure them much renown. Nothing, therefore, remained but to write classical English, which, though exceedingly difficult to men who spoke their mother-tongue without disguise, was greatly facilitated by the enthusiastic ardour with which they studied the best English authors.' The distinction drawn between classical English and the mother-tongue is vital to an understanding of the Scottish Augustans. They acquired English as Wordsworth acquired Greek and Latin. His view of the process, and its results, is relevant and illuminating:

In fine,
I was a better judge of thoughts than words,
Misled in estimating words, not only
By common inexperience of youth,
But by the trade in classic niceties,
The dangerous craft of culling term and phrase
From languages that want the living voice
To carry meaning to the natural heart;
To tell us what is passion, what is truth,
What reason, what simplicity and sense.

[*The Prelude*]

Their prose models were excellent, and the Scots learned to write good English prose. 'The Scotch write English wonderfully well,' Johnson commented in sending thanks to Dr. Blair for his sermons. One need look no further than Burns's letters (not, of course, his stilted and pretentious letters to Clarinda) for proof of this. But it was the result of constant vigilance. 'In all their essays at composition, it behoved them to avoid everything that could be called a Scotticism or solecism.' Intelligence, care and enthusiasm did much, but they could not defeat nature. Lord Mansfield told Alexander Carlyle that when he read Hume and Robertson 'he did not think he was reading English.'

One cannot doubt that the effort to attain an English prose style was right and necessary. The 'literature of knowledge' must be expressed with as little obstruction as possible, as much lucidity. The eighteenth-century Scots were responding, as the English had done in the sixties of the seventeenth century—and for much the same reasons—to 'the imperious need of a fit prose'. But constant watchfulness, nervous fear of the instinctive and spontaneous phrase, uneasy unfamiliarity and reference to the dictionary (Boswell even consults it in writing his love letters!) make an atmosphere unpropitious to poetry. The living word of 'race' and character is struck out in favour of the safe one. The temptation to write about it and about is overwhelming: many words will surely include the right one. Sometimes they do so, but the result is usually tiresome and distracting over-painting. The writing of familiar verse is impossible in an unfamiliar tongue, and the Scots poets give us little corresponding to the easy, natural verse of Swift or Prior. Burns in his verse epistles, even Beattie in 'To Mr. Alexander Ross', show how admirably they could do it in dialect. Their native fun and humour, so characteristic of their *native* verse, is paralysed by the strain of writing English. [Burns writes in the letter to G. Thomson of October 19, 1794]: 'These English Songs gravel me to death.—I have not that command of the language that I have of my native tongue.' Burns does not merely state the problem; he illustrates the strangling effect in his passages of English verse—'A Winter Night' might have been specially written to display the contrast between the quick and the dead. What is bad in Burns is worse in Beattie, Smollett, Wilkie—all his many compatriots so incomparably less gifted with poetic power. To neglect the mother-tongue is to attain frigidity, or rhetoric, or dull tameness. The appropriate criterion of the Scottish Augustan verse is not, perhaps, the English verse of contemporary Englishmen, but their *poemata*.

In a study on this scale it would be pointless to resurrect what is dead, and what indeed never had genuine life, whether it be conventional inanity, like the mechanical lyrics which so strangely contrast, in Smollett's novels, with the vital prose of their context, or whether it be the painful effort of misdirected zeal, like Wilkie's classical epic on the siege of Thebes. Nothing would be easier or more entertaining—at least for the writer—than to poke fun at Wilkie's *Epigoniad*—and nothing could be more useless. It is bad, and everyone has always thought so, except for the Dundas clique who seized it as a stick to beat John Home, and for David Hume, who largely confines himself to retelling the story more clearly than Wilkie does, and whose description of it as 'a performance which may, perhaps, be regarded as one of the ornaments of our language' is remarkable for its judicious qualifying word. The writer devoid of poetic gift, who nevertheless wrote verse for exercise or amusement, offers only the interest of curiosity—and this will be sufficient notice of Boswell's verse output, such as 'The Cub, at Newmarket: a Tale', the undergraduate wit of his metrical effusions to Andrew Erskine, or his nightly five couplets in Holland. But the Scottish Augustans include not merely poetasters. Some were poets, and this preliminary view of the common predicament may help towards an understanding of the imperfect and unsatisfactory nature of much of their work.

Most of the defects and virtues of these Scottish poets are apparent in Thomson. His 'outset', to borrow one of Ramsay's favourite terms, was typical—a son of the manse, a manse set in the austere and beautiful Border countryside, he found

> Caledonia stern and wild,
> Meet nurse for a poetic child.

He was fifteen before he left Southdean for Edinburgh University, to study classics and theology, and almost twenty-five before he left Scotland for London. In Edinburgh he had belonged to a club for the study of English. In London he was helped by friendly Scots. The pattern of education, poverty, courage, ambition, emigration and success is familiar, although Macpherson and Beattie visit England after achieving success, and Blair, Wilkie and Blacklock remain in Scotland. But, in intention and aspiration at least,

> Frae the cottar to the laird
> We a' rin South.
> [Beattie, "To Mr. Alexander Ross"]

Thomson met with immediate recognition (there were four editions of *Winter* in 1726) and a widespread popularity which lasted throughout the century and beyond. This popularity sprang from his tactful blending of the familiar with the strange. The themes which Wordsworth was to present in their own right are served by Thomson as dressings rather than as main dishes. His autobiographical references, for example, are rare and brief. We read of his cheerful morn of youth by the banks of Jed, and wish he had told us more. It is possible to feel that Wordsworth has told us more than we desire or deserve. The contemporary reader who opened *The Seasons* found nothing to startle or repel. He found a descriptive and meditative poem which acknowledged its debt to the *Georgics* and to 'Pomona's bard' (and was indeed written, like Philips's *Cider*, in blank verse, which, being '*English* Heroic Verse without Rime', was clearly appropriate where the ultimate model was in hexameters). He found, too, something not unlike *Coopers Hill, Claremont* and *Windsor Forest*, majestically defined by Johnson [in his *Lives of the Poets* (1779-81)] as '*local poetry*, of which the fundamental subject is some particular landscape, to be poetically described, with the addition of such embellishments as may be supplied by historical retrospection, or incidental meditation.' Thomson's 'particular landscapes' are many, his survey is global rather than local, but the rest of the definition beautifully covers *The Seasons.* The 'embellishments' are added with a hand so ungrudging that the poem becomes a miscellany—and the eighteenth century loved miscellanies.

The groundwork is of course natural description, and in the context of Wordsworth's undisputed dictum that 'excepting the nocturnal Reverie of Lady Winchilsea, and a passage or two in the "Windsor Forest" of Pope, the poetry of the period intervening between the publication of the "Paradise Lost" and the "Seasons" does not contain a single new image of external nature' [Wordsworth, "Essay, Supplementary to the Preface"], one may realize the novelty and attraction of the poem. The familiar—the revolution of the year, the effects of the changing seasons on every form of life—is presented with fidelity. The truth of Thomson's descriptions is a critical truism. His memory was stored with closely observed images; his familiar scenes are full of life and movement. Imagination supplements these with others which are sometimes, as in the incident of Sir Hugh Willoughby's ship icebound in the Arctic seas (*Winter,* ll. 925-35), powerfully rendered.

This incident is a very favourable specimen of another ingredient of Thomson's mixture, the inserted tales. Like the narrative papers which diversified the contemporary periodical essay, these gratified the universal love of a story. Thomson's tales, diffuse and sentimental, are in the sharpest contrast with Pope's. The story of Sir Balaam is *merum sal;* only the reader who knows the Book of Job will fully realize its point and power, and the implication of its climax, 'sad Sir Balaam curses God'. Thomson's stories can be read with relaxed attention, and their point—such as it is—is obvious. Easy and undemanding reading, they gave mild and widespread pleasure for a time. They appeared in anthologies. The story of Palemon and Lavinia, for example (*Autumn,* ll. 177-310), was one of Goldsmith's *Beauties of English Poesy,* though Goldsmith claims little responsibility for this: 'It is rather given here for being much esteemed by the public, than the editor.' Wordsworth attributes much of Thomson's popularity to these tales. 'In any well-used copy of the "Seasons" the book generally opens of itself with the rhapsody on love, or with one of the stories (perhaps "Damon and Musidora").' If the celebrated copy found in the inn at Linton thus opened of itself, there may have been some irony in Coleridge's exclamation, '*That* is true fame!'

The sugary flavour of the tales is offset by the more solid fare of Thomson's learning. His interest in Newtonian physics is deep and genuine, he *knows* how natural appearances are created, and he loves to instruct his reader. 'The swain' wonders at the bright enchantment of the rainbow, but Thomson knows its woof, its texture:

> Here, awful Newton, the dissolving clouds

> Form, fronting on the sun, thy showery prism;
> And to the sage-instructed eye unfold
> The various twine of light, by thee disclosed
> From the white mingling maze.

Thomson had already treated the subject in *A Poem, Sacred to the Memory of Sir Isaac Newton,* where thirty lines of accurate description of the composition of the rainbow reach a climax in 'How just, how beauteous, the *refractive law.*' The catalogue of spring flowers contains a botanical note:

> From family diffused
> To family, as flies the father-dust,
> The varied colours run.

To the cause of instruction Thomson sacrifices much—too much. With

> Sudden the fields
> Put on their winter-robe of purest white

he had evoked a visual image of the swift transformation wrought by snow; it was the simple, the inspired stroke of an artist. But it gave no information about the function of snow, so the image was blurred in favour of 'The cherished fields'. In the description of the hunted hare he spoils a passage of simple and vivid writing by one didactic touch:

> The fallow ground laid open to the sun
> Concoctive.

The poet had fixed our attention on the plight of the hare; we can only resent the interference of the scientist.

Thomson is a preacher as well as a teacher:

> These, as they change, Almighty Father! these
> Are but the varied God. The rolling year
> Is full of Thee.

His religious feeling is related rather to the dignity and gentlemanliness of Addison than to the emotionalism of Isaac Watts. But Thomson is impressed not only by the spacious firmament on high. He notes

> where gloomily retired
> The villain spider lives, cunning and fierce,
> Mixture abhorred!

He watches the sleeping dogs, and guesses their dreams.

> Nor shall the muse disdain
> To let the little noisy summer-race
> Live in her lay and flutter through her song;
> Not mean though simple.

He accepts them all with affection and appreciation, and is quite unstirred by them to 'thoughts that do often lie too deep for tears'. *His* train of thought is easy enough to follow:

> Behold, fond man!
> See here thy pictured life: pass some few years,
> Thy flowering Spring, thy Summer's ardent
>   strength,
> Thy sober Autumn fading into age,—
> And pale concluding Winter comes at last
> And shuts the scene.

Such thinking is neither original nor profound. It has the qualities which Johnson noted in Gray's *Elegy,* and it helps to explain Thomson's popularity. Beside the awful universality of 'Man that is born of a woman', and the piercing, immediate particularity of 'It is Margaret you mourn for' [G.M. Hopkins, "Spring and Fall"], Thomson's moralizing is conventional and trite. It is politely in keeping with a general poem addressed to the general reader, dedicated to a patron and nicely blended to suit all tastes.

In his choice of theme for his first considerable poem Thomson draws on Scottish tradition. Henryson's description of winter in 'The Preiching of the Swallow', the opening of his *Testament of Cresseid* and Douglas's Prologues are unforgettable in their intensity. They point forward to Burns,

> While winds frae aff Ben Lomond blaw,
> And bar the doors wi' driving snaw,
>   And hing us owre the ingle;

and Thomson, though he has (alas!) denied himself their unfettered expression of elemental feeling, yet writes as one having authority. Winter in Scotland can still be harsh and paralysing; in the eighteenth century 'in the more remote parts of the country, for five or six months in the year, social intercourse was almost impossible'. Smollett comments that 'there is no such convenience as a waggon in this country'—because there was scarcely a road fit to bear wheeled traffic. The effect of winter's rigour was to isolate its victims in small, self-contained groups, thrown each upon itself for mutual comfort and support. The sorrows of each member were shared, in sympathy, by all. Thomson's picture of the shepherd lost in the snow, of his family awaiting him in vain, is based on knowledge and is full of feeling, as are his studies of the sufferings inflicted by winter upon birds and animals. Within the isolated groups an intense social intercourse flourished, all the more precious for the misery without. Beside the brilliance and hilarity of 'The Farmer's Ingle', 'The Jolly Beggars' and 'Tam o' Shanter', Thomson's description of village night-life in winter is decorous, yet it suggests what that life meant to the people, and how rich it must have been in inspiration to the young poet, with its jests and games, its traditional music and dancing, and the 'goblin story' arousing superstitious horror. There is vitality here, in contrast to the preachifying and abstract passage, immediately following, on the city's night life. Thomson's studies of peasant life, slight as they are in bulk, and given neither local habitation nor name, initiate a tradition which includes Gray, Goldsmith and Cowper, and culminates in Wordsworth. With the peasants he associates the supernatural, obviously too crude an element

to be presented directly in the Age of Reason. It is a *shepherd* of the Hebrid Isles who sees the miraculous vision.

Winter brought an intensified and concentrated social life. Further, it threw each man upon his own resources. Thomson's response [in *Testament and Winter*] to the fierce and isolating season recalls Henryson's:

> I mend the fyre, and beikit me about,
> Than tuik ane drink my spreitis to comfort,
> And armit me weill fra the cauld thairout:
> To cut the winter nicht and mak it schort,
> I tuik ane Quair, and left all uther sport.
>
>   Be my retreat
>   . . . . .
> A rural, sheltered, solitary scene,
> Where ruddy fire and beaming tapers join
> To cheer the gloom. There studious let me sit,
> And hold high converse with the mighty dead.

The contrast between them is more significant than the superficial resemblance. Henryson writes in the confidence and power of a native tradition; his 'Quair', moreover, is the mainspring and inspiration of his poem. But Thomson's 'high converse with the mighty dead' is but an excuse for a catalogue of Greek and Roman worthies, a hundred lines long, in the manner of *Liberty*. It is as creditable to the author's reading and general knowledge as it is otiose and irrelevant to his poem.

Summer, Spring and *Autumn* resulted from the success of *Winter,* which is unique in its Scottish character and in the fact that Thomson wrote it with no thought of making up a set. The others are sequels, assembled, if not constructed, after the manner of the prototype. *Summer,* for example, includes an excursion to the tropics, as *Winter* has one to the far North. The poem suffers from its length; matter which in a single 'season' might have passed as relevant is instantly seen to be padding. How far from organic much of it is is clear from Thomson's transferring sections from one 'season' to another. *Winter* is a fair specimen of *The Seasons,* in the variety of its content, its accurate natural description, humanitarian exhortation, anecdotal spicings, classical references, contemporary ideas, moralizing reflections and piety. There is something for everyone, and Thomson fed the appetite he created. For *Winter* may finally be taken as representative in the fact that Thomson revised it unceasingly. The first edition (1726) contained 405 lines; in the first complete edition of *The Seasons* (1730), *Winter* had 781 lines, and in Thomson's final edition (1746) it had 1069. The figures are striking, but only a first-hand comparison of the many editions can give any idea of the nature and extent of Thomson's rewriting. *The Seasons* was a different poem at different times, as Wordsworth found to his satisfaction when he maintained that 'the true characteristics of Thomson's genius as an imaginative poet' were by no means those which were earliest or most widely recognized.

Thomson's fundamental weakness, both in content and in style, is his inability to discriminate. A true Augustan, he is alive to the poet's responsibility to teach, to exhort, to be actively a man of his time. Thus he loads his Muse with luggage so heavy and so awkward that movement is difficult and soaring impossible. *The Castle of Indolence,* which relates the destruction of sensuous pleasure by respectable industry, is a convenient symbol of his whole poetic output. The reader swallows—or skips—the didactic passages of *The Seasons* for the sake of the descriptive; but *Liberty* is a purely didactic poem with narrative illustrations. In the tradition of Addison's *A Letter from Italy,* the first three parts provide a condensed classical education, a synopsis of the history and culture of Greece, with a sermon on the reasons for its decay and fall, an approving précis of early Roman history with moralizings on Patience, Hope, Moderation and Independence. The history of Britain, with its extremely unfavourable view of the Stuarts and its adulation of William III—'Than hero more, the patriot of mankind!'—makes the reader feel that it was lucky for Thomson that Johnson so early desisted from his perusal of *Liberty.*

Part V is a summary and restatement of Thomson's purpose, a lecture on the excellence of the British constitution:

> Then was the full, the perfect plan disclos'd
> Of Britain's matchless constitution, mixt
> Of mutual checking and supporting powers,
> King, lords and commons.

Only luxury can hurt it:

> Britons! be firm!—nor let corruption sly
> Twine round your heart indissoluble chains!

For luxury, 'Rapacious, cruel, mean, Mother of vice', caused the fall of Rome and its 'softer shackles' destroyed Venice. Like the preacher on sin, Thomson is 'agin' luxury. It is the peroration of *Britannia,*

> Oh, let not then waste Luxury impair
> That manly soul of toil,

and the burden (in every sense) of *Liberty,* whom he invokes at the close of Part I:

> While I, to nobler than poetic fame
> Aspiring, thy commands to Britons bear.

This is an explicit admission that Thomson has served two masters, and has preferred one of them to poetry. Poetry has taken its revenge.

Thomson's patriotic zeal for industry and commerce, which fills such vast tracts of his work, has one permanent memorial. Britons may no longer read his injunction to venerate the plough, or gratify themselves with the thought that the Knight of Arts and Industry chose their island as his favourite spot, in which, having approved the soil, the climate and the genius of the land, he 'Bade social com-

merce raise renownèd marts', and to which he then called the drooping muses. But more than two centuries after the publication of *Alfred, a Masque* they can still sing 'Rule, Britannia' with a vigour and feeling before which 'criticism is suspended.'

Thomson has always been the poet of *The Seasons.* This is unfortunate, for, despite the abiding worth of some parts of that monumental miscellany, *The Castle of Indolence* is finer and more sustained poetry. Thomson wrote it at leisure over the last years of his life, when he was no longer a writer on his probation; he wrote it when he was relatively at ease with English, and in any case his model is Spenser's 'no language'. Here he has spared himself the effort of striving after a grand style in an idiom partly contemporary and partly Miltonic. The first canto reads like Spenser himself, or like Keats:

> The rooms with costly tapestry were hung,
> Where was inwoven many a gentle tale,
> Such as of old the rural poets sung
> Or of Arcadian or Sicilian vale.

Sometimes he anticipates one of Coleridge's lovelier effects:

> He ceased. But still their trembling ears retained
> The deep vibrations of his 'witching song.

Some vibrations of *The Castle of Indolence,* with its bickering streams and woods in summer moonlight, may be audible in *The Ancient Mariner.*

The Seasons tends to exhaustiveness. It would be a captious reader who complained that some aspect of any season, dear and familiar to him, had been ignored in Thomson's survey. In *Spring,* the list of 'the tuneful nations' includes ten different kinds of bird in sixteen lines. Thomson has indeed been 'prodigal of harmony'. In *The Castle of Indolence* he mentions only two bird-songs among the natural sounds which bring sleep:

> And now and then sweet Philomel would wail,
> Or stockdoves 'plain amid the forest deep,
> That drowsy rustled to the sighing gale.

He has learned to select. He is no longer straining every nerve, and his poem in consequence has free and spontaneous life. The memories of boyhood—

> What transport to retrace our boyish plays,
> Our easy bliss, when each thing joy supplied,—
> The woods, the mountains, and the warbling
>   maze
> Of the wild brooks!

—and the personal references to his friends, emphasize the poem's informality. With infectious gaiety he celebrates that indolence which was his natural bent and of which he officially disapproved. In the first canto he neither teaches nor preaches. He is as far removed from his didactic and edifying self as is the shepherd of the

Hebrid Isles in the astonishing thirtieth stanza which moved Joseph Warton to rapture and can surely never be read without emotion. He is on holiday, but holidays must end. He pulls himself together and reassumes the familiar rôle of moralist and sage. The Knight of Arts and Industry triumphs, the colour and light are extinguished, the enchantment disappears, 'Then all at once in air dissolves the wondrous show'.

Eighteenth-century verse as a whole suffers from the habit of deliberately clothing thought with style. The clothes are often ill-chosen and ill-fitting, despite Pope's warning that they are 'more decent, as more suitable' ["An Essay on Criticism"]. Thomson is an outstanding example, and from the first his readers have drawn a clear distinction between what he says and how he says it. [In his "Epistle to Mr. Thomson"] Somervile considered his faults mere spots in the sun, but advised their removal:

> Read Philips much, consider Milton more;
> But from their dross extract the purer ore.
> To coin new words, or to restore the old,
> In southern bards is dangerous and bold;
> But rarely, very rarely, will succeed,
> When minted on the other side of Tweed.
> Let perspicuity o'er all preside—
> Soon shalt thou be the nation's joy and pride.

Joseph Warton called him 'a favourite author, and who would have been a first-rate poet, if his style had been equal to his conceptions'. Coleridge judged that 'Thomson was a great poet, rather than a good one; his style was as meretricious as his thoughts were natural', and Wordsworth that 'notwithstanding his high powers, he writes a vicious style.'

This formidable chorus, from which but a few voices have been selected, had been opened by the Professor of Divinity at Edinburgh who rebuked Thomson for the 'poetically splendid' language he used in explaining a psalm. He seems to have been incapable of effective self-criticism. His fault was not carelessness—far from it. He did not need Somervile's hint—

> Why should thy Muse, born so divinely fair,
> Want the reforming toilet's daily care?

—or, rather, he misapplied it, and added cosmetics where an astringent or a sponge would have met the case. His rhythms are monotonous. Even the notorious 'O Sophonisba! Sophonisba, O!' is paralleled by 'No, fair illusions! artful phantoms, no!' Too often he repeats the effect of

> See where the winding vale its lavish stores,
> Irriguous, spreads!

and

> 'Mid the bright group Sincerity his front,
> Diffusive, rear'd.

These phrases illustrate his fondness for the Latin poly-syllable, especially for opening the line, and for adjectives ending in -*ive* (effusive, amusive, afflictive, conjunctive) and -*ous* (sequacious, auriferous, umbrageous, ovarious). Thomson's respect for Latin—and for Milton—leads to some frigidity and obscurity in his English. If 'in cheerful error let us tread the maze', or 'the latent Damon', give nothing more than a moment's regretful amusement, 'inspect sage' has to be deliberately translated to 'wise insight'. 'Ceres void of pain' (crops produced without trouble) evokes memories of one of the tenderest passages of human feeling in *Paradise Lost:*

> . . . . Which cost *Ceres* all that pain
> To seek her through the world. . . .

The grief of the bereaved mother is real to Milton, and Ceres is a living and suffering creature. She is real and alive, too, the triumphant embodiment of natural vitality, in Pope: 'laughing Ceres re-assume the land'. Thomson's phrase is mechanical, dead and literary.

He overloads his line with epithet—'Her full-assembled youth innumerous swarm'd'—and with compound words:

> Foul ministers, dark-working by the force
> Of secret-sapping gold.

There is too much rhetorical question, exclamation, exhortation and apostrophe: too much for the reader's patience, or to need illustration. Occasionally, and with an unintended comic effect, Thomson answers his rhetorical questions:

> 　　　　—was there no father, robbed
> Of blooming youth to prop his withered age?
> No son . . . no friend, forlorn?

> 　　　. . . . .

> No:—Sad o'er all profound dejection sat.

He closes *Liberty V* with a long series of *Lo! See! Behold! Hark!* as the prospect of future times unrolls before him. His poetic diction—'plumy people', 'finny race', 'glossy kind'—is notorious. But even into such conventionalities as these he can sometimes infuse feeling, as when he describes the sheep driven into the pool as 'the soft fearful people', or when, writing of the silkworm, he provides a kind of crossword-puzzle clue:

> And let the little insect-artist form,
> On higher life intent, its silken tomb.

This highly characteristic blend of periphrasis, accurate description and tenderness of heart is present also in his injunction to the fisherman to throw back into the stream 'the speckled infant.' The faults of Thomson's style—verbosity, declamation, the piling-up of epithet, insensitivity and monotony—are cruelly and conveniently obvious in his 'Paraphrase on the latter part of the sixth chapter of St. Matthew':

Say, does not life its nourishment exceed?
And the fair body its investing weed?
Behold! and look away your low despair—
See the light tenants of the barren air:

. . . . .

Observe the rising lily's snowy grace,
Observe the various vegetable race. . . .

Even his variation on the theme in *The Castle of Indolence* (i. 73-90, where 'the merry minstrels of the morn' have a vitality denied 'the light tenants of the barren air') is long-winded and clumsy beside the simplicity of the original.

But Thomson is capable of felicities; he notes the redbreast's 'slender feet', and the 'many-twinkling leaves of aspen'. His wallflower is deservedly famous, and there is an equal precision in

auriculas, enrich'd
With shining meal o'er all their velvet leaves.

He is notably successful in rendering the sound and movement of water. The sea in all its moods resounds in his poetry, from 'The murmuring main was heard, and scarcely heard, to flow' to

Where the Northern Ocean in vast whirls
Boils round the naked melancholy isles
Of farthest Thule, and the Atlantic surge
Pours in among the stormy Hebrides.

The closing phrase, with its echo of 'Lycidas', suggests the poet to whom Thomson is indebted for some of his finest effects—including his splendid use of place-names— as well as some of his worst. Under the impact of grief he writes the language of the heart. His significantly named 'Verses. Occasion'd by the Death of Mr. Aikman, a particular friend of the Author's' may stand with Johnson's 'On the Death of Mr. Robert Levet' as an unaffected, deeply felt expression of sorrow:

As those we love decay, we die in part,
String after string is sever'd from the heart;
Till loosen'd life, at last, but breathing clay,
Without one pang is glad to fall away.
Unhappy he, who latest feels the blow,
Whose eyes have wept o'er every friend laid
    low,
Drag'd ling'ring on from partial death to death,
Till, dying, all he can resign is breath.

Among the earliest of the Scottish Augustans, Thomson is incomparably the most important. He showed his compatriots that success could be won, and how it could be won. His boldness in using blank verse and the Spenserian stanza encouraged others. His themes were taken up by other writers, and it would be difficult to name any notable Scottish contribution to eighteenth-century English poetry which does not owe its hint to Thomson.

True, he writes few genuine epistles, but there is little that is noteworthy in those of Armstrong, Mickle, Blacklock or Beattie; he writes no formal verse translations, though here and there he embeds a passage of translation in his own work. His rendering in *Liberty* of the close of the great Regulus ode is diffuse and weak, but what translation in an uninflected tongue could match that original? Thomson writes very little satire, but what he does (for example, the lines in *The Castle of Indolence* on earthly vanity) is well done, which is more than can be said for Mallet's 'Of Verbal Criticism', Falconer's 'The Demagogue', Smollett's *Advice* and *Reproof,* Blacklock's 'Advice to the Ladies' or Beattie's wretched attack on Churchill's memory. The vein which Thomson opened in the treatment of Scottish scenes and the supernatural was to be exploited with increasing confidence by his successors. Of more immediate effect was his lead in didactic verse.

Arbuthnot, more than thirty years older than Thomson, may have composed [*Know Yourself*] before Thomson could write at all; 'wrote several years before', it was published in 1734. It is convenient to group it with Scottish didactic verse, but it is more philosophical than instructive, related to *De Rerum Natura* rather than to the *Georgics.* The author is concerned with the hybrid and enigmatical nature of man, part animal and part divine. His poem is valuable, not so much for its literary quality as for the light it throws on the serious interests of Arbuthnot, and on his character. He was one of the most attractive figures of the age, witty, kind and unassuming. Swift found in him 'every quality and virtue that can make a man amiable or useful', and the news of his death 'struck [him] to the heart.' Pope's Epistle is but the most celebrated of the tributes paid him by the discerning, such as Berkeley, Gay and Chesterfield. But no member of the Scriblerus Club was safe from attack, and though James Moore Smyth's *One Epistle to Mr. A. Pope, occasion'd by Two Epistles, lately published* (1730) is merely entertaining in its abuse of Arbuthnot as a quack, and a 'puzzling, plodding, prating, pedant Scot', there is some justification for his couplet on

The grating scribbler! whose untuned Essays
Mix the Scotch Thistle with the English Bays.

Arbuthnot, unlike Thomson, paid little attention to style. He is strenuously occupied with the subject of *Know Yourself,* and where the printed text varies from his original manuscript it is for the purpose of expressing his thought with greater clarity and precision. There are incidental stylistic improvements: for example, in his account of metabolism 'The Fabrick changd; the Tenant still remains' becomes 'The mansion changed, the tenant still remains', where the kinship of the words from an identical root (*maneo*) sharpens the antithesis of the thought. More characteristic of the poem as a whole is his rewriting of the passage on the Bible:

Stupendous is thy power; O light divine
The sons of darkness tremble at each Line.
Black doubt, & Hell-Born error shun thy Ray

As tardy sprights are startled at the day.
Thow cleard the secret of my high descent,
Thow told me what those Motly tokens meant.

This appeared in the printed version as:

Thus the benighted traveller that strays
Through doubtful paths, enjoys the morning
   rays;
The nightly mist, and thick descending dew,
Parting, unfold the fields, and vaulted blue.
'O truth divine! enlightened by thy ray,
I grope and guess no more, but see my way;
Thou clear'dst the secret of my high descent,
And told me what those mystic tokens meant.'

The reader may regret the elimination of the sprights, while admitting their merely decorative character. The image of the benighted traveller clarifies the thought, and directly recalls *Religio Laici,* which the poem so closely resembles in its honest attempt to measure a problem of vital significance, and to reach a solution. Like Dryden too, Arbuthnot might have said:

Thus have I made my own Opinions clear:
Yet neither Praise expect, nor Censure fear:
And this unpolish'd, rugged Verse, I chose;
As fittest for Discourse, and nearest Prose.
               [Dryden, *Religio Laici*]

Johnson's comment on lines by Richard Bentley the elder is wholly applicable to Arbuthnot's poem: 'they are the forcible verses of a man of a strong mind, but not accustomed to write verse; for there is some uncouthness in the expression.'

There is uncouthness of expression in Armstrong too, despite his more extensive practice in verse. (We cannot guess, of course, how many of Arbuthnot's papers, handed to his children for kite-making, may have been poetical compositions.) Both men, like Grainger and Smollett, were doctors of medicine. The first of Dr. Theobald's two Odes, 'Ad ingenuum Virum, tum medicis, tum poeticis, facultatibus praestantem, Johannem Armstrong, M.D.', opens with a neatly turned variant of the common compliment on a twofold kinship with Apollo:

Artisque Coae O et Citharae sciens,
Utroque mirè dexter Apolline!

The Art of Preserving Health is admirable in its seriousness, its effective organization and the power of much of its writing. Armstrong was conscious of the intractability of his material. He invokes Hygeia's help to steer him 'Thro' paths the Muses never trod before', because

'Tis hard, in such a strife of rules, to choose
The best, and those of most extensive use;
Harder in clear and animated song
Dry philosophic precepts to convey.

In the subject of diet he sees

A barren waste, where not a garland grows
To bind the Muse's brow.

Forced to make his own garlands, he weaves them of classical mythology, of passages on flowers and sunlight and music, of resounding rhetoric on the inevitability of old age and the transience of all things. Like Thomson, he uses place-words with rich effect:

the Babylonian spires are sunk;
Achaia, Rome and Egypt moulder down.

Like him, and indeed like most of these Scottish Augustans, he is moved by Scots place-names to tender autobiographical writing; his lines on the 'romantic groves' and 'fairy banks' of Liddel where he bathed and fished 'when life was new' stand with Smollett's 'To Leven-Water' as evidence of feeling unaffected by distance, absence or time.

With Armstrong, vocation and avocation are one. His verse is penetrated by his professional zeal. *A Day*—an epistle to Wilkes—is full of advice on matters of health, and the four stanzas which end Canto I in *The Castle of Indolence* were contributed by him. The portrait of Armstrong (I. lx) in this poem is that of a shy and silent man, and Alexander Carlyle, who noted his 'sarcastical vein', tells us that he 'was naturally glumpy'. Clearly he had nothing of Arbuthnot's happy charm; but he shared his power and honesty. His contemporaries admired him—except for Churchill, who found in him 'the vain stiffness of a *letter'd* Scot.' Hume thought he received less fame than he deserved; Lord Monboddo judged his diction more splendid than that of Milton's *Paradise Lost;* Boswell found it 'impossible to translate into French his force of style, a force remarkable even in English.' These men have a common factor which may render their praise a little suspect, and Hume's kindly feeling for a fellow-Scot was celebrated. Graham notes [in his *Scottish Men of Letters in the Eighteenth Century* (1901)] that, 'with him blind Blacklock, mildest of poetasters, was a Pindar; Wilkie, dullest of versifiers and most grotesque of mortals, was a Homer; Home was a Shakespeare "without his barbarisms"'. But Goldsmith was unbiased. Though he finds Thomson 'in general, a verbose and affected poet', he gives discriminating praise to Armstrong's occasional verbal felicities. John Nichols, in a friendly and discursive note on the poet, predicts of *The Art of Preserving Health* that it will transmit Armstrong's name to posterity as one of the first English writers.

Falconer's *The Shipwreck* transcends its didactic 'kind' through its tragic theme and the passionate sincerity of its handling. The writer, in boyhood 'condemned reluctant to the faithless sea', knew his subject intimately. Alexander Chalmers quotes an expert's opinion that *The Shipwreck* 'is of inestimable value to this country, since it contains within itself the rudiments of navigation: if not sufficient to form a complete seaman, it may certainly be considered as the grammar of his professional science.' Falconer would have rejoiced in this tribute. He took his seamanship with intense seriousness. Each of the three editions published in his lifetime carries a detailed diagram of a ship; he added explanatory notes on his many technical terms; not only action, but time and place are exactly indicated. He would, he says in the Advertisement to the second edition, have referred his readers to dictionaries, but 'he could by no means recommend their explanations, without forfeiting his claim to the character assumed in the Title-Page, of which he is much more tenacious than of his reputation as a poet'. The character is that of 'a sailor', and Falconer guards it jealously. He does not tamper with fact, though he may vary its expression. His accuracy and reliability are shown, for example, in the details of the fate of the crew. A single couplet is changed from

> As o'er the surf, the bending main-mast hung,
> The shrouds still grasping, thirty Seamen clung

to

> As o'er the surf the bending main-mast hung,
> Still on the rigging thirty seamen clung

and finally to:

> As o'er the surge the stooping main-mast hung,
> Still on the rigging thirty seamen clung.

These two 'characters', of seaman and poet, Falconer deliberately cultivates and cherishes. The revisions of the poem show him taking increasing trouble to make his facts crystal clear; he removes no technical terms, but he expands and elucidates his explanations. Anything less than the truth and the whole truth would insult the 'dreadful grandeur of [his] theme'. The reader, to whom such terms are not unfamiliar through experience or reading ('Here a sheer hulk lies poor Tom Bowling'!) accepts with fortitude their excessive use. It is otherwise with Falconer's second 'character'. His attempts to embellish the poem are, like much of Thomson's revision, the unhappy result of not letting well alone. The second edition is almost twice as long as the first; the third is yet longer. The characters at first are distinguished by their function alone; they are brave men, bearing each his share of responsibility, facing danger and death. But 'the master' of the first draft becomes 'Albert'; romantic love and friendship motives are added; Falconer adds a comparison of the master's grief to that of Priam at the fall of Troy. The first draft ends with a concise and simple narrative; this is expanded in the second edition by the introduction of a lengthy dying speech and an apostrophe; matter which filled sixteen lines is spun out to fill over a hundred and fifty. 'The design and power (or influence) of poetry' is a subject of much importance, but Falconer has seriously underestimated the power of his own narrative in supposing any reader would welcome a digression on poetry—or on anything else—at the opening of Canto III. The arrival of the Muses from the shores of light to tame the savages of old (third edition) is of even less immediacy to the story than the contrast (in itself pathetic) between Homer and himself with which Falconer opens the canto

in his second draft. He could not, and he did not, improve on the original edition:

> Now from the side the cumbrous ruins clear,
> The falling prow at last begins to veer.

Alterations in language show a similar straining after elegance. In the first draft the second paragraph of Canto I ends:

> The fate, in lively sorrow, to deplore,
> Of wand'rers shipwreck'd on a leeward shore.

To this is added, in the second edition:

> And, while my lines the nautic theme display,
> Dissolve in sympathy the weeping lay!

The 'melting' numbers (l. 22) become 'sadly-social' in the second draft.

Falconer's additions and 'improvements' emphasize the literary quality which is prevalent in eighteenth-century writing, and in no writing more than that of the Scots. But his poem is rooted in experience. Its epigraph is literally true of the writer:

> —quaeque ipse miserrima vidi,
> Et quorum pars magna fui.

At least one added literary touch of intensely personal appeal is the quotation inserted in the third edition: 'A shipboy on the high and giddy mast.' He must have been an extraordinary shipboy. But admiration for his struggles after self-education, to which his poem freely bears witness, is mingled with regret that these struggles led him so far afield. The finest of all stories of wrecks in that classic sea is not in Pope's *Homer;* it lay to his hand in the Acts of the Apostles. In spite of all his well-meant efforts to improve his poem, Falconer's shipwreck is not unworthy to be named beside St. Paul's.

The first poem of James Grainger, 'Solitude. An Ode', proclaimed his belief: 'The height of virtue is to serve mankind'. This he did in the practice of his profession, in his prose *Essay on the more common West India Diseases* (1764), where he urges planters to treat their slaves with humanity, for 'they must answer before the Almighty for their conduct toward their Negroes', and this he conscientiously attempted to do in *The Sugar-Cane: A Poem* (1764), supplementing instruction in verse with copious footnotes in prose. He makes some effort, in Thomson's manner, to embellish his work: he inserts the tale of Junio and Theana; he digresses on Commerce; he touchingly refers to Shenstone, 'my too, too distant friend', and to his childhood:

> O might the Muse
> Tread, flush'd with health, the Grampian hills
> again!

Grainger adapts, without improving, lines from Shakespeare, Milton and Gray, and varies his verse, doubtless in honour of 'lofty Maro', with many a pathetic half-line; he does what he can, but his decorations are so ill-matched with his subject and its technical terms that the result reads like merciless parody:

> Six times the changeful Moon must blunt her
>   horns,
> And fill with borrowed light her silvery urn;
> Ere thy tops, trusted to the mountain-land,
> Commence their jointing; but four moons suffice
> To bring to puberty the low-land cane.

This blend of scientific accuracy with elegant expression reminds the reader of Blackmore's *Creation* and of *The Loves of the Triangles;* but *that* poem was meant to be funny.

Grainger's passion for the whole truth is his undoing. Somervile admitted rabies into *The Chace,* but 'Of lesser ills [his] Muse declines to sing'. Not so Grainger's; she can sing of composts, dung-heaps, yaws, 'nor soil her heavenly plumes'. The cocoa-bean too

> In future times, the enraptur'd Muse may sing:
> If public favour crown her present lay.

The condition was not fulfilled. Boswell's amusing account of Grainger's reading aloud of *The Sugar-Cane,* and his report of Johnson's remark, 'What could he make of a sugar-cane? One might as well write the "Parsley-bed, a Poem"; or "The Cabbage-garden, a Poem",' suggest that his contemporaries, despite their love of the man (and Percy thought him 'one of the most generous, friendly and benevolent men [he] ever knew') felt that his Muse should rest. She had achieved the *reductio ad absurdum* of didactic poetry.

Robert Blair's *The Grave* is secure of immortality through the drawings of Blake. It went through many editions; its blank verse was turned into rhyme by Henry Lemoine (1790); it was frequently reprinted with Young's *Night Thoughts* or Gray's *Elegy,* and figures in the sombre collection printed by Thomas Tegg in 1823, of 'The Grave. By R. Blair. Death. By Beilby Porteus, D.D. The Day of Judgment. By Robert Glynn, M.D. The Last Day. By E. Young, D.D. Deity. By Samuel Boyse.' Blair's theme and tone are so grim that it is no surprise to find Alexander Carlyle avoiding the manse of Athelstaneford, since its occupant 'was so austere and void of urbanity as to make him quite disagreeable to young people.' *The Grave* bears obvious marks of Jacobean drama, but with all its apparatus of mattock, worm and skull, its morality is a mere expansion of Thomson's 'Behold, fond man!' Slight as it is, it conveniently illustrates some of the most striking characteristics of the Scottish Augustans: their respect for what preceded 'the reform of our numbers'; their love of preaching and teaching; their sense of responsibility (Blair describes his poem in a letter to Dr. Doddridge as 'written, I hope, in a way not unbecoming my profession as a minister of the gospel'); their nervous anxiety to please London (in the same letter Blair refers to the arts he has

used, sometimes against his inclination, 'to make such a piece go down with a licentious age, which cares for none of those things'). It is characteristic of them, too, in its unevenness of style, and the flashes of poetry which illumine the most unpromising theme:

> Thus, at the shut of ev'n, the weary bird
> Leaves the wide air, and in some lonely brake
> Cow'rs down.

Finally, it associates wild natural conditions with the supernatural. *The Grave* is full of ghosts: twice they are used in similes; they are reported by fame to perform their mystic rounds, to rise grisly at the sound of the wind and the screaming owl, to shriek from the tomb and ring the church bell—even to forewarn men of their death. The schoolboy in the moonlit churchyard

>   hears, or thinks he hears,
> The sound of something purring at his heels;
> Full fast he flies, and dares not look behind him.

Half-a-century later Blair's terrifying image was to receive perfect expression at the hands of Coleridge.

Their treatment of the supernatural is the most fruitful and the most individual contribution made by these Scots to English literature. Addison, speaking for the Age of Reason, had dismissed it with polite contempt: 'Our Forefathers looked upon Nature with more Reverence and Horrour, before the World was enlightened by Learning and Philosophy, and loved to astonish themselves with the Apprehensions of Witchcraft, Prodigies, Charms, and Enchantments.' But in Scotland the forces of learning and philosophy had to contend, not only with the talk

> In rangles round, before the ingle's lowe,
> Fra guid-dame's mouth

but with the authority of the popular *Satan's Invisible World Discovered . . . proving . . . that there are Devils, Spirits, Witches and Apparitions.* The evidence of the power and prevalence of superstition in eighteenth-century Scotland is so rich that quotation is almost unnecessary. Alexander Carlyle tells a touching little story of his having settled with a dear friend

> that whoever should die first, should appear to the other, and tell him the secrets of the invisible world. I walked every evening for hours in the fields and links of Prestonpans, in hopes of meeting my friend; but he never appeared. This disappointment, together with the knowledge I had acquired at the Logic class, cured me of many prejudices about ghosts and hobgoblins and witches, of which till that time I stood not a little in awe.

Relatively few had Carlyle's advantages of proof by experiment and attendance at the Logic class. Burns's letter to Dr. Moore shows, not only the range and variety of Scottish superstitions and their effect on a poetic imagination, but also their lasting influence even on a sceptic.

The passage is of supreme importance for the full under-standing of any eighteenth-century writer who spent his boyhood in Scotland. Burns writes of

> tales and songs concerning devils, ghosts, fairies, brownies, witches, warlocks, spunkies, kelpies, elf-candles, dead-lights, wraiths, apparitions, cantraips, giants, inchanted towers, dragons and other trumpery.— This cultivated the latent seeds of Poesy; but had so strong an effect on my imagination, that to this hour, in my nocturnal rambles, I sometimes keep a sharp look-out in suspicious places; and though nobody can be more sceptical in these matters than I, yet it often takes an effort of Philosophy to shake off these idle terrors.

In the earlier years of the century the Scots poets' deal-ings with the supernatural were sparing and discreet, and their reception was cool. Arbuthnot removed the 'sprights' when he printed *Know Yourself*, but Chesterfield still found that 'his good understanding could not get the better of some prejudices of his education and country. For he was convinced that he had twice had the second sight, which in Scotch signifies a degree of nocturnal inspiration, but in English only a dream.' Thomson was careful to assign supernatural experience to uneducated peasants. David Mallet, a very minor Thomson, is in this respect a little more daring. His claim to 'William and Margaret' stands no longer, but *The Excursion* is his own, with its picture of Night, who

> calls her train
> Of visionary fears; the shrouded ghost,
> The dream distressful, and th'incumbent hag,
> That rise to Fancy's eye in horrid forms,
> While Reason slumbering lies.

His description of the 'place of tombs' is a foretaste of Blair:

> All is dread silence here, and undisturb'd,
> Save what the wind sighs, and the wailing owl
> Screams solitary to the mournful Moon,
> Glimmering her western ray through yonder isle,
> Where the sad spirit walks with shadowy foot
> His wonted round, or lingers o'er his grave.

Moving in imagination, like Thomson, to the far North, Mallet finds a land of fears where

> night by night, beneath the starless dusk,
> The secret hag and sorcerer unblest
> Their sabbath hold, and potent spells compose,
> Spoils of the violated grave.

Armstrong, like Thomson, associates superstition with the peasant. His youthful imitation of Shakespeare 'helped to amuse the solitude of a winter passed in a wild romantic country; and, what is rather particular, was just finished when Mr. Thomson's celebrated poem upon the same subject appeared'. His 'hinds' by the winter fire talk

> Of prodigies, and things of dreadful utterance,

> That set them all agape, rouse up their hair,
> And make the ideot drops start from their eyes;
> Of churchyards belching flames at dead of night,
> Of walking statues, ghosts unaffable,
> Haunting the dark waste tower or airless
>   dungeon;
> Then of the elves that deftly trip the green,
> Drinking the summer's moonlight from the
>   flowers;
> And all the toys that phantasy pranks up
> T'amuse her fools withal.

The talk of these unlettered folk, reported no matter how apologetically, kept the subject before the educated, and, as the century advanced, poets grew bolder. Mickle has ghosts and spectres, wailing or 'ungrav'd', gliding not only on Eskdale Braes but (in simile) in the Siege of Marseilles and ('as the hoary villagers relate') on Almada Hill. His ballad, 'The Sorceress', is lavish in supernatural trappings:

> And thrice the witch her magic wand
>   Wav'd o'er the skeleton;
> And slowly, at her dread command,
>   Up rose the arm of bone.

In his 'Dissertation on the Lusiad' he defines the marvel-lous as 'the very soul of poesy'. Logan's 'Ode written in Spring', in characteristic rocking-horse metre, depicts the lonely milkmaid who

> sees the Fairies with their queen,
> Trip hand-in-hand the circled green,
> And hears them raise at times, unseen,
>   The ear-enchanting lay.

Poets grew bolder, and critics, such as Hurd and Warton, grew warmer. Gray, writing to Stonehewer (29 June 1760) about the 'nature and noble wild imagination' of *Ossian,* and the wind that sounds like the voice of a spirit, re-marks that 'Thomson had an ear sometimes: he was not deaf to this; and has described it gloriously, but given it another different turn, and of more horror. I cannot repeat the lines: it is in his *Winter*.' The lines Gray had in mind are probably (191-4):

> Then too, they say, through all the burdened air
> Long groans are heard, shrill sounds, and distant
>   sighs,
> That, uttered by the demon of the night,
> Warn the devoted wretch of woe and death.

This enthusiasm set Beattie researching 'to gratify [Gray's] curiosity and love of superstition', and Beattie sympathet-ically traces the Highland superstitions to the silence and solitude of a wild country. 'Nor is it wonderful, that per-sons of lively imagination, immured in deep solitude, and surrounded with the stupendous scenery of clouds, prec-ipices, and torrents, should dream, even when they think themselves awake, of those few striking ideas with which their lonely lives are diversified' [Beattie, *On Poetry and Music*]. For evidence that wild scenery and the associated supernatural were especially identified with Scotland, one need look no further than Langhorne's *Genius and Valour* or Collins's *Ode on the Popular Superstitions of the Highlands.*

Interest in the legendary and marvellous, and its appropriate scenery, was fed and raised to fever-pitch by Macpherson's *Ossian.* Shenstone both explains and illustrates its effect [in a letter of September 24, 1761, to McGowan]: 'The public has seen all that art can do, and they want the more striking efforts of wild, original, enthusiastic genius. . . . Here is, indeed, pure original genius! The very quintessence of poetry.' We may allow it to be the quintessence of opportunism. Macpherson's way had been prepared by Jerome Stone, schoolmaster of Dunkeld, who published a translation of Gaelic poetry, 'Albin and the Daughter of Mey', in the *Scots Magazine* (January 1756). This, says Ramsay, 'though a pretty wild tale, yet being in *verse,* it attracted little notice, being classed with magazine poetry.' Macpherson's measured prose, suggested to him by John Home, is certainly not verse; and he avoided Stone's fate by the independent, though anonymous, publication of his *Fragments* in 1760. Success enlarged his plans and his ambition. Unchecked by the doubts of the judicious and sceptical, the fame and influence of

Ossian grew and spread till, as Arnold says, all Europe felt the power of its melancholy.

Thoughtful contemporaries were perplexed by the problem of originality or forgery. Johnson's comment is, on the whole, confirmed by later scholarship: 'He has found names, and stories, and phrases, nay passages in old songs, and with them has blended his own compositions, and so made what he gives to the world as the translation of an ancient poem.' Macpherson himself neatly posed their dilemma: 'Those who have doubted my veracity have paid a compliment to my genius.' His 'genius' is still our concern; his originals may be 'a non-existing non-existence,' but that need not discourage the study of Macpherson's printed pages.

The pages themselves provide their own discouragement. The didactic poets, however dull, do at least teach, and there are worse ways of spending time than in learning from an enthusiastic professional who knows his subject, even if his subject is elephantiasis or a compost-heap; the absence of humour which permitted so much instruction to be imparted in verse, so earnestly and so ingeniously, is in itself funny. But there is neither instruction nor amusement in *Ossian*—there is wind. Vague scenes of mist and shadow, moonlight and whirling leaves, bearded thistles, floating beards, white-bosomed females, moss, single trees, shielded warriors, harps, caves, tombs, meteors, rainbows, eagles and above all and everywhere ghosts, dissolve into each other with the ease but without the purpose of Shelley's Cloud. Everything is blurred and indistinct. The many epithets ending in -*y* point to and emphasize this vagueness: *beamy, streamy, foamy, wavy, woody.* Epithets are piled on one another so that phrases like 'the wan cold moon', or 'the breeze—that flies dark-shadowy over the grass', which have, in themselves, both feeling and charm, are smothered in their context. Rhetorical questions abound: 'Whence is the stream of years? Whither do they roll along?' Biblical phrase and image there is in plenty: 'The mighty have fallen in battle', 'We decay like the grass of the hill; our strength returns no more', 'Let none tell it in Selma, nor in Morven's woody land. Fingal will be sad, and the sons of the desert mourn.'

It is impossible to feel any interest in the story. Macpherson's heroines, disguised as men, follow their lovers to battle, as Cassandra follows Diomede in *The Epigoniad*; thus oddly are the least prosaic prose and the most prosaic verse of the century connected. Everyone, white-bosomed, grey-bearded or ghost, talks alike, in a mournful recitative. A favourable specimen of a recurring theme is: 'Happy are they who fell in their youth, in the midst of their renown. They have not beheld the tombs of their friends, or failed to bend the bow of their strength.' Beside Thomson's lines on Aikman, painfully wrung from him by a real grief, this is exposed for the fluent, facile and ready-made thing that it is. To this fragment of talk we may add some lines of narrative. Selection is easy, for though Macpherson's cakes are of different sizes and have different names they are all baked from the same mixture. Early in Book II of *Fingal* we find:

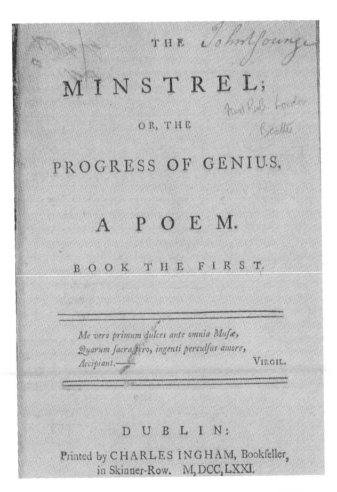

THE *Johnsoung*

MINSTREL;

OR, THE

PROGRESS OF GENIUS.

A POEM.

BOOK THE FIRST.

Me vero primum dulces ante omnia Musæ,
Quarum sacra fero, ingenti perculsus amore,
Accipiant.—   VIRGIL.

DUBLIN:

Printed by CHARLES INGHAM, Bookseller,
in Skinner-Row. M,DCC,LXXI.

Title page of Beattie's The Minstrel, *volume one (1771).*

As the dark shades of autumn fly over the hills of grass, so gloomy, dark, successive came the chiefs of Lochlin's echoing woods. Tall as the stag of Morven, moved stately before them the king. His shining shield is on his side, like a flame on the heath at night, when the world is silent and dark, and the traveller sees some ghost sporting in the beam! Dimly gleam the hills around, and shew indistinctly their oaks! A blast from the troubled ocean removed the settled mist. The sons of Erin appear, like a ridge of rocks on the coast; when mariners, on shores unknown, are trembling at veering winds!

Dr. Hugh Blair, in that *Critical Dissertation on the Poems of Ossian* in which, after comparing him to his advantage with Homer, Virgil and the romances of chivalry, he assigns him 'a place among those whose works are to last for ages', warns the reader 'that the beauties of Ossian's writings cannot be felt by those who have given them only a single or hasty perusal'. The present writer's perusals have been two, and as patient as possible. They have ended, like the Marriage Service, in amazement. Never, one feels, has so much excitement been roused, in so many, by such fustian.

The seventies of the eighteenth century, unlike the decades immediately preceding and following, produced so little that historians of literature have been thankful to mention Beattie's *The Minstrel; or, the Progress of Genius*. (Mickle's translation of *The Lusiad* is a much more creditable performance.) *The Minstrel* had its day. Cowper, poor as he was, felt that he 'must afford to purchase at least the poetical works of Beattie', and Burns, presenting a copy to Miss Logan, sent

> more than India boasts
> In Edwin's simple tale.

Beattie claims Spenser as his master, but *The Minstrel* seems rather a watered-down and emasculated version of *The Castle of Indolence*. With little of Thomson's poetic gift, Beattie has some of his ability to compound a popular mixture, and he attempts to 'be either droll or pathetic, descriptive or sentimental, tender or satirical, as the humour strikes.' Edwin's simple tale is the progress of a Poetical Genius, from fancy and love of nature (Book I) to an interest in education and the betterment of mankind (Book II). The hero, ('no vulgar boy'), is advised by a sage hermit. The poem peters out before anything much can happen, and the modern reader wonders, not so much that Beattie did not finish it, as that he could bear to amble along as far as he did. Thomson's influence is clear in Beattie's stern attitude to luxury; it is clear too in his idea of progress:

> What cannot Art and Industry perform,
> When Science plans the progress of their toil!

If this stanza directly recalls the hero of *The Castle of Indolence*, the following one is *Liberty* in a nutshell. The moralizing, and there is much moralizing, is all of the 'Behold, fond man!' kind:

> Yet such the destiny of all on Earth:

So flourishes and fades majestic Man.

Like Thomson, Edwin is humanitarian and hates field sports.

But *Fingal* had appeared since *The Castle of Indolence,* and the vogue for mist and mountain is clear in *The Minstrel.* Edwin the child feeds on old wives' tales in winter, and dreams of fairy warriors and dames. True, the superstitions are exploded by Reason, but they have been described.

The Minstrel was composed while Beattie was working on his *Essay on the Nature and Immutability of Truth*— they are commemorated together by Burns in 'The Vision.' The *Essay* won him royal favour and a pension (the King kept one copy at Kew and another in town), an honorary doctorate of the University of Oxford, an allegorical portrait by Reynolds and a popularity and respect hardly to be described. Some of his admired anti-sceptical reflections break into his verse too, and this may help to explain why it was so popular. It is awkward, unmusical stuff. Beattie strings words and phrases together in groups of three:

> Is glory there achieved by arts, as foul
> As those that felons, fiends, and furies plan?
> Spiders ensnare, snakes poison, tigers prowl.

His pages are littered with ejaculation—*lo! alas! oh! ah!;* with archaism—*besprent, wight, imp, shene;* and with personification. There is nothing in *The Minstrel* so 'glossy and unfeeling' as the diction of his translation of Virgil's *Eclogues* ('flexile osiers', 'my yielding fair', 'fostering Zephyrs fan the vernal skies'), but Beattie truly 'writ no language'. Only his dialect poem 'To Mr. Alexander Ross' is vital and vigorous. His English verse was patiently scrutinized by Gray, but it bears little sign that Beattie laid to heart his celebrated advice, 'Remember Dryden!'

Beattie's verse, nerveless as it is, has the interest of foreshadowing better work. Though the hero of *The Progress of Genius* has the advantage of beginning life among the beauties of Nature, it is only the accident of title that links it with *Growth of a Poet's Mind;* but Beattie's description of the Minstrel of old—

> His waving locks and beard all hoary grey:
> While from his bending shoulder decent hung
> His harp, the sole companion of his way,
> Which to the whistling wind responsive rung

—points forward unmistakably to a later and far more potent Minstrel.

The Scots poets, while freely using the stock measures of the time (they nearly all write heroic and octosyllabic couplets and some form of ode or lyric) were ready to experiment, and to revive disused forms. Their blank verse speaks for itself, and so, in its way, does Macpherson's measured prose. Mickle's sonnets, two of which were inspired by the passion for Camoëns which sustained his greater labour, are more easily overlooked. The imitations of Spenser are really important. Pope made a jest of him in his youthful parody, 'The Alley'. Prior was obviously deaf to his music, and *An Ode, humbly inscribed to the Queen on the glorious success of Her Majesty's Arms. MDCCVI,* is a travesty. In the Preface he explains that he is following 'our great countryman Spenser . . . having only added one verse to his stanza, which I thought made the number more harmonious'. (Only!) He makes no mention of the fact that he has also eliminated Spenser's linking rhyme, and that for Spenser's total of three rhymes in the stanza he has substituted five. Hamilton of Bangour's idea of Spenser's style (*On Seeing Lady Mary Montgomery sit to her Picture*) is a Gray's *Elegy* quatrain with *whilom, algates* and *couth* sprinkled on it.

But Thomson's true Spenserians are followed, however feebly, by Armstrong, in his stanzas on disease inserted in *The Castle of Indolence,* and by Wilkie, in 'A Dream. In the Manner of Spenser', with which he cheered himself at the close of *The Epigoniad.* Saintsbury shows how Beattie's idiosyncratic treatment of the form reappears in Byron, who studied *The Minstrel.* Mickle seems to have had a special feeling for Spenser: 'The Concubine', later named 'Syr Martyn', is 'in the manner of Spenser', as is the unfinished 'Hence, vagrant minstrel', with which he closes the 'Observations upon Epic Poetry' which make part of the prolegomena to *The Lusiad.*

For evidence that the imitation of Spenser was connected especially with the Scots poets, one may turn to Nathan Drake's account of Johnson's critical papers in *The Rambler.* He agrees with Johnson that 'the obsolete words of this amiable poet, indeed, it would be pedantry to attempt to revive; but who, that has read the productions of Mickle and Beattie, would wish the structure of the stanza of Spenser, and the occasional use of his more polished diction, laid aside?'

The lead given by Thomson towards didactic verse was decisive with the more gifted of the Scots poets; Armstrong and Falconer have some power; Beattie and Blacklock are feeble. But didactic verse was a dying 'kind'. In his fable 'The Wilding and the Broom', a dispute on the importance of ethical teaching in verse, Langhorne shows Thomson pointing to the broom-flowers and saying:

>   Shepherd, there
> Behold the fate of song, and lightly deem
> Of all but moral beauty,

—but he gives Hamilton of Bangour the last word. The Preface to Joseph Warton's *Odes* (1746) states explicitly that their author 'is convinced that the fashion of moralizing in verse has been carried too far' at the expense of invention and imagination. The future belonged to the more romantic elements of superstition and legend, wild scenery and haunting place-names, discreetly introduced by Thomson and lavishly exploited by Macpherson. These are the elements which were to make Scott's lays so captivating to his contemporaries, and to form a contrasting strand in the richer and more lasting fabric of his novels. 'The rude sweetness of a Scotch tune' sounds in English fitfully through the century, from Thomson's 'Tell me, thou soul of her I love' and Mallet's 'The Birks of Endermay' to Logan's 'The Braes of Yarrow' and 'To the Cuckoo'. Whether this poem was his own or by Michael Bruce, Logan certainly wrote the autumn ode from which Dorothy Wordsworth quotes: 'We have been reading the life and some of the writings of poor Logan since dinner. "And everlasting longings for the lost." It is an affecting line. There are many affecting lines and passages in his poems' [*The Grasmere Journal*]. There are indeed, and in the poems of many of the Scottish Augustans, lines and passages which were seminal of the sustained poetry in this kind which they could not themselves achieve. [In his *Observations on the Faerie Queen of Spenser* (1754)] Thomas Warton describes Scotland as a nation 'which amidst a variety of disadvantages has kept a constant pace with England in the progress of literature.' No one intimate with the general run of average eighteenth-century English poetry will think it an extravagant claim. The satires of Pope, the lyrics of Blake are not average, and if eighteenth-century Scots produced, in English verse, nothing that should be named in the same day with these, there is comfort in the thought that one at least of their compatriots, working in the native tradition and in the mother-tongue, wrote poetry which needs no apology.

SCOTTISH BALLADS

John Speirs

SOURCE: "The Scottish Ballads," in *The Scots Literary Tradition: An Essay in Criticism,* second edition, Faber & Faber, 1962, pp. 131-141.

[*A former lecturer at the University of Exeter, Speirs has written a number of studies of poetry, including books on Medieval poetry and Chaucer. In the following essay, originally published in the first edition of* The Scots Literary Tradition *(1940), Speirs discusses the folk tradition in relation to Scottish Ballad poetry.*]

As we have them in the Collections, the Scottish Ballads are poems chiefly of the eighteenth century. That they are quite different from other poems of that century may at first occasion surprise, but has its explanation. On the other hand it has been denied (by the primitivists) that they are poems of that century at all. It has been argued that there is no reason to suppose they did not come into being centuries earlier than the century in which they were written down. It has also been observed that a good deal of the 'material' used is 'medieval'. But a poem and the language it is in are one and the same. Translated, it either becomes a new poem or ceases to be a poem at all. It is sufficient therefore to point to the language the ballads are in, which in most cases is at the point of development it was in the eighteenth century. (This is not merely a matter of language, but of sensibility. The ballads taken down after the beginning of the nineteenth century show a distinct modification of sensibility.) Certainly the ballads are traditional. But so also is every poem—in its own degree.

I have isolated the Scottish Ballads from the other ballads in Child's Collection for the purposes of this consideration. Child includes several: *Judas, St. Stephen and King Herod,* which belong with medieval verse. *Robyn and Gandelyn* is fifteenth century, and the finer of the Robin Hood Ballads also are rather earlier than the Scottish Ballads. The broadsheets that fluttered across the English country from the printing presses of 'the town' are more nearly contemporaneous with the Scottish Ballads. Scotland seems to have suffered less than England from the broadsheet contagion, being at that time less exposed, though nowadays newspapers, in Scotland as in England, have long since superseded ballads and broadsheets both. There are comparatively few Scottish Ballads in Percy's *Reliques.* But it was in Scotland that the Collectors of the eighteenth century found their finest poems.

The Scottish Ballads and the English Ballads are not wholly distinct from each other, but both are distinct from 'literary' English verse. The simultaneous existence of two distinct types of verse points to the simultaneous existence of two distinct traditions. But that is no reason for supposing, as has been done, that the oral tradition (represented by the ballads of the Collections) and the 'literary' tradition were distinct to begin with, since an examination of the ballads themselves, their metre, their conventions, shows them to be not medieval verse certainly, but a development, a 'popular' development, from medieval verse. They were the verse which entertained the largely unlettered 'people', and they posses in themselves a life distinct and apart both from the 'literary' verse they were contemporaneous with and from the medieval verse they are a development from.

The Scottish Ballads therefore are, as every poem is, new and at the same time old. They are late (later, I think, than has been held) in that they belong mostly to the eighteenth century, but late also in that they bear on themselves the mark of a long ancestry. They are stiff with a

Poetic Diction. To illustrate this Poetic Diction with an exhaustive list of phrases—*yellow hair, cherry cheeks, lily-white, rose-red, clay-cauld*—would be superfluous; the ballads themselves are the composite illustration of it; any analysis of the ballads is necessarily an analysis of it. Its strength is that it is to a considerable extent a stylization of popular speech. It is simple: it is sensuous: and it retains something of the passion of popular speech. Its most evident 'limitation' as an artistic medium is perhaps its intractability to the expression of subtle shades of perception, its ready formation of simple, and at moments brutally effective, contrasts:

> And clear, clear was her yellow hair
> Whereon the red blood dreeps,

not only in colour:

> Shool'd the mools on his yellow hair.

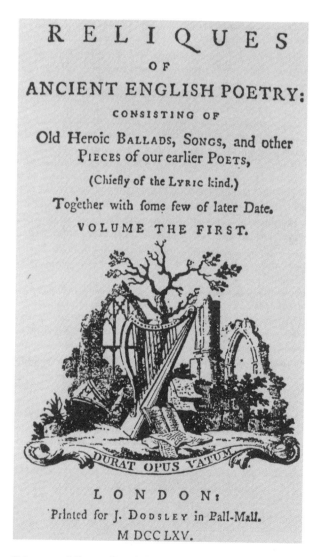

Title page of Thomas Percy's Reliques of Ancient English Poetry
(1765), part of the Scottish vernacular revival.

When therefore the late eighteenth century began looking for a poetry which should be 'simple, sensuous, and passionate', it certainly found such in the ballads. What fascinated the late century were these 'natural' qualities and not merely that here was a Poetic Diction different from the prevailing Poetic Diction and therefore 'fresh'. Bishop Percy in his introduction to his *Reliques* (1765) is still apologetic, but he indicates clearly enough what he, and his contemporaries, supposed were the merits of the ballads.

> In a polished age, like the present, I am sensible that many of these reliques of antiquity will require great allowances to be made for them. Yet have they, for the most part, a pleasing simplicity, and many artless graces, which in the opinion of no mean critics have been thought to compensate for the want of higher beauties, and, if they do not dazzle the imagination, are frequently found to interest the heart.

The description is to a certain extent just. We can all of us recall lines in the ballads which affect us suddenly and sharply (to express it more strongly than the Bishop) with an apparent utmost economy of means. Yet once the stylization of the diction, especially in certain of the Scottish Ballads, is perceived the impression is more generally one of 'conventionality'. It will be sufficient to refer the reader to the finer of the *Twa Sisters* (*Binnorie*) variations. But the precise degree of conventional richness of one couplet from one ballad—

> The bride cam tripping down the stair
> Wi' the scales o' red gowd on her hair,

—cannot of course be appreciated unless one remembers the recurrences in other ballads of 'brides', ladies who 'cam tripping down the stair', 'red gowd' and adorned 'hair'.

This Poetic Diction is built into a Rhetoric—partly by means of repetitions. The *Gil Brenton* (*Cospatrick*), the *Cruel Brother* and the *Babylon* variations come first to my mind as exemplifying it. What it indicates is the adaptation of speech to something outside itself, to declamation or to song. This also imposes upon it a certain rigidity which arrests any development from it, such as there was in Elizabethan dramatic verse from its earliest rhetorical 'simplicity' to its later close-down-to-speech complexity. But what in the ballads is lost in simplification is gained in effectiveness of dramatic presentation:

> 'What news, what news?' said young Hind Horn;
> 'No news, no news,' said the old beggar man,

> 'No news,' said the beggar, 'No news at a',
>   But there is a wedding in the king's ha'.'

What the repetition does is to increase the expectancy. This is resolved into a surprise. 'A conversation' seems to be reproduced in what seems a hard, unyielding medium, but with (as also, and more especially, in *Lamkin*) quite astonishingly effective results. The ballad dialogue is both itself stylized and an integral part of the stylization. 'All imaginative art', writes Yeats (in his remarkable essay *Certain Noble Plays of Japan*), 'remains at a distance, and this distance once chosen must be firmly held against a pushing world. . . . The arts which interest me, while seeming to separate from the world and us a group of figures, images, symbols, enable us to pass for a few moments into a deep of the mind that had hitherto been too subtle for our habitation' . . . seem, in fact, 'to recede from us into some more powerful life. . . . ' The ballads are more than the beginnings of such an art.

When the eighteenth century found the ballads artistically 'rude' and 'unpolished' it may have been simply that the variations are for the most part very fragmentary, so that anything like a completely formed poem in the literary sense is rare. The ballads are sets of variations, fragmentary indeed, but in the extremely conventionalized medium I have spoken of. It is in this sense they are 'impersonal' apart altogether from their anonymity as to authorship.

Not that this medium itself remains constant. Even the Scottish Ballads, considered as a group by themselves, break up into lesser groups as soon as one looks at them closely enough. *Hughie the Graeme, Dick o' the Cow, Jamie Telfer, Jock o' the Side, Kinmont Willie,* for example, form a group possessing robust characteristics of its own, considerably apart from what I have taken to be the central group. But these lesser groups retain a vital relation with each other and with the whole, which evidences a homogeneous community, in vital contact also with its neighbours but not dependent on imported stuff.

The mere existence of this ballad poetry among the largely unlettered Scottish 'people' in the eighteenth century is evidence also of the existence then of a popular taste that there is no equivalent of now among the lettered 'people' either in Scotland or in England. The contemporary popular taste as represented by the contemporary popular entertainment (popular fiction, popular films, jazz music) is of a very much lower order. There is now such a gap between it and the literary tradition that it is difficult to know how long the literary tradition itself, deprived of sustenance from beneath, can persist.

But more particular evidence of the quality of popular taste a generation or two ago is provided by a comparison between the variations of any ballad. . . . Between the eight variations of the two opening lines of the *Unquiet Grave* . . . there is indeed very little to choose. This is the case also with an astonishingly large proportion of the ballad variations. Whether they were always the result of forgetfulness or not (it is very doubtful) they exhibit an astonishingly high degree of artistic competence to have been so widespread. Whoever was responsible for them could substitute lines as good as the lines which were either forgotten or not. They exhibit in practice a popular taste acquired, quite unconsciously, through long familiarity with ballads. My reason for doubting whether the variations arose simply from the necessity for filling up gaps in memory, rather than from some deeper necessity, may become clear from a comparison between two passages from two variations of the *Cruel Mother*:

> CHILD B. As she was going to the church,
> She saw a sweet babe in the porch.
>
> O sweet babe, and thou were mine,
> I wad cleed thee in the silk so fine.
>
> O mother dear, when I was thine,
> You did na prove to me sae kind.
>
> CHILD C. She has howked a hole baith deep
>   and wide,
> She has put them in baith side by side.
>
> She has covered them oer wi a marble stane
> Thinking she would gang maiden hame.
>
> As she was walking by her father's castle wa,
> She saw twa pretty babes playing at the ba.
>
> O bonnie babes, gin ye were mine,
> I would dress you up in satin fine.
>
> O cruel mother, we were thine . . .

These variations are in fact two independent poems. There is here a difference of vision.

This suggests also the nature of what, I think, one learns to look for in the Scottish Ballads. When the fragments belonging to the group are set together (not that one supposes they were ever anything else than fragmentary) portions of the outlines of a pattern within that of the conventionalized medium become discernible. What these form the very fragmentary revelation of is a folk-mythology. It is, I wish tentatively to suggest, the central thing

---

Allan Ramsay defends his use of the Scots vernacular:

There is nothing can be heard more silly than one's expressing his *Ignorance* of his *native Language;* yet such there are, who can vaunt of acquiring a tolerable Perfection in the *French* or *Italian* Tongues, if they have been a Forthnight in *Paris* or a Month in *Rome:* But shew them the most elegant Thoughts in a *Scots* Dress, they as disdainfully as stupidly condemn it as barbarous. But the true Reason is obvious: Every one that is born never so little superior to the *Vulgar,* would fain distinguish themselves from them by some Manner or other, and such, it would appear, cannot arrive at a better *Method.* But this affected Class of Fops give no uneasiness, not being numerous; for the most part of our Gentlemen, who are generally Masters of the most useful and politest *Languages,* can take Pleasure (for a Change) to speak and read their own.

Allan Ramsay, in the preface to
The Ever Green, *1724.*

---

in the Scottish Ballads, from which a complete understanding of them must proceed. It is here:

> She's gane into the Jew's garden
> Where the grass grew lang and green:
> She powd an apple red and white
> To wyle the young thing in.

It is also here:

> I'll show you where the white lilies grow
> On the banks of Italie.

And later in the same poem:

> 'O what hills are yon, yon pleasant hills,
> That the sun shines sweetly on?'
> 'O you are the hills of heaven,' he said,
>   'Where you will never won.'
>
> 'O whaten a mountain is yon,' she said,
> 'All so dreary wi frost and snow?'
> 'O yon is the mountain of hell,' he said,
>   'Where you and I will go.'

and it is, wizened, here:

> She's turned me into an ugly worm
> And gard me toddle about the tree.

It is a symbolism which is unmistakable wherever it occurs—the green garden, the apple, the braid, braid road across the lily leven (*Thomas the Rhymer*) or down by yon sunny fell (*Queen of Elflan's Nourice*), the rose broken from the tree (*Tam Lin*), the nut broken from the tree (*Hind Etin*), the place 'at the foot of our Lord's knee' 'set about wi gilly-flowers' where women go who die in childbirth (*Sweet William's Ghost*). I find what corresponds with it in Bunyan, whose work is the expression of a folk-mythology which is not merely derivative from the Authorized Version. But I seem to find the same quality of vision, individualized, in Blake.

It is at this point that it becomes necessary to stress the fundamental difference between the Scottish Ballads and the Romantic Poetry of the nineteenth century (with which work Blake is also, I think, wrongly associated). That poetry took over for its own purposes a quantity of what may be described as the 'machinery' of the ballads. Its Poetic Diction is derived, through Coleridge and *La Belle Dame Sans Merci,* almost as much from that of the ballads (chiefly because of their apparent 'picturesque' medievalism) as from Spenser and Milton. But this Poetic Diction is cut off from the vigour—

> She stickit him like a swine

—of the popular speech which the Poetic Diction of the ballads is to a considerable extent a stylization of. Correspondingly there is nothing in common between the vital, if very fragmentary, vision of the Scottish Ballads, and the insubstantial dream of nineteenth-century poetry.

The ballad art, like other art, seems 'to separate from the world and us a group of figures, images, symbols' and thereby 'enables us to pass . . . into a deep of the mind'. It is difficult to resist the conclusion that nineteenth-century 'appreciation' subtly externalized (and sentimentalized) the significance of these 'figures, images, symbols', even those which most appealed to it:

> And he saw neither sun nor moon
> But he heard the roaring of the sea.

has a 'definite' significance in its context.

> 'Get dancers here to dance', she said,
>   'And minstrels for to play,
> For here's my young son, Florentine,
>   Come here wi me to stay . . .'
>
> For naething coud the companie do,
>   Nor naething coud they say,
> But they saw a flock o' pretty birds
>   That took their bride away.

There is more than a nursery-tale significance in, for example, the birds—that is to say, in *Cow-me-doo* as well as in the *Twa Corbies*; rather, there is the significance there often is, latent, in a nursery-tale which has been folk-tale.

If the symbolism of which I have spoken is kept in mind, the other images too assume, in varying degrees, a symbolical value in relation to it. The images of finery, for example, particularly of dress, which are so frequent in the Scottish Ballads, are then recognized to possess a symbolical value as profound as in Bunyan (' . . . he that is clad in Silk and Velvet'). That finery is associated with folly, pride and death. It is Vanity.

> Fair Margaret was a rich ladye
>   The king's cousin was she;
> Fair Margaret was a rich ladye
>   As vain as vain could be.
>
> She ward her wealth on the gay cleedin
>   That comes frae yont the sea,
> She spent her time frae morning till night
>   Adorning her fair bodye.
>
> Ae night she sate in her stately ha,
>   Kaimin her yellow hair . . .

This religious sense is behind the peculiar satiric element (a fierce exultant derision almost) in the lines:

> O our Scots Nobles were richt laith
>   To weet their cork-heild schoone;
> Bot lang owre a the play wer playd,
>   Thair hats they swam aboone.
>
> O lang, lang may their ladies sit,
>   Wi thair fans into their hand,
> Or ere they se Sir Patrick Spence

Cam sailing to the land.

> O lang, lang may the ladies stand
>   Wi thair gold kems in their hair,
> Waiting for their ain deir lords,
>   For they'll se thame na mair.

And this religious sense is present also, pityingly and wonderingly, in

> But she put on the glistering gold
>   To shine through Edinburgh town,

in its *Marie Hamilton* context—a poem which seems to me charged with this religious sense.

The ballads are concerned, it is true, almost entirely with the circle of the life of the body, with birth, instinctive action, death (often violent death), and the decay of the body. Again, they present on the one hand . . . images of a princely grandeur erected out of earth, and on the other hand, its counterpart, the earthiness of death and decay. These images are contrasted and associated, if not explicitly, by their mutual presence. The total effect is thus sombre. It has been customary to speak of the 'paganism' of the Scottish Ballads. I suppose I mean the same thing, but I should prefer to describe them (keeping in mind the symbolism I have spoken of) as, in a profound sense, 'religious'. They embody, in any case, very fragmentarily indeed, but with startling immediacy, a tragic vision of human life which sprang, apparently, from the imagination of the 'folk'.

THE SCOTS VERNACULAR REVIVAL

H. J. C. Grierson

SOURCE: "The Problem of the Scottish Poet," in *Essays and Studies,* Vol. XXI, 1936, pp. 105-23.

[*Formerly a professor of English and rector at the University of Edinburgh, Grierson wrote and edited a number of books on Sir Walter Scott. In the following excerpt, Grierson discusses the limited role of the Scottish dialect since the eighteenth century and asserts that Burns and Scott were the last representatives of a genuine Scottish poetic tradition.*]

Throughout the seventeenth, the eighteenth, and even part of the nineteenth century the cultured, educated Scot spoke, among his fellow Scots, his Scottish vernacular; but if he wrote—philosophy, history, theology, poetry, economics, whatever the theme—he wrote in English. The position today is reversed. He speaks English, a northern English certainly, *lingua inglese in bocca scozzese* (unless early education or social ambition has further polished and disguised his speech), but he may, if he is literary, compose verses in Scots or write a novel of Scottish life in which the dialogues are in Scots or in what passes as Scots. The late Professor Mair wrote Scots poems no better if no worse than those of many others. His Greek renderings of some Scots poems are, or seem, better than the originals.

The interaction between the two varieties of one language, which is what they are, the standard English of the southern kingdom and the northern English, Inglis, which had established itself as the speech of the Kingdom of Scotland (so far as this was not Gaelic), began early. The Scottish poets, from Barbour to Montgomery, wrote in their own northern tongue, and a very noble tongue it is. But these Scottish Makars were no forerunners of Wordsworth. The speech of the poet was not for them the language of every day, but a nobler rhetoric, composed like the chorus of a Greek tragedy in an artificial, decorative diction, the aureate style which was the fashion in various countries in the fifteenth century, the diction of the French *rhétoriqueurs,* the 'schuim' or 'foam' of the *Rederijkers* of the Low Countries. And some of the Scots poets' 'rhetorike' was borrowed from the English poets:

> O moral Gower, and Lydgate laureate,
> Your sugarit lippis and tongues aureate
>> Been to our earis cause of great delite.
> Your angelic mouthis most melifluate
> Our rude language has clear illuminate
>> And faire ourgilt our speche, that imperfyte
>> Stude or your goldin pennis shope to write:
> The Isle before was bare and desolate
>> Of rhetorike or lusty fresh endite.

That is at once an express statement, and a fair example, of the Scottish poet's ideal of his art, his rhetoric; and also an indication of his respect for the poetry of his southern neighbour, the 'auld enemy'. The chief feature, indeed, of Scottish rhetoric, of aureate diction, was the Latinized phraseology, for which Scottish writers have never quite lost a predilection; but these early poets borrowed also syntactical features of the southern tongue. None the less their language remained in its chief traits, pronunciation, vocabulary, idiom, our northern Scottish tongue.

With the migration to London of the Scottish Court in 1603 the process of change began at once and has gone on with ever-increasing rapidity. The Scottish poets of the seventeenth century set themselves, almost as one man, to learn and to write Southern English—Drummond of Hawthornden, a disciple of Spenser and Sidney and of their French and Italian models; Robert Kerr, Earl of Ancram; Sir David Murray of Gorthy (*The Tragicall Death of Sophonisba,* a poem in the metre and manner of *The Rape of Lucrece*); William Lithgow (*The Pilgrimes Farewell to his native country of Scotland,* 1618), Simeon Graham (*The passionate Sparke of a relenting minde,* 1604), Alexander Craig (*Amorose Songs, Sonets and Elegies,* 1606, and *Poeticall Recreations of Alexander Craige, Scoto-Britane,* 1604). Scotticisms abound in such poems, but of the manner of the old Makars the only feature which these poets retain is their fondness for

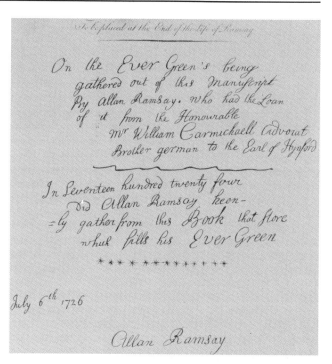

Facsimile of a note Ramsay placed with the Bannatyne Manuscript of 1568, from which he drew most of the Middle Scots poetry contained in The Ever Green *(1724).*

Latinized words:

> Thou steepie hill, so circling piramiz'd,
>> That for a prospect serves East Lothian
>> landes,
> Where ovile flockes doe feed half enamiz'd
>> And for a trophee to North Berwicke
>> standes,
> So mongst the marine hills growes didemiz'd,
>> Which curling plaines and pastring Vales
>> commaundes:
> Out from thy poleme eye some sadnesse borrow,
> And deck thy listes with streames of sliding
>> sorrow.

So Lithgow addresses North Berwick Law, familiar to generations of golfers. One can understand why a century later Thomson of *The Seasons* cultivates the new poetic diction so ardently and writes of 'the plumy race', 'ovarious food', 'th'inspective glass', 'prelusive drops', 'th' amusive arch' (rainbow), &c. Even the Scottish common people love a Latinized diction. A friend's caddy on St. Andrews links, directing his shot, asked: 'Do you see yon castellated mansion?'

These poets wrote in English, but they quite certainly spoke Scots. In fact the anglicization of their work was not infrequently the work of the printer—Vautrollier a Frenchman or Waldegrave an Englishman, or even good Scotsmen like Robert Charteris and Andro Hart. The English is not always pure. To unlearn the use of Scotticisms was a great concern of every writer and teacher till well into the nineteenth century. Sinclair's *Scotticisms* or properly *Observations on the Scottish Dialect* by John

Sinclair, Esq., M.P. (later Sir John Sinclair or in Scott's letters 'Sir John Jackass'), 1782, includes 'Scots' itself as a Scotticism for 'Scotch' or 'Scottish', so low had we sunk. Some of the words he lists are still pure Scots, as 'gar', 'sib', 'sicker', 'drumly', but others have either passed into English or never were entirely Scots, e.g. 'restrict', 'sweet-blooded', 'midges', 'a pier', 'suet', 'so soon as', but perhaps these are still Scottish to a purer ear than mine.

The seventeenth century did produce a few poems in the vernacular, the anonymous *Philotas* at the beginning of the century—a survival of the poetic manner of the 'Makars'; *Ane Godlie Dreame,* by Lady Culross; the poems of Alexander Hume 'in a curious blend of the Scots and the English idiom'. The best and best known of these, *Of the Day Estivall* (which is an aureate phrase for *A Summer's Day*), is as delightful for its vivid rendering of the atmosphere of such a day as its decorated Scots is quaint:

> The gloming comes, the day is spent,
> The sun goes out of sight,
> And painted is the Occident
> With purpour sanguine bright.
>
> The Skarlett nor the golden threid
> Who would their beauty trie,
> Are naething like the colours reid
> And beautie of the skie.
>
> Our west Horizon circuler
> Fra time the sun be set
> Is all with rubies (as it were)
> Or roses reid ou'rfret.

But the poets who wrote Scots as spoken were the Sempils of Beltrees (Sir James but especially Robert) and the anonymous authors of some of our oldest songs, 'Todlen Ben', 'Maggie Lauder', 'The Barrin' o' the Door', 'O waly, waly', &c. These are poems, however, like the earlier *Christ's Kirk* or *Peebles to the Play,* about, or for, the people. The cleavage is already complete—English for serious purposes, Scots for humour or sentiment.

What is true of poetry is also true of prose. 'The literary Scots dialect practically disappears from prose in the seventeenth century', says J. H. Millar. The English Bible is read in the pulpit, rolled doubtless through a Scottish mouth, and commented on in the vernacular. The relation between the two tongues, that which one spoke and that one wrote, is well brought out, as Miss Bald shows, by the fact that Lepreuik prints David Ferguson's *Answer to an Epistle written by Renet Benedict* (1563) in English, but a sermon by the same author (1572) in Scots. 'This proves that English or Anglicized Scots was regarded quite early as the correct diction for academic works, but unadulterated Scots continued to a later period as the usual speech of the preacher facing his congregation'; and so it continued to be for two centuries and more—the speech of the preacher in the pulpit, of the advocate at the bar, of the judge upon the bench, of the people high and low

in the intercourse of every day. As late as the closing years of the eighteenth century 'no Englishman could have addressed the Edinburgh populace without making them stare and probably laugh. We looked upon an English boy at the High School as a ludicrous and incomprehensible monster. . . . Still however Scotch is pretty deeply ingrained into the people, but among the gentry it is receding shockingly. Among families spending £700 or even £500 a year it seems to me that there is a majority of the modern children to whom Burns is a sealed book . . . Scotch has ceased to be the vernacular of the upper classes.' So Lord Cockburn in 1844, who deplores the fact. 'Old Scotland can only live in the character of the people, in its native literature and in its picturesque and delightful language. The gradual disappearance of the Scotch accent and dialect is a national calamity.' One can understand that things have not improved. For most of the students in a university class Burns needs as careful study with a glossary as Chaucer. Things stand much as follows. The people, especially in the country, speak Scots among themselves. In the elementary schools the children speak Scots among themselves, if in the towns a debased Scots. In the secondary public schools, or some of them in the smaller towns, this is also so, and a good English accent may expose one to ridicule. It was so at the Grammar School in Aberdeen twenty years ago, and at King's College, Aberdeen, many spoke Scots. But as one goes up in the social scale, to public schools in Edinburgh, the use of Scots becomes more and more a sign of social inferiority. The highest class socially are careful to send their sons to school and university in England for fear, as Sir Herbert Maxwell states, they should acquire the slightest tincture of the native accent. I have no doubt that during his early years at Aberdeen Byron spoke the local dialect perfectly. He knows the difference between the general Scottish word for 'school', viz. 'Schüle', and the same word *Aberdonice,* 'Squeel'. In later years he was very sensitive to any suggestion of a Scottish flavour in his speech, yet some of his rhymes are Scottish or northern:

> then howl your idle wrath
> While she [the Muse] still silvers o'er your
> gloomy path.

We can recall more than one Scottish student who has gone to Oxford or Cambridge with a definite brogue and has returned without the consonant 'r' and with few distinguishable vowels, all replaced with what sounds to a Scottish ear like 'er', 'er'. A few robuster souls, like the late Master of Emmanuel, have scorned such flunkeyism and remained as faithful to their native bur, even in speaking southern English, as Professor Barker to that of Lancashire.

What then was the significance of the revival in the eighteenth century of the Scottish vernacular in the poetry of Allan Ramsay, of Robert Fergusson, of quite a galaxy of song-writers, and finally of Burns and those whom he inspired? What of the Scottish novel, Scott and Galt—their pictures of Scottish life and manners and reproduction of Scottish speech? The movement was both a consequence and a symptom of a revival of patriotic feeling, of feeling outraged by the method by which the union of the Parliaments had been achieved, and unassuaged by the economic compensation which materialized slowly. Nor can it be doubted that Burns and Scott, in whom the movement found its fullest expression, did much both to restore national self-confidence and to restore Scotland to a place on the map of Europe. They completed what had been begun by James Macpherson's *Ossian,* emphasized by the work and fame of Hume, Robertson, and Adam Smith, and they gave this revived picture a more native imprint than could be done by the English of Macpherson and Robertson and Hume. But the movement did not restore in any appreciable way the balance as between the two tongues. The cleavage was complete—English for serious compositions on learned themes, Scots for compositions dealing with the life, the sentiments, the humours of the common people. The new poetry and the new novel were to confine the use of Scots to this narrower channel. Not one of the poets but would write in English too, and in the novel the vernacular would be used only for dialogue. Whatever they thought of England politically—and till the French Revolution quickened new passions Burns was a sound British imperialist, Scott was always passionately so—the Scottish writers had as unbounded an admiration for contemporary English writers as had the Makars of the fifteenth century. They admired Pope and Addison and Sterne and Gray just as Dunbar had revered Gower and Lydgate. No; as Burns's life illustrates, the revival of Scottish national sentiment became a power only as it merged itself in the larger democratic movement of the century. The passions of the Scottish people were gradually roused, not for any restoration of Scottish independence, but for the delivery of Scotland from the domination of the landed Tory party. When the Reform Bill was passed they would be ejected *uno pede.* If Burns became the hero, almost the patron saint, of the Scottish people, the middle classes and the peasantry (not the West End, who have always sniffed a little), it was because they saw in him a combination of two ideals which were gaining in importance and appeal: the inspired poet and the great man of the people.

A Man of the People—'The dignity, the spirit, the indignation of Burns', writes Scott, 'was that of a plebeian—of a high-souled plebeian indeed—of a citizen of Rome or Athens; but still a plebeian, untinged with the slightest shade of that spirit of chivalry which since the feudal times has pervaded the higher ranks of European society.' So justly does Scott distinguish between the spirit of his own work and Burns's: his own aristocratic, in the spirit of the romantic and historical ballads, of the romances, of the courtly poetry of the Middle Ages; Burns's in the spirit of the songs in which the people sang of their own joys and sorrows and loves and hates, and of such old Scottish poems as *Christ's Kirk on the Green* and *Peebles to the Play.* In only one of Burns's songs is the note of chivalry audible:

> It was a' for our rightfu' king
> We left fair Scotland's strand,

and it was so unlike a song by Burns that Scott took it for

an old song revived and borrowed the stanza and the refrain for a song of his own in *Rokeby.* One of themselves the Scottish people have felt Burns to be both as man and poet—one of the peasantry, that is, for the Industrial Revolution had not yet made of us a nation of artisans. For a glimpse of town life in the Edinburgh of the eighteenth century—dirty, noisy, convivial, immoral, and pious—one must turn to Ramsay and Fergusson. The background to Burns's poetry is the country-side seen through the eyes of the working peasant. Wordsworth and Angellier have expressed surprise that there is nowhere in Burns's poems a reference to the beautiful view from Mount Oliphant or Mauchline of the sea and the Isle of Arran and Ailsa Craig. Burns was no landscapist, no Gilpin or Wordsworth or even Scott. What filled his vision was the fields in which he worked, the streams and hills, the farms and cottages with, a little farther in the background, the neighbouring villages, Mauchline and Tarbolton, with their kirks and taverns:

> O sweet are Coila's haughs and woods
> Where lintwhites chant amang the buds,
> And jinkin hares, in amorous whids,
>   Their loves enjoy;
> While through the braes the cushat croods
>   With wailfu' cry!

That is one aspect. The other is:

> When chapman billies leave the street
> And drouthy neebors neebors meet;
> As market days are wearin' late
> An folk begin to tak the gate:
> While we sit bousing at the nappy
> An' getting fou and unco happy.

Burns is not a Clare, a Shelley born by accident a peasant. He is a peasant who found his inspiration in the life and work, the joys and sorrows, the prejudices and passions of the peasantry, but raised these in his expression of them to a higher power. Burns's temperament was his great gift to poetry, and one which none of his followers has inherited. The glowing eye and the passionate temperament of which it was the index are what Scott recalls in all he has to say of Burns.

What then are the native themes of popular poetry, poetry addressed to and dealing with the common people and their lives? A little reflection, a little study, of Scottish poetry of the kind or of Dutch painting, or better still a little acquaintance with any small peasant or fishing community, will soon show. It is not work. Of the interest of that the common man is apt to become aware only when he is out of work. It is the onlooker, the philosophic, reflective poet, a Wordsworth or a Tolstoi, who is aware of the beauty, the sublimity, of his stern, wearing, unambitious, regular (as recurrent as the seasons themselves) struggle for a livelihood with the soil or with the sea. He does not reflect on this himself. It is a necessity. The peasantry of Westmorland did not understand Wordsworth. They preferred Hartley Coleridge, who would join them in a glass of beer at the tavern. Nor is it war. The glories of war are the theme of aristocratic poetry, for to the aristocrat goes most of the glory. The chief interests of the peasant are threefold—love in various moods but never with courtly or metaphysical sophistication; revelry (the scenes and incidents in which the Dutch and Flemish painters delighted); and lastly satire. A small community's knowledge of each other is very close, and the satirical mood which close contact breeds finds expression in many ways including nicknames and practical jokes.

Now the great—what I may, following Mr. Dover Wilson, call the 'essential' Burns, is just the poet of these themes. His verse epistles are fresh, ardent, and reflective. The poems in the sentimental tradition of the English poets, Gray, Shenstone, and others, as *The Cottar's Saturday Night, To a Mouse, To a Mountain Daisy,* are charming. They are the sources of later Scottish sentimental poetry. But the great Burns, the Burns who has had no successor, is the poet of the gaiety of *Halloween,* the rollicking fun of *Tam o' Shanter,* and the combination of fun and satire, fast and furious, of *The Holy Fair.* That poem and *Halloween* are in the tradition of *Christ's Kirk* and *Peebles to the Play,* and also of such a Dutch poem as *Arent Pieter Gysen* by Brederode, and the paintings of the Flemish masters. Has any English poet rendered the zest of life and movement as Burns has in *The Holy Fair?*—

> Now butt an' ben the Change-house fills
>   Wi' yill-caup commentators;
> Here's crying out for bakes an' gills,
>   An' there the pint-stowp clatters;
> While thick an' thrang, an' loud an' lang,
>   Wi' Logic an' wi' Scripture,
> They raise a din that, in the end,
>   Is like to breed a rupture
>   O' wrath that day.

As a satirist, a satirist whose satire is at once searching and yet also steeped in laughter, Burns's place is with the greatest. Is there a better piece of satiric verse in the language than *Holy Willy's Prayer?*—

> O Thou that in the Heavens dost dwell,
> Wha, as it pleases best Thysel,
> Sends ane to Heaven, an' ten to Hell
>   A' for Thy glory,
> And no for ony guid or ill
>   They've done before Thee!

>   . . . . .

> When from my mither's womb I fell
> Thou might hae plung'd me deep in Hell,
> To gnash my gooms, and weep and wail
>   In burning lakes,
> Whare damnèd devils roar and yell
>   Chain'd to their stakes.

> Yet I am here, a chosen sample,
> To show Thy grace is great and ample;
> I'm here a pillar o' Thy temple

> Strong as a rock,
> A guide, a buckler, and example
>   To a' Thy flock.

> But yet, O Lord, confess I must,
> At times I'm fash'd wi' fleshly lust;
> And sometimes, too, in warldly trust,
>   Vile self gets in;
> But Thou remembers we are dust,
>   Defil'd wi' sin.

> O Lord—yestreen—Thou kens—wi' Meg—
> Thy pardon I sincerely beg—
> O may't ne'er be a living plague
>   To my dishonour!
> And I'll ne'er lift a lawless leg
>   Again upon her.

>   . . . . .

> Maybe Thou lets this fleshly thorn
> Buffet Thy servant e'en and morn,
> Lest he owre proud and high should turn
>   That he's sae gifted:
> If sae, Thy han' maun e'en be borne
>   Until Thou lift it.

Calvinism as popularly understood—carnality, hypocrisy, unction—all combine in one felicitous stream of wit and poetry.

In his love-songs, too, Burns is pre-eminently the peasant, the plebeian. There is no Petrarchan or Donnean sophistication. Here are just the sentiments of the common country people with their daffings and night-courtings and wholesome blend of sense and heart, passion and affection. The tragic notes are few but piercing. Burns's sadder love-songs are good in parts rather than as a whole. If they had survived, like Sappho's, in single lines or stanzas, posterity might have imagined a greater poet lost:

> The pale moon is setting behind the white wave,
>   And time is setting wi' me, O.

or

> Had we never loved sae kindly,
> Had we never loved sae blindly,
> Never met or never parted
> We had ne'er been broken-hearted.

The rest of that song, as Scott says, is verbiage. The fact is, the peasant poet can hardly give to the elaboration of his grief the subtlety, metaphysical or decorative or ironical, of the cultured poets as Shakespeare in

> Take, O take those lips away
> That so sweetly were forsworn,

or Rochester or Shelley or Heine, though Heine has no finer stroke of penetrating irony than Burns's

George Douglas on the endurance of Scots vernacular poetry:

For all prose purposes other than those which are purely dramatic—the dialogue, for instance, or, in rare cases, the narrative in a work of fiction—the vernacular has completely passed into disuse. For it is safe to prophesy that no history, no philosophic or scientific treatise, will ever be composed in Scots again. And this was as true in the Eighteenth Century as it is true to-day. But, for poetry, the vernacular survived—as it still survives. But poetry is the intimate language of the heart and of the soul: the language alike of ease and of elevation: of a man discharged from care, on pleasure bent, among his equals; and of one alone, or in a twofold solitude, expressing his love, his longing, his ideal—uttering as if to one he knows and trusts the things that are most sacred and most dear to him. To such purposes as these, then, has the Scottish Doric been dedicated; of such uses as these gifted men have deemed it worthy. And, speaking to us through that tongue, these men have seemed to come nearer to us in their own persons than have others who have spoken only in alien or in artfully acquired words.

George Douglas, in Scottish Poetry: Drummond of Hawthornden to Fergusson, *James Maclehose and Sons, 1911.*

We're a' dry wi' drinkin' o' it,
We're a' dry wi' drinkin' o' it,
The minister kiss'd the fiddler's wife
An' couldna preach for thinkin' o' it.

But where Burns has no superior is in songs of mutual contented love: 'O my luve is like a red, red rose', 'Of a' the airts the wind can blaw', 'Go fetch to me a pint o' wine', the classically perfect

When o'er the hills the eastern star
    Tells buchtin' time is near, my Jo.

In *Tam Glen* he blends humour with real affection, and so in 'Last May a braw wooer cam' doun the lang glen'. In one of the most delightful poems written:

In simmer when the hay was mawn
    And corn waved green in ilka field,

Burns has blended lyrically and dramatically the feelings of the 'old struggler' (as the Irish woman described herself to Scott), the old woman who knows the real, harsh facts of life, and the more reckless spirit of the generous, warm-hearted young girl.

Burns then is the plebeian, the last and greatest of genuinely peasant poets, his work in a tradition that goes back to the fifteenth century in Scottish poetry. But Burns was bilingual, and though the poems he wrote deliberately in English and in the fashionable manner of the day, Odes, &c., are a failure, yet he blends Scots and English in almost all his poems, just as the old Makars had done, and when he wishes to rise to a higher strain of reflection passes in *Tam o' Shanter* from broad Scots to pure English:

But pleasures are like poppies spread, &c.

Sir Walter Scott was also the inheritor and last genuine representative of a tradition in Scottish poetry, not one confined to Scottish poetry, for it is the tradition of medieval romantic and courtly poetry. For him the ballads, romantic and historical, to which Burns preferred the songs and poems of peasant revelry, were his first and great inspiration, and the reason is clear, for scholarship has established the fact that the ballads, like the verse romances, were courtly, aristocratic in origin and spirit. The chivalrous was his passion, though blended with a sober realism due to his Scottish blood and the influence of the great novelists of the eighteenth century and a due regard for his audience. He had no wish like Chatterton, or Morris later, to archaize and so limit his audience. Like Shakespeare, Scott wrote for gain, not glory. In his collective work the tradition of ballad, romance, drama, and prose fiction were combined to produce the genuine historical novel. But with this I am not concerned, only with his poetry and his use of Scots and English.

In all his work Scott is a reviver to some extent of old moods of feeling and old modes of expression, and he is most a poet when this is most true, when there is least of accommodation to the manner of his own day. The essential Scott the poet is to be found, not in the longer lays, but in the songs and fragments scattered through these poems and the novels, and all the best of these are in some older manner. Every one remembers the Lyke-Wake Dirge printed by Ritson and then by Scott:

This ae night, this ae night,
    Every night an' all,
Fire and sleet, and candle-light,
    And Christ receive thy saul.

That is clearly the inspiration of Meg Merrilies' song:

Wasted, weary, wherefore stay,
Wrestling thus with earth and clay?
From the body pass away:—
        Hark, the mass is singing, &c.

and also of Claud Halcro's:

And you shall deal the funeral dole:
    Aye, deal it, mother mine,
To weary body and to heavy soul,
    The white bread and the wine.

And you shall deal my horses of pride;
    Aye, deal them, mother mine;
And you shall deal my lands so wide,
    And deal my castles nine.

But deal not vengeance for the deed,

And deal not for the crime;
The body to its place, and the soul to Heaven's
grace,
And the rest in God's own time.

That is old in tone, and yet strangely modern in its suggestion of meaning that is not fully defined. The ballad which Scott puts into the mouth of Old Elspeth in *The Antiquary* is in a purer ballad tradition and style than many of those in the *Minstrelsy*. All the snatches of song put into the mouth of Meg Merrilies are of the same traditional character—a harvest song; a hymn in the manner of Addison and the earlier eighteenth century; a tragic song of love:

Cauld is my bed, Lord Archibald,
And sad my sleep o' sorrow;

and the lovely *Proud Maisie*. The same is true of 'Look not thou on beauty charming', or 'Soldier, wake, the day is peeping', or 'Woman's faith and woman's trust, Write the characters in dust', and 'An hour with thee', the last song he wrote. Scott can catch with equal ease the note of a Catholic dirge:

Dust unto dust,
To this all must;
The tenant has resigned
The faded form
To waste and worm—
Corruption claims her kind.

or that of a Scottish metrical Psalm:

When Israel of the Lord belov'd
Out from the land of bondage came, &c.

I need not refer to the mottoes he invented, echoes of Elizabethan and later drama. Scott began his literary work as a translator, and he wrote to the end as one who was in a way translating—translating an older world of sentiment and song into a language understood of his contemporaries.

Burns and Scott have had no genuine successors. Each was the last representative of a long line of tradition in life and poetry, if each was also a contributor to the revolution that was in progress. Burns is the last genuine peasant poet, for the peasant life of Scotland was in a process of rapid disintegration. And Burns was also a voice of the new democratic spirit that was quickening in Scotland, the spirit of equalitarianism so much stronger in France and Scotland than in England:

A man's a man for a' that.

Scott was the last poet who took the aristocratic tradition of life and feeling quite seriously, and even he had his doubts, for the aristocracy which Scott loved and to find a place among whom he laboured and dreamed was on the verge of disappearing before the advent of democracy and, still more powerful, of plutocracy. Scott's own life is

a strange blend of aristocratic and plutocratic ambitions. Nor did Burns or Scott do anything to re-establish the Scottish vernacular as a medium for serious literature. They are both bilingual and make in different ways effective use of the two. What they did do, however, was to vindicate the claims of Scots to be something more than a vulgar *patois* such as that of the English yokels who insulted Jeanie Deans in a far worse speech than her own at which they laughed. For theirs had never been, as her vernacular had been, the language of cultured men and women, and of both poetry and prose. Neither Burns nor Scott—and Scott's vernacular is purer than Burns's—could have written as they did, could have made Meg Merrilies or Jeanie Deans speak as they do at great moments, in a *patois* that had no history and no literature. But no Scot was prepared to forgo the use of English for work in philosophy, history, economics, any more than at an earlier period they would or could have dispensed with the use of Latin. And so Scottish poetry has continued in the narrow channel prescribed for it, a medium for occasional popular use in such farm-servants' ballads as the late Mr. Gavin Greig collected, and for the poems of cultured writers on similar themes, and the dialogue of novels on Scottish life.

David Craig

SOURCE: "The Old Communal Culture," in *Scottish Literature and the Scottish People: 1680-1830,* Chatto & Windus, 1961, pp. 19-39.

[A professor of literature and creative writing at the University of Lancaster, Craig utilized a cross-disciplinary perspective in such books as The Real Foundations: Literature and Social Change *(1973). In the following excerpt, he analyzes the social themes of eighteenth-century Scottish poetry and discusses the Edinburgh society that influenced such poets as Ramsay and Fergusson.]*

[Scottish poetry] is peculiarly rich in all that has to do with social life. In the 17th and 18th centuries it is taken up almost exclusively with that, but socialness of a kind very different from, say, the equally 'social' English poetry of that time. Dryden and Pope lived amidst and wrote for an upper-middle and upper class metropolitan world of coffeehouse, town mansion, and country estate, a milieu of politicians and landowners growing rich (or bankrupt) on investments, and the artists to whom they gave commissions and hospitality. Pope especially writes as one accustomed to shine in the company of the sophisticated and important; this forms not only his subject-matter (the conditions of a genuine literary culture; 'the use of riches'), but his manner also, which turns to creative uses the poise of a conscious conversationalist. The Scottish contemporaries, Allan Ramsay, Robert Fergusson, and later, Burns, could hardly differ more. They inhabit the ordinary pubs and market places, centres of gaming, drinking, eating, small business deals, the coming and going of farmers, chapmen (pedlars), and lawyers looking for work—but not, apparently, of literary connoisseuring and the discussion of new publications which could seriously influence a central government. They write in the manner of popular wiseacres, masters of repartee, in a language little different from that of the mass of their countrymen, not in that of an educated upper crust. 18th-century Scotland is of course famous for such an 'élite': men of letters such as Hume, Adam Smith, Henry Mackenzie, and (a little later) Scott, and the cultured law lords (Kames, Hailes, and later Jeffrey). But as far as these men were concerned, at least in the 18th century, the creative literature of the country—the poetry of Ramsay, Fergusson, and Burns—was virtually underground, or in the backwoods. Its comedy embodied a social life beneath the dignity of the 'polite' class. Yet that stratum of social life—lived out in the howffs (pubs), street markets, and tenement stairs—was in fact shared, even in the capital city, by all classes, aristocracy, bourgeoisie, and working folk alike, to an extent unthinkable in any later age. The society was close-knit in its physical conditions of life, if not in education, property, and outlook.

Why was it, then, that the expression of Scottish socialness was carried on so exclusively by the vernacular writers? Why did the communications represented by the national poetry stay so insulated from the more refined manners and ideas which the educated classes were learning from France and England? The town of Edinburgh, in its expansion from a congested, narrow, filthy medieval settlement to a geometrically planned model city, is not only a symbol of this two-sided Scottish culture, it is the very soil in which it grew. In exploring the town and village communities of pre-19th-century Scotland, we are to a great extent examining the immediate conditions which made the literature what it was, and made it distinctive.

The line of poetry which culminates in Burns represents the last phase in Scottish history in which a distinctively native mode of expression held together through several generations. It will be as well to form a concrete sense of what that poetry was like, before going further into the social conditions behind it. This line of poetry got its nickname, 'the matter of Habby Simson', from Robert Sempill's poem of the mid-17th century, 'The Piper of Kilbarchan' (a poem which Grierson and Bullough were catholic enough to put into the *Oxford Book of Seventeenth Century Verse*). This poem seems authentically popular, with no taint of *arrière-pensée* about the ordinary village fun. It gives the effect, though written by a landed gentleman, of sharing directly and artlessly in a village life whose high moments were signalled by music:

> Now who shall play, the Day it Daws?
> Or Hunts Up, when the Cock he craws?
> Or who can for our Kirk-town-cause,
>   Stand us in stead?
> On bagpipes (now) no body blaws,
>   Sen Habbie's dead.
>
> Or wha will cause our shearers shear?
> Wha will bend up the brags of weir,
> Bring in the bells, or good play meir,

In time of need?
Hab Simson cou'd, what needs you spear?
    But (now) he's dead.

. . . . .

> At Clark-plays when he wont to come,
> His pipe play'd trimly to the drum,
> Like bikes of bees he gart it bum,
>   And tun'd his reed.
> Now all our pipers may sing dumb,
>   Sen Habbie's dead.

Such sociable music seems to have been in the bones of the people. [In *The Tea-Table Miscellany* (1724-37),] Allan Ramsay says affectionately of the popular song tunes: "They are, for the most part, so cheerful, that on hearing them well played or sung, we find a difficulty to keep ourselves from dancing . . . such as are not judges of the fine flourishes of new music imported from Italy and elsewhere, yet will listen with pleasure to tunes that they knew, and can join in the chorus." The familiar rhythms, indeed, get into the very metre of the poetry. Such snatches as this from the probably 16th-century 'Peblis to the Play',

> Sum said the quene of may——wes cumit
> Of peblis to the play,

move with just the beat of the foot checking and setting off again in a country dance.

Such a poem as 'The Piper of Kilbarchan' is still purely of the old village way of life, that enacted in 'Peblis to the Play' and 'Christis Kirk on the Green' (to name two of the early models for Ramsay, Fergusson, and Burns). By Ramsay's time, the vernacular poet—even if he thinks of himself as popular—is no longer immersed in the country life. When Ramsay imitates 'Christis Kirk', he forces his jocosity onto us:

> But mony a pawky look and tale
>   Gaed round when glowming hous'd them;
> The ostler wife brought ben good ale,
>   And bad the lasses rouze them . . .

In contrast the poet of the 16th century (or earlier) loses himself in the momentum of the fun:

> Stewin come steppand in with stendis
> No renk mycht him arrest
> Platfut he bobbit up with bendis
> for mald he maid requeist . . .
>
> Than thai come to the townis end
> withouttin more delay
> He befoir and scho befoir
> To se quha wes maist gay.
> all that luikit thame upon
> leuche fast at thair array
> Sum said that thai wer merkat folk
> Sum said the quene of may—wes cumit
> Of peblis to the play.

In this, much the better of these two festivity poems, the action is relieved from the monotonous wallowing in muck and brutal horseplay by the extraordinary vivacity of every movement, for example,

> Be that the bargan was all playit
> The stringis stert out of thair nokkis . . .

And once an extra delicacy that the fun takes on is plainly in touch with a very old vein of folk symbolism, apparently related to the strange imagery of heavenly beauty in the Border ballad 'The Wife of Usher's Well':

> The carline wife's three sons came hame,
> And their hats were o' the birk.

> It never grew in syke nor ditch,
> Nor yet in ony sheugh;
> But at the gates o' Paradise,
> That birk grew fair eneugh.

'Peblis to the Play' expands the motif into something like a Pan figure or god of growth, and the stanza springs like a green shoot out of the poem:

> Ane young man stert in to that steid
> als cant as ony colt
> ane birkin hat upon his heid
> with ane bow and ane bolt

> Said, mirrie madinis think nocht lang
> The wedder is fair and smolt
> He cleikit up ane hie ruf sang
> Thair fure ane man to the holt—quod he
> of peblis to the play.

The suggestion that there is some *arrière-pensée,* or self-conscious rusticity, in this poetry has been made by the recent editor of Fergusson, Matthew P. MacDiarmid [in *The Poems of Robert Fergusson* (1954)]. He calls 'The Piper of Kilbarchan' "a comic play with undignified language, a species of burlesque", and regarding 'Peblis to the Play' he speaks of "burlesque" and "clownish caricature." But such poetry, in its rhythm and in the unforced flow of action, reads more like a perfectly straight celebration of unbridled community-fun in which the whole village is caught up. Allan Ramsay, who took up this poetry in the 18th century, reprinting, garbling, and imitating it, catches onto only its possibilities for pawky farce, for example he misses the running-on dance rhythm got by the bob that ends each stanza and cuts it down to one short line:

> She'd gar them a' be hooly
> Fou fast that day.

His people are individuals, unlike the scarcely-differentiated villagers of the old anonymous poetry. But this is not pure gain, for, as we have seen, his jocosity is put in, not the spontaneous emotion of primitive village life. As David Daiches has noted [in his "Eighteenth-Century Vernacular Poetry" (1955)], he is self-conscious, unintegrated, in his feelings about 'low life'. For one thing, he cannot but feel that the sayings of the townsfolk at play are quaint— vernacular gems or plums. Thus his proverbial phrases are visibly forced into his poetry for their own sake, rather than turned into genuine metaphor, for example:

> . . . Now they may mak a kirk and mill
> O't, since he's dead,

> We drank and drew, and fill'd again,
> O wow but we were blyth and fain!
> When ony had the Count mistain,

> O it was nice,
> To hear us a' cry, Pike yer Bain
> And spell yer Dice.

Such phraseology—proverbs, favourite metaphors, gambling jargon—were indeed the natural idiom for Scots poetry, for they were the favourite usage of a country still accustomed to the old oral literature and vernacular habits of speech and thought. 'A round of Scots proverbs'. . . was a regular amusement amongst parties of ordinary folk. . . . The same fun was had at the tea- and dinner-tables of the middle and upper classes. There was a craze for repeating proverbs at the tea-tables of the Edinburgh gentlefolk in the 1820's—some people could quote dozens. . . . Ramsay, however, picks such sayings out of natural speech and exploits them for local colour. He edited a collection of proverbs which circulated very widely in the late 18th century, especially in the form of the chapbooks or pamphlets which the chapmen sold at the farmhouse door. In his Preface he even sells the country people their own speech, on the lines of a conversation course:

> Ye happy herds, while your hirdsels are feeding on the flow'ry braes, you may eithly make yoursells masters of the hale ware. How usefull will it prove to you (wha have sae few opportunities of common clattering) when you forgather with your friends at kirk or market, banquet or bridal?

Although Ramsay thus belongs to an age in which an interest in Scottish culture was all too prone to turn it into (at best) folk-lore, nevertheless the vernacular, and the 'Habbie Simson' style, do supply the one mode which seems to suit his experience, in which he becomes at all interesting or vivid. Whereas in most of his other works he is blatantly aspiring to Literature, in his mock-elegies and verse epistles he is writing close to life. They give a sense of being in the thick of a social kind of life, not only in content but at those specially vivid points at which he expresses appreciation of simple convivial zest, as in "We drank, and drew, and fill'd again" or another couplet from the mock-elegy on Maggy Johnstoun, a popular pub-keeper:

> Sae brawly did a pease-scon toast
> Bizz i' the queff, and flie the frost . . .

This is a characteristic feeling of the Scots poetry in this tradition. It is rich in passages in which food and drink are revelled in as part of the fellow-feeling and brisk, busy coming-and-going of pub celebrations, often worked up into a sort of extravaganza which we would call caricature if the poet were not so wholeheartedly *with* the feeling he evokes. In Fergusson's 'Caller Oysters', money whirls round with the party:

> When auld Saunt Giles, at aught o'clock,
> Gars merchant lowns their chopies lock,
> There we adjourn wi' hearty fock
>   To birl our bodles

Handing round the common cup is described in words which richly evoke a sort of ideal luxury:

> Auld Reikie! thou'rt the canty hole,
> A bield for mony caldrife soul,
> Wha snugly at thine ingle loll,
>   Baith warm and couth;
> While round they gar the bicker roll
>   To weet their mouth.

In Burns, the drink itself takes on a super-animated life:

> When Vulcan gies his bellows breath,
> An' ploughmen gather wi' their graith,
> O rare! to see thee fizz an' freath
>   I' th' lugget caup!
> Then Burnewin comes on like death
>   At ev'ry chaup.

Burns also, with his genius for making something poetic of the familiarity natural to the people in a small community, has striking phrases which concentrate the sense of accustomed well-being and comradeliness which are part of such life, for example his emphatic use of "stand":

> At kirk or market, mill or smiddie,
> Nae tawted tyke, tho' e'er sae duddie,
> But he wad stand, as glad to see him,
> An' stroan'd on stanes an' hillocks wi' him.

Or, again, the passage at the beginning of 'Tam o' Shanter':

> . . . Ae market night,
> Tam had got planted unco right,

Sketch of the College Wynd, a street in the Old Town section of Edinburgh.

Fast by an ingle, bleezing finely,
Wi' reaming swats, that drank divinely . . .

In the weight of "stand" and "planted", we feel that the very posture embodies the heart of the contentment, the social rightness and well-being.

This characteristic socialness is seen at its best in the habit of making poetry from the high moments in the life of the community, whether ceremonies or festivities. Fergusson does the motley town scene almost for its own sake, or for its surface ludicrousness, as in 'The Election':

The MAGISTRATES fu' wyly are,
　　Their lamps are gayly blinking,
But they might as leive burn elsewhere,
　　Whan fock's *blind fu'* wi' drinking.
Our DEACON wadna ca' a chair,
　　The foul ane durst him na-say;
He took SHANKS-NAIG, but, fient may care,
　　He ARSELINS kiss'd the cawsey
　　　　Wi' BIR that night.

Burns, however, transforms such rollickings into a satirical image of Presbyterian extremist heat and sectarianism; the rhythm and extravagance of the mode are *used* to hit off, farcically, the other kind of extravagance indulged in by the bigot:

Kilmarnock wabsters, fidge and claw,
　　An' pour your creeshie nations;
An' ye wha leather rax an' draw,
　　Of a' denominations.

Swith! to the Laigh Kirk, ane an' a',
　　An' there tak up your stations;
Then aff to Begbie's in a raw,
　　An' pour divine libations
　　　　For joy this day.

. . . Mak haste an' turn King David owre
　　And lilt wi' holy clangor;
O' double verse come gie us four,
　　An' skirl up 'the Bangor':
This day the kirk kicks up a stoure,
　　Nae mair the knaves shall wrang her,
For Heresy is in her pow'r,
　　And gloriously she'll whang her,
　　　　Wi' pith this day.

We can see how much pointedness the social poetry has taken on since Ramsay's imitations of the old jocundity. A related characteristic is coining phrases which amount to a whole notation for the life of a community, for example Fergusson's "stair-head critics", Burns's "yill-caup commentators"—equivalent of 'bar-room politicians'—and Hamilton of Gilbert-field's "send them a' right sneaking hame / Be Weeping-Cross". At every point in this poetry it is the focal points and familiar symbols of a community way of life that are used for the basic idiom.

It is true that the conviviality runs also to a dismayingly silly cult, for it is really too slight to give the impulse of a whole poetry, or of a poetry sufficiently removed from light verse. In the end one's heart sinks at the everlasting 'homely' moral-swopping about drink:

A wee soup drink dis unco weel
　　To had the heart aboon,

or the bravado of

Leeze me on drink! it gies us mair
　　Than either school or college;
It ken'les wit, it waukens lear,
　　It pangs us fou o' knowledge . . .

We must remember that at that time a pre-occupation with drink was something like inevitable in the people's poetry. Engels (writing in [*The Housing Question*], 1872) refers very justly to "The fact that under the existing circumstances drunkenness among the workers is a necessary product of their living conditions, just as necessary as typhus, crime, vermin, bailiff and other social ills, so necessary in fact that the average figures of those who succumb to inebriety can be calculated in advance"; and figures and comments from Scotland in the late 18th and early 19th century bear this out. The literary fact, however, is that the very copious poetry of drink is usually inferior, seemingly a reaction part defensive, part self-surrendering to an evil social fact. I have concentrated on the feeling of pure convivial enjoyment because that is so often what is there at the most vivid points of wording in this poetry. Sometimes such feeling is self-conscious, and tries to rationalise itself. But when it is straight-forward, it is one of the poetry's most genuine emotions. It seems to represent the amazing energy and animal spirits of the common people, coming out in a poetry which helps to put us in the thick of the life they led in public.

A literature so strongly 'social' brings home to us what it meant to live in a society so thrown upon its own devices as the Scottish—in particular, so compact a capital. Living conditions in Edinburgh before the modern replanning have often been described, but more often than not for the gossip, or for the sake of 'old Edinburgh' itself, than as a way to understanding the national culture. Here the make-up of the town is to be considered in so far as it directly influenced the literature, both as a positive inspiration and as a cause of the alienation of the Scottish cultivated class from the 'typically Scottish'.

Scotsmen were used to very small, close communities, even in their main cities. Glasgow's population had gone up from 12,700 at the Union (1707) to 20,000 by mid-century, and its commercial expansion had begun. Yet carriers still built their haystacks in front of their doors, and the town herd went round every morning with his horn calling the cattle from the Trongate and the Saltmarket (where early in the century the wealthiest merchants lived) to the common meadows nearby. Edinburgh too was very compact, clustered round two parallel main streets, and it had, for a capital, unusually few communications with the rest of the country. Roads were very bad, and settlements (unlike those of England) were set far apart from each other. The first Scottish bank, the Bank of Scotland, failed in several early attempts to circulate its paper money in the provinces because so little trade came and went between the capital and the country. . . .

Because of the way Edinburgh had grown up on a narrow ridge of volcanic rock, it had had to build perpendicularly, squeezing lofty, narrow buildings (as in Manhattan) onto the slim pier of building space available. The main streets, High Street and Cowgate, ran east and west along the ridge, and the poorer streets were tunnel-like wynds and closes piercing the ground floor of the lofty tenements or 'lands' and dropping in slopes and steps down the cliff to either side. Behind the lands—some of whose façades were well enough built and even, if inhabited by the aristocracy, carved with arms and decorations—were those courts, deep wells of dirty stonework, where nowadays old air-raid shelters stand surrounded by dustbins and the dwellers hang out their washing on gallows-like spars projecting from the upper windows. Thus Edinburgh was not quartered off between the classes until the end of the century. This Scottish town housing was until the 1780's unique in the way it mixed the classes. In England even the poor usually had separate dwellings, whereas old Edinburgh was the only important British town in which tenement dwelling had been normal time out of mind, a condition it shared at this time with other old walled towns such as Stirling, and also with Glasgow, where most of the well-known, well-off citizens lived in tenement flats. As a result, leading tradesmen squeezed their families into quarters as cramping and unhygienic as the poor had elsewhere: one eminent goldsmith lived above his shop in Parliament Square, his nursery and kitchen in a cellar. . . . The lands were such warrens that in places people could step from one upper window to another across the street. Early census-takers were unable to track down every family living in the maze of stairs, closes, and cellars. Yet in these buildings the wealthiest and most elegant people in the country had apartments. Sweeps or messengers and odd-job men from the Highlands lived in the cellars, aristocrats or professional people on the first floor, shopkeepers and clerks on the higher floors, and poor skilled workmen in the attics.

So conditioned by this small community were the townsfolk that their social life, even that of the cultivated, was very close. As late as the '90's, the first planned extension to the old High Street nucleus, Brown and Argyle Squares, south of the Castle ridge, formed "a little world of their own, and had their own Assembly-rooms, and society of an excellent quality, in some degree apart from the rest of Edinburgh". Brown Square, indeed, was occupied by the set who produced the *Mirror,* Scotland's *Spectator*: Henry Mackenzie, William Craig (later a judge), Lord Woodhouselee, the 'great' Dundas (when an advocate), Islay Campbell, and Jeannie Elliot of Minto, author of 'The Flooers o' the Forest'. A man could live and die on that south side of the town without seeing the New Town to the north, beyond the pit of the Nor' Loch which became Princes Street Gardens after drainage. Adam Ferguson the historian's house at Sciennes, a couple of miles

from the Town Cross, was called by the other *literati* 'Kamchatka'; and lawyers were alarmed that the move to the New Town would lose them their *clientèle*.

Primitive conditions would by their nature throw people together. [In the *Gentleman's Magazine* of 1766], an Englishman observed of the narrow main street: "So great a crowd of people are nowhere else confined in so small a space, which makes their streets as much crowded every day as others are at a fair". There was no piped water until the '70's. Water was drawn from five public wells, which must thus have been great gathering points for the working-class. The gregarious habit was so strong that the modern Exchange, begun in 1754, was for some time little frequented because "the merchants always chuse standing in the open street, exposed to all kinds of weather". Although their stance, the Cross, was removed from the Canongate (the eastward extension of the High Street) in 1765, the lawyer-historian of Edinburgh, Hugo Arnot, writing in [his *History of Edinburg* in] 1779, observed that "Public proclamations continue to be made there. There also company daily resort, from one to 3 o'clock, for news, business, or meeting their acquaintances, nobody frequenting the exchange". Before the Bank of Scotland was founded, even important business would be done in little back shops or pubs and hardly any elsewhere. In Glasgow this was so widespread that the Council had to rule that town funds would not be liable for expenses incurred in this way.

This hugger-mugger living affected the vernacular poetry through the kind of popular culture—the network of institutions, habits of mind and behaviour, styles of expression—engendered by the compact town. The celebrations and gatherings which so fascinated the poets were bound to be enacted in the very midst of the city. Funerals and processions were elaborate shows; and the Company of Archers, in gorgeous costume, and (till the Union) Parliament paraded through the High Street. Leith Races, celebrated in Fergusson's poem of that name, was "a species of carnival to the citizens of Edinburgh". Every morning one town officer walked down to Leith with the 'City Purse' on a pole richly decked with flags and streamers, accompanied by the City Guard in full uniform and their drummer. Quacks and mountebanks put up stages in the High Street itself to sell remedies with comic patter; acrobats performed there; and quakers preached at the Cross to large audiences. The Edinburgh of Ramsay and Fergusson recalls, not contemporary London, but the London of Shakespeare and Ben Jonson.

The arts, too, were carried on amidst the people's daily life. For example, Fergusson himself had fun seeing how many sheets of ballads he could sell in two hours in the High Street, plying as a street singer. Before the Musical Society was formed, gentlemen met weekly in a pub whose proprietor was a great lover of music, and a good singer of Scots songs, and played Handel and Corelli. In the great hall of Parliament House which was used as a common promenade, there were bookstalls against one wall, just as there were jewellers' booths against one wall of St Giles's Cathedral. The better bookshops were, like the coffee-houses of Dryden's and Addison's London, the centres of literary society. James Donaldson's shop was the resort of the wits of Edinburgh during the time of Boswell. The leading bookseller in the '70's and '80's, William Creech, made his shop a 'lounge' and held literary breakfasts at his house. Its situation near the Parliament House was convenient as so many of the literary men were lawyers. . . . Also, the comparative poverty of the place tended to keep amusements popular and informal. Theatre after theatre failed, out of all proportion to the population, because trade around the mid-century brought in so little that [as Arnot notes] even "ordinary gentle-women, or the wives and daughters of shopkeepers or mechanics" were reluctant to go to the theatre unless they heard that it was packing for some performance; and their menfolk preferred the pubs.

The Edinburgh of Ramsay and Fergusson recalls, not contemporary London, but the London of Shakespeare and Ben Jonson.

—*David Craig*

Such conditions affected literature quite directly. Scots town literature of this period is, like English, highly social, but in a way very different from *Spectator* prose or Augustan poetry—products of a metropolitan fashionable society which, as F. R. Leavis puts it [in his *Revaluation* (1936)], "thought of poetry in general as of something that ought to be social . . . as belonging to the province of manners." Not a hint of 'correct' behaviour, of the cultivated manner and clever wit that belong to it, or indeed of a *conscious* code of any kind appears in the Scots work of that time. Its impulse, as has been suggested, comes directly out of the *mêlée* of common life; and this life was so formed that the bourgeoisie and ruling-class were not aloof from popular amusements any more than from the popular haunts. Ramsay's vernacular 'elegies' were modelled on cheap broadside-verse, yet at least one of them was handed round in manuscript among the gentry who were fellow-members of the Easy Club. Fergusson speaks familiarly of the various kinds of sociable group, the popular debating and drinking clubs, as an essential part of his town:

> Siclike in ROBINHOOD debates,
> Whan twa chiels hae a pingle;
> E'en-now some couli gets his aits,
> An' dirt wi' words they mingle,
> Till up loups he, wi' diction fu',
> There's lang and dreech contesting;
> For now they're near the point in view;
> Now ten miles frae the question
>   In hand that night.

Fergusson was himself the 'Precentor'—seemingly the recognised wit, singer, reciter—of the Cape Club, whose members included smiths and barbers as well as advo-

John Speirs on the Scots poetry of Ramsay, Fergusson, and Burns:

Allan Ramsay, Fergusson and Burns—in that chronological order—are the three outstanding makers of Scots verse in the eighteenth century. These poets are not remarkable as innovators. They work within the narrowly defined limits of a comparatively few modes, conventions and attitudes which they have inherited from the past of Scots verse. Their resemblances to each other are partly to be explained by the fact that they share the same modes, conventions and attitudes, and do not move outside them. It was perhaps in some ways to the advantage of their poetry that it was thus somewhat sharply defined and shaped. The spontaneous life and character of their poetry, for which it is indeed remarkable, are those of their spoken Scots out of which, within these definite limits, their poetry was made.

Ramsay, Fergusson and Burns were perhaps less ready than their predecessors to assume that the practice of Scots verse would continue to be kept up without a conscious determination on their part that it should be. Such an attitude implies some recognition of the danger (which had certainly become real) that it might not continue to be kept up. The one sure and certain way by which that might happen would be by the destruction of the Scottish community whose spoken language was the language of Scots poetry. The Industrial Revolution did virtually destroy the old Scottish community which is implied in the poetry of Ramsay, Fergusson and Burns.

John Speirs, in The Scots Literary Tradition: An Essay in Criticism, *Faber and Faber, 1962.*

cates and middle-class men of letters. In his 'The Daft-Days' drinking is evoked in rough vernacular—"While round they gar the bicker roll". Yet Lord Kames records that in *any* company, as late as 1730, one common cup was used by everybody for the whole evening, and it was thought fussy when people began to wish for separate glasses. Likewise Ramsay writes as a poor workman in 'Maggy Johnstoun':

> When in our pouch we found some clinks,
> And took a turn o'er Bruntsfield Links.

In fact the *habitués* of Maggy Johnstoun's howff included a judge (Lord Cullen) and a "well-employed advocate". In contrast the English clubs of the period were the preserve of the upper classes, whether literary or political, and the aristocracy were beginning to split off into their own exclusive societies with their own premises.

It is never easy precisely to define how such social conditions—so broad, so mixed, so varying in their effect on individuals—impinge on literature, or the writers of literature. But it is not uncommon for lines of force and limitations in the society to set broad limits which literature will be at least likely to keep to. We cannot account for all there is to Metaphysical poetry simply by referring to the make-up of the Court and country-house circles in which so much of it was written. Yet consider its kind of satirical wit, its mingled courtliness and indecency, the sophistication which is so conscious of itself, the close co-presence (in poems like Donne's 'Sunne Rising' and 'Canonization') of an intimate personal passion and a busy, mercenary, place-seeking Court *milieu,* felt as surrounding almost oppressively the personal life. These features show plainly enough the marks of the Stuart court, with its community of cultured nobility and arranged marriages, diplomats who were also scholars and poets, and officials living on perquisites. The style of the courtly poets—Wyatt, Raleigh, Donne, Carew, Herbert of Cherbury, Ben Jonson, Wotton—is both dignified and idiomatic, combining "the candour and naturalness of conversation among equals with the grace of a courtly society". When they are wittily amorous, they often (notably Carew) give the effect of vying with their fellows in the tradition of the elaborate compliment so ready to turn into indecency. Here again we see the marks of the reading-public or social set in which the poets functioned: gentlemen writing for gentlemen, circulating their work in manuscript, and certainly not exposing it for public sale.

The richer the literature, the less straightforward is the problem of making out the process whereby social forces had their conditioning effects. At the very least, however, a precise knowledge of history can forbid those covertly idealising speculations or assumptions about past communities to which modern critics often succumb. John Speirs, for example, has argued [in *The Scots Literary Tradition* (1940)] that Fergusson's poetry is "fundamentally rustic": the "town community . . . was still distinctly rural in character and speech", its legal side superficial. According to Mr Speirs the rural affiliations come out in a poem such as 'The Rising of the Session':

> . . . The wylie *writers,* rich as Croesus,
> Hurl frae the town in hackney chaises,
>   For country cheer . . .

This by itself, however, might be no more rustic fundamentally than London professional men holidaying on their dairy farms in Sussex. [In *Peter's Letters to His Kinsfolk* (1819)], Lockhart describes how the judges and advocates prepared for their summer week-ends in the country at farm or villa, wearing gorgeous informal clothes in court on Saturday, their horses lined up in parade in the Parliament Close. It is hard to see how such habits connect with the hurly-burly of common folk which gave Fergusson his impulse, especially as many farming lawyers of those days were of the new 'improving', scientific type. Lord Auchinleck, Boswell's father, was an early cultivator of root crops in the south-west. Cockburn of Ormiston, father of the great farming pioneer and a Lord Justice Clerk of Scotland, gave his tenants long leases enabling them to drain and hedge their ground. Sir James Montgomery, a Lord Advocate, was an improver of crops and livestock and sponsored a Bill to alter the law of entail in favour of improvers. Lord Kames, author of the *Elements of Criticism,* experimented in every branch of farming, especially root vegetables, green crops, sown grass, summer fallowing, and drainage, and wrote an expert

book on these subjects. An East Lothian advocate, Michael Menzies, invented a threshing machine. Such legal landowners hardly belonged to the ancient country round Mr Speirs apparently has in mind. One judge, Lord Hermand, is described by Cockburn as spending whole days on his farm hoeing in his old clothes, but he was famous for his eccentrically broad and old-fashioned ways. What we know of community life in the 17th and 18th centuries amounts to a strong presumption that the Edinburgh *town* community was, by itself, the natural basis for poetry such as Ramsay and Fergusson's. Certainly it is striking that their comedy should be so akin to the country-living Burns's. But that is surely because in Scotland at that time even the central cities were villagey in their smallness, their closeness, and their informal, rough-and-ready social habits.

We must also remember that old Edinburgh was in many ways a nasty warren, and so close-packed that none could get away from it. The sociable wells and stairheads made inevitably for filth. Workmen and lords alike had heaps of slops and excrement on the landings outside their flats; and shopkeepers sometimes had to cut a passage from shop door to street through piles of garbage. Much of the most brutal life of the place was out there in the main streets. One of the marts, the Grassmarket, is succinctly called by Pennant (who toured in 1767) the place "where cattle are sold, and criminals executed" [William Cobbett, *Rural Rides* (1853)]; and there are descriptions of the crowds buying and selling farm produce at one end of the Market while they watched the gallows being put up at the other. Yet in spite of the "inconvenience, and exceeding nastiness" of the market places, new ones were not begun till 1774 [Arnot]. At the end of the 17th century (fifteen years before Ramsay started to write), specimens were provided for the early anatomy classes from "unclaimed bodies of persons dying in the streets" [Robert Chambers, *Domestic Annals of Scotland* (1861)]. In 1700 floggings were carried out at several points on the High Street; in 1709 there were beheadings at the great gathering-place, the Cross; and petty offenders stood in the jougs and pillory at the Tron. Cock-fighting on the streets had to be prohibited by the Town Council to stop the disturbances it caused. Although so much of the social life centred in the pubs, their "equivocal character" made it unwise for women of "delicacy and propriety" to go into them [Arnot]. Scotland still suffers from the lack of a natural, integrated social life (in comparison with, for example, France and England) because there are so few pubs where women are welcomed on equal terms with the men.

Scott had good reason to know the miserable side of Old Town life—his parents lost four sons and two daughters in seven years, probably because the College Wynd at the foot of the Canongate, where they had their house, was so insanitary. Hence, perhaps, the actuality of his description, in *Provincial Antiquities,* of the wear and tear of that old close life. "Each inhabitable space was crowded like the under deck of a ship. Sickness had no nook of quiet, affliction no retreat for solitary indulgence." He emphasises the darkness of the interiors; the bother and labour for the porters who had to carry all water up many flights of stairs; and the lack of space for furniture in the cramped rooms.

The buoyant energy which tided people through such a life is felt in the non-stop flow of action and the caricaturing idiom, hearty and familiar, of the vernacular poetry. But we must equally note the wear and tear, the loss and curtailment of life, and the brutal attitudes to one another inevitable in such conditions. Much of the action in poems such as Ramsay's 'Christis Kirk', Fergusson's 'The King's Birth-Day in Edinburgh' or 'Hallow Fair', is horse-play, gross and dirty, and the poet's attitude is to revel in the discomfiture of the butt who falls down in the gutter or gets a swipe from a dead cat. Such is the counterpart of a life in which the festivities at Leith Races ended in a "promiscuous free fight" all up and down Leith Walk as the crowds returned to Edinburgh on the last evening of race week [James Grant, *Old and New Edinburgh* (1882)]. The real destructiveness and brutality of such a life is, of course, lost sight of in Fergusson's or the old anonymous poets' kind of rollicking comedy.

Such conditions were bound to cause a recoil. For one thing, the bourgeois men of letters—the spokesmen of the 'polite' culture which grew up as the century wore on—themselves lived on top of the dirt and confusion. Grant, the historian of Edinburgh, remarks that "within the narrow compass of this wynd [the College Wynd, Scott's birthplace] . . . were representatives of nearly every order of society, sufficient for a whole series of his Waverly novels". This also meant that there was a filthy byre at the foot of the street (not far from the University), and a well-known town idiot, Daft Bailie Duff, died in a "little den" there, in 1788. Yet late in the century the Cowgate, for example, was still reckoned an aristocratic locality. Henry Mackenzie, connected with the landed upper-class, was born in a wynd off the Cowgate, and later lived with his wife and family in a land at the junction of the Cowgate and the Grassmarket. Hume wrote his *History of England* in a land in the Canongate before moving to James's Court in the Lawnmarket (the continuation of the High Street towards the Castle), where Boswell also lived. William Robertson, the historian and leader of the Moderate clergy, lived in the Principal's house in the College, near the foot of the Canongate. His house was stormed by mobs rioting against the 1779 Bill to repeal the Catholic Penal Laws, his library was burned, and he had to take refuge in the Castle. Yet well on in the century the Canongate was still the fashionable quarter for "the better aristocracy of letters and science", including Adam Smith, Lord Kames, Lord Hailes, Cullen, Dugald Stewart, Lord Monboddo, and Sir John Dalrymple [*The Book of the Old Edinburgh Club* (1925)].

Such conditions were bound to force them out. When the English poet Rogers visited Edinburgh in 1789, Adam Smith told him that the Old Town "deserved little notice"—it had a bad name for filth, and he himself wanted to move to George Square (another of the model extensions to the south). Hugh Blair, the Moderate minister and fashionable writer on rhetoric, moved from the Lawn-

market to Argyle Square; Robertson moved to Grange (a near-rural district where the law lords built their villas, between Edinburgh and the Pentland Hills), for his health, not long before he died; and Hume died in the house he had built himself in St Andrew Square, then the most fashionable quarter of the New Town. St David's Street, still the name of the connection between the Square and Princes Street, is supposed to have got its name from a jibe chalked by a town humorist on the notorious atheist's front door.

The *literati* thus participated in a general change. The town was becoming conscious of its obligations as a capital. By the 1780's hotels were being built to replace [what Arnot calls] the "noisy, dirty, and incommodious" pubs in which travellers of all ranks had lodged like waggoners or carriers. Tradesmen's daughters "blushed to be seen in a market" [William Creech, *Edinburgh Fugitive Pieces* (1815)]. A new ideal of civic dignity came to the fore. [Arnot writes that] the Exchange was founded to fill the want of "public buildings necessary for accommodating those societies which assemble in populous cities, to direct the business of the country, and provide for its general welfare". "Proper accommodation" was wanted for the Musical Society, it being "for the interest of the town to give countenance for such polite amusements as might encourage strangers of rank to reside in the city" [*Book of the Old Edinburgh Club*]. The final outcome was a clean split in the said city, for the New Town was not a plan for Edinburgh as a whole. The ruling-class simply moved out into their "brilliant aristocratic quarter" on the other side of the Nor' Loch (so grand that some at first feared it would be impractically expensive) and left the Old Town to become, in the 19th century, a crammed slum of 80,000 people, living in quarters meant for nearer 30,000 [Chambers]. At precisely the same period Edinburgh ceased to have its own literature. Scott, living in the New Town, looked out to the whole of the country for his subject-matter; and the Edinburgh of his novels is either historical, intelligently so, as in *The Heart of Midlothian,* or indulged in for its bygone charm, as in *The Chronicles of the Canongate.* Ramsay and Fergusson had written out of the thick of Edinburgh. After the removal of the cultivated class from the Old Town, contemporary 'socialness' entirely ceases to figure in Scots literature. In this case the affiliations of literature and social change were decisive.

David Daiches

SOURCE: "Eighteenth-Century Vernacular Poetry," in *Scottish Poetry: A Critical Survey,* edited by James Kinsley, Cassell and Company Ltd., 1955, pp. 150-184.

[A prominent critic, historian, and editor, Daiches has written a number of important studies of Scottish literature and culture, including The Paradox of Scottish Culture: The Eighteenth Century Experience *(1964) and* Robert Burns and His World *(1971). In the following essay, Daiches explores the works of Ramsay, Fergusson, and Burns in relation to the problem of "[how] to use the*

vernacular as a language in serious literature."]

The seventeenth century saw Scottish poets moving away from the older Scots literary tradition: from Sir Robert Aytoun to Montrose the trend was towards a courtly English idiom, and Scots was rapidly ceasing to be a literary language and becoming merely a spoken dialect. The most important Scots poem of the seventeenth century is the vulgar, vigorous, rollicking vernacular 'Life and Death of the Piper of Kilbarchan', better known as 'The Epitaph of Habbie Simson', by Robert Sempill of Beltress. Scots is now a vernacular, drawing on popular speech rather than on an artistic tradition. And in the early eighteenth century there is a growing interest in popular, vernacular Scots verse, represented by both imitations of it and collections of it. The first volume of James Watson's *Choice Collection of Comic and Serious Scots Poems* (1706) shows this new interest, the interest of a printer and anthologist; and that line follows on through Allan Ramsay and David Herd to Johnson's *Scots Musical Museum* (1787 ff.). The editorial line of collectors and improvers leads on the one hand to new appreciation of ballad and folk-song and on the other to curiosity about the older artistic tradition that flourished before first the Reformation and then the Union of the Crowns altered or at least obscured the nature of Scottish culture. This appreciation and this curiosity helped to provide the cultural climate in which Fergusson wrote his Scots poems and Burns drew the lines together to produce the grand culmination of an Indian summer of Scottish poetry.

But the second Temple was not like the first. Going back to Alexander Scott, we find a stanza like this:

> For nobillis hes not ay renown
> Nor gentillis ay the gayest goun,
> Thay cary victuallis to the toun
>> That werst dois dyne:
> Sa bissely to busk I boun [*I get to the bush*]
> Ane uthir eitis the berry doun [*another eats the berry*]
>> That suld be myne.

The opening of 'Habbie Simson' has the same stanza form:

> Kilbarchan now may say alas!
> For she hath lost both game and grace,
>
> Both *Trixie* and *The Maiden Trace;*
>> But what remead?
> For no man can supply his place:
>> Hab Simson's dead.

There is a difference in weight here; though both Scott and Sempill use images and expressions from popular speech, Scott's language is more highly charged, it has more gravity and greater reverberation. 'Habbie Simson' is sprightly popular verse written for amusement by a member of the landed gentry and written in a language which by this time few educated people felt to be suitable for the highest kind of art. The poem is important historically, both for drawing attention to the possibilities of folk-humour as a way of bringing the vernacular back into current poetry and for reviving a stanza form which was to play such an important part in eighteenth-century Scottish poetry; but it lacks a dimension. Between Sempill of Beltrees and Burns Scottish vernacular poetry had to learn how to be the product of the whole man, how to achieve scope and density—in short, how to recover the lost dimension. Where it did so, it was by transmuting antiquarian, patriotic and patronizing gestures towards the vernacular into something deeper, something with an organic connexion with contemporary sensibility; and that transmutation was itself made possible by the re-establishment of living contact with certain important currents in Scottish literature and Scottish folk-poetry.

How to use the vernacular as a language in serious literature (that is, in literature that was more than an antiquarian exercise, a jest, or a *tour de force*) was the problem faced by Ramsay, Fergusson and Burns, and it was never permanently solved.

— *David Daiches*

A literary language, arising out of the different forms of the spoken language and transcending them, reflects back on the spoken language and gives it a steady relationship to the national culture. Once the literary tradition is broken, once there is no literary language growing out of the spoken language (however different from it it may be, and however many artificial elements may have been added), the spoken language is bound to disintegrate into a series of regional dialects. Scots became a vernacular only after the literary language of its serious writers had ceased to be Scots. How to use the vernacular as a language in serious literature (that is, in literature that was more than an antiquarian exercise, a jest, or a *tour de force*) was the problem faced by Ramsay, Fergusson and Burns, and it was never permanently solved.

'Habbie Simson' is a vernacular squib; 'Holy Willie's Prayer' is a Scots poem, written in a literary language in which English and Scots reinforce each other. Yet the latter is not quite the same kind of thing that Alexander Scott or Montgomerie wrote. Burns only re-established contact with the Scots literary tradition by looking at it through the spectacles provided by folksong and other kinds of popular art, and as a result the tradition as he uses it is a composite one, in which the satiric boisterousness of Lindsay's *Satyre of the Thrie Estaits,* the happy artifice of Montgomerie, the stark clarity of the ballads, the richness and warmth and earthiness of folk-song, the pious beat of Scottish psalmody, combine to produce a precarious but—while it lasted—a brilliant unity. It was Burns's predecessors who made that synthesis possible; it was his own genius that made it brilliant; it was the cultural context of his time that made it precarious.

At the opening of the eighteenth century Scotland had preserved an oral literary culture which had deep roots in the past, while both broadsides and private manuscripts were playing their different parts in another kind of preservation. How far that culture would have survived into the eighteenth century without the deliberate encouragement of those who had by now become self-conscious about it, is impossible to say; the chances are that it would not have survived long. The growing prestige of English culture, together with the closer political and economic ties between England and Scotland, would have been likely to force the native popular tradition into nooks and corners. But fortunately, by some happy shift of attention after the political hopes of Scottish patriots had been finally ruined by the Union of Parliaments, Scotland turned from politics to investigate her literary claims to nationhood.

In 1706, the year before the union was finally voted, James Watson, an Edinburgh printer of skill and enterprise, brought out the first of his three volumes entitled *A Choice Collection of Comic and Serious Scots Poems both Ancient and Modern.* Watson apparently edited the collection himself, and in a prefatory note to the first volume he explained his motives:

> As the frequency of Publishing Collections of Miscellaneous Poems in our Neighbouring Kingdoms and States, may, in a great measure, justify an undertaking of this kind with us; so 'tis hoped, that this being the first of its Nature which has been publish'd in our native *Scots* dialect, the Candid Reader may be the more easily induced, through the Consideration thereof, to give some Charitable Grains of Allowance, if the Performance come not up to such a Point of Exactness as may please an over nice Palate. . . .

It is clear that Watson saw himself as a pioneer, producing for the first time a collection of poems 'in our own native *Scots* dialect' to rival the many English collections. The preface also makes clear that he was dependent on 'Generous Helps' from 'the Repositories of some Curious and Ingenious Gentlemen' who collected 'Comic and Diverting Poems'. Watson also claimed to have printed his poems 'from the most Correct Manuscripts that could be procured of them'. The flavour of antiquarian jest still hangs a little round the project; yet the patriotic intention is real, and his ambition to print accurate texts (however faintly realized) is genuine.

With its mixture of poems of popular revelry, laboured exercises in courtly English, macaronics, mock elegies, serious sixteenth-century Scots poems, trivial epigrams and epitaphs, poems by Drummond and Montrose, flytings, laments and miscellaneous patriotic pieces, Watson's collection appears at first sight to represent the casual putting together of whatever the editor found to his hand. Yet (except for ballads, which it lacks, and song lyrics, which are few, and the perhaps surprising lack of any-

thing by Sir David Lindsay) the collection represents with a fair degree of accuracy the different kinds of material available for the development or reconstruction of the Scottish poetic tradition in the eighteenth century. The tradition of the makars was represented by Montgomerie (we must wait until Ramsay to find the earlier poets made available); the courtly tradition in English by Drummond and Aytoun; the older popular tradition by 'Christis Kirk on the Grene' and the newer by 'Habbie Simson' and other pieces; various kinds of popular and semi-popular Scottish song were represented, some in Scots and some in English; the characteristic Scottish humour and Scottish violence are represented in several ways, as is the goliardic tradition as it developed in Scotland and the tradition of macaronic humour associated with it. Watson printed the best texts he could find, though these were often poor broadsides. Perpetuation in broadsides at least denotes vitality. Throughout the seventeenth century the line between folk-song and 'art' poem was often obscured in Scotland; poems even by courtly poets found their way to popular singers and printers of broadsides, as well as to private collectors; and changes, corruptions, emendations and additions were the natural result. What Watson printed represented things that were still going on in Scotland, though often not on the surface. In bringing them to the surface he prevented them from being obscured completely by the new face of Scottish culture and at the same time helped to divert patriotic attention from politics to literature. Scotland became concerned about its literary past and about the possibilities of continuity with that past. It is true that that concern was mixed up in many quarters with confused ideas about the vernacular and primitive poetry and the natural man, and this confusion made serious difficulties for Burns. But it also provided an environment which encouraged the writing of an enriched vernacular poetry under certain circumstances and at certain levels: and that was decisive for the course of eighteenth-century Scottish poetry.

Meanwhile, the practice of rewriting or imitating traditional Scottish songs grew among ladies and gentlemen. To John Hay, tenth Lord Yester, for example, is attributed a version of 'Tweedside.' Lady Grizel Baillie (1665-1746) wrote the simply lilting 'Werena my heart licht, I wad dee', which first appeared in Ramsay's *Tea-Table Miscellany.* Lady Wardlaw (1677-1722) presented her 'Hardyknute' as part of an old ballad; it is difficult to see now how this too smoothly running piece, with its carefully chosen echoes of common ballad phrases, could have been accepted (as it was) as a genuine old ballad. But the poem has speed and vigour, and helped to familiarize genteel Scottish ears with a polished version of the ballad cadence.

A more important character, as far as the Scottish literary tradition in the eighteenth century is concerned, is William Hamilton of Gilbertfield (to be distinguished from his younger contemporary, William Hamilton of Bangour) whose modernized version of Blind Harry's *Wallace* was to fire Burns's patriotism. His 'Last Dying Words of Bonnie Heck' continued the 'Habbie Simson' tradition, but with a difference. 'Habbie Simson' was an elegy on a piper, himself a representative of popular festivity, and in recalling his life Sempill recalls the folk-customs of rural Scotland:

> At Clark-plays when he wont to come;
> His Pipe play'd trimly to the Drum,
> Like Bikes [*hives*] of Bees he gart [*made*] it
>   Bum,
>   and tun'd his Reed.
> Now all our Pipers may sing dumb,
>   sen Habbie's dead. . . .
>
> He was convoyer of the Bride
> With Kittock hinging at his side:
> About the Kirk he thought a Pride
>   the Ring to lead.
> But now we may gae but a Guide
>   for Habbie's dead. . . .

Hamilton's poem is more definitely a *mock* elegy, and, further, it is a lament for an animal, which links it with 'The Mare of Colintoun' and that Scottish tradition of animal poetry that was to come alive so splendidly in Burns. True, in his dying reminiscences Bonny Heck, too, gives a picture of popular festivities, but it is the mixture of the comic and pathetic deriving from the notion of a dying animal speaking like a human that links the poem with Burns's 'Death and Dying Words of Poor Maillie'.

Hamilton is at least as important in the history of Scottish vernacular poetry for the epistles which he exchanged with Ramsay. This is the beginning of a tradition of familiar verse letters in the vernacular which was again to be magnificently exploited by Burns. It provided a medium for 'occasional' poetry, a kind of verse to which the vernacular was particularly suited, for its endeavour was to capture the accent of conversation. With literary prose always English and not Scots, and the vernacular allowed in verse only for the familiar, the popular, the comic or the mock-antique, the verse letter provided a fine new form for vernacular Scots. If the novel had been developed in Scotland by the early eighteenth century, dialogue in prose fiction might have effectively employed the spoken Scots speech of the time—this is how Galt and Scott were later to use dialogue. But lacking a tradition of colloquial prose, the eighteenth-century Scottish writer turned happily to the tradition of familiar Scots verse which Hamilton of Gilbertfield helped to establish.

With Allan Ramsay the scene becomes more complex. To the editorial function of Watson he added that of reviser, popularizer, experimenter, poet, *entrepreneur,* clubman, satirist, general busybody and spokesman for Scotland before the Queen Anne wits. In 1712 he joined with other young men in Edinburgh in founding the Easy Club, 'in order that by a Mutual improvement in Conversation they may become more adapted for fellowship with the politer part of mankind and Learn also from one another's happy observations'. (Burns was to found the Tarbolton Bachelors' Club with similar ends in view.) The members of this club all had pseudonyms, and Ramsay's was first Isaac Bickerstaff and later Gavin Douglas, a pair of names

which reflect Ramsay's dual interest in the Queen Anne wits and in older Scottish literature. The Easy Club is important in Ramsay's career because it shows him in training to become a gentleman in the early eighteenth-century sense and also because it provided him with an audience for 'occasional' poetry for which he soon began to display his talent. Ramsay was far from being a great poet, but he was a facile versifier with certain happy flashes, and when circumstances were propitious he could turn out admirable specimens of familiar verse. The Easy Club provided the environment which encouraged this gift; it also provided a background of patriotic sentiment against which Ramsay's nationalism flourished vigorously. Isaac Bickerstaff and Gavin Douglas; a gentleman of the Augustan Age and an ardent Scottish patriot; an admirer of Pope and Gay and Matthew Prior and a devoted champion of the older Scottish makars and of the use of vernacular Scots by contemporary Scottish poets; a seeker after polish and good breeding and a vulgar little gossip whose schoolboy snigger spoils many of his poems and songs; a sentimental Jacobite and a prudent citizen who cannily absented himself from Edinburgh when Prince Charlie held court in Holyrood in 1745; a champion of Scottish folk-song and a wrecker of scores of such songs by turning them into stilted would-be neo-classic effusions—the dualism in Ramsay's life and character was deep-seated and corresponded to a dualism in the Scottish culture of his day. He could defend the coarsest and frankest language in poetry and yet dress up a Scottish song in intolerable false elegancies. At the same time he could demonstrate that he possessed the Horatian elegance of the English gentleman by rendering Horace's 'Vides ut alta stet nive candidum' in vivid and homely Scots verse:

> Look up to *Pentland*'s towring Taps,
> Buried beneath great Wreaths of Snaw,
> O'er ilka Cleugh [*glen*] ilk Scar and Slap
>   [*breach in a fence*],
> As high as ony *Roman* Wa'.
>
> Driving their Baws [*balls*] frae Whins or Tee,
> There's no ae Gowfer to be seen,
> Nor dousser [*soberer*] Fowk wysing a Jee
>   [*guiding on a bending course*]
> Thy Byas Bouls on *Tamson's* Green.

Ramsay's first published works were single poems in English heroic couplets in the contemporary English style; these are no better if no worse than the work of many a minor English versifier of the day. 'The Morning Interview', described as 'An Heroi-Comical Poem', derives from *The Rape of the Lock,* but has none of Pope's metrical cunning, fineness of texture, or subtle shifts in tone. Waggish jocularity strives with self-conscious elegance to take control, and the result is not happy, though the poem has its moments. In 1718 Ramsay first showed his interest in older Scottish literature by bringing out, anonymously on broadsides, several editions of 'Christis Kirk on the Grene' (with the same stanza form as Watson had printed—different from the text he was to use in *The Ever Green* in 1724) with first one and then two new cantos of his own. Ramsay's new cantos have verve and ingenuity, and capture something of the spirit of the original while adding his own brand of vulgarity. In the Elegies on Maggy Johnston, John Cowper and Lucky Wood (which all appeared in 1718) Ramsay displayed his best vernacular vein. These poems are in the tradition that Ramsay himself, in a verse epistle to Hamilton of Gilbertfield, called 'Standart *Habby*', the comic elegy tradition of the 'Epitaph on Habbie Simson' and 'Bonny Heck'. The elegy on Maggy Johnston, famous for her cheap and good ale, moves from lament to reminiscences of conviviality. The poem on Cowper, Kirk Treasurer's Man and expert at 'sa'ring [smelling] sculdudry out', is interesting as one of the earliest pieces of Scots verse to laugh at what Burns was to call the 'holy beagles'. The 'Elegy on Lucky Wood' laments the loss of an honest and hospitable ale-house keeper in the Canongate, and again it turns from elegy to reminiscent conviviality. There is a fine sense of atmosphere in the poem, with the scenes etched in warm and lively colours like a Breughel painting of a village celebration.

About the same time also appeared 'Lucky Spence's Last Advice' (first called 'Elegy on the Death of an Auld Bawd'), where Ramsay uses the 'death and dying words' device to put grimly ironical advice to prostitutes into the mouth of a dying brothel keeper. This kind of humour does not wear well, particularly when accompanied by Ramsay's variety of vulgar coyness (for example, he draws attention to an obscene phrase by a footnote in which he declines to explain it). But the poem uses the vernacular vigorously, with a fine proverbial forcefulness.

Of the other poems which Ramsay published separately, *Tartana: Or, The Plaid* deserves mention for its strong patriotic feeling and warm defence of Scottish customs against foreign innovations, even though the poem is in stilted English couplets. And two pastorals are of some importance: 'Richy and Sandy', a pastoral elegy on the death of Addison, and 'Patie and Roger', the germ of *The Gentle Shepherd*. 'Richy and Sandy' (i.e. Richard Steele and Alexander Pope) is a dialogue between two shepherds who lament the death of a third of their number, Edie (Addison). It is a ludicrous enough mixture—Steele, Pope and Addison transformed into Scots shepherds talking in a Theocritean convention, yet Ramsay's combination of conversational idiom with classical allusion comes off better than one might expect, and the piece has something of the same 'faded charm' that critics have found in *The Gentle Shepherd*. 'Patie and Roger' is likewise a dialogue between two shepherds, but this time the theme is love. The vernacular flows easily and the accent of conversation is audible beneath the flow of the verse. The images are fresh and effective, and altogether the piece succeeds in putting a little life into the worn-out convention of pastoral dialogue, in spite of its faded properties. Ramsay's basic uncertainty of taste, which could lead him into the most hideous vulgarities, was less of a liability in this kind of writing: the touches of rustic realism make for freshness, not vulgarity, and the idiom and cadence of popular speech embedded in the slow-moving iambic line waters the aridity of a stock situation, as in Patie's advice to Roger on how to get his girl:

> Daft Gowk [*fool*]! Leave aff that silly whindging [*whining*] Way,
> Seem careless, there's my Hand ye'll win the Day.
> Last Morning I was unco [*uncommonly*] airly out,
> Upon a Dyke I lean'd and glowr'd about;
> I saw my *Meg* come linkan [*tripping*] o'er the Lee,
> I saw my *Meg,* but *Maggie* saw na me:
> For yet the Sun was wafing [*wandering*] throw the Mist,
> And she was closs upon me e'er she wist.
> Her Coats were kiltit, and did sweetly shaw
> Her straight bare Legs, which whiter were than Snaw:
> Her Cockernony [*gathered hair*] snooded up fou [*full*] sleek,
> Her haffet Locks hung waving on her Cheek [*side*]:
> Her Cheek sae ruddy! and her Een sae clear!
> And O! her Mouth's like ony hinny Pear.
>
> Neat, neat she was in Bustine [*fustian*] Wastecoat clean,
> As she came skiffing o'er the dewy Green:
> Blythsome I cry'd, My bonny *Meg* come here,
> I fairly wherefore ye'er sae soon a steer:
> But now I guess ye'er gawn to gather Dew.
> She scour'd awa, and said what's that to you?
> Then fare ye well, *Meg Dorts,* and e'en 's ye like,
> I careless cry'd and lap [*leapt*] in o'er the Dyke.
> I trow, when that she saw, within a crack
> With a right thieveles Errand [*improper*] she came back;
> Miscau'd [*abused*] me first,—then bade me hound my Dog
> To weer [*stop*] up three waff [*wandering*] Ews were on the Bog.
> I leugh, and sae did she, then wi' great Haste
> I clasp'd my Arms about her Neck and Waste . . .

Finally, we must mention the verse letters between Ramsay and Hamilton of Gilbertfield. The series begins with a letter to Ramsay from Hamilton:

> O Fam'd and celebrated ALLAN!
> Renowned RAMSAY, canty Callan [*merry fellow*],
> There's nowther Highlandman nor Lawlan,
> 　In Poetrie,
> But may as soon ding [*cast*] down *Tamtallan*
> 　As match wi' thee. . . .

And Ramsay replies in similar strain:

> Sonse fa me, witty, wanton *Willy* [*happy*],
> Gin blyth [*if*] I was na as a Filly;
> Not a fow [*full*] Pint, nor short Hought Gilly [*small glass of spirits*],
> 　Or Wine that's better,

Cou'd please sae meikle [*much*], my dear Billy,
    As thy kind Letter.

Before a Lord and eik a Knight,
In Gossy *Don's* be Candle Light,
There first I saw't, and ca'd it right,
    And the maist feck [*greatest number*]
Wha's seen't sinsyne [*since*], they ca'd as tight
    As that on *Heck.*

The poems run on with an apparent effortlessness, given form by the demands of epistolary courtesy for an opening of compliment and a concluding benediction or invitation to the recipient to visit and make merry with the writer. From compliment to news to invitation is the commonest course of these letters, and they set a pattern which Fergusson and Burns were to follow. This is not, of course, great poetry; but it represents a craftsmanlike handling of the 'familiar' style, an exercising of the vernacular which was to stand Burns in good stead, and it further helped to provide both a social and a metrical convention for Scots verse.

Ramsay's preface to the 1721 volume of his poems gives us some important clues to his own view of the nature and significance of his poetry. He cheerfully admits that he is no classical scholar ('I understand Horace but faintly in the Original') and claims that many eminent men of letters have assured him 'That my small Knowledge of the dead or foreign Languages is nothing to my Disadvantage. King David, Homer and Virgil, say they, were more ignorant of the Scots and English Tongue, than you are of Hebrew, Greek and Latin: Pursue your own natural Manner, and be an original.' The use of vernacular Scots is thus associated with ignorance of Latin and Greek: Scots is no longer a literary language employed by poets with a European perspective and a rich background of classical culture which they draw on for vocabulary, imagery and subject-matter. We have come a long way from the aureate Middle Scots poems of Dunbar. Ramsay's classical knowledge comes through the strainer of neoclassic elegance; Greek and Roman gods and goddesses are for him useful ornamental devices which he has learned about from the English poets. Burns, too, was to pose as a heaven-taught ploughman and claim superiority to the college-educated who 'gae in stirks and come oot asses', but Burns was in fact fundamentally better educated than Ramsay, though he was faced by some of the same problems.

Ramsay warmly defends the expressive capacities of Scots, yet he is on the defensive about his 'Scotticisms'. 'The *Scotticisms,* which perhaps may offend some over-nice Ear, give new Life and Grace to the Poetry, and become their Place as well as the *Doric* dialect of *Theocritus,* so much admired by the best Judges.' He is writing, after all, for a genteel audience, both English and Scottish, who might be expected to lift their eyebrows at his use of the Doric. He dedicates his book 'To the most Beautiful, the Scots Ladies' and quotes Prior to the effect that he writes only for the young and fair. Clearly Ramsay's role as he saw it was, if not confused,

at least multiple.

In writing songs, Ramsay's favourite procedure is to take a popular Scottish song and to the same air set a new version which retains the opening line or the chorus or some other part of the original, but in all other respects is a wholly different poem deriving in tone and idiom from English love-lyrics of the period. Thus 'The last time I came ower the moor' becomes 'The happy Lover's Reflections':

The last Time I came o'er the Moor,
    I left my Love behind me;
Ye Pow'rs! What Pain do I endure
    When soft Idea's mind me:

Soon as the ruddy Morn display'd
    The beaming Day ensuing,
I met betimes my lovely Maid,
    In fit Retreats for wooing.

The phrases here are a mass of *clichés,* a parody, almost, of neo-classic idiom. 'The Lass of Peattie's Mill', on the other hand, begins with a lilting stanza in the true folk-idiom, then falls away into frigid artificialities, to return to the folk-idiom again in the third and last stanza. Ramsay has been blamed for ousting the old songs by his pseudo-genteel substitutes, and indeed many of his more outrageous rewritings appear not only in his own *Tea-Table Miscellany* but also in David Herd's *Ancient and Modern Scottish Songs* (where they appear anonymously), in the *Scots Musical Museum* and in *Select Scotish Airs.* It is of course possible, if not probable, that if Ramsay had not printed his versions the old versions would have died out anyway and the tunes would also have been lost: most of the original words of Ramsay's songs were irrecoverable later in the century even by such a conscientious collector as David Herd, and perhaps in many cases only the melody and the refrain were known to Ramsay. 'Of many of the songs in these volumes', wrote Herd in his preface to the second edition of his collection (1776), 'the chief merit will be found to consist in the musical air, while the poetry may appear much below mediocrity. For this the Editor has no other apology to offer, than that these were the only words existing to the tunes in question, the original words which gave rise to these tunes being irrecoverably lost.' It is important to remember that 'the musical air' was the more significant element in most of these songs; indeed, it is impossible to get any proper idea of this phase of Scottish literature without taking the music into consideration and treating the songs as songs and not as poems which happen to have been set to music.

How far Ramsay can go in the direction of pseudo-elegance in language can be seen in his song 'Delia', which is set to the tune of 'Greensleeves':

Ye watchful Guardians of the Fair,
Who skiff on Wings of ambient Air,
Of my dear *Delia* take a Care,
    And represent her Lover . . .

Many of his songs contain an impossible mixture of folk-idiom and self-conscious classical allusion. He can write a song with the simple Scots title 'Bonny Jean' (the title of the old air) and open it thus:

> Love's Goddess in a Myrtle Grove
> Said, *Cupid,* bend thy Bow with Speed,
> Nor let the Shaft at Random rove,
> For *Jeanie*'s haughty Heart must bleed. . . .

And his version of 'Auld Lang Syne' (entitled 'The Kind Reception') begins:

> Should auld Acquaintance be forgot,
>   Tho they return with Scars?
> These are the noble Heroe's Lot,
>   Obtain'd in glorious Wars:
> Welcome my *Varo* to my Breast,
>   Thy Arms about me twine,
> And make me once again as blest,
>   As I was lang syne.

We never know what Ramsay is going to do. 'Peggy I must Love Thee' becomes the conventional English 'Love's Cure'; 'Bessy Bell and Mary Gray' lilts happily along in true folk-style until suddenly we find

> When *Phoebus* starts frae *Thetis'* Lap
> The Hills with Rays adorning . . .

(One is reminded of Burns's outrageously obscene parody of this style of poetry.) 'The Young Laird and Edinburgh Katy' is lively Scots throughout and sticks to a single idiom:

> Now [*know*] wat ye what I met Yestreen
> Coming down the Street, my Jo,
> My Mistress in her Tartan Screen,
> Fou' bonny, braw and sweet, my Jo. . . .

'Mary Scot' combines a refrain about Yarrow with such a line as 'When in soft Flames Souls equal burn'; but 'O'er Bogie' keeps to a lilting folk-style throughout, beginning with the traditional refrain, 'I will awa' wi' my Love'. 'O'er the Moor to Maggy' is the mixture again, but 'Polwart on the Green' is effective, simple Scots throughout. 'Up in the Air' is one of Ramsay's few real masterpieces, a lively drinking-song in roaring Scots. The refrain is old, and perhaps some other lines are too, but Ramsay has got into the spirit of the original magnificently:

> Now the Sun's gane out o' Sight,
> Beet the Ingle [*mend the fire*], and snuff the
>   Light:
> In Glens the Fairies skip and dance,
> And Witches wallop o'er to *France,*
>   Up in the Air
>   On my bonny grey Mare.
> And I see her yet, and I see her yet,
>   Up in, &c.

> The Wind's drifting Hail and Sna'

O'er frozen Hags [*mosses*] like a Foot Ba',

> Nae Starns keek throw the Azure Slit,
> 'Tis cauld and mirk [*dark*] as ony Pit,
>   The Man i' the Moon
>   Is carowsing aboon,
> D'ye see, d'ye see, d'ye see him yet.
>   The Man, &c.

The fireside interior, with its warmth and conviviality, is contrasted with the winter weather outside, a contrast characteristic of much Scottish poetry, from the opening of Henryson's *Testament of Cresseid* to the beginning of 'Tam o' Shanter'.

'Patie and Pegie', which was later incorporated into *The Gentle Shepherd,* has been much praised, but it is not in fact a happy performance; the deliberately cultivated sentimentality clashes with the Scots frankness. A leering or even pawing eroticism, mixed with affected sensibility, has a tendency to crop up in Ramsay, and it is not attractive.

Ramsay's songs are most successful when he sticks to the folk-idiom and enters with verve and spirit into the atmosphere of the original refrain. 'An thou wert my ain Thing', in spite of an occasional false touch, has an effective strain of lyrical simplicity; 'For the Sake of Somebody' is a fine lilting piece in true folk-style; 'The Widow can bake, and the Widow can brew' has speed and liveliness and no trace of a false sensibility; 'O Mither dear, I 'gin to fear' is a skilful and unspoiled reworking of a folk-song, and the same is true of 'The Carle he came o'er the Croft', 'This is No my ain Hoose', 'Clout the Caldron' and some others.

It is not, of course, true that all folk-songs are good or that simplicity is necessarily a good quality in a song and that any kind of stylization is bad. But it is true that Ramsay's attempt to add a dimension to Scots vernacular poetry by sprinkling bits of English neo-classic convention or other evidence of a deliberately induced genteel sensibility over a verse that is basically a realistic Scots was misguided. Realistic Scots does not necessarily produce good poetry, any more than elegantly stylized English necessarily produces bad; but whatever the language a poet uses, it must be used organically, it must be the fully realized medium of the whole man at work, and this cannot be said of Ramsay's strange mixtures of Scots and English. Sometimes (like Burns) he is successful in an English tipped with Scots; more often, in his songs at least, he succeeds when he uses the vernacular in a fairly short, lilting line, as in the one wholly successful song (with the possible exception of 'My Patie is a lover gay') in *The Gentle Shepherd:*

> My Peggy is a young thing,
>   Just enter'd in her teens,
> Fair as the day, and sweet as May,
> Fair as the day, and always gay:

> My Peggy is a young thing,

And I'm not very auld,
Yet well I like to meet her at
The wauking [*watching*] of the fauld [*fold*]. . . .

Ramsay experimented in older Scottish metres other than 'Standart *Habby*'. One of his epistles to Hamilton uses the same ten-line stanza as 'The Claith Merchant', a poem which he printed in *The Ever Green*. In 'Edinburgh's Salutation to the Most Honourable, My Lord Marquess of Carnarvon' he uses the stanza of 'Christis Kirk on the Grene' in Watson's form. In 'The Poet's Wish' he uses *The Cherrie and the Slae* stanza for exactly the same purpose as Burns was to use it for in his 'Epistle to Davie'—which is in fact based in many respects on Ramsay's poem, even to the point of quoting a line from it, 'Mair speir na, nor fear na'. Ramsay's description of the contented but simple life shows one of his most appropriate uses of the vernacular. Indeed, in subject-matter, language and stanza form 'The Poet's Wish' is historically one of the most important of Ramsay's poems: it showed how an older Scottish tradition could be put to contemporary poetic use, and its influence on Burns was of the greatest significance. Ramsay could make good use of octosyllabic couplets when he stuck to a Scots conversational idiom, as his epistles to James Arbuckle and to the Earl of Dalhousie testify. His renderings of Horace in octosyllabic couplets have less force and weight than the original demands: *'Horace to Virgil, on his taking a Voyage to Athens',* for example, though it has speed and verve, is altogether too happy-go-lucky. But 'To the Ph——an Ode' ('Look up to Pentland's towring Taps') is an admirable domesticating of the Horatian mood in an Edinburgh setting, and easily the best of his renderings from the Latin.

The Gentle Shepherd was an expansion of 'Patie and Roger' into a five-act pastoral comedy. It is the best known of all Ramsay's works, and, in spite of its artificially contrived plot and rather stiff movement, it manages to retain a certain freshness. The first edition contained only four songs—'Peggy, now the King's come', 'By the delicious warmness of thy mouth', 'Jocky said to Jenny', and 'My Patie is a lover gay'—but many more were added in 1728, when the play was changed into a ballad opera for the pupils of Haddington Grammar School. This is the version that has been printed ever since, which is a pity, because these editions print both the original dialogue and those parts of it which Ramsay turned into lyrics to be sung, with the result that there is much irritating duplication in the text. We gain 'My Peggy is a Young Thing' from these alterations, but otherwise the only advantage of the change was that it enabled *The Gentle Shepherd* to be sung, and this helped to keep it alive and popular.

The language is a somewhat anglicized Scots, showing on the whole a greater sureness of touch than Ramsay generally displayed in such mixed modes. Details of rural labour and rural festivity are handled with observant precision, and though there are some melodramatic moments connected with the return of the Royalist laird Sir Will-

iam Worthy, there is an atmosphere of country work and play pervading the whole which the pastoral had long lost in England and elsewhere in Europe. The first part of the play, when rustic love is displayed against a lively background of rustic labour, is better than the latter part, where the action is manipulated unconvincingly in the interests of the proper *dénouement* and a happy ending; Jenny and Peggy are up early to lay their linen out for bleaching, and that gives them an opportunity of talking together, and when Patie detains Peggy, after the day's work, for some amorous words, Peggy knows that she should be at home helping to prepare supper:

O Patie! let me gang; I mauna [*must not*] stay;
We're baith cry'd hame.

Altogether, this pastoral drama represents a precarious equilibrium for Ramsay; he has found a way of combining vernacular realism and a rather tired convention without incongruity or vulgarity. The tiredness is not altogether banished, and the plot limps. But a Scottish breeze blows through this countryside, freshening the air and blowing away at least some of the languors of a stale tradition.

Ramsay produced thirty-one verse fables and tales, of which twenty are adaptations from La Motte and three are from La Fontaine. These are lively performances in Scots, done in fast-moving octosyllabic couplets, lacking the grace and polish of the French, but with a vigorous vernacular humour of their own. He consistently expands his original, filling it out with realistic and occasionally vulgar detail; he is nearer the *fabliau* than either La Motte or La Fontaine, and the Scots tradition of low-life comedy comes alive again in his hands. Again, this is not the greatest kind of poetry, but it is a kind to which the Scots vernacular at this stage of its life was appropriate, and it provided exercise for the vernacular in a setting where it could be used without constraint or affectation.

More important in some respects than Ramsay's original work was his work as an editor. In *The Tea-Table Miscellany* he collected songs and ballads, and in *The Ever Green* he printed the work of the 'Scottish Chaucerians' and others from the Bannatyne MS. In his preface to one of the many later editions of *The Tea-Table Miscellany* Ramsay wrote:

My being well assured how acceptable new words to known tunes would prove, engaged me to the making verses for above sixty of them, in this and the second volume: about thirty more were done by some ingenious young gentlemen, who were so well pleased with my undertaking, that they generously lent me their assistance; and to them the lovers of sense and music are obliged for some of the best songs in the collection. The rest are such old verses as have been done time out of mind, and only wanted to be cleared from the dross of blundering transcribers and printers; such as, *The Gaberlunzieman, Muirland Willy,* &c., that claim their place in our collection for their merry images of the low character.

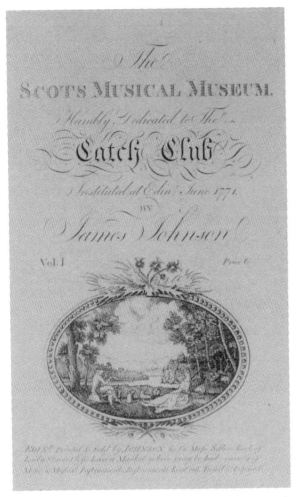

Title page of James Johnson's The Scots Musical Museum, *volume one (1787), which Robert Burns helped compile and to which he contributed a number of poems.*

Ramsay had thus none of the modern scholar's respect for the original text, and it may be hard to tell exactly what has happened to a song that appears in his collection. Ramsay's sources are often obscure, and a full inquiry into the history of many of the songs he prints, and indeed into the whole question of song collections in eighteenth-century Scotland, has still to be made. But, whatever their history, here the songs are, some 'improved', some rewritten, some printed as Ramsay found them. Ramsay provided some index to what had happened to the songs by marking some of them with letters. 'The SONGS marked C, D, H, L, M, O, &c., are new words by different hands; X, the authors unknown; Z, old songs; Q, old songs with additions.' But the system is not used consistently, and many songs have no letter at all.

The Ever Green is an easier collection to deal with; it takes most of its material from the Bannatyne MS. As Ramsay put it in a set of doggerel verses he wrote in the manuscript on 6 July 1726:

In Seventeen hundred twenty four

Did Allan Ramsay keen
—ly gather from this Book that store
which fills his Ever Green. . . .

Ramsay's patriotic intention is made clear by his remarks in the preface:

When these good old *Bards* wrote, we had not yet made Use of imported Trimming upon our Cloaths, nor of foreign Embroidery in our Writings. Their *Poetry* is the Product of their own Country, not pilfered and spoiled in the Transportation from abroad: Their *Images* are native, and their *Landskips* domestick; copied from those Fields and Meadows we every Day behold.

The *Morning* rises (in the Poets Description) as she does in the *Scottish* Horizon. We are not carried to *Greece* or *Italy* for a Shade, a Stream or a Breeze. The *Groves* rise in our own Valleys; the *Rivers* flow from our own Fountains, and the *Winds* blow upon our own Hills. I find not Fault with those Things, as they are in *Greece* or *Italy:* But with a *Northern Poet* for fetching his Materials from these Places, in a Poem, of which his own Country is the Scene; as our *Hymners* to the *Spring* and *Makers* of *Pastorals* frequently do.

The collection introduced eighteenth-century readers to the literature of their country's golden age. Dunbar and Henryson are both represented, the former by 'The Thistle and the Rose', 'Lament: Quhen he was Sek', 'The Goldyn Targe', 'Dunbar's Dregy', the 'Flyting', 'The Dance of the Sevin Deidly Synnis' and seventeen others. This selection gives a fair picture of Dunbar's range both in style and theme, including examples of the ceremonial, the aureate, the elegiac, the satiric, the moralizing, the humorous and the confessional. The poems from Henryson include 'Robene and Makyne', 'The Garmont of Gud Ladeis' and two of the fables. Among other pieces from the Bannatyne MS. are 'Christis Kirk on the Grene'; 'The Battle of Harlaw', one of the best known of the Scottish historical ballads; 'The Wife of Auchtermuchty', a lively verse-tale of husband and wife reversing roles to the former's discomfiture, attributed to Sir John Moffatt; several poems by Alexander Scott; a group of coarse satires on loose women by the sixteenth-century Robert Sempill, and other poems by minor sixteenth-century writers. Ramsay changes spelling, punctuation, word order and even stanza form where it suits him; and where he cannot understand a word or a phrase he is liable to rephrase the passage.

Ramsay occasionally inserts stanzas of his own into older poems. He adds two stanzas to Dunbar's 'Tydingis fra the Sessioun', containing his own friendly opinion of the Edinburgh judges and advocates, and gives no indication that these stanzas are not by Dunbar; he slips a stanza full of elaborate classical allusions into the midst of Alexander Scott's simple, singing love lyric, 'Return thee, hairt, hamewart agane' (whose first line, incidentally, Ramsay characteristically 'regularizes' to 'Return Hamewart my Hart again'); and, most notorious, he adds his own preposterous conclusion to Dunbar's 'Lament':

Suthe I forsie, if Spae-craft [*gift of prophecy*]
   had,
Frae Hethir-Muirs sall ryse a LAD,
Aftir twa Centries pas, sall he
    Revive our Fame and Memorie.
Then sall we flourish EVIR GRENE:
All thanks to carefull *Bannatyne*,
And to the PATRON kind and frie,
    Qhua lends the LAD baith them and me.
Far sall we fare, baith Eist and West,
Owre ilka [*every*] Clyme by *Scots* possest;
Then sen [*since*] our Warks sall nevir die,
    Timor mortis non turbat me.

To which monstrous conclusion Ramsay calmly appends the words, 'Quod Dunbar'.

The two poems attributed to 'Ar. Scot' are both anti-English patriotic poems (though 'The Eagle and Robin Red-breist' is veiled in allegory) and apparently Ramsay thought that they would have more force if put in antique dress—perhaps, too, he thought it safer so to disguise them. 'The Vision' is subtitled: *'Compylit in Latin be a most lernit Clerk in Tyme of our Hairship and Oppression, anno 1300, and translatit in 1524.'* It bewails the oppressed condition of Scotland and ends by prophesying successful battle for the re-establishment of an independent Kingdom of Scotland. The stanza is that of *The Cherrie and the Slae*. 'The Eagle and Robin Red-breist' tells how the robin, singing loyal songs to the royal eagle, is maligned by the other birds, jealous of his merit and of the king's regard for him, and driven from court. Here also the language is deliberately antique, though the verse form is the octosyllabic couplet. For Ramsay, Scots as a serious literary medium belonged to the past.

The Ever Green had nothing like the popularity of *The Tea-Table Miscellany*. There were no reprints in Ramsay's lifetime, and only four later reprints between 1761 and 1876. It was the popular vernacular tradition and the tradition of the late sixteenth-century poets, rather than the mediaeval makars, that influenced Fergusson and Burns. And though both the popular tradition and the tradition of Montgomerie and his contemporaries derived from and in their own way continued the mediaeval Scottish tradition, the fifteenth-century makars did not directly influence subsequent eighteenth-century Scottish poetry. The relatively homogeneous national culture of the Scotland of the early Stuarts was too far away; the Reformation, the Union of the Crowns and the Union of Parliaments had between them created too wide a gulf between past and present, and complicated the Scottish cultural situation to the point where no full, unselfconscious contact could any longer be made with Henryson and Dunbar. Both Watson and Ramsay had shown other ways and made other material available; ballad and folk-song remained alive, certain late mediaeval themes and stanza forms had been popularized, the goliardic tradition survived in the universities, and Scottish national sentiment was increasingly turning from politics to literature.

The 'ingenious young gentlemen' whose help Ramsay

acknowledges in the preface to *The Tea-Table Miscellany* included several amateur versifiers who are remembered for a song, or a handful of songs, which took the popular fancy. This was the age of amateur poetizing among Scottish ladies and gentlemen. Their productions were as likely to be in neo-classic English as in Scots, as the artificial versions of Robert Crawford witness. Crawford's 'Tweedside', 'Bush abune Traquair', 'Broom of Cowdenknows', 'My Deary, if thou die' (to the air of 'Down the Burn, Davie') and 'One day I heard Mary say' (to the air 'I'll never leave thee') are uninspired English texts written for older Scottish song tunes, yet they remained popular throughout the century. But not all the minor song-writers of the period wrote in neo-classic English. Sir John Clerk of Penicuik is the reputed author of a lively elaboration of an old folk-song, 'O merry may the maid be' (to the tune to which 'Mary Morison' is now sung). Alexander Pennecuik wrote in a variety of styles, covering much of Ramsay's ground: his 'Elegy on Robert Forbes' is reminiscent of Ramsay's 'Elegy on John Cowper', while 'The Merry Wives of Musselburgh's Welcome to Meg Dickson' (if it really be his) is a colourful and spirited piece as good as Ramsay's best in this vein. William Hamilton of Bangour wrote mostly in English, but he contributed a remarkable, melodious elaboration of a folk-theme to *The Tea-Table Miscellany* in 'The Braes of Yarrow'. Alexander Ross whose *Helenore, or the Fortunate Shepherdess* derives from *The Gentle Shepherd* and presents a rather faded Buchan version of Scottish pastoral, wrote the lively songs, 'Wooed and Married and A'' and 'The Rock and the Wee Pickle Tow'. John Skinner's rollicking 'Tullochgorum' was considered by Burns to be 'the best Scotch song ever Scotland saw', and his 'Ewie wi' the Crookit Horn', an elegy on a favourite ewe, combines humour and tenderness with considerable skill. Alexander Geddes wrote 'Lewis Gordon', a simple and effective Jacobite song (and it should be remembered that the Jacobite Rebellion of 1745 provided Scotland with a folk-emotion, as well as a set of symbols with which to evoke a variety of feelings from the simply patriotic to the elegiac, the passionate and the mocking, and so gave new impetus to the interest in real and imitated folk-song and retarded the sophistication of the folk-tradition by about fifty years). Geddes was perhaps also the author of 'The Wee Bit Wifukie', a masterpiece in the rollicking vein. Jean Elliot produced her version of 'The Flowers o' the Forest', an effective rendering of the popular note of lament for Flodden, more successful than Mrs. Cockburn's more deliberately artful, and more English, poem with the same title and refrain. And Lady Anne Barnard's 'Auld Robin Gray' passed for some times as an old song.

There were other songs of the period whose authorship is uncertain or unknown, among them 'There's Nae Luck about the House' (probably by William Julius Mickle), 'O weel may the Boatie Row' (probably by John Ewen, 1741-1821), the full version of 'Aye Waukin' O', 'Logie o' Buchan' (perhaps by George Halket, *d.* 1756), 'The Drunken Wife of Gallowa' (also known as 'Hoolie and Fairly') and many of those found in Herd's collection.

Ramsay's *Tea-Table Miscellany* was by no means the only

collection of songs published in Scotland at this time. The interest in 'primitive' poetry which prompted the publication of Percy's *Reliques* in England in 1765 and which later helped to determine the terms of the Ossian controversy, began earlier in Scotland and was there mixed up with patriotic motives. Collections of songs and ballads, with and without music, were numerous in Scotland from *The Tea-Table Miscellany* to Thomson's *Select Scottish Airs* (1795 ff.). In 1726 the *Orpheus Caledonius* was published in London, containing about fifty Scottish songs with the music, and it was followed in 1733 by an enlarged edition in two volumes. Similar collections followed in Scotland, culminating in James Johnston's *Scots Musical Museum,* of which the first volume appeared in 1787 and to whose subsequent volumes Burns contributed so much. Of the books of Scots songs without music, the most important was David Herd's *Ancient and Modern Scots Songs.* There were also many collections of the tunes alone, arranged for a variety of instruments. The pioneer volume here was the *Collection of Scots Tunes* made by the violinist Adam Craig in 1730, and the most impressive collection was James Oswald's *Caledonian Pocket Companion,* of which the first of many volumes appeared in 1740. Antiquarians, folk-lorists and romantic lovers of the past joined the procession as the century advanced; and between Herd's first edition in 1769 and John Finlay's *Scottish Historical and Romantic Ballads* in 1808, a whole tribe of collectors (including John Pinkerton, Joseph Ritson, Walter Scott and Robert Jamieson) were at work. This was, of course, far from being a purely Scottish movement, but in Scotland it took on special significance and sprang from special motives.

Herd's two volumes of 1776 constitute a remarkable collection. He reprinted a fair number of pieces that had appeared in Watson and in *The Tea-Table Miscellany,* together with much that had not appeared before, and he printed almost everything anonymously without any indication of age. But he never tampered with his material; he printed the pieces as he found them, and he was content to let many of the older songs appear in fragmentary form. Unlike Percy and most other editors of his time, he had no urge to complete and improve. Herd is thus an important figure in the transmission of the Scottish popular tradition in poetry. Scholarly, accurate and modest, he never put his own name to his work (neither of his editions mentions an editor), and in his preface to the two volumes of 1776 he 'anticipated the censure of the severe, by confessing them a work of slight importance'.

The kind of interest in Scottish literature represented by Ramsay's original and editorial work, and by that of the collectors and imitators of older Scottish songs who followed him, must be seen in its true perspective. The general cultural current was still flowing strongly towards England, and the Edinburgh historians, philosophers, scientists and literary critics who contributed so much to Scotland's second 'golden age' wrote in English and studiously avoided 'Scotticisms' in their speech. In 1761 the Irishman Thomas Sheridan (father of the dramatist) delivered twelve lectures on the 'correct' speaking of English at St. Paul's Episcopal Church, Edinburgh, and about three hundred of the city's most distinguished citizens attended. In the issue of *The Mirror* for 22 February 1780, Henry Mackenzie explained to his readers why Scotsmen, writing an English they did not speak and speaking a dialect they did not write, were incapable of writing humorously in English or seriously in their native dialect:

> When a Scotsman . . . writes, he does so generally in trammels. His own native original language, which he hears spoken around him, he does not make use of; but he expresses himself in a language in some respects foreign to him, and which he has acquired by study and observation. . . . Hence Scottish writers may have been prevented from attempting to write books of humour. . . . In confirmation of these remarks it may be observed, that almost the only works of humour which we have in this country, are in the *Scottish* dialect. . . . The *Gentle Shepherd,* which is full of natural and ludicrous representations of low life, is written in broad *Scotch.* . . .

Scots thus remained a vernacular, and there was no tradition of written Scots prose in the eighteenth century. Anyone who had claims to international fame in dealing with general matters of scientific or philosophic interest wrote in English for the same reason that he would have written in Latin in an earlier age. And in poetry the vernacular established itself as a vehicle only for exercises in the mock-antique or for humorous or convivial or skittish or condescending verses. Ramsay had not enlarged the potentialities of the Scottish vernacular; still less had he re-created Scots as a full-blooded literary language. Nobody, in fact, achieved that in the eighteenth century or later: it is one of the ideals of the modern Lallans movement. But one eighteenth-century Scottish poet did achieve a Scots idiom which combined ease, weight, variety and cunning, and which pointed the way towards the re-establishment of Scots as a literary language (though it was a way that nobody was to take). This was Robert Fergusson, not the greatest of the eighteenth-century Scottish poets but perhaps the most assured in his use of Scots.

Fergusson was fortunate in not having the multiple motivations that confused the careers of both Ramsay and Burns. Unlike Ramsay, he was not a half-educated country boy trying in the city to be both genteel and patriotic, and unlike Burns he was not tempted to parade a self-conscious primitivism before the eyes of the Edinburgh literati. He was an Edinburgh man and an Edinburgh poet, who rendered the life of the city with warmth and colour. But his student days had made him well acquainted with Fife, and he had also paid visits to his mother's people in Aberdeenshire. Further, the Edinburgh of the 1760s and 1770s was not, in spite of its bustling city life, an urban area in the modern sense: the countryside extended right up to its doorstep, and there were fishing-towns and a seaport right beside it. To be an Edinburgh man did not mean, therefore, that one was ignorant of the cycles of agricultural activity or of the life of the fisherfolk (both of which Fergusson had also known in Fife), or that one was deprived of the pleasures of scrambling over hills and moors. If we think of Fergusson as a figure belonging to the closes and howffs of Edinburgh, a convivial companion at Lucky Middlemass's or with members of the Cape Club at James Mann's tavern in Craig's Close, we must not forget that he knew other scenes too. He knew the spoken Scots of Lothian, Fife and Aberdeenshire, and he knew Lowland Scottish life in both town and country: he was at home in Scotland in a quietly assured way. Further, he had received a reasonably good formal education, so that he had no inferiority complex about his knowledge of the classics. He was free to laugh at the literati if he wanted to, and when Dr. Johnson insulted the Scots he could cheerfully satirize the Grand Cham in lively and uninhibited verse. He did not have to declare defensively that he understood Horace but faintly in the original, or to present himself to the genteel world as a remarkable example of the natural man.

The Cape Club provided a better atmosphere for a poet than the self-conscious young would-be gentlemen of the Easy Club provided for Ramsay. Members of this Club—The Knights Companions of the Cape, as they called themselves—included David Herd, the painters Alexander Runciman, Alexander Nasmyth and (later) Sir Henry Raeburn; the actors Thomas Lancashire and William Woods, and Stephen Kemble, manager of the Theatre Royal; James Sibbald, the historian of Scottish poetry; the later notorious Deacon Brodie; Stephen Clarke, the musician who was to help Burns; a large number of tradesmen of convivial, literary or musical inclination; and some lawyers and other professional men. It was a democratic, informal, friendly group, having none of the genteel pretensions of the more formal societies attended by the literati yet with nothing of the coarse debauchery of the lower Edinburgh taverns. Eighteenth-century Edinburgh was a city of clubs and taverns, and Fergusson easily found his level among them. He was at home in the Cape Club (to which he was admitted in October 1772), and he was equally at home 'o'er oysters and a dram o' gin' at Lucky Middlemass's or with a dish of rizzard haddock and a bicker of tippeny at this or some other Edinburgh howff. He was also a frequenter of the theatre, the friendship of Woods the actor obtaining for him free admission.

Members of the Cape Club took knightly titles. David Herd was Sir Scrape-Greysteil, Alexander Runciman was Sir Brimstone, and Fergusson was admitted as Sir Precentor, presumably because of his good voice and his fondness for singing. He attended the meetings regularly throughout 1733.

Fergusson's first appearance as a poet was not promising. He wrote three poor English songs to Scottish airs for a performance of the opera *Artaxerxes* at the Theatre Royal in 1769. Two years later he began contributing to Ruddiman's *Weekly Magazine,* starting with three English pastorals entitled 'Morning', 'Noon' and 'Night'. But as a poet in English Fergusson never achieved anything more than a certain dexterity in the manipulation of English words. Only when he uses English in parody of the genteel literary tradition of his day does he achieve any spark at all. His poem, 'The Sow of Feeling'—the lament of a pig of sensibility whose husband and children have been slaughtered for the table—is an amusing satire of Henry Mackenzie's *The Man of Feeling* and the fashion which is started. It is also a parody of the kind of English poetic style which eighteenth-century Scottish poets tended to fall into when they wanted to be genteel:

> Thrice happy, had I lived in Jewish time,
> When swallowing pork or pig was deem'd a
>   crime;
> My husband long had blest my longing arms,
> Long, long had known love's sympathetic
>   charms!
> My children too—a little suckling race,
> With all their father growing in their face,
> From their profile dam had ne'er been torn,
> Nor to the bloody stalls of butchers borne.

And in his 'To Dr. Samuel Johnson, food for a new edition of his Dictionary', he parodies the lexicographer's vocabulary. Such poems are significant only as indicating Fergusson's educational independence, as compared with Ramsay or Burns.

It was the issue of the *Weekly Magazine* for 2 January 1772 that introduced Fergusson to the public as a Scots poet. The poem was 'The Daft-Days', the period of convivial celebration at the end of the old year and the beginning of the new; it opens with a memorable picture of Edinburgh in December:

> Now mirk [*dark*] December's dowie [*doleful*]
>   face
> Glours our the rigs [*ridges*] wi' sour grimace,
> While, thro' his *minimum* of space,
>   The bleer-ey'd sun,
> Wi' blinkin light and stealing pace,
>   His race doth run.
>
> From naked groves nae birdie sings,
> To shepherd's pipe nae hillock rings,
> The breeze nae od'rous flavour brings
>   From *Borean* cave,
> And dwyning [*drooping*] nature droops her
>   wings,
>   Wi' visage grave.

The picture of winter laying its frozen hand on Edinburgh and its rural environs is done with a gravity (far from the same thing as solemnity) of language that shows us at once that Fergusson took the vernacular more seriously than Ramsay had done. The Latin *minimum* and the adjective *Borean* take their place naturally in a descriptive verse whose tone and accent demonstrate its hospitality to any legitimate devices for adding weight and scope. A line such as 'And dwyning nature droops her wings' is stylized in an altogether appropriate way: it is not a conventional image thrown inappropriately on top of a colloquial style in the way that Ramsay so often did, but a formal handling of Scots.

After building up the atmosphere of the winter exterior, the poet turns to the contrasting interior:

Auld Reikie [*Edinburgh*]! thou'rt the canty
    [*cheerful*] hole,
A bield [*shelter*] for many a caldrife [*sensitive to
    cold*] soul,
Wha snugly at thine ingle [*fireside*] loll,
    Baith warm and couth [*comfortable*];
While round they gar [*make*] the bicker
    [*drinking-cup*] roll
      To weet their mouth.

As the poem develops, it becomes clear that its true theme is conviviality—brilliantly localized Edinburgh conviviality. The patriotic theme emerges naturally from the convival; when the capital of Scotland celebrates, it must be in an appropriately Scottish way:

Fidlers, your pints in temper fix,
And roset [*rosin*] weel your fiddle-sticks,
But banish vile Italian tricks,
    From out your quorum:
Nor *fortes* wi' *pianos* mix,
      Gie's *Tulloch Gorum.*

It may be that Fergusson's touchiness about foreign influences in Edinburgh (which he demonstrates more than once) shows a parochial spirit, which the Middle Scots poets, who were Europeans as well as Scots, wholly lacked; but it must be remembered that not only was the Italianizing of Scottish song seriously threatening an important part of Scotland's musical heritage in Fergusson's day, but the uncertainty and obsequiousness about the nature and status of Scottish culture shown by so many of Fergusson's contemporaries were bound to make an initial defence of Scottish traditions take a form that would seem merely xenophobic to a more assured generation.

The theme suggested in the stanza attacking 'vile Italian tricks' in music is developed in 'Elegy, On the Death of Scots Music', which appeared in the *Weekly Magazine* on 5 March 1772. This is a serious patriotic poem, a lament for the swamping of the native Scottish tradition in music by foreign influences. The mock elegy form (which Fergusson had used with great spirit and considerable skill in his 'Elegy on the Death of Mr. David Gregory, late Professor of Mathematics in the University of St. Andrews', one of his earlier works) has here shed its note of rather self-conscious humour and is sublimated into something more formal and more *whole.* Fergusson takes his epigraph from Shakespeare's *Twelfth Night,* with an easy appropriateness that once again shows his poetic assurance:

Mark it Cesario; it is old and plain,
The spinsters and the knitters in the sun,
And the free maids that weave their thread with
    bones,
Do use to chant it.

This sets the tone, and the poem opens with an elegiac stateliness:

On Scotia's plains, in days of yore,
When lads and lasses *tartan* wore,

Saft music rang on ilka [*every*] shore,
    In hamely weid;
But harmony is now no more,
      And *music* dead.

Three more stanzas develop the mourning theme in fairly general terms, and then, in a manner characteristic of him, Fergusson begins to narrow his subject with increasing particularization:

Nae lasses now, on simmer days,
Will lilt at bleaching of their claes;
Nae herds on *Yarrow's* bonny braes
    Or banks of *Tweed,*
Delight to chant their hameil [*home-bred*] lays,
    Since music's dead.

At glomin now the bagpipe's dumb,
Whan weary owsen [*oxen*] hameward come;
Sae sweetly as it won't to bum,
    And *Pibrachs* skreed
We never hear its warlike hum;
      For music's dead. . . .

A reference to his favourite song 'The Birks of Invermay' finishes the particularization, and the poem then moves at once to its formal conclusion:

O SCOTLAND! that cou'd yence [*once*] afford
To bang the pith of Roman sword,
Winna your sons, wi' joint accord,
    To battle speed?
And fight till MUSIC be restor'd,
      Which now lies dead.

Fergusson's next poem, 'The King's Birthday in Edinburgh', was a full-blooded performance in the Scottish tradition of poems of popular revelry though lacking what might be called the broadside accent of so many of such poems. It is a description of Edingburgh's celebration of the King's birthday, and, significantly, has as epigraph a line from Drummond's Scots macaronic, *Polemo-Middinia,* 'Oh! qualis hurly-burly fuit, si forte vidisses'. The style of the poem is familiar but not vulgar. The opening is humorous in a new way for eighteenth-century Scottish poetry:

I sing the day sae aften sung,
Wi' which our lugs [*ears*] hae yearly rung,
In whase loud praise the Muse has dung
    [*wearied*]
      A' kind o' print;
But wow! the limmer's [*rogue*] fairly flung;
      There's naething in't. . . .

O *Muse,* be kind, and dinna fash [*trouble*] us
To flee awa' beyont Parnassus,
Nor seek for *Helicon* to wash us,
    That heath'nish spring;
Wi' Highland whisky scour our hawses [*throats*],
    And gar [*make*] us sing.

Begin then, dame, ye've drunk your fill,

You woudna hae the tither [*other*] gill?
You'll trust me, mair wou'd do you ill,
   And ding you doitet [*stupid*];
Troth 'twou'd be sair agains my will
   To hae the wyte [*blame*] o't.

The poet's mischievously familiar attitude to the Muse is not vulgarity, but controlled high spirits. It sets the tone for the ensuing description:

Sing then, how, on the *fourth* of June,
Our *bells* screed aff a loyal tune,
Our antient castle shoots at noon,
    Wi' flag-staff buskit,
Frae which the soldier blades come down
    To cock their musket.

And off he goes, describing the noise, the pranks, the brulzies with the City Guard, with artful verve. The poet's self, introduced in the very first line, is present throughout, both as observer and as celebrant, and the introduction of his own comments adds to the spontaneity of the tone, as when he addresses the old cannon, Mons Meg:

. . . Right seldom am I gi'en to bannin
  [*swearing*],
But, by my saul, ye was a cannon,
Cou'd hit a man, had he been stannin
   In shire o' Fife,
Sax long Scots miles ayont *Clackmannan*,
   And tak his life.

The note of personal wonder, rising to a climax in a line which opens with four emphatic monosyllabic words— 'Sax long Scots miles ayont Clackmannan'—represents technique of a high order, from which Burns was to learn. At the end of the poem he returns to the Muse, reminding himself that the final stages of riotous celebration are not fit themes for her, who is accustomed to more conventionally poetic aspects of the day's proceedings:

She'll rather to the fields resort,
Whare music gars [*makes*] the day seem short,
Whare doggies play, and lambies sport,
    On gowany [*daisied*] braes,
Whare peerless Fancy hads her court,
    And tunes her lays.

'Peerless Fancy' is deliberate, almost ironic, English poetic diction: the pastoral aspects of the celebration are more suitable for conventional poetic treatment than the more violent urban goings-on that he has been recounting. And on that note of mingled pastoral cheerfulness and ironic poetizing the poem concludes.

'Caller [*fresh*] Oysters' is another of Fergusson's convivial poems. Its opening, a fine tribute to the Forth and its fishermen, shows him handling the 'Standart *Habby*' stanza with a slowness and openness not often found in this verse form:

Of a' the waters that can hobble [*toss*]

A fishin yole [*yawl*] or salmon coble [*flat-bottomed boat*],
And can reward the fishers trouble,
   Or south or north,
There's nane sae spacious and sae noble
   As Firth o' *Forth*. . . .

He moves inland from the sea, from the Forth coast to Auld Reekie's oyster cellars, and soon we have one of his cosy Edinburgh interiors again:

Whan big as burns the gutters rin,
Gin ye hae catcht a droukit [*drenched*] skin,

To *Luckie Middlemist's* loup in,
   And sit fu snug
Oe'r oysters and a dram o' gin,
   Or haddock lug. . . .

On 3 September 1772 there appeared in the *Weekly Magazine* a Scots poem signed 'J. S.', dated from Berwick, hailing Fergusson as Ramsay's equal and successor. The following week Fergusson's reply appeared, following the tradition of the verse epistle as developed by Hamilton of Gilbertfield and Ramsay. It is a skilful enough occasional piece, but his predecessors had done as well in this mode. More original in both style and content is 'Braid Claith', which appeared on 15 October. It is a satire, whose theme is that clothes make the man: with a good suit of braid claith a man, whatever his natural endowments, commands respect and is sure to get on in the world. The conclusion illustrates both the tone of the poem and the comic-ironic ingenuity of some of Fergusson's rhymes:

Braid Claith lends fock [*folk*] an unco heese
  [*strange lift*],
  Makes mony kail-worms [*caterpillars*] butterflies,
Gies mony a doctor his degrees
    For little skaith [*trouble*]:
In short, you may be what you please
    Wi' gude Braid Claith.

For thof ye had as wise a snout on
As *Shakespeare* or Sir *Isaac Newton*,
Your judgment fouk wou'd hae a doubt on,
   I'll tak my aith,
Till they cou'd see ye wi' a suit on
   O' gude Braid Claith.

In October appeared 'Geordie and Davie, an Eclogue to the Memory of Dr. Wilkie'. Wilkie had been professor of Natural Philosophy at St. Andrews, and had taken an interest in Fergusson when he was a student there. The eclogue is modelled on Ramsay's pastoral elegies, but it is an altogether more assured performance than anything Ramsay did in that style. He uses heroic couplets with gravity and flexibility (though the lines are as a rule end-stopped) and the Scots appears completely at home in this verse form. This is something new in eighteenth-century Scottish poetry:

. . . Tho' simmer's gane, an' we nae langer view
The blades o' claver wat wi' pearls o' dew.
Cauld winter's bleakest blasts we'll eithly
   [*easily*] cowr,
Our eldin's [*fuel*] driven, an' our har'st is owr;
Our *rucks* fu' thick are stackit i' the yard,
For the *Yule-feast* a sautit [*salted*] mart's
   prepar'd;

The ingle-nook supplies the simmer fields,
An' aft as mony gleefu' maments yields.
Swyth [*quickly*] man! fling a' your sleepy
   springs awa',
An' on your canty [*cheerful*] whistle gie's a
   blaw:
Blythness, I trow, maun [*must*] lighten ilka eie
   [*every eye*],
An' ilka canty callant sing [*fellow*] like me.

The language here is integrated and confident, and does not halt between genteel English and vulgar Scots. But a brief quotation loses the effect: one must read the whole poem to appreciate Fergusson's control and assurance.

'Hallow-fair' is another poem which develops a Scottish tradition that Ramsay and others had already made popular. It is an account of the lively scenes that took place at the annual market held in November in the outskirts of Edinburgh, done in that form of 'Christis Kirk on the Grene' stanza that Watson had printed and which Burns was to use. The life and colour and movement of the poem are magnificent, and the way Fergusson manages to use the short four-syllable ending to each stanza (always with the same two last words, 'that day', except for 'that night' on two occasions) shows a firm control over his medium. The poet is the mere observer here; he is not himself implicated as in 'The King's Birthday' and 'Caller Oysters'; and the poem moves from scene to scene picking out the liveliest and most striking activities. Here again Fergusson can play with classical deities without any feeling of either vulgarity or pretentiousness:

When *Phoebus* ligs [*lies*] in *Thetis* lap
   Auld Reikie [*Edinburgh*] gies them shelter,
Whare cadgily [*gaily*] they kiss the cap [*Wooden
   cup*],
   An' ca't [*knock it*] round helter-skelter.
Jock Bell gaed furth to play his freaks,
   Great cause he had to rue it,
For frae a stark Lochaber aix
   He gat a *clamihewit*, [*blow*]
      Fu' sair that night.

The last of the 1772 poems is 'To the Tron-kirk Bell', a magnificent piece of studied abuse directed at the 'wanwordy [*worthless*] crazy, dinsome thing' whose 'noisy tongue' was 'sair to thole [*endure*]'. Here Fergusson demonstrated a virtuosity that had not been seen in Scots poetry since the makars. The mixture of skill and gusto with which the riven bell is abused is reminiscent of Dunbar in his best flyting style; the poem, however, is not a satire on bells but on baillies: the conclusion is that the city fathers allow this scandal because they live out of its hearing:

But far frae thee the *bailies* dwell,
Or they wud scunner [*be disgusted*] at your
   knell. . . .

The 1773 poems began on 21 January with 'Caller Water', a poem in praise of fresh water which, deftly handled and cunningly constructed, turns out to be a poem in praise of the Edinburgh lasses. Water kept 'father Adie' healthy in Eden (Fergusson uses that familiar tone to scriptural characters that Burns was to exploit so happily); it is prescribed by doctors who confuse their patients' noddles by giving it a pretentious Latin name; it provides healthful swimming; it cures the colic; it keeps the lasses trig and bonny. The poem, which moves trippingly throughout, comes to a neat and happy conclusion:

O may they still pursue the way
To look sae feat [*neat*], sae clean, sae gay!
Than shall their beauties glance like *May*,
   And, like her, be
The goddess of the vocal Spray,
   The Muse, and me.

A more ambitious work is 'Mutual Complaint of Plainstanes and Causey', a dialogue in flexible octosyllabic couplets between the main road of the High Street (causey) and its sidewalk (plainstanes). Each complains of what it has to bear and thinks it has a worse lot than the other—causey with wagons, horses, coaches, Highland chairmen and the Luckenbooths, plainstanes (designed for nothing heavier than 'sole of shoe or pump') trod by 'burden-bearers heavy shod' and loutish rustic characters. The result is both a picture of Edinburgh street life and a

---

David Craig on the legacy of Scotland's golden age of literature:

We have to recognise, then, that there did not emerge along with modern Scotland a mature, 'all-round' literature. Sheer social forces—centralisation, emigration, the widespread wasting away of the regional and the vernacular—were against the sustained output of anything like a *separate* literature for Scotland. By the close of this period that has become, simply, something it would be unreasonable to look for. In the 17th century the mental talents of Scotsmen had run to the intense but one-track activity of Church and theological debate. In the 18th, this talent was, apparently, released for wider work—research, study, and experiment in science, farming, technology, philosophy, poetry—as a result of peace, more rational religion, new markets and increased investment. . . . But though David Hume could marvel that "we should be the people most distinguished for literature in Europe," all that the famous Golden, or Athenian, Age could show for imaginative literature was a very striking dearth.

David Craig, in Scottish literature and the Scottish People, 1680-1830, *Chatto & Windus, 1961.*

satire on snobbery.

'The Rising of the Session', which appeared in March, should be considered together with 'The Sitting of the Session', which did not appear until 4 November. These poems remind us of the important part that the law played in Edinburgh life: the rising of the Court of Session at once diminished the city's activities, and the first of these two poems is a sharply etched series of pictures of the denuded city, with empty taverns and change-houses, shot through with a running satire on lawyers. 'The Sitting of the Session' presents the other side of the picture: it shows in brilliant detail the revived life of the city, with bar-keepers and litigators in full cry. The poem begins with one of Fergusson's fine seasonal portraits of Edinburgh in November: he then moves through the city, as the slightly ironical observer, and describes what he sees. Sometimes he ironically encourages the activities he is describing:

> Now at the door they'll raise a plea;
> Crack [*abuse*] on, my lads!—for flyting's
>   [*scolding*] free;
> For gin ye shou'd tongue-tacket be,
>   The mair's the pity,
> Whan scalding but and ben [*arguing hither and
> yon*] we see
>   PENDENTE LITE.

The macaronic tough here, with its ironical humour, is in an old Scottish tradition.

On 13 May the *Weekly Magazine* printed 'The Farmer's Ingle', one of Fergusson's two real masterpieces (the other is 'Auld Reekie'). Hitherto Fergusson had excelled as an urban poet, as the bard of Edinburgh, but here he celebrates the agricultural life in a rich, slow-moving verse of a kind that Scottish poetry had not seen for centuries. The stanza is a modified Spenserian; the tone is that of affectionate observation, without a trace of sentimentality; the structure, moving from the vivid description of evening settling over the countryside to the interior domestic scene and then taking the farmer and his family through their evening's activities until they retire to rest, to conclude on a note of peaceful benediction, is perfectly controlled throughout. 'The Farmer's Ingle' is a finer poem than Burns's 'The Cotter's Saturday Night', which, in spite of some magnificent passages, is confused in tone, motive and diction. Fergusson's very title indicates the superiority: Burns's title sounds as though he is about to show off some model rustics to benevolent genteel observers, whereas Fergusson is describing, with knowledge and affection, what he sees. Here at last is a full-blooded Scots poem, written by the whole man, rich and musical and assured:

> Whan gloming grey out o'er the welkin
>   [*twilight*] keeks,
>   Whan *Batie* ca's his owsen [*oxen*] to the byre,
> Whan *Thrasher John,* sair dung [*wearied*], his
>   barn-door steeks [*shuts*],
>   And lusty lasses at the dighting [*winnowing*]

tire:
> What bangs [*defeats*] fu' leal [*truly*] the e'enings
>   coming cauld,
>   And gars snaw-tapit [*makes snowtopped*]
>   winter freeze in vain;
> Gars dowie [*melancholy*] mortals look baith
>   blyth and bauld,
>   Nor fley'd [*affrighted*] wi' a' the poortith
>   [*poverty*] o' the plain;
>   Begin, my Muse, and chant in hamely strain.

The second stanza describes the gudeman coming home, the third shows the gudewife making everything ready for his arrival, the fourth moves to an unforced moralizing on the superior healthfulness of hard work and simple fare to idleness and drugs, and the fifth develops this into a tribute to the achievements of Scotsmen of old, brought up on simple fare. Then, in the sixth stanza, he turns again to the scene before him:

> The couthy cracks [*friendly chats*] begin when
>   supper's o'er,
>   The cheering *bicker* [*drinking cup*] gars them
>   glibly gash [*talk*]
> O' simmer's *showery blinks* and winters sour,
>   Whase floods did erst their mailins [*small
>   farms*] produce hash [*destroy*]
> 'Bout *kirk* and *market* eke their tales gae on,
>   How *Jock* woo'd *Jenny* here to be his bride,
>
> And there how *Marion,* for a bastard son,
>   Upo' the *cutty-stool* [*stool of repentance*] was
>   forc'd to ride,
>   The waefu' scald [*castigation*] o' our *Mess*
>   [*Minister*] *John* to bide.
>
> The fient [*devil*] a chiep's [*squeak*] amang the
>   bairnies now;
>   For a' their anger's wi' their hunger gane:
> Ay maun [*must*] the childer, wi' a fastin mou'
>   [*mouth*],
>   Grumble and greet, and make an unco mane
>   [*great noise*],
> In rangles [*clusters*] round before the ingle's
>   [*flame*] low:
>   Frae *gudame's* mouth auld warld tale they
>   hear,
> O' *Warlocks* [*wizards*] louping round the
>   *Wirrikow,* [*hobgoblin*],
>   O' gaists [*ghosts*] that win in glen and kirk-
>   yard drear [*dwell*]
>   Whilk [*which*] touzles a' their tap, and gars
>   [*makes*] them shak wi' fear.

And so the evening wears on. In the tenth stanza we have an attractive picture of the gudeman relaxing, and in the eleventh he is shown discussing the next day's work with the lads. In the twelfth they all retire to bed, and the final stanza asks a blessing on them all:

> Peace to the husbandman and a' his tribe,
>   Whase care fells [*supplies*] a' our wants frae

year to year;
Lang may his sock and couter turn the gleyb,
    [*ploughshare*],
        And bauks [*ridges*] o' corn bend down wi'
            laded ear.
May SCOTIA's simmers ay look gay and green,
    Her yellow har'sts frae scowry blasts
        decreed;
May a' her tenants sit fu' snug and bien
    [*prosperous*],
        Frae the hard grip of ails and poortith freed,
        And a lang lasting train o' peaceful hours
            succeed.

The ending is perfectly modulated, in contrast to the more rhetorical conclusion of 'The Cotter's Saturday Night'.

'The Farmer's Ingle' is a Scots poem, but this does not mean that it derives entirely and solely from Scottish literary traditions. On the contrary, the stanza form, the tone and even the subject show English influence; the significant point is that these influences have been thoroughly assimilated, and are used in an assured Scots way. The strength of a national art does not lie in its refusal to borrow from other national arts, but in its ability to domesticate its borrowings properly in its own medium. This is what Fergusson does in 'The Farmer's Ingle', and it is something that no Scottish poet in the eighteenth century had yet done.

'The Ghaists: a Kirkyard Eclogue' is a dialogue between the ghosts of George Heriot and George Watson (Edinburgh merchants who had left bequests to found 'hospitals'—now schools—in the city), who deplore the effect in Scotland of the proposed 'Mortmain Bill' introduced in Westminister. The bill (which, owing to Scottish opposition, was eventually restricted in scope to apply to England only) was intended to enable charitable foundations in Britain to realize their assets and invest the proceeds in three per cent. funds, which would be the future source of their income. This would have impoverished certain Scottish foundations, and Scottish national feeling was aroused. Fergusson's poem was a contribution to the debate, and at the same time a defence of the national integrity of Scotland. The verse is the heroic couplet, handled with deliberate *gravitas*:

    Think na I vent my well-a-day in vain,
    Kent ye the cause, ye sure wad join my mane
        [*complaint*].
    Black be the day that e'er to England's ground
    Scotland was eikit [*added*] by the UNION's
        bond;
    For mony a menzie [*company*] of destructive ills
    The country now maun brook frae *mortmain
        bills,*
    That void out test'ments, and can freely gie
    Sic will and scoup to the ordain'd trustee,
    That he may tir our stateliest riggins bare,
    Nor acres, houses, woods, nor fishins spare,
    Till he can lend the stoitering [*stumbling*] state a
        lift

    Wi' gowd in gowpins [*gold in handfuls*] as a
        grassum [*free*] gift; . . .
        Hale interest for my fund can scantly now
    Cleed [*clothe*] a' my callants backs, and stap
        their mou'.
    How maun [*must*] their weyms [*bellies*] wi'
        sairest hunger slack,
    Their duds [*rags*] in targets [*tatters*] flaff upo'
        their back,
    Whan they are doom'd to keep a lasting Lent,
    Starving for England's weel at *three per cent*.

This kind of patriotic poetry, dealing boldly with contemporary affairs, is both more poetic and more effective than the oblique pseudo-historical contrivances of Ramsay.

The next two poems, 'On Seeing a Butterfly in the Street' and 'Hame Content, a Satire' (like the 'Ode to the Bee', which had appeared earlier), are moral pieces in octosyllabic couplets, starting from a particular situation and moving outwards to illustrate what it means in terms of the way people live. They are vigorous enough, and show Fergusson's competence and confidence if not the height of his genius. 'Leith Races', which appeared in July, is in the mood and stanza form of 'Hallow Fair'. It is another of Fergusson's Edinburgh poems, and the model for Burns's 'The Holy Fair'. A short quotation cannot suggest its quality; it is the carefully handled sequence of scenes that builds up into an impressive poem. 'Ode to the Gowdspink', in the same general style as the butterfly poem, appeared in August, and 'The Election', another Edinburgh poem with all the life and speed of 'Hallo Fair' and 'Leith Races', in September. 'To the Principal and Professors of the University of St. Andrews, on their superb treat to Dr. Johnson' is a skilful and high-spirited fling at the doctor in octosyllabic couplets. After describing the elaborate foreign dishes at the feast, he says that if he had been there he would have filled the anti-Scottish lexicographer with humble Scottish fare, which he proceeds to catalogue. It is a satire, which emerges as a patriotic poem.

The 'Elegy on John Hogg' also appeared in September: it is perhaps the most brilliant, certainly the most technically accomplished, of all the mock elegies in the 'Habbie Simson' tradition. 'A Drink Eclogue', a dialogue in heroic couplets between 'Landlady, Brandy and Whisky', is a piece of skilful flyting between the two liquors, with the landlady intervening at the end. Finally, 'To my Auld Breeks' (25 November), a ruefully comic address to his worn-out trousers in octosyllabic couplets, brings the *Weekly Magazine* series of Fergusson's Scots poems to a close.

There are a few other Scots poems by Fergusson which did not appear in the *Weekly Magazine*. They include another 'Hallow Fair', a song this time. There is also an accomplished Scots translation of an ode of Horace (I. xi), which first appeared in the 1779 edition of his poems. But most important of all the poems first published outside the *Weekly Magazine* is 'Auld Reekie', published separately in 1773 and included, in a later version, in the 1779 volume. It is the Edinburgh poet's fullest and most accomplished celebration of his city. The octosyllabic couplets, shifting in tempo in accordance with the particular scene before the poet's eye, carry the expressive Scots forcefully to the ear, while the imagery, fixing the scene with its most significant component or appropriate symbol, builds up the Edinburgh sights, sounds and smells. This is more than a Dickensian exploration of urban oddities or the search for the striking scene or incident: the whole poem is set in a framework of acceptance—acceptance of the whole of life, with its colour, gaiety and debauchery, dreariness and pretentiousness and weakness, companionship, loneliness and sheer unadulterated humanity. He is not exhibiting Edinburgh to a sniggering or an admiring audience; he is savouring its full quality because he enjoys doing so. The whole Edinburgh scene passes under his eye. Gossips, schoolboys, housemaids, lawyers, thieves, whores, tavern-haunters, Sunday walkers, corrupt politicians, each against their appropriate background, are picked out and described; and there is an undercurrent of satire directed against those who through laziness or selfishness neglect the city's welfare or actively contribute to its harm. The contrasts are frequent and impressive:

> Near some lamp-post, wi' dowy [*melancholy*]
>   face,
> Wi' heavy ein, and sour grimace,
> Stands she that beauty lang had kend,
> Whoredom her trade, and vice her end.
>
> But see whare now she wuns her bread
> By that which nature ne'er decreed;
> And sings sad music to the lugs, [*ears*],
> 'Mang bourachs [*clusters*] o' damn'd whores and
>   rogues. . . .

And here is another:

>   In afternoon, a' brawlie buskit, [*grandly
>   dressed up*],
> The joes and lasses [*sweethearts*] loe to frisk it:
> Some tak a great delight to place
> The modest *bon-grace* [*bonnet*] o'er the face;
> Tho' you may see, if so inclin'd,
> The turning o' the leg behind.
> Now Comely-garden, and the Park,
> Refresh them, after forenoon's wark;
> Newhaven, Leith, or Canon-mills,
> Supply them in their Sunday's gills. . . .

The conclusion, where the poet retires across the Forth to look at his city whole, across the water from Fife, rounds the poem off perfectly:

>   REIKIE, farewell I ne'er cou'd part
> Wi' thee but wi' a dowy heart;
> Aft frae the *Fifan* coast I've seen,
> Thee tow'ring on thy summit green;
> So glowr the saints when first is given
> A fav'rite keek o' glore [*glory*] and heaven;

> On earth nae mair they bend their ein,
> But quick assume angelic mein;
> So I on *Fife* wad glowr no more,
> But gallop'd to EDINA's shore.

Perhaps the measure of Fergusson's technical success as a Scots poet is that he can (requiring the brevity and formality) call Edinburgh 'Edina' in the last line of this poem, and get away with it: Burns, in 'Edina! Scotia's darling seat', could not. If there is something of John Gay in this poem, it is not, as it often is in Ramsay, a vulgar aping of a metropolitan wit beyond his ken, but an influence happily assimilated.

Was Fergusson's Scots a homogeneous literary language? It was certainly more than a regional dialect, for it contained, in addition to its Edinburgh base, elements from Fife and from Aberdeenshire as well as from older literary Scots. Does this mean that Fergusson raised the status of Scots from a vernacular to a literary language? Hardly; because it takes more than a single poet to achieve such a task. Fergusson was the only Scots poet of his century to be able to look contemporary civilization in the eye. He knew where he stood and what he wanted to do. But he founded no school. The future lay with Burns and the rustic tradition.

SCOTTISH POETRY AFTER BURNS

T. C. Smout

SOURCE: "The Golden Age of Scottish Culture: Poetry and Novels," in *A History of the Scottish People, 1560-1830*, Charles Scribner's Sons, 1969, pp. 489-500.

[*A professor of Scottish history at the University of St. Andrews, Smout has written several important historical studies of Scotland, including* Scottish Trade on the Eve of the Union, 1660-1707 *(1963) and (with I. Levitt)* The State of the Scottish Working Class in 1843 *(1979). In the following excerpt, Smout discusses the culmination and subsequent decline of Scottish poetry.*]

Why should Scottish imaginative literature of the eighteenth century . . . beat up to a crescendo of achievement and then break off into a silence broken only by staccato outbursts? This is a problem to which there is perhaps no simple answer, but traditions in poetry and fiction both appeared to lead into a cul-de-sac from which it was difficult to make further meaningful advance.

In poetry the cul-de-sac was a linguistic one. In the early sixteenth century practically the only medium for any kind of serious expression in prose or in poetry was the Scottish language, which was, in its vocabulary, its constructions and its rhythms plainly distinct from English, though allied to it closely enough for a Scotsman and an Englishman to converse without an interpreter. Sixteenth-century

Scottish was rather more distinct from English than modern Danish is from Norwegian, but not so distinct as those two languages are from Swedish. From the Reformation onwards, however, there were more and more pressures to replace Scottish by English. The Reformer's Bible was in English, for the Scots from the start used translations prepared in the south and eventually adopted the Authorised Version of James VI and I. Politicians and civil servants after the Union of the Crowns in 1603 began to use standard English for official documents. The National Covenant itself was written in English, and at the end of the century the two greatest exponents of Scottish nationalism, Andrew Fletcher of Saltoun and Lord Belhaven, even if they spoke with a Scottish accent, wrote and published their speeches against the Union of Parliaments in beautifully measured English. It would not have occurred to anyone to do otherwise who wished to receive attention from the political public. The courtly poets of the mid-century, like Drummond of Hawthornden and Montrose, wrote their polished and melancholy verse in English just as their forebears a hundred years earlier would have written in Scottish. The only Scottish verse of any vigour after about 1630 was found in the bucolic celebrations of the Sempills, like Robert Sempill's 'Piper of Kilbarchan':

> Now who shall play, the Day it Daws
> Or Hunts Up, when the cock he craws
>
> Or who can for our Kirk-town-cause
> Stand us in stead?
> On bagpipes now no body blaws
> Sen Habbie's dead.

By the opening of the eighteenth century, therefore, Scottish had become merely the language of the poor, the uncouth and the humorous, and even in its common usage it was being constantly modified and diluted by English. The landed classes and the middle-class intelligentsia wrote English, and increasingly after the Union sought the most perfect English forms. To speak with a Scottish inflexion was to betray one's provincial origins, and all who aspired to polite society tried to get rid of their dialect in both written and spoken form. Lord Monboddo said of David Hume that he died confessing not his sins but his Scotticisms. One of the most popular books of the third quarter of the century was James Beattie's *Scotticisms, arranged in Alphabetical Order designed to correct Improprieties of Speech and Writing,* written 'to put young writers and speakers on their guard against some of those Scottish idioms which, in this country, are liable to be mistaken for English.' Some of the most popular lectures in the same period were those of Thomas Sheridan who 'lectured in his Irish brogue to entranced members of the Select Society of Edinburgh on the proper pronunciation of English' [David Daiches, *The Paradox of Scottish Culture: the Eighteenth Century Experience* (1964)].

Scottish, nevertheless, survived as an acceptable language for poetry, or at least, for certain types of poetry. This was partly because of tradition: some Scots poems, for example John Barbour's *Brus,* Blind Harry's *Wallace* and some of Sir David Lindsay's, remained as part of the normal national cultural background which even peasants' children heard recited by their elders. Songs in the vernacular also had a grip on all classes of society, both as ballads and lyrical folksong: they were handed on within the household, and the fact that they were written in the vernacular did not make them unacceptable even to the genteel. The work of Allan Ramsay (1686-1758), too, went a long way towards ensuring the survival of Scottish as a vehicle for poetry; not only was the best of his own verse vigorous and unaffected, in the Sempill tradition, but his two collections of older Scottish poetry, *The Ever Green* (1724) and the *Tea-Table Miscellany* (1724-1737), deliberately tried to recall intellectual Scotsmen to a recollection of the past poetic achievements of their language. On the other hand, Ramsay was so apologetic about reprinting old vernacular verse that he appeared to imply it really was suitable only for the archaic, the rollicking and the sentimental; a vehicle for song and humour but not for 'serious' modern expression.

Nevertheless, narrowed though it was to this particular constricting channel, Scottish poetry could draw for its life upon the expressive language that was still spoken in the farmtouns and taverns of eighteenth-century Scotland, and that was still written in prose or verse in bawdy and trivial chapbooks which church and gentry so much objected to, but which found a ready sale from hawkers' packs throughout the land. Undoubtedly its most original voice before Burns's was Robert Fergusson, the dissipated son of an Edinburgh clerk, who died in 1774 at the understandably early age of twenty-four. Poems like 'Tron-Kirk Bell' showed the peculiar suppleness and glow of the vernacular:

> Wanwordy, crazy, dinsome thing,
> As e'er was fram'd to jow or ring . . .

But nothing more serious than the celebration of food and drink was ever his business. Alcohol is the greatest good of the greatest number:

> The tinker billies i' the Bow
>   Are now less eidant clinking,
> As lang's their pith or siller dow,
>   They're daffin', and they're drinking.
> Bedown Leith-walk what burrochs reel
>   Of ilka trade and station
> That gar their wives an' childer feel
> Toom weyms for their libation
>   O' drink thir days.

With Robert Burns (1759-1796) Scottish poetry reached a peak that it had not approached for two hundred years, and which it was hardly to approach again in the following two hundred years. There was, of course, a great deal of the traditional explosive joy in eating, drinking and wenching. It can be boring, but at best it lifts his lyrical verse high above conventional levels of insipid sentiment. There is, for instance, much happiness but no false chastity in 'Rigs o' barley':

I have been blythe wi' comrades dear;
I hae been merry drinking;
I hae been joyfu' gath'rin gear;
I hae been happy thinking:
But a' the pleasures e'er I saw
Tho' three times doubl'd fairly
That happy night was worth them a',
Among the rigs o' barley.

In Burns there was more than mere rustic celebration. There was his ability, unequalled among either Scottish or English poets, to write marvellous songs. There was his one epic ballad, 'Tam o' Shanter' that would have made his reputation if he had written nothing else. There was his ability to take a pedestrian observation—the unearthing of a mouse's nest, the sight of a louse on a lady's bonnet—and make it memorable. There was his brilliant gift of satire, at its sharpest impaling the religiosity of his fellow men of Ayrshire in 'Holy Willie's Prayer' or 'The Holy Fair'. Whenever he is successful it is the virtuosity of his use of the Scottish language that makes him so. Sometimes it pours out of him, lavish, yet exact and expressive, as in his address to the louse:

Swith, in some beggar's hasset squattle
There ye creep, and sprawl and sprattle
Wi' ither kindred, jumping cattle . . .

Sometimes it is used with spare cunning to exploit the double meaning of religious language in the two-faced talk of a hypocrite:

O L . . d yestreen, Thou kens, wi' Meg—
Thy pardon I sincerely beg—
O! may't ne'er be a livin plague
    To my dishonour,
An' I'll ne'er lift a lawless leg
    Again upon her.

In Burns the Scottish tongue was always unforced and natural. Even if it was no longer quite the same as it had been in the sixteenth century, one cannot escape the knowledge that it was the language of the Ayrshire peasant society into which he was born and in which he remained for the greater part of his life. That society, however, was changing rapidly at the end of the century. Rich peasants were becoming capitalist farmers, members of a genteel class that spoke English. Poor peasants were becoming farm-workers. Everyone was exposed to purer English from their employers, from the church and from the schools.

Consequently, at about the time of Burns's death there occurred a triple crisis in Scottish poetry. Firstly, nobody could excel Burns in the particular use to which he had put his language, for his genius was impossible to outshine. There were many imitators mesmerised by his achievements who dug their own poetic graves trying to do what he did. Also, poets were increasingly cut off from the linguistic base of a Scottish tongue. Only twenty years after the agricultural revolution the vernacular had become something largely remembered from the past,

quaint: and the poet's use of it was increasingly derivative, forced and folksy.

On the other hand, Scottish poets of this twilight time simply could not use English properly, and thus could not investigate at all those realms of poetry that lay beyond the song, the rural celebration and the satire. Burns himself usually went along with the eighteenth-century conviction that Scottish was unsuitable for a serious poem, and when he wanted to write solemnly he wrote in English. Sometimes the result was insipid, sometimes it was absurd. Thus in 'The Cottar's Saturday Night';

But now the Supper crowns their simple board,
    The healsome *Porritch*, chief of SCOTIA's food . . .

Almost all his contemporaries and successors also found themselves tongue-tied in a language that even yet did not seem to come naturally from their own hearts. The only eighteenth-century Scot who did not was James Thomson (1700-1748) author of that fine English classical poem *The Seasons,* which had considerable influence upon Wordsworth. He was the son of a Roxburghshire minister, and lived entirely in England from the age of twenty-five.

It is right at least to mention that the eighteenth century also saw the greatest achievements of Gaelic poetry. It is difficult for one who is not a Gaelic speaker to judge how great these were, but those who know are inclined to rank Alexander Macdonald (?1700-1768), Duncan Ban MacIntyre (1724-1812), Rob Donn (1714-1778) and Dugald Buchanan (1716-1768) among the finest poets Scotland has produced writing in any tongue at any time. Macdonald was the poet of war and love, moved by the landing of Prince Charles to splendid martial verse, and moved by many different loves in a way that makes all translators timorous. . . . MacIntyre was also a Jacobite bard, and a poet of love-songs and satires. Donn was strongly influenced by the verse of Pope, which he had heard in Gaelic translation from his local minister. Buchanan was a writer of hymns and religious poetry of great power. If in this diversity there was anything common to all of them it was perhaps their ability to describe nature. Macdonald did it by creaming his noun with adjectives that no doubt sound even better in the Gaelic original than they do in English. That other Celt, Dylan Thomas, would have seen the point and envied the power:

It is most lovely to hear from the fold the faint
    low of the calf,
vigorous, piebald, handsome, white-backed,
    short-haired, merry,
white-headed, keen-eyed, red-eared, white-
    bellied, lively, young,
shaggy, soft-hoofed, well-grown, as it leaps to
    the lowing of the cows.

All the time this ferment of genuine poetry was taking place in the Highlands, the Lowlands remained obvious to it. The S.P.C.K. charged Macdonald, who was one of their schoolmasters, with 'composing and singing indecent songs.' Ironically enough, however, Lowland society was simultaneously very excited about bogus Gaelic poetry. James Macpherson of Kingussie had produced what purported to be a translation of an ancient Highland manuscript dealing with the mythical Celtic heroes Fingal and Ossian, but which was in fact a very inferior epic of his own in which echoes of Highland tradition were interlarded with slabs of mock-Milton and mock-Homer. Dr. Johnson made himself unpopular by calling it a fraud: Britain as a whole took it very seriously, and it passed from thence into the bloodstream of European romanticism to become the inspiration of countless poets and composers from William Blake to Mendelssohn. The latter's overture 'Fingal's Cave' is today the best-known memorial to one of the most successful forgeries in the history of literature. . . .

There was also a cultural change beginning to come over Edinburgh's own society at the end of the first quarter of the nineteenth century. James Boswell's only rival in the private art of autobiography, Henry Cockburn (1779-1854), sensed it and expressed it in his *Journals* and *Memorials of His Own Time*. He saw many things that were purely Scottish in the capital's society passing away, and manners and fashions becoming increasingly assimilated to those of polite society throughout the United Kingdom. He believed too that it was largely inevitable. The world was getting smaller, and people were more easily drawn to London. Economic change, by affecting England and Scotland simultaneously and in the same way, was bound to make the societies of the two countries more alike. But he also regretted that Scottish national characteristics should be thrown into this rough melting-pot after so many centuries of proud differentiation. He spoke for many when he wrote in his *Journal*:

> The prolongation of Scotch peculiarities, especially of our language and habits, I do earnestly desire. An exact knowledge and feeling of what these have been since 1707 till now would be more curious five hundred years hence than a similar knowledge and feeling of the old Greeks. But the features and expression of a people cannot be perpetuated by legislative engraving. Nothing can prevent the gradual disappearance of local manners under the absorption and assimilation of a far larger, richer and more powerful kindred adjoining kingdom. Burns and [Sir Walter] Scott have done more for the preservation of proper Scotland than could ever be accomplished by law, statesman or associations.

Scott deliberately, and Burns unwittingly, thus provided the public with the nostalgic stability and sense of nationhood in the past that it sensed it was losing in the present. The result, however, was catastrophic to literature, as it twisted its head back to front—its poetry looking always to Burns and a dead language, in prose to Scott and a past society. In this frozen posture it was obliged to walk on into the nineteenth century seeing nothing of the real world about it.

It was, incidentally, hardly less catastrophic to the study of Scottish history which became, in the popular mind only an extension of imaginative literature, bound up with myth and a safely remote and anti-English past. It was not, indeed, Scott's fault that his later followers were much less competent historians than he. The start that had been made in the eighteenth century with such professionals as William Robertson to see history as connected with explaining the development of society up to the point of contemporary existence was lost. By common consent the Victorians placed history beneath a rose-coloured glass, and everyone who beheld Scotland's Romantic Story was expected to exclaim 'here's tae us, whaur's like us'.

Alas, the answer to those most mindless words may change over the centuries.

FURTHER READING

Buchan, John. "Certain Poets: Scots Vernacular Poetry." In *Homilies and Recreations*, pp. 261-72. 1926. Reprint. Freeport, N.Y.: Books for Libraries Press, 1969.
    Chronicles the evolution of Scots, focusing on its revival and preservation in eighteenth-century Scottish literature and its subsequent deterioration.

Craig, David. *Scottish Literature and the Scottish People, 1680-1830*. London: Chatto & Windus, 1961, 340 p.
    Cross-disciplinary "'social history' of literature" exploring especially the cultural environment that produced the vernacular revival.

Crawford, Thomas. "Scottish Popular Ballads and Lyrics of the Eighteenth and Early Nineteenth Centuries: Some Preliminary Conclusions." *Studies in Scottish Literature* 1, No. 1 (July 1963): 49-63.
    Surveys Scottish manuscripts, broadsides, and songbooks of the eighteenth and early nineteenth centuries to explore the popular song of Scotland during that time.

Cunningham, Allan. *The Songs of Scotland, Ancient and Modern*. 1825. Reprint. 4 vols. New York: AMS Press, 1975.
    Four-volume anthology of Scottish poetry, including an extensive introduction and critical discussion of Scotland's major poets from King James V to Sir Alexander Boswell.

Freeman, F. W. "The Intellectual Background of the Vernacular Revival before Burns." In *Studies in Scottish Literature*, vol. XVI, edited by G. Ross Roy, pp. 97-109. Columbia: University of South Carolina Press, 1981.
    Views the Scots Vernacular Revival as a movement typical of eighteenth-century European thought.

Henderson, T. F. *Scottish Vernacular Literature, a Succinct History*. 3d rev. ed. Edinburgh: John Grant, 1910, 462 p.
    History of Scottish vernacular literature from its beginnings in the thirteenth century to its "death" in the mid-nineteenth century.

MacQueen, John. "Literature, Science and Improvement: Ramsay, Thomson and Smollett." In *The Enlightenment and Scottish Literature, Volume 1: Progress and Poetry*, pp. 55-

66. Edinburgh: Scottish Academic Press, 1982.
    Argues that the literature of Ramsay, Thomson, and Smollett reveals a celebration of the industrial revolution and a strain of animosity toward rural Scotland.

Speirs, John. *The Scots Literary Tradition, an Essay in Criticism*. Reprint. London: Faber and Faber, 1962, 229 p.
    Discussion of Scottish literature from the fifteenth through the twentieth centuries. Each chapter focuses on a specific movement, figure, or work; the chapter on "The Scottish Ballads" is included in the above entry.

Robert Fergusson

1750-1774

Scottish poet.

The following entry contains criticism published from 1897 through 1992.

INTRODUCTION

Known chiefly for his poems employing the forms, subjects, and language of his native Scots, Fergusson is widely recognized as the most influential predecessor of Scotland's most famous poet, Robert Burns.

Biographical Information

Fergusson was born in Edinburgh in 1750, the youngest of four children. His father earned a modest income as a clerk-copyist. Fergusson received an early education from his parents and a tutor, and in 1758 he enrolled in Edinburgh High School, where he received a strong classical education. He then transferred to the Grammar School of Dundee, where he obtained a scholarship which also entitled him to four years of support at the University of St. Andrews. Following the death of his father, Fergusson left school without taking a degree in order to help his mother. In 1769, he took the position of copyist in an Edinburgh law firm, where he earned a meager salary. He found his employment tedious, but became active in the cultural life of Edinburgh during this time. A friendship with the famous opera singer Giusto Ferdinando Tenducci led to the performance of three pastoral songs composed by Fergusson in the opera *Artaxerxes* at the Edinburgh theatre. Fergusson's first published poetry appeared in 1771 in the *Weekly Magazine, or Edinburgh Amusement*, a publication for which he became a regular contributor. While his early poems were written in conventional English verse forms, the 1772 publication of "The Daft Days" marked the beginning of a series of poems written in the Scottish vernacular. Fergusson's familiarity with both the common people and the cultural elite of Edinburgh enhanced the local color and realism of his works. His first book of poetry, *Poems by Robert Fergusson*, appeared in 1773, followed by the long poem *Auld Reikie*, published in the same year. In 1774, however, Fergusson fell seriously ill with a nervous disorder associated with his congenitally weak constitution and the effects of alcohol and what may have been an advancing case of syphilis. His condition became critical following a fall down a flight of stairs, from which he suffered a concussion. He was subsequently confined for a brief period to the "Schelles," the Edinburgh asylum, where he died soon after his twenty-fourth birthday.

Major Works

Although generally considered inferior to his verse written in the Scots language, critics have observed that some of Fergusson's early English-language poems such as "An Eclogue," reveal a unique use of humor, dialogue, characterization, and natural description. These qualities were further developed in the Scots vernacular poems that secured Fergusson's reputation. Characterized by conviviality, wit, local color, realism, and linguistic facility, many of the vernacular poems are occasional. "The Daft Days," for example, describes life in Edinburgh during the holidays between Christmas and the New Year. "Caller Oysters," another noted vernacular poem, celebrates the fresh oysters which were consumed in the Edinburgh taverns and surrounding countryside. In his vernacular poems, Fergusson frequently employed the six-line stanza form known as the "Standard Habbie," which was also used by Ramsay. Other forms successfully adapted by Fergusson were heroic couplets in "An Eclogue, to the Memory of Dr. William Wilkie," and the nine-stanza "Christis Kirk" form in "Hallow Fair." Widely considered one of Fergusson's best works, the long poem *Auld Reikie* is written in octosyllabic couplets. This work chronicles a week in the city of Edinburgh, vividly describing the shops, markets, taverns, clubs, and diverse characters that move through the streets. Another of Fergusson's landmark poems is "The Farmer's Ingle," which uses a nine-line Spenserian stanza to depict a small farm household, evoking the traditional lifestyle and language of the Scottish countryside.

Critical Reception

Despite his popularity, Fergusson received little critical attention during his lifetime and immediately following his death. This lack of critical response has been attributed to the brevity of his career, the popularity of his immediate successor, Robert Burns, and his resistance to the dominant literary style of his era. James A. Roy commented: "By remaining a realist and a satirist at a time when sentiment was the fashion and by insisting on writing in the vernacular, "Fergusson missed the way that led to recognition by the literary élite of his country." Fergusson has predominantly been viewed by critics as either an "unrealized possibility," or an important transition figure who served as a link between the achievements of Ramsay and those of Burns. Recent decades have witnessed increasing attention to the originality and skill of Fergusson's writings, and the extent of his important influence on Robert Burns. Many agree with A.M. Kinghorn and Alexander Law, who commented that "without Fergusson, more fertile in original conceptions, Burns would not have found the forms that . . . made him Scotland's national poet."

PRINCIPAL WORKS

Poems by Robert Fergusson (poetry) 1773
Auld Reikie: A Poem (poetry) 1773
Poems on Various Subjects: Part II (poetry) 1779
The Unpublished Poems of Robert Fergusson (poetry) 1955

CRITICISM

Henry MacArthur (essay date 1897)

SOURCE: "Robert Fergusson," in *Realism and Romance and Other Essays,* 1897. Reprint by Kennikat Press, 1970, pp. 204-25.

[*In the following excerpt, MacArthur briefly discusses Fergusson's strengths and weaknesses as a poet and compares his work with that of Robert Burns.*]

In our estimate of Fergusson's poetry his English pieces do not count. 'These English songs,' said Burns, 'gravel me to death,' and it is easy to imagine Fergusson saying the same thing.

> No choiring warblers flutter in the sky;

> Phœbus no longer holds his radiant sway;
> While Nature, with a melancholy eye,
>   Bemoans the loss of his departed ray.

That is a measure of Fergusson's English performance; and for most people it will be quite enough. Clearly, had Fergusson written always in this fashion, one would not be talking of him at this time of day. Indeed, if there is one thing more than another specially noticeable in Fergusson, it is the rich feast of the Doric which in every one of his best poems he sets before us. Such phrases as 'gust your gab' and 'weet your thrapple' ought to be dear to the heart of every patriotic Scot, and of such phrases Fergusson is full. Not Burns himself has a greater command over the resources of our kindly Scots tongue. If we valued our poets in proportion to the difficulty which the base Southron finds in reading their works, then would Fergusson be elevated far above Burns. Without going quite so far as that, one has a certain malicious satisfaction in trying to guess what one who has the misfortune not to be a Scotsman would make of this address **"To the Tron-Kirk Bell"**:—

> Wanwordy, crazy, dinsome thing,
> As e'er was framed to jow or ring!
> What gar'd them sic in steeple hing,
>   They ken themsel;
> But weel wat I, they couldna bring
>   Waur sounds frae hell.
>
>   . . . . .
>
> Oh! were I provost o' the toun,
> I swear by a' the powers aboon,
> I'd bring ye wi' a reesle doun;
>   Nor should ye think
> (Sae sair I'd crack an' clour your crown)
>   Again to clink.
>
>   . . . . .
>
> But, far frae thee the bailies dwell,
> Or they would scunner at your knell;
> Gie the foul thief his riven bell,
>   And then, I trow,
> The byword hauds, "The deil himsel
>   Has got his due."
>
>   . . . . .

This familiar way of treating the august personage referred to is, I think, very characteristic of our Scots poets. And the reason seems clear. It is not hard to hate the Devil, but, in spite of yourself, you cannot but have a friendly, neighbourly sort of feeling for one whom you call, familiarly, the Deil.

Fergusson has been called the Laureate of Old Edinburgh, and the title is richly deserved. There he had been born, there he spent most of his life, and he came, as most do, to love the old grey city right well. With his quick eye and his true descriptive power he contrives to give us, in a wonderfully vivid fashion, an idea of what life in the chief of Scottish cities was like in the last years of the eighteenth century. **"Auld Reekie," "The Daft Days," "The King's Birthday," "The Election," "Caller Oysters," "Leith Races"**—how picturesquely these bring before us the old, quaint town, with all the bustle and humours of the streets, the dirt, the smells, the merry din of the change-houses, and the drunkenness, the cheerful, the deliberate drunkenness, of its douce citizens.

Here, then, lay Fergusson's strength, in describing in his quietly humorous and satirical fashion the city scenes he knew so well, and had joined in so often. He was not without a feeling for Nature, of course—witness the idyllic close of that rollicking poem, **"The King's Birthday,"**—but he had been born among the high lands of Edinburgh, and it was of Edinburgh that he wrote best. Dealing with such themes as the street scenes suggested, his verse naturally lacked dignity and elevation, but at least—and this was much—it was true to life; he described only what he saw, always he wrote 'with his eye on the object.'

Fergusson had neither the fire nor the pathos of Burns; love had not come to him as it came to Burns, causing spontaneous bursts of song. His experience was not mature; seriousness, that deep and true view of life which only the progress of the years can bring, was wanting; dying at twenty-four, how could it have been otherwise? But through all his best poems there runs a tone of genuine humour and sarcasm, always pleasant and sometimes pungent. Thus he sings satirically the praises of **"Gude Braid Claith"**:

> Braid claith lends fouk an unco heeze;
> Maks mony kail-worms butterflees;
> Gies mony a doctor his degrees,
>   For little skaith:
> In short, you may be what you please,
>   Wi' gude braid claith.
>
>   . . . . .
>
> For tho' ye had as wise a snout on,
> As Shakespeare or Sir Isaac Newton,
> Your judgment fouk wad hae a doubt on,
>   I'll tak my aith,
> Till they could see ye wi' a suit on
>   O' gude braid claith.

Let me conclude my quotations with one which shows how sweet a strain Fergusson was master of once in a while. It occurs in the **"Elegy on the Death of Scots Music."** He complains, a hundred years before Professor Blackie, of the neglect of our national airs, and asks—

> Could lavrocks, at the dawnin' day,
> Could linties, chirmin' frae the spray,
> Or todlin' burns, that smoothly play
>   Owre gowden bed,
> Compare wi' "Birks o' Invermay"?
>   But now they're dead. . . .

What Fergusson might have achieved had he lived it is idle to speculate. He died, insane, at twenty-four; but already his work was done. In his habit of dealing directly with the subjects that lay nearest to his hand—dealing with them faithfully and freely in the homely tongue he so well knew how to use,—in this habit he had shown the way to Burns, he had marked out the path which he who had the good fortune to come after was to tread with a firmer, a more assured step. He is thus linked with that great movement in English poetry of which Wordsworth was—not so much the originator as—the first wholly conscious exponent. . . .

W. J. Courthope (essay date 1910)

SOURCE: "Democracy and Lyric Poetry, Scottish and English," in *A History of English Poetry, Vol. VI,* Macmillan & Co., 1910, pp. 52-83.

[In the following excerpt, Courthope briefly summarizes Fergusson's poetic achievement, focusing on his use of the Scots vernacular.]

Fergusson, like Ramsay, wrote both in literary English and in the vernacular. The former class of his poems comprises Odes, Pastorals, Elegies, Mock-heroics, in all of which the predominant influence of the Classical Renaissance is not less plainly visible than is the imitation of such English writers as Collins, Gray, and Shenstone. In many of his "Scots Poems" there is also an unmistakable English manner, shown by the frequent use of the heroic couplet and the coupling of substantives and adjectives; while the element of what would now be called "particularism" is marked simply by the choice of the subject and the distinction of dialect. Fergusson was in a special sense the poet of Edinburgh, the manners of which city he reproduced in verse with as much liveliness as Smollett had shown in the prose of *Humphrey Clinker.* He had, however, a model for his **"Auld Reekie"** in the "Trivia" of Gay, whose minutely detailed manner he copies in descriptions of the lighting and the law-courts, the "Bucks" and "Maccaronis," the street-cries and even the smells, of the Scottish Capital. Gay gives the necessary mock-heroic air to his subject by a lofty classical style: Fergusson, on the other hand, shows his affection for his native city by his appropriate use of a colloquial vocabulary which allows touches of homely humour and sentiment. His classical training was of good service to him in his patriotic verse; and the genuine spirit of the Renaissance breathes in his Eclogues, **"The Mutual Complaint of Plainstanes and Causey,"** the **"Dialogue between Brandy and Whisky,"** and **"The Ghaists,"** poems which Burns has imitated in his "Brigs of Ayr," without (if an Englishman may presume to venture on a comparison of two Scottish poets) attaining an equal measure of artistic success. Fergusson's Elegies, written in *rime couée,* are better than Ramsay's, and though his lyrical description of manners in **"Leith Races"** and **"The Election"** does not equal Burns's "Hallowe'en," **"The Farmer's Ingle"** seems to me to have a more genuine classical movement than "The Cotter's Saturday Night":

The fient a cheep's amang the bairnies now;
    For a' their anger's wi' their hunger gane:
Ay maun the childer, wi' a fastin' mou',
    Grumble, and greet, and mak' an unco
mane.
In rangles round, before the ingle's lowe,
    Frae Gudame's mouth auld-warld tales they
hear,
O' warlocks loupin' round the wirrikow:
    O' ghaists that win in glen and kirkyard
drear;
    Whilk touzles a' their tap, and gars them
shake wi' fear.

For weel she trows that fiends and fairies be
    Sent from the deil to fleetch us to our ill;
That kye hae tint their milk wi' evil e'e;
    And corn been scowdered in the glowin'
kill.

O mock na this, my friends! but rather mourn,
    Ye in life's brawest spring wi' reason clear;
Wi' eild our idle fancies a' return,
    And dim our dolefu' days wi' bairnly fear:
    The mind's ay cradled when the grave is
near.

But both Ramsay and Fergusson use the vernacular as if it were something exterior to themselves, a material useful for producing metrical effects proper to poetic diction: language is not with them, as it is with Burns, a lyrical instrument responsive to every inward movement of passion and imagination: in range of fancy, geniality of humour, and fineness of artistic taste, they stand on a level much below their great disciple, generous though the latter was in exalting their merits as the first explorers of the poetical region which he made so peculiarly his own.

Sir George Douglas (essay date 1911)

SOURCE: "Robert Fergusson," in *Scottish Poetry: Drummond of Hawthornden to Fergusson,* James Maclehose & Sons, 1911, pp. 157-93.

[*In the following excerpt, Douglas discusses the artistic temperament evidenced by Fergusson's life and poetry.*]

It was in 1771, at the age of twenty, that [Fergusson] contributed his English Pastorals: **"Morning," "Noon,"** and **"Night,"** to an Edinburgh Weekly Magazine, conducted by a son of that Dr. Ruddiman who had been one of Allan Ramsay's first patrons. These pastorals, deft and pretty though they be, are obviously the work of a writer who as yet has nothing to say. But his apprenticeship to poetry was brief. Next year he published **"The Daft Days,"** a Christmas poem, in the Doric; which he proceeded to follow up regularly with similar contributions. Fergusson had now found himself; and ere long was hailed as the true successor to Ramsay, who had died fourteen years before. But this recognition, dearly gratifying as it must have been to him, was limited to a small and entirely

uninfluential circle, not extending much beyond his own drinking acquaintance. To live by poetry was for him, of course, out of the question; but he is said to have been paid for his magazine contributions, whilst a small volume of collected poems which he issued in 1773 brought him in £50. This was the climax of his career,—the highest point of appreciation, or remuneration, to which those verses which are now an integral part of Scottish literature ever carried him whilst he lived. For it was now that the catastrophe arrived.

A life passed mainly betwixt the tavern and the copyist's desk can scarcely have been favourable whether to bodily health or mental serenity. Nor was his constitution adapted to bear the slightest strain. His mind had been at all times open to religious impressions of the gloomier kind; and it is probable that, justly or unjustly, the Furies of Conscience were by this time on his track. His native melancholy—the constitutional complement of his wild sportive humour—began to deepen perceptibly, and it was noticed that mere trifles now upset him. He committed his cherished manuscripts to the flames, and ceased to read in any book save a Bible which his mother had given him when he first left home. About this time the shock sustained by a fall downstairs increased the mischief already done, and, his reason becoming unhinged, it was found necessary to place him in the asylum known by the sinister name of The Schelles, or Cells. There he lingered for some two months—two months of which the story is intensely painful; for it is the story of the gradual extinction of a soaring mind—an extinction rendered only the more harrowing by the interruption from time to time of stray gleams of reason and feeling—of flashes of the old Fergusson.

And there, amid ghastly surroundings, not wholly unconscious of his own awful position, he died on October 16th, 1774, aged twenty-four years and one month. Surely, I have not exaggerated in claiming for Fergusson the saddest fate recorded in Scottish letters! . . .

It has not yet ceased to be customary—even in Scotland, where we should know better—to regard Fergusson as the mere forerunner of Burns, whose glory Burns eclipsed. And this is easily explicable; for many things that were done well by Fergusson were much better done by Burns. And, yet, it is not as it ought to be. For not only was Fergusson the favourite model to whom Burns owed the first idea, or the form, of many well-known passages—there is a list of these in Dr. Grosart's book on Fergusson [*Robert Fergusson,* 1898]: not only this, but, independently of this, the Scottish poems of Fergusson are well worth study for their own sake. And, as I have already hinted, one of the most surprising things about them is that, miserable as was Fergusson's short life, there is little or nothing of sadness in his poems. But for reported speech of his, only too unmistakably sincere, we might indeed believe him callous—insensibly content.

But that is not the real explanation of the case. No; Fergusson was proud—was not the man, young as he was, to wear his heart upon his sleeve: he was too guileless, and perhaps too self-respecting, to take the public into his confidence and to parade his griefs in print. It was the instinct of a brave man and a gentleman which bade him wear a jaunty air under misfortune's buffets; and, though his heart were heavy, carry his head erect. He would have no man's pity. And so, when he speaks of himself at all in verse, his attitude becomes defiant.

But there is this to be remembered, too: that, despite indifferent health and straitened circumstances, Fergusson was no moping, or cloistered poet, but very much the reverse. Indeed the character in which he most readily rises before us is that of a brisk walker of the streets, a busy frequenter of public places, an infinitely arch and observant commentator on whatever met his eye.

He sought company as a means of forgetting his sorrows, no doubt often with success. For, wherever a crowd was gathered—were it on Leith Sands for the Horse-races, in the Meadows or King's Park of a Sunday, or in Edinburgh streets upon a Birthday—there was Fergusson in the midst. So that the impression produced by reading his best-known poems is very much that of walking in a crowded thoroughfare with a sprightly, malicious companion on one's arm, whispering remarks. For example: this comment on the barber's apprentice, playing the gentleman after shop-hours:—

> On Sabbath-days, the barber spark,
> When he has done wi' scrapin' wark,
> Wi' siller broachie in his sark,
>   Gangs trigly, faith!
> Or to the Meadows, or the Park,
>   In gude braid claith.
>
> Weel might ye trow, to see him there,
> That he to shave your haffits bare,
> Or curl and sleek a pickle hair,
>   Would be right laith—
> When pacin' wi' a gawsy air
>   In gude braid claith.

This little picture lives: a fragmentary survival from the Edinburgh of one hundred and forty years ago, and an anticipation of our "Church Parades."

Or take this thumb-nail sketch of the card-tout on Leith race-course:—

> Now mony a scawd and bare-back'd loon
>   Rise early to their wark:
> Eneuch to fley a muckle toon
>   Wi' dinsome squeel and bark:—
> 'Here is the true and faithfu' list
>   O' noblemen and horses;
> Their eild, their weight, their height, their grist,
>   That rin for plates and purses,
>   Fu' fleet this day!'

He hits off the Buchan and the Highland accents with equal fidelity, breathing the breath of life into his puppets. And, not only this, but the tone of his comments throughout is infinitely genial: his fine irony never degenerates into harsh or ugly satire.

In 1726, the painter Hogarth had dedicated certain of his plates to Allan Ramsay. The compliment was a gratifying one, and the discrimination shown in the choice of its recipient is surprising. But, in his magic power of seizing and communicating the humours of streetlife, Fergusson, in his own day, came much nearer the spirit of Hogarth than ever Ramsay had done. Where the stripling poet falls short of the maturer painter is in depth and tragic significance; as well as in the power of combining distinct and diverse traits of character so as to make them unite in contributing to a single artistic effect. Fergusson's sketches in such poems as **"The Election,"** his most elaborate attempt in this style, as **"Hallowfair,"** the **"Rising of the Session,"** and others already named, are too often isolated and dispersed; with the result that, notwithstanding their vivacity, their effect fails to be cumulative, and evaporates as we read. In this sense, the term improvisation, which I applied to Ramsay's work, is applicable also to much of Fergusson's.

The faculty of observation is, however, by no means rare in young people, in whom it is likewise pretty often associated with that of reproduction, by mimicry. A much rarer attribute of Fergusson's genius is the precocious grasp of character exhibited in his dialogues, and in his **"Elegy on John Hogg the College Porter,"** a northern Sancho Panza, whose estimate of the comparative utility of money and of learning, the poet thus sums up:—

> For John aye lo'ed to turn the pence—
> Thought poortith was a great offence:—
> 'What recks tho' ye ken mood and tense?
>   A hungry wame
> For gowd would wi' them baith dispense,
>   At ony time.
>
> 'Ye ken what ails maun aye befall
> The chiel that will be prodigal;
> When, wasted to the very spaul
>   He turns his tusk
> (For want o' comfort to his saul)
>   To hungry husk.'

And it is remarkable in a poet at once so youthful and so forcible as Fergusson that he never overdoes his effects, never condescends to caricature. The label "Laureate of Auld Reekie" has been affixed to him; and, though it falls short of including the whole man, it is just in so far that he has done more than any other poet to paint the life and manners of the Scotch metropolis. With all its imperfections, to which he was by no means blind, he loved that noble city with a perfect filial love: a love which tempers, very winningly, his denunciation of such a distressing public nuisance as the local Tron Kirk Bell; and which turns a distant prospect of the town into a revelation of opening Paradise. And yet he paints unsparingly: his night-scenes are Hogarthian; their atmosphere is heavy with stench and with the fumes of drink. And it is a drunken Silenus, rather than a vine-crowned Bacchus, who presides over their orgies. But from the age of Ramsay on to that of North, Scots drink is the bane, the blight, of Scottish literature.

Town-bred and known to superficial students as a town poet, Fergusson has never yet received due praise as a poet of the country. His knowledge of country ways and of country character speaks to his rapidity of "up-take"; for it must have been mainly acquired during visits to his uncle's house and to Professor Wilkie's farm: and yet, so far as it goes, it is as close, and as spontaneously exhibited, as that of Burns himself. In his Odes addressed to the Bee and to the Gowdspink, he already shows interest in country themes, and readiness to deal with them.

But Fergusson's overmastering interest was an interest in man and character: immature and undeveloped as his talent was, it was before all things else dramatic. Of that we may be certain. And so, though the sight of a butterfly in the street might lead him to philosophize—and, incidentally, to supply the model of Burns's verses to the Field-Mouse; the one thing which really interested him was humanity, in its various shapes, its contrasts and its conflicts. Even when the speakers in his dialogues are presumedly non-human, his humanity still gets the better of his art; and he gives us, in place of Plainstanes and Causey, of Brandy and Whisky, two contrasted human types. He was human to the finger-tips—much more in sympathy with his kind than Keats had shown sign of being; and I venture to say that, by his early death, Scotland lost a great dramatic talent.

And it is this human sympathy which gives to his poem of **"The Farmer's Ingle"** its essential value, its essential charm. I do not claim that this interior equals "The Cotter's Saturday Night," the later poem which it suggested; for Burns's strain is loftier, his emotion deeper, his characters are more typical, more powerfully etched in. But Burns at the age at which Fergusson wrote this poem had as yet done nothing comparable to it. Judged on its merits, **"The Farmer's Ingle"** possesses a quiet penetrative charm, recalling that of a Dutch *genre* painting, or of one by our own Scottish master, Wilkie. But Fergusson has done what painter scarce could do: he has suffused the scene with a warm glow of sympathy, touching the farmer, grandam, children—all, with a humanizing touch, which lifts them from the sphere of alien things and makes them kindred with ourselves. . . .

[Poems] in which Fergusson speaks directly in his own person . . . are but two or three in number: namely, **"To My Auld Breeks," "My Last Will,"** and the **"Codicil"** thereto; but to students of Fergusson they are of the very highest interest for the self-revelation which they contain. Fergusson was, like Villon, a "gangrel" poet. Well! we have poets of respectability enough and to spare. Not, by the way, that there is any offence in Ferguson's rhymes; but that his attitude is that of a man with whom life has dealt hardly (can we wonder at this?), a man at odds with the world. And yet Fergusson has no quarrel with the world: he is too sweet-tempered for that. Nor does he ask its sympathy: he is too proud for that. He is content to

snap his fingers at it, thus:—

> While sober folk, in humble prose,
> Estate, and goods, and gear dispose,
> A poet surely may disperse
> His movables in doggerel verse;
> And fearing death my blood will fast chill,
> I hereby constitute my last will.
>
> Then, wit ye me to have made o'er
> To Nature my poetic lore;
> To her I give and grant the freedom
> Of paying to the bards who need 'em
> As many talents as she gave,
> When I became the Muse's slave.
>
> Thanks to the gods, who made me poor,
> No lukewarm friends molest my door;
> Who always show a busy care
> For being legatee or heir.
> Of this stamp none will ever follow
> The youth that's favour'd by Apollo.
>
> But, to those few who know my case,
> Nor thought a poet's friend disgrace,
> The following trifles I bequeath,
> And leave them with my kindest breath;
> Nor will I burden them with payment
> Of debts incurred, or coffin raiment.

On this follows a ludicrous list of burlesque legacies: to one friend he bequeaths his snuff-box; to another his manuscripts; to a third his outstanding debts. The verse is hastily dashed off, but is well worth reading for the wit that flashes through it. But there is something more than wit: something which it were unjust to designate bitterness; something which I can speak of only as heartbreak. Brave hearts break cheerfully to all appearance, with jest upon the lips. And so it was with Fergusson. There comes a time when the gallant show can be kept up no longer. From himself—from his writings, that is—we know not a word of what he endured. But we know what sort of nature he had, and we know what sort of life he had. Surely it does not require an expert to explain the catastrophe!

That Fergusson's Scotch was archaistic we may gather from his rhymed **"Epistle to J. S.,"** his Berwick correspondent, in which he describes his Muse as having found

> a knack,
> To gar *auld-warld wordies* clack
> In hamespun rhyme.

His Doric was purer than that of Ramsay; though, in this respect, still leaving somewhat to be desired. In poetic rank, as in time, he stands mid-way between Ramsay and Burns. But, more than all else, he remains to us a great unrealized possibility.

A. Montgomerie Bell (essay date 1923)

SOURCE: "Robert Fergusson, 1750-1774," in *The Cornhill Magazine,* Vol. LV, No. 326, 1923, pp. 179-88.

[In the following excerpt, Bell offers an overview of Fergusson's life and career and comments on some of the poems that established the poet's reputation.]

Robert Fergusson, the Scottish poet, was born in Edinburgh on September 5, 1750, and died in the same city on October 16, 1774; a brief life, yet worthy of long remembrance. His parents, William Fergusson and Elizabeth Forbes, both children of the farm-house, in 1746 left Tarland in Aberdeenshire, and settled in the metropolis, where William Fergusson showed considerable business capacity, and, after a hard struggle with poverty, obtained a good and permanent position with the British Linen Company. Young Robert early displayed an aptitude for letters, and in 1758 joined the High School. In 1762 he was appointed to the Fergusson Bursary, which provided 'maintenance and education' for two poor children at the Grammar School of Dundee and the College of St. Andrews. So selected, he received his schooling in Dundee from 1762 to 1764, and from 1765 to 1768 was a redgowned student at St. Andrews University.

Of these, his boyish years, few memorials remain, yet enough to reveal, that in his case, as in others, the boy was father to the man. His mother, always described as 'a woman of great worth and piety,' was wont to call him 'our darling gentle Robert,' just as Miss Ruddiman, the last survivor of his friends, loved in her old age to name him 'a dear, modest, gentle creature.' Taught by his mother to read, he was quick to envisage the meaning of the printed page. One day he burst into his mother's room in tears, exclaiming 'Oh, mother, whip me! whip me!' Astonished by the request, his mother asked his reason, and found that he had just read the words 'He that spareth the rod, hateth the child.'

In 1764, before joining the University, in company with his mother he paid a visit to Mr. John Forbes, his maternal uncle, at Round Lichnot, in Aberdeenshire, where Mr. Forbes was factor to the Earl of Finlater, and, undoubtedly, in good circumstances. This visit was of importance to the future poet. His poems fall into two classes, those of the city and those of country life. While the poems on city life are more numerous, more humorous also, and witty, those of the country display a higher imaginative power, and more intimately reveal the poet's heart. Whence came the first impressions which gave birth to these poems, unless from this visit to Round Lichnot?

With the life of St. Andrews the report of the young lad becomes clearer; he was a competent Latin scholar—usually with a Virgil or Horace in his pocket; 'a considerable proficient,' also, 'in mathematics.' His biographer possessed a copy of the 'Anabasis,' with *'Ex libris Rob. Fergusson'* written on the fly-leaf, and a rude drawing of a harp sketched below. Three traditions from this time are constant: first, that he began to write verses at St. Andrews, *vers d'occasion,* playful skits on a professor or other celebrity—fugitive pieces, of which none have been

preserved; secondly, he was much esteemed by Dr. William Wilkie, the able though eccentric Professor of Natural Philosophy, in whose house he was a frequent guest, and, during one summer, was engaged by the Professor to copy out his lectures; thirdly, his genial and friendly disposition made him beloved by some of his fellow-students, while his wit and gaiety brought general popularity. Young men at Scottish Universities are entirely left to themselves at an age when the judicious guidance of an elder friend or tutor is peculiarly helpful. Hence popularity is apt to be a path to regrettable indiscretions, and it was so with Fergusson. An incident which occurred in his fourth year may be narrated. He had a beautiful voice, so noticeable in the College Services that he was frequently asked to officiate as Precentor, or leader of the singing. Far from regarding the selection as an honour, the boy considered that he was too often called upon to perform another's duty. It was then customary in Scotland for persons, prevented by illness or other necessary cause from attending public worship, to give in a *line,* to be read by the Precentor, asking for the prayers of the congregation on their behalf. Fergusson, rising in the desk, with assumed nasal whine and ultra solemnity of voice— his powers of mimicry were great—pronounced the words: 'Remember in prayer *John Adamson,* for whom, from the sudden effects of inebriety, there appears but small hope of recovery.' An ill-repressed titter arose from the many students present, John Adamson among them, and Fergusson was justly and severely reprimanded. Yet not repressed, for shortly afterwards another incident occurred, of which details are not given, but Fergusson was extruded from the College for four days, after which he was 'received in again,' Professor Wilkie speaking warmly in his cause.

Hardly had he left College, when, by similar folly, he damaged his prospects in the home circle. His father had died in 1767, and, from lack of means, the son could not continue his education at the University. His mother's brother invited his fatherless nephew to Round Lichnot, presumably with the intention of lending him a helping hand. One day, Lord Finlater, through whose good word Fergusson had received his bursary, was expected to dinner, Mr. Forbes asked the Laird of Meldown to meet him, and young Robert was to be of the party. The guests were late in arriving, the boy slipped off to a neighbouring wood, climbed trees birdnesting, and finally came in late for dinner, his clothes torn and ruffled, and green with tree-dust. His uncle, in great anger, ordered him from the room, the boy, in as deep dudgeon, went to his bedroom, packed up his little bundle, and started for Aberdeen, without bidding his uncle, or any inmate of the house, farewell. The two stories reveal an excess of boyish thoughtlessness, and may easily be exaggerated *in malam partem;* juster criticism of this part of his life may be found in the words of the College janitor: 'Remember Bob Fergusson? that I do! Many a time I've put him to the door. Ah! he was a tricky callant, but *a fine laddie for a' that.*'

With his return, in 1769, to his widowed mother in Edinburgh, his real difficulties and his real life began. Further study was impossible, whether for the Church, Medicine, or Law; for the profession of a 'Dominie' he felt no call; yet something he must do, both to maintain himself and, if possible, to aid his mother. After some delay he was offered a copying-clerkship in the office of the Deputy Commissary-clerk; the duties were irksome, copying legal documents, and the emolument was small—one penny per page copied. Yet he accepted the post with gladness, rejoiced to secure the prospect of subsistence, however humble. Whatever the income which he received, possibly £25 or £30 a year, he never, until his death in 1774, had any other regular employment. Evidence that with his appointment his mind was more at ease is visible in this, that his first published verses appeared in the winter of 1769. A year, however, elapsed before he began to write frequently.

In 1770 Edinburgh society was acting on the resolution no longer to speak, much less to write, in the Scots tongue which they had learned from their fathers. Fergusson accepted the ruling, and his first essays were written in classical English, his models being the smart couplets of Pope, and the flowing quatrain of Shenstone; and, be it said, he did no dishonour to either of his originals. In 1768 the brothers, Walter and Thomas Ruddiman, had started the *Weekly Magazine, or Edinburgh Amusement,* and early in 1771 Fergusson began to be one of their regular contributors. His first published poems were pastorals, where Corydon sings to Timanthes of Delia's virtues, and one only wonders why both editors and public found reason to praise them as they did. One early poem, however, is of a different stamp, it is an **'Ode to Hope,'** and was probably written in 1770, and reflects a manly resolve to exercise his powers to the full.

> O smiling Hope! in adverse hour
> I feel thy influencing power;
> Though frowning fortune fix my lot
> In some defenceless lonely cot,
> Where Poverty, with empty hands,
> In pallid, meagre aspect stands,
> Thou canst enrobe me, 'midst the great,
> With all the crimson pomp of state;
> What cave so dark, what gloom so drear,
> So black with horror, dead with fear,
> But thou canst dart thy streaming ray,
> And change close night to open day?

Towards the close of 1771 he made the discovery that he could express his thoughts more naturally, with fresher humour and more lively verve, in the old dialect, which still persisted throughout Scotland. Among the first 'hameil' (homely) poems so published was **"The Daft Days,"** or Holidays of Christmas and New Year; it has these verses:

> Fiddlers! your pins in temper fix,
> And roset [rosin] weel your fiddle sticks,
> But banish vile Italian tricks
> 　　　From out your quorum,
> Nor fortes wi' pianos mix,
> 　　　Gie's Tullochgorum

> For nought can cheer the heart sae weel
> As can a canty Highland reel:
> It even vivifies the heel
> 　　　To skip and dance;
> Lifeless is he who cannot feel
> 　　　Its influence.

In a few weeks followed **"The King's Birthday,"** a favourite poem of Sir Walter Scott; it tells, *inter alia,* how Mons Meg, the great cannon of Edinburgh Castle, was burst in the rejoicings, and thus describes her:

> Right seldom am I gi'en to banning [swearing],
> But, by my saul, ye was a cannon;
> Could hit a man, had he been stannin'
> 　　　In shire o' Fife,
> Sax lang Scots miles ayont Clackmannan,
> 　　　And tak' his life.

The City Guard of Edinburgh, now best remembered from *The Heart of Midlothian,* as the Porteous Riot was directed against their captain, are so well described by Fergusson, that Scott calls him their Poet-Laureate. He begs them to be gentle:

> O soldiers, for your ain dear sakes,
> For Scotland's, alias Land o' Cakes,
> Gie not her bairns sic deadly paiks [thrusts],
> 　　　Nor be sae rude,
> Wi' firelock or Lochaber aix.
> 　　　To spill their blude.

The poem ends with a stanza prompted by the writer's gentler genius; his Muse refuses to record the evening misdeeds, of which some of the holiday-makers were proud; she

> Will rather to the fields resort,
> Where Music gars [makes] the day seem short,
> Where doggies play, and lambkins sport
> 　　　On gowany braes,
> Where peerless Fancy hads [holds] her court,
> 　　　And tunes her lays.

Is there not an inbred quality, what Johnson called *race,* in these verses? Do they not evince descriptive powers, quaint humour, captivating rhymes, and a higher strain of poetic feeling? His contemporaries thought so, for the poem from which the quotations are taken was read with delight from one end of Scotland to the other, and the author was hailed as a welcome successor to Allan Ramsay.

The result was natural, and for two reasons. First, for the merit of the verse. The stanza employed was familiar to Scottish readers from Allan Ramsay, as it is familiar now from Burns. It has great capacity for picturesque description, humorous phrasing, and rhyme-surprises, and, in the writer's judgment, Fergusson's chief success in the technique of poetry is his use of this stanza, in which he is not surpassed either by his predecessor or by his successor. The stanza is an old one, and, like many other good things, entered Scotland from the south. It is frequently employed in the Yorkshire Mystery Plays, written in the fourteenth century, though with this difference: the religious writers used it as a medium for the expression of pathos, whereas the Scottish writers look to it for humour. The second reason for approval lay with the audience. Eighteenth-century Scotland is ill conceived as a land of sour faces and cold hearts; far rather was it a land of music and song. A lyric inspiration yet hung over the country, like a refreshing dew, ready to fall on all homely things, and clothe them in new and bright shapes. Had the housewife too much on her hands? She went on with her duties, singing 'Women's wark will ne'er be dune.' Was she overburdened by sorrows? She did not give way, but sang 'Werena my heart licht, I wad die.' Did a lazy maid stickle over the allotted 'stent' of wool to be carded? She did not down tools, but changed her grievance into song: 'The weary pund, the weary pund, the weary pund o' tow.' Was there a lazy hind who would rather lie abed on a wintry morning than be up at his work! He too found solace with the verse:

> Up in the mornin's 's no' for me,
>   Up in the mornin' early:
> When a' the grund is covered wi' snaw,
>   I'm sure it's winter fairly.

These rural singers were under no compact to speak or write in southern English, and Fergusson's verses at once reached their hearts.

In Edinburgh society also the young poet quickly became popular. 'For social life,' his friend Ruddiman wrote, 'he possessed an amazing variety of qualifications. He was always sprightly, always entertaining. His powers of song were very great. When seated with some select companions, over a friendly bowl, his wit flashed like lightning, striking the hearers irresistibly.' The Cape Club was a famous convivial, at times high-spirited, society of the time: the name was taken from the Cape, or head-dress, worn by the president, or 'sovereign,' on state occasions. Thomas Lancashire, a famous actor, was the first sovereign; David Herd, editor of 'Old Ballads,' was the second; other members were Alexander Runciman and Henry Raeburn, the artists. Each member received a club name, with a knightly addition: Herd was Sir Scrope; Runciman, Sir Brimstone. On October 10, 1772, Fergusson, under the sobriquet Sir Precentor, was admitted as a member of the Club, and touching the mace, or 'Holy Poker,' with his right hand, took the oath of allegiance:

> I swear devoutly by this light
> To be a true and faithful Knight,
>   With all my might
>   Both day and night,
>   So help me Poker.

He was then touched thrice by the royal hand, and the sovereign, uttering the letters C. F. D., explained that they stood for *Concordia Fratrum Decus,* the motto of the Club.

Lithograph based on a sketch by a member of the Cape Club, an Edinburgh literary and drinking society to which Fergusson belonged.

Admitted a member, 'Sir Precentor' was a popular knight, and much taken out in society. These acquaintanceships unfortunately led him into convivialities, too much alike for his purse and his constitution. Amid many an evening spent in gaiety, his heart was ill at ease, as his thoughts returned to his mother, working at her needle with aching fingers. Nevertheless, his industry was great and unbroken; rarely a week passed without some contribution to the *Magazine;* and the pieces sent were of high quality. It has been said that he received no remuneration for his poems: it was not so; the brothers Ruddiman gave him a small sum for each contribution, and, such was the simplicity of the times, two suits of clothes annually, 'one for week-day, the other for Sabbath wear.'

At the close of 1772 he was encouraged, by subscriptions of many friends, to publish a small volume, containing nine of his Scottish poems; the edition sold rapidly, and the author, £50 in pocket, sang with unwonted joy that

> Damon was master of gold.

Nor was his vein dulled, for in 1773 some of his best verses followed in quick succession. Among them was **"The Farmer's Ingle,"** justly considered his best composition. It consists of thirteen nine-lined stanzas, and contains a lively description of an autumn evening in the farm-house, the occupations of Gudeman and Gudewife, Granny, Oë (grandchild), and servants being touched upon with singular sympathy and felicity:

> Weel kens the gudewife that the pleughs
>   [ploughmen] require
>   A heartsome maltith [meal], and refreshing
>   synd [draught]
> O' nappy liquor, o'er a bleezing fire;
>   Sair wark and poortith douna [cannot] weel
>   be join'd;
> Wi' buttered bannocks now the girdle [baking-
>   plate] reeks.
>   I' the far nook the bowie [milk-pail] briskly
>   reams,
> The readied kail stand by the chimley cheeks,
>   And had [keep] the riggin [rafters] het wi'
>   welcome streams,
> Which than the daintiest kitchen [sauce] nicer
>   seems.'

The poem, confessedly, suggested to Burns the "Cottar's Saturday Night," and, though not framed in so lofty a strain, is yet free from an affectation which mars some lines in Burns' masterpiece.

Another poem of the year, set in a merrier key, is **"Caller Water,"** which enjoins the pussy-foot practice, with quaint humour, and no little good sense.

> When father Adie first put spade in
> The bonny yeard of antient Eden,
> His amry [cupboard] had nae liquor laid in
>   To fire his mou',
> Nor did he thole [endure] his wife's upbraidin'
>   For being fou [tipsy].

On the contrary,

> A caller [fresh] burn o' siller sheen
> Ran cannily [gently] out ow're the green,
> And when our gutcher's [grandsire's] drouth had
>   been
>   To bide right sair,
> He loutit doun [stooped], and drank bedeen [at
>   once]
>   A dainty skair [share].

He closed with praise of the fair damsels of Edinburgh:

> On May-day in a fairy ring
> I've seen then round St. Anton's spring
> Frae grass the caller dewdrops wring
>   To wet their ein [eyes];
> And water clear as chrystal spring,
>   To synd them clean.
>
> Oh may they still pursue the way
> To look sae feat, sae clean, sae gay!
> Then shall their beauties shine like May,
>   And, like her, be

> The goddess of the vocal spray,
>   The Muse, and me.

To the same year belong two poems, the Odes to the Gowdspink (Goldfinch) and the Bee, both dear to lovers of the poet. They were written in the country, the second at least, when Fergusson was staying at Broomhouse, a guest of the Laird; and, while both are attractive, the **"Ode to the Gowdspink"** is of a slightly melancholy cast, as, undoubtedly, in the caged bird,

> steekit [barred] frae the gowany field,
> Frae ilka fav'rite howff and bield [lodging and
>   shelter],

the poet sees an image of himself, condemned to sit at the desk and drudge over dreary documents. The **"Ode to the Bee"** has no such note of sadness; it describes brightly the Bee's habits and haunts, and this brief account of Fergusson's poetry may well close with a quotation which reflects his naturally joyous spirit, and also records his claim to be, as in truth he was, one of the sweet singers of his native land.

> Like thee,—[the Bee],—by fancy wing'd, the
>   Muse
> Scuds ear' [early] and heartsome o'er the dews,
> Fu' vogie [delighted] and fu' blythe to crap
> The winsome flowers frae Nature's lap;
> Twining her living garlands there,
> That lyart [greyhaired] Time shall ne'er impair.

He was indeed on the verge of what might have been a prosperous life, had he but known it. [In a footnote, the critic adds: "A few days after the poet's death, a letter addressed to him reached his mother. Enclosed was a note for £100, and the request that Fergusson would join the writer in India, where a suitable appointment awaited him. The donor, on bearing the truth, gave the money to Mrs. Fergusson."] He also had the wish, and on one occasion made a strong resolution, to flee from the temptations which the convivial habits of the time threw in his way. The resolution was not kept; he returned to his previous mode of life and paid the severest penalty—the loss of reason and of life. In 1774 his physical strength was already affected, when his mind, now over-sensitive, was well-nigh unhinged by an accidental circumstance. A favourite starling, caged in his bedroom, was one night worried by a cat, which had crept down the chimney. The poet at once saw in the fate of the bird an image of what might befall himself: as suddenly might he be called away. He rose with the morning, resolved to alter his course of life; never again to write verses, never to associate with the thoughtless and the gay. Like Collins, whose end was similar, and due to the same cause, he took the Bible for his only book; and his constant companion was the Rev. Dr. Erskine, of the Grey Friars' Church. The words, that he was to blame for something, 'And for many, many other follies,' were often on his lips. His mental balance was indeed shaken; still, with the quieter regimen, there was improvement and hope, when an untimely accident hastened the close. He fell from the head of a staircase, striking his head severely at the bottom, and was carried home insensible, to awake raving. His poor mother had no resource save to take him to the public asylum; as he entered, his mind returned, and he raised a piteous cry of anguish. With morning he was calmer, his mother and sister came to see him; he thanked them for their affection, and besought his sister to 'bring her seam, and sit beside him.' As they replied with tears, he sought to console them, saying that he hoped ere long to be restored to them. He was in the institution for two months, daily visited by his mother and sister; at times his mind wandered; at others he would sing Scottish melodies, especially his old favourite, the 'Birds of Endermay,' and he sang with a pathos which he had never reached before.

On the day after his death he was buried in the Canongate Churchyard, and many mourners were present. Thirteen years later, Robert Burns, in his visit to Edinburgh, sought out the grave, and found it but 'a green mound and scattered gowans.' Uncovering his head, he shed tears, and obtained leave from the Managers of the Kirk and Kirkyard to raise a headstone over the grave, on which he had this inscription engraved, which, the writer can testify, is still legible, and eloquent of the poet:

> No sculptur'd marble here, nor pompous lay,
>   No storied urn, or animated bust:
> This simple stone directs pale Scotia's way,
>   To pour her sorrows o'er her poet's dust.

James A. Roy (essay date 1948)

SOURCE: "Robert Fergusson and Eighteenth-Century Scotland," in *University of Toronto Quarterly,* Vol. XVII, No. 2, January, 1948, pp. 179-89.

[*Roy is a Scottish critic and educator. In the following excerpt, he argues that Fergusson's critical reception was impeded by his use of satire and traditional Scottish dialect during "an age when sentimentalism was the vogue."*]

Fergusson made his first appearance as an author by contributing three songs to the opera *Artaxerxes,* which was a translation of Metastasio's work of that name. The English version, which was produced at the Theatre Royal, Edinburgh, in 1769, was a miserable travesty of the original, and Fergusson's songs were on a par with the rest of the work. Although Tenducci sang them, the author was so ashamed of the versicles that he never acknowledged them. But he had at least the satisfaction of actually seeing his name in print, and the very fact that he had been asked to write verses for the opera at all, and that they had been sung by Tenducci, is proof that Fergusson was already known as a writer to a small literary and artistic circle and that his talents were recognized. The publication of **"The Daft Days"** in Ruddiman's *Weekly Magazine,* on January 2, 1772, first showed the public, especially that part of it which understood and habitually spoke the vernacular, that a new poet had arisen in Scotland and that the Scottish Muse was not only not dead but capable of high utterance. **"The Daft Days"** is full of pawky humour and has the smack and intimacy of Old Edinburgh in its every stanza.

> Auld Reikie! thou'rt the canty hole;
> A bield [*shelter*] for mony caldrife [*cheerless*]
> Wha snugly at thine ingle loll, [*fire-side*]
>   Baith warm and couth; [*comfortable*]
> While round they gar the bicker roll, [*kind of
>   wooden dish*]
>   To weet their mouth.

Two months later appeared the **"Elegy on the Death of Scots Music,"** an appealing little thing that is full of pathos, poetry, and patriotism.

> At glomin now the bagpipe's dumb,
> Whan weary owsen hameward come;
> Sae sweetly as it wont to bum,
>   And *Pibrach's* skreed;
> We never hear its warlike hum,
>   For music's dead. . . .
>
> Now foreign sonnets bear the gree
> And crabbit queer variety
> Of sounds fresh sprung frae *Italy,*
>   A bastard breed!
> Unlike that saft-tong'd melody
>   Which now lies dead. . . .
>
> O Scotland! that cou'd yence afford
> To bang the pith of Roman sword,
> Winna your sons, wi' joint accord,
>   To battle speed?
> And fight till Music be restor'd,
>   Which now lies dead?

On June 4, 1772, appeared (again in Ruddiman's *Weekly Magazine*) the jolly, witty verses on **"The King's Birthday in Edinburgh,"** when

> fock of ilka age and name,
>   Baith blind and cripple,
> Forgather aft, O fy for shame!
>   To drink and tipple.

On August 27 Ruddiman's published **"Caller Oysters,"** another intimate poem with a rich vernacular and pungent but wholesome humour. It contains what is perhaps Fergusson's best bit of interior description:

> Whan big as burns the gutters rin,
> Gin ye hae catcht a droukit [*wet*] skin,
> To *Luckie Middlemist's* loup [*jump*] in,
>   And sit fu snug
> Oe'r oysters and a dram o' gin,
>   Or haddock lug.
>
> When auld Saunt Giles, at aught o'clock
> Gars merchant lowns their chopies lock,
> There we adjourn wi' hearty fock
>   To birle our bodles,

And get wharewi' to crack our joke,
    And clear our noddles.

When *Phoebus* did his windocks steek, [*windows
    shut*]
How aften at that ingle cheek [*fire-place*]
Did I my frosty fingers beek, [*warm*]
    And taste gude fare?
I trow there was nae hame to seek
    When steghin there.

While glakit fools, o'er rife o' cash,
Pamper their weyms wi' fousom trash,
I think a chiel [*a young fellow*] may gayly pass,
    He's no ill boden [*provided for*]
That gusts [*tastes*] his gabb [*mouth*] wi' oyster
    sauce,
    And hen weel sodden.

"Braid Claith," "Hallowfair," "To the Tron Kirk Bell,"
"Mutual Complaint of Plainstanes and Causey," "The
Rising of the Session," "The Farmer's Ingle," and other verses followed in rapid succession. There is admirable
satire in the first of these works:

Braid Claith lends fock an unco heese, [*lift*]
Makes mony kail-worms butter-flees,
Gies mony a doctor his degrees
    For little skaith;
In short, you may be what you please
    Wi' gude Braid Claith.

For thof ye had as wise a snout on;
As *Shakespeare* or *Sir Isaac Newton*
Your judgment fouk wou'd hae a doubt on,
    I'll tak' my aith,
Till they cou'd see ye wi' a suit on
    O' gude Braid Claith.

For condensation of language and ideas, for accuracy of
description and truth of detail, for firmness and strength
of line, we must go back to Dunbar to find anything in
the vernacular like **"The Farmer's Ingle."**

Whan gloming grey out o'er the welkin keeks,
    [*peeps*]
        When *Batie* ca's his owsen [*oxen*] to the
    byre,
Whan *Thrasher John,* sair dung, [*worsted*] his
    barn-door steeks, [*closes*]
        And lusty lasses at the dighting
    [*threshing*] tire:
What bangs fu' leal the e'enings coming cauld,
        And gars snaw-tapit winter freeze in vain:
Gars dowie mortals look baith blyth and bauld,
        Nor fley'd wi' a' the poortith o' the plain;
        Begin, my Muse, and chant in hamely
    strain.

In another poem, **"Auld Reikie,"** one may discover not
only Fergusson's love for his own city but his indignation
at the denationalizing of his country.

While dandring cits delight to stray
To Castlehill, or public way,
Whare they nae other purpose mean,
Than that fool cause o' being seen;
Let me to *Arthur's Seat* pursue,
Whare bonny pastures meet the view;
And mony a wild-lorn scene accrues,
Befitting *Willie Shakespeare's* muse.
If fancy there would join the thrang,
The desart rocks and hills amang
To echoes we should lilt and play,
And gie to *Mirth* the lee-lang day.

    Or shou'd some canker'd biting show'r
The day an' a' her sweets deflow'r,
To Holyrood-house let me stray,
And gie to musing a' the day;
Lamenting what auld *Scotland* knew,
Bien [*plentiful*] days for ever frae her view.
O Hamilton, for shame! the muse
Would pay to thee her couthy vows,
Gin ye wad tent the humble strain,
An' gie's our dignity again!
For, O, wae's me! the Thistle springs
In *domicile* o' ancient kings,
Without a patriot to regret
Our *palace,* and our ancient *state.*

In this same poem Fergusson strikes the note that was
presently to be heard so frequently in the poetry of
Burns, the note of protest against the dullness of Scots
religion and the hypocrisy of many of its practitioners.
Fergusson was thinking of the Scottish sabbath when
he wrote:

    On Sunday here, an alter'd scene
O' men and manners meets our ein:
Ane wad maist trow, some people chose
To change their faces wi' their clo'es. . . .
But there's an unco dearth o' grace,
That has nae mansion but the face. . . .
Why should religion make us sad

If good frae Virtue's to be had?
Na, rather gleefu' turn your face,
Forsake hypocrisy, grimace;
And never have it understood
You fleg mankind frae being good.

Fergusson knew his Edinburgh as Cockburn and Scott
knew theirs; but he had no Henry Mackenzie to act as his
sponsor. Perhaps he was partly to blame himself. By remaining a realist and a satirist at a time when sentiment
was the fashion and by insisting on writing in the vernacular when men like "Jupiter" Carlyle and Principal Robertson were struggling to rid their prose of the least trace
of it, Fergusson missed the way that led to recognition by
the literary *élite* of his country. When he was writing
there were actually three varieties of English in Scotland:
the English English of the nobility, the acquired English
of men like Robertson and Carlyle whose native speech
was the Scots idiom, and the dialect of the common peo-

ple who spoke only the vernacular. It is the same in Scotland today. There are in this year of Our Lord 1948 still many people like Dr. James Beattie, author of the harmonious but forgotten *Minstrel,* who believe that the words "vernacular" and "vulgar" are synonymous. It is the endeavour of these people to speak what they believe is "correct" English; they merely succeed, in many instances, in acquiring what Lord Jeffrey was said to speak, a "nippity nippity English." Beattie explained that the main difficulty for Scottish writers was

> to give a vernacular cast to the English we write. . . . We who live in Scotland are obliged to study English from books like a dead language. Accordingly, when we write, we write it like a dead language, which we understand but cannot speak. Our style is stately and unwieldy, and clogs the tongue in pronunciation, and smells of the lamp. We are slaves to the language we write, and are continually afraid of making gross blunders, and when an easy, familiar idiomatical phrase occurs, dare not adopt it if we recollect no authority, for fear of Scotticisms. . . . An English author of learning is the master, not the slave of his language, and wields it gracefully because he wields it with ease and with full assurance that he has the command of it. . . . At Edinburgh it is commonly said by your critical people that Hume, Robertson, etc. write English better than the English themselves: than which in my judgment there cannot be a greater absurdity. I would as soon believe that Thuanus wrote better Latin than Cicero or Caesar, and that Buchanan was a more elegant poet that Virgil or Horace.

Beattie's remedy for Scotticisms was to read Addison, Swift, and Lord Lyttleton, and for the better guidance of his countrymen he and Hume compiled a list of Scotticisms to be avoided. But to little avail. The Scots still speak of "coarse" instead of "bad" weather. They still pay their tailor's "account" instead of his "bill." They still "feel a smell" and ask for "a clean plate." And some of them still feel "no dubiety" while the English have "no doubt." But even if Fergusson had followed the fashionable trend of the times and written his verses in English, it would have made little or no difference; even if he had not written **"The Sow of Feeling,"** which gave mortal offence to "the Man of Feeling," it still would have made little or no difference. Robert Fergusson was one of those men who do not rise above their own level and who, even if they are appreciated after their death, are never given full and wide credit for their achievement. Yet for a short time he was immensely popular throughout the length and breadth of his native land. One brother poet, "J.S.," wrote:

> Is Allan risen frae the deid,
> Wha aft has tun'd the aiten reed,
> And by the Muses was decreed
>   To grace the thistle?
> Na; Fergusson's cum in his stead
>   To blaw the whistle.

John Mayne, who wrote the celebrated "Siller Gun," which was praised by both Burns and Scott, describes the young poet's amazing popularity:

> 'Twas than, as now, your fame gaed roun'
> To sic a pitch thro' ilka toun,
> That the postboy cou'd nowther soun'
>   Nor blaw his horn,
> But heeps o' fouk wad him surroun'
>   Be'teen or morn. . . .

> . . . sair we miss our ain braid measure
> Sin Rabie die't. . . .

We cannot tell what Robert Fergusson would have given us if he had lived longer. He was a better technician than Allan Ramsay, a greater stylist in the language which Scottish kings had been proud to speak. Yet Fergusson could never have written "A Man's a Man for a' That", or "The Cotter's Saturday Night." Apart from **"The Farmer's Ingle,"** there was nothing that Burns did not do as well as Fergusson. Carlyle underrated him; Burns overrated him. The truth about Fergusson is somewhere between the estimates of these two men. Andrew Lang called attention to his real claims and long neglect when he spoke these words at a Burns anniversary dinner in Edinburgh in 1891. "Some people are inclined to ask—Are we quite sure that we are worshipping the right poet? It is true that there are many poets, and I sometimes yield so far to the suggestion as to think that we might worship some of them a little more than we do. There is Fergusson, Burns's master . . . a true poet, but so unfortunate after death as in life, that I doubt if we have a proper critical edition of [him.]"

The reason why Fergusson holds such a lowly place in the esteem of his countrymen is that he was a satirist and not a sentimentalist in an age when sentimentalism was the vogue. Edinburgh was no place for satirists, and Fergusson made the mistake of offending Henry Mackenzie, "the Man of Feeling," a dangerous man to offend. Burns was a man of feeling; that is one reason why Mackenzie took him up. Burns appealed to Mackenzie's vanity. Had not the "Ayrshire ploughman" worn out two copies already of a pocket edition of *The Man of Feeling?* Had he not written to a friend that his favourite authors were "of the sentimental kind"?

True, Fergusson had written a few things like the **"Ode to Pity"** and **"Retirement,"** poems touched with sentiment; but he had also ridiculed sentiment and its most influential Scottish practitioner. That finished Fergusson; there was no chance for him of a posthumous paper in the *Mirror* or the *Lounger* or a tardy recognition of his genius. In Mackenzie's eyes he was nothing but a guttersnipe, an ignorant vulgarian who did not know his proper place and had not learned to treat his betters with fitting respect. Even when he was a very old man, hovering "on the very brink of human dissolution," to use Scott's phrase, Mackenzie was unable to forget the insult to his dignity and penned these bitter and libellous words: "Fergusson, dissipated and drunken, died in early life, after having produced poems faithfully and humorously describing scenes of Edinburgh, of festivity and somewhat of blackguardism. Burns['s] . . . great admiration of Fergusson showed his propensity to coarse dissipation."

We can do little now to change matters. Fergusson must be content to be remembered by a minority of his countrymen; but those of them who take the trouble to understand his language can appreciate his humour, his keen observation, his faculty of graphic description, and the undertone of sadness that runs through much of his verse. And it cannot be too often repeated that Fergusson was the poet to whom Burns most gladly acknowledged his indebtedness.

Herbert J. C. Grierson and J. C. Smith (essay date 1947)

SOURCE: "The Revival of Scottish Poetry," in *A Critical History of English Poetry,* Chatto & Windus, 1947. Reprint by Chatto & Windus, 1965, pp. 263-67.

[*A Scottish critic and educator, Grierson was considered a leading authority on Milton, Donne, and Scott. In the following excerpt from* A Critical History of English Poetry, *originally published in 1944, Grierson and Smith offer a brief summary of Fergusson's contribution to the Scottish literary tradition.*]

Robert Fergusson (1750-1774) wrote no songs in Scots, but in other forms of poetry he has left a body of work remarkable in one who died so young. . . . In poetry other than song Fergusson is the chief link between Ramsay and Burns. He was not so versatile a metrist as Ramsay, but he was a sounder and more original poet. He broke new ground in **"The Farmer's Ingle"** and in the dialogues of **"Plainstanes and Causey"** and **"The Ghaists"**. He was the laureate of Auld Reekie, whose jollifications he celebrated with cleanly glee in **"The Daft-Days,"** and **Hallow-Fair,"** and **Leith Races"**. In **"The Farmer's Ingle"** he went afield for his subject: his odes to the caged goldfinch and the butterfly seen in the street bring Nature into the city, and show the same sympathy for the lower creation as charms us in Cowper and Burns. He had not Burns's gift of phrase, nor his virility—his impetuous blood; but he blazed the trail for him in several directions: his **"Leith Races," "Plainstanes and Causey,"** and **"Farmer's Ingle"** were the models which Burns 'emulated' in "The Holy Fair, "The Twa Brigs," and "The Cotter's Saturday Night"—rough diamonds, no doubt, beside Burns's polished gems, but diamonds for all that.

This is how **"Leith Races"** opens:

> In July month, ae bonny morn,
>   Whan Nature's rokelay green
> Was spread o'er ilka rigg o' corn
>   To charm our roving een;
> Glouring about I saw a quean,
>   The fairest 'neath the lift;
> Her EEN ware o' the siller sheen,
>   Her SKIN like snawy drift,
>   Sae white that day.

And here is the opening of "The Holy Fair":

> Upon a simmer Sunday morn,
>   When Nature's face is fair,
> I walk-ed forth to view the corn,
>   An' snuff the caller air.
> The rising sun, owre Galston Muirs,
>   Wi' glorious light was glintin';
> The hares were hirplin' down the furs,
>   The lav'rocks they were chantin
>   Fu' sweet that day.

We see at once how much Burns owes to Fergusson and how quickly his "emulating vigour" carries him beyond his original.

Allan H. MacLaine (essay date 1963)

SOURCE: "Robert Fergusson's *Auld Reikie* and the Poetry of City Life," in *Studies in Scottish Literature,* Vol. 1, No. 2, October, 1963, pp. 99-110.

[*MacLaine is a Canadian critic who specializes in Scottish poetry. In the following excerpt, he discusses Fergusson's description of eighteenth-century Edinburgh in "Auld Reikie," comparing the style and form of the poem with that of John Gay's "Trivia."*]

The most famous poem in British literature devoted wholly to description of city life is John Gay's *Trivia*. But this fascinating work stands by no means alone; rather it is representative of a vast body of little-known poetry in this genre, extending from the time of Chaucer to the present. William H. Irving in the final chapter of *John Gay's London* (Cambridge, Mass., 1928), an encyclopedic and eminently useful study of this kind of verse, notes that prior to the Romantic movement which brought more personal, humanitarian, symbolic, or even mystic poetic interpretations of the city into fashion, the city poetry of earlier eras is marked by more or less objective descriptive technique: the poet observes the life of the city and describes it for purposes of eulogy (as in Dunbar's *The Flour of Cities All*, or in passages of Spenser or Herrick); or for purposes of satire and exposure of folly (as in Swift's savage little sketches of street life); or for the sheer fun and fascination of it all (as in *Trivia*). A long-neglected work in this earlier tradition and a direct successor of *Trivia* chiefly concerns us here. This is ***Auld Reikie***, an extraordinary portrait of life in eighteenth-century Edinburgh by the brilliant Scots poet Robert Fergusson (1750-1774). Fergusson, whose career was tragically cut short in the first flush of his genius by death in the Edinburgh mad-house at the age of twenty-four, is remembered as the author of some thirty Scots poems (mostly graphic sketches of life in his beloved city) which were destined, a decade later, to have a profound and decisive impact upon the creative imagination of Burns. ***Auld Reikie*** a poem of 368 lines in tetrameter couplets, is Fergusson's longest and most ambitious treatment of the Edinburgh scene, and deserves to be recognized as one of the finest poetic renderings of city life in our literature.

Matthew P. McDiarmid, in the notes to his splendid edition of Fergusson, declares curtly of *Auld Reikie* that "the main suggestion for the poem came from Gay's *Trivia*." This statement is unquestionably accurate, since it is clear that Fergusson was thoroughly familiar with the work of Gay (and, also with that of Dryden, Pope, and Swift), and that in *Auld Reikie* he was obviously trying to do for Edinburgh something on the order of what Gay had already done for London. But *Auld Reikie* bears the stamp of Fergusson's distinctive originality, and is anything but a servile imitation of Gay; in fact, the differences between the two poems are more striking than their similarities. At this point, then, a brief comparison of the two, in structure, subject matter and style, will help to elucidate the characteristics of both poems, before we turn to a more detailed analysis of *Auld Reikie*.

Gay evidently conceived *Trivia* partly as a sort of "town-georgic" adapted from the Virgilian rural georgics, and partly as a burlesque on the versified "Arts," the habit, very popular in his day, of composing pompous poetic treatises on the most mundane of arts. Accordingly, he provides his poem with a subtitle, "The Art of Walking the Streets of London," though Gay's original satiric motive seems soon to have become subordinated to his zest for his subject matter. The idea of burlesquing the "Arts" poems, however, supplied Gay with a convenient framework for his material which is nearly organized in three books: "Of the Implements for Walking the streets, and Signs of the weather"; "Of Walking the Streets, by Day"; and "Of Walking the Streets, by Night." Within this overall scheme, the structure of *Trivia* is firm and satisfying.

Auld Reikie on the other hand, suffers from a certain looseness of structure. Dealing with the same kind of miscellaneous, kaleidoscopic materials, Fergusson's poem lacks an overall structural bond such as Gay's street-walking device which gives to *Trivia* a logical pattern. Fergusson simply shifts his focus from one vignette to another without reference to any single scheme, although it is possible that a more definite structure would have emerged had Fergusson completed his original conception. The fact is that *Auld Reikie* as we have it, is essentially a fragment. The first 328 lines were published separately in 1773, "for the author," in a slim pamphlet, with a dedication to Sir William Forbes in some of the copies, and the subtitle "Canto I" which suggests that further installments were to follow. The original design was never completed, however, presumably because Fergusson met with no encouragement from Sir William Forbes. After publication of his first "Canto," the poet merely added forty lines to round off the work, and it was reprinted in its final from five years after Fergusson's death in the 1779 edition of his poems. Hence the total design for the poem, if Fergusson had one, remains unknown.

Nevertheless, this apparent lack of an overall unifying structure in the poem as we have it does not mean that *Auld Reikie* is altogether without organization. Actually, the first half of the poem, after the introduction, is neatly divided into morning, afternoon, and night scenes (lines 23-58, 59-66, and 67-194 respectively). This arrangement

was no doubt suggested to Fergusson by Gay's separation of day from night scenes in Books II and III of *Trivia*. But at line 194 there is an abrupt break in the smooth development of *Auld Reikie* as Fergusson abandons his morning-afternoon-night scheme, and turns to treatment of other aspects of Edinburgh life which do not fit into this scheme. The second half of the poem falls into five sections on the following topics: contrasted description of the attractive vegetable market and the repulsive meat market (lines 195-230); Sunday in Edinburgh (lines 231-270); Holyrood House and poverty (lines 271-312); tribute to the late George Drummond as contrasted to the present corrupt civic leaders (lines 313-350); and a concluding eulogy on Edinburgh (lines 351-368). It should be noted, however, that the three central sections of this second half of the poem—on Edinburgh Sundays, on Holyrood and poverty, and on the city government—are ingeniously linked, one developing naturally out of the other. The section on the markets is the weakest part of the poem from a structural point of view, being more or less unrelated to what precedes and follows it. Thus, although *Auld Reikie* contains long passages which are carefully organized around related themes and linked by smooth transitions, the poem as a whole suffers from lack of an overall structural principle.

As for subject matter, *Trivia* and *Auld Reikie* show inevitable similarities. Many of the characters to be encountered in the streets of any eighteenth-century city are treated in both poems—bullies, fops ("macaronis" in Fergusson), housemaids, chairmen, link-boys ("caddies" in Fergusson), whores, and so forth. One brief passage on funerals in *Auld Reikie* (lines 163 ff.) is clearly modelled on *Trivia* (III, lines 255 ff.). Apart from this instance of direct indebtedness and one or two other minor hints, however, Fergusson's treatment of the same characters or scenes is entirely independent of Gay's in detail and phrasing. In general, it may be said that the far greater length of *Trivia* (over three times that of *Auld Reikie*) enables Gay to present more wealth of cumulative illustration and detail than is possible to Fergusson within the scope of *Auld Reikie*. At the same time, Gay's use of the street-walking device limits his material mainly to outdoor scenes, whereas Fergusson is able to move indoors to portray the lively tavern life of old Edinburgh. For this reason, Fergusson's poem is more comprehensive than Gay's in that it attempts to recreate the whole life of the city, not just its street scenes. Finally, whereas Gay includes several extended and detailed scenes, a large proportion of his poem is taken up with brief, undeveloped illustrations or suggestive glimpses. Fergusson, on the other hand, within his narrower space tends to concentrate upon a few sharply realized vignettes.

More striking than the differences in structure and subject matter, however, are the differences in the style of these two poems. Gay chose the mock-heroic technique for *Trivia* probably for two reasons: the mock-heroic was then very much in vogue; furthermore, this style enabled his neo-classical sense of decorum to remain inviolate. He could thus render poetically a subject which might otherwise seem to his fashionable readers intrinsically unpoet-

ic and unpleasant. For purposes of outright satire or burlesque the mock-heroic style, especially in the hands of a
master like Pope (in *The Rape of the Lock,* for example),
may do wonderfully well. But *Trivia,* though it does contain satiric elements, is not basically a satire. The poem is
too long and too miscellaneous in subject matter, and
Gay's attitudes toward his material are too varied for a
consistent mock-heroic technique. As a result there is a
certain sense of strain in *Trivia,* or at least so it seems to
modern readers accustomed to realistic treatment of city
themes. But the delicately artificial quality of his style is
doubtless part of Gay's conscious purpose. Through copious use of classical allusion, myth, and pseudo-myth,
together with Latinate diction and euphemisms, Gay deliberately softens the harsh realities of his subject matter
and achieves a gently ironic, urbane, and pleasantly humorous effect.

Fergusson's aim in **Auld Reikie** is very different. Though
he brings in touches of mock heroic here and there in
comic or satiric passages, for the most part Fergusson
employs a far more direct and unvarnished style to render
his brilliant vision of eighteenth-century Edinburgh. The
contrast can be illustrated by the fact that Fergusson introduces only eight classical allusions and eight personified abstractions, whereas Gay's poem is filled with scores
of these devices. Moreover, Fergusson employs a stylistic
method based upon dramatic contrast, thereby achieving
a style which is wholly his own and which may be unique
in the poetry of city life. A detailed examination of this
style will be given later. In summary, it may be said that
although **Auld Reikie** was clearly suggested by *Trivia* and
in several ways resembles it (being like *Trivia* neither
wholly satiric nor wholly eulogistic in point of view),
Auld Reikie is distinguished from it and from other city
poems chiefly by the method of dramatic contrast which
Fergusson uses. And this method is perfectly suited to the
unique city which Fergusson celebrates—Edinburgh.

In Fergusson's day Edinburgh was a relatively small city,
squeezed within ancient walls with open country on all
sides. The overflow of population to the New Town was
just barely beginning in 1773; the Old Town, dramatically perched upon its narrow ridge from the Castle to Holyrood House was still the focal center of Edinburgh life.
The old capital was an incredibly crowded place, a gray
stone jungle of tall tenements (called "lands") huddled on
either side of a single mile-long street, penetrated by a
fantastic network of narrow, evil smelling closes and
wynds which gave access to the High Street. So cramped
were housing conditions, whole families often living in
single rooms, that most of the business and social life of
the city had to be carried on in the High Street or in the
many taverns. Tavern life was, in fact, the heart and soul
of eighteenth-century Edinburgh. Despite the filth and
squalor, the city had a strange and impressive kind of
beauty which coexisted with this ugliness. No doubt its
dramatic location on a narrow ridge with magnificent views
of high hills nearby and the Firth of Forth glistening in
the distance, has much to do with this impression. At any
rate, this unique juxtaposition of beauty and squalor has
always fascinated visitors to Edinburgh, and continues to

do so. Unfortunately much of the Old Town, the ancient
closes of the High Street and the Cowgate, has degener-
ated since Fergusson's time into something of a slum.
This fact is graphically expressed by the contemporary
Scots poet Maurice Lindsay in his poem entitled *In the
High Street, Edinburgh*:

> Warriston's Close, Halkerston's Wynd!
> Crookit and cramped, dim, drauky, blind. . . .
>
> Fegs, and you're gey romantic places
> for thae wha ainly pree your faces!

In Fergusson's day, however, the Old Town was anything
but a backwater. It was a dynamic community, bustling
with energy, full of stirring life. Unlike London with its
sprawling suburbs, Edinburgh was a compact and homogeneous kind of community in which all classes lived
together in very close contact. Its intellectual as well as
its social life was lively and generally uninhibited. Smollett in *Humphrey Clinker* characterized it as "a hotbed of
genius." This, then, was the city full of bewildering contradictions which Fergusson attempted to recreate in all
of its contrasting moods, its robust and dissipated life, in
Auld Reikie.

In a poem of this length it is, of course, manifestly impractical to attempt to treat all of its noteworthy passages
and lines in detail, but a few typical examples will perhaps be enough to illustrate the important features of
Fergusson's style and method. He opens, appropriately,
with a rousing salute to Edinburgh:

> AULD REIKIE, wale o' ilka Town [*best; every*]
> That SCOTLAND kens beneath the Moon;
> Where couthy Chiels as E'ening meet [*sociable
>   fellows*]
> Their bizzing CRAIGS and MOUS to weet;
>   [*parched; throats; mouths*]
> And blythly gar auld Care gae bye [*make*]
> Wi' blinkit and wi' bleering Eye . . .

These lines are notable for their warmth and vigor, expressing as they do Fergusson's hearty and unchanging
love for the old gray city. It is significant that he begins
his poem with this reference to drinking, always a dominant feature of Edinburgh social life in his time.

The next section of the poem, on morning scenes, begins
with a splendid couplet portraying sunrise over the city,
followed by lines describing the early activities of housemaids and the foul morning smells of sewage (which
Fergusson ironically refers to as "Edina's *Roses*"). This
passage is photographic in its terse and impressive realism, as the following extracts will show:

> Now Morn, with bonny Purpie-smiles,
>   [*purple*]
> Kisses the Air-cock o' St. Giles; [*weathervane*]
> Rakin their Ein, the Servant Lasses [*rubbing;
>   eyes*]
> Early begin their Lies and Clashes . . . [*gossip*]

. . . . .

> On Stair wi' TUB, or PAT in hand [*pot*]
> The Barefoot HOUSEMAIDS looe to stand, [*love*]
> That antrin Fock may ken how SNELL
>   [*strangers; strong*]
> Auld Reikie will at MORNING SMELL.
>
>   (lines 23-6, 33-6)

This passage is typical of Fergusson's comprehensive realism: he does not allow his profound affection for Auld Reikie to blind him to the city's more obnoxious characteristics; while, at the same time, his description of the foul smells and of the sordid side of Edinburgh social life and customs is softened and modified by his emotional response to the strange and unique beauty of this grimy old city, a beauty which coexists with its squalor. It is this balance, this double vision which distinguishes Fergusson's style in *Auld Reikie* from that of Swift in his fiercely realistic satires on London life. Fergusson perceives that the unique atmosphere, the essence of old Edinburgh, lies in the startling and unusual contrasts, both physical and social, which the city presents; and he recreates that atmosphere, with remarkable precision and intimacy, in terms of these contrasts. This double vision, reconciling beauty and uglyness, and unifying thought and feeling so that each modifies the other, is ever present in *Auld Reikie* and is the basic artistic principle of the poem. This principle is clearly discernible in the lines quoted above, where Fergusson, in a single charming couplet, suggests the fragile, fleeting loveliness of sunrise over the ancient spire of St. Giles, and follows it immediately with lines on the slovenly housemaids and the nauseous morning smells of the city.

In his fifth verse paragraph Fergusson makes a direct and trenchant attack on the vanity and small-mindedness of the idle "wits" of the town who gather at the Luckenbooths [a narrow range of buildings which once stood in the middle of the High Street near St. Giles Cathedral.] to observe the passing crowds and sneer at all they see. The passage is worth noting for its biting sarcastic force:

> Now Stairhead Critics, senseless Fools,
> CENSURE their AIM, and PRIDE their Rules,
> In Luckenbooths, wi' glouring Eye,
> Their Neighbours sma'est Faults descry:
>   [*smallest*]
> If ony Loun should dander there, [*fellow;
>   wander*]
> Of aukward Gate, and foreign Air,
> They trace his Steps, till they can tell
> His PEDIGREE as weell's himsell.
>
>   (lines 51-8)

Fergusson, it will be seen, has no sympathy with sham, affectation, false pride, or meanness of soul; and these are the qualities which become the objects of his severest satire whenever he observes them, as in these lines and elsewhere in the poem.

The section on Edinburgh night life is perhaps the most brilliantly executed part of the poem. Here Fergusson describes in sharp, vivid detail typical characters and scenes of the city, when "Night, that's cunzied [invented] chief for Fun," begins. Out of doors in the narrow streets the "cadies" and Highland chairmen go about their respective businesses, the latter working hand in glove with prostitutes. Next we are shown the belligerent ramble of a drunken "Bruiser" or pugilest, in a passage which is a brilliant example of Fergusson's descriptive method, of his balanced realism. It begins as follows:

> FRAE joyous Tavern, reeling drunk,
> Wi' fiery Phizz, and Ein half sunk, [*face; eyes*]
> Behad the Bruiser, Fae to a' [*behold; foe*]
> That in the reek o' Gardies fa': [*reach; arms;
>   fall*]
>
> Close by his Side, a feckless Race [*feeble*]
> O' Macaronies shew their Face,
> And think they're free frae Skaith or Harm,
>   [*injury*]
> While Pith befriends their Leaders Arm:
>   [*strength*]
> Yet fearfu' aften o' their Maught, [*might*]
> They quatt the Glory o' the Faught [*quit; fight*]
> To this same Warrior wha led
> Thae Heroes to bright Honour's Bed . . . [*these*]
>
>   (lines 99 ff.)

In these lines Fergusson portrays the "Bruiser" from a satiric point of view, emphasizing the coarseness of the man, his crude, primitive instincts and blind brutality. The picture of him being egged on to "Glory" by the "feckless Race" of cowardly toadies is disgusting enough in itself. But Fergusson does not allow this feeling of disgust at the bruiser to develop any further in the reader's mind. He immediately modifies it in the the very next couplet, and places the bruiser's behavior in another light:

> And aft the hack o' Honour shines [*often; scar*]
> In Bruiser's Face wi' broken Lines . . .

This is a brilliant and sensitive stroke; Fergusson, in this single couplet, controls his reader's reaction to the whole scene, and reveals his own attitude toward and judgment on the conduct of both bruiser and macaronies. The point that Fergusson is making here is that whereas the behavior of the bruiser is far from admirable, that of the macaronies who have goaded him on is a great deal worse. The bruiser is an ignorant and barbarous creature, but at least he has courage and a certain sense of honor; he is not contemptible. The macaronies, on the other hand, who take advantage of the bruiser and leave him in the lurch, have neither courage nor honor and are wholly despicable. Fergusson exposes this "feckless Race" of parasites and frauds, while at the same time he elicits sympathy for the bruiser. The passage is remarkable both for the moral judgment it implies and for the brilliant way in which Fergusson modifies and changes our original impression of the bruiser by contrasting his conduct with that of the macaronies. Fergusson's realism here, as elsewhere, is of a sane and comprehensive kind, involving both rational

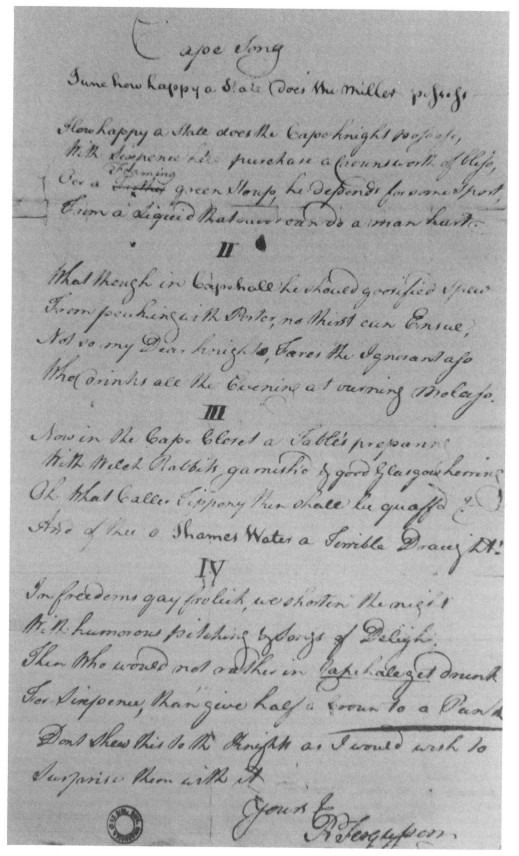

Manuscript for a song Fergusson wrote for a meeting of the Cape Club.

and emotional response to the situation, the one balancing and modifying the other.

In his next verse paragraph Fergusson portrays the macaroni in another situation. For relentless realism and sharp satiric power these lines are unsurpassed in Fergusson:

> Whan Feet in dirty Gutters plash, [*splash*]
> And Fock to wale their Fitstaps fash: [*choose; footsteps; take care*]
> At night the Macaroni drunk,
> In Pools or Gutters aftimes sunk:
> Hegh! What a Fright he now appears,
> When he his Corpse dejected rears!
> Look at that Head, and think if there
> The Pomet slaister'd up his Hair! [*pomatum; plastered*]
> The Cheeks observe, where now cou'd shine
> The scancing Glories o' Carmine? [*shining*]
> Ah, Legs! in vein the Silk-worm there
> Display'd to View her eidant Care; [*busy*]
> For Stink, instead of Perfumes, grow,
> And clarty Odours fragrant flow. [*filthy*]
>   (lines 117-130)

As John Speirs very acutely observes of this passage [in *The Scots Literary Tradition*] "the richness of this magnificent comic poetry arises from its unusual combinations of images and sharp contrasts." The "Corpse" and "Gutter" associations contrast with the idea of pomatum and rouge, suggestive of elegance and finery; while at the same time Fergusson's choice of word and idiom, especially "slaister'd up his Hair" and "scancing Glories o' Carmine," conveys an impression of the messiness and unpleasantness of these cosmetics, as well as of their "Glories." These contrasts culminate, as Speirs points out, in the last two couplets, in the superbly restrained and suggestive "Ah, Legs!" image, and in final juxtaposition of "Stink" and "Perfumes," "clarty" and "fragrant." Through his skillfull use of these contrasts Fergusson succeeds, without explicity describing the scene, in rendering an astonishingly precise and powerful impression of its filth and loathsomeness as seen from a satiric and semi-humorous point of view. Perhaps the most striking thing about the passage is its admirable restraint. At least half of the power and vividness of this description lies in what Fergusson does *not* tell the reader. He merely suggests certain aspects of the scene in such a way that the reader's imagination is stirred and induced to fill in the rest of the details.

The principle of contrast operates in *Auld Reikie* on two levels: in the imagery of individual passages, as in the lines just cited, where it is an inherent characteristic of the style; and, on a larger scale, in the overall arrangement of the poem. The way in which this principle of contrast works out on the structural level may be illustrated from Fergusson's arrangement of his night scenes in this major section of the poem and of the morning scenes which follow. In his verse paragraphs on the bruiser and on the drunken macaroni rising from the gutter Fergusson

is treating the more sordid and disgusting aspects of Edinburgh night life. Yet in his next passage, when he begins to tell of the clubs and societies, the mood suddenly changes as Fergusson starts to develop another side of the picture. Here the emphasis is on a more wholesome conviviality:

> Now mony a Club, jocose and free,
> Gie a' to Merriment and Glee . . . [*give all*]
>   (lines 135 ff.)

At the end of this same verse paragraph, however, Fergusson introduces a rather ominous note in commenting on the inspiriting qualities of liquor:

> It makes you stark, and bauld, and brave, [*stout; bold*]
> Ev'n whan decending to the Grave.

This reference to "the Grave" casts only a momentary shadow on this generally sunny part of the poem. In his next two paragraphs Fergusson describes and commends the activities of two famous Edinburgh social societies, the Pandemonium Club, and his own Cape Club. But the genial, light-hearted mood of these passages abruptly changes once again at the end of the lines on the Cape Club where Fergusson suddenly pauses to describe in gruesome detail a passing funeral (lines 161-194). Even though the poet has partially prepared for this passage in his previous incidental reference to "the Grave," it comes as a shock to the reader, especially since Fergusson lays on the horrid details with rather too heavy a hand. These lines, with their references to "a painted Corp" and the "Dead-deal" (a board for laying out corpses), and their excessive emphasis on the frightfullness of death, smack of morbidity and are suggestive of that neurotic streak in Fergusson which caused him to feel an unnatural terror at the thought of sickness and death and which undoubtedly contributed to his final mental collapse. Yet this ghastly funeral scene is immediately followed by a charming description of the vegetable market which was in those days held in the High Street between St. Giles and the Tron-kirk. He then touches on the bits of pastoral freshness, the trees and greenery, which brighten even the grimy old city and "Ca' [*drive*] far awa' the Morning Smell." Next comes an extraordinary lyrical outburst apostrophizing "Nature":

> O Nature! canty, blyth and free, [*happy*]
> Whare is there Keeking-glass like thee? [*looking-glass*]
> Is there on Earth that can compare
> Wi' Mary's Shape, and Mary's Air,
> Save the empurpl'd Speck, that grows
> In the saft Faulds of yonder Rose? [*soft folds*]
>   (lines 209-214)

The lyric tone and emotional quality of these lines are unusual in Fergusson and are strongly suggestive of the lyrical style of Burns. They are followed, significantly, by a passage on the filth and nauseating smells of the Edinburgh "flesh-market."

The summary given above of two major sections of the poem should be enough to show how basic is the method of dramatic contrast in *Auld Reikie*. Fergusson is attempting to catch the essential spirit of the old city and to fix it forever in terms of its strangely contrasting moods. He shows the sordidness and bestiality of Edinburgh night life side by side with its friendliness, its genial goodfellowship and spirited conviviality; he contrasts the greenery of the vegetable stalls in the High Street and the sweet freshness of trees and flowers with the foul stink and filth of the "flesh-market." The constant shifting of scene and mood and the bold juxtaposition of ugliness and beauty give the poem a high degree of actuality and dramatic force. The imagination of the reader is excited by the sharpness and suggestiveness of the poem's details, as one keenly-etched portrait after another flashes before his eyes and the whole bustling, colorful panorama of eighteenth-century Edinburgh gradually takes shape.

Two or three passages of the latter part of the poem demand special comment. Fergusson's attack on Sunday hypocrisy is one of the most biting satiric passages in the poem. It reads, in part, as follows:

> On Sunday here, an alter'd Scene
> O' Men and Manners meets our Ein: [*eyes*]
> Ane wad maist trow some People chose [*almost*]
> To change their Faces wi' their Clo'es,
> And fain wad gar ilk Neighbour think [*make;*
> *each*]
> They thirst for Goodness, as for Drink:
> But there's an unco Dearth o' Grace, [*strange*]
> That has nae Mansion but the Face,
> And never can obtain a Part
> In benmost Corner of the Heart. [*innermost*]
>   (lines 231-240)

Fergusson here uses a more direct method of attack than is usual with him. The effectiveness of the passage is undeniable, however, and lies chiefly in its sharply satiric phrasing, skillful use of rime, and, above all, in its imaginative force, especially in the brilliant simile, "They thirst for Goodness, as for Drink." The same kind of direct, keen-edged satire is evident again a few lines later in the poem, where Fergusson derides the pretentious Sunday strollers:

> While dandring Cits delight to stray
> [*strolling citizens*]
> To Castlehill, or Public Way,
> Whare they nae other Purpose mean,
> Than that Fool Cause o' being seen . . .
>   (lines 259-262)

The terse, biting, epigrammatic quality of these touches of direct satire in *Auld Reikie* remind one of the polished couplets of the great English neo-classical satirists, especially of Pope, Swift, and Gay, to whom Fergusson is unquestionably indebted in a general way.

The poem ends fittingly on a note of inimitable wit in a short verse paragraph which is worth quoting in full:

> Reikie, farewel! I ne'er cou'd part
> Wi' thee but wi' a dowy heart; [*sad*]
> Aft frae the *Fifan* coast I've seen, [*often*]
> Thee tow'ring on thy summit green;
> So glowr the saints when first is given
> A fav'rite keek o' glore and heaven; [*peek;*
> *glory*]
> On earth nae mair they bend their ein, [*eyes*]
> But quick assume angelic mein;
> So I on *Fife* wad glowr no more,
> But gallop'd to EDINA'S shore, [*Edinburgh's*]
>   (lines 359-368)

The humorous force of this farewell is irresistible. Fergusson's affection for the old gray city is here given comical, half-satiric expression through his use of a mock epic simile. In its irrepressible waggery and imaginative daring the passage seems to epitomize Fergusson's whole poetic personality. The scintillating wit of the passage, its richness in humorous suggestiveness, arise from the comic irony of Fergusson's comparison of Edinburgh and heaven in the light of what has gone before, and from the impish tone of his phrasing in such superb lines as "A fav'rite keek o' glore and heaven." The ironical force of the comparison, it may be noted, is underlined by his happy choice of the adjective "angelic." Yet, in spite of the conscious irony of his praise of Auld Reikie, Fergusson manages to convey in these lines the impression that he sincerely loves this strangely beautiful, historic, battered, incredibly crowded and squalid old city of his birth,

Auld Reikie is an extraordinarily attractive and powerful poem and, as Fergusson's last major work, forms a fitting climax to his poetic career. It ranks as one of his four or five very best poems, and is certainly the most comprehensive and impressive of Fergusson's many treatments of eighteenth-century life in Edinburgh. As we have seen, the poem owes much to *Trivia*, but its overall effect is strikingly different, its style far more vividly realistic though no less sophisticated than that of Gay's pleasantly artificial work. Had Fergusson been given the time and encouragement to complete his original design of the poem, it would probably have developed to epic proportions; and, in view of the quality of what he actually did get on paper, it might well have become one of the major classics of eighteenth-century poetry. As it stands, *Auld Reikie* is a little classic, and deserves to stand beside *Trivia* as one of the most distinguished treatments of city life in British poetry.

Allan H. MacLaine (essay date 1965)

SOURCE: "Fergusson and the Tradition," and "Fergusson and Burns: Conclusion," in *Robert Fergusson*, Twayne Publishers, Inc., 1965, pp. 15-21, 152-63.

[*In the following excerpt, MacLaine offers an overview of the Scots poetic tradition and discusses Fergusson's place in the Scots poetic revival of the eighteenth century, summarizing his achievement "from both the historical and purely literary points of view."*]

The Scots Poetic Tradition:

When Robert Fergusson burst upon the literary scene of Scotland in the 1770's, the native poetic tradition was in a rather precarious state. In the early part of the century, a group of writers and editors, led by Allan Ramsay, had attempted with partial success to revive interest in the ancient and honorable Scots literary tradition, and to bridge an almost fatal gap in the development of a distinctive national literature. This gap, separating medieval from modern Scots literature, resulted from the long barren period of about 1570 to 1700, during which time the strong and bright current of poetic writing in Scots had been reduced to an intermittent trickle. So long and severe had been the blight upon Scots literature that, by the opening of the eighteenth century, the very names of the great makers of the medieval past—William Dunbar, Robert Henryson, King James I—were half forgotten, while many of their works survived only in obscure and scattered manuscripts. It was as though Scotland had chosen not to remember that she had once had a proud and distinguished literature.

In the fifteenth and early sixteenth centuries, the "golden age" of the old tradition, the situation had been very different indeed. Then the Scottish court had been the center for a brilliant, versatile national literature held in high esteem throughout Europe, and far surpassing in artistic quality the work produced in England during the same period. The Scots poetry of this fruitful age can be divided into three broad classification. First, there was the sophisticated courtly poetry with its "termes aureate," its dream-visions, love lyrics, and elaborate moral allegories. This poetry was essentially medieval and international in character, though expressed in a distinctively Scots literary language. In the fifteenth century this "aureate" tradition is represented by such poems as "The Kingis Quair" of James I, "The Testament of Cresseid" of Henryson, and "The Goldyn Targe" of Dunbar, and in the sixteenth century by the graceful lyrics of Alexander Scott, "The Cherrie and the Slae" of Alexander Montgomerie, and the courtly poems of Sir David Lindsay and Sir Richard Maitland. Second, at the other end of the scale, there was the folk poetry, consisting of popular ballads and songs of the common people. Finally, there was a third and very important type of poetry: the artistic treatment of folk themes. Into this broad category fall such poems as the fifteenth-century "Christis Kirk on the Green" and "Peblis to the Play" (attributed to James I); Henryson's "Fables"; Scott's "Justing and Debait"; much of the best work of Dunbar, Lindsay, and Maitland; and a great bulk of poems by unknown authors.

What happened in Scotland to account for the sudden withering of this vigorous poetic tradition toward the close of the sixteenth century? Among many possible causes, three may be adduced as certain. One was the triumph of Knoxian Calvinism, which proscribed poetry along with other "lewd" entertainments and brought such powerful social and moral pressure to bear that it succeeded in virtually stifling poetic creation in Scotland except among a handful of the aristocracy. A second severe blow was

the removal in 1603 of the court, which had always been the center of poetic patronage, from Edinburgh to London. Finally, the overwhelming influence of the great English poetry of the late sixteenth and seventeenth centuries persuaded the few Scottish gentlemen who (like Drummond of Hawthornden) continued to practice the art to turn their backs upon the old native tradition and to follow the Elizabethan English style. The result was an almost complete break in the development of sophisticated poetry in the Scots tongue, though the folk poetry did continue to thrive obscurely in oral transmission through the long winter of the seventeenth century despite the Kirk's disapproval. From the whole seventeenth century only a handful of new art poems in Scots have come down to us, written by country gentlemen of the type of Drummond or the Sempills of Beltrees. Among these sporadic efforts "The Life and Death of Habbie Simson" (ca. 1640) by Robert Sempill of Beltrees should be mentioned as the prototype of the comic-elegy genre which became immensely popular in the next century. But, generally speaking, the seventeenth century is a dismal and almost fatal hiatus in the history of Scots poetry.

The revival of interest in the native poetic tradition, which took place in the early decades of the eighteenth century, came in the wake of a renewed sense of Scottish nationalism. The parliamentary Union of 1707, which reduced Scotland politically to the status of a British province, provoked a profound cultural reaction. Many Scots, suffering from a feeling of injured dignity and political betrayal, were stirred to reassert their country's ancient cultural identity and to resist assimilation by England. The result was an extraordinary cultural resurgence, which produced an imposing array of internationally famous philosophers, physicians, architects, lawyers, historians, and men of letters; and this renaissance turned Edinburgh into "the Athens of the North," one of the most dynamic intellectual centers in Europe. In literature, some (like Thomson and Boswell) tried to outdo the English in their own literary idiom; others (like Ramsay and his followers) attempted to reinvigorate the native poetic language and tradition.

The Scots poetic revival in the eighteenth century, then, was essentially a nationalistic movement, the effort of some sections of a small and economically poor nation to reaffirm its cultural integrity. It was heralded by the publications of James Watson's epoch-making anthology, *A Choice Collection of Comic and Serious Scots Poems, both Antient and Modern* (Edinburgh, 1706, 1709, 1711), and pioneered by the versatile Allan Ramsay. Ramsay's work as an editor and publicist of Scots poetry (*The Ever Green,* 1724; *The Tea-Table Miscellany,* 1724) met with instantaneous success; moreover, his original poetry in the vernacular—though by no means first-rate—restored to vigorous life several traditional Scots genres. In the latter respect, however, Ramsay's achievement was limited. The Scots tongue had been so long in disuse as a vehicle for serious poetry that Ramsay felt able to use it, for the most part, only for comic verse and songs; in his serious poetry, Ramsay usually reverted to labored neo-Classical English. Even so, Ramsay's many-faceted and untiring effort as a restorer of literary Scots was of great historical importance and formed an indispensable foundation for the later work of Fergusson and Burns.

The personal influence and example of Allan Ramsay stimulated several younger writers to follow his lead; but, during the long period from about 1730 to 1770 (Ramsay himself virtually stopped writing in 1728), no Scots poet of comparable stature appeared. As a result, the vernacular revival, so auspiciously launched in the first quarter of the century, seemed to be in serious danger of petering out altogether for lack of adequate leadership. This danger, however, was fortunately averted by the sudden emergence in 1772 of a compelling new voice in Scots poetry—that of an obscure Edinburgh legal clerk, Robert Fergusson. . . .

The tragic brevity of Fergusson's career—he did all of his best work in two short years—has tended to obscure the true nature of his achievement. Eclipsed as he was almost immediately by Burns, Fergusson has usually been relegated by historians of literature to the anomalous position of a "forerunner"; seldom has he been treated as a poet in his own right. This approach has encouraged the view of Fergusson as a boy-poet with a lucky gift, who dashed off a few vivid sketches of Edinburgh life and then died and whose only importance is that he happened to have stimulated Burns. But Burns knew better; his poetic instinct recognized the astonishing power and maturity of Fergusson's work which he valued above Ramsay's as, up to his own time, the finest Scots poetry of the century. And Burns was right.

With Auld Reikie—Fergusson's final and climactic masterpiece of comprehensive realism—his significant poetical career came to an end. It is worthwhile at this point to look back over the Scots poems of 1772-73 and to summarize as concisely as possible the distinguishing features of Fergusson's work and to come to some general conclusions as to the true nature of his achievement from both the historical and purely literary points of view.

Fergusson's Qualities as a Poet:

The historical importance of Fergusson's work is two-fold: it lies both in his innovation and development of forms and genres and in the intrinsic quality of his performance within these forms and genres. The changes and innovations he made in particular Scots poetic forms not only represent an original contribution to the growth of the tradition in general, but are of more specific interest for their profound effect upon the work of Burns. In the first place, Fergusson was the first Scottish poet to exploit the full potentialities of the "Habbie" stanza, a form which had come to be used exclusively for the comic elegy and the rimed epistle. Perceiving the possibilities of this stanza, Fergusson broke through the narrow limitations and stereotyped formulas of the "Habbie" tradition, and applied the stanza to several new purposes and kinds of subject matter. In **"The Daft-Days," "The King's Birth-Day," "Caller Oysters," "Caller Water,"** and other pieces, he developed an original type of Scottish poem: the

poem of humorous social description in the six-line stanza. In **"Braid Claith"** he used the same meter for pure satire, while in the **"Elegy on Scots Music"** he adapted the "Habbie" stanza as a vehicle for serious rather than comic poetry. Finally, in **"To the Tron-Kirk Bell"** he revived the ancient "flyting" tradition and used the Habbie stanza for the first time in Scottish poetry for a "flyting" poem. In all of these ways Fergusson's development and extension of the "Habbie" tradition led directly to Burns's even more versatile use of the form.

Fergusson brought about almost equally important developments in other genres, especially in the "Christis Kirk" tradition and in Scottish pastoralism. In **"Hallow-fair"** and **"Leith Races"** he introduced a modification of the traditional stanza, a modification which was to be adopted by Burns in "The Holy Fair" and in "Hallowe'en." In **"The Election"** he extended the subject matter of the genre to include political as well as social satire, and in so doing gave Burns the hint for his further development of the "Christis Kirk" form as a vehicle for clerical satire. In the realm of Scottish pastoralism, Fergusson departed even more radically from eighteenth-century tradition. Though his first effort in this genre, the **"Eclogue on Wilkie,"** is conventional enough (being closely modeled on the pastoral eclogues of Ramsay), in **"An Eclogue"** Fergusson went far beyond Ramsay in the direction of realism and developed a new type of Scottish pastoralism, treating country life from a humorous point of view, with intimate, homely details and convincing character types, yet remaining within the conventional form of the pastoral eclogue. In **"The Farmer's Ingle"** he portrayed Scottish farm life with the same kind of unpretentious realism, but with a serious rather than a comic emphasis, while his daring and successful experiment with Spenserian stanzas determined Burns's choice of the same form for his "Cotter's Saturday Night." Fergusson demonstrated in these two poems that interesting and meaningful poetry could be made out of the most ordinary and homely details of rural life, and Burns was quick to take the hint.

Several other innovations which Fergusson introduced may be listed briefly. In **"Plainstanes and Causey"** and in **"A Drink Eclogue"** he created an entirely new poetic form, the "flyting eclogue," by combining the old Scottish "flyting" genre with the pastoral eclogue form; and, in so doing, he provided Burns with the models for his "Brigs of Ayr." Furthermore, in several of his poems Fergusson treated themes of satire which had been virtually untouched by earlier eighteenth-century poets in Scotland. He introduced legal satire in **"Plainstanes and Causey,"** the **"Rising"** and **"Sitting of the Session,"** and other poems, and a sharp element of political satire in **"The Ghaists"** and **"The Election."** In Auld Reikie, moreover, there is a very suggestive passage of religious satire, a theme which Ramsay had already touched upon in his "Elegy on John Cowper," and which Burns was to develop brilliantly. The theme of Scottish patriotism, also touched upon by Ramsay, was given far more conspicuous emphasis by Fergusson in such poems as **"Elegy on Scots Music," "The Ghaists," "To the Principal and Professors," "Hame Content,"** and **"A Drink Eclogue"**; and so it passed on to Burns. Finally, Fergusson was chiefly responsible for domesticating the English meditative nature poem in Scottish eighteenth-century verse. He attempted this genre with increasing success in the odes to the **"Bee,"** **"Butterfly,"** and **"Gowdspink"**; and he supplied Burns with Scottish precedent for his "To a Mouse," "To a Mountain Daisy," and other works of this type.

In one respect Fergusson stands alone among Scottish poets: no other comes near him in his brilliant poetic treatment of city life. It was, of course, perfectly natural and appropriate that he should find the materials for his poetry in the life of the Edinburgh he loved and knew intimately, just as it was natural for Burns to write about the rural community in which he lived. But Fergusson's Edinburgh poems form a class by themselves; there is nothing comparable to them in Scottish poetry; and, indeed, in their scope, their vividness, their penetrative, many-sided vision, they must rank among the finest poetic treatments of city life in all British literature. What Fergusson did for Edinburgh life, Burns was presently to do for Scottish farm life; and Burns was to follow Fergusson's lead in building his poetry out of the stuff of everyday experience.

In all of these ways, then, Fergusson was breaking new ground, making his individual contributions to the growth of the great vernacular tradition of which he is a part, and preparing the way for Burns. But Fergusson did more than this: he wrote poems which are important, not merely because they broke with the tradition or modified the tradition in the several ways noted above, but also because they are permanently valuable in themselves as works of art. Fergusson's work has never received adequate recognition for its own sake. Most historians of literature and commentators on Fergusson tend to neglect the intrinsic quality of his work, or to brush over it with brief, uncritical appraisals; they speak as though Fergusson's poems had no life and being of their own—as though they existed only because of Burns. Yet, as I have tried to demonstrate in previous chapters, Fergusson's vernacular poetry, aside from its historical significance or its influence on Burns, is vitally interesting, often powerful, and eminently readable for its own sake. It has, moreover, a unique and highly personalized flavor which sets it apart from the work of any other Scottish poet.

Several characteristics of Fergusson's work distinguish it from that of Hamilton of Gilbertfield, Ramsay, Ross, and other eighteenth-century predecessors. In the first place, there is his bold poetic imagination, essentially a comic imagination, revealing itself both in his daringly original conceptions of entire poems and in his shrewd, penetrating grasp of significant detail. Such poems as the sharp-edged and powerful **"Braid Claith"**; the delightful fantasies, **"Plainstanes and Causey"** and **"To My Auld Breeks"**; and such brilliant comic extravaganzas as **"Hallowfair," "Leith Races," "The Election,"** and *Auld Reikie*—all these show that he possessed creative powers of a high order. Fergusson's imagination, though narrower in its range than Ramsay's, is infinitely finer in quality, more daring and, at the same time, more sensitive and

perceptive. His humor has greater depth and richness than Ramsay's, and certainly more delicacy. His view of life is predominantly comic: he has the rare faculty of finding humor everywhere in the life around him, and, what is even rarer, the ability to select, organize, and communicate his experience through poetic art. He far surpasses Ramsay in his unerring choice of significant details, in his keen eye for humorous incongruities, and, consequently, in his ability to make the most unpromising materials richly suggestive and meaningful.

Fergusson's poetry is, furthermore, remarkable for its pictorial qualities and for its sane and comprehensive realism. Many of his poems are series of vivid little pictures, each illustrating a different aspect of the whole subject and contributing to the total effect. Particularly deft at using dramatic contrast as a satiric method, he shows in poem after poem a surprisingly mature insight into human motives and behavior and an unfailing skill at revealing human incongruities. Fergusson's satire, moreover, is generally good-natured and tolerant in tone, except when he is dealing with sham or meanness of soul. His reaction to a situation is usually two-fold, both intellectual and emotional, the one modifying the other; his keen-eyed satiric vision is often balanced by a degree of sympathy with the human failings of others or by his recognition of compensatory good qualities. This broad-minded attitude in Fergusson, his clear-sighted, yet comprehensive, balanced realism, is one of the most fundamental and attractive features of his work.

Fergusson's style is an inseparable part of his poetic imagination and personality. When we consider the tragic brevity of Fergusson's career, the high degree of technical skill and the distinctive personal style which he managed to develop are equally astonishing. His craftsmanship is generally precise and finished, yet he does not allow his disciplined attention to form and technique to inhibit the vitality of his expression. His mastery of particular verse forms, as we have seen, increased rapidly and steadily during his two most prolific years, until he was producing toward the end almost consistently brilliant poems, little masterpieces of conscious, skilled artistry. Fergusson's technical superiority to Ramsay shows most clearly in such poems as **"The King's Birth-Day,"** **"Braid Claith," "Hallow-fair," "Leith Races," "The Election,"** and **"To My Auld Breeks,"** in which he succeeds in reproducing the natural, vigorous rhythms of actual speech, while remaining within the rigid limitations of the verse form. Fergusson handles difficult and exacting stanza forms with ease and fluency, especially in the later poems. For vigor combined with perfection of form, many passages in Fergusson are unsurpassed in Scottish poetry, even by Burns. Burns's work was, in fact, greatly benefited by the examples of technical brilliance set by Fergusson.

The personal flavor of Fergusson's style is more difficult to define than its technical virtues. Though he seldom brings himself directly into his writings, Fergusson's poetry communicates a sense of his buoyant and attractive personality, characterized by audacity, irreverence, impish waggery, geniality, shrewdness, tolerance, sensitivity, keen observation, dry penetrating wit, and abounding vitality. He has a wonderfully rich and suggestive command of Edinburgh vernacular, the "brave metropolitan utterance," as Stevenson called it; and he exploits the subtle possibilities of that language as Ramsay never did. In his command of his own vigorous mother tongue, Fergusson shows the imaginative instinct of the true poet. He has a fine feeling for words, an unerring sense of the right word, for the precise, expressive idiom. The sharpness and conciseness of his imagery, its rich suggestiveness, may be easily illustrated from any of his better poems. Take, for example, these lines from **"Hallow-fair"**—

> Upo' the tap o'ilka lum
> The sun began to keek . . .

or these from **"To My Auld Breeks,"**—

> As mony a time
> Wi' you I've speel'd the braes o' rime . . .

or from **"To the Principal and Professors,"**—

> Mair hardy, souple, steive an' swank,
> Than ever stood on SAMY'S shank.

Fergusson's style, as may be seen from the last lines cited above, has not only muscular vitality and precision, but a peculiar kind of "pawkiness," a quietly humorous flavor. He has a way of giving droll and original expression to almost any idea. This "pawkiness" is an integral part of Fergusson's style and of his distinctive, lovable poetic personality.

Something should be said, finally, about Fergusson's precocious grasp of characterization. As we have seen, he became adept at revealing character briefly and vividly, both through direct description and through dialogue. He shows, in such portraits as those of the barber in **"Braid Claith,"** Robin Gibb in **"The Rising of the Session,"** the cobbler in **"The Election,"** and the bruiser" in Auld Reikie, an almost Chaucerian ability to suggest the whole character of the man in a few bold strokes through highlighting significant details. He manages in a few trenchant lines to reveal the essence of characters and scenes in a flash, without stooping to caricature. Perhaps his greatest successes in characterization, however, are achieved through dialogue in which the poet, instead of describing the character, makes the character reveal himself. The speakers in Fergusson's brilliant duologues—Sandie and Willie, Plainstanes and Causey, Brandy and Whisky—are all made real and convincing by this method. Plainstanes, in particular, is a triumph of humorous and dramatic characterization. Similarly, the speeches of Sawny and Jock Bell in **"Hallow-fair,"** of the captain in **"Leith Races,"** and of "John" and "cooper Will" in **"The Election"** are superbly effective in giving concrete, precise, and vivid impressions of the several speakers. Fergusson's mastery of poetic dialogue is, in fact, unsurpassed in eighteenth-century Scottish verse for vigor, naturalness, and power of sug-

gestion. The depth of understanding Fergusson shows in his delineation of character, his clear-sighted perception of the essential elements and motives in human behavior, are extraordinary in so young a poet.

Influence on Burns:

The intrinsic excellence of Fergusson's best work has historical importance as well as purely esthetic value. His poems appeared just in time to save the vernacular revival from dying out altogether. Their sprightliness, craftsmanship, and broad popular appeal served to refresh the lagging vernacular tradition in poetry and to give renewed impetus to the whole movement. Fergusson's sudden emergence, moreover, helped to reassemble and restimulate a popular reading public for Scots verse, without which the tremendous success of Burns would have been impossible. But the intrinsic brilliance of Fergusson's poems did more than this: it provided Burns with examples of high quality in vernacular poetry such as he could never have found in the works of Ramsay. Fergusson's careful workmanship, his mastery of language, and, above all, the boldness and brilliance of his poetic imagination opened Burns's eyes to the full possibilities of the vernacular as a poetic medium.

Fergusson showed Burns that he need not go far afield for the subject matters and language of his poetry, that the light of imagination could be thrown over the humblest objects of the life around him; and, above all, he demonstrated to him, as Ramsay never could, how to make finely wrought, interesting, and meaningful poetry out of such homely subjects from everyday life as "braid claith," "caller oysters," and "auld breeks." Ramsay, too, had treated common life vigorously in some of his works, but he lacked the bold imagination and the artistry necessary to give such subjects permanent value as works of art. Within the relatively narrow range of his best work, Fergusson gave Burns examples of high quality, power, and precision in vernacular poetry; and Burns never forgot the lesson or underestimated its value to him in his own creative practice.

We know from Burns's autobiographical letter to Dr. Moore and from a notation in his *First Commonplace Book* that he "discovered" Fergusson's poems for the first time about August, 1784. As Frank Beaumont has pointed out, the contrast between Burns's poems written before and after his reading of Fergusson attests to the impact of Fergusson's poems upon Burns's creative imagination. The experimental poems of the Mount Oliphant period (1766-1777) are mostly feeble imitations of the genteel English poets—Pope, Addison, Shenstone, Gray, and others—and of Shakespeare. During Burns's residence at Lochlea farm, though he was still very much under the spell of Shenstone's "Elegies," his powers began to mature steadily, as evidenced by such promising pieces as "The Death and Dying Words of Puir Mailie," and two good songs, "Mary Morison" and "The Rigs o' Barley." Despite these promising indications, the bulk of Burns's work during these early years is definitely inferior and imitative.

Then, in late 1784, he discovered Fergusson; and a new and vital development of Burns's genius was almost immediately apparent. Shenstone, the "divine Shenstone," his former bosom favorite, was eclipsed and forgotten; for Burns, stimulated by the brilliance and suggestiveness of Fergusson's poems, turned his energies toward the native poetic tradition where his real strength lay, and began to pour out, with breathtaking speed and fecundity, that magnificent series of vernacular masterpieces written in 1785 and 1786, beginning with the "Epistle to Davie"; "Holy Willie's Prayer"; "Death and Doctor Hornbook"; the epistles to Lacraik, Simson, Goldie, and M'Math; "Hallowe'en"; "To a Mouse"; "The Jolly Beggars"; "Address to the Deil"; and so on to "The Twa Dogs", "The Holy Fair," and many others. Fergusson was unquestionably the primary literary force behind Burns's upsurge of creative activity during these, his greatest and most fruitful years.

In poem after poem Fergusson's influence can be seen operating on Burns's imagination, suggesting themes, ideas, verse forms, satiric devices, descriptive methods, expressive words and phrases which stuck in Burns's subconscious memory. So profound and interpenetrative was this influence that we must conclude that Burns read and reread his Fergusson, virtually memorizing the poems until they became a part of his own thought and feeling. In almost every major poem that Burns wrote during these two wonderful years, traces of Fergusson can be discerned—stimulating, suggesting, and, to some extent, directing Burns's creative activity.

The many different ways in which Fergusson's poems operated on Burns's imagination have already been touched on and need only be summarized briefly. In the years before he met with Fergusson's work, Burns had used the "Habbie" stanza very seldom, in some three or four poems. Fergusson's brilliant handling of the form, however, seems to have opened Burns's eyes to its possibilities since, shortly after his reading of Fergusson, he began to use it with increasing frequency in poem after poem. Similarly, Fergusson's work in the "Christis Kirk" stanza prompted Burns to try his hand at the form; and it is significant that in his first attempt, "Hallowe'en," Burns used Fergusson's special form of the stanza. Other Scottish poetic forms used by Fergusson in his own original way were soon taken over by Burns, including the rimed epistle, the duologue form ("The Twa Dogs" and "Brigs of Ayr"), the serious description of farm life in Spenserian stanzas ("The Cotter's Saturday Night"), the meditative nature poem ("To a Mouse"), and Fergusson's original "flyting eclogue" ("Brigs of Ayr"). Besides taking over these poetic forms and genres developed by the Edinburgh poet, Burns modeled several poems directly and, no doubt, consciously on Fergusson: "The Cotter's Saturday Night" on **"The Farmer's Ingle,"** "Scotch Drink" on **"Caller Water"** and **"A Drink Eclogue,"** "The Holy Fair" on **"Leith Races"** and **"Hallow-fair,"** "Brigs of Ayr" on **"Plainstanes and Causey,"** and so forth.

But Fergusson's influence was far more diffuse and inter-

penetrative than these obvious manifestations would indicate. We find Burns taking up again and again themes and methods of satire which he found in Fergusson, and re-working them in the light of his own experience. Traces of Fergusson's style; of Fergusson's quietly humorous tone; of Fergusson's distinctive kind of insinuative, "pawky," satiric humor; of his actual phraseology—all of these crop up in poem after poem of Burns, often in poems which are generally unlike anything that Fergusson ever wrote. Sometimes too, Burns made use of suggestions from Fergusson's worthless English poems, a fact which proves how thoroughly saturated his mind was with all of Fergusson's works, good and bad.

On the whole, however, Fergusson's example was of incalculable value to Burns; no other poet had so decisive an effect upon his work. Fergusson seems to be ever-present in Burns himself, his influence operating just beneath the surface of Burns's conscious mind, acting as a kind of poetic catalyst, prompting and stimulating Burns to creative activity. Burns, in fact, found himself in Fergusson; he saw in Fergusson's unfulfilled career the key to his own poetic ambitions and desires, and he set to work with a will to continue and complete what Fergusson had so brilliantly begun.

In comparing the poetry of Fergusson and Burns, one must recognize the greater range and maturity of Burns's imagination. There is no hint in Fergusson, for example, of the spontaneous and powerful lyric impulse which made Burns one of the great song writers of all time, nor of Burns's deep feeling of kinship with nature so movingly expressed in such poems as "To a Mouse." Moreover, for all Fergusson's imaginative audacity, he shows little of Burns's social and political radicalism, of the sweep and passion of Burns's art. Burns's essentially passionate nature, bursting the bonds of restraint that the Kirk would have imposed upon him, leads him to attack the Kirk itself and to a freer and franker expression in a greater variety of matters than Fergusson would have dared to undertake. Burns dares to go to the roots of his own being and to speak his heart out in his poetry. He feels compelled to do so. There is none of this intense subjectivity in Fergusson; rather, he tends to be reticent about himself in his writing.

Fergusson is, in fact, essentially conservative in his attitudes. He was living in times which, notwithstanding the unrest in Scotland resulting from the Union of 1707 and the Jacobite rebellion of 1745, were generally stable, politically and socially. Though Fergusson is quick to satirize the abuses and shortcomings he perceives in the society of his day, he never goes so far as to attack the social structure itself. The American and French revolutions, however, coming a few years after Fergusson's death, and accompanied by a general upheaval of European society, acted as direct and potent stimuli upon the imagination of Burns; and they partially account for the radical, and defiantly democratic elements in his poetry. Burns's naturally rebellious nature and the fact that he was a peasant rather than a graduate of St. Andrews also had much to do with the intensity of his political views.

Fergusson lived in less exciting years, but he seems also to have possessed a kind of genial tolerance, a willingness to accept the world as he found it, without feeling compelled to change it. Thus the vivid little world of his art is generally undisturbed by current philosophical questions. Fergusson excels at humorous social description, and within this relatively narrow range the vitality and artistry of his work has seldom been surpassed in Scots poetry, even by Burns.

In coming to a final evaluation of Fergusson's achievement, we must never forget his youthfulness, the extreme brevity of his career, and the crushing difficulties under which he worked. All of his best poetry was produced during a period of twenty-four months, and his poetical career was ended when he was twenty-three. Burns during the first twenty-three years of his life produced nothing comparable to Fergusson's achievement. Fergusson, then, like his English contemporary Chatterton, is one of the unfulfilled possibilities of our literature. Up to the moment of his collapse, as we have seen, Fergusson was increasing in stature and maturity as a creative artist. Had he lived, there is little doubt that he would have seriously rivaled Burns, at least as a satirist and as a writer of humorous descriptive poetry, if not as a lyricist. Additionally, it may safely be said that, had it not been for Fergusson's achievement, Burns would not have been the Burns that we know as the great national poet of Scotland. Part of Burns's glory belongs, in a very real sense, to Robert Fergusson.

But judged on merit alone, Fergusson's poetry deserves higher rank and recognition than it has hitherto received. Though small in bulk and relatively narrow in scope, his work is unquestionably the finest body of poetry produced in Scotland during the eighteenth century before Burns. Fergusson deserves a permanent place among the classics of Scottish poetry, ranking not too far below Dunbar and Burns. In the wider field of British literature, he remains necessarily a minor poet—but a minor poet of extraordinary quality and interest. He breaks new ground in poetry, not by breaking with the established poetic traditions, but by putting the traditions to new uses. As the English Romantic poets a generation later were to exploit such older forms as the Spenserian, stanza, blank verse, and the heroic couplet, so Fergusson revitalized the traditional forms of Scottish verse.

Aside from a place in literary history, Fergusson's work has a perennial freshness and enduring appeal. He makes old Edinburgh live again as no other writer has ever done. Fergusson's objective realism; the sharpness, vividness, and finished artistry of his style; the genial, insinuative tone of his humor; and the bold, yet sensitive and highly personal quality of his imagination combine to make his poetry especially attractive to modern tastes. It is to be hoped that in the years to come his reputation will increase, that there will be a rediscovery, a new and more genuine appreciation of Fergusson as one of the little masters.

Alexander Manson Kinghorn (essay date 1974)

SOURCE: An introduction to *Poems by Allan Ramsay and Robert Fergusson,* edited by A. M. Kinghorn and A. Law, Rowman & Littlefield, 1974, pp. vii-xxxiv.

[*An English critic, Kinghorn is widely considered an authority on Scottish poetry. In the following excerpt, he and Law, a Scottish writer who co-edited with Kinghorn* The Works of Allan Ramsay (1961-74), *discuss Fergusson's innovative use of language and poetic form, praising "his ability to associate language and locale in unexpected ways."*]

Fergusson did not live long enough to attract attention outside his immediate circle, which was unlucky, since it is unlikely that he would have long remained without wider recognition at a time when all but the most conventional Scottish tastes were veering towards the home-bred, and when there was a dearth of significant poets. His premature departure from the scene left the role of upholder of the native tradition to Burns, whose Kilmarnock preface made tactful overtures to the *literati,* while not neglecting to mention the names of Ramsay and Fergusson, "these two justly admired Scotch poets", as his particular inspiration.

In his attitude to Scots as a poetic medium, limiting it to informal styles and the matter that best suited these, Burns is more like Ramsay than he is like Fergusson. Yet, though it was Ramsay that the critics held up to him as an example, mainly as the author of "The Gentle Shepherd", it was Fergusson whom Burns, understandably, preferred to imitate. In his First Commonplace Book, mentioning "The excellent Ramsay and the still more excellent Fergusson", he regrets that so little has been written about his own west country, and this suggestion of a regional poetry has plainly come from Fergusson's Edinburgh poems. Burns's larger purpose of being a patriot poet had the same source. It is evident that he appreciated how much more original a creator was Fergusson "the bauld and slee" than "honest Allan"; the resemblance in title, or theme and conception, between Fergusson's and Burns's better-known poems can hardly be missed.

Fergusson's innovations show genius. Ramsay transmitted to him the fifteenth-century comic tradition of "Christ's Kirk on the Green" but the younger poet rejected the mere farce of its narrative and altered its jingling rhyme scheme to allow a more varied and poetic comedy. His experiments with 'standart Habbie' which Ramsay had employed for humorous poetry only, show the same impatience with limiting convention; thus the serious, imaginative uses that he found for the stanza in the **"Elegy on the Death of Scots Music"**, **"To the Tron-kirk Bell"**, and within the mainly comic **"Hallow-Fair"**, **"Leith Races"**, **"The Election"**, discovered a range of effects that Burns was to emulate. Even in the pastoral *genre,* where Ramsay had been so effective, his originality appears: **"An Eclogue"** represents a considerable advance on the older poet's less decided realism. Of this poem Matthew McDiarmid observes that it is "unique in the whole range of pastoral or rural poetry . . . One can only compare its admirable keeping of decorum with *The Twa Dogs.*" Fergusson's innovating artistry is most remarkable, however, in the form of the Spenserian stanza that he invented to convey the sensitive but objective scenes of his masterpiece, **"The Farmer's Ingle."** Burns in his less convincing imitation, "The Cotter's Saturday Night", injudiciously reverts to the original stanza, too leisurely and above all too literary for such a subject.

All Fergusson's variations on satirical themes—legal, political or religious, as suited him—were either freshly conceived or represented transformations of familiar material. From the publication of **"The Daft-Days"** he struck sparks from his audience but because he supplied Burns with so many precedents, and because his poetic life was so short, he has been regarded as a torch-bearer, a transition-figure. He is thus too often measured by the Burns yardstick, as an influence or even as a premature explosion of Burnsian talent, perhaps a talent that, if it had been allowed, would have won to the heights of the Scots Parnassus.

For this last speculative opinion something may be said. Assuredly Burns had a more powerful and matured imagination than his "elder Brother", and his range was far wider. But, without Fergusson, more fertile in original conceptions, Burns would not have found the forms that expressed him and made him Scotland's national poet. Mr Allan MacLaine argues

> Though small in bulk and relatively narrow in scope his (Fergusson's) work is unquestionably the finest body of poetry produced in Scotland during the eighteenth century before Burns.

There was in fact little competition apart from that of Ramsay's work. It might be more to the point to suggest that if English poets too were considered, Fergusson, as a portrayer of town life, would then find rivals only in Pope and the more comparable Gay, whose *Trivia* did for London something of what Fergusson's Auld Reikie did for Edinburgh - though *Trivia* is an objective description of street activity, without those personal, picturesque insights which distinguish the Scotsman's poem. But in general the 'genteel', refining tendencies of the English masters make such comparisons unprofitable. Of Fergusson's English contemporaries, Gray, Shenstone and Collins, it may be said that they seem to wish to contribute more to literature than to life.

Moreover, discussion of English and Scots poetry in the same terms and according to a defined set of criteria is bound to fall short of the fair or adequate in literary criticism. To take but one example from Fergusson, his lashing of Johnson in **"To the Principal and Professors of the University of St Andrews, on their superb treat to Dr Samuel Johnson"** is animated by a fiery wit quite alien to Johnson's own devastating common-room ironies. Fergusson says that had he himself been put in charge of the culinary arrangements, he would have seen to it that this Scotophobe, this inveterate critic of his host

country, was fed on "gude hamel gear" and not treated as though he were royalty—

> For ne'er sic surly wight as he
> Had met wi' sic respect frae me.

This is the old Scots flyting tradition, which in style and character is quite different from any convention that Johnson could have recognised.

The same kind of distinction applies to all Scottish writing for the late eighteenth-century English market, for the Northern temperament had to be sickled over if it were to have any real appeal in London. Fergusson made no concession to Augustanism as a man like Goldsmith understood the term; he betrayed no interest in seeking fame 'furth of Scotland'. He wrote for his friends, not for established critics or for a foreign audience, and in his day there was no accepted standard of criticism upon which contemporary Scots vernacular verse might be evaluated, other than the sentimentalist assessments for which Fergusson had no respect.

In this volume only two English poems are included, the ten-line vignette, **"The Author's Life"**, and the fourteen-line impression, **"On Night"**, illustrating Fergusson at his best in a southern style, in the second case not unlike that of Collins. They display something of the feeling for form and the significant word that is more evident in the Scots poems. To mention his other English poems, however, is only to cite echoes, borrowed felicities. Naturally the want of an individual style in English versifying is felt even more in his comic work. Dr Johnson shivering in a kilt is a splendid conception (**"To Dr. Samuel Johnson: Food for a new Edition of his Dictionary"**, ll. 61-67), and a 'Sow of Feeling' that laments husband and children sent to the *abattoir* is an admirable response to Henry Mackenzie's lachrymose novel *The Man of Feeling*, but the inflated English of these burlesques is only mildly amusing. A much more comic effect would have been given by the reductive Scots idiom.

All the significant verse of Fergusson is developed from a base of local vernacular. The latter enables him to give his Horace a convincingly homespun character. It was an appropriate use of Scots that he had learned from Ramsay; thus one notes the similarity of colloquial phrasing and economical expression in Fergusson's version of Horace, Book I, Ode XI, and Ramsay's spirited Ode, "To the Phiz", stanzas I to 8. The genius of Scots for burlesque, the ridiculous, as in the comic elegy, Fergusson seems to have appreciated early; if the subject is an index to the date his **"Elegy on the Death of Mr. David Gregory"** was composed in his fourteenth year. Here the passing of a famous mathematician is made amusing - "He'll till the resurrection sleep / As sound's a tap". Each of the Professor's ludicrously detailed accomplishments gets the very final comment, "But now he's dead".

Like Douglas, the Renaissance translators, Thomas Ruddiman, Ramsay and his circle, Fergusson had patriotic motives in seeking to revivify the Scots literary language.

Eighteenth-century Scots poets, however, seeing the shadow of England lengthen over the national destiny, felt compelled to take up a defensive posture that the late-mediaeval *makars,* with no sense of nation and tradition under attack, did not have to adopt. Ramsay was inclined to limit his Scots, Fergusson to make the most of his mother-tongue, which he used stridently, even aggressively, though never carelessly or uneasily. With Dunbar he is now acknowledged as a model for modern Scots-writing poets. The linguistic verve exhibited by both men is largely traceable to the fact that their vocabularies were grounded in living speech and owned a wealth of communal and conventional expression. Fergusson's language is fundamentally the Scots of Edinburgh Old Town, which he enriched by importing words from other dialects, notably that of his Aberdeenshire parents, and also by creating new words upon the analogy of older ones. His idiom mingled urban with rural strains and reflected the persisting mediaeval identity of the crowded city and its hinterland.

Fergusson's genius not only appropriates 'language at large' as did the *makars* but also displays some of their architectonic qualities. His method is mainly narrative, a personal account related in a series of independent images, each one bold and standing out against a diffuse, crowded backdrop. The panoramic Auld Reikie is an excellent instance of this technique. Built up in brisk tetrameter couplets, the poem contrasts light and shade and mingles impressions of sight, sound, memory and even smell. The sketch of the 'bruiser' or pugilist emerging from the tavern

> . . . reeling drunk,
> Wi' fiery phizz, and ein half sunk

is made to follow hard upon the night-scene of the exharlot singing in the street near a lamp-post, too old to ply her former trade, while the glimpse of convivial gatherings that, like Fergusson's own Cape Club,

> . . . jocose and free,
> Gie a' to merriment and glee,
> Wi' sang and glass

marks the gradual decline of street activity as the town settles down for yet another night.

Fergusson did not idealise the denizens of the wynds and closes. 'Embro' has blemishes to match its beauties, but, as he states, "without souring nocht is sweet"; having previously shown how the delights of the morning landscape over St Giles are quickly banished by the bickerings of barefooted maidservants and the stink from their emptied chamber-pots, whereby

> They kindly shower Edina's roses,
> To quicken and regale our noses.

The absence of holograph MSS. makes it difficult to decide how the poet worked. It is tempting to discern in his verse the brilliance of insobriety, but whatever the source of his inspiration the product is plainly no careless screed.

In celebration, as of the Firth of Forth, than which

> There's nane sae spacious and sae noble

or ironic commendation

> Braid Claith lends fock an unco heese,
> Makes mony kail-worms butter-flies,
> Gies mony a doctor his degrees
>   For little skaith

or recollection of country peace

> Beneath the caller shady trees,
> Far frae the din o' Borrowstoun,
> Whar water plays the haughs bedoun

or commiseration with his Auld Breeks, like himself heirs to the human condition—

> Still making tight wi' tither steek,
> The tither hole, the tither eik,

or in so many other attitudes, Fergusson is always the craftsman, the 'maker'.

Like the English poets he imitated or prefigured, Fergusson put most of the stock classical forms to work as frames for contemporary modes, but his ability to associate language and locale in unexpected ways gave his eclogues, elegies, epistles, odes and epodes an individual quality which a stereotype lacks. A clear instance of this originality is the **"Elegy on the Death of Scots Music"**. This beautifully modulated Scots poem exploits English formulae; superficially it invites comparison with certain of Ramsay's works, but the alliance here of Augustan formalism with a familiar Scottish terrain is not derived from Ramsay's prescription of native images and domestic landscapes. Fergusson is making the point that the vogue for Italianate musical settings, embellished with trills and other inessential ornaments, threatened to spoil a taste for the simpler excellence of Scots song, and merely provided instrumentalists with opportunities to show off technique. His **"Elegy"** draws attention to the incongruities produced by juxtaposing foreign and home-bred elements in poetry, and invites the reader to arrive at similar conclusions in the case of music. The poem has ironic tones.

This ability to blend the lyrical with the satirical is Fergusson's most consistently perceptible poetic talent. It was also possessed in great strength by Dunbar. Both poets devoted much time to recording what purported to be solitary musings on life as it was being lived before their eyes. Thus, when Fergusson contemplates Auld Reikie he peers at his city in various perspectives, weighing, as we have noted, her good and bad points. Again, in **"The Farmer's Ingle"** the grandmother's fondness for tales of superstitious terror occasions the comment—

> O mock na this, my friends! but rather

mourn,
    Ye in life's brawest spring wi' reason clear,
Wi' eild our idle fancies a' return,
    And dim our dolefu' days wi' bairnly fear;
The mind's ay cradled when the grave is near.

in the manner of Horace dwelling on the bitter-sweet quality of all human existence. The *pallida mors* of the Roman poet is never far away, though in Scots garb Death and the De'il are intimates. There is a vast difference between the image of

    . . . Death, grim Death! with all his ghastly train

and the nuisance-figure, almost practical joker (for life itself can seem a joke) addressed here—

    Death, what's ado? the de'il be licket,
        Or wi' your stang, you ne'er had pricket,
    Or our Auld Alma Mater tricket
        O' poor John Hogg.

This attitude, at once sardonic and reflective, grasps contrasting aspects of the same entity, each as tangible as its co-existing opposite. When Fergusson concludes **"The Election"** by predicting the early demise of the hard-drinking deacons, who will soon be

                            . . . in a truff,
    Inrow'd in the lang leet
            O' death yon night

what affects us is the satirical insight into the ephemeral character of mortal concerns, the ultimate unimportance of what the deacons are met to discuss, their insensitivity to the consequences of that festive night, which will be to create further vacancies in the Town Council, making necessary a further succession of elections, thus completing the ridiculous circle. Something more has been provided than the naïve Horatian epicureanism promised by the introductory tag, *nunc est bibendum.*

Fergusson shared with Ramsay and Burns that quality of intimacy which, as we have noted, linked the first-named with his early audiences. But he is more clinical in his observations than the other poets, and his named characters, though they are presented in greater detail than familiars like Lucky Wood and Lucky Spence, are much less 'cosy'. Capable of a deeper interpretation of life than Ramsay, he is also capable of seeing it at a greater remove. A Dunbar-like detachment touches his art at times, as in the fantasy of **"Plainstanes and Causey"** which serves to convey only the factual and functional. Here the sun

                taks his leave of Thetis,
    And comes to wauken honest fock,
    That gang to wark at sax o'clock.

This slight aloofness shows also in his poetic *persona*, which rarely offers real information about himself, grave or gay. We learn little about his own despair, though in **"Ode to the Gowdspink"** he comes close. In the 'Job' version, of course, the revelation is in the overtones. We know that he had his 'Stella' as Burns had his Clarinda, but he kept her out of his published verse. He left only one serious lovesong, **"The Lee Rigg"** (which Burns admitted he could not better), and his complaints about the harshness of reality are general. Unlike 'canty Allan', who is almost a period-piece, Fergusson, though never a poetical wraith, lacks physical presence. He is to be seen as a face in the old Embro crowd through whose "real livan words" we are given glimpses of the pulsating life about him.

David Daiches (essay date 1982)

SOURCE: "Chapter III," in *Robert Fergusson,* Scottish Academic Press, 1982, pp. 39-110.

[*Daiches is an English critic. In the following excerpt, he offers a chronological discussion of Fergusson's poetry, with a view to describing the poet's artistic development.*]

On 7 February 1771 *The Weekly Magazine* printed anonymously the first of three pastoral poems, entitled respectively **"Morning"**, **"Noon"** and **"Night"**. The latter two appeared in the issues of the 14th and 21st, and they were all anonymous. But the first had an introductory note by Walter Ruddiman: "We have been favoured with three Pastorals, under the titles of Morning, Noon and Night, written by a young Gentleman of this place, the stile of which appears as natural and picturesque as that of any of the modern ones hitherto published." The young gentleman was Fergusson, and the poems are written in a somewhat vapid style imitative of a strain of English pastoral poetry that flourished in the eighteenth century and was well represented by William Shenstone, though Shenstone's pastoral poetry was more varied both metrically and in mood than these efforts of Fergusson's. (It is unfair to Shenstone to say, as Fergusson's editor Matthew McDiarmid says in his preface, that the poems are "just as tinkling and as amiably vapid as those of their models, the pastorals of William Shenstone". It is true that Shenstone could be sententious and pretentious, as sometimes in his posthumously published *Elegies,* which certainly influenced Fergusson, but he was a genuine connoisseur of country scenery and of landscape; he had a gift for epigram as well as meditative description, and he could display a kind of mocking humour.) Fergusson's first Pastoral, **"Morning"**, is a dialogue between two shepherds, Alexis and Damon. Alexis begins in highly stylised verse:

    'Tis thine to sing the graces of the morn,
    The zephyr trembling o'er the ripening corn:
    'Tis thine with ease to chant the rural lay,
    While bubbling fountains to your numbers play.

This is pretty mechanical stuff, written in a dead or dying tradition. But it is interesting that in his highly stylised language, put into the mouths of shepherds with names from Greek pastoral poetry, Fergusson introduces a familiar Edinburgh landscape:

> Behold Edina's lofty turrets rise,
> Her structures fair adorn the eastern skies;
> As Pentland cliffs o'er top yon distant plain,
> So she the cities on our north domain.

So we have Edinburgh, classicised into "Edina", and the Pentland Hills, as well as invocations to Ceres, Pan and Apollo and an abstract vocabulary of natural objects that trembles on the absurd:

> Ye balmy breezes, wave the verdant field,
> Clouds all your bounties, all your moisture yield;

This is reminiscent of W. S. Gilbert's poem where the speaker addresses the world and tells it to roll on, and a concluding direction adds, "It rolls". The second Pastoral, **"Noon"**, is in a similar style; it is a dialogue between the shepherds Corydon and Timanthes set at the time of day when "the sun the summit of his orb hath gained". The only flash of interest in the poem is the reference to the conflict between Lord North's government and "Wilkes and Liberty". Fergusson was a Scottish nationalist Tory (the phrase will become clearer later) and was very conscious of Wilkes's anti-Scottish attitude. Corydon laments that his love Delia is now in England, wandering "o'er the *Anglian* plain",

> Where civil discord and sedition reign.
> There Scotia's sons in odious light appear,
> Tho' we for them have wav'd the hostile spear:
> For them my sire, enwrapp'd in curdled gore,
> Breath'd his last moments on a foreign shore.

The sentiment—protest against anti-Scottish attitudes in England in spite of the fact that Scots had died in England's imperialist wars—is more interesting than the language. But it is of some interest to note "Edina" and "Scotia"—Burns was to use both these terms with conspicuous lack of success—as attempts by Fergusson to classicise aspects of Scotland. He was to show the benefits of a classical education in more effective ways in some of his Scots poems. The third Pastoral, **"Night"**, is characterised by a graver sententiousness and more edifying sentiments as Amyntas and Florellus moralise in the dusk. The style is something of a jumble, beginning with an evening scene reminiscent of Gray's "Elegy" and ending with something a little more Elizabethan:

> Now *owls* and *batts* infest the midnight scene,
> Dire snakes, invenom'd twine along the green; . . .

Another pastoral poem, entitled **"The Complaint"**, is written in the lilting rhythms of Shenstone's "Pastoral Ballad in Four Parts". It did not appear in *The Weekly Magazine* but in the volume of Fergusson's poems published in 1773. It has some biographical interest, for Damon is represented singing of his unrequited love for Stella, and Stella was a real person (she wrote a poem on

Fergusson after his death) who married someone else but retained an interest in the poet. Shenstone's poem opens:

> Ye shepherds give ear to my lay,
>   And take no more heed to my sheep:
> They have nothing to do but to stray;
>   I have nothing to do but to weep.

Damon's lament, in Fergusson's poem, begins:

> O Cupid! thou wanton young boy!
>   Since, with thy invisible dart,
> Thou hast robb'd a fond youth of his joy,
>   In return grant the wish of his heart.

There is nothing in Fergusson's poem that could not have been written by a minor English versifier of the period. But it is interesting that Fergusson was attracted to this metrical pattern, which is very like the metrical pattern of some older Scots poems of popular revelry which he used later in his **"Hallow Fair"**. (We do not know the date of **"The Complaint"**, but it must have been composed some time in 1772 at latest to have appeared in the 1773 volume. **"Hallow Fair"** did not appear in Fergusson's lifetime, but was communicated by him to David Herd, who printed it in volume II of his *Scots Songs*, 1776. It was first attributed to Fergusson in the index of James Johnson's *Scots Musical Museum*, volume V, 1797.) Another of Fergusson's early pastoral poems in the English Shenstonian mode is **"Written at the Hermitage of Brand, near Edinburgh"**, which appeared in *The Weekly Magazine* on 10 October 1771. It has the same lilting metre, used by other eighteenth century English poets besides Shenstone, sometimes to suggest an almost ballad note. But there is nothing of the ballad in Fergusson's poem:

> Would you relish a rural retreat,
>   Or the pleasure the groves can inspire?
> The city's allurements forget,
>   To this spot of enchantment retire. . . .

These early poetic essays of Fergusson are of no great interest, but it is perhaps worth noting that although he wrote them in a conventional English poetic diction he clearly pronounced the words with a Scots accent. In **"Noon"**, for example, Corydon complains of his poverty, since

> *Tay* bounding o'er *his* banks with awless sway,
> Bore all my corns—all my flocks away.

"Corns" is clearly disyllabic, with a long rolled "r".

"On the cold Month of April 1771", which appeared in *The Weekly Magazine* on 16 May 1771, is written in the style of Shenstone's *Elegies,* but at least it describes the real weather, having been provoked, apparently, by a poem entitled "April" that had appeared in the previous issue of the magazine giving a poetic account of spring weather as it is supposed to be and not as it was that year. Fergusson uses the unseasonable weather to moralise pretentiously about life:

> Life! What art thou? a variegated scene
>   Of mingl'd light and shade, of joy and woe;
> A sea where calms and storms promiscuous
>   reign,
>   A stream where sweet and bitter jointly
> flow.

He goes on to describe how the plains are mute, the shepherd pipes no more, and winter still bestrides the blast, concluding with an appeal to Boreas to relent and allow spring to come. The language is almost ridiculously stylised, even when it tells the truth about the weather.

On 1 August 1771 a rather different sort of poem by Fergusson appeared in *The Weekly Magazine*. This was **"A Saturday's Expedition. In Mock Heroics"**, written in the mock-Miltonic style popularised by John Philips' "The Splendid Shilling" and employed also, although with less comic intent if often with similar comic effect, in John Armstrong's "The Art of Preserving Health" and John Dyer's "The Fleece". This kind of style appealed to Fergusson's sense of humour, and he reverted to it more than once in the course of his short poetic career. The poem describes an expedition across the Forth to Fife, and Fergusson clearly relished the combination of a high-pitched epic style with local references:

> After regaling here with sober cann,
> Our limbs we plied, and nimbly measur'd o'er
> The hills, the vales, and the extensive plains,
> Which form the distance from *Burntisland*'s port
> To *Inverkeithing*. Westward still we went,
> Till in the ferry-boat we loll'd at ease;
> Nor did we long on Neptune's empire float,
> For scarce ten posting minutes were elaps'd
> Till we again on *Terra Firma* stood,
> And to M'Laren's march'd, where roasted lamb,
> With cooling lettuce, crown'd our social board. . . .

A "pastoral elegy" in seventeen quatrains, entitled **"The Decay of Friendship"**, appeared in *The Weekly Magazine* on 19 September 1771. It is a moralising poem in the style of Shenstone's *Elegies,* and still shows no sign of where Fergusson's real strength lay. Nor did his poem **"A Burlesque Elegy on the amputation of a Student's Hair, before his Orders"**, which appeared on 21 November. This rather faint echo of "The Rape of the Lock" also owes something to Allan Ramsay's "On the most Honourable The Marquess of Bowmont's Cutting off his Hair". . . .

None of the poems by Fergusson or indeed anybody else that had hitherto appeared in *The Weekly Magazine* could have prepared the readers for **"The Daft Days"** on 2 January 1772. At a stroke Fergusson now defined his position as a Scottish poet and an Edinburgh poet; he brought together his reading in English poetry, his knowledge of earlier Scots poetry and his classical education; he placed himself in a Scottish tradition that he revived and altered while drawing on it; he anchored the poem

solidly in his own time and place while at the same time harking back to older styles and modes; and he created an enthusiastic audience for this kind of poetry without whom Burns would not have had the success he did have.

He did not, however, give up writing poems in Shenstonian and other English modes, but these, though sometimes showing a certain imitative skill, are so vapid in comparison with his Scots poems that the reader is not tempted to stay with them long. **"Fashion. A Poem"** appeared in *The Weekly Magazine* on 27 February 1772, and readers must have been bitterly disappointed when, instead of finding a successor to **"The Daft Days"**, they read the opening:

> O Nature, parent goddess! at thy shrine,
> Prone to the earth, the muse, in humble song,
> They aid implores: . . .

But on 5 March they could read Fergusson's **"Elegy on the Death of Scots Music"**. This is a belligerently nationalistic poem, yet it has as epigraph a quotation from Shakespeare's *Twelfth Night* that makes it clear that his interest is in the genuine, the native and the traditional rather than in Scottishness for its own sake:

> Mark it, Caesario; it is old and plain,
> The spinsters and the knitters in the sun,
> And the free maids that weave their thread with
> bones,
> Do use to chant it.

This sets the tone, and the poem (although it uses a traditional Scots stanza more associated with lively humour than with serious elegy) opens with an elegiac stateliness:

> On Scotia's plains in days of yore,
> When lads and lasses *tartan* wore,
> Saft Music rang on ilka [*every*] shore,
>   In hamely weid; [*simple
>   dress*]
> But harmony is now no more,
>   And *music* dead.

"Scotia's plains" (rather than "Scotland's plains") gives evidence of a formality in the Scots language, and in its context the phrase comes off. Yet the formality is used to give weight to the subject rather than to distance it from the ordinary and the colloquial. Indeed, in some degree the subject is precisely regret at the disappearance of the ordinary and the colloquial, the loss of music that rang "in hamely weid" [dress]. And "weid" give notice that "dead", though spelt in the conventional English manner, is to be pronounced in Scots, "deid".

The next stanza employs the conventional neo-classic English phrase "feather'd choir" and the equally conventional "zephyrs", but accompanies them with the adverbs "bonnily" and "sleely" which domicile these phrases in a Scottish context. It is a remarkably bold combination, as is the use in the following stanza of "ilka nymph" and "ilka swain" (making "nymph" and "swain" into Scots words by prefixing "ilka") and the introduction of Na-iads.

> Round her the feather'd choir would wing,
> Sae bonnily she wont to sing,
> And sleely [*skilfully*] wake the sleeping string,
>> Their sang to lead,
> Sweet as the zephyrs of the spring;
>> But now she's dead.
>
> Mourn ilka [*every*] nymph and ilka swain,
> Ilk sunny hill and dowie [*gloomy*] glen;
> Let weeping streams and *Naiads* drain
>> Their fountain head;
> Let echo swell the dolefu's strain,
>> Since music's dead. . . .

After four stanzas of lament in fairly general terms, Fergusson, in a manner characteristic of him, begins to narrow the subject with increasing particularisation . . . :

> Nae lasses now, on simmer days,
> Will lilt at bleaching of their claes;
> Nae herds on *Yarrow's* bonny braes,
>> Or banks of Tweed,
> Delight to chant their hameil [*home-bred*] lays,
>> Since music's dead.
>
> At glomin now the bagpipe's dumb,
> When weary owsen [*oxen*] hameward come;
> Sae sweetly as it wont to bum[*play*]
>> And *Pibrachs* skreed; [*lively playing*]
> We never hear its warlike hum;
>> For music's dead.

A reference to his favourite song, "The Birks of Inver-may", finishes the particularisation, and the poem then moves at once to its formal conclusion:

> O SCOTLAND! that cou'd yence [*once*] afford
> To bang [*overcome*] the pith of Roman sword,
> Winna your sons, wi'joint accord,
> To battle speed?
> And fight till MUSIC be restor'd,
>> Which now lies dead.

The poem shows an interesting combination of influences and attitudes. The nostalgic Scottish patriotism, that he found in some of Ramsay's poems, can accommodate a reference of Shakespeare and an echo of Gray ("What weary owsen hameward come"). Friend of Tenducci though he was, he deplores the influence of Italian music on the native Scots tradition. (It is quite true that the Italianising of Scottish folk song went on increasingly in the latter years of the eighteenth century and can be seen in the excessive trills and ornaments in the accompaniments in Thomson's *Select Scottish Airs,* but the situation was more complex than that, and Fergusson's enthusiasm for his native tradition led him to over-simplify.) In one stanza he laments the death of Macgibbon (or McGib-bon):

> *Macgibbon's* gane: Ah! was my heart!
> The man in music maist expert,
> Wha cou'd sweet melody impart,
>> And tune the reed,
> Wi' sic a slee and pawky art; [*skilful; cunning*]
>> But now he's dead.

The violinist and composer William McGibbon was born in Edinburgh about 1695 and died there in 1756. Though Fergusson contrasts McGibbon's native skills with imported Italian trash—

> Now foreign sonnets bear the gree, [*prize*]
> And crabbit queer variety [*perverse*]
> Of sounds fresh sprung frae *Italy,*
>> A bastard breed!
> Unlike that saft-tongu'd melody
>> Which now lies dead—

the fact is that McGibbon seems to have modelled his early career on Corelli, although after 1740 he became more and more interested in Scots fiddle music. Like Corelli, he made a name for himself both as a composer and as a violinist, and was Scotland's leading composer in the first half of the eighteenth century. Fergusson seems to have been less interested in his trio sonatas, his sonatas for flute and violin or two flutes and his other compositions in the Italian tradition of Corelli, and more interested in his settings of Scots folk tunes, of which he published one hundred and twenty-eight between 1742 and 1755. Yet even these combined, with remarkable success, the idiom of Scots folk music with the idiom of Italian baroque. Matthew McDiarmid has asserted that the idea of introducing McGibbon into the poem "though with a serious and not a comic purpose, certainly came from Hamilton of Gilbertfield's *The Life and Death of the Piper of Kilbarchan* and Ramsay's "Elegy on Patie Birnie", 'the Famous Fiddler of Kinghorn'". There is of course a continuous tradition working here, but the differences between the earlier poems and Fergusson's are more marked than the similarities. Fergusson's poem is about the dwindling integrity of Scottish culture, and it is part of his response to the fate of Scotland after the Union. The concluding apostrophe to Scotland (not, interestingly enough, to "Scotia") founded a special kind of rhetorical tradition in Scots poetry that Burns drew on in the conclusion of "The Cotter's Saturday Night".

On 7 May 1772 *The Weekly Magazine* published Fergusson's **"Conscience. An Elegy"**, a rather feeble moralising poem in the Shenstonian tradition, but this was followed on 4 June by one of his finest pieces in Scots, **"The King's Birth-Day in Edinburgh"**. This is a full-blooded performance in the Scottish tradition of poems of popular revelry through lacking what might be called the broadside accent of so many of such poems. It is a description of Edinburgh's celebration of George III's thirty-sixth birthday, of which an account was given in sober prose in *The Weekly Magazine* of 12 June, which describes both the official celebrations on the Castle Hill and in Parliament House and the rowdy activities of sections of the populace in the evening when "the lower class of people" became "perfectly licentious" and "after their ammunition of squibs and crackers was exhausted, they employed dead cats, mud &c. which they discharged very plentifully on the city guard; and, when threatened to be chastised or apprehended, they betook themselves to the more dangerous weapons of stones and brickbats &c. in this encounter several of the guard were wounded, and they in return dealt their blows pretty liberally, by which, amid the confusion, some innocent persons suffered along with the guilty."

Fergusson's poem begins with an epigraph from that exuberant and very popular macaronic (or rather for the most part-Latin) poem by William Drummond of Hawthornden, "Polemo-Middinia", which appeared in the first volume of Watson's *Choice Collection* and was also included in a one-volume folio edition of Drummond's works in 1711. This kind of jocular use of the classics seems to have appealed to Fergusson from his student days: it is a taste that distinguished him sharply from both his predecessor Ramsay and his successor Burns, neither of whom was equipped by education, as Fergusson was, to relish this sort of student humour. The flavour of Drummond's poem can be judged from its opening lines:

Nymphae, quae colitis highistima monta *Fifaea,*
Seu vos *Pitenwema* tenent, seu *Crelia* crofta,
Sive *Anstraea* domus, ubi nat *Haddocus* in
     undis,
Codlineusque ingens, & *Fleucca* & *Sketa*
     pererrant
Per costam, & scopulos, *Lobster* manifootus in
     udis
Creepat, . . .

The combination of Latin, dog-Latin and Latinised Fife place names had a special appeal for Fergusson. But in fact, though his quotation from Drummond's poem reflects his knowledge of and interest in it, Fergusson is not here writing in this style at all. The epigraph consists of but one line from Drummond:

Oh! qualis hurly-burly fuit, si forte videsses.

The poem then proceeds in a style that is familiar but not vulgar. The opening is humorous in a new way for eighteenth-century Scottish poetry:

I sing the day sae aften sung,
Wi' which our lugs [*ears*] hae yearly rung,
In whase loud praise the Muse has dung [*poured
     forth*]
          A'kind o' print;
But wow! the limmer's fairly flung; [*wench;
     baffled*]
          There's naething in't. . . .

O *Muse*, be kind, and dinna fash [*trouble*] us
To flee awa' beyont Parnassus,
Nor seek for *Helicon* to wash us,

That heath'nish spring;
Wi' Highland whisky scour our hawses, [*throats*]
          And gar us [*cause us to*] sing.

Begin then, dame, ye've drunk your fill,
You wouldna hae the tither gill?
You'll trust me, mair wou'd do you ill,
          And ding you doitet; [*drive you
     crazy*]
Troth 'twou'd be sair agains my will
          To hae the wyte o't. [*blame*]

To rhyme the Scots phrase "dinna fash us" ("don't bother us") with "Parnassus" shows a certain boldness in claiming the right to use classical references in a rollicking Scots poem, and this is what Fergusson must have learned, directly or indirectly, from the tradition of vernacular Humanism associated with Pitcairn and the older Ruddiman. He addresses the Muse as "dame" with cheerful familiarity, using a language that is more consistently Scots than most other parts of the poem. This mischievously familiar attitude to the Muse is not vulgarity, but controlled high spirits. It sets the tone for the ensuing description:

Sing then, how on the *fourth* of June,
Our *bells* screed [*played*] aff a loyal tune,
Our antient castle shoots at noon
          Wi' flag-staff buskit,
Frae which the soldier blades come down
          To cock their musket.

(Note that "down", in spite of the spelling, is clearly to be pronounced in the Scots way, "doon".)

So off he goes, describing the noise, the pranks, the brulzies with the City Guard, with artful verve. The poet's self, introduced in the very first line, is present throughout, both as observer and as celebrant, and the introduction of his own comments adds to the spontaneity of the tone, as when he addresses the old cannon, Mons Meg:

Right seldom am I gi'en to bannin, [*swearing*]
But, by my saul, ye was a cannon,
Cou'd hit a man, had he been stannin
          In shire o'Fife,
Sax long Scots miles ayont *Clackmannan,*
          And tak his life.

The note of personal wonder, rising to a climax on a line which opens with opens with four monosyllabic words—"Sax long Scots miles ayont Clackmannan"—represents technique of a high order, from which Burns was to learn. At the end of the poem he returns to the Muse, reminding himself that the final stages of riotous celebration are not fit themes for her, who is accustomed to more conventional poetic aspects of the day's proceeding:

She'll rather to the fields resort,
Whare music gars [*makes*] the day seem short,
Whare doggies play, and lambies sport
          On gowany braes, [*daisy-covered*]

Whare peerless Fancy hads her court,
And tunes her lays.

"Peerless Fancy" is deliberate, almost ironic, English poetic diction: the pastoral aspects of the celebration are more suitable for conventional poetic treatment than the more violent urban goings-on that the he has been recounting. And on that note of mingled pastoral cheerfulness and ironic poetizing the poem concludes. (The diminutives "doggies" and "lambies", so characteristic of northeastern Scottish speech, Fergusson probably picked up from his parents.)

Fergusson's next contribution to *The Weekly Magazine* was an epigram in English verse **"On the Death of Dr Toshack of Perth, a great homourist"**, and two Shenstonian pastoral poems, **"The Simile"** and **"Damon to his Friends"**. More interesting, though still not in Scots, was his **"Burlesque Poem"** entitled **"The Canongate Playhouse in Ruins"**. This opens in the burlesque style we have already seen him use, but soon a rhetorical seriousness takes over and the poet's genuine regret for the loss of the playhouse and his nostalgic recollection of the plays that were performed there express themselves in a derivative but yet genuinely felt English poetic style:

O Shakespeare! where are all thy tinsell'd kings,
Thy fawning courtiers, and thy waggish clowns?
Where all thy fairies, spirits, witches, fiends,
That here have gambol'd in nocturnal sport,
Round the lone oak, or sunk in fear away
From the shrill summons of the cock at morn?
Where now the temples, palaces, and towers?

The Shakespearean echoes here—from *Julius Caesar, Hamlet* and *The Tempest*—are not in the least burlesque. He remembers with emotion Tenducci's singing, and concludes the poem, more moved, we feel, than he set out to be, with a tribute.

To the blest memory of happier times.

Sincerity of emotion does not in itself, however, make great poetry, and at best this is interesting and competent verse.

Fergusson's **"Caller Oysters"** appeared in *The Weekly Magazine* on 27 August 1772. It is another of his convivial poems. Its opening, a fine tribute to the Forth and its fishermen, shows him handling the "Standart *Habby"* stanza with a slowness and an openness not often found in this verse form:

Of a' the waters that can hobble
A fishin yole or salmon coble, [*yawl; flat-
bottomed boat*]
And can reward the fishers trouble,
Or south or north,
There's nane sae spacious or sae noble
As Firth o' *Forth*

He moves inland from the sea, from the Forth coast to Auld Reekie's oyster cellars, and soon we have one of his cosy Edinburgh interiors again:

Whan big as burns the gutters rin,
Gin ye hae catcht a droukit [*wet*] skin,
To *Lucky Middlemist's* loup in,
And sit fu snug
O'er oysters and a dram o' gin,
Or haddock lug.

Lucky Middlemist or Middlemass kept a tavern in the Cowgate ("where the south pier of the bridge now stands", Chambers informs us in his *Traditions of Edinburgh* which was a popular venue for "oyster parties" in Fergusson's day. The Forth was then renowned for its oysters, the largest and best being the "pandours", those caught near Prestonpans at the doors of the salt pans.

At *Musselbrough,* and eke *Newhaven.*
The fisher-wives will get *top livin,*
Whan *lads* gang out on Sunday's even
To treat their *joes,*
And tak of fat pandours a prieven, [*large
oysters; taste*]
Or *mussel brose*: . . .

the poem is more than an Edinburgh poem: it is a Forth poem. The language is a lively colloquial Scots, yet not too colloquial to refuse to admit classical references. he follows the stanza about Lucky Middlemists with this:

When auld Saunt Giles, at aught
o'clock,
Gars merchant lowns their chopies
lock, [*causes to; fellows; shops*]
There we adjourn wi' hearty fock [*people*]
To birle our bodles,
[*spend our coppers*]
And get wharewi'to crack our joke,
And clear our noddles.

"Chopies" has the north-eastern diminutive again; "birle our bodles" is vividly colloquial, as is "clear our noddles". Yet the very next stanza introduces the sun as Phoebus:

When *Phoebus* did his windocks steek, [*shut*]
How aften at that *ingle* cheek [*fireside*]
Did I my frosty fingers beek, [*warm*]
And taste gude fare?
I trow there was nae hame to seek
Whan steghin there.
[*gorging*]

Phoebus is easily domiciled in a racy Scots. Fergusson deliberately uses the Scots "windocks" for "windows", "steek", "beek" and the expressive "steghin" with its emphatic guttural to end the stanza. It might be asked how he gets away with it, how he can associate Phoebus with windocks and ingle cheeks and the rest without sounding absurd. The answer lies surely in his simple confidence that it can be done. He is not showing off, he

Title page for Fergusson's first collection of poetry.

The rhymes "sicker", "bicker", "liquor","vicar" add an air of merriment to the verse. Fergusson was highly skilled in using rhyme for a variety of purposes, often comic. In an earlier stanza he had summoned the reader to "prie" ("taste")an oyster as a cure for sickness in these words:

> Come prie, frail man! for gin thou *art sick*
> 　　[*taste; if*]
> The oyster is a rare cathartic,
> As ever doctor patient gart lick
> 　　　　　　To cure his ails;
> Whether you hae the head or heart-ake
> 　　　　　　It ay prevails.

The comic rhymes give notice here that the poet's recommendation fo oysters as a sovereign remedy for all kinds of illness is made in a fit of high spirits and is not to be taken as solemn truth. . . .

"Braid Claith" appeared in *The Weekly Magazine* on 15 October. It is a social satire, making the point that as far as public opinion is concerned clothes make the man:

> Ye wha are fain to hae your name
> Wrote in the bonny book of fame,
> Let merit nae pretension claim
> 　　　　　　To laurel'd wreath,
> But hap ye weel, baith back and wame, [*clothe
> 　yourself*]
> 　　　　　　In gude Braid Claith.

The third stanza shows him using outrageous rhymes for ironic rather than purely comic purposes:

> Waesuck for him wha has na fek o't! [*alas;
> 　amount*]
> For he's a gowk [*fool*] they're sure to
> 　　geck [*scoff*] at,
> A chiel [*fellow*] that ne'er will be respekit
> 　　　　　　While he draws breath,
> Till his four quarters are bedeckit
> 　　　　　　Wi' gude Braid Claith.

The poem proceeds through a series of sharply etched scenes illustrating the poet's point, until it reaches its penultimate stanza and broadens out into generalizations:

> Braid Claith lends fock an
> 　　unco heese, [*remarkable lift*]
> Makes mony kail-worms [*caterpillars*] butter-
> 　flies,
> Gies mony a doctor his degrees
> 　　　　　　For little skaith; [*effort*]
> In short, you may be what you please
> 　　　　　　Wi' gude Braid Claith.

The concluding stanza appears to derive from a passage in the Life of Richard Boyse in Colley Cibber's *Lives of the Poets:* "His extreme carelessness about his dress was

is not self-consciously and exhibitionistically drawing on a genteel classical tradition as Burns sometimes does. There is for him no reason why a vivid colloquial Scots should not be enriched by whatever classical dimension he feels inclined to add at any given moment. The run of the verse is the guarantee of the naturalness and appropriateness of that dimension. The flow is never stopped or altered, there is no pause of wonder or special attention.

The poem ends with advice to those who cannot stand very firmly after having twice emptied "the big ars'd bicker" (a splendid vulgarity): mix oysters with your drink and you'll carry it as well as any greedy priest or vicar:

> A'ye wha canna stand sae sicker, [*so firmly*]
> Whan twice you've took'd the
> 　　big ars'd bicker, [*emptied; drinking cup,*]
> Mix *caller oysters* wi' your liquor,
> 　　　　　And I'm your debtor,
> If greedy *priest* or drouthy *vicar*
> 　　　　　Will thole it better.

a circumstance very inauspicious to a man who lives in that city [Edinburgh]. They are such lovers of this kind of decorum, that they will admit of no infringement upon it; and were a man with more wit than Pope, and more philosophy than Newton, to appear in their market-place negligent in his apparel, he would be avoided by his acquaintances, who would rather risk his displeasure than the censure of the public, which would not fail to stigmatize them, for associating with a man seemingly poor; for they measure poverty and riches, understanding, or its opposite, by exterior appearance."

Here is how Fergusson turned this thought in ending his poem:

> For thof [*though*] ye had as wide a snout on
> As *Shakespeare* or Sir *Isaac Newton*,
> Your judgment fouk wou'd hae a doubt on,
>   I'll tak my aith,
> Till they cou'd see ye wi'a suit on
>   O'gude Braid Claith.

"Snout" and "doubt" are clearly to be pronounced "snoot" and "doot". To introduce "Sir Isaac Newton" as a rhyme between "snout on" and "doubt on" and follow it with "suit on" has of course the comic effect associated with rhyming two monosyllabic words and one disyllabic one and, as we have seen, it is the sort of thing Fergusson liked to do. But the effect is not simply that of a comic trick; the comedy adds to the irony to sum up the point of the poem in mocking laughter.

Fergusson's next poem in *The Weekly Magazine* appeared on 29 October 1772, **"An Eclogue To the Memory of Dr William Wilkie, late Professor of Natural Philosophy in the University of St. Andrews"**. Wilkie, whose kindness to Fergusson when he was a student has already been discussed, died on 11 October, so the poet lost no time in commemorating him. This time he did not write in "Standart *Habby*" or adopt the comic elegy tradition of the **"Epitaph on Habbie Simson"** and **"Bonny Heck"** to more serious purposes, nor did he write in neoclassic English in imitation of Shenstone. The poem is modelled on Ramsay's pastoral elegies, but it is an altogether more assured performance than anything Ramsay did in that style. Fergusson uses heroic couplets with gravity and flexibility (though the lines are as a rule end-stopped) and the Scots appears completely at home in this verse form. This is something new in eighteenth-century Scots poetry:

> . . . *Tho' simmer's* gane, [*summer's gone*] an'
> we nae
>   langer view
> The blades o' claver [*clover*] wat wi' pearls
>   o' dew.
> Cauld winter's bleakest blasts we'll
>   eithly cow, [*easily recover from*]
> Our eldin's driven, an' our har'st
>   is owr; [*fuel; harvest*]
> Our *rucks* fu' thick are stackit i'
>   the yard,

> For the *Yule-feast* a sautit mart's [*salted cow*]
>   prepar'd;
> The ingle-nook [*fireside*] supplies the simmer
>   fields,
> An' aft as mony gleefu' maments yields.
> Swyth man! [*quick!*] fling a' your sleepy
>   springs awa,
> An' on your canty whistle gie's a
>   blaw: [*merry; give us*]
> Blythness, I trow, maun lighten
>   ilka eie, [*every eye*]
> An' ilka canty callant [*every cheerful lad*] sing
>   like me.

This is Davie, replying to Geordie's announcement of his as yet unexplained sorrow. Scots names now replace classical names. Geordie answers Davie, explaining why he cannot sing cheerfully:

> Na, na; a canty spring wad now impart
> Just threefald sorrow to my heavy
>   heart.
> Thof to the *weet* my ripen'd aits
>   had fawn, [*though; wet; oats*]
> Or shake-winds [*strong winds*] owr *my rigs wi'*
>   pith
>   had blawn,
> To this I cou'd *hae* said,
>   "I carena by," [*I don't care*]
> Nor fund occasion now *my* cheeks
>   to dry.
> Crosses like thae, or lake of warld's
>   gear, [*goods*]
> Are naething when we tyne [*lose*] a friend
>   that's dear.

Fergusson is exercising his Scots in a new way, continuing his search for appropriate ways of using and extending it. This particular route proved a blind alley. The pastoral convention had really had its day by this time, and to lament Wilkie by having two shepherds mourn the death of a poetic and astronomically minded fellow shepherd is hardly the most effective way of writing a Scots elegy. Geordie explains to Davie:

> 'Twas na for weel tim'd verse or
>   sangs alone,
> He bore the bell frae ilka shepherd
>   swain.
> *Nature* to him had gi'en a kindly lore,
> Deep a' her mystic *ferlies* [*wonders*] to explore:
> For a' her secret workings he could gie
> Reasons which wi' her principles agree. . . .

And Davie replies:

> They tell me, Geordie, he had sic [*such*]
>   a gift
> That scarce a starnie blinkit [*glanced;*] frae
>   the lift, [*sky*]
> But he wou'd some auld warld name
>   for't find,

As gart [*caused him to*] him keep it freshly in
    his mind: . . .

The conclusion tries to lift the poem to classical heights
with a formal (and conventional) reference to Virgil:

Scholars and bards *unheard of yet* shall come,
And stamp memorials on his grassy tomb,
Which in yon antient kirk-yard shall remain,
Fam'd as the urn that hads the mantuan *swain*.

The speaker is hardly a shepherd now, and in spite of the
reference to "you antient kirk-yard" and the Scots "hads"
for "holds" the tone has moved away from any sort of
Scottish rural expression to something more conventionally "poetic" in the eighteenth-century English manner.
The poem is interesting for what it tries to do. Parts of it
are remarkably successful, as in such lines as

Whase sangs will ay in Scotland be
    rever'd,
While *slow-gawn owsen* [*slow-moving oxen*] turn
    the flowr'ry swaird;
While bonny *lambies* lick the dews of
    spring,
While *gaudsmen* [*ploughmen*] whistle, or while
    birdies sing.

The lambies and birdies take their place quite naturally in a landscape which, though Scottish, owes something to Gray and Shenstone. But this note is not
consistent in the poem, and as a whole it does not
quite come off.

On 17 November 1772 *The Weekly Magazine* published
Fergusson's **"Hallow Fair"**. This was a conscious attempt
by Fergusson to revive an older Scottish tradition of poetry of popular celebration as represented by "Peblis to
the Play" and "Christ's Kirk on the Green". The latter is
the first poem in the first volume of Watson's Choice
Collection: it is in a nine-line stanza, alternating iambic
octosyllables and iambic trisyllables, with the last line
consisting of four emphatic beats, always ending with the
words "that day". Here is its opening stanza as Watson
printed it:

Was ne'er in Scotland heard nor seen
    such Dancing and Deray; [*boisterous mirth*]
Neither at *Faulkland* on the Green,
    nor *Peebles* at the Play,
As was of Wooers as I ween
    at *Christ's Kirk* on a day:
For there came *Katie* washen clean
    with her new Gown of Gray,
        Full gay that day.

Fergusson's **"Hallow Fair"** celebrates a market that has
held about the time of Hallowmas (All Saints' Day, 1
November), generally in the first week of November but
in 1772 beginning on 9 November, in the outskirts of
Edinburgh. It opens:

At *Hallowmas,* when nights grow lang,

And *starnies* [*stars*] shine fu' clear,
What fock, the nippin cauld to bang, [*people;*
    cold; overcome]
    Their winter *hap-warms* [*wraps*] wear,
Near Edinbrough a fair there hads, [*is held*]
    I wat [*know*] there's nane whase name is,
For strappin dames and sturdy lads,
    And cap and stoup, [*bowl and flagon*] mair
        famous
                Than it that day.

The poem follows the tradition in its lively descriptions
of individual encounters. . . . .

After eight stanzas of lively description in a racy Scots,
Fergusson unexpectedly introduces—without abandoning
his Scots diction—classical references:

Whan *Phoebus* ligs [*lies*] in *Thetis* lap,
    Auld Reikie gies them shelter,
Whare cadgily they kiss the cap, [*gaily; drink*]
    An' ca't round helter-skelter.
Jock Bell gaed furth to play his
    freaks,
    Great cause he had to rue it,
For frae a stark Lochaber aix
    He gat a *clamihewit,* [*severe blow*]
        Fu' sair that night.

This playful and confident introduction of classical deities into a Scots poem is something that Fergusson could
do and neither Ramsay nor Burns could. Burns could be
funny about Latona and Thetis, but not in the middle of
a Scots poem, only in a deliberately obscene parody of
formal neo-classic language, as in his "Ode to Spring" set
to a traditional Scots air but using for the most part a far
from traditional Scots language. . . .

Fergusson's classicism was more inward and more spontaneous, and though, as we have seen, he enjoyed burlesque and mock-heroic, his relation to the older Scottish
vernacular humanist tradition enabled him to accommodate Phoebus and Thetis in Scots verse without making a
self-conscious bawdy joke of it.

The "clamihewit", which Fergusson glossed as "severe
blow", received by Jock Bell from a Lochaber axe,
must have been delivered by a member of the City
Guard, who carried these weapons. His first readers
would have recognized the incident as a further illustration of Fergusson's by now well known personal war
against that body of elderly Highland policemen. In a
later stanza he describes the victim lying in the street
after the assault, while members of the City Guard,
speaking in a parody of a Highland accent, decide to
take him into custody:

He peching [*panting;*] on the cawsey [*street*] lay,
    O'kicks and cuffs weel sair'd; [*served*]
A *Highland* aith [*oath*] the serjeant gae, [*gave*]
    "She maun [*must*] pee see our guard."
Out spak the weirlike [*warlike*] corporal,

"Pring in ta drunken sot."
They trail'd him ben, an' by my saul,
He paid his drunken groat
For that neist [*next*] day.

"To the Tron-kirk Bell" appeared in *The Weekly Magazine* in 26 November 1772. This is a poem in the old Scottish flyting tradition, a splendid piece of studied abuse directed at the "wanwordy [*worthless*], crazy, dinsome thing" whose "noisy tongue" was "sair to thole [*endure*]". Here Fergusson demonstrates a virtuosity that had not been seen in Scots poetry since the makars. The mixture of skill and gusto with which the bell is abused is reminiscent of Dunbar in his best flyting style. The poem, however, is not a satire on bells but on bailies: the conclusion is that the city fathers allow this scandal because they live out of its hearing:

If magistrates wi' me wad 'gree,
For ay *tongue-tackit* [*tongue-tied*] shud you be,
Nor fleg [*frighten*] wi' *antimelody*
Sic honest fock, [*folk*]
Whase lugs were never made to dree [*suffer*]
Thy doolfu' shock.

But far frae thee the *bailies* dwell,
Or they wud scunner [*feel disgust*] at your knell,
Gie the *foul thief* his riven bell,
And then, I trow,
The by-word hads, [*holds*] "the de'il himsel'
"Has got his due."

An earlier stanza had described the bell as a trick of the Devil to scare people from church, and the concluding stanza comes round to the Devil again in a neat turn. Fergusson's ability to move a poem from its ostensible subject to a logical yet surprising conclusion becomes increasingly apparent in his Scots poems.

By the time "To the Tron-kirk Bell" appeared, Fergusson had already assembled a group of poems for publication in book form, so this poem was too late to be included in it. The publication date was probably January 1773; the title was simply Poems by Robert Fergusson. The book contained twenty-seven poems in English and nine in Scots ("Sandie and Willie", "Geordie and Davie", "Elegy on the Death of Mr David Gregory", "The Daft-Days", "The King's Birth-Day in Edinburgh", "Caller Oysters", "Braid Claith", "Elegy on the Death of Scots Music" and "Hallow-fair").

"Sandie and Willie, an Eclogue" had not appeared in *The Weekly Magazine*. The poem is a dialogue between two Scots farmers, Sandie complaining to Willie that his wife, who seemed so modest and pretty and quiet when they were courting, has turned out to be an idle scold. The opening sets the scene in an assured Scots, domiciling the English pastoral tradition firmly in Scotland. . . .

This poem ["Sandie and Willie"] is one of several that remind us that Fergusson, though a city poet, also knew and loved the country and was in touch with the rhythms of country life. He had seen farm life in Fife and Aberdeenshire, but, more important, he saw it all the time in the countryside around Edinburgh, for Edinburgh was still a small city with quick and easy access to its pastoral surroundings, as the ending of "The King's Birth-Day in Edinburgh" makes clear. It was not only the physical countryside that he was in touch with; it was also the spirit of rustic festivities and seasonal celebrations. In some respects these celebrations were common to town and country, and Fergusson can present them in either context. In his later poems "The Rising of the Session" and "The Sitting of the Session" he evokes vividly the effect on city life of the cessation and renewal of legal activity in that very legal city, and in "The Daft-Days" he describes the seasonal winter festivities of Edinburgh. But his more elemental feelings about seasonal change were both traditionally oriented and associated with the countryside.

Among the English poems in the 1773 volume that had not appeared in *The Weekly Magazine* was the ambitious Ode entitled "The Rivers of Scotland", which was set to music by John Collett. This is in the tradition of the eighteenth-century English ode, with different sections in different rhythms. Incidental songs are punctuated by choruses, some of the latter being set to traditional Scots airs ("Tweedside" and "Gilderoy"). It is all rather forced and over-rhetorical. "Fortha's shores" harbour "Naiades", "Pan from Arcadia to Tweda came", while

From the dark wombs of earth Tay's waters
spring,
Ordain'd by Jove's unalterable voice;
The sounding lyre celestial muses string,
The choiring songsters in the groves rejoice.

There are patriotic outbursts, addresses to "Ye powers" to protect "Scotia's ample fields" (Burns was to remember "Ye Powers") and to Jove to keep foreign foes from Caledon. The Ode seems to have been popular; it was reprinted in three Edinburgh publications, *The Nightingale* (1776), *The Goldfinch* (1777) and *The Scots Nightingale* (1778), appealing as it did to a patriotic-topographical-rhetorical taste, but it is pretty empty stuff really.

Another English poem in the 1773 volume that had not previously appeared is "The Town and Country Contrasted. In an Epistle to a Friend". Fifty-five lines of blank verse contrasting in highly formal neo-classic English the health-giving countryside with the smelly city end with a moral appeal for "temperance, health's blyth concomitant". It is all very derivative, and "literary" in the more dubious sense of the word.

The English poems in the 1773 volume also include an "Ode to Hope" and an "Ode to Pity", the former alternating heroic couplets with quatrains and the latter entirely in octosyllabic couplets: there are echoes of both Gray and Milton. There is also "A Tale", an amusing anecdote in octosyllabic couplets where the major influence seems to be Matthew Prior. And there are a number of poems in anapaestic or dactylic quatrains with the lilting movement found in so many early eighteenth-century lyrics. These and other English poems in the volume show Fergusson aping a variety of styles, sometimes ingeniously, sometimes with a fair degree of craftsmanship, but never with the authority of his Scots poems.

That Walter and Thomas Ruddiman should have been prepared to issue a volume of young Fergusson's poems shows the esteem in which they held him by the end of 1772 and argues some degree of popularity for Fergusson's *Weekly Magazine* contributions. We know from other sources that his Scots contributions were widely esteemed, but there is no such evidence for the popularity of his English verses. . . .

The volume was on the point of publication when Fergusson's poem **"Good Eating"** appeared in *The Weekly Magazine* on 17 December 1772. It is in the now familiar burlesque, mock-heroic style, which continued to have a fatal fascination for him. It opens:

Hear, O ye host of Epicurus! hear!
Each portly form, whose overhanging paunch
Can well denote the all-transcendent joy
That springs unbounded from fruition full
Of rich repast; to you I consecrate
The song advent'rous; . . .

He hails roast beef as "monarch of the festive throng", especially when accompanied

By *root Hibernian,* or *plumb-pudding* rare,

and ends by recommending the reader to work up an appetite by walking by Arthur's Seat to Duddingston (then famous for its sheep-head dinners and today still boasting the Sheep-Heid Inn) or to Lawson's tavern on the shore at Leith:

Ye who for health, for exercise, for air,
Oft saunter from *Edina's* smoke-capt spires,
And, by the grassy hill or dimpl'd brook
An appetite revive, should oft-times stray
O'er *Arthur's seat's* green pastures to the town,
For *sheep-heads* and bone-bridges fam'd of yore,
That in our country's annals stands yclept,
Fair *Duddingstonia,* where you may be blest
With simple fare and vegetative sweets,
Freed from the clamours of the busy world.
    Or, if for recreation you should stray
To *Leithian* shore, and breathe the keener air
Wafted from Neptune's empire of the main;
If appetite invite, and cash prevail,
Ply not your joints upon the homeward track,
Till LAWSON, chiefest of the Scottish hosts!
To nimble-footed waiters give command
The cloth to lay. . . .

At this point the poem, which begins in a large general manner, becomes very much an Edinburgh affair, and that must have been part of its appeal to its first readers. It is

perhaps surprising that Fergusson should have continued to celebrate his city in this English burlesque style after he had found and so successfully employed a Scots style so much more vigorous and authentic.

1773 opened with the publication in *The Weekly Magazine* of **"The Delights of Virtue"**, a moralising piece in English quatrains whose movement suggests Gray's "Elegy". But on 21 January he returned to Scots, with one of his finest poems, **"Caller Water"**, a poem in praise of fresh water which, deftly handled and cunningly constructed, turned out to be a poem in praise of the Edinburgh lasses. Water kept "father Adie" healthy in Eden (Fergusson uses that familiar tone in talking of scriptural characters that Burns was to exploit so happily); it is prescribed by doctors who confuse their patients' noddles by giving it a pretentious Latin name; it provides healthful swimming; it cures the colic; it keeps the lasses trig and bonny. The opening has a fine humorous directness:

Whan father *Adie* first pat spade in
The bonny yeard of antient Eden,
His amry [*cupboard*] had nae liquor laid in
    To fire his mou',
Nor did he thole [*suffer*] his wife's upbraidin'
    For being fou [*drunk*] . . .

In the tenth stanza of this fifteen-stanza poem he turns to the beneficial effect of fresh water on "the bonny lasses" and he stays with this aspect until the end, concluding with a deft little turn to the poet himself, who modestly ends the final line:

O may they still pursue the way
To look sae feat, [*pretty*] sae clean, sae gay!
Than shall their beauties glance
    like *May,*
        And, like her, be
The goddess of the vocal Spray,
        The Muse, and me.

The language has become almost standard English now, and a phrase such as "goddess of the vocal Spray" taken out of context might sound like a high formal neo-classic English. Yet Fergusson's Scots can accommodate this kind of language; it is fluent and confident enough to allow him to include English in more ceremonial moments of the poem, as in this conclusion. A poem like **"Caller Water"** shows clearly how Fergusson found a way of developing a poetic vocabulary larger and more versatile than either a limited regional Scots or a standard neo-classic English, and this indeed is always an advantage open to a Scots poet. Fergusson did not invent this ability to move freely within both languages: the Middle Scots poets, too, could draw on an English vocabulary to enrich their Scots at appropriate moments. Burns was to do this too.

Fergusson's next Scots poem to appear in *The Weekly Magazine* was **"Mutual Complaint of Plainstanes and Causey in their Mother-tongue"**. It is a dialogue in octosyllabic couplets. (In content though not in verse-form this clearly influenced Bruns's "The Brigs of Ayr"; the verse form is seen in Burns's "The Twa Dogs".) Each party in the dialogue complains of what it has to bear and thinks it has a worse lot than the other—causey with wagons, horses, coaches, Highland chairmen and the Luckenbooths, plainstanes (designed for nothing heavier than "sole of shoe or pump") trod by "burden-bearers heavy shoe" and loutish rustic characters. The result is both a picture of Edinburgh street life and a satire on snobbery. Each suggests taking his case before the Town Council, which gives Fergusson the opportunity to show off his knowledge of legal terminology:

> I dinna care a single jot
> Tho' summon'd by a shelly-coat, [*sheriff's officer*]
> Sae leally I'll propone [*vigorously; put forward*] defences,
> As get ye flung [*baffled*] for my expences;
> Your libel I'll impugn *verbatim*
> And hae a *magnum damnum datum;* . . .

They finally agree to take the matter to the Robin Hood debating society, and the poem ends with Plainstanes agreeing to the suggestion just before dawn brings the first pedestrians and puts an end to the night-time conversation:

> Content am I—But east the gate is
> The sun, wha taks his leave of Thetis,
> And comes to wauken honest fock,
> That gang to wark at sax o'clock;
> It sets us to be dumb a while,
> And let our words gie place to toil.

The appearance of Thetis, emphasized in the half-comic rhyme, is yet another example of ease in introducing such classical references in a wholly familiar manner in a Scots context. . . .

Fergusson's next poem in *The Weekly Magazine* appeared on 8 April. It is in his familiar burlesque style, mock-heroic couplets, but the interest lies less in its somewhat undergraduate humour than in its subject: he is taking off Henry Mackenzie, the celebrated and popular author of the sentimental novel *The Man of Feeling,* a book that was to be passionately admired by Burns on whom it did not have a good influence. But Fergusson was more confident in his attitude to contemporary literary fashion than Burns was able to be, and he could laugh equally at Henry Mackenzie and Dr. Johnson, representatives of two very different strains in the literary culture of his day. A few weeks before the appearance of Fergusson's poem, Mackenzie's tragedy *The Prince of Tunis* was performed in Edinburgh to great applause, though there was some criticism of its excessive feeling. Fergusson gleefully mocks the whole cult of feeling associated with Mackenzie, putting the monologue into the mouth of a sensitive sow mourning the destruction by butchers of her husband and children:

> Thrice happy, had I liv'd in Jewish time

> When swallowing pork or pig was doom'd a crime;
> My husband long had blest my longing arms
> Long, long had known love's sympathetic charms!

"Love's sympathetic charms", a phrase that Burns would have swallowed whole, is rendered ludicrous when put into the mouth of a pig, as indeed is the whole concept of a "man of feeling" when applied to an animal that resigns life in sorrow, "to be number'd 'mongst the *feeling swine*". **"The Sow of Feeling"** is not a poem of any distinction, any more than Fergusson's poem "To Dr Samuel Johnson: Food for a new Edition of his Dictionary". But both are significant declarations of independence. . . .

Nothing that Fergusson had yet written prepared his readers for **"The Farmer's Ingle"**, which appeared in *The Weekly Magazine* on 13 May, 1773. This poem has long been known as the inspiration of Burns's "The Cotter's Saturday Night", but it is a remarkable work in its own right and in some respects is a better poem than Burns's. The Spenserian stanza in which it is written he got from James Thomson and Shenstone, but he uses it with his own kind of Scots *gravitas*. The line and a half from Virgil's fifth Eclogue, which he uses as epigraph, describing indulgence in the joys of Bacchus by the fireside in cold weather, is perhaps an unnecessary classical flourish, but it gives evidence of the poet's working in an assured literary tradition. It is strange that Burns, who really was a peasant while Fergusson was not, wrote "The Cotter's Saturday Night" to show off some model rustics to benevolent genteel observers whereas Fergusson describes, with knowledge and affection, what he sees. Here at last is a full-blooded Scots poem, written by the whole man, rich and musical and confident:

> Whan gloming grey out o'er the
>   welkin keeks, [*looks*]
>   Whan *Batie* ca's his owsen to
>   the byre,
> And *Thrasher John* sair dung, [*exhausted;*] his
>   barn-door steeks, [*shuts*]
>   And lusty lasses at the dighting
>   tire: [*winnowing grain*]
> What bangs fu'leal the e'enings
>   coming cauld, [*overcomes; thoroughly*]
>   And gars snaw-tapit [*makes; snow-topped*]
>   winter freeze
>   in vain;
> Gars dowie [*gloomy*] mortals look baith blythe
>   and bauld,
>   Nor fley'd wi' a'the poortith o'
>   the plain; [*frightened; poverty*]
> Begin, my Muse, and chant in hamely
>   strain.

The slow, sonorous movement of the opening line effectively transforms into Scots the kind of feeling we get at the opening of Gray's "Elegy", but the stanza moves at once into particularization of Scots names that make the rural activities real and local, not part of the sentimental reverie of the observer. The invocation to "my Muse" in the last line of the stanza might be expected to be pretentious or in some way out of place, but it is carried by the movement of the verse and the tone of the whole stanza without strain.

The second stanza describes the gudeman coming home with a deliberate dropping of Scots words where they fall most effectively—

> Sods, peats, and *heath'ry trufs* [*turfs*] the
>   chimley fill,
>   And gar their thick'ning smeek salute
>   the lift;. . . .

The third stanza shows the gudewife making everything ready for her man's arrival, with a relish of rustic fare that is effortlessly tied to a generalization about hard work requiring good food and drink (there is an echo back to the epigraph from Virgil, but the difference between the Virgilian and the Scottish festivity is as important as any similarity):

> Weel kens the *gudewife* that the
>   pleughs [*ploughs*] require
>   A heartsome *meltith*, [*meal;*] and refreshing
>   synd [*drink*]
> O' nappy liquor, [*strong ale*] o'er a bleezing
>   fire:
>   Sair wark and poortith douna weel be
>   join'd.
> Wi'butter'd *bannocks* now the girdle
>   reeks, [*smokes*]
>   I' the far nook [*small barrel;*] the *bowie*
>   briskly reams; [*rises like cream*]
> The readied *kail* stand by the chimley
>   cheeks,
>   And had the riggin het wi' welcome
>   steams, [*keep the roof hot*]
>   Whilk than the daintiest kitchen
>   nicer seems.

The inversion of the last line here seems a bit forced, but then this is a formal poem, using a carefully wrought structure, and the kind of formality, even artificially, represented by this inversion, even though we may suspect that the verb is put at the end of the line for the sake of the rhyme, is not wildly out of place.

The fourth stanza moves to an unforced moralizing on the superior healthfullness of hard work and simple fare to idleness and drugs (a theme developed in the second canto of Thomson's *Castle of Indolence,* but handled here in tones of proverbial rustic wisdom rather than of genteel moralising) and the fifth develops this into a tribute to the achievements of Scotsmen of old, brought up on simple fare. Then, in the sixth stanza, he turns again to the scene before him:

> The couthy cracks [*sociable talk*] begin whan
>   supper's o'er

> The cheering *bicker* [*drinking cup;*] gars
>   them glibly gash [*freely talk*]
> O'simmer's *showery blinks* [*moments of
>   sunshine*] and winters sour,
>   Whase floods did erst their mailins [*farm;*]
>   produce hash: [*damage*]
> 'Bout *kirk* and *market* eke their tales gae on,
>   How *Jock* woo'd *Jenny* here to be his
>   bride,
> And there how *Marion,* for a bastard son,
>   Upo'the *cutty-stool* was forc'd to ride,
>   The waefu'scald o'our *Mess John* [*parish
>   minister*] to bide.

The last line of this stanza, like the last line of many of the stanzas, including the first, does not employ the Spenserian Alexandrine but uses the shorter pentameter. He uses the Alexandrine in only four stanzas, including the final one, in order to round the stanza off with a special weight or in some other way to involve the reader in the movement of a longer line, as in the description of the children quaking with fear when they hear stories of ghosts and warlocks:

> The fient a chiep's amang the bairnies [*devil a
>   (i.e., not any)*] now;
>   For a'their anger's wi'their hunger gane:
> Ay maun the childer, wi'a fastin mou',
>   Grumble and greet, [*cry*] and make an
>   unco mane, [*great moan*]
> In rangles [*groups*] round before the ingle's
>   low [*fire's blaze*]:
>   Frae *gudame's* mouth auld warld tale
>   they hear,
> O' *Warlocks* [*wizards*] louping round the
>   *Wirrikow,*
>   O' gaists that win [*live*] in glen and
>   kirk-yard drear,
> Whilk touzles [*tousles*] a'their tap [*top*] and gars
>   [*makes*] them shak wi'fear.

And so the evening wears on. In the tenth stanza we have an attractive picture of the gudeman relaxing, stretched out on a wooden settle with his cat and collie dog, and in the eleventh he is shown discussing the next day's work with the lads. In the twelfth stanza they all retire to bed, and the final stanza sounds an eloquent note of benediction:

> Peace to the husbandman and a'his tribe,
>   Whase care fells a'our wants [*supplies*] frae
>   year to year;
> Lang may his sock and couter turn the
>   gleyb, [*ploughshare; coulter; glebe*]
>   And bauks o'corn bend down wi'
>   laded ear.
> May SCOTIA's simmers ay look gay and
>   green,
>   Her yellow har'sts [*harvests*] frae scowry
>   blasts decreed;
> May a'her tenants sit fu'snug and
>   bien, [*prosperous*]

Frae the hard grip of ails and
  poortith [*poverty*] freed,
And a lang lasting train o'peaceful
  hours succeed. . . .

Except for "lang" and perhaps "o'" this line could take its place easily in an English poem. But it is a tribute to Fergusson's mastery of his medium that it takes its place with equal ease in a poem written in Scots. For though **"The Farmer's Ingle"** is a Scots poem, this does not mean that it derives entirely and solely from Scottish literary tradition. On the contrary, the stanza form, the tone and even the subject show English influence; the significant point is that these influences have been thoroughly assimilated, and are used in an assured Scots way. The strength of a national art does not lie in its refusal to borrow from other national arts, but in its ability to domesticate its borrowings properly in its own medium. This is what Fergusson does in **"The Farmer's Ingle"**, and it is something that no Scottish poet of the eighteenth century had yet done.

"The Ghaists: A Kirk-yard Eclogue" appeared in *The Weekly Magazine* on 27 May 1773. It is a dialogue between the ghosts of George Heriot and George Watson (Edinburgh merchants who had left bequests to found educational "hospitals"—now schools—in the city), who deplore the effect in Scotland of the proposed "Mortmain Bill" introduced in Westminster. The bill (which, as a result of Scottish opposition, was eventually restricted in scope to apply to England only) was intended to enable charitable foundations in Britain to realize their assets and invest the proceeds in three per cent funds, which would be the future source of their income. This would have impoverished certain Scottish foundations, and Scottish national feeling was aroused. Fergusson's poem was a contribution to the debate, and at the same time a defence of the national integrity of Scotland. . . . The verse is the heroic couplet, handled with considerable weight and flexible enough to accommodate such extremes as an echo of Hamlet ("But look, the Morn, in russet mantle clad . . . ")—

For tho' the eastern lift betakens day,
Changing her rokelay [*cloak*] black for mantle
  grey—

and the spitting irony of

Starving for England's weel at *three per cent.* . . .

For all his successes with Scots poetry by this time, Fergusson was still enamoured of the English burlesque, mock-heroic style, and he returned to it again with **"The Bugs"**, which appeared in *The Weekly Magazine* on 10 June 1773. What was it that so fascinated him about this rather childish form of poetic humour? Was it that he was most at home in an English poetic style when it contained an element of parody? Was there a streak of the incorrigible under-

graduate persisting in him? The traditions handed down about Fergusson's life in Edinburgh suggest that there is certainly some truth in the latter diagnosis; he was a great practical joker and he liked to abandon himself to the moment of convivial celebration. And he was still a very young man: he was only twenty-four when he died. But it may well be true that there was a more serious element in his constant recurring to English mock-heroic burlesque, that he wanted to keep the English poetic tradition at arm's length and that he could best do this by employing an English style in which he could simultaneously exhibit a certain virtuosity and mock the very style he was successfully employing. Of course it might be asked why English poets of the first half of the eighteenth century employed such a style—it was, after all, from them that Fergusson learned it. This is a complex question, and part of the answer seems to be that on the one hand neo-classic critical theory postulated the epic or heroic as the highest poetic mode while on the other hand the social tone of the age of Queen Anne, and the "Queen Anne Wits" who dominated London literary culture in the early years of the century, and who were really responsible for the emergence of the English eighteenth-century mock-heroic style, were a group of urban sophisticates who theoretically worshipped Homer as the great father of poetry while living in a world as far removed from the Homeric age as could be imagined. Fergusson's Edinburgh was different; but Fergusson had his own cultural reasons for employing a mode developed earlier in the century by English poets to cope with the difference between their poetic theory and their cultural situation. It was not, however, the mode in which he realised his true poetic potential. . . .

Fergusson's next poem in *The Weekly Magazine* was **"On Seeing a Butterfly in the Street"**, written in octosyllabic Scots couplets. It is a skilful translation into Scots of an early eighteenth century English poetic mode, describing a butterfly—"Daft gowk in MACARONI dress"—that has flown from the country into the city, "To cast a dash at REIKIE's cross", and there finds itself quite out of place. The moral is that people should mind their own business and not stray into inappropriate places. "Hame Content. A Satire", which appeared on 8 July, is also in octosyllabic Scots couplets, but though it is in its way a moral poem it is more complex than the butterfly poem. One of its main themes is his determination to celebrate his native country rather than write of classical scenes:

The ARNO and the TIBUR lang
Hae run fell clear in Roman sang;
But, save the reverence of schools!
They're baith but lifeless dowy [*gloomy*] pools,
Dought they compare wi'bonny Tweed,
As clear as ony lammer-bead? [*amber-bead*]
Or are their shores mair sweet and gay
Than Fortha's haughs or banks o'Tay? [*low
  ground at riverside*]. . . .

In **"Hame Content"** this tone is achieved as a final turn to a poem that moves through a series of moods, some of them satirical rather than elegiac, and very colloquial in accent:

> Unyoke then, man, an'binna sweer [*don't be reluctant*]
> To ding a hole in ill-haind gear; [*drive; uselessly hoarded*]
> O think that ELID, wi'wyly fitt, [*old age; cunning foot*]
> Is wearing nearer bit by bit;
> Gin yence [*if once*] he claws you wi'his paw,
> What's siller for? Fiend haet awa, [*money*]
> But GOWDEN playfair, that may please
> The second SHARGER till he dies.

The concluding two-and-a-half lines of this passage (saying that once a man is dead his money will only go to the "sharger", the weakling, who inherits his wealth, until he in turn dies—"dies" to be pronounced "dees", as the rhyme indicates), and the ironic question "What's siller for?" that precedes them, show Fergusson master of a lively, colloquial satirical mood, which he skilfully modulates as the poem proceeds to move through patriotic celebration of elegy. Fergusson is in control throughout the poem, and knows precisely what he wants to do, and does it effectively.

Fergusson's next poem to appear in *The Weekly Magazine,* on 22 July, was **"Leith Races"**, in the old Scottish tradition of poetry of popular festivity and using the same old stanza form he had used in **"Hallow-Fair"**. It is best known today as the model for Burn's "Holy Fair", but it is a fine celebratory poem in its own right.

The poem begins with an encounter. This is very much in the ballad tradition, as Matthew McDiarmid has noted, but it is also in a tradition that is much more widespread than the ballad, the old mediaeval tradition of the poet beginning by narrating his going forth into a wood or the fields and meeting with someone who provides the reason for the poem. Where Fergusson got this from we cannot precisely say; it may be that he thought it up for himself and thus unconsciously made contact with an age-old poetic mode. The poem begins with a meeting in a July country setting:

> In JULY month, ae [*one*] bonny morn,
>   Whan Nature's rokelay [*cloak*] green
> Was spread o'er ilka rigg [*every ridge*] o'corn
> To charm our roving een; [*eyes*]
> Glouring about I saw a quean, [*girl*]
>   The fairest 'neath the lift; [*sky*]
> Her EEN ware o'the siller sheen,
> Her SKIN like snawy drift,
>   Sae white that day.
> Quod she, "I ferly unco sair, [*marvel very much*]
>   "That ye sud musand gae, [*should musing*]
> "Ye wha hae sung o'HALLOW-FAIR,

> "Her winter's pranks and play:
> "Whan on LEITH-SANDS the racers rare,
>   "Wi' Jocky louns are met,
> "Their orro [*spare*] pennies there to ware, [*spend*]
>   "And drown themsel's in debt
>   "Fu' deep that day."

The use of the old Scots present participle in "musand" gives notice that this is to be a very Scottish—one might say a fiercely Scottish—poem. . . .

The poem is essentially a series of brightly coloured pictures, each one drawn vividly and jocularly and each succeeding the other in rapid movement. The effect is like the translation of a Breughel picture into a moving film. There is a sense of openness to life, an amused tolerance of follies and excesses, a satirical tone that is at the same time friendly and participatory, that make this poem more than an exercise in an old tradition of poetry of popular merry-making. Burns was to recapture precisely this combination of qualities in his **"Holy Fair"**. How far below this Fergusson could fall when, instead of drawing on a lively old Scots tradition, he drew on a somewhat debased English tradition of poetry of conviviality, can be seen if we set a poem such as **"Leith Races"** beside a song he wrote (to the air, "Lumps of Pudding") about the same time:

> HOLLO! keep it up, boys—and push round the glass,
> Let each seize his bumper, and drink to his lass:
> Away with dull thinking—'tis madness to think—
> And let those be sober who've nothing to drink.
>   Tal de ral & c.

As Dr. Johnson said of Macpherson's Ossian, a man could write such stuff for ever if he would abandon his mind to it.

Fergusson had not yet done with the English burlesque, mock-heroic mode. He was at it again in *The Weekly Magazine* of 5 August 1773 in a poem entitled **"Tea"**. It opens with one enormous sentence:

> YE maidens modest! on whose sullen brows
> Hath weaning chastity her wrinkles cull'd,
> Who constant labour o'er consumptive oil
> At midnight knell, to wash sleep's nightly balm
> From closing eye-lids, with the grateful drops
> Of TEA's blest juices; list th' obsequious lays
> That come not with Parnassian honours crown'd
> To dwell in murmurs o'er your sleepy sense,
> But fresh from ORIENT blown to chace far off
> Your LETHARGY, that dormant NEEDLES rous'd
> May pierce the waving MANTUA's silken folds:
> For many a dame, in chamber sadly pent,
> Hath this reviving liquid call'd to life;
> And well it did, to mitigate the frowns
> Of anger reddening on *Lucinda*'s brow

With flash malignant, that had harbour'd there,
If she at masquerade, or play, or ball,
Appear'd not in her newest, best attire,
But VENUS, goddess of th' eternal smile,
Knowing that stormy brows but ill become
Fair patterns of her beauty, hath ordain'd
Celestial Tea. . . .

On 2 September 1773 Fergusson returned to Scots with a poem in *The Weekly Magazine* entitled **"To the Principal and Professors of the University of St Andrews, on their superb treat to Dr Samuel Johnson"**. This was a characteristic piece of nose-thumbing at the Establishment. Dr Johnson, starting on his famous tour of the Western Isles with Boswell, was first proceeding up the east coast of Scotland. They visited St. Andrews where, as Boswell duly noted, "the professors entertained us with a very good dinner" on 19 August. Fergusson had an affection but no great veneration for his *alma mater,* while his feelings about Johnson were affected by Johnson's known anti-Scottish views. Here was an opportunity to write a satiric poem in assertive Scots putting the great man and his hosts in their place. The tone is deliberately disrespectful: Dr. Johnson is "Sammy":

St Andrews town may look right gawsy, [*stately*]
Nae GRASS will grow upon her cawsey, [*street*]
Nor wa'flow'rs of a yellow dye,
Glour dowy h'er her RUINS high, [*gaze*]
Sin SAMY's head weel pang'd wi' lear
    [*crammed; learning*]
Has seen the ALMA MATER there:
Regents, my winsome billy boys!
'Bout him you've made an unco noise;
Nae doubt for him your bells wad clink,
To find him upon EDEN's brink,
An' a' things nicely set in order,
Wad keep him on the Fifan border:
I'se arrant now frae France an' Spain
Baith COOKS and SCULLIONS many ane
Wad gar the pats [*make; pots*] an'kettles tingle
Around the college kitchen ingle [*fire*]
To fleg frae a' your craigs the roup, [*frighten; throats;*]
Wi' reeking het and crieshy [*greasy*] soup;
And *snails* and *puddocks* [*frogs*] many hunder
Wad beeking lie the hearth-stane under,
    [*warming*]
Wi' roast and boild, an' a'kin kind,
To heat the body, cool the mind.

But if he had been there, the poet would have arranged a purely Scottish diet. He remembers that Johnson had defined oats in his Dictionary as a food given to horses in England and eaten by men and women in Scotland. Let him then learn something more about Scottish food. His proposed menu begins with

        a haggis fat,
Weel tottl'd [*boiled*] in a seything pat, [*boiling*

pot]
Wi' *spice* and *ingans* [*onions*] weel ca'd thro', . . .

and continues with "a gude sheep's head", then some "gude fat brose", washing it down with "the contents o' sma' ale quegh".

Then let his wisdom girn an' snarl [*grimace*]
O'er a weel-tostit girdle farl, [*oat cake*]
An' learn, that maugre o' his wame, [*in spite of his stomach*]
Ill bairns are ay best heard at hame.

The poem proceeds to lament that Scotland "maun stap ilk birky's mow" with foreign "eistacks" (dainties) when her native peasantry made do with "cog o' brose an' cutty spoon". If, he concludes, critics accuse him of being unfair to Fife (not, significantly, of being unfair to Dr. Johnson), then let them come and drink with him, and the process will improve their prose "and heal my rhyme".

The poem races along with high satiric exuberance, the Scots words almost shouting their native vigour at the anti-Scottish doctor. It is a joke, a show of high spirits, a Scottish nationalist exhibition piece, an "occasional" poem. It is not the finest kind of poetry of which Fergusson was capable, but it is first-rate of its kind.

On 16 September *The Weekly Magazine* published Fergusson's poem on the Town Council elections, entitled simply **"The Election"**. It is in the old Scottish stanza he had used in **"Leith Races"** and gives a humorously mocking account of the activities of election day. Burns was to remember some of Fergusson's vivid phrases:

The DEACONS at the counsel stent [*hasten*]
    To get themsel's presentit:
For towmonths twa their saul is lent [*two years; soul*]
    For the town's gude indentit: . . .

The last phrase is echoed in Burn's "The Twa Dogs":

Wha aiblins, thrang a-parliamentin' [*perhaps; busy*]
For Britain's gude his saul indentin . . .

Fergusson's next poem to appear in *The Weekly Magazine,* **"Elegy on John Hogg, late Porter to the University of St Andrews"**, is very much a St. Andrews poem, full of local allusions and university reminiscences. It is in the "Standart *Habby*" form, and again it shows Fergusson adapting a tradition of mock elegy to a more serious mood, though here the tone of jovial reminiscence overcomes the note of loss and the mood is almost that of a wake, combining mourning and festivity. It is a deftly poised poem, and shows how fluently Fergusson could now handle this old Scottish verse form.

The Weekly Magazine of 21 October published Fergusson's second poem laughing at Dr. Johnson, **"To Dr

Samuel Johnson: Food for a new Edition of his Dictionary". Here Fergusson's fondness for burlesque finds vent in a somewhat schoolboyish parody of Dr. Johnson's fondness of a Latinized vocabulary. . . .

On 11 November *The Weekly Magazine* printed Fergusson's poem **"A Drink Eclogue. Landlady, Brandy and Whisky"**. This is a flyting, in Scots heroic couplets, between Brandy and Whisky. Brandy sneers at Whisky as the drink of "porters, chairmen, city-guard" (all of whom tended to be Highlanders: chairmen were the men who carried sedan chairs) and boasts of its own superior breeding; Whisky complains that the gentlefolk nowadays despise their native spirit and prefer imported stuff:

> Yet I am hameil, [*home-bred*] there's the sour
>   mischance!
> I'm no frae Turkey, Italy, or France;
> For now our Gentles gabbs [*mouths*] are grown
>   sae nice,
> At thee they toot, [drink] an' never speer [*ask*]
>   my price:
> Witness—for thee they hight their
>   tenants rent,
> And fill their lands wi' poortith, [*poverty*]
>   discontent;
> Gar them o'er seas for cheaper mailins [*farms*]
>   hunt,
> An' leave their ain as bare's the
>   Cairn-o' mount.

There is social criticism here, as well as the same kind of complaint about the rejection of native traditions that we find in the **"Elegy, On the Death of Scots Music"**. Brandy replies that the drinking of brandy by landlords is not the cause of tenants' poverty, which is caused by the tenants' love of whisky:

> For love to you, there's mony a tenant
>   gaes
> Bare-ars'd and barefoot o'er the
>   Highland braes:
> For you nae mair the thrifty gudewife
>   sees
> Her lasses kirn, [*chorn*] or birze [*press*] the
>   dainty cheese;
> CRUMMIE nae mair for Jenny's hand
>   will crune
> Wi' milkness dreeping frae her teats
>   adown:
> For you o'er ear' the ox his fate
>   partakes,
> And fa's a victim to the bludey aix.

This passage contains an echo of Gray's "Elegy":

> For them no more the blazing hearth shall burn,
>   Or busy housewife ply her evening care;
> No children run to lisp their sire's return,
>   Or climb his knees the envied kiss to share.

Yet Fergusson's tone is not Gray's, and there is nothing in the mournful flow of Gray's lines to compare with Fergusson's harsh line

> And fa's a victim to the bludey aix.

Whisky retorts that it is Brandy that makes greedy bankers embezzle the maiden's dowry; Brandy abuses Whisky as a "haveril Scot"

>   that for ay maun dwell
> In poet's garret, or in chairman's
>   cell,
> While I shall yet on bien-clad [*well-furnished*]
>   tables stand,
> Bouden [*laden*] wi' a' the daintiths o' the
>   land.

Whisky replies by boasting of the inspiration it has given to poets, notably Allan Ramsay ("Allie"), and then Brandy summons the landlady to decide the issue between them. The landlady points out that

> Inlakes [*deficiencies*] o' BRANDY we can soon
>   supply
> By WHISKY tinctur'd wi' the SAFFRON's
>   dye,

and turns on Brandy:

>   Will you your breeding threep, ye
>   *mongrel loun*!
> Frae hame-bred liquor dy'd to colour
>   brown?
> So FLUNKY braw, whan drest in master's
>   claise,
> Struts to Auld Reikie's cross on sunny
>   days,
> Till some auld comerade, ablins [*perhaps*] out o'
>   place,
> Near the vain upstart shaws his meagre
>   face;
> Bombaz'd he loups frae sight, and jooks
>   his ken, [*gets quickly out of the way*]
> Fley'd to be seen amang the tassel'd
>   train.

This is an unexpected turn at the end. Not only is Brandy dismissed as an upstart, merely whisky died yellow or brown ("brown", by the way, is clearly to be pronounced "broon"), but the analogy is then made with upstart flunkies parading at the Cross of Edinburgh, and the poem ends on a note of social satire. We have already seen Fergusson's skill at moving a poem round from its ostensible subject to its sure subject; here the movement is done with great speed and neatness.

Two poems by Fergusson appeared in *The Weekly Magazine* of 25 November 1773, **"To my Auld Breeks"**, a ruefully comic address to his worn-out trousers in Scots octosyllabic couplets, and **"Rob. Fergusson's Last Will"**, in English octosyllabic couplets. A **"Codicile to Rob. Fergusson's Last Will"**, also in English octosyllables but interlarded with Latin legal phrases, appeared on 23 December. It was his last contribution, and the poem itself, like the previous one, though sounding a note of rather forced humour, is some indication of his foreboding of death. A letter to a friend written in October 1773 is subscribed "Your afflicted humble servant", while a verse letter addressed to Charles Lorimer refers to his gloomy state, says that he has given up drink in the fear that he would be attacked by "new horrors", but looks forward to the time when he will be restored to health and be sociable again.

Jerry O'Brien (essay date 1984)

SOURCE: "The Sonsie Muse: The Satiric Use of Neoclassical Diction in the Poems of Robert Fergusson," in *Studies in Scottish Literature,* Vol. XIX, 1984, pp. 165-76.

[*In the following excerpt, O'Brien discusses Fergusson's satirical use of neoclassical conventions in his pastoral verse.*]

Modern criticism of Scots literature has provided us with many fine studies on the poetry of Robert Fergusson. Among the revelations disclosed, the influence of Fergusson's Scots poems on the imagination of Robert Burns is of great significance. We know now with certainly that Burns's discovery of Fergusson's poems toward the latter part of 1784 marked the turning point in the development of his poetic sensibility from the neoclassical and sentimental strains of the eighteenth century to the forms and subjects of his native Scots. By the spring of 1785 the influence of Fergusson can be clearly felt in Burns's work, and the intensity of his creative development during the next twelve months at Mossgiel to the spring of 1786 brought forth the greatest poems of the Kilmarnock edition and some which were not printed until later. Although Burns's letters have helped little in fixing the exact date of his introduction to Fergusson (his poems provide us with more reliable evidence), they do indicate the dramatic importance the poems had for him. In his letter to Dr. Moore of August 2, 1787, Burns wrote, "Rhyme, except some religious pieces which are in print, I had given up; but meeting with Fergusson's Scotch Poems, I strung anew my wildly-sounding, rustic lyre with emulating vigour." And in verse, Burns remembered the debt he owed to Fergusson: "O thou, my elder brother in Misfortune, / By far my elder Brother in the muse."

Both Burns and Fergusson faced the dilemma in their creative lives of having to choose between English and Scottish poetic models. Both were keenly aware of the neoclassical tradition—Fergusson through his education at St. Andrews, Burns through his intense self-education—and both had come under the spell of the Scots literary revival initiated by Allan Ramsay in the first two decades of the century. But Ramsay himself had stopped writing by 1728, and until Fergusson's emergence no other poet had managed to keep alive the verse forms and language that Ramsay had retrieved from the medieval "makaris" with equal success. Edinburgh itself symbolized the conflicting allegiances of literary artists: on the one hand, Watson's and Ramsay's popular anthologies of Scots verse brought the native tradition back to life, and on the other, the continued popularity of Pope and the sentimentalist Shenstone made English the only acceptable language for the genteel literati.

One of the many traces of the poetic diction and sensibility of the neoclassical can be found in Fergusson's use of classical imagery. In his Scots poems these images are invariably used for satiric purposes; the artificial language of the English poets becomes a witty, self-conscious statement on the inadequacies of that language for true expression. The self-important grandeur of the classical figures of speech contrasts strongly with the "hamely" subjects and style of Scots vernacular verse. A tension is created between the two modes which could not go unnoticed and unappreciated by the poet's audience. But it also has the inverse effect at times: it can be a way of creating a formalized continuity between the two, bestowing a mock literary validity on the Scots verse by uniting it with an "approved" longstanding tradition. Fergusson's personal battles with neoclassicism as an inappropriate language for his unique creative impulses were Burns's battles, too. For each of them, the satiric use of these images becomes one way of exorcising the neoclassical demon.

Fergusson's first surviving attempt in Scots is a translation of "Horace, Ode 11, Lib. I" from Latin, and the deft juxtaposition of Scots colloquial expressions with the exalted regard demanded of the ancient model creates a delightful tension which seems to comment upon both:

> Ne'er fash your *thumb* what *gods* decree
> To be the *weird* o' you or me,
> Nor deal in *cantrup's* kittle cunning
> To speir how fast your days are running.
>
> (*ll.* 1-4)

And later:

> The day looks *gash,* toot aff your *horn,*
> Nor care yae *strae* about the *morn.*
>
> (*ll.* 13-14)

The poem may be derivative in its choice of language, but it reveals a keen awareness of alliteration, assonance, and the beauty of a smooth and easy rhythm.

Fergusson's next Scots poem, **"Elegy, on the Death of Mr David Gregory, Late Professor of Mathematics in the University of St Andrews,"** is a comic elegy in the line of Robert Semphill's "Life and Death of Habbie Simson," and like its model is written in the Habbie stanza. There are two classical references in the poem, and in each case the effect is one of contrast for the sake of gentle satire on the late professor. In the third stanza, Gregory's abilities are compared to those of Euclid, the

Greek master of geometry, but only to reveal that Gregory could divine "That *three* times *three* just made up nine; / But now he's dead" (*ll.* 17-18). In the fifth stanza, the effect is the same; we are told that Gregory can lecture equally well in architecture and "the nature o' the sector," and that "Of geometry he was the *hector;* / But now he's dead" (*ll.* 26, 29-30). The association of Euclid and Hector with Gregory is used to upbraid him in a mocking but affectionate way. In each case, part of the tension rests in the incongruity of the classical reference with the more common subject of the poem. . . .

The titles alone give us an idea of the nature and scope of Fergusson's English verse: there are pastorals in one part and pastorals in three parts; there are pastoral dialogues and pastoral monologues; there are pastoral elegies; there is an ode to hope, an ode to pity, an ode to horror, and an ode to disappointment; there are dirges, lyrics, and songs. His later English poems are pointedly satiric in general, but in most of these earlier poems it is hard to find where sentiment stops and unintentional satire begins, so labored and insincere is the effect.

Compare, for example, these sections from Fergusson's **"Pastoral III. Night"** (which appeared anonymously in Ruddiman's *The Weekly Magazine, or Edinburgh Amusement* on February 21, 1771) with his first published poem in Scots, **"The Daft-Days"** (which appeared in the same publication, and with his name, on January 2, 1772), for a dramatic instance of his real poetic affinities:

> 1. While yet gray twilight does his empire hold,
> Drive all our heifers to the peaceful fold;
> With sullied wing grim darkness soars along,
> And larks to nightingales resign the song.
>
>   (*ll.* 1-4)

> 2. Now mirk December's dowie face
> Glours our the rigs wi' sour grimace,
> While, thro' his *minimum* of space,
>   The bleer-ey'd sun,
> Wi' blinkin light and stealing pace,
>   His race doth run.
>
>   (*ll.* 1-6)

> 1. The grassy meads that smil'd serenely gay,
> Cheer'd by the everburning lamp of day,
> In dusky hue attir'd, are cramp'd with colds,
> And springing flow'rets shut their crimson folds.
>
>   (*ll.* 9-12)

> 2. From naked groves nae birdie sings,
> To shepherd's pipe nae hillock rings,
> The breeze nae od'rous flavour brings
>   From *Borean* cave,
> And dwyning nature droops her wings
>   Wi' visage grave.
>
>   (*ll.* 7-12)

> 1. The weary ploughman flies the waving fields,
> To taste what fare his humble cottage yields:
> As bees that daily thro' the meadows roam,

Feed on the sweets they have prepar'd at home.

                                            (*ll.* 5-8)

> 2. *Auld Reekie!* thou'rt the canty hole,
>   A bield for mony caldrife soul,
> Wha snugly at thine ingle loll,
>   Baith warm and couth;
> While round they gar the bicker roll
>   To weet their mouth.
>
>   (*ll.* 19-24)

Could any contrast be more telling than this? To think that an artistic sensibility as unique and as confident as Fergusson's could be wasted for over three years on a poetic mode and language whose only redeeming value is his increasing dissatisfaction with it, is almost unbelievable. When we consider that he would live less than three more years, it becomes surely tragic. . . .

Fergusson's English verse is not without some quality; Burns incorporated quite a few of his lines into his own poetry, especially into "The Cottar's Saturday Night," and **"The Epilogue"** was a favorite in Edinburgh circles into the nineteenth century. But it always seems that either Damon or Strephon is stealing away to some green umbrage, or Alexis is counting her pearly dew-drops, or some whispering zephyr sweetly echoes from the banks, the hills, or the dells. If Fergusson learned nothing else through these dismal exercises, he learned the vocabulary of insincerity; he transformed it, with a gentle and even-handed satiric twist, into Scots verse of great humor and directness.

Further examples bear equal witness to the true source of Fergusson's poetic inspiration. Here is the opening stanza of his English poem, **"Retirement,"** a piece modelled on Horace, and with the traditional invocation to the muse:

> Come inspiration! from thy vernal bow'r,
>   To thy celestial voice attune the lyre;
> Smooth gliding strains in sweet profusion pour,
>   And aid my numbers with seraphic fire.
>
>   (*ll.* 1-4)

This becomes expressed in Scots in **"The King's Birth-Day in Edinburgh,"** in the glorious third stanza:

> O *Muse,* be kind, and dinna fash us
> To flee awa' beyont Parnassus,
> Nor seek for *Helicon* to wash us,
>   That heath'nish spring;
> Wi' Highland whiskey scour our hawses,
>   And gar us sing.
>
>   (*ll.* 13-18)

The "seraphic fire" is now usquabae, and the neoclassical muse is begged to be kind (Parnassus is too high and the Helicon too wet); the association between poetic inspiration and its ancient source is here parodied by the poet's faith in the proven and more immediate efficacy of **"Highland Whiskey."** Again, the comic effect turns upon the artificiality of the neoclassical models, and its contrast with the realistic details of Scottish life. The gods are being dragged down to earth, but seem the better for it.

As if this were not enough, Fergusson's playful wit leads us into a tavern where the poet sits, plying the muse with liquor in an attempted seduction:

> Begin then, dame, ye've drunk your fill,
> You woudna hae the tither gill?
> You'll trust me, mair wou'd do you ill,
> > And ding you doitet;
> Troth 'twou'd be sair agains my will
> > To hae the wyte o't.
> > > (*ll.* 19-24)

We can imagine the opening phrase, "Begin then, dame," recited with appropriate classical solemnity as we recall the "begin, my muse" of the Homeric, Virgilian, and Miltonic epics, but then the unexpected "ye've drunk your fill," spoken with the feigned naiveté of the experienced ladies' man. The effect is powerful, and in characteristic economy of expression Fergusson manages to undermine an entire literary tradition. "The limmer's fairly flung" (*l.* 5), but so are we: in his treatment of the traditional compliment to the king, the king is never even mentioned.

Our sonsie muse re-emerges in the last two stanzas, however, as the traditional austere muse of the neoclassical pastoral. Rather than hear the hyperbolic renderings of the day's events by "each hero" (*l.* 85),

> She'll rather to the fields resort,
> Whare music gars the day seem short,
> Whare doggies play, and lambies sport
> > On gowany braes,
> Whare peerless Fancy hads her court,
> > And tunes her lays.
> > > (*ll.* 91-96)

Her "reversion" back to the traditional form is strikingly ironic; after having been introduced to the drinking muse, the conventional pastoral ending further questions the validity of the whole pastoral and ceremonial modes. She'd rather to the fields, and we'd rather let her go.

The facetious treatment of traditional poetic conventions is, of course, not new with Fergusson; it informs the artistic strategy of many poets throughout literary history. The Elizabethan sonneteers, for example, often tested the limits of the Petrarchan and classical conventions in an attempt to redefine the possibilities of a specific poetic mode. Sonnet I of Philip Sidney's "Astrophel and Stella" finds the poet unmoved by artificial sources of inspiration—the genuine source is elsewhere: "'Fool,' said my Muse to me, 'look in thy heart and write.'" And Sidney's sonnet XV suggests that poetic inspiration cannot be found in Parnassus, or the dictionary, or Petrarch, sighs, or wit; only the contemplation of the beloved can provide the satisfaction of love and fame. The beauty of this poem rests in the tension between the explicit criticism of the traditional conventions and the implicit establishment of Stella as an equally artificial source. Sidney well knows,

as Fergusson himself would learn, that the true source of inspiration is within the poet himself. . . .

We see, then, in Fergusson's English verse, an increasing dissatisfaction with the rigid and artificial trappings of the pastoral, and with the false and humorless morality of the sentimentalists. His increasing interest and experimentation in vernacular Scots forms and subjects during 1772 and 1773 paralleled his lack of interest, his satiric attacks, and his almost complete rejection of English as a language fit for sincere poetic expression. Further, the situations, themes, and techniques in which Fergusson showed interest in his early Scots poems and more significant English poems had a long tradition in Scots vernacular verse. He most certainly found affinity with the *Christis Kirk* poems of the fifteenth century, particularly in their attention to characteristic detail, their tone of mild satire, and their fast-paced rhythms and economic expression. Fergusson's heart spoke in Scots; he had to learn to write in Scots, or more properly, he had to acquire the courage to do so. His early successes gave him the confidence, and with the publication of **"The Sow of Feeling"** Fergusson effectively kissed goodbye any chance he may have had at finding acceptance in the more genteel circles of Edinburgh—Mackenzie was simply too popular. So at some point, probably by the end of 1772, Fergusson returned to where he had begun: plain, braid Scots.

Fergusson's **"Elegy, On the Death of Scots Music"** shows the influence of the poet's trials with the neoclassical pastoral and his finer poetic bond with the Scots experience. The classicism is most clear in the second and third stanzas, in which the poet describes "the feather'd choir," "the zephyrs of the spring," and "the sunny hill and dowie glen" (*ll.* 7, 11, 14). But the lament for lost music becomes a means for something much greater, as evidenced in the ninth stanza:

> Now foreign sonnets bear the gree,
> And crabbit queer variety
> Of sound fresh sprung frae *Italy,*
> > A bastard breed!
> Unlike that saft-tongu'd melody
> > Which now lies dead.
> > > (*ll.* 49-54)

The poet has developed the influence of the "foreign sonnets" himself in the opening stanzas; the poem then becomes a self-contained piece of literary criticism, almost a poem about writing poems, or, more to the point, about the creative dilemma of the contemporary Scoto-English artist. It is an extraordinary poem in its deft handling of the Scots and the English poetic experiences. As Allan H. MacLaine has written, "the '**Elegy**' is a self-conscious expression of the eighteenth-century Scots revivalist spirit, of a culture in danger of being overwhelmed from outside—a culture fighting for its life, so to speak, wishing to preserve intact its ancient heritage and identity."

Fergusson's assimilation of the pastoral tradition to his

native Scots received one of its finest expressions in **"Caller Water."** In the first three stanzas Fergusson depicts the prelapsarian golden age of the pastoral garden in terms of Scots rural life: "The bonny yeard of antient Eden" (*l.* 2). The careful juxtaposition of Christian and classical imagery with the distinctive, natural flavor of the Scots dialect creates a tension that is wry and humorous, but that tends to humanize the classical rather than expose its inadequacies. And playfully, the rhyme of "their lays / *Anacreontic*" with "As big's the Pontic" indeed suggests the pretensions of those "fuddlin' Bardies now-a-days" (*ll.* 21-22, 24, 19). . . .

Fergusson is Burns's source for the satiric application of classical imagery, and though this may be a lesser point of similarity between the two poets, it represents in miniature the greater tension that both felt in the most important crises in their artistic careers—the decision to abandon English in favor of Scots. Fergusson's rejection of the neoclassical mode taught him a lesson that only a mortal muse could provide: to look into his heart and write.

Alan T. McKenzie (essay date 1984)

SOURCE: "Two 'Heads Weel Pang'd Wi' Lear': Robert Fergusson, Samuel Johnson, and St. Andrews," in *Scottish Literary Journal,* Vol. 11, No. 2, December, 1984, pp. 25-35.

[*In the following excerpt, McKenzie discusses Fergusson's satirical verse epistle, "To the Principal and Professors of the University of St Andrews on their Superb Treat to Samuel Johnson," in which Fergusson expressed his resentment of English influence over Scottish literature*].

On August 19th, 1773 the eight Professors at the University of St Andrews entertained two distinguished visitors with what one of the visitors later called 'a very good dinner' and the other described as 'all the elegance of lettered hospitality'. Two weeks later the lively and mildly nationalistic *Weekly Magazine* published a poem, [**"To the Principal and Professors of the University of St Andrews on Their Superb Treat to Samuel Johnson,"** by Robert Fergusson], in which a recent, and somewhat less distinguished, St Andrews graduate [Fergusson] scolded his former teachers for their hospitality. He offered to Scottify the palate of one of the visitors in retaliation for a lexicographic jibe at the Scottish diet he had published nearly twenty years earlier. Like most of Robert Fergusson's best poems, this one is occasional and satirical, and in the lively and responsive Scots dialect he had fashioned for his own poetical purposes. His indirect and good humoured abuse produced a mild literary confrontation, a triumph of nationalism, and a clever piece of linguistic polemics. A few items from Fergusson's biography heighten the occasion, and several thematic devices invite more comment than they have received.

One biographical consideration certainly underlies Fergusson's sardonic reaction to the enthusiastic welcome St Andrews gave to Samuel Johnson: Fergusson himself had been a student—a fairly irreverent student—there from 1764 to 1768. He left behind him a reputation for pranks and a trail of sarcasm that lingered many years after he left. He had directed his sarcasm at his classmates, the faculty (**"Elegy on the Death of Mr David Gregory, Late Professor of Mathematics in the University of St Andrews"**), the staff (**"Elegy on John Hogg, late Porter to the University of St Andrews"**), and the food (see his mock grace for rabbit, Rogers, *Leaves,* p. 15). He took away with him a strong grounding in the classics, especially Horace and Virgil, recollections of the meagre repasts he himself had survived upon as a bursar, and a special affection for the Professor of Natural Philosophy, William Wilkie.

The strong academic grounding in the classics is evident in the urbane tone of most of Fergusson's best poems, including this one, and in his bent for satire and his fondness for the detachment available in the form of the epistle. It may well have something to do with his frequent employment, as here, of the Horatian themes of hospitality, excess, and pride. It certainly gave him the confidence to face the literati—a confidence not often evident in Ramsay or Burns. . . .

I need hardly add that Fergusson was by no means the only one to take exception to the fanfare over Johnson's visit. Resentment lingered long after Johnson had gone on to the Highlands and Islands, and Boswell was at pains to reply to a 'very absurd and ill natured story' that Johnson had insulted the Professors by insisting on reinforcing their Scottish grace with a Latin one. It seems highly probable that some such rumour reached Fergusson's ear. Such a rumour would have heightened the aptness of Fergusson's harping on the food over which the grace was said.

Johnson's tour was obviously a topic of conversation in the various Edinburgh literary circles—circles to which Fergusson had regular access. Suffice it to say that, however Fergusson heard about it, his own alma mater, an institution for which he seems to have retained some fondness, and from which he seems to have expected some effort to champion the national culture and pride, had made too big a fuss over a polysyllabic Southron who had insulted the Scots language and cuisine. Some or all of these personal considerations must have figured in the pique that led Fergusson to heighten so remote a social occasion into so good a satire. His eye for public display and civic formality was sharpened by just enough personal interest and good humoured antipathy to produce a poem that survives its occasion without drawing all of its own strength from its target.

It might be diverting to point out how many things the Scottish Horatian had in common with the Augustan humanist he had attacked: precocity, learning, poverty, pride, melancholy, urbanity, etc. Let Robert Sommers' (who knew him well) description of Fergusson's clubability serve as an indication of how alike the two might be made to seem:

I passed many happy hours with him, not in *dissipation* and *folly,* but in useful conversation, and in listening to the more inviting and rational display of his *wit, sentiment* and *song;* in the exercise of which, he never failed to *please, instruct,* and *charm.*

        (Sommers, *Life,* p. 46)

It would be more to the point to enumerate their differences—in age, nationality, politics, appearance, manner, etc. Such a survey might well concentrate on their attitudes toward language, the more so because this was the issue that Fergusson himself chose to raise. Johnson's gift for forcible abstraction relied on his capacious mind, his vast reading, and his years as a lexicographer. Lampoons like those of John Campbell, a later, and equally irreverent student at St Andrews, indicate some of its elements: "'Shall I snuff the candle, Dr Johnson?' 'Sir, you may deprive the luminary of its superfluous eminence'"(Rogers, *Leaves,* p. 16).

Fergusson, in contrast, placed his pen at the service of the Scots language, more specifically, of the supple and 'plastic' idiom he had fashioned from what he heard from his Aberdeenshire parents, his Edinburgh companions, his fellow students at St Andrews, and the vigorous and outspoken Wilkie, along with the printed Scots he found in chapbooks and the poems of Allan Ramsay. On the substantial issues of which language to use and what uses to put that language to, then, the two men differed radically. Fergusson chose to embody these cultural and linguistic differences in the selection and nomenclature of cuisine, for it is in the names of its foods that a language retains its most direct connections with native culture. Every time Fergusson names one of the fierce local dishes he would like to have stuffed down Johnson's gullet instead of the fancy French cuisine his hosts did provide, he strikes a linguistic blow for the independence of his own culture. And he does so in response to Johnson's definition of 'oats'. This fusion of language, diet, culture, and argument sharpens his polemic and embellishes his poem. . . .

The defence of his native and threatened culture was one of Fergusson's favourite themes. In addition to his recurrent concern for the Scots language, he alerted his countrymen to threats to Scottish music, fashion, and cuisine. He cultivated national and traditional word forms and served them to his metropolitan audience in exactly the way that he urged the cooks at St Andrews to be more sparing and authentic in their menu. Humility, too, was a recurrent theme. He was equally unable to receive or offer flattery (See **"Answer to Mr J. S.'s Epistle"**). And he reverts again and again to the inflated sense of themselves that civic functionaries seek occasion to display. A drift into satire is perhaps the occupational hazard of every occasional poet, but few occasional poets are presented with a word as perfectly suited to their purpose as 'gawsy'. (The glossary of the 1773 edition of Fergusson's poems defines 'gawsy air' as 'Looking big'.) The 'Horatian philosophy of the independent mind content with the simple, home-bred pleasures' which Fergusson read in Ramsay and revered in Wilkie, indeed the numerous special affinities the Scots have always

felt with Horace, are, as we have seen, evident throughout this **Epistle.** The conversational gaiety and the urbane, satirical, and classical manner which Sydney Goodsir Smith finds in Fergusson is equally and effectively evident, as is the 'astonishing power of direct statement' which McDiarmid identified as Fergusson's hallmark. The 'uncommon, often temporary' subject, the 'lively and striking' images and sentiments, and the sprightly and entertaining 'genius and vivacity' which his obituary claimed for all of his work are also to be found here in gratifying abundance.

Having decided to pick this quarrel, Fergusson chose his form for it shrewdly. He selected the 'familiar verse letter in the vernacular', the most successful Scottish verse form of his age. It was a form well established by Horace and well developed for occasional poetry by Hamilton of Gilbertfield and Ramsay. The certainty that there will be no reply enhances (a little) Fergusson's impudence, as does his use of the blunt octosyllabic couplet, a metre whose abruptness made it especially suitable for scoffing. He achieves the 'integrated and confident' language (especially in the opening 22 lines and lines 71-82), and he maintains his special controlled and assured tone—a tone without which the epistle would have discredited its author and its cause.

A few other features may be mentioned. The use of rivers to localise was, of course, a poetic commonplace (one of the few conjunctions of poetry and military history). The resonant 'Eden' (line 10) is everywhere else overshadowed by the Forth, the Tweed, and the Tay, especially in **"The Rivers of Scotland: An Ode"** and **"Hame Content: A Satire"**. The recourse to proverb in line 60 is a frequent ploy of Fergusson, who embedded many such nuggets in his works. The same bells that 'clink' for Johnson (line 9) 'mourn and clink' for John Hogg ('late Porter to the University of St Andrews'). In fact, bells seem regularly to have caught, and sometimes to have offended, Fergusson's very musical ear (**"To the Tron-Kirk Bell"**, **"On the Music-bells"**). Fergusson takes a little advantage of a linguistic dilemma in rhyming 'wame' (belly) with both time (line 35) and hame (line 60). And while it sometimes diverts Scottish patriots to compare the plaid to the toga, they do not often suggest that these national costumes sharpen one's eye for the shape of a man's leg. Fergusson certainly glanced at other shanks than Johnson's (line 38; cf. **"Caller Water"**, l. 15; **"The Ghaists"**, l. 141; and Horace, *Satires,* I, ii, 25-26, iii, 47-49, vi, 27-30). Allan Maclaine has aligned Fergusson's repeated, and to me somewhat adolescent, resorting to nicknames to the typical Scottish fondness for them (p. 75; cf. l. 5). Fergusson is certainly the only one I know of to have called Dr Johnson 'Samy', even if he never did so to his face. The opponent he had chosen was a mighty one, mighty in size, in language, and in reputation. Fergusson did well to challenge him from a distance.

But it is the repeated application to Johnson's 'wame' and the insistent attention to food and drink that mark the poem as Fergussonian in its very essence. Few other poets offer work after work in which the dishes are piled so high and the liquor flows so freely. Food and drink abound in most of his poems, and many of them are emblems of hospitality and evocations of kindred spirits: **"Caller Oysters"**, **"Hame Content"**, **"The Farmer's Ingle"**, and **"The Sitting of the Session"**, not to mention **"Good Eating"** and **"A Drink Eclogue"**. When Andrew Gray wrote a poem to praise Fergusson and to ingratiate himself with him, he included in it an invitation to a congratulatory repast of barley bannocks, cabbage kail, and, not just for the sake of the rhyme, much 'guid ale' (see Fergusson, Poems, II, 151-52). He knew his man.

There is something decidedly right, then, in Fergusson's hurling at Johnson the names of food that has grown or grazed in the countryside or under the waters over which Johnson had just passed—landscape from which Johnson's origins, manner, attitudes, and above all, language, cut him off. Fergusson withheld from the menu the 'caller oysters' which were just coming into season, and whose praises he had sung a year earlier. Nor did he include potatoes, a staple just recently added to the Scottish diet, partly through the efforts of Fergusson's mentor Wilkie, who had acquired the nickname of 'the potato minister' (Bennett, *Student*, p. 29). Each of the foods Fergusson cites enters the poem redolent of the field or the sea from which it has just been taken, or the kitchen where it was prepared. This will remind us that the Edinburgh audience for whom the poem was really intended inhabited a town that mingled its urbanity with the surrounding agricultural community far more than it does now, and that it had seen its haggis on the hoof. And finally, Fergusson's objections to the extravagance, as well as the disloyalty, of the 'superb treat' remind us that 'Patriotism and a sense of social justice go together with him' (Smith, *Essays*, p. 43). . . .

It remains only to remark that . . . Fergusson's poem was not successful in its retaliation. On 29 September 1773, in a passage entered into his Journal, but omitted from the published version, Boswell recorded Johnson's reaction to the poem:

> I mentioned to him a droll Scottish poem which I had just seen on occasion of his being entertained by the professors at St. Andrews. He desired to hear it. I read all but two lines about *skait* which were rather indecent, and explained it. He laughed, but said nothing.

F. W. Freeman (essay date 1984)

SOURCE: "The Substitute Life (City)," in *Robert Fergusson and the Scots Humanist Compromise*, Edinburgh University Press, 1984, pp. 123-78.

[*In the following excerpt, Freeman discusses the political views that influenced Fergusson's poetry, characterizing Fergusson as a resolute Scots Tory, Jacobite and nationalist who was often "openly anti-England, Hanover, and Whig," and a "most uncompromisingly political poet."*]

When the Scots humanist pondered the nation that Scotland had become after the ousting of the Stewarts, the eclipse of the older religions and the church hierarchy, the dissolution of the Scots parliament, the severance of old continental alliances, and the change from a classical to a neoclassical culture, he saw discontinuity, an unnatural break in his nation's culture and history effected for an alleged utility. In his mind the Whigs built a new Scotland at the expense of its past. Certainly this is the feeling one gets in reading the local historians of the time, like Hugo Arnot, and, indeed, it is most directly stated by at least one local Edinburgh poet, Claudero, in his many ruined building poems.

> *What is my crime? Oh! what my blot?*
> AULD REIKIE Cry'd, *Thou'rt an old* SCOT.
> *What then?* my Echo loud did cry,
> *Must* Scots *antiquity now die?*
> Yes, cry'd AULD REIKIE, *die you must.* . . .

Claudero, like any good humanist, believed a sense of history indispensable for the proper exercise of the will and, like all humanists, accounted it one of the chief qualities in distinguishing man from beast.

In the two or more poems about the loss of an historical sense and the inanity of living for the moment, Fergusson impugns modern society in the mock heroic vein, the accustomed mode of the eighteenth-century Augustan humanist satirist. Scots humanist literature, as we have observed, carried on the tradition of the kirk knight; Whig society was in the humanist imagination a 'continual war' . . . so mock heroics, the language of battle and epic, naturally became the conventional means of aspersing the Whigs.

Fergusson's views of the modern are summed up in his **"Epilogue . . . in the Character of an Edinburgh Buck"** which possesses some of the more important elements that make up the greater satire, **"King's Birth-Day in Edinburgh"**. The **"Epilogue"** enumerates the frivolous misadventures of the buck 'whose sole delight / Is *sleep* all day, and *riot* all the night' (ll.3-4). Here we find 'Lethe's cup' (l.1), 'lusty *Bacchus*' (l.7), *'Argus'* eyes' (l.33), 'Phoebus' (l.38) and Helen of *'Troy'* (l.52), 'Doomsday' (l.36) and 'fate' (l.41), 'war' (l.27) and 'val'rous champions . . . O deed unequall'd (ll.43-4)—all this to describe the bucks' flight from a City Guardsman before vandalising lamps on George Square (ll.13-40). The irony of the heroic language and classical reference sets off the folly of modern experience and, placed in the mouth of the buck, corroborates his avowed irreverence for, and misapprehension of, history.

> What are your far fam'd warriors to us,
> 'Bout whom historians make such mighty fuzz:
> Posterity may think it was uncommon
> That *Troy* should be pillag'd for a woman;
> But ours your ten years sieges will excel,
> And justly be esteem'd the nonpareil.
> Our cause is slighter than a dame's betrothing,
> For all these mighty feats have sprung from
>   nothing.
>
> (ll.49-56)

"The King's Birth-Day in Edinburgh", a parody of the birthday ode, paints a very droll picture of a wider cross section of contemporary society. Though not obviously so in terms of overt statement, this is another work in the old Scots humanist tradition of satire. The motto itself, . . . by Drummond of Hawthornden, foreshadows very much what amounts to a seventeenth-century style satire on the perverse and ignorant rabble though in practice the poem is less heavy handed or didactic. It has some basis in fact, in the real disorders of 4th June 1773, during the celebration of his majesty's birthday; nonetheless, the allusions prove it to be more a conventional, than an occasional, piece. . . .

Whiggism, in the guise of the mechanisms of progress or, more frequently, in that of sentimentalism, which treated man as a machine of natural impulse—a common animal, always elicited [Fergusson's] contempt. **"The Sow of Feeling,"** the early burlesques, **"A Burlesque Elegy on the amputation of a Student's Hair, before his Orders"** and **"The Canongate Play-House in Ruins. A Burlesque Poem,"** are satires explicitly on the eighteenth-century man of feeling and his false sentiment. Less explicit are the satires on the Whig sentimentalist which rely heavily upon the mock elegy and the stanza often associated with that form: the Habbie stanza. In a very thorough treatment of the subject, *The Funeral Elegy and the Rise of English Romanticism,* John Draper traces the evolution of the funeral elegy from its beginnings as a seventeenth-century Episcopalian form, serious and political in nature, to its gradual modification, still by the Episcopalians, as a satirical weapon against the Puritans and Presbyterians, who had borrowed the original form, albeit making it more macabre and sentimental, for their own purposes. Draper identifies a polarisation of the funeral elegy by the late seventeenth century into an affectedly grave Presbyterian genre and the Episcopalian parody of the same. The funeral elegy in Scotland followed the same pattern of development from Royalist politics as it had in England: starting with serious elegies like Bishop Patrick Forbes of Corse's *Funerals* (1635) and reaching its high water mark in the broadside elegies of Ninian Paterson, another Episcopalian divine. Though Draper claims that the satiric elegy in Scotland seems not wholly to have been the tool of any one party, it is clear that from its origins at the hands of the Royalist lairds, like Sir Robert Sempill—who were well aware of the English clergy—that it was most often used to parody the sanctimonious funeral elegy: works like Basil Hamilton's "The Mournful Muse" (1701), which dwells on the horrors of the grave, and the later poetry of Robert Blair and the graveyard school. Certainly Fergusson adopts the mock elegy form and the Habbie stanza to satirise the affected nature and the acquisitiveness of the Calvinist or the forced emotionalism of the Whig. He otherwise uses elegy unaffectedly for elegiac action, just as it had been employed in the seventeenth century, or, later by Alexander Nicol, as in "An Elegy on Johnie Galla" and "An Elegy on Auld Use and Wont", that is, as a vehicle for political propaganda. In so doing he was like Ruddiman and the humanist critics, swimming against the tide of sentimental aesthetics in Scotland.

The notion that Fergusson began as a sentimentalist poet in English and later recanted his sentimentalism in his Scots verse is mistaken. With the exception of a very few poetic exercises . . . there are few 'sorrows', 'gushing tears', or exclamation marks in the early poetry: far fewer than is generally accepted that there were. Satiric poetry aside, his vein is more that of a genuine melancholy retrospect as he ponders changes in his society and holds up the past in an attempt to frustrate these changes. The towering city (**"Pastoral I. Morning,"** ll.31-4), 'civil discord' (**"Pastoral II. Noon."** ll.19-28), a decaying Britain (**"On the Month of April"**), are recurring themes more akin to those of Goldsmith than to those of Shenstone and the sentimental school. Furthermore the English poems in the period 1769-1771 are related to the later works in Scots and English rhetorically, through the humanist rhetoric of winter or the society of the bees; hence with the opposing tradition to sentimentalism.

Among his first pieces were in fact burlesques of the sentimental elegy and the graveyard poem. **"A Burlesque Elegy on the Amputation of a Student's Hair, before his Orders"** is one such piece, written, M. P. McDiarmid notices, in the tradition of Pope's 'The Rape Of The Lock', and metrically and rhythmically parodying Gray's "Elegy". The profusion of exclamation marks and overstatements in the introduction sets the mock moral tone.

> O sad catastrophe! O event dire!
> 　　How shall the loss, the heavy loss be born?
> Or how the muse attune the plaintive lyre,
> 　　To sing of *Strephon* with his ringlets shorn?
> 　　　　　　　　　　　　　　　(ll.1-4)

'Solemn sounds', 'sad echoes' (ll.13-14), 'bitter anguish sighs' (l.29), mourning and grief (ll.25, 20) make light of sentimentalism and obliquely disparage a dour Kirk: those who must know

> Why such oppressive and such rigid laws
> 　　Are still attendant on religious things?
> 　　　　　　　　　　　　　　　(ll.7-8)

Another early satire on sentimentalism, but also on graveyard verse and the morbid elements of the Whig elegy, is **"The Canongate Play House in Ruins. A Burlesque Poem."** Here everyday scenes at the theatre, trivialised through parody and through narrowing the compass of King Richard and Shakespeare (ll.29-50), idyllic shepherds (ll.51-6), Jove and Olympus (ll.60-8) to the Canongate stage,—as it were, through suspending the suspension of disbelief—are set in the verbose sentimental/graveyard framework, beginning with 'feeling hearts' (l.I) and closing with the 'church-yard's gloom' (l.69).

> Ye few whose feeling hearts are ne'er estrang'd
> 　　From soft emotions: Ye who often wear
> The eye of pity, and oft vent her sighs,
> 　　When sad *Melpomene,* in woe-fraught strains,
> Gains entrance to the breast; or often smile
> When brisk *Thalia* gayly trips along
> Scenes of enlivening mirth; attend my song.

And Fancy, thou! whose over-flaming light
Can penetrate into the dark abyss
Of chaos, and of hell: O! with they blazing torch
The wasteful scene illumine, that the muse,
With daring pinions, may her flight pursue,
Nor with timidity be known to soar,
O'er the *theatric world,* to chaos chang'd.
     Can I contemplate on those dreary scenes
Of mould'ring desolation, and forbid
The voice elegiac and the falling tear!

                (ll.1-17)

These two early satiric strains, on false sentiment and morose graveyard musing, remained with Fergusson to the end of his short career as a poet, there being swipes at the sentimental elegy in **"Good Eating"** (ll.10-52) and full-fledged satires on the entire cult of sentiment in **"The Sow of Feeling"** and **"Mutual Complaint of Plainstanes and Causey, in their Mother-tongue."** In the latter two instances the myth of the man of feeling is taken apart piece by piece: myth of that genteel figure, created by Hutcheson and the new light of Presbyterian moderate philosophers and literateurs, whose moral sense and heightened sensibilities infallibly led him to right action, and whose tears and gesticulations were the surest signs of that infallibility.

The motto to **"The Sow of Feeling,"** the **"Epilogue"** to Henry Mackenzie's 'Prince of Tunis', tells us clearly what is to follow.

> *Well! I protest there's no such thing as dealing*
> *With these starch'd poets—with these* MEN *of*
> FEELING!

But beyond ridiculing men of feeling, **"The Sow"** is a genuine burlesque of the sentimental elegy. From the mouth of a feeling sow, who laments her recently slaughtered husband, are spoken the elegiac words of a Presbyterian divine on the subjects of blighted innocence and pure love (ll.5-6, 33-40), the perversion of the laws set down in the Old Testament (ll.7-8, 72-5), luxury (ll.15-16, 76-81), and the sorrows and horrors of the grave (ll.13-14, 51-71). This is underpinned by a fine sprinkling of sentimental and pious expressions: 'pitiless oppression—cruel case!' (l.3), 'cruel hands' (l.5), 'innocence . . . fled!' (l.6), 'doom'd a crime' (l.8), 'blest my longing arms' (l.9), 'love's sympathetic charms!' (l.10), 'bloody stalls' (l.14), 'load of misery . . . load of woes!' (l.16), 'heavy heart' (l.17), 'tender infants' (l.33), 'flame divine' (l.34), 'No deadly, sinful passion' (l.37), 'warmest vows' (l.43), 'Happiness, a floating meteor thou' (l.49), 'gloomiest *horrors* (l.51), 'deep-dy'd *sanguinary tide*' (l.52), 'blood-distilling ear!' (l.57), 'many a briny tear!' (l.59), 'weep till sorrow shall my eye-lids drain' (l.60), 'base murd'rers' (l.63), 'mournful voice!' (l.64), 'Had melted any hearts—but hearts of stones!' (l.65), 'The blood-stain'd blade' (l.68). Lines 1-14 introduce the theme of a blasted innocence and the decline of religious law.

    MALIGNANT planets! do ye still combine
      Against this wayward, dreary life of mine!

Has pitiless oppression—cruel case!
Gain'd sole possession of the human race?
By cruel hands has ev'ry virtue bled,
And innocence from men to vultures fled!
     Thrice happy, had I liv'd in Jewish time,
When swallowing pork or pig was doom'd a
    crime;
My husband long had blest my longing arms,
Long, long had known love's sympathetic
    charms!
My children too—a little suckling race,
With all their father growing in their face,
From their prolific *dam* had ne'er been torn,
Nor to the bloody stalls of butchers borne.

Lines 15-48 start with a summary condemnation of luxury and proceed, in the wonted humanist fashion, to the sow's reveries on sacred love, always masking, of course, more earthy, animal passions.

    Ah! luxury! to you my being owes
Its load of misery—its load of woes!
With heavy heart, I saunter all the day,
Gruntle and murmur all my hours away!
In vain I try to summon old desire,
For favourite sports—for wallowing in the mire:
Thoughts of my husband—of my children slain,
Turn all my wonted pleasure into pain!
How oft did we, in Phoebus warming ray,
Bask on the humid softness of the clay?
Oft did his lusty *head* defend my *tail*
From the rude whispers of the angry gale;
While *nose-refreshing* puddles stream'd around,
And floating odours hail'd the dung-cled ground. . . .

    In early times the law had wise decreed;
For human food but reptiles few should bleed;
But monstrous man, still erring from the laws,
The curse of heaven on his banquet draws!
Already has he drain'd the marshes dry
For *frogs,* new emblems of his luxury;
And soon the *toad* and *lizard* will come home,
Pure victims to the hungry glutton's womb:
Cats, rats and *mice,* their destiny may mourn,
In time their carcasses on spits must turn;
They may rejoice to-day—while I resign
Life, to be number'd 'mongst the *feeling swine.*

                (ll.72-83)

The last two lines are especially pungent in their deliberate ambiguity, referring, of course, to the *'feeling swine'* of society, the men of feeling. This underlies his choosing for his persona a sow; animals in humanist terms, especially pigs, being lowly creatures of feeling, impulse and passion:instinctive machines. Through the sow, Fergusson holds up to ridicule the moral sense, a notion, which as in Swift's *Mechanical Operation Of The Spirit,* deflects man's attentions from good sense and reason.

"Mutual Complaint of Plainstanes and Causey, in their Mother-tongue" belongs to the humanist tradition of anti-Whig legal satire, setting out, as it does, to expose the man of feeling as a cold fish, a legalist; discrediting the Whig notion of legislating progress and improvement; and deprecating the idea of law as a substitute life. The structure itself is built round the Enlightenment philosophy of utility and compromise for the general good, as expressed, for example, in parts of Kames *Sketches Of The History Of Man* (1774), where the subject also is highways, the weight of traffic on them, and their appropriate tolls. The dialogue of legal debate between Plainstanes and Causey is a travesty of the just compromise, social betterment being in no way the ultimate end of the compromise that is struck. The simple structure falls into three divisions: the argument between Plainstanes and Causey over who suffers the greater abuse (ll.21-62); the exchange of legal threats and subsequent compromise (ll.63-128); the agreement to place the issue before the local debating society and final resolution, it would seem, to do nothing about it whatsoever (ll.29-42).

Undoubtedly, characterisation and the topical issues under fire are more important than structure in the work. These are indeed caricatures of two Whig personalities: Plainstanes, the man of feeling, and Causey, the would-be man of law. The former is a prototype of the ideal man Mackenzie had in mind in *The Man Of Feeling,* an individual whose sole defence against Causey is on grounds of gentility and heightened sensibilities. He is, avowedly, a preserver of love (ll.30-42), 'a weak and feckless creature . . . moulded by a safter nature' (ll.72-2), a man of affection (ll.79-82), a protector of ladies and children and the elderly (ll.88-92).

> Had sae, and lat me get a word in,
> Your back's best fitted for the burden;
> And I can eithly tell you why,
> Ye're doughtier by far than I;
> For whin-stanes, howkit frae the craigs,
> May thole the prancing feet of naigs,
> Nor ever fear uncanny hotches
> Frae clumsy carts or hackney-coaches,
> While I, a weak and feckless creature,
> Am moulded by a safter nature. . . .

In the same breath he unmasks himself as uncharitable, calculatingly rational and legalistic.

> Take then frae me the heavy load
> Of burden-bearers havy shod,
> Or, by my troth, the gude auld town shall
> Hae this affair before their council.
>
> (ll.93-6)

Later Plainstanes recommends a purely utilitarian compromise, in the fashion of Hutcheson, hardly made more palatable by the lip service he pays to aiding the poor (ll.121-8).

> Gin we twa cou'd be as auld-farrant
> As gar the council gie a warrant,
> Ilk lown rebellious to tak,
> Wha walks not in the proper track,
> And o' three shilling Scottish suck him;

> Or in the *water-hole* sair douk him;
> This might assist the poor's collection,
> And gie baith parties satisfaction.

In fact, Plainstanes is cast as a social climber and a snob who, in the beginning lines of his defence (ll.63-70), damns himself, as he did in his earlier arguments against associating with the lower orders.

> Speak, was I made to dree the laidin
> Of Gallic chairman heavy treadin,
> Wha in my tender buke bore holes
> Wi' waefu' tackets i' the soals
> O' broags, whilk on my body tramp,
> And wound like death at ilka clamp.
>
> (ll.43-8)

The point throughout is that the man of feeling masks his real sentiments behind a parade of emotions. There is a marked discrepancy between his soft nature and his legalism; his unanalysed emotional outbursts and his rational presence of mind. Additionally, as that other Whig protagonist, the man of action—right feeling implied correct action—he is unable to act. A man given to emotional outburst rather than action, Plainstanes is really bent on forgetting the matter altogether.

> Content am I—But east the gate is
> The sun, wha taks his leave of Thetis,
> And comes to wauken honest fock,
> That gang to wark at sax o'clock;
> It sets us to be dumb a while,
> And let our words gie place to toil.
>
> (ll.137-42)

Again note, Fergusson is exceedingly close here to Butler's *Hudibras, The First Part,* Canto III, where Hudibras waxes verbose on the subject of whether Presbyterians are beasts, and finds a handy excuse to drop the issue.

> But I shall take a fit occasion
> T' evince thee by Ratiocination,
> Some other time, in place more proper
>
> Then this w'are in: Therefore let's stop here,
> And rest our weary'd bones awhile,
> Already tir'd with other toile.
>
> (I,p.268)

Plainstanes, like Hudibras, is bogged down in empty words, like 'chiels' in their 'ROBINHOOD debates' driven 'ten miles frae the question / In hand that night' (**"Leith Races,"** ll.163-74).

Causey, on the other hand, the budding man of law, is an unwitting mouthpiece for Whig values, misgovernment, incompetence, and the foolhardy belief in mechanisms. It is through him that the thematic matter of the introduction develops from the very oblique satire on futile improvements (ll.1-4), the bungling puppets of state (ll.7-8), the law and its jargon (ll.15-20). Moreover, he fulfils the stereotype in humanist literature of the rising middle class cit, now able to challenge the upper classes in law; he is cast from the same dye as the Bull and Frog in Arbuthnot's *The History of John Bull* (Chapter III) adopting completely their style of rhetoric and manner of reconciling differences with opponents.

> I dinna care a single jot,
> Tho' summon'd by a shelly-coat,
> Sae leally I'll propone defences,
> As get ye flung for my expences;
> Your libel I'll impugn *verbatim*,
> And hae a *magnum damnum datum* . . .
>
> (ll.97-102)

It is Causey who gives 'sentiments' (l.120) a new meaning for Plainstanes, in his threat redefining it as legal impulses—

> The deil's in't gin ye dinna sign
> Your sentiments conjunct wi' mine.
>
> (ll.119-20)

—impulses once again, but not actions, as his challenges give way to the fatuous suggestion

> To bring it to the *Robinhood,*
> Whare we shall hae the question stated,
> And keen and crabbitly debated . . .
>
> (ll.130-2)

Causey, like Plainstanes, is ineffectual. The similarity does not end here. Plainstanes actually treats of himself as a mechanism of feeling with a programmed sense of appropriate responses to situations. But Causey too acts and thinks as if people were controlled by unintended effects of circumstances, as for example in his platitudes about social mechanisms: the notion,

> . . . coachman never trow they're sinning,
> While down the street his wheels are spinning . . .
>
> (ll.57-8)

—the prevalent idea that every action has unforeseen effects. Similarly, he is a singularly insentient critic—like Willie in **"An Eclogue"**—of the very cause he wishes to promote. Aside from certain ironical comments about the provost and baillies (ll.133-4), Causey voices the well-aired complaints of Whig maladministration and 'improvement' regarding the Royal Exchange and the removal of the centuries old Mercat Cross, removed for incommoding the street.

> Tho' magistrates the *Cross* discard,
> It makes na whan they leave the *Guard,*
> A lumbersome and stinkin bigging,
> That rides the sairest on my rigging.
> Poor me owr meikle do yet blame,
> For tradesmen tramping on your wame,
> Yet a' your advocates and braw fock
> Come still to.me 'twist ane and twa clock,
> And never yet were kend to range

> At *Charlie's Statue* or *Exchange.*
>
> (ll.107-16)

The solution of dismantling the Cross manifestly did not work; convention was stronger than utility as crowds continued to aggregate round the area where the Cross had been.

Graveyard poetry sprang from the same roots as sentimental poetry: from the Whig elegy, emotional, gloomy, and horrific, with its 'tears of blood', 'sorrows', 'wormes and slime'. This poetry had, of course, been brought into popular acclaim by the poets of the graveyard school, men like Robert Blair, author of *The Grave*. And, as always, and this partially explains his repudiation by the literati, it was parodied in the spirit of Colvil and Pitcairne by diehard humanists like Robert Fergusson. A parody of Blair, and even Gray, is at its most vivid in the early social satire on the beaux and fops at the theatre, **"The Canongate Play-house in Ruins. A Burlesque Poem,"** with its heavy trappings of the graveyard poem: 'feeling hearts' (l.1), 'soft emotions' (l.2), 'pity', 'sighs' (l.3), 'woe-fraught strains' (l.4), 'the dark abyss / Of chaos, and of hell' (ll.9-10), 'dreary scenes / Of mould'ring desolation' (ll.15-16), 'The voice elegiac and the falling tear!' (l.17), 'silver light' (l.68), 'churchyard's gloom' (l.69), 'cypress shades' (l.70), 'this sad mansion' (l.71), 'Unconsecrated paths' (l.72), 'the unhallow'd spade' (l.80), 'this ruin'd fane' (l.84), 'the tragic tear' (l.86), 'pensive shadow' (l.90). That Fergusson's imagination continued to run counter to the sentimental elegy and the graveyard poem throughout his career is evident in the later light pieces, like **"Rob Fergusson's Last Will,"** a Hudibrastic using pompous sounding Latin legal terms and irreverent metaphors.

> parting breath's a sneeze
> To let sensations all at ease.
>
> (ll.37-8)
> As I in health with him wou'd often
> This clay-built mansion wash and soften . . .
>
> (ll.68-9)

His later odes, which have an element of horror in them, derive, rather, from a humanist tradition which owes much to Drummond of Hawthornden, and which dwells upon mutability and the limitation of the senses.

"On James Cumming" satirises the graveyard imagination, quite incidentally, through linking it with a satire on the antiquarianism of the age. In making light of the antiquary's obsession with old things, Fergusson, again with a humour of scale, pokes fun at graveyard conventions as he localises the exotic, places the eternal in a momentary context. In this instance the antiquary becomes, notably, a 'knight' and his familiar grounds of research the typical setting of the graveyard poem.

> Just now in fair Edina lives,
> That famous Antient Town
> At a known place hight Blackfry'rs Wynd
> A knight of Odd renown

A Druids sacred from he bears
 With Saucer Eyes of Fire
An Antique Hat on's head he wears
 Like Ramsays the Town Cryer

Down in the Wynd his Mansion Stands
 All gloomy dark within
Here mangled Books like blood and Bones
 Strew'd in a Giants Den

Crude indigested half devour'd
 On groaning Shelves theyr thrown
Such Manuscripts no Eye can read
 No hand Wrote but his own

No Prophet he like Sydrophel
 Can future times explore
But what has happened he can tell
 Five hundred years and more

Butler hovers in the background as usual—Sydrophel was the astrologer in *Hudibras*—and the sentimental elegy does not elude the final banter of the last impious lines on 'Sin'(l.30), death and the solemnity of the church (ll.40-1).

This wight th' outsides of Churches loo'd
 Almost unto a Sin
Spires gothic of more use he prov'd
 Than Pulpits are within

  . . . . .

When e'er the fatal day shall come
 For come alas it must
When this good knight must stay at home
 And turn to antique dust

The solemn Dirge ye Owls prepare
 Ye Bats more hoarsly skreak
Croak all ye Ravens Round the bier
 And all ye Church Mice Squeak

Fergusson's most effective counter to sentimentalism and the related concept of determined mechanisms were his mock elegies in the Habbie stanza, recalling its seventeenth-century usage and thus constituting an integral part of the meaning of the poem. One of his very first literary efforts was probably composed during his first year at university: the **"Elegy, On the Death of Mr David Gregory, late Professor of Mathematics in the University of St Andrews."** It possesses elements of the tradition passed down from Robert Sempill's *Epitaph On Sanny Briggs*, which are visible in phrases like "Without remeid' (l.4) and, more especially, in the tone of mock horror, tearful sentiment, irreverence of death and the resurrection.

NOW mourn, ye college masters a'!
 And frae your ein a tear lat fa',
Fam'd *Gregory* death has taen awa'
 Without remeid;

The skaith ye've met wi's nae that sma',
 Sin Gregorys dead.

        (ll.1-6)

Great 'casions hae we a' to weep,
An' cleed our skins in mourning deep,
For Gregory *death* will fairly keep
 To take his nap;
He'll till the resurrection sleep
 As sound's a tap.

        (ll.37-42)

Fergusson's contempt of mathematics was a strictly orthodox humanist distaste for reducing men to statistical principles and disbelief, as the politico mathematicians of the time would have it, in controlling destiny through calculations. Gregory is, therefore, cut down to size as something less than a flesh and blood hero; as a geometrical *'bector'* (l.29), no doubt harried by the Achilles of his own miscalculations. His mathematical powers, ability to 'divine' the obvious (ll.15-17), and his awesome knowledge, despite which, death takes the hindmost part, make him a Hudibrastic figure of uncommon banter, as the following quotes illustrate.

He could, by *Euclid*, prove lang sine
A gangin *point* compos'd a line;
By numbers too he cou'd divine,
 When he did read,
That *three* times *three* just made up nine;
 But now he's dead.

In *Algebra* weel skill'd he was,
An' kent fu' well *proportion's* laws;
He cou'd make clear baith B's and A's
 Wi' his lang head;
Rin owr surd roots, but cracks or flaws;
 But now he's dead.

Weel vers'd was he in architecture,
An' kent the nature o' the *sector*,
Upon baith globes he weel cou'd lecture,
 An' gar's tak heid;
Of geometry he was the *hector*;
 But now he's dead.

        (ll.13-30)

He was in *Logick* a great Critick,
Profoundly skill'd in Analytick.

  . . . . .

He'd undertake to prove by force
Of Argument, a Man's no Horse.

  . . . . .

In *Mathematicks* he was greater
Then *Tycho Brahe* or *Erra Pater*:
For he by *Geometrick* scale
Could take the size of *Pots of Ale*;
Resolve by Sines and Tangents straight,

If *Bread* or *Butter* wanted weight;

And wisely tell what hour o' th' day
The Clock does strike, by *Algebra*.
                    (*Hudibras,* The First Part, Canto I,)

**"Elegy on John Hogg, late Porter to the University of
St Andrews"** is a better example of humanist satire on
the sentimental elegy and Whig values. It is a mock elegy
on one of those greedy Puritanical merchants, so common
to seventeenth-century humanist literature and prominent
in **"Hallow-Fair"** and **"Leith Races,"** and, generally, a
satire on religious hypocrisy, though not serious or ven-
omous: in this respect Fergusson's good nature and humanity are the compromising factors which soften the
most grotesque of his caricatures.

Lines 1-30 convey us, with the couthy village intimacy of
eavesdroppers, before an irreverently familiar meeting with
death, where the eternal becomes the commonplace or
absurd, and an exaggerated fit of mourning; they open
with a loose conversational address to 'DEATH', in feminine rhymes, and with the imagery of 'wicket' and 'log'
(II.5-6), more suggestive of a winter's wood-chopping at
a cottar's house than of entering St Peter's gates.

> DEATH, what's ado? the de'il be licket,
>   Or wi' your *stang,* you ne'er had pricket,
> Or our AULD ALMA MATER tricket
>   O' poor John Hogg,
> And trail'd him ben thro' your mark wicket
>   As dead's a log.
>
> Now ilka glaikit scholar lown
> May dander wae wi' *duddy gown;*
> KATE KENNEDY to dowy crune
>   May mourn and clink,
> And steeples o' Saint Andrew's town
>   To yird may sink.
>
>   (II.1-12)

The passing taunt at the learned, 'ilka glaikit scholar lown'
(I.7), leads naturally into mock praise of the rigours of an
education under *'Pauly Tam'* (I,13), Thomas Tullidelph,
Principal of the Varsity, and, more pertinently, former
Professor of Divinity at St Mary's College and Moderator
of the General Assembly of the Kirk: a man noted for
strict discipline. Pauly Tam represents the more dour side
of the Kirk; with his 'canker'd snout' (I.13), his stringent
rules requiring the students to wear black (I.15), his 'common schools' for discipline and moral reflection (I.19),
and his formidable railing (I.28). Moreover, the same
informal address, pawkily, puts *'Pauly Tam'* or 'auld *Tam'*
(II.13,20) on an equal footing with 'DEATH' and rhetorically equates him with an insect, 'Like ony emmack' (I.22).

> Sin' *Pauly Tam,* wi' canker'd snout,
> First held students in about
> To wear their claes as black as soot,
>   They ne'er had reason,
> Till death John's haffit ga'e a clout
>   Sae out o' season.

> Whan *regents* met at common schools,
> He taught auld *Tam* to hale the dules,
> And eidant to row right the bowls
>   Like ony emmack;
> He kept us a' within the rules
>   Strict academic.
>
> Heh! wha will tell the students now
> To meet the *Pauly* cheek for chow,
> Whan he, like *frightsome wirrikow,*
>   Had wont to rail,
> And set our stamacks in a low,
>   Or we turn'd tail.
>
>   (II.13-30)

Lines 31-60 shift the attention to John Hogg as he was;
carrying out his porter's duties like a lay preacher; threatening hell and damnation and citing biblical saws. We see
him larger than life, a total caricature of the Auld Licht
minister: a knight of the kirk; a cit too well versed in the
language of the law (I.33); a gloatingly proud spouter of
scriptures (II.39-42, 55-60); an overzealous lay minister
outdoing the dominies and preachers in admonishing students against their evil ways (II.43-8); an ignorant, un-
imaginative fundamentalist (II.49-58); an avid debater, like
Causey, more interested in the 'contesting' than in the
substance of the issue (II.59-60).

> Ah, Johnny! aften did I grumble
> Frae cozy bed fu' ear' to tumble;
> Whan art and part I'd been in some ill,
>   Troth I was sweer,
> His words they brodit like a wumill
>   Frae ear to ear.
>
> Whan I had been fu' laith to rise,
> John than begude to moralize:
> 'The TITHER NAP, the *sluggard* cries,
>   'And turns him round;
> 'Sae spake auld Solomon the wise
>   'Divine profound!'
> Nae dominie, or wise mess John,
> Was better lear'd in Solomon;
> He cited proverbs one by one
>   Ilk vice to tame;
> He gar'd ilk sinner sigh an' groan,
>   And fear hell's flame.
>
> 'I hae nae meikle skill, quo' he,
> 'In what you ca' philosophy;
> 'It tells that baith the earth and sea
>   'Rin round about;
> Either the Bible tells a lie,
>   'Or you're a' out.
>
> 'It's i' the *psalms* O' DAVID writ,
> 'That this wide warld ne'er shou'd flit,
> 'But on the waters coshly sit
>   'Fu' steeve and lasting;
> 'An was na he a head o' wit
>   'At sic contesting!'
>
>   (II.31-60)

Above all, John was a business-man, a 'bien body', as one contemporary described him: in the poem, another one of those Puritanical merchants whose religion was money.

> For John ay lo'ed to turn the pence,
> Thought poortith was a great offence . . .
>
> (II.79-80)

After a few lines on 'Johnny's lodge' (I.62), where the students were wont to drink as long as there was 'siller on us' (I.64), the poem concludes with a mock morale on the virtues of money making (II.73-96). The edges of the caricature are sharpest in the biblical language describing John's secular, business pursuits and the metaphysical vindication of his money-making practises.

> Wi' haffit locks, sae smooth and sleek,
> John look'd like ony antient Greek;
> He was a Nazarene a' the week,
>   And doughtna tell out
> A bawbee Scots to straik his cheek
>   Till Sunday fell out.
>
> For John ay lo'ed to turn the pence,
> Thought poortith was a great offence:
> 'What recks tho' ye ken *mood* and *tense*
>   'A hungry *weyme*
> 'For GOWD wad wi' them baith dispense
>   'At ony time.
>
> 'Ye ken what ails maun ay befal
> 'The chiel that will be prodigal;
> 'Whan wasted to the very spaul
>   'He turns his tusk,
> 'For want o' comfort to his saul
>   'O' hungry husk.'
>
> (II.73-90)

Waxing affectedly moralistic in tone himself while, ironically, extolling money-grubbing, in the vein of John Hogg, the poet finally exhorts the students to follow in the footsteps of John and his 'canny' (I.95) widow.

> Ye royit lowns! just do as he'd do;
> For mony braw green SHAW and MEADOW
> He's left to cheer his dowy widow,
>   His winsome *Kate*,
> That to him prov'd a canny she-dow,
>   Baith ear' and late.
>
> (II.91-6)

"To the Tron-Kirk Bell" is not one of the mock elegies but should be grouped with them as a satire, also in the Habbie stanza, on determinist mechanisms and Whig misgovernment. The title is in fact not what it suggests; the poet is not writing 'To', or eulogising, **"The Tron-Kirk Bell"** so much as directing his flyting to the same; actually, decrying new disturbances and nuisances in the town after the fashion of Juvenal's 'Third Satire', the basis of so many humanist town satires by D'Urfey, Gay, Swift, Fergusson and others.

> Here want of rest a' nights more people
>   kills
> Than all the college, and the weekly bills;
> Where none have privilege to sleep, but those
> Whose purses can compound for their repose.
> In vain I got to bed, or close my eyes,
> Methinks the place the middle region is,
> Where I lie down in storms, in thunder rise;
> The restless bells such din in steeples keep,
> That scarce the dead can in their churchyards
>   sleep . . .

The Tron Kirk, it must be affirmed, was not just any bell. The Tron itself was a symbol of the Presbyterian ascendancy, the edifice having been built in 1647 and completed in 1673, as a classic piece of post-Reformation architecture. But no doubt seventeenth- and eighteenth-century humanists compared it to what the reformers had destroyed, and remarked, as does one twentieth-century literary historian on its amateurish spire and, generally, on the decline of church architecture in Scotland after the Reformation. The Tron had other associations as well for the eighteenth-century humanists, for during temporary occupation by Jacobites in 1745 Reverend Neil M'Vicar had the audacity to pray for a heavenly, rather than earthly, crown for Bonnie Prince Charlie. At the time of the satire's publication John Drysdale was the Tron's minister. A friend and staunch disciple of William Robertson in religious affairs, he was, in the following year, 1773, himself Moderator of the General Assembly.

The Tron Kirk, then, was a bastion, and, in Fergusson's own mind, much like Old St Paul's for the Episcopal Circle, a symbol of Presbyterian moderate culture: in this poem, of moderate notions of determinism and the inevitability of progress, which the poet depicts as a rationale for controlling the masses and serving the self-interests of the moderates.

Throughout the first half of the poem (II.1-36) the speaker, like so many of Fergusson's comic characters, is the unwitting observer and critic of all that is happening around him; like Willie in **"An Eclogue"** he draws connections suppressed from his desensitised consciousness. In the introductory lines he is punch-drunk with the bell's noise—effectively evoked by the 'thing - ring - hing - sel' - bring -hell' (II.1-6) rhymes—and cannot fathom what end it serves.

> Wanwordy, crazy, dinsome thing,
> As e'er was fram'd to jow or ring,
> What gar'd them sic in steeple hing
>   They ken themsel',
> But weel wat I they couldna bring
>   War sounds frae hell.
>
> What de'il are ye? that I shud ban,
> Your neither kin to pat nor pan;
> Not *uly pig,* nor *master-cann*
>   But weel may gie
> Mair pleasure to the ear o' man
>   Than stroak o' thee.

Fleece merchants may look bald, I trow,
Sin a' Auld Reikie's childer now,
Maun stap their lugs wi' teats o' woo,
    Thy sound to bang,
And keep it frae gawn thro' and thro'
    Wi' jarrin twang.

                      (II.1-18)

His bewilderment is conveyed in humanising and flyting with the inanimate bell, rather than with the politicians behind it, and in providing more information to the reader than he is actually aware of. He mentions the bell 'was fram'd' (I.2) and refers to 'them' (I.3) and 'They' (II.4-5) while indirectly satirising their utilitarian notions—for the bell is useless (II.7-9)—and the well-known economic principle of the time that the creation of one mechanism creates a demand for others: his playful assertion that the bell's noise will generate a desire for wool ear plugs, a particularly germane comment as the wool industry was thought by the Whigs to have contributed the most to luxury.

Lines 19-36 shift the attention to the townsman's battle with the bell for peace of mind at home. The bell is personified as a nagging wife responsible for leaving her husband in a senseless state.

Your noisy tongue, there's nae abideint,
Like scaulding wife's, there is nae guideint:
Whan I'm 'bout ony bus'ness eident,
    It's sair to thole;
To deave me, than, ye tak a pride in't
    Wi' senseless knoll.

                    (II.19-24)

In agonising over his one-sided communication with the bell, he intimates who is accountable for the disturbance; stumbles—still without recognising it—into an implication as to who ultimately is beyond the reach of hearing his protests.

O! war I provost o' the town,
I swear by a' the pow'rs aboon,
I'd bring ye wi'a reesle down;
    Nor shud you think
(Sae sair I'd crack and clour your crown)
    Again to clink.

                    (II.25-30)

Still bedazed and, miraculously, unaware of his own implications, the town dweller stops his flyting to mull over a recent dream, linking the kirk—moderates in point of fact—with the local government in insidiously restricting the awareness of, and cowing, the masses in order to control them. The passage is neatly handled. In two stanzas (II.37-48) the poet makes economical use of the rhetoric of the more fanatical kirk sects in representing the long held humanist picture of Presbyterian preaching, and the old Hudibrastic association of the kirk minister—his frightening 'Oratory'—and the 'Devil' (e.g. *Hudibras, Third Part,* Canto I,). The lines read like a footnote to H. T. Buckle, the Victorian historian, on seventeenth-centu-ry Scots Presbyterian preaching.

> They (kirk ministers) kept the people in a worse than Egyptian bondage, inasmuch as they enslaved the mind as well as body . . .

> Of all the means of intimidation employed by the Scotch clergy, none was more efficacious than the doctrines they propounded respecting evil spirits and future punishment. On these subjects, they constantly uttered the most appalling threats. The language, which they used, was calculated to madden men with fear, and to drive them to the depths of despair . . . And, what made it more effectual was, that it completely harmonized with those other gloomy and ascetic notions which the clergy inculcated, and according to which, pleasures being regarded as sinful, sufferings were regarded as religious.

> It was generally believed, that the world was overrun by evil spirits, who not only went up and down the earth, but also lived in the air, and whose business it was to tempt and hurt mankind . . . At their head was Satan himself, whose delight it was to appear in person, ensnaring or terrifying every one he met . . . His strategems were endless. For, in the opinion of the divines, his cunning increased with his age . . .

I dreamt ae night I saw Auld Nick;
Quo he, 'this bell o' mine's a trick,
    'A wylie piece o' politic,
        'A cunnin snare
'To trap fock in a cloven stick,
        ' 'Ere they're aware.
'As lang's my dautit bell hings there,
'A' body at the kirk will skair;
    'Quo they, gif he that preaches there
        'Like it can wound,
'We douna care a single hair,
        'For joyfu' sound.'

                    (II.37-48)

By the closing lines (II.49-60) the town dweller's own submerged awareness, which has logically reinforced his assertions regarding a benighted populace, comes to the fore, and he is able to recognise that the magistrates and baillies are to blame for his disturbance. Like the magistrates of **"The Election,"** so complacently indifferent to the *'blind fu'* (II.73-6) of the town, the magistrates leave the townsmen to their own devices by legislating for them at a safe distance.

If magistrates wi' me wud 'gree,
For ay *tongue-tackit* shud you be,
Nor fleg wi' *antimelody*
    Sic honest fock,
Whase lugs were never made to dree
    Thy doolfu' shock.

But far frae thee the *bailies* dwell,
Or they wud scunner at your knell,
Gie the *foul thief* his riven bell,
    And than, I trow,

The by-word hads, 'the de'il himsel'
    'Has got his due.'

(II.49-60)

The satire closes significantly on notes of *'antimelody'* and 'doolfu' shock' (II.51, 54), the persistent bell's jarring twang preventing communication: in simple humanist terms, noise, as in **"Hallow-Fair,"** the hallmark of the city of chaos.

"The Ghaists: A Kirk-yard Eclogue" stands as a bridge between the mock elegies or graveyard pieces and the unsentimental humanist elegies. It both burlesques the graveyard elegy and genuinely laments the passing of Scots traditions, advocating, in the humanist vein, elegiac action. In **"The Ghaists"** Fergusson is most unashamedly and resolutely the Scots Tory, Jacobite and nationalist; most openly anti-England, Hanover, and Whig; most uncompromisingly political poet. The very lines subscribed to the title leave this in no doubt.

> *Did you not say, on good* ANN'S *day,*
>   *And vow and did protest, Sir,*
> *That when* HANOVER *should come o'er,*
>   *We surely should be blest,* Sir?
>   An auld Sang made new again.

This is the political message that the dialogue is designed to put across. The poem is, in an immediate sense, a piece against the Mortmain Bill, which threatened the charitable trusts of Heriot's and Watson's schools for the sons of poor burgesses and merchants, and is, more generally, a piece of Scots Tory propaganda.

Technically speaking, two things occur in lines 1-78. There is, firstly, the burlesque of the conventional setting and horrors of the graveyard. Second, the pastoral device is employed, more idealistically than in **"Hallow-Fair"** and **"Leith Races,"** to contrast the two Scotlands, past and present. The two techniques complement one another. In lines 1-18 the setting is replete with 'dowy murmurs' (I.1), 'the cald, clad grave' (I.2), 'ghaists, sae grizly and sae wan' (I.5), 'lanely tombs' (I.6), 'douff discourse' (I,6), 'mirkest hour' (I,9), 'Bogles and spectres' (I,10), 'hidden cairns' (I,11), 'hamlocks wild, and sun-burnt fearns' (I,12), 'dern mansions of the midnight tomb' (I,14), 'the black hours' (I,18): in short, with the trappings of the sentimental elegy and graveyard poem. The satire resides in the turgidity of the passage and, equally, in the awe diminishing localisation of the description; the silly intrusion of Geordie Girdwood, the late sexton, and the particularised image of the evil spirits 'Harlin' the pows and shanks to hidden cairns' (I.11), flouting the ghostly atmosphere as did 'DEATH' in **"Elegy on John Hogg"** (II.5-6).

> WHARE the braid planes in dowy murmurs wave
> Their antient taps out o'er the cald, clad
>   grave,
> Whare *Geordie Girdwood,* mony a lang-spun
>   day,
> Houkit for gentlest banes the humblest clay,
> Twa sheeted ghaists, sae grizly and sae wan,

> 'Mang lanely tombs their douff discourse began.

Watson

>   Cauld blaws the nippin north wi' angry
>   sough,
> And showers his hailstanes frae the Castle
>   Cleugh
> O'er the Greyfriars, whare, at mirkest hour,
> Bogles and spectres wont to tak their tour,
> Harlin' the pows and shanks to hidden cairns,
> Amang the hamlocks wild, and sun-burnt fearns,
> But nane the night save you and I hae come,
> Frae the dern mansions of the midnight tomb,
> Now whan the dawning's near, whan cock maun
>   craw,
> And wi' his angry bougil gar's withdraw,
> Ayont the kirk we'll stap, and there tak bield,
> While the black hours our nightly freedom yield.

Heriot goes on to relate the false literary setting of the Whig elegy, the Scotland in which he awakens, to a changed 'NATURE' (1.25), and, in so doing, introduces the pastoral device, implying that modern Scotland is not—and stating that Scotland under the Stewarts was—the natural ideal. When recounting the unnatural changes of these new physical surroundings (ll.19-28)—in terms reminiscent of the unnatural reversals in **"An Eclogue"**(ll.51-5)—he uses the language of the graveyard poem (e.g. 'owlets round the craigs . . . And bludy bawks'—ll.27-8); immediately afterwards, his remarks, despite the exclamations, cease to be so affectedly morbid and stilted, and are obviously intended as a genuine lament. In humanist rhetorical terms, Heriot's nostalgic outpourings follow the formula: 'JAMIE' (1.32) (Scotland under the Stewarts) = nature = civilisation or, rhetorically, shelter ('stately turrets'—1.36), growth, natural protection (his statue brawly 'busk(ed) wi' flow'rs ilk coming year'—1.40). And conversely: Whiggism = anti-nature = barbarity, the destruction of shelter ('tow'rs are sunk'—1.41), security and growth ('lands are barren now, / . . . flow'rs maun dow'—ll.41-2).

Herriot

> I'm well content; but binna cassen down,
> Nor trow the cock will ca' ye hame o'er soon,
> For tho' the eastern lift betakens day,
> Changing her rokelay black for mantle grey,
> Nae weirlike bird our knell of parting rings,
> Nor sheds the caller moisture frae his wings.
> NATURE has chang'd her course; the birds o'day
> Dosin' in silence on the bending spray,
> While owlets round the craigs at noon-tide flee,
> And bludey bawks sit singand on the tree.
> Ah, CALEDON! the land I yence held dear,
> Sair mane mak I for they destruction near;
> And thou, EDINA! anes my dear abode,
> Whan royal JAMIE sway'd the sovereign rod,
> In thae blest days, weel did I think bestow'd,
> To blaw thy poortith by wi' heaps o' gowd;
> To mak thee sonsy seem wi' mony a gift,

And gar thy stately turrets speel the lift:
In vain did Danish Jones, wi' gimcrack pains,
In Gothic sculpture fret the pliant stanes:
In vain did he affix my statue here,
Brawly to busk wi' flow'rs ilk coming year;
My tow'rs are sunk, my lands are barren now,
My fame, my honour, like my flow'rs maun
    dow.

                        (ll.19-42)

Watson's response does little more than keep the dialogue moving while parodying the graveyard style in the mention of local wizards and superstitions and the hamely images of 'corbie fleeing' and 'croupin' craws' (l.51).

    Sure *Major Weir*, or some sic warlock wight,
    Has flung beguilin' glamer o'er your sight;
    Or else some kittle cantrup thrown, I ween,
    Has bound in mirlygoes my ain twa ein,
    If ever aught frae sense cou'd be believed
    (And seenil hae my senses been deceiv'd
    This moment, o'er the tap of Adam's tomb,
    Fu' easy can I see your chiefest dome:
    Nae corbie fleein' there, nor croupin' craws,
    Seem to forspeak the ruin of thy haws,
    But a' your tow'rs in wonted order stand,
    Steeve as the rocks that hem our native land.

Again using the pastoral scheme, lines 55-114 broach the issue of the Mortmain Bill, which was virtually to deprive the two schools of their endowments. Herriot relates not only the Mortmain Bill but the 1707 Union to the new capitalist lairds and the demise of the former pastoral state of the nation. In the passage England is the repressive landlord; Scotland the dispossessed tenantry. The Union is said to have brought 'destructive ills' (l.59), and Scotland is depicted as full of servile trustees who carry out the demands of their laird, England, paying 'gowd in gowpins as a grassum gift' (l.66): the fee paid to the landlord by the new tenant. England, as the cruel masters who 'Yoke hard the poor' (l.71), reminds us of the 'Gentles' for whose delicacies

    . . . they hight their tenants rent,
  And fill their lands wi' poortith, discontent . . .
          ("A Drink Eclogue", ll.65-6)

and of starving farmers of The Rising of the Session, ll.25-48.

    Think na I vent my well-a-day in vain,
  Kent ye the cause, ye sure wad join my mane,
  Black be the day that e'er to England's ground
  Scotland was eikit by the UNION's bond;
  For mony a menzie of destructive ills
  The country now maun brook frae *mortmain
    bills,*
  That void our test'ments, and can freely gie
  Sic will and scoup to the ordain'd trustee,
  That he may tir our stateliest riggins bare,
  Nor acres, houses, woods, nor fishins spare,
  Till he can lend the stoitering state a lift

Wi' gowd in gowpins as a grassum gift;
In lieu of whilk, we maun be weel content
To tyne the capital at three *per cent.*
A doughty sum indeed, whan now-a-days
They raise provisions as the stents they raise,
Yoke hard the poor, and lat the rich chiels be,
Pamper'd at ease by ither's industry.
  Hale interest for my fund can scantly now
Cleed a' my callants backs, and stap their mou'.
How maun their weyms wi' sairest hunger slack,
Their duds in targets flaff upo' their back,
Whan they are doom'd to keep a lasting Lent,
Starving for England's weel at *three per cent.*

                        (ll.55-78)

Note too those images of decline, those 'stateliest riggins bare' and devastated 'acres, houses, woods . . . fishins' (ll.63-4). Watson reinforces the metaphor in an eighteenth-century moral vein, claiming that Edinburgh in the past—'the golden times' (l.79)—embodied ideal moral values and social responsibility. Under the present Whig administration vice prevails: moral values are inverted to serve, ironically, 'a back-gaun king' (l.84); 'honesty and poortith baith are crimes' (l.80); a Hanoverian king connives at 'vice' and never frets over the 'price o'sin' (ll.85-9), crushing the 'pious' among the poor—again the rhetoric of barbarity—with 'ruthless, ravenous, and harpy laws' (ll.91-4).

                  Watson
  AULD REIKIE than may bless the gowden times,
  Whan honesty and poortith baith are crimes;
  She little kend, whan you and I endow'd
  Our hospitals for back-gaun burghers gude,
  That e'er our siller or our lands shou'd bring
  A gude bien living to a back-gaun king,
  Wha, thanks to ministry! is grown sae wise,
  He douna chew the bitter cud of vice;
  For gin, frae Castlehill to Netherbow,
  Wad honest houses baudy-houses grow,
  The crown wad never spier the price o' sin,
  Nor hinder younkers to the de'il to rin;
  But gif some mortal grien for pious fame,
  And leave the poor man's pray'r to sane his
    name,
  His geer maun a'be scatter'd by the claws
  O' ruthless, ravenous, and harpy laws.
  Yet, shou'd I think, altho' the bill tak place,
  The council winna lack sae meikle grace,
  As lat our heritage at wanworth gang,
  Or the succeeding generations wrang
  O' braw bien maintenance and walth o' lear,
  Whilk else had drappit to their children's skair;
  For mony a deep, and mony a rare engyne
  Ha'e sprung frae Herriot's wark, and sprung frae
    mine.

                     (ll.79-102)

Herriot's rejoinder makes the old division between England, the unnatural, the barbaric, the bestial, as court, and Scotland as country, sold by bribery. But there is another telling theme superimposed upon this one, one that we have seen before in **"The Election"**: the humanist idea that though individuals either act freely or choose to deny their own will, they can be limited in their decision making through coercion, especially by enforced poverty or hunger. Thus Herriot uses the metaphor of England as the fishermen who 'need only bait the line' (1.109); the trustees as feckless creatures who snap at 'the prevailing flee, the gowden coin' (1.110); and the flagging nation as 'sport' (1.113), men whose limited will makes them an easy catch.

Herriot

> I find, my friend, that ye but little ken,
> There's einow on the earth a set o' men,
> Wha' if they get their private pouches lin'd,
> Gie na a winnelstrae for a' mankind;
> They'll sell their country, flae their conscience
>   bare,
> To gar the weigh-bauk turn a single hair.
> The government need only bait the line
> Wi' the prevailing flee, the gowden coin,
> Then our executors, and wise trustees,
> Will sell them fish in forbidden seas,
> Upo' their dwining country girn in sport,
> Laugh in their sleeve, and get a place at court.
>
> (ll.103-114)

The poem closes (ll.115-34), notably, with that recurrent winter image and with the antidote to Whig hegemony. Watson, who first awakened to 'the nippin north wi' angry sough' and 'showers' of 'hailstanes' (ll.7-8) threatens to see the reversals of nature to their ultimate end, should the bribery Herriot deprecates persist.

Watson

> 'Ere that day come, I'll 'mang our spirits pick
> Some ghaist that trokes and conjures wi' Auld
>   Nick,
> To gar the wind wi' rougher rumbles blaw,
> And weightier thuds than ever mortal saw:
> Fire-flaught and hail, wi' tenfald fury's fires,
> Shall lay yird-laigh Edina's airy spires:
> Tweed shall rin rowtin' down his banks out o'er,
> Till Scotland's out o' reach o' England's pow'r;
> Upo' the briny Borean jaws to float,
> And mourn in dowy saughs her dowy lot.
>
> (ll.115-24)

Herriot's final prescription for the nation's ills constitutes one of Fergusson's most explicit party-political statements, for the Mackenzie to whom they are about to appeal for help was a notorious Royalist and Episcopalian stalwart. As M.P.McDiarmid rightly notices, he was known by Presbyterians as the 'Bluidy Advocate' for his prosecution of the Covenanters; as the opponent of Charles II's proposal to unite the two kingdoms; and as the author of the Royalist *The Defence of the Antiquity of the Royal Line of Scotland* (1685). Mackenzie represented the spirit of the early Vernacular Revival in his scholarship—he founded the Advocate's Library—, his defence of Scot-

tish traditions, legal, social, linguistic and literary, and in his religious and political opinions. That founding father of the Revival, Watson, published Mackenzie's *Works* (1716-20), and it was notably to him that Freebairn, Pitcairne, the Ruddimans, the Fraser-Tytlers, Meston, Fergusson and their circle naturally turned for inspiration. He was one of the last defenders of a Scots humanist culture. Herriot's answer to Whiggism would not have sat so easily on Ramsay's tongue.

Herriot

> Yonder's the tomb of wise *Mackenzie*
>   fam'd,
> Whase laws rebellious bigotry reclaim'd,
> Freed the hail land frae covenanting fools,
> Wha erst ha'e fash'd us wi' unnumber'd dools;
> Till night we'll tak the swaird aboon our pows,
> And than, when she her ebon chariot rows,
> We'll travel to the vaut wi' stealing stap,
> And wauk Mackenzie frae his quiet nap:
> Tell him our ails, that he, wi' wonted skill,
> May fleg the schemers o' the *mortmain-bill*.
>
> (ll.125-34)

The prospect of waking 'Mackenzie frae his quiet nap' (1.132), of describing death in this off-hand manner, makes a fitting closure to this burlesque of the graveyard poem.

The impulse to compose mock elegies and burlesques of the graveyard remained with the poet to the end of his short career; nevertheless, he did turn his hand to serious elegiac verse; not the stilted sentimental drivel of the mid-eighteenth century. There was an ongoing tradition of elegiac satire and elegiac verse, which Fergusson inherited, thematically centring on the decline of Scotland's towns and the erosion of Scottish culture. Dunbar himself, the father of the 'local poem' or city poem 'in English', had written "The Devillis Inquest", "Tydingis frae the Sessioun"—published in popular eighteenth-century collections like Ramsay's *Ever Green* and Hailes' *Bannatyne Poems*—and "To the Merchantis of Edinburgh". These were satires in the Juvenalian vein. Then there were the seventeenth-century Latinist poets: John Johnston, whose town poems, included in "Camden's Britannia", and Arthur Johnston, whose *Epigrams (upon the City of Aberdeen)*, adopted the elegiac mood, at times, in pondering the rise and fall of Scotland's towns. . . .

This mood appealed to the humanists of the post-Union period; it was tailored to their sentiments. In 1741, for example, appeared the anonymous *Lamentation for E— Na in Thraldom,* taking the form of Oldham and Dryden's translations of Juvenal's 'Third Satire', but bewailing the now politically emasculated capital city.

> Once famed *Metropolis!* wretched is thy Doom,
> In abject Ruines sunk, and ruthless Gloom:
> Senate's meer Shadow, but without a Soul,
> What can thy swift, approaching Fate controul?

Fergusson's friends and contemporaries published elegiac

verse and satire that influenced him a good deal: works like Dougal Graham's 'Turinspike'; Mercer's 'Arthur's Seat', lamenting 'many a ruin'd port' on the once prosperous Fife coast and 'the wheel of ceaseless change', crushing empires beneath it; and Claudero's many Edinburgh ruin poems. The keynotes of these works was Scotland rebuilding over the crumbling foundations of its past; Scotland changing for the sake of utility or mere modishness, and without a sense of continuity or benefit from the lessons of history: again themes which see the poet oscillating back to his more stringent humanist models.

Fergusson's elegiac verse falls into two categories: those works in which fashion, mainly clothing, is a metaphor for regrettable social changes, and those quite generally about the ebbing culture. The fashion metaphor is an important one in humanist poetry. As Paul Fussell astutely observes, 'To the Augustan humanist, clothes, like buildings, are static, public, social, completely controllable . . . ; they are symbols of conventions and institutions, as with Swift's use of the torn coat poorly repaired to symbolise Episcopacy's replacement in Scotland by the Presbytery, and the subsequent impoverishment of the ousted clergy.' Clothes distinguish man from other similar species, thus the humanist insists that one should neither, as Fussell has it, oversymbolise, mistaking clothing for the wearer, nor undersymbolise, conceiving of the individual as distinct from his clothing. By this definition the town fop is as uncivilised as the savage. More often than not Fergusson's characters are guilty of oversymbolising, like Swift's corrupt sect who worship tailors, conceiving of man as a '*Micro-Coat,* or rather a compleat Suit of Cloaths with all its Trimmings' (*A Tale of a Tub*). The poet upholds the ancient humanist imperative:

> . . . let all finery not suitable to a man's
> dignity be kept off his person . . .

The idea of fashion in Fergusson's poetry is part of a systematic, interlocked network of imagery: another segment of the rhetorical formula used in **"The Ghaists"**: Nature (the pastoral state) = Appropriate Clothing (proper symbolising) = Time-worn institutions and conventions = Shelter (protection) = Adaptability to Seasons = *Civilisation;* Art (counterpastoral) = Fashion (oversymbolising / undersymbolising) = Changing values and institutions = Destruction (Winter rules) = Bestiality and *Barbarism.* This, we may recall, was the central art/nature tension in **"On seeing a Butterfly in the Street,"** where the natural laird, simply clad, represents old loyalties and harmonious living as against the fop, the laird turned politician, traitor to his tenants, unable to weather life's storms.

> For they war' never made to dree
> The adverse gloom O' FORTUNE'S eie . . .
>
> (ll.35-6)

The poet's own **"Fashion. A Poem,"** though by no means one of his better efforts, makes just such rhetorical distinctions. In it we find 'Nature', as she appears in **"Leith Races,"** cloaking 'ilka rigg o' corn' (ll.1-3), the parent and protector; figuratively the shelter to those who de-

pend upon her—'O Nature, parent goddess!' (l.1); Nature as pastoral in her 'bright form! in thy effulgence pure' (l.4); Nature, obviously imagined in a 'simple garb' as in 'HAME CONTENT' (l.102), 'regardless of vain fashion's fools' (l.7), accompanying 'Wisdom in sober contemplation clad' (l.10); Nature in a simple dress superior to the finest Art, representing physical and spiritual wellbeing.

> Nature! to thee alone, not Fashion's pomp,
> Does beauty owe her all-commanding eye.
> From the green bosom of the wat'ry main,
> Array'd by thee, majestic Venus rose,
> With waving ringlets carelessly diffus'd,
> Floating luxurious o'er the restless surge.
> What *Rubens* then, with his enliv'ning hand,
> Could paint the bright vermillion of her cheek,
> Pure as the roseat portal of the east,
> That opens to receive the cheering ray
> Of Phoebus beaming from the orient sky?
> For sterling beauty needs no faint essays,
> Or colourings of art, to gild her more:
> She is all perfect. And, if beauty fail,
> Where are those ornaments, those rich attires
> Which can reflect a lustre on that face,
> Where she with light innate disdains to shine?
>
> (ll.51-67)

We must add that Fashion (Art) as 'foreign weeds' (l.79) is portrayed as something of an Orange or Hanoverian figure, especially if, in our reading, we bear in mind that the motto of the poem is again from Butler.

> Bred up where discipline most rare is,
> *In Military Garden* Paris.
>
> (*Hudibras*)

In fact throughout the poem the language has the flavour of Royalist propaganda about it in depicting the rise of fashion and consequent overthrow of old values: 'vain fashion's fools' (l.7) loom large as the rebellious mob— 'those vile enormities of shape / That croud the world' (l.9), 'those bold usurpers' (l.11); while 'FASHION her empire holds . . . amidst the *Millenarian* train / On a resplendent throne exalted high' (ll.14-16). In relation to the Nature—Art tension, fashion's empire, like Hanover's in **"The Ghaist,"** is a treacherous force against well being: her

> . . . dear bought treasures o'er their native isle
> Contagious spread, infect the wholesome air
> That cherish'd vigour in Britannia's sons.
>
> (ll.21-3)

She is destined to wreak havoc and to make of the Eden of the past a barren, putrefying waste.

> By pride, by luxury, what fatal ills
> Unheeded have approach'd thy mortal frame!
> How many foreign weeds their heads have rear'd
> In thy fair garden? Hasten 'ere their strength
> And beneful vegetation taint the soil,
> To root out rank disease, which soon must

spread,
If no bless'd antidote will purge away
Fashion's proud minions from our sea-girt isle.
(ll.77-84). . . .

Fergusson's other pieces in the elegiac strain, and the elegies themselves, concentrate on the receding culture. Of the former group is the satire **"To the Principal and Professors of the University of St Andrews, On their superb treat to Dr Samuel Johnson,"** and parts of **"An Expedition to Fife and the Island of May"** and **"The Bugs"**. The satire on Johnson is elegiac in that it mourns the national disgrace of Scotland, and subsequent loss of national pride, in the wake of a strong anti-Scottish campaign begun during Lord Bute's, a Scottish prime minister's, administration.

Fergusson's disdain for Samuel Johnson and, equally, for the regents of St Andrews University who welcome him, is, in good Augustan fashion, conveyed through making food—the food prepared for Johnson—a moral issue. Like the landlady in **"A Drink Eclogue,"** he deplores the advent of anti-Scots upstarts, the people who cater to them, and the delicacies bought for them from afar, which threaten to change the staple diet of the nation, and its lifestyle in the process.

> Ah! willawins, for Scotland now,
> Whan she maun stap ilk birky's mow
> Wi' eistacks, grown as 'tware in pet
> In foreign land, or green-house het,
> When cog o'brose an' cutty spoon
> Is a' our cottar childer's boon,
> Wha thro' the week, till Sunday's speal,
> Toil for pease-clods an' gude lang kail.
> Devall then, Sirs, and never send
> For daintiths to regale a friend,
> Or, like a torch at baith ends burning,
> Your house'll soon grow mirk and mourning.
> (ll.71-82)

Another grievance the poet bemoans, despite his avowed intention of assuaging the ill-will between himself and the citizens of Fife, is adverted to in lines 83-98: his malevolence towards the country for its Covenanting activities in the seventeenth century, and, as Thomas Ruddiman notes, the 'misunderstanding he had with a Gentleman, a native of Dunfermline, who took amiss at the concluding reflection in the **"Expedition to Fife"** so much, that he sent him a challenge; but which our Author treated with great contempt'.

> What's this I hear some cynic say?
> Robin, ye loun! it's nae fair play;
> Is there nae ither subject rife
> To clap your thumb upon but Fife?
> Gi'e o'er, young man, you'll meet your corning,
> Than caption war, or charge o'horning;
> Some canker'd surly sour-mow'd carline
> Bred near the abbey o'Dumfarline,
> Your shoulders yet may gi'e lounder,
> An'be of verse the mal-confounder.

Come on ye blades! but 'ere ye tulzie,
Or hack our flesh wi' sword or gulzie,
Ne'er shaw your teeth, nor look like stink,
Nor o'er an empty bicker blink:
What weets the wizen an' the wyme,
Will mend your prose and heal my rhyme.

Bearing this in mind, recalling that Fergusson makes light of a ruinous St Andrews University at the beginning, which had been purged several times of its Jacobites and Episcopalians; noting those very significant passing references to the arch seventeenth-century Scots humanist, 'Drummond, lang syne, o' Hawthornden, / The wyliest an'best (ll.61-2) and to his *Polemo-Middinia;* we may read into the poem something of a lament for a lost Episcopal and Stewart past. Certainly this is what the poet has in mind in **"An Expedition to Fife and the Island of May"** when his misgivings on time and decay lead to the following lines. M.P.McDiarmid states, in fact, that Fergusson 'has chiefly in mind the enthusiasm of the country for the Covenant in the reign of Charles I, and the murder of Archbishop Sharp by men of Fife on Magus Muir in 1679'; and that, 'In such lines the poet voices not only the Episcopalian tradition of the North-East, from which his family came, but also his own Deistical opinions'.

> To FIFE we steer, of all beneath the sun
> The most unhallow'd 'midst the SCOTIAN plains!
> And here, sad emblem of deceitful times!
> Hath sad hypocrisy her standard borne.
> Mirth knows no residence, but ghastly fear
> Stands trembling and appall'd at airy sights.
> ONCE, only *only once!* Reward it, O ye powers!
> Did HOSPITALITY, with open face,
> And winning smile, cheer the deserted sight,
> That else had languish'd for the blest return
> Of beauteous day, to dissipate the clouds
> Of endless night, and superstition wild,
> That constant hover o'er the dark abode.
> (ll.107-19)

Parabolically, **"The Bugs"** bewails the undoing of old Edinburgh in a counterpastoral vision. 'The rude ax . . . / Of daring innovation' (ll.29-30) razes the umbrageous forests of the 'DRYADS' (l.21), destroying the 'shade' of 'Pan' and 'his rural train' (ll.21-6). Edinburgh, 'Edina's walls' (l.21), 'Edina's mansions' (l.33), her once 'spacious' and 'gay' streets (l.37), is portrayed as a moribund civilisation through the rhetoric of counterpastoral: the devastation of the forest, the intrusion of black night and disease, the end of summer, the removal of shelter.

> Of old the DRYADS near Edina's walls
> Their mansions rear'd, and groves unnumber'd
> rose
> Of branching oak, spread beech, and lofty pine,
> Under whose shade, to shun the noontide blaze,
> Did Pan resort, with all his rural train
> Of shepherds and of nymphs.—The Dryads
> pleas'd,
> Would hail their sports, and summon echo's
> voice,

To send her greetings thro' the waving woods;
But the rude ax, long brandish'd by the hand
Of daring innovation, shav'd the lawns;
Then not a thicket or a copse remain'd
To sigh in concert with the breeze of eve.
    Edina's mansions with lignarian art
Were pil'd and fronted.—Like an ARK she
    seem'd
To lie on mountain's top, with shapes replete,
Clean and unclean, that daily wander o'er
Her streets, that once were spacious, once were
    gay.
To JOVE the Dryads pray'd, nor pray'd in vain,
For vengeance on her sons.—At midnight drear
Black show'rs descend, and teeming myriads rise
of BUGS abhorrent, who by instinct steal
Thro' the diseased and corrosive pores
Of sapless trees, that late in forest stood
With all the majesty of summer crown'd.
                        (ll.21-44)

Of paramount importance is the chaffing of the moral meagreness of the new town cit. Engaging in battle with the bugs, the upholsterer and the housemaid are cut down in stature—and we must note the swipe at sentimentalism—in exactly the same manner as were the burghers of **"The Election,"** who 'fleg awa the vermin' from their coats (ll.28-36).

    Ev'n so befalls it to this creeping race,
This envy'd commonwealth—For they a while
On Cloe's bosom, alabaster fair,
May steal ambrosial bliss—or may regale
On the rich *viands* of luxurious blood,
Delighted and suffic'd. But mark the end:
Lo! WHITSUNTIDE appears with gloomy train
Of growing desolation.—First UPHOLSTERER rude
Removes the waving drapery, where, for years,
A thriving colony of old and young
Had hid their numbers from the prying day;
Anon they fall, and gladly would retire
To safer ambush, but his merciless foot,
Ah, cruel pressure! cracks their vital springs,
And with their deep-dy'd scarlet smears the
    floor.
    Sweet pow'rs! has pity in the female breast
No tender residence—no lov'd abode?
To urge from murd'rous deed th' avenging hand
Of angry house-maid—She'll have blood for
    blood!
For lo! the boiling streams from copper tube,
Hot as her rage, sweep myriads to death.
Their carcases are destin'd to the urn
Of some chaste Naiad, that gives birth to floods,
Whose fragrant virtues hail Edina, fam'd
For yellow limpid—Whose chaste name the
    Muse
Thinks too exalted to retail in song.
                      (ll.92-117)

"Elegy, On the Death of Scots Music"—music in the wider sense of music and poetry—is one of the historicist

works on a declining Scottish way of life and art, and its replacement by adopted English or Italian styles. Fergusson's elegy is obviously modelled on Nicol's *An Elegy on Auld Use and Wont (Rural Muse)* and is not, then, as one scholar has it, the first example after Ramsay 'of the use of the six-line stanza in a poem of serious intent'. Nicol's elegy is fraught with themes familiar to much of Fergusson's poetry, and particularly to **"Elegy, On . . . Scots Music"**: themes on unnatural changes in 'church and state' (p.12); the loss of 'A race of kings . . . / Twa thousand years' old, and of 'baith parliament and king' (p.13); 'peers and gentrie (once) content / To bide at hame and spend their rent', 'Landlords (who) didnae grudge to see / Their tenants thrive' (p.13); 'nae foreign wines nor tea'; 'poets too that cou'd mak lines'; 'browsters (who) made good nappie ale, / And sald it cheaper a good dale'; oppressive 'taxes on our ale and maut'; the rescinding of 'ancient rights and liberties'; the banning of 'ane auld gun' or 'rusty blade' for defence. Aside from being a serious elegy composed in the Habbie stanza, Nicol's *Elegy on Auld Use and Wont* resembles Fergusson's poem in singling out fashion too as a symbol of cultural erosion.

A farmer ween'd himself fu bra',
When he had plaiden hose like sna',
A good gray hodden coat, and a
    Gray plaid aboon,
Warm mittens on his hands, and twa
    Strong pointed shoon:

But now ilk chiel that wins a fee,
Maun hae bra blues; and wha but he?
Wi' buckles at's neck, feet and knee,
    Well scour'd and clean,
As new coach harness use to be;
    He looks nae mean.
Our lairds and lords, yea e'en our king,
For grab sought never ony thing
But what our ain land forth did bring;
    Ladies at a'
For foreign segrims didnae fling
    Their gou'd awa'.

        . . . . .

Our native garb aside is laid,
The ancient tartan coat and plaid;
Nane o' them a'dares now be had
    Sin' Wont's awa;
Poor Scotland now maun a' be sway'd
    By English law.

And both poems address themselves once to the nation itself: Nicol in the first line of his first stanza—'OH Scotland, Scotland!', and Fergusson in the first line of his last stanza—'O SCOTLAND!'.

This said, Fergusson's is a far more sophisticated composition which ingeniously sets in opposition different poetic forms to underpin his structure. In lines 1-18 the *Elegy* begins with a straightforward Scots pastoral, equating older, simple fashions with traditional music and, implicitly, with an ideal society and gives way to the stylised form of the English neoclassical pastoral elegy: the 'feather'd choir' (l.7), 'weeping streams and *Naiads*' (l.15), etc.

> On Scotia's plains, in days of yore,
> 　　When lads and lasses *tartan* wore,
> Saft Music rang on ilka shore,
> 　　　　In hamely weid;
> But harmony is now no more,
> 　　And *music* dead.
>
> Round her the feather'd choir would wing,
> Sae bonnily she wont to sing,
> And sleely wake the sleeping string,
> 　　　　Their sang to lead,
> Sweet as the zephyrs of the spring;
> 　　But now she's dead.
>
> Mourn ilka-nymph and ilka swain,
> Ilk sunny hill and dowie glen;
> Let weeping streams and *Naiads* drain
> 　　　　Their fountain head;
> Let echo swell the dolefu' strain,
> 　　Since music's dead.

The effect is not only to make the Scots past, devoid of superfluities and extravagant dress, the true measure of nature and culture but, even more, to equate the vernacular Scots pastoral form with Nature, and the English neoclassical form with Art. Taking the point a step further; if language, as the humanist Pope puts it, is the 'dress of thought' then this overdone neoclassical verse, like gaudy dress or over-ornate Baroque architecture, is improperly attired, and reflects declining standards of culture.

Lines 19-48 follow a similar thesis—antithesis pattern, where the first corresponds to the Scots pastoral elegy form and the second, this time, to a different form altogether: to the Scots mock elegy which, with its conscious over-emoting, recalls the earlier lines of the English sentimental elegy—the 'weeping streams' (l.15) and the like—in order to deflate them. A great deal appears in the thesis. There is firstly a Ramsayesque lament for pastoral song followed by several supportive allusions to vernacular poetry and song: allusions to Ramsay's *Gentle Shepherd*, Hamilton of Bangour's 'The Braes Of Yarrow', Robert Crawford's 'Tweed-Side': in short, allusions to a pastoral tradition seen as departing along with an old communal, bucolic way of life.

> Whan the saft vernal breezes ca'
> The grey-hair'd Winter's fogs awa',
> Naebody than is heard to blaw,
> 　　　　Near hill or mead,
> On chaunter, or on aiten straw,
> 　　Since music's dead.
>
> Nae lasses now, on simmer days,
> Will lilt at bleaching of their claes;
> Nae herds on *Yarrow*'s bonny braes,

> 　　　　Or banks of *Tweed,*
> Delight to chant their hameil lays,
> 　　Since music's dead.
>
> 　　　　　　　　　　　　(ll.19-30)

The lines that follow are pregnant with suggestion.

> At glomin now the bagpipe's dumb,
> Whan weary owsen hameward come;
> Sae sweetly as it wont to bum,
> 　　　　And *Pibrachs* skreed;
> We never hear its warlike hum;
> 　　For music's dead.
>
> 　　　　　　　　　　　　(ll.31-6)

The bagpipes, pibrochs, and the pipes 'warlike hum' (l.35), like the mention of tartan before, conjure up romantic notions of Jacobites and the spirit of the '15 and the '45, while, in drawing together the pipes' muteness and the flagging military spirit with outdated farming methods—'weary owsen' (l.32)—which were discarded by the new capitalist lairds, the poet looks nostalgically back upon a Highland culture antedating the two late rebellions: though, of course, he does so less explicitly than had Nicol in his *Elegy.* The lines on Macgibbon are more an excuse to interpose the Standard Habbie mock elegy form for reductive effect than to celebrate the noted fiddler, classical composer—who actually composed in the Italian style—and Scots tune collector.

> *Macgibbon*'s gane: Ah! waes my heart!
> The man in music maist expert,
> Wha cou'd sweet melody impart,
> 　　　　And tune the reed,
> Wi' sic a slee and pawky art;
> 　　But now he's dead,
>
> Ilk carline now may grunt and grane,
> Ilk bonny lassie make great mane,
> Since he's awa', I trow there's nane
> 　　　　Can fill his stead;
> The blythest sangster on the plain!
> 　　Alake, he's dead!
>
> 　　　　　　　　　　　　(ll.37-48)

Moving logically from the pattern of sections I and II, the final lines (49-66) posit an apology of Scots national poetry and music with an implicit denunciation of English neoclassical verse.

> Now foreign sonnets bear the gree,
> And crabbit queer variety
> Of sound fresh sprung frae *Italy,*
> 　　　　A bastard breed!
> Unlike that saft-tongu'd melody
> 　　Which now lies dead.
>
> Cou'd *lav'rocks* at the dawning day,
> Cou' *linties* chirming frae the spray,
> Or todling *burns* that smoothly play
> 　　　　O'er gowden bed,
> Compare wi' *Birks of Indermay?*

But now they're dead.

O SCOTLAND! that cou'd yence afford
To bang the pith of Roman sword,
Winna your sons, wi' joint accor,
    To battle speed?
And fight till MUSIC be restor'd,
    Which now lies dead.

The cliche language and imagery of lines 55-60—'dawning day', 'the spray', 'smoothly play', 'gowden bed'—express false sentiment; hence, counterpastoral, a state in which false feelings and empty pastoral rhetoric mask nature. In this case art does not mirror nature; it obscures it. Nor is the neoclassical pastoral subtle like the Scots pastoral was, which could 'sleely wake the sleeping string' (l.9); 'cou'd sweet melody impart, / And tune the reed, / Wi' sic a slee and pawky art' (ll.39-41). The romanticised closing lines, reminding Scotland of her once glorious defeat of the Romans, recapitulate the subject of the waning military spirit, now lost with the moderns' commercial pursuits. Apropos of this, the word 'afford' (l.61) possesses a touch of irony: now that Scotland has wealth she cannot 'afford' to defend her identity. Ancient simplicity and superfluities, as the literati stated repeatedly, could not co-exist. Fergusson's final appeal supporting historicist over commercial interests couched, as it is, in military terms, couples a hard pastoral, however romantic—independent, fighting—Scotland with the preservation of her musical traditions.

Again we see pastoral in Fergusson united with vernacular traditions; again we see him close to his humanist touchstones, as in **"The Daft-Days,"** published 2nd January 1772, which is an unusually subtle and well crafted poem for so young a poet. A seasonal piece in the classical tradition of Epicurean withdrawal it is. But the seasonal framework has a particular Scottish humanist context.

In lines 1-18 two aspects of nature during the Christmas season in the country are envisaged.

NOW mirk December's dowie face
    Glours our the rigs wi' sour grimace,
While, thro' his *minimum* of space,
    The bleer-ey'd sun,
Wi' blinkin light and stealing pace,
    His race doth run.

From naked groves nae birdie sings,
To shepherd's pipe nae hillock rings,
The breeze nae od'rous flavour brings
    From *Borean* cave,
And dwyning nature droops her wings,
    Wi' visage grave.

Mankind but scanty pleasure glean
Frae snawy hill or barren plain,
Whan Winter, 'midst his nipping train,
    Wi' frozen spear,
Sends drift owr a' his bleak domain,

And guides the weir.

As the prevailing power of 'Winter' (l.15), nature is a fierce chieftain: a primitive warrior ''midst his nipping train, / Wi' frozen spear', lording over his 'bleak domain', determining his own fate in battle (ll.15-18). Simultaneously, nature exhibits the opposite qualities as the powerless victim fleeing for his own survival; the sun runs his race in hiding, with a 'stealing pace' confined to a *minimum* of space (ll.3-6); nature's hopeless 'wings' droop impotently in a state of sad decay (l.11). Moreover, the unmitigated personification of the passage brings home the two aspects of nature to man. Imperial December, the warrior, 'Glours' with a 'dowie face' and 'sour grimace' (ll.1-2); appears with 'visage grave' (l.12). The sun, like a snow-blind Antarctic explorer, 'bleer-ey'd', nervously 'blinkin'', paces cautiously to safety (ll.4-6). Here then are two pictures of natural man—hardly the sentimentalist's noble savage—living like a savage out of doors, without shelter, warmth, or civilisation: the one a picture of a ruthless barbarian fighting with his fellow man in survival-of-the-fittest circumstances, and the other, of an unadaptable victim of his environment.

Lines 19-42 transport us from the bleak outdoors into the age-old festivities of the old town, which, in humanist terms, is a fortification—the last line of defence—against winter's rage.

Auld Reikie! thou'rt the canty hole,
A bield for mony caldrife soul,
Wha snugly at thine ingle loll,
    Baith warm and couth;
While round they gar the bicker roll
    To weet their mouth.

When merry *Yule-day* comes, I trow
You'll scantlins find a hungry mou;
Sma' are our cares, our stamacks fou
    O' gusty gear,
And kickshaws, strangers to our view,
    Sin Fairn-year.

Ye browster wives, now busk ye bra,
And fling your sorrows far awa';
Then come and gies the tither blaw
    Of reaming ale,
Mair precious than the well of *Spa,*
    Our hearts to heal.

Then, tho' at odds wi' a' the warl',
Amang oursells we'll never quarrel;
Tho' Discord gie a canker'd snarl
    To spoil our glee,
As lang's there's pith into the barrel
    We'll drink and 'gree.

Indoors we find a mirror image of the outdoor conflict in the opposition of formidable determinist forces and humanist ideals, as vital and as natural to survival as protection from winter's cold. Fergusson, in attempting to combat modernity, goes back to first principles, describing his ideal city, his receptacle of civilisation, in stark terms. He is like the social historian Lewis Mumford who discerns

> . . . in the rites of the cave the social and religious impulses that conspired to draw men finally into cities, where all the original feelings of awe, reverence, pride, and joy would be further magnified by art, and multiplied by the number of responsive participants.

The poet's 'canty hole' (1.19) is like the cave to which the first communities sought shelter, and it, being the proper refuge for a 'caldrife soul' (1.20), is Auld Reikie, symbol of traditional Scotland; a magnification of the Scots rural cottage, with a snug 'ingle', 'Baith warm and couth', plenty of heart warming drink in celebration of the Yule festivities (ll.21-4). The smoke of Auld Reikie becomes, in this image, that welcoming 'smeek'—with all that it implies—that saluted the gudeman in **"The Farmer's Ingle"** (1.13). Outside the ambit of the cottage, beyond the confines of Auld Reikie and its Christmas celebrations, are the perilous conditions of winter which introduced the poem. 'Discord('s) canker'd snarl' (1.39), reminiscent of December's 'sour grimace' (1.2), and the phrase 'tho' at odds wi' a' the warl" (ll.37-9) signal a state of turmoil; 'caldrife soul' (1.20), 'sorrows' (1.32), 'Our hearts to heal' (1.36), infer that man, without his town and culture, like the rest of nature victimised by December, does not guide his own struggles. Bearing in mind Reikie as a cave from the wind and cold, this refuge is what civilises and humanises man; what distinguishes his plight from the rest of nature in winter. In essence, culture defends and protects; heals and harmonises; rebuffs the powers that would control the individual.

It is, beyond this, the source of his power to act and the well-spring of his original innocence and happiness; the restorer of Eden, the first civil society. Hence lines 43-66 are an entreaty back to the native culture; back to the original pastoral state of harmony, healing, and fullness of life.

> *Filders,* your pins in temper fix,
> And roset weel your fiddle-sticks,
> And banish vile Italian tricks
> 　　　　From out your quorum,
> Nor *fortes* wi' *pianos* mix,
> 　　Gie's *Tulloch Gorum.*

> For nought can cheer the heart sae weel
> As can a canty Highland reel,
> It even vivifies the heel
> 　　　　To skip and dance:
> Lifeless is he wha canna feel
> 　　　　Its influence.

> Let mirth abound, let social cheer
> Invest the dawning of the year;
> Let blithesome innocence appear
> 　　　　To crown our joy,
> Nor envy wi' sarcastic sneer
> 　　　　Our bliss destroy.

> And thou, great god of *Aqua Vitae!*
> Wha sways the empire of this city,
> When fou we're sometimes capernoity,
> 　　　　Be thou prepar'd
> To hedge us frae that black banditti,
> 　　　　The City-Guard.

The supplication is to the fiddlers' pins in 'temper' (1.43)—equal musical temperament or harmony—to banish foreign influences. Highland music enables Scots to overcome winter's gloom. It 'can cheer the heart' (1.49). It 'vivifies' the listener (1.51). It 'influence(s)' those who can 'feel' (ll.53-4); those not numbed 'Lifeless' (1.53), beyond a natural response to the national traditions of their forefathers. The second supplication calls upon traditional joys to 'Invest the dawning of the year' (1.56), and this coupled with the reappearance of 'blithesome innocence' and 'bliss' (ll.57, 60)—Eden—heralds a renewal of original control, freedom, civilisation. In the image, man clothes—'Invest' (1.56), being from the Latin, *investire,* to clothe in or to surround—nature's cold season. He makes winter livable; adapts himself to the season; controls his environs; builds upon nature. . . .

From the cave onwards this is what the national tradition is all about. It is a civilising agent. The last supplication, in a lighter vein, calls upon the 'great god of *Aqua Vitae!',* who 'sways the empire of this city' (ll.61-2), to protect the revellers—'hedge us' (1.65)—from the ill powers that be. However tongue-in-cheek, this is a genuine Bacchanalian tribute to the social and festive drink that brings the old community together, and makes man once again the central, or, dominant, figure in his setting. With this, then, the imagery of the introduction has moved from nature as ruler to man as ruler.

"The Daft-Days" is a particularly good representation of eighteenth-century Scots humanist poetry. Winter and pastoral shelter, we have seen so often before, are rhetorically two means the humanist poet employs in differentiating between Whig and humanist cultures respectively. On continuing to use this conventional humanist rhetoric, Fergusson naturally bore in mind such works as Pitcairne's *Babell,* in which the General Assembly of the Kirk is excoriated for bringing to Scotland a state of barbarity, a 'politique brute' (1.134), 'constant war' (1.125), perpetual winter, 'frost and snow' (1.9). Fergusson writes here from exactly the same point of view, for the daft-days held little favour among Presbyterians, being the derogatory epithet they gave to the Episcopal celebration of the Yule. John Ramsay of Ochtertyre says in a footnote, 'Whilst the Episcopals called Christmas-week the *holidays,* the Presbyterians gave it no better name than the *daft days.* When very young, I was reprimanded by an old gentleman for using that expression. He told me very gravely it was a Whiggish phrase.' Meston, for example, says in *The Knight of the Kirk—*

> Our *Knight* will neither *preach* nor *pray,*
> Nor sing a psalm on *Christmas* day . . .
> Quoth he (Andrew Cant), 'You call it good old

Yool-day,
'But I say, it is good old *Fool-day*,
'O! But you say, 'tis a brave *halie* day,
'I tell you, *Sirs*, 'tis a brave *belly* day.'

The holiday festivities and *joie de vivre* of **"The Daft-Days"** are very much in keeping, then, with an older Scots culture. At the same time the poem is grounded in the classical literature of Horace and Virgil, and has many Latinate touches—*'minimum'* (l.3), 'quorum' (l.46), 'Invest' (l.56), *'Aqua Vitae!'* (l.61)—which remind us of the Latinist tradition in Scotland. And Fergusson's penultimate stanza, part of which reads—

Let blithesome innocence appear
        To crown our joy,
Nor envy wi' sarcastic sneer
        Our bliss destroy.

(ll.57-60)

—has more than a hint of Alexander of Struan's last stanza in *The 20th Psalm imitated from Buchanan,* a lament for the Stuarts.

O! let our party Hearts have Peace,
        And Innocence restore,
Then shall thy sacred Law take Place,
        And Faction rule no more.

The various elements make up a very complete Scots humanist poem.

F. W. Freeman (essay date 1987)

SOURCE: "Robert Fergusson: Pastoral and Politics at Mid Century," in *The History of Scottish Literature: 1660-1800, Vol. 2,* edited by Andrew Hook, Aberdeen University Press, 1987, pp. 141-56.

[*In the following excerpt, Freeman discusses Fergusson's defense of Scottish traditions that were threatened by radical social change during the eighteenth century, observing that his poems oppose themes of "shelter, nature, pastoral," and "artifice, false appearance, counter-pastoral."*]

Robert Fergusson, whom Burns pronounced 'By far, my elder brother in the Muses', Wordsworth greatly admired, and Scott, Stevenson, Muir and MacDiarmid, recognized as one of the foremost of Scottish poets, was dismissed by literary worthies in his own day as 'dissipated and drunken', 'coarse', tending to the representation of 'blackguardism'. . . .

Culturally, he was wholly out of step with the Anglicized, Whig, Moderate Presbyterian Scotland of the mid-eighteenth century, however nationalistic it could be in its support of militia movements, Ossianic heroes, or such native literary figures as Thomas Blacklock, John Home, Henry MacKenzie and—Fergusson's friend—William Wilkie. If for MacDairmid in this century 'back to Dun-

bar' was the slogan pointing the way to the revival of a flagging poetic tradition, it was for Fergusson back to vernacular classicism, to the Scots Renaissance art of Gavin Douglas. Generally, Fergusson aspired to classical cultural ideas and values. He composed town poems and pastorals after the models of Juvenal, Horace and Virgil, and, at some point, planned his own translation of the *Georgics* into Scots. Politically, he was a romantic Jacobite, a Scots Tory, as Dr Johnson would have defined one, a Counter-Enlightenment apologist, and if not a regular member of any church (despite short bouts of religious gloom among the small Presbyterian sect called the anti-Burghers), an artist with Episcopal sympathies. . . . He had close ties with his publishers, the Ruddimans, and their circle, whose spiritual home was that Jacobite stronghold, Old St Paul's in Edinburgh's Old Town, and he typified as M P McDairmid aptly describes it, a Northeast Episcopal outlook. What is manifest is that he often wrote in the style and tradition of the Scots Episcopal (and Catholic) satirists and elegists, most of whom were published by the Ruddiman press: Samuel Colvil, Archibald Pitcairne, Alexander Nicol, James Wilson (Claudero) and others.

As a Tory traditionalist, Fergusson at his most idealistic upheld a hierarchical view of the cosmos and of society: what the Episcopal royalist, Sir George Mackenzie of Rosehaugh, called the 'Order of nature which God has established': the Stuart king, courtiers and merchants in the town; the laird, gudeman and tenants in the countryside. Expressions of such a view occur in his poems concerning the demise of the old rural order: the displacement of the gudeman by the new capitalist farmer, the creation of an alienated urban poor drawn from the unemployed of the country, the old laird's abandonment of his tenants for a legal career in the town. Certainly in his country verse he espouses the Tory ideal of a well-regulated rural society through the skilful use of pastoral or, more broadly speaking, *la belle nature,* in terms reminiscent of Sir John Denham's "Cooper's Hill" or Pope's "Windsor Forest", with its notions of "Order in Variety" (l.15), "Rich Industry . . . on the Plains, / And Peace and Plenty" under a "STUART" (ll.41-2).

From his first literary efforts the poet creates and resolves tension between the pastoral world and its opposite, or between nature and art, where the latter represents the agrarian revolution and the forces of change, and the former the traditional way of life. **"Pastoral II. Noon"**, a rather hackneyed neoclassical lament, written in the style of Cunningham or Shenstone but for its stronger, albeit gentle, political overtones, is the earliest example of this kind of poem. According to the dejected shepherd, Corydon, his Delia no longer enjoys the 'embowering solitary shade' (l.20) but

. . . wanders o'er the *Anglian* plain,
Where civil discord and sedition reign.

(ll.23-4)

—a reference to the turmoil between the government headed by Lord North and the Whigs. Later the lover reveals that he and his opponent, Delia's father, are two different men of the soil, he being a subsistence farmer (with 'the weak fences of a scanty fold', l.45) who has not yet assimilated more widely-accepted techniques of enclosure, and the father ('a thousand fleeces numbers o'er / And grassy hills increase his milky store', ll.43-4) obviously a gentleman farmer, and prosperous Whig laird. Agrarian reforms have driven a social wedge between the lovers. With a contrived happy ending it is left to Corydon's elder friend, Timanthes, the model stay-at-home laird, to save the day, providing ample pasturage for Corydon's flock and—consistent with the natural metaphor—leading him away from the sharp rays of the sun, safe from the ill-effects of change.

The themes of the good and the bad laird and, especially, the survival of the gudeman, a substantial tenant whose existence was doomed by the new class of rack-renting lairds, were common to Fergusson's anti-Improving poems: works written after the fashion of the early vernacular revival protest poems, like **"The Speech of a Fife Laird, Newly come from the Grave"**, or, later, Alexander Nicol's "An Elegy on Auld Use and Wont". In this genre Fergusson characteristically upholds staunchly royalist models of social class, and appears to be propounding a solution to the plight of the subsistence farmers put forward years earlier by the Scots Jacobite, William Mackintosh, who, having been out in the 1715 and 1719 rebellions, published from his prison cell a very un-Whiggish improving guide, *An Essay on Ways and Means for Inclosing, Planting etc . . . Scotland* (1729), which appealed to the landlords for longer leases and fewer services to the landowners so that the tenant could properly enclose his land and survive.

Fergusson's best known and most elaborate pastoral, **"The Farmer's Ingle",** is a piece of cosmic Toryism which employs classical and modern (Enlightenment) concepts to idealize the wholly outmoded gudeman system of farming—especially with respect to the techniques of ploughing and winnowing—and of living: the diet, clothing made and worn, the general conditions within the old world thatched cottage which is portrayed: This idealization is effected through neatly fitting the gudeman into the microcosmic scheme of the classical bucolic and, at the same time, into the macrocosmic pattern of *concordia discors,* the ancient cosmology of harmony through balanced opposition which became a cosmic rationale for the Tory ideal. . . .

How we view him is in great measure determined by what we choose to look at: the narrow nationalist, bewailing the Union (**"The Ghaists"**) and deprecating foreign influences, whether in the new taste for French delicacies (**"A Drink Eclogue"**), Italian music (**"The Daft Days"**) or English neoclassical verse (**"Elegy, On the Death of Scots Music"**); or, the internationalist, friend of the Italian tenor, Tenducci, and admirer of William McGibbon, the noted fiddler and classical composer (who actually wrote in the Italian style); friend of Thomas Mercer, who dedicated his anthology of poetry, *The Sentimental Sailor* to Rousseau; afficionado of the theatre, thoroughly enjoy-

ing the Elizabethan revival of the period and especially Shakesperian drama; Augustan man of letters, relishing (and imitating) the poetry of Pope, Gay, Gray and Collins and, equally, the Anglo-Scottish poetry of Drummond of Hawthornden and James Thomson; Fergusson the Counter-Enlightenment artist or, as we have observed, the advocate of industry and industrial reform.

An identical dualism or division occurs in Fergusson's urban poetry: the town poems frequently contain pastoral elements and rhetorical devices used in a political context. Nothing could be more backward-looking than the idealization of a very medieval Edinburgh as rural village in the pastoral sections of **"Hallow-Fair"**, for example. . . .

Like Claudero, an Edinburgh Catholic poet who wrote numerous ruined building poems which voiced the unpopular opinion that the Whigs were building a new Scotland on the crumbling foundations of its traditional past, Fergusson often expresses a strain of pessimism wholly out of step with the forward looking attitude of the Scottish Enlightenment.

If in so many of the town poems Auld Reikie is equated with order and tranquility, purity and health, fair weather or indoor warmth, modern Edinburgh is its antithesis: counterpastoral, or, specifically, as in **"Hallow-Fair"**, **"Babylon"** (l.71), an image familiar to the reading public since the days of Roundhead and Cavalier. Modern Whig Edinburgh, was, in the rhetoric of Mackenzie of Rosehaugh, Colvil, Pitcairne and William Meston, the new Babylon: 'Babel', 'Babylon of Confusions', 'Whore of Babylon', 'Whore of Babel', and so on. Archibald Pitcairne, Thomas Ruddiman's boon companion, simply named his satire on the Church of Scotland's General Assembly, "Babell," and the relation between Kirk and city satire is obvious in moving from "Babell," or Colvil's "Mock Poem," with its screeching and buzzing streets, to Fergusson's **"Hallow-Fair"**, **"Leith Races"** or **"The Election"**. . . .

Caricature is used effectively to ridicule the society of modern Edinburgh as the prominent city of the day act out a travesty of the Tory social order. In this caricature, form is all important. At least part of **"Hallow-Fair"**, and the song of the same title, **"Leith Races",** and **"The Election",** satirize the brutalized poor as well as the new merchant class through relating their immediate living conditions to those Tory principles regarding the mob, and through making those conditions part of an old literary pattern. All of these poems are cast in the Christis Kirk stanza which was initially—and subsequently—used to burlesque peasant rites and customs, from a royalist point of view. . . .

In using this old stanzaic form Fergusson, in part, subtly upholds royalist notions of a debased commons.

Within the Babylon framework some of Fergusson's caricature draws upon the tradition of Episcopal religious satire, especially the idea of mock order, typified by the would-be knight or cavalier, like Samuel Butler's *Hudibras* or Meston's *Sir John Presbyter,* attempting unsuccessfully to be what he clearly is not. Relevant here is the starving, vermin infested poor of **"The Election"** whose pretense of 'order' (l.46) and 'nobility' (ll.52, 62) highlights ironical comparisons between nobleman and peasant and reminds us of the Episcopal literary background (e.g. Pitcairne's play *The Assembly,* 'Act III. Scene I'). The caricature is sharper in depictions of the City Guard, an abusive Whig police, formed after the 1715 rebellion for maintaining order, and comprised mainly of dispossessed Highlanders. Fergusson treats of them in the light vein of Dougal Graham, another little known Glasgow poet, but with some intent to show how far they had strayed from the vigorous, militant Highlanders of Ossianic legend (legend which Fergusson probably believed). In Episcopal literature, Whig society was in a 'continual war' (e.g. "Babell", ll.1337-51); mock heroics were the conventional means of aspersing it. In **"Hallow-Fair"** the combatants, the mischievous Jock Bell and the Town Guard, hail directly from Butler's knights and their battles of bruises rather than blood.

As we have observed, in **"Hallow-Fair"** and **"Leith Races"** Fergusson makes a clear demarcation between two cities in the pastoral-counterpastoral structures of the poems. Nonetheless one senses that the poet does not fully believe that humanity can be confined within the idealization of a frozen pastoral dream. Within Fergusson the rigid moralist co-exists with the iconoclast. His New Babylon is much like Swift's Dublin or Gay's London, a kaleidoscopic rendering of people and events, possessing moral and amoral dimensions. It is manifestly his intention in the town poems to represent principles of order against which to measure the buffoonery of human activity, but, at the same time, to depict an exciting movement of colour and light, sound and motion which, in its spontaneity, has little regard for order. In this portrayal lies a clash of intentions, as the rhetoric tells us one thing and the energetic movements, something else. It is an inclusive compromise based more on inventiveness and doubt. Characteristically, Fergusson portrays classical models of human behaviour, satirizes their irrelevance to human experience; sketches, like Daumier, the vileness of everyday urban living, and, somehow, allows stumbling humanity, as in Auld Reikie, a place in the grand design.

In several of the poems the forces of change and creativity, diversity and unrest, both within the poet and the poem, appear to be forging themselves into a new order. If, for instance, we again find in **"Dumfries"** the familiar formula in which pastoral implies anti-Whig (part of the poem satirizes Charles Churchill in these terms), the idyllic portrayal is not of an idealized medieval village but of a technologically and architecturally sophisticated place, a bustling old royal burgh known as the 'Queen of the South'. This must be borne in mind in interpreting Fergusson's pastoral vision of Dumfries as a Scots Eden, a garden of the 'caller [fresh] flow'r', clear 'stream' (ll.3-4), 'beauties' (l.8), health (ll.21-4) and plenty. It is an ordered ('ilka thing's sae trig and feat' [smart and pretty], l.11), modern town set in opposition to Churchill's Lon-

don. Likewise, **"Caller Oysters"** focuses on modern Edinburgh as it commends the successful fishing industry which saw Leith merchants selling huge quantities of oysters to London by 1773. In a subtle interlacing of visions Fergusson restates the formula, the traditional culture of Auld Reikie equals pastoral (Luckie Middlemists is a 'hame' with 'gude fare' and life centring on the *'ingle',* ll.50-3), while attributing the fisherwives' *'top livin'* (l.62), the 'blyth faces' of 'September's merry month' (ll.13-14), to commercial prosperity Progress and tradition, as in **"Ode to the Bee"**, walk hand-in-hand.

Auld Reikie is the most elaborate reconciliation of the two cities. In an emotional and psychological working through *concordia discors,* the town is in turn part of the natural cycle—hence the pastoral muse moves easily from SIMMER's Green (ll.7-8) to its sociability (ll.3-4) and protection ('whase biggin stands / A Shelter to surrounding Lands', ll.21-2)—and, the city of chaos, home of 'Lies and Clashes' (l.26), dirt, 'stinking Air INUNDATION BIG' (ll.30, 37, 44), darkness and 'DEATH' (l.165). Throughout, the rhetoric of pastoral and shelter is solidly underpinned by an exact architectural balance of themes in harmonious opposition: an interplay of light and dark, sweet scents and stinks, sorrow and joy, growth and death, poverty and prosperity, civilization (rhetorically, shelter, nature, pastoral) and savagery (artifice, false appearance, counterpastoral). In the end Reikie is transfigured into a new pastoral entity, 'tow'ring on thy summit green' (l.362). Conceived in a vision from across the Forth it is like the rural retreat of the opening, but has become a genuine city of the imagination; a heavenly city (ll.363-66), and, to use Kenneth Clark's expression, a 'landscape of symbols'. All energy has been reconciled into order by a superior unifying power: as Fergusson puts it in an early poem

> That righteous Power, before whose heavenly
>   eye
> The stars are nothing, and the planets die;
> Whose breath divine supports our mortal frame,
> Who made the lion wild, and lambkin tame.
>   **("Pastoral III. Night"**, ll.29-32)

A. M. Kinghorn (essay date 1992)

SOURCE: "Watson's Choice, Ramsay's Voice and a Flash of Fergusson," in *Scottish Literary Journal,* Vol. 19, No. 2, November, 1992, pp. 5-23.

[*In the following excerpt, Kinghorn praises Fergusson's use of language, and asserts that the poet's critical reception was impeded during his lifetime by widespread prejudice against the Scots vernacular.*]

In comparison [with the poet Allan Ramsay], Fergusson was neglected, though with him and through him literary Scots assumed a comparatively stable form, the more familiar 'Lallans' used by Burns and his imitators. Analysis shows that it was rooted chiefly in the vernacular of Edinburgh with some additions from older Scots and owning considerable freedom to adopt or reject dialect or anglicised elements according to the demands of rhyme or context. Though loosely referred to as a dialect, 'literary convention' is a better description of this Burnsian compromise, a legacy from Ramsay and Fergusson.

Initially, anti-English politics had helped to fuel Ramsay's patriotic fire and mandarin rejection of the 'Doric' as a language in which it was now unthinkable to write was not such a great obstacle during his active lifetime as it later became. In his forties, long after the first blush of youthful radicalism had faded, Ramsay received support from titled friends and prosperous acquaintances. This well-connected coterie foreshadowed the better-known bourgeois literati of the second half of the century but, like Ruddiman, it was more openly tolerant of Scots while maintaining neo-classical humanist preferences. It has been argued that they would rather have written in Latin following the tradition of Buchanan had not history and the pressures of politics forced English upon them.

Prejudice against current Scots, spoken as well as written, increased. Clear record exists of acute sensitivity in matters of accent and pronunciation during the second half of the eighteenth century. However, lists of 'Scotticisms' printed to guide the unwary were not designed to convert Scotsmen into Englishmen; there is no suggestion of lack of patriotism or confusion of identity (even if James Boswell, politically conscious of his accent, did claim to have been born a 'North-Briton') and although the material benefits of Union had been grudgingly recognised, at least in the towns and ports. These guides to language-traps might be thought cynical but they represented sound social advice. David Hume's, James Beattie's and James Elphinstone's were different types of example. Hume, together with Adam Smith reproved by English readers for his Scotticisms, ironically regretted his inability to change. Beattie was simply fastidious and wished Scots eliminated, but Elphinstone tried to set a standard of Scoto-English and admired 'the braudest Scotch' as indeed the majority who spoke it did, though the pressures of provincial snobbery prevented them from admitting their feelings, at least in 'polite' circles.

This increased self-conscious element goes some way to explain why Fergusson's own handling of the convention is much more uncompromising, flexible, pointed and vivid than Ramsay's; he made sharper pictures out of it, flowing past in a series of 'shots'. **"Leith Races"** is packed with examples; this one is of the ancient Town Guard heroes, to whom their captain gives the order to fix bayonets in a Highland accent:

> 'Come hafe a care (the captain cries),
>   On guns your bagnets thraw;
> Now mind your manual exercise,
>   An marsh down raw by raw.'
> And as they march he'll glowr about,
>   Tent a' their cuts and scars:
> 'Mang them fell mony a gausy snout
>   Has gusht in birth-day wars,

>   Wi' blude that day

and Sawney, selling hose in **"Hallow-Fair"**, hails 'frae Aberdeen':

> 'Come ye to me fa need:
> The brawest shanks that e'er were seen
>   I'll sell ye cheap an' guid'

where *w* becomes *f* and *guid* rhymes with *need*. The Highland NCOs patrol to keep order and the corporal commands 'Pring in ta drunken sot' when they find Jock Bell 'peching on the causey'.

Albert Mackie's essay on Fergusson's Scots [in *Robert Fergusson*, edited by Sydney Goodsir Smith] shows how far Fergusson's basic Edinburgh dialect was laced with recognisable Aberdeenshire and Fife elements. In order to secure the effects he sought, he moved from one dialect of Scots to another, casting about for rhyme, crossing the border for English, reaching back to Middle Scots to suit his drift.

> The Buchan bodies thro' the beech
>   Their bunch of Findrums cry,
> An' skirl out baul', in Norland speech,
>   'Gueed speldings, fa will buy.'

is again unmistakably far Nor'-Eastern. Fergusson's direct appeal as 'a laureate of low life' is oral and in experiment he appears as a true *makar,* more of a Dunbar or Gavin Douglas than a follower of Ramsay's track. He was no editor or antiquary deliberately reviving the past but an original poet who naturally looked to his immediate surroundings for inspiration and to the living legacy of his sixteenth-century poetic ancestors for a suitable means of expressing it. He had no interest in the English market nor in scraping acquaintance with touring London writers as Ramsay had tried to do with Steele and Gay; he wrote no poems corresponding to "Richi and Sandy." On the contrary, he scorned the 'treat' given by his old University of St Andrews to Samuel Johnson, an undeserving case whose professed contempt for Scotsmen was notorious, and he parodied the style of Henry Mackenzie's popular *Man of Feeling* in **"The Sow of Feeling"**, probably without realising that Mackenzie's intent was itself satirical. Fame such as Mackenzie's 'English' novel brought was not for him.

Fergusson's experiments in language and verse form were dazzling (compare **"The Farmer's Ingle"**). His vocabulary was more extensive and his use of Scots more concentrated than Ramsay's or, for that matter, Burns's. His death at twenty-three (by which age Ramsay had hardly started to write) closes speculation on what Fergusson might have achieved. His lifespan was less than a third of Ramsay's, yet only ten years after he died the sheer merit of Fergusson's work was perceived by Burns. With excessive modesty Burns placed himself below Ramsay, Hamilton of Gilbertfield and Fergusson, 'a deathless name' whose

>   glorious parts

Ill suited law's dry, musty arts!
My curse upon your whunstane hearts,
    Ye Enbrugh gentry!

Through his membership of the Cape Club and his flood
of contributions to Walter Ruddiman's *Weekly Magazine*
Fergusson became a local celebrity but nothing more. The
high Professoriate (with the possible exception of William Wilkie of *Epigoniad* fame) seems to have ignored
him, and most of his Cape Club cronies failed to realise
the quality of his achievement. The gulf between Fergusson and the Edinburgh *bon ton* towards modern literary
Scots had widened since Ramsay's day, and the greater
prosperity of 'North Britain' in the second half of the
century was accompanied by a leaning towards genteel
culture as represented in London society. Along with this
went a hardening of prejudice against home-grown traditions and in particular a denial of the 'polite' use of contemporary Scots, which under the *aegis* of the Select
Society and ornaments of their respective professions like
Blair and Robertson became almost official.

In such an atmosphere, explicit critical approval of Fergusson was rarely recorded. There were exceptions, notably one made by his friends the Ruddimans. Thomas
Ruddiman was well qualified to provide a just estimate
of Fergusson and he did, but only after the poet had
died:

> His talent for versification in the Scots dialect has
> been exceeded by none, equalled by few . . . Had he
> enjoyed life and health to a maturer age, it is probably
> he would have revived our ancient Caledonian Poetry,
> of late so much neglected and despised. His works are
> lasting monuments of his genius and vivacity.

FURTHER READING

Biography

"Fergusson, Tannahill, and Pollock." In *Dublin University
Magazine* LXXXVIII, No. DXXIV (July, 1934): 324-25.
    Offers a descriptive interpretation of Fergusson's life
    and artistic sensibility.

Grosart, Alexander B. *Famous Scots Series: Robert Fergusson.*
Edinburgh: Oliphant, Anderson & Ferrier, 1898, 160 p.
    Discusses Fergusson's life, career, and works. Considered
    by some critics to be a well-researched biography of
    occasionally questionable accuracy.

Criticism

MacLaine, Allan H. "The *Christis Kirk* Tradition: Its
Evolution in Scots Poetry to Burns. Part III: the Early Eighteenth
Century: Allan Ramsay and his Followers." *Studies in Scottish
Literature* 2, No. 3 (January 1965): 163-82.
    Discusses the surge of activity in the ancient *Christis
    Kirk* genre during the first half of the eighteenth century
    and Fergusson's important contribution to Scottish
    poetry. Examines the technique of several poems by
    Fergusson.

Smith, Sydney Goodsir, ed. *Robert Fergusson: 1750-1774:
Essays by Various Hands to Commemorate the Bicentenary
of his Birth.* Edinburgh: Thomas Nelson and Sons, 1952,
210 p.
    Collection of critical essays discussing Fergusson's life
    and poetry in relation to the Scottish literary tradition.

**Additional coverage of Fergusson's life and career is contained in the
following source published by Gale Research:** *Dictionary of Literary
Biography,* **Vol. 109.**

James Macpherson

1736-1796

Scottish poet, translator, essay writer, and historian.

INTRODUCTION

In the 1760s Macpherson perpetrated one of the most famous frauds in English literary history by publishing what he claimed were translations of poetry by an ancient Gaelic poet named Ossian. His efforts began as fragments of ballads and lyrics, based very loosely on actual Gaelic sources, and the success of these encouraged him to publish two longer poems, *Fingal* (1762) and *Temora* (1763), also presented as the work of the third-century epic poet Ossian. The poems were enthusiastically received by almost all of Scotland for celebrating the Gaelic, Highland heritage that was then rapidly being obliterated by changing economic and political conditions, contributing to the dominance of the English language. Samuel Johnson, however, almost immediately declared Macpherson's "translations" of Ossian a fraud, and others, such as the Scottish philosopher David Hume, soon began to question their authenticity as well. But these doubts had no effect on the popularity of the poems, which swept not only Scotland but also England and the whole of Europe. They were rapidly translated into German, French, and Italian, and Ossian was ranked second in poetic greatness only to Homer, with some critics even arguing that his works surpassed the *Iliad* and the *Odyssey*. Johann Wolfgang von Goethe was an admirer, along with many other German Romantics, and Napoleon Bonaparte carried an Italian translation of the poems on his military campaigns. Macpherson's Ossianic poems were one of the great literary sensations in Europe during the eighteenth century, and his influence continued well into the next century, long after his claims of authenticity had been proven false.

Biographical Information

Macpherson was born on October 27, 1736, in the village of Ruthven, between Perth and Inverness, where his father was a farmer. He began his university studies in Aberdeen, entering King's College in 1752 and transferring to Marischal College in 1754; he then studied at Edinburgh University for a year. In 1756 he returned to teach school in Ruthven, where he wrote *The Highlander* (1758), an epic. He then went back to Edinburgh and accepted a position as a private tutor. In 1759, while staying with a student of his at a fashionable resort, he met John Home, a famous Scottish dramatist of the time. Impressed with Macpherson's knowledge of Gaelic, Home

asked him to translate some poetry; Macpherson returned a few days later with several poems he had translated. Impressed, Home brought them back to Edinburgh and within a year arranged for Macpherson to publish *Fragments of Ancient Poetry Collected in the Highlands of Scotland* (1760).

Following a much-publicized trip around the Scottish Highlands to collect more Gaelic manuscripts, Macpherson published the two epics *Fingal* and *Temora*. For years after their publication, Macpherson conducted a public debate with Johnson over the authenticity of his Ossianic poetry. The controversy was perpetuated by Macpherson's unwillingness to produce the originals of the poems he claimed to have translated; he continued to insist on his integrity while refusing to offer any evidence to support his claims. "Stubborn audacity," Johnson finally wrote, "is the last refuge of guilt." Macpherson, meanwhile, made a great deal of money from his publications, and his fame as the translator of Ossian also brought him opportunities in business and politics. He became extensively involved in the growing trade with India, served in the House of Commons, and purchased an estate in Scotland. He died on his estate in 1796, leaving an endowment of a thousand pounds to fund the publication of the Gaelic originals he still insisted existed for his poetry.

Major Works

In *Fingal* Macpherson attempted to provide Scotland with a national epic, as Homer did for the Greeks, or Vergil for the Romans. *Temora* describes the raising of a monument to honor Fingal's victories in battle. Macpherson's Ossianic poems were all written in a style intended as an exact rendering of Gaelic verse. As Robert Fitzgerald has noted, quoting from the *Fragments*, Macpherson deliberately reordered his syntax to sound like a word-for-word translation of an ancient language: "Bent is his head of age, and red his tearful eye. Alpin, thou son of the song, why alone on the silent hill?" Widely praised for their natural descriptions of the Scottish highlands, the poems anticipated many aspects of Romantic poetry. They also appealed to a growing European interest in an idealized primitive society. Robert Folkenflik has attributed Macpherson's popularity in Scotland to his ability to create a heroic and poetic past that his countrymen wanted to believe had existed: "The general reception of the Ossianic works, with . . . Highland Scots by the score prepared to state under oath that they had learned these poems as boys, shows that the country was crying out for such a past and such a poet." Many scholars believe this was the basis of Macpherson's appeal throughout Europe. The poetry not only captured a pre-Romantic mood, it authenticated and legitimized it; people found some of their most popular beliefs embodied in what they believed was an artifact from an ancient civilization, and they took comfort in the discovery of an ancient poet who had expressed ideas with which they were familiar.

Critical Reception

At the height of the controversy concerning Macpherson's sources, Johnson proclaimed that the Ossianic poems "never existed in any other form than that which we have seen. The editor, or author . . . doubtless inserted names that circulate in popular stories, and may have translated some wandering ballads, if any can be found." By the nineteenth century this verdict was widely accepted, and Ossian was less frequently and less widely read. "The extraordinarily fashionable almost inevitably becomes the irreconcilably unfashionable," George Saintsbury wrote of Macpherson at the turn of the twentieth century. But critics since then have been interested in rehabilitating Macpherson. Though the poems often had no exact originals, scholars have shown that they did rely on Gaelic sources; many have identified Gaelic sources for Macpherson's poetry and have established the existence of stylistic and structural similarities. For most critics, fraud is now too strict or harsh a verdict. Though the poems were not what Macpherson claimed, they still remain an important contribution to Scottish, English, and European culture, and critical discussion has turned from the issue of authenticity to exploration of the poetry itself. As Peter T. Murphy has written of Macpherson: "What he did with the inheritance of the

Highlander is nothing worse than absorption, that respectable bardic activity . . . He adapted the Gaelic tradition to the modern world."

PRINCIPAL WORKS

The Highlander (poetry) 1758

Fragments of Ancient Poetry Collected in the Highlands of Scotland (poetry) 1760
Fingal, an Ancient Poem, in Six Books (poetry) 1762
Temora, an Ancient Epic Poem, in Eight Books (poetry) 1763
The Poems of Ossian (poetry) 1765
The Iliad [translator; from *The Iliad* by Homer] (poetry) 1773
The History of Great Britain (history) 1775
Original Papers (essays) 1775

CRITICISM

Rudolf Tombo, Jr. (essay date 1901)

SOURCE: "General Survey and First Notices: General Considerations upon the Reception of the Ossianic Poems in Germany," in *Ossian in Germany*, 1901. Reprint by AMS Press, 1966, pp. 66-75.

[*In the following excerpt from his landmark study of Macpherson's influence on German Romantic poetry, Tombo surveys the history of the poet's popularity in that country.*]

Almost a century and a half has elapsed since the literary world of Europe bowed to a new offspring of the poetic muse that many thought would be immortal. The poems of Ossian were assigned to a 'natural genius,' whom men of unquestioned literary sagacity placed next to and even above Homer. Now they are almost forgotten, and their interest lies mainly in the influence they exerted upon some of the greatest minds of the 18th century.

It was in the year 1760 that James Macpherson, a Scotch youth of twenty-four, published in Edinburgh some *Fragments of Ancient Poetry, Collected in the Highlands of Scotland, and Translated from the Gallic or Erse Language*. Neither Macpherson nor his friends anticipated the tremendous sensation these fragments were destined to make, not only in Scotland and England, but on the whole continent of Europe. But Macpherson was not the man to underestimate the position which he had suddenly attained, and accordingly, emboldened by his initial success, he published in 1761 *Fingal,* an epic poem in six books, and in 1763 *Temora* in eight books. With the dispute over the authenticity of the poems we are not here concerned. The researches of modern Celtic scholars have cast much light upon the long-disputed question. They have accorded Macpherson the place that in justice belongs to him, the place of a 'skillful artificer,' who took a few crude scattered fragments of Irish—not distinctively Scotch—folk-songs as his foundation, and not only lengthened them into more elaborate and refined poems, but built up long epics, which, although accepted as genuine by a credulous age in a moment of blind enthusiasm, have not been able to withstand the scrutiny of the unprejudiced scholar.

Macpherson's *Ossian* was not the first literary product of England that was received with favor by the Germans in

---

William Wordsworth faults the "spurious" nature of Macpherson's poetry:

If it be unbecoming, as I acknowledge that for the most part it is, to speak disrespectfully of Works that have enjoyed for a length of time a widely-spread reputation, without at the same time producing irrefragable proofs of their unworthiness, let me be forgiven upon this occasion.— Having had the good fortune to be born and reared in a mountainous country, from my very childhood I have felt the falsehood that pervades the volumes imposed upon the world under the name of Ossian. From what I saw with my own eyes, I knew that the imagery was spurious. In nature everything is distinct, yet nothing defined into absolute independent singleness. In Macpherson's work, it is exactly the reverse; everything (that is not stolen) is in this manner defined, insulated, dislocated, deadened,— yet nothing distinct. It will always be so when words are substituted for things. To say that the characters never could exist, that the manners are impossible, and that a dream has more substance than the whole state of society, as there depicted, is doing nothing more than pronouncing a censure which Macpherson defied; when, with the steeps of Morven before his eyes, he could talk so familiarly of his Car-borne heroes;—of Morven, which, if one may judge from its appearance at the distance of a few miles, contains scarcely an acre of ground sufficiently accommodating for a sledge to be trailed along its surface. . . .

William Wordsworth, in an Essay Supplementary to the Preface of the 1815 edition of his Collected Poems, *in* William Wordsworth's The Prelude, *edited by Carlos Baker, Holt, Rinehart, and Winston, 1954.*

---

the 18th century, but no other made its influence felt so strongly. . . . There was scarcely a writer of note who did not at some time or other fall under the spell. First came Klopstock, who, regarding Ossian as a German, found the songs of the bard a fit vehicle for the transmission of his patriotic ideas. Gerstenberg wrote a long drama in the Ossianic vein. Denis translated the poems of the bard and imitated him zealously. Kretschmann and many so-called 'bards' of smaller caliber fell into line. Herder hailed the advent of the songs with delight and based his theories of popular poetry largely upon them. Goethe, inspired by Herder, took a passing but deep interest in the literary curiosity, which left its impress upon a portion of his work. Schiller's earliest dramas show traces of Ossian's influence. The *Storm and*

Stress writers found nourishment in the writings of a genius who observed no rules. Merck edited an English edition of the poems. Lenz translated **Fingal**. The poets of the *Göttinger Bund*—Bürger, Hölty, Voss, Fried. Stolberg, Cramer—have all left testimony of their admiration for the Gaelic Homer. Then there were Claudius and Matthisson and Kosegarten, all influenced by Ossian. Even Gessner shows his indebtedness in some of his later idyls. Weisse and Haller wrote detailed reviews. Adelung strongly opposed the authenticity of the poems. Wilhelm Schlegel seconded the latter's efforts. Friedrich Schlegel seriously discussed the authenticity. Jacob Grimm was extremely anxious to appear as their champion. The melancholy of Novalis sought consolation in the Ossianic 'joy of grief.' Tieck produced several imitations in his youth. Hölderlin also read the poems with ardor. Freiligrath wrote a ballad "Ossian." . . . Schubert and Brahms, Zumsteeg and Dittersdorf, Seckendorff and Löwe, and other German composers, have set portions of the poems to music. German artists have tried their hand at illustrating Ossianic scenes and depicting Gaelic heroes. But why pursue the subject further? It were almost impossible to overestimate the favor which the poems of Ossian once enjoyed in Germany. The baptismal name Oskar, so common in Germany, and those of Selma and Malvine, still found there, serve as perpetual reminders of the proud rôle that Ossian, son of Fingal, once played on German soil.

In order to comprehend this wide-spread influence, let us glance at the literary condition of Germany in the seventh decade of the 18th century. As far as their success in Germany is concerned, the poems of Ossian could not have been ushered in at a more opportune moment. We may safely assert that at no time before were the chances of a favorable reception so good; and had they been published in the 19th century, their influence would have been nil. And it was fortunate in many respects that the songs appeared when they did, for although we have long ceased to regard Ossian as a classic, we have no reason to consider his influence pernicious. Of course the danger of drawing false conclusions and exaggerating the value of the poems was great, and that they worked a certain amount of mischief no one will deny. Yet the indisputable facts remain, that the poems of Ossian aroused a wide-spreading interest in the 'tales of the times of old,' that they helped to draw the attention of the Germans to their own rich store of popular poetry; that they aided in eradicating the general idea that German literature depended for its prosperity upon imitation. Themselves artificial, by a strange paradox they helped to dispel artificiality, and we really owe to Macpherson a debt of gratitude for making us acquainted with those 'deeds of the days of other years' when 'Fingal fought and Ossian sung.' The controversy that arose over the genuineness of the songs was instrumental in calling general attention to them. A fight usually attracts a crowd, and it did not fail to do so in this instance. Aspirants for critical honors were allured into the polemical arena like moths into the flame. The majority of the German critics came nobly to Macpherson's defense, and their decided views as to the authenticity and beauty of the poems had a marked effect upon the opinions of their readers.

And then the poems appeared in English, a language that had become interesting to the Germans, especially after the Seven Years' War drew Prussia and England closer together. It did not require a thorough knowledge of English to read Ossian. The periods were short and simple, involved constructions were almost entirely lacking, and repetitions of the same thought in terms virtually similar were of frequent occurrence. The episodes themselves were simple and called for no serious application of the reasoning powers; any complications that might arise were explained away by a careful argument preceding each poem, and those who were curious to know more about the origin and age of the poems found abundant material to satisfy them in the various dissertations prefixed to many of the editions and translations. On the whole, nothing in the entire range of English literature could have been found that better met the demand for a text shorn of the most common difficulties. The number of English reprints that appeared in Germany is incontrovertible evidence of the frequency with which these poems were read in the original. And it is patent that this circumstance contributed in some measure to their popularity. A German of the 18th century, possessed of a moderate knowledge of English, would be less drawn to *Paradise Lost* than to Ossian. While the nature of the subject is the primary cause for the large number of German translations of Ossian, the apparent simplicity of the material no doubt induced more than one person to present his countrymen with a new translation. And thus it came about that Ossian was in more cases than one translated into German by men who absolutely lacked poetic talent. The earliest translations were in rhythmic prose, a fact that did much to increase the popularity of this style of writing in Germany at that time. About the time of Klopstock's entrance upon the literary stage, and for some time afterwards, the theory widely prevailed, that the poet enters into more direct contact with nature by clothing his thoughts in prose. This prose, however, was to be a poetic prose, poetic and at the same time natural; for prose was regarded as the most natural expression of the soul. Surely the sensation that Ossian made in Germany would not have been so prodigious had his poems appeared in meter. An indignant protest arose on all sides when Denis introduced an innovation by publishing a translation in hexameters. Had the poems of Ossian appeared originally in the measures of the so-called Gaelic originals, they might have found readier acceptance with scholars, but scarcely with the reading public. There was something in Macpherson's abrupt but pompous, rhapsodical, measured prose *per se* that won the hearts of the admirers of 'these glorious remains of antiquity.'

Two distinct tendencies stand out prominently on the literary horizon of Germany in the middle of the 18th century: imitation of the ancients, and the return to nature as preached by Rousseau and his disciples. It is a signal coincidence that Macpherson's poems and Rousseau's

Nouvelle Héloïse appeared about the same time. It is well known with what acclaim Rousseau's doctrines were hailed in Germany. To a people professedly longing for a return to the delights of savage life, nothing could have been more opportune than the practical illustration of Rousseau's theories in the account of the crude civilization depicted by Macpherson, whose characters, while leading a life of freedom in the wild fastnesses of the mountains, far from the haunts of civilized man, had been supplied by Macpherson with a veneer of nobility and refinement that would have better befitted a powdered and perfumed gallant of the 18th century. There are some points of resemblance between the panegyrists of Thomson's *Seasons,* who sang the beauties of the sunrise but never rose before noon, and those followers of Rousseau who never wearied of sighing for the advantages of savage life, but would have indignantly declined to be taken at their word and transported among a tribe of Patagonians. The heroes of Ossian were more to their taste: these at least made some pretension to refinement of manners, even if they did not powder their hair nor use snuff. We can vividly picture to ourselves the immense stir that the sudden appearance of Ossian must have made in a society that was ready to embrace Rousseau's cause with such alacrity. To a certain extent the return to nature went hand in hand with the awakening of a love for wild and lonely scenery, and here, also, Macpherson gave all that could be demanded, even by the most fastidious. Rousseau was a true lover of nature; he was passionately fond of the Alps, and his example inspired the Germans with a new love for mountain scenery. His writings did much to bring on the era of nature-worship in Germany, and they were nobly seconded by Macpherson's descriptions of the Scottish Highlands.

In an age when it was considered good taste to imitate the ancients, Ossian could not fail to arouse more than passing interest. From imitation of the French and English, the Germans had, in accordance with the ideas of Lessing, come back to the Greek source. But even in imitation of the Greeks there was no real salvation. It needed a Klopstock to arouse an interest in Germanic antiquity, in a civilization that was less alien to the specifically German *Anschauung.* And here Ossian's beneficent influence enters, for his works undoubtedly increased the interest that was beginning to be taken by the Germans in their own antiquity. Klopstock regarded Ossian as a German, and Herder based many a theory of the folk-song upon the lays of the Gaelic bard. The influence, then, that Ossian had in this respect was rather an indirect one. When we regard his direct influence in the matter of imitation, the outlook is not so encouraging. Ossian's world is encompassed by narrow bounds, the field of his images and descriptions is small, the emotions and sentiments expressed by his actors are confined to a limited sphere; and all this, coupled with the continual repetitions, greatly simplifies the process of direct imitation. And this very simplicity proved an irresistible temptation and a snare to many not at all qualified to enter the lists. Thus we find sorrowful examples of attempts at Ossianic imitation in the work of some of the so-called 'bards' and elsewhere. One thing Ossian did, however: he aided Klopstock in his attempt to elevate the personal rank of the poet. At a time when Klopstock was making strenuous efforts in this direction, it was a great gain for those similarly minded to be able to point to the times of old, when the bard was placed upon an equal footing with the warrior and held in extraordinary esteem by the people. If Macpherson involuntarily contributed his mite to the spread of the idea that the poet's vocation is a noble one, he deserves our sincere gratitude.

The influence exercised in Germany by Shakspere and by Bishop Percy's *Reliques* in several particulars goes hand in hand with that of Ossian. Herder grasped all three in close connection, but we shall postpone our account of their inter-relation to the paragraphs on Herder. A few words are due, however, to Young's *Night Thoughts* and his *Conjectures on Original Composition,* in the latter of which the poets of the *Storm and Stress* found much fuel for their fire. Original genius is a shibboleth frequently met with in the German literature of the time. In Shakspere the Germans believed they had discovered a true original genius, and he came to be regarded as the perfect type of the natural poet, who, throwing aside existing rules and conventionalities, became a law unto himself. But when they came to Ossian, they discovered a man that really stood in much closer communion with nature than even Shakspere, for the former lived in surroundings that precluded the establishment of fixed rules of poetical composition. If the poems of Ossian were genuine—and it took a very long time to convince the Germans of the fact that they were not—here they had certainly to deal with a poet who was a genius born not made—an undeniable original. Dr. Blair had in his "Critical Dissertation" undertaken to make a comparison of the characteristics of the work of Ossian and Homer, and nowhere did his conclusion fall upon more willing ears than in Germany. Soon a most delightful controversy arose over the relative excellence of Homer and Ossian, and it was intensified by the appearance of Robert Wood's *Essay on the Original Genius and Writings of Homer* (1769), in which, too, Homer was proclaimed as a product of the soil. Homer generally came out second best in the comparison, critics vieing with one another in discovering some new phase wherein Homer could with apparent justice be placed beneath Ossian. And how many German translations of Ossian had appeared before one respectable version of Homer came into being! The latter's heroes were branded not only as cruel and artful, but as possessed of other unattractive qualities that relegated them to a lower level than the characters depicted by Ossian, who never failed to develop the attributes that distinguish the true hero, and so on *ad absurdum.* Fortunately the aberration was only temporary. No doubt the frequent comparisons are responsible for the Homeric dress occasionally given to Ossian's warriors in illustrations; *e.g.,* in No. 14 of Ruhl's sketches, Oscar wears a Greek helmet, coat-of-mail, etc.

A translation of the *Night Thoughts* by Johann Arnold Ebert (1723-95) had appeared in 1760 and its influence soon began to manifest itself in the odes of Klopstock and his pupils. The profound melancholy underlying the *Thoughts* was the leading cause of its popularity in Ger-

many and in a measure paved the way for the related strain that runs through Ossian. In this respect, then, the influence of the one accentuated that of the other, although the popularity of Young waned noticeably after the appearance of Ossian. Closely bound up with the spirit of melancholy is that of sentimentality, and here again Ossian's sway is unmistakable. Before the appearance of *Werthers Leiden* (1774), the influence of Ossian had been felt in several directions, but it was reserved for Goethe to open up a new field for the Gaelic bard. Feeling began to enter the arena, and Ossian's 'joy of grief' began to symbolize for many a German youth and maiden "the shower of spring, when it softens the branch of the oak, and the young leaf rears its green head." Goethe, through his incomparable translation of **"The Songs of Selma"** in *Werthers Leiden,* served to increase the admiration that had so willingly been offered on the shrine of Ossian. But we must not anticipate the paragraphs on Goethe.

And now that the famous bard had once been started upon his triumphal career, nothing of importance occurred for some years to disturb the general tenor of his fame. The work of translation and imitation went on and there was always some one prepared to enter the lists as his champion. For a long time it was considered bad form for a German critic to doubt the authenticity of the poems. Not one had the courage of his convictions, not one was prepared to damn with faint praise. A number of literati had their private doubts as to the genuineness of the poems, but they feared to share their opinions with the public. . . . Ossian filled so many long-felt wants, that it was not to be expected that the Germans would give him up easily, and yet this one-sided chorus of praise could not satisfy perpetually.

When the poets of the Romantic School arrive upon the scene, Ossian has, to be sure, lost some of his old-time glory, yet he is still ready to respond to the cells made upon him. Macpherson died in 1796, and soon afterwards steps were taken looking towards the publication of the supposed Gaelic originals. Rumors of the circumstance reached Germany and called forth wide-spread interest. The dying embers were for the last time blown into a bright flame, to which fact the mass of Ossianic literature which appeared from 1800 to 1808 clearly attests. Much of the renewed interest must be ascribed to the influence of Ahlwardt, who prepared a translation from the original Gaelic (1811). The excellence of this translation was trumpeted throughout the land long before its appearance, a specimen was published as early as 1807 and widely reviewed, so that when the complete translation finally appeared, little was left to be said. Ahlwardt's translation really marks the beginning of the end. What a lowering from their former position the poems had suffered even at the beginning of the century, is shown by a statement made by Schröder in the preface to his translation of **Fingal** (1800), where he refers to Ossian as one of those poets that are praised more than read. We still meet with an occasional translation and imitation, to be sure, but they are of little weight when compared with the hold the Ossianic craze once had on the German people. Ossian came generally to have more interest for the philologist than for the man of letters. More than one critic no longer concealed his doubts of the authenticity, until finally Mrs. Robinson's (Talvj's) work upon the non-genuineness of the poems was published (1840), which treatise marks the turning-point in German Ossian criticism. Since Talvj's days the Celtic scholars of Germany have sought to make good the errors into which their predecessors of the previous century had fallen, and to them we owe much of the light that has been shed upon the long-mooted question in comparatively recent years. At the present day Ossian is read but little in Germany, and where he is known attention has generally been called to him by Goethe's famous translation of **"The Songs of Selma."** He still attracts the average reader if read in snatches, but few will be found who can derive pleasure from the reading of his entire works. Macpherson's Ossian has become the property of the literary historian, and the genuine old folk-songs connected with his name that of the Celtic scholar.

George Saintsbury (essay date 1916)

SOURCE: "The Fugitives from the Happy Valley," in *The Peace of the Augustans: A Survey of Eighteenth Century Literature as a Place of Rest and Refreshment*, Oxford University Press, 1946, pp. 286-334.

[*In the following excerpt from an essay first published in 1916, Saintsbury discusses the poetic merit of Macpherson's Ossianic poems apart from the issue of their authenticity.*]

It has been said that it requires considerable critical exercise or expertness to appreciate, in any critical fashion, the charm of Gray's *Elegy*. It may be added that even greater preparation is required before any modern man can really appreciate *Ossian*. The penalty of enthusiastic and unhesitating acceptance, at once, of such a work of art as this by any generation has—not quite universally but almost so—been future distaste if not disgust. The extraordinarily fashionable almost inevitably becomes the irreconcilably unfashionable. With singular felicity or singular cleverness (he showed himself, in fact, in all relations of life, except his exceedingly foolish and rash attempt to bully Johnson, a very clever man indeed) Macpherson managed to shoot his bolt with just that aim, a little ahead of the object, which is sure to hit as the object itself progresses. His recipe (to change the metaphor) was exactly what the crude and indiscriminate but greedy appetite of the last third of the century demanded without knowing its own demand, and consumed ravenously when it was presented with the supply. But this very description implies a certainty of satiety, and its usual consequences, later.

To the modern reader, then, for some generations past, *Ossian* has been a shot bolt—a fashion out of fashion—a food which is turned from, if not exactly with loathing, at any rate with no appetite. Even such things as 'Celtic renascences' have done it little if any good, because of its less than doubtful genuineness and its perfectly certain adulteration, even if there is any genuineness in it at all.

For readers of some reading its countless bad imitations, and the trail which these imitations left upon succeeding literature, have put it still more out of favour; and to the comparatively illiterate (no disrespect to them) it offers few present delights.

These considerations can hardly lose their force; and many as are the changes which the student of the history of literature has seen, it is very difficult to imagine eager and intense enjoyment of *Ossian* reappearing at any time. Yet the person who neglects it entirely, loses something. For the actual student—not a 'researcher', but an intelligent reader—whom we have frequently had in view, the immense influence of the book or books, the evidence given of the desires and needs of the time, and other such things, would make *Ossian* readable, even if it were savourless in itself. But it is not. Actual forger as Macpherson may have been and probably was; charlatan and 'faker' as he was beyond all doubt—he was, after all and before all, an actual Highlander: he had, at a time when not many had done so, traversed and observed the Highlands pretty thoroughly, and he had, beyond all question, if only by the combined instincts of the native and the 'literary gent', succeeded in grasping and expressing the local colour in a singularly effective and original way. His history is patched and colourless myth; he has no connected romantic story to tell, and does not show much sign of being able to tell it if he had; while his characters are hardly even shadows. But no one who has watched the snakes of mist coil and twine and mock round the summits of the Coolins; no one who has seen the black rocks sleep and the brown rivers plunge and foam; no one who has trudged over leagues of moor and peat-hag in search of some 'Burn of the Deceivers', which is almost impossible to find, and acts up to its name as a guide when found,—can admit that the scenery and atmosphere of *Fingal* and *Temora* and the rest are merely theatrical. There is more in it than any scene-painter, even if he be a very Stanfield, can give; more even than the most accomplished artist, with no taint of the theatre about him, has given—the charm of 'the word' expressing the experience and the emotions of the senses and the soul.

This, though the gift referred to may perhaps have obtruded itself in too overwhelming measure, and have been made to do duty for a great many other gifts, the want of which is only too much felt, is a great thing to say of any book or book-writer. There may be added to it another and more questionable attraction—that of the curious verse-prose in which the composition is couched. To different persons—even to the same person in different moods—this will of course appeal differently. It will sometimes tease; it will very frequently seem, what the scenery has been denied to be, theatrical; it must be admitted to be unequally managed. But it sometimes suits the peculiar description itself very well; and it must be admitted to be a very clever mask and 'pass' for the shadowiness of figure, the insufficiency of character, and the absence of story, which plain prose would set ruthlessly in the daylight, and to which almost any regular form of verse would be almost equally dangerous. Of course any one may say that this brings us back to the central fact that

Ossian is after all (as somebody once punned it) a mere 'mistification'. It is, except for some definite purpose, an impossible book to read through; and in any case a very unlikely book to which to recur often. But almost everybody who cares for the Humanities of modern as well as ancient literature should read it, or a good part of it, at least once; and it would be surprising if some such readers did not sometimes turn to it again, if only as to a shrine (to talk in the vein of its own century), desolate and unlit now, but once thronged with worshippers and fragrant with glowing incense.

Derick S. Thomson (essay date 1952)

SOURCE: "Fingal: The Garbh mac Stàirn and Magnus Ballads" and "Fingal (contd.)," in *The Gaelic Sources of Macpherson's "Ossian,"* Oliver and Boyd, 1952, pp. 13-20, 21-41.

[*In the following excerpt from his book-length study, Thomson offers a detailed examination of the Gaelic verses Macpherson used to create some of the central scenes in his epic* Fingal.]

Fingal is probably to be regarded as Macpherson's *magnum opus*. Some of the shorter pieces may claim a greater felicity, and indeed the lack of architectonic power which [Matthew] Arnold attributed, with some justice, to the Celts, and particularly to Ossian, may be attributed to Macpherson also. But when *Fingal* is compared with Macpherson's other essay in epic, *Temora,* the measure of his success in the former becomes more apparent. His theme, at least, was heroic, although his treatment of the theme was at times arbitrary. W. A. Craigie, writing on *Fingal,* remarks,

> Had the same thing been done by one of equal genius at an earlier date there might have been a great Gaelic epic, not inferior in interest to those of Greece or later Europe.

The theme of *Fingal* may be described briefly in the words of Macpherson's own *Dissertation,*

> The subject of it is an invasion of Ireland by Swaran, king of Lochlin, which is the name of Scandinavia in the Galic language. Cuchullin, general of the Irish tribes in the minority of Cormac, king of Ireland, upon intelligence of the invasion, assembles his forces near Tura, a castle on the coast of Ulster. The poem opens with the landing of Swaran, councils are held, battles fought, and Cuchullin is, at last, totally defeated. In the meantime Fingal, king of Scotland, whose aid was solicited before the enemy landed, arrived and expelled them from the country. This war, which continued six days and as many nights, is including the episodes, the whole story of the poem.

The episodes take up a greater part of the poem than might be inferred from Macpherson's passing reference to them, but they are in some cases very skilfully dovetailed into the poem, whose main action is fairly clear.

We are justified in thinking that Macpherson took considerable pains in constructing *Fingal*.

Macpherson's dependence on his sources for what, at the most conservative estimate, we may call hints for his plot, and the vagueness of his work when it rests on no such sources, cannot be better illustrated than by the contrast between *Fingal* and *Temora*. It is true that in Macpherson's notes *Temora* has a convincing, if often unhistorical, background. But the plot of *Temora* remains vague, so that the reader, through no fault of his own, may often be quite at a loss to understand what is happening. The best explanation of this difference between the two 'epics' may be found, it seems to me, in the fact that whereas in *Fingal* we can point to twelve passages in which Macpherson drew on Gaelic sources, in *Temora* we can point only to one. Further, the part of *Temora,* namely Book I, which has a ballad source, is comparatively free from the fault of vagueness noticed above.

To proceed, then, to an examination of the actual Gaelic sources of *Fingal,* we find that Macpherson fused two ballads, those of 'Garbh mac Stairn' and 'Magnus' or 'Manus' in order to construct the main outlines of his plot. Also he draws on three ballads for his main episodes. These are 'Fingal's Visit to Norway', 'Duan na h-Inghinn' (The Maid of Craca), and 'Ossian's Courtship'. In a more restricted way he makes use of the ballads 'Sliabh nam Ban Fionn', the 'Praise of Goll', and possibly of a ballad about Cù Chulainn's chariot. Finally he uses either a ballad or a prose story about Ferdiad and the 'Táin Bó Cùalnge' generally, together with other traditions concerning the Ulster and Fenian heroes, which he may have derived from oral sources or from historical works, such as the histories of Keating and O'Flaherty.

The chief sources used in *Fingal,* Bk. I, are the Garbh mac Stairn ballads. Maclagan's version of this, 'Duan a' Ghairibh', is one of the ballads which Macpherson acknowledges in his letter to Maclagan. In this same letter, which was written in January, 1761, Macpherson indicates that he has in his hands other versions of the ballads sent to him by Maclagan—'It is true, I have most of them from other hands, but the misfortune is that I find none expert in the Irish orthography so that any obscure poem is rendered doubly so, by their uncouth way of spelling'. We have two other early versions of this ballad, one in Fletcher's collection and another in MacNicol's. The text of Maclagan's version is given in Reliquiae Celticae. Later versions are those of Campbell, two versions by Irvine and one by Stewart, but the ballads of Irvine and Stewart are different from the others, and are probably influenced to a certain extent by Macpherson's work. A comparison of the versions of Fletcher and MacNicol with that of Maclagan may be said to bear out, in a general way, Macpherson's assertion that their orthography is more 'uncouth' than that of Maclagan, but this is not advanced as an argument that Macpherson had either of these versions in his possession, as neither Fletcher nor MacNicol can be thought to have had a monopoly in 'uncouth' Gaelic spelling at this time, while Fletcher's version, as we have it in the MS., is, of course, a considerably later production.

The hero Garbh mac Stairn, although he has been assimilated to the Fenian cycle, and especially to the Norse element in that, belongs to the older Irish invasion-legends. Thus in Fletcher's version Garbh is said to have come from Greece. The Fenian Cycle of tales and ballads has, however, gathered much extraneous material into its net, and it is not surprising that an early and probably mythical Greek invader should in latter days have changed his nationality to fit in with a better-remembered scheme of things. Garbh is also associated with Cù Chulainn in the ballads, so that here, as in other instances, Macpherson had some justification for introducing characters from both the Cù Chulainn and the Finn cycles into the same work.

Macpherson's *Fingal* begins, 'Cuchullin sat by Tura's wall. . . . ' As he sat there the 'scout of ocean' came, Moran the son of Fithil,

> 'Rise', said the youth, 'Cuchullin, rise; I see the ships of Swaran. Cuchullin, many are the foe: many the heroes of the dark-rolling sea.'

> 'Moran!' replied the blue-eyed chief, 'thou ever tremblest, son of Fithil: Thy fears have much increased the foe. Perhaps it is the king of the lonely hills coming to aid me on green Ullin's plains.'

(A note in the 1762 edn. says that the king here referred to is Fingal.)

With this may be compared the two opening stanzas of Maclagan's version,

> Erigh a Chuth na Teimhridh
> Chi mi Luingishe do-labhradh
> Lom-lan nan Cuan Clannach
> Do luingishe nan Albharach.

> Breugach thus Dhorsair go Muadh
> Breugach thu'n diu sgach aon uair
> She than Loingis mor nan Maogh
> 'S iad teachd Chugainne gar Cobhair.

> (Arise, Hound of Tara, I see an untold number of ships, the undulating seas full of the ships of the strangers.

> A liar art thou, excellent doorkeeper, a liar art thou today and at every time; that is but the great fleet of Moy(?), coming to bring help to us.)

The last line in Fletcher's second stanza is

> San Fhiann a teachd d'ar cobhair.

> (. . . And the Fian coming to bring help to us.)

The resemblances are clear. Tura is Teamhra or Tara. A messenger or watchman addresses Cuchullin, and gives news of the approach of ships in great numbers. Cuchullin belittles the danger, and says that it is Fingal coming to help them. The resemblance may be noticed between Macpherson's 'thou ever tremblest' and 'A liar art thou today and at every time'. This is the sort of distant echo which Macpherson continually achieves. . . .

Before leaving *Fingal*, Bk I., some reference may be made to the description therein of Cù Chulainn's chariot. Only three ballads are extant describing Cù Chulainn's chariot, and these all belong to later collections than those we have been considering above. The versions of MacCallum (1813) and Grant (1814) are almost identical, while that in Sir George Mackenzie's collection differs considerably in detail from those two. This latter version was transmitted to the Highland Society before their Report was published in 1805. Macpherson's version bears only a general resemblance to that of the ballads, and is very much abbreviated. Donald Macleod, minister of Glenelg, wrote in 1764,

> It was in my house that Mr. Macpherson got the description of Cuchullin's horses and car in Bk. I, p. II (i.e. the 1762 edn. of *Fingal*) from Allan MacCaskie, schoolmaster, and Rory Macleod, both of this glen: he has not taken in the whole of the description; and his translation of it (spirited and pretty as it appears, as far as it goes) falls so far short of the original in the picture it exhibits of Cuchullin's horses and car, their harness and trappings, etc., that in none of his translations is the inequality of Macpherson's genius to that of Ossian so very conspicuous.

The Rev. Donald MacQueen of Kilmuir writes, also in 1764, of the same description,

> . . . it is very grand in the original; there are four horses described in it, with a long string of epithets applied to each, of which the translator dropped a few through his fingers.

It is perhaps unnecessary to enter into all the details. Macpherson's description, which is to be found on pp. 11-12 of *Fingal,* begins with an account of the chariot which is embossed with stones, replenished with spears, etc. Then he passes on to a description of the two steeds, one being called Sulin-Sifadda, the other Dusronnal. Each is given several epithets, such as 'thin-maned', 'high-headed', 'bounding'. After this he gives a description of Cù Chulainn within the chariot. The ballads describe the spectacle in a similar framework, and certain similarities can be detected. Thus MacCallum and Grant use the adjective *clochara,* 'studded with stones or gems'. The horses are *Liath maiseach* (Irish *Liath Macha*) and *Dubh-Seimhlinn* (Irish *Dubh-Sailend*), the latter having a distant resemblance to Macpherson's Dusronnal.

If it be objected that the Gaelic ballads mentioned above are too late to have evidential value, it can be shown that they bear a fairly close resemblance to much older Irish material. Thus in the *Táin,* Cù Chulainn's chariot is described, with its horses *Liath Macha* and *Dubh Sithleann* (or *Sailend*) while the adjectives 'bounding', 'broad-chested', 'long-maned', and 'gaily-prancing' may be compared with Macpherson's 'bounding', 'broad-breasted', 'high-maned', 'thin-maned' and 'high-leaping'. In the *Táin* much attention is paid to the description of Cù Chulainn's hair. He is also said to have seven toes on each foot, and seven fingers on each hand. It may be confusion with this, or merely the 'magical' quality of the number seven, which is responsible for two occurrences of this number in the Gaelic ballads, where Cù Chulainn is said to have seven eyes, or seven glances from his eyes, and seven white hairs on his head. Also in the *Táin* version the chariot is said to be 'studded with dartlets, lancelets, spearlets and hardened spits . . . ' Macpherson in merely saying that it is 'replenished with spears', is more modest, or less tautological.

. . . . .

Passing on to *Fingal,* Bk. II, we find Macpherson making fairly extensive use of another ballad dealing with a Norse hero and an attack made by him on the coast of Ireland. The ballad of Mànus or Magnus was very popular in the Highlands, and a large number of versions are extant. The name first appears in Fenian tradition as Mane in *Acallam na Senórach,* where he comes into the story of Caoilte's visit to Assaroe. Doubtless the historical character Magnus Barelegs, who was killed in Ireland in 1103, is referred to. . . .

Macpherson has made use of this ballad in four different passages in *Fingal,* first in Bk. II, and afterwards in Books IV, V and VI. He has, however, changed the tenor of the story. In the ballad the heroes of the Fian are out hunting when they see a thousand sails approaching. They send messengers to ask what the strangers want, and Mànus replies that he wants Finn's wife and his hound Bran. Macpherson, however, has introduced his Norse leader, whom he has called Swaran, at the beginning of Bk. I, and when we first see him in Bk. II, the Irish have already fled, and Morla is sent with an ultimatum, not to Finn, but to Cuchullin—

> Take Swaran's peace, the warrior spoke, the peace he gives to kings when the nations bow before him. Leave Ullin's lovely plains to us, and give thy spouse and dog. Thy spouse high-bosomed, heaving fair. Thy dog that overtakes the wind. Give these to prove the weakness of thine arm, and live beneath our power.

Cuchullin refuses these terms, saying,

> But never shall a stranger have the lovely sun-beam of Dunscaich, or ever deer fly on Lochlin's hills before the nimble footed Luath.

(Macpherson here names the dog Luath, but elsewhere, e.g. in Bk. VI, p. 81, Bran is mentioned.)

With the above passage may be compared stanza 20 in Stone's version (and similar stanzas in the others)—

> Choidhe cha tugamsa mo Bhean
> Do dh'aon neach a ta fuidh'n Ghrein
> 'S cha mho mheir mi Bran gu brath
> Gus an teid am Bas 'na Bheil.

> Never shall I give my wife to any man under the sun, nor shall I ever give away Bran until death comes to him.

The reference to the sun may possibly have suggested to Macpherson the epithet 'sun-beam of Dunscaich.' . . .

Now we move on to Bk. V.

Swaran and Fingal meet at last in single combat:

> Such were the words of Connal, when the heroes met in the midst of their falling people. There was the clang of arms. There every blow, like the hundred hammers of the furnace! Terrible is the battle of the kings, and horrid the look of their eyes. Their dark brown shields are cleft in twain; and their steel flies, broken, from their helmets. They fling their weapons down. Each rushes to his hero's grasp. Their sinewy arms bend round each other, they turn from side to side and strain and stretch their large spreading limbs below. But when the pride of their strength arose, they shook the hill with their heels; rocks tumble from their places on high; the green-headed bushes are overturned. At length the strength of Swaran fell; and the king of the groves is bound.

The corresponding passage in Stone's ballad consists of stanzas 31 and 33-7:

> Rinneadar an Uirnigh theann
> Budh Cosmhulach re Grian na'n Ord
> Cath fuileach an da Righ
> Gu ma ghuinneach bridh an Colg.

> Thachuir Macumhail na'n Cuach
> Is Manus na'n Ruag gun Agh
> Re cheile an tuitim an t sluaigh
> Chlerich nach budh chruaidh an dail.

> Air briseadh do Sgiath na'n Dearg
> Ar eirigh dhoibh Fearg is Fraoch
> Theilg iad a'm Buil air Lar
> 'S thug iad Sparnne 'n da Laoch.

> Cath fuileach an da Righ
> 'S an leunne budh chian an Clost
> Bha Clachan agus Talamh trom
> Ag moisgeala faoi Bhonn na'n Cois.

> Leagadh Righ Lochlin gun Agh
> An fiadhniuse Chaich air an Fhraoch
> Dho sa's cho b' Onar Righ
> Chuirt air Ceangal na'n tri Chaol.

> They made a fierce onset (lit. 'descent'). Like to the collision of hammers was the bloody battle of the two kings—venomous was the sting (lit. 'power') of their swords.

> There met together Macumhail of the goblets and unfortunate Manus of the routs, in the falling of the host—O cleric, was not that a hard meeting.

When the shields of the red warriors were broken, and when their wrath and fury had arisen, they threw their weapons to the ground, and took to heroes' wrestling.

Far and wide, methinks, could be heard the noise of the bloody battle of the two kings. Stones and heavy earth were mashed up under the soles of their feet.

The unfortunate king of Lochlin was struck down on the heather in the sight of all around, and upon him—no honorable fate for a king—was put the binding of the three slender parts i.e. neck, wrists and ankles.

Between these two passages there are many close correspondences of phrase and idea, while the progress of the fight is similar in both versions. Some interesting details emerge. The phrase 'in the falling of the people,' which Macpherson seems to render at the beginning of the passage quoted from *Fingal*, occurs in Stone's, but not in the other versions of the ballad, and is probably a mistaken rendering. Turner gives *ntosach na nsluadh*, 'in the forefront of the hosts', and MacNicol has *ann an tiugh an tsluaigh*, 'in the thick of the host.' It seems likely, therefore, that Macpherson was using Stone's version, although it is improbable that this was the only version which he had. The order of stanzas in MacNicol is slightly different to that in Stone's version, and is closer to Macpherson's sequence of ideas. Thus MacNicol's version makes the heroes meet in the thick of battle before he mentions the pounding of the hammers. Stone has mentioned the 'hammers' before formally saying that MacCumhail and Mà- nus met face to face. Macpherson's 'dark-brown shields' is derived from some such phrase as Stone's 'Sgiath na'n Dearg', although it is very doubtful if this is what the Gaelic means to convey. This whole passage shows Macpherson wrestling with his sources.

Robert P. Fitzgerald (essay date 1966)

SOURCE: "The Style of Ossian," in *Studies in Romanticism*, Vol. VI, No. 1, Autumn, 1966, pp. 22-33.

[*In the following essay, Fitzgerald shows how Macpherson's literary style was shaped both by his exposure to Gaelic sources and the necessity of making the poetry sound like a translation.*]

When James Macpherson published his *Fragments of Ancient Poetry, Collected in the Highlands of Scotland* in 1760 at Edinburgh, he presented them in a form that undoubtedly had a good deal to do with the remarkable success of the little volume. His rhythmic prose, with its simple syntax and exotic and profuse imagery, had the appeal of novelty; and this style was easily preserved in translation, thus accounting for some of the vogue of Ossian on the continent. But most important of all, the rhythmic prose gave the impression of authenticity. Hugh Blair noted in his Preface to the *Fragments* that "the translation is extremely literal. Even the arrangement of the words in the original has been imitated"; and to those who, like Blair, believed in Macpherson the peculiar rhet-

oric of a passage like the following derived from the effort to be literal:

The wind and the rain are over: calm is the noon of day. The clouds are divided in Heaven. Over the green hills flies the inconstant sun. Red through the stony vale comes down the stream of the hill. Sweet are thy murmurs, O Stream! but more sweet is the voice of Alpin the son of the song, mourning for the dead. Bent is his head of age, and red his tearful eye. Alpin, thou son of the song, why alone on the silent hill? why complainest thou, as a blast in the wood; as a wave on the lonely shore?

This was thought to be an exact rendering of the Gaelic original, with only very minor liberties taken by the translator.

Indeed, it was not unreasonable for Macpherson's readers to think that he was only a translator. His unusual style was like nothing seen before in English prose or verse. George Saintsbury [in *A History of English Prosody*, 1908] has given an accurate description of one of its central features: "His chief special secret . . . is the sharp and absolute isolation of sentences of unequal length. There is hardly anywhere, in verse or prose, a style so resolutely *cumulative,* while maintaining such complete want of connection between the constituents of the heap. Each sentence conveys its meaning completely—as far as it goes." Because Macpherson used the short clause or phrase as a unit, his prose easily resolves itself into a series of short lines, many of which show the rhetorical device which Biblical critics call *parallelism,* that is, stating the same general idea in different images (as in the three clauses at the beginning of the quotation), or repeating words or syntactic structures in successive clauses. The lines usually have from three to six accents and can be scanned as a mixture of common metrical feet, particularly iambs and anapests, with a frequent substitution of dactyls. Sometimes there are fourteeners, or octosyllabic couplets, or even common measure, but regularity was never consistently pursued, and the distinctive rhythm derives from the use of lines with a varying number of accents. In this "measured prose" (Macpherson's term for it) the use of imagery is notable. The epithets ("dark-bosomed ships," "White-armed Foinabragal") and the genitives of description ("the son of the song," "hill of storms," "dweller of battle's wing") are reminiscent of Homer or the Bible but no English poet had consistently employed them. Taken singly, the similes, metaphors, and personifications could be paralleled in many eighteenth-century poems, but their profuseness and the fact that they are almost all drawn from simple natural objects set off Macpherson's own practice. For his later collections, *Fingal* (1762) and *Temora* (1763), Macpherson used the same style, and all of the characteristics mentioned above can be illustrated from any page of the Ossian poems.

If Macpherson did not translate literally from Gaelic originals, then where did he get the idea for the poetic prose? The answers to this question that are given in standard accounts assume that Macpherson either invented it himself or derived it from English or classical models, the Bible being the one most frequently mentioned. In this respect modern commentators have advanced little beyond the approach of Malcolm Laing, the most perversely dedicated of those contemporaries who sought to expose Macpherson as a complete fraud. Besides attempting to discover every plagiarism that Macpherson might have committed, Laing also argued that the poetic prose was inspired by Bishop Lowth's explanation of the principle of parallelism in Hebrew verse; his argument is the ultimate source of the common idea that in some way Macpherson stole his style from that of the Biblical poetry. But this theory, and any others that do not take into account the influence of genuine Gaelic poems, are highly improbable when we consider the facts of Macpherson's career and the light that scholars of Gaelic have shed upon it. The remainder of this paper will be concerned with showing how this evidence helps to explain the origin of Macpherson's poetic prose, and, incidentally, with reviewing some aspects of the Macpherson problem about which there are widespread misconceptions. The paper's conclusion would probably not surprise specialists in Gaelic literature, but it is one which they themselves have not presented in any specific or developed way.

It has been clear for a long time that the inspiration for Macpherson's poems came from the genuine Ossianic ballad, a comparatively late development in the cycle of stories, poems, and legends concerned with the Irish hero Fionn Mac Cumhaill and his band of warriors, the Fian. Assuming a standard form in the fifteenth-century, the ballads entered into the folk tradition of Scotland and Ireland, versions of them to be heard even today in the Western Islands. They employed a variety of meters and rime schemes but were almost always in quatrains of short end-stopped lines, with the simple syntax and the use of formulas characteristic of the genuine ballad in any culture. In subject matter they celebrated the significant events of the Fionn cycle and incidental adventures of the members of the Fian: the battle of Gabhair, for example, at which the great hero Osgar died; or the combat that occurred when a maiden fled to the Fian for protection from a pursuer. Some of the ballads are recited by Oiséan, the son of Fionn and the father of Osgar. He survives the Fian and, old and blind, sadly relates the great deeds of an heroic age that has disappeared. Sometimes he encounters St. Patrick, who, although sympathetic to the Fian, represents a new, non-heroic, Christian scheme of values. Before Macpherson wrote there was little public interest in the ballads in Scotland. The only version in print was a metrical English paraphrase of the story of Fraoch that the collector Jerome Stone published in *The Scots Magazine* in 1758. However, the manuscript collections that have survived show that the ballads were well known and frequently recited in those areas where Gaelic was still a living language. Campbell's *Leabhar na Feinne (Book of the Fian)* lists sixty-three versions of ballads that derive from the period between 1739 and 1760. And later authentic versions give greater evidence of the vitality of the ballad tradition. Anyone of Macpherson's age who knew Gaelic and who went among the Gaelic-speak-

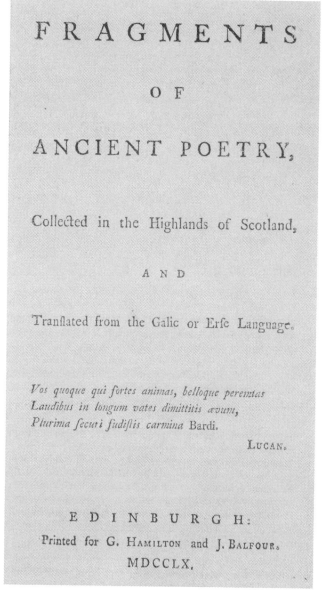

FRAGMENTS

OF

ANCIENT POETRY,

Collected in the Highlands of Scotland,

AND

Translated from the Galic or Erse Language.

Vos quoque qui fortes animas, belloque peremtas
Laudibus in longum vates dimittitis ævum,
Plurima secuti fudistis carmina Bardi.

LUCAN.

EDINBURGH:
Printed for G. HAMILTON and J. BALFOUR,
MDCCLX.

Title page for Macpherson's first collection of poems, which he claimed to have translated from Gaelic verses.

ing population could easily have heard the old ballads of Fionn and the Fian.

That Macpherson in fact knew some of the ballads and used them as sources has been known to objective students of the controversy since 1805, when the Highland Society published its Report of the Committee . . . Appointed to Inquire into the Nature and Authenticity of the Poems of Ossian. A recent study, Derick S. Thomson's "The Gaelic Sources of Macpherson's Ossian" [see essay dated 1951], affirms the validity of the Committee's conception of Macpherson's procedure and spells out in a detailed way exactly what ballads Macpherson knew and when and how he used them. According to Thomson, "We can prove, in most cases conclusively, that Macpherson in the course of his writings made use of some fourteen or fifteen Gaelic ballads." Thomson also reviews what has been long known from contemporary accounts, that Macpherson, after the success of his *Fragments* and after he was subsidized to go to the Highlands to find an epic, became a close student of the ballads and was an eager collector of them, both from manuscripts and from oral recitation. One little-known fact is relevant here: in spite of many assertions in print to the contrary, there are Gaelic "originals" for many of Macpherson's poems. When he published the epic *Temora* in 1763, he included a Gaelic version of its seventh book; and in his last years he worked on a Gaelic edition of the complete works of Ossian. This version, about two-thirds complete, appeared posthumously in 1807, edited by friends from his manuscripts and notes. The two specimens of Gaelic poetry are known on philological and other grounds to be fraudulent, but in subject matter, style, and metrics they show their derivation from genuine ballads. Even if Macpherson had a good deal of help in composing them, they still prove his direct acquaintance with the ballad tradition.

An excerpt from Macpherson's preface to *The Poems of Ossian*:

The eagerness with which these poems have been received abroad, is a recompense for the coldness with which a few have affected to treat them at home. All the polite nations of Europe have transferred them into their respective languages; and they speak of him who brought them to light, in terms that might flatter the vanity of one fond of fame. In a convenient indifference for a literary reputation, the author hears praise without being elevated, and ribaldry without being depressed. He has frequently seen the first bestowed precipitately; and the latter is so faithless to its purpose, that it is often the only index to merit in the present age. Though the taste which defines genius by the points of the compass, is a subject fit for mirth in itself, it is often a serious matter in the sale of a work. When rivers define the limits of abililities, as well as the boundaries of countries, a writer may measure his success, by the latitude under which he was born. It was to avoid a part of this inconvenience, that the author is said, by some who speak without any authority, to have ascribed his own productions to another name. If this was the case, he was but young in the art of deception. When he placed the Poet in antiquity, the Translator should have been born on this side of the Tweed. . . .

James Macpherson, in his translation of The Poems of Ossian, *Bernhard Tauchnitz, 1847.*

But did Macpherson know much about the ballads before it became profitable for him to do so? This is the question that is central to our concern. To approach it we had best review the circumstances of the meeting with John Home that directly led to the publication of the *Fragments*. In the summer of 1759 Macpherson, an obscure tutor, and Home, famous in Scotland for his *Douglas*, were both at

the spa Moffatt. The son of a farmer, Macpherson had grown up in the Highlands in the district of Badenoch, and had, as a boy, spoken Gaelic as well as English. His epic *The Highlander* (1758) had had no success. It and some juvenilia that have survived show Macpherson to have been a mediocre poet. Conventional in style, using clumsy blank verse or heroic couplets, too strongly influenced by Blair's *Grave* and Thomson's *Seasons,* his poems are of a kind that any young Scot with moderate talents might have written. Home struck up an acquaintance with Macpherson and, interested to find that he knew some of the vernacular literature of the Highlands, asked for translations, Macpherson at first refusing. But Home, as he reported later to the Highland Committee, persisted:

> Mr Home, with some difficulty, persuaded him to try, and in a day or two he brought him the poem on the death of Oscar; with which Mr Home was so much pleased, that in a few days two or three more were brought him, which Mr Home carried to Edinburgh, and shewed them to Dr Blair, Dr Fergusson, Dr Robertson, and Lord Elibank. . . .

Encouraged by Home, Macpherson went to Edinburgh, and with the support of Blair and others his *Fragments* were printed.

Of the fifteen *Fragments* (sixteen in the second edition), two have obvious ballad sources. Fragment VI parallels the popular ballad in which the Fian protect a maiden who flees to them for help. Macpherson later incorporated it into *Fingal,* the Fragment version being, according to Thomson, more faithful to the tradition. Fragment XIII is also not completely invented, following one of the Garbh mac Stairn ballads that describes the coming of a foreign invader to Ireland. It too is less distorted than Macpherson's later adaptation of it for *Fingal.* None of the other Fragments closely follows any known ballad source, although the heroes and their names are taken from the Fionn cycle, Fingal (i.e., Finn of the Gaels) being based of course upon Fionn himself, Oscur upon Osgar, Oscian upon Oiséan, Gaul upon Goll, and so on. The first poem that Macpherson brought Home, **"The Death of Oscur"** (printed as Fragment VII—Macpherson later changed *Oscur* to *Oscar*), was probably largely Macpherson's own invention, for it has Osgar lose his life in a way completely unknown to tradition. Instead of falling at Gabhair, Oscur here dies because of the fatal effects of love: both he and the warrior Dermid fall in love with the daughter of the slain chieftain Dargo, and the conflict of love and friendship leads to the death of all three. From the beginning, then, Macpherson never literally translated genuine ballads, but he did know something about them. And this knowledge is certainly relevant to the style of his English poems.

When one compares the *Fragments* with ballads of the kind that Macpherson might have known, it seems obvious that many of the peculiar features of his poetic prose result from an attempt to imitate the style of the ballads. What follows will point out some of the similarities between the two, with particular attention to examples from

"**The Death of Oscur,**" the first of the Ossian poems, and, by Home's testimony, in the printed version substantially the same poem that he had seen at Moffatt.

To begin with, the sharply paratactic and episodic quality of the poetic prose can be easily paralleled in any one of the ballads. Consider this passage from a "Lay of Osgar" that relates the traditional death at Gabhair:

Osgar
"Raise me now with you, Eanna [the Fian],
Never before have you lifted me;
Take me now to a clear mound,
That you may strip off me my armour."

Oiséan
"There was heard at the northern strand,
Shouts of people and edge of arms;
Our warriors suddenly started,
Before that Osgar was yet dead."

("Togaibh leibh mi nis Fhianna,
Nior thog sibh mi roimhe riamh;
Thugaibh mi gu tulaich ghlain,
Ach gu'm buin sibh dhiom an t-aodach."

"Chualas aig an traigh mu thuath
Eibheach sluaigh a's faobhar arm,
Chlisg ar gaisgich gu luath
Ma'n robh Osgar fhathasd marbh.")

But examples are hardly necessary here. The quality that Saintsbury thought to be Macpherson's "chief special secret" and that has often been traced to the influence of the Bible is clearly to be found in the Gaelic. In fact, as Bertrand H. Bronson has clearly explained [in *The Traditional Tunes of the Child Ballads*, 1949], it is a part of any genuine ballad style: "The textual line of the ballad, in singing, is seized by the ear as a *musical phrase:* it is this which has discouraged suspensions of meaning and kept the sentence-structure uncomplex. Each typical line of a ballad yields its total content as it is sung: . . . the conjunctions between phrase-lines are habitually progressive; *and, or, for, nor, till;* and *if* is likely to come before, not after, the apodosis." Any literal translation of the Gaelic ballads will give a sense of an original that has short, syntactically independent lines, the very quality that Macpherson's prose gives.

Moreover, because such a style so clearly limits discursiveness and development, the Gaelic ballads, like other ballads, proceed by repetition with variation (i.e., by *parallelism*), change abruptly from one scene to another, and avoid discursive or analytical transitions. Macpherson has certainly caught some of this. His obvious parallelisms ("The warriors saw her, and loved; / Their souls were fixed on the maid." "They reaped the battle together. / Their friendship was strong as their steel") represent the kind of variation upon a single idea that is typical of ballad literature. His piling up of similes is an aspect of this. More generally, in the *Fragments* one often notices the abruptness of the shift from speaker to speaker, from scene to scene, that also characterizes the genuine ballad.

The rhetorical pattern of question and response so common in the *Fragments* is also imitated from the Gaelic. "Why openest thou afresh the spring of my grief, O son of Alpin, inquiring how Oscur fell?" asks Ossian at the beginning of "**The Death of Oscur,**" the whole poem being a dramatic reply to the implied question. "The son of Alpin" is a traditional epithet for St. Patrick in the ballads, many of them developing as Oiséan replies to Patrick's questions about the Fian. For example, in a ballad from the sixteenth-century Dean of Lismore's Book, Patrick asks to be told of the battle of Gabhair and Osgar's death: "O Oiséan, tell me tidings: when you fought the stout battle, when thine own son fell in the strife,— or didst thou attain speech with him?" And Oiséan's reply is the poem. In the twenty-nine poems in the Dean's Book there are six which proceed completely in a dialogue framework, the others often using dialogue within some other kind of framework. Macpherson's practice here seems close to the ballad tradition. Four of his *Fragments* are completely in dialogue form, and others make frequent use of the dialogue, the dialogues in "**Oscur**" between Oscur and Dargo's daughter being typical of the ballad style: "Why that gloom, son of Oscian? what shades thy mighty soul?" "Though once renowned for the bow, O maid, I have lost my fame."

In his tracing of sources Thomson has pointed out one specific stylistic parallel: "Again, in style, Macpherson is sometimes close to the ballads, especially in his use of parenthetical or descriptive phrases. . . . In the ballads these phrases and lines have no particular relevance to the context, but are used to fill out the stanza, or to provide a rhyme." By this he appears to have in mind such phrases as *"son of Ronan," "Goll, the Foe of Fionn," "Caoilte, the stout warrior," "Oiséan of brave deeds"*; "The warrior ceased not from his warlike work, *Conlaoch the furious and over-whelming*"; "Think not but to resist him, *O King of blue blades and terrible.*" In "**The Death of Oscur**" there are such comparable examples as *"O son of Alpin," "Prince of the warriours,* Oscur my son," *"son of Morny,"* and from others of the *Fragments,* "Gaul, *the tallest of men,*" "Crimora, *bright in the armour of man,*" "*gloomy son of Mugruch,* Duchommar." Here the use of the "son of" epithet is obviously taken from the Gaelic *mac* formula. And Macpherson in the epithets sometimes follows traditional ascriptions. Tallness is ascribed to Goll in the Dean's Book—"a warrior fierce and tall," and just as the maidens in Macpherson always have "breasts, as the new-fallen snow," so are they often in the ballads "fair-breasted" (*uchtgheal*) or "white bosomed" (*gealocht*). Incidentally, Macpherson's frequent use of the "O" of address before names and epithets is taken from the Gaelic *a* form—*a Phádraig* (O Patrick), *a Ghuill* (O Goll).

The profuseness of Macpherson's imagery is not typical of the ballads, but the use of imagery from nature and simple objects is something the two have in common. And occasionally the ballad writers were profuse. Here, for example, is a stanza from the Fraoch ballad that Stone collected about 1750:

> Blacker than the raven was the growth of his hair.
> Redder was his cheek than the blood of the fawn;
> Smoother than the foam of streams,
> Whiter than snow was the skin of Fraoch.

One can see how a description like this from the Dean's Book—"Brighter her radiance than the sun, and her disposition yet nobler than her form. The maiden who came from afar, we too met her graciously."—parallels the more elaborated description of Fragment VI: "Her breast was like the snow of one night. Her cheek like the bud of the rose. Mild was her blue rolling eye: but sorrow was big in her heart." Both describe the maiden who fled to the Fian, and Macpherson's practice here gives some insight into how he put together **"The Death of Oscur."** The comparable description of Dargo's daughter—"His daughter was fair as the morn; mild as the beam of night. Her eyes, like two stars in a shower: . . . her breasts, as the new-fallen snow . . ."—show Macpherson using in an original story the traditional ballad technique of describing a beautiful maiden in terms of images from nature.

Two final parallels can be easily demonstrated. The ballads abound with genitives of description in the Gaelic *na* form: "the Hill of the Fian" (*Tulach na Féine*); "Sons of the Craftsman" (*Clann na Cearda*); "O cleric of the fair croziers" (*A chléirigh na mbachall mban*). This form is the source of Macpherson's incessant genitives, for his "Prince of the warriors," "brook of the mountain," "brook of the hill," "sons of the mountain." Finally, we may note the inversions. Macpherson is particularly fond of beginning a line with an adjective or verbal ("Fixed on a tree by the brook of the hill," "Blessed be that hand of snow," "Sightless are his aged eyes"). Because of the nature of the Gaelic line any attempt to translate literally would result in such inversions. In this respect Hugh Blair's Preface to the *Fragments* presented a half-truth when it observed that the literalness of the translation caused "some inversions in style, that otherwise would not have been chosen."

These examples are sufficient, I think, to show how in both general and specific ways Macpherson's style derives from the genuine ballads. If he had been called upon to do so, Macpherson could probably have turned any one of the *Fragments* into a Gaelic poem that would have resembled a genuine poem, in something like the way Coleridge's *Rime of the Ancient Mariner* resembles a genuine English ballad. In fact, this is exactly what Macpherson later did when he, perhaps with the help of some collaborator, created the Gaelic Ossian, in which some of those parts of the *Fragments* that were incorporated into the *Fingal* and *Temora* collections can be found in ballad form. Fragment XIII, for example, which became the beginning of *Fingal,* can be found in Gaelic in the volume of 1807.

What all this points to is that if Macpherson, after Home's demand, had conceived or even worked out in detail a Gaelic ballad that imitated the genuine ballad style, conventions, and atmosphere, while giving the hero Osgar a novel fate; and if he had put this into English prose, attaining a kind of rhythm by avoiding clusters of accented and unaccented syllables; then the result would be very much like what we have in **"The Death of Oscur."** The problem is, of course, not solved that simply. The ballads are primarily heroic, not romantic. They contain details of daily life, sometimes have a satiric or comic tone, and often simply narrate the deeds of the warriors. In contrast, the fifteen *Fragments* are all elegiac and thirteen of them are concerned with unhappy love. Macpherson must have approached Gaelic poetry with a taste already formed, a taste like that of many young men of his time. The elegiac tone of those ballads attributed to Oiséan and the occasional romantic love stories told in the ballads are what must have appealed to him. His juvenilia and the sources he plagiarized from show a fondness for the graveyard school of poetry, a practice of the kind of poetic diction used by Gray, a passion for sentiment, and an appreciation of striking images, whether found in the Bible, Homer, Virgil, or Milton. The process of selection that such a taste would impose upon his originals and the proviso that the translation be in prose give the simplest explanation of the origin of his style.

That Macpherson used prose has inspired some of the searching for English models. But why he did so can be explained in a straightforward way. This was really not his own idea. In the Preface to the 1773 *Works of Ossian,* he observed that his original intention had been to publish in verse, but "he had yielded to the judgment of others in a mode which presented freedom and dignity in expression instead of fetters, which cramp the thought, whilst the harmony of language is preserved." There have been some advantages to using traditional poetic forms, but "it is, however, doubtful, whether the harmony which these poems might derive from rhyme . . . could atone for the simplicity and energy which they would lose." It is unlikely that he was lying about this when we consider that Home and Blair would have seen the lie. That they encouraged him to work in this form is the result, I think, of the qualities they wanted in the translations, something literal, true, genuine, close to the Gaelic, and yet also "poetic," smooth, capable of stirring emotion. These indeed were the general demands of the admirers of exotic literatures, very few of whom could read the original poetry of the Scots, the Welsh, the Scandinavians, the Lapps, the Arabs, and the Iroquois (a not unusual concatenation in the 1760s). Such an audience would not have been satisfied by the old scholarly tradition of translations into Latin, as used, for example, in George Hickes' *Linguarum Veterum Septentriolum Thesaurum* (1705), nor by translations in the tradition of Dryden or Pope. Enthusiasts like Blair and Bishop Percy were strongly interested in the culture portrayed in the exotic poetry and wanted translations that did not distort it. Besides the poems of Ossian, such works as Evan Evans' *Specimens of the Poetry of the Antient Welsh Bards* (1764) and Bishop Percy's *Song of Solomon* (1764) are translations that satisfied these demands of the age. We may note also that before Macpherson the literal prose translation had been practiced and had the support of some critics. In this respect the close relationship between the Edinburgh circle and French thought and culture is probably important. It was common in France to publish prose translations of foreign poetry, and the influential Abbé Batteux had argued in his *Cours de Belles Letters* that the only satisfactory way to translate poetry was by prose. It is perhaps not irrelevant that the section of the *Cours* dealing with translation was published in Edinburgh a few months before the **Fragments** came out.

Given Macpherson's sensibility, his knowledge of the authentic ballads, and the interests of his supporters, one can see clearly the genesis and continuation of the style of the Ossian poems. What must have been a sudden inspiration to satisfy Home's demand was "approved," and Macpherson had found an instrument that would take him from obscurity to fame. That he did in fact reflect and adapt some of the qualities of Gaelic originals is at least a partial clue to his success, and also helps to explain some of the faith of his supporters, most particularly of those who had some acquaintance with Gaelic literature. And, in this respect, his friends must be given credit for being more nearly right about Macpherson than those who thought that nothing in the Ossian poems derived from an authentic native tradition.

Derick Thomson (lecture date 1963)

SOURCE: "'Ossian' Macpherson and the Gaelic World of the Eighteenth Century," in *The Aberdeen University Review*, Vol. XL, No. 129, Spring, 1963, pp. 7-20.

[*In the following essay, originally delivered as a lecture at the University of Aberdeen, Thomson relates both Macpherson's Ossianic poetry and the controversy over its authenticity to social and political circumstances in Scotland during the eighteenth century.*]

What we mark today by these bicentennial celebrations is not a single, isolated occasion, but a series of events which brought James Macpherson, a young man from the Eastern Highlands and an alumnus of both King's and Marischal Colleges, prominently on to the literary stage. 1962 is a sufficiently central date for such celebrations: although James Macpherson made his first timid appearance as a translator in 1760, and although the first edition of **Fingal** appeared in December 1761, his epic task was not completed until 1763, with the publication of **Temora**, and the year 1762 can in many ways be regarded as his *annus mirabilis*.

The Ossianic Controversy has something of the air of an antiquarian puzzle. It is not easy to disengage one's mind from the present, or from more concrete problems, to reconsider the improbable chain of events which led Macpherson to the publication of **Fingal**, and to the greater eccentricity of defending his own translations for more than thirty years afterwards. Yet the effort may be worth

making, not only for the curiosity of the story itself, but also because of the light that is shed, incidentally, on eighteenth-century conditions and attitudes.

We in Aberdeen have an additional, pious interest in Macpherson and his work. He was an alumnus of both Aberdeen Universities and a graduate of neither, but we have no evidence that he was an "unsatisfactory student." Indeed we have very little evidence of his activities at Aberdeen. He entered King's College in 1752. In 1754 he migrated to Marischal College, probably because the session at King's was lengthened in that year. From Marischal he went to Edinburgh University, possibly with the intention of studying Divinity. Perhaps he was fortunate enough to discover in time that the Church was not his bent: at any rate he retired once again without receiving the University accolade.

In a description of his appearance in 1761, Ramsay of Ochtertyre says that he was "a plain-looking lad, dressed like a preacher. What he said was sensible, but his manner was starch and reserved." All this changed: a ferryman on the Spey later described his appearance in his prime, saying that he was "a great man from London and the Court, bedizened with rings, gold seals, and furs." He was described in retrospect as "a handsome man—six feet three inches in height, of a fair and florid complexion, the countenance full, and somewhat inclining to the voluptuous in expression, but marked by sensibility and acuteness." The portraits by Romney and Reynolds support this description, if indeed they are not in part the origin of it. From what we know of his life we have no reason to suppose that it was an over-fastidious conscience which deflected him from his studies in Divinity.

On leaving college Macpherson returned to his birthplace, Ruthven, south of Kingussie, to take charge of the Charity School there. This was in 1756, and Macpherson was verging on twenty years of age. Like many another student he had dabbled in verse-making at college, and he must have continued this pastime in Ruthven. In 1758 he published a poem called **The Highlander,** which attracted very little attention. By then he had returned to Edinburgh, and was earning a livelihood as a tutor, undertaking some light literary hackwork in his spare time. In 1759, when visiting Moffat with his pupil, a son of Graham of Balgowan, Macpherson met John Home, author of the play Douglas, and in the course of discussions about the Highlands Macpherson mentioned (to quote Home himself) "that he had in his possession several pieces of antient poetry. When Mr. Home desired to see them, Mr. Macpherson asked if he understood the Gaelic? 'Not one word.' 'Then, how can I show you them?' 'Very easily,' said Mr. Home; 'translate one of the poems which you think a good one, and I imagine that I shall be able to form some opinion of the genius and character of the Gaelic poetry.'"

This conversation may justly be regarded as the beginning of the Ossianic industry. The chance meeting with Home, and the literary contacts which Home provided for him, determined the course of Macpherson's activities for the next three years, and much else besides.

The Rev. Dr. Alexander Carlyle, writing in 1802, recalled a visit he had paid to Moffat on 2 October 1759. He spent the day with John Home, who told him excitedly of his meetings with Macpherson, and of the translations which he had persuaded Macpherson to make. Carlyle goes on: "I was perfectly astonished at the poetical genius displayed in them. We agreed that it was a precious discovery, and that as soon as possible it should be published to the world. Mr. Home carried the manuscript with him soon after to Edinburgh; and having shown it to Dr. Blair, and other good judges, they were so much pleased that they encouraged Mr. Macpherson to publish them without delay, which he did early in the year 1760, with the title of *Fragments of Ancient Poetry collected in the Highlands.*"

Even after an interval of forty-two years, Carlyle's words retain some of the excitement he felt on reading these translations. This excitement was widespread in literary circles. There were some critics, certainly, who woke up next morning and wondered why they had been so merry the night before; but with many the early enthusiasm lasted. This new prose poetry had an exotic air, even if on closer contact it turned out to be Scotch mist. Its grandiloquent periods seemed to reverberate in the ancient corries of history. To some it must have seemed poetic justice that such majesty could survive in the land where Cumberland had butchered to make a Hanoverian holiday.

The success of the *Fragments* was such that plans were soon laid for Macpherson to make an extensive tour of the Highlands to collect more Gaelic poetry for translation. Dr. Hugh Blair, the Professor of Rhetoric at Edinburgh University, took a leading part in making the arrangements for financing this expedition, and the Faculty of Advocates contributed generously. About the end of August 1760 Macpherson set out, proceeding through Perthshire and Argyllshire to the north-west of Invernessshire, and thence to Skye, North and South Uist and Benbecula. This journey lasted approximately six weeks, half of the time being spent in the Islands.

Macpherson was back in Ruthven in late October, as appears from a letter dated the twenty-seventh of the month. Sometime between then and early January 1761, he made a second trip, via Glenorchy to the Argyllshire coast, and on to the Island of Mull.

A good deal of evidence survives to show how he spent his time during these two expeditions. We have accounts of his collecting poems in various places in Glenelg, Skye, South Uist, Benbecula, Glenorchy, and Mull; and of his receiving Gaelic MSS. in Skye and S. Uist. We see him at work on his collections in Brae Badenoch and Edinburgh, and copies of a few of his letters to the Rev. James McLagan of Blair Atholl survived, showing that he was busy collating versions of poems, and still anxious, after his return to Edinburgh, to gather more. Some of the men

who wrote accounts of Macpherson's activities at this time were much better Gaelic scholars than he was, and the picture we build up of Macpherson is not entirely flattering. He finds some of the handwriting and spelling of the manuscripts uncouth and mysterious, is puzzled by words and phrases, and often by whole passages in poems, sometimes curses the old scribes and poets. Captain Morrison, one of his collaborators, says of Macpherson: "(that) he had much merit in collecting, and arranging, and translating; but that he was no great poet, nor thoroughly conversant in Gaelic literature. . . . "

But the picture is by no means unflattering to Macpherson's integrity. This evidence suggests that he was struggling to understand his Gaelic originals, and to arrange them in a coherent pattern. It is crucial to an understanding of what Macpherson was trying to do. What he did is in some ways a different story.

The first fruits of these labours appeared with the publication of *Fingal,* late in 1761. It was published early in December, in London, and a few days later in Edinburgh, but the edition bears the date 1762. Boswell, writing from Edinburgh to Andrew Erskine, on 17 December 1761, refers to the book, and says: "I will not anticipate your pleasure in reading the Highland bard; only take my word for it, he will make you feel that you have a soul." Erskine had obviously profited from reading *Fingal* over Christmas and New Year, for we find him writing thus to Boswell on 10 January 1762:

> The storms of night descended, the winds rolled along the clouds with all their ghosts, around the rock the dark waves burst, and showed their flaming bosoms, loud rushed the blast through the leafless oaks, and the voice of the spirit of the mountains was heard in our halls; it was Saturday, when lo! at once the postman came, mighty was his striding in the kitchen, and strong was his voice for ale. In short, I have as yet received no letter from you. . . .

On 22 January Boswell wrote to say: "Fingal has been very warmly received at London. A second edition of it is just now come out." And on 8 May Boswell wrote: "Derrick, a London author, whom you have heard me mention, has sent me his verifications of the battle of Lora, and some of the Erse fragments." Even earlier, in February, Ferdinando Warner's *Remarks on the History of Fingal* had appeared.

By now the Ossianic industry was getting merrily into gear.

One or two further critical reactions may be quoted, before we move on to consider briefly the Controversy which arose.

Dr. Hugh Blair had from an early date in the proceedings become deeply interested and implicated in Macpherson's work. He had helped to write the Preface to the *Fragments* in 1760, and after having treated his Edinburgh students to a series of lectures on Ossian, he published an enlarged version in 1763, with the title of *A Critical Dissertation on the poems of Ossian.* This was frequently reprinted in editions of the translations. Some of Blair's remarks are apposite, however unsound his premises are. "The two great characteristics of Ossian's poetry", he says, "are, tenderness and sublimity. It breathes nothing of the gay and cheerful kind; an air of solemnity and seriousness is diffused over the whole. Ossian is perhaps the only poet who never relaxes, or lets himself down into the light and amusing strain; which I readily admit to be no small disadvantage to him, with the bulk of readers." Ossian's scenery, says Blair, is "wild and romantic. The extended heath by the sea-shore; the mountain shaded with mist; the torrent rushing through a solitary valley; the scattered oaks; and the tombs of warriors overgrown with moss; all produce a solemn attention in the mind, and prepare it for great and extraordinary events."

Some other critics were more detached than Blair, but were strongly attracted to Macpherson's work. Thomas Gray was charmed with the early *Fragments,* and seemed anxious to be assured that the translations were from authentic Gaelic poetry. David Hume was cautious in his assessment, and more interested in the question of authenticity than in the poetry: "It is vain to say that their beauty will support them, independent of their authenticity: No; that beauty is not so much to the general taste, as to insure you of this event." Boswell, who had been inclined to enthusiasm in 1761, had perhaps attuned his opinions more to Dr. Johnson's by the time he wrote his Journal of the Tour to the Hebrides. Hinting at a certain monotony in the poetry he likens it to "the paper with which a room is finished, where you have a number of birds and a number of figures and a number of trees and a number of flowers; and as there is a variety of objects, one does not at once perceive that the finishing is composed of pieces all exactly the same. By the time your eye has made the round of the pattern, you forget what you first looked at. So is it with Ossian's poetry to a considerable degree." Johnson, of course, "used to boast that he had, from the first, resisted both Ossian and the Giants of Patagonia." When Dr. Blair asked him whether he thought any man of a modern age could have written such poems, Johnson replied: "Yes, Sir, many men, many women, and many children." No doubt this was going too far, but in his critical assessment of Macpherson's work, Johnson's sturdy common sense was in happy enough accord with his prejudices.

It is of particular interest to turn to the opinions expressed by a Marischal College professor, James Beattie. Writing to Robert Arbuthnot on 29 March 1762, Beattie says:

> I have now read *Fingal;* but I am at a loss to know whether I should give you my opinion of it or not. My humble tribute of praise (were I disposed to praise it) would be lost amidst that universal deluge of approbation poured upon it, both from critics of London and of Scotland. And were I inclined to censure it, my suffrage would be as little regarded as the loitering javelin which

palsied Priam threw against the heaven-tempered shield of Pyrrhus—*telum imbelle sine ictu.* The particular beauties of this wonderful work are irresistibly striking, and I flatter myself that I am as sensible of them as another. But to that part of its merit which exalts it, considered as a whole, above the *Iliad* or *Aeneid,* and its author above Homer or Virgil, I am insensible.

Beattie concludes that Ossian is defective in the highest species of poetry. "Ossian", he says, "seems really to have very little knowledge of the human heart; his chief talent lies in describing inanimate objects. . . . "

It is clear from another letter of Beattie's that it was out of conversations about Ossian, "while the rage of extolling the Highland bard continued", that Beattie had formed the design of writing his Essay on Poetry, composed in 1762, but not published until 1776.

The vogue of Macpherson's translations abroad was even more remarkable than at home. English editions appeared, e.g. in Germany (1773-75), France (1783) and Austria (1801). Foreign translations had appeared earlier, as Cesarotti's into Italian verse in 1763, and Engelbrecht's and Wittenberg's into German prose in 1764. Goethe began his translation in 1770, and a French translation of *Temora* appeared in 1774. The poems had a greater influence in Germany than elsewhere, as on the *Sturm und Drang* movement; they inspired *The Sorrows of Werther.* In several European countries Ossianic odes and plays and musical scores drew their inspiration, at first or second hand, from Macpherson's work. Napoleon is said to have carried about with him Cesarotti's Italian translation, and to have given practical proof of his enthusiasm by founding a Celtic academy in Paris. Ossianic names, such as Oscar and Malvina, were given to French children, and the royal Oscars of Norway and Sweden owed their name to the same source.

The fame and influence of Macpherson's prose-poems remained buoyant for forty to sixty years. Only a few, out of many publications, have been mentioned, and were one to produce maps or diagrams they would be thickly pin-pointed for the period 1762-1820, and for the countries of Britain, France and Germany. But there would be many outliers also, both in time and space, as for instance the Czech translation of 1827, the Danish one of 1850, the Polish verse translation of 1830, and the Russian one of 1891. Almost from the very beginning of the period there would be a variety of critical contributions to record: some of them taking the form of burlesques, others appearing as reviews, pamphlets and books. For even before *Fingal* had appeared, the Ossianic Controversy had begun.

It is probably fair to say that at first Macpherson intended no serious deception. His "translations" in the *Fragments* were either very free, or in some cases practically fictitious, but this was not in violent disagreement with the literary ethics of the time. It is also clear that he was cajoled by men such as Home and Blair to undertake a systematic search for further Gaelic materials, and perhaps encouraged by Blair to find a grand epic original—the story of the wars of Fingal. It is not unlikely that Macpherson set out, in the autumn of 1760, to find this epic, and he may well have thought he had found it in Skye, when Alexander Macpherson, a blacksmith, gave him the quarto manuscript which he had procured at Lochcarron in his youth: a manuscript which Macpherson found very difficult to read, but which apparently treated at length of the exploits of Fingal and his fellow heroes. This was the Book of the Dean of Lismore, a manuscript written about 1520 in an eccentric orthography which still in part defies interpretation. He also gained possession of other manuscripts, written in the old Irish hand, and using the classical bardic language. Since neither Macpherson nor his collaborators had been trained to read or write this language it must have teemed with obscurities for them, and it must have been at this point, during the winter of 1760 or the spring of 1761, that the bold decision was taken to use imagination where scholarship failed, and to produce an epic in "translation." It is quite unlikely that the whole blame or credit for this deception and achievement should go to Macpherson. Two of his fellow-clansmen helped him in various ways: Ewan Macpherson, a Badenoch schoolmaster, and Lachlan Macpherson, the laird of Strathmashie, a competent Gaelic poet and wit.

Fingal claimed to be a translation of a Gaelic epic which had been composed by the poet Ossian in the third century A.D. This contention was supported by an ingenious assemblage of introductory material and notes in which a considerable mass of pseudo-learning was deployed. The study of Celtic history and Celtic philology was in its infancy, and Macpherson and his close friends apparently judged that their work would not be seriously challenged. But some critics thought it inherently improbable that a third century Gaelic work, however much changed by time, should survive in the eighteenth century. The only European languages then known to have as ancient a literary tradition were Latin and Greek. It is only in modern times that it has been demonstrated that the manuscript tradition in Celtic goes back to the sixth century A.D., and the oral literary tradition much farther.

There was a variety of opinions as to Macpherson's claim of a third century origin for his epic, ranging from implicit belief to complete scepticism. Those who accepted the claim proceeded to study the work as though it were an ancient text, thus producing an excellent parody of academic method.

Macpherson was asked to submit his originals to scrutiny, and his refusal to do this on demand threw doubt on his *bona fides.* In fact Macpherson had deposited manuscripts at the shop of Becket the publisher, in London, and claimed that no one took any interest in them. But there is no doubt that he was evasive in this matter, and with good reason. For many years he was under pressure to publish the Gaelic originals in book-form, and eventually a subscription of £1,000 was raised, in India, to defray the expenses. When Macpherson died in 1796 he bequeathed this £1,000 to pay for the printing of the Gaelic. The matter had long been on his conscience, but he was in

genuine difficulties, for the alternatives which lay before him were both unpalatable and daunting. He could choose to edit the Gaelic ballads which he had from a wide variety of sources, oral and manuscript (including manuscripts which he could not read), demonstrating, if he wished to be honest, that he had not been honest in his earlier claims. Alternatively he had to produce a fabricated Gaelic original to match his "translations." To do the latter he had to learn to write Gaelic verse, or find trusty henchmen to undertake this laborious and thankless task. He found it too much to throw away even the tarnished reputation he had acquired as a translator, and evidently decided to get the originals fabricated. He was no doubt encouraged to make this decision because part of the task had already been done. A Gaelic original of the seventh book of *Temora* had already been published (in 1763), and other isolated parts appeared later. But Lachlan Macpherson, to whom posterity has accorded the honour of having fabricated the Gaelic of the seventh book of *Temora,* had died in 1767, and some of his other collaborators may not have had an equal facility. And it must be remembered that James Macpherson had led a busy life since 1763, employed largely in the service of Bute's government in the capacity of what we should now call a P.R.O. or a Press Officer, but dabbling also in the writing of history, parliamentary duties, and the lucrative activities of London agent to the Nabob of Arcot. He had engaged lavishly in dalliance with the daughters of John Bull, and in his later years had acquired an estate north of Kingussie, and built a handsome villa there. His eventful life had taken him a long way from that hastily acquired expertise in Gaelic language and literature in the years 1760-62.

Somehow or other the compilation of the Gaelic "original" grew, and of this there was vivid evidence in Macpherson's own hand. After his death, the Rev. Mr. Anderson, minister of Kingussie, sent to the Highland Society of Scotland a transcript of notes which Macpherson had written in a copy of *Fingal,* and which were discovered at his home, Bellville. These memoranda referred to his delivering specific parts of the Gaelic versions of his poems to John Mackenzie of the Temple, Secretary of the Highland Society of London. The first of these memoranda runs: "Delivered the 3 Duans (i.e. books) of Cathloda to Mr. Jno. Mackenzie, as complete as the translation." It was a curious turn of phrase: one might expect rather to talk about a translation being as complete as the original. But if we take "translation" to mean "original," the memorandum makes excellent sense. What we have here is a record of Macpherson gradually fulfilling what he regarded as his obligations: namely to provide a Gaelic original, since his friends expected it of him, and since he had accepted a subscription for publishing it.

It was not until 1807 that this "original" appeared in print. Macpherson had been dead for eleven years, and one might wonder at the delay. Some of his collaborators survived him, and honoured the dubious trust he had bequeathed to them. But we must also make an allowance of time for other features of that remarkable edition of 1807, for it contained not only elaborate and sometimes useful editorial apparatus but also a complete Latin metrical translation of the Gaelic poems. No expense, and no pains (if we except the readers) were spared.

There are ample grounds for saying that the Gaelic "originals" of 1807 constitute a more complete forgery than the "translations" of 1760-63. There were passages in the latter which were more or less what they purported to be—translations from Gaelic. But the Gaelic of 1807 was all composed in 1760 or afterwards.

It may be useful at this point to try to summarize briefly what Macpherson did in putting the poetry of Ossian before the public. He collected a considerable quantity of Gaelic Ossianic ballads from oral and manuscript sources, and used characters and stories, related traditions and history, as and when it suited him, sometimes following the gist and sequence of the ballads but more often altering these, always adding ideas and incidents which have no Gaelic counterpart, and imposing on the whole a style which bears very little resemblance to anything in Gaelic literature. In *Fingal* he made varied use of a fairly large number of Gaelic ballads, whereas in *Temora* he seems to have used only one. In writing *Temora* he was largely working out a vein that had proved lucrative. By then the imposture had gone too far; to retract a little might have been to lose all. For that reason he continued to compose history which harmonized with the scheme of his "translations," and he refused to give reasonable opportunities to his critics to investigate his sources. Instead he set about providing Gaelic sources which would be "as complete as the translation."

Much of what has been said places Macpherson in a bad light. But there were extenuating circumstances which should be considered, and Macpherson's work was as productive of good as of bad effects. Sometimes his critics were as wrong, and as obstinate, as he was. And there was much in the Gaelic world of the eighteenth century which neither Macpherson nor his critics appreciated. We may turn now from the antiquarian puzzle to a brief inquiry into that world, hoping that the result of the inquiry will be not to whitewash Macpherson but to understand him more adequately.

Some of the difficulties in the way of understanding that world, from the outside, appear in the series of letters written in the late 1720s by Thomas Burt, an Englishman and a Captain of Engineers. Burt was nearer to the Jacobite risings of 1715 and 1719 when he wrote these letters than we are now to the Second World War, and he was somewhat in the position of a British officer in Germany in the late 1940s, except that the twentieth-century officer might know something about Beethoven and Goethe and Thomas Mann, whereas Burt knew nothing of the art of the Gaels. But his curiosity was probably greater. His ignorance of Highland conditions, on arriving in Inverness, was shared with the vast majority of Scottish Lowlanders. "The Highlands," he says, "are but little known even to the Inhabitants of the low Country of Scotland, for they have ever dreaded the Difficulties and Dangers of Travelling among the Mountains; and when some extraordi-

nary occasion has obliged any one of them to such a Progress, he has, generally speaking, made his Testament before he set out, as though he were entering upon a long and dangerous Sea Voyage, wherein it was very doubtful if he should ever return."

The early letters show a good deal of prejudice against Scotland in general and the Highlands in particular, but later his interest increases and some of his prejudices are dropped. He learnt a good deal of Gaelic and had taken pains to find out about Highland modes of dress and arms, social organization, the place of music, and literary orders. Despite an assumption of superiority, even to the chiefs of whom he frequently writes, there is a genuine desire to understand the Highlands. He underlines his own fair-mindedness, as though he were acutely conscious that it is unusual, and almost needs an apology.

The spectacular events of the '45 Rising brought the Highlands into an unhappy prominence again—unhappy because of the repressive measures that were taken to punish the Jacobites, and prevent further civil strife. These measures were founded on the simple-minded assumption that what is English is best, so that the Highlands as a whole suffered, and not only the Jacobite clans. The Highland dress was proscribed, the possession of firearms was prohibited, heritable jurisdictions were abolished, and the language and way of life associated with the Gaelic area were discouraged. But this was merely an attempt to complete a process begun long before, and directed from the Scottish Lowlands. The attempt to bring the Gaelic area fully within the sphere of Scottish government had been in progress at least since the second half of the fifteenth century. Politicians of one sort or another had for long cherished the prosaic ambition of making all the subjects alike, in language and in allegiance. Now, in the first half of the eighteenth century, a band of evangelical churchmen jumped on the same disreputable waggon. The Society for the Propagation of Christian Knowledge devoted considerable effort to the holy task of extirpating Irish and Popery in the Highlands, thus perhaps obscuring the racial issue which had seemed clearer earlier.

For propagandist purposes, and through simple ignorance, the Highlands had long been designated a barbaric area, and its inhabitants were sometimes called savages. This had the natural result of arousing the curiosity of people who had anthropological interests, and the second half of the eighteenth century brought a long succession of intrepid explorers to the Highlands. We may conclude with some confidence that James Macpherson was instinctively aware of the climate of opinion concerning the Highlands, and took some advantage of it. The warlike character of the clans, and the defeat of Culloden coloured his account of the wars of Fingal; he must have known the fatalism that he projects on to his Ossianic heroes; he must have resented the calumny and repression which his fellow-countrymen were subjected to. He was attempting to restore the honour of his race. The attempt in itself shows a chink in his armour: he had partly accepted the viewpoint of his adversaries.

Macpherson's translations in their turn undoubtedly reinforced the curiosity of strangers concerning the Highlands. They certainly aroused once more Johnson's curiosity, earlier stirred by reading Martin Martin's account of the Western Isles. Since Johnson's *Journey* and Boswell's *Journal* are such famous contributions to the literature of Highland exploration it may be useful to consider the attitudes, methods and results of these two adventurers.

By 1773 Dr. Johnson had left far behind him the hardships of his early life in London, and his anthropological zeal was tempered by a liking for amenities, both material and intellectual, to which he had grown accustomed. London was the centre of his life, and he was at the centre of London's literary life. The decision to tour the Highlands was therefore a bold and generous one. Many of his reactions to what he saw and heard were bold and generous also. His impressions of the Highlanders might in some quarters have been regarded as treasonable: "Civility," he says, "seems part of the national character of Highlanders. Every chieftain is a monarch, and politeness, the natural product of royal government, is diffused from the laird through the whole clan." [Johnson was talking about the pre-Clearance period.] Perhaps, however, he did not fully appreciate the flavour of the minister's comment which he quotes in the following passage:

> By their Lowland neighbours they would not willingly be taught, for they have long considered them as a mean and degenerate race. These prejudices are wearing fast away; but so much of them still remains, that when I asked a very learned minister in the islands, which they considered as their most savage clans: "Those," said he "that live next to the Lowlands."

He sums up the Lowland attitude to the Highlands in a telling passage:

> To the southern inhabitants of Scotland, the state of the mountains and the islands is equally unknown with that of Borneo or Sumatra: of both they have only heard a little, and guess the rest. They are strangers to the language and the manners, to the advantages and wants of the people, whose life they would model, and whose evils they would remedy.

The Highlanders' pride, he says, had been "crushed by the heavy hand of a vindictive conqueror." His comment on Highland depopulation reminds us of the consistency of much Government policy: "To hinder insurrection, by driving away the people, and to govern peaceably, by having no subjects, is an expedient that argues no great profundity of politicks."

Johnson had come to Scotland, to quote his own words, to "hear old traditions, and see antiquated manners." He had come to discover what Gaelic society consisted of. He made several errors of judgment which seriously impeded this enquiry. In the first place, like a modern cabinet minister or a member of the royal family, he restricted his acquaintance unduly, staying with the people whose outlook and amenities most closely resembled his own.

Secondly, he did not reach the Outer Hebrides; he was conscious of this gap in his itinerary, saying: "If we had travelled with more leisure, it had not been fit to have neglected the Popish Islands." Thirdly, he seems to have arrived with certain fixed notions which he found hard to dislodge, and he spent much time pontificating about matters of which he knew little, instead of patiently gathering information.

Yet he asked many pointed questions, and gleaned much information. He enjoyed listening to Gaelic songs: "After supper the ladies sung *Erse* songs, to which I listened as an *English* audience to an *Italian* opera, delighted with the sound of words which I did not understand." Unlike many Englishmen, he was prepared to be civil about bagpipe music—he does not seem to have his tongue in his cheek even when he says: "The solace which the bagpipe can give, they have long enjoyed." But it is noteworthy that even within earshot of the MacCrimmon College of Piping near Dunvegan he does not seem to have discovered that a highly distinctive musical system was associated with the pipes. All he says is "The tunes of the bagpipe are traditional." But it is in his investigation of the Gaelic language and its literary traditions that his enquiry is least satisfactory and his conclusions most untrustworthy. He concluded that "the Earse never was a written language" and that "there is not in the world and Earse manuscript a hundred years old." "The nation was wholly illiterate", he says. "Neither bards nor Senachies could write or read"; "no Earse genealogy was ever written": and he concluded "Thus hopeless are all attempts to find any traces of Highland learning." In these passages Johnson falls into a host of errors, through lack of systematic enquiry. He seems to have expected the small cross-section of lairds and ministers he met to have the answers to all possible enquiries he could make. They were his ultimate encyclopaedia for Gaelic topics, and when they did not know of the existence of something, Johnson seemed too ready to conclude that it did not exist.

Boswell, with his journalistic genius, is less open to such charges. Infinitely more adaptable than his stately mentor, Boswell danced and sang Gaelic songs, and by the time they got to Coll had picked up, he supposed, thirty words of Gaelic. Although this may seem a modest enough linguistic achievement it is symptomatic of Boswell's approach and attitude. On the question of Gaelic literacy and the existence of Gaelic manuscripts Boswell's attitudes are much more reasonable than Johnson's, as appears from a letter he wrote to Johnson from Edinburgh, on 8 February 1775. "It is reasonable to suppose," he says, "that such of the inhabitants as acquired any learning, possessed the art of writing as well as their Irish neighbours, and Celtick cousins; and the question is, can sufficient evidence be shown of this?" Boswell goes on to say that "There is now come to this city Ranald Macdonald from the Isle of Egg, who has several MSS. of Erse poetry, which he wishes to publish by subscription. I have engaged to take three copies of the book . . . as I would subscribe for all the Erse that can be printed be it old or new, that the language may be preserved. This man says, that some of his manuscripts are ancient; and, to be sure, one of them which was shewn to me does appear to have the duskyness of antiquity." Johnson replied: "The dusky manuscript of Egg is probably not fifty years old; if it be an hundred, it proves nothing. . . . There are, I believe, no Erse manuscripts." His mind was made up.

We may now turn to consider what lay beyond the radius of the feeble searchlight that was beamed from the English-speaking parts of Scotland, and from England, on the Gaelic area. The inquiry may be largely confined to evidence of literary life in the Gaelic area, since this has some relevance to the Controversy we have been considering. The evidence is of two main kinds: (I) factual and contemporary evidence, that is for example, evidence of and concerning literary works, authors, scholars and manuscripts; and (2) inferential evidence, whereby we can argue, for example, that an oral tradition which was alive in the nineteenth and twentieth centuries, and which has roots in the Middle Ages, may be presumed to have been alive in the eighteenth century also. Although our knowledge of some of these matters is much fuller than in Macpherson's time, a good deal remains to be done in this field still, while the missed opportunities of the eighteenth century must invitably arouse feelings of sadness.

In 1775, the year in which Dr. Johnson confidently announced that he believed there were no Erse manuscripts, John Walker, Professor of Natural History in the University of Edinburgh, obtained a statement from Neil MacMhuirich in South Uist, testifying that members of his family had for nineteen (*recte* seventeen) generations been bards to the MacDonalds of Clanranald and the MacDonalds of the Isles, and he recited fifteen generations of his pedigree. It must have seemed both a large and a curious claim to make, but the more the history of the MacMhuirich family is investigated the more honourable does the claim appear to be. References to this long line of bards are found in a number of Scottish and Irish documents, such as the Irish Annals of the Four Masters, the Acts of the Scottish Parliament, the Register of the Privy Council and the Charter Chest of the Clanranald family. The progenitor of the family came from Ireland to Scotland, probably about the year 1213, and two Gaelic poems which he addressed to the Earls of Lennox survive. Eight of his poems are included in the early sixteenth-century anthology known as the Book of the Dean of Lismore, while others survive only in Irish manuscripts. One of his putative descendants appears as a witness to a grant of land in 1259; another is said to have composed an incitement to battle for the MacDonalds, before the Battle of Harlaw in 1411. (This may have been the nearest a MacMhuirich ever got to Aberdeen until the family changed its name to Currie.) Lachlan MacMhuirich is described as *Archipoeta* to MacDonald of the Isles in 1485. John MacMhuirich held lands in Kintyre in the sixteenth century, and a branch of the family stayed there, although the main poetic branch migrated about that time to the Outer Hebrides, holding lands in Benbecula and South Uist in virtue of their office as bards and historians to Clanranald. Niall Mór MacMhuirich wrote of a famous dynastic wedding in Dunvegan in 1614. Neil MacMhuirich wrote in Gaelic an account of the Montrose Wars, and

survived to compose elegies on the death of Allan of Clanranald at Sherriffmuir. Donald MacMhuirich was composing poems and witnessing documents in the 1730s. Donald's son Neil gave Gaelic manuscripts to James Macpherson in 1760, and told of his family's pedigree in 1775. His son Lachlan recited his pedigree in 1800, but deponed that he could not write. The policy of the Anglicizers was at last showing results, and five hundred years of Gaelic literary history were at an end. All Dr. Johnson knew of was the last inglorious period of fifty years.

The earliest Gaelic in a surviving Scottish manuscript is that in the Book of Deer. The Gaelic entries were probably made in the middle of the twelfth century. Manuscript remains are scanty for the succeeding centuries, although thirteenth- and fourteenth- and fifteenth-century poems survive. Records become more abundant from the seventeenth century onwards. In the year 1700, Edward Lhuyd, Keeper of the Ashmolean Museum, met John Beaton, descendant of the Beatons who had been hereditary physicians to the Lords of the Isles, and later to the Scottish kings, and noted down the titles of a score of Gaelic manuscripts which Beaton had in his private library. It is only within the last three or four years that Lhuyd's evidence has come to light again. It serves to remind us of the scantiness of our sources for the literary history even of the seventeenth and eighteenth centuries in Gaelic Scotland. But it serves also to make us more critical of such contemporary sources of evidence as Dr. Johnson's *Tour*. Our sources are so scanty because native archives had been abandoned, native institutions had atrophied, and the archives and institutions in non-Gaelic Scotland were not interested in time. The lack of intellectual curiosity shown by the Scottish Universities is a remarkable case in point (although this extended to languages and subjects other than Gaelic).

Gaelic alumni and graduates of the Scottish Universities were beginning to make amends in the eighteenth century, but in some ways it was too late. Such efforts were responsible in part for the preservation of the Gaelic manuscripts now held by the National Library of Scotland, and for the collection of much poetry in particular from oral sources, but the native Gaelic academies (the bardic schools and monastic scriptoria, such as that of Iona) had not passed on their treasures and their traditions to Scottish colleges and libraries. Manuscripts were burnt, lost, and cut up to be used as tailors' tapes. The first University official to study Gaelic manuscripts seriously was Ewen MacLachlan, Librarian in King's College in the early years of the nineteenth century.

James Macpherson made contact with some of the survivors of the old orders. He did this most obviously when he went to see Neil MacMhuirich in South Uist in 1760, but other contacts were significant also. His collaborator Captain Morrison was almost certainly a descendant of the ñ Muirgheasáins who had once been bards to the MacLeods of Harris and Dunvegan; Lachlan Macpherson was a worthy representative of the class of lairds who were Gaelic poets and scholars; the MacNicols of Glenorchy, from whom he got Gaelic ballads, came of a long line of tradition-bearers; by an odd chance he acquired in Skye the Gaelic poem-book of a sixteenth-century Perthshire ecclesiastic.

But he does not seem to have contacted the MacLachlans of Kilbride, who passed on Gaelic manuscripts to the Highland Society and the Faculty of Advocates in the late eighteenth and early nineteenth centuries, nor the descendants of the O'Connachers of Lorn, hereditary physicians and scribes, nor the heirs of the Beatons, hereditary physicians and secretaries. He does not seem to have met Alasdair Mac Mhaighstir Alasdair, the eighteenth-century poet who was deeply knowledgeable in Gaelic literary tradition, and whose son published a Gaelic anthology in 1776. Macpherson does not seem to have known of the comparatively rich tradition of Gaelic song, going back to the fifteenth century, and he was perhaps not interested in the tradition of classical pipe-music, while the art of harp-music was practically dead before his time. Although he listened to some prose tales about Ossianic heroes he cannot have known how extensive the corpus of oral prose literature was. It was in the mid-nineteenth century that this began to be investigated, and investigation still continues. If he had known to look for it, he might have found a manuscript version of the Old Irish prose epic, the *Tain Bó Cuailnge,* in the library of the Dukes of Athol: he might also have found oral versions of it in the Hebrides, where a fragmentary one was recorded three years ago. We cannot criticize him for knowing nothing of these matters: the common-rooms of the Universities he attended scarcely knew of their existence; political and ecclesiastical policy strove to expunge such lore from the national memory, and to replace it by ill-natured, ill-informed gibes.

From our standpoint, two centuries later, when Gaelic studies have regained some of their former status in their native environment, we may instead, quixotically perhaps, but quite sincerely, salute James Macpherson.

John J. Dunn (essay date 1971)

SOURCE: "James Macpherson's First Epic," in *Studies in Scottish Literature,* Vol. LX, No. 1, July, 1971, pp. 48-54.

[*In the following essay, Dunn argues that* The Highlander, *a long poem Macpherson published as a young man under his own name, demonstrates a commitment to Gaelic history and his Highland heritage that predates his "discovery" of Ossian.*]

In June of 1760, Macpherson's *Fragments of Ancient Poetry* was published anonymously with a short preface by Dr. Hugh Blair, who was then at work preparing his lectures on *belles lettres.* A warm commendation from the pastor of the High Church of St. Giles assured the volume attention at least in the North, for at that time "Blair was one of the most signally honored men in Edinburgh"; furthermore, the poems had already been circulated among the Edinburgh *literati* and had received praise

from such distinguished figures as Hume, Robertson, Ferguson, and Home. In view of the strong nationalistic feelings current in Scotland at the time, it would not have been difficult to predict the popularity in the North of the first published volume of what purported to be a translation of Highland poetry; but probably no one, least of all Macpherson himself, would have anticipated the great vogue these poems were to enjoy in England and throughout Western Europe.

How different was the reception that had awaited Macpherson's first volume, *The Highlander,* published in Edinburgh by Walter Ruddiman, Jr., just two years earlier. It too was anonymous, but on that occasion there was no commendatory preface. *The Scots Magazine* made note of its existence and its cost (one shilling) but failed to review it. *The Edinburgh Magazine,* also published by Ruddiman, ignored the poem completely. Macpherson suffered the most bitter fate of any artist: he was completely ignored.

The Highlander, an epic poem in six cantos, deals with the rising fortunes of Alpin, the Scottish protagonist; he begins as an unknown youth of obscure lineage but, as the poem progresses, he distinguishes himself through acts of courage and generosity. Ultimately he emerges as the new Scottish king. The first three cantos show his excellence during time of war, the final three during peace.

At the outset we learn that Sueno has led a band of Scandinavian invaders against the Scots, who are governed by Indulph. Alpin first shows signs of his daring by instigating and leading a bold and successful night raid against the powerful enemy. During the course of this action he overcomes the young champion of the Danes, Haco; but in recognition of his valor and prowess Alpin befriends his adversary, and the two young men exchange gifts. On the following day (Canto II) the two armies struggle heroically for supremacy, and, though victory flits from one side to the other, the day ends without either side emerging victorious. Alpin again shows himself as an uncommonly skillful and courageous warrior. That night (Canto III) Alpin leads a carefully chosen band of valiant Scots to destroy the enemy fleet. Their purpose is accomplished, and the alarmed invaders are put to rout. Alpin generously allows Haco to escape with his bride Aurelia, who has come on the expedition disguised as a warrior.

The war over, Alpin once more displays his heroism by rescuing Culena, the daughter of Indulph, from a base attacker (Canto IV). The Highlander, furthermore, shows himself as adept in courtly athletics as he was in battle. In Canto V the noble ancestry of Alpin is revealed; he is in fact a prince, the son of the murdered King Malcom. Subsequently he assumes his true name, Duffus. Although Indulph immediately offers to restore the throne to the rightful heir, Duffus refuses because he recognizes his inexperience in affairs of state. He seeks and wins the hand of Culena (Canto VI), ensuring the union of the two dynasties. When the King is unexpectedly murdered by Danish pirates, Duffus assumes the throne with the prospect of a long and benevolent reign over a loving people.

It is obvious that certain major aspects of *The Highlander* are later reflected in Ossian, particularly in the first epic, *Fingal*. The setting is Scotland in the remote past, and the central action revolves around the people's defense of their homeland against Scandinavian invaders, led in *The Highlander* by Sueno, in *Fingal* by Swaran. The heroes of both poems defeat the invading force and restore peace to the land.

The Highlander no less than Ossian expresses a plea for Scots national feeling, which reached its peak during the half-century following Culloden. Largely because of its Scottish theme, John Home's tragedy, *Douglas,* kept Edinburgh in an ecstasy of praise, and made its author a celebrated literary figure; in the North he was frequently called the "Scottish Shakespeare." Probably because of its utter conventionality, *The Highlander* received little attention despite its patriotic appeal.

Macpherson drew upon details from the recent past in his epic. With bagpipes playing, the kilted Scots, proudly wearing their tartans, go into battle:

> To show invaders that they dar'd to die,
> For barren rocks, for fame and liberty.
>
> (III, 31)

Not only do the Scots repeatedly express fervent national sentiments, but their generous patriotism and heroic valor, which serve to keep their nation free, are in marked contrast to the conduct of their southern neighbors:

> England's subdu'd, the Saxons are o'ercome,
> And meanly own a Danish Lord at home.
>
> (I, 8)

There is also a marked tendency to idealize the past, and to reflect the conviction that man in a more primitive state acted from more disinterested motives. In Ossian such an assumption is never stated explicitly since the poems are supposed to be a direct reflection of a primitive mind, but as readers we are struck by the generosity and compassion of these ancient people. By listing faults not shared with contemporary times, Macpherson in passages of *The Highlander* more explicitly suggests the nobility of an early period. The Caledonian court is a model of openness based on benevolence, honesty, and trust; in the event of private oppression, the court will seek to remedy it:

> No frowning spear-man guards the awful door;
> No borrow'd terror arms the hand of pow'r:
> No cringing bands of sycophants appear,
> To send false echoes to the monarch's ear.
> Merit's soft voice, oppression's mournful groan,
> Advanced, unstill'd, to th' attentive throne.
>
> (I, 6)

The art and architecture reflect the manly simplicity of the people's martial lives:

> The royal hall, in simple nature great.
> No pigmy art, with little mimickry,

> Distracts the sense, or pains the weary eye:
> Shields, spears and helms in beauteous order
>   shone,
> Along the walls of uncemented stone.
>
> (III, 38)

Like the description of the court, the details of the Caledonian council meeting are an almost explicit condemnation of the contemporary state of affairs and reaches the proportions of a catalogue of current political abuses:

> Within the high-arch'd hall the nobles sat,
> And formed in council the reviving state;
> For instant peace solicitous prepare,
> And raise a bulwark 'gainst the future war.
> No high-flown zeal the patriot hurl'd along,
> No secret gold engag'd the speaker's tongue,
> No jarring seeds are by a tyrant sown,
> No cunning senate undermines the throne.
> To public good their public thoughts repair,
> And Caledonia is the gen'ral care.
> No orator in pompous phrases shines,
> Or veils with public weal his base designs.
> Truth stood conspicuous, undisguis'd by art,
> They spoke the homely language of the heart.
>
> (IV, 49)

In *The Highlander* and in Ossian the characters are conceived with the same uniformity. There is no one in either work that could be described as a complex character. Some of the figures in the latter work might be called compound in that they are, for instance, courageous but proud, or fierce in war *but* generous in peace; but in general the delineation is between the good and the bad. The view of hero and villain is usually as stereotyped as in the American Western before the discovery of psychological realism. Alpin, who is the epitome of the noble warrior, reflects the general over-simplification of character when he comments that his rescue of Culena deserves no special recognition, for he

> But frightened from his prey a sensual slave,
> The gloomy sons of guilt are never brave—
> Whoe'er would seize on a defenceless fair,
> Wou'd shun the sword and fly amain from war.
>
> (IV, 48)

In addition to these similarities to Ossian, there are three features of *The Highlander* which are later developed into major themes: the convention of female disguise (always as a warrior), the interest in violent, forboding landscapes, and the central role of the courtly bard.

We are told that Aurelia and Haco were married, but even before the marriage could be consummated, he was called to war. She was supposed to remain at home, but in her determination not to be parted from her lover, she disguises herself as a young warrior and joins the expedition. Variations on this same device occur in Ossian with such frequency that they become as monotonous as they are incredible.

The natural settings in *The Highlander* are not nearly so prominent as in Macpherson's later work, and are usually brought in as epic similes. However, in this use they are almost always depictions of nature in a violent and threatening state:

> Thus, on a night when rattling tempests war,
> Thro' broken clouds appears a blazing star;
> Now veils its head, now rushes on the sight,
> And shoots a livid horror thro' the night.
>
> (I, 9)

Finally, when we are given a description of the bards at court, their function is conceived of in terms identical with those of Ossian:

> Harmonious bards exalt the tuneful voice:
> A select band by Indulph's bounty fed,
> To keep in song the mem'ry of the dead!
> They handed down the ancient rounds of time,
> In oral story and recorded rhyme.
>
> (V, 69)

After recognizing that there are a number of similarities between *The Highlander* and Ossian, we must hasten to add that the total artistic effect of the two works is vastly different, and it is this difference that to a large degree explains the fact that the earlier poem was almost completely neglected, not only by the general British reading public, but even in Edinburgh, where works by Scots dealing with a native scene were so rare that when they did appear they were apt to be accorded lavish praise.

The Highlander is clearly the work of an inexperienced writer, who is trying his hand at employing the conventions of neo-classical epic verse as derived from Dryden's and Pope's translations, but who is unable to use the convention in an imaginative or creative way. The use of periphrasis is stock. The sun is referred to as "the beam of day," "the flaming lord of day," and "the occidental light." Waves are "liquid mountains," and the seabirds are the "songsters of the spray." Compound epithets abound and though more original are no more fortunate. We find "steel-clad ridges" (i.e. lines of warriors), "tree-set vale," "tear-distilling maids," and "favor-speaking mein." The fashionable "y" adjectives derived from nouns are also common: "ridgy sea," "spumy waves," "healthy wild," and "pearly grass."

The heroic couplets are generally managed with little vigor, though there are passages that suggest Macpherson might have learned to handle the form with flexibility and even grace:

> Thus when devouring hatchet-men invade,
> With sounding steel, the forest's leavy head,
> The mountains ring with their repeated strokes;
> The tap'ring firs, the elms, the aged oaks,
> Quake at each gash; then nod the head and
>   yield;
> Groan as they fall, and tremble on the field.
> Thus fell the men; blood forms a lake around,

> While groans and spears hoarse harmony
>   resound.
> The mountains roar, and thunder back each
>   noise,
> And eccho [sic] stammers with unequal voice.
>
> (II, 20-21)

More commonly, however, we find lines that suggest an inexperienced poet straining to sustain the form and fiction of his work. Cliches abound and are often placed in a stressed position; Alpin,

> Resolved to offer to his king and lord,
> The gen'rous service of his trusty sword.
>
> (1,14)

There are even examples of what might be called a mixed cliche:

> Yet hear this thought.—Within the womb of
>   night,
> Confirm the troop, and arm the youth for fight.
>
> (I, 10)

Unconscious puns sometimes produce ludicrous effects:

> Whence is the youth? I see fierce Denmark
>   warms
> Each gen'rous breast, and fires 'em into arms.
>
> (I, 6)

And an extension of a metaphor results in an image that borders on the grotesque:

> At length returning life her bosom warms,
> Glows in her cheeks and lights up all her
>   charms.
>
> (IV, 46)

There are indications of Macpherson's laboring to find rhymes. We find inversion and padding often:

> Silent and slow she moves along the main,
> Behind, her maids attend, a modest train!
>
> (IV, 44)

Language is sometimes forced for the sake of rhyme:

> Slow-curling waves advance upon the main
> And often threat the shore, and oft abstain.
>
> (IV, 45)

Similarly words are forced into unnatural syntactical structures for the sake of rhyme:

> Th' astondished chiefs congeal'd in dumb amaze,
> Stiffen'd to silence, on each other gaze.
>
> (V, 67)

Such specific weaknesses in the management of the poem are indicative of more than technical inadequacy. There is rarely an indication that the author has thought or felt very deeply about the subject. Despite the praise given to simple emotional diction—"the homely language of the heart"—the poem itself is better described in terms of the "pompous phrases" that it ostensibly condemns. The pervasive torpor of the lines suggests the efforts of an earnest young man rather dispiritedly completing a poetic exercise by sticking doggedly at it. Macpherson's comment on imitative poets, made some fifteen years later in his preface to *The Iliad*, may well be based on his own youthful experience; it is at any rate an astute commentary on his own early work:

> The greatest genius, when employed merely in copying, must be unhinged; The fancy, which should animate genuine poetry, is curbed and depraved; and the judgment, which ought to preconcert the whole frame of a perfect work, becomes languid for want of employment.

The question of why Macpherson wrote Ossian in the extraordinary manner in which he did affords no simple explanation; those who seek to portray him either as a well-meaning adapter or as a thorough-going charlatan fail to take into account the whole of the evidence, for at each stage in the composition of the poems he was probably something of both. What is evident from a reading of *The Highlander* is that Macpherson was not a mere literary opportunist; he had a genuine and serious desire to fashion an epic on a Scottish theme long before the publication of *Fingal* and *Temora.*

Robert Folkenflik (essay date 1974)

SOURCE: "Macpherson, Chatterton, Blake and the Great Age of Literary Forgery," in *The Centennial Review*, Vol. XVIII, No. 4, Fall, 1974, pp. 378-91.

[*In the following essay, Folkenflik argues that eighteenth-century English culture made literary forgery both practically and imaginatively useful for several different writers, including Macpherson.*]

It is no accident that the later eighteenth century was the great age of literary forgery. Macpherson, Chatterton, Pinkerton and Ireland (Steevens is perhaps another case) share a world which made forgery an innovative answer to a difficult series of questions which faced the would-be artist. The circumstances are fairly familiar, but the problems they posed have only recently been receiving any attention.

The chief question consciously or unconsciously asked by the ambitious was, "How can I be a great poet now?" In what follows I shall be concerned primarily with Macpherson, for though we do not consider him to be among the first rank of poets of his day, he was the first among them to provide a striking answer to the question, and his solution was immediately successful and influential. I shall then consider Chatterton's solution briefly in relationship to Macpherson, and end with a short account of a non-forger, Blake, who was a better poet than either and whose achieve-

ment may be best seen in the context of late eighteenth-century dilemmas.

Macpherson's "Preface to *Fingal*" reveals a mind finely attuned to the implications of his enterprise. Throughout it his comments are far more appropriate to his own situation than to Ossian's:

> Poetry, like virtue, receives its reward after death. The fame which men pursued in vain, when living, is often bestowed upon them when they are not sensible of it. This neglect of living authors is not altogether to be attributed to that reluctance which men shew in praising and rewarding genius. It often happens, that the man who writes differs greatly from the same man in common life. His foibles, however, are obliterated by death and his better part, his writings remain: his character is formed from them, and he that was no extraordinary man in his own time, becomes the wonder of succeeding ages.—From this source proceeds our veneration for the dead. Their virtues remain, but the vices, which were once blended with their virtues, have died with themselves.

This is a suitable apologia for a living man who has written a book supposedly by a dead man, for a profligate who has written a morally uplifting work. Ossian's living fame is rather beside the point, and his "foibles" as they cannot be known are hardly available for speculation. Macpherson displays in this preface an urge to confess which seems just barely to become part of his defense of the work's authenticity. In the next paragraph he continues,

> This consideration might induce a man, diffident of his abilities, to ascribe his own compositions to a person, whose remote antiquity and whose situation, when alive, might well answer for faults which would be inexcusable in a writer of this age.

Describing his own practice he emphasizes the gain, the comparative freedom such a writer might have from anxieties about modern critical judgment and its demands on the writer. Attributing this last view to an "ingenious gentleman" of his acquaintance, he goes on to say that upon reading the poems themselves the gentleman was convinced of their authenticity and adds—with perhaps a sly recognition of his own real originality—"it would be a very uncommon instance of self-denial in me to disown them, were they really of my composition."

If we step back, some of Macpherson's achievements should come into focus: the acceptance of the age's demands for literary excellence, the development of significant new genres, the innovative adoption of ancient and modern literary tradition. Macpherson's achievement was in the genre most admired by eighteenth-century critics, and least successfully written by eighteenth-century poets, the epic. It is worth noting that his first book, the *Fragments of Ancient Poetry* (1760), anticipated that characteristic Romantic genre, the fragment, which became a norm as poets and critics began to consider the long poem a contradiction in terms. Macpherson also anticipates another Romantic development, the prose poem.

As Malcolm Laing observed in 1805, he probably was indebted to Lowth's recent praise of the sacred poetry of the Hebrews (1753) for his choice of rhythmical prose as a medium for ancient epic poetry. The success of King James's committee of translators made such an alternative a distinct possibility, and Macpherson's account of his decision sounds like a diffident Milton defending blank verse in *Paradise Lost*. He considers the use of prose a novelty, yet he intended to rhyme until others (Macpherson's whole achievement is hedged round with nameless others) convinced him of the rightness of his final choice, "a mode which presented freedom and dignity of expression, instead of fetters, which cramp the thought. . . ." He, too, would free the heroic poem from what Milton called "the troublesome and modern bondage of rhyming." Like Milton and the Bible, Ossian was greatly praised for his sublimity.

As Schiller notes in his "On Naive and Sentimental Poetry," the opposition of the moderns to the ancients is generally put in terms which take the genres and tones of the ancient's literary achievements as highest in the scale. By becoming an ancient, Macpherson placed that Herculean burden of the past on other shoulders. He made of all the major impasses that faced the modern poet a broad highway that took him back to the ancients for a solution. But there was a price: it consisted of fame for his creation at the partial expense of his own fame and even, in certain quarters, of his reputation.

Many critics of the time insisted that the great poet must be original, and this brought in its wake the kind of self-consciousness that Walter Jackson Bate has recently discussed as the burden of the past. One could praise Shakespeare's woodnotes wild and despair of equaling his achievement, but one could hardly go about his innocent plot-pilfering and expect to be great. One *could* imitate, but, as Johnson put it, "no man was ever great by imitation."

The age was interested not only in originality but in original *genius*. There was a steadily developing fascination with the poet as person and a shifting emphasis from the work he produced to the poem as expressive of his personality. Part of the difficulty critics have with Johnson's *Life of Milton* comes from a failure to recognize that Johnson assumes the poet should accommodate himself to his audience whereas we assume that the reader should accommodate himself to the poet. This attitude is part of a legacy, probably deriving from Longinus, that the late eighteenth and early nineteenth centuries have left us. The development of print culture, the independence of the artist that came with the decline of patronage and the rise of professionalism, the burgeoning (an effect which became a cause) of literary biography: these were a few of the reasons why poets began to supersede poetry as an object of inquiry.

The primitivism of the eighteenth century was pervasive and far-reaching in its implications, though usually treated with suspicion by critics such as Johnson, Hume and Gibbon. The most important aspect of primitivism for Macpherson derives from Thomas Blackwell's *Enquiry into the Life and Writings of Homer* (1735)—Blackwell was one of Macpherson's professors at Aberdeen—and continues as a distinctly though not exclusively Scottish concern. It identified poetry as the natural language of primitive man and suggested that only among primitive men was genius to be found. And even Johnson, on empirical grounds, could come to some of the same conclusions. In a famous passage in *Rasselas* Imlac notes that "in almost all countries, the most ancient poets are considered as the best," surveys some of the possible reasons for this preference and concludes, "whatever be the reason, it is commonly observed that the early writers are in possession of nature, and their followers of art. . . ." Where there such agreement on the virtues of the early writers, Macpherson's decision to become an ancient seems, biding the question of authenticity, a fairly obvious choice.

And his work was doubly primitive. Ossian was not only a member of an ancient primitive society, but his native Scotland remained partly primitive in modern times. This association of Scotland with primitivism would later spur on the cult of the poetical plowboy, Bobbie Burns, partly at the expense of that excellent Scots poet, Robert Burns. Just five years after Macpherson's fragments appeared, Percy explained why most of the minstrels in his *Reliques of Ancient English Poetry* came from the "North Countrie" by saying "the civilizing of nations has begun from the South: the North would therefore be the last civilized, and the old manners would longest subsist there." The Romantic associations of modern Scotland may have had something to do with the European vogue of the Ossian poems.

The complement to primitivism was the belief that, to take the phrase of Milton's to which Samuel Johnson objected so strenuously, it was an age too late for poetry. This was a favorite theme of the mid- and late eighteenth century. (In fact for the last few hundred years a number of our greatest poets have been writing superb poems about the impossibility of writing poetry.) Milton's example should have been sufficient to show the fallacy of such thinking, but instead Milton ironically became the last possible great poet. In Collins's "Ode on the Poetical Character" the would-be poet attempts to reach the poetic Eden, the place where Milton is to be found, but though Collins's "trembling feet his guiding steps pursue," the attempt is a failure:

> In vain—such Bliss to One alone,
> Of all the Sons of Soul was known,
> And Heav'n, and Fancy, kindred Pow'rs,
> Have now o'erturn'd th'inspiring Bow'rs,
> Or Curtain'd close such Scene from ev'ry future
>   View.

Gray was no more sanguine: "The Bard," which was to become the most popular ode of the next generation (if Robert Southey's testimony in his *Life of Cowper* is reliable) shows a medieval prophet-poet, at odds with the political rulers, committing suicide, though not before prophesying the triumph of poetry and prophecy in the age of Elizabeth. Though the poem is set in the past, the application, as other poems by Gray make evident, is certainly contemporary. "Oh! Lyre divine," he asks in "The Progress of Poesy," "What daring Spirit / Wakes thee now?" And in the unpublished "Stanzas to Mr. Bentley," he regrets that

> . . . not to one in this benighted age
> Is that diviner inspiration giv'n
> That burns in Shakespear's or in Milton's page,
> The pomp and prodigality of heav'n.

Several reciprocal influences were at work here. The rise of literary history was directly related to the rise of historical thinking generally and an intensification of nationalism. Nationalism demanded a great literature, and English literary history, at least from the time of Dryden, made much of the greatness of national achievement. Perhaps Scottish nationalism and the Golden Age of Scottish literature were paradoxically a product of the Union that made Scotland a part of Great Britain. In any case the general reception of the Ossianic works, with Hugh Blair declaring Ossian the equal of Homer and Highland Scots by the score prepared to state under oath that they had learned these poems as boys, shows that the country was crying out for such a past and such a poet. Hume, who had given early support to Macpherson, soon began to regard his productions skeptically. He gave Blair some good advice (unheeded) on how to determine the authenticity of the works, and in an interview with Boswell after Johnson's tour of the Hebrides offered a number of objections, including the difficulty of oral transmission (a hurdle that no longer exists for modern scholars). He viewed the fame of the Ossianic poems as a product of their putative antiquity, for he thought that if Macpherson had published them under his own name they would not have been read through. He ascribes the Highlanders' support of Macpherson to the flattery of having a great poet among their warlike ancestors. Boswell told him that Johnson claimed

> that he could undertake to write an epic poem on the story of Robin Hood which the half of the people of England should say they heard in their youth. Mr. Hume said the people of England would not be so ready to support such a story. They had not the same temptation with the Highlanders, there being many excellent English Poets.

Hume's observation is acute; national consciousness demands literary history. The Ossian affair illustrates the need for myth at its broadest level. Macpherson may be said, in at least several ways, to have forged the uncreated conscience of his race in the smithy of his soul.

And the immediate success of Macpherson's Ossian poems, whatever our own judgment of his achievement, is indisputable. It can perhaps be best seen in the chapter headings of William Duff's *Critical Observations on the Writings of the Most Celebrated Original Geniuses in Poetry* (1770). Duff devotes a chapter apiece to seven poets, Homer, Ossian, Shakespeare, Spenser, Milton, Ariosto and Tasso. The sixty-page chapter on Ossian is long-

er than those on Spenser and Milton, and only two pages shorter than that on Homer.

There were likenesses between Macpherson and the better artist whose undisputed forgeries helped to give the age something of its characteristic tone, Thomas Chatterton. Both poets were provincials who turned their provincialism to poetic gain. The works of both were precocious achievements, and both poets led the world to believe that they were even more precocious than they were in fact. Chatterton was, as has been noted by Meyerstein and others, an imitator of Ossian, and one wonders if his first ill-fated letter to Walpole was also in imitation of Macpherson's successful application to the antiquarian of Strawberry Hill. At any rate, Chatterton had before him not only the example of Macpherson's success, but also the question of authenticity. An Ossianic imitator was still burdened with the tag of unoriginality, so to show that he had truly learned Macpherson's trick, Chatterton had to come up with an original though analogous solution to the problem. This was a game that could only be played by one at a time.

The primary influences on Chatterton's medieval poems were Percy's *Reliques* and Elizabeth Cooper's *The Muses' Library*. Though Percy in his Preface to the *Reliques* makes rather modest claims for his minstrels, more was at stake. The poets he introduced to the public tended to be an anonymous lot, but Thomas Rowley, a putative contemporary of John Lydgate, arguably would be among the first great English poets, as secure in his sphere as Homer and Ossian in theirs—such at least, I suggest, was the logic behind the Rowley poems. Chatterton's creation, like Macpherson's, made his conquests. A quarter of a century after Chatterton's death, Lancelot Sharpe, in his preface to *Poems, Supposed to have been written at Bristol, by Thomas Rowley and others* (1794), mentions the controversy over authenticity, but goes on to rank the poet, whoever he may be, "in the fourth place among our British poets." Whether it is Chaucer, Spenser, Shakespeare or Milton who is pushed from his pedestal, we are not told.

There were, of course, other exemplars for Chatterton. As he pointedly asks Walpole in a satire his sister talked him out of sending,

> thou mayst call me Cheat—
> Say, didst thou ne'er indulge in such Deceit?
> Who wrote Otranto?

The long ago and far away Gothic of *The Castle of Otranto,* like the contemporary bourgeois novels of Richardson, was nominally the presentation of a self-effacing editor. And Collins, who adumbrates both the problems and solutions of Macpherson and Chatterton in less assertive fashion, indulged in such deceit in his *Persian Eclogues* thirty years before the appearance of Rowley. The "Preface" claims that these oriental poems, which according to Johnson he later liked to call his "Irish eclogues," were the product of "the Beginning of *Sha Sultan Hosseyn's* Reign."

This is not yet the end of the story. Ossian became one of the great figures for the rising generation and has retained a place, if a small one, in world literature. I say world literature, not English, for if there are only about five articles published on Macpherson in a given year, they are likely to be in four languages. This is one more of Macpherson's lingering achievements that has paled. Unlike most of the writers and critics of the eighteenth century, we are wary of poetry which can be successfully translated. Those who believed, like Addison early in the century, that the very test of true wit was translation, probably viewed the European vogue of Ossian as the final seal of poetic excellence. Macpherson himself was quick to seize on this evidence of his achievement in the preface to a later edition (1773):

> Genuine poetry, like gold, loses little, when properly transfused; but when a composition cannot bear the test of a literal version, it is a counterfeit which ought not to pass current. The operation must, however, be performed with skilful hands. A Translator, who cannot equal his original, is incapable of expressing its beauties.

Macpherson seems to have enjoyed some of the ironies of his position. Here the "counterfeit" is the poem which cannot be translated, and the translator must "equal his original" if he is to make it live in another language. Far from being a humble drudge, the translator must be on a par with the great poet who wrote the poem. Though Macpherson's comments refer to the continental translators of Ossian, he is taking the last step in overcoming if not fulfilling the conditions of greatness that the age demanded. After giving of necessity to Ossian what was really his, he finds a way of getting equal billing with his own creation.

The real moral of Macpherson's innovation can best be seen in the words which Richard Hurd, whose writings contain a congeries of the themes I have been discussing, quotes to refute contemporary critics in letter ten of the *Letters on Chivalry and Romance: "they, who deceive, are honester than they who do not deceive; and they, who are deceived, wiser than they who are not deceived."* Take this remark as a gloss on Blake's "I Believe both Mac-pherson & Chatterton, that what they say is Ancient Is so. . . . I own myself an admirer of Ossian equally with any other Poet whatever Rowley & Chatterton also": the importance of Macpherson's solution of the dilemmas of the late eighteenth-century poet should become clear. The factually false became imaginatively true, and the poets of the early nineteenth century generated their own myths.

The topic of Blakean inspiration is an intricate one, and I cannot do much more here than point to some of the implications of what I have been saying in the context of his work. Blake had his own version of the poetic wasteland found in Collins and Gray; it appears, significantly, in the poem "To the Muses":

> How have you left the antient love
> That bards of old enjoy'd in you!

> The languid strings do scarcely move!
> The sound is forc'd, the notes are few!

Collins practically stops at such a position, but for Blake it is a starting point. One of the "memorable fancies" of *The Marriage of Heaven and Hell* is a little symposium on becoming a prophet-poet. Blake asks Isaiah and Ezekiel, who had come to dine with him, "how they dared so roundly to assert that God spake to them," and Isaiah replies:

> I saw no God, nor heard any, in a finite organical perception; but my senses discover'd the infinite in every thing, and as I was then perswaded, & remain confirm'd that the voice of honest indignation is the voice of God, I cared not for consequences, but wrote.

And to Blake's question, "does a firm perswasion that a thing is so, make it so?" Isaiah replies:

> All poets believe that it does, & in ages of imagination this firm perswasion removed mountains; but many are not capable of a firm perswasion of any thing.

This advice from a master would suggest that the recovery of nerve (to adopt the phrase Peter Gay applies to the *Philosophes*) must come from within, especially during a period when the culture would seem to offer little support. It also suggests that the poet, who has become *déclassé,* can only find his proper society in those avatars, the prophet-poets of the past.

At this point we may see the solutions of Macpherson, Chatterton and Blake side by side. When writing to his friend Thomas Butts of his epic *Milton,* Blake could say, "I may praise it, since I dare not pretend to be any other than the Secretary; the Authors are in Eternity." Although this letter may not describe the poem we now know as *Milton,* it is consistent with Blake's emphasis in the completed poem and in *Jerusalem* as well on "dictation" as the means by which he writes. Macpherson was the translator; Chatterton, the discoverer's middleman; Blake, the secretary: by such mediations were poems written during this period.

Blake's *Milton* may provide us with one last clue to the problems the poet faced at this time. In typically perplexed fashion Henry Crabb Robinson reports of Blake that "the oddest thing he said was that he had been commanded . . . to write about Milton, and that he was applauded for refusing—he struggled with the Angels and was victor. . . . " Here, through the dark glass of Crabb Robinson's perception, is an emblem of the relation of the poet to his literary past: it is burden and blessing. He may wrestle with the angel of poetry, but he dare not let it go unless it bless him.

In an age when the best poets (with the notable exception of Johnson) believed that it was hardly possible to write great poetry, and when they also believed (including Johnson) that the greatest poetry had been written in previous historical periods, the first task of the literary artists we sometimes think of as forgers was to create "poets" capable of producing great poetry, to find voices which did not exist in their own culture, and we rightly think first not of Macpherson's Caledonian epics, but of Ossian; not of Chatterton's medieval poetry, but of Rowley. Staggering problems often require radical solutions; getting out from under the burden of Atlas may take some undignified trickery. Only consider: Blake, the poet who solved these problems by the most radical means while preserving his own integrity, produced epics whose idiosyncracies made them only twenty-five years ago, according to their foremost modern admirer, Northrop Frye, "what is in proportion to its merits the least read body of poetry in the language. . . . " By putting himself in direct imaginative contact with Homer and Milton, Isaiah and Ezekiel, Blake obtained his metaphors for poetry. And his contemporaries thought him mad rather than dishonest.

John L. Greenway (essay date 1975)

SOURCE: "The Gateway to Innocence: Ossian and the Nordic Bard as Myth," in *Studies in Eighteenth-Century Culture*, Vol. 4, 1975, pp. 161-70.

[*In the following essay, Greenway offers a reinterpretation of Macpherson's* Fingal, *maintaining that the poem functions as a "mythic narrative."*]

Few now tremble at the dauntless heroism of Fingal, and none of us, I fear, are tempted to don Werther's yellow vest and share the misty signs of Temora. Indeed, the noble passions of this Last of the Bards have been treated with a neglect less than benign. Though we no longer read Ossian, we do read writers who, convinced of his authenticity, attempt to recapture what they imagine to be that synthesis of vigor and sentiment possessed by their Northern ancestors. As I have already implied, I propose to take Ossian seriously, and to suggest that he functioned as a mythic narrative for a modern era—"mythic" not in the Enlightenment sense of "falsehood," but in the more recent sense of "symbolic apprehension of reality." But what can Ossian have to do with reality?

Let us consider for a moment the nature and function of mythic narrative. The myths of a culture provide an orientation for man's moral experience in that they bestow an objective status upon values of the present, preserving them from relativism. Myths of gods and heroes show that the paradigms for human action not only exist outside man, but can be a part of genesis itself; that is, present values are legitimized, transferred from the profane world to the sacred by projecting them *in illo tempore* (to use Mircea Eliade's term): a static time of creation when a culture's truths were established. I see Ossian and his imitators as doing essentially the same thing, and on a pre-rational level of cultural consciousness—legitimizing the val-

ues of sentimental primitivism through a mythic narrative (the Ossianic poems) which showed that sentimental views of human nature, virtue, and vice were really present at the dawn of Northern, *non*-classical civilization.

From Hugh Blair, *A Critical Dissertation on the Poems of Ossian*:

The manner of composition [of Ossian's poems] bears all the marks of the greatest antiquity. No artful transitions; nor full or extended connexion of parts; such as we find among the poems of later times, when order and regularity of composition were more studied and known; but a style always rapid and vehement; in narration concise even to abruptness, and leaving several circumstances to be supplied by the reader's imagination. The language has all that figurative cast which, . . . partly a glowing and undisciplined imagination, partly the sterility of language and the want of proper terms, have always introduced into the early speech of nations; and, in several respects, it carries a remarkable resemblance to the style of the Old Testament. It deserves particular notice, as one of the most genuine and decisive characters of antiquity, that very few general terms, or abstract ideas, are to be met with in the whole collection of Ossian's works. The ideas of men, at first, were all particular. They had not words to express general conceptions. These were the consequence of more profound reflection, and longer acquaintance with the arts of thought and of speech. Ossian, accordingly, almost never expresses himself in the abstract. His ideas extended little further than to the objects he saw around him. A public, a community, the universe, were conceptions beyond his sphere. Even a mountain, a sea, or a lake, which he has occasion to mention, though only in a simile, are for the most part particularized; it is the hill of Cromla, the storm of the sea of Malmor, or the reeds of the lake of Lego. A mode of expression which, while it is characteristical of ancient ages, is at the same time highly favourable to descriptive poetry. For the same reasons, personification is a poetical figure not very common with Ossian. Inanimate objects, such as winds, trees, flowers, he sometimes personifies with great beauty. But the personifications which are so familiar to later poets, of Fame, Time, Terror, Virtue, and the rest of that class, were unknown to our Celtic bard. These were modes of conception too abstract for his age.

All these are marks so undoubted, and some of them too so nice and delicate, of the most early times, as put the high antiquity of these poems out of the question. . . .

Hugh Blair, in The Poems of Ossian, *translated by James Macpherson, Bernhard Tauchnitz, 1847.*

This brings us to a second point about myth, one which in a sense distinguishes modern myths such as Ossian from pre-scientific myths. The anthropologist Malinowski has noted that while we see myth, rite, and ritual as symbolic, the believer does not: to him, the constructs of myth are empirically real. Modern man, however, defines truth in terms of rational thought, and either tends to see myth as falsehood, or as symbolizing an empirical or conceptual content. But, as Cassirer and others have shown, the impulse to myth-making is not negated by reason, for modern myths must maintain their objectivity in two realms: first, as narratives expressing spontaneously the world of feeling, and second, as historical, empirical fact. As an illustration of this, the assumed literary merit of Ossian was predicated upon his historicity; indeed, this was the most important single fact about the forgeries, in that Ossian's status as historical document objectified values, much as ritual validates rites by presenting them to a receptive audience as reenactments of sacred paradigms of the *illud tempus*. As a means of organizing values, myth is neither true nor false—it is expressive or inexpressive.

Ossian validated and gave factual status to several primitivist fantasies of the Nordic past. Basically, the Ossianic poems fused in one symbolic universe what had been a paradox since the first humanist attempts to build a national past upon Tacitus' *Germania,* first edited in the fifteenth century. This paradox, simply stated, was that enthusiasts for Germanic valor such as Conrad Celtis could admire our heroic ancestors for their martial vigor and, at the same time, following Tacitus, point to tribes of chaste, democratic, freedom-loving (Humanist) Teutons. Obviously, one part of this mythic construct ran counter to another, older view, which helps to give substance to the paradox; that is, this very martial vigor destroyed classical culture, and brought on what Renaissance scholars called those dark "Ages in the Middle." In the eighteenth century, Shaftesbury was not alone in identifying "Gothic" with "barbaric," and the dual nature of the myth continued even into the next century.

Before Ossian, the "nobler qualities of the mind" necessary to complement the fascinating barbarity of the North in a primitivist myth had to be supplied by conjecture. In 1763, the year of *Temora*'s appearance, Bishop Percy complained that "many pieces on the gentler subjects" must exist, but that they simply have not been edited. With the appearance of the Ossianic poems, however, there was no longer need for apologies or conjectures such as the German Humanists of the sixteenth- and Swedish historians of the seventeenth-century Great Power Era had had to make, for the mythic imagination had received its document.

As myth, Ossian was more expressive than Homer, his southern counterpart, in that his poems expressed no moral ambivalence. The Humanists had seen history in terms of a struggle between virtue and vice (witness the popularity of Virgil), but this makes a balanced conflict difficult to portray in a moral narrative. In *Temora,* Macpherson is ingenious; in the first book he kills off the villain, whose noble brother Cathmor is obliged by honor to oppose the mighty Fingal. Macpherson was then able to sustain his narrative by more than token opposition to Fingal's moral (hence, martial) invincibility.

Fingal fights only defensive wars (*Fingal*), or he fights the *bellum justum* to further social justice (*Temora*). "My arm was the support of the injured," he says, "but the weak rested behind the lightning of my steel." Fingal thus functioned paradigmatically, in fulfillment of one of the great Enlightenment axioms that emancipated valor must triumph over tyranny and idolatry. This Fingal does, always.

The legacy of barbarism, which was an integral part of the myth of the Nordic past, is also present in the Ossianic poems. Macpherson assigns this role to the Scandinavians; and Starno, in the poem "Cath-Loda," is a repository for all the pejorative connotations of "Gothic." But even though we find that his Scandinavians are barbaric, tyrannous idolaters, Macpherson's "Caledonians" are not, as his notes make clear. And though Ossian believes in spirits, Fingal's defeat of the Scandinavian chimera "Cruth-Loda" indicates that neither Fingal nor Ossian was an idolater nor obnoxiously superstitious.

Within this large universe legitimizing truths that the Enlightenment held to be "self-evident," Ossian also validated several other literary myths, among them that of the spontaneous perception of nature by the primitive poet. W. K. Wimsatt has pointed out that in eighteenth-century literature it was not easy to express a sense of animate or "souled" nature, for the conscious use of mythology was generally restricted to decorative, intellectual allegory. When the setting of the poem was temporalized, however, and the narration placed in the *illud tempus* of the Nordic past, it was possible to create the illusion of the naive experience of Northern nature for the modern reader, by giving him the impression that the poem is being narrated by a naive *Volksdichter* as the reader reads it. Northrop Frye calls this technique that of "poem-as-process," saying that "Where there is a sense of literature as process, pity and fear become states of mind without objects, moods which are common to the work of art and the reader, and which bind them together psychologically instead of separating them aesthetically." Herder used this technique in his *Abhandlung über den Ursprung der Sprache* to recreate for the reader the illusion of the creative process of the primitive mind:

> Since all of nature sounds, nothing is more natural to a sensuous human being than to think that it lives, that it speaks, that it acts. That savage saw the tall tree with its mighty crown and sensed the wonder of it; the crown rustled! There the godhead moves and stirs! The savage falls down in adoration! Behold, that is the story of sensuous man, the dark link by which nouns are fashioned from verbs.

Herber was not the only critic attempting to convey the illusion of process in essays describing the creative process of the primitive, though what others did was sometimes derivative; for example, certain data concerning the "wild" Nordic nature appear to have been taken from *The Castle of Otranto*. But Macpherson employed the illusion in what became mythic narratives. The belief in Ossian's authenticity implied that "poem-as-process" had been an actual technique of the primitive Northern poet.

Macpherson's creation of the illusion of process and his validation of the technique are actually rather sophisticated—sophisticated in that the reader is taken through time by several devices. The first element is his use of the mythic figure of the naive *Volksdichter,* the Bard. Bishop Percy and Thomas Gray had been central in establishing this persona in the 1760's. Here I will mention only briefly Thomas Gray's ode "The Bard" (1757), which was central to the establishing of the *Volksdichter* as a narrative persona in the 1760's. Gray employs the knavish Edward I and the naive national Bard of the Golden Age, and as the last of the bards "plunged to endless night," the Golden Age ended and the modern, fallen world began.

Ossian as Bard was a principal part of Macpherson's mythmaking, establishing a psychological tie from the historical present to the mythic past, and part of the success of the "ancient epics" was owing to Macpherson's structuring of these poems. By means of a fairly complex point of view, he managed to create the illusion that the reader was experiencing directly the "raw nature and noble passion" of his ancestors. Ossian, near death, a death that will mark the end of the Golden Age (it always does, in these cases), is singing to Malvina, the fiancée of his dead son Oscar, "a song of the days of old," in which Fingal, Ossian's father, is the principal character. In all this, the illusion of the spontaneous process is maintained by several devices: Ossian can make himself a character in his own poem and by doing so remind one that there is a narrator ("I walked over the heath"); or he can remind one of the narrator by breaking his own narration ("Malvina! Why that tear? Oscar is not dead yet"). We participate in the Golden Age through the naive songs of the Bard, yet we are constantly made aware that it is coming to an end, and our own unheroic time is beginning.

Ossian as myth legitimized as being "Nordic" not only the naive Bard and the illusion of process, but a particular kind of imagery used to express this spontaneous relationship to nature. Indeed, one of the merits of Ossian, and one of the inadequacies of his imitators, was just this use of sympathetic imagery (where nature is an extension of character or mood) to integrate landscape into the action. For instance, when things are going badly for the noble Cuchullin, Macpherson's use of sympathetic imagery both amplifies the impending disaster and isolates the warrior by focusing down upon him: "The winds came down on the woods. The torrents rushed from the rocks. Rain gathered round the heads of Cromla. And the red stars trembled between the flying clouds. Sad by the side of a stream whose sound was echoed by a tree, sad by the side of a stream the chief of Erin sat." (One of the facts that had filtered out of Antiquarian editing was that Northern poetry was alliterative.)

Macpherson's notes are an integral part of Ossian-as-myth, for they provide a constant empirical commentary, emphasising the historicity and verisimilitude of the poems. They also make of Ossian an epic counterpart to Homer, Virgil, and Milton, showing that though Ossian expressed a superior Northern morality, he obeyed the "general rules" of the epic. A growing accretion of appended commentary elaborated upon this, beginning with Hugh Blair's

essay. In Germany, Denis translated the poems into hexameters, adding his own notes and those of Cesarotti to the poems and to Blair's essay as well.

Initially, then, Ossian served to provide an epic Northern counterpart to Homer, unifying the genesis of the primitive Nordic genius in the minds of the primitivists, as Madame de Staël illustrates in *De la littérature*. Secondly, and more importantly, Ossian's mythic function as the objectification of the Northern muse helped break down the stigma of Northern barbarity, in that he either modified the view of the Nordic past or shaped reactions to it. Ossian could animate the nostalgia of Denis for the lost Lieder of Charlemagne, while in Denmark, Blicher saw the same virtues celebrated in Ossian and in the Icelandic sagas. Ossian's main function, however, was as a mythic paradigm, a touchstone for contemporary poets. If we look at the Ossianic poems and those they inspired, we see that Macpherson enjoyed a relationship to the Golden Age unavailable to other moderns. He was actually a kind of modern folk poet, transmitting primal truth in a quasi-oracular form, not creating on his own. In the Swedish poet Thomas Thorild we can see this difference between Macpherson and his imitators. Though Thorild felt himself to be part of Ossian's Golden Age ("You should have seen me . . . when I first saw the sun set in Glysisvall, when with Ossian I can feel [*sic*] the shades of heroes about me"), his creativity was limited to incantation, not recreation of the naive experience:

> Stream exultation! To You, ah, You immortal, gentle,
> All-elevating; you Nature, my trembling harp is tuned.
> Silently weave about me, spirit of Ossian!

The Ossianic muse came to dubious fruition in Germany with the "Bardic Movement," sustained by a group of mediocre poets who were primed by a bowdlerized version of Herder's concept of *Volkspoesie,* but who were not galvanized into imitation until they encountered the paradigms of Ossian, the Bard, and Germania. Most of these poets exist today only in literary histories and dissertations, for their poetry functioned as myth for only a few years in the 1760's—during the first Ossianic craze—and was particularly vulnerable to the dialectic process that ultimately overtook Ossian himself.

The mythic aspect of the Bardic lyrics was almost immediately inadequate; as it not only objectified contemporary literary values (Ossian being the paradigm), but also depended upon an assumption of historical objectivity, the Bards' myth was fatally vulnerable in two areas. First, it succumbed to the revolutionary effects of Herder's conjectures concerning the literary imagination; second, to philology.

The idol of the Germanic Bards was Klopstock, who read Ossian before reading about Norse mythology: Klopstock's "Nordic" poems and dramas are predicated upon the superiority of an Ossian-constituted Teutonic muse to that of the artificial South. In "Der Hügel und der Hain" (1767), the Southern poet is defeated in the battle for a modern poet's soul by a Bard who sings of "souled nature," and whose Telyn (a musical instrument) sounds "Fatherland."

Though Klopstock is widely cited as inaugurating a new sensibility of nature into German poetry, it is clear that his poetic convention could not assimilate a subject matter intrinsically "Teutonic," not even such a Teutonic subject matter as the Golden Age of Ossian's invention. In 1767, for instance, Klopstock "Nordicized" his ode "An des Dichters Freunde" (1747), merely by removing Apollo and plugging in Braga: "Would you be verses, O song? Or, / Unsubmissive, like Pindar's songs, / Like Zeus' noble, intoxicated son, / Whirl free from the creating soul?" became "Would you be verses, O heroic song? / Would you soar lawless, like Ossian's flight, / Like Uller's dance upon sea-crystal, / Free from the poet's soul?"

But such was the momentary power of this myth to constitute reality that Lessing could praise lines like the following from Klopstock's drama *Hermanns Schlacht* (1769) as being "completely in the ancient German manner" (Hermann speaks): "Noble lady of my youth! Yes, I live, my Thusnelda! Arise, you free princess of Germany! I have not loved you before, as today! Has my Thusnelda brought me flowers?" Klopstock, too, was convinced that this was pretty accurate dialogue, and footnotes the morality of his Teutons. The central role of Ossian in this drama is obvious, except that Klopstock has choruses of Bards chanting "Höret Thaten der vorigen Zeit!" whereas Macpherson had been content with Ossian's beginning "A song of the days of old!"

The most common effect of the Ossianized Nordic muse was what Northrop Frye calls "psychological self-identification." As an example we may consider the otherwise forgettable masterpiece of K. F. Kretschmann, *Gesang Ringulph des Bardens, als Varus geschlagen var* (1768). Again, the mythic world here derives much of its texture from the defeat of Southern tyranny by Northern freedom, thanks both to the hero Hermann and to the Ossianic Bard, Ringulph, who implements the transition to the sacred *illud tempus.* "Ha!" Ringulph begins, giving the sense of process by recalling the scene in present tense, "There they lie, yes! / The legions lie slain!" "Ha's" and "Ach's" dot the narrative to support the illusion of spontaneity. But the fundamental contradiction in the Bardic myth is obvious; that is, despite the ostensible epic purpose of the poem—"Allvater" tells Ringulph to quit singing about his beloved Irmgard and sing about Hermann— only a small part of the fourth *Gesang* (out of five) concerns the battle. The rest is mostly about Ringulph himself.

Central to the "poetics" of the Bards was that their function as poets and their literary products were reincarnations of an actual Teutonic genius, Ossian, of course, being the paradigm. Denis emphasizes in his well-informed essay "Vorbericht von der altern vaterlaendischen Dichtkunst" that the modern Bard must not betray his muse through anachronisms. But it is a singular commentary on the power of this myth to regulate rational inquiry that Denis, the most philologically oriented of any of the Bards, cites the poems of Klopstock and Kretschmann as exemplary for those who wish a "complete transition of oneself into other times." Denis was correct in a sense he did not intend, for the mythic world given symbolic form by Ossian, Klopstock, and Kretschmann was for a time *more real* to the general perception of the age than historical fact.

Even though myth's truths are not primarily validated by reason, a modern myth must maintain a factual superstructure to complement that part of it which operates extra-rationally. This requirement implies a separation of Faith and Reason, which in fact worked to render the Bardic myth inexpressive. And the separation was ultimately to undermine Ossian himself. Concerning Denis, Gleim wrote to Jacobi in 1768, "my Herder, who has long sighed deeply for such a Bard, will rejoice." But Herder, though unaware of Ossian's role as myth, sensed the great discrepancy between the lyrics of the Bards and those of his idol: they are not *Volkspoesie,* but *about Volkspoesie,* he maintained. His response to lines such as these by Kretschmann is also telling:

> I crept in the forest
> . . . . .
> In the high peaks roared
> The spirits of airy night;
> Then a chill broke out on my brow,
> And strongly beat my heart.
> And look! It seemed to me
> As though there stood a man . . . Are you a
>   man? An elf
> Of midnight?

Herder sensed the great flaw in Kretschmann's myth: "Where Ringulph, the Bard, sings well, he sings modern."

If one thinks of them in the context of eighteenth-century primitivism, *Fingal* and *Temora* were indeed folk-epics, but because of their pretense to historicity, both Ossian and the Bardic Movement were vulnerable to the latent sundering of the temporary accommodation between myth and reason. In 1800, Kretschmann in effect defended the myth in an article asking "Did the Germanic Peoples have Bards and Druids or Not?" He supported his affirmative argument with sources dating from the days of the Humanists. The next month, H. Anton argued persuasively that "The Germanic Peoples had no Bards and no Druids," attacking not only Kretschmann's methodology (argument by analogy), but the veracity of his sources—his "factual" base: "I assumed," Anton says, "That we in our criticism at the end of the century must be more advanced than we were at the beginning." His view heralds the Twilight of the Bards.

Herder and others were able to dispatch the Bardic lyrics by the sheer force of individual critical acuity. More theoretical criticism of the Bards was taken up by philologists, who tested the paradigm of the myth with an informed methodology. That basis was Ossian himself. Earlier assaults on Ossian, Hume's, for example, had been based upon aesthetic distaste. But these empiricist attacks were philogical. In the 1780's, John Pinkerton concentrates what he terms the "fierce light of Science" upon the vision of the Nordic past and finds error wherever he looks. Conversant with the recent Scandinavian scholarship of Suhm, Schøning, and others, Pinkerton demolishes the Ossianic universe by showing the Norse myths to be "merely" myths, and not real at all. He then attacks Ossian's "costume." Since historicity was an integral part of Ossian's mythic significance, the exposure of anachronism was mortal: "Eternal ladies in mail, where no mail was known," writes Pinkerton, "sicken one at every turn."

In 1817, the Swedish poet and critic Erik Gustaf Geijer could look back upon this period as closed, and describe it as an unsuccessful attempt to "return to ourselves." His comments upon the ineffectiveness of the Klopstock method of studding manuscripts with "By Thor!" are an index to the increased sophistication with which a new generation viewed the Nordic past. Though the figure of the Bard, perched at the end of the sacred Golden Age and at the beginning of profane, historical time, continued (Hugo, Scott, and Geijer himself, among others, used the persona), the assault on Ossian was symptomatic of a larger process, the calling into question of the whole moral universe of sentimental primitivism. Geijer and others saw that the simple structure of good *vs.* evil, virtue *vs.* vice was inadequate to explain the colliding contraries of moral experience. For a later generation Ossian was, in important ways, dead. Yet, in the myth of Ossian's synthetic spontaneity we can see a lasting legacy—the genesis of the contemporary attempt to merchandise both electronic Bards and the sentimental naive.

Kirsti Simonsuuri (essay date 1979)

SOURCE: "Notions of Poetry and Society in the Controversy about Ossian," in *Homer's Original Genius: Eighteenth-Century Notions of the Early Greek Epic (1688-1798),* Cambridge University Press, 1979, pp. 108-18.

[*In the following excerpt, Simonsuuri examines some of the literary and philosophical preconceptions that underlay the enormous popularity of Macpherson's Ossianic Poems in the eighteenth century.*]

The view that folk poetry and popular culture have an interest of their own and are worthy of serious attention gained acceptance during the middle years of the eighteenth century. Scholars hunted for genuine folk epics. They looked for evidence for the workings of the spontaneous genius of simple peoples, not only in the past productions of northern nations, but also in the earliest works of classical antiquity. The prevalent eagerness to find evidence for certain theoretical presuppositions about early stages of civilization, an eagerness most marked in Scotland, can partly explain the fact that the inauthenticity of the Ossianic poems was not immediately realized. Ossian, Homer and the Bible were utilized almost indiscriminately as evidence by the primitivists when they formulated their theories of man and society; and this

meant, in the first place, that Homer had come to attract notice as a representative of the primitive poets.

James Macpherson established his poetic reputation with *The Poems of Ossian* (1760-73) and with his prose translation of the *Iliad* (1773). The primary problem about the poetry of the third-century Gaelic poet Ossian, the son of Fingal, King of Morven, is admittedly its inauthenticity. To say this is not to deny the existence of authentic Highland poetry, some of which had survived orally for several centuries, but what Macpherson did was to claim the veracity of a translation for poems which were largely the offspring of his own imagination. Among educated Englishmen, he commonly passes for an audacious imposter who published his own compositions as the work of an ancient writer. Knowledge of the existence of authentic Gaelic poetry on the one hand, and knowledge about the northern parts of Europe that had been gradually accumulating since the sixteenth century on the other, certainly helped the success of Macpherson's publications, but the impact of Ossian's poems in England, Scotland and then all over Europe must be understood, in the final analysis, in the context of a moment when the influence of Graeco-Roman culture was temporarily spent, and the ideas of the Enlightenment were being transformed into those which we associate with Romanticism. For the interesting fact from the point of view of literary history is that the body of literature attributed to Ossian, Orran, Ullin and other ancient Scots bards succeeded in arousing the interest and admiration of the best eighteenth-century minds throughout Europe, and it is relevant to ask if Ossian would have aroused this interest, had his work appeared in its genuine form. Macpherson's achievement was to have linked the primitivist interest with a keen awareness of contemporary taste as it was exemplified during the century in the ideas of the *modernes*.

James Macpherson (1736-96) was born of an old Highland family of the clan of Macpherson (Celtic Mac Mhuirich), who inhabited the southern parts of the county of Inverness. In his early youth he saw the rising of 1745. His education was by no means exceptional, but was as good as a boy whose native tongue was Gaelic was likely to receive at that time. He entered King's College, Aberdeen, in 1752, where he benefited from the teaching of Thomas Reid, the philosopher, and Thomas Blackwell. But he took no degree there, moved later to Marischal College, and then spent a year at the University of Edinburgh in 1755-6. Having written from a very early age verses which were of a mediocre and imitative kind, he came into contact with popular Gaelic poetry and began to translate it while he was a schoolmaster at Ruthven, and a lucky encounter with John Home brought early specimens of his translations to the notice of the Edinburgh literati. Macpherson's motives in publishing translations of his Gaelic 'ancestors' must be regarded as patriotic and political. He believed in the existence of a complete Scottish epic, and his extremely free adaptations of some authentic manuscripts expanded, in the course of continuing success, into the ambitious project of producing a large body of ancient Scottish literature in order to demonstrate the glory of Highland culture.

The translations appeared between 1760 and 1773 in Edinburgh and London. While unreserved enthusiasm was shown in Scotland by Blair, Ferguson and others, they were viewed with suspicion by such eminent contemporaries as David Hume and Dr Johnson. Hume, basing his arguments on the nature of oral tradition deemed them inauthentic, and Dr Johnson's rational mind could not appreciate nationalistic poetry, which he regarded as downright silly. Later, Wordsworth, although he had a taste for the productions of 'the philosophical peasants', expressed the opinion that the natural sentiment of Ossian's poems rang false and contrived. The diversity of opinion led to impartial research, and the poems were conclusively proved inauthentic in the course of an examination undertaken by the Highland Society of Scotland in 1805, a view which modern scholarship has reaffirmed.

But what was the nature of the poetry that struck a chord in the hearts of men throughout Europe? An excerpt from Ossian's poems from the *Songs of Selma,* which was translated into Germany by Goethe, will suffice as illustration.

> When bards are removed to their place; when the harps are hung in Selma's hall; then comes a voice to Ossian, and awakes his soul! It is the voice of years that are gone! they roll before me, with all their deeds! . . . Roll on, ye dark-brown years! ye bring no joy on your course! Let the tomb open to Ossian, for his strength has failed. The sons of song are gone to rest. My voice remains, like a blast that roars, lonely, on a sea-surrounded rock after the winds are laid. The dark moss whistles there; the distant mariner sees the waving trees!

The imagery is banal, while the pathetic fallacy, nature echoing the personal feelings of the poet, is obvious. The sentences are extremely simple and the narrator uses only a few crude descriptive techniques to produce the impression of a poet unrolling his song at the moment of inspiration. The appeal is to the emotions, not to the intellect, of the reader.

When the Ossianic poems spread, directly or through translations, to Europe, they aroused an enthusiasm that far surpassed the impact they had made in England, where their reception remained moderately cool. Taken out of their cultural and linguistic context, the poems more immediately yielded their essential message, conveying a natural sentiment and a genuine feeling which had been lacking from the literary productions of the early eighteenth century. Contemporary taste found its expression in Ossian. If we try to determine why we still continue to read Homer, Goethe or Wordsworth, whereas the poems of Ossian strike us as virtually unreadable, we are bound to raise the issue of aesthetic taste. It is unlikely that the taste that was prevalent at the time of the Ossianic movement was so unusual that it cannot be understood by any other age. But the taste for Ossian was something of an excess and was backed by evident intellectual factors present in Europe at that time.

In Germany, which proved the most receptive ground for Macpherson's inventions, four complete and 34 partial translations were published between 1762 and 1800, and nine complete and 22 partial translations between 1800 and 1868. Ossianic poetry was admired by Klopstock, Voss, Schiller and Goethe. The *Sturm und Drang* movement owed its origins largely to Ossian. Herder utilized Ossianic poetry for his theories of the epic as an expression of national spirit. Schiller, in his essay *Über das Erhabene,* spoke of Ossian, declaring that a truer inspiration lay in the misty mountains of Scotland than in the fairest of meadows and gardens. Goethe, initiated into Ossian by Herder in Strasbourg in 1770-1, included his translation of the *Songs of Selma* and a passage of 'Berrathon' in *Werther.* In France too, Ossian enjoyed both popularity and serious attention. A translation appeared almost immediately after Macpherson's publication of 'Two fragments of ancient poetry' in 1760. Minds as diverse as the Marquis de Saint-Simon, Diderot, Voltaire, Chateaubriand, Napoleon, Mme de Staël and Lamartine were interested in Ossianic poetry. Mme de Staël gave expression to the popular view in saying that in Ossian were contained all the essential characteristics of northern literature; and it is well known that Ossian was the favourite reading of Napoleon during his military campaigns. Elsewhere, in Scandinavia, in Italy and in Spain, the repercussions, either through translations such as Cesarotti's Italian version or through imitations, remained largely poetical and sentimental, and Europe's infatuation with Ossian was echoed in nineteenth-century art and music.

Philosophical preoccupations characterized the reception of the poems in Scotland, France and Germany. The discovery of Ossian's poems and the Ossianic movement can be seen as an inevitable outcome of the interest in the origins and nature of poetry and the epic in Scotland in the middle of the eighteenth century. It is not entirely cynical to say that if the poems of Ossian had not existed, it would have been necessary to invent them. Documentary evidence about the early stages of poetry was welcome to theorists who had begun to realize that the existing examples provided by classical antiquity did not fit into the current conceptions of the primitive. The genuineness of the texts attributed to Homer's predecessors, such as the half-mythical poets Orpheus and Musaeus, was already much in doubt. The Homeric epics themselves, especially the *Odyssey,* when carefully read, could be seen to portray a society of considerable complexity and refinement, and the moral values of the *Iliad* were thought to be barbaric and applicable merely to a war situation. Moreover, the language of Homer was beginning to reveal to scholars layers of poetic composition, and the text itself was understood to have undergone several changes from its first appearance at the time of Pisistratus to the considerable revisions suggested by the Alexandrian scholars. The eighteenth century had reappraised Homer and had largely rejected the neoclassical view that he was the father of epic rules; but he appeared to many to have possessed a kind of artistic sophistication that was alien to a truly primitive poet who, they thought, had also existed.

The theoretical assumption that poetry is an authentic record of its society and that it has a historical meaning which may surpass in importance the primarily poetic content, marks a decisive departure in eighteenth-century thought. Isolated expressions of the idea can be found in French writers like the abbé Dubos, Saint-Evremond and Mme Dacier, but not until the primitivists began to work on what they believed to be native material offered by their own popular poetry were its methodological implications fully developed in practice.

Macpherson had been influenced by the ideas current in primitivist circles in the 1750s and 1760s, but his own arguments, it must be remembered, remained naively non-theoretical. He was influenced by a genuine and life-long enthusiasm for the Scots cause and had a certain poetic sensibility. He translated Homer with the conviction that the simplicity which he had found in the popular poetry of his own ancestors was also the primary virtue of the Greek poet, and that there existed in the histories of Greece and Scotland an analogous cultural level of which their bards had given a record. Consequently, in his translation of the *Iliad* (1773), he replaced Homer's concrete and vivid descriptions with the same vague and high-sounding phrases that he had previously employed in the old Highland ballads; and in fact his Homeric translation illustrates not a little his practice in dealing with the Ossianic poems.

The preface to his translation of the *Iliad* makes two points. First, we are told that Homer was the greatest of poets because of his simplicity and ease of style, which was the result both of his individual genius and of his being conditioned by the age and society in which he wrote. Second, we are to bear in mind that Homer could be translated with the original simplicity, but this meant essentially that considerable liberties had to be taken with the text. The translation had to be in prose instead of verse, the hexameter was certainly barred; and the characteristic Homeric language had to be translated so as to fit an analogous cultural level in the history of an English-speaking audience.

Macpherson's idea that Homer was a poet who had lived and worked in a society similar to the third-century Ossian's was derived from his own experience as a translator of early Gaelic poetry rather than from study or understanding of the nature of the Homeric epic. Although the translation of the *Iliad* was inspired by the current enthusiasm for Homer and by a conviction of the similarity of Ossian and Homer, it also reveals the cynicism and depravity of the author. The energy Macpherson spent on his forgery and on his poor translation of Homer has few parallels in literary history, and it shows how easily fashionable literary issues can be exploited by someone who is responsive to the interests of his day but wishes only to play his solitary game with them.

Macpherson regarded his Homeric enterprise as a side issue; his poetic talents were better suited to the production of Ossian's poems, and his historical and political interests were focused on his ***History of Great Britain and Ireland*** (1771-3). In this work he delineated the society that he conceived to have been Ossian's: an original, uncorrupted state of humanity where social norms were created spontaneously because man had a natural will to imitate virtue, not vice.

> The ancient British nations heard their poems with such rapture and enthusiasm, that they formed their character and manners upon the model of the virtues which the Bards recommended in their songs. In an age unacquainted with science men became disinterested, generous, noble, as individuals . . . (A publication which the Author of the Introduction has already given to the world establishes the justness of the above observation . . .)

Macpherson's contemporaries preferred Ossian to Homer exactly because he was thought to represent an older and more primitive, hence more virtuous and original, stage of social development. He had sung about heroism without military glory. John Gordon came to Macpherson's support for these reasons: 'Ossian's skill was superior to *Homer*'s; as the great simplicity and attention to nature in them [i.e. his poems] shew . . . they were written in a period of greater antiquity, than the *Iliad* . . . I mean in an earlier state of civilization; before art had reached that height, to which it had attained in *Homer*'s time.' The artlessness, the straightforward imperfection of Ossianic poetry was to the eighteenth-century English critics, at home with verse composed on rigorous neoclassical principles, a mark of originality in itself. By many the age was felt to have lost contact with originality because the classics had imposed a model for imitation in the genres of epic, lyric and drama. The curious fact about the Ossianic poetry was that the critics could not come to an agreement even as regards its genre. Hence we find in England, side by side with the major trends of Augustan and neoclassical literature, a counter-movement that called for the exercise of individual genius even at the expense of reason. Ossian was 'a complete instance of first poetry' and corresponded to the ideal of those literary men who saw that poetry 'ought to give raptures' and not merely please. It was this condition of immediacy and spontaneity, supposedly characteristic of primitive poetry, that Macpherson offered to his contemporaries.

Was then the enthusiasm with which these poetic fakes were received, especially in France and Germany, an indication of a greater malaise with the achievements of western civilization than has so far been realized by historians of eighteenth-century culture? The ideas we associate with the Enlightenment, which were based on the great scientific advances of the seventeenth and early eighteenth centuries, were felt to be insufficient by many who were searching for the principles of that unattainable condition, happiness in the world of here and now. Spinoza's motto, 'non ridere, non lugere, neque detestari, sed intelligere', appealed little to those who thought that man, as an individual and as a social being, need not only apply his reason but also laugh, grieve and feel delight and disgust, as an integral part of his human happiness. Moreover, despite the similarities between the Homeric epics and the Ossianic poetry, Ossian seemed to offer a better model of the ideal poet because he was entirely free from the burden of tradition. The Homeric text had come to us weighed down with commentaries and the poems had close associations with later Greek culture, which could not be regarded as spontaneous or as representing the infancy of mankind. Ossian, on the other hand, corresponded to men's nostalgia for paradisiac spontaneity; and he depicted the sort of simple heroic behaviour that could be seen as a viable attitude in the fight against the evils of civilization. Macpherson had hit upon a telling formula: he offered a poetry that had an air of historical authenticity, that was easy, even insipid by all aesthetic standards, and that yet carried with it the promise of salvation through a new individual and collective heroism.

The idea that a primitive society represented a state of perfection, which refinement, prosperity and scientific advance could only make worse, runs through Macpherson's writings. Moreover, like the poetic theorists of his time, he thought that primitive societies which were relatively free despite the ritual organization of their way of life were the best possible matrices of creativity. William Duff stated that in early periods of society 'original Poetic Genius will in general be exerted in its utmost vigour.' Macpherson argued that the era of Ossian was such an instance of an ideal ancient society: 'The nobler passions of the mind never shoot forth more free and unrestrained than in the times we call barbarous. That irregular manner of life, and those manly pursuits from which barbarity takes its name, are highly favourable to a strength of mind unknown in polished times. In advanced society the characters of men are more uniform and disguised.' Macpherson's direct support in Scotland came from Hugh Blair, a theorist with a speculative interest in the origins of folk literature. He regarded Ossian as a poet without parallel either among the classical authors or among the Hebrew prophets because the Gaelic bard was unhampered by any form of sophisticated reasoning, and because the Celtic tribes naturally accorded great importance to poetry in their primitive environment.

> Irregular and unpolished we may expect the productions of uncultivated ages to be; but abounding, at the same time, with that enthusiasm, that vehemence and fire, which are the soul of poetry. For many circumstances of those poetic times which we call barbarous, are favourable to the poetical spirit. That state, in which human nature shoots wild and free, though unfit for other improvements, certainly encourages the high exertions of fancy and passion.

> ["A Critical Dissertation on the Works of Ossian"]

Like Macpherson, Blair claimed that primitive society creates a totally satisfying environment because it is an environment coherent in its values—it combines the great achievements of poetry with virtues such as magnanimity and heroism; and this harmony between aesthetic and moral excellence was thought to be the natural state of man.

These ideas found a response not only in England and Scotland, in the numerous writings of Macpherson's con-

temporaries, but also in France. In vain did Voltaire try to remind men that early ages of civilization undoubtedly represented barbarism, vileness and moral degradation, and that progress was in every sense humanity's imperative. In vain also did he try to ridicule the Ossianic poems. The primitivist arguments found their way to the Continent in connection with Ossianism. Ancient Scotland was held to represent a historically verifiable model of an ideal society, and England, together with the rest of Europe, was classed among civilization's malcontents.

An indication of the way primitivist thinking spread in France can be found in an essay by the translator of *Temora,* the Marquis de Saint-Simon. He evaluates Ossianic poetry and the Highland societies at a universal level and sees their parallels in ancient Greece; he argues without hesitation that the 'Scottish Homer' has found in Macpherson its Pisistratus. The present age has exhausted its poetic genius and spent its force. . . . He goes on to maintain that the secret of Ossian's greatness lay in the ancient society that had produced him. There was a radical difference between that primitive state of natural freedom and the confining existence that modern civilization had brought in its course. . . . Saint-Simon emphatically took the view that civilization in its higher forms had resulted in a dichotomy of theory and practice: though philosophers preached virtue, its natural vitality in society had been lost. The opposition between ignorance and self-awareness, between the primitive and the civilized state of man, could not be resolved, for once humanity opted for progress it also opted for alienation. Saint-Simon had none of the optimism that characterized Rousseau's redemptive programmes. But the poems of Ossian seemed to offer mankind useful lessons, and he was convinced that Macpherson's pioneering work had a lasting value as material evidence on which a philosophical theory could be based. . . .

Moreover, it was exactly Ossian's paganism that appealed to enlightened thinkers on the Continent such as Saint-Simon. Unlike the Scots philosophers who had close ties with the Church and were influenced by the Protestant climate of their country, men on the Continent felt free to stress Ossian's lack of religion. The Ossianic poetry portrayed a ritualistic and myth-centred society liberally governed by its Druids and poets, but one that seemed completely to lack a clerical hierarchy and dogma. The anti-religious argument drew its evidence from the historical fact that the third-century Ossian wrote before the arrival of Christianity, and this was additional proof of the purity and virtue of his society. A pagan society had been capable of producing poetry that equalled in sublimity the works of the Hebrew prophets and surpassed in vigour those of the present century. In this way the Ossianic poetry served thinkers with a far more radical programme than young Macpherson could have envisaged.

In conclusion, we must consider the basic issues to which the Ossianic controversy gave expression. Ossian's poetry instigated men's opposition to ideas which they felt to be outdated, the dead wood of the preceding centuries, and also inspired them to discover some new solutions to

current problems. It is ironical that these records of ancient poetry should have proved to be inauthentic. But to
cite a parallel case, what is the degree of genuineness of
the poems collected by Lönnrot for the Finnish national
epic *Kalevala*—poems which are to be held responsible
for the spiritual revival of a whole people?

During the Ossianic controversy there appeared to be
four main clusters of ideas on which criticism was focused. First, there was a clearly expressed opposition to
civilization as it existed. The grandeur of ancient poetry
served men as proof of the inherent virtues of a primitive, uncultivated age. Secondly, there was the opposition to war and military glory with their false heroic
ideals. The Ossianic poems seemed to advocate a natural
vitality of a basically pacifist kind. Thirdly, where Ossian was compared with Homer, the opposition to the
values of classical antiquity, perpetuated through the
classical tradition in contemporary literature with its
servile imitation of the classics, became more pronounced.
And lastly, where Ossian was compared with the Bible,
men discovered that sublimity could be found in a totally pagan and non-clerical context—a fact which provided further evidence for the anti-religious philosophers of
the Enlightenment.

Some of the new sentiments and ideas that Ossian inaugurated can be seen to have provided a foretaste of Romanticism. The interest in the past and in ancient cultures that explains much of the preoccupation with Homer
and the Bible shown by eighteenth-century poets and
critics was transformed, in connection with Ossian, into
an enthusiasm for the remote and the exotic that had a
distinctly Romantic colour. Ossian seemed to have provided an archetypal model of the Romantic poet who
could give free expression to the nature of his environment and to the history of his people; he was not merely
the creative genius of a primitive society such as the
primitivist thinkers wanted him to have been, but also a
type of poetic genius that appealed to contemporary taste.
For the body of lyrical and imitative poetry that Ossian
inspired all over Europe can be understood in the context of Goethe's *Werther*: it was no coincidence, perhaps, that the poet who inspired the social utopias of
sophisticated thinkers was also the favourite of all those
sensitive young men whose vision proved their own
destruction.

Richard B. Sher (lecture date 1980)

SOURCE: "'Those Scotch Imposters and their Cabal':
Ossian and the Scottish Enlightenment," in *Man and
Nature: Proceedings of the Canadian Society for Eigh-
teenth-Century Studies, Vol. 1,* Roger L. Emerson, Gilles
Girard, Roseann Runte, eds., The University of Western
Ontario 1982, pp. 55-63.

[*In the following essay, originally delivered as a lecture
in 1980, Sher argues that Macpherson's "translations"
of Gaelic poetry were in some part the product of a group
of literary figures in Edinburgh with whom Macpherson*

*was associated and who provided the financial and intel-
lectual support that made the project possible.*]

Although the name of Ossian was heard a great deal during
the late eighteenth and early nineteenth centuries, it has
since become little more than a historical curiosity. We
are amazed and amused that so many intelligent, well-
educated people could have sincerely believed that the
works of Ossian were both completely authentic and (what
is perhaps more astounding) aesthetically unsurpassed—
even by Homer. We have become accustomed to regarding this strange phenomenon as a case of deliberate deception: the public was simply fooled by James Macpherson, a brash young Highlander who cleverly tricked the
literary world into accepting compositions that were in
part distortions of genuine Gaelic poems and ballads, in
part his own creation, as the original poetry of a legendary third-century Highland bard called Ossian. The world
of letters fell for the ruse, so the story goes, because
Macpherson was shrewd enough to endow his Ossianic
poetry with the primitivism and pathos for which a vast
audience of pre-romantics yearned. Ossian was Homer
cleaned up for eighteenth-century tastes and then sold to
an unsuspecting public by an unscrupulous entrepreneur.

This literary "confidence-man" explanation for the genesis and vogue of Ossian is not exactly false, but neither
is it entirely true. For one thing, while Macpherson alone
produced the Ossianic "translations" themselves, in a very
real sense his Ossian was also the product of a "cabal" of
Edinburgh literary men who provided the necessary inspiration, incentive, financial support, editorial assistance,
publishing connections, and emotional encouragement. At
the heart of this Ossianic "cabal" stood a coterie of Presbyterian clergymen affiliated with the Moderate party in
the Church of Scotland—John Home, Hugh Blair, Adam
Ferguson, William Robertson, and Alexander Carlyle—
but these "Moderate literati" were at various times assisted by other Scottish literati and gentlemen, the most
important of whom seem to have been Robert Chalmers
and Patrick Murray, Lord Elibank. Furthermore, the sentimental, pre-romantic, primitivist component in Ossianic
poetry, while very possibly the most important factor in
accounting for the success of Ossian abroad, was only
one of several features that made Ossianic poetry so attractive to the Edinburgh "cabal." It is to other, peculiarly
Scottish factors that we must turn in order to understand
how and why Ossian came to be.

Our account begins in the critical year 1757, shortly before Macpherson introduced Ossian to the Scottish literary community. In July of that year, when David Hume
made his famous boast about the Scots being "the People
most distinguish'd for Literature in Europe," the literati
of Edinburgh were experiencing a sense of national pride
and expectation difficult for us to grasp fully today. The
Select Society was in full bloom. There was much talk of
"improvement." Attempts to censure Hume and Kames in
the General Assembly of the church had been decisively
defeated by the Moderate party. John Home's *Douglas*
and William Wilkie's *Epigoniad* had just proven—at least
to the satisfaction of Edinburgh literary men like Hume—

that Scotsmen could write first-rate tragedies and epic poems, and several other young Scottish authors, such as Adam Smith, William Robertson, and Adam Ferguson, were soon to publish works of history and philosophy that would give Scotland an enduring name in the republic of letters. There was a growing sense among the cultural elite of Edinburgh that Scotland was on the verge of a new era of civilization and enlightenment which would compel Englishmen to forget past differences and to embrace their northern neighbors as equal partners in a truly united kingdom. The outbreak of the Seven Years War in the previous year had encouraged this spirit of British unity by pitting the Scots and English against a common enemy. In a significant speech in Home's *Douglas,* Lady Randolph articulated the view that England and Scotland were like two foolish sisters who habitually waste their energies fighting each other instead of joining forces against "foreign foes":

> A river here, there an ideal line,
> By fancy drawn, divides the sister kingdoms.
> On each side dwells a people similar,
> As twins are to each other; valiant both;
> Both for their valour famous thro' the world.
> Yet will they not unite their kindred arms,
> And, if they must have war, wage distant war,
> But with each other fight in cruel conflict.

After half a century of animosity and prejudice it appeared that the time had finally come to "compleat the Union."

Two issues that came to a head in the first half of 1757 demonstrated that Scottish dreams of obtaining political and literary equality in English eyes were not soon to be realized. First, Scotland was excluded by Parliament from the provisions of Pitt's militia bill, ostensibly because of English fears that Scotland would be unable to finance a militia but probably more because of English fears about the danger of arming potential Jacobites, as the Scots were widely perceived to be. To loyal Whigs like the Moderate literati of Edinburgh, who had fought and preached against the Jacobite menace posed by Bonnie Prince Charlie twelve years earlier, this was a devastating blow not only to Scottish pride but also to Scottish defense. The feeling of vulnerability which had so upset these men during the Forty-Five returned, only this time the immediate threat came from France rather than the Highlands. When a French squadron under Admiral Thurot headed for the North Sea late in 1759 and then actually appeared in Scottish waters early in 1760, Presbyterian Whigs like William Robertson joined with Jacobites like Lord Elibank in proclaiming the militia question the most important issue since the Union. Yet efforts to extend the provisions of the English militia act to Scotland were handily defeated in the House of Commons in April 1760.

The second instance of Anglo-Scottish tension was literary rather than political. It was thought to be bad enough that Home's *Douglas* had been rejected as "unfit for ye Stage" by London's leading actor and theatrical manager, David Garrick. What rankled the Scottish literati still more

was the fact that even after *Douglas* had triumphed gloriously in Edinburgh in December 1756 and then enjoyed a successful run at London's Covent Gardens three months later, some English literary critics, including Samuel Johnson, refused to recognize Home's tragic genius. The same pattern occurred when Wilkie's *Epigoniad* put the Scottish literary world "in raptures" during the spring of 1757, only to be either panned or ignored by English critics. The following winter Home's second play, *Agis,* was savagely attacked as a mere party piece—the party being that of Pitt, Bute, and Leicester House that was then associated with the cause of martial virtue—and in 1759 a London edition of Wilkie's *Epigoniad* failed miserably despite the efforts of David Hume to make it less offensive to English readers.

Thus, even before the Earl of Bute's rise to political power in the early 1760s touched off the century's biggest outburst of anti-Scottish sentiment in England, Scottish men of letters were feeling bitterly resentful towards John Bull for denying Scotland her due in military and literary affairs. The Bute era seriously intensified that resentment, especially since Bute himself was so closely connected with the Scottish literati as personal and literary patron. Meanwhile the Scots militia agitation continued, and early in 1762 the Moderate literati, Elibank, and other members of the Edinburgh literary community established the Poker Club for the express purpose of stirring up support for a Scots militia. As in 1760, however, the Scots militia scheme had little political support in England, and in March 1762 Bute and the Scottish members of Parliament decided to shelve a Scots militia bill rather than incur another humiliating defeat in the Commons.

It is surely no accident that the same Edinburgh literati who took the lead in the cause of Scottish literary nationalism, spearheaded the Scots militia campaigns of 1759-60 and 1762, and established the closest relations with the Earl of Bute were the very men who encouraged—one might almost say commissioned—the Ossianic endeavors of James Macpherson. In 1759 Macpherson was an obscure young poet working as tutor to the son of a Highland laird. His first contact with the Edinburgh literati may have been with Adam Ferguson, a fellow-Highlander who is said to have supplied him with a letter of introduction to John Home. At the resort town of Moffat, in early autumn 1759, Home met Macpherson, saw several of his Ossianic fragments in English "translation," and showed them to Alexander Carlyle and another Moderate clergyman, Rev. George Laurie of Loudon. Home and Carlyle then carried their "precious discovery" to Blair, Robertson, and Elibank, and in June 1760 these literary men published at Edinburgh a modest collection of fifteen of Macpherson's little Ossianic poems under the title *Fragments of Ancient Poetry, collected in the Highlands of Scotland,* with an anonymous preface by Hugh Blair.

Two crucial factors should be noted in regard to the events leading to publication of Macpherson's *Fragments.* First, we must be aware that when Ferguson, Home, and Carlyle met Macpherson in 1759 they were obsessed with fear about Scotland's vulnerability in the event of a French invasion and resentment towards England for making such a situation possible. Shortly before his critical meeting with Macpherson at Moffat, Home articulated this theme in a characteristically vehement letter [26 August 1759] to Lord Bute:

> I am sorry to say My Lord that this country is in the most wretched situation that ever any country was in which the people were allowed to talk of Liberty. The ignorance of the English and I don't [know] what name to give to the conduct of the Scotch has reduced us in the midst of alarms, to a state totally defenceless. No Poet that ever foamed with inspiration can express the grief and indignation of those Scots that still love their country, to find themselves disarmed.

The same obsession characterizes much of the extant correspondence from this period of Ferguson, Carlyle, Elibank, and Robertson. Indeed, Ferguson was only half joking when he told Gilbert Elliot in September 1759 that he and Home actually hoped for a French invasion in order to horrify people into realizing the need for a Scots militia! The attraction of Macpherson's Ossianic *Fragments* to these Edinburgh literary men seems to have derived largely from its depiction of a race of heroic Scottish warriors that formed an obvious contrast with their disarmed and sometimes indifferent descendants of the eighteenth century. This militaristic aspect was made all the more appealing because it was sheathed in the polite veneer of sentimental neo-classicism. Here were poems that spoke of noble deeds but little bloodshed, rude manners mixed with lofty sentiments, much weeping and dying but no physical pain. Here, too, were poems with a pedigree, and a pedigree far older than anything the English could produce. English critics could sneer and scoff at Home's tragedies and Wilkie's *Epigoniad,* but could they possibly deny the importance of an authentic third-century Highland bard? In short, Macpherson's Ossianic *Fragments* served Home and his friends both in their ongoing propaganda war against John Bull for recognition of Scotland's literary accomplishments and in their program to encourage martial virtue and a Scots militia.

Secondly, we must realize just how passive Macpherson was in the events leading to publication of the *Fragments.* He did not come to Edinburgh with grandiose claims of a major discovery. On the contrary, he was "entreated and dragged" into the project, as Hugh Blair reminded a skeptical David Hume some years later. John Home had actually been looking for examples of ancient Gaelic poetry long before his visit to Moffat, and it was only "with some difficulty" that he had prevailed upon young Macpherson to provide him with several short specimens in English translation. The idea to publish a collection of Macpherson's Ossianic fragments had originated with Hugh Blair, and "much and repeated importunity" had been required before Macpherson would agree to it. Blair had secured a publisher and written an enthusiastic preface. Even the style of the fragments had probably been suggested to Macpherson by his Edinburgh backers, for it seems more than likely that they were the unnamed per-

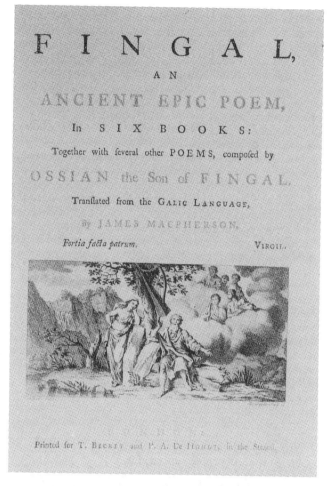

Title page for Macpherson's "translation" of the first part of an epic poem he claimed to have found on an expedition to the Scottish Highlands in 1760-1761.

sons whom Macpherson later credited with persuading him to render Ossian in "what is called a prose version" instead of verse.

The factors and individuals that were chiefly responsible for the *Fragments of Ancient Poetry* were also the driving forces behind Macpherson's later and better known Ossianic endeavors, *Fingal* (1761) and *Temora* (1763), only the scale of the enterprise was enlarged and the stakes increased. After the success of the *Fragments,* Macpherson displayed his usual reluctance to participate in any further Ossianic exertions and once again had to be "entreated and dragged" into action by the Edinburgh literary "cabal." This time Blair organized a special dinner party in Macpherson's honor, to which Robertson, Elibank, Home, Sir Adam Fergusson and others came for the specific purpose of persuading Macpherson to undertake a Highland jaunt in search of an epic about the heroic exploits of Ossian's father, an ancient Scottish king called Fingal. Since Macpherson's meager income as a tutor could not provide the necessary funds for such a jaunt, Blair also organized a systematic collection (under the supervision of Robert Chalmers) which is said to have raised £100 for the Ossianic cause. We must imagine a poor, proud, previously unknown young Highland lad being feted and funded by some of Edinburgh's leading literary figures and men of affairs. The pressure to comply with their wishes must have been enormous, certainly more than Macpherson could withstand. Considering these circumstances, the notion of a slick confidence man single-handedly hoodwinking the Edinburgh literati begins to appear untenable. It would be closer to the truth to say that Macpherson was as much the victim as the victimizer of the Edinburgh literary community.

Macpherson was smart enough to know what was expected of him. The initial Ossianic fragments had been a source of great pride to Edinburgh literary men, but only a complete Gaelic epic, dressed, of course, in neo-classical English garb, could possess the scope and grandeur necessary to elevate Scotland to a new place in the national history of poetry. It is significant that long before Macpherson had even begun to search for *Fingal* and *Temora* Blair was privately referring to those works as "our epics." After Macpherson returned from his first Highland excursion early in 1761, Blair kept a watchful eye on his "translating" progress; Robert Chalmers escorted him to London to secure a publisher there; John Home accompanied him on a second Highland jaunt in the spring and summer of 1761; and Lord Bute was persuaded to become Ossian's foremost patron. By the time *Fingal* actually appeared, the Edinburgh literary "cabal" had invested far too much time and energy in the project to tolerate much skepticism about Ossian's authenticity, and they angrily attributed such skepticism to the anti-Scottish prejudices and machinations of the English. "Who but John Bull could entertain the belief of an imposture so incredible as this?", Blair asked David Hume with undisguised hostility in 1763. Yet testimony submitted to the Highland Society indicates that Blair, Carlyle, and Ferguson suspected all along that Macpherson had taken "liberties" in piecing together "separate or broken fragments" to create his Ossianic epics. Those epics were apparently considered too important for nationalistic reasons to be discredited simply because they had never really existed!

Scottish literary nationalism was not the only cause for which Fingal's sharp sword did strike. By bravely performing his duty as king and warrior in a world of continual adversity, by fighting only for public virtue, and above all by successfully defending Scotland against armies of foreign invaders, Fingal raised to epic proportions the theme of martial virtue in the service of national defense that had been suggested in a fragmentary way by Macpherson's first book of Ossianic poetry. By contemporary standards Fingal's forces were in fact nothing but a "Raw Militia"—as Alexander Carlyle later termed the army of Highlanders that had beaten Cope's regulars at Prestonpans in 1745—and it seems likely that *Fingal* was read by its Scottish patrons as a pro-militia statement. How else can we explain the fact that the men who formed the nucleus of the Edinburgh "cabal" responsible for *Fingal* also constituted the nucleus of the Poker Club, which came into existence within weeks of *Fingal's* publication for the purpose of spreading Scots militia propaganda? Elibank, Carlyle, and Ferguson (who gave the club its

name) head the Poker's membership list, and Home, Robertson, and Blair were also early members. The only other man known to have attended the important Ossianic dinner party of June 1760, Sir Adam Fergusson, was a member, as was Robert Chalmers, the Edinburgh merchant who directed the Ossianic collection drive and accompanied Macpherson to London to secure a publisher for *Fingal*. Attendance figures for the period 1774-1784 show that Home, Ferguson, Robertson, Carlyle, Blair, and Elibank (until his death in 1778) continued to be among the club's most active participants, and Robert Chalmers attended more meetings during those years than any other member.

Hostile contemporary English critics like Samuel Johnson and Horace Walpole employed such phrases as "those Scotch imposters and their cabal" (Walpole) and "Scotch conspiracy in national falsehood" (Johnson) when privately discussing the Ossian affair. This line of thought would seem to suggest that those contemporary English critics were closer to the truth than they themselves could have known. Ossian *was* a group effort on the part of James Macpherson and a "cabal" of Edinburgh literati who were motivated, largely by topical issues which were in turn situated within the broader context of Scottish aspirations and disappointments in relations with England during the era of the Seven Years War and the political "reign" of the third Earl of Bute.

Such considerations do not render Ossian any less fraudulent, but they do suggest a new view of Macpherson's personality and role in the Ossian affair. Beneath his cocksure exterior, Macpherson now appears to have been an insecure young man who found himself pushed along by the leaders of the Edinburgh literary community, whom he greatly admired and did not wish to disappoint. He perceived what they were after and was manipulated by them into producing it. Far from being merely a "confidence man", he was himself conned into playing a game whose rules and stakes he probably never completely understood until play had already begun. By that time his only alternatives were failure or fraudulence. After some hesitation he opted for the latter and never looked back.

Peter T. Murphy (essay date 1986)

SOURCE: "Fool's Gold: The Highland Treasures of Macpherson's Ossian," in *ELH*, Vol 53, No. 3, Fall, 1986, pp. 567-91.

[*In the following essay, Murphy places both Macpherson's accomplishments and the controversy surrounding them in the context of the Scottish sense of national heritage in the eighteenth century.*]

James MacPherson was once a famous man, famous for translating Ossian's poems. If he is remembered now, it is for forging the Ossian poems, with the emphasis on the forgery rather than the poetry; but mostly he is hardly remembered at all. If literary memory is founded on quality, then the turgid prose of these "poems," with its thick syntax and grand, vague gestures, certainly encourages forgetfulness. But if we think of him as a literary event, as a writer who generated a great deal of interest (regardless of the source of that interest), then he seems more deserving of attention. The Ossian books figure in the education of all major writers through about 1830, most often as a fond memory of youth (just as Walter Scott's novels will for the later nineteenth century); Ossian gave to these youths that adventure, mystery and romance that is still, to some extent, the clearest association of the Scottish Highlands. To the literary scholar MacPherson offers an interesting example of the literary criminal, a kind of malefactor whose faults are at best vaguely defined. In MacPherson's case the difficulties are exacerbated by the genuine complexity of the facts, the source of the surprising duration and interest of the "Ossianic Controversy," which lasted for almost fifty years. The definition of MacPherson's crime, and the delineation of the attractive (to the eighteenth century) qualities of the poems themselves, are parallel problems that lead to the same problematic place: the mysterious, unavailable Highlands, source of treasure and terror. To talk about the Ossian poems, one must start by sorting through the odd collection of Highland materials that the poems bring with them, and then turn to the poetry itself.

The Jacobite rebellions of 1715 and 1745 are marks of the entrance of the Highlands into British culture. At the beginning of the eighteenth century, the Gaelic-speaking people of northern Scotland were a mystery to the rest of the population of the island, though their periodical descents to prey on the Lowlanders made them a feared mystery. At the end of the eighteenth century they were a different kind of mystery: a culture whose strange ways were a subject of great curiosity—mystery made into a cultural commodity, and a culture that was rapidly disappearing into the legends of history. It is common to fix the date of the Highland's decline at 1745, and certainly there is reason to do this. The martial spirit of the clans had made its one, final, all-too-conspicuous appearance, the Hanoverian establishment had noticed it, and decided to eliminate it. The policy of elimination took several paths, but all focussed on destroying the functioning of the clan, which they took (correctly) to be the central feature of the Highland culture.

The policies actually put into practice aimed at reducing the isolation of the Highlands, at mixing this durably foreign culture in with the rest of Britain. The hereditary jurisdiction of the chiefs was abruptly ended, curbing their despotic control over their clans, and the substitution of British law was accomplished by the quartering of troops in the region and the large-scale construction of the military roads. It is important to remember that the isolation of the Gael was compounded by their very foreign tongue, which has no connection at all with what we call "Scottish." Early on, in 1716, the teaching of English was seen as a way of "reducing" the country. The problem with Gaelic, what made it so "foreign," was not that it was especially difficult to learn, but rather how it had to be learned. In the mid-eighteenth century there were no Gaelic grammars or dictionaries, and the only textual support

was a New Testament. Gaelic had to be learned from the mouth of an actual speaker (an actual Highlander), and, because the upper classes so eagerly abandoned their native ways as they mixed with British society, the only reward for learning Gaelic was the ability to talk with lower-class Highlanders.

Both of these methods of including the Gael (building roads and attempting to suppress Gaelic) sought to rend the shroud of secrecy that surrounded, or seemed to surround them. So it is not a simply gratuitous pun on my part to include in this category the outlawing of "Highland garb" as one of the most effective methods of eliminating the crucial and dangerous difference of Highland culture. The distinctive way in which the Highlanders shielded themselves from the elements provided a sort of badge of culture, separating them from others and identifying them with each other. Scott explains the purpose of this tactic best:

> The system of disarming the Highlands had been repeatedly resorted to upon former occasions, but the object had been only partially attained. It was now resolved, not only to deprive the Highlanders of their arms, but of the ancient garb of their country; a picturesque habit, the custom of wearing which was peculiarly associated with use of warlike weapons. The sword, the dirk, the pistol were all as complete parts of the Highland dress as the plaid and the bonnet, and the habit of using the latter was sure to remind the wearer of the want of the former. It was proposed to destroy this association of ideas, by rendering the use of the Highland garb, in any of its peculiar forms, highly penal. [*Tales of a Grandfather*]

As Scott describes, the government cannily fixed upon a kind of metonymical lynchpin of Highland culture: not crucial in itself, but through its connections, its association, leading to the very heart of Highland identity. In terms of its specific goals, this law was very effective, for though it was repealed only four decades later, the tartan did not reappear.

If this disappearance is a mark of the disappearance of a culture, we should be surprised, I think, that it happened so quickly. This surprise is justified, and the '45 and its aftermath are not enough to account for the state of Gaelic culture by the end of the eighteenth century. The legal repression of Gaelic culture was terribly successful, but the Highlands were opened to this repression by internal causes, and the success must be at least partly attributable to this vulnerability. And as with any cultural subjection, it is important to remember that what was being destroyed was fully a way of life, culture in all senses—economic, social and artistic. It is the last sense I wish to emphasize here, but the way to it is through the first two, the economic and the social.

The close-knit, purposefully cohesive and isolated social structure of the clan had been under pressure throughout the seventeenth century, and in the early eighteenth century this pressure intensified and expanded. Chiefs had begun to feel the attractions of Lowland life (sons were being sent out of the Highlands for their education). The old communal economy, where rent was paid in kind, and in blood in the form of periodic military service, was not designed to satisfy the needs of this new way of life. The chiefs needed a transportable medium of exchange, something to translate their local wealth into a true British wealth. They wanted to live in Edinburgh or London; they wanted the accoutrements of the British manor house; they wanted to travel to the continent. This translation, of course, is effected by money, and the eighteenth-century Highland chief began to feel the need for it. There were a number of ways to get more money out of a given estate, all of which involved "improvement," methods of increasing cash return through increasing productivity or changing the product itself. Improvement usually implied enclosure of previously communal land, and the new product was (in most cases) wool, which implied not only enclosure but depopulation. These methods were entirely destructive of the old communal life, and substituted for it a new focus on the individual and individual holdings.

One of the casualties of this disruption of the old communal culture was the literary tradition associated with the bards ("bard" is a Welsh word that came to be the name for this feature of Celtic culture). This tradition was intimately connected to the institutions of the clan, for the bards were hereditary retainers who farmed their memories and spirits instead of the soil (though they were often given farms in return for their pains). Everything about this tradition indicates that it was a classical tradition: the poetry developed a particular vocabulary, was extremely aware of an inherited corpus, and depended on the forms associated with patronage (eulogies, elegies, and depictions of military exploits). The transmission of poetry was largely oral, though manuscripts were kept by certain bards in certain cases. Throughout its lifetime, this tradition maintained close links with Ireland, even after Scottish Gaelic diverged from Irish as a separate Gaelic dialect. Bards were routinely trained in Ireland, returning to Scotland to ply their trade.

The bards were responsible for the transmission and development of the (verse) Ossianic cycles, and for their retention in long form, though the popular tradition also contained Ossianic material in the form of tales. There was a sharp distinction between a poetic tradition associated with learning and a popular tradition; the bards did not write popular verse, and they could not be described as being part of a folk tradition. There was a strong folk culture, vernacular in the sense that the works were in the local dialect instead of the literary dialect of the bards, in which the Ossianic legends had a large place. The folk tradition tended to erase the identities of individual artists, as folk traditions always do, while the bardic tradition was obsessed with the transmission of such data. The bards often functioned as genealogists for the clan, and they transmitted their own information along with that of their chiefs. In the mid-eighteenth century, the son of a bard, illiterate and incapable of carrying on the tradition, was still able to recite the sixteen generations of bards before him. This thematization of their own history, and of their place in recording it, is a major feature of bardic

poetry, and certainly the feature that interested people like MacPherson. He describes the importance of the Ossianic poetry as linked to this interest in history, for the chiefs loved to hear of the exploits of the heroes, and to hear how they were descended from such heroes. The bardic succession projects the song of origins forward:

> bards were employed to repeat the poems, and to record the connection of their patrons with chiefs so renowned. . . . By the succession of these bards, the poems concerning the anscestors of the family were handed down from generation to generation.

This is a structure of interlocking fame, with the fame of the ancestors being gathered up by the fame of a poem and projected into the future. The bard thus occupies a historical middle ground, handing the past to the future by virtue of his verse. That the succession of bards created a self-consciously perpetuating tradition points out that this middle ground is a good place to be; that is, the activity of "handing on" is regarded as one definition of poetic activity. This structure is absolutely central to MacPherson's project, and I will return to it later.

In the seventeenth century this tradition fell into decline from a variety of causes, among them the continuing disintegration of clan structure and the (consequently) decreasing number of clans who retained bards; by the early eighteenth century it was largely moribund. In its place developed a thriving vernacular poetry, not a folk-tradition but poetry of the sort we are familiar with from English literature; we feel comfortable calling the practitioners "poets" instead of bards. This movement, generally regarded as the true flowering of Gaelic verse, peaks in the mid-eighteenth century and then disappears. These poets are not part of the bardic continuity. The decline that Gaelic had undergone by the middle of the eighteenth century was not the loss of culture or of high-quality verse, but the loss of a classical tradition that had very strong historical associations: it was an inheritance that got misplaced.

This is the situation that MacPherson found on his tours in the early 1760s. Because no sense of their value had been retained, MacPherson was able to obtain several manuscripts from the ClanRanalds, precious relics of a forgotten age. The present generation of the bardic family (MacVuirich, or MacMhuirich), Lachlan, was unable to read the manuscripts and had no real idea what they contained; he says that some pages had been used for tailor's measures. The poetry itself survived on the tongues of people who were able to remember it, with remnants of bardic poetry mixed with remnants of folk tradition. Bardic poetry survived, literally, in fragments. One could still find people who could recite (continuously) for days, but they were becoming increasingly rare.

The Highlanders were very well aware that things had changed, and their descriptions make the Highland Society's *Report* fascinating reading. The report itself offers this explanation for the fugitive condition of the Ossianic tradition:

[There has been] a change of manners in the Highlands, where the habits of industry have now superseded the amusement of listening to the legendary narrative or heroic ballad, where consequently the faculty of remembering and the exercise of repeating such tales or songs, are altogether in disuse, or only retained by a few persons of extremely advanced age and feeble health, whom . . . it is not easy to discover.

This passage does what I am trying to do: it links poetics to a social and economic argument. The phrase about the new "habits of industry" euphemistically describes the destruction of the old communal order; it also implies that the old order was one of indolence and primitive laziness (one can find this notion in Hugh Blair). These new habits have caused the traditional inheritance to lose its way, and as a result the poems are only available from very old people who may pass on at any time, without passing on their verse. Old age, clinging to old habits in the face of new ones, isolated and on the verge of dissolution, is a central figure in the Ossian poems, and so this theme too will return.

Industry is described in a more partisan way by a Highlander from the Western Isle of South Uist:

We can easily prove, that the noblest virtues have been ruined, or driven into exile, since the love of money has crept in amongst us; and since deceit and hypocrisy have carried mercenary policy and slavish, sordid avarice into our land. Before this modern change, our Chiefs cherished humanity.

The profound sense of loss that this man feels overwhelms all writing about the Highlands at this time, and it is the *articulation* of this sense of loss—rather than the actual circumstances of decline—that seems to begin around 1745. This is not the "joy of grief" that will become a fashion through MacPherson's efforts, but real grief over the destruction of a culture, arising from the sudden realization that things have passed away. This lament finishes my historical picture by confirming that Highland culture was under the pressures I have been describing and by emphasizing that the theme of money and avarice has a way of popping up when talking about the Ossian books.

When I say that a sense of loss overwhelms writing about the Highlands, I mean to include MacPherson's Ossian poems as well, overwhelmed as they are by a sense of lateness. It is the subject of Ossian's familiar call:

Soon shall he lie in the narrow house, and no bard shall raise his fame! Roll on, ye dark-brown years; ye bring no joy on your course! Let the tomb open to Ossian, for his strength has failed. The sons of song are gone to rest. My voice remains, like a blast, that roars, lonely, on a sea-surrounded rock, after the winds are laid.

In many ways this is the "historical" Ossian found in Gaelic tradition, but MacPherson has modified him to his taste. The son of Fingal (of Finn), he is the last of the race

of heroes founded by Fingal. This eminence is of a special kind, for he was not the last-born of the Finns, but has been cut off before and after: Fingal his father and Oscar his son die before him, leaving him, as he says, on a temporal island isolated from both past and future. He compensates for his isolation through his singing, his verse, and this compensation works in both directions. His memory returns the past to him, and his voice, which through the metaphor of song is the name for his poetic faculty, pours it forth in the form of poetry, which overleaps Oscar and lives on.

This compensation is the obsessive subject matter of the stories, and forms the substance of what makes them "heroic" poems: heroes are strong people, famous because they have survived, and famous people have poems sung about them. Because all heroes, even the strongest, pass on, survival by personal strength is replaced by survival in heroic verse. Fingal says this to one of his vanquished enemies, whom he has forgiven:

Swaran . . . to-day our fame is greatest. We shall pass away like a dream. No sound shall remain in our fields of war. . . . Our names may be heard in song. What avails it, when our strength hath ceased? O Ossian . . . you know of heroes that are no more. Give us the song of other years.

Fingal questions the value of living on in song instead of in body, as a way of expressing the evanescence of his prowess, but he also takes comfort in the songs of past heroes. The moment of comfort underwrites the present (shielding it from the future) by summoning up the past; we are compensated for our losses by the depiction of past loss. We hear of this moment from Ossian, of course, and this moment of song is also recorded in song: past and future needs meet in the activity of the bard, with future songs (those composed now, in the spontaneous present) singing of the use of the past in the present. This is the moment of "handing on," when tradition generates itself. Imitating the self-referential tradition he mined his ideas from, MacPherson dramatizes the compensation fame offers for loss: to be embedded in a heroic poem, a poem that perpetuates the memory of heroes (this is a more detailed way of saying that the most popular subject matter in these songs is the subject of singing itself). These poems are thus about continuity, but continuity as highlighted by discontinuity. Ossian is a runner in the bards' continuous race toward the future, but he has no one to hand his baton to, no ear to pour his poems into: he must entrust them to the wind. He goes through the motion of handing, the composition of song, without the cultural machinery that the singing is part of. No chiefs are gathered to hear him—there are no more chiefs. He is an oxymoronic bard, a bard famous for having no successor.

The popularity of these poems hints that there must be some powerful profit to be derived from this depiction of a lonely singer. The phrase contemporaries applied to it, a phrase taken from the songs themselves, is "the joy of grief." Ossian is ruled by oxymoron, and this is another example. What is the joy of being the last of the Finns?

It is the joy of memory, the business of the bards, but it is also, in Ossian's case, the joy of having things behind him. He is old, he is blind, he has nothing left to him, but he is also beyond anxiety; he has no heroic activity left to him except to mine the heroism of his age, the age that will pass away with him. Because of his weakness, because of his utter dependence on his past for his poetic activity, Ossian is infinitely close to being overwhelmed by his past, made small by it, but because he is part of the past recalling it is exhilarating instead of sickening. He cannot repeat the heroism of Fingal (he is old and weak), but he was himself a hero, his son was a hero, so his inferiority is the subject of lament but not anxious reflection.

As the frequent exclamations and "O"s indicate, Ossian's song is a spontaneous one, one of the benefits of having his subject matter be a part of his soul, his memory:

> then comes a voice to Ossian, and awakes his soul! It is the voice of years that are gone! they roll before me, with all their deeds! I seize the tales, as they pass, and pour them forth in song.

He makes his poems from the past, from a simple excavation of the materials of the past, but this past is also part of him. His extreme age energizes this scene. He is ready to depart; like Gray's, MacPherson's bard is the last, and with his extinction the last easy link to the past will be pushed forever out of reach. Ossian was praised as a poet of the sublime, and this is an example of his sublimity. A whole tradition, a history of singing and victory, of heroism and great deeds, concentrates itself in the person of Ossian, and trembles on the precipice of extinction. His job is to translate these deeds into permanence, to give them a form that will convey them into the future, to keep them from being lost in dark time. This is the bard's job: but again, Ossian has no audience but the air; alone on his rock, he sings only to the mysterious forces (into the blast) that preserve some things and obliterate others. The immediate, staged drama of these poems is that this dying effort worked: the poems are presented as having succeeded, as having made the trip, dropping into the modern world with the scent of the ancient still miraculously fresh. Whether Ossian's last song, thus preserved, is a curse (like the song in Gray's poem) or a treasure remains to be seen.

As I have described them so far, these poems, or prose-poems, are the works of a poet called Ossian; and so they are, in an important sense, and the drama they invoke depends on that authorship. Equally important to the success of these works, though, is the dramatic presence of MacPherson, the editor-translator, who is part of the machinery that presents Ossian to us in his simple guise. As editor, MacPherson constantly makes himself known to us through notes, and he imposes two hefty "dissertations" on us before we begin the actual poems. His presence as translator continually returns to us through his careful style of translation, his use of a style that connotes translation. The most common and the most effective feature of this style is its inversions, things like "bent is

his head of age" instead of "his aged head is bent." (This has the added advantage of being something English readers would be likely to call poetic diction.) The other obtrusive feature of his style is also illustrated by my example: the use of clumsy "of" phrases instead of simple possessives. Added to this, of course, is the "measured prose" itself, labelled as "poetry" by the titles of the books and of the individual pieces. By calling this prose poetry, MacPherson conjures up the shadowy original, marching dim Gaelic feet through unknown Gaelic meters, and at the same time his humble refusal to recreate this meter is always before our eyes.

This style has been described as derived from features of the Gaelic originals MacPherson worked from, and this may well be true; but the important fact is that MacPherson has retained them, and has depicted himself as avoiding one of the tasks of the translator, that of turning things into good English. It is a rhetorical trick designed to express literality, faithfulness, and its advantages for MacPherson are obvious. If his office is that of the humble translator, then anything which reinforces that humility reinforces his position as translator, the position he is trying to hold onto in the controversy.

The apparent literality of the translation becomes part of an argument for the merit of the poetry in Hugh Blair's "Critical Dissertation," a quaintly fervent work almost invariably attached to editions of Ossian after 1763. Blair cheers MacPherson's choice of prose over verse because it lets the "spirit" of Ossian come through (the mechanics of foreign meter would interfere with spirit), and goes on to describe translation as a test of poetic merit:

> Elegant, however, and masterly as Mr. MacPherson's translation is, we must never forget, whilst we read it, that we are putting the merit of the original to a severe test. For we are examining a poet stripped of his native dress: divested of the harmony of his own numbers. We know how much grace and energy the works of the Greek and Latin authors receive from the charm of versification in their original languages. If, then, destitute of this advantage, exhibited in a literal version, Ossian still has power to please as a poet . . . we may very safely infer, that his productions are the offspring of true and uncommon genius.

Setting aside for the moment the nice figure of the undressed Highlander, here we see Blair effectively erasing form as a critical ingredient in poetry. The genius of poetry is something that informs form, that underwrites the grace and charm of form. That this meshes so well with MacPherson's tactics is one of the marks of MacPherson's skill; as a principle of poetics, the test of translation not only supports his rhetoric of translation, but it enthusiastically supports the metaphor of song and Ossian's spontaneity. The voice that calls to Ossian (inspiration, the spirit of genius) is the important part of the poems, and it will be heard even through the veil of English.

MacPherson picks up this argument himself. He says of his poems:

That they have been well received by the Public, appears from an extensive sale; that they shall continue to be well received, he may venture to prophecy without that gift of that inspiration, to which poets lay claim. Through the medium of version upon version, they retain, in foreign languages, their native character of simplicity and energy. Genuine poetry, like gold, loses little, when properly transfused; but when a composition cannot bear the test of a literal version, it is a counterfeit which ought not to pass current.

The counterfeit poem would be one in which there is no real gold, no real poetry, and this hollowness is revealed by the bite of a literal version; here form is something which could actually hide the presence of true poetry. Echoing Blair (this was written after Blair's "Dissertation"), MacPherson insists that poetry needs to be undressed in order to test for essential quality. This undressing, which occurs when the poems are translated, absorbed into another language, has a suspicious resonance that I will take up shortly. In this passage MacPherson also thematizes the difficulties of his own project: to convince the public of the value of his gold, his poems, so that they will let them pass current. He does this constantly, especially in his footnotes (where he will often berate certain poems as "forgeries of a later age"), and this is all part of his tactics of truthfulness, of frankness, which make up so large a part of the Ossian books.

Inspiration, in this passage, is curiously linked to the sale of books, or negatively linked (sales eliminate the need for inspiration), which is at least congruent with Blair's general thought that spirit and inspiration are things that go along with quality; since sales are an affirmation of quality too, we may bypass the need for inspiration of vision. This inspiration also corresponds to Ossian's inspiration, the power that projects his songs into the future, and (again) to this power as it is described by Blair, the true spirit of genius that shines through even in a foreign tongue and culture. Something has happened here, though, for MacPherson is confident that he has evaded passing time without the benefit of inspiration; he feels sure that he and his poems are projected safely into the future (become famous as heroes are famous). His sureness is based on money, sales, on the gold that has been exchanged for poems in the commercial economy of Britain. This is veiled self-congratulation on MacPherson's part, of course, but it is also part of a picture that includes Blair's disrobed Highlander. This picture absorbs many elements, and I want to describe it here, and go on, in the next section, to follow out some principles of its composition.

Gold is a mark of purity, of something that resists diminution and counterfeit through its individual integrity. It also has an abiding relationship to money, being sometimes actual currency and sometimes the guarantor of the value of currency (MacPherson seems to use both qualities above). MacPherson says that his poems are gold, and hence good, but we also remember that gold (figurative gold: money) is what he got in return for them. This association makes the part about inspiration troubling, as

if some mercenary spirit had replaced true poetic quality with monetary reward, and as if MacPherson were insisting that he did all this without that quality which is essential to true poetry, throwing his crime in our faces. His boldness exploits the associations of translation, for the translator creates poetry without inspiration, simply mining the riches of a poem in a different language; this is what makes us think of "mere" translators. True quality is that which can survive this process (which both Blair and MacPherson seem to feel is rather brutal—a test) without deformation. If we put into this pot the undressed Highlander, the Ossianic poem in English, then we may follow the monetary thread out of poetics into the society of the Highlander in 1760, forbidden to wear his national dress, and forbidden to live the way his ancestors had lived. Behind this transition is gold too, in the form of avarice (gold as a metaphor) and in the form of money, the invasion of commercial economy. This is translation in another form, the translation of a culture, which threatens to become dislocation, and makes up the pathetic part of the picture.

Today what is best remembered about the Ossian poems is that people argued so much about them. The fascination of the "Ossianic controversy" has all but pushed the poems themselves from view, and one might argue that this has happened because the controversy is more interesting than the poems. But the controversy is not a gratuitous addition; it is intimately bound up with the complex genealogy and exotic subject matter of the poems. Even the simplest facts about them tended to add to their mystery. The argument against MacPherson's claims is most often represented by Samuel Johnson [in "A Journey to the Hebrides and the Western Isles"]:

> I believe that [the Ossian poems] never existed in any other form than that which we have seen. The editor, or author, never could show the original; nor can it be shown by any others. . . . He has doubtless inserted names that circulate in popular stories, and may have translated some wandering ballads, if any can be found.

He goes on to add, using our familiar money-metaphor:

> It is said, that men of integrity profess to have heard parts of it, but they all heard them when they were boys. . . . They remember names, and, perhaps, some proverbial sentiments; and, having no distinct ideas, coin a resemblance without an original.

The positive side of the controversy is perfectly represented by Blair in the quotation above. So far this is clear and understandable enough, and the only puzzle is why the controversy lasted so long, from 1760, when the *Fragments* were published, until 1805, when the Highland Society's *Report* came out. Part of the solution to this puzzle can be found in MacPherson's own behavior. When people request his originals, he invariably replies with a lament that the orthography of the manuscripts was so idiosyncratic that only he could comprehend it, and that he simply did not have time to do what only he was capable of. This defense is ingenious, and very difficult to argue with. At this time, Gaelic was singularly unavailable to those out of earshot. Spoken by thousands, it had lapsed out of texts. Even the Highland ministers, who delivered sermons in Gaelic, were largely illiterate in Gaelic itself; they were taught to read and write in English. Amongst those who could read Gaelic texts, the standards of orthography were not fixed, and would not be for another century. MacPherson could thus plausibly say that he had a manuscript that only he could read.

On the other side, these same factors strengthened Johnson's assertion that the Ossian poems had to be fakes because Gaelic was a language without texts, unwritten; it merely "floated in the breath of the people." Without the refinement generated by the presence of writing (a polished language, or literary language), Johnson says, all development is short-circuited: "diction, merely vocal, is always in its childhood." This is the unique quality about the case of Ossian. Both sides of the controversy are curiously insulated, insulated by the now-outlawed tartan plaid, the secrecy of the Highlander. This difficulty crops up in any discussion of Ossian, even in the attempt to define MacPherson's crime.

It should be clear by now that calling MacPherson a forger is true only in a qualified sense, as has been shown many times by the rehearsal of the following facts: in the eighteenth century, there were many poems in Gaelic that contained a persona called Ossian (*Osein*), most of which were in oral form, but some of which were in manuscript. MacPherson had some of these manuscripts, or at least one major manuscript, referred to as "The Red Book." Many parts of many of these poems make their way into MacPherson's **Ossian** books, translated fairly faithfully. Thus when Highlanders said that they heard the Ossian poems in their youth, they were telling the truth, as far as they knew, for MacPherson's poems were at least partly made up of the poems they had heard. The problem of identity, which Johnson touches on above, is a *real* problem, and should not be dismissed as simplemindedness or stubborn national pride. The Highland Committee, attempting to discover exactly what poems MacPherson had in his possession, was faced with answers like this from their Highland correspondents:

> I shall make no difficulty of thinking that the editor of Ossian's works has translated those parts of the original which were repeated in my hearing, I will not say with servile exactness, but on the whole inimitably well.

Inimitable, not servile: those terms are repeatedly applied to MacPherson's efforts. Calling a translation servile bolsters the authority or integrity of the *function* of the translator, even while condemning an actual instance of translation. The use of such a term implies that a strong or manly translator is not servile to his original, but somehow asserts his own integrity in the process of turning one language into another. He is not a mere functionary under the thumb of the original, but a writer in his own right; not simply handing the poem from one language to another, invisible, but adding transformation to translation. In MacPherson's case, there seems to be an air of

present fame to the term, as if one should not be too servile to the past, but respect and use the past. This becomes one way of defending MacPherson. Lord Webb Seymour, who took a tour in the Highlands and dabbled in Ossianic research, had poems recited to him in Gaelic and then translated, and spoke with people who claimed to have compared the English and Gaelic versions; but all he was able to say was that "in slight outline" the versions corresponded, or that he "found them to vary but little." The investigator, instead of confidently dividing sheep from goats as he would like, the false and derivative from the true, finds himself confronted with a curious mixed breed, neither one nor the other. If the task is not one of matching words, what is left of the problem?

This vexing and unavoidable confusion fueled the controversy. MacPherson's crime always threatened to degenerate into a matter of the theory of translation. This removes the focus of the critical eye from MacPherson's originals to his relationship to his originals, from forgery to skill. The role of the editor was, at this time, a large one; he was free to work over the materials, even to add things when this seemed appropriate (as Bishop Percy did). Was this MacPherson's crime? Was he just a bad translator? If he was a bad translator, it was not his actual text that was at fault, but the relationship of that text to the original. His problem would be that he had been too independent (hadn't been servile enough), that he had not let the original guide him completely enough but had added parts of himself to someone else's work. He would be guilty of not having enough respect for the inheritance of tradition, of not being a faithful part of the long chain of passing-on that delivers the past to the present. To this could be answered, as above, that the twist MacPherson puts in the chain of tradition is just the translator's job: he produces not a copy but a literal *version*, a version that another culture can absorb.

This problem, though not solvable in any clear way, would have disappeared quietly enough if the originals had been available; people could have made their own decisions, but at least they would have been arguing a question of poetics and not one of morality. MacPherson's refusal to produce his originals, however, was taken as proof of their forgery, as well as of the general perversity of the man. He did have originals, in some form, which some people knew, so that his answer that it was simply too complicated to put them into a form appropriate for inspection sounded plausible. This is the center of the voiced controversy, but this textual matter is only a ruse, a diversion from the real problems, which Johnson illustrates so well, and which is summed up by the thoughts of another Highland visitor, William Shaw. In his "Enquiry into the Authenticity of the poems ascribed to Ossian" (1782), he describes asking some Highlanders to produce some poems of Ossian. He expects his witnesses to produce manuscripts,

> but instead of going to their cabinet for manuscripts, or copies of them, as I expected, application was made to some old man, or superannuated fiddler, who repeated over again the tales of the 15th century.

Here again is the old man, the repository of tradition, and Shaw's disgust is the disgust of the foreigner, the outsider, to whom this tradition is meaningless, as well as the disgust of the literate for the illiterate and the young for the old. As Johnson says, Gaelic floats on the breath of the Highland peasant, and he and Shaw find the presence of poetry in these circumstances simply unbelievable, or simply silly, not worth considering if it exists (it is not really poetry). For them, "original" means "written": they wanted manuscripts, not memories. It seems as though Johnson would have been satisfied with transcripts of the original recitals, but even these were not available. The possibility, in an oral tradition, for variation or mutability obliterates any meaning Johnson might recognize in the word "original." As he says, he thinks that people, when they recognize Ossian, coin a resemblance without an original, like people using an unsound currency. He is disturbed, in fact, by the shadowy presence of the cognate "originality" (what Ossian has, the voice that comes to him), and the possibility that the Ossian poems could be a record of someone else's originality, even MacPherson's. Chasing these poems would seem to be as fruitless as chasing the wind, a wind that threatens to be simply the inspiration of whomever you are talking to. To someone who had not found his poems being recited, MacPherson could always answer, "well, I heard them, but the people who told them to me have died; so perhaps their poetry died with them." What could be said to this? MacPherson could claim that his poems are themselves originals, the first capture of oral materials.

Part of the reason people distrusted oral poetry was that they had difficulty believing that an oral tradition could be resilient and sturdy enough to survive the hundreds of years between composition and capture. The cusp of transmission bothers Johnson, for instance; diction is always in its childhood in a nonliterate society because transmission of the past is impossible, and each generation must start from scratch. This was a popular subject for speculation, and most of the explanations for successful transmission went something like this:

> Language is changed from its use in society, as coins are smoothed by their currency in circulation. If the one be locked up among a rude, remote, and unconnected people, like the other when it is buried in the earth, its great features and general form will be but little altered.

This invokes a principle of mixture (or circulation), and the accurate transmission of past language depends on the culture remaining pure, in an unmixed state:

> At a distance from the seat of government, and secured, by the inaccessibleness of their country, [Highlanders] were free and independent. As they had little communication with strangers, the customs of their ancestors remained among them, and their language retained its original purity.

These are familiar *topoi* of the eighteenth century, where purity is associated with the primitive, and where the

retention of the qualities of the primitive, the qualities of Ossian, depends on the parallel retention of purity. These *topoi* extend as far as poetics, and primitive people are said to "display themselves to one another without disguise: and converse and act in the uncovered simplicity of nature," making them naturally poetic. This state is usually described as coming before commerce, and before Art, and here it also comes before the need for translations of any kind. Mixture, we could say, would be easy, unimpeded by the difficulties of modern language. The refreshing qualities of the primitive were what the Ossian poems seemed to bring with them from the past, true remains, communicating their freshness and especially their simplicity to an age that had grown beyond such things. This simplicity is always tied to boldness, boldness of imagination, and in the anthropomorphic historical model, this boldness is attributed to the youth of mankind, just as it is the domain of actual youth:

> The powers of imagination are most vigorous and predominant in youth; those of the understanding ripen more slowly, and often attain not to their maturity, till the imagination begin to flag. Hence, poetry, which is the child of the imagination, is frequently most glowing and animated in the first ages of society. As the ideas of our youth are remembered with a peculiar pleasure on account of their liveliness and vivacity; so the most ancient poems have often proved the greatest favorites among nations. [Blair]

In the language I applied to the poems, the losses of age are compensated by the memories of youth, and the natural result is that the memories of youth are contained in the oldest of poems, as old Ossian contains his past.

The other ancient poems are, of course, those of Homer, and Ossian is compared to Homer in a very specific way by Blair. When describing the Aristotelean regularities of Ossian, he dismisses any astonishment over their existence by insisting that Ossian is nature, like Homer, and that "Aristotle studied nature in Homer". Ossian is pre-rule, part of the basis from which rules are derived. This explanation of the disturbingly western features of Ossian (that he got them from the original, nature) was a popular one, as popular as attacking MacPherson on these grounds. Malcolm Laing, in the last year of the controversy, brought out an edition of the poems in which he claimed to trace "every simile, and almost every poetical image" to sources in western tradition. The bizarre energy of Laing's effort is a perfect example of the power of rule as it is embodied in tradition, and of the release MacPherson could obtain by exploiting a manipulated history. MacPherson's picture of inheritance is conservative but enriching, ancient but refreshing. Opposed to this is the tradition of the West, which produces a mind like Laing's, where the present and the future are obliterated by their original, the past. Originality is defined as simply that quality that generates rules, and makes for its own extinction. Transmission of a culture like the one Laing reflects turns all composition into translation, and his edition of Ossian is an example, where he decodes MacPherson to find the original language "with which the author's mind was previously impregnated," impregnated by the winds of tradition.

Here I need to collect my metaphors again. Ossian is praised for his "originality," meaning his presence at the origin, and he is placed, in the hierarchy of tradition, at the very top, the place where rules begin. These rules are the definition of a classical tradition: they define what poetry is and can be. It is the circumventing of the power of rules, the bold and the simple, that reasonable moderns find so pleasing in the poems. Their simplicity is the simplicity of gold, which refreshes us by its refusal to compromise with baser material, by its permanence. It is this simplicity that MacPherson insists makes for the possibility of translation, that makes it possible to appreciate the poems even when they are robbed of their native dress. Their simplicity has been retained by their lack of circulation, by the impregnable Highlands, and so their simplicity is a result of their being unknown. They are a treasure, which MacPherson can rescue from non-circulating burial in the secrecy of the Highlands, and translate into the modern world.

Those who criticize MacPherson say one of two things: either that he refused to be guided by the rules of inheritance, and deformed and re-forged what he received by "translating" it into something else, or that the whole ethos of earliness is nonsense, that "primitive poetry" is an oxymoron, and that MacPherson is only trying to escape the consequences of the lateness of the age by palming his own originality off as primal simplicity. In both cases he violates what we might call laws of currency, laws of a system in which something stands in for an original. In the first, he undermines the value of the translation by not properly fixing the relationship of representative to original, and in the second he is guilty of pretending that he has a gold original when in fact all he has is the translation.

Tied to this is a contradictory, or oxymoronic, arrangement of youth and age. Because of their extreme age, the Ossian poems are productions of humanity's youth, and remind us of that youth; because of his extreme age, Ossian is reduced to singing about his youth. Because the Highlands remained retarded, youthful, these productions of old age were preserved from the deformations of younger times. The oxymoron appears on the simplest of levels, in the fact that the person behind the hoary persona is the twenty-five-year old MacPherson. Linked to this is the social problem the Highland Committee encountered: that the tradition that underwriters MacPherson's effort is in the memories of the superannuated, those who have lived beyond the destruction of their culture, or, worse yet, *was* in their possession, for they may have died.

To admit that the retrieval of these poems is an exhumation is to admit that the refusal on the part of the Highlanders to mix with the rest of Britain retained the purity that transmits the freshness of youth to us. For loyal British subjects, this might be hard to admit, for this very purity, this resistance to the impregnation of western culture, was the danger that lurked in the Highlands until it appeared openly in 1745. Even the appealing parts of Ossian, his boldness, loyalty, martial vigor, and romance, were the qualities so strongly attached to Bonny Charlie and the '45. By retaining their "early" culture, the Highlanders remained free from the "toil and business, which engross the attention of a commercial people." That we have come to know these poems is a sign that what preserved them has passed, and that the Highlanders, wrapped up in their new habits, absorbed by a commercial people, have in some way been robbed of their treasure. To have them at all is completely sufficient to describe the mixture that destroys things like them.

As a way of starting to conclude, I re-ask the most important questions about the Ossian episode. What was MacPherson's crime? And why did he do it, what profit did he stand to gain? In the way of answering the second question first, I offer a different formulation of it, put in the form of an objection to questions about MacPherson's honesty:

> none but a madman, or a wild enthusiast, could think of forfeiting his honesty, and disclaiming the merit of his own compositions, merely to gratify the imaginary honour of having been born in the corner of a country which, perhaps, 1500 years ago, chanced to produce a bard of some merit.

The simplest answer to this riddle is money. MacPherson stood to gain a lot of money as a result of his fame, and indeed he did, from the various positions he was able to obtain (most notably, agent for the Nabob of Arcot). This is perhaps to be guilty of the same lack of imagination that the above writer is guilty of, to ignore the way such a ruse could ease the burden of the past, to ignore the possibility that MacPherson perpetrated his scheme in order to find his way into a canon otherwise (apparently) closed. But fame is another name for the canon, and money is just the material and modern representative of fame, a palpable expression of why people want to be famous. Money does what we so often think modernity does, reducing things to their basal materialities: "living on" in fame becomes a statement about estates and everyday material concerns. Fame and money were hard to come by in the depths of the North, which seemed to offer only its own peculiarities as a possible commodity, and so MacPherson's course appears clever, even inspired.

From here we can answer the other question. MacPherson was guilty of fraud, but not the simple fraud he has become famous for. What he did with the inheritance of the Highlander is nothing worse than absorption, that respectable bardic activity; and his manipulations might also be called bardic, an exploitation of the possibilities of tradition. He adapted the Gaelic tradition to the modern world. Even modern scholars thank him for saving "The Red Book" from the tailor's scissors, and he was largely responsible for the explosion of activity in the nineteenth century that did in fact save many parts of Gaelic culture from complete disappearance. His crime is apart from these scholarly matters.

MacPherson's activity stands as an emblem for the movement of his culture into Britain, and his picture is one of ease and humility, of handing the dark past to the present, the mountain people to the Lowlanders, with one easy gesture. This, he says, is possible because of the golden integrity of his originals, for gold is always easy to circulate: its virtues are pan-cultural, recognized by every eye. This gold is the inheritance of every Gael, but, as the eighteenth century wears on, it becomes painfully clear that the golden part is just a metaphor, and that it is in fact a mark of danger, something to be obliterated (what it represents, the integrity of the Highlander, is dangerous). The Ossian poems make it equally clear that this obliteration can take the form of a feast on the remnants of Highland culture. MacPherson's crime is the preparation of this feast, and his fraud is in his ease. He substitutes simplicity for nakedness, and in doing so he makes it seem that the mixing of the Highlander with the rest of Britain, the whisking away of the tartan, is painless, or even joyful (the joy of grief). He pretends that it does not leave the humble Highlander simply naked. He (and here he is standing as a representative of many, including Blair) covers over the essential immiscibility of the Highlander, and the destruction that would have to take place before mixture.

His arguments about poetry are versions of this fraudulent ease, and here the fraud is plainly an underhanded way of portraying his own genius. The Ossian poems, products of genius, easily pass from version to version, in the hands of genius. Form is erased, essence is transmitted, and the forms of culture, the Gaelic rhyme or the tartan plaid, are left as tokens of locality, unimportant and unnecessary. The ease of mixture, of absorbtion, is utterly dependent on this erasure of distinguishing form. Thus another way of defining the fraud is to say that MacPherson pretends that the magic of the ancient can be separated from its material form, which returns us to saying that MacPherson fraudulently claims that the Highlander, be it Ossian or his descendants, can be translated with primitive virtues intact: that the poems can be divested of foreignness without loss. The potion thus prepared is an imperial elixir, a cure for the ills that a highly wrought culture develops, and preparation of the elixir does not damage the source of the cure. A crime this complex needs a name, or a category; we may call it the crime of Pastoral: "Pastoral" to describe the way the virtues of the primitive are depicted as translatable, and the way this translation pretends that the resulting mixture is not unstable or exploitive; and "crime" because, as I have been saying, this picture cannot be realized without pain.

Of course the poems have a bad conscience, and the drama of Ossian, the old blind bard, is the drama of the extinction of a culture. I have traced other features of this bad conscience, particularly in MacPherson's replacement of inspiration with money. This bad conscience can, tentatively, be associated with the failure of MacPherson's vision, the general and complete lapsing of the Ossian poems from the canon. This gives a rather constructive interpretation to the power of the canon, which seems at least partly suspect, but we can say that the charms of

Ossian, the charms of the primitive, gradually lost their magic, and the fraud, as I have described it, became, eventually, all too clear.

Maurice Colgan (lecture date 1986)

SOURCE: "Ossian: Success or Failure for the Scottish Enlightenment?" in *Aberdeen and the Enlightenment: Proceedings of a Conference Held at the University of Aberdeen,* edited by Jennifer J. Carter and Joan H. Pittock, Aberdeen University Press, 1987, pp. 344-49.

[*In the following essay, originally delivered as a lecture in 1986, Colgan traces some of the contemporary influences on Macpherson's poetic vision and argues that Scottish intellectual culture bears at least some responsibility for his literary deceptions.*]

Literary historians do not find it difficult to explain the European-wide interest in James Macpherson's 'translations' from the Gaelic of the ancient bard, Ossian. The Enlightenment, still very interested in the classical world, did not want to be confined to it. Non-classical cultures offered varieties of literary diet and alternative insights into human nature and society: they were part of the expanding consciousness of the age. Primitive cultures appeared to have most to offer, with their imagination and feeling uninhibited by belief in rationality as the essence of humanity, and by classical rules of composition. One of the most influential works taking this viewpoint was Thomas Blackwell's *An Enquiry into the Life and Writings of Homer* (1735). Blackwell lectured at Marischal College, Aberdeen, where Macpherson studied. The question of the relationship between primitive society and genius was one of those discussed at meetings of the Aberdeen Philosophical Society, founded in 1758.

The germination of these theories in Macpherson's mind led him to the belief that in his native Highlands there had existed such a primitive society. Could it have produced a poet of Homeric quality? In 1755, the headmaster of Dunkeld Academy, Jerome Stone, wrote to the *Scots Magazine* to arouse the interest of its readers in the great number of poems which he claimed were available in Gaelic, 'some of them of great antiquity.' To his communication he added as an example a translation of one poem. After Stone's death Macpherson gained access to some of his manuscripts, and also to the Dean of Lismore's collection, in which several of the poems are headed, 'Auctor hujus Ossin.' This was that Ossian whom Macpherson later was to claim flourished in the third century A.D.

Edinburgh Enlightenment circles were aware of the primitivist theories of Blackwell and his followers, but Highland Gaelic culture was a closed book to them. John Home, the minister-playwright, had his interest aroused when he was a prisoner of the Jacobite army after the Battle of Falkirk in 1746. Through a fellow-prisoner, an English officer with whom he became friendly, he later met William Collins. Their reminiscences of the Jacobite Highlanders inspired Collins to write his 'Ode on the Popular

Superstitions of the Highlands of Scotland,' which was an admonition to Home to leave the metropolitan literary world and delve more deeply into Gaelic culture. Knowing Home's interest, Adam Ferguson, the only Gaelic speaker in Enlightenment circles, gave Macpherson a letter of introduction to him.

Travelling as tutor to a gentleman's son, Macpherson caught up with Home at Moffat, Dumfries, which was then a spa. He had copies of the poems in his possession, which he translated for Home, who was impressed. Alexander Carlyle, who was introduced to Macpherson on the Moffat bowling green a few days later, was 'perfectly astonished at the poetical genius displayed' in the translations. Next to be contacted was the Rev. Hugh Blair, who was just about to become Professor of Rhetoric and Belles Lettres in the University of Edinburgh. Blair found himself in the rare and advantageous situation of being able to announce the discovery of a literature hitherto unknown to the civilized world. Most astonishing of all was that it had been found, not in remotest Tahiti or Ceylon, but almost on Edinburgh's doorstep. The *Fragments of Ancient Poetry Collected in the Highlands of Scotland* was published in 1760, and in the preface Macpherson claimed that the poems were probably part of an epic. Blair organised a subscription to finance an expedition to the Highlands by Macpherson to search for the epic, which was found and published as *Fingal* (1761). A second expedition, on which Home accompanied Macpherson, was partly financed by the Earl of Bute, the King's favourite, who was shortly to become Prime Minister. This resulted in the discovery of another epic, *Temora,* published in 1763.

Translations into Italian, German, French, and other languages excited even greater interest in Ossian in Europe than in Britain, and inspired the recovery and dissemination of other national literatures. Artists and composers throughout the Continent created visual and musical equivalents of ideas and emotions released by reading Ossian, of which Mendelssohn's 'Fingal's Cave' is only the best known. Nationalism, as an ideology, owes much to Macpherson. The great philosopher of nationalism, J. G. Herder, collaborated with Goethe on a work entitled *Von Deutscher Art und Kunst* (1773), to which he contributed an essay, 'On Ossian and the Songs of Ancient Peoples.' This, and another essay on Shakespeare in the same volume, are described by a recent editor as displaying 'a degree of imaginative historical understanding hitherto unprecedented in the German Enlightenment.' It was that expansion of historical understanding, and the new appreciation of non-classical cultures that resulted from it, that marked the success of Ossian.

When the particular effect of Ossian on the appreciation of Gaelic literary culture is studied, however, the story is a different one. Samuel Johnson, who appears to have been immune to the vogue for the primitive, regarded Ossian from the start as a forgery. The Highlanders, as a mainly illiterate people, were, he believed, incapable of an epic, or, indeed, of any worthwhile poetry. They were even incapable of remembering anything:

In an unwritten speech, nothing that is not very short is transmitted from one generation to another. Few have opportunities of hearing a long composition often enough to learn it, or have inclination to repeat it so often as is necessary to retain it; and what is once forgotten is lost forever.

But most preferred to believe Hugh Blair, whose *A Critical Dissertation on the Poems of Ossian, the Son of Fingal,* often reprinted with the poems, guaranteed both the authenticity of Ossian and the superlative moral and aesthetic qualities of primitive Highland society. *Critical Observations on the Poems of Ossian* by another formidable scholar, Lord Kames, added weight to the cause. When pressed to show his originals, Macpherson said that they had already been displayed in his publisher's window, but his critics had not bothered to look there. After his death, the Highland Society of Scotland set up a Committee of Inquiry into Ossian. After eight years of investigation, the committee reported in 1805 that Ossianic poetry existed in the Highlands in great abundance; that Macpherson had added and suppressed passages and changed the general tone; and that it was unable to find any one poem 'the same in title and tenor with the poems published by him.' Stated thus baldly, these conclusions sound damning, but in the body of the report, hedged about with qualifications, and preceded by the evidence of witnesses who believed in Macpherson's authenticity, they appear much less emphatic. During his lifetime, Highlanders in the service of the East India Company raised a thousand pounds to publish the original Gaelic poems of Ossian. Such a gesture by well-wishers could not be rejected, and Macpherson himself wrote that no excuse, 'but want of leisure,' could prevent him from commencing the work in 'a very few months.' That was in 1784.

At the time of his death in 1796, the supposed preparation of the originals was still incomplete, but in 1805 the Highland Society of London was able to publish the Gaelic Ossian in three volumes, with a Latin translation on facing pages. This helped to bolster Macpherson's reputation in the nineteenth century, but modern scholarship has demonstrated that the Gaelic is a translation of Macpherson's *English* Ossian.

The appearance of the 'Gaelic' Ossian was the finishing touch to an episode that must be regarded as the most successful forgery in literary history. Macpherson's audacious mode of operation was to take poems which he sometimes imperfectly understood, and alter them radically in 'translations' tailored to meet the demands of those eager to read the compositions of a bard of ancient times. When the originals, which he himself had used, were presented as evidence of his inaccuracy, he denounced them as spurious fifteenth-century Irish versions of his third-century poems. A minister in Argyll and Mull, the Rev. Archibald MacArthur, stopped collecting Gaelic poems because he came to believe that those he was finding were of the kind Macpherson had denounced as spurious. Even before the publication of Macpherson's *Frag-*

ments, Archibald Fletcher of Glenorchy, who was illiterate, had recited Ossianic poems to neighbours, who wrote them down. The manuscript eventually found its way to the Advocates' Library in Edinburgh, where the cover was marked 'Corrupt copies'—corrupt because they did not tally with Macpherson's versions! It took John Francis Campbell, the great nineteenth-century collector of folklore, thirty years to convince himself that Macpherson was a forger. His *Leabhar na Feinne* (1872) printed all known Ossianic poems in Gaelic, but included nothing by Macpherson. Macpherson's supporters—and he still had many—ignored Campbell's work. Others had become so sceptical that *any* Ossianic poetry was associated with the bogus, and, like the work of another famous Scot, *Leabhar na Feinne* fell still-born from the press. Because of lack of interest the second volume, which was to have given the English translations, was never published.

Some of the texts Campbell used were from Ireland, the original homeland of Gaelic culture, and one of these was Charlotte Brooke's *Reliques of Irish Poetry* (1789). Aware of the controversy surrounding Macpherson, Miss Brooke was careful to give the sources of her translations. A later development in Ireland was the bringing together of a small group of Gaelic scholars between 1834 and 1837 to work on the historical and topographical aspects of the Irish Ordnance Survey. One of them, Eugene or Eoin O'Curry, devoted the rest of his life to the listing and study of ancient Irish manuscripts both literary and historical, some of which had been discovered during the survey. An Irish Ossianic Society was founded in Dublin in 1853 to publish these manuscripts, but the language was often so archaic that many words and even sentences could not be understood. Enough, however, was revealed to inspire the Irish Literary Renaissance at the turn of the century. W. B. Yeats and the other writers involved used Standish James O'Grady's *History of Ireland,* published between 1878 and 1880. As his title implies, O'Grady believed that the literature was recounting historical facts. Because his sources were still fragmentary, he made major additions and revisions, but at least he knew that the Ossianic and Ulster epic cycles, which Macpherson had confused, were different.

The breakthrough which enabled the old manuscripts to be understood and assessed came neither in Scotland nor in Ireland. A German philologist, Johann Caspar Zeuss, was looking at some early medieval Irish manuscripts in the monastery of Würzburg when he was struck by the number of root-words similar to some in Sanskrit, and by the archaic nature of the language. He decided to study old Gaelic and the result was the publication in 1853 of *Grammatica Celtica,* a landmark in Indo-European philology. He was followed by several generations of scholars who had come to the conclusion that the language was Western Europe's oldest vernacular. One of them, Kuno Meyer, asked himself, if the language were so archaic, would not the literature be so, too? In the introduction to his *Selections from Ancient Irish Poetry* (1911) he wrote:

Slowly . . . the fact is becoming recognised . . . that the vernacular literature of ancient Ireland is the most primitive . . . among the literatures of Western Europe . . . its importance as the earliest voice from the dawn of West European civilisation cannot be denied.

This point was taken up by Kenneth Jackson when he delivered a public lecture in Cambridge in 1964 on the earlier of the two Gaelic epic cycles, the *Táin Bó Cuailnge* ('The Cattle Raid of Cooley') to which he gave the subtitle, 'A Window on the Iron Age'. His point was that the *Táin,* believed by some scholars to date as far back as the first century B.C., is our only literary evidence for the culture of Iron Age Europe, which is otherwise known only from archaeology. Publication in 1969 of an English translation of the *Táin* by Thomas Kinsella has demonstrated to the world that it is also great literature. These developments, from Zeuss to Kinsella, have passed Scotland by. Apart from a handful of Celtic scholars, everyone's vision is still blinkered by Macpherson. In a work entitled *History of Scottish Literature,* which typically ignores any Gaelic writing, Maurice Lindsay says, 'No amount of high-toned purist condemnation gets over the fact that Macpherson's influence in Europe was immense.' There is no mention that the same Macpherson frustrated for nearly 150 years the recovery of an indigenous literary culture of greater antiquity and quality than even he had claimed! If, as his nineteenth-century biographer, Bailey Saunders [in *The Life and Letters of James Macpherson*], 1894 and the more recent writer, Richard Sher [in *Church and University in the Scottish Enlightenment,* 1985], have claimed, Macpherson was led into the path of deception by the demands of the Edinburgh literati of the time, the failure is as much theirs as his.

Leah Leneman (lecture date 1986)

SOURCE: "The Effects of Ossian in Lowland Scotland," in *Aberdeen and the Enlightenment: Proceedings of a Conference Held at the University of Aberdeen,* edited by Jennifer J. Carter and Joan H. Pittock, Aberdeen University Press, 1987, pp. 357-62.

[*In the following essay, originally delivered as a lecture in 1986, Leneman describes how Macpherson's poetry influenced the Scottish perception of the Highlands.*]

In the first half of the eighteenth century the Highlands held no appeal for Lowland Scots. The scenery had no attraction, as evidenced by descriptions such as Daniel Defoe's 'frightful country full of hidious desert mountains.' The language was considered barbarous and the people were seen as superstitious and incorrigibly idle. Indeed, their whole way of life seemed an offence against the Calvinist work ethic.

The only attraction which the Highlands had at this time was *potential.* If the Highlanders could be remade in the image of Lowlanders—learn to speak English, become honest, hardworking, and industrious, discover the delights of true religion, and become imbued with the principles of the Glorious Revolution—then the area might become peaceful and prosperous instead of warlike and poor.

As far as the reformers were concerned there was nothing to be weighed in the balance against these benefits. If someone had suggested to them (no one did) that perhaps there was much joy to be gained from singing songs and reciting poetry in a language rich in such productions; that a conviction of kinship with the chief of the clan might give a feeling of worth to every man however poor and lowly; that hospitality, generosity and loyalty were virtues not to be despised; and that hardiness, endurance and the ability to withstand extremes of cold and hunger were in any way admirable, the response would have been utter incomprehension. The Highlanders were 'savages'; no one in the early eighteenth century was interested in observing them or in learning more about them. The aim was to 'civilise' them.

After the '45 it became necessary to get to grips with the Highlands. The strand of thought which dominated the pre-1745 attitude toward the Highlands—that the whole of the *Gaidhealtachd* should be refashioned in the image of the Lowlands—can be found in the aftermath of the rising, particularly in the debate which took place within the pages of the *Scots Magazine* in 1746. One writer enjoined compassion on the 'poor ignorant men, whose whole way of life rendered them incapable of enjoying the benefit, and insensible of the blessing of a mild and gracious government, and so more liable to be drawn into the snare by the subtle insinuations of their chiefs'. The notion of the common people as slaves who could be redeemed and rendered respectable citizens if only they were removed from the sway of their chiefs is one which recurs frequently in this period.

The idea of 'civilising' the Highlands could be illustrated from many other sources, but the theme of this paper is the very different stream of thought which became prevalent after the publication of James Macpherson's 'Ossianic' poems in the early 1760s. This stream of thought also started from the premise that the Highlanders were 'savage', but it came to a different conclusion, because the primitivist ideas which were so intrinsic to Enlightenment thinking saw virtue in 'savage' societies. Important seeds were sown by the publication of Jerome Stone's translation (or, rather, adaptation) of a fine old Gaelic elegy in the *Scots Magazine* in January 1756, for it made it feasible to consider the possibility of more fine ancient poetry emanating from the 'savage' Highlands. Clearly it was this belief that made John Home, and later Hugh Blair and others, so eager to accept the fragments and then the 'epic' which James Macpherson presented to them. Similarly, the belief already in existence, that primitive societies were not just braver and bolder than modern societies but also somehow more refined and nobler of spirit, made it easy for the literati to accept the type of society which Macpherson pictured for them in the Ossianic poems. The frequency with which Ossian was subsequently invoked to 'prove' such theories is evidence enough of this.

A great deal of attention has been given to the effect of Ossian on Germany and other Continental countries but very little to how it affected Lowland Scots. The effects were threefold, but they coalesced to form a new image of the Highlands.

First of all, Ossian provided a new way of looking at wild and desolate scenery. 'Sublimity' is the key concept here. Hugh Blair's writing enlarged the theme considerably and his ideas gained wide credence. A sublime object, according to Blair, 'produces a sort of internal elevation and expansion; it raises the mind much above its ordinary state; and fills it with a degree of wonder and astonishment'. Flowery fields were not conducive to sublimity, 'but the hoary mountain, and the solitary lake; the aged forest, and the torrent falling over the rock'. The way in which so much of the scenery of the Highlands conforms to these ideas of the sublime is an important element in the impact of Ossian.

The question of whether Blair's ideas about sublimity preceded or post-dated Ossian is an interesting one and can probably best be answered by saying, 'both'. Blair's published material appeared after **Fingal** and **Temora,** and he used Ossianic examples to illustrate his points. Blair's biographer summed up the situation: 'Macpherson's stuff was meat for Blair's theories, and Blair's theories were, one suspects, the food on which Macpherson's poetical efforts throve and flourished' [R.N. Smitz, *Hugh Blair,* 1948].

The new way of looking at Highland scenery may be illustrated by the following passage from a book entitled *Observations relative chiefly to Picturesque Beauty made in the year 1776, on several parts of Great Britain; particularly the High-Lands of Scotland* by William Gilpin. Referring to remarks made by Samuel Johnson about his tour of the Highlands, Gilpin writes [in *Observations Relative Chiefly to Picturesque Beauty . . . ,* 1789]:

> It is true indeed, that an eye, like Dr Johnson's, which is accustomed to see the beauties of landscape *only in flowery pastures, and waving harvests,* cannot be attracted to the great, and sublime in nature . . . Dr. Johnson says, the Scotch mountain has the appearance of matter *incapable of form, or usefulness . . . as for it's being incapable of form,* he can mean only that it cannot be formed into cornfields, and meadows. Its form as a mountain is unquestionably grand and sublime in the highest degree. For that poverty in objects, or *simplicity,* as it may be called, which no doubt injures the beauty of a Scottish landscape; is certainly at the same time the source of *sublimity.*

Not everyone was able to respond to Highland scenery in this way, but in the post-Ossianic era every visitor knew how he or she was expected to respond. This is beautifully captured in the following remarks by Mrs Anne Grant of Laggan, who was born in the Highlands but spent most of her childhood in America, before returning in 1773:

> When I came . . . to Scotland, Ossian obtained a

complete ascendant over my imagination . . . Thus determined to like the Highlands; a most unexpected occurrence carried me, in my seventeenth year, to reside there, and that at Abertarfe, the most beautiful place in it; yet it is not easy to say how much I was repelled and disappointed. In vain I tried to raise my mind to the tone of sublimity. The rocky divisions that rose with so much majesty in description, seemed like enormous prison walls, confining caitiffs in the narrow glen. These, too, seemed like the dreary abode of solitude and silence. These feelings, however, I did not even whisper to the rushes. [*Essays on the Superstitions of the Highlanders of Scotland,* 1811]

After she had lived there for some time, Anne Grant became a passionate advocate of the Highlands and Highlanders, but her initial reaction is certainly revealing.

Apart from the supposed appeal of the sublime in general, the enormous success of Ossian also gave the Highlands specific associations. When Charles Cordiner, a minister from Banff who was asked by Thomas Pennant to draw some picturesque scenes of Highland Scotland, visited a locality connected with Ossian, he not only described the scene at length, with appropriate quotations from **Temora,** he also included a blind harper in the foreground of his picture of the waterfall.

Robert Burns certainly fell under the Ossianic spell. In September 1786, when he returned to Edinburgh after a tour which included Highland Perthshire, he wrote to his brother Gilbert, hardly mentioning the last stages of his journey for, as he put it, '[wa]rm as I was from Ossian's country where I had seen his very grave, what cared I for fisher-towns and fertile carses?'

In Tobias Smollett's novel, *Humphry Clinker,* the character of Jery, who is depicted as a very ordinary, down-to-earth young man, writes to a friend from the Highlands: 'I feel an enthusiastic pleasure when I survey the brown heath that Ossian wont to tread; and hear the wind whistle through the bending grass—When I enter our landlord's hall, I look for the suspended harp of that divine poet, and listen in hopes of hearing the aerial sound of his respected spirit.'

However, for Lowland visitors to the Highlands it was not simply a question of losing themselves in associations with a literary past; they also saw present-day Highlanders in a new light. The surroundings in which they lived were said to have had a profound effect on the Ossianic heroes, and those surroundings had not changed significantly over the centuries, so it followed that eighteenth-century Highlanders possessed many of the same qualities as their noble ancestors. Anne Grant writes of 'the hold which long-descended habits of thinking, heightened by wild poetry and wilder scenery, took of even the more powerful intellect, giving to the whole national character a cast of "dreary sublimity" as an elegant critic has happily expressed it, altogether unique and peculiar'.

This new perception made Highlanders acceptable in a way which would hitherto have been unimaginable. It is significant to note that one of Anne Grant's books was

entitled *Essays on the Superstitions of the Highlanders,* for in the Romantic era superstitions were not to be despised; they added to the mystical aura of primitive societies. It is fascinating to recall that Anne Grant actually lived among Highlanders, and her books do reveal a good deal of perception about them. For example, she writes of the Highlander that 'he perfectly comprehends that we know many things of which he is ignorant; but then he thinks, first, that in his situation, none of those things would make him better or happier, though he did know them; and, next, that he possesses abilities to acquire all that is valuable in knowledge, if accident had thrown him in the way of culture'. This is all very commonsensical, yet at the same time she can turn them into living exemplars of the primitivist idea, as in the following extract:

The importance and necessity, in a country thus enervated by luxury, thus lost in frivolous pursuits and vain speculations, to cherish in whatsoever remote obscurity they exist, a hardy manly Race, inured to Suffering, fearless of Danger, and careless of Poverty, to invigorate Society by their Spirit, to defend it by their Courage, and to adorn it with those Virtues that bloom in the shade, but are ready to wither away in the sunshine of prosperity. [*The Highlanders and Other Poems,* 3rd. ed., 1810]

It seems to me that Anne Grant is inhabiting two worlds simultaneously, a real one and a mythological or idealised one. She did in fact become proficient enough at the Gaelic language to translate some old poems, and her translations, while versified to suit current taste, are close enough to the originals to be recognisable. However, when she switched to writing her own poetry it became full of sentimental clichés. Here are just three lines from *The Highlanders:*

Where ancient Chieftains rul'd those green
    retreats,
And faithful Clans delighted to obey
The kind behests of patriarchal sway.

It is noteworthy that in the course of half a century clan chiefs have been transformed from ruthless oppressors to kindly patriarchs.

Anne Grant was by no means the only person capable of inhabiting the two worlds simultaneously. Patrick Graham, who contributed one of the century's numerous essays on the 'authenticity' of Ossian, observed that 'the prospect which perpetually engages the eye of the Highlander, of barren heath, lofty mountains, rugged precipices, and wide stretched lakes, has a natural tendency to call forth sentiments of sublimity, which are unfavourable to frivolousness of thought'. Now Patrick Graham was in fact minister at Aberfoyle, and one can scarcely credit that he did not come into contact with some 'frivolousness of thought' in his daily contact with parishioners. Indeed, in the same publication quoted above he wrote: 'to such scenery as the Trossachs exhibit, the natives attribute no beauty. They consider such scenes as horrible; and however attached they may be to their native soil, they sigh after an exchange of such abodes, for the rich and level plains of the low-country. To enjoy these scenes, the culture of taste is requisite'. If the 'culture of taste' is necessary, then what becomes of the natural tendency of the scenery to call forth sentiments of sublimity?

A final quotation—from Francis Jeffrey's review of *The Lady of the Lake* [*Edinburgh Review*, August, 1810]—seems to me to encapsulate the new view of the Highlands. It will be noted that all the things which everyone wanted to destroy before, and immediately after, the '45 are the very things which are here being lauded:

> There are few persons, we believe, of any degree of poetical susceptibility, who have wandered among the secluded vallies of the Highlands, and contemplated the singular people by whom they are still tenanted—with their love of music and of song—their hardy and irregular life, so unlike the unvarying toils of the Saxon mechanic—their devotion to their chiefs—their wild and lofty traditions—their national enthusiasm—the melancholy grandeur of the scenes they inhabit—and the multiplied superstitions which still linger among them,—without feeling, that there is no existing people so well adapted for the purposes of poetry, or so capable of furnishing the occasions of new and striking inventions.

I am certainly not arguing that Ossian led to a greater understanding of Gaelic culture on the part of Lowlanders. The eighteenth century was the era of some of the finest Gaelic poetry ever composed, but this genuine poetry was largely ignored by the Lowlanders who lapped up Ossian. Ossian was eagerly accepted because it chimed in so well with Enlightenment ideas about primitive societies, and because it fulfilled a genuine need by transforming a hitherto unacceptable section of the Scottish population into one which was universally admired.

Ian Heywood (essay date 1986)

SOURCE: "Ossian: The Voice of the Past," in *The Making of History: A Study of the Literary Forgeries of James Macpherson and Thomas Chatterton in Relation to Eighteenth-Century Ideas of History and Fiction*, Fairleigh Dickinson University Press, 1986, 73-100.

[*In the following excerpt from his book-length study of literary forgeries, Heywood examines the evolution of Macpherson's fictitious historical vision.*]

To understand fully Macpherson's making of history, it is necessary to look at his forgery as it evolved. Like Chatterton, the historical vision manifested itself accumulatively with each new item. The forgeries were a process. The focus of our analysis in this [essay] will be on method: the mode of access to the past; the authenticating procedures used. The manner in which each new forged work related to previous ones and in hindsight to later ones was a crucial aspect of this method. Both forgers were extremely skilled in using devices such as interallusion, anticipation, and fulfillment. Macpherson began

with "fragments" of ancient Erse poetry and progressed to complete and finished epics. Macpherson was given a free rein as to how his forgery appeared in print. It is possible then to study the evolution of his vision by taking each text in the order of original publication.

In 1760 appeared *Fragments of Ancient Poetry, Collected in the Highlands of Scotland, and Translated from the Gaelic or Erse Language*. The anthology was fronted by a short preface. This text, then, introduced the forgeries to the world. Its importance requires a substantial amount of time to be spent on its study.

The opening of the preface established Macpherson's central strategy: "The public may depend on the following fragments as genuine remains of ancient Scottish poetry." One might wonder why, if the poems were genuine, such a statement was needed. But Macpherson's aim was authentication. The preface was the first part of the scholarly apparatus of authentication that was to be erected around the imaginative text. Authenticity was of greater priority than commentary on the literary quality of the poems: "Of the poetical merit of these fragments nothing shall here be said. Let the public judge, and pronounce." It would have been a cunning move to have simply assumed authenticity and to have had the preface serve as literary criticism. The fact that Macpherson did the opposite shows his fascination with process, with the act of making.

Most of the preface, then, was ostensibly designed to prove the validity of the opening statement. The first paragraph told us that the exact date of composition of the fragments was not known. But Highland tradition "refers them to an aera of the most remote antiquity." . . . Macpherson was not being duplicitous in not giving precise dates, or in not saying how remote "remote" was. Added to external proof of the poems' ancientness, Macpherson noted "the spirit and strain of the poems themselves; which abound with those ideas, and paint those manners, that belong to the most early strata of society." So Macpherson used external and internal information. Not only did he predict the approach that participants in the controversies about the forgeries were to commonly take to the issue. Macpherson also anticipated the essentially dualistic format of his own and later historical fiction: the text (internal) and the annotation (external). Actually, as will be shown, there was no properly distinct border between the two. Both were controlled by the overall vision.

The reference to "manners" alluded to the view of ancient literature as social history. As yet this correlation was being used only as part of the dating exercise. We were not told what those "manners" consisted of. Authentication was weak. A few sentences later however, two verifiable and authentic institutions were brought into the argument: the Highland clans and Christianity. Because there was no mention of either in the poems, we are told, the poems necessarily predated these institutions. However suspect the logic, Macpherson cleverly incorporated an authenticating perspective. Once more Macpherson demonstrated a pioneering awareness of how history was made by ancient literature. He knew there were no rules as to the amount or type of social history a poem should embody. Thus he could make capital out of what was left out of the poems as much as what was included. As with so much else in the preface, the omission had an imaginative role to play in the vision. The rise of clans and Christianity signified the end of Ossian's pagan golden age. Hindsight could be applied here, because one of the ways the preface operated was to predispose us in certain ways to our reading of the texts. The relevance of these statements only became apparent later. A hint of a potential culture clash came in the remark that the poems were "coeval with the very infancy of Christianity in Scotland." Literate history rose from the ashes of prehistory. Note also that we are being taken back to the roots of society—the "very infancy." Macpherson was concerned with elemental history.

Macpherson's understanding that authentication did not rely on a plenitude of verifiable references within the text (indeed, many of them could function just as well in the notes) was shown in the reaction of two early commentators. Patrick Graham believed the Ossianic poems were literally like historical fragments that could be pieced together:

> these poems occasionally furnish many interesting views of the manners and mode of living which prevailed in that period of society, to which they relate. It would be amusing, and perhaps instructive, to collect these scattered traits, and to form from them a more precise picture of that state of society, in those ages, than has hitherto been exhibited.

In Graham's eyes, Ossian made superlative social history. Lord Kames, on the other hand, put himself in the mind of the eighteenth-century writer of historical fiction:

> Can it be supposed, that a modern writer could be so constantly on his guard, as never to mention corn, nor cattle? . . . a man of such talents inventing a historical fable, and laying the scene of action among savages in a hunter-state, would naturally frame a system of manners the best suited in his opinion to that state. What then could tempt him to adopt a system of manners so opposite to any notion he could frame of savage manners? The absurdity is so gross, that we are forced, however reluctantly, to believe, that these manners are not fictitious, but in reality the manners of his country, coloured perhaps, or a little heightened, according to the privilege of an epic poet.

When Joseph Warton asked for history to be used as the theme of national poetry, it is very likely he had in mind narrative. It is doubtful whether he understood the complexity that the essentially non-narrative issue of social history would create, and that Kames's comments reflect. The "manners" in Ossian's poetry, according to Kames, had replaced the historical fable that was unanimously regarded as the basis of an epic poem. Macpherson, to stimulate such a response, must have understood the different kinds of historical value Ossian's verse could create. Indeed, Patrick Graham's view of Ossian as social

history was not put forward as the principal way history was made in Ossian. Ossian's main task, claimed Graham,

> was to relate, in verse, indeed, or in measured diction, for the ease of the memory, subjects of true history. . . . Fictitious circumstances were altogether denied to him. The bard was, in fact, more properly a *historian* than a *poet*.

Ossian only "seldom" descended to the details of everyday life. For Graham, Ossian was authentic history both at the level of events and of non-narrative social history.

Macpherson's "proof" that the fragments were of an age contiguous with the rise of Christianity constituted the crucial and most remarkable component in the preface. The source of the relevant information was literary: "a fragment of the same poems, which the translator has seen." The use of "seen" rather than "heard" implied the translator was working from MSS. The transition from oral to literate culture was precisely what this fragment was about. Its content was reported to us:

> a Culdee or Monk is represented as desirous to take down in writing from the mouth of Ossian, who is the principal personage in several of the following fragments, his warlike achievements and those of his family. But Ossian treats the monk and his religion with disdain, telling him, that the deeds of such great men were subjects too high to be recorded by him, or by any of his religion.

The subject of this imaginary poem was nothing less than the making of history. The first point to note is that the poem was being cited as history—that is, for its information relating to the age of the ***Fragments***. History and poetry were fused at this level. Second, Macpherson was drawing on the real Ossianic poems of the Irish Fenian cycle. From Samuel Johnson's remarks to the proof by Derrick Thomson in 1952, it was known that Macpherson worked from genuine Gallic (presumably oral) sources. In such poems, a confrontation between Ossian (or Oisin) and Saint Patrick was common. Their meetings could be violent. As Alfred Nutt says: "Ossian, in the ballads, is a pagan, defiant and reckless, full of contempt and scorn for the howling clerics and their churlish low-bred deity." The relationship between Macpherson's Scottish vision and his Irish sources was to be worked out imaginatively and polemically with great subtlety in the later poems. The important point to note here is how Macpherson had modified the ethnically abrasive encounter between Ossian and the Christian. The context of the meeting was very interesting. The monk wished to record Ossian's songs, which chronicle "his warlike atchievements and those of his family." Ossian's verse was bardic history, the recording of felt experience, empirical data of the past—a Humean regression. The literate monk wished to preserve bardic history. He wanted to make a MS, a contemporaneous "voucher," the most authentic historical source possible. The monk would, if successful, have made a transition from oral to literate culture. It is striking therefore that Macpherson had Ossian refuse the request, thus denying the possible existence of a contemporary voucher (the MSS Macpherson supposedly discovered were never given dates, but they were meant to be a transcription from oral tradition made at some time after Ossian's demise). But Ossian's refusal prepared for the essential feature of the bardic voice—its spontaneity. The bard's poetry was stimulated by painful experiences; it could not be requisitioned, recited under artificial conditions. The empirical nature of bardic history ran deep. The monkish MS would have been impure. In these terms should Ossian's "disdain" be interpreted.

Even more important was the focus of the encounter: "the *mouth* of Ossian." The bardic voice: the voice of the past. The point where history and poetry fused, and history was created. This was the preparation we were given in the *Fragments,* which were to present us with Ossian's voice. It should be appreciated already how Macpherson exhibited a high degree of historiographical reflexivity—an understanding of the processes of history regarded specifically in terms of the role of literature in that making. Note that it was in the context of an imaginary poem that Macpherson chose to introduce Ossian to the world.

Also significant is the fact that the eschatology of Macpherson's vision was introduced in the figure of Ossian: "the last of the heroes." As the last of the Fingalian heroes, Ossian was also the last of his species of bard. The notion of a poetic Fall concomitant with the historical one was undermined by the fourth paragraph, where it was argued that "the Bards" who composed the poems continued to exist uninterrupted through many centuries. In later poems, this sloppiness was cleared up. Macpherson's aim here was to construct a perspective of transmission, by which "such poems were handed down from race to race; some in manuscript, but more by oral tradition." Unadulterated transmission relied on purity of culture. The Highlands were pure—"a country so free of intermixture with foreigners"—and thus the poetic remains were "in a great measure incorrupted to this day." Macpherson provided an answer to those doubts that untainted literary records could be preserved.

The last salient feature of the preface was that it looked directly beyond the *Fragments* to as yet unwritten (or "undiscovered") material. Macpherson hoped that "many more remains of ancient genius" might be recovered. In particular, "an heroic poem," which related how Fingal rescued the Irish from the invading Danes. The last three fragments were extracts from this epic. One of Macpherson's intentions was clearly to stimulate a public demand for Ossian. If the *Fragments* were well received, readers' appetites for more Ossianic verse would be whetted by the samples of the epic. The technique was repeated in *Fingal* (1762), in which an extract from *Temora* was presented. But there was also an imaginative level to the posturing. It was hinted, in the third paragraph, that all the *Fragments* may actually be part of the unrecovered epic: "there is ground to believe that most of them were originally episodes of a greater work which related to the wars of Fingal." A unity was suggested. That unity was

Macpherson's historical vision, the imagined Ossianic world and its transmission. Ultimately, the unity was Ossian, who was the author of the "greater work." A key feature of the forthcoming epic was given: "the author speaks of himself as present in the expedition of Fingal." Such was the pressure for empirical data of the past that Macpherson found a new genre: the memoir-epic. Ossian's bardic history "might serve to throw considerable light upon the Scottish and Irish antiquities." The preface closed with the Ossianic poem as history. We have been given essential clues as to how that history was made.

Fragment I was a dialogue between two lovers, Shilric and Vinvela. The dramatic nature of the poetry was immediately established: voices from the past: "What voice is that I hear?" is Shilric's first utterance. The mood of the conversation was mournful. Shilric left to fight in the "wars of Fingal" and was not expected to return. Loss and grief were imminent. Shilric desired, as any warrior did, to be remembered—by a monument and in memory. This situation was realized in the next fragment, though strikingly inverted. It is important to note that the dialogue was a recreation of a spontaneous present in the past—the white-hot presentation of history as it happened, the "first original." As yet there was no place for the bard in the making. Although Macpherson eventually incorporated all the fragments into the Ossianic repertoire, at the outset, he used the poems to build up accumulatively the features of the bardic voice.

One such trait was established in Fragment II:

> I sit by the mossy fountain; on the top of the hill of winds. One tree is rustling above me. Dark waves roll over the heath. The lake is troubled below. The deer descend from the hill. No hunter at a distance is seen; no whistling cow-herd is nigh. It is mid-day: but all is silent. Sad are my thoughts as I sit alone.

This self-dramatizing resembled a soliloquy. The poetic genre most comparable to it is the dramatic monologue. In the sense that the voice of the past we hear was clearly not meant to be the poet's (Macpherson's), the fragments were dramatic monologues. It is preferable however to dispense with the term in favour of a descriptive apparatus more relevant and contemporary. In other words, the terms that have been presented so far in this study. Ossian made history through the bardic voice. That voice was an innovation in poetic form.

The voice in Fragment II was Shilric's. The poem was a sequel to Fragment I. Surprisingly, it was Shilric who mourned the loss of Vinvela. She died of grief at hearing, mistakenly, of his loss in battle. Her spirit returned: "She speaks: but how weak her voice!" Instead of the artificial dialogue form, which always suggests the poet is a presence outside of the poem, imposing the form, Fragment II was created before us. The maker was the speaker. Other voices had to be reported, subsumed in the spontaneous voice. In terms of the imaginative vision Macpherson was creating, the voice was taking on an authoritative status, an authenticity. Shilric was left, at the end of Fragment II, mourning his lover: "Let me hear thy voice, as thou pass-est, when mid-day is silent around!" Macpherson imagi-natively recreated oral culture from the inside.

The experimental nature of the *Fragments* was demon-strated in the number of times the "authentic" form of making—the spontaneous utterance—was transgressed. Fragments I, IV, XII, and XIV were dialogues. Fragments III, XIII, and VIII had a past tense, third-person editorial framework. Fragment XIII, the opening of the forthcom-ing epic, perhaps understandably maintained an orthodox narrative form (though in *Fingal* it was made apparent eventually that the whole of the narration was being ut-tered by Ossian; most of the fragments were eventually transformed in this manner). Fragments III and VIII, however, were less excusable. The first four sentences of Fragment III were a present-tense description of the land-scape, identical to the opening of Fragment II. But then we read

> Sad, by a hollow rock, the grey-hair'd Carryl sat. Dry ferns wave over his head; his seat is an aged birch. Clear to the roaring winds he lifts his voice of woe.

The rest of the poem which is Carryl's utterance, should, strictly, have been in quotation marks, like Gray's *The Bard*. This was not to be the form of Ossian. Macpher-son's role as a modern historical poet did not in later verse enter the poem, and such an imposition, was alien to his imaginative program. The reason he transgressed in Fragments III and VIII was to give us a privileged exter-nal view of the speaker. The ageing, bereaved Carryl was a type of the Ossian described in Fragment VIII. The engraving of Ossian, which acted as frontispiece to *Fin-gal* (1762), followed that description closely.

Carryl, like Shilric before, and like Ossian later, mourned the loss of a loved one. Malcolm had been drowned sail-ing to or from the wars. The emphasis on voice remained dominant. Carryl pleaded with the returned spirit "let me hear thy voice," but agonizingly could not make out any words. Malcolm's loss was the loss of his voice, which gave him identity: "No more from the distant rock shall his voice greet thine ear." Now Carryl's utterance had to speak for Malcolm's: "Hear my voice, ye trees! as ye bend on the shaggy hill. My voice shall preserve the praise of him, the hope of the isles." The most celebrated func-tion of the ancient bard was his preservation of the fame of the warriors he served.

Fragment IV was a dialogue between two such warriors, Connal and Crimora. (She was the first of several ver-sions of Virgil's female warrior, Camilla.) The motivat-ing force was again the Fingalian wars. Connal's return home was first heard: "Whose voice is that, loud as the wind, but pleasant as the harp of Carryl?" The inter-allu-sions of the vision began to accumulate. The process of internal authentication was underway. We had just heard Carryl's voice. Also the first three fragments acted as a foil to the Fingalian wars. The cost of the wars to those left behind had been counted. Now Connal informed his lover "the war, my love is near." An invasion threatened

the homeland itself. The preface had informed us that Fingal, his family (which included Ossian) and his mili-tary achievements were the central topics of Ossianic poetry. So far Fingal had been a presence in the back-ground. Now he was brought tantalizingly close. Battle would take place on the morrow. We expect the next fragment to be a sequel, to show us finally the wars at first-hand.

The fulfilment of this expectation in Fragment V incorpo-rated new elements into the voice, which prepared the reader for the ultimately "authentic" utterance of Ossian in Fragment VI. For the first time, history became a topic. The poem was the utterance of an anonymous friend of Connal. The reader had leapt in time beyond the battle prophesied at the end of Fragment IV. That battle, and the fall of Connal and Crimora, were now history. Specifical-ly, they were now the memory of the speaker, who had been an eyewitness:

> Here was the din of arms; and here the groan of the dying. Mournful are the wars of Fingal. O Connal! it was here thou didst fall. Thine arm was like a storm. . . .

Here was a past-tense narration existing within the voice of the past. Macpherson broke through the conventions of past-tense narrative. His primary concern was to create the spontaneous experiencing of the past. Within this spontaneity, regression took place. History was a deeply felt emotion springing from personal loss: empirical data. The dramatic situation of the speaker of Fragment V was one that Ossian was often to be in—seated, alone, by the graves of loved ones:

> The grass grows between the stones of their tomb; I sit in the mournful shade. The wind sighs through the grass; and their memory rushes on my mind.

We see now why Ossian could not create poetry for the monk. Bardic verse was, to borrow Wordsworth's famous dictum, "the spontaneous overflow of powerful feelings." These feelings, however, were always about the loss of the past. "Memory" was the first word Ossian uttered in Fragment VI:

> Memory, son of Alpin, memory wounds the aged. Of former times are my thoughts; my thoughts are of the noble Fingal. The race of the king return into my mind, and wound me with remembrance.

Unlike the bard of Fragment I, Ossian was more than a spectator of the Fingalian wars. He was a participant, the "Son of the noble Fingal," as the opening of Fragment VI told the reader. Or rather, he had been these things. The Ossian the reader was to know as poet had "the cheeks of age." To him the glory of Fingal could only be history, it could not be the immediate present of the first four Frag-ments. From now on, the material promised in the pref-ace—"the wars of Fingal"—was bardic history. Fingal and others were recalled by Ossian, they were made by his voice. As the wars resulted in many real wounds, now the wounds were inflicted on Ossian's memory. He remembered the family:

> One day, returned from the sport of the mountains, from pursuing the sons of the hill, we covered this heath with our youth. Fingal the mighty was here, and Oscur, my son, great in war.

The situation quickly turned to tragedy. A fugitive maiden implored their aid. Their response was immediate, but in the ensuing mayhem she was killed. The mini-plots of the *Fragments* were sensationalist and repetitive, though Macpherson used this repetition to explore different ways of making the past. Ossian's first memory then was not of the Fingalian wars proper. Rather, he remembered the heroism of his son Oscur, who felled the pursuing villain. Oscur was given precedence, because "Oscur my son was brave; but Oscur is now no more." Oscur was Ossian's only son. His death accounted for the situation of Ossian as "last of the heroes."

Little wonder then that the next poem (Fragment VII) related "the mournful death" of Oscur. It is significant that this poem was the first item of the forgery produced by Macpherson. The essence of Ossian's position and his bardic utterance was revealed in the second paragraph:

> He fell as the moon in a storm; as the sun from the midst of his course, when clouds rise from the waste of the waves, when the blackness of the storm inwraps the rocks of Ardannider. I, like an ancient oak on Morven, I moulder alone in my place. The blast hath lopped my branches away; and I tremble at the wings of the north.

The change in tense marked a causal connection. Ossian was driven to a past that reminded him of his forlorn situation in the present

Oscur's death was not in battle, but in the star-crossed conflict of rival love. Oscur killed his best friend in a dual over Dargo's daughter. Unable to bear the responsibility, he deceived the maiden into killing him, and on realizing this, she committed suicide. More important than the fatuity of these events was the authenticating capital Macpherson made out of them. The moment of Oscur's death ("Her arrow flew and pierced his breast") was momentous enough to stimulate the first footnote:

> Nothing was held by the ancient Highlanders more essential to their glory, than to die by the hand of some person worthy or renowned. This was the occasion of Oscur's contriving to be slain by his mistress, now that he was weary of life. In these early times suicide was utterly unknown among that people, and no traces of it are found in the old poetry. Whence the translator suspects the account that follows of the daughter of Dargo killing herself, to be the interpolation of some later Bard.

Much can be said about this footnote. Macpherson wrote as an editor. The *Fragments* were, of course, a spurious anthology of ancient poetry. . . . Macpherson authenticat-

ed the veracity of Oscur's death by bringing in historical information. A detail of Scottish social history was given. As no source was cited, of course, the details could not be checked. It was suggested that ancient poetry was itself a source. A logical circle was set up, uniting history and poetry ever more firmly. Macpherson anticipated footnotes used by real anthologists and by historical writers, including Chatterton and Scott. The ostensible purpose of the notes was to illustrate further the Fingalian custom of dying an honorable death at the hand of a worthy killer. Macpherson's conclusion that the suicide of Dargo's daughter must be an interpolation was a remarkable one. Macpherson was aware of the inevitability of forgery in ancient MSS, as Toland, Locke, and Innes were. Macpherson's interpolation was therefore realistic, and also had the effect of authenticating the interpolation-free remainder of the text. Also, the whole question of a modern editor's interference in the received MS text was shot through with the notion of imposture. Macpherson himself was eventually branded a duplicitous interpolator and embellisher. His fake interpolation in Fragment VII was a forgery-in-forgery.

Macpherson put complete faith in oral tradition, even though he was aware of its pitfalls. Ossian was usually but not always a protagonist in his own narrative. Some information, such as Oscur's death, must have been transmitted to him. Similarly, the "son of Alpin," who had been Ossian's companion in Fragments VI and VII, was the "authentic" equivalent of the monk of the preface: the mode of transmission. Such listeners were not always present in Ossian's poems, though there were enough of them to carry the point.

Fragment VIII was the final poem acknowledged to be Ossian's. (Macpherson had not yet informed the reader directly that the forthcoming epic *Fingal* was Ossian's.) So the reader was permitted to see the bard from the outside:

> By the side of a rock on the hill, beneath the aged trees, old Ossian sat on the moss; the last of the race of Fingal. Sightless are his aged eyes; his beard is waving in the wind. Dull through the leafless trees he heard the voice of the north. Sorrow revived in his soul: he began and lamented the dead.

Like Homer, Ossian was blind. Unlike Homer, he was perched on the brink of an historical abyss: "the last of the race of Fingal." One of the jobs of *Fingal* (1762) and *Temora* (1763) was to fill out this eschatalogical model with much more historical detail. The job of the *Fragments* was to establish the authenticity of the bardic making of history. Ossian spoke to the reader. The past spoke to him: at the end of this fragment, Ossian lamented "no more I hear my friends." In the poem Ossian recalled for the first time the martial valor of Fingal, and described him defeating the rebel Gaul. Ossian's final poem prepared us for the extracts from *Fingal* that comprised the final three fragments. The end of the narrative celebrated Fingal's compassion and mercy (which for many early readers of Ossian meant an ascendancy over

Homer's heartless heroes). He gave up the captive Gaul to his suppliant daughter. Ossian's parting words were cleverly engineered:

> Such, Fingal! were thy words; but thy words I hear no more. Sightless I sit by thy tomb. I hear the wind in the wood; but no more I hear my friends. The cry of the hunter is over. The voice of war is ceased.

"The voice of war" was an artfully ambiguous phrase referring to Fingal's voice and to Ossian's own, which was making a temporary disappearance, having established its proper form. The next four fragments (up to the first extract from *Fingal*) had non-martial themes. Macpherson used the sequence of his poems to experiment with authentication and modes of access into the past.

Several features of Fragment IX suggested a break with its predecessors. The narrative was not spontaneous or requested, but demanded. The bard was an employee:

> Why seek we our grief from afar? or give our tears to those of other times? But thou commandest, and I obey, O fair daughter of the isles!

The young Ossian was also the bard of Fingal, and in later poems he was ordered to sing. Another way in which Fragment IX was different was in the datum from a footnote: "This fragment is reckoned not altogether so ancient as most of the rest." Macpherson had cleared a space for himself in which he could attempt some virtuoso maneuvers with his voices and plots. In Fragment IX, the story was told of a tragic misunderstanding. Two friends were deceived into dueling over the lover of one of them. In Fragment X, the same plot situation occured. But this time it was created from the inside by the maiden. She awaited her lover (they were to elope) only to discover he and her brother had killed each other in a duel. This fragment, like the early ones, was wholly in the spontaneous present, with no recalled narrative. The maiden ended by prophesying the return of her spirit to this spot: "sweet shall my voice be; for pleasant were they both to me." In Fragment XI, the maiden's plight became part of a narrative again. Her voice was transmuted from spontaneity to recreation by a bereaved narrator; we were given now a quoted speech rather than the speech itself. Her death was the death of her voice: "Before morning appeared, her voice was weak. It died away. . . . Spent with grief she expired." The father's agony on seeing his children's spirits was also described in terms of voice: "they walk in mournful conference together. Will none of you speak to me?" Armyn, as "the last of his race" recalling the loss of his family, was a type of Ossian.

Ossian's presence was also prepared for in the hoary, aged father of the dead Morar in Fragment XII. Morar had "left no son," making his father the last of the line. Fragment XII, a dialogue, had neither a romantic nor martial narrative. The focus was purely on personal loss, a situation in which the past dominated the present.

The most notable feature of the three extracts from *Fin-* *gal* (Fragments XIII, XIV, XV) was their seeming incongruity and inconsequentiality. Fragment XIII had no spontaneous bardic voice, and Fragments XIV and XV had themes unrelated to Fingal's expedition to Ireland (they would in fact be introduced into *Fingal* as episodes). Moreover, Fragment XIV contained bizarre anti-authenticating stage directions inserted between speeches in the dialogue: "[He gives her the sword: with which she instantly stabs him.]" As an editor's interpolation, suggesting what might be supposed to have happened in a lost part of the text, it is difficult to decipher Macpherson's intention, other than to conclude he was trying out a disastrous experiment. Fragment XIV ended like Fragment XV, abruptly. But if Macpherson was trying to create an unfinished poem, a "fragment," the parenthesis that ended Fragment XIV failed to accomplish this. It has been apparent, of course, that none of the fragments resembled genuine, incomplete relics, other than in name and shortness. Fragment XIII would probably have served its purpose of advertising and authenticating *Fingal* better if it had been the only extract. Though the Irish leader Cuchulaid went to give battle to the invading Scandinavian Garve, it was the arrival of Fingal that everyone awaited. He "alone can fight with Garve." Only Ossian's "voice of war" could tell us of this fight.

FURTHER READING

Biography

Saunders, Bailey. *The Life and Letters of James Macpherson.* London: Swann and Sonnenschein and Co., 1894, 327 p.
　　Relates the facts of Macpherson's life, as well as the reception of his literary works, and the course of the controversy they engendered.

Smart, J.S. *James Macpherson: An Episode in Literature.* London: David Nutt, 1905, 224 p.
　　A biographical and critical study of Macpherson's career, in which the author argues that he possessed "a sensitive and poetic mind, and a shrewd capacity for business."

Criticism

Barratt, Glynn R., "The Melancholy and the Wild: A Note on Macpherson's Russian Success." In *Studies in Eighteenth-Century Culture: Racism in the Eighteenth Century,* edited by Harold E. Pagliaro, pp. 125-35. Cleveland: The Press of Case Western Reserve University, 1973.
　　An overview of Macpherson's popularity in Russia.

Bysveen, Josef. *Epic Tradition and Innovation in James Macpherson's "Fingal."* Stockholm: Uppsala, 1982, 145 p.
　　A book-length study of the epic elements in Macpherson's poem.

Gaskill, Howard. "German Ossianism: A Reappraisal?" *German Life and Letters* XLII, No. 4 (July, 1989): 329-41.

A discussion of some of the questions left unanswered by Rudolf Tombo's *Ossian in Germany* (see excerpt dated 1901).

Grobman, Neil R. "James Macpherson, Ossian, and the Revival of Interest in Bardic Traditions in Eighteenth-Century Scotland." *Midwestern Journal of Language and Folklore* VI (Spring / Fall, 1980), pp. 51-55.

An examination of both the positive and negative effects Macpherson had on the preservation of Scotland's "oral antiquities."

Hutchinson, T. Review of *The Life and Letters of James Macpherson,* by Thomas Bailey Saunders. *The Academy* 46, No. 1167 (September 22, 1894): 205-07.

A detailed review of the circumstances surrounding the Ossianic controversy in which the author faults Saunders for an inadequate understanding of the subject.

Keith, Christiana. "Second Thoughts on Ossian." *Queen's Quarterly: A Canadian Review* LVIII, No. 4 (Winter, 1951-52): 551-57.

A defense of Macpherson's achievement.

Krause, David. "The Hidden Oisìn," in his *The Profane Book of Irish Comedy,* pp. 59-104. Ithaca: Cornell University Press, 1982.

An examination of the distinction between Oisìn, the figure in Irish folklore, and the alleged author of Macpherson's poems.

Malek, James S. "Eighteenth-Century British Dramatic Adaptations of Macpherson's *Ossian." Restoration and Eighteenth-Century Theatre Research* XIV, No. 1 (May, 1975): 36-41, 52.

An exploration of Macpherson's influence on British drama.

Metzdorf, Robert F. "M'Nicol, Macpherson, and Johnson." In *Eighteenth-Century Studies in Honor of Donald F. Hyde,* edited by W.H. Bond, pp. 45-61. New York: The Grollier Club, 1970.

A discussion of the extended debate between Johnson and Macpherson, combined with an account of another Scottish foe of the English critic's, Donald M'Nicol.

Parnell, Arthur. "James Macpherson and the Nairne Papers." *The English Historical Review* XII, No. 46 (April, 1897): 254-84.

Examines Macpherson's relationship to an eighteenth-century political scandal that turned on questions of the authenticity of another set of documents.

Wain, John. "Alternative Poetry." In his *Professing Poetry,* pp. 13-44. New York; The Viking Press, 1978.

Discusses Macpherson's work in the context of the nineteenth-century revival of the Fenian story cycle.

Walsh, W. E. "Macpherson's Ossian." *Queen's Quarterly: A Canadian Review* XLV, No. 3 (Autumn, 1938): 366-76.

An historical overview of the controversy surrounding the publications of Macpherson's Ossianic poetry.

Additional coverage of Macpherson's life and career is contained in the following source published by Gale Research: *Dictionary of Literary Biography,* Vol. 109.

Allan Ramsay

1684(?)-1758

Scottish poet and editor.

INTRODUCTION

Through his own poetry and his editions of works by earlier writers, Ramsay played a major role in reviving the Scots poetic tradition that had languished since the late sixteenth century. Although he wrote both in English and in vernacular Scots, he is most remembered for his verses in Scots, which demonstrated the viability of the Scots language and of traditional Scottish genres and verse forms as vehicles for contemporary literary expression. He is considered an important predecessor of Robert Burns and a precursor of the Romantic movement of the later eighteenth century.

Biographical Information

Ramsay was born in Leadhills in Lanarkshire, Scotland, some fifty miles from Edinburgh, in 1684 or 1685 (some sources say 1686). His father, the manager of a lead mine, died soon after his son's birth, and Ramsay spent most of his youth on a small farm belonging to his stepfather. In about 1700, Ramsay left Lanarkshire for Edinburgh, where by 1710 he was a master wigmaker and a burgess of the city. Two years later he married Christian Ross, daughter of a law clerk; the eldest of their several children, Allan, would become a noted portrait painter and essayist. From 1712 to 1715, Ramsay was a member of the Easy Club, a small group of young Scottish nationalists who wrote poetry and letters to the press and discussed relations between England and Scotland, which had been joined under the Parliamentary Union of 1707. He gradually gave up wigmaking in favor of bookselling, and in 1725 opened the first circulating library in the United Kingdom in his Edinburgh bookshop. He also opened a theater in 1936, but was forced to close it three years later by the opposition of the more conservative members of Edinburgh society and by the passage of the 1737 Licensing Act, which prohibited the production of plays outside of London without the permission of the lord chamberlain. He died in Edinburgh in 1758.

Major Works

Ramsay's first poems were apparently written for the Easy Club, including his first poem in Scots, "Elegy on Maggie Johnston, who died Anno 1711." Over the next several years, his poems in Scots and English circulated in the form of broadsides and small collections. His reputation as a poet spread with his publication in 1721 of a collection of his verse which he issued to nearly five hundred subscribers, including a number of aristocrats and prominent literary figures, merchants, and profession-

als. Ramsay's poetry, written in both Scots and English, included work in a wide variety of genres, but he was particularly known for his depictions—sometimes humorous, sometimes sentimental—of Scottish rural and urban "low life." His pastoral drama *The Gentle Shepherd* appeared in 1725; three years later, he added some twenty songs to his original text, expanding it into a "ballad-opera" which became popular in England and the American colonies as well as in Scotland, where it was produced regularly into the nineteenth century. Ramsay also collected and published older Scots poetry in his anthologies *Ever Green* (1724) and *Tea-Table Miscellany* (four volumes, 1723-37), at times—to the dismay of later scholars—with his own unacknowledged additions or amendments.

Critical Reception

While Ramsay has long been credited with revitalizing the Scots poetic tradition, his stature as a poet was eclipsed by the enormous popularity of Burns in the latter years of the eighteenth century. His reputation was particularly tarnished by the comments of two late-eighteenth century editors of Scots poetry, Lord Hailes (1770) and John Pinkerton (1786); both severely criticized Ramsay's free-handed editorial methods, and Pinkerton dismissed Ramsay's own verse as crude in both content and execution. The tendency to view Ramsay as a very minor talent whose primary contribution to literature was—despite his editorial shortcomings—his popularization of earlier Scots verse culminated in the assessment of T. F. Henderson, whose *Scottish Vernacular Literature* (1898) remained influential well into the twentieth century. The pattern for more positive evaluations of Ramsay was set by a long critical essay by Alexander Fraser Tytler, Lord Woodhouselee, published in the 1800 Chalmers edition of the poet's works. While admitting that many of Ramsay's poems lack polish, Tytler praised the vitality of his best verse and defended him against charges of vulgarity with the argument that his language and style were suited to his true-to-life depictions of rural and city life. In Tytler's essay and in much subsequent nineteenth-century criticism, *The Gentle Shepherd* was singled out as Ramsay's most important work and was praised for its emotional veracity and its adaptation of the pastoral mode to a native British setting. More recent critics, while continuing to recognize the importance of Ramsay's editorial work and of *The Gentle Shepherd,* have turned increased attention to his other poetic accomplishments. Allan MacLaine, in particular (1985), argues that Ramsay produced admirable work in a wide variety of genres and in so doing not only won popular and critical acceptance of vernacular Scots verse, but also revived or created the verse forms and genres that would dominate the Scots literary revival throughout his century.

PRINCIPAL WORKS

Poems (poetry) 1721
Fables and Tales (fables and short stories) 1722
The Tea-Table Miscellany 4 vols. [editor] (poetry) 1723-37
Ever Green 2 vols. [editor] (poetry) 1724
The Gentle Shepherd (drama) 1725
Poems 2 vols. (poetry) 1728
A Collection of Scots Proverbs [editor] (aphorisms) 1737
The Poems of Allan Ramsay 2 vols. (poetry) 1800
The Works of Allan Ramsay 6 vols. 1945-74

CRITICISM

John Pinkerton (essay date 1786)

SOURCE: "John Pinkerton," in *The Gentle Shepherd: A Pastoral Comedy,* William Gowans, 1852, pp. lxiv-lxvi.

[*Pinkerton was a noted late-eighteenth century editor of poetry in the Scots language. In the following excerpt, originally published in his collection* Ancient Scotish Poems *in 1786, he belittles Ramsay's poetic accomplishments and knowledge of Scots.*]

ALLAN RAMSAY. The convivial buffoonery of this writer has acquired him a sort of reputation, which his poetry by no means warrants; being far beneath the middling, and showing no spark of genius. Even his buffoonery is not that of a tavern, but that of an ale-house.

The *Gentle Shepherd* all now allow the sole foundation of his fame. Let us put it in the furnace a little; for, if it be gold, it will come out the purer. Dr. Beattie, in his Essay on Laughter and Ludicrous Composition, observes, that the effect of the *Gentle Shepherd* is ludicrous from the contrast between meanness of phrase, and dignity or seriousness of sentiment. This is not owing to its being written in the Scotish dialect, now left to the peasantry, as that ingenious writer thinks; for the first part of Hardy-knute, written in that very dialect, strikes every English reader as sublime and pathetic to the highest degree. In fact this glaring defect proceeds from Allan Ramsay's own character as a buffoon, so evident from all his poems, and which we all know he bore in private life; and from Allan's total ignorance of the Scotish tongue, save that spoken by the mob of Mid Lothian. It is well known that a comic actor of the Shuter or Edwin class, though highly meritorious in his line, yet, were he to appear in any save *queer* characters, the effect would even be more ludicrous than when he was in his proper parts, from the contrast of the man with his assumed character. This applies also to authors; for Sterne's sermons made us laugh, though there was nothing laughable in them: and, had Rabelais, or Sterne, written a pastoral opera, though the reader had been ignorant of their characters, still a something, a je ne sçai quoi, in the phraseology, would have ever provoked laughter. But this effect Ramsay has even pushed further; for, by his entire ignorance of the Scotish tongue, save that spoken by the mob around him, he was forced to use the very phraseology of the merest vulgar, rendered yet more ridiculous by his own turn to low humour; being himself indeed one of the mob, both in education and in mind. So that putting such *queer* language into the mouth of respectable characters—nay, pretending to clothe sentiments, pathos, and all that, with such phraseology—his whole *Gentle Shepherd* has the same effect as a gentleman would have who chose to drive sheep on the highway with a harlequin's coat on. This radical defect at once throws the piece quite out of the class of good compositions.

. . . . .

Allan was indeed so much a *poet,* that in his *Evergreen* he even puts rhyming titles to the old poems he publishes; and by this silly idea, and his own low character, has stamped a kind of ludicrous hue on the old Scotish poetry, of which he pretended to be a publisher, that even now is hardly eradicated, though many editors of great learning and high respectability have arisen.

. . . . .

I have been the fuller on this subject, because, to the great discredit of taste in Scotland, while we admire the effusions of this scribbler, we utterly neglect our really great poets, such as Barbour, Dunbar, Drummond, &c. There is even a sort of national prejudice in favour of the *Gentle Shepherd,* because it is our only drama in the Scotish language; yet we ought to be ashamed to hold prejudices so ridiculous to other nations, and so obnoxious to taste, and just criticism. I glory in Scotland as my native country; and, while I try to root up all other prejudices out of my mind, shall ever nourish my partiality to my country; as, if that be a prejudice, it has been esteemed an honest and a laudable one in all ages; and is, indeed, the only prejudice perfectly consonant to reason, and vindicable by truth. But Scotland has no occasion to recur to false history, false taste, false science, or false honours of any kind. In the severest light of truth she will stand very conspicuous. Her sons, in trying to adorn her, have shown remarkable defects of judgment. The ancient history of the Picts, so splendid in the page of Tacitus, is lost in our own fables. We neglect all our great poets, and are in raptures with Allan Ramsay. Our prejudices are as pitiful as strong; and we know not that the truth would make us far more illustrious, than all our dreams of prejudice, if *realized,* to use an expression of impossibility. Good sense in antiquities, and good taste in poetry, are astonishingly

---

Hugh Blair's comments on *The Gentle Shepherd*, 1783:

I must not omit the mention of another *pastoral drama,* which will bear being brought into comparison with any composition of this kind, in any language; that is, Allan Ramsay's **Gentle Shepherd**. It is a great disadvantage to this beautiful poem, that it is written in the old rustic dialect of Scotland, which, in a short time, will probably be entirely obsolete, and not intelligible; and it is a farther disadvantage that it is so entirely formed on the rural manners of Scotland, that none but a native of that country can thoroughly understand or relish it. But, though subject to these local disadvantages, which confine its reputation within narrow limits, it is full of so much natural description, and tender sentiment, as would do honour to any poet. The characters are well drawn, the incidents affecting; the scenery and manners lively and just. It affords a strong proof, both of the power which nature and simplicity possess, to reach the heart in every sort of writing; and of the variety of pleasing characters and subjects with which *pastoral poetry,* when properly managed, is capable of being enlivened.

Hugh Blair, quoted in The Gentle Shepherd: A Pastoral Comedy, *William Gowans, 1852.*

---

wanting in Scotland to this hour.

The Scots Magazine (essay date 1797)

SOURCE: "Letter First on Ramsay's Gentle Shepherd," in *The Scots Magazine,* Vol. LIX, February, 1797, pp. 76-78.

[*In the following excerpt, the anonymous critic, who signs himself "Philo-Scoticus," praises Ramsay's characterization and rendering of Scottish country life in* The Gentle Shepherd *and defends the poem against charges of vulgarity.*]

Sir,

Before I enter particularly upon the **Gentle Shepherd,** I beg leave to make a few observations upon the poem in general, as is customary with the greatest ancient as well as modern critics; I shall, in doing this, have an eye upon Aristotle's method of examining epic poetry, poetry, which Addison has adopted in that excellent critique upon Milton's *Paradise Lost.* He *first* considers the fable; *secondly,* the characters; *thirdly,* the sentiments and behaviour of the actors; and *fourthly,* the language.

1st, The fables of all dramatic works must be probable, but those of the pastoral drama must be peculiarly so; nay these last must consist chiefly of common incidents, subservient to one interesting event, which is the end and occasion of the whole. Exactly such is the pastoral before us; almost all the scenes in it are familiar to the Scotchman, who hath passed his days on this side the Tweed; and there is one leading circumstance, one principal occurrence, which all the rest (nicely organized) approximate, at their several distances. This great and happy event is no less than the safe return of Sir William Worthy from the wars, and his arrival at his paternal seat.

There are few, very few of my countrymen, I believe, who have not perused the **Gentle Shepherd** again and again, with increased satisfaction and delight; and from whence, let me ask, arise these pleasing emotions? are they not occasioned by the affinity which we observe between this comedy and nature, and its uniform concordance with what we have seen and experienced in the world?

2d, Of the characters. These are perhaps as well diversified as the pastoral life will admit of. The incidents in it are supposed to be few, and those uninteresting. We imagine that the pipe and crook alternately engage the shepherd's attentions; in every season of the year he spends to-day as he did yesterday, with little or no variation. In like manner, the son (making allowance for the difference in natural dispositions) grows up in the very footstep of his father, his ambition ends with the boundaries of his pasture; his affections are fixed on some coy shepherdess, whose praises he sings with unwearied affinity, or whose cruelty he laments in such feeling strains, that the sympathetic rocks and vallies resound his tale of woe.

We further suppose, that these happy people formed themselves into convenient societies, where they did and received good offices to and from one another; and who, from the nature of their profession, and from their situation in life, we may conclude were remarkable for the innocency of their lives, and simplicity of their manners.

Such is a sample of the golden age, which is no more to be met with in these iron times.

In the *third* place, the sentiments and behaviour of the actors are perfectly correspondent to their respective conditions. All of them, except the knight, are placed in an humble sphere of life, and their opinions and actions are such as befit persons who have not received a liberal education; yet notwithstanding, they (tutored by nature, and uncorrupted by the world) make use of similes drawn from objects immediately surrounding them, which come home with greater force to the feeling heart, than any thing which can be effected by the choicest language, or most elaborate phraseology. Part of these it shall be my business hereafter to point out, when I consider each act particularly by itself.

In the mean time, I shall conclude the present communication by remarking, in the *fourth* place, of the language: that by some it hath been reprobated for its vulgarity and meanness; that there are some vulgarisms in this poem which it would certainly have been better without, I am not disposed to deny, but that these, abound throughout, or that the language on the whole is mean, I can on no account admit: it is seldom (if ever) unsuitable to the quality of the speakers, who it may be proper here to observe, most not be considered as every way the same with the primitive shepherds spoken of before, or as exactly of that cast which Pope describes to be the fittest characters for pastoral poetry, but in a great degree below both; they may be said to be their equals in facility; their inferiors in birth, riches, and mental qualifications; viewing them in this light, we ought not to be out of humour with the poet, when we meet with one or two unpolished phrases in the mouths of any of his *dramatis personae;* because, 1*st,* they are taken from real life; 2*d,* they render the poem more ludicrous; and lastly, the author meant they should please. In short I am of opinion, that if such naturalities do not always beautify, they seldom disfigure a work of this kind.

I may finally remark . . . that the speeches of the good old Knight are happily characteristic. They possess a degree of dignity, tempered with affability, which is exceedingly agreeable to the reader, and which is highly meritorious in the author. . . .

Alexander Fraser Tytler (essay date 1800)

SOURCE: "Remarks on the Genius and Writings of Allan Ramsay," in *The Poems of Allan Ramsay, Vol. I,* Alex. Gardner, 1877, pp. xliii-cii.

[*Tytler's commentary, which first appeared in the 1800 edition of Ramsay's poems edited by George Chalmers, represents the first extended critical analysis of Ramsay's works. In the following excerpt, Tytler assesses Ramsay's contributions to Scottish literature in the Scots vernacular and in English, as well as his stature as a poet, particularly with regard to the elegies, the satires, and the pastoral poem* The Gentle Shepherd.]

As the writings of Allan Ramsay have now stood the test of the public judgment during more than seventy years, and in the opinion of the best critics, he seems to bid fair to maintain his station among our poets, it may be no unpleasing nor uninstructive employment to examine the grounds on which that judgment is founded, to ascertain the rank which he holds in the scale of merit, and to state the reasons that may be given for assigning him that dis-

tinguished place among the original poets of his country to which I conceive he is entitled.

The genius of Ramsay was original; and the powers of his untutored mind were the gift of nature freely exercising itself within the sphere of its own observation. . . .

Inheriting that ardour of feeling which is generally accompanied with strong sentiments of moral excellence, and keenly awake even to those slighter deviations from propriety which constitute the foibles of human conduct, he learned, as it were from intuition, the glowing language which is best fitted for the scourge of vice, as well as the biting ridicule which is the most suitable corrective of gross impropriety without deviating into personal lampoon.

A consciousness of his own talents induced Ramsay to aspire beyond the situation of a mere mechanic; and the early notice which his first poetical productions procured him was a natural motive for the experiment of a more liberal profession, which connected him easily with those men of wit who admired and patronized him. As a bookseller, he had access to a more respectable class in society. We may discern, in the general tenor of his compositions, a respectful demeanour towards the great and the rich, which, though it never descends to adulation or servility, and generally seeks for an apology in some better endowments than mere birth or fortune, is yet a sensible mark that these circumstances had a strong influence on his mind.

As he extended the sphere of his acquaintance, we may presume that his knowledge of men and acquaintance with manners were enlarged; and in his latter compositions we may discern a sufficient intelligence of those general topics which engaged the public attention. The habits of polite life and the subjects of fashionable conversation were become familiar at this time to the citizens of Edinburgh from the periodical papers of Addison and Steele; and the wits of Balfour's Coffee-house, Forrester, Falconer, Bennet, Clerk, Hamilton of Bangour, Preston, and Crawfurd, were a miniature of the society which was to be met with at Will's and Button's.

The political principles of Ramsay were those of an old Scotsman, proud of his country, delighted to call to mind its ancient honours, while it held the rank of a distinct kingdom, and attached to the succession of its ancient princes. Of similar sentiments at that time were many of the Scottish gentry. The chief friends of the poet were probably men whose sentiments on those subjects agreed with his own; and the Easy Club, of which he was an original member, consisted of youths who were anti-unionists. Yet, among the patrons of Ramsay were some men of rank, who were actuated by very different principles, and whose official situation would have made it improper for them openly to countenance a poet whose opinions were obnoxious to the rulers of his country. Of this he was aware; and putting a just value on the friendship of those distinguished persons, he learned to be cautious in the expression of any opinions which might risk the forfeiture of their esteem: hence he is known to have suppressed some of his earlier productions which had appeared only in manuscript; and others, which prudence forbade him to publish, were ushered into the world without his name, and even with false signatures. Among the former was a poem to the memory of the justly celebrated Dr. Pitcairne, which was printed by the Easy Club, but never published; and among the latter is **"The Vision,"** which he printed in the *Evergreen,* with the signature of "Ar. Scot."

In Ramsay's **"Vision,"** the author, in order to aid the deception, has made use of a more antiquated phraseology than that which we find in his other Scotish Poems; but it evidently appears from this attempt, and from the two cantos which he added to King James the First's ludicrous satire of **"Christ's Kirk on the Green,"** that Ramsay was not much skilled in the Ancient Scotish dialect. Indeed, the Glossary which he annexed to the two quarto volumes of his Poems, wherein are many erroneous interpretations, is of itself sufficient proof of this assertion. In compiling the Glossary to his *Evergreen,* Lord Hailes has remarked that he does not seem ever to have consulted the Glossary to Douglas's Virgil; "and yet, they who have not consulted it cannot acquire a competent knowledge of the Ancient Scotish dialect, unless by infinite and ungrateful labour." A part of this labour, undoubtedly, may be ascribed to Ramsay, when he selected and transcribed from the Bannatyne Manuscript those Ancient Poems which chiefly compose the two volumes of his *Evergreen*; and hence, it is probable, he derived the most of what he knew of the older dialect of his country. His own stock was nothing else than the oral language of the farmers of the Lothians and the common talk of the citizens of Edinburgh, to which his ears were constantly accustomed. A Scotsman, in the age of Ramsay, generally *wrote* in English,—that is, he imitated the style of the English writers; but when he *spoke,* he used the language of his country. The sole peculiarity of the style of Ramsay is that he transferred the oral language to his writings. He could write, as some of his compositions evince, in a style which may be properly termed English verse; but he wrote with more ease in the Scotish dialect, and he preferred it, as judging, not unreasonably, that it conferred a kind of Doric simplicity which, when he wished to paint with fidelity the manners of his countrymen and the peculiarities of the lower orders, was extremely suitable to such subjects.

From these considerations, one cannot but wonder at the observation which is sometimes made, even by Scotsmen of good taste, that the language of *The Gentle Shepherd* disgusts from its vulgarity. It is true that in the present day the Scotish dialect is heard only in the mouths of the lowest of the populace, in whom it is generally associated with vulgarity of sentiment; but those critics should recollect that it was the language of the Scotish people which was to be imitated, and that, too, of the people upwards of a century ago, if we carry our mind back to the epoch of the scene.

If Ramsay had made the shepherds of the Lowlands of Scotland, in the middle of the seventeenth century, speak correct English, how preposterous would have been such a composition! But, with perfect propriety, he gave them the language which belonged to them; and if the sentiments of the speakers be not reproachable with unnecessary vulgarity, we cannot with justice associate vulgarism with a dialect which in itself is proper and in its application is characteristic. After all, what is the language of Ramsay but the common speech of Yorkshire during the last century? . . .

The **"Elegy on Maggy Johnston"** was, it is probable, among the first compositions which the author allowed to appear in print. It is in that style in which certainly lay his chief talent—ludicrous and natural description of low life. It is written in the character of a good-humoured, joyous toper, lamenting in burlesque but cordial strains of regret, the privation of an accustomed haunt where he and his cronies were wont to resort for the purpose of enjoying a country dinner and a social bowl. Maggy Johnston lived at a small hamlet, called Morning side, about a mile to the south-westward of Edinburgh. Of a similar character with this composition is the **"Elegy on Lucky Wood,"** who kept an alehouse in the suburbs; and who is celebrated as a rare phenomenon, an upright and conscientious hostess. Both these poems are characteristic of times and of manners. The concluding stanza of the latter exhibits a stroke of genuine poetry:

> O Lucky Wood! 'tis hard to bear
> Thy loss:—but oh! we mum forbear:
> Yet sall thy memory be dear,
> 　　While blooms a tree;
> And after-ages' bairns will speer
> 　　'Bout thee—and me.

In the same strain of burlesque composition is the **"Elegy on John Cowper, the Kirk-Treasurer's Man,"** which is dated in 1714. The hint of this *jeu d'esprit* was probably taken from Pope and Swift's account of the death of Partridge, the Almanack-maker, for John Cowper survived this intimation of his decease, and must have had his ears frequently stunned with this ludicrous encomium on his merits! which was hawked about the streets in a halfpenny sheet. The Kirk-Treasurer and his man, who were personages of signal importance in those days, when the discipline of the Kirk favoured strongly of Puritanism and the stool of repentance was in habitual use, were fair objects of satire to the rakish wits who suffered from the vigilant discharge of their duty. Pennycuik, the younger,—a poet of no mean talents,—in ludicrous Scotish verse has an elegy in the same strain on "Robert Forbes," who was probably John Cowper's successor in office. This bard, who was a contemporary of Ramsay, and who appears frequently to have chosen from emulation to celebrate the same topics of the day, has satirised the Kirk-Treasurer in a composition entitled "The Presbyterian Pope" in strains of great humour and drollery.

"Lucky Spence's Last Advice" is from the same mint with the preceding compositions, and of its most perfect coinage. The subject being the last words of a dying bawd,

I grant, is scarcely fit "for modest ear or eye;" but the moral is strong pointed. . . . Even a deathbed to the hardened sinner brings no repentance. The old procuress instructs her pupils, with her latest breath, in the arts of their vocation, and dies with a glass of gin in her hand. . . .

Of a similar character, and of a tendency more strongly moral, is **"The Last Speech of a Wretched Miser,"**—a satire of very high merit, whether we consider the intimate knowledge of human nature which it displays, the force of humorous description, or the salutary lesson which it inculcates. The character of a miser, even from the pencil of a Moliere, is not drawn with greater force of expression or truth of colouring; nor has the power of this most odious vice to extinguish every moral feeling and sentiment of natural affection ever been set in a stronger light of reprobation:

> O Gear! I held you lang thegither;
> For you I starv'd my guid auld mither,
> And to Virginia sald my brither,
>   And crush'd my wife:
> But now I'm gaun I kenna whither,
>   To leave my life.
>
> My life! my God! my spirit yearns,
> Not on my kindred, wife, or bairns;
> Sic are but very laigh concerns,
>   Compar'd with thee;
> When now this mortal rottle warns
>   Me, I man die.

It seems to have been a favourite whim of Ramsay's, as it was the practice of the age, to write elegies on the living: a fancy in which there is fully as much propriety as in familiar letters from the dead to the living: the former is a harmless jest; the latter, however well intended, an awful and presumptious fiction. We may freely amuse ourselves with **"The Life and Acts,"** or

> An Elegy on Patie Birnie,
>   The famous fidler of Kinghorn,
> Wha gart the lieges laugh and girn ay,
>   Aft till the cock proclaim'd the morn.

This catgut-scraper, like the minstrels of old, was a poet as well as a musician; a rogue, too, of infinite humour; in short, completely versant in the arts of his profession. From the mention of this Scotch Crowdero, we are led to remark that the strongest test of the merits of Ramsay, as a characteristic painter of nature, and of his peculiar excellence in humorous description, is the compliment paid him by the inimitable Hogarth, who dedicated his twelve plates of Hudibras "To Allan Ramsay of Edinburgh, and William Wood of Great Houghton in Northamptonshire." . . .

In the two supplemental cantos of **"Christ's Kirk on the Green,"** the poet appears again in the style in which he peculiarly excelled—humorous description of vulgar life. The first canto is one of the many compositions of that most accomplished Prince, James the First of Scotland. . . . It de-

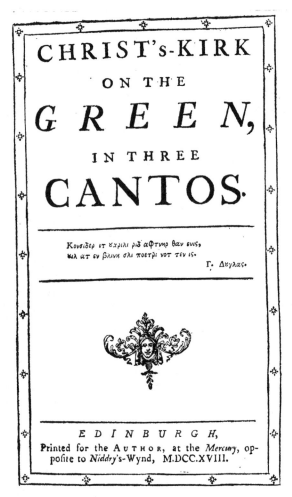

CHRIST's-KIRK
ON THE
GREEN,
IN THREE
CANTOS.

*Κονσιδερ ιτ ὑκριλι ρἰ αφτυηρ θαν ενις,
Ιλ ἱτ εν βλινη ὁλι ποετρι νοτ τεν ις.*
            Γ. Δυγλας.

EDINBURGH,
Printed for the AUTHOR, at the *Mercury*, opposite to *Niddry's*-Wynd, M.DCC.XVIII.

Title page of a 1718 edition of Christ's Kirk on the Green.

scribes with great humour and pleasantry a brawl at a country wake or dancing bout, probably on occasion of a wedding. "The King," says Ramsay, "having painted the rustic squabble with an uncommon spirit, ambitious to imitate so great an original, I put a stop to the war, called a congress, and made them sign a peace, that the world might have their picture in the more agreeable hours of drinking, dancing, and singing." This was a bold attempt; but the poet knew his own powers, and has executed his part in a most masterly manner. The quarrel is put an end to in the first stanza by the intervention of a tremendous figure. . . . It is not

> ——the blue-ey'd maid,
> Who to its sheath returns the shining blade.

But a personage equally awful:

> But now the bauld gude wife of Baith,
>   Arm'd wi' a great kail-gully,
> Came belly-flaught, and loot an aith,
>   She 'd gar them a' be hooly
>   Fou fast that day.

Terrified into good order, after a slight skirmish between

a noisy poltroon and a termagant, the parties with one consent shake hands, adjust their dishevelled locks, tye their cravats, and call in the fiddler. A scene ensues of frolic and jolity which furnishes a picture that Hogarth could not easily have improved. The variety of humorous characters and their several employments in the piece evince the most thorough acquaintance with rustic life and manners. The bold and sturdy hostess, the bragadocio, who lay quiet while the fray was at its height and whose courage rises when the danger is over; the priggish taylor, who affects the airs of a courtly dancer, Falkland bred; the little short-legged gentleman, who makes up in pride what he wants in stature, and who damns the fiddle and calls for the pipes; Tam Lutter, who scorns all amusement but the tankard; the self-important parish-clerk, ("the letter-gae of haly rhyme"), who sits at the head of the board, and whose opinions it was unlawful to contradict or question—all are painted with exquisite humour; each with the strongest characters of discrimination and with the strictest consonance to nature, from which the poet drew.

The two supplemental cantos of **"Christ's Kirk"** were written, the one in 1715 and the other in 1718. The latter is of equal merit with the former. It opens with a description of the morning as rising on the jolly villagers, who are unusually drowsy from the last night's debauch. Here let us, by the way, remark the difference between witty and humorous composition. Butler and Ramsay were each possessed of both wit and humour in no ordinary measure; but the former quality predominated with the English bard, the latter with the Scotish. Butler thus describes the morning, ludicrously, but wittily:

> The sun had long since in the lap
> Of Thetis taken out his nap,
> And, like a lobster boil'd, the morn
> From black to red began to turn.

This pleases as an ingenious piece of wit. The whimsicalness of the comparison makes us smile; but it is no just picture of nature, and therefore it is not humorous. Now, mark the humour with which Ramsay describes the dawn as rising upon his jolly company at the bridal: a little coarseness must be excused; the picture, otherwise, had not been faithful:

> Now frae th' east nook of Fife, the dawn
>   Speel'd westlines up the lift;
> Carles, wha heard the cock had crawn,
>   Begoud to rax and rift;
> And greedy wives, wi' girning thrawn,
>   Cry'd, 'Lasses, up to thrift.'
> Dogs barked, and the lads frae hand
>   Bang'd to their breeks like drift,
>   Be break o' day.

Humour must be consonant to nature: it is nature seen in absurd and ludicrous aspects. Wit gives an apparent and fanciful resemblance to nature, but it requires, for its very essence, a real contrariety. This canto describes the events of the day following the marriage. The friends of the

young couple bring each his present of some utensil or piece of furniture, which is laid down on the bed, with a compliment or a banter. The morning is spent in receiving these tokens of kindness, the day in frolic and sports peculiar to the occasion, and it is concluded with a hearty carousal, where the main object is to send the new-married man to bed as drunk as possible, that his wife may know at once the best and worst of her bargain.—Such is the plan of Ramsay's **"Christ's Kirk on the Green,"** a composition of very high merit, in its own particular style, and which will preserve the memory of customs and manners long after they have ceased to be observed or are known in actual life. . . .

"Wealth, or the Woody;" a poem on the South Sea, written June, 1720. At a time when this fascinating project was at its height, and the nation seemed intoxicated to the utmost pitch, Ramsay appears to have entertained a just suspicion of the solidity of a scheme which promised boundless wealth to a people, without the smallest exertion of talents or of industry; and this composition is evidently intended to put his credulous countrymen on their guard against a delusion which he foresaw would entice thousands to their ruin. After a poignant description of the effect produced by a sudden change of prosperous fortune on native meanness of soul,—the insolence and pride attending undeserved elevation,—and painting, with the pencil of satire, the fastidious airs assumed by those who, a few months before, were the tenants of a garret:

> And only durst, in twilight or the dark,
> Steal to a common cook's with half a mark.

How prophetic is the following anticipation of what a similar term of time might probably produce!—

> This I foresee, and time shall prove I'm right,
> (For he's nae poet wants the second sight):
> When Autumn's stores are ruck'd up in the yard,
> And sleet and snaw dreeps down cauld Winter's
>   beard,—
> When bleak November's winds make forests
>   bare,
> And with splenetic vapours fill the air,—
> Then, then, in gardens, parks, or silent glen,
> When trees bear nothing else, they'll carry—
>   men.

"The Prospect of Plenty" follows. To the chimerical hopes of inexhaustible riches from the project of the South Sea, the poet now opposes the certain prospect of national wealth from the prosecution of the fisheries in the North Sea,—thus judiciously pointing the attention of his countrymen to the solid fruits of patient industry, and contrasting these with the airy projects of idle speculation. Of industry the certain consequence is plenty, a gradual enlargement of all the comforts of society, the advancement of the useful, and the encouragement of the elegant arts, the cultivation of talents, the refinement of manners, the increase of population,—all that contributes either to national prosperity or to the rational enjoyments of life. The composition and structure of this piece are less deserving of encomium than the wisdom of its precepts. An unskilful use is made of the Heathen Mythology. *Amphitrite* claims the song; *Nereus* rises from his watery bed; and *Oceanus,* with pleasure, hears him sing—of herring-busses filling the Northern Seas—"in order rang'd before the muse's eye." The measure, which is heroic, is at variance with the dialect and phraseology, which are provincial and burlesque.

The elapse of a few months completely justified the poet's foresight in the preceding composition; and in an Epistle to Lord Ramsay, intitled **"The Rise and Fall of the Stocks,"** he relates the origin and progress of the South Sea bubble till its burst into air. This piece is dated the 25th March, 1721. It is a strong and vivid picture, contrasting the tumultuous infatuation that prevailed while the project was at its height, with the deep despondency that attended its dissolution. He cautions his countrymen from giving way to this despondency. He labours to teach them the best improvement of their misfortunes, and presents to their minds the prospect of a bright sunshine which is to break forth after a gloomy morning.

On the same subject, in a happy and frolicsome moment, our poet wrote **"The Satyr's Comic Project for recovering a young bankrupt Stock-jobber."** It is a parody of the well-known ballad of "Colin's Complaint."

> By the side of a murmuring stream,
>   A shepherd forsaken was laid, &c.

> On the shore of a low ebbing sea,
>   A sighing young jobber was seen
> Staring wishfully at an old tree
>   Which grew on the neighbouring green.

The project, if it want the merit of novelty, has the superior recommendation of constant repetition with complete success. The young stock-jobber in despair of retrieving his broken fortune and meditating to purchase a halter, is addressed by a satyr:

> A satyr that wander'd along,
>   With a laugh to his raving reply'd;
> The savage maliciously sung,
>   And jok'd while the stock-jobber cry'd.
> Come, hold up thy head, foolish wight!
>   I'll teach thee thy loss to retrieve;
> Observe me this project aright,
>   And think not of hanging, but live.

> Hecatissa, conceited and old,
>   Affects in her airs to seem young;
> Her jointure yields plenty of gold,
>   And plenty of nonsense her tongue.

> Lay siege to her for a short space,
>   Ne'er mind that she's wrinkled and grey;
> Extol her for beauty and grace,
>   And doubt not of winning the day, &c. . . .

"The Tale of Three Bonnets" is rather a dramatic dialogue than a proper tale. It is a severe political satire against his countrymen for agreeing to the Union of the kingdoms. Had our author lived to the present age he would have confessed the absurdity of his prejudices, and borne testimony to the falsehood of his own predictions. Abstracting from the error of its opinions, we see the genius of the author in the characteristic painting, the knowledge of life and manners, and the keen edge of satire, which are conspicuous in this performance. It was among those compositions which the author, perhaps grown wiser as a politician, did not admit into the collection of his works, though it appears in a separate pamphlet along with the two tales before-mentioned,—"Printed for the author and sold at his shop, Edinburgh."

On the same or a kindred subject, on which it appears that the mind of our author had taken a keener interest than he dared to avow, is **"The Vision,"** printed by him in *The Evergreen,* with a misleading signature. This fine poem, under the affected disguise of being "Compylit in Latin be a most lernit clerk in tyme of our hairship and oppression, Anno 1300, and translatit in 1524," is ascertained to have been composed by Ramsay about the period of the Rebellion, 1715. During half a century, it imposed itself upon the public as an ancient composition. . . .

"The Vision" has great poetical merit. The allegorical personage of the *Genius of Scotland* is drawn with great power of imagination and characteristic propriety of attribute. The sentiments are suitable to the dignity of the theme, and the diction is highly energetic. It is a pity that the poem is not possessed of uniform excellence. In the description of the carousal of the gods, the author has indulged his talent for the ludicrous at the expense of his propriety.

A few of the poems of Ramsay are written, as we have before remarked, in what may properly be termed English verse. It is in these attempts, which are generally of a graver species of composition than is suitable to his genius, that our Scotish Poet chiefly fails. He is evidently not at his ease. He is in a dress of ceremony; and, from want of use, he feels it sit awkwardly upon him. He is constantly falling back into his accustomed habits. He mistakes the quantities and sometimes the proper sense of English words,—as we see in his **"Content,"** and in his poem on **"Friendship."** When he clothes the same sentiment in Scotish and in English phraseology, its inferiority in the latter dress is most remarkably conspicuous. Thus, in the beautiful dialogue between *Peggy* and *Jenny* in the *Gentle Shepherd* the latter paints, with genuine humour, the distresses incident to a married life:

> O 'tis a pleasant thing to be a bride—
> Syne whinging gets about your ingle side,
> Yelping for this or that wi' fasheous din;
> To make them brats then ye man toil and spin:

> Ae wean fa's sick, ane scads itsell wi'brue,
> Ane breaks his shin, anither tines his shoe;
> The de'il gangs o'er Jock Webster, hame grows

hell,
And Pate miscaws you war than tongue can tell.

In the poem intitled **"Content,"** we find the same sentiment in English; but how poor, how mean, in comparison
is the expression!

    The pregnant matron's grief as much prevails;
    Some of the children always something ails;
    One boy is sick, t'other has broke his head;
    And nurse is blam'd when little miss is dead.

Yet, from this censure of his pieces in English verse, we
must except the poem intitled **"Health,"** which is a composition of superior merit. Its form is that of satire; and
its purpose is to inculcate the attainment and preservation
of the inestimable blessing of health by the delineation of
a series of characters in which the effects of sloth, effem-
inacy, gluttony, ebriety, and every species of debauchery,
are contrasted with those of activity, temperance, and
sobriety. The effects of the passions on the bodily tem-
perature are likewise judiciously estimated; the peevish,
the envious, and the malignant characters, are opposed to
the cheerful, the contented, and the benevolent; and the
preservation of a just equilibrium of mind, and benignity
of heart, is shown to be eminently promotive of the vigour of the animal frame. The characters are drawn with
a bold spirit and a powerful hand, while the satire has all
the keenness of the Juvenalian school.

Of lyric poetry, one of the most difficult species is the
song. It is one of those mental exertions that require, not
so much a superiority either of genius or of poetic fancy,
as a certain native address; so, in the intercourse of life,
there is an elegance of manner, which pleases, independently, either of worth or ability. Some of the best songs in
the English language were written by contemporaries and
countrymen of Ramsay; by Crawfurd, Hamilton of Bangour,
and Lord Binning: for we have nothing more perfect in
that species of composition than "Tweedside," "What beauties does Flora disclose;"—"Go, plaintive sounds;" and,
"Did ever swain a nymph adore." The elegant author of
"Essays on Song-writing" has arranged his collection under three different classes—ballad and pastoral—passionate and descriptive—ingenious and witty. As the talents of
Ramsay were conspicuous in all of these departments, it
might be presumed that he should particularly excel in song
composition. And in reality he has displayed, in that species of writing, a high portion of merit; though perhaps not
reaching that degree of eminence at which other writers,
who are in other respects of inferior talents, have arrived.
This appears to have arisen from his haste rather than his
incapacity to give his compositions that perfect polish which
seems to be particularly requisite in a song. Philips has
observed justly, that "a song loses all its lustre if it be not
polished with the greatest accuracy. The smallest blemish
in it, like a flaw in a jewel, takes off the whole value of it.
A song is as it were a little image in enamel, that requires
all the nice touches of the pencil, a gloss and a smoothness
with those delicate finishing strokes which would be superfluous and thrown away upon larger figures, where the
strength and boldness of a masterly hand gives all the grace."

This delicate finishing Ramsay's hasty pencil could not
always bestow; yet, as the beauty and propriety of sentiment are still more material than the elegance of the dress,
. . . we find many of his songs, wherein there is everything
to praise in the thought, and fortunately very little in the
expression, that diminishes its power of pleasing. An excellent judge has declared his opinion, that "'**The Lass of
Patie's Mill,' 'The Yellowhair'd Laddie,' 'Farewell to
Lochaber,'** and some others, must be allowed to be equal
to any, and superior, in point of pastoral simplicity, to most
lyric productions, either in the Scotish, or any other language." Among those others, I would mention, **"The last
time I came o'er the Moor," "Bessy Bell and Mary
Gray," "Now wat ye wha I met yestreen," "Through
the Wood, Laddie," "The Highland Laddie," "My Patie
is a Lover gay."** His ballad on **"Bonny Kate,"** (Lady
Catherine Cochran), which is written in the stanza of Shenstone, has uncommon vigour and hilarity, propriety and
polish. Such, then, are the lyric merits, which, notwithstanding their attendant imperfections, must for ever give
Ramsay a very high place among the writers of Scotish and
English song. . . .

In the year 1725, Ramsay published his pastoral comedy
of *The Gentle Shepherd,* the noblest and most permanent
monument of his fame. . . .

The story of the *Gentle Shepherd* is fitted to excite the
warmest interest, because the situations into which the
characters are thrown, are strongly affecting, whilst they
are strictly consonant to nature and probability. The whole
of the fable is authorized by the circumstances of the
times in which the action of the piece is laid. The era of
Cromwell's usurpation, when many a loyal subject, sharing the misfortunes of his exiled sovereign, were stripped
of their estates, and then left to the neglect and desolation
of forfeiture; the necessity under which those unhappy
sufferers often lay of leaving their infant progeny under
the charge of some humble but attached dependent till
better days should dawn upon their fortunes; the criminal
advantages taken by false friends in usurping the rights of
the sufferers, and securing themselves against future question by deeds of guilt; these circumstances, too well founded in truth and nature, are sufficient to account for every
particular in this most interesting drama, and give it perfect verisimilitude. . . .

The persons of the Scotish pastoral are the actual inhabitants of the country where the scene is laid—their manners are drawn from nature with a faithful pencil. The
contrast of the different characters is happily imagined,
and supported with consummate skill. *Patie* of a cheerful
and sanguine temperament; spirited, yet free from vain
ambition; contented with his humble lot; endowed by
nature with a superior understanding, and feeling in himself those internal sources of satisfaction which are independent of the adventitious circumstances of rank and
fortune. *Roger,* of a grave and phlegmatic constitution; of
kind affections, but of that ordinary turn of mind, which
is apt to suppose some necessary connection between the
possession of wealth and felicity. The former, from native
dignity of character assuming a bold pre-eminence, and

acting the part of a tutor and counsellor to his friend, who bends, though with some reluctance, to the authority of a nobler mind. The principal female characters are contrasted with similar skill, and equal power of discrimination. *Peggy,* beautiful in person as in mind, endowed with every quality that can adorn the character of woman; gentle, tender-hearted, constant in affection, free from vanity as from caprice; of excellent understanding; judging of others by the criterion of her own innocent mind, and therefore forming the most amiable views of human nature. *Jenny,* sensible and affectionate, sprightly and satirical; possessing the ordinary qualities of her sex,—self-love, simulation, and the passion of conquest; and pleased with exercising a capricious dominion over the mind of a lover; judging of mankind rather from the cold maxims of instilled prudential caution, than from the native suggestions of the heart.—A contrast of characters strongly and skilfully opposed, and therefore each most admirably fitted to bring the other into full display.

The subordinate persons of the drama are drawn with equal skill and fidelity to their prototypes. *Glaud* and *Symon* are the genuine pictures of the old Scotish yeomanry, the Lothian farmers of the last age, in their manners, sentiments, and modes of life; humble, but respectable; homely, yet comfortable. The episode of *Bauldy,* while it gives a pleasing variety, without interrupting the principal action, serves to introduce a character of a different species as a foil to the honest and simple worth of the former. It paints in strong colours, and exposes to merited reprobation and contempt, that low and sordid mind which seeks alone the gratification of its own desires, though purchased by the misery of the object of its affection. *Bauldy* congratulates himself on the cruel disappointment of *Peggy's* love;—"I hope we'll a' sleep sound, but ane, this night;"—and judges her present situation of deep distress to be the most favourable moment for preferring his own suit. His punishment, as it is suitable to his demerits, gives entire satisfaction. . . .

The charm of the **Gentle Shepherd** arises equally from the nature of the passions which are there delineated, and the engaging simplicity and truth with which their effects are described. The poet paints an honourable and virtuous affection between a youthful pair of the most amiable character; a passion indulged on each side from the purest and most disinterested motives, surmounting the severest of all trials—the unexpected elevation of the lover to a rank which, according to the maxims of the world, would preclude the possibility of union; and crowned at length by the delightful and most unlooked for discovery that this union is not only equal as to the condition of the parties, but is an act of retributive justice. In the anxious suspense that precedes this discovery, the conflict of generous passions in the breasts of the two lovers is drawn with consummate art, and gives rise to a scene of the utmost tenderness and the most pathetic interest. Cold, indeed, must be that heart, and dead to the finest sensibilities of our nature, which can read without emotion the interview between *Patie* and *Peggy,* after the discovery of *Patie's* elevated birth, which the following lines describe:

> PATIE.
>   —My Peggy, why in
> tears?
> Smile as ye wont, allow nae room for fears!
> Tho' I'm nae mair a shepherd, yet I'm thine.
>
> PEGGY.
>   I dare not think sae high.—I now repine
> At the unhappy chance that made not me
> A gentle match, or still a herd kept thee.
> Wha can withoutten pain see frae the coast
> The ship that bears his all like to be lost;
> Like to be carried, by some rever's hand,
> Far frae his wishes to some distant land?
>
> PATIE.
>   Ne'er quarrel fate, whilst it wi' me remains
> To raise thee up, or still attend these plains.
> My father has forbid our loves, I own;
> But love's superior to a parent's frown:
> I falsehood hate. Come, kiss thy cares away;
> I ken to love, as weel as to obey.
> Sir William's generous; leave the task to me,
> To make strict duty and true love agree.

. . . . .

In intimate knowledge of human nature Ramsay yields to few poets either of ancient or of modern times. How naturally does poor *Roger* conjecture the insensibility of his mistress to his passion, from the following simple, but finely-imagined circumstances:

> My Bawty is a cur I dearly like,
> Even while he fawn'd she strak the poor dumb
>   tyke;
> If I had fill'd a nook within her breast,
> She wad have shawn mair kindness to my beast.
> When I begin to tune my stock and horn,
> Wi' a' her face she shaws a cauldrife scorn;
> Last night I play'd, ye never heard sic spite;
> "O'er Bogie" was the tune, and her delight,
> Yet tauntingly she at her cousin speer'd
> Gif she could tell what tune I play'd, and
>   sneer'd.

The counsel which *Patie* gives his friend to prove with certainty the state of *Jenny's* affections, is the result of a profound acquaintance with the human heart:

> Daft gowk! leave aff that silly whining way;
> Seem careless; there's my hand ye'll win the
>   day.
> Hear how I serv'd my lass, I love as weel
> As ye do Jenny, and wi' heart as leal.

Then follows a picture so natural, and at the same time so exquisitely beautiful, that there is nothing in antiquity that can parallel it:

> Last morning I was gay, and early out,
> Upon a dyke I lean'd, glow'ring about;

I saw my Meg come linkan o'er the lee;
I saw my Meg, but Meggy saw na me,
For yet the sun was wading thro' the mist,
And she was close upon me ere she wist.
Her coast were kiltit, and did sweetly shaw
Her straight bare legs that whiter were than
    snaw;
Her cockernony snooded up fu' sleek,
Her haffet locks hang waving on her cheek;
Her cheeks sae ruddy, and her een sae clear,
And oh! her mouth like ony hunny pear.
Neat, neat she was in bustine waistcoat clean,
As she came skiffing o'er the dewy green.
Blythsome I cry'd, "My bonny Meg, come here,
I ferly wherefore ye're sae soon asteer!
But I can guess, ye're gawn to gather dew."
She scowr'd awa, and said, "What's that to
    you?"
"Then fare ye weel, Meg dorts, and e'en's ye
    like,"
I careless cry'd, and lap in o'er the dyke.
I trow when that she saw, within a crack,
She came wi' a right thieveless errand back;
Misca'd me first; then bad me hound my dog
To wear up three waff ewes stray'd on the bog.
I leugh, and sae did she; then wi' great haste
I clasp'd my arms about her neck and waist,
About her yielding waist, and took a fowth
Of sweetest kisses frae her glowing mouth.
While hard and fast I held her in my grips,
My very saul came lowping to my lips.
Sair, sair she flet wi' me 'tween ilka smack,
But weel I kend she meant na as she spake.
Dear Roger, when your jo puts on her gloom,
Do ye sae too, and never fash your thumb;
Seem to forsake her, soon she'll change her
    mood;
Gae woo anither, and she'll gang clean wood. . . .

The principal difficulty in pastoral poetry, when it attempts an actual delineation of nature (which we have seen is too seldom its object), lies in the association of delicate and affecting sentiments with the genuine manners of rustic life; an union so difficult to be accomplished, that the chief pastoral poets, both ancient and modern, have either entirely abandoned the attempt, by choosing to paint a fabulous and chimerical state of society, or have failed in their endeavour, either by indulging in such refinement of sentiment as is utterly inconsistent with rustic nature, or by endowing their characters with such a rudeness and vulgarity of manners as is hostile to every idea of delicacy. It appears to me that Ramsay has most happily avoided these extremes; and this he could the better do from the singularly fortunate choice of his subject. The principal persons of the drama, though trained from infancy in the manners of rustic life, are of generous birth; to whom, therefore, we may allow, from nature and the influence of blood, an elevation of sentiment, and a nobler mode of thinking, than to ordinary peasants. To these characters the poet has, therefore, with perfect propriety and knowledge of human nature given the generous sentiments that accord with their condition, though

veiled a little by the manners and conveyed in the language which suits their accidental situation. The other characters, who are truly peasants, are painted with fidelity from nature; but even of these, the situation chosen by the poet was favourable for avoiding that extreme vulgarity and coarseness of manners which would have offended a good taste. The peasantry of the Pentland hills, within six or seven miles of the metropolis, with which, of course, they have frequent communication, cannot be supposed to exhibit the same rudeness of manners which distinguishes those of the remote parts of the country. As the models, therefore, from which the poet drew were cast in a finer mould than mere provincial rustics, so their copies, as drawn by him, do not offend by their vulgarity, nor is there any greater degree of rusticity than what merely distinguishes their mode of life and occupations.

In what I have said of the manners of the characters in the *Gentle Shepherd,* I know that I encounter the prejudices of some Scotish critics, who allowing otherwise the very high merits of Ramsay as a poet, and giving him credit in particular for his knowledge of human nature and skill to touch the passions, quarrel with him only on the score of his language, as they seem to annex inseparably the idea of coarseness and vulgarity to everything that is written in the native dialect of their country; but of this I have said enough before. To every Englishman, and, I trust, to every Scotsman not of fastidious refinement, the dialect of the *Gentle Shepherd* will appear to be most perfectly consonant to the characters of the speakers and the times in which the action is laid. To this latter circumstance the critics I have just mentioned seem not to have been sufficiently attentive. The language of this pastoral is not precisely the Scotish language of the present day: the poet himself spoke the language of the beginning of the century, and his persons were of the age preceding that period. To us their dialect is an antiquated tongue, and, as such, it carries with it a Doric simplicity. But when we consider both the characters and the times, it has an indispensable propriety; and to have given the speakers in the *Gentle Shepherd* a more refined and polished dialect, or more modern tone of conversation, would have been a gross violation of truth and nature.

In the faithful painting of rustic life, Ramsay seems to have been indebted to his own situation and early habits, as well as to the want of a learned education. He was familiarly acquainted with rural nature from actual observation; and his own impressions were not weakened or altered by much acquaintance with the classical commonplaces, or with those artificial pictures which are presented by the poets. It is not, therefore, the general characters of the country which one poet can easily draw from the works of others that we find in his pastoral; it was the country in which he lived, the genuine manners of its inhabitants, the actual scenes with which he was conversant, that fixed his observation, and guided his imitative pencil. The character which, in the preface to his *Evergreen,* he assigns to the Scotish poetry in general, is in the most peculiar manner assignable to his own:—"The morning rises in the poet's description, as she does in the Scotish horizon; we are not carried to Greece and Italy for a shade, a stream, or a breeze; the groves rise in our own valleys, the rivers flows from our own fountains, and the winds blow upon our own hills." Ramsay's landscapes are drawn with the most characteristic precision; we view the scene before us, as in the paintings of a Claude or a Waterloo; and the hinds and shepherds of the Pentland hills, to all of whom this delightful pastoral is as familiar as their catechism, can trace the whole of its scenery in nature, and are eager to point out to the inquiring stranger—the waterfall of *Habbie's* howe—the cottages of *Glaud* and *Symon*—*Sir William's* ancient tower, ruinated in the civil wars, but since rebuilt—the auld avenue and shady groves still remaining in defiance of the modern taste for naked, shadeless lawn. And here let it be remarked, as perhaps the surest criterion of the merit of this pastoral as a true delineation of nature, that it is universally relished and admired by that class of people whose habits of life and manners are there described. Its sentiments and descriptions are in unison with their feelings. It is recited with congenial animation and delight at the fireside of the farmer, when in the evening the lads and lasses assemble to solace themselves after the labours of the day, and share the rustic meal. There is not a milk-maid, a plough-boy, or a shepherd, of the Lowlands of Scotland, who has not by heart its favourite passages, and can rehearse its entire scenes. There are many of its couplets that, like the verses of Homer, are become proverbial, and have the force of an adage when introduced in familiar writing or in ordinary conversation.

I have thus endeavoured to accomplish what I proposed in the beginning of this Essay, which was, by an examination of the writings of Ramsay, to ascertain the character of his genius, and vindicate his title to that rank which, I conceive, it is his right to hold among our classical poets. I have shewn that his genius was original, inasmuch as he drew from nature with a vivid imagination and a vigorous pencil; that he inherited, in an uncommon measure, the knowledge of the human heart, the detail of life and manners; and though more prone to discern the weaknesses of mankind, the mean and the absurd in human conduct, and to apply to them the scourge of satire; yet, that he possessed the power of touching the finer passions, and was eminently skilled in the pathetic of nature. Of his power of invention, the drama of the **Gentle Shepherd,** and his **"Comic Tales,"** afford indisputable evidence; as does **"The Vision"** of his imagination. In variety of talents he yields to few poets either of ancient or of modern times.

The writings of Ramsay, as of every uncultivated genius, abound with blemishes. Even the **Gentle Shepherd,** tender and affecting as it is in the general strain of its sentiments, displays some strokes of coarseness; and his smaller pieces are frequently tarnished with improprieties, both of thought and expression. A harsh and fastidious critic may find abundant room to gratify a splenetic disposition; and such will not fail to remark, that, in this short review of his writings, I have been much less solicitous to point out those imperfections of my author than to display his beauties. I acknowledge the justness of this

observation; but I take no blame to myself. On this subject I have ever been of an opinion, in which I am warranted by the best of the English critics, Dryden and Addison, that it is much easier, in all works of taste, to discover faults, which generally float upon the surface, and are therefore obvious to the meanest understanding, than to discern those beauties which are delicate in their nature, and operate only on our finer sensibilities; and, as the task is the nicer, so is it incomparably the more pleasing. . . .

Leigh Hunt (essay date 1848)

SOURCE: "Leigh Hunt," in *The Gentle Shepherd: A Pastoral Comedy,* William Gowans, 1852, pp. lxviii-lxxii.

[*Hunt is recognized for his articulation of the principles of the Romantic movement. In the following excerpt from an essay originally published in* A Jar of Honey from Mount Hybla *(1848), he praises* The Gentle Shepherd *for its descriptions of nature and depiction of the emotional lives of its characters.*]

Poetical expression in humble life is to be found all over the south. In the instances of Burns, Ramsay, and others, the north also has seen it. Indeed, it is not a little remarkable, that Scotland, which is more northern than England, and possesses not even a nightingale, has had more of it than its southern neighbour.

Allan Ramsay is the prince of the homely pastoral drama. He and Burns have helped Scotland for ever to take pride in its heather, and its braes, and its bonny rivers, and be ashamed of no honest truth in high estate or in low; an incalculable blessing. Ramsay is entitled not only to the designation we have given him, but in some respects is the best pastoral writer in the world. There are, in truth, two sorts of genuine pastoral—the high ideal of Fletcher and Milton, which is justly to be considered the more poetical,—and the homely ideal, as set forth by Allan Ramsay and some of the Idyls of Theocritus, and which gives us such feelings of nature and passion as poetical rustics not only can, but have entertained and eloquently described. And we think the **Gentle Shepherd,** 'in some respects,' the best pastoral that ever was written, not because it has anything, in a poetical point of view, to compare with Fletcher and Milton, but because there is, upon the whole, more faith and more love in it, and because the kind of idealized truth which it undertakes to represent, is delivered in a more corresponding and satisfactory form than in any other entire pastoral drama. In fact, the **Gentle Shepherd** has no alloy whatsoever to its pretensions, *such as they are*—no failure in plot, language, or character—nothing answering to the coldness and irrelevances of 'Comus,' nor to the offensive and untrue violations of decorum in the 'Wanton Shepherdess' of Fletcher's pastoral, and the pedantic and ostentatious chastity of his Faithful one. It is a pure, healthy, natural, and (of its kind) perfect plant, sprung out of an unluxuriant but not ungenial soil; not hung with the beauty and fragrance of the productions of the higher regions of Parnassus; not waited upon by spirits and enchanted music; a dog-rose, if you will; say rather, a rose in a cottage-garden, dabbled with the morning dew, and plucked by an honest lover to give to his mistress.

Allan Ramsay's poem is not only a probable and pleasing story, containing charming pictures, much knowledge of life, and a good deal of quiet humour, but in some respects it may be called classical, if by classical is meant ease, precision, and unsuperfluousness of style. Ramsay's diction is singularly straightforward, seldom needing the assistance of inversions; and he rarely says anything for the purpose of 'filling up;'—two freedoms from defect the reverse of vulgar and commonplace; nay, the reverse of a great deal of what pretends to be fine writing, and is received as such. We confess we never tire of dipping into it, 'on and off,' any more than into Fletcher or Milton, or into Theocritus himself, who, for the union of something higher with true pastoral, is unrivalled in short pieces. The *Gentle Shepherd* is not a forest, nor a mountain-side, nor Arcady; but it is a field full of daisies, with a brook in it, and a cottage 'at the sunny end;' and this we take to be no mean thing, either in the real or the ideal world. Our Jar of Honey may well lie for a few moments among its heather, albeit filled with Hybla. There are bees, 'look you,' in Habbie's How. Theocritus and Allan shake hands over a shepherd's pipe. Take the beginning of Scene ii., Act i., both for description and dialogue:

A flowrie howm between twa verdant braes,
Where lasses use to wash and spread their
    claiths,
A trotting burnie wimpling thro' the ground,
Its channel peebles, shining, smooth, and round;
Here view *twa barefoot beauties* clean and clear;
First please your eye, next gratify your ear,
While Jenny *what she wishes discommends,*
And Meg, with better sense true love defends.

JENNY

Come, Meg, let's fa' to wark upon this green,
The shining day will bleech our linen clean;
The water's clear, the lift unclouded blew,
Will make them *like a lilly wet with dew.*

PEGGY

Go farer up the burn to Habby's How,
Where a' the sweets of spring and summer grow;
Between twa birks, out o'er a little lin
The water fa's, and makes a singand din;
A pool breast-deep beneath, as clear as glass,
Kisses with easy whirles the bordring grass:
We'll end our washing while the morning's cool,
And when the day grows het, we'll to the pool,
There wash our sells—'tis healthfu' now in May,
And sweetly cauler on sae warm a day.

This is an out-door picture. Here is an in-door one quite

as good—nay, better.

While Peggy laces up her bosom fair,
With a blew snood Jenny binds up her hair;
Glaud by his morning ingle takes a beek,
The rising sun shines motty thro' the reek,
A pipe his mouth; the lasses please his een,
And now and than his joke maun interveen.

We would quote, if we could—only it might not look so proper, when isolated—the whole song at the close of Act the Second. The first line of it alone is worth all Pope's pastorals put together, and (we were going to add) half of those of Virgil; but we reverence too much the great follower of the Greeks, and true lover of the country. There is more sentiment, and equal nature, in the song at the end of Act the Fourth. Peggy is taking leave of her lover, who is going abroad:

At setting day, and rising morn,
    With soul that still shall love thee,
I'll ask of Heaven thy safe return,
    With all that can improve thee.
I'll visit aft the Birken Bush,
    Where first thou kindly told me
Sweet tales of love, *and hid my blush,*
    Whilst round thou didst enfold me.
To all our haunts I will repair,
    By Greenwood-shaw or fountain;
Or where the summer-day I'd share
    With thee upon yon mountain.
There will I tell the trees and flowers,
    From thoughts unfeign'd and tender,
By vows you're mine, *by love* is yours
    A heart which cannot wander.

The charming and so (to speak) natural flattery of the loving delicacy of this distinction—

By vows you're mine, *by love* is yours,

was never surpassed by a passion the most refined. It reminds us of a like passage in the anonymous words (Shakspeare might have written them) of the fine old English madrigal by Ford, 'Since first I saw your face.' Perhaps Ford himself wrote them; for the author of that music had sentiment enough in him for anything. The passage we allude to is—

What, I that *loved,* and you that *liked,*
Shall *we* begin to wrangle?

The highest refinement of the heart, though too rare in most classes, is luckily to be found in all; and hence it is, that certain meetings of extremes in lovers of different ranks in life are not always to be attributed either to a failure of taste on the one side, or unsuitable pretensions on the other. Scotish dukes have been known to meet with real Gentle Shepherd heroines; and everybody knows the story of a lowly Countess of Exeter, who was too sensitive to survive the disclosure of the rank to which her lover had raised her.

J. Logie Robertson (essay date 1886)

SOURCE: "Allan Ramsay," in *Macmillan's Magazine,* Vol. LV, No. 325, November, 1886, pp. 19-26.

[*In the following excerpt, Robertson views Ramsay's poetry as a transitional link between the medieval tradition of Scots poetry and that of later Scots poets, such as Fergusson and Burns.*]

Two hundred years ago, in October, 1686, Allan Ramsay was born in the upland village of Leadhills; and one hundred years ago last July, the first edition of Burns's poems made its appearance in the weaving-town of Kilmarnock. For the greater part of the century prior to the latter event Ramsay was universally regarded as the national poet of Scotland, and *The Gentle Shepherd* was believed to be the most consummate flower of Scottish poetical genius; for just a century since, and in virtue of that latter event, his name and fame have suffered more or less partial eclipse. He has not been forgotten,—his reputation was too firmly rooted in the popular heart for that; but he has been undeservedly neglected; his poetical power has been growing more and more traditional, and is now, we fear, very largely taken on trust. His name, we have said, has not been forgotten—it is, indeed, a household word throughout the Scottish Lowlands. There, and more especially in the rural parts of that district, they talk familiarly, in the Scottish manner, of Allan; "that's ane o' Allan's sangs" they will say. But if they speak of Allan Cunningham, who was also in his way successful in touching the national heart, they never fail to give him his full name. Ramsay has a prescriptive right to the simple and unsupported *prenomen*. Sometimes they vary the expression by prefixing honest; "honest Allan!" they will say in the excess of a proud familiarity with his name. And then they will most likely follow up the words by a quotation, said to be from Burns, which probably reveals the origin of the adjective:

> Yes! there is ane—a Scottish callan;
> There's ane—come forrit, honest Allan!
> Thou needna jouk behint the hallan,
>   A chiel sae clever;
> The teeth o' time may gnaw Tantallan,
>   But thou's for ever!

Yet it may well be doubted whether they appreciate at its proper value the epithet which they repeat so glibly. Ramsay was not unduly bold; but bashfulness was no feature of his disposition, and he was the last person of the men of his day to be found "jouking behint the hallan" [ducking behind the door]. If Burns did not write the lines, and it is only Burns's brother Gilbert who denies the authorship, somebody else of Burns's day did, who saw and lamented the neglect into which Ramsay was falling as the brighter orb of Burns's genius rose on the literary horizon. If Burns did write them, a supposition to which we decidedly incline, they are in his mouth a singularly graceful acknowledgment of the excellence of his first and best model and master, and at the same time express or imply a sentiment which is quite in harmony with the frequent and just confessions of his indebtedness to Ramsay. Ramsay's name marks an epoch in the history of Scottish poetry. Before him were "the Makkaris," who reached their lofty culmination in William Dunbar, and who may be said to have terminated in some obscurity in the Sempills. The era of modern Scottish poetry began with Ramsay. His is the style, the treatment of a subject, the language, which, with modifications and development of a perfectly natural and organic growth, Fergusson, and Burns, and Scott (in those of his novels which describe purely Scottish character), and all the many minor writers of distinctively Scottish literature, Hogg being the most notable exception, have since adopted and used. But though he began a new era, he was not altogether independent of the old. He links on, at the outstart of his literary career, to the middle Sempill, whose humorous elegy on the death of the Piper of Kilbarchan was the standard of his imitation, as it had previously been that of his contemporary and correspondent, Hamilton of Gilbertfield. Not less sympathetic was his sense of humour with the comic vein of the royal poet, James the First, as exemplified in **"Christ's Kirk on the Green,"** and his two cantos of continuation to that famous poem are an acknowledgment of the inspiration which he drew from the ancient "Makkaris." He was, however, essentially original. Cowper was not more original, excepting only in the matter of language. The poets of Scotland have from time to time employed a conventional and artificial phraseology; but no age, and scarcely a writer in the long line of their history, has been quite deficient in the use of a vigorous vernacular, sufficient to bring them into living touch with the men of their generation. Ramsay's originality did not, therefore, chiefly show itself in his adoption of the current and conversational speech of his day. It is, however, to be noticed that by the voluminousness of his poems and their immense popularity, continued without a break for three generations, he may be said to have fixed the standard of modern Scotch, by blending his mother-tongue with antique expressions of the past, and proving the capability of the mixture for large and varied poetical representation. "Thy bonnie auld words gar (make) me smile," was part of a complimentary epistle addressed to Ramsay by a contemporary, himself an adept in the use of Scotch and considerably older than the person whom he was addressing. The fact would seem to be, that modern Scotch is very much what Ramsay made it; and we question if there are many expressions in the rural Scotch of to-day, with all Burns's cultivation of the language, which Ramsay, if he were living now, would not readily recognise.

But it is not in the humour of his delineations that Ramsay is really most original. The humour, though in one sense it was his own, that is, unaffectedly sincere and genuine as a personal possession, was, notwithstanding, what one might almost call a national property, in which such of the elder poets as Dunbar and Lyndsay, and such of their successors as Fergusson and Burns, could claim at least an equal share. Yet it may well be allowed that he deepened and widened the national sense of humour by the use which he made of his own share, and turned it with greater emphasis and effect upon the follies and minor immoralities of social life than any had ever done before him. He set the example of humorous portraiture and address to Burns; and even in that dangerous, though legitimate, field for satirical humour, which since Lyndsay's time has been the exclusive walk of Burns, namely, religious bigotry and hypocrisy, he was meditating entrance and onslaught at the age of seventy—too late an age! Hear his own words:

> I have it even in my poo'er
> The very Kirk itself to scour,
> An' that ye'll say 's a brag richt bauld!
> But did not Lyndsay this of auld?
> Wha gave the scarlet harlot strokes
> Sneller [keener] than all the pelts of Knox.

Ramsay's originality lies much in the unromantic and yet fascinating realism of his natural descriptions. He brings no lime-light effects to bear upon his scenery; neither does he present us with mere photographic copies. It is Nature, her naked self, but never presented except when in perfect harmony with the lyrical mood to which she is accessory, or the dramatic situation to which she is subordinated. It is very much the nature to which Cowper introduces us, allowance being made for difference of locality—healthy, every-day, commonplace nature; only, we think, more vividly, more completely and harmoniously presented. A brief quotation or two will in a general way exemplify what we mean. "This sunny morning," says the Gentle Shepherd,

> This sunny morning, Roger, cheers my
> blood,
> And puts all Nature in a jovial mood.
> How heartsome is't to see the rising plants,
> And hear the birds chirm owre their pleasing
> rants!

The description of Habbie's How (Hollow) is another case in point—

> Gae farer up the burn to Habbie's How
> Where a' the sweets of Spring and Simmer
> grow.
> Between twa birks, out o'er a little linn,
> The water fa's and maks a singand din;
> A pool breast-deep, beneath as clear as
> glass,
> Kisses with easy whirls the bordering grass;
> We'll end our washing while the morning's
> cool,
> And, when the day grows het, we'll to the
> pool,
> There wash oursels—'tis healthfu' now in
> May,
> And sweetly cauler on sae warm a day.

It is, however, in his delineation of human nature that Ramsay is most genuine; but he is less so in his earlier and somewhat exaggerated descriptions of low life, than in his later and cheerfully serious representations of commonplace rural character. The pastoral drama of *The*

Gentle Shepherd is not only a masterpiece, but an original creation. There was nothing like it, nothing to suggest it, in all the antecedent literature of Scotland. It is to this day the poem that most successfully represents Scottish rural life. The 'Farmer's Ingle' of Fergusson and Burns's 'Cotter's Saturday Night' are kindred poems, similar in subject, and approached with the same serious spirit. But the form is different; they are narrative poems, each descriptive of a common phase of rustic life within doors. None the less are they pendents to *The Gentle Shepherd*; for *The Gentle Shepherd* is less a rustic drama in which the interest depends on the plot, than a rustic idyll, the form of which happens to be dramatic, with the interest dependent on the author's views of rustic human life. It is to the credit of Ramsay that, living in close and actual contact with the artificial school of poets of whom Pope and Gay were the representatives of his acquaintance, and rather welcoming than seeking to withdraw himself from their influence, he had yet within himself an instinct of true poetic feeling and a power of true poetic art, sufficient to lift him above their blandishments, and to anticipate by half a century that return to nature which in England was inaugurated by Cowper and finally consummated by Wordsworth.

Nor should it ever be forgotten that Ramsay was, in fact, the first in point of time of Scottish song-writers. He may be called the inventor of that species of song which is regarded as distinctively Scottish. Burns's songs have in much more abundant measure the true lyrical quality, the inspiration and the utterance, but they are of identically the same species as Ramsay's. To the green and but half-opened buds of Ramsay they offer the contrast of the full-blown blossoms of June, gorgeous with dyes and breathing a paradise of fragrance, but they are yet the development of those buds, grown on the same stem and drawing nourishment from the same soil. Much was to be expected from a country which had already given the rich promise of **"Polwarth on the Green," "Lochaber no more," "The last time I came o'er the Muir,"** and a really charming love-song beginning somewhat coldly with the question, "Now wat ye wha I met yestreen?" They were the genuine forerunners of "Bonnie Jean," "The gloomy Night is gath'ring fast," and even of "Highland Mary." . . .

It was about [1712 that] he first began to write verses in emulation of Hamilton, and it was in that same year he was admitted into a very select social coterie of twelve, self-styled the Easy Club, and numbering among its members a university professor, a doctor in large practice, and the well-known scholar and printer, Thomas Ruddiman. His connection with this club was of the utmost importance in drawing out and directing his poetical talent. He became its laureate, entertained its gatherings with his compositions, profited by its criticisms, and acquired something of its professional culture. It was for the Easy Club he wrote his humorous descriptions of low life, such as the elegy on the death of Maggie Johnston, a suburban ale-wife well known to all Edinburgh. This was really his first poem, his earlier pieces being merely the essays of an apprentice learning the art of literary expression. It was much applauded, and encouraged him to renewed

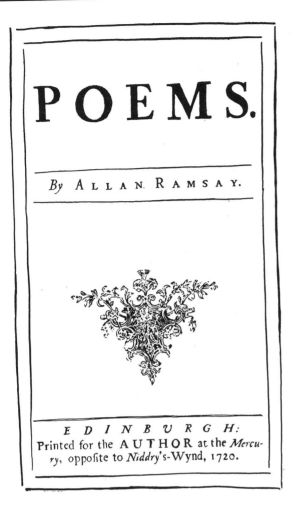

Title page of a 1720 collection of Ramsay's poems.

efforts which were still more successful. The companion elegy on the death of Lucky Wood, the cleanly ale-wife of the Canongate, and his additions to the ancient poem of **"Christ's Kirk on the Green,"** mark his highest achievements as a humorist in the department of low life. His situations in these compositions are intensely comical, and the language that depicts them is correspondingly blunt and broad. Coarse, indeed, they are, but their coarseness is neither morbid nor prurient. It is the natural healthy coarseness of Chaucer. Hogarth found in Ramsay a brother artist, and in token of his delight at the discovery, dedicated to him the twelve plates of his illustrations of 'Hudibras.' But after his thirty-sixth year most of this coarseness disappears, and the result is a style of composition not less effective and much more refined, and more distinctly on the side of virtue. Ramsay however, it should be noticed, claimed in his earlier compositions the credit of a moralist, and attributed to the spiritual purblindness of his critics their failure to perceive the satire of his representations.

The members of the Easy Club were suspected of sympathy with Jacobitism, and the suspicion becoming warm, the club broke up in some alarm. Ramsay steered pretty clear of politics, but there is good ground for believing that his political leanings were towards the exiled Stuarts. The famous Countess of Eglinton, who accepted the dedication of **The Gentle Shepherd,** was no politically indiscriminate patroness of literature; and there can be no doubt that community of political sentiment would be a recommendation, if not a requisite, to the friendship of Pope, Gay, and Arbuthnot—a friendship which Ramsay enjoyed. On the dissolution of the club, which occurred shortly after the fiasco of "The Fifteen," Ramsay resolved on an appeal to the public for confirmation of his claim to rank as a poet. He went about the matter with characteristic prudence. Specimens of his poetry were printed on broad sheets and circulated about the town by street-vendors, for the purpose of testing or stimulating the popular taste. The plan succeeded so well that it became a practice of the citizens' wives to send out for "Allan Ramsay's last piece," and discuss it with their afternoon tea. He next opened a subscription list for purchasers' names, and finally a handsome quarto of four hundred pages made its appearance from the press of his friend Ruddiman, and was speedily taken up. An analysis of the subscription list shows, to the credit of the Scottish nobility, that about one-seventh of his patrons were of aristocratic birth. It is pleasant to find Pope's name in the list. The result of the publication was to extend his fame, and to improve his fortunes by about four hundred guineas. At the same time it determined him to a literary career, and from the moment of that determination wig-making languished, and the more leisurely occupation of bookselling filled his vacant hours. A period of great industry followed. Scarcely a year passed for the next decade but he was before the public with one or more offerings of original or editorial work. His editorial work was the collection of selected songs, both Scottish and English, into **The Tea-Table Miscellany,** and a series of Scottish poems, purporting to have been "wrote by the ingenious, before 1600," brought together into **The Evergreen**. These collections contained compositions of his own, which were either too free morally or too dangerous politically to be owned amongst his authorised productions. Of these anonymous poems the best is, undoubtedly, **"The Vision,"** which may, indeed, be regarded as Ramsay's most ambitious effort, and certainly reveals an unusual sweep and power of imagination. In creative work he ventured unfortunately into fields foreign alike to his genius and his art; he took to imitating Pope, and produced some very laborious essays in English verse, and a few sad but unsorrowful elegies. His true sphere and talent lay in the use of the Scottish language upon themes of national interest. Of this he was well aware; but he could not altogether resist the temptation to enter the lists with his English contemporaries and encounter them with their own weapons. His English verses, of which he wrote far too many, may show his culture, but they give no indication of his genius.

The quarto of which we have spoken appeared in 1721. Seven years later he published a companion quarto containing the pieces written in the interval, and then he rested from poetical labours. The period of his literary activity altogether extended over twenty years, of which the first five were the years of his apprenticeship. He gave over when he ceased to write with facility,—when, as he said, he found his muse beginning to be "dour and dorty," [loth and sulky]. He had, however, used the pen too long and too assiduously to be able entirely to forego the luxury of its use, and an occasional epistle in verse towards the end of his life showed that if he composed with more effort he also composed with more pith.

The second quarto established Ramsay's fame. It contained the composition which gave him the most satisfaction, and which best illustrates the true character of his genius, the charming pastoral drama of **The Gentle Shepherd**. It became instantly popular, and so excited the envy of enemies who had hitherto identified him with the school of art which delights to minister to immorality, that they absurdly refused him the authorship. The germ of the play will be found in two detached pastoral poems in the first quarto, where they seem to have attracted little attention. Ramsay ran them together as the first and second scenes of a drama which beautifully and naturally evolves the story they half suggest. No more pleasing and effective moral agency than this dramatic pastoral, the Bible alone excepted, ever entered the cottages of the Scottish peasantry. Its morality is of the best type; it is the morality of common sense, practicable, honest, and cheerful. . . .

Satirist, of course, he was, but his satire was of that genial and even gentle kind, that aims at institutions rather than individuals, at manners rather than men, and is content with simple exposure. Ramsay, either as a poet or a man, needs no great critic to interpret him for us. His life, and his writings, which afford the best commentary on his life, are open to all who have eyes to see. But if we must find a critic of authority with whom our own opinion shall agree, we shall hardly find a better than Walter Scott, who brought the essential quality of the man into a single word when he called him "the joyous Ramsay."

John Veitch (essay date 1887)

SOURCE: "Modern Period: Alan Ramsay (1686-1758)," in *The Feeling for Nature in Scottish Poetry, Vol. II*, William Blackwood and Sons, 1887, pp. 24-38.

[*In the following excerpt, Veitch praises Ramsay's depiction of the natural scenery of the Scottish Lowlands.*]

Allan Ramsay (1686-1758) is by far the most interesting and influential literary personage in Scotland in the first half of the eighteenth century. To his example, impulse, and suggestions of new lines of poetry, we owe much of all that is best in Scottish poetry and literature since his time. Fergusson and Burns could not have done what they did, unless as coming after Ramsay, and being thus enabled to start from the high level both of feeling and of accomplished versification which he had attained. Ramsay had the courage, in a conventional time both in English and Scottish poetry, to recognise and be true to the manners, the simple everyday life, the rural character,

and the scenery of his native land. . . .

Ramsay came to Edinburgh in 1701, where he was apprenticed to a wig-maker—then a business higher in the social scale than anything corresponding to it in these days. Here he came under the influence, in the first place, of the older Scottish poetry, through the publication of *Watson's Choise Collection of Comic and Serious Scots Poems, both Ancient and Modern, by several hands,* which appeared in three parts, in 1706, 1709, and 1711. Ramsay was an apprentice lad of seventeen when Watson printed the first part of his *Collection.* The second edition appeared in 1713, "printed and sold at his shop, next door to the *Red Lyon,* opposite to the *Luckenbooths.*" The preface to the First Part bears that this was the first collection of its kind in the vernacular.

Among other poems, Watson's *Collection* contains "Christ's Kirk on the Green," "The Cherry and the Slae" of Montgomerie, "Cælia's Country House" by Sir George Mackenzie, "Forth-Feasting" by Drummond of Hawthornden, "Three Poems" by Sir Robert Aytoun. Among Ramsay's first efforts was that of adding a canto to "Christ's Kirk on the Green." Watson's *Collection* not only influenced him greatly, but led him to form collections of the same kind. Ramsay's **Tea-Table Miscellany** appeared in January 1724, and his **Evergreen** in October of the same year. The latter is founded chiefly on the Bannatyne MS., then in the possession of William Carmichael, brother of the Earl of Hyndford, and lent by him to Ramsay. Ramsay was not a good editor of the older poems. He was not well skilled in the language, and he took unwarrantable liberties with the text. But he himself profited in his poetical growth by his labour. The study of these older national pieces fixed the bent of Ramsay's genius. They recalled historical incidents and scenes, suggested the manners of rural and everyday life, were written many of them in the vernacular; and if they did not contain descriptions of scenery for their own sake, they yet suggested localities, contained pictures by the way, and allusions to nature for purposes of simile and illustration. Out of these rose the suggestions and the inspiration which, when fused in a whole, gave birth to **The Gentle Shepherd** in 1725.

Of the general merits of this poem, as a pastoral, this is not the place to speak. These are now definitely and permanently recognised. A Scotsman who retains his nationality cannot read it without feeling its truth and its power. Properly enough it does not pause on descriptions of scenery, nor does it unduly prolong them; but they are there as the groundwork of the piece, constantly recurring, well woven into the progress of the incidents; and truer or more apt pictures of certain aspects of the Scottish landscape we have not in the language. Ramsay overleaps the garden limits, so common and tiresome in the older poets; goes out into the meadows, the fields, and the pastoral moorlands; daunders by the burn, climbs the hillside, and tells us what he finds there at first hand—what the eye sees and the ear hears—and tells it so deftly, so briefly often, that a few lines contain a complete picture. His painting is thoroughly realistic, taken straight from nature, and yet it is completely typical of the scene. Ramsay first revealed the power and the beauty of the Lowland and pastoral landscape of Scotland. To grandeur or sublimity he never rises. We have nothing of mountain power, beetling crag, deep corrie, or unfathomable glen—nothing of the stern and the wild in our scenery. His somewhat toned-down and timid spirit, always tending to the golden mean in action and even imagination, shrank from this; and it was as yet hardly recognised in the feeling of the time. The sympathy with and depicting of this side of things came much later. It is neither in Fergusson nor in Burns. Leyden probably was the first after Ramsay to feel it; and it comes to its climax in Scott. Withal, Ramsay's work in this direction is invaluable; and one of its merits is, that it first led a native artist—David Allan—in 1788, to illustrate with the pencil those native scenes which Ramsay had so well portrayed in words. This gave a direction to Scottish art, the fruits of which the country has reaped richly since the last quarter of last century.

The key-note to Ramsay's mode of dealing with nature is in these lines [from **"Epistle to W. Somerville,"** 1729]:

> I love the garden wild and wide,
> Where oaks have plum-trees by their side;
> Where woodbines and the twisting vine
> Clip round the pear-tree and the pine;
> Where mixed jonquils and gowans grow,
> And roses 'midst rank clover blow
> Upon a bank of a clear strand,
> In wimplings led by Nature's hand.
> Though docks and brambles here and there
> May sometimes cheat the gardener's care,
> Yet this to me's a paradise
> Compared with prim-cut plots and nice,
> Where Nature has to Art resigned,
> Till all looks mean, stiff, and confined.
>
> . . . . .
>
> Heaven Homer taught; the critic draws
> Only from him and such their laws:
> The native bards first plunge the deep
> Before the artful dare to leap.

This was the new spirit, the very spirit of Scott himself, carried in him to a greater height and freedom [in *Marmion*]:

> On the wild hill
> Let the wild heath-bell flourish still;
> Cherish the tulip, prune the vine;
> But freely let the woodbine twine,
> And leave untrimmed the eglantine.

In **The Gentle Shepherd** the pictures of scenery, complete and rounded, are too numerous to quote; but it is only by reference to some of these that we can understand the change which has now come over the mode of dealing with the Scottish landscape. The Prologue to each scene contains a perfect image. Thus, to Act I., Scene 1, we have the following Prologue:

> Beneath the south side of a craigy bield,
> Where crystal springs the halesome waters yield,
> Twa youthfu' shepherds on the gowans lay,
> Tenting their flocks ae bonny morn of May.
> Poor Roger granes [groans], till hollow echoes ring,
> But blither Patie likes to laugh an' sing.

Patie and Roger

Pat. This sunny morning, Roger, cheers
>   my blood,
> And puts all nature in a jovial mood.
> How heartsome 'tis to see the rising plants,
> To hear the birds chirm o'er their pleasing
>   rants!
> How halesome 'tis to snuff the cauler air,
> And all the sweets it bears, when void of care!
> What ails thee, Roger, then? What gars thee
>   grane?
> Tell me the cause of thy ill-season'd pain.

In Scene II., Prologue, we have:

> A flowrie howm atween twa verdant braes,
> Where lasses use to wash and spread their claes;
> A trotting burnie wimpling thro' the ground,
> Its channel pebbles, shining, smooth and round;
> Here view twa barefoot beauties, clean and
>   clear;
> First please your eye, then gratify your ear.

Peggy and Jenny

Jen. Come Meg, let's fa' to wark upon
>   this green,
> This shining day will bleach our linen clean;
> The water's clear, the lift unclouded blue,
> Will make them like a lily wet with dew.
>
> *Peg.* Gae farer up the burn to Habbie's How,
> Where a' the sweets of spring and summer grow;
> Between twa birks, out o'er a little lin,
> The water fa's and makes a singin' din;
> A pool breast-deep beneath as clear as glass,
> Kisses with easy whirls the bord'ring grass:
> We'll end our washing while the morning's cool;
> And when the day grows het, we'll to the pool,
> There wash oursells—'tis healthfu' now in May,
> And sweetly cauler on sae warm a day.

The Lowland burn here appears lovingly in poetry. Montgomery had noted it in its more forcible features; but here it is taken to the heart, as a thing to be affectionately pictured and cherished as a familiar inspiration. It is fused, moreover, with simple everyday feeling, which is yet one of the primary human emotions.

In Act II., Scene 1, the Prologue gives us a picture of a small farmhouse of last century, which almost makes one long for a turning back of the dial for a hundred and fifty years, and wish now there were a world of Glauds:

> A snug thack-house, before the door a green;
> Hens on the midden, ducks in dubs are seen:
> On this side stands a barn, on that a byre;
> A peat-stack joins, and forms a rural square.
> The house is Glaud's;—there you may see him
>   lean,
> And to his divot-seat invite his frien'.

Again, in Act II., Scene 2, we have as Prologue:

> The open field; a cottage in a glen;
> An auld wife spinning at the sunny end.
> At a small distance, by a blasted tree,
> With faulded arms, and half-rais'd look, ye see
>   Bauldy his lane.

In Scene III., Prologue:

> A green kail-yard; a little fount
>   Where water poplan springs;
> There sits a wife with wrinkled front,
>   And yet she spins and sings.

These extracts show that we are now in a wholly new field of observation and description—the simple homely scenes and objects of everyday rural life—away from cities and the artifice of man, in the free moorland air by the wimpling burn of the Lowlands. Ramsay felt with Virgil:

> Pallas, quas condidit arces
> Ipsa colat; nobis placeant ante omnia sylvæ.

In his songs Ramsay is very unequal, being often merely sentimental and affected. But he emphasised, though he did not introduce into our Scottish songs of love, the courtship in the open air, with all its tender associations of natural scenery—hillside and wood, the water and the glen, the hawthorn and the gowan, and the notes of birds; and thus fused with the feeling for nature the emotion most sacred to lyrical poetry. This fusion has since his time become the almost universal characteristic of the Scottish love-songs, adding immensely to their charm.

The key-note of those songs is in such stanzas as these:

> Oh, Katie, wilt thou gang wi' me,
>   And leave the dinsome toun a while?
> The blossom's sprouting frae the tree,
>   And a' the simmer's gaun to smile.
> The mavis, nightingale, and lark,
>   The bleeting lambs and whistling hynd,
> In ilka dale, green, shaw, and park,
>   Will nourish health and glad your mind.
>
> Sune as the clear gudeman o' day
>   Does bend his morning draught o' dew,
> We'll gae to some burn-side and play,
>   And gather flowers to busk your brow.
> We'll pou the daisies on the green,
>   The lucken-gowans frae the bog;

> Between hands, now and then, we'll lean,
>   And sport upon the velvet fog.

Ramsay's feeling for scenery is very good up to its limit; but the sterner side of Scottish nature he neither knew nor felt. Ramsay was quite at home by the side of the trotting wimpling burnie; he would hardly have followed it with equal delight to its wild source—through, say, the peat-hags of Winterhope to where the crags beetle and the mists hover over the dark grey waters of Loch Skene. The poet of the sweets of Habbie's How and the agreeable green slopes of the Pentlands would not have felt much inspiration from being

> alone
> Amid the heart of many thousand mists,
> That came to him, and left him on the heights.

Well did Burns sum up the characteristics of Ramsay in those stanzas:

> Thou paints auld Nature to the nines,
> In thy sweet Caledonian lines;
> Nae gowden stream thro' myrtles twines,
>   Where Philomel,
> While nightly breezes sweep the vines,
>   Her griefs will tell!
>
> In gowany glens thy burnie strays,
> Where bonnie lasses bleach their claes;
> Or trots by hazelly shaws and braes
>   Wi' hawthorns grey,
> Where blackbirds join the shepherd lays
>   At close o' day.

This is true: though there was, indeed, in Ramsay just the lingering touch of the Philomel spirit,—the old conventional feigning,—yet the power and the soul of his poetry are to be found in an essentially direct feeling for the living people around him, and the world of nature which he saw and loved. And we should not omit to notice that Ramsay gave most manly, and at the same time most pathetic, voice to that love of one's place of birth, and thence of country, which is so strong in the Scot, and which has grown in a great measure out of the scenery of the land and its associations. I refer, of course, to the touching strains of **"Lochaber no more"**:

> Farewell to Lochaber, farewell to my Jean,
> Where heartsome wi' thee I ha'e mony a day
>   been;
> To Lochaber no more, to Lochaber no more,
> We'll maybe return to Lochaber no more.

T. F. Henderson (essay date 1910)

SOURCE: "Ramsay to Burns," in *Scottish Vernacular Literature: A Succinct History*, revised edition, John Grant, 1910, pp. 400-26.

[*Henderson's* Scottish Vernacular Literature: A Succinct

History *was the first book-length study of Scots literature. In the following excerpt, Henderson credits Ramsay with reviving interest in the Scots literary tradition, but typifies most of his verse as coarse in content and crude in execution.*]

If not the victim of the contradictory poetic models, English and Scots, which he sought combinedly to imitate, Ramsay, except in the case of *The Gentle Shepherd*, was nothing advantaged, either as Scots or English versifier, by any compensating result of the twofold influence. His familiarity with the vernacular song and some of the verse of the old Scots 'makaris,' in no wise tended to modify the pompous commonplace of his more ambitious essays in English verse, while his acquaintance with the English classics exercised little truly educative influence on his vernacular method. But this twofold acquaintanceship assisted him to construct a species of Scoto-English song which was rampantly popular both in Scotland and England. While his vernacular pieces won him universal fame among the lower classes of his native land, and his English verse was read with something resembling admiration by the more enlightened classes of both countries, his songs—as is abundantly testified by the song-books and sheet music of the period—were warbled, to rapturous applause, by the favourite vocalists at the London 'gardens,' and other places of popular resort. Familiar with the old popular songs of both countries, he utilised them for his own purposes with much superficial cleverness. His manner was exactly that which the masses could thoroughly appreciate, and the Scottish flavour, comparatively mild as it was, conferred on them a piquancy which in England greatly aided their popularity.

Some of them—as **"Nany," "O, Bony Jean," "I'll never leave Thee", "Clout the Caldron,"** and **"Through the Wood, Laddie"**—were reminiscent of old English broadsides. A great many more, usually published as his own, are founded on older Scottish songs, some of them poetically much superior, and all of them at least equal to Ramsay's versions. They include **"Bessy Bell and Mary Gray," "Auld Lang Syne," "The Bob of Dunblane,"** . . . in addition to many old songs which he merely amended. Indeed, Ramsay can claim comparatively few songs as wholly his own. Among his best are **"The Lass of Patie's Mill"**—which some assert is not wholly his—and **"Lochaber No More,"** and both are marred by solecisms. Yet he has written one admirable lyric, perfectly faultless in its simplicity, **"My Peggy is a Young Thing"**. His worst defect is his *penchant* for the grovelling, and when not grovelling, he is too apt to be stalely commonplace.

"The Soger Laddie," for example, which used to create a *furore* at Mary'bone Gardens, and other popular London resorts of the eighteenth century, but expresses the unadorned sentiments of Mary Jane, in language even more prosaic and banal than many a Mary Jane would employ:

My soger laddie is over the sea

And he will bring gold and money to me;
And when he comes hame, he'll make me a
    lady;
My blessing gang with my soger laddie.
My doughty laddie is handsome and brave,
And can as a soger and lover behave;
True to his country, to love he is steady,
There's few to compare with my soger laddie.

Shield him, ye angels, frae death in alarms,
Return him with laurels to my langing arms;
Syne frae all my care he'll pleasantly free me,
When back to my wishes my soger ye gie me.

O soon may his honours bloom fair on his brow,
As quickly they must, if he get his due:
For in noble actions his courage is ready,
Which makes me delight in my soger laddie.

Nor even in the best of his convivial songs does he embody the true rapture of good fellowship. **"Up in the Air"** begins fairly well, and stanza ii contains a rather picturesque allusion to a snowy night; but the piece is wholly lacking in poetic glamour, while the last stanza is but stiffly wooden:

Steek the doors, keep out the frost;
Come, Willy, gie's about ye'r toast,
Fill it lads, and lilt it out,
And let us hae a blithsome bout.
        Up wi't there, there,
        Dinna cheat, but drink fair;
Huza, huza, and huza, lads, yet,
        Up wi't there.

But as the comic satirist of low life Ramsay evidenced the possession of a strong vein of clever clownish humour. The **"Elegy on John Cowper"** and **"Lucky Spence's Last Advice,"** are caustic and graphic enough after their own rancid fashion; and the elegies on **"Maggy Johnstone"** and **"Lucky Wood"** supply us with a curious photographic picture of the tavern life of Old Edinburgh. The portrait of Lucky Wood, the pattern ale-wife of the Canongate, is indeed quite admirable:

She ne'er gae in a lawin fause,
Nor stoups a' froath aboon the hause,
Nor kept dow'd tip [stale tipple] within her
    waws
        But reaming swats [new ale];
She ne'er ran sour jute, because
        It gees the batts [colic].

She had the gate sae well to please,
With gratis beef, dry fish, or cheese,
Which kept our purses ay at ease,
        And health in tift;
And lent her fresh nine gallon trees
        A hearty lift.

She gae us oft hail legs o' lamb,
And did nae hain her mutton-ham;

Then aye at Yule whene'er we cam,
   A braw goose-pye;
And was na that good belly-baum?
   Nane dare deny.

The writer-lads fow well may mind her;
Fruthy was she, her luck design'd her
Their common mither; sure nane kinder
   Ever brake bread!
She has na left her mak behind her,
   But now she's dead.

But the most elaborate effort of Ramsay's in expounding the humours of common life is his two additional cantos to **"Christis Kirk,"** which, while lacking the vivid conciseness of the earlier piece, and indeed little better than a mere vulgar parody of its method, depict realistically enough the more sordid aspects of Scottish mirth. The first canto of Ramsay describes a wedding-feast, ending with the bedding ceremony; and in the second the rejoicings are renewed on the morrow until all the men reach the becoming condition of brutal intoxication. It is all true to nature and all most grotesquely comic, but not all quite quotable. Here, however, are some quaint stanzas depicting the arrival of the gossips on the morning after the marriage:

Be that time it was fair foor days,
   As fou's the house could pang,
To see the young fouk ere they raise,
   Gossips came in ding-dang.
And wi a sos aboon the claiths
   Ilk ane their gifts down flang:
Twa toop-horn-spoons down Maggy lays,
   Baith muckle-mow'd and lang
      For kale or whey.

Her aunt a pair of tangs fush in,
   Right bauld she spake and spruce:
'Gin your goodman shall make a din,
   And gabble like a goose,
Shorin whan fou to skelp ye're skin,
   Thir tangs may be of use;
Lay them enlang his pow or shin,
   Wha wins syn may make roose
      Between you twa.'

Auld Bessie, in her red coat braw,
   Came wi her ain oe Nanny,
An odd-like wife, they said, that saw
   A moupin' runckled granny;
She fley'd the kimmers ane and a',
   Word gae'd she was na kanny;
Nor wad they let Lucky awa,
   'Till she was fou wi' branny,
      Like mony mae.

Ramsay's **Tales and Fables** call for little comment. A good many are in English or in Scoto-English, and the majority in the octo-syllabic couplet. Some, he states, were 'taken from Messieurs la Fontaine and la Motte,' and those which are his 'own invention with respect to

the plot as well as the numbers' he leaves the reader 'to find out,' or if any one thought 'it worth his while to ask' him, he professed his willingness to tell him. Ramsay is now beyond interrogation; but one may venture to affirm that **"The Monk and the Miller's Wife,"** which was long credited to him, was neither his own invention nor 'taken from Messieurs la Fontaine and la Motte,' but is merely a modernised and vulgarised reading of 'The Freiris of Berwick;' and that his most elaborate tale, **"The Three Bonnets,"** a long-winded, complicated, and occasionally gross satire on the Union, is most probably all his own.

Ramsay's satires entitle him to rank as at least a cleverly comic vernacular Zola, but for the author of *The Gentle Shepherd* something more than this may be claimed. If not quite poetry, it is at least admirable 'kailyaird.' A most pleasing because a quite unaffectedly homely and simple sketch of rustic courtship—somewhat idealised—it almost by mere accident reveals a literary talent which had been partly smothered by his imperfect training and untoward circumstances. Here his twofold course of poetic study stood him in much better stead than usual. The English pastorals, which he so far made his model, exercised a certain restraining influence on his rather too realistic Scottish method, while by electing to write in the vernacular he avoided the worst pitfalls of artificiality. It has given him a certain acknowledged position in literature, and not undeservedly; but though also as a vernacular satirist his strenuity and wit—often too much tinged with squalidity—are undeniable, and though he contrived one excellent and one or two passably good lyrics, it is rather as editor than author that he occupies his peculiar place in the vernacular revival. The results of his editorial enterprise were twofold: (1) *The Tea Table Miscellany*—dedicated gallantly (and pawkily)

To ilka lovely British lass,
   Frae Ladies Charlotte, Anne, and Jean,
Down to ilk bony singing Bess,
   Wha dances barefoot on the green—

in conjunction with Thomson's *Orpheus* aroused—curious patchwork of old and new, of Scots, English, Scoto-English, and Anglo-Scots, though it be—in a new fashion the old interest in popular song among the bulk of the Scottish people; and (2) by *The Evergreen*—which he described as 'a Collection of Scots Poems wrote by the Ingenious before 1600,' and which included, besides a few ballads such as "Hardyknute," "Johnie Armstrang," and "The Battle of Harlaw," and **"The Vision"** (which may be wholly or partly his own), and one or two of *The Gude and Godlie Ballates,* a large number of the best productions (often very freely altered) of the old 'makaris' preserved in the Bannatyne MS.—he was the first to rescue from oblivion the old vernacular poetry of the fifteenth and sixteenth centuries, which, thus resurgent after a trance of some century and a half, was found to have lost comparatively little of its ancient vitality, and by its vivifying effects partly rekindled in the eighteenth century the old vernacular poetic flame.

J. W. Mackail (essay date 1924)

SOURCE: "Allan Ramsay and the Romantic Revival," in *Essays and Studies,* Vol. X, 1924, pp. 137-44.

[*In the following excerpt, Mackail argues that "[Ramsay's] importance in letters is less in respect of his own poetry, vital and even excellent as some of it is, than as having given the first clearly assignable impulse to the romantic movement of the eighteenth century."*]

[Sir John] Steel's statue of Ramsay [in West Princes Street Gardens, Edinburgh] has nothing romantic about it. It is the presentment of the sleek little tradesman of the Luckenbooths, burgess and *bon vivant,* and the presentment is true to life. But it is incomplete. Here, as often elsewhere, a man stands in the history of his country and of his art not merely for what he obviously was and consciously did, but also for what he in effect, and perhaps unconsciously, originated; for the turn he gave, recognizable only in the backward perspective of distance, to the movement of a whole age. Portrait and biography have to be supplemented by a larger and more searching interpretation.

Thus with Allan Ramsay; his importance in letters is less in respect of his own poetry, vital and even excellent as some of it is, than as having given the first clearly assignable impulse to the romantic movement of the eighteenth century. That movement is generally thought of as having begun much later. Its effective development is dated from the publication of Macpherson's *Ossian* in 1762, and of Percy's *Reliques* in 1765. But these, important and decisive as their influence was, appeared when the soil was already prepared and the new growth was well started. Quite twenty years earlier, the re-emergence of romanticism is clearly marked in the two Wartons. No less remarkably, though more confusedly, does it appear at about the same date in the *Castle of Indolence.* That was the work of a Scotsman, though one denizened in England and hardly counting as a Scottish poet. But for its first beginnings we have to go earlier still, and to go to the northern kingdom. We shall find them (so surprising and unexpected are the ways of the Muses) in the little Edinburgh wig-maker; and not so much in his idylls and lyrics, or in the pastoral drama by which his name is chiefly known, as in *The Evergreen,* that collection of older Scottish poetry which holds in germ, forty years before the *Reliques,* the rediscovery of romance and the recapture for poetry of the submerged or dormant lyrical instinct.

Ramsay's original poetry is not negligible. It had a wide fame even beyond his native country; and it retained for a full century a hold not merely on the partial judgement of Scottish critics but on the heart of the Scottish people. It is true that much of it is not original, and a good deal of it is not poetry. *The Gentle Shepherd* itself is an amorphous structure. The absurdities which are so easy to find in it are perhaps no greater, though they are more patent, than those of the *Aminta.* The point to be emphasized is that they arise in the course of a real attempt to rescue the pastoral convention from classicism and re-connect it with life. This was what had been the unique triumph of Theocritus; but with the instinctive Greek tact, Theocritus kept within the manageable field of the detached idyll. The idyllic drama of Guarini and Tasso was only made possible by narrowing the convention. *The Gentle Shepherd*—and the courage, even the daring, of the attempt is remarkable—aimed at widening it. Success was not attained, and was not attainable; the return to nature had to be made through other channels.

Praise may be given, with little or no qualification, to several of the distinct and still separable idylls which were pieced together as scenes in one idyllic drama. This holds good for the originating idyll of **"Patie and Roger,"** with its beautiful opening lyric of **"My Peggy is a Young Thing,"** which now stands as Act I, scene i, of *The Gentle Shepherd;* it had in fact been printed as a separate piece years before. It holds good even more fully of the two idylls of **"Peggy and Jenny"** (now Act I, scene ii), and of **"Roger and Jenny"** (now Act III, scene iii). It is in the former of these that the beautiful lines come,

> Gae farer up the burn to Habbie's How
> Where a' that's sweet in spring and summer
>   grow;
> Between twa birks out ower a little lin
> The water fa's and makes a singan din;
> A pool breast-deep beneath, as clear as glass,
> Kisses wi' lazy whirls the borderin grass:

which give perfect expression to the native quality of the North, the 'delicate spare soil', the 'slender and austere landscape' where 'through the thin trees the skies appear'. Nor would it be easy to overpraise several of the interposed songs, of which there are more than twenty in the whole piece. The one, for instance, beginning:

> O dear Peggy, love's beguiling,
> We ought not to trust his smiling;
> Better far to do as I do
> Lest a harder luck betide you:

or the other beginning:

> Hid from himself, now by the dawn
> He starts as fresh as roses blawn,
> And ranges o'er the heights and lawn
>   After his bleating flocks:

or one which may be given in full:

> Jock said to Jenny, 'Jenny wilt thou do't?'
> 'Ne'er a fit', quoth Jenny, 'for my tocher-good;
> For my tocher-good I winna marry thee.'
> 'E'ens ye like,' quoth Jocky; 'ye may let it be.
>
> 'I hae gowd and gear; I hae land eneugh;
> I hae seven good owsen ganging in a pleugh,
> Ganging in a pleugh and linkan o'er the lea;
> And gin ye winna tak me, I can let ye be.
>
> 'I hae a good ha' house, a barn and a byre,

A peatstack fore the door, will mak a rantin fire.
I'll mak a rantin fire, and merry sall we be;
And gin ye winna tak me, I can let ye be.'

Jenny said to Jocky, 'Gin ye winna tell,
Ye sall be the lad, I'll be the lass mysell.
Ye're a bonny lad, and I'm a lassie free;
Ye're welcomer to tak me than to let me be.'

But the group of idyllic sketches lose a good deal of their effectiveness by embodiment in the cumbrous framework of a regular drama constructed according to rule, 'the time of action within twenty-four hours', and with a conventional plot. The historical or quasi-historical setting for the action in this queer stageland Arcadia is preposterous. To a generation for whom the Killing Time was well within living memory, the representing of the Restoration as inaugurating an era of peace and happiness could only, one would think, be an unconvincing and repellent fiction. Sir William Worthy is a figure whose only possible place is in the naked and shameless innocence of melodrama. But even in that atmosphere he is not much of a success. It is curious that the name 'Sir William' is, throughout the fiction of the eighteenth century, whether in prose or verse, a danger-signal to the reader. Sir William Thornhill in *The Vicar of Wakefield,* Sir William Honeywood in *The Good-Natured Man,* are no less than Ramsay's Sir William, in the apt phrase of Sir Robert Ayton's, 'fond impossibilities'. But more largely, it was the weakness of Ramsay's 'return to nature' that it sought expression here in the vehicle of the *favola boschereccia* which had gone hopelessly out of date. Just so, in his production on the wedding of the Duke of Hamilton, he had attempted with even scantier success to revive the Elizabethan Masque which had expired in a blaze of splendour with Milton's *Comus.*

But the artistic defects of *The Gentle Shepherd,* no less than its real excellences, just hit popular taste. It made him a popular poet in the most genuine sense of the term. The assertion made in 1800, that 'there is not a milkmaid, a ploughboy, or a shepherd of the lowlands of Scotland, who has not by heart its favourite passages and can [*sic*] rehearse its entire scenes', was no doubt a flight of rhetoric; but it was the exaggeration of a substantial truth. Sir Archibald Geikie, when making a geological survey of the Pentland range in 1856, 'was much interested to find that the custom still prevailed among the peasant population of acting Allan Ramsay's pastoral play of *The Gentle Shepherd* in the midst of the very scenery which had inspired the poet. The Scottish language of the dialogue was given by the rustic actors with full Doric breadth, and even sometimes with creditable dramatic power. That the poem which was published in 1725 should survive in the affections of the peasantry is strong evidence of the force and fidelity of its picture of Scottish rural life. Its survival in this form has probably kept much of the old Scots tongue still in use throughout the district.' But when a later editor wrote, as recently as 1877, that 'to this day it is as much read and as often quoted by many of the peasantry as any of the poems of Burns', the exaggeration is excessive. For the Lothians it may have had a grain of

truth; *The Gentle Shepherd* no doubt remained alive longest among its native Pentlands, though the occasional performances of recent years have only been artificial antiquarian revivals. But as regards Ayrshire, which that editor specifically mentions, it cannot be accepted. Allan Ramsay's name was a lingering household word there, but that was about all.

It is, however, with full truth that the same editor claims for Ramsay that he 'was the pioneer of a new era, and gave an impulse to the study and cultivation of the poetic art'. He was a germinal force. His own lyrical gift, though genuine, was slender. His dramatic sense, notwithstanding that devotion to the theatre which got him into so much trouble with the Edinburgh Town Council and very nearly ruined him financially, was weak. When he 'gets to his English', he is only a minor and provincial Augustan. Only in his admirable *Fables and Tales* can he take rank beside those Southern contemporaries of whom he writes, that

Swift, Sandy, Young, and Gay
    Are still my heart's delight.

With Swift he had little or nothing in common. With Gay, that thin but sweet voice of poetry (himself too connected with Scotland through the fostering friendship of the Queensberrys), he had much. There is a certain kinship between *The Gentle Shepherd* and *The Beggar's Opera;* and Gay and Ramsay are the two best British fabulists. Their debt to la Fontaine and la Motte is of course, in both, patent and confessed, but their own skill of handling was much alike and was very great. Gay's own *Shepherd's Week* (1714), though primarily a burlesque, touches here and there, in virtue of his delicate and never fully disengaged poetical instinct, the authentic Theocritean note. 'Though only half intending it,' Mr. E. K. Chambers says [in *English Pastorals*], in words which, though with some hesitation, may be accepted, 'he produced a genuine work of pastoral art, the nearest approach to a realistic pastoral which our literature had yet seen.' But he lacked the intention; his touch on those strings was light and transitory.

It was presumably through Gay, whose acquaintance he made in Edinburgh, that Ramsay came to the knowledge of the other members of the group. It should be borne in mind that it was the Young of the *Satires,* not the later and more famous Young of the *Night Thoughts,* in whom he delighted. And Sandy likewise—one cannot help wondering how Pope liked being called Sandy—is the Pope of the *Pastorals* and *Windsor Forest,* not the Pope of the *Essay on Man* and *The Dunciad.* It brings the whole eighteenth century into closer perspective to remember that the Countess of Eglinton, to whom, then in the prime of her age and beauty, *The Gentle Shepherd* was dedicated, lived on to receive the homage of Dr. Johnson during his tour in Scotland half a century later.

But Pope's known and recorded admiration of *The Gentle Shepherd* shows how 'the return to nature' was a real motive, a sincere aim, even at the time and among the circle in which poetry was most artificial, and most heavily fettered by a classicist tradition. And to many readers Ramsay's *Evergreen* must have come, when it appeared in 1724, as something like a new revelation. His texts are deplorable; the liberties he took with his originals are monstrous; and he had little flair for distinguishing genuine antiquity from recent or contemporary forgery. Yet, in the words of his Preface, 'the groves rise in our own valleys, the rivers flow from our own fountains, and the winds blow upon our own hills'. With all its defects, a collection which begins with **"Christ's Kirk on the Green"** and ends with "Hardyknute," and thus traverses the whole field of Scottish poetry for nearly three centuries, is memorable as having reopened the springs of poetry. Though the released stream ran turbid, it had not lost its quickening and refreshing power. And as it ran on, it cleared itself, as streams do, in the open air.

It was in the generation after Ramsay's that Edinburgh first put forward the boast of being the modern Athens, and that Scottish writers took a leading place in British letters. But the most famous of these were writers of prose; historians, essayists, or philosophers. Among Edinburgh poets, Allan Ramsay may still claim the foremost place but one; and indeed, if we set Scott apart as belonging less to Edinburgh than to Scotland, and less to Scotland than to the world, he might claim the foremost; for Ferguson's fame rests more on the generous and over-generous praise of Burns than on his own substantive merits. Ramsay when still a young man was made poet-laureate of the Easy Club. He became in effect for the rest of his life poet-laureate of the city. He received no public honours; in the eyes of authority he was only one of 'the playhouse comedians who debauch all the faculties of our rising generation'; but he had a secure place in popular affection, and his wreath still remains green. His house has for many years been merged in a students' hostel; a better use, one may judge, than to be preserved like Abbotsford as a show-place filled with ghostly memories. Something of his gay spirit, of his love for nature and for books, of his devotion to the national poetry of his country, may still linger there to inspire new generations of students.

Burns Martin (essay date 1931)

SOURCE: "The Reputation and the Influence of Ramsay," in *Allan Ramsay: A Study of His Life and Works,* Cambridge, Mass.: Harvard University Press, 1931, pp. 124-35.

[*Martin's 1931 biography of Ramsay was considered definitive until it was supplanted by Alexander Kinghorn in 1970 with his* The Works of Allan Ramsay. *In the following excerpt, Martin discusses Ramsay's reputation among his contemporaries and in the latter half of the eighteenth century.*]

There is no reason for thinking that before 1719 Ramsay was known beyond the city of Edinburgh. But in that year we have his correspondence with Hamilton of Gil-

bertfield, the englishing of **"Richy and Sandy"** by Josiah Burchet, and the exchange of riming epistles with the Irishman, James Arbuckle. From this time Ramsay's fame spread rapidly beyond the walls of the *Good Town,* not without the help of his friends. Before Steele went to Edinburgh on government business in 1720, he instructed James Anderson to find him lodgings. The latter in reporting to his superior concluded his letter thus: "I enclose you a poem of Mr. Ramsay's, whose performances, I presume, you are not a stranger to." This specimen must have found favour with the Englishman, for he subsequently subscribed for two copies of the quarto of 1721. About a year later, Sir William Bennet of Grubet wrote the Countess Dowager of Roxburghe: "I send your ladyship Allan Ramsay's essay one [*sic*] the cutting of my Lord Bowmont's hair." Whatever we may think of the tradition that the housewives of Edinburgh were in the habit of sending their children to buy Allan Ramsay's latest piece to be read over a dish of tea, we must grant, in the light of these letters, that the citizens of Edinburgh looked upon a new poem by him as somewhat of an event to be communicated to friends abroad. The congratulatory verses and the list of subscribers published in *Poems* (1721)—at least one copy went to New England—gives the same impression of an ever-growing and widening popularity. Indeed, one feels that during his life Ramsay must have received homage in verse from every poetaster in Scotland and many of those in England. Dublin had an edition of his works in 1724, seven years before London; and when in 1727 a rumour spread through the Irish capital that Ramsay had died, a broadside elegy of the usual quality was hawked in the streets. In 1726 Ramsay subscribed for thirty copies of a new edition of *Hudibras* with illustrations by Hogarth. When the artist shortly afterwards republished twelve of the plates, he dedicated the edition jointly to William Ward of Great Houghton and Allan Ramsay of Edinburgh. Gratitude may have induced Hogarth's action—or, possibly, a feeling of kinship with the satiric observer of Edinburgh low-life.

There is a tradition that Ramsay's shop, admirably situated as it was on the High Street near the Cross, was the rendezvous for the wits of the city. Southerners seem to have found it a pleasant place to while away the time. William Tytler remembered having seen Gay there. We have already noted that the Earl of Oxford visited Ramsay while in Edinburgh. There can be little doubt, in view of the above quotation, that Steele found his way to Ramsay's shop when he was in the north. But it is uncertain that Tom D'Urfey and Ramsay met, for when D'Urfey was young enough to make the long journey to Edinburgh, Ramsay had not yet become so prominent. Englishmen did not need, however, to travel to Edinburgh to hear of Ramsay, for his works were in the London bookshops, and his name in the journals. The *British Journal* for March 9, 1723, published a translation of a short passage in Vergil purported to have been made by the Scottish poet Allan Ramsay for which the translator had received the sum of twenty marks. In the issues of October 3 and 24, 1724, the same journal had a version of Ramsay's elegy on the Duchess of Hamilton, contributed by an ardent admirer; but the text being abbreviated and debased, Ramsay sent the editor a true copy with a letter, both of which were published in the issue of November 14. About the same time (November 2, 1724), the *Plain Dealer* had a letter in defence of Scottish as a poetic medium; the writer thought "Our *Allan Ramsay*, a living Versifier in Old-Style, uses few words that are not to be met with in *Shakespear, Spencer*, &c . . . except, when he coins Words, by virtue of his *extra-judicial* Poetick Privileges, that never were, and never will be, used by any Mortal, besides Himself." But if Ramsay's friends were doing their best to keep his name before the London reader, his critics also had their turn. In the *Weekly Journal or Saturday's Post* for September 14, 1723, appeared what seems to be a covert attack on the poet. The writer of an essay on Fortune, bemoaning the human failing of deserting a tried and proved trade for one less suitable, remarks that he has known "a good Taylor turn an ignorant Chymist and an expert Barber become a miserable Poet." Then under the guise of friendliness he delivers his blow:

> I do not say this in the least to reflect upon Mr. *Allen Ramsey* of *Edinburgh*, whose Works I have read with Pleasure; I understand he uses Poetry like a Gentleman, that is, only plays with it at leisure Hours, when the more important Business of his Trade is over, he smooths a Verse and a Chin with the same Facility; I have seen of his Work in both Capacities, and confess I can't help thinking his Perriwigs and his Poetry both very good.

Incidentally, we have here for the first time the mistaken idea, which was to have such a long history, that Ramsay was a barber. As late as 1745 we find Ramsay's name dragged into an attack on Curll in a pamphlet, *Remarks on 'Squire Ayre's Memoirs of the Life and Writings of Mr. Pope. In a Letter to Mr. Edmund Curl, Bookseller, etc.* Perhaps a quotation will be pardoned, as it shows the eighteenth-century method of carrying on literary quarrels:

> *Allen Ramsay*, the *Scotch* Poet, whose Works you have, with your usual Propriety, forc'd in, to the great Assistance and Amplification of your own, you treat in another manner. No malicious Critic's Censure, no witty Sneer, nor boisterous Mirth will you permit to keep down his rising Honours, but all is Praise, all Fame, all Glory, and *Allen Ramsay*, any one must think, who would be taught to judge from you, has more Merit, and deserves more Fame than *Pope*, or *Gay*, than *Tasso* or *Guarini*. . . . Why do you praise? For what peculiar Beauties is it he has run away with such a double Portion of your Encomiums? Why, for no peculiar Beauties at all, (except indeed those of the Binding) but for a Reason worth a Million such, because you have forty Sets of them (a dead Stock) upon your Hands, and would be very glad, by a worse Means than this Puff, as it is call'd, to sell some of them.

This use of Ramsay as a means of attacking some other person we have already seen in connection with the *North Briton's* campaign against Lord Bute.

But the criticism of Ramsay in London was naught compared with the vituperation poured on him by enemies at home. [Wodrow attacked] his library as corrupting the youth and servant women of the city. The author of "The Flight of Religious Piety from Scotland" . . . has Piety describe Ramsay's influence in these terms:

> The Pulpits there did represent
> The Glories of the Lord of Hosts
> Until the Devil sow'd the Seed
> Of Poetry in *Ramsay's* Brain,
> Who never for God's Glory stood,
> But only for his private Gain.
> I strove in vain to gain the Youth
> Whose Reason Ramsay hath debauch'd.

Indeed, the poet's critics never could forget that he, a mere wigmaker, had become wealthy. In the same poem the devil addresses Ramsay thus:

> Now Ramsay my brave Adjutant,
> Which I once took from picking Hair,
> I told thee, that thou shouldst not want,
> If thou but with me wouldst take Fare.
> Have I once fail'd, at thy Request,
> To grant more than thy Heart could wish?
> Herrings and Fardles did please thy Taste;
> Now thou canst get a dainty Dish:
> Thou heldst an House then but for Hire,
> And glad to poll a Teat of Hare;
> To face the Cross, thy Nest and Fire,
> Thy House I have procur'd thee there;
> Thy piss-brown Wig, thou us'd to wear
> I have turn'd to a three-tail'd Buckle;
> I have procur'd thee all thy Gear,
> Thy Block-Head then to me must truckle.

A cleverer method of attack was used by the anonymous author of "Allan Ramsay Metamorphosed to a Heather-Bloter Poet in a Pastoral between Aegon and Melibae": one character praises Ramsay on various accounts only that the other may turn the seeming eulogy to censure. Aegon finds that Ramsay uses the vernacular because he was bred in either the Braid or the Pentland Hills; he criticizes the poet's choice of themes and his writings for the stage. His closing lines have a familiar ring:

> Then Melibae, If you praise his Deeds,
> Provide a Block unto his high flowing Wigs.

The criticism of Ramsay's use of the vernacular in the last writer is interesting, for as the century moves along, we find that it is this characteristic of Ramsay's work that wins most praise. In 1746 there was published in London a poem entitled "The Saddle put on the right Horse . . . A Poem in the Stile of Allan Ramsay's Poetical Works." The author of the poem, which is in Scots, says that he has been induced to publish it because his friends have pronounced it the equal of Ramsay's. In 1750 "Orestes" contributed a poem to the *Scots Magazine*, entitled "To a Gentleman, upon saying he had in vain attempted to answer a few lines sent him in Scots verse; and that he feared, either that Allan was dead, or that I had borrowed his muse." The poet tells of a talk with the Scottish muse ("landart lass"), who says she has well nigh lost her strength since Allan sits at home and writes no more verse. "Orestes" tries to cheer her with the hope that Ramsay will again turn to poetry. This poem, like so many others addressed to Ramsay, is in Scots, and herein lies its significance. To those who were interested in the vernacular at a time when the more ambitious were painfully trying to drop all Scotticisms from their speech Ramsay seemed a pillar of strength.

Ramsay's death in 1758 produced, despite statements to the contrary, a number of tributes. The *Scots Magazine* published an elegy, "To the Memory of Mr. Allan Ramsay." Another appeared in the columns of the *Caledonian Mercury,* and a broadside was published in Dublin. We have also noticed that in 1758 several performances of *The Gentle Shepherd* were given. In other words, by the time of his death Ramsay had become a minor national figure, especially to those who were proud of the native dialect. When Smollet wished to exalt Scottish humorous verse in *Humphrey Clinker* (1771), he had a Scot vaunt of Ramsay's *Ever Green*. It became the fashion to mention Ramsay in praising a new poet. So we find "Geordie Buck" writing "Claudero":

> When Allan dy'd, the muses then
> Did mourn aloud baith butt and ben;
> Apollo sigh'd! but spoke up then,
>   I've still a hero
> In Caledon—Syne took his pen,
>   And wrote Claudero.

To this the recipient answered:

> But thou has screw'd my muse so high,
> Like Daedalus, in air to fly,
> She dreads his fate, and must implore,
> Beneath fam'd Allan's wings to soar.

In the latter part of the century Ramsay's and Fergusson's names were linked together. John Learmont wrote "An Encomium on Allan Ramsay and Robert Fergusson, without, however, trying to decide their relative merits." On April 14, 1791, a debate took place at the Pantheon, a literary club in Edinburgh, to decide which of the two poets had done the more for Scottish poetry. R. Cummings and E. Picken read poems in Ramsay's praise. The former devoted his time to *The Gentle Shepherd,* while the latter stressed Ramsay's work in reviving the vernacular, and the naturalness and simplicity of his style. A. Wilson, who upheld Fergusson's claims, maintained his superiority in virtue of his greater realism; with his conclusion we cannot but agree:

> It's my opinion, John, that this young fallow,
> Excels them a', an' beats auld Allan hallow,
> An' shews, at twenty-twa, as great a giftie
> For painting just, as Allan did at fifty.

With the advent of Burns we have his name linked with his predecessors by all aspirants to poetic fame. One of many examples is [by George Galloway]:

> O cou'd I sing as Ramsay sung
>   And far-fam'd Fergesson
> Or if my lyre it were but strung
>   Like Rab's the Mauchline clown.

Such allusions to the Scottish trinity continue through the first decade of the nineteenth century, but after that they become rare, the cause of the change being most probably a just realization of the superiority of Burns. At the same time a new form of respect was paid Ramsay. The events of his life began to attract attention, the first biography being published in 1797. Then arose the celebrated dispute about the site of *The Gentle Shepherd*. It was inevitable that a monument should be suggested, but whether it should be erected in Edinburgh or on the site of Ramsay's pastoral was not easily decided. Some years passed, and in 1820 a tablet was placed on the south wall of Greyfriars Church. About 1850 a proposal was advanced to build a great stone terrace in front of Ramsay Gardens with a statue of Ramsay thereon. Although there was adverse criticism, the work proceeded until it fissured and collapsed. In 1865, through the generosity of Lord Murray, the present handsome monument in Princes Street Gardens was erected. Throughout the century writers on romantic old Edinburgh busied themselves in collecting or making anecdotes about Ramsay, and the Society of Antiquarians of Scotland began to collect relics. The "Goose-Pie" became a university residence. By all these tokens Ramsay had become a classic, and the time for reading and enjoying him had passed.

Little need be said here about Ramsay's influence. *The Gentle Shepherd* . . . did much to break down the prejudice against the stage, and it also served as a model for certain writers. We [note] Ramsay's service to the vernacular by his use of it at a time when it was rapidly passing out of favour. Poets and poetasters of the century were inspired by his example to write in Scots. We need not attempt to trace the influence of Ramsay on Burns, as that has been done adequately elsewhere. To show his influence on minor writers of the period we shall mention two instances. The following passage from Thomas Blair's "Gibbie and Wattie" should be compared with Ramsay's **"Robert, Richy, and Sandy"**:

> He held out his snout forgainst the peat-stack
>   'now,
> Wi' mony a lengsome elrich wough, wough,
>   wow,
> I ran to chase him but a' was in vain.
> He fletted frae his seat, and yowld again.
> I cry'd 'isk 'isk poor Batie, hae tak a piece, but
>   the grumbling tyke
> Ran farther off and yowl'd at the fauld dyke.

David Bruce, a political writer in Pennsylvania in the last decade of the eighteenth century, imitated Ramsay in both diction and stanza. His opponents, who soon saw the source of his inspiration, called him "Allan Ramsay degenerated into a rough, dull, shrill, reminiscence of his former greatness." It is a far cry from the streets of Edinburgh to the frontiers of Pennsylvania, but the voice of Allan Ramsay was heard in both places.

David Daiches (essay date 1955)

SOURCE: "Eighteenth-Century Vernacular Poetry," in *Scottish Poetry: A Critical Survey,* edited by James Kinsley, Cassell and Company Ltd., 1955, pp. 150-84.

[*In the following excerpt, Daiches surveys Ramsay's contributions to Scottish literature as a poet and as an editor of Scots verse.*]

In 1712 [Ramsay] joined with other young men in Edinburgh in founding the Easy Club, 'in order that by a Mutual improvement in Conversation they may become more adapted for fellowship with the politer part of mankind and Learn also from one another's happy observations'. (Burns was to found the Tarbolton Bachelors' Club with similar ends in view.) The members of this club all had pseudonyms, and Ramsay's was first Isaac Bickerstaff and later Gavin Douglas, a pair of names which reflect Ramsay's dual interest in the Queen Anne wits and in older Scottish literature. The Easy Club is important in Ramsay's career because it shows him in training to become a gentleman in the early eighteenth-century sense and also because it provided him with an audience for 'occasional' poetry for which he soon began to display his talent. Ramsay was far from being a great poet, but he was a facile versifier with certain happy flashes, and when circumstances were propitious he could turn out admirable specimens of familiar verse. The Easy Club provided the environment which encouraged this gift; it also provided a background of patriotic sentiment against which Ramsay's nationalism flourished vigorously. Isaac Bickerstaff and Gavin Douglas; a gentleman of the Augustan Age and an ardent Scottish patriot; an admirer of Pope and Gay and Matthew Prior and a devoted champion of the older Scottish makars and of the use of vernacular Scots by contemporary Scottish poets; a seeker after polish and good breeding and a vulgar little gossip whose schoolboy snigger spoils many of his poems and songs; a sentimental Jacobite and a prudent citizen who cannily absented himself from Edinburgh when Prince Charlie held court in Holyrood in 1745; a champion of Scottish folk-song and a wrecker of scores of such songs by turning them into stilted would-be neo-classic effusions—the dualism in Ramsay's life and character was deep-seated and corresponded to a dualism in the Scottish culture of his day. He could defend the coarsest and frankest language in poetry and yet dress up a Scottish song in intolerable false elegancies. At the same time he could demonstrate that he possessed the Horatian elegance of the English gentleman by rendering Horace's 'Vides ut alta stet niva candidum' in vivid and homely Scots verse:

Look up to *Pentland's* towring Taps,

Buried beneath great Wreaths of Snaw,
O'er ilka Cleugh, ilk Scar and Slap,
As high as ony *Roman* Wa'.

Driving their Baws [balls] frae Whins or Tee,
There's no ae Gowfer to be seen,
Nor dousser [soberer] Fowk wysing a Jee
Thy Byas Bouls on *Tamson's* Green.

Ramsay's first published works were single poems in English heroic couplets in the contemporary English style; these are no better if no worse than the work of many a minor English versifier of the day. **"The Morning Interview",** described as "An Heroi-Comical Poem", derives from *The Rape of the Lock,* but has none of Pope's metrical cunning, fineness of texture, or subtle shifts in tone. Waggish jocularity strives with self-conscious elegance to take control, and the result is not happy, though the poem has its moments. In 1718 Ramsay first showed his interest in older Scottish literature by bringing out, anonymously on broadsides, several editions of **"Christis Kirk on the Grene"** (with the same stanza form as Watson had printed—different from the text he was to use in *The Ever Green* in 1724) with first one and then two new cantos of his own. Ramsay's new cantos have verve and ingenuity, and capture something of the spirit of the original while adding his own brand of vulgarity. In the Elegies on Maggy Johnston, John Cowper and Lucky Wood (which all appeared in 1718) Ramsay displayed his best vernacular vein. These poems are in the tradition that Ramsay himself, in a verse epistle to Hamilton of Gilbertfield, called 'Standart *Habby*', the comic elegy tradition of the 'Epitaph on Habbie Simson' and 'Bonny Heck'. The elegy on Maggy Johnston, famous for her cheap and good ale, moves from lament to reminiscences of conviviality. The poem on Cowper, Kirk Treasurer's Man and expert at 'sa'ring [smelling] sculddry out', is interesting as one of the earliest pieces of Scots verse to laugh at what Burns was to call the 'holy beagles'. The **"Elegy on Lucky Wood"** laments the loss of an honest and hospitable ale-house keeper in the Canongate, and again it turns from elegy to reminiscent conviviality. There is a fine sense of atmosphere in the poem, with the scenes etched in warm and lively colours like a Breughel painting of a village celebration.

About the same time also appeared **"Lucky Spence's Last Advice"** (first called **"Elegy on the Death of an Auld Bawd"**), where Ramsay uses the 'death and dying words' device to put grimly ironical advice to prostitutes into the mouth of a dying brothel keeper. This kind of humour does not wear well, particularly when accompanied by Ramsay's variety of vulgar coyness (for example, he draws attention to an obscene phrase by a footnote in which he declines to explain it). But the poem uses the vernacular vigorously, with a fine proverbial forcefulness.

Of the other poems which Ramsay published separately, **"Tartana: Or, The Plaid"** deserves mention for its strong patriotic feeling and warm defence of Scottish customs against foreign innovations, even though the poem is in stilted English couplets. And two pastorals are of some importance: **"Richy and Sandy"**, a pastoral elegy on the death of Addison, and **"Patie and Roger"**, the germ of *The Gentle Shepherd*. **"Richy and Sandy"** (i.e. Richard Steele and Alexander Pope) is a dialogue between two shepherds who lament the death of a third of their number, Edie (Addison). It is a ludicrous enough mixture—Steele, Pope and Addison transformed into Scots shepherds talking in a Theocritean convention, yet Ramsay's combination of conversational idiom with classical allusion comes off better than one might expect, and the piece has something of the same 'faded charm' that critics have found in *The Gentle Shepherd*. **"Patie and Roger"** is likewise a dialogue between two shepherds, but this time the theme is love. The vernacular flows easily and the accent of conversation is audible beneath the flow of the verse. The images are fresh and effective, and altogether the piece succeeds in putting a little life into the worn-out convention of pastoral dialogue, in spite of its faded properties. Ramsay's basic uncertainty of taste, which could lead him into the most hideous vulgarities, was less of a liability in this kind of writing: the touches of rustic realism make for freshness, not vulgarity, and the idiom and cadence of popular speech embedded in the slow-moving iambic line waters the aridity of a stock situation, as in Patie's advice to Roger on how to get his girl:

> Daft Gowk [fool]! Leave aff that silly whindging
>   Way,
> Seem careless, there's my Hand ye'll win the
>   Day.
> Last Morning I was unco airly out,
> Upon a Dyke I lean'd and glowr'd about;
> I saw my *Meg* come linkan o'er the Lee,
> I saw my *Meg*, but *Maggie* saw na me:
> For yet the Sun was wafing throw the Mist,
> And she was closs upon me e'er she wist.
> Her Coats were kiltit, and did sweetly shaw
> Her straight bare Legs, which whiter were than
>   Snaw:
> Her Cockernony [gathered hair] snooded up fou
>   sleek,
> Her haffet Locks hung waving on her Cheek:
> Her Cheek sae ruddy! and her Een sae clear!
> And O! her Mouth's like ony hinny Pear.
> Neat, neat she was in Bustine Wastecoat clean,
> As she came skiffing o'er the dewy Green:
> Blythsome I cry'd, My bonny *Meg* come here,
> I fairly wherefore ye'er sae soon a steer:
> But now I guess ye'er gawn to gather Dew.
> She scour'd awa, and said what's that to you?
> Then fare ye well, *Meg Dorts*, and e'en 's ye
>   like,
> I careless cry'd and lap in o'er the Dyke.
> I trow, when that she saw, within a crack
> With a right thieveles Errand she came back;
> Miscau'd me first,—then bade me hound my
>   Dog
> To weer up three waff Ews were on the Bog.
> I leugh, and sae did she, then wi' great Haste
> I clasp'd my Arms about her Neck and Waste . . .

Finally, we must mention the verse letters between Ram-

say and Hamilton of Gilbertfield. The series begins with a letter to Ramsay from Hamilton:

> O Fam'd and celebrated ALLAN!
> Renowned RAMSAY, canty Callan [merry fellow],
> There's nowther Highlandman nor Lawlan,
>   In Poetrie,
> But may as soon ding down *Tamtallan*
>   As match wi' thee. . . .

And Ramsay replies in similar strain:

> Sonse fa me, witty, wanton *Willy,*
> Gin blyth I was na as a Filly;
> Not a fow Pint, nor short Hought Gilly,
>   Or Wine that's better,
> Cou'd please sae meikle, my dear Billy,
>   As thy kind Letter.

> Before a Lord and eik a Knight,
> In Gossy *Dom's* be Candle Light,
> There first I saw't, and ca'd it right,
>   And the maist feck
> Wha's seen't sinsyne, they ca'd as tight
>   As that on *Heck.*

The poems run on with an apparent effortlessness, given form by the demands of epistolary courtesy for an opening of compliment and a concluding benediction or invitation to the recipient to visit and make merry with the writer. From compliment to news to invitation is the commonest course of these letters, and they set a pattern which Fergusson and Burns were to follow. This is not, of course, great poetry; but it represents a craftsmanlike handling of the 'familiar' style, an exercising of the vernacular which was to stand Burns in good stead, and it further helped to provide both a social and a metrical convention for Scots verse.

Ramsay's preface to the 1721 volume of his poems gives us some important clues to his own view of the nature and significance of his poetry. He cheerfully admits that he is no classical scholar ('I understand Horace but faintly in the Original') and claims that many eminent men of letters have assured him 'That my small Knowledge of the dead or foreign Languages is nothing to my Disadvantage. King David, Homer and Virgil, say they, were more ignorant of the Scots and English Tongue, than you are of Hebrew, Greek and Latin: Pursue your own natural Manner, and be an original.' The use of vernacular Scots is thus associated with ignorance of Latin and Greek: Scots is no longer a literary language employed by poets with a European perspective and a rich background of classical culture which they draw on for vocabulary, imagery and subject-matter. We have come a long way from the aureate Middle Scots poems of Dunbar. Ramsay's classical knowledge comes through the strainer of neoclassic elegance; Greek and Roman gods and goddesses are for him useful ornamental devices which he has learned about from the English poets. Burns, too, was to pose as a heaven-taught ploughman and claim superiority to the college-educated who 'gae in stirks and come oot asses', but Burns was in fact fundamentally better educated than Ramsay, though he was faced by some of the same problems.

Ramsay warmly defends the expressive capacities of Scots, yet he is on the defensive about his 'Scotticisms'. 'The *Scotticisms,* which perhaps may offend some over-nice Ear, give new Life and Grace to the Poetry, and become their Place as well as the *Doric* dialect of *Theocritus,* so much admired by the best Judges.' He is writing, after all, for a genteel audience, both English and Scottish, who might be expected to lift their eyebrows at his use of the Doric. He dedicates his book 'To the most Beautiful, the Scots Ladies' and quotes Prior to the effect that he writes only for the young and fair. Clearly Ramsay's rôle as he saw it was, if not confused, at least multiple.

In writing songs, Ramsay's favourite procedure is to take a popular Scottish song and to the same air set a new version which retains the opening line or the chorus or some other part of the original, but in all other respects is a wholly different poem deriving in tone and idiom from English love-lyrics of the period. Thus 'The last time I came ower the moor' becomes **"The happy Lover's Reflections"**:

> The last Time I came o'er the Moor,
>   I left my Love behind me;
> Ye Pow'rs! What Pain do I endure
>   When soft Idea's mind me:
> Soon as the ruddy Morn display'd
>   The beaming Day ensuing,
> I met betimes my lovely Maid,
>   In fit Retreats for wooing.

The phrases here are a mass of *clichés,* a parody, almost, of neo-classic idiom. **"The Lass of Peattie's Mill"**, on the other hand, begins with a lilting stanza in the true folk-idiom, then falls away into frigid artificialities, to return to the folk-idiom again in the third and last stanza. Ramsay has been blamed for ousting the old songs by his pseudo-genteel substitutes, and indeed many of his more outrageous rewritings appear not only in his own *Tea-Table Miscellany* but also in David Herd's *Ancient and Modern Scottish Songs* (where they appear anonymously), in the *Scots Musical Museum* and in *Select Scotish Airs.* It is of course possible, if not probable, that if Ramsay had not printed his versions the old versions would have died out anyway and the tunes would also have been lost: most of the original words of Ramsay's songs were irrecoverable later in the century even by such a conscientious collector as David Herd, and perhaps in many cases only the melody and the refrain were known to Ramsay. 'Of many of the songs in these volumes', wrote Herd in his preface to the second edition of his collection (1776), 'the chief merit will be found to consist in the musical air, while the poetry may appear much below mediocrity. For this the Editor has no other apology to offer, than that these were the only words existing to the tunes in question, the original words which gave rise to these tunes being irrecoverably lost.' It is important to remember that 'the musical air' was the more significant element in most of these songs; indeed, it is impossible to get any proper idea of this phase of Scottish literature without taking the music into consideration and treating the songs as songs and not as poems which happen to have been set to music.

How far Ramsay can go in the direction of pseudo-elegance in language can be seen in his song **"Delia"**, which is set to the tune of 'Greensleeves':

> Ye watchful Guardians of the Fair,
> Who skiff on Wings of ambient Air,
> Of my dear *Delia* take a Care,
>   And represent her Lover . . .

Many of his songs contain an impossible mixture of folk-idiom and self-conscious classical allusion. He can write a song with the simple Scots title **"Bonny Jean"** (the title of the old air) and open it thus:

> Love's Goddess in a Myrtle Grove
> Said, *Cupid,* bend thy Bow with Speed,
> Nor let the Shaft at Random rove,
> For *Jeanie*'s haughty Heart must bleed. . . .

And his version of "Auld Lang Syne" (entitled **"The Kind Reception"**) begins:

> Should auld Acquaintance be forgot,
>   Tho they return with Scars?
> These are the noble Heroe's Lot,
>   Obtain'd in glorious Wars:
> Welcome my *Varo* to my Breast,
>   Thy Arms about me twine,
> And make me once again as blest,
>   As I was lang syne.

We never know what Ramsay is going to do. 'Peggy I must Love Thee' becomes the conventional English **"Love's Cure"**; **"Bessy Bell and Mary Gray"** lilts happily along in true folk-style until suddenly we find

> When *Phoebus* starts frae *Thetis'* Lap
> The Hills with Rays adorning . . .

(One is reminded of Burns's outrageously obscene parody of this style of poetry.) **"The Young Laird and Edinburgh Katy"** is lively Scots throughout and sticks to a single idiom:

> Now wat ye what I met Yestreen
> Coming down the Street, my Jo,
> My Mistress in her Tartan Screen,
> Fou' bonny, braw and sweet, my Jo. . . .

"Mary Scot" combines a refrain about Yarrow with such a line as 'When in soft Flames Souls equal burn'; but **"O'er Bogie"** keeps to a lilting folk-style throughout, beginning with the traditional refrain, 'I will awa' wi' my Love'. **"O'er the Moor to Maggy"** is the mixture again, but **"Polwart on the Green"** is effective, simple Scots throughout. **"Up in the Air"** is one of Ramsay's few real masterpieces, a lively drinking-song in roaring Scots. The refrain is old, and perhaps some other lines are too, but Ramsay has got into the spirit of the original magnificently:

> Now the Sun's gane out o' Sight,
> Beet the Ingle, and snuff the Light:
> In Glens the Fairies skip and dance,
> And Witches wallop o'er to *France*,
>   Up in the Air
>   On my bonny grey Mare.
> And I see her yet, and I see her yet,
>   Up in, &c.
>
> The Wind's drifting Hail and Sna'
> O'er frozen Hags like a Foot Ba',
> Nae Starns keek throw the Azure Slit,
> 'Tis cauld and mirk as ony Pit,
>   The Man i' the Moon
>   Is carowsing aboon,
> D'ye see, d'ye see, d'ye see him yet.
>   The Man, &c.

The fireside interior, with its warmth and conviviality, is contrasted with the winter weather outside, a contrast characteristic of much Scottish poetry, from the opening of Henryson's *Testament of Cresseid* to the beginning of "Tam o' Shanter".

"Patie and Pegie", which was later incorporated into *The Gentle Shepherd*, has been much praised, but it is not in fact a happy performance; the deliberately cultivated sentimentality clashes with the Scots frankness. A leering or even pawing eroticism, mixed with affected sensibility, has a tendency to crop up in Ramsay, and it is not attractive.

Ramsay's songs are most successful when he sticks to the folk-idiom and enters with verve and spirit into the atmosphere of the original refrain. **"An thou wert my ain Thing"**, in spite of an occasional false touch, has an effective strain of lyrical simplicity; **"For the Sake of Somebody"** is a fine lilting piece in true folk-style; **"The Widow can bake, and the Widow can brew"** has speed and liveliness and no trace of a false sensibility; **"O Mither dear, I 'gin to fear"** is a skilful and unspoiled reworking of a folk-song, and the same is true of **"The Carle he came o'er the Croft"**, **"This is No my ain Hoose"**, **"Clout the Caldron"** and some others.

It is not, of course, true that all folk-songs are good or that simplicity is necessarily a good quality in a song and that any kind of stylization is bad. But it is true that Ramsay's attempt to add a dimension to Scots vernacular poetry by sprinkling bits of English neo-classic convention or other evidence of a deliberately induced genteel sensibility over a verse that is basically a realistic Scots was misguided. Realistic Scots does not necessarily produce good poetry, any more than elegantly stylized English necessarily produces bad; but whatever the language a poet uses, it must be used organically, it must be the fully realized medium of the whole man at work, and this cannot be said of Ramsay's strange mixtures of Scots and English. Sometimes (like Burns) he is successful in an English tipped with Scots; more often, in his songs at least, he succeeds when he uses the vernacular in a fairly short, lilting line, as in the one wholly successful song (with the possible exception of **"My Patie is a lover gay"**) in *The Gentle Shepherd*:

> My Peggy is a young thing,
>   Just enter'd in her teens,
> Fair as the day, and sweet as May,
> Fair as the day, and always gay:
> My Peggy is a young thing,
>   And I'm not very auld,
> Yet well I like to meet her at
>   The wauking of the fauld. . . .

Ramsay experimented in older Scottish metres other than 'Standart *Habby*'. One of his epistles to Hamilton uses the same ten-line stanza as "The Claith Merchant", a poem which he printed in *The Ever Green*. In **"Edinburgh's Salutation to the Most Honourable, My Lord Marquess of Carnarvon"** he uses the stanza of **"Christis Kirk on the Grene"** in Watson's form. In **"The Poet's Wish"** he uses *The Cherrie and the Slae* stanza for exactly the same purpose as Burns was to use it for in his "Epistle to Davie"— which is in fact based in many respects on Ramsay's poem, even to the point of quoting a line from it, 'Mair speir na, nor fear na'. Ramsay's description of the contented but simple life shows one of his most appropriate uses of the vernacular. Indeed, in subject-matter, language and stanza form **"The Poet's Wish"** is historically one of the most important of Ramsay's poems: it showed how an older Scottish tradition could be put to contemporary poetic use, and its influence on Burns was of the greatest significance. Ramsay could make good use of octosyllabic couplets when he stuck to a Scots conversational idiom, as his epistles to James Arbuckle and to the Earl of Dalhousie testify. His renderings of Horace in octosyllabic couplets have less force and weight than the original demands: **"Horace to Virgil, on his taking a Voyage to Athens"**, for example, though it has speed and verve, is altogether too happy-go-lucky. But **"To the Ph—an Ode"** ('Look up to Pentland's towring Taps') is an admirable domesticating of the Horatian mood in an Edinburgh setting, and easily the best of his renderings from the Latin.

The Gentle Shepherd was an expansion of **"Patie and Roger"** into a five-act pastoral comedy. It is the best known of all Ramsay's works, and, in spite of its artificially contrived plot and rather stiff movement, it manages to retain a certain freshness. The first edition contained only four songs—**"Peggy, now the King's come"**, **"By the delicious warmness of thy mouth"**, **"Jocky said to Jenny"**, and **"My Patie is a lover gay"**—but many more were added in 1728, when the play was changed into a ballad opera for the pupils of Haddington Grammar School. This is the version that has been printed ever since, which is a pity, because these editions print both the original dialogue and those parts of it which Ramsay turned into lyrics to be sung, with the result that there is much irritating duplication in the text. We gain **"My Peggy is a Young Thing"** from these alterations, but otherwise the only advantage of the change was that it enabled *The Gentle Shepherd* to be sung, and this helped to keep it alive and popular.

The language is a somewhat anglicized Scots, showing on the whole a greater sureness of touch than Ramsay generally displayed in such mixed modes. Details of rural labour and rural festivity are handled with observant precision, and though there are some melodramatic moments connected with the return of the Royalist laird Sir William Worthy, there is an atmosphere of country work and play pervading the whole which the pastoral had long lost in England and elsewhere in Europe. The first part of the play, when rustic love is displayed against a lively background of rustic labour, is better than the latter part, where the action is manipulated unconvincingly in the interests of the proper *dénouement* and a happy ending; Jenny and Peggy are up early to lay their linen out for bleaching, and that gives them an opportunity of talking together, and when Patie detains Peggy, after the day's work, for some amorous words, Peggy knows that she should be at home helping to prepare supper:

> O Patie! let me gang; I mauna stay;
> We're baith cry'd hame.

Altogether, this pastoral drama represents a precarious equilibrium for Ramsay; he has found a way of combining vernacular realism and a rather tired convention without incongruity or vulgarity. The tiredness is not altogether banished, and the plot limps. But a Scottish breeze blows through this countryside, freshening the air and blowing away at least some of the languors of a stale tradition.

Ramsay produced thirty-one verse fables and tales, of which twenty are adaptations from La Motte and three are from La Fontaine. These are lively performances in Scots, done in fast-moving octosyllabic couplets, lacking the grace and polish of the French, but with a vigorous vernacular humour of their own. He consistently expands his original, filling it out with realistic and occasionally vulgar detail; he is nearer the *fabliau* than either La Motte or La Fontaine, and the Scots tradition of low-life comedy comes alive again in his hands. Again, this is not the greatest kind of poetry, but it is a kind to which the Scots vernacular at this stage of its life was appropriate, and it provided exercise for the vernacular in a setting where it could be used without constraint or affectation.

More important in some respects than Ramsay's original work was his work as an editor. In *The Tea-Table Miscellany* he collected songs and ballads, and in *The Ever Green* he printed the work of the 'Scottish Chaucerians' and others from the Bannatyne MS. In his preface to one of the many later editions of *The Tea-Table Miscellany* Ramsay wrote:

> My being well assured how acceptable new words to known tunes would prove, engaged me to the making verses for above sixty of them, in this and the second volume: about thirty more were done by some ingenious young gentlemen, who were so well pleased with my undertaking, that they generously lent me their assistance; and to them the lovers of sense and music are obliged for some of the best songs in the collection. The rest are such old verses as have been done time out of mind, and only wanted to be cleared from the dross of blundering transcribers and printers; such as, *The Gaberlunzieman, Muirland Willy,* &c., that claim their place in our collection for their merry images of the low character.

Ramsay had thus none of the modern scholar's respect for the original text, and it may be hard to tell exactly what has happened to a song that appears in his collection. Ramsay's sources are often obscure, and a full inquiry into the history of many of the songs he prints, and indeed into the whole question of song collections in eighteenth-century Scotland, has still to be made. But, whatever their history, here the songs are, some 'improved', some rewritten, some printed as Ramsay found them. Ramsay provided some index to what had happened to the songs by marking some of them with letters. 'The SONGS marked C, D, H, L, M, O, &c., are new words by different hands; X, the authors unknown; Z, old songs; Q, old songs with additions.' But the system is not used consistently, and many songs have no letter at all.

The Ever Green is an easier collection to deal with; it takes most of its material from the Bannatyne MS. As Ramsay put it in a set of doggerel verses he wrote in the manuscript on 6 July 1726:

> In Seventeen hundred twenty four
> 　　Did Allan Ramsay keen
> —ly gather from this Book that store
> 　　which fills his Ever Green. . . .

Ramsay's patriotic intention is made clear by his remarks in the preface:

> When these good old *Bards* wrote, we had not yet made Use of imported Trimming upon our Cloaths, nor of foreign Embroidery in our Writings. Their *Poetry* is the Product of their own Country, not pilfered and spoiled in the Transportation from abroad: Their *Images* are native, and their *Landskips* domestick; copied from those Fields and Meadows we every Day behold.

> The *Morning* rises (in the Poets Description) as she does in the *Scottish* Horizon. We are not carried to *Greece* or *Italy* for a Shade, a Stream or a Breeze. The *Groves* rise in our own Valleys; the *Rivers* flow from our own Fountains, and the *Winds* blow upon our own Hills. I find not Fault with those Things, as they are in *Greece* or *Italy:* But with a *Northern Poet* for fetching his Materials from these Places, in a Poem, of which his own Country is the Scene; as our *Hymners* to the *Spring* and *Makers of Pastorals* frequently do.

The collection introduced eighteenth-century Scottish readers to the literature of their country's golden age. Dunbar and Henryson are both represented, the former by "The Thistle and the Rose", "Lament: Quhen he was Sek", "The Goldyn Targe", "Dunbar's Dregy", the "Flyting", "The Dance of the Sevin Deidly Synnis" and seventeen others. This selection gives a fair picture of Dunbar's range both in style and theme, including examples of the ceremonial, the aureate, the elegiac, the satiric, the moralizing, the humorous and the confessional. The poems from Henryson include "Robene and Makyne", "The Garmont of Gud Ladeis" and two of the fables. Among other pieces from the Bannatyne MS. are "Christis Kirk on the Grene"; "The Battle of Harlaw", one of the best known of the Scottish historical ballads; "The Wife of Auchtermuchty", a lively verse-tale of husband and wife reversing rôles to the former's discomfiture, attributed to Sir John Moffatt; several poems by Alexander Scott; a group of coarse satires on loose women by the sixteenth-century Robert Sempill, and other poems by minor sixteenth-century writers. Ramsay changes spelling, punctuation, word order and even stanza form where it suits him; and where he cannot understand a word or a phrase he is liable to rephrase the passage.

Ramsay occasionally inserts stanzas of his own into older poems. He adds two stanzas to Dunbar's "Tydingis fra the Sessioun", containing his own friendly opinion of the Edinburgh judges and advocates, and gives no indication that these stanzas are not by Dunbar; he slips a stanza full of elaborate classical allusions into the midst of Alexander Scott's simple, singing love lyric, 'Return thee, hairt, hamewart agane' (whose first line, incidentally, Ramsay characteristically "regularizes" to "Return Hamewart my Hart again"); and, most notorious, he adds his own preposterous conclusion to Dunbar's "Lament":

> Suthe I forsie, if Spae-craft had,
> Frae Hethir-Muirs sall ryse a LAD,
> Aftir twa Centries pas, sall he
>   Revive our Fame and Memorie.
>
> Then sall we flourish EVIR GRENE:
> All thanks to carefull *Bannatyne,*
> And to the PATRON kind and frie,
>   Qhua lends the LAD baith them and me.
>
> Far sall we fare, baith Eist and West,
> Owre ilka Clyme by *Scots* possest;
> Then sen our Warks sall nevir die,
>   *Timor mortis non turbat me.*

To which monstrous conclusion Ramsay calmly appends the words, "Quod Dunbar".

The two poems attributed to 'Ar. Scot' are both anti-English patriotic poems (though **"The Eagle and Robin Red-breist"** is veiled in allegory) and apparently Ramsay thought that they would have more force if put in antique dress—perhaps, too, he thought it safer so to disguise them. **"The Vision"** is subtitled: '*Compylit in Latin be a most lernit Clerk in Tyme of our Hairship and Oppression, anno 1300, and translatit in 1524.*' It bewails the oppressed condition of Scotland and ends by prophesying

successful battle for the re-establishment of an independent Kingdom of Scotland. The stanza is that of *The Cherrie and the Slae.* **"The Eagle and Robin Red-breist"** tells how the robin, singing loyal songs to the royal eagle, is maligned by the other birds, jealous of his merit and of the king's regard for him, and driven from court. Here also the language is deliberately antique, though the verse form is the octosyllabic couplet. For Ramsay, Scots as a serious literary medium belonged to the past.

The Ever Green had nothing like the popularity of *The Tea-Table Miscellany.* There were no reprints in Ramsay's lifetime, and only four later reprints between 1761 and 1876. It was the popular vernacular tradition and the tradition, of the late sixteenth-century poets, rather than the mediaeval makars, that influenced Fergusson and Burns. And though both the popular tradition and the tradition of Montgomerie and his contemporaries derived from and in their own way continued the mediaeval Scottish tradition, the fifteenth-century makars did not directly influence subsequent eighteenth-century Scottish poetry. The relatively homogeneous national culture of the Scotland of the early Stuarts was too far away; the Reformation, the Union of the Crowns and the Union of Parliaments had between them created too wide a gulf between past and present, and complicated the Scottish cultural situation to the point where no full, unselfconscious contact could any longer be made with Henryson and Dunbar. Both Watson and Ramsay had shown other ways and made other material available; ballad and folksong remained alive, certain late mediaeval themes and stanza forms had been popularized, the goliardic tradition survived in the universities, and Scottish national sentiment was increasingly turning from politics to literature.

Alexander M. Kinghorn (essay date 1970)

SOURCE: "Biographical and Critical Introduction: *The Gentle Shepherd,*" in *The Works of Allan Ramsay, Vol. IV,* edited by Alexander M. Kinghorn and Alexander Law, William Blackwood & Sons Ltd., 1970, pp. 90-108.

[*Kinghorn's introduction to the fourth volume of Ramsay's works includes what is widely considered the most accurate and complete biographical information on the poet. In the following excerpt from the critical portion of Kinghorn's introduction, the critic discusses Ramsay's use of the Scots language and the place of* The Gentle Shepherd *in Scots literary history.*]

The work by which Ramsay achieved an immediate reputation among his own contemporaries and in the eyes of succeeding generations was *The Gentle Shepherd, a Pastoral Comedy,* published in 1725. Woodhouselee refers to it as "the noblest and most permanent monument of his fame" [In *The Works of Allan Ramsay,* 1800]. The play springs out of two eclogues, **"Patie and Roger"** and **"Jenny and Maggy"**, probably written in 1720 and 1723 respectively, and both incorporated in the finished drama. *The Gentle Shepherd,* which obviously owed its title to Spenser, was dedicated to Susanna, Countess of Eglintoun, in a spirit of heavy flattery. Ramsay concluded his inscription by striking an attitude of intimate self-doubt succeeded by a weak confidence:

> *I write this last Sentence with a Hand that trembles between Hope and Fear: But if I shall prove so happy as to please your Ladyship in the following Attempt, then all my Doubts shall vanish like a Morning Vapour; I shall hope to be class'd with Tasso and Guarini, and sing with Ovid,*
>
> > If 'tis allowed to Poets to divine,
> > One half of round Eternity is mine.

His reference to European pastoralists as the standard at which he has aimed is misleading, for the most obvious comparison is with Gay's *Shepherd's Week,* printed in 1714, which, more than any other work in the genre, links Spenser with Ramsay. *The Shepherd's Week,* a skit on the pastoral eclogue probably conceived at the expense of Ambrose Philips, went into five London editions before 1742. The delicately ironic "proeme" suggests the intention and temper of the six-day "Week", for Gay draws a fine distinction between actual shepherds and the pastoral variety, writing, after the manner of Spenser, in stylised "old" dialect:

> Thou wilt not find my shepherdesses idly piping on oaten reeds, but milking the kine, tying up the sheaves, or if the hogs are astray driving them to their styes. My shepherd gathereth none other nosegays but what are the growth of our own fields, he sleepeth not under myrtle shades, but under a hedge, nor doth he vigilantly defend his flocks from wolves, because there are none, as maister Spenser well observeth.

Like Greene over a century earlier, Gay applied the stock conventions of the pastoral form to what he knew of actual rustic life and manners so that the Virgilian shepherd seen against the English country background is revealed as an amusingly incongruous personage.

Woodhouselee said of *The Gentle Shepherd* that

> There is not a milk-maid, a plough-boy, or a shepherd, of the Lowlands of Scotland, who has not by heart its favourite passages, and can rehearse its entire scenes.

and that

> The *persons* of the Scotish pastoral are the actual inhabitants of the country where the scene is laid

a fact which distinguished it from the pastoral drama of the mid-sixteenth century, like Tasso's *Aminta* and Guarini's *Pastor Fido* with which Ramsay's play was occasionally compared, as we have noted, by himself and his contemporaries. The coy nymphs and swains and the brutal satyrs of Italian originals had no foundation in real life, whereas Glaud and Madge apparently stepped directly from the ranks of the old Scottish yeomanry, respectable, homely and comfortable figures.

Ramsay's pastoral was not intended to be satiric but its character probably owes something to this attempt of Gay's to domesticate the style and to ridicule the fastidious pose affected by writers like Rowe and Philips. The Scottish shepherds seemed to be flesh-and-blood creatures and their vitality was communicated in large part by the authentic-sounding (rather than authentic) speech which English pastoral personages lacked. To the metropolitan theatre-goer Ramsay's figures were convincing and if they were not quite real, they were close enough to reality to be accepted by those sophisticates who sought symbols of a bygone age in Ramsay's stage-versions of still-living primitives. In its ballad-opera form, the play itself was re-issued practically every year from 1725 to the last quarter of the nineteenth century. Pope, Boswell, Burns and Leigh Hunt all praised it and it undoubtedly seems to have filled a need in the lives of townsfolk whose lives were changing as industrialisation grew. *The Gentle Shepherd* helped to create from among such people a reading public for whom the Scottish countryside held a glamour and whose desire for literary entertainment had not yet been satisfied by a spate of popular novels. It also helped to break down prejudice against the theatre and, as the first native drama since Lyndsay's *Ane Satyre,* occupied a unique position in Scotland's literature; it represented a genre which neither Fergusson nor Burns attempted and partly for that reason Ramsay's comedy, slight in itself, survived as a monument to an otherwise minor poet.

The action of the play is presented, in heroic couplets, against a rustic setting and is introduced by a song, **"My Peggy is a young Thing"**, sung by Patie, first printed in *Tea-Table Miscellany* (5th ed., 1729), together with twenty other ballads intended, according to Ramsay's directions, to be sung in their proper order within the play itself. The poet had been asked to make a "ballad-opera" out of *The Gentle Shepherd* by the pupils of Haddington Grammar School who had witnessed a performance of Gay's *Beggar's Opera* in October, 1728. Ramsay's efforts on their behalf were soon represented by a public performance of *The Gentle Shepherd,* with musical accompaniment, given on 22nd January, 1729 "in Taylor's Hall, by a *Set of Young Gentlemen*". In this way Ramsay demonstrated the fusion of an old literary tradition, adapted to Scottish urban tastes, with a new musical fashion, that of Italian light opera. Ramsay's biographer in the MS. *Life* informs us that the poet soon regretted this conversion and would have retracted the songs if he could have done so; however, "he comforted himself with the thought that the contagion had not infected his second Volume in Quarto, where *The Gentle Shepherd* is still to be found in its original purity". Nevertheless, the play was quite successful as a ballad-opera until the early nineteenth century, in London as well as in Scotland. In the latter country, the combination of a performance with a musical concert, together with the frequent introduction of songs and dances into the body of the play, circumvented the Licensing Act.

The historical background of *The Gentle Shepherd* is that of Restoration times. The laird, Sir William Worthy, who had fought with Montrose in the period of Cromwell's

Protectorship, had been compelled to go into exile, leaving his son Patrick to be brought up as the son of an old shepherd, Symon, free of the contaminations of court life abroad. About the same time, Mause, a loyal nurse in the service of Sir William's sister, had saved Peggy, the infant daughter of that house from being smothered by relatives who wanted the estate to come to them. Mause had taken the child fifty miles to the doorstep of Glaud, an old shepherd, and since that time had lived in a cottage close by, in order to maintain an interest in her one-time charge. Eventually, the Restoration makes it possible for Sir William to reclaim his birthright, and the action of the play begins. With the songs, the performing time would be about two hours, representing about twenty hours of "stage time". . . .

The final Act is ushered in with an amusing passage in which we find Bauldy turning up at the crack of dawn in a state of funk and complaining that Mause had raised up a ghost to torment him: Sir William promises to look into the matter and makes some observations, straight from the body of sophisticated opinion, concerning village superstitions and the absurdity of rustic beliefs in the supernatural which a want of formal education encourages. This weighty rationalism does not affect the success of the scene as a whole, for it is full of a home-spun vitality and contains flashes of vivid description in Scots that are convincing as Burns was later to be convincing in "Tam o' Shanter". Bauldy's tale of his encounter with

> . . . a Ghaist or Diel, I kenna whilk,
> Like a dead Corse in Sheet as white as Milk,
> Black Hands it had, and Face as wan as Death,
> Upon me fast the *Witch* and *it* fell baith,
> And gat me down; while, I, like a great Fool,
> Was laboured as I wont to be at School.
> My Heart out of its Hool was like to lowp;
> I pithless grew with Fear, and had nae Hope,
> Till, with an Elritch Laugh, they vanish'd quite:
> Syne I, haff dead with Anger, Fear and Spite,
> Crap up, and fled straight frae them, Sir, to you,
> Hoping your Help, to gi'e the Deil his Due.
> I'm sure my Heart will ne'er gi'e o'er to dunt,
> Till in a fat Tar-barrel *Mause* be burnt.

and Sir William's gently ironic reply to Symon's question about the possibility of supernatural tricks really taking place:

> Such as the Devil's dancing in a Moor
> Amongst a few old Women craz'd and poor
> Who are rejoic'd to see him frisk and lowp
> O'er Braes and Bogs, with Candles in his Dowp;
> Appearing sometimes like a black-horn'd Cow,
> Aftimes like *Bawty, Badrans* or a *Sow*:
> Then with his Train thro' airy Paths to glide,
> While they on Cats, or Clowns or Broom-staffs ride,
> Or in the Egg-shell skim out o'er the Main,
> To drink their Leader's health in *France or Spain*:
> Than aft by Night, bumbaze Hare-hearted Fools,

> By tumbling down their Cup-board, Chairs and Stools.
> Whate'er's in Spells, or if there Witches be,
> Such Whimsies seem the most absurd to me.

both share something of Burns's ability to convey in a stream of vital images, each clear-cut and at the same time evaporating rapidly, the picture of frenzied movements, sudden appearances, objects flung past the eye by an invisible hand and the whole shifting kaleidoscope of the dance, the flight, the uncontrolled fall and individual terror to which the Scots tradition of dramatic poetry-making is so well suited.

Sir William's knowing attitude to the supernatural as the absurdities believed in only by the credulous or ignorant is complemented by his own reliance on the power of such credulity; he assumes the role of a fortune-teller of whom Elspa says

> . . . a Warlock, or possest
> With some nae good—or second Sight at least:

and Symon thinks he must have made a bargain with the Devil. Ramsay builds up the emotional tension surrounding Mause by making Bauldy describe her considerable repertoire of magic tricks and menacing spells:

> Here *Mausy* lives, a Witch, that for sma' Price
> Can cast her Cantraips, and give me Advice.
> She can o'ercast the Night, and cloud the Moon
> And mak the Deils obedient to her Crune.
> At Midnight Hours, o'er the Kirk-yards she raves,
> And howks unchristen'd We'ans out of their Graves;
> Boils up their Livers in a Warlock's Pow,
> Rins withershins about the Hemlock Low;
> And seven Times does her Prayers backward pray,
> Till Plotcock comes with Lumps of *Lapland* Clay,
> Mixt with the Venom of black Taids and Snakes;
> Of this unsonsy Pictures aft she makes
> Of ony ane she hates—and gars expire
> With slaw and racking Pains afore a Fire;
> Stuck fu' of Prins, the devilish Pictures melt,
> The Pain, by Fowk they represent, is felt.

Of course the supernatural elements in the play are all rationally explainable, and in the end the ghostly atmosphere is dissipated—Sir William has been playing a part, Mause is a witch only in the eyes of those less well-informed than herself and Bauldy's "ghaist" is part of a trick. Nevertheless, the dramatic power of *The Gentle Shepherd* is largely rooted in passages like these. The eighteenth century discussed the question of the existence of ghosts with considerable enthusiasm, and Ramsay's play was published eleven years before the old Witchcraft Act was repealed; in fact, the year 1727 saw the carrying out of the last capital sentence for witchcraft in England, so that Ramsay's references were to a topic of the moment. Generally speaking, the supernatural was to be rejected by the enlightened and Ramsay, speaking through the *persona* of Sir William, comes to the rational conclusion that such beliefs are "silly Notions". At the same time, his handling of it testifies to his poet's fascination for "graveyard" writing of the kind which became more popular than it deserved to be in the hands of Robert Blair, Edward Young, Mark Akenside, William Collins and the elder Warton. In Scotland, James Beattie's *The Minstrel* showed this same combination of rationality and emotional delight which determined Ramsay's attitude in *The Gentle Shepherd*. But when Ramsay was composing his play the rural clergy were still assiduous witch-hunters—and there were enthusiastic laymen like Sir James Steuart of Goodtress and Professor William Forbes of the University of Glasgow who were only too ready to put pressure on clergymen in order to satisfy their own consciences in the matter of suffering witches to live. In Edinburgh there was much more enlightenment than in the rural parishes so that we may expect Ramsay to follow the liberal trend and to introduce ghosts, use them for effect, and then explain them away patronisingly as absurd whimsies.

In the hands of Burns the supernatural is exploited simply for its comic effects; the "Address to the Deil" and "Tam o' Shanter" both keep the traditional terrors under control by keeping up a constant mockery while Fergusson's "bogles and spectres" in "The Ghaists" strike no terror, nor is his kirk-yard setting ever permitted to become more than a setting. Nevertheless, it is with such poems in mind that the action in *The Gentle Shepherd* has to be considered. Ramsay lacks Burns's range, technical skill, and power of maintaining effects, but passages like these in *The Gentle Shepherd* draw attention to precisely what it was that Ramsay did for Scots poetry in the eighteenth century and indicate his place as a link between a late mediaeval *makar* like Dunbar and Scottish Augustans like Fergusson and Burns. . . .

The action of *The Gentle Shepherd* is certainly not original. The pattern of lovers, the foundling complications, and the device of disguise are all stylised descendants of classical comedy. Attic new comedy included many examples of this carefully-patterned and thoroughly predictable development of situation and the "froth" of a Heliodorus anticipated many stereotypes in Roman comedy and eventually in English plays of the sixteenth century. Direct ancestry is untraceable, for the influence of the *genre* touched the Renaissance at many points. What should interest us, therefore, is not source-hunting, but the way in which Ramsay adapted the old form in order to make a fresh Scots play. The first part of *The Gentle Shepherd* is more original than the second part; in the latter the action dominates the background and there is only a limited appeal in the conventional gathering of the threads. The manipulations in the interest of a standard *denouement* are not particularly ingenious, nor is there much attempt on Ramsay's part to make the principal characters individual. The laird speaks largely

standard English, with an occasional lapse into the Doric when he is addressing a rustic like Symon. His sententious observations about the elevating value of education for peasants as well as for gentlemen read rather quaintly nowadays, as do his ponderous moral statements delivered in his role as patron of the rustics. In his guise as a *spaeman*, the laird speaks a braid Scots that totters uneasily on the brink of anglicisation. One moment he is saying:

> Whisht, doubtfu' Carle; for ere the Sun
> Has driven twice down to the Sea,
> What I have said ye shall see done
> In part, or nae mair credit me.

and shortly afterwards:

> Delay a while your hospitable Care;
> I'd rather enjoy this Evening calm and fair,
> Around you ruin'd Tower, to fetch a Walk
> With you, kind Friend, to have some private
>   Talk.

Patie and Roger, the rustic swains, are conventional pastoral figures whose sayings, like Sir William's, veer from Scots to English in accordance with their changes in status. The Patie of the finale is a young gentleman; he of the opening scene is a young hind. The same, more or less, applies to Peggy, who sheds her Scots vocabulary with her station as a milkmaid. The other personages are more attractive, on the whole, largely because they are and never cease to be lowland countrymen and women, speaking a heightened form of braid Scots. It is here that Ramsay breaks away from his established models and by a skilful use of the Doric manages to paint scenes descriptive of the real countryside, not the romanticised one of urban English poets, put a recognisably faithful reflection of what he himself knew at first hand. The editor of the 1808 edition of *The Gentle Shepherd* made out a case for Newhall as the original setting of the play, but wherever Ramsay had in mind, his background is consistently naturalistic and his slices of "low life", if not so close to reality as Fielding's, are at the least persuasive to all but the most critical. Consider Symon's account of his preparations for the banquet in *II, i*, or Roger's brief statement of his assets in *III, iii*, or the references to peasant superstitions made, for example, in Bauldy's soliloquy in *II, ii*, or, best of all, perhaps, the hints of the less-pleasant side of the rustic's precarious existence dropped here and there throughout the play, as in Jenny's observations on poverty and destitution in *I, ii*:

> But Poortith, *Peggy*, is the warst of a',
> Gif o'er your Heads ill Chance shou'd Beggary
>   draw:
> But little Love, or canty Chear can come,
> Frae duddy Doublets, and a Pantry toom.
> Your Nowt may die—the Spate may bear away
> Frae aff the Howms your dainty Rucks of
>   Hay.—
> The thick blawn Wreaths of Snaw, or blashy
>   Thows,

> May smoor your Wathers, and may rot your
>   Ews.
> A Dyvour buys your Butter, Woo and Cheese,
> But, on the Day of Payment, breaks and flees.
> With glooman Brow the Laird seeks in his Rent:
> 'Tis no to gi'e; your Merchant's to the bent;
> *His Honour* mauna want, he poinds your Gear;
> Syne, driven frae House and Hald, where will ye
>   steer?

With these in mind it is easier to perceive, as his contemporaries did, the nature of Ramsay's unique originality as a writer of pastoral drama.

The Gentle Shepherd was not intended as a mask for political allegory, and apart from Sir William's position as an exiled supporter of Montrose (who is actually mentioned in the Laing MSS.), there is nothing in the way of political nationalism expressed anywhere in the play. Ramsay's deep-rooted patriotism is contained in his choice of setting and selective use of Scots idiom. He recognised that the language was not an adequate vehicle for expressing sophisticated ideas; Hamilton of Gilbertfield, author of an abridged *Wallace* (1722), together with Thomas Ruddiman, with his earlier publication of Douglas's *Aeneid,* had drawn attention to the potentialities of a literary Scots, or rather, of a heightened vernacular, arbitrarily spelled and made up of borrowings from various regional dialects. What modern critics hold against Ramsay is his confinement of Scots to low-life and convivially comic subjects or, at its most dignified, to antiquarian pastiche like his extension to **"Christ's Kirk on the Green"**. At the same time, it is admitted, by Daiches and others, that he was the first to pursue the idea that Scots had literary potentialities and to practise making poetry in it. Unfortunately its range was severely limited by his efforts, so that the language suffered an eventual loss of integrity and descended to Burns and through him to Stevenson as a medium fit only for the crudest of emotional expression. Certainly Ramsay had no notion of the way in which his juxtaposition of Scots with English actually undermined the strength of the former by showing it to be unsuited to the complexities of modern communication. He gave authority to the belief, already well-established, that education, the outward trappings of a gentleman, excluded Scots, a yokel tongue which, if in some respects attractive, was not really a sign of good breeding and ought to be excised by right-minded teachers. Ramsay's longest and most ambitious work emphasised the poverty of Scots for all purposes save that of describing the speech and activities of a "North British" agricultural community, and the appearance of his home-bred Muse in ancient garb must now be reckoned a severe setback to the cause of the revivifiers of Scots as a language of literature. Though its merit as a dramatic work of art is slight, **The Gentle Shepherd,** as an example of what could, and could not, be achieved in Anglo-Scots, mirrors its author and his times faithfully, and is therefore historically significant. In other respects it is a little-read curiosity, too superficial and lacking in emotional force to bear more than a rare revival on the stage; there are no characters like Captain Macheath or Polly Peachum, no

atmosphere like that of Newgate is created to fascinate the audience, and no strong sentiments of any kind are evoked by the situations of the shepherds, who have no conflicts to resolve. The sub-plot involving Madge, Mause and Bauldy is trivial and peters out when the audience are denied the promised comic scene in which Bauldy meets the "ghaist"; Ramsay makes no attempt to explore the dramatic possibilities of this and rests content to report it in Bauldy's own words. Their graphic character, already commented upon as successful verse, is in fact a substitute for stage action. Ramsay does not really know how to write for the stage, and lacks the true dramatist's consciousness of the power of witnessed as distinct from reported action.

Ramsay's published views on drama and the value of the stage were liberal, and we have a number of statements, in prose and verse, revealing him to have been an alert critic of the practical effects and uses of the theatre as a reforming agent. His **"Prologue to Aurenzebe"** and **"The Drummer,"** performed "by the young Gentlemen of the Grammar School of Haddington, August, 1727" is typical of his published views on the subject:

> . . . we speak to those can hear
> The nervous Phrase, which raises Thoughts more
>   hy,
> When added Action leads them thro' the Eye.
> To paint fair Vertue, Humours and Mistakes,
> Is what our School with Pleasure undertakes,
> Thro' various Incidents of Life, led on
> By DRYDEN, and immortal ADDISON:
> Those study'd Men, and knew the various
>   Springs
> That mov'd the Minds of *Coachmen* and of
>   *Kings.*
> Altho' we're young—allow no Thought so mean,
> That any here's to act the *Harlequin*:
> We leave such dumb-show Mimickry to Fools,
> Beneath the Sp'rit of *Caledonian Schools.*
> Learning's our Aim, and all our Care, to reach
> At Elegance and Gracefulness of Speech,
> And the Address, from Bashfulness refin'd,
> Which hangs a weight upon a worthy Mind.

There is nothing original about this statement since Ramsay is merely echoing the sentiments of the average critic of the time, who believed that extremism such as moralists of the Jeremy Collier school represented needed tempering. Between 1719 and 1736 Ramsay printed or drafted a number of "prologues" and "epilogues" intended to be delivered to a live audience, sometimes on a specific occasion; all of them try to convey the role of the dramatist as social reformer. When his theatre was opened in Carrubber's Close, Mr Bridges introduced the offerings of the first night with a recitation written by Ramsay which began

> Long has it been the Bus'ness of the Stage
> To mend our Manners, and reform the Age

a couplet which echoes the eighteenth stanza of his **"Ad-**

dress to Lord Provost Drummond", printed in the 1728 *Poems*. . . . In the 1721 *Poems* appears a **"Prologue, Spoke by one of the young Gentlemen, who, for their Improvement and Diversion, acted The Orphan, and Cheats of Scapin, the last Night of the year 1719"**. The tone is scathingly satirical at the expense of the canting enemies of the play, who are made to engage in mock dialogue:

> Stage-Plays, quoth Dunce, are unco' Things
>   indeed!
> He said,—he gloom'd,—and shook his thick boss
>   Head.
> They're *Papery, Papery*!—cryed his Nibour
>   neist,
> Contriv'd at *Rome* by some malignant Priest,
> To witch away Fowks Minds frae doing well,
> As saith *Rab Ker, M'Millan* and *M'Neil.*

Ramsay changes his method of attack and becomes contemptuous of such criticism:

> But let them tauk.—In Spite of ilk Cadaver,
> We'll cherish Wit, and scorn their Fead or
>   Favour;
> We'll strive to bring in active Eloquence,
> Tho for a while upon our Fame's Expence.—
> I'm wrang.—Our Fame will mount with metled
>   Carles,
> And for the rest, we'll be aboon their Snarls.—
> Knock down the Fools, wha dare with empty
>   Rage
> Spit in the face of Virtue and the Stage.
> 'Cause Hereticks in Pulpits thump and rair,
> Must naithing orthodox b'expected there;
> Because a Rump cut off a Royal Head,
> Must not anither Parli'ment succeed.
> Thus tho the *Drama's* aft debauch'd and rude,
> Must we, for some are bad, refuse the good:

In **"An Epilogue for a Scoolplay"**, written in 1729, he informs his audience that

> To day our Scenes have to your View desp(l)ayd
> The consequence of cruelty & pride
> The Tyrant falls while one Heroick chief
> to groning Nations gives a brave relief
> such beautyous Painting should engage each
>   mind
> to all thats generous noble just & kind
> Then since Improvement now is all our aim
> we surely may your smiles & praises claim
> which if obtain youl Quickly see each Boy
> spring throw his Learning up to man with Joy.

and his several recorded connections with performances by young people suggest that he was keen to emphasise an active relationship between drama and the upbringing of boys—a theme touched upon by many critics later in the century, like Beattie, Blair, Mackenzie and Richardson, all of whom argued on behalf of the stage as an instrument of moral education.

Alexander M. Kinghorn (essay date 1970)

SOURCE: "Biographical and Critical Introduction: Ramsay as 'Translator,'" in *The Works of Allan Ramsay, Vol. IV*, edited by Alexander M. Kinghorn and Alexander Law, William Blackwood & Sons, 1970, pp. 109-127.

[*In the following excerpt, Kinghorn discusses Ramsay's imitations of the Latin poet Horace and the French fabulists La Fontaine and La Motte.*]

Ramsay's renderings from Horace show how much, and how little, he had in common with the Roman, whose poetic character, with its urbanity and worldly-wise sophistication, held an understandable attraction for the Scot. The MS. *Life* is one authority for judging the extent of the language barrier separating Ramsay from his originals, both in French and Latin. The biographer writes:

> He had made himself very much master of the French language, and his imitations of the Fables of La Motte are excellent. He much lamented his deficiency in the Latin; of which, however, he had pickt up so much, as, by the help of Dacier, to catch the spirit of the Odes of Horace; which, even by this twilight, he, above all writings, admired; and, supplying, by congenial fancy, what he wanted in erudition, has imitated some of them with a truly Horatian felicity.

Ramsay's 1721 **"Preface"** contains several references to Horace, who is made the second of a triumvirate of poets, "Anacreon, Horace *and* Waller", inferior to Virgil in sustained effort but with the souls of true poets. The reader is encouraged to think of Ramsay as in this class and company. He goes on to defend his ignorance of Latin in a slightly aggressive tone, saying:

> *I understand* Horace *but faintly in the Original, and yet can feast on his beautiful Thoughts dress'd in* British; *and do not see any great occasion for every Man's being made capable to translate the Classicks, when they are so elegantly done to his Hand.*

and at the conclusion of his **"Preface,"** referring to the "five or six Imitations of Horace", Ramsay describes his re-creation of certain *Odes*:

> *I have only snatched at his Thought and Method in gross, and dress'd them up in* Scots, *without confining my self to no more or no less; so that these are only to be reckoned a following of his Manner.*

It is evident, therefore, that Ramsay's acquaintance with the authentic Horatian spirit came through translations. . . .

"Translating" is a misnomer for what Ramsay tried to do to Horace. He would have agreed and called his poems "imitations" or "renderings" from the Latin. Ramsay's "imitations" are uneven. In many of them there is only a diluted Horace, but here and there the Roman's "true Poetick flame" flickers in the Scotsman's versions. **"To** the Ph—an Ode" is one of the best examples of a successful attempt on Ramsay's part to recreate the naive Horatian Epicureanism. The original is *Odes,* I, ix:

> Vides ut alta stet nive candidum
> Soracte . . .

paralleled in Ramsay by:

> Look up to *Pentland's* tow'ring Taps
> Buried beneath great Wreaths of Snaw . . .

Soracte, a mountain twenty-six miles from Rome, can be seen from the city, as can the Pentlands from Edinburgh. What Horace omits or achieves by suggestion, Ramsay handles directly and unsubtly. His octosyllabic line is less forceful and lacks the weight of the original though in this particular case it is more appropriate to the subject than in some of the other exercises:

> dissolve frigus ligna super foco
> large reponens, atque benignius
> deprome quadrimum Sabina
> O Thaliarche, merum diota.

becomes

> Then fling on Coals and ripe the Ribs,
> And beek the House baith Butt and Ben,
> That Mutchken Stoup it hads but Dribs,
> Then let's get in the tappit Hen.

The spectacle of "gowfers" dodging the Edinburgh winter winds and thudding hailstones is a strongly visual intrusion into Horace's urbane moralisings. Horace's popular Epicureanism takes effect through its stylish and concise presentation, but Ramsay's version strains each point almost to excess. Scots poets from Henryson and Douglas onwards have excelled at painting pictures of bad weather and Ramsay's "blattering winds" have an authenticity about them which tends to dominate the poem, making it un-Horatian and markedly domestic. . . .

Ramsay's versions of the Vth and VIIth *Odes* follow his usual method of domestication. In the former he adapts the customs of an antique civilisation in order to comment on a similar Scottish situation. Horace is talking of Pyrrha's artful preparations for a lover; the imagery refers to Pyrrha as the beguiling but dangerous sea, and the poet compares himself in the final stanza to a shipwrecked sailor, who escaped to tell the tale and dedicated a votive tablet to Neptune. He has ventured and now wishes to warn others. Ramsay preserves this situation though he loses much of the smooth irony of his model. His poem is a clever take-off on the theme of the fickle woman but is far away from the sophisticated mood affected by Horace, for he is never more than sentimental. Renderings like

> with hair unsnooded and without thy Stays.

for

> cui flavam religas comam,
> simplex munditiis?

signal a much cruder vision on Ramsay's part than the poetically fruitful comparison of Pyrrha with the sea.

The VIIth *Ode* opens with references to the rivalry of taste between Grecian and Italian cities; Ramsay transmutes this to Scotland and draws a parallel between the woods and orchards of the Tiber, twenty miles from Rome, and the beauty spots of his own countryside, Arthur's Seat, for example, and

> Clyds Gow'ny Howms & Watter faws
> the Louthian rigs & Leader Haughs
> and Ed'nburghs high and hewn stain Waws.

which delight him more than do any cities of past glory. At this point the resemblance ends, for Horace's poem is chiefly concerned with invoking the sentiments of the soldier, always on the move from one place to another:

> . . . nunc vino pellite curas;
> cras ingens iterabimus aequor

Ramsay finishes rather lamely with an oblique reference to "Rugh plains wher Cannons rair" and a line "O—Drink—and drive aff Care" which suggests that he had lost interest in what he was doing or possibly that his inspiration had momentarily deserted him. Neither of these two poems was printed during his lifetime. . . .

In contrast, and by way of a departure from his usual method of nationalising, or "naturalising" Horace by changing all classical references and European place-names to Scots ones, Ramsay's **"Horace to Virgil, on his taking a Voyage to Athens"** represents an attempt to render *Ode* III without dependence on contemporary allusion or local topography. Both poems are prayers for a safe journey, but Ramsay has changed Horace's lofty sentiments out of all recognition. The original theme and form is conventional—that of an envoi to a friend turned into an *indignatio,* or cursing, of the primal inventor of some dangerous practice or skill, in this case sea-voyaging, which violates the natural order of things.

> Nil mortalibus ardui est:
> caelum ipsum petimus stultitia neque
> per nostrum patimur scelus
> iracunda Iovem ponere fulmina

becomes

> What is't Man winna ettle at?
> E'en wi' the Gods he'll bell the Cat:
> Tho *Jove* be very Laith to kill,
> They winna let his Bowt ly still.

The verses are superficial and his "Scottification" ill-adapted to his subject, for he is very far from being the "Gawain Douglas" whose name he borrowed. Daedalus contradicting Nature and "keeking" in at Jove's high winnocks is barely acceptable but when

> . . . Hercules, wi's Timber Mell,
> Plays rap upo' the Yates of Hell

the level has dropped sharply to that of buffoonery. The first half of the Scots poem is better than the second if only because it tries to maintain a serious tone, but the whole is interesting chiefly as an illustration of the difficulty Ramsay had in trying to employ Scots for serious purposes. Tytler condemns this one on the grounds that it is ludicrous to treat the topic of the origin of evil, which Horace attributes to the crime of Prometheus in stealing fire from Heaven, in such gross phraseology. It is hard to disagree. . . .

Ramsay's **"The Conclusion, After the Manner of Horace"**, "ad librum suum" is the last poem in the 1721 volume. His original is *Epistles* I, xx, an *envoi* to Horace's book, involving in its last section a conventional literary self-portrait of the author. The *envoi* is light and playful, containing an extended irony, in this case a risqué *double-entendre,* for the "liber" to whom the letter is addressed is not the book alone but is also, etymologically, the word for "a freed slave". Horace cleverly exploits this ambiguity; the slave is a "puer delicatus" who, like the book, will "stand for sale" in the forum, with his skin smoothed by pumice, like the papyrus and who will fall into many hands until his sated lovers tire. Then, old and worn, he will retire to the provinces and become a tutor of school-children, where he will call back memories of the one who set him free. Ramsay's rather literal adaptation weakens Horace's succinct irony, for the Scot's tone is not really ironic at all. He is beset first by fears, but he banishes them by an effort of will and concludes on a naively hopeful note. The effect is that of an imitation of a well-known stereotype such as was fairly frequently employed by Roman poets such as Ovid and Martial, and it rounds off Ramsay's volume neatly.

> Gin ony want to ken my Age,
> See *Anno. Dom.* on Title Page;
> This year when Springs by Care and Skill
> The spacious leaden Conduits fill,
> And first flow'd up the *Castle-hill*
> When *South-Sea* Projects cease to thrive,
> And only *North-Sea* seems alive,
> Tell them your Author's Thirty five.

In spite of his professed ignorance of the Latin language, Ramsay seems to understand Horace quite well and displays far more precise knowledge of poetic detail than critics usually hold to his credit. There is nothing in this, however, which he could not have acquired through the study of translations and the advice of friendly Latinists, such as Ruddiman and John Ker. It is in any case well-known that many Augustan poets, like Pope and Prior, not to mention the minor stars of London literary coteries, whom Ramsay held in respect and indeed envy, compared the age of Horace with their own eighteenth-century "age of Reason". Horace, with his patronage, his townsman's view of the country, his Sabine farm and his

philosophy of popular Epicureanism provided the school of Pope with a mentor having the highest authority who seemed to show them an example of defence against growing materialism, and the gross worship of wealth, and furthermore, appealed to their rationalism as though he were an understanding relative, not blocked from them by centuries of time or by Renaissance deification of the kind given to Virgil. Ramsay, perhaps without more than a vague notion of what he was doing, adapted certain of these attitudes as part of his pose as a young Scottish gentleman, and found in Horace an ancient who was also a modern and as such a suitable model for a self-styled descendant of Dalhousie to imitate. He gave Horace's sentiments a distinctively Scottish cast and colouring, and on the whole his versions have much to recommend them. In a poem addressed **"To Maevis Junior"**, he defies a contemporary Horatian who, like Maevius of old, obtruded his nonsense on the world:

> Translations, Pedant, be thy task
>   it is beneath me to Translate
> but in Clear Rays I loo to Bask
>   and shining paterns imitate.
>
> . . . Let Horace sleep!—he neer could tire
>   touch not his ashes!—he has none
> he's all oer Brightness life and fire
>   too dazling for sae dul a drone

and in the final stanza refers to his own renderings:

> I'll Rowze the Prophet that forsaw
>   Langsyn in the Augustan days
> that I shoud Chaunt oer Dale & Law
>   his notes in Calidonian Lays. . . .

Ramsay's classicism was self-conscious and emphasises the association of vernacular Scots with an ignorance of Greek and Latin, but his "Horatianism", that is, his posing as a homespun philosopher who distrusted modern fads and fashions, a wise country mouse who looked good-naturedly but with misgivings upon the more feverish activities of his urban counterpart, was well served by his colloquial, prosaic style. The satirical genius of Horace lurked in Scots poetry, and if one wishes to estimate the extent of Ramsay's debt to the Roman poet one must go beyond his "translations" to his moral epistles, which set a high value on middle-aged *bourgeois* virtues like thrift, "canniness", economy in all things. Like Horace, Ramsay strums his lyre in a tranquil garden. A late poem, **"An Epistle Wrote From Mavisbank March 1748 To A Friend In Edr"**, is a concentrated statement suggesting what Horace meant to Ramsay "in his Grand Climaterek", as he puts it.

He starts off, like Horace, with a salutation. He is addressing a friend "to smoak and noise confine'd" in the town from the security of a quiet retreat in the country and advises him "to leave the chattering, Stinking city" where politics, the pressure of foreign affairs daily reported in the newspapers, and the thousand things that conspire to perpetuate a worried state of mind in the city-dweller can never be forgotten. He concludes that the advantages of entertainment which the town provides have the effect of dulling the rational faculties, and should not be indulged in too much. The poet then urges his friend to return to the contemplation of nature:

> come view with me the golden Beams,
> which, Phebus, every Morning pours
> upon the plains, adorn'd with flowers,
> with me o'er springing verdures stray,
> where wimpling watters make their way,
> here from the Oak with Ivy bound
> you'll hear the soft melodious Sound
> of all the Choiresters on hy
> whose notes re-echoe through the skie
> better than concerts of your Town,
> yet do not cost you half a crown,
> here Blackbirds, Mavises & Linnets
> excell your fidles, flutes, & Spinnets. . . .

a passage which reveals several of the "pre-romantic" influences at work on the elderly Ramsay and mingling with the exaggerated figures beloved of the Augustan Miltonic school of verse-making. The longing for rural scenery, the concern for precise details of nature's creations, the calling-up of attention to her sound effects and the sharp rejection of man-made equivalents are obvious signs of the transition phase represented by the poetry of Gray and Collins. The harsh satirical note struck in the last four lines was learned from Dryden, but rough satire was unacceptable in the baroque age and the dominating influence is Horatian:

> If Zyphers, and the radiant bleeze
> invite you to the Shady Trees,
> some hours, in indolence, to pass
> extended on the velvet gras,
> with Milton, Pope, & all the Rest,
> who smoothly coppy Nature best. . . .
>   This is the Life, all those have sung,
> most to be wish'd by old, and young,
> by the most Brave, and the most ffair,
> where Least Ambition, least of Care,
> desturbs the Soul, where virteous Ease,
> and Temperance, never cease to please.

Ramsay liked to pose as an escapist from city pleasures, and the Horatian attitude of retreat, with the sting of cynicism taken out by mellowed feelings of home contentment, affected many of his later poems. If his Horatianism was superficial, it was certainly at home in the tradition which Ramsay sought to continue and in which he found significant things to say.

Of less significance than his Horatianism, though in the same spirit linguistically, is Ramsay's "Europeanism", reflected in his efforts to versify the fables and tales of La Motte and La Fontaine. Like Gay, he followed current fashions and there is a great similarity in their handling of these stories, though Gay's versions are more sophisticated and his animals too human, so that the spontaneity of this kind of writing is less within his grasp than within

Ramsay's. Nevertheless, Gay and Ramsay remain the two best-known British fabulists. Gay's *Fables* (1722) were written to instruct the young Duke of Cumberland; they fitted the tastes of the age, preached obvious morals and were thought by their author to be his most important contribution to a "polite" age. La Motte's *Fables* (1719) were the work of a libertarian modernist who rewrote the old stories according to contemporary forms. La Fontaine's *Fables et Contes* (1668, 1678), taken from Aesop and Marot, reflected life in Paris in *le grand siècle*. La Motte was translated into English in 1720, but La Fontaine had to wait until 1734 for an English prose version, justified, according to the translator, by an interest in La Fontaine shown in the schools.

Ramsay's preface to his own ***Fables and Tales*** makes his intention plain:

> Some of the following are taken from Messieurs Fontaine and La Motte, whom I have endeavoured to make speak Scots with as much Ease as I can.

By "some", Ramsay meant the majority, since of the thirty fables, three are drawn from La Fontaine and twenty from La Motte. What has been said about his renderings from Horace applies also to his adaptations from the French, which are much expanded in length and lack the sophisticated veneer of their originals. Ramsay is coarser and more vigorous than La Motte. . . .

There is nothing in La Fontaine to parallel Ramsay's forceful description of the Whig wife, which falls just short of ludicrous.

> But *Bess,* the *Whig,* a Raving Rump,
> Took Figmaliries, and wald jump,
> With Sword and Pistol, by her Side
> And Cock-a-stride arowing ride,
> On the Hag-riden Sumph, and grapple
> Him hard and fast about the Thraple;
> And with her furious Fingers whirle,
> Frae youthfu' Black ilk Silver Curle.
> Thus was he serv'd between the twa,
> Till no ae Hair he had ava.

This looks forward to Burns and back at Dunbar and shows forth a side of Ramsay's poetical technique which makes sporadic appearances in ***The Gentle Shepherd***—the ability to create the impression of acceleration and rapid movement, like Dunbar's dancing poems and Burns' "Tam o' Shanter." On the other hand, the high polish and the hard brilliance of La Fontaine's wit is not found in Ramsay's narrative. What he did, in the main, was to borrow European themes and "Scottify" them. **"The Clever Offcome"** is close to La Fontaine's *Le Mari Confesseur,* which had a source in Conte XXXXVIII of *Les Cent Nouvelles Nouvelles* but for no obvious reason Ramsay sets his scene during Francis I's Italian wars, not Louis XIV's wars, and burlesques the plot at the expense of the finer touches. The story is essentially the same, but in Ramsay's version there is the familiar device of "a vile ratrime of nasty names", probably taken from real-life exchanges in the

Chalk study of Allan Ramsay by his son, the painter Allan Ramsay, 1729.

Grassmarket and which does much to convey this unpolished character. This separates it from modern France but not so much from late mediaeval Europe, where indeed many of these old narratives had currency in one form or another.

Thomas Crawford (essay date 1979)

SOURCE: "The Gentle Shepherd," in *Society and the Lyric: A Study of the Song Culture of Eighteenth-Century Scotland,* Scottish Academic Press, 1979, pp. 70-96.

[*In the following excerpt, Crawford examines the political and social context and implications of* The Gentle Shepherd.]

According to Ramsay's own statement *The Gentle Shepherd* was written in the years 1724 and 1725. When the first edition came out in 1725 there were only four songs, **"Peggy, now the King's come"**, II, iii; the duet between Patie and Peggy, **"By the delicious warmness of thy mouth"**, II, iv; Bauldy's snatch of song, **"Jenny said to Jocky, 'Gin ye winna tell'"**, IV, i; and the conclusion to the whole work, Peggy's **"My Patie is a lover gay"**. Although it is most unlikely, as is sometimes claimed, that the first edition, containing a mere handful of songs,

had any influence on *The Beggars' Opera,* it is nevertheless certain that there was at first some interaction between these almost opposite works. Gay's ballad opera was performed in Edinburgh by Tony Aston's company in October 1728 and seen by the pupils of Haddington Grammar School, who thereupon asked Ramsay to do the same with his drama; the upshot was a 'public performance of *The Gentle Shepherd,* with musical accompaniment, given on 22 January, 1729 "in Taylor's Hall, by a *Set of Young Gentlemen*"', in which the four songs were expanded to twenty-one. The 1734 printed edition describes itself as 'the sixth edition with the songs'. A manuscript life of the poet, ascribed to his son, Allan Ramsay the painter, claims that he soon became unhappy with the expanded form and wished the songs away, but 'comforted himself with the thought that the contagion had not infected his second Volume in Quarto, where *The Gentle Shepherd* is still to be found in its original purity'. Nevertheless, it was in its ballad opera form that it was widely known, in both Scotland and England, until the early nineteenth century; and it was through the reprints of the songs in the later editions of *The Tea-Table Miscellany,* other song-books, and chapbooks that it most influenced the popular lyrical tradition.

The Gentle Shepherd is set at the time of the Restoration of 1660, and its plot is of the slightest. In a village at the foot of the Pentland Hills, near Edinburgh, the poor but independent Patie is in love with Peggy, who requites his passion; his rich friend Roger dotes on Jenny, who slights him. The foundling Peggy, brought up by a shepherd called Glaud, is actually a laird's daughter; and Patie, reared in his turn by Symon, is the son of Sir William Worthy, exiled during the Cromwellian interregnum. Sir William returns disguised as a fortune-teller, reveals himself to Symon and covertly observes young Patie, with whom he is well pleased. The shepherd's real identity is disclosed to him; he is truly 'gentle' (i.e. one of the upper classes), and it behooves him, now that his restored father is about to enjoy his own again, to give up the low-born Peggy. This is the cue for Mause, who had at one time been Peggy's nurse, to reveal the truth about the heroine. All this time the action has been counterpointed by a subplot. In her flouting of Roger, Jenny coquettishly appears to favour the boorish Bauldy. But Bauldy (who once courted Neps) now wants Peggy; believing that Mause is a witch he asks her to use her eldritch skills to make Peggy dote on him and transfer Patie's affections to his own former sweetheart, Neps. In IV, i Madge (Glaud's sister) accuses Bauldy of being a heartless jilt and drives him off the stage in the style of crude popular farce, while Mause and Madge plot to scare Bauldy out of his wits, by his unseemly passion, by dressing up as ghosts. At the end Patie and Peggy are betrothed, as are Roger and Jenny while the sadder and wiser Bauldy goes back to Neps, and there is general rejoicing.

The plot is so trite and conventional that, as A. M. Kinghorn has put it, [in *The Works of Allan Ramsay*, Vol. IV, 1970] 'direct ancestry is untraceable . . . the pattern of lovers, the foundling complications, and the device of disguise are all stylised descendants of classical comedy':

it goes right back through the Renaissance to Roman comedy and Attic new comedy. But the structure of the action, deriving so obviously from written, even learned forms, and couched in the form of a regular neo-classic drama observing the unities, nevertheless manages to preserve some of the responses aroused by the folk-tale. After a minute examination of a hundred Russian fairy tales, Vladimir Propp concluded [in *Morphology of the Folktale*, 1970] that the total number of 'structural functions' never exceeded thirty-one, and that whatever the number of such functions in a given tale, they always appear in the same order. Examples of such structural functions are Propp's nos. 21, 22 and 23—'the hero is pursued', 'rescue of the hero from pursuit' and 'the hero, unrecognised, arrives home from another country'. No less than twenty-one of Propp's functions appear in *The Gentle Shepherd,* only they are not always assigned to a single hero, but are split between Patie and his father, and they do not always appear in the same order as in narrative folk-tale. When *The Gentle Shepherd* is scrutinised with Propp's categories in mind, some of the functions which in a simple Fairy Tale are given to hero or villain, are in Ramsay embodied in the historic process itself: for example, 'the hero acquires the use of a magical agent'. Because History is on the side of Sir William's return and therefore, unknown to him, of Patie, History usurps the function of a magical agent. I shall come back to this point in a moment. In the meantime, it is worth observing that at the level of structure Ramsay's pastoral attempts to synthesise different traditions; and that it does exactly the same at the level of texture.

This is exemplified in the first four lines of the piece, in the six-lined Prologue which sets the scene:

> Beneath the south side of a craigy beild,
> Where crystal springs the halesome waters yield,
> Twa youthful shepherds on the gowans lay,
> Tenting their flocks ae bonny morn of May.

Not only is the plain directness of the first line, moving from the neutral 'south side' to the downright Scots of 'craigy beild', contrasted with the Augustan balance of the second, but the counter-pointing within the figure is heightened by the way the Scots 'halesome' offsets the English 'crystal', at the same time as Scots and English are linked between the lines by the cross alliteration of '*c*raigy' and '*cr*ystal'. In the ballad-opera the Prologue is followed immediately by one of Ramsay's best pastoral lyrics, **"My Peggy is a young thing"**, sung by Patie, and first printed in the 1729 edition of the *Tea-Table Miscellany*. This lyric shows exactly the same contrasts as the Prologue. Its thin sprinkling of Scots is dramatically appropriate for Patie, one of nature's gentlemen who also happens to be socially a gentleman, although he does not yet know it; and a Scots expression in the second stanza, 'To a' the lave I'm cauld' is paralleled in the last stanza by its English translation, no doubt to provide the medial rhyme: 'By a' the rest, it is confest / By a' the rest that she sings best'. In this first song, too, we are presented with a genuine contemporary ideal that is one of the positives of the play. The songs Peggy sings best are

informed 'With innocence the wale o' sense'; she is loved for her own personal qualities which are those of nature's gentlewoman; she excels others not only in singing but in true womanly qualities, as a Scots lady should. In the whole of the following eclogue, which does duty for Act I, sc. i, the movement is at first from the contrast between Patie's joyous mood, perfectly in tune with the sunny morning, and Roger's despair at Jenny's scorn, towards the more permanent difference between their inherent characters. Patie, cheerful but impoverished, is popular with all; Roger, despairing though wealthy, is unpopular—especially with the girls. The notions of innate excellence, of its opposite, innate meanness, and of 'Slow rises Worth, by poverty depressed', are brought out by the rhetoric of Roger's very first couplet:

> I'm born, O Patie! to a thrawart fate;
> I'm born to strive with hardships sad and great.
>
> (I, i, 15-16)

The stars and his forbears have given Patie a slow, solid, stoical common-sense that can be found in all classes, but is particularly suitable in a landowner or community leader:

> The bees shall loath the flower, and quit the
>   hive,
> The saughs on boggie-ground shall cease to
>   thrive,
> Ere scornful queans, or loss of warldly gear,
> Shall spoil my rest, or ever force a tear.
>
> (I, i, 21-4)

The transition to the second part of the scene, where the topic is Jenny's coquettishness, is made by means of superstition, a subsidiary theme of the whole work; . . . such folk-beliefs were a debating point in the theoretical discussions over pastoral. Roger says:

> I dream'd a dreary dream this hinder night,
> That gars my flesh a' creep yet with the fright
>
> (lines 63-4)

which Patie counters with 'Daft are your dreams' (line 67)—the very voice of common-sense and the Enlightenment; but when Roger begins to tell how badly Jenny has treated him, he uses another allusion to rural superstition—'she fled as frae a shellycoat (spectre clad in a rattling coat) or kow (goblin)' (line 78), thus consolidating the difference between the character-types of the two men. Patie advises him to give over his 'silly whinging way' (line 103) and use amorous tactics, seeming to forsake her. After all, it worked for him with Peggy:

> Blythsome, I cry'd, my bonny Meg, come here,
> I ferly wherefore ye're sae soon asteer;
> But I can guess, ye're gawn to gather dew:
> She scoured awa, and said, 'What's that to you?'
> 'Then fare ye well, Meg Dorts, and e'en's ye
>   like',
> I careless cry'd, and lap in o'er the dike.
> I trow, when that she saw, within a crack,

She came with a right thievless errand back;
Misca'd me first,—then bade me hound my dog
To wear up three waff ews stray'd on the bog.
I leugh, and sae did she; then with great haste
I clasp'd my arms about her neck and waste,
About her yielding waste, and took a fouth
Of sweetest kisses frae her glowing mouth.

(lines 121-34)

This is a completely new voice in British poetry. The pentameter couplet is now naturalised in Scotland and has become something quite different in the process. It has acquired a colloquial vigour not found in [Thomas] Purney or [Ambrose] Philips, let alone in [Alexander] Pope's Pastorals: and the passage quoted, so admirably conveying the cut and thrust of everyday flyting ('What's that to you?', 'Fare ye well, Meg Dorts, and e'en's ye like'), and so full of action-verbs, is preceded by a beautifully sensuous description that is again far more effective than any similar passage from Ramsay's southern predecessors:

I saw my Meg come linkan o'er the lee;
I saw my Meg, but Meggy saw na me:
For yet the sun was wading thro' the mist,
And she was close upon me ere she wist;
Her coats were kiltit, and did sweetly shaw
Her straight bare legs that whiter were than
    snaw;
Her cockernony snooded up fou sleek,
Her haffet-locks hang waving on her cheek;
Her cheek sae ruddy, and her een sae clear;
And O! Her mouth's like ony hinny pear.

(lines 109-18)

In the ballad-opera, Patie expands his advice given in the following couplet

Seem to forsake her, soon she'll change her
    mood;
Gae woo anither, and she'll gang clean wood

into the song **"Dear Roger if your Jenny geck"**, which quite charmingly embroiders the meaning of the preceding couplets: unlike some of the later songs, though it may be superfluous, it still manages to be effective as decoration. The first scene—the eclogue—is resolved in a new friendship and understanding between Roger and Patie. Roger agrees to follow the advice of his natural superior (Patie) and will celebrate the change in their relationship with the gift of a tartan plaid of his mother's making. Patie caps this with the offer of his own greatest treasure, his new flute, in a marvellous couplet that triumphantly blends the idiomatic with the concise:

My flute's be your's, and she too that's sae nice
Shall come a will, gif ye'll tak my advice.

(lines 157-8)

In an equally fine and simple couplet, Roger refuses the flute—

As ye advise, I'll promise to observ't;
But ye maun keep the flute, ye best deserv't.

(lines 159-60)

The scene ends with an anticipation of breakfast which gives Ramsay an opportunity to restate in Scots the old pastoral preference for homely fare and the traditional condemnation of luxurious dishes:

Be that time bannocks, and a shave of cheese,
Will make a breakfast that a laird might please;
Might please the daintiest gabs, were they sae
    wise,
To season meat with health instead of spice.

(lines 165-8)

The contrast and linking of Scots and English language, of the simple with the sophisticated, which we noted in the Prologue, are again present here, and aptly synthesised in the last line quoted, balancing 'health' against 'spice': an abstract noun standing for a whole way of life against the concrete symbol of an opposite complex of values. A Scots colouring is delicately imparted by the pronunciation; the normally voiced 'wise' becomes voiceless to rhyme with 'spice'.

The second scene—and it too, we remember, was originally a separate eclogue—is formally parallel to the first. It is a debate between Peggy and Jenny where

. . . Jenny what she wishes discommends,
And Meg with better sense true love defends

(lines 7-8)

to such effect that, just like Pate in the preceding scene, she converts her friend to her own view. Their friendship is re-established under the dominance of the natural leader, Peggy: she is as superior in her feminine sphere as Patie is in his masculine one.

For the girls, any debate about love is automatically a debate about marriage. Jenny scorns her own lover out of fear because of what she has seen and heard of the 'perils' of marriage, but Peggy utterly rejects her suggestion that Pate will tire of her after a fortnight, 'And think he's tint his freedom for your sake' (line 85). His innate male superiority is her guarantee that he will respect her type of female superiority for life: 'His better sense will lang his love secure' (line 106). Jenny next paints a grim picture of the trouble of family life—'whindging getts about your ingle-side, / Yelping for this or that with fasheous din', toiling and spinning from morn to night, and the inevitable sick and fractious children:

The deel gaes o'er John Wobster, hame grows
    hell,
When Pate misca's ye war than tongue can tell.

(lines 116-17)

We have come a long way from the deliberate idealisation demanded by Fontenelle [in "Discours sur la nature de l'eclogue," 1688], or the contention in *Guardian* 22 that true pastoral writing represents only the simplicity and hides the misery of country life. In her next statement, Jenny gives a stark picture of rural poverty in a period of general economic crisis:

> Gif o'er your heads ill chance shou'd beggary
> draw:
> But little love, or canty chear can come,
> Frae duddy doublets, and a pantry toom.
> Your nowt may die—the spate may bear away
> Frae aff the howms your dainty rucks of havy. . . .
> A dyvour buys your butter, woo and cheese,
> But, or the day of payment, breaks and flees.
> With glooman brow the laird seeks in his rent:
> 'Tis no to gi'e; your merchant's to the bent;
> His Honour mauna want, he poinds your gear:
> Syne, driven frae house and hald, where will ye
> steer?
>
> (lines 129-33, 136-41)

In reply, Peggy avers that Jenny's mistake has been to ignore the *mental* aspects of love (line 190) and she wins the minx over in a beautiful, if traditional, extended simile:

> Bairns, and their bairns, make sure a firmer try,
> Than ought in love the like of us can spy.
> See yon twa elms that grow up side by side,
> Suppose them, some years syne, bridegroom and
> bride;
> Nearer and nearer ilka year they've prest,
> Till wide their spreading branches are increast,
> And in their mixture now are fully blest.
> This shields the other frae the eastlin blast,
> That in return defends it frae the west.
> Sic as stand single,—a state sae liked by you!
> Beneath ilk storm, frae ev'ry airth, maun bow.
>
> (lines 191-201)

Ramsay does not just set a glib idealism over against a brutal 'real world' of battered babies, battered wives and unfaithful husbands. His vision of married happiness is far from idyllic; he well knows the storms of life are fierce; but it is a matter of simple observation that the friendship and companionship of a happy marriage are the surest safeguards against such storms. The values in this scene are the highest point in the drama, and they are precisely those which Burns was later to express in four of his most hackneyed lines [in 'To Dr Blacklock']:

> To make a happy fireside clime
> To weans and wife,
> That's the true *Pathos* and *Sublime*
> Of Human Life.

The extended, musical version has three songs summing up the girls' respective positions in the debate: Sang iii, given to Peggy ('The dorty will repent / If lover's heart grows cauld'); Sang iv, given to Jenny ('O dear Peggy, love's beguiling'); and Sang v, which is again Peggy's ('How shall I be sad when a husband I hae / That has better sense then any o' thae'). In Sang vi ('I yield, dear lassie, ye have won'), Jenny acknowledges her defeat.

While all are lyric expansions of what is more pithily expressed in the dialogue, only the third and the sixth songs are completely mechanical: the fourth and the fifth add some nuances of emotional tone to what is said in the preceding passages.

One function of the two eclogues which Ramsay put together to form Act I is to set the pastoral firmly in *place*. We only gradually become aware of its exact locale, and this arouses in us a distinct sense of movement inwards towards a center. When Patie tells us he has bought a new flute in the West-port, we deduce, if we are watching a performance without a printed programme, that the action probably takes place near Edinburgh (I, i, 56). And it is only in the second scene, when Peggy says 'Go farer up the burn to Habby's How', that we know the little community is situated in a particular corner of the Pentland Hills (I, ii, 13).

The parallel function of II, i, where Glaud and Symon crack about politics, is to fix the play solidly in *time*, using the Scots reductive idiom to bring national politics within the compass of a rustic mind. Symon brings the news:

> Now Cromwell's gane to Nick; and ane ca'd
> Monk
> Has play'd the Rumple a right slee begunk,
> Restor'd King Charles, and ilka thing's in tune. . . .
>
> (II, i, 29-31)

The two main political themes of the scene, that political revenge is sweet and that the ideal landlord, epitomised in the character of Sir William Worthy, does not 'stent' his tenants in a 'racket rent', are singled out by the seventh and eighth songs in the opera version:

> (1) Cauld be the rebels cast,—
> Oppressors base and bloody;
> I hope we'll see them at the last
> Strung a' up in a woody.
>
> (Sang vii, 1-4, Tune
> 'Cauld Kail in Aberdeen')

> (2) The laird who in riches and honour
> Wad thrive, should be kindly and
> free,
> Nor rack the poor tenants who labour
> To rise above poverty. . . .
>
> (Sang viii, 1-4, Tune
> 'Mucking o' Geordy's byre')

The social paternalism of the last lines is no isolated observation but connects with Peggy's conviction that a tenant's first duty is to his landlord:

> A flock of lambs, cheese, butter, and some woo,
> Shall first be sald to pay the laird his due;
> Syne a' behind's our ain.
>
> (I, ii, 157-9)

II, ii and II, iii develop the sub-plot and prepare the way for the discomfiture of the wretched Bauldy. Mause's fine song 'Peggy, now the King's come' to the tune of 'Carle and the king come', one of the four lyrics in the original drama, allows the audience to anticipate the final resolution by informing them that Peggy is herself 'gentle', at the same time as it relates Mause to the main plot.

These scenes connect obviously and even obtrusively with Burns. Ramsay's Enlightenment condemnation of witch-beliefs and also much of his detail are taken over bodily into 'Tam o' Shanter'. In II, iv the action shifts to a lovers' meeting between Patie and Peggy, and lines 57-68 of the original, describing how they became acquainted, are in the opera expanded into a courtship dialogue song of three stanzas in anapaestic couplets to the tune of 'Winter was cauld, and my claithing was thin'. The first two stanzas are surely as good as the corresponding couplets, and the whole song is aesthetically pleasing in itself:

PEGGY

When first my dear laddie gaed to the green hill,
And I at ewe-milking first sey'd my young skill,
To bear the milk bowie no pain was to me,
When I at the bughting forgather'd with thee.

PATIE

When corn-riggs wav'd yellow, and blue
    heather-bells
Bloom'd bonny on moorland and sweet rising
    fells,
Nae birns, brier, or breckens, gave trouble to
    me,
If I found the berries right ripen'd for thee.

(Sts. i, ii)

It is a lyric community that surrounds Patie and Peggy, where songs are sung at work and at evening ceilidhs, forming part of the very texture of daily life:

Pat. Jenny sings saft *The Broom of Cowden-*
    knows,
    And Rosie lilts *The Milking of the Ews;*
    There's nane like Nanise, *Jenny Nettles*
        sings;
    At turns in *Maggy Lauder,* Marion dings:
    But when my Peggy sings, with sweeter
        skill,
    The Boat-man, or *The Lass of Patie's Mill;*
    It is a thousand times mair sweet to me:
    Tho' they sing well, they canna sing like
        thee.

(II, iv, 69-76)

At the end of the scene there is a duet, **"By the delicious warmness of thy mouth"**, sung 'to its own tune', that ends with a kiss upon the stage. The lyric puts forward once again the official ideal of this society—long devotion and no sex before marriage, though some sensuality is permitted:

Sung by both
Sun, gallop down the westlin skies,
Gang soon to bed, and quickly rise;
O lash your steeds, post time away,
And haste about our bridal day:
And if ye're wearied, honest light,
Sleep, gin ye like, a week that night.

(II, iv, 120-5)

This song at least, which was in the text from the start, is dramatically appropriate.

Since III, i introduces Sir William Worthy, who speaks English as a matter of social decorum, except when disguised, the prologue is in Scots-English with a modicum of Scots vocabulary, the pronunciation being indicated by the orthography. Sir William's English couplets are not sign of a split national consciousness but a matter of realism and decorum. His long soliloquy of fifty-two lines, taking up the entire scene, presents the stock 'happier than kings' ideal, the simple life to which he has consigned his son during exile; in the opera, these ideas are repeated in the nondescript Sang xii. The scene as a whole connects what the audience has come to accept as a real community of homely peasants with an almost mythic ideal; it presents the little hamlet or village as a microcosm of the Golden Age *within* a society menaced by the 'dinsome town', revolutionaries like Cromwell, and corrupt self-seeking money-grubbers. The conclusion, not stated directly but implicit in the feeling-tone of the drama as a whole, is that the closest we can come to realising the pastoral ideal is when the worthy, epitomised by Sir William, enjoy their own—when the best rule, and the entire country is governed by a natural aristocracy who are in practice identical with the traditional aristocracy of property and blood.

In the next scene (III, ii) the hint that Peggy is a natural aristocrat, given in II, iii by Mause's song **"Peggy, now the King's come"**, is strengthened by Symon, when the repeats the rumour that Peggy was a foundling. We are now in the second part of the play, which A. M. Kinghorn finds decidedly less attractive than the first: 'the action dominates the background and there is only a limited appeal in the conventional gathering of the threads. The manipulations in the interests of a standard *dénouement* are not particularly ingenious, nor is there much attempt on Ramsay's part to make the principal characters individual.' Surely Dr Kinghorn is less than fair to Ramsay. Surpassing ingenuity is not required by the genre and truly realistic character-presentation would necessitate a kind of historical drama nowhere produced in early eighteenth-century Europe. Although it is true, as Dr Kinghorn says, that *The Gentle Shepherd* 'was not intended as a mask for political allegory', its great achievement was to give expression to both the social and national character of early eighteenth-century Scotland: an achievement of which Ramsay was partly conscious, and partly unconscious. In the remainder of III, ii, disguised as a spaeman peddlar, Sir William offers to tell fortunes—and does so, in good vernacular Scots. When the strange 'warlock' prophesies that Patie will be a laird, Patie is the identical stalwart sceptic of Act I:

> A laird of twa good whistles, and a kent,
> Twa curs, my trusty tenants, on the bent,
> Is all my great estate—and like to be:
> Sae, cunning carle, ne'er break your jokes on
>　　me.
>
> 　　　　　　　　　　　　　　(lines 94-7)

The rationality of the natural aristocrat is identical with the shrewd common-sense of the more solid and experienced peasants, for both Glaud and Symon are sceptical of spaemen. There is some simple but effective stage-business. Sir William 'looks a little at Patie's hand, then counterfeits falling into a trance, while they endeavour to lay him right'; when he 'starts up and speaks' it is to foretell his own return and Patie's transformation into 'Mr Patrick', *via* an allegorical tale about 'A knight that for a Lyon fought, / Against a herd of bears' (III, ii, 112-24). In a strongly contrasting love scene, Jenny—despite her decision to accept love and its obligations—repeats a real fear to Roger, the tyranny of a soul-destroying domestic drudgery:

> When prison'd in four waws, a wife right tame,
> Altho' the first, the greatest drudge at hame.
>
> 　　　　　　　　　　　　　　(lines 38-9)

Roger retorts that woman's slavery is caused by money and arranged marriages: it is different in a love-match. Love—as in a hundred lyrics of 'the common pursuit'—is supreme, and—should Jenny's father deny,

> 　　　　. . . I carena by,
> 　　He'd contradict in vain;
> Tho' a' my kin had said and sworn,
> 　　But thee I will have nane.
> 　　　　　　　　　(Sang xiv, lines 9-12,
> 　　　　　　　　　　tune 'O'er Bogie')

In III, iv, the recognition scene between Sir William and Symon, Symon praises Pate to his father. As befits a natural aristocrat, he is the acknowledged leader of the other shepherds, and studious too, buying books every time he goes to Edinburgh. To say, as A. M. Kinghorn does, that the laird's 'sententious observations about the elevating value of education for peasants as well as for gentlemen read rather quaintly nowadays', and that his 'ponderous moral statements delivered in his rôle as patron of the rustics' are equally uninteresting, is to give less than due attention to *The Gentle Shepherd* in its historical context. When we are told that Roger reads Shakespeare, Ben Jonson, Drummond, William Alexander, and Cowley (lines 73-6), we are being told what sort of *traditions* ought to mould Scottish culture: Anglo-Scottish ones, uniting the best from both countries. And when (lines 84-5), Sir William says

> Reading such books can raise a peasant's mind
> Above a lord that is not thus inclin'd

he is in fact expressing a national ideal, the 'social char-

acter' of the Good Scotsman implicit in John Knox's free school in every parish, looking forward to the later myth of the 'lad o' pairts'. In the opera, the only song from this scene (Sang xv), to the tune 'Wat ye wha I met yestreen', which occurs at the end of the act just before the curtain falls, no more than paraphrases the soliloquy that precedes it, where Sir William says that 'Mister Patrick' must now forget his 'rustic business and love' and go abroad to improve his 'soul' in 'courts and camps'. In other words, the leading classes must be not just Scottish; they must be *international,* experiencing the practical introduction to European culture and manners, which only the grand tour can give.

In IV, i, when Maud and Madge tell us how the community rejoiced at Sir William's restoration, there is one highly significant line which 'nationalises' the values of pastoral, identifying them with the heroic age of the War of Independence. Without giving away anything about Peggy's birth, Mause hints that she may, after all, be able to marry 'Mr Patrick':

> Even kings have tane a queen out of the plain:
> And what has been before, may be again.
>
> 　　　　　　　　　　　　　　(lines 36-7)

To which Madge retorts:

> Sic fashions in King Bruce's days might be;
> But siccan ferlies now we never see.
>
> 　　　　　　　　　　　　　　(lines 40-1)

The artificial plot, by ensuring that this 'ferly' takes place after all, identifies Sir William's restoration, and therefore, by extension, the restoration of the Stuarts in 1660, with 'King Bruce's days'. When Bauldy comes on, singing the magnificent 'Jocky said to Jenny, Jenny wilt thou do't', of which only four lines were printed in the 1728 text, follows a vigorous vernacular flyting between Madge and Bauldy, leading on to the slapstick already mentioned, where Madge bloods his nose and drives him off the stage.

The hero's dilemma when he is expected to give up Peggy, is the subject of IV, ii, formally organised in two dialogues-the first between Roger and Patie, the second between Patie and Peggy—separated by a brief soliloquy in which Patie beautifully sums up her conflicting emotions and, by implication, his own:

> With what a struggle must I now impart
> My father's will to her that hads my heart!
> I ken she loves, and her saft saul will sink,
> While it stands trembling on the hated brink
> Of disappointment.—Heaven! support my fair,
> And let her comfort claim your tender care.
> Her eyes are red!
>
> 　　　　　　　　　　　　　　(lines 106-12)

At the purely formal level the scene parallels both the first eclogue (I, i) between the two shepherds, and the first love-meeting of Peggy and Pate (II, iv). And at the level of meaning the two halves of the scene set before us

(1) ideological tensions which run through the whole drama—love against duty, rural simplicity against the 'monkey-tricks' of aristocrats in capital cities where Mammon rules, and (2) the concepts we are to see as 'positives'—inborn uncomplicated innocence, the improving power of education and book-learning (lines 91-4) and life-long sincere love whose centre is marriage and the family. The first part of the scene is a debate in which Roger, though in a muted and subordinate manner, as befits one of the 'lower orders', shows exactly the same solid common-sense as Patie did in I, i; the second is an emotional dialogue about parting, full of contrasting satirical thrusts at the affectations of upper-class life (lines 178-85). In the opera text four songs are added, which merely embellish crucial parts of this dialogue, and give the actress who plays Peggy a chance to captivate the audience still further with her singing. They are set to such popular tunes as 'Wae's my heart that we should sunder', 'Tweedside' and 'Bush aboon Traquair'; the second of these, . . . is a ludicrously naïve expression of female submissiveness. Peggy has no doubts whatever about her rôle: the husband is superior, the upper classes are superior, 'virtue' and common-sense are woman's highest qualities. The best of the three (Sang xix) has one delightful quatrain:

> I'll visit aft the birken bush
>   Where first thou kindly told me
> Sweet tales of love, and hid my blush
>   Whilst round thou didst enfold me.
>
> (lines 5-8)

In the fifth act two recognition scenes flank an interchange between Glaud, Jenny, Peggy and Madge that concludes on a note both stoical and fatalistic:

> Gif I the daughter of some laird had been,
> I ne'er had notic'd Patie on the green:
> Now since he rises, why should I repine?
> If he's made for another, he'll ne'er be mine:
> And then, the like has been, if the decree
> Designs him mine, I yet his wife may be.
>
> (V, ii, 71-6)

The first recognition (V, i, continued at the beginning of V, iii) sees folk-superstition firmly vanquished by civilised reason, and Sir William's sophisticated ridicule finds an echo in Glaud's peasant common-sense:

> 'Tis true enough, we ne'er heard that a witch
> Had either meikle sense, or yet was rich.
>
> (V, i, 76-8)

The lyric which ends V, i in the opera is the once popular 'The bonny grey-ey'd morn begins to peep', given to Sir William, expressing the Horatian ideal of 'health and quietness of mind' in country retirement 'plac'd at a due distance from parties and state', untroubled by either ambition or avarice blind, and (in lines 3-4) anticipating some of the language of Gray's *Elegy*:

> The hearty hynd starts from his lazy sleep,
> To follow healthfu' labours of the day.

In V, iii, when Peggy is revealed as Sir William's niece, she and Pate embrace and kneel to him in a visual emblem of the play's utterly orthodox values. Reunion is to be followed by social reconstruction: pastoral is now subsumed in the improvements and rational planning of enlightened landlords:

> I never from these fields again will stray:
> Masons and wrights shall soon my house repair,
> And bussy gardners shall new planting rear. . . .
>
> (V, iii, 163-5)

Dynastic restoration of the Stuarts and political Toryism are identical with 'building' and 'planting'; the magical agent of fairy-tale, the Warlock, is identified with the social class and the ethic of sober reason which will dominate the next hundred years, and therefore with the historic process itself. The last word is *almost* left to Sir William:

> My friends, I'm satisfied you'll all behave,
> Each in his station, as I'd wish or crave.
> Be ever virtuous, soon or late you'll find
> Reward, and satisfaction to your mind.
>
> (V, iii, 222-5)

But not quite. The final note, in both play and opera, is lyrical, a song on the supreme value of 'virtuous love' from the lips of an attractive singer, to the tune of 'Corn rigs are bonny':

> Let lasses of a silly mind
>   Refuse what maist they're wanting:
> Since we for yielding were design'd,
>   We chastly should be granting.
> Then I'll comply, and marry Pate,
>   And syne my cockernonny,
> He's free to touzel air or late,
>   Where corn-riggs are bonny.
>
> (st. iii)

The song is yet another instance of the formal balance of the whole work; it is the counterpart of Pate's 'My Peggy is a young thing' which begins the operatic version. But thematically it by no means negates Sir William's adjuration. 'Each in his station' and 'chaste granting' are of equal value, and it is towards the effect achieved by putting them so closely together that the entire play has been moving.

How, then, does Ramsay's drama fit in with the early eighteenth-century debate about pastoral which is part of its background? It must be seen as 'practical criticism' of the more nostalgic forms of pastoral idealisation. Symon, Glaud, Bauldy, Madge, Elspa, Roger and Jenny are not courtiers in masquerade, with ladies' and gentlemen's feelings below their shepherds' clothing: and when Pate and Peggy turn out to be from the upper classes, this is acceptable because their 'natural aristocracy' is an extension and embellishment of peasant virtues and peasant common-sense. If **The Gentle Shepherd** does not idealise, as the *fêtes galantes* of Watteau idealise, it nevertheless presents a model to be imitated—a simplified silhouette of the type of man Ramsay admired. Although there are passages which unmask bad landlords and urban affectation as well as oafish superstition, its main effect is not *socially* critical but a bodying forth of the social character of early eighteenth-century Scotland. It reveals and builds on some of the main tensions of contemporary society—between, for example, man and woman in a money-economy, between realistic and idealistic views of marriage, between superstition and sceptical common-sense, between the urge for refinement and the brutal inheritance of the past: thus Bauldy is punished by Mause, not because he is a fool, but because he broke good-breeding's laws (V, iii, Prologue). The social character, which produces its ideal man and woman for innumerable citizens to emulate, is manifest above all in Sir William Worthy, restored royalist and ancestral Tory; in Pate, the man of independent, rational common-sense who may be found in any social class; and in his female counterpart, Peggy. These idealised embodiments are transitional between upper-class Augustan paradigms of 'the happy and the good' man or woman, and Burns's man of independent mind, perhaps self-educated, who 'looks and laughs at a' that'. The Burnsian ideal is a democratisation of the image held up by Ramsay for our approval; in the following century he formed a pattern for innumerable lowlanders to imitate—self-made men, godly fathers of families, radical Chartists, pioneer settlers in Canada and Middle America, in Brisbane and Otago and the African veldt. Kipling's Macandrew and Conrad's McWhirr in *Typhoon* were among his descendants, and countless non-Scots—humble artisans, democrats, evangelical Christians, radicals and socialists of every persuasion, identified themselves with the archetypal figure behind [what Auguste Angellier terms] the '*Marseillaise* of Equality' [in *Robert Burns: la vie, les oeuvres,* 1893].

Not for nothing does the statue of Burns in Canberra bear as its inscription Pope's line 'An honest man's the noblest work of God', quoted in *The Cotter's Saturday Night* (line 166) and, on the statue, wrongly ascribed to Burns himself. For there is a direct line of evolution between the enlightened hard-headedness of a Pope or a Swift, the ideology of the Scottish Vernacular Revival, and colonial democracy.

Carol McGuirk (essay date 1981)

SOURCE: "Augustan Influences on Allan Ramsay," in *Studies in Scottish Literature,* Vol. XVI, 1981, pp. 97-109.

[*In the following excerpt, McGuirk compares Ramsay's selective use of the Scots vernacular "to match the elevation of his chosen genre" with the use of colloquial English dialects by London's neo-classical Augustan poets.*]

Allan Ramsay's pastorals, songs, elegies, satires and epistles, in which neoclassical and dialect elements were mixed, had established him by 1720 as Edinburgh's most popular poet. The whole spectrum of Edinburgh's literate and semi-literate population supported Ramsay's work, which was extensively circulated in broadside sheets. By 1719 he was so well known even outside Scotland that a pirated edition of one of his pastorals was printed at London. By 1720 an octavo collection of Ramsay's most popular pieces was issued at Edinburgh, and the following year a more ambitious quarto edition was published there.

The subscription list for Ramsay's 1721 *Poems* included what must have been nearly every nobleman who was even a part-time resident in Edinburgh (such as the Duke of Queensberry), as well as a large contingent of advocates and doctors from Edinburgh's formidable professional classes. Yet Ramsay's appeal was not exclusively local: also among his subscribers were Alexander Pope, John Arbuthnot, Richard Savage and (for two copies) Sir Richard Steele.

The London writers who subscribed to Ramsay would have had little difficulty understanding his poems. As with Ramsay's successors Robert Fergusson and Robert Burns, many of the poems were written entirely in neoclassical English and the vernacular usage in the "Scots" poems varied in density. Comic poems were broadly vernacular, love songs less so. Ramsay used Scots in no verse form an Augustan would think incompatible with his "Doric" diction. Like the London writers who also experimented with colloquial diction in their poetry, Ramsay used vernacular in the Augustan occasional genres such as epistle and complimentary song, and in pastoral. In the "Index" to his 1721 *Poems,* genre-conscious Ramsay categorized his pieces as Serious [meaning elegiac], Comick, Satyrick, Pastoral, Lyrick, Epistolary, Epigrammatick: an extensive range of the Augustan occasional genres.

Like the London Augustans, Ramsay modulated his diction to match the elevation of his chosen genre. Augustanism did not always express itself in elaborate productions like *The Hind and the Panther, Cato,* and *The Essay on Man:* there were verse-forms "below" allegory, tragedy and "ethic epistle" in which a non-heroic, colloquial diction had its proper place. In using a selectively Scots diction in forms such as verse-epistle, pastoral and satire, Ramsay was emulating (and extending) the work of the popular London Augustans Matthew Prior and John Gay, who had pioneered in the use of English rustic diction to spice up the "lower" literary kinds. It is certain that Ramsay had been impressed by Prior and Gay before 1721, because his collection for that year was sprinkled with epigraphs from their occasional poetry. And it is clear from Ramsay's 1721 "Preface" that he viewed his work as part of the neoclassical mainstream, though he acknowledged his lack of epic ambition:

> Whether Poetry be the most elevated, delightful and generous Study in the World, is more than I dare affirm; but I think so. Yet I am afraid, when the following Miscellany is examined, I shall not be found to deserve the eminent Character that belongs to the Epick Master, whose Fire and Flegm is equally blended.—But *Anacreon, Horace* and *Waller* were Poets, and had

Souls warmed with true Poetick Flame, altho their Patience fell short of those who could bestow a Number of Years on the finishing one Heroick Poem, and justly claim the Preeminence.

Although Ramsay did not aspire to the top echelon of poetry—epic masters claimed the "Preeminence"—he was careful to place his work in the solid second rank. And although Ramsay did not cite Gay or Prior (or any living poet) in his "Preface," he did cite as his models Anacreon, Horace and Waller—the three predecessors to whom Gay and Prior were most indebted.

Ramsay achieved two different effects by using vernacular diction in his chosen "kinds." In pastoral he was chiefly influenced by Gay, and a Scots vocabulary made the characters seem ingenuous. In epistle, epigram and—to a certain extent—satire, however, his model was Prior and his predominant air was one of literate craftiness. Ramsay's deployment of vernacular, like Prior's and Gay's use of colloquial English, heightened the premises of his chosen genre. The "realism" of vernacular diction made the country landscape of pastoral seem more gentle and simple; it made the urban landscape of satire more complex and seamy.

For Augustan pastoral poets the classical models were Theocritus, Anacreon and the bucolic Vergil of the *Eclogues* and *Georgics.* Both Theocritus and Anacreon had written of country matters in dialect variants of literary Greek (Doric and Ionic, respectively) which classical tradition had sanctioned for use in pastoral and related types of poetry; and Ramsay was aware of this from the *Guardian* papers on pastoral. John Gay's *The Shepherd's Week* (1714), which was suggested by the *Guardian* controversy on pastoral diction, was a major influence on Ramsay's best-known work, ***The Gentle Shepherd*** (1725). Both for Ramsay and Gay, a rural vocabulary was used to evoke an attractive, sometimes comical, naivete. It was, however, also essential for both to avoid the fate of Ambrose Philips, who (as Pope pointed out in *Guardian* 40) had achieved such an air of blissful provinciality in his pastorals that he seemed to be just such a bumpkin as the people he wrote about. Gay and Ramsay both underscored the deliberateness of their use of rustic dialect: Gay in a series of comic footnotes and in an "Alphabetical Catalogue" (an Index) to *The Shepherd's Week;* Ramsay in the glossary attached to his 1728 ***Poems,*** a collection in which ***The Gentle Shepherd*** was included. Gay provided page references for every country thing mentioned in his pastoral, from "endive" to "udder." Ramsay glossed his special words, including even well-known Scottish expressions like "bony" and "wee," whose currency throughout contemporary Britain seems certain, since they were used casually by many popular song-writers, like Londoner Thomas D'Urfey. This critical apparatus of index and glossary in Gay and Ramsay certified the authenticity of the landscape and the people in the poem while it emphasized the self-consciousness of the writers' use of words. When reading Ramsay and Gay we are encouraged to distinguish them from their artless characters.

To say that Gay suggested techniques to Ramsay is not to say that their creative procedures were identical. For one thing, the burlesque undercurrent or undertow in *The Shepherd's Week* was not emulated by Ramsay; and Gay's poem is nimbler than ***The Gentle Shepherd***. Yet Gay's rural diction, realistic narrative and naive (yet not oafish) characterization did show Ramsay how to achieve for his own pastoral a dynamic middle ground between artificiality and mere stockishness.

The Gentle Shepherd is often both easy and vivid:

> For yet the Sun was wading thro' the Mist,
> And she was closs upon me ere she wist;
> Her Coats were kiltit, and did sweetly shaw
> Her straight bare Legs that whiter were than
>   Snaw;
> Her Cockernony snooded up fou sleek,
> Her Haffet-Locks hang waving on her Cheek;
> Her Cheek sae ruddy, and her Een sae clear;
> And O! her Mouth's like ony hinny Pear.
> Neat, neat she was, in Bustine Waste-coat clean,
> As she came skiffing o'er the dewy Green.
> Blythesome, I cry'd, my bonny *Meg,* come here.

The rustic English diction that Gay used for a mixed effect of comedy and realism is transposed in Ramsay's Scottish version to promote a concentrated visual descriptiveness which has its own definite charm. Gay was careful to encircle his bucolic vignettes with references to the current debate over pastoral's properties as a genre. (His "Proeme," for instance, is an unmistakable parody of the hapless Philips' "Preface" to his *Pastorals* [1710].) Ramsay, too, assumes an authorial voice in the peripheries of his pastoral (especially in such features as his glossary) but he remains essentially unjudicial in his treatment of the pastoral characters themselves (rejecting Gay's burlesque nomenclature, for instance, in favor of more natural rustic names). Ramsay's pastorals evoke non-ironic images of country freshness, healthful youth and accurate, if rather idealized, Scottish landscape.

Ramsay's non-pastoral work is different. In his epistles, epigrams and satires, Scots words produce effects of urban realism and a Ramsay *persona* generally dominates the narrative. The classical model for these urbane poems is Horace (Ramsay's 1721 ***Poems*** includes a series of Scots poems paraphrased from Horace), and the English poems in this manner which most influenced Ramsay were Prior's colloquial verse-epistles of the 1709 *Poems on Several Occasions* and some of the writings of the Tory satirists, especially Gay's *Trivia* (1716). The poetry of Alexander Pope was regarded almost with reverence by Ramsay, but Pope's influence was less salutary than Prior's or Gay's, perhaps because Pope was less likely than they to infuse his poems with casual colloquialism. (Swift's vivid poems on town-life also come to mind as a possible influence on Ramsay, but Ramsay seldom quoted from Swift, as he did from Prior, Gay and Pope. It is also worth bearing in mind that Swift's model in his urban output was Juvenal, not Horace: many of Swift's poems were written in explicit "imitation" of the later Roman poet.)

From Horace on, the characteristic tone of the verse-epistle had been a canny, ironic casualness. Its typical chemistry had combined topical references with general principles; and its proper subjects had included current affairs, trends in literature and literary theory, and the debate over the comparative merits of town and country living. Allan Ramsay's Horatian poetry holds to these traditions of the genre. Like his chief English model Matthew Prior, Ramsay achieved the desired ironic flavor by juxtaposing elevated or heroic diction with colloquial words. The verbal interplay conveys distrust of static (non-ironic) forms of expression. The following passage from Prior's "Epistle to Fleetwood Shephard" (1689) is a good example of the Horatian ironic texture achieved through the manipulation of "high" and "low" diction:

> From me, whom wandring Fortune threw
> From what I lov'd, the Town and You;
> Let me just tell You how my Time is
> Past in a Country-life.—*Imprimis,*
> As soon as PHOEBUS' Rays inspect us,
> First, Sir, I read, and then I Breakfast;
> So on, 'till foresaid God does set,
> I sometimes Study, sometimes Eat.
> Thus, of your Heroes and brave Boys,
> With whom old HOMER makes such Noise,
> The greatest Actions I can find,
> Are, that they did their Work, and Din'd.

Prior has undercut the noble connotations of "Heroes" by preceding it with a slang use of "your" and by following it with that cliche of popular war songs, "brave Boys." The passage presents its classical allusions (wandering Fortune, Phoebus' rays, Homer) in a decidedly conversational way ("Let me just tell you"). "Old Homer" is undermined not only by the disrespectful epithet but by the reference to his epics as "such Noise." Any reader familiar with the important eighteenth-century Scottish vernacular epistles, from those of Ramsay's lively correspondent Hamilton of Gilbertfield to those of Robert Burns, will see the resemblance of Prior's ironic diction in poems like "Epistle to Fleetwood Shephard" to the verbal intricacies of Scottish vernacular epistles. This influence of Prior was transmitted chiefly by Allan Ramsay, in whose urbane poems vernacular diction replaces Prior's English slang as the leveller of high-flown references: "Horace, / Was a bauld Bragger."

One sustained example of Prior's influence on Ramsay is **"Epistle Wrote from Mavisbank"** (1748). This epistle opens with an attack on city life, but juxtaposes its generalized praise of a country existence with semi-comic descents into doggerel and coarseness. As in Prior's epistles, the "gentleman" is shown to have an extensive repertoire of firmly ordinary images and words:

> Dear friend to smoak and noise confine'd [sic]
> which Soils your Shirt, and frets your mind,
> and makes you rusty look, and crabbed,
> as if you were bepoxed, or Scabbed,
> or had been going through a dose
> of Mercury, to save your Nose,

> Let me advise you, out of pity,
> to leave the chattering, Stinking city.

Such corrosive, yet not abusive, diction has often been said to be peculiar to Scots writers: because of such diction, eighteenth-century Scottish writing is sometimes called earthier or more realistic than English writing. Yet it takes only a moment's reflection to think of many non-vernacular writers of Ramsay's time who were anything but effete: the range extends from bad writers like D'Urfey to perhaps the best of all, Jonathan Swift. And it takes only a cursory knowledge of Matthew Prior's work to know how frequently Ramsay's emphases on the "low" as an index of the "real" were supported by the writings of an Augustan predecessor.

Prior and Ramsay—and Gay—came from middle class families, which must have contributed to their commonly vexed relationships with high diction, high genres and high seriousness. Early in his literary career, Prior collaborated on an astute parody of Dryden's high-toned allegory *The Hind and The Panther;* and throughout his life he maintained his distance from heroic views of life or art. A judicial deflation of the grandiose can be seen everywhere in Prior, from his offhand summary of the indiscriminately idolized *Iliad* ("The whole Quarrel is concerning three harlots") to his best elegy "Jinny the Just," in which a woman of "low" quality is affectionately perceived as a woman of "real" quality:

> Releas'd from the Noise of the Butcher and
>   Baker,
> Who, my old friends be thanked, did seldom
>   forsake Her
> And from the soft Duns of my Landlord the
>   Quaker
>
> From chiding the footmen and watching the
>   lasses,
> From Nel that burn't milk too, and Tom that
>   brake glasses
> (Sad mischeifs thrô which a good housekeeper
>   passes!)
>
> From some real Care but more fancied vexation
> From a life party: color'd half reason half
>   passion
> Here lyes after all the best Wench in the nation.

Although Ramsay could not have read "Jinny the Just," which did not come to light until 1907, it is a good example of the easy diction that Prior made respectable in succeeding volumes of his *Poems on Several Occasions* and that Ramsay emulated as he revived the use of vernacular Scots in published verse, expanding the dialect from local to relatively cosmopolitan status.

Ramsay's 1721 *Poems* has as its epigraph a paraphrase of Anacreon by Matthew Prior which begins: "Let them censure, what care I?/The Herd of Criticks I defy" before proceeding to court the untutored but instinctively correct judgment of the ladies. Ramsay's choice of this epigraph suggests both the support he derived from the London Augustans who favored a non-pedantic style and his important divergences from these Augustan models. When Prior disdained the "Herd of Criticks," he had in mind specific critics like Gildon and Dennis who were trying to align British literature with the purist theories of French neoclassicism. When Prior wrote in a volume of Montaigne, "No longer hence the GALLIC Style preferr'd, / Widsom in ENGLISH *Idiom* shall be heard," . . . he stated a resistance to French influences that he could be sure most English readers would share during those years of war with France.

Ramsay's defiance of "Criticks" was less certain to find a sympathetic audience. He knew that the native idiom which made Prior seem patriotic might in his case strike readers as provincial. The last major poet to publish in vernacular Scots had died a century before Ramsay initiated the eighteenth-century vernacular revival. Although Ramsay revered the achievements of the distant Makars, he looked to contemporary Augustan writing for ways to reintroduce Scots in forms "higher" than the bawdry and comic elegy in which it had continued to be used. Ramsay's "Herd of Criticks" was not a small group under the spell of Continental neoclassicism, but the large segment of people in Edinburgh itself that regarded the Scots as a moribund dialect. Ramsay disarmed the criticism of such people by asserting—in his prefaces and epigraphs as well as within his poems—that his Scots diction was validated by its use as a "Doric" counterpoint to neoclassical English. In replying to contemporaries who deplored his vernacular renditions of Horace, for instance, Ramsay took the London Augustan line. True poets are inspired, not legislated, by classical models; idiomatic imitation is preferable to literal translation; "taste" is demonstrated not by artificial correctness of grammar but by the emulation of admirable models:

> Translation be the Pedandts task
>   it is beneith me to Translate
> but in fair Rays I like to Bask
>   and shining paterns Imitate
>
> Thus I sometimes sic masters view
>   and with delight their Beautys see
> And can up hill the steps pursue
>   faster than thou crawls after me
>
>   . . . . .
>
> Let Horace sleep!—he near coud tire
> Touch not his ashes! he has none
> he's all oer Brightness, Life & fire
>   too dazaling for a drivling dron
>
> I'll Rouze the Prophet who forsaw
>   far back in the Agustan days
> that I should sing oer Dale & Law
>   his notes in Calidonian Lays

Though Ramsay presents himself in this rebuttal as a direct descendant of the Roman Augustans, his relationship was really collateral: through the contemporary writers who translated the Roman poet and made Horatian "imitation" fashionable. And beyond the examples of genre, style and subject offered by poets like Prior and Gay was a factor hardly less significant in the shaping of Ramsay's career. This was the influence on both Ramsay and his readers of the Augustan periodicals, especially *The Spectator* and *The Guardian.*

The Spectator was the arbiter of urbanity throughout Britain and was highly popular in early and mid-eighteenth-century Edinburgh. The memoir-writer Ramsay of Ochtertyre began his account of eighteenth-century Edinburgh by noting that the "prodigious run" of those essays "had done more to diffuse true taste than all the writers, sprightly or serious, that had gone before them." In 1712 when Allan Ramsay, still a wigmaker, co-founded the Easy Club, he chose as his club-name Isaac Bickerstaff—the *persona* Addison and Steele had appropriated for *The Spectator* from some earlier pamphlets by Swift. A paper of *The Spectator* was read at every meeting, or so the members claimed in a letter to Addison and Steele on which the Easy Club collaborated on 22 May 1712. The beginning of Ramsay's literary career coincides with this Easy Club—and Edinburgh—cult of *The Spectator.* Direct influence cannot be proved, but it is notable that Ramsay's work was most popular with his readers when it followed most closely the literary dictates of the London periodicals.

Of the major Augustan influences on Ramsay's work, however, that of *The Spectator* and *The Guardian* was least personal to Ramsay and most often productive of weak poetry. Much of Ramsay's poorest work might be ascribed not to his inability to understand the English language per se, but to his failure to achieve the balance of naturalness and gentility which the periodical writers, particularly Addison, considered the ideal for contemporary poetry. In *Spectator* 70, for instance, Addison praises the anonymous author of "Chevy Chase," who used a native subject-matter and, instead of depending on classical models, "found out an Hero in his own Country." This praise of ballads, with its implicit support for native as well as classical literary forms, must have encouraged Ramsay in his efforts to preserve a Scots diction in Scots writing. Yet Addison's endorsement of an archaic or provincial diction in ballads, lyric poetry and pastoral led Ramsay to more mannered effects than the idiomatic ease encouraged by Prior and Gay; and when emulating Addison, Ramsay was less likely to exploit his individual talent for descriptive, concentrated verse.

The author of *Guardian* 30—probably Addison's protege Thomas Tickell—thought that "pretty rusticity" should be the typical Doric effect. Ramsay, although appealing enough in **The Gentle Shepherd,** was seldom at his best when cultivating the pretty. *Guardian* 28 did praise rugged Theocritus over polished Vergil as a poet of nature, yet undercut its preference for nature when it added: "There is indeed sometimes a grossness and clownishness in Theocritus, which Vergil . . . hath avoided." Realism was served to some extent in such passages as the following:

> There are some things of an established nature in pastoral, which are essential to it, such as a country scene, innocence, simplicity. Others there are of a changeable kind, such as habits, customs, and the like. The difference of the climate is also to be observed, for what is proper in Arcadia, or even in Italy, might be very absurd in a colder country. By the same rule the difference of the soil, of fruits and flowers, is to be considered. And in so fine a country as Britain, what occasion is there for that profusion of Hyacinths and Paestan roses, and that Cornucopia of foreign fruits, which the British shepherds never heard of!

But this selective realism could only serve idealism. British trappings were proper to British pastoral, but only insofar as they advanced a classical effect of "innocence, simplicity." Otherwise, the realist was likely to lapse, like Theocritus, into that undirected explicitness the contemporary mind labelled as "grossness."

The virtue Tickell perceived in naturalistic diction and detail was its fresh, spirited "softness" (*Guardian* 28). Ramsay's readers were always more responsive to those of his poems and songs which used the vernacular to promote a "soft" effect in which innocence rather than urbanity prevailed: hence the popularity of *The Gentle Shepherd* and Ramsay's best-selling songbook *The Tea Table Miscellany,* which were both popular throughout Britain. Even when Ramsay used Scottish models and a partially vernacular vocabulary, an Addisonian ideal of central softness could debilitate his lyrics, as the Ramsay version of "Auld lang syne" demonstrates:

> Should auld Acquaintance be forgot,
> Tho they return with scars?
> These are the noble Heroe's Lot,
> Obtain'd in glorious Wars:
> Welcome my *Varo* to my Breast,
> Thy Arms about me twine,
> And make me once again as blest,
> As I was lang syne.

When creating **"The Kind Reception"** (his title for the above), Ramsay drew on a lyric preserved in the sixteenth-century *Bannantyne Manuscript.* In "Auld Kyndness Forgett," however, the sentiment is presented declaratively, not subjunctively, with all the Old Testament pessimism of Job or Ecclesiastes:

> This warld is all bot fengeit fair
> and als vnstable as the wind
> Gud faith is flemit I wat not quhair
> Trest fallowschip is evill to find
> gud conscience is all maid blind
> and cheritie is nane to gett
> Leill loif and lawte lyis behind
> and auld kyndnes is quyt forgett

Ramsay's distortion of this noble model shows what happened to his writing when his descriptive energy was diverted into the sententious formulas encouraged by *The*

Spectator and *The Guardian.*

Yet sometimes the pursuit of prettiness did result in a decent lyric. **"Lochaber No More"** uses the same dramatic situation as **"The Kind Reception"**—the wartime separation of lovers which forces an outburst from the speaker in the song—yet here the formula produces good results:

> Farewell to *Lochaber,* and farewell, my *Jean,*
> Where heartsome with thee I've mony Day been;
> For *Lochaber* no more, *Lochaber* no more,
> We'll may be return to *Lochaber* no more.
> These Tears that I shed, they are a' for my Dear,
> And no for the Dangers attending on Weir,
> Tho' bore on rough Seas to a far bloody Shore,
> May be to return to *Lochaber* no more.

"Lochaber No More" corresponds closely to the standards of Addison and his friends. It shows a sophisticated use of realistic detail in its repetition of the place-name Lochaber and in the Scots cognates—picturesque but not puzzling—scattered throughout ("heartsome," "mony," "a'," "weir"). Yet the effect of these details is to heighten, not to contain, the mood of evocative generalization. The phrase "dangers attending on weir" refers to the probability of violent death in such a general way that the reader is struck only by the pathos of this prospect; what Addison might have called its "pleasing anguish." This is successful lyric writing as defined in *Guardian* 22, in a passage that also suggests why "The Kind Reception" fails: "[Pastoral or lyric writing] must give us what is agreeable in . . . [the] scene, and hide what is wretched. . . . It is sometimes convenient not to discover the whole truth, but that part only which is delightful."

"The Kind Reception," for all its insistence on glory and heroes, is unconvincing because it has concealed so little of what is wretched about war. Its occasion is inherently unpleasant: a maimed soldier returns home to a mistress who is immediately struck by his alteration for the worse, and who proceeds to sing a song about it. On the other hand, **"Lochaber No More,"** which sounds more real because it is more conversational, actually conceals more of "what is wretched" about war. The violence, scars, separation all are hypothetical: the warrior-speaker has not yet left home. The departing hero of **"Lochaber No More"** has an aura of unearned glamour which was exactly what attracted Addison to folk song. And the song "please[s] the imagination," to quote further from *Guardian* 22, by concentrating on feelings—devotion for Jean and Lochaber—that mitigate a reader's share in the anxiety also expressed by the speaker.

If Ramsay's success were just a function of the density of vernacular words in his work, both "The Kind Reception" and "Lochaber No More" should be equally failures as they are equally mediated by Augustan aesthetic standards. But Allan Ramsay is like other poets: his success has to do with the depth achieved by his lyrics, not the impression created by his vocabulary. Ramsay failed, like any poet, when he used words, Scots or English, to force rather than to create effects. Because, following Augustan guidelines, he tended to write in vernacular to achieve descriptive rather than exalted effects—using an Anacreontic rather than Homeric template—he achieved his more defined goal more often than when using neoclassical English, which he saw as a vehicle for top-flight efforts. Ramsay's deficiencies seem more glaring in his English verse, but that is because he could not assert a judicial authority for himself, not because he could not understand English. He read and admired the didactic poetry of Pope and Dryden, but he could not imitate it effectively. He was, on the other hand, a clever adapter of the lyric and satiric techniques of Gay, Prior and (with less consistent success) Addison. Although Augustan influences sometimes led Ramsay astray, it should also be noted that Augustanism gave Ramsay a context for using vernacular when it established a vogue for folk song and revived the classic rustic genres such as pastoral.

Allan H. MacLaine (essay date 1985)

SOURCE: "Scots Satires," in *Allan Ramsay,* Twayne Publishers, 1985, pp. 14-41.

[*MacLaine's 1985 study of Ramsay was the first book-length critical treatment of Ramsay's work. In the following excerpt, MacLaine analyzes the poet's satiric verses, crediting them with reviving interest in ancient Scottish verse forms and setting the precedent for modern Scots satire.*]

At the very beginning of his poetic career Allan Ramsay made the conscious but risky decision of writing in his native Scottish tongue and of attempting to breathe new life into the moribund Scots poetic tradition. That tradition, as we have noted in the previous chapter, had become so impoverished that by Ramsay's time the Scots language was used only for humorous treatments of low life. It was, therefore, wholly natural if not inevitable that Ramsay should launch his career as a Scots poet by turning to various types of comic verse at the outset. He began with two major efforts in satiric verse—social satire in his continuations of **"Christis Kirk on the Green"** and political satire in **"A Tale of Three Bonnets."** At about the same time he moved into another popular comic form, the Scots comic elegy, producing no fewer than six of these from 1712 onward. Another traditional Scots satiric form, the "mock testament," attracted him also, and he tried his hand at two or three other types of comic verse in the vernacular. Altogether, Ramsay produced over fifteen satiric poems in Scots, most of them early in his career, including several of his finest efforts.

"Christis Kirk on the Green," Cantos 2 and 3

Ramsay's two supplemental cantos of **"Christis Kirk on the Green,"** nearly 400 lines in all, are his most sustained effort in Scots except for *The Gentle Shepherd* and **"A Tale of Three Bonnets."** Of his many poems in English, only **"Content"** and **"Health"** are longer. These cantos, therefore, must be regarded among his major works, and

yet they have been strangely neglected by the critics. Lord Woodhouselee, it is true, devotes some four laudatory pages to them—"a composition of very high merit"—but his discussion is largely summary, with minimal critical analysis [in *The Works of Allan Ramsay,* 1848]. Among modern critics, Burns Martin [in *Allan Ramsay,* 1931] praises Ramsay's handling of the stanza form, David Daiches [in *Scottish Poetry: A Critical Survey,* ed. James Kinsley, 1955] and David Craig [in *Scottish Literature,* 1961] stress the self-conscious antiquarianism of the work, but none of them pays more than cursory attention to it. Most unaccountably, Kinghorn in his otherwise admirable critical treatment of Ramsay's poetry [in *The Works of Allan Ramsay,* Vol. 4, 1970] ignores **"Christis Kirk"** altogether. Yet the two cantos represent, as we shall see, an ambitious and solid achievement.

For his inspiration Ramsay looked backward some three centuries to the original "Christis Kirk on the Green." George Bannatyne, the Edinburgh lawyer who compiled in 1568 a massive and invaluable manuscript anthology of Middle Scots poetry, ascribed the poem to King James I of Scotland (died 1437) and it probably is by him. At any rate, the fifteenth-century "Christis Kirk" became the prototype of an extremely popular, distinctively Scottish genre. In this type of poem we have a genial, satiric depiction of a lower-class celebration, such as a wedding, a fair, or a country dance, as seen from the point of view of an amused, superior onlooker. The poem normally begins with a panorama of the whole uproarious scene of merry-making, drunkenness, and horseplay, followed by a series of vignettes highlighting the antics of individual characters amid the general confusion. There is considerable use of dialogue in the separate scenes, scenes that have a cumulative effect in building a vivid impression of the affair as a whole. In "Christis Kirk" and its companion piece, "Peblis to the Play," this formula is embodied in a distinctive and rollicking verse form, the "Christis Kirk" stanza, consisting of eight lines of alternating iambic tetrameter and trimeter with a rhyme scheme of *a b a b a b a b,* followed by a "bobwheel" of a very short line (monometer) and a trimeter refrain at the end. In the fifteenth-century prototypes a fairly consistent pattern of alliteration is superimposed, adding to the intricacy of this very difficult verse form.

The original "Christis Kirk" became very popular during the Middle Scots period, influencing the work of William Dunbar, Sir David Lindsay, Alexander Scott, and others of the Scots makars. In his hilarious poem called "The Justing and Debait" (ca. 1575), Scott fused the "Christis Kirk" tradition with another medieval genre, the "mock tournament," and modified the basic verse form slightly by using a refrain line ending always in the words "that day" or "that night." During the long winter of the seventeenth century "Christis Kirk," almost alone among Middle Scots art poems, retained its popularity and was reprinted several times. It was only natural, then, that this famous poem should be a favorite of the eighteenth-century revivalists. James Watson gave "Christis Kirk" the place of honor in his *Choice Collection* (1706), and Allan Ramsay took it under his wing a few years later.

Ramsay's earliest known editions of "Christis Kirk" are both dated 1718; the first of these reprints the old poem as canto 1 with a sequel by Ramsay as canto 2; the second repeats these cantos and adds a further sequel, canto 3. In his prefatory note to canto 2 in the three-canto edition, Ramsay states that he composed canto 2 in 1715 and canto 3 in 1718, so that it seems probable that there was an earlier publication (now lost) of the two-canto version before 1718. Ramsay further asserts in his introductory note to canto 1 that he took the text of the fifteenth-century poem "from an old Manuscript Collection of *Scots Poems* written 150 Years ago"—that is, from the Bannatyne Manuscript. This statement is clearly inaccurate since the text Ramsay printed is not the Bannatyne version but is basically the corrupt text published in Watson's *Choice Collection*. What certainly happened is that Ramsay prepared his two-canto edition before he had access to Bannatyne, and he simply copied the old poem straight from Watson, including Watson's erroneous attribution of the work to King James V. Sometime between the publication of the two-canto and the three-canto versions Ramsay was able to borrow the Bannatyne Manuscript; from it he changed the authorship to King James I and made some other (largely minor) revisions. But even in his final three-canto version the text of canto 1 is still predominantly Watson's rather than Bannatyne's. One evidence of this is the fact that Ramsay, both in his printing of the old poem and in his own sequels, adopted the simplified stanza form that he found in Watson—a shortening of the two-line "bobwheel" into a single dimeter tag line ending in "that day." Watson undoubtedly derived his text from one of the corrupt seventeenth-century printings of the poem, such as that of Bishop Edmund Gibson (1691) where the shortened bobwheel also appears. Where and when this version of the stanza originated remains a mystery, though it surely was suggested by Alexander Scott's "that day" refrain in "The Justing and Debait." Kinghorn and Law are mistaken in asserting [in *The Works of Allan Ramsay,* Vol. 6, 1974] that Ramsay himself "altered" the stanza, he just took it as he found it in Watson.

The original "Christis Kirk" describes a gathering of rustics on some festive occasion. A fight breaks out between two of the young men over a girl, leading to a kind of burlesque archery contest to decide the issue, and finally to a barbarous and drunken free-for-all involving the entire male population of the village. The poem seems to be a fragment, though the final stanza (there are twenty-four in all) begins with the words "When a' was done." Ramsay assumes that the work is incomplete and that the occasion of the festivities described was a wedding, though there is no indication of this in the text. His attempt to "complete" a famous poem such as this, already three centuries old, was indeed a daring one, fraught with potential pitfalls. Fortunately, Ramsay did not try to imitate the language and to write in Middle Scots. (His knowledge of that tongue was certainly shaky, as nearly all critics have noted, though not nearly so bad as some have suggested.) Rather, Ramsay's sequels are in more or less contemporary Scots, but sprinkled with proverbial sayings or "quaint" phrases that detract from its naturalness.

Beyond that, Ramsay drags into the poem descriptions of old-fashioned folk rituals, such as the "bedding of the bride" and the "riding of the stang," to such an extent that he felt it necessary to add a set of footnotes to his poem to explain these old customs and quaint sayings. Daiches, Craig, and others are right in deploring the studied antiquarianism of Ramsay's sequels; his cantos suffer artistically from this sort of forced folklore in precisely the same way that Burns's "Halloween" suffers. But that is not the whole story of Ramsay's **"Christis Kirk"**; his cantos have some fine redeeming qualities, as a close look at the text will show.

Ramsay opens canto 1 with a really brilliant transitional stanza:

> But there had been mair Blood and Skaith,
> Sair Harship and great Spulie,
> And mony a ane had gotten his Death
> By this unsonsie Tooly [unhappy fight]:
> But that the bauld Good-wife of *Braith*
> Arm'd wi' a great Kail Gully [cabbage knife],
> Cam bellyflaught, and loot an Aith [oath],
> She'd gar them a' be hooly
>   Fou fast that Day.

Here Ramsay takes skillful advantage of the rollicking rhythm of the "Christis Kirk" stanza to bring the general brawl to a swift and dramatic end. The light, tricksy effect of the feminine rhymes in the trimeter lines helps with this, as does the sudden slowing down of the tempo in the final tag-line. At the same time, the formidable figure of the "Good-wife of *Braith,*" with amusing folklore associations, is an ideal means of bringing about the truce. In this stanza Ramsay succeeds in catching much of the rambunctious and witty spirit of the original. It would indeed be difficult to imagine a more effective way of bridging the gap between the old poem and the new.

Though the rest of canto 2 does not quite live up to the brilliance of the opening stanza, Ramsay does maintain a brisk and entertaining pace. In stanzas 3 and 4 he presents contrasting vignettes of two characters carried over from the old poem, *"Hutchon"* (brave) and *"Tam Taylor"* (cowardly), in their different reactions to the truce. As in the Middle Scots original, Ramsay makes effective satiric use of the themes of peasant cowardice and bungling. In the next stanza a minstrel is brought in to provide music for dancing, and then, in stanza 6, Ramsay gives us a scene of uproarious farce as one of the young men approaches a girl with strenuous directness:

> *Claud Peky* was na very blate [shy]
> He stood nae lang a dreigh;
> For by the Wame he gripped *Kate,*
> And gar'd her gi'e a Skreigh:
> Had aff, quoth she, ye filthy Slate,
> Ye stink o' Leeks, O figh!
> Let gae my Hands, I say, be quait;
> And wow gin she was skeigh [skittish],

And mim [affectedly modest] that
Day.

This stanza probably owes something to a passage in Chaucer's *Miller's Tale* (lines 3271-87) where Nicholas's initial wooing of Alisoun is described; but in any case Ramsay's handling of the scene is very skillful. He strikes just the right note of hilarious burlesque, with swift movement and funny dialogue.

In his next dozen stanzas or so Ramsay presents a series of dancing scenes that are lively and convincing. The middle lines of stanza 10, for example, are wonderfully vivid:

The Lasses bad'd about the Reel,
    Gar'd a' their Hurdies [buttocks] wallop,
And swat like Pownies whan they speel
    Up Braes, or when they gallop. . . .

What better way to suggest the sensual, sweaty bouncing of a reel than in these brief lines? This is Ramsay at his earthy, colloquial best. Many more such examples could easily be drawn from canto 2, but the passages cited above are perhaps enough to suggest the vigorous quality of the whole. In the latter part of this canto Ramsay goes on to depict various excesses of eating and drinking at the party, and finally the coming of evening and the ceremonial "bedding" of the bride.

Canto 3 opens with a whimsical description of daybreak the next morning when the sleepy villagers "Begoud to rax and rift" (began to stretch and break wind), many with hangovers. They soon reenter the cottage where the newly married couple are still abed, and lay their simple wedding gifts on the coverlet. Two of the local girls are given contrasting sketches: one is lighthearted and "kanty" (happy), but "*Mause* begrutten [in tears] was and bleer'd" because she had lost her virginity the night before. One of the older women, Maggy, consoles her with the thought that this is a common occurrence and not the end of the world, with an amusingly worded example from her own experience (stanza 9):

Or Bairns can read, they first
    maun spell,
    I learn'd this frae my Mammy,
And coost a Legen-girth [lower hoop] my sell,
    Lang or I married *Tammie*.

Then the celebration begins all over again, even more wildly than on the previous day.

Ramsay is generally effective in portraying these scenes of drunkenness, horseplay, and bickering between husbands and wives. He manages the complex verse form skillfully throughout. But this last part of his **"Christis Kirk"** is not quite so strong or delightful as canto 2, mainly because of the labored effect of the folklore. In stanza 12, for example, we have the "creeling of the groom," a custom Ramsay has to explain in a footnote: "For Merryment, a Creel or Basket is bound, full of Stones,

upon his Back; and if he has acted a manly Part, his young Wife with all imaginable Speed cuts the Cords, and relieves him from the Burthen. If she does not, he's rallied for a Fumbler." Similarly, in stanzas 16 and 17, he gives us "The Riding of the Stang on a Woman that hath beat her Husband," an even more elaborate ritual that is artistically obtrusive and boring. These episodes, self-conscious and strained, detract from canto 3, but do not nullify its effectiveness otherwise.

On the whole, Ramsay's continuations of **"Christis Kirk on the Green"** are a notable achievement, a sustained effort of rollicking action, humorous caricature, and realistic dialogue that is mainly successful. He cleverly bridges the gap from the old poem, and he catches much of its spirit and flavor—though not its wild comic momentum. In doing this, and in doing it so well, Ramsay gave a vital new impetus to the "Christis Kirk" tradition; he showed its adaptability to modern times, and he paved the way for the more brilliant exploitation of the form by Fergusson and Burns. His cantos are no small achievement.

Ramsay's only other poem in the "Christis Kirk" form is dated May 1720, **"Edinburgh's Salutation to the Most Honourable, My Lord Marquess of Carnarvon,"** consisting of six stanzas in a kind of Scoto-English style—that is, the language is basically standard English with a thin sprinkling of Scots words or spellings. This is a fairly competent effort, though the personification of Edinburgh welcoming a distinguished visitor is somewhat strained, and the piece as a whole comes nowhere near the spriteliness and vigor of Ramsay's earlier cantos.

"A Tale of Three Bonnets"

This dramatic poem in four cantos and 669 lines is Ramsay's longest original work in Scots or English, apart from *The Gentle Shepherd*. Like Ramsay's continuations of **"Christis Kirk,"** it has suffered from unaccountable neglect at the hands of the critics. Woodhouselee, himself an ardent Unionist, did not appreciate Ramsay's strong anti-Unionist views (which he calls "absurd") in this work; as a result he devotes to it only a sentence or two of faint praise as a work of art. Of recent critics, Martin, Daiches, and Lindsay ignore the poem altogether, while Kinghorn barely mentions it, and that only in connection with Ramsay's political ideas. Surely, as Ramsay's second longest work the tale deserves some discussion—and it has more positive merits, as we shall see.

The date of **"A Tale of Three Bonnets"** is problematic, but it is generally thought to be an early work that Ramsay did not dare to publish until 1722, and then only as an anonymous pamphlet. It did not appear among his official collected works until 1729. Most probably Ramsay composed the tale for the amusement of his radical friends in the Easy Club; if so, the year 1715 will have to suffice as an educated guess. In any event, this dramatic poem is a hard-hitting political satire on the Act of Union, in the form of transparent allegory that would have been instantly clear to all of Ramsay's readers. In form the work is a series of dramatic dialogues among various characters, enclosed within a narrative framework spoken by "Bard" (Ramsay himself). The framework arrangement anticipates the structure of Ramsay's **The Gentle Shepherd,** where each scene is introduced by a chatty, colloquial prologue. For his verse form Ramsay employs another traditional Scots meter, the tetrameter couplet.

The characters in **"A Tale of Three Bonnets"** are listed at the beginning, with descriptive phrases, and their allegorical significances become quickly apparent. Following "Bard" we have "Duniwhistle, *Father* to Bristle, Joukum, *and* Bawsy," who represents the old historic independence of Scotland. "Bristle, *A Man of Honour and Resolution*" is clearly the contemporary, independent, patriotic son of Scotland of the type of Andrew Fletcher of Saltoun who led the fight against the parliamentary Union of Scotland and England. Next comes "Joukum, *In love with Rosie,*" the Anglophile Scot seduced by "English gold"; followed by "Bawsy, *A Weak Brother*" whose epithet is self-explanatory. "Rosie, *An Heiress*" is obviously the red rose of England, loaded with wealth. Finally, there is "Ghost, *Of* Duniwhistle," and, amusingly, "Beef, *Porter to Rosie.*"

In the opening canto Duniwhistle, on his deathbed, bequeaths to his sons the three bonnets which represent the ancient virtues and integrity of Scotland, a proud heritage that has been handed on from generation to generation for many centuries. He admonishes them never to surrender their birth-right:

> And if ye'd hae nae Man betray ye,
> Let naithing ever wile them frae ye,
> But keep the BONNETS on your Heads,
> And Hands frae signing foolish Deeds.

All three sons swear never to give up their bonnets. "Bard" then intrudes to tell us that Duniwhistle was scarcely in his grave before the promise was broken by two of the sons (Joukum and Bawsy) as a consequence of Joukam's falling in love with the flamboyant Rosie. The description of Rosie who lives, of course, south of the border hills, is especially entertaining, including two lines ("She was a winsome Wench and waly, / And cou'd put on her Claiths fu' brawly") that were to stick in the memory of Burns and to affect a famous passage in "Tam O'Shanter" ("But *Tam* kend what was what fu' brawlie, / There was ae winsome wench and wawlie"). The remainder of canto 1 is taken up with Joukum's crass wooing of Rosie—a strong satiric scene in which the mercenary motives of both characters are stressed. Rosie finally agrees to marry Joukum on condition that he break his father's will and turn over to her the three bonnets of Scotland.

In canto 2 Joukum approaches Bristle with promises of riches if he will give up his ancestral bonnet. Bristle explodes in righteous anger at the suggestion of this base deal, and attacks Joukum in a passage of cutting vigor:

> Thou vile Disgrace of our Forbeers,
> Wha lang with valiant Dint of Weirs,
> Maintain'd their Rights 'gainst a' Intrusions

> Of our auld Faes the
> 　　*Rosycrucians,*
> Do'st thou design at last to catch
> Us in a Girn [snare] with this base Match,
> And for the hading up thy Pride,
> Upon thy Breether's Riggings ride?
> I'll see you hang'd and her thegither. . . .

This is followed in canto 3 by Joukum's approach to the slovenly Bawsy, whom he easily bribes into giving up his bonnet. In this section the Bard's extended description of Bawsy's filthy cottage is particularly rich in comic realism.

In canto 4 Joukum delivers two of the three bonnets to Rosie. They are interrupted by the "Ghaist" (ghost) of Duniwhistle who denounces them both and so frightens Joukum that Rosie has to "soup him up with Usquebae" (whisky) to revive his courage. The marriage of Joukum and Rosie then takes place, with the understanding that Rosie will now have a free hand with the resources of Scotland. It should be noted that Rosie gets two out of the three bonnets, a proportion that roughly corresponds to the actual vote in the Scottish parliament in 1707 in favor of the Union.

In the last part of Ramsay's allegory the disastrous results of the marriage are shown. Rosie and Joukum squander Rosie's wealth until they are deeply in debt and Rosie must send Joukum back to *"Fairyland,"* that is, Scotland, to raise rents and taxes a mere thirty percent to support their high living. Ramsay's satire here is devastating:

> Away, with strict Command, he's sent
> To *Fairyland* to lift the Rent,
> And with him mony a *Catterpillar*
> To rug from *Birss* and *Bawsy* Siller [silver],
> For her braid Table maun be serv'd,
> Tho' Fairy-fowk shou'd a' be starved.

Bristle is furious, but legally helpless; Bawsy, greedily expecting riches, is treated with contempt and ridicule by Beef (Rosie's flunky) and is easily placated with false promises from Rosie and Joukum. And thus the seduction and humiliation of Scotland is accomplished.

Though **"A Tale of Three Bonnets"** is seldom brilliant in style, it is consistently well written, with a few passages of "hamely" colloquial imagery that are very effective. This dramatic poem is a daring, patriotic attack upon the Union which Ramsay depicts as a shameful surrender of independence for supposed economic benefits that prove to be illusory. Bawsy, for instance, is forced to pay for the extravagances of Rosie and Joukum, and is despised by them in the bargain. Like most of his countrymen Ramsay mistrusted the Union; he was indeed passionately opposed to it, and in this tale he frankly says so. That does not mean that Ramsay was a radical—politically, economically, or socially. On the contrary, he was fundamentally conservative, and leery of what seemed to him to be drastic and untrustworthy solutions such as the Union. His anti-Union sentiment is part of his special Scottish conservatism; he wished to preserve traditional Scottish values and the main thrust of his literary career is in that direction. He was prudent enough, however, to publish **"A Tale of Three Bonnets"** anonymously; there was no need to give offense to some of his powerful friends who happened to be on the other side of this issue. Nevertheless, **"A Tale of Three Bonnets"** is a courageous, outspoken, and quite remarkable satire that has been undervalued or totally ignored in Ramsay scholarship. It deserves to be recognized as one of his major works.

Comic Elegies

The Scots comic elegy tradition was inaugurated about 1640 by a talented Renfrewshire laird, Robert Sempill of Beltrees, in his celebrated poem "The Life and Death of Habbie Simson, the Piper of Kilbarchan," followed by a second elegy in the same style called "Epitaph on Sanny Briggs." For his verse form Sempill adopted a stanza that was fairly common in late medieval poetry in Scotland and northern England, consisting of six lines rhymed *a a a b a b,* with tetrameter lines for the *a* rhymes and dimeters for the *b*' s. This stanza in the next century was christened "Standart Habby" by Allan Ramsay, became the favorite of both Fergusson and Burns, and in more recent times has often been called the "Burns stanza." The witty, clinching effect of the final rhyme makes it well suited for comic or satiric purposes, as the opening stanza of Sempill's "Habbie Simson" will show:

> Kilbarchan now may say alas!
> For she hath lost her game and grace,
> Both *Trixie* and *The Maiden Trace,*
>   But what remead?
> For no man can supply his place:
>   Hab Simsons dead.

Sempill's poem became the prototype of a new Scots satiric genre. In it the subject is usually an eccentric local character who has in fact died. The narrator expresses comically exaggerated grief as he describes the past life of the departed with good-natured satire, in such a way as to leave the final impression that the subject was a worthy person in spite of peculiarities, or because of them. "Habbie Simson" itself is by no means a great comic poem; though it has several flashes of genuine wit, on the whole it is no more than competent. Yet this poem, perhaps partly by virtue of its effective verse form, caught the popular imagination to such an extent that by Ramsay's time it was no doubt the most widely known and loved of Scots comic pieces. It was, therefore, inevitable that the young Ramsay should be drawn to this genre.

Altogether, Ramsay composed six comic elegies in the "Habbie" stanza; the four that he thought fit to publish—those on Maggy Johnston, John Cowper, Lucky Wood, and Patie Birnie—were all products of the first phase of his career. The dates of composition of some of these elegies are slightly uncertain. The historical Maggy Johnston died in 1711, and there is evidence that Ramsay's elegy in some form existed in 1712, which makes it one of the very earliest of his surviving works. The poem

on John Cowper is dated "Anno 1714" by Ramsay himself. Lucky Wood died in 1717, and Ramsay dated his poem in May of that year. All three of these early elegies were published together in pamphlet form in 1718. The one on Patie Birnie was first published in 1720. Ramsay's last two elegies, unpublished during his lifetime, were certainly later. That on Magy Dickson, who was hanged in 1724, could not have been written earlier than that year; the final elegy, on Samuel Clerk, is wholly uncertain as to date but is probably still later.

"Elegy on Maggy Johnston, who died *Anno* 1711" celebrates a famous alewife who kept a tavern on a small farm about a mile south of Edinburgh on the southern edge of the ancient golf course of Bruntsfield Links. Maggy was popular among all classes, Ramsay tells us, because of her low prices, genial disposition, and, above all, her "Pawky [cunning] Knack / Of brewing Ale amaist [almost] like Wine." Ramsay's poem is, of course, based solidly on the tradition established by Sempill's comic elegies, even to the extent that he echoes in his thirteenth stanza the "remead—dead" rhyme from "Habbie Simson." But Ramsay departs from his model in one significant respect: whereas Sempill's tributes to Habbie Simson and Sanny Briggs are taken up with amusing descriptions of those characters, Ramsay devotes only four of his fifteen stanzas to Maggy Johnston herself. The bulk of his elegy consists of fond reminiscences of happy times in Maggy's "Howff" (tavern), including hearty drinking parties, the playing of "Hyjinks" (a drunken game similar to the modern "chug-a-lug"), the enjoyment of tasty snacks, a personal account of falling into a drunken sleep in a nearby field on a summer night, and so forth. Stanza 4 is typical:

> When in our Poutch we fand some Clinks
>   [coins],
> And took a Turn o'er *Bruntsfield-Links,*
> Aften in *Maggy's* at Hy-jinks,
>   We guzl'd Scuds,
> Till we cou'd scarce wi hale out Drinks
>   Cast aff our Duds.

The poem is full of this kind of youthful bravado; its real subject is conviviality, Ramsay and his friends having fun at Maggy's, rather than Maggy herself.

Ramsay's **"Elegy on Maggy Johnston"** is one of the most frequently anthologized of all his poems, but it is far from his best. As we have seen, it is one of his very earliest writings, and it suffers from immaturity in substance and in technique. Now and then there is a flash of wit or an effective trick rhyme, as in the tenth stanza:

> Syne down on a green Bawk [bank], I trow
>   I took a Nap,
> And soucht a' Night Balillilow
>   As sound's a Tap.

Such imaginative touches, however, are rare in **"Maggy Johnston."** On the whole, it is competent in style, but lacking in subtlety and spark; it is a promising but relatively crude specimen of Ramsay's earliest verse in Scots.

His next effort in this genre, **"Elegy on John Cowper Kirk-Treasurer's Man, Anno 1714,"** is much better and is historically very important. Ramsay's long prefatory note to this poem defining for the benefit of "Strangers" the functions of the Kirk-Treasurer and his man is interesting evidence that even at this early stage in his career he hoped to interest readers beyond the borders of Scotland. Obviously, for Scottish readers this kind of information would have been wholly unnecessary; from the beginning Ramsay was aiming at London as well as at Edinburgh. He explains that in each town a Kirk-Treasurer is appointed each year to oversee the private morals of the parishioners, especially in matters of fornication and prostitution. "The Treasurer being changed every Year, never comes to be perfectly acquainted with the Affair; but their general Servant continuing for a long Time, is more expert at discovering such Persons, and the Places of their Resort, which makes him capable to do himself and Customers both a good or an ill Turn. *John Cowper* maintain'd this Post with Activity and good Success for several Years."

Ramsay begins with a powerful stanza expressing mock grief:

> I wairn ye 'a to greet [weep] and drone,
> *John Cowper's* dead, Ohon! Ohon!
> To fill his Post, alake there's none,
>   That with sic Speed
> Cou'd sa'r Sculdudry out like *John,*
>   But now he's dead.

Two things should be noted about this remarkable opening of a remarkable poem. For one thing, Ramsay deviates sharply from the typical comic elegy pattern by lamenting the death of a wholly unworthy, if not despicable, character—a slimy informer and extortionist of the type of Chaucer's Summoner, not at all comparable to the genial and entertaining figures of Habbie Simson, Sanny Briggs, or Maggy Johnston. Secondly, the narrator *seems* to approve of John Cowper. Though his point of view is slightly ambiguous, the speaker consistently praises Cowper as an efficient enforcer of kirk discipline. He deplores the passing of this hypocritical officer as a disaster for the municipality—"The Loss of him is publick Skaith" (injury)—and in stanza 6, he curses Death as the malevolent instrument of Edinburgh's deprivation:

> Fy upon Death, he was to blame
> To whirle poor *John* to his lang Hame;
> But tho' his Arse be cauld, yet Fame,
>   Wi' Tout of Trumpet,
> Shall tell how *Cowper's* awfou Name
>   Cou'd flie a Strumpet.

The voice here, and throughout, is surely not Ramsay's, but rather that of a bigoted prude, one of Edinburgh's evangelical Calvinists.

In short, Ramsay's method in this elegy is that of lively burlesque, an important and daring innovation in the "Habbie" tradition. He adopts the voice of the "enemy" in order to make his point of view as ludicrous and loathsome as possible in his grief for the reprobate Cowper. As John C. Weston has pointed out in a very perceptive essay [in *Scottish Literary Journal,* December, 1974], Ramsay's use of the ironic voice in this poem provided a crucial hint for Burns's brilliant exploitation of the burlesque technique in such poems as "The Holy Tulzie," "The Ordination," and "Holy Willie's Prayer." Further, Ramsay's addition of a witty "Postscript" to the elegy may have suggested to Burns the same device in "Tam Samson's Elegy" and "Epistle to William Simson."

On the whole, the **"Elegy of John Cowper"** is the most original and historically important of Ramsay's comic elegies. Artistically, it is far superior in technique and imagination to the one on Maggy Johnston. It is also one of the most underrated of his Scots poems.

Ramsay's third effort in this genre, **"Elegy on Lucky Wood in the Canongate, May 1717"** is, like his poem on Maggie Johnston, a celebration of a local tavern keeper, but this time with the more traditional emphasis on the character of the woman herself. In Ramsay's day the Canongate (now part of central Edinburgh) was a separate municipality, a suburb of the city extending from the Nether-bow Port, the city gate at the eastern end of the High Street, down the slope to the palace of Holyroodhouse. The elegy contains several allusions to local matters which Ramsay has to explain in footnotes, including an amusing reference to Aikenhead (stanza 10), the porter at the Nether-bow who customarily locked up the city gate at midnight. Late drinkers at Lucky Wood's, like Ramsay and his friends, returning in the wee hours of the morning, would have to bribe Aikenhead with gills of whisky to open the gate and let them back into the city.

Ramsay opens his elegy with the usual expressions of comically exaggerated grief, including the notable second stanza:

> Hear me ye Hills, and every Glen,
> Ilk Craig, ilk Cleugh, and hollow Den,
> And Echo shrill, that a' may ken
>   The waefou Thud,
> Be rackless Death, wha came unsenn
>   To Lucky Wood.

This strong and witty stanza must have impressed Burns, since echoes of it crop up in phrases and in the overall conception of his "Elegy on Captain Matthew Henderson." Most of Ramsay's elegy, however, is taken up with spritely and humorous praise of Lucky Wood's general excellence and neatness as an alewife, and especially of her generosity with free food. Stanza 7 is typical:

> She had the Gate sae weel to please,
> With *gratis* Beef, dry Fish, or Cheese;
> Which kept our Purses ay at Ease,
>   And Health in Tift [good order]
> And lent her fresh Nine Gallon Trees [barrels]
>   A hearty Lift.

The final "Epitaph" on Lucky Wood also anticipates the endings of Burns's elegies on Henderson and on Tam Samson. Moreover, the entire poem was destined to influence Robert Fergusson's sparkling description of Lucky Middlemist's oyster cellar in "Caller Oysters."

As a whole, the **"Elegy on Lucky Wood"** is a skillful and delightful poem. It gives us a genial satiric view of night life in old Edinburgh, with the emphasis on the lighthearted and more wholesome aspects of that world, with nothing of the crudity or immaturity of **"Maggy Johnston."** Though it lacks the imaginative boldness of **"John Cowper,"** it is at least its equal in craftsmanship, and it shows Ramsay steadily increasing in stylistic control as a comic poet in vernacular Scots.

"The Life and Acts of, or An Elegy on Patie Birnie," composed about 1720, is the longest (twenty-one stanzas) of Ramsay's comic elegies and the last of them that he chose to publish; it is also, at least in terms of style and craftsmanship, the most accomplished. Here, even more than in **"Lucky Wood,"** Ramsay follows the pattern of Sempill's "Habbie Simson" very closely, partly because his subject, a famous fiddler of Kinghorn (on the coast of Fife across from Edinburgh), is a similar sort of eccentric local musician as the immortal Habbie. But Ramsay's elegy is by no means a servile imitation; it is wholly original in its details and is, in fact, a much superior poem when compared to Sempill's. As might be expected, **"Patie Birnie"** strongly influenced Burns in at least two respects, as we shall see.

After the usual amusing expressions of grief, Ramsay plunges into a series of anecdotes of the career and character of Patie Birnie. Though it takes some annotation by Ramsay to make several of Birnie's escapades clear, on the whole they are highly entertaining. In stanzas 3 to 5, for example, we see Birnie's standard trick to gain employment as a fiddler: whenever he saw wealthy looking strangers enter an inn he would rush breathlessly up to them, pretend that he had been sent for, apologize for being late, whip out his fiddle, and immediately start playing, with all kinds of ingratiating lies and hilarious antics—all expressed in a rich, colloquial Scots, with touches of burlesque.

In stanza 8 we learn that Patie began as a fiddler with a home-made instrument with strings attached to a mare's skull. Ramsay then draws a whimsical analogy from Greek mythology:

Sae some auld-gabet [old-fashioned] Poets tell,
Jove's nimble Son and Leckie snell [lackey
    sharp]
Made the first Fiddle of a Shell,
            On which *Apollo*,
With meikle Pleasure play'd himsel
            Baith Jig and Solo.

This clever stanza obviously suggested Burns's passage on another fiddler in "The Jolly Beggars":

            The wee Apollo
    Set off wi' ALLEGRETTO glee
            His GIGA SOLO—

Ramsay next introduces (stanza 10) Birnie's pal "Jonny Stocks," identified in a footnote as "A Man of a low Stature, but very broad, a loving Friend of his, who used to dance to his Musick":

O *Jonny Stocks* what comes o' thee,
I'm sure thou'lt break thy Heart and die;
Thy *Birnie* gane, thou'lt never be
            Nor blyth nor able
To shake thy short Houghs merrily
            Upon a Table.

And in the following stanza Ramsay's ludicrous picture of Jonny dancing with a much taller girl ("With Nose forgainst a Lass's Midle") gave yet another hint to Burns for his brilliantly farcical sketch in "The Jolly Beggars" of the tiny fiddler smitten with love for the huge female pickpocket—"Her strappan limb an' gausy middle, / (He reach'd nae higher)." Similarly, Ramsay's surprise ending for the elegy in which he tells his readers to wipe away their tears because Patie Birnie, after all, is still alive ("He is not dead"), became the model for Burns's final stanza in "Tam Samson's Elegy" where the same kind of reversal is effected (*"Tam Samson's livin!"*).

Of the several escapades in Birnie's career that Ramsay recalls in this poem perhaps the most entertaining is the final one (stanzas 19 and 20). Here Ramsay explains that Patie went to the battle of Bothwell-Brig in 1679, but decided, Falstaff-like, that discretion was the better part of valor; he saw no point in risking injury to his eyesight or to his precious "Fidle-Hand":

Right pawkily [craftily] he left the Plain
Nor o'er his Shoulder look'd again,
But scour'd o'er Moss and Moor amain,
            To Riecky [Reekie (Edinburgh)] straight,
And tald how mony Whigs were slain
            Before they faught.

The smooth technique and wry wit of these lines are typical of the poem as a whole. Incidentally, the "straight-faught" rhyme in this stanza is an interesting illustration of the kind of compromise with standard English spelling that Ramsay felt obliged to make in his Scots poems, a pattern that was to be followed by both Fergusson and Burns later in the century. In those poems that he left unpublished during his lifetime Ramsay tended to use a more or less phonetic spelling, as we shall see, a spelling that tried to approximate the actual sounds of Scots speech in his day. But in the Scots poems that he revised for publication Ramsay adopted, somewhat inconsistently, a sort of semi-Anglicized spelling in order to make his work more easily accessible to non-Scots readers. In his "Preface" to *Poems,* 1721, he derides those pedants who "are ignorant of the Beauties of their Mother Tongue," defends his use of Scots, argues that Scots blended with English provides richer vocabulary and sound effects, and states that even his poems in standard English are meant to be read with a Scots pronunciation. The Scots pronunciation of the word "straight" in this instance would be "straught," providing an identical rhyme with "faught" in the last line. Why, then, would Ramsay use the English spelling for the one word and the Scots for the other? He probably feared the "straught" might present a problem for English readers, whereas "faught" would be clear enough to all. Nevertheless, the inconsistency creates a slightly confused effect, an effect that Ramsay must have felt was the lesser of two evils, preferable to making himself incomprehensible to members of that wider audience that he hoped to interest.

In any event, the **"Elegy on Patie Birnie"** is a remarkably good poem, lively in its humor, consistently skillful in its style. It is not only his longest comic elegy, but also, artistically speaking, his best.

Ramsay's last two efforts in this genre are much less substantial and may be treated briefly. In 1724 he produced **"Magy Dickson,"** a rather slapdash poem in the comic elegy tradition, inspired by the incredible adventure of a local character who became an Edinburgh celebrity as "half-hangit Maggie Dickson." Kinghorn and Law in their note on this poem summarize the whole affair neatly and eloquently: "In 1724, Margaret Dickson of Fisherrow, Musselburgh [a fishing village near Edinburgh], who had been separated from her husband for ten months, was hanged for concealing the birth of an illegitimate child. Cut down from the gallows, she recovered as she was being taken home for burial, and was none the worse for the experience except, as the *Caledonian Mercury* felicitously expressed it, for a pain in the neck." Ramsay's opening stanza will suffice to illustrate the quality as well as the phonetic spelling of this unpublished piece:

> Assist ye Creil wives ane & a'
> of Musselbrugh & fisher Raw
> in souching sang the sooth to shaw
>   of that slee wife
> that after she was hangit staw
>   again to Life.

On the whole, **"Magy Dickson"** is a rather careless occasional poem, mildly amusing but seldom more than competent in style. The actual facts of this grotesque case are, indeed, funnier than Ramsay's poem about them; so that his mock elegy can hardly be called an artistic success.

"An Elegy on Mr. Samuel Clerk Running Stationer," also unpublished by Ramsay and of uncertain date, is much better. Clerk was another local Edinburgh character, a "running stationer"—that is, a street vendor of books and pamphlets with no fixed place of business, or, as Ramsay puts it (stanza 3), "A Stationer without a Station." In this lively poem Ramsay focuses on three aspects of Clerk's character, beginning with his usefulness and courage as an impartial seller of controversial and sometimes treasonous political pamphlets (stanzas 3-5). Then we learn (stanzas 4-6) that his parents had intended him for a career in the ministry, "But his wise Head— /

To Arts mair usefou was inclined." Ramsay wryly explains in stanza 5 that Clerk was ill suited to the ecclesiastical life because his tender soul could not stand the petty bickering of theological disputes:

> His Saul sublimer could na bear,
> The Sturt, the Struggle, strife, and Steer,
> Hair-cleaving, *grano-salis* weir,
>   About the Creed;
> And calling ane annither Liar,
>   But now he's Dead.

This is witty enough, but even more entertaining is the last part of the elegy (stanzas 8-13) on Clerk's addiction to strong drink ("Delicious Drams were his Delight") and on his rumored liaison with his hard-drinking landlady (stanza 11):

> What else he acted with this Lady,
> The Muse say'th not, tho some are ready,
> To swear he try'd to be a Dady,
>   But came nae speed;
> He being not o'er stout or steady,
>   For sic a Deed.

The elegy on Samuel Clerk is a relatively polished performance, in contrast to **"Magy Dickson,"** with more or less orthodox spelling and capitalization, a fact which leads us to suspect that Ramsay prepared it for publication but never got round to it, or changed his mind for some reason. However that may be, it is a charming piece of good-natured wit, well worth reading.

Ramsay's comic elegies, taken together, are a significant achievement. Starting with a very popular seventeenth-century poem, Sempill's "Habbie Simson," as his inspiration, Ramsay developed the form far beyond the limitations of his model. In **"John Cowper"** he introduced a burlesque method wholly new to this genre, as well as a sharper edge of satire. In **"Patie Birnie"** and to a lesser extent in **"Lucky Wood"** and **"Samuel Clerk"** he surpassed Sempill in general wittiness and sophistication of style. Looked at chronologically, Ramsay's elegies show a steady improvement (except for the sloppy **"Magy Dickson"**) from the relative awkwardness of **"Maggie Johnston"** to the smooth and skillful effects of the later pieces. For the eighteenth-century Scots revival Ramsay himself, in fact, *created* the comic elegy as an important genre which he passed on to Fergusson and Burns.

Mock Testaments and Other Satiric Genres

Ramsay's Scots satires include two notable specimens of the "mock testament" or "last dying words" type. This genre has medieval roots, but Ramsay's immediate model was undoubtedly Hamilton of Gilbertfield's "Last Dying Words of Bonny Heck" which he found in Watson's *Choice Collection*. For this poem Hamilton used the "Habbie" stanza and also the beast fable method; his speaker is a dog, "A Famous Greyhound in the Shire of Fife," so that his "Bonny Heck" provided the obvious precedent for Burns's "The Death and Dying Words of Puir Mailie" where the speaker is a sheep. For his own purposes Ramsay omitted the animal speaker, but adopted the verse form and "last dying words" device of Hamilton's work.

Ramsay's earliest effort in this genre is **"Lucky Spence's Last Advice,"** apparently composed in 1718. Lucky Spence was another well-known Edinburgh character, the keeper of a brothel near the palace of Holyroodhouse. In an opening stanza of narrative Ramsay depicts the old bawd, about to expire, calling her team of young whores to her bedside to hear her final admonitions; the rest of the poem, sixteen "Habbie" stanzas, presents her dying words. The second and third stanzas typify the flavor of the whole:

> My loving Lasses, I maun leave ye,
> But dinna wi' ye'r Greeting grieve me,
> Nor wi' your Draunts and Droning
>   deave me,
>   But bring's a Gill;
> For Faith, my Bairns, ye may believe me,
>   'Tis 'gainst my Will.
>
> O Black Ey'd *Bess* and mim Mou'd *Meg,*
> O'er good to work or yet to beg;
> Lay Sunkots up for a sair Leg,
>   For whan ye fail,
> Ye'r Face will not be worth a Feg,
>   Nor yet ye'r Tail.

This is fairly spirited stuff; the poet exploits his verse form with skill, making deft satiric use of the end-rhymes in each stanza. Ramsay portrays the way of life of the prostitute with relentless realism, stressing the appalling risks of disease and imprisonment as well as the cash rewards that result from utterly unscrupulous methods. In stanza 6, for example, Lucky Spence gives sage advice on rolling a helpless drunk:

> Cleek [grab] a' ye can be Hook or Crook,
> Ryp ilky Poutch frae Nook to Nook;
> Be sure to truff his Pocket-book,
>   Saxty Pounds *Scots*
> Is nae deaf Nits: in little bouk
>   Lie great Bank-Notes.

"Lucky Spence," in general, affords vivid pictures of low life in Ramsay's Edinburgh. It is moderately successful as a comic treatment of the oldest profession, presenting glimpses of squalid human degradation in a way that makes us laugh rather than cry—with humor and some lively wit. Artistically, this is fairly effective comic poetry, though not among Ramsay's very best pieces.

Ramsay's other effort in this genre, **"The Last Speech of a Wretched Miser,"** is more impressive. First published in 1724 and probably written in that year, this poem is notable in at least three respects. For one thing, it is Ramsay's most sustained work in the "Habbie" verse form, with twenty-nine stanzas and 174 lines. Secondly, it differs from most of Ramsay's Scots satires in that it appears to be a generalized attack upon a human type rather than a personal satire on an individual—though, of course,

the poet may have had one or more actual men in mind. Finally, and somewhat surprisingly, it is a remarkably good poem, a piece of comic grotesquerie, full of extravagantly earthy but effective images that make it one of Ramsay's most imaginative works.

Ramsay's **"Miser"** is totally unrepentant; in his dying words he simply explains and graphically illustrates his obsession, and his only regret is that he cannot take his money with him but must leave it to a spendthrift son. He compares his long, painful struggle to amass wealth to that of Tantalus ("Chin deep into a Siller Flood"), or to the self-denying vigilance of eunuchs guarding Oriental harems (stanza 4):

> Or like the wissen'd beardless Wights,
> Wha herd the Wives of Eastern Knights,
> Yet ne'er enjoy the saft Delights
>   Of Lasses bony;
> Thus did I watch lang Days and Nights
>   My lovely Money.

After this brilliant analogy the Miser goes on to detail the incredible economies to which he gladly subjected himself. He tells us in the seventh stanza that "I never wore my Claiths [clothes] with brushing, / Nor wrung away my Sarks [shirts] with washing," and in the ninth—

> Nor kept I servants, Tales to tell,
> But toom'd my Coodies [emptied my chamber
>   pots] a' my sell;
> To hane [save] in Candle I had a Spell
>   Baith cheap and bright,
> A Fish-head, when it 'gins to smell,
>   Gives curious Light.

There are several passages in the poem as telling as these, but one more must suffice to demonstrate its power. Toward the end of his speech (stanza 24) the Miser sums up the terrible sacrifices he has made:

> O Gear! I held ye lang thegither
> For you I starv'd my good auld Mither,
> And to *Virginia* sald my Brither,
>   And crush'd my Wife:
> But now I'm gawn I kenna whither;
>   To leave my Life.

All things considered, **"The Last Speech of a Wretched Miser"** is one of Ramsay's finest poems. Despite its generalized subject, it is full of bold, concrete images that give it a kind of imaginative force that is unusual in Ramsay's work. The unabashed confessional quality reminds one of Chaucer's *Pardoner's Prologue;* the speech's strong, gritty comedy is an impressive achievement, generally underrated by the critics.

Two or three others of Ramsay's Scots satires deserve mention, including **"The Rise and Fall of the Stocks, 1720."** This piece in tetrameter couplets is in the form of an epistle to Lord Ramsay, dated 25 March 1721, and is a moderately witty satire on foolish speculations on the

South Sea Bubble. Ramsay uses as his motto four lines from Samuel Butler's *Hudibras* and his work is clearly modeled on that poem. The opening paragraph with its comic personification of the nation is especially spritely (lines 4-8):

> Viewing our poor bambousl'd Nation,
> Biting her Nails, her Knuckles wringing,
> Her Cheek sae blae, her Lip sae hinging;
> Grief and Vexation's like to kill her,
> For tyning [losing] baith her Tick and Siller.

Unfortunately, Ramsay fails to maintain this level of style through the 196 lines of his topical epistle. It is generally competent and mildly amusing, but lacks imaginative spark; Maurice Lindsay is correct in characterizing this piece as a kind of "versified journalism" [in *History of Scottish Literature,* 1977].

"The Marrow Ballad" is a very different story. This trenchant satire on religious bigotry, never published during Ramsay's lifetime, bears the subtitle "On Seeing a Stroling Congregation Going to a Field Meeting, May 9th, 1738," and is written to the tune of the popular seventeenth-century song "Fy let us a' to the Bridal." In their notes to this poem Kinghorn and Law quietly assert that the "poem has resemblances, in style and attitude, to Burns's *Holy Fair.*" That is surely an understatement, since the resemblances are quite astonishing, not only in style and attitude but also in the structural method of highlighting the dramatic contrasts between the pious preaching and the profane behavior of lads and lasses in the congregation. The general resemblances are indeed so striking that one would be tempted to see in Ramsay's poem the catalyst for Burns's, were it not for the fact that it is improbable in the extreme that Burns could ever have seen this poem in manuscript.

In **"The Marrow Ballad"** Ramsay launches an ironic attack upon the extreme Presbyterian position as represented by such popular preachers as Erskine and Mair of the breakaway Associate Synod. The opening lines set the tone very deftly:

> O fy let us a' to the meeting
>   for there will be canting there
> Wher some will be laughing some greeting
>   [weeping]
>   at the preaching of Erskine and Mair.

In his next stanzas Ramsay goes on to suggest, as Burns does in "The Holy Fair," not only that these religious revival meetings provide opportunities for boys and girls to get together for lovemaking, but also that the mood of spiritual exaltation induced by the sermons leads directly into sexual passion. Ramsay's speaker throughout is a young man on the way to the field meeting (stanza 3):

> The sun will be sunk in the west
>   before they have finished the wark
> then behind a whin Bush we can rest—
>   ther's mekle good done in the dark.

> There Tammy to Tibby may creep
>   Slee Sandy may mool in with Kate
> while other dowf sauls are asleep
>   we'll handle deep matters of State.

Later, in the opening lines of the final stanza, the speaker gives ironic thanks to the ministers for providing such ideal conditions for love, and then slips in an incisive thrust at their rigid fanaticism:

> Then up with the Brethren true blew
>   wha lead us to siccan delight
> and can prove it altho they be few
>   that ther is naebody els wha is right.

That last line, in its context, is wonderfully devastating.

Why did Ramsay leave this fine poem unpublished? Discreet as he was in this late stage of his career (1738), after he had made his fortune, Ramsay no doubt was reluctant to give offense; perhaps also he worried about libel suits, since the poem names the names of distinguished churchmen. In any case, he held it back, and **"The Marrow Ballad"** remained buried in an obscure manuscript for well over two centuries. It ranks high among his satires and deserves to be widely known.

Summary

Obviously, Ramsay's Scots satires constitute a major part of his significant poetry. One striking fact about them is that, with the exception of the **"Christis Kirk"** cantos, parts of **"A Tale of Three Bonnets,"** and one or two others, all of these satires deal with town life—especially with Edinburgh, "Auld Reekie," the old greystone jungle of narrow wynds and closes flanking the High Street and Canongate, the crowded, battered, squalid, vibrant city he lived in all of his adult life and clearly loved. The vivid impressions of that unique world that we get in these poems look back two centuries to the incisive Edinburgh satires of William Dunbar, and they provided a solid modern precedent for the brilliant Edinburgh poems of Robert Fergusson fifty years later.

Another point worth noticing in these satires is that in them Ramsay limited himself to three verse forms: the "Christis Kirk" stanza, the "Habbie" stanza, and the tetrameter couplet—all traditional Scottish meters. The only exception to this, **"The Marrow Ballad,"** is composed in a pattern very closely related both in form and spirit to the "Christis Kirk" tradition. In so doing Ramsay succeeded in showing that these ancient native poetic forms were still alive and adaptable to modern themes, and he passed them on, reinvigorated, to his successors. At the same time, he revealed the possibilities of the burlesque method for modern Scots satire in **"John Cowper,"** **"Lucky Spence,"** and **"Wretched Miser"**—a development that was to have a profound effect on Burns.

How good are Ramsay's Scots satires intrinsically? As we have seen, their quality is uneven, and we should not claim too much for them. **"Maggy Johnston"** is awkward and immature, **"Magy Dickson"** is sloppy, others are no more than competent. But in the best of them—including the second canto of **"Christis Kirk,"** the bold experiment of **"John Cowper,"** the skilled, genial satire of **"Lucky Wood"** and **"Patie Birnie,"** the imaginative power of **"Wretched Miser,"** and the cutting wit of **"The Marrow Ballad"**—Ramsay shows an impressive talent. Kinghorn, in the most recent and in many respects most valuable biographical and critical work on Ramsay, largely ignores these remarkable satires, preferring to focus on his pastoral poetry, adaptations of Horace, and editorial labors. But the Scots satires cannot be ignored; they belong to the vital, central part of Ramsay's life work.

FURTHER READING

Fairchild, Hoxie Neale. "Sentimentalism—Severer Cases." In his *Religious Trends in English Poetry,* pp. 424-87. New York: Columbia University Press, 1939.

    Includes a brief discussion of Ramsay's relation to the Romantic Movement and the political and religious beliefs reflected in his poetry.

Gibson, Andrew. *New Light on Allan Ramsay.* Edinburgh: William Brown, 1927. 152 p.

    The first modern biographical and bibliographical study of Ramsay.

Kinghorn, Alexander Manson. "Watson's Choice, Ramsay's Voice and a Flash of Fergusson." *Scottish Literary Journal* 19, No. 2 (November 1992): 5-23.

    Examines Ramsay's use of contemporary and Middle Scots in his poetry.

——, and Alexander Law. Introduction to *Poems by Allan Ramsay and Robert Fergusson,* pp. vii-xxxiv. Totowa, N.J.: Rowman and Littlefield, 1974.

    A brief biographical sketch and critical analysis of Ramsay's work, focusing on his writing in Scots.

——. "Allan Ramsay and Literary Life in the First Half of the Eighteenth Century." In *The History of Scottish Literature,* Vol. 2, edited by Andrew Cook, pp. 65-79. Aberdeen: Aberdeen University Press, 1987.

    An overview of Ramsay's life, works, and place in Scottish Literature.

MacLaine, Allan H. "The Christis Kirk Tradition: Its Evolution in Scots Poetry to Burns. Part III: The Early Eighteenth Century: Allan Ramsay and His Followers." *Studies in Scottish Literature* 2, No. 3 (January 1965): 163-82.

    Analyzes Ramsay's contributions to the "Christis Kirk" genre as an editor and as an original poet.

McClure, J. Derrick. "Language and Genre in Allan Ramsay's 1721 Poems." In *Aberdeen and the Enlightenment: Proceedings of a Conference Held at the University of Aberdeen,* edited by Jennifer J. Carter and Joan H. Pittock, pp. 261-69. Aberdeen: Aberdeen University Press, 1987.

    Examines the association between language, metrical form, and genre in the 1721 edition of Ramsay's poems and the influence of Ramsay's use of Scots on later writers.

Smeaton, Oliphant. *Allan Ramsay.* Edinburgh and London: Oliphant, Anderson & Ferrier, 1896. 160 p.

    An early biography of Ramsay that includes three chapters of critical commentary on his works.

Tennant, William. "The Life of Allan Ramsay" and "Remarks on the Writings of Ramsay." In *The Gentle Shepherd: A Pastoral Comedy,* by Allan Ramsay, pp. xi-xxx. New York: William Gowans, 1852..

    A biographical sketch and brief critical comments on *The Gentle Shepherd* and Ramsay's other writings.

James Thomson

1700-1748

Scottish poet and dramatist. For further information on Thomson's career, see *LC,* Vol. 16.

INTRODUCTION

Regarded as one of the leading poets in eighteenth-century European literature, Thomson is primarily known for *The Seasons* (1726-30), a four-part poetic work about nature and its transformations during the course of the year. Considered Thomson's masterpiece, *The Seasons* had a significant influence on eighteenth-century English and Continental literature, reflecting the period's fascination with nature, and establishing a paradigm for pastoral poetry throughout Europe. Thomson is also known for his patriotic poem "Rule Britannia," from the masque *Alfred* (1740), written with David Mallet and set to music by Thomas Augustine Arne. Since its debut in 1740, "Rule Britannia" has been the emblematic song of Great Britain.

Biographical Information

Born the son of a clergyman in southern Scotland, Thomson was raised in the picturesque rural environment depicted in his most famous poems, and later studied for the ministry at Edinburgh University. In 1725, he went to London to pursue a literary career. While employed as a tutor, he worked on *The Seasons,* publishing *Winter* in 1726, *Summer* the following year, *Spring* in 1728, and *Autumn* in 1730. Even after publishing the collected cycle that same year, Thomson continued reworking and revising his masterpiece, introducing significant changes and additions and eventually publishing a revised edition in 1744. The poem was received enthusiastically, resulting in literary fame and the attractive position of travelling companion and tutor to Charles Talbot, son of the future Lord Chancellor. Thomson held this post, which provided him with the opportunity to visit France and Italy, until 1733, when he became Secretary of Briefs in the Court of Chancery. In 1737, he lost the secretarial appointment, owing to the death of the Lord Chancellor. The following year, upon the intervention of his friend George Lyttelton, the poet received an annual pension from the Prince of Wales. His financial situation became quite comfortable in 1744, when he was named Surveyor-General of the Leeward Islands. Highly esteemed by literary London, surrounded by loyal friends, and the recipient of sinecures, royalties, and a royal pension, Thomson spent his last years quietly, in a fine house in Kew Lane, Richmond, not far from his friend Alexander Pope. As many commentators—including Thomson himself—have noted, Thomson's life, though closely bound to writing, was characterized by a certain degree of indolence, which is one of the themes of his poetic oeuvre, notably the last poem completed before his death, *The Castle of Indolence* (1748).

Major Works

Described by some critics as a precursor of Romanticism, Thomson is nevertheless firmly rooted in the traditions of Classicism and Rationalism, his worldview being clearly defined by the paramount significance he accorded science. Thomson venerated the scientist and philosopher Sir Isaac Newton, whose philosophy of nature represented the dominant intellectual paradigm of the period. "Newton," as Douglas Bush as written, "sees everywhere in the universe the proofs not only of design, both majestic and minute, but of God's continuously active care." The Newtonian conception of God as architect and guardian of the universe constitutes the religious and philosophical foundation of *The Seasons.* Related to Newton's theology, and also incorporated into the intellectual framework of *The Seasons,* is the idea of the Great Chain of Being, ultimately traceable to Platonic idealism, which postulates a hierarchical gradation of beings, from the lowest to the highest. Thomson also turned to Newton for accurate poetic description, as did many other poets; the seminal scientific work from which Thomson benefited was Newton's *Opticks* (1704), a treatise explaining the nature of color and light. "With Newtonian eyes," Marjorie Hope Nicholson has explained, "the poets discovered new beauties in the most familiar aspects of nature, which had always been the stuff of poetry in individual colors seen through the prism, the rainbow, in sunrise and sunset, in the succession of colors throughout the day." But no poet of the mid-century, Nicholson has asserted, "responded to Newtonian color and light more fully than did Thomson in *The Seasons,* and no other poet so well used the new techniques."

Characterized as a descriptive work lacking a narrative structure, *The Seasons,* with its stately blank verse construction and Latinate vocabulary, harks to the poetry of John Milton. Yet Thomson, while emulating Milton, superimposed his idiosyncratic diction onto an archaic poetic form, thus creating striking and highly suggestive images and harmonies. Thomson's descriptions are eminently pictorial, evoking the characteristic atmosphere encountered in the works of such landscape artists as Nicolas Poussin, Claude Lorrain, and Salvator Rosa. "Thomson and Dyer," wrote Mario Praz in *The Romantic Agony,* "with their descriptions which translate into terms of literature the pictorial manner of Claude Lorrain and Salvator Rosa, are the godfathers of the Picturesque." Influenced by visual artists, the author of *The Seasons* in turn inspired the English painter J. M. W. Turner, who honored the Scottish poet in his 1811 work, *Thomson's Aeolian Harp.* However, as critics have argued, *The Seasons* is more than a purely descriptive poem, considering that Thomson extends his interest to include not only nature but the observer, as well as the gamut of feelings elicited by the contemplation of nature's majesty. Thomson's concern for feelings, as commentators remark, reflects the spirit of the time, pointing to the Romantic sensibility of later poets. As such, Thomson is considered a forerunner of such poets as William Cowper and William Wordsworth.

In *Liberty* (1735-36), a five-part poetical panorama of various countries and their governments and mores, Thomson drew from the optimistic moralism of Anthony Ashley Cooper, Lord Shaftesbury, to extol the unrivalled virtues of Britain's political system. Indicative of Thomson's British patriotism, *Liberty,* as well as the poem *Britannia* (1729), also reveals the poet's sympathies for the political opposition—headed by the Prince of Wales—to the Whig prime minister Sir Robert Walpole, known for his feuds with writers. *The Castle of Indolence,* a verse allegory detailing, in Spenserian diction, the ills of indolence and the blessings of industry, has been hailed by critics as a brilliant and highly suggestive recreation of an old poetic mode. Thomson's other writings include incidental poems, exemplified by gentle love lyrics, and five dramas, which seldom rise above rhetorical bombast, according to critics. Thomson did gain some measure of fame as a playwright, however, particularly with his 1745 tragedy *Tancred and Sigismunda,* which is based on an episode from Alain-René Lesage's popular picaresque novel *Gil Blas.*

Critical Reception

Thomson gained an international reputation primarily as a result of the success of *The Seasons.* Accessible to readers in translation, the poem became immensely popular shortly following its publication in England, eliciting praise from both the reading public at large and litterateurs, and exerting an extraordinary influence on writers. In the German-speaking world, Thomson's admirers included Albrecht von Haller, author of the poem *Die Alpen (The Alps),* Ewald von Kleist, who wrote *Frühling (Spring),* the lyric poet Johann Peter Uz, and Gotthold Ephraim Lessing. In an adaptation by Gottfried van Swieten, the poem served Franz Joseph Haydn as a text for his celebrated oratorio *Die Jahreszeiten.* In France, Thomson was praised by Voltaire and emulated by poets. His influence can also be seen in the pastoral poetry of the Spaniard Juan Melendez Valdés. Thomson's English critics appreciated his originality but also expressed certain technical concerns. For example, such eminent contemporaries as Pope and Samuel Johnson, while recognizing *The Seasons* as a remarkable literary accomplishment, noted its compositional weakness. William Hazlitt thought highly of Thomson, naming him the foremost descriptive poet of the time. Anticipating a theme in later criticism, Wordsworth recognized Thomson's talent but complained about his "vicious style." Indeed, such later nineteenth-century commentators as George Saintsbury and Edmund Gosse focused on the formal structure of Thomson's poetry, identifying technical and stylistic faults and placing his diction under careful scrutiny. Twentieth-century critics have attempted to offer a balanced assessment of Thomson's poetry, noting that stylistic imperfections and dissonances in diction hardly diminish his poetic voice. "Despite the general and particular flaws," affirmed Douglas Grant in his acclaimed 1951 biography of Thomson, "*The Seasons* is a great if not a good poem, and it would be impossible to exaggerate its influence on English poetry." Commentators have also questioned earlier evaluations of Thomson's diction and style, arguing that some of his cadences may sound awkward because they are heard outside the natural context of Scottish speech. Finally, as the work of a Scottish poet who spent his productive years in England, Thomson's poetry has inevitably attracted the attention of scholars interested in Anglo-Scottish literary relations.

PRINCIPAL WORKS

Winter. A Poem (poetry) 1726
Summer. A Poem (poetry) 1727
A Poem Sacred to the Memory of Sir Isaac Newton (poetry) 1727
Spring. A Poem (poetry) 1728
Britannia. A Poem (poetry) 1729
Autumn. A Poem, (poetry) 1730
The Seasons. A Poem (poetry) 1730
The Tragedy of Sophonisba (drama) 1730
Antient and Modern Italy Compared: being the first Part of Liberty, a Poem (poetry) 1735
Greece: being the Second Part of Liberty, a Poem (poetry) 1735

Rome: being the Third Part of Liberty (poetry) 1735
Britain: being the Fourth Part of Liberty (poetry) 1736
The Prospect: being the Fifth Part of Liberty (poetry)
    1736
Agamemnon. A tragedy (drama) 1738
The Works of Mr. Thomson (poetry, dramas) 1738
Edward and Eleonora. A Tragedy (drama) 1739
Alfred. A Masque (drama) 1740
Tancred and Sigismunda. A Tragedy (drama) 1745
*The Castle of Indolence: an Allegorical Poem. Written in
    Imitation of Spenser* (poetry) 1748
Coriolanus. A Tragedy (drama) 1749

CRITICISM

Alan Dugald McKillop (essay date 1961)

SOURCE: "*A Poem Sacred to the Memory of Sir Isaac
Newton:* Introduction" and "*Britannia:* Introduction," in *The
Castle of Indolence and Other Poems* by James Thomson,
edited by Alan Dugald McKillop, University of Kansas
Press, 1961, pp. 128-47, 157-64.

[*In the excerpt below, McKillop critically examines two
of Thomson's major poems, providing historical background for each.*]

Thomson's poem, linked in various ways, like all his work,
with tendencies already clearly defined in the feeling and
thought of his age, still conveys a fresh and authentic
response to Newtonian science. Like the physico-theolog-
ical pieces, it seeks some degree of precision, and in the
tradition of philosophical panegyric it takes the highest
ground. Among Thomson's shorter pieces it preëminently
illustrates Miss [Josephine] Miles' excellent description
of his mode as "an exceptionally panoramic and panegyric verse, emotional, pictorial, noble, universal, and tonal,
rising to the height of heaven and of feeling in the style
traditionally known as grand or sublime." Or, using the
terms of an earlier age, we may apply to this poem Dryden's description of his *Eleonora* (1692): "It was intended . . . not for an Elegie, but a Panegyrique. A kind of
Apotheosis, indeed; if a Heathen Word may be applyed to
a Christian use." . . .

Newton is the central figure in a drama of revelation—
almost a second creation, the theme epigrammatically
expressed in Pope's "Epitaph intended for Sir Isaac Newton":

> Nature, and Nature's Laws lay hid in Night.
> God said, *Let Newton be!*—and All was Light.

Other poems close in time to Thomson's lines apply the
formula of John Hughes' *The Ecstacy* to the theme of
Newton's soul in the future life. Allan Ramsay's elegy,
An ode to the memory of Sir Isaac Newton, published at
Edinburgh (without date, but almost certainly 1727), shows
how naturally the heavenly journey and the apotheosis
could be combined in a memorial poem:

> The God-like *Man* now mounts the sky,
>   Exploring all yon radiant Spheres;
> And with one View can more descry,
>   Than here below in eighty Years.

> Tho' none, with greater Strength of Soul,
>   Could rise to more divine a Height,
> Or range the *Orbs* from *Pole* to *Pole,*
>   And more improve the humane Sight.

> Now with full Joy he can survey
>   These Worlds, and ev'ry shining Blaze,
> That countless in the *Milky Way*
>   Only through glasses shew their Rays.

> Thousands in thousand Arts exceil'd,
>   But often to one Part confin'd;
> While ev'ry Science stood reveal'd
>   And clear to his capacious Mind.

> His Penetration, most profound,
>   Launch'd far in that extended Sea,
> Where humane Minds can reach no Bound,
>   And never div'd so deep as he.

A

POEM

Sacred to the MEMORY of

SIR ISAAC NEWTON.

By JAMES THOMSON.

His Tibi me Rebus quædam divina Voluptas
Percipit, atque Horror ; quòd fic Natura tuâ Vi
Tam manifefta patet ex omni Parte retecta.   LUCRETIUS.

LONDON:

Printed for J. MILLAN, at *Lock's Head* in *New-ftreet,* between
Marybone-ftreet and *Piccadilly* ; and Sold at his Shop near *Whiteball.*
MDCCXXVII.   (Price One Shilling.)

N. B. *Lately Publifh'd* ; *By* JAMES THOMSON. 1. WINTER, *a Poem. The 4th
Edition. Price* 1 s. 2. SUMMER, *a Poem. Price* 1 s. 6 d.

First-edition title page of Thomson's
Poem Sacred to the Memory of Sir Isaac Newton.

Edward Young's *Cynthio* (June 1727), a poem on the death of the Marquis of Carnarvon, shows how naturally the Newtonian theme entered into contemporary elegy:

> Tho' well the Sun may hide his Head,
> And each Star mourn *their Newton* dead;
> Who travell'd, with them, *Nature* round;
> Who fathom'd all the *blue Profound;*
> New Worlds of *Science* did explore
> And *Light* upon the *Planets* pour;
> Had not his Soul like these been blest,
> Of every *tender Grace* possest,
> To *learned Pride* this Truth I tell,
> We less had lost, when *Newton* fell.

Andrew Motte's frontispiece to his translation of the *Principia* (1729) represents Newton as a prophet or apostle translated on a cloud, enveloped in celestial light, and further instructed or inspired by the naked figure of Truth with a pair of compasses in her hand.

The slighting reference to Descartes appears in somewhat sharper form in the first edition of Thomson's poem than in the version of 1730. All who concerned themselves with Newtonian physics would of course, like Newton himself, have occasion to condemn Descartes' theory of vortices. Farther in the background was the old campaign against Descartes as a mechanist, tarred with the same brush as Hobbes, and as a speculative rather than an experimental scientist, whose method was opposed to the fruitful Baconian way. The popular literature was left with the idea that Descartes was a purveyor of "physical Romance," with the theory of vortices as the prime illustration. So in Swift: "*Cartesius* reckoned to see before he died, the Sentiments of all Philosophers, like so many lesser Stars in his *Romantick* System, rapt and drawn within his own *Vortex.*"

The one current theme which is strikingly absent from Thomson's poem is the emphasis on the limitations of human powers at their best. Great as Newton was, the argument might run, he had left much to do, and finally the most powerful genius will be brought to a stand in humility and ignorance. This was an almost inevitable development of the religious approach to the theme, as in Henry Grove's *Spectator* No. 635, already noted. And the tribute to Newton in *Mist's Journal,* April 8, 1727, had ended on this note.

> We are not intimately acquainted even with the Objects that are within our Reach, they seem to mock our Enquiries, and flee from us as fast as we pursue: But when we would look into the Immensity of the Universe, the Mind starts back at the amazing Prospect, our Presumption is immediately check'd and baffled, and our Imagination loses it self in the boundless Reflection. I shall conclude in the Words of M. Paschall: *Tho' our Sight,* says he, *is limited, let our Thoughts at least pass beyond; yet even then we may sooner exhaust the Power of conceiving, than Nature can want a new Store to furnish out our Conceptions.*

In *Summer* Thomson had already said that the structure of

the universe is beyond the ken, not merely of the captious and ignorant, but of the most sweeping vision; he had given Newton a high and honorable place among British sages, but had not assigned to him solitary eminence.

It is *Summer,* however, which gives us Thomson's first specific treatment of Newtonian themes, and the relation of the Newton poem to the poet's main line of development in *The Seasons* may be briefly considered here. Gravitation and projection appear in the opening passages of *Summer:*

> With what a perfect, World-revolving Power
> Were first th' unweildy Planets launch'd along
> Th' illimitable Void!—

and in the address to the sun:

> 'Tis by thy secret, strong, attractive Force,
> As with a Chain, indissoluble, bound,
> Thy System rolls entire; from the far Bourn
> Of slow-pac'd *Saturn,* to the scarce-seen Disk
> Of *Mercury,* lost in excessive Blaze.

One senses the possibility of a catalogue of the planets, and Thomson also moves toward his catalogue of the colors:

> The vegetable World is also thine,
> Parent of Seasons! from whose rich-stain'd Rays,
> Reflected various, various Colours rise.

This leads a few lines farther on to the great catalogue of gems, already brilliantly expounded by Miss Nicolson [in *Voyages to the Moon* (1948)], but which we may quote here in the original text as the pioneer and exemplary Newtonian color passage of the period:

> Th' unfruitful Rock, itself, impregn'd by Thee,
> In dark Retirement, forms the *lucid Stone,*
> Collected Light, compact! . . .
> At Thee the *Ruby* lights his deepening Glow,
> A bleeding Radiance! grateful to the View.
> From Thee the *Saphire,* solid Aether! takes
> His Hue cerulean; and, of evening Tinct,
> The Purple-streaming *Amethyst* is thine.
> With thy own Smile the Yellow *Topaz* burns.
> Nor deeper Verdure dies the Robe of *Spring,*
> When first she gives it to the Southern Gale,
> Than the green *Emerald* shows. But, all
>   combin'd,
> Thick, thro' the whitening *Opal,* play thy
>   Beams;
> Or flying, several, from his Surface, form
> A trembling Variance of revolving Hues,
> As the Site changes in the Gazer's hand.

The stage is further set for Newton at the end of *Summer,* after the long passage on the popular terror caused by the aurora borealis:

> Not so the Man of *Philosophic* Eye,

And Inspect sage, *the waving Brightness,* He,
Curious surveys, inquisitive to know
The Causes, and Materials, yet unfix'd,
Of this Appearance beautiful, and new.

Miss Nicolson has demonstrated the special influence on contemporary poets of Thomson's lines on the solar spectrum, beginning with Richard Glover's imitative but remarkable "Poem on Sir Isaac Newton" prefixed to Pemberton's *View of Sir Isaac Newton's Philosophy* (1728). Thomson indeed imitates himself in the description of the rainbow in *Spring* (1728):

Mean-time refracted from yon Eastern Cloud,
Bestriding Earth, the grand aetherial Bow
Shoots up immense! and every Hue unfolds,
In fair Proportion, running from the Red,
To where the Violet fades into the Sky.
Here, mighty *Newton,* the dissolving Clouds
Are, as they scatter round, thy numerous Prism,
Untwisting to the Philosophic Eye
The various Twine of Light, by Thee pursu'd
Thro' all the mingling Maze.

One of the central questions in Thomson criticism is how far these scientific findings are merged or fused into a genuine imaginative view of the world. In the poet's best and most characteristic work the treatment of special effects and laws is drawn into a larger movement. The beauty of natural law appears in the gravity-passage in *Summer* and the spectrum-passage in *Newton,* but it is never a static beauty; there is the cosmic procession, the drama of revelation in which mind and spirit participate; and in connection with the emphasis on color there is always the special association of color with pervasive vitality and energy. Thomson's tribute to Newton is centered about his emphasis on the beauty and simplicity of the divine scheme as revealed by the master, who

from MOTION's simple Laws,
Could trace the boundless Hand of PROVIDENCE,
Wide-working thro' this universal Frame.

O unprofuse Magnificence divine!
O WISDOM truly perfect! thus to call
From a few Causes such a Scheme of Things,
Effects so various, beautiful, and great,
An Universe compleat!

The same principle appears in *The Seasons:*

Unlavish *Wisdom* never works in vain.
Mysterious round! what skill, what force divine,
Deep-felt, in these appear! A simple train,
Yet so harmonious mix'd, so fitly join'd,
One following one in such inchanting sort,
Shade, unperceiv'd, so softening into shade,
And all so forming such a perfect whole,
That, as they still succeed, they ravish still.

The scheme connects the simple with the boundless, the

unprofuse with the various. Unity and diversity appear together in Hutcheson's statement of the principle:

There is another *Beauty* in Propositions, which cannot be omitted; which is this, When one *Theorem* shall contain a vast Multitude of Corollarys easily deducible from it. . . . In the search of *Nature* there is the like *Beauty* in the Knowledge of some great *Principles,* or universal *Forces,* from which innumerable Effects do flow. Such is *Gravitation,* in Sir ISAAC NEWTON's Scheme; such also is the Knowledge of the Original of Rights, *perfect* and *imperfect,* and *external; alienable* and *unalienable,* with their manner of *Translations;* from whence the greatest Part of moral Dutys may be deduc'd in the various Relations of human Life.

The conception of simplicity as applied to the arts moves in a somewhat different direction, emphasizing limitation and proportion, or design rather than color. But in Thomson's practice the central simplicity or economy is easily connected with an infinite diversity of effect, and the endless pageant of nature is impelled by vital, not merely mechanical, forces. . . .

Britannia shows us the young poet moved to sharp political and patriotic utterance under circumstances which are not yet entirely clear. The lines on Newton . . . had been dedicated to Walpole. *Britannia* expresses Opposition sentiment which perhaps had its origins in the year 1727, when Spain declared war on England and threatened Gibraltar. Admiral Hosier's death in that year, while in command of the British fleet in the West Indies, came in the minds of many to symbolize the Government's ineffective support of vigorous naval measures. Spain, so the general complaint went, continued to violate the freedom of the seas. Thomson's personal response can be inferred only from his verse; it has been suggested that since Bubb Dodington was one of his chief patrons after 1727, and since relations between Walpole and Dodington had been strained since the middle of that year, when Dodington paid court to the King's new favorite, Sir Spencer Compton, Thomson might now feel that he was free to follow his own inclination in criticizing Walpole.

The publication of *Britannia* seems to have been timed to coincide exactly with the opening of Parliament on January 21, 1729 (*Daily Journal* of that date). The verses open with a reference to the arrival of Prince Frederick on English soil; after having been detained at Hanover by his father since 1727, he had landed at Harwich on December 3, 1728. According to the court poets, his arrival was eagerly awaited:

See! with impatience to the wide sea-shore
They croud, and long to ken
His *Navy,* whit'ning o'er the deep,
And bounding o'er the surge to the expecting
strand.

Britannia was the only one of Thomson's works to be published anonymously, and the only one during his early period to appear without a dedication. . . .

Britannia is a modification and to some extent a reversal

of the praise of Britain in *Summer* (1727):

> HAPPY BRITANNIA! where the Queen of Arts,
> Inspiring Vigour, LIBERTY, abroad,
> Walks thro' the Land of Heroes, unconfin'd,
> And scatters Plenty with unsparing Hand. . . .
>
> Bold, firm, and graceful, are thy generous
>   Youth,
> By Hardship sinew'd, and by Danger fir'd,
>
> Scattering the Nations where They go; and first,
> Or on the listed Plain, or wintry Seas.
> Mild are thy Glories too, as o'er the Arts
> Of thriving Peace thy thoughtful Sires preside;
> In Genius, and substantial Learning high;
> For every Vertue, every Worth renown'd.
> Sincere, plain-hearted, hospitable, kind,
> Yet like the mustering Thunder when provok'd;
> The Scourge of Tyrants, and the sole Resource
> Of such as under grim Oppression groan. . . .
>
> Island of Bliss! amid the Subject Seas,
> That thunder round thy rocky Coasts, set up,
> At once the Wonder, Terror, and Delight
> Of distant Nations; whose remotest Shore
> Can soon be shaken by thy naval Arm.
> Not to be shook Thy self, but all Assaults
> Baffling, like thy hoar Cliffs the loud Sea-Wave.

In the optimistic exuberance of *Spring* (1728), Britain's overseas commerce is blended with the general theme of Nature's fecundity.

> Ye generous *Britons* cultivate the Plow!
> And o'er your Hills, and long with-drawing
>   Vales,
> Let *Autumn* spread his Treasures to the Sun,
> Luxuriant, and unbounded. As the Sea,
> Far thro' his azure, turbulent Extent,
> Your Empire owns, and from a thousand Shores
> Wafts all the Pomp of Life into your Ports,
> So with superior Boon may your rich Soil,
> Exuberant, Nature's better Blessings pour
> O'er every Land; the naked Nations cloath,
> And be th' exhaustless Granary of the World.

But in 1729 Thomson reaches the point at which one line of "Whig panegyric," to use a convenient though possibly overworked term, diverges into "dissident Whig panegyric," and thus points forward ominously to the editorial vein which reaches its height in *Liberty*. [In *The Varied God: A Critical Study of Thomson's "The Seasons"* (1959)] Mrs. Spacks has recently described this tendency with considerable precision as a shift from interest in "man in nature" to "man in society." On the positive side, this patriotic poetry exalts the peaceful spread of British power through commerce, as Cecil A. Moore long ago demonstrated in a classic essay ["Whig Panegyric Verse, 1700-1760: A Phase of Sentimentalism," originally published in *PMLA* XLI (1926)]. Current benevolism, fusing then

as now in a strange way with Anglo-Saxon politics, delighted to dwell on peace as an international blessing conferred by a righteous nation. Ideally the panegyrist would lay equal stress on peace, prosperity, and power. But power is always accompanied by "mustering Thunder." This theme appears at the end of the description of the port of London in *Autumn* (1730), after a glowing account of warehouse, river, and shipping—

> While deep the various voice of fervent toil
> From bank to bank increas'd; whence ribb'd
>   with oak,
> To bear the BRITISH thunder, black, and bold,
> The roaring vessel rush'd into the main.

Yet an indefatigable panegyrist like Edward Young was eager to see the war clouds roll away and to celebrate peaceful imperialism, as in his *Imperium Pelagi,* inspired by the Treaty of Seville at the end of 1729:

> Trade springs from Peace, and Wealth from
>   Trade,
> And Power from Wealth.
>
>   . . . . .
>
> Then perish War!—Detested War!

But *Britannia* strikes a different note. Though the poem still formulates the ideal of peaceful imperialism, it reverts to the contrast between the unique and glorious situation and mission of Britain and the present state of things—the pattern that had been set in the dying speech of John of Gaunt in *Richard II.* The goddess in *Britannia,* no longer the triumphant sea-born figure of earlier iconography, contemplates "her degenerate Sons" on a melancholy coast, and is not at all certain that she rules the waves. Britain is the last resort of Liberty, "the World almost in slavish Sloth dissolv'd." The poem *Liberty* elaborates the same framework: in each poem the goddess appears and speaks movingly and at length of the visualized situation while the Muse records her words, then vanishes, leaving the poet in the desolate scene presented at the beginning—the wild coast in *Britannia,* the ruins of Rome in *Liberty.* In both poems, past glories are contrasted with the present shameful decline; the opposition between luxury and liberty is emphasized; tendentious political utterances merge with universally acceptable political, moral, and social generalizations. Except in the passage on the Armada, and perhaps the lines on the sources of the Nile, reflecting the geographical reading which underlies part of *The Seasons,* Thomson is far from being at his best here. Yet his remarkable feeling for public opinion and public sentiment should not go unnoticed; his sensitiveness to the winds that were blowing is as evident here as in the *Newton,* though it appears in a less engaging form.

Patricia Meyer Spacks (essay date 1965)

SOURCE: "Vision and Meaning in James Thomson," in *Studies in Romanticism,* Vol. IV, No. 4, Summer, 1965, pp. 206-19.

[*An American essayist, biographer, and educator, Spacks has written extensively on eighteenth-century poetry. In the following essay, she demonstrates that, as is evidenced in* The Seasons, *Thomson possesses "clear physical vision, and the ability to reproduce its perceptions," as well as "the vital gift of transforming imaginative vision."*]

Although James Thomson's **The Seasons** was early admired for its fine sentiments, its greatest influence was clearly as a work of natural description. Thomson himself, however, soon became aware of the essential impossibility of recording actuality in poetry. **Spring** (1728) contains a revealing passage (quoted here in its slightly altered final form):

> But who can paint
> Like Nature? Can imagination boast,
> Amid its gay creation, hues like hers?
> Or can it mix them with that matchless skill,
> And lose them in each other, as appears
> In every bud that blows? If fancy then
> Unequal fails beneath the pleasing task,
> Ah, what shall language do?
>
> (ll. 468-475)

That the eye can discriminate more colors than language can define was an eighteenth-century truism. Thomson, however, here goes further, to suggest that the limitation exists in the imagination—the human re-creative power—as well as in language. The task of accurate poetic description, in other words, is by definition impossible. Yet this is the task Thomson set himself, and for its accomplishment he was widely praised; indeed, John Aikin, late in the eighteenth century, asserted that the success of **The Seasons** proves the value of description as "the sole object of a poem." Early in the century Fénelon, after insisting that "The Perfection of Poetry itself . . . depends on a full and lively Description of Things in all their Circumstances," had been concerned to point out that this truth does not imply that reality should be described in all its individual circumstances. "We shou'd represent nothing to the Hearers but what deserves their Attention; and help's [*sic*] to give a clear and just Idea of the Things we describe." But before 1800 particularity of description had become a poetic ideal, and for this shift in taste Thomson was at least partly responsible. "Some Criticks have supposed, that poetry can only deal in generals," wrote John Scott of Amwell; "or in other words, that it cannot subsist with any very minute specification of particulars. To such, this passage [the description of birds building their nests, from **Spring**] might well be produced as a proof, that their opinion is erroneous." Joseph Warton, another admirer of Thomson, is yet more emphatic: "A minute and particular enumeration of circumstances judiciously selected, is what chiefly discriminates poetry from history, and renders the former, for that reason, a more close and faithful representation of nature than the latter." Thomson is repeatedly used as the supporting example for such a point of view. He is praised because, in a passage of landscape description, "It is as if the range of the eye were, at once enlarged by the aid of the telescope, and

every object magnified by the microscope." As early as 1739, a rhetoric intended for school boys defines the figure of "vision" as "a Representation of Things distant and past as if seen and present," and advises its readers to see **The Seasons** for the best examples of the figure.

If there was little disagreement in Thomson's own century about his skill at detailed, accurate description (only more recently has it been argued that his skill is really the evocation of general scenes rather than the delineation of particularity), there was yet room for dissatisfaction with Thomson specifically as a descriptive poet. The case against him is eloquently put by John Pinkerton:

> The objects which he exhibits appear in those lights exactly in which their forms and colours have the most pleasing effect which they can produce to the eye. *But,* to say the truth, *I do not see that he has improved their beauties with too much of that magic colouring with which the fancy of the impassioned inamorato often gives to the object of his fondness, a perfection of beauty which none but himself can discover.* Yet, the power of doing this, is that which, above all other qualities, constitutes the Poet.

The critic's italics emphasize the graveness of his indictment; it amounts to an accusation that Thomson possesses clear physical vision, and the ability to reproduce its perceptions, but that he lacks the vital gift of transforming imaginative vision. The charge has been echoed in modern times; it raises fundamental questions about the poetic value of Thomsonian description—and the even more basic question: what, exactly, does such description consist of?

In a letter written in 1730 Thomson remarked, "Travelling has been long my fondest wish for the very purpose you recommend: the storing one's Imagination with Ideas of all-beautiful, all-great, and all-perfect Nature. These are the true materia poetica, the light and colours with which Fancy kindles up her whole creation, paints a sentiment, and even embodies an abstracted thought." If these comments suggest the poet's conviction that perception and the memory of perception must be the source of his art, they also imply that he proposes to move, somehow, from perception to "sentiment" and even to "abstracted thought." His descriptions in **The Seasons** are characteristically dominated by semiphilosophical ideas and emotions derived from them. If the "insight" they offer is not the sort we usually desire from nature poetry, still far more than mere "sight" has been provided.

A characteristic descriptive passage in **Spring** begins, "And see . . . " and ends, ". . . shuts the scene" (l. 47): it is offered as a visual panorama. It opens, characteristically, with a personification:

> And see where surly Winter passes off
> Far to the north, and calls his ruffian blasts:
> His blasts obey, and quit the howling hill,
> The shattered forest, and the ravaged vale;
> While softer gales succeed, at whose kind touch,
> Dissolving snows in livid torrents lost,

The mountains lift their green heads to the sky.

(ll. 11-17)

Despite the command to "see," only the last line of the seven is predominantly visual. Stress is rather on "character" than appearance. The passage creates an impression of Winter as fierce, disagreeable, "surly" criminal, attended by "ruffian blasts," in the role almost of cosmic highwayman, victimizing the natural world; it does not, on the whole, evoke physical images. Nature is personalized without being quite personified, through such modifiers as *howling, ravaged, kind.* To treat inanimate nature thus as closely akin to sentient beings is vital for Thomson, as for most writers in the pastoral or georgic tradition. In the lines quoted above, the reader must be made aware of nature's insistent vibrancy in order to sense the philosophic underpinnings of the passage.

With "green" introduced in the description of mountains, the tone is set for the remainder of the passage, with its emphasis on the "bright," "light," "white," "shining" quality of spring. As typical of Thomson as his introduction of the personification is his quick abandonment of it.

> As yet the trembling year is unconfirmed,
> And Winter oft at eve resumes the breeze,
> Chills the pale morn, and bids his driving sleets
> Deform the day delightless; so that scarce
> The bittern knows his time with bill engulfed
> To shake the sounding marsh; or from the shore
> The plovers when to scatter o'er the heath,
> And sing their wild notes to the listening waste.
>   At last from Aries rolls the bounteous sun,
> And the bright Bull receives him. Then no more
> The expansive atmosphere is cramped with cold;
> But, full of life and vivifying soul,
> Lifts the light clouds sublime, and spreads them
>   thin,
> Fleecy, and white o'er all-surrounding heaven.

(ll. 18-31)

The loose metaphoric foundation of the description begins to emerge: it is based on the antithesis between the "expansive atmosphere," "full of life and vivifying soul," and the state of being "cramped with cold." Martin Price has pointed out that all Thomson's "best landscapes involve tension and movement," adding that such tensions, "like an abstract form—musical or pictorial— . . . articulate patterns of tension that underlie or are embedded in much of our experience." In this instance, the sense of tension clearly focuses most of the details of the scene and supplies the atmosphere of significance. While the year trembles, "unconfirmed" ("Not fortified by resolution; not strengthened; raw; weak," as Dr. Johnson defines the word), Winter, vaguely personified once more, takes control of natural energies ("resumes the breeze") in order to remove vitality and warmth from the scene, to "Deform" (literally destroy the form of) the day. Opposed to winter are the forces of movement and of life. The bittern tries to "shake the sounding marsh"; the plovers, which "scatter o'er the heath," sing to a "waste" which is nonetheless, in this time of

approaching vitality, "listening."

Now man is introduced, as part of the natural scene; Thomson describes the plowing and sowing of spring (ll. 32-47). The beginning of this description (ll. 32-38) lays heavy stress on participles which recall their opposites, thus continuing the emphasis on winter's rigidity versus spring's energy. *Unconfined, unbinding, relenting, loosened, unrefusing:* such modifiers insist on the antithesis, heighten the impression of spring's vitality by reminding one of winter's confinement. The pattern Thomson outlines is clear. Man "Winds [*Wind:* "To regulate in action" (Johnson)] the whole work" (l. 43), controls the agricultural activity which fulfills spring's fertility, but master, sower, and "lusty steers" (l. 35: the "lust" of the steers is perceived as redirected toward a nonsexual form of creativity) also participate in the simple assertion of life which is spring's triumph: cheered by the lark (l. 40), cattle affirm as importantly as birds the essentially celebratory activity which defies and destroys the binding force of winter. The passivity of earth suggested at the outset in such phrases as "howling hill" and "ravaged vale," when earth is the victim of winter, becomes ultimately the source of fruition, as "the faithful bosom of the ground" (l. 46)—a metaphor faintly ludicrous in the context, but clearly intended to enforce the thematic statement of the entire passage—receives the sower's grain. The total pattern of nature is Thomson's real subject; this fact is emphasized by the succeeding lines (48-52), an invocation to Heaven, which leads to moral generalizations about the value of rural poetry and rural virtue—"morals" which the poet appears to find implicit in his view of natural pattern.

In spite of his insistence that he is offering us something to "see," then, Thomson controls his descriptive passage through idea rather than through visual detail. Not only are the actual "scenes" highly generalized, much of the presentation is not visual at all, hardly even sensuous. We may be reminded of a curious fact revealed by Josephine Miles's tabulation of the words which Thomson uses more than ten times in a thousand lines: *eye* and *scene* are among the most frequently used nouns (although *man* and *soul* occur twice as often, and *life* three times as frequently); *see* is one of the eight favorite verbs; but of the twelve adjectives listed, only four are at all visual, and even they are very general (*deep, fair, long, wide*). The more characteristic Thomsonian adjective, these statistics suggest, points to the emotional or spiritual: *fierce, gay, great, happy, mighty, pure, sad, wild.*

Even the passages of *The Seasons* most famed as descriptive set-pieces reveal the same preoccupation with significance at the expense of appearance. The well-known description of a garden is a case in point, although it is misleading to isolate it from its context. (A persistent problem in dealing with *The Seasons* is that its effects usually depend on units about a hundred lines long: too long for quotation or detailed analysis.) The passage is introduced, in the final version of the poem, by an invocation to "Amanda" and an appeal that she join the poet in his walk (*Spring,* ll. 480-493). Then she is invited to "see" how the vale is irrigated, the lily watered; to appreciate "The negligence of nature wide and wild" (l. 505); to contemplate the "busy nations" of bees (l. 510) at "their delicious task" (l. 508).

> At length the finished garden to the view
> Its vistas opens and its alleys green.
> Snatched through the verdant maze, the hurried
>   eye
> Distracted wanders; now the bowery walk
> Of covert close, where scarce a speck of day
> Falls on the lengthened gloom, protracted
>   sweeps;
> Now meets the bending sky, the river now
> Dimpling along, the breezy ruffled lake,
> The forest darkening round, the glittering spire,
> The ethereal mountain, and the distant main.
>   (ll. 516-525)

This is all introductory to the famous description of garden flowers, part of the same verse paragraph. Its emphasis is double: on the viewer, and on the curious power of nature. Thomson does not offer this scene simply as a description of what he himself has seen; he presents it, rather, as something *to be* seen. His use of the definite article ("the view," "the hurried eye") depersonalizes and universalizes the presentation, but that presentation depends upon the context of the broad appeal to Amanda to see and understand what nature has to offer. "The hurried eye" is the grammatical subject of the sentence which extends from line 518 to line 525; the eye sweeps the bowery walk, meets the bending sky, the lake, the forest, and the main. Yet the eye is not the active agent here. It is "snatched" through the maze, as though the scene itself had power and energy. The eye itself, "distracted," can only wander. Energy resides in the river which dimples, the forest which darkens, the breezy lake; the eye is led, without volition, from one object to another. And the abstracted viewer must be recalled by the poet to the immediate scene:

> But why so far excursive? when at hand, . . .
> Fair-handed Spring unbosoms every grace.
>   (ll. 526, 529)

In the account of the flowers which immediately follows (ll. 530-555), nature, examined near-at-hand, seems far more passive than in the more general prospect. Yet its power remains, conceived now in more abstract terms; the reader is reminded of it every few lines. [In *The Fields of Light: An Experiment in Critical Reading* (1962)] Reuben Brower has pointed out that these lines "loosely compose a metaphor—of Spring, and beyond that of the vaguely benign Thomsonian Nature." The presented pattern alternates between what is visible to the eye and what is only imaginable, or perceptible by what Thomson often terms "the eye of reason." There is the mass of flowers, which the observer may even perceive as a "wilderness" (l. 528); there is also the *source* of these flowers, consciousness of which turns wilderness to order. The aesthetically satisfying vision of colorful flowers and the emotionally satisfying awareness of meaning in those flowers together comprise

the image of Spring and of Nature.

"Fair-handed Spring unbosoms every grace": this first reminder that the garden is significant primarily as the product of Spring recalls the personification which presides over the whole poem (see ll. 1-4). There are subsequent, subsidiary hints that Spring is the presiding deity: anemones are shed from the "wing" of spring breezes (ll. 335-336); auriculas are "enriched" with their "shining meal" (ll. 336-337): the participle (as opposed to the obvious adjective *rich*) defines the flowers as passive recipients of Spring's bounty. In the description of "the tulip-race" (ll. 339-344), where the vocabulary insists upon the connection between the animate and inanimate worlds, emphasis on the *sources* of visual effects virtually excludes actual description: personalized beauty herself is a cause of the tulips' colors (ll. 339-340); so is "the father-dust" (l. 341); so, the "exulting florist" believes, is he (ll. 343-344). But the ultimate cause, as the total context makes clear, is Spring, and beyond Spring, the natural order.

"The charmed eye" (l. 343) now has replaced the "hurried eye" with which the sequence began; Nature exerts her power over the observer, to hurry or to charm. But visual perception is by no means the most significant kind, as two lines added only in 1744 clearly suggest ("No gradual bloom is wanting—from the bud First-born of Spring to Summer's musky tribes" [ll. 345-346]). Crocuses and carnations do not actually bloom together, as they seem to in this description, but the summary lines quoted above suggest the irrelevance of any such objection to Thomson's grouping of flowers. The poet wishes to present not an actual scene but an imagined panorama of the garden's progress from early spring to summer. [In *James Thomson: Sa vie et ses oeuvres* (1895)] Léon Morel has said of Thomson, "Les objets . . . se montrent surtout au poète comme partie d'un vaste tableau, et lors même qu'il les observe séparêment, ils lui apparaissent toujours comme animés, mobiles at changeants; c'est là une condition qui exclut la notation précise de formes arrêtées." The garden passage strongly supports this thesis. In it the "vast tableau," the *pattern,* is above all important, and description provides only a metaphor for this pattern. In the concluding section of the garden passage, Thomson recapitulates briefly the possible modes of flower description: by color (the hyacinths; ll. 548-549), fragrance (jonquils; ll. 549-550), mythological association (narcissus; ll. 550-551), form (carnations and pinks; l. 552). Then he reminds us once more that description is, paradoxically, impossible: there remain "hues on hues expression cannot paint" (l. 554), but this fact matters little, since the importance of flowers is not their indescribable colors but the fact that they are "The breath of Nature, and her endless bloom" (l. 555).

In even so "descriptive" a passage as this, then, Thomson is clearly far more concerned with insight than with sight. His realization that observation of nature could be used to express nature's grand significance marks an important step toward true romantic nature imagery, which has been well defined by W. K. Wimsatt [in "The Structure of Romantic Nature Imagery," *The Age of Johnson: Essays*

Presented to Chauncey Brewster Tinker (1949)]:

> The common feat of the romantic nature poets was to
> read meanings into the landscape . . . characteristically
> . . . concerning the spirit or soul of things. . . . And
> that meaning especially was summoned out of the very
> surface of nature itself. It was embodied imaginatively
> and without the explicit religious or philosophic
> statements which one will find in classical or Christian
> instances.

In Thomson's imagery meaning does not really inhere in
the landscape; it is felt as the product of human imagination or intelligence contemplating the natural scene. And
the eighteenth-century poet felt obliged to make his meanings explicit. The passage immediately following the garden scene begins, "Hail, Source of Being! Universal Soul
Of heaven and earth!" (ll. 556-557), and elaborates the
relation between the Deity and natural process, stating
directly the meanings implicit in the earlier description.
Yet one's sense that nature is genuinely important to
Thomson derives not from his insistent didacticism but
from his ability to convey meaning directly through imagery.

The aesthetics of *The Seasons* is based not on Wordsworthian principles but on ideas widely current in Thomson's
own time. Mark Akenside's *The Pleasures of Imagination*
was published in 1744, the year that *The Seasons* received its final major revision. Much of it is merely ponderous versification of Addison's essays on the imagination, with some broadening of Addison's principles. But
Akenside's aesthetics conforms precisely with that implied by *The Seasons*. Beauty, asserts *The Pleasures of
Imagination,* resides first in color alone, then in shape,
then in color and shape combined. The addition of growth
produces an object yet more aesthetically satisfying (the
flowers of a garden, for example); sentient life is more
appealing still; and the greatest beauty is in beings combining life and mind. "In nature's fairest forms, is aught
so fair   As virtuous friendship?" enquires Akenside, rhetorically. The implications of this position are important
in understanding Thomson's poem. A modern reader can
easily feel that its long sections praising famous men or
glorifying some such human activity as plowing or prison
reform are excrescences on a poem which would do far
better to concentrate entirely on nature, its true subject.
But if Thomson, like Akenside, believed that description
of peasants (or, for that matter, of city folk) almost by
definition offered aesthetic pleasure of a higher order than
description of nature, and that the presentation of such
themes as "virtuous friendship" was necessarily superior
to either kind of description, superior in *beauty* and in
power over the imagination, aesthetically as well as morally more pleasurable, he would conceive it a necessary
part of his poetic responsibility to record, for the sake of
aesthetic effect, his impressions of humanity as well as of
the natural world, to use description of nature as a method for approaching discussion of man.

The most successful descriptions of human activities in
The Seasons are much like the poem's typical nature
descriptions in technique and in apparent purpose. The
harvest scene in *Summer* is a case in point. The "ruddy
maid" is described as "Half naked, swelling on the sight"
(l. 356); however unfortunate the faint prurience of the
point of view, it reminds one (like equivalent constructions in the garden scene) of the actual presence of an
observer. Here, as in the nature descriptions, the diction
insists on some essential identity between man and nature: the mead is "jovial" (l. 352); the maid resembles a
summer rose (ll. 354-355); the voices of the workers are
heard "Waking the breeze" (l. 369). If the garden provides a metaphor for natural order, the haying scene supplies an image of man in nature, a functioning part of the
universal pattern. The poet's greater concern with function than with scene is suggested by his use of the metonymy of abstract for concrete: "stooping age" (l. 358), "kind
oppression" (l. 360; here the oxymoron may even recall
Thomson's frequent insistence that good and evil are inextricably intertwined in the great universal pattern, where
partial evil will ultimately be revealed as universal good),
and by the generalizing, unrealized personifications at the
very end ("happy labour, love, and social glee" [l. 370]).
The activity of the haymakers provides a visual pattern of
order, as they advance, wheel, "drive the dusky wave
along the mead" (l. 366), and leave behind them hay-
cocks "in order gay" (l. 368). But the visual pattern, like
the aural one suggested by "the blended voice   Of happy
labour, love, and social glee," is primarily important in
reflecting a vital philosophic pattern. Here again, scenic
is subordinated to conceptual in what purports to be a
descriptive passage; the poet's "vision" is more significantly internal than external.

The view that human activity must be aesthetically interesting of course encouraged descriptive presentation of
human affairs. Another of the aesthetic principles which
Akenside versified, however, could justify the inclusion
of material presented without physical objectification. An
outgrowth of the Lockean concept of association of ideas,
this held that the imagination receives greater pleasure
according to the perceiver's lot in life. Akenside offers
these examples: spring is more delightful to one who has
been ill; the rainbow is more beautiful to one who understands it; consciousness of divine wisdom makes the spectacle of nature more compelling. They are very Thomsonian instances. The beauty of the rainbow to the educated
observer is discussed in *Spring* (ll. 203-217); *Summer*
contains a similar treatment of the joy which the sight of
a comet gives "the enlightened few" (l. 1714). And discussions of the role of divine wisdom in relation to the
beauties of nature is a recurrent—*the* recurrent—theme of
The Seasons. Akenside provides an important aesthetic
rationalization for Thomson's characteristic pattern of alternating description and commentary, which does not come
merely, as Jean Hagstrum suggests, from the fact that
Thomson's material forced him to "the picture-gallery
method of 'see and respond.'" Akenside also suggests why,
throughout *The Seasons,* commentary is typically embedded in description. The richest aesthetic satisfaction can be
achieved by a presentation which suggests not only visual
actuality but its meaningful associations, the importance of
that actuality in some larger context. To establish contexts

appears to be one of Thomson's principal purposes in virtually all his descriptions; this is one reason why their visual detail frequently evaporates under close examination, which reveals how much the visual is actually subordinated to the rational.

The persistence with which Thomson attempted to achieve the union of sensuous and intellectual response is suggested by his frequent use of perceptual metaphors for intellectual activity. Both reason and imagination are strongly and repeatedly associated with vision. Early in *Spring,* for example, at the end of a description of rainfall, the poet points out that the falling rain is the bounty of heaven, producing fruits and flowers.

> Swift fancy fired anticipates their growth;
> And, while the milky nutriment distils,
> Beholds the kindling country colour round.
> (ll. 183-185)

Fancy can "behold" a scene which does not yet exist, "see" simultaneously the reality of the present and that of the future. This capacity justifies the adjective *milky,* which presumably refers either metaphorically to the nourishing quality of rain or literally to the appearance of the unseen sap working in the plants: in either case it derives from imaginative rather than actual perception. Thomson frequently uses this device of presenting, as though visual, images which can only be the products of the fancy. Thus, contemplating a mass of flowers,

> the raptured eye
> Hurries from joy to joy, and, hid beneath
> The fair profusion, yellow Autumn spies.
> (*Spring,* ll. 111-113)

Again, Amanda is invited to "See how the lily drinks The latent rill, scarce oozing through the grass" (ll. 495-496). The eye, asserted able to see the unseeable, is totally identified with the imaginative process.

Indeed, the capacity of imagination to enlarge the bounds of physical perception appears to be its chief value for Thomson. In a rhapsodic passage on the sources of water, he relies heavily on the analogy between imagination and sight. "Oh! lay the mountains bare, and wide display Their hidden structure to the astonished view" (*Autumn,* ll. 779-780), he begs:

> Give opening Hemus to my searching eye, . . .
> Unveil
> The miny caverns. . . .
> Amazing scene! Behold! the glooms disclose!
> I see the rivers in their infant beds!
> Deep, deep I hear them labouring to get free!
> I see the leaning strata. . . .
> (ll. 785, 799-800, 807-810)

The poet thus gives tacit assent to the view that reality can only be grasped in images. He asks his fancy to "view the wonders of the torrid zone" (*Summer,* l. 632), begs his readers to "see" what goes on there (l. 635), reminds

them repeatedly throughout his travel-book descriptions that he is offering "scenes," something to "behold." "To every purer eye," Thomson maintains, "The informing Author in his works appears" (*Spring,* ll. 859-860). That "purer eye" is presumably the eye of fancy, which, in association with reason, can lead the soul, under the guidance of Philosophy, to God. Fancy's eye receives

> The whole magnificence of heaven and earth,
> And every beauty, delicate or bold,
> Obvious or more remote, with livelier sense,
> Diffusive painted on the rapid mind.
> (*Summer,* ll. 1748-1752)

With livelier sense than what? The phrase suggests the poet's conviction that the impressions of fancy are more vivid, more intense, than literal sense impressions. "The mind's creative eye" (*Autumn,* l. 1016) has mysterious powers; it can exalt thought "Beyond dim earth" (l. 1013), can even "anticipate those scenes / Of happiness and wonder" (*Winter,* ll. 605-606) which the afterlife will provide.

Thomson recognizes that the eye of imagination can be so powerful as even to control physical vision. His description of human love stresses the extent to which the lover exists in an imaginary world, "Wrapt in gay visions of unreal bliss" (*Spring,* l. 988). When the youth despairs, all natural beauty disappears (ll. 1009-1013). Under the influence of jealousy, "internal vision" is "tainted" (l. 1084), and imaginary perceptions dominate love's victim. The visions of imagination can be dangerously as well as rewardingly compelling.

The peroration of *Winter,* which is, in a sense, the resolution of *The Seasons* as a whole, depends heavily on a visual metaphor. The reader is invited to "see" with his mind's eye the glories of the future, as "The great eternal scheme . . . To reason's eye refined clears up apace" (ll. 1046, 1049). As Thomson asserts triumphantly the supremacy of good in the universe, the ultimate benignity of the universal scheme, he relies on the antithesis between the unlimited vision which reason may, in some future dispensation, provide, and the "bounded view" which sees only "A little part" of the universe (ll. 1066-1067). The same antithesis has operated throughout the poem, with emphasis sometimes on the limitations of human vision, metaphorically or literally conceived, and sometimes on the infinite possibilities of reason's view. The "sage-instructed eye" can see the colors of the prism in the rainbow (*Spring,* ll. 210-211), but the botanist, even when he tries to number the kinds of herbage, only "Bursts his blind way" through the forest (l. 228). Not even the power of education and reason is sufficient to enable human beings fully to see what nature offers. Even the smallest part of Creative Wisdom's works exceeds the narrow vision of the mind of Ignorance (*Summer,* ll. 321-323), but not the wisest of men possesses the "universal eye" which can sweep "at once the unbounded scheme of things" (ll. 329-330). No one has *seen* the Great Chain of Being; man can only draw analogies from the evidence of his senses, recognize that God's wisdom "shines as lovely on our minds / As on our smiling eyes his servant-sun" (ll. 340-341). Yet to the "exulting eye" of those with philosophic minds, "a fairer world" than the vulgar can know "Displays its charms" (*Summer,* ll. 1385-1388). If fancy's eye provides the panorama of heaven and earth which leads man to awareness of his Creator, reason's eye can trace "The chain of causes and effects to Him, . . . who alone Possesses being" (ll. 1746-1748). It becomes finally irrelevant, then, that no one has literally seen the Great Chain of Being: reason, like imagination, provides a capacity closely analogous to sight. The philosophic man is "intent to gaze Creation through" (*Summer,* ll. 1784-1785); the "inward view" (l. 1788) of Philosophy provides visions even of "the ideal kingdom" (l. 1789), although it cannot penetrate where God has set obscuring cloud (ll. 1788-1789). The poet begs Nature to "show" her workings, to allow him to "scan" her laws, to light his "blind way" through the deep and upward, to open all the universe to his "ravished eye" (*Autumn,* ll. 1357-1366).

The eye, then, provides for Thomson an image for man's pettiness and for his greatness. The *significance* of sight is, characteristically, at least as important to him as the actual revelations the sense provides; those revelations, to be really meaningful, must, Thomson clearly feels, be immediately commented on by the reason as an organizing or an analytical faculty. At the beginning of *Winter,* the poet expresses his desire to fill the "judging ear / With bold description and with manly thought!" (ll. 28-29). His attempts to unite the two, to express his sense of how necessarily they must be related, to a large extent controls both the structure and the selectivity of *The Seasons.*

A. S. P. Woodhouse (essay date 1965)

SOURCE: "Religion and Poetry, 1660-1780," in *The Poet and His Faith: Religion and Poetry in England from Spenser to Eliot and Auden,* The University of Chicago Press, 1965, pp. 123-59.

[*In the excerpt below, Woodhouse finds Thomson's poetry to represent the synthesis of several religious and aesthetic strands which eventually saw their culmination in William Wordsworth's* Prelude.]

With the spaciousness of the *Georgics* as precedent, James Thomson writes his poem on the seasons, mingling scenes from nature and rural life with philosophic reflections on nature and the God of nature. In these reflections the influence of Shaftesbury is dominant, but it is joined by that of Newton. Indeed, as McKillop has shown, all the major currents of religio-philosophic thought as applied to nature meet in *The Seasons*; and the reflections are supported by a more immediate response to the variety, grandeur, and beauty of nature than is found in the rather labored paragraphs of Shaftesbury. Though the subject is well worth pursuing in detail, we can afford here no more than a quotation from *A Hymn,* in which various currents of thought mingle and merge: a Shaftesburian sense of God's immanence, a Newtonian sense of his direction

and control, the older traditions of God's power and goodness as revealed in the work of his hand, and of all his creatures as owing and paying him praise, and a sense of progression as the mark of nature's life, culminating in an apocalyptic note.

These, as they change, Almighty Father! these
Are but the varied God. The rolling year
Is full of thee. Forth in the pleasing Spring
Thy Beauty walks, thy Tenderness and Love. . . .

Then comes thy Glory in the Summer months,
With light and heat refulgent. Then thy sun
Shoots full perfection through the swelling year,
And oft thy voice in dreadful thunder speaks. . . .

Thy Bounty shines in Autumn unconfin'd,
And spreads a common feast for all that lives.
In Winter, awful thou! with clouds and storms
Around thee thrown, tempest o'er tempest roll'd.
Majestic darkness! On the whirlwind's wing
Riding sublime, thou bidst the world adore. . . .
Mysterious round! what skill, what force divine,
Deep-felt in these appear! . . .
But wandering oft with brute unconscious gaze,
Man marks not thee, marks not the mighty hand
That, ever busy, wheels the silent spheres,
Works in the secret deep, shoots streaming
      thence
The fair profusion that o'erspreads the Spring,
Flings from the sun direct the flaming day,
Feeds every creature, hurls the tempest forth,
And, as on earth this grateful change revolves,
With transport touches all the springs of life.

  Nature attend! join, every living soul
Beneath the spacious temple of the sky,
In adoration join, and ardent raise
One general song. . . .
Still sing the God of Seasons as they roll. . . .
Since God is ever present, ever felt
In the void waste as in the city full,
And where he vital spreads there must be joy.
When even at last the solemn hour shall come,
And wing my mystic flight to future worlds,
I cheerful will obey. . . .
            I cannot go
Where universal love smiles not around,
Sustaining all yon orbs and all their sons
From seeming evil still educing good,
And better thence again, and better still,
In infinite progression. But I lose
Myself in him, in light ineffable!
Come then, expressive Silence, muse his praise.

Here natural religion has taken the place of revealed; nature is itself a sufficient revelation; and with revealed religion has disappeared that realistic—sometimes even excessive—sense of evil, which finds expression in the Christian dogma of man's Fall, accompanied by nature's dislocation, and of the imperative need of redemption by Christ. Fallen man can find in fallen nature, so runs the orthodox reply, only a snare and pitfall; what Shaftesbury, Thomson, and their fellows attribute to man in general can be truly experienced only by the redeemed: for the regenerate—and for them alone—nature itself is transfigured. This is the burden of William Cowper's criticism of such lines as I have quoted. It is significant, however, that Cowper writes under the influence of the Evangelical revival. More moderate Anglicans were less inclined to attack the excesses of Shaftesburian natural theology and natural ethics than tacitly to recognize allies in the struggle against materialism, mechanism, and the atheism (as they did not scruple to call it) of the tradition of Hobbes and Mandeville.

Thomson was but one of a series of poets who responded to the influence of Shaftesbury, but he will serve as sufficient example. In *The Seasons* he established the tradition of the long descriptive and reflective poem in blank verse which centered in nature and reached out from the individual scene to contemplate the scheme of things in its larger aspects: the tradition which culminates in Wordsworth's *Prelude*.

John Chalker (essay date 1969)

SOURCE: "Thomson's *Seasons,*" in *The English Georgic: A Study in the Development of a Form,* The Johns Hopkins Press, 1969, pp. 90-140.

[*In the following essay, Chalker examines the influence of Virgil's* Georgics *upon* The Seasons *"in order to show more clearly how Thomson's 'unspectacular competence' works, in other words to consider more fully the form of the poem."*]

Thirteen years after the publication of *Windsor Forest* Thomson brought out *Winter* and by 1730 *The Seasons* in its first version was complete. It was a poem which achieved and long retained an extraordinary popularity. There were often more than eight editions a year until the mid-nineteenth century, and there was a total of considerably more than three hundred separate editions in the

hundred years from 1750-1850. It was frequently illustrated, and the illustrations range from grand designs by William Kent to humble woodcuts by obscure artists. After nearly a century Hazlitt wrote that Thomson was, perhaps, the most popular of English poets because,

> he gives most of the poetry of natural description . . . treating a subject that all can understand, and in a way that is interesting to all alike, to the ignorant or the refined, because he gives back the impression which the things themselves make upon us in nature.

Yet what strikes the modern reader is not so much Thomson's faithful reflection of 'impressions' as the variety and complexity of the responses that nature evokes in the poet. Because of this variety *The Seasons* is one of the most difficult of works to characterize at all briefly, or to represent adequately by a passage in an anthology. Asked to choose some typical lines, one might, for example, select from *Spring* a picture of domestic fowl which is detailed, sharply etched, almost heraldic in its vividness, and which characteristically owes something to Milton's picture of the cock in *L'Allegro:*

> The careful Hen
> Calls all her chirping Family around,
> Fed and defended by the fearless Cock
> Whose Breast with Ardour flames, as on he walks
> Graceful, and crows Defiance. In the Pond
> The finely-checker'd Duck before her Train,
> Rows garrulous . . .
>
> (*Spring,* 1728, 714-20)

But it might be thought that sublimity is a commoner Thomsonian mood, the spacious sweep of emotion and style that is found so often in *Winter* and that produces great elevation:

> Thro' the black Night that sits immense around,
> Lash'd into Foam, the fierce-conflicting Brine
> Seems o'er a thousand raging Waves to burn.
> Meantime the Mountain-Billows, to the Clouds
> In dreadful tumult swell'd, Surge above Surge,
> Burst into Chaos with tremendous Roar,
> And anchor'd Navies from their Stations drive,
> Wild as the Winds, across the howling Waste
> Of mighty Waters . . .
>
> (*Winter,* 1746, 158-66)

Here again there is a strong Miltonic note, this time recalling *Paradise Lost,* which is heard in the syntax, the handling of the blank verse, and especially in the repetition of the phrase 'Surge above Surge'. The sense here of man's insignificance in the face of natural forces is common enough in *The Seasons:* it occurs dramatically, for example, in the episode of Celadon and Amelia in *Summer* where Thomson tells the story of an innocent girl who was struck by lightning. On the other hand some readers might argue that the most common and characteristic note in *The Seasons* is that of winning pastoral softness and lush sensuous description. This is perhaps the dominant tone in **Spring,** as, for example, in Thomson's description of the flowers of the season which owes something to 'I know a bank whereon the wild tyme blows':

> Then seek the Bank where flowering Elders
> 　crowd,
> Where scatter'd wild the Lily of the Vale
> Its balmy Essence breathes, where Cowslips hang
> The dewy Head, where purple Violets lurk,
> With all the lowly Children of the Shade . . .
> 　　　　　　　　　(**Spring**, 1746, 446-50)

These are three very different moods, each of which might be thought of as typical, and obviously the list could be made much longer without any danger of overlapping. Most importantly there is no example so far of the feature of Thomson's verse which seems most clearly to point forwards to Wordsworth, the moralizing passages in which man is transformed by the power of nature,

> And all the Tumult of a guilty World,
> Tossed by ungenerous Passions sinks away.
> 　　　　　　　　　(**Spring**, 1744, 936-7)

This variety of styles points to one of the crucial questions that has to be faced in any attempt to give a critical account of **The Seasons**. What sort of poem is it that can contain such stylistic diversity, and is the diversity 'contained' in the sense that it is kept under control, or is it just contained in that everything is piled into an expandable suitcase of a poem?

A second question is raised by an apparent flabbiness in the structure of the work. Dr. Johnson said that 'the great defect of **The Seasons** is want of method'. Like *Tristram Shandy*, Thomson's poem is 'progressive and digressive too' and it sometimes seems that the digressive element is so strong as to inhibit progression altogether. The reader easily gets lost (or at least loses his sense of direction), and when he reaches the end he may have difficulty in ordering his memories of the ground that has been covered: the various episodes of the poem are not linked by an easily perceived structural thread. There is also some difficulty in deciding what the basic mode of the poem is. Is it fundamentally descriptive, reflective or didactic? Is there, in other words, a modal organization which in any way takes the place of a structural one?

Finally, **The Seasons** sometimes appears inconsistent in its enthusiasms. The most frequently criticized example is Thomson's apparently conflicting praise of pastoral innocence on the one hand and commercial progress on the other, and this conflict recurs in a way that cannot be ignored.

These are some of the critical problems put at their baldest, and they point to real qualities in the work itself, indeed to central elements in its make-up. In this chapter these problems will be examined in the light of **The Seasons'** relationship to the Virgilian tradition, and it may be suggested in anticipation that, although Thomson's poem lacks the formal Virgilian structure that is so prominent in *Cyder* or *The Fleece*, it is at once the most thoroughgoing, the most complex, and the most sensitively serious eighteenth-century imitation of the *Georgics*.

Writing in *The Background to Thomson's Seasons* A. D. McKillop remarked that

> we often overlook the unspectacular competence of the eighteenth century in adapting or even creating literary genres for its own needs. The L'Allegro/Il Penseroso model, the more expository parts of *Paradise Lost* and the *Georgics* gave Thomson his scheme.

More recently, [in the chapter "The Smiling God" in *The Happy Man, Vol. II: Studies in the Metamorphoses of a Classical Ideal, 1700-1760* (1958)] Maren-Sofie Røstvig accepted the main lines of this account of **The Seasons'** origins, but introduced some modifications:

> Thomson's true originality consisted in creating a new poetic form for already well-known poetic themes. While Sir John Denham had hit upon a new loco-descriptive genre (following the example of Casimire Sarbiewski) by expanding the limits of the Horatian philosophic lyric, James Thomson went even further by merging the Horatian ode (in the form established by Milton's companion poems as well as in the expanded form popularized by Denham and Pope) with the classical Georgic and with the new type of philosophical poem on the Creation which grew so popular in the eighteenth century.

Although both critics acknowledge the Virgilian influence (as indeed Durling had previously done) they do not attempt to show, because their preoccupations are otherwise, how widely pervasive the Georgic influence is or how it affects the form and feeling of the poem. I propose first to trace the influence of the *Georgics* in order to show more clearly how Thomson's 'unspectacular competence' works, in other words to consider more fully the form of the poem.

As early as the Preface to the second edition of **Winter** (June, 1726) Thomson specifically acknowledged his use of the *Georgics* as a model:

> I know no Subject more elevating, more amusing; more ready to awake the poetical Enthusiasm, the philosophical Reflection, and the moral Sentiment, than the Works of Nature. . . . It was this Devotion to the Works of Nature that, in his Georgicks, inspired the rural Virgil to write so inimitably. . . .

Here Thomson is thinking primarily of subject matter, but the question arises of the formal relationship between the *Georgics* and Thomson's poem.

To make a list of the passages in **The Seasons** which were written under direct Georgic influence is a reasonably straightforward exercise. In **Spring,** for example, a list would include:

> 1. The description of the onset of Spring (1728, 32-43).

2. The exaltation of agriculture (1728, 65-75).

3. Some of the practical advice, for example that on destroying insects (1728, 112-35).

4. The account of the signs of the weather (1728, 169-210).

5. The account of the Golden Age and the contrast with 'these Iron Times' (1728, 259-379).

6. The fishing section (1744, 377-440).

7. The account of the 'Passion of the Groves' and the loves of the beasts (1728, 534-776).

8. The sections in praise of rural retirement (1744, 901-59 and 1158-62).

These are the most important passages and there are others that have a decided although less pronounced Georgic colouring. However, even taken on their own these passages form a very substantial section of the poem: 402 lines are directly modelled on the *Georgics* themselves and a further sixty-two (those on fishing) on material which belongs directly to the Georgic tradition. That is to say that in a poem of 1,170 lines 464 are recognizably Georgic in kind and the character of the poem that Thomson is writing is thus overwhelmingly established. It is also significant that some of the characteristically Georgic materials (that on fishing and a passage on the pleasures of retirement near the end of the poem) were added only in 1744. In other words the poet continued, even when revising the work, to emphasize its Georgic origins. This was not a phase that Thomson grew out of, nor was it a decorative impulse that came to him late in the poem's development. The Georgic influence is important from beginning to end of *Spring's* composition.

In *Summer*, *Autumn* and *Winter* the Georgic influence does not dominate the poems so completely but it remains very considerable. In *Summer* five extended passages show direct Virgilian influence: the haymaking and sheep-shearing episodes (1744, 352-422); the account of the plague (1744, 1044-94); the signs of the weather (1744, 1108-35); the formal praise of England (1744, 1430-1593), and, finally, the contrast of the Golden and Iron Ages (1727, 1104-24). In addition the influence of the *rerum cognoscere causas* notion, and consequent enthusiasm for scientific speculation, from the second *Georgic* is clear at two points (1727, 21-30 and 1125-46). The retirement passage (1744, 1371-1429) also derives ultimately from Georgics II (although certainly with a good deal of modification by Thomson) and it leads, in lines already cited above, into a section in praise of England which is in places a paraphrase of Virgil's praise of Italy:

> Rich is thy Soil, and merciful thy Clime;
> Thy Streams unfailing in the Summer's Drought;
> Unmatch'd thy Guardian-Oaks; thy Valleys float

> With golden Waves. . . .
>
> 　　　　　　　　　　(1744, 1438-41)

Finally the exotic digressions in ll. 663/1040 probably have their structural justification with reference to Virgil. One remembers, for example, that Somerville later introduced the exotic digressions of *The Chace* with an appeal to Virgilian precedent. In *Summer*, then, it is true to say that the *Georgics* are continuously brought to the reader's mind and that remembrance of Virgil's poem is an important factor in determining his response to Thomson's work.

In *Autumn* there occurs (1730, 1131/1269) the most extended piece of Virgilian paraphrase in the whole of *The Seasons*—the version, almost a translation, of the passage *O fortunatos agricolas* (O happy husbandmen) from *Georgics II*. This is a positive and detailed statement of Thomson's attitude to country life, and the fact that he bases himself so closely on Virgil (and that the section is placed at a most emphatic point, at the end of *Autumn*) shows how seriously he looked upon his relationship to his major source. The treatment of retirement here is reinforced by further passages at lines 641-70 (on Dodington's estate) and lines 902ff:

> *Thus* solitary, and in pensive guise,
> Oft let me wander o'er the russet mead,
> *And* thro' the *sadden'd* grove. . . .

In terms of the number of examples *Winter* is less obviously influenced by the *Georgics* than other sections of the *Seasons*, but even so the debt is clear. First, lines 118-194 (1726) deal with signs of the weather; more extensively lines 794-949 (1744) give, often with close approximation to Virgil, an account of the Scythian Winter; and, more generally, there is the long retirement passage beginning at line 424 (1744). And, in discussing *Winter*, of course, one also has the supporting evidence of Thomson's Preface which has already been quoted.

This extensive use of derivative thematic material is supported by direct references to Virgil's example, and by occasional echoing of individual lines. In lines which form part of the original 1728 version of *Spring* Thomson defends the agricultural aspect of his work by reference to Virgil:

> 　　　　Nor, Ye who live
> In Luxury and Ease, in Pomp and Pride,
> Think these lost Themes unworthy of your Ear.
> 'Twas such as these the Rural Maro sung
> To the full Roman Court, in all it's height
> Of Elegance and Taste. The sacred Plow
> Employ'd the Kings and Fathers of Mankind,
> In antient Times.
>
> 　　　　　　　　　　(1728, 52-9)

Very early in the final form of *The Seasons*, therefore, the Virgilian reference is made explicit. In effect the reader is told to be aware of this influence as he reads. And in the final version of *Spring*, in the passage on fishing which Thomson added in 1744, this explicit acknowledgement is supported by a further reference:

> Then seek the Bank where flowering Elders
>   croud,
> Where scatter'd wild the Lilly of the Vale
> It's balmy Essence breathes . . .
> There let the Classic Page thy Fancy lead
> Thro' rural Scenes; such as the Mantuan Swain
> Paints in immortal Verse and matchless Song . . .
>   (1744, 444-55)

By his revision Thomson makes it even more difficult to
ignore Virgil. The lines are also interesting because they
look back very clearly to *Rural Sports* and, taken in conjunction with a reference to Phillips' *Cyder* in **Autumn,**
they show Thomson as aware that he is writing not only
with Virgil in mind, but also in a tradition of English
Georgic verse.

Echoes of individual lines occur frequently: many have
been noted by Zippel and it is sufficient to give one or
two examples. Compare, for example,

> Forth fly the tepid Aires; and unconfin'd,
> Unbinding Earth, the moving Softness strays . . .
>   (*Spring,* 1728, 32-3)

with

> parturit almus ager Zephyrique tepentibus auris
> laxant arva sinus;
>
>   (II, 330-1)

The bountiful land brings forth, and beneath the West's
warm breezes the fields loosen their bosoms.

or

>   his lusty Steers
> Drives from their Stalls, to where the well-us'd
>   Plow
> Lies in the Furrow, loosen'd from the Frost.
>   (*Spring,* 1728, 35-7)

with

> Vere novo, gelidus canis cum montibus umor
> liquitur et Zephyro putris se glaeba resolvit,
> depresso incipiat iam tum mihi taurus aratro
> ingemere, et sulco attritus splendescere vomer.
>   (I, 43-6)

In the dawning Spring, when icy streams trickle from
snowy mountains, and the crumbling clod breaks at
the Zephyr's touch, even then would I have my bull
groan over the deep driven plough, and the share glisten
when rubbed by the furrow.

This sort of echoing would not be particularly significant
were it not for the more extended and explicit Virgilian
references elsewhere. But, taken in conjunction with the

material that has already been cited, its importance (as an
element in the total scheme of the poem) is clearly greater.

What has been said so far has established that the Georgic
influence on *The Seasons,* calculated in terms of derivative thematic material, direct reference and echoing of
details, is continuous, that the reader is constantly made
aware of Virgil while he is reading the poem, and that he
is invited to compare Virgil's treatment of the themes
with Thomson's. The rest of this discussion will involve
an attempt to estimate the importance of this influence
and the way in which full recognition and acceptance of
it may be expected to modify our critical attitude to the
poem.

The main discussion will be divided into three sections
dealing in turn with three themes which are central to
Thomson's purpose. These are: the contrast between the
Golden and Iron ages; the theme of patriotic exaltation;
the theme of retirement. A consideration of these three
leading ideas and their relation to the *Georgics* will be
found to lead to a consistent interpretation of the poem as
a whole.

But first it will be as well to formulate as explicitly as
possible the kind of critical problem that this discussion
can be expected to illuminate. The problem is met acutely
in lines like these in praise of agriculture:

> Ye generous Britons, venerate the Plow!
> And o'er your Hills, and long withdrawing
>   Valves,
> Let Autumn spread his Treasures to the Sun,
> Luxuriant and unbounded. As the Sea,
> Far thro' his azure, turbulent Domain,
> Your Empire owns, and from a thousand Shores
> Wafts all the Pomp of Life into your Ports,
> So with superior Boon may your rich Soil,
> Exuberant Nature's better Blessings pour
> O'er every Land; the naked Nations cloath,
> And be th'exhaustless Granary of the world!
>   (*Spring,* 1744, 65-75)

The lines make an immediate impression by their complete assurance (a hostile critic might say by their bland
complacency). This assurance is felt, in the first place,
through the firm control that Thomson retains in handling
the extended comparison: 'As the Sea, etc. . . . . So with
superior Boon, etc.' The Miltonic expansiveness of syntax reflects the vastness of the idea itself, and, although
this is a fairly obvious effect it is an obviousness that
works, especially in the second half of the comparison
where a rising rhythm is maintained, first by the adjecti-
val form and placing in its line of *exuberant*

>   may your rich Soil,
> Exuberant, Nature's better Blessings pour. . . .

and secondly the rhythmic effect of the syntactic catalogue
('Blessings pour/O'er every Land, the naked Nations cloath,
etc.') which allows a sense of complete rhythmic resolu-

tion, a full close in the last line. Rhythmic emphasis is given by the frequent alliteration: 'Pomp . . . Ports; superior . . . Soil; better Blessings; naked Nations', and this emphasis is increased by the juxtaposition, in the last two cases, of the alliterating words. Finally a sense of the spontaneity of the prosperity that is described, of man as the passive recipient, is induced by the words themselves: the sea *wafts;* the soil *pours* and this sense of gratuitous vitality is increased by *boon, exuberant, exhaustless.*

The problem is that, taken by themselves, the lines seem to breathe a spirit of jingoistic patronage. Britain is the end towards which all Creation ministers and she must treat outsiders with benevolent compassion. There is difficulty in deciding whether this is the true or the only feeling in the lines, how they relate to the rest of the poem, and how far they are justified both intrinsically and in relation to the work as a whole. And the same sort of question is constantly arising: it occurs, for example, in *Summer:*

> Happy Britannia! where the Queen of Arts,
> Inspiring Vigour, Liberty, abroad,
> Walks thro' the Land of Heroes unconfin'd,
> And scatters Plenty with unsparing Hand.
> Rich is thy Soil, and merciful thy Skies . . .
> (1727, 498-502)

Writing on this passage one of Thomson's most recent critics, Patricia Spacks, says:

> The fact that the digression was 'noble' and that it was undoubtedly agreeable to Thomson's contemporaries, in no way lessens its digressiveness or the sense of inappropriateness with which one plods through it. The scheme of values upon which the passage is based has virtually no relation to the scheme underlying the rest of the poem.

This condemnation forms part of an extended discussion of an alleged inconsistency in Thomson in his attitude to Primitivism and Progress and Miss Spacks concludes that Thomson's centre of interest gradually changed from Nature to Man during the poem's various revisions and that this change 'was marked by the development of emotional and intellectual confusion'. This idea is a fundamental and common one, and I quote Miss Spacks here simply because she is its most recent and most cogent proponent. But it seems to me to show a failure to sympathize with Thomson's own attitudes and intentions and also seriously to underestimate the emotional content of passages like that in praise of Britain, just quoted.

These may be taken as typical of many intransigent passages in *The Seasons* and it is with their interpretation, with difficulties having to do with the consistency and coherence of the poem as a whole that this discussion is now concerned. The starting point will be Thomson's attitude to Primitivism and to the Golden Age.

The vision of the Golden Age that we get in the *Seasons* is essentially literary: it is a traditional imaginative experience which is necessarily conceived by Thomson in terms of Virgil, Ovid and Milton. The Miltonic frame of reference—largely that of *Paradise Lost,* Books, IV, V and IX—is the most obvious, because it is reinforced by the Miltonic suggestions of Thomson's blank verse. Adam's sleep was 'from pure digestion bred, / And temperate vapours bland'; Thomson's primal men rise "vigorous as the sun' when their light slumbers are 'gently fum'd away'. In Milton's Eden all the beasts of the wood play together in happy amity; in Thomson's Golden Age

> The Herds and Flocks, commixing, play'd
> secure.
> (*Spring*, 1728, 287)

Just as in Paradise 'Blossoms and Fruits at once of golden hue / Appeerd', so, Thomson says, Spring once

> Green'd all the Year; and Fruits and Blossoms
> blush'd
> In social Sweetness on the self-same Bough.
> (*Spring*, 1727, 366-7)

And the reader may be reminded at this point not only of Milton, but also of Spenser's Garden of Adonis:

> There is continuall spring and harvest there
> Continuall, both meeting at one time:
> For both the boughs do laughing blossoms bear . . .
> And eke attonce the heavy trees they clime,
> Which seem to labour under their fruits load.
> (*Faerie Queene, III,* VI, xlii)

One constantly feels the pressure of analogues like these when reading Thomson's poem, and, because he works so much in terms of literary reference, it is important, if one is to define Thomson's attitude to the Golden Age, to establish what general attitudes to primitivism and progress he is drawing upon. What general ideas is Thomson referring to?

For the polar viewpoints one can most usefully take Lucretius and Ovid. In *De Rerum Natura* the balance is heavily weighted in favour of the Age of Iron: the notion of a progression from a state of nature to one of civilization is very clearly marked. It is true that the men of ancient days were strong and healthy and were pleased to eat nuts and berries that Nature provided in abundance: there was then no need of regular work. But the disadvantages were overwhelmingly greater. In his primitive state Man was unsociable, a solitary hunter, and his life was nasty, brutish and short. It was only in the course of time that communal feeling developed, but eventually men did begin to build huts and to use skins and fire, marriage was established and the human race began to mellow.

> tunc et amicitiem coeperunt iungere aventes
> finitimi inter se nec laedere nec violari. . . .
> (*De Rerum Natura*, V, 1019-20)

> Then also neighbours began eagerly to join friendship amongst themselves to do no hurt and suffer no violence.

The line of development from native simplicity to a sophisticated social contract is straightforward and all that is valuable in life is thought of as springing from men's efforts. Sea-faring, laws, defence, the arts, all were acquired gradually:

> sic unumquicquid paulatim protrahit aetas
> in medium ratioque in luminis erigit oras.
> namque alid ex alio clarescere corde videbant
> artibus, ad summum donec venere cacumen.
>
> (*De Rerum Natura*, V, 1454-7)

So by degrees time brings up before us every single thing, and reason lifts it into the precincts of light. For their intellect saw one thing after another grow famous amongst the arts, until they came to their highest point.

Sometimes, for example in **Autumn**, when he describes the rewards of industry, Thomson's thought seems to take on an almost entirely Lucretian cast. At first Man was 'naked, and helpless'

> . . . the sad barbarian, roving, mix'd
> With beasts of prey; or for his acorn-meal
> Fought the fierce tusky boar: a shivering wretch!
> Aghast, and comfortless. . . .
>
> (**Autumn**, 1730, 57-60)

but as he developed the social virtues progress became possible until

> . . . every form of cultivated life
> In order set, protected, and inspir'd,
> Into perfection wrought. Uniting all,
> Society grew numerous, high, polite,
> And happy.
>
> (**Autumn**, 1730, 110-14)

The progressive point of view could hardly be put more clearly.

For the opposite attitude one can turn to Ovid who, in the *Metamorphoses,* emphasizes the excellence, both material and moral, of primitive Man:

> Aurea prima sata est aetas, quae vindice nullo,
> sponte sua, sine lege fidem rectumque colebat.
>
> (*Metamorphoses*, I, 89-90)

Golden was that first age, which, with no one to
  compel,
without a law, of its own will, kept faith and did
  the right.

Then rivers flowed with milk and nectar and honey dripped from the green oak tree. When this ideal, harmonious, state was succeeded by the Age of Iron there was a complete moral disaster: modesty, truth and faith disappeared from the earth and in their place came tricks, plots, violence and greed. The Iron Age is certainly seen as one of tremendous energy. Only now did men begin to build ships and sail the seas, to farm and discover the use of

minerals, but all this power led to evil because the moral harmony of the Golden Age had been completely shattered:

> victa iacet pietas, et virgo caede madentis
> ultima caelestum terras Astraea reliquit.
>
> (*Metamorphoses*, I, 149-50)

Piety lay vanquished, and the maiden Astraea,
  last of
the immortals, abandoned the blood-soaked earth.

The contrast with Lucretius is complete, yet, just as one can find Lucretian passages in Thomson, so one can find sections which seem purely Ovidian. When, for example, Thomson turns in **Spring** from the Golden Age to 'these Iron Times, / These Dregs of Life!' and describes the psychology of fallen Man, the picture that he gives is a despairing one:

> . . . the Human Mind
> Has lost that Harmony ineffable,
> Which forms the Soul of Happiness; and all
> Is off the Poise within; the Passions all
> Have burst their Bounds; and Reason half
>   extinct,
> Or impotent, or else approving, sees
> The foul Disorder. Anger storms at large,
> Without an equal Cause. . . .
>
> (**Spring**, 1728: 327-34)

Obviously there is a conflict here, but it is not one which Thomson left unresolved, and he found the resolution in his major source, Virgil's *Georgics*. On the subject of the Golden and the Iron Ages we find in Virgil attitudes of greater complexity than in either Lucretius or Ovid. There is a vivid contrast presented in *Georgics* I between the two Ages, but it is not a straightforward shift from idyllic pleasure to unrewarding labour, or from brutality to social sophistication. Certainly the Golden Age was a time when the Earth 'yielded all, of herself', and when material prosperity was matched by moral harmony: it was unlawful even to divide the fields and men worked for the common good. But this idyllic harmony passed and then Jove made life hard and difficult:

> ille malum virus serpentibus addidit atris,
> praedarique lupos iussit pontumque moveri,
> mellaque decussit foliis, ignemque removit,
> et passim rivis currentia vina repressit. . . .
>
> (*Georgics*, I, 129-32)

'Twas he that in black serpents put their deadly venom,
bade the wolves plunder and the ocean swell; shook
honey from the leaves, hid fire from view, and stopped
the wine that ran everywhere in streams. . . .

However, this change in Man's condition was not purposeless. Jove acted as he did for a reason, and it is a reason that rendered the movement from a Golden to an Iron Age ambivalent. Jove made Man's life difficult in order that all the arts of civilization might be developed:

ut varias usus meditando extunderet artis
paulatim et sulcis frumenti quaereret herbam,
et silicis venis abstrusum excuderet ignem.
(*Georgics*, I, 133-35)

so that practice, by taking thought, might little by little
hammer out divers arts, might seek the corn-blade in
furrows, and strike forth from veins of flint the hidden
fire.

Now men could learn how to make boats, to hunt, to fish
and to build:

labor omnia vicit
improbus et duris urgens in rebus egestas.
(*Georgics*, I, 145-46)

Toil conquered the world, unrelenting toil, and want
that pinches when life is hard.

In other words an age of naïve, effortless and therefore
morally neutral happiness was succeeded by a time of
moral triumph in which Man, by his own efforts, became
the master of the world. Clearly there can be no simple
attitude to the change of values described by Virgil because the ideas themselves are complex.

The fourth *Eclogue,* in its forecast of the passing of the
Iron Age and the return to the Golden, has a similar
ambiguity of attitude, and Virgil is clearly unwilling to
give up or utterly condemn either Age. On the one hand
the birth of the wonder-child which the poet celebrates
will be heralded by a bounteous nature, and this excites
Virgil's imagination. Everywhere there will be spontaneous abundance and a new natural harmony in which,

ipsae lacte domum referent distenta capellae
ubera, nec magnos metuent armenta leones;
ipsa tibi blandos fundent cunabula flores.
(*Eclogues*, IV, 21-3)

Uncalled, the goats shall bring home their udders
swollen with milk, and the herds shall not fear huge
lions; unasked, thy cradle shall pour forth flowers for
thy delight.

But despite the excitement which this forecast generates
Virgil is not prepared to give up too easily his satisfaction
in Man's Iron Age triumphs. For a time, he says, some
few traces of sin will remain to urge men to sail the seas,
to build walled cities and to cultivate the earth:

alter erit tum Tiphys, et altera quae vehat Argo
delectos heroas; erunt etiam altera bella
atque iterum ad Troiam magnus mittetur
   Achilles.
(*Eclogues*, IV, 34-6)

A second Tiphys shall then arise, and a second Argo
to carry chosen heroes; a second warfare, too, shall
there be, and again shall a great Achilles be sent to
Troy.

Finally, after these, the ultimate products of Man's state
of sin, the Golden Age really will return in all its spontaneous magnificence. The very wool itself will no longer
need to be dyed: the ram will change his colour at will
from 'blushing purple' to 'saffron yellow', and

sponte sua sandyx pascentis vestiet agnos.
(*Eclogues*, IV, 45)

of its own will shall scarlet clothe the grazing
   lambs

Obviously there is a conflict of values in Virgil's mind,
and there is no question, in the *Eclogue* or in the *Georgics,* of either the Golden or the Iron Ages being given
automatic precedence. Nostalgia for an idyllic past (or
future) is entirely blended with pride in a vigorous present.
The benefits that work can bring are in some ways greater
than those accessible in a prelapsarian state, but, of course,
the cost too is high. Consequently a man is forced to
entertain contradictory feelings; there is no simple solution.

When one turns again to Thomson one finds that, despite
the Lucretian and Ovidian elements that have already been
illustrated, his central position is a Virgilian one. He has
intense nostalgia for the Golden Age (and therefore feels
very acutely the occasional golden manifestations of external nature), but he is also very much aware of the
potentialities of the Iron Age in which he lives. Man in
the historical period is a worker and organizer capable of
transforming his environment, and the comparative stability and prosperity of modern life is due to his efforts.
In the past Britain was disunited and disrupted by internecine warfare, but now, because of organized labour and
the will to prosperity,

. . . Wealth and Commerce lift their golden
   Head,
And o'er our Labours Liberty and Law
Illustrious watch, the Wonder of a World!
(***Spring***, 1728, 792-4)

The basis of social and political unity is economic success. This is made clear many times: for example, in
Thomson's comment on the sheep-shearing scene in ***Summer*** (an episode added in 1744), that 'hence Britannia
sees / Her solid Grandeur rise.' (423-4) It is important,
critically, to accept that when Thomson writes in this way
he is not gratuitously adulterating a descriptive genre. The
combination of pastoralism and progressivism, and consideration of the relationship between them, was one that
he found in his formal model, and it was because the
combination was important to him that he introduced it
into his poem. The motif of *labor omnia vicit* is fundamental to the interpretation of life presented in ***The Seasons,*** and in it Thomson, following Virgil, finds a resolution for many of the apparent contradictions of his subject
matter.

In the description of the tropics we find the idea treated

from an original point of view. The tropics are shown as luxuriating in a prelapsarian fertility, so rich indeed that it is 'beyond whate'er / The Poets imag'd in the Golden Age' (**Summer**, 1744, 678-9). The picture is completely idyllic in its atmosphere of casual abundance:

> . . . Gardens smile around, and cultur'd Fields;
> And Fountains gush; and careless Herds and Flocks
> Securely stray; a World within itself,
> Disdaining all Assault . . .
> A Land of Wonders! which the Sun still eyes
> With Ray direct, as of the lovely Realm
> Inamour'd, and delighting there to dwell.
>
> (**Summer**, 1744, 762-75)

But the defects of this tropical paradise are seen just as clearly:

> But what avails this wondrous Waste of Wealth?
> . . . the softening Arts of Peace,
> Whate'er the humanizing Muses teach;
> The Godlike Wisdom of the temper'd Breast;
> Progressive Truth, the patient Force of Thought;
> Investigation calm, whose silent Powers
> Command the World; the Light that leads to Heaven;
> Kind equal Rule, the Government of Laws,
> And all-protecting Freedom, which alone
> Sustains the Name and Dignity of Man:
> These are not theirs.
>
> (**Summer**, 1744, 852-76)

The easy (although, of course, inaccessible) delights of innocence are rejected for the hard-won pleasures of experience. But this does not preclude intense longing for what is being given up—the 'odorous Woods, and shining Ivory Stores'. Indeed it is a condition of the paradoxical subject-matter which Thomson is dealing with that neither choice can be made without regret.

It is the same paradox that underlies apparent contradictions of attitude in **Winter**. Two remote northern races are described. First the Lapps who, after an idealized account of the northern summer, are described as a

> Thrice happy Race! by Poverty secur'd
> From legal Plunder and rapacious Power:
> In whom fell Interest never yet has sown
> The Seeds of Vice; whose spotless Swains ne'er knew
> Injurious Deed, nor, blasted by the Breath
> Of faithless Love, their blooming Daughters Woe.
>
> (**Winter**, 1744, 881-6)

This race, uncorrupted by contact with more progressive peoples, continues to live in a state of perfect moral harmony. Thomson is frequently criticized for including also in **Winter** a very different account of a primitive northern race. The remote Russians, 'the last of men', are present-

ed with an emphasis which is very far from idyllic:

> Here Human Nature wears it's rudest Form.
> Deep from the piercing Season sunk in Caves,
> Here by dull Fires, and with unjoyous Chear,
> They waste the tedious Gloom. Immers'd in Furs,
> Doze the gross Race. Nor sprightly Jest, nor Song,
> Nor Tenderness they know . . .
>
> (**Winter**, 1744, 940-54)

Here again the primary problem—for both Thomson and the reader—is the complexity of the subject itself. A life of remote and diligent labour cannot be given a single and immutable value. What Thomson does is to take the two extremes of near Arctic experience—the happiness of summer and the misery of dead winter—to express two possible but opposed values. The different significance of the two passages is clearly marked. The Lapps are thought of as living a frugal but adequate existence. Life is hard, but they are not destitute:

> They ask no more than simple Nature gives
>
> (**Winter**, 1744, 845)

and this is sufficient. The Russians, on the other hand, live where 'Human Nature wears it's rudest Form' in a state of almost total privation. After contemplating this Thomson reacts against the harshness of Scythian life and returns, quite legitimately, to his staple theme:

> What cannot active Government perform,
> New-moulding Man?
>
> (**Winter**, 1744, 950-1)

and to praise of Peter the Great's government.

Had Thomson presented contrasting passages of this kind in a straightforwardly descriptive poem they would undoubtedly have been confusing. But he is not being merely descriptive, and the whole tendency of his concern with primitivism and progress has to be seen in relation to the literary kind that he is fashioning. Since he has established the Georgic intentions of his work so clearly he is able to use Virgil's own resolution of the Golden/ Iron Age antithesis as the basis for an attitude which might be described as that of nostalgic progressivism.

Virgilian practice is also the inspiration behind a good deal of the overtly patriotic and political material. The most important source here is naturally Virgil's memorable passage in praise of Italy in *Georgics* II. In that passage Virgil finds four main reasons for the intensity of his patriotic feeling. First there is a rhapsodic appreciation of the natural beauty of the country, in which the Italian scene is interpreted in terms of Golden Age imagery. Italy is a country of eternal spring and summer: all is fruitful and nothing evil threatens the land, 'ravening tigers are far away, and the savage seed of lions.' Secondly, as might be expected, Virgil is proud of what Man has done to the country. Think too, he says, of all the noble cities that have been built by men. Thirdly, and springing from the first point, Virgil points to the country's abundant material wealth, her silver, copper and gold. Finally, he praises his countrymen and their martial triumphs and, greatest of all, Caesar himself who has been victorious in the farthest extremities of Asia. This last theme, praise of the present government of the country, is, as we have seen before, a recurrent one which is found, for example, in the opening invocation and also in the concluding lines.

In *Summer* Thomson has a fairly direct paraphrase of Virgil's patriotic section. The opening lines have already been quoted:

> Happy Britannia! where the Queen of Arts,
> Inspiring Vigour, Liberty, abroad,
> Walks thro' the Land of Heroes, unconfin'd,
> And scatters Plenty with unsparing Hand.
> Rich is thy Soil, and merciful thy Skies;
> Thy Streams unfailing in the Summer's Drought:
> Unmatch'd thy Guardian-Oaks: thy Vallies float
> With golden Waves; and on thy Mountains
>   Flocks
> Bleat, numberless: while, roving round their
>   Sides,
> Bellow the blackening Herds, in lusty Droves.
> Beneath, thy Meadows flame, and rise unquell'd,
> Against the Mower's Sythe. On every Hand,
> Thy Villas shine. Thy Country teems with
>   Wealth;
> And Property assures it to the Swain,
> Pleas'd, and unweary'd, in his certain Toil.
>   Full are thy Cities with the Sons of Art;
> And Trade, and Joy, in every busy Street,
> Mingling, are heard: even Drudgery, Himself,
> As at the Car He sweats, or dusty, hews
> The Palace-Stone, looks gay. Thy crowded Ports,
> Where rising Masts an endless Prospect yield,
> With Labour burn, and echo to the Shouts
> Of hurry'd Sailor, as He, hearty, waves
> His last Adieu, and, loosening every Sheet,
> Resigns the spreading Vessel to the Wind.
>
> Bold, firm, and graceful, are thy generous
>   Youth,
> By Hardship sinew'd . . .
>   (*Summer*, 1727, 498-524)

From this point Thomson gives an extended account of British heroes (and, more briefly, heroines), and ends with lines which owe something to Virgil and something to Shakespeare's John of Gaunt:

> Island of Bliss! amid the Subject Seas,
> That thunder round thy rocky Coasts, set up,
> At once the Wonder, Terror and Delight
> Of distant Nations . . .
>   (*Summer*, 1727, 585-8)

Again some difficulty may be felt in reconciling the notions of casual, Golden, abundance on the one hand and, on the other, riches won by hard labour; and there is no

doubt that Thomson does sometimes attribute to external nature a prelapsarian quality. In *Spring,* for example, there is a long list of flowers which gives a strong sense of the idyllic bountifulness of nature—a sense which is reinforced by pastoral echoes from Browne, Milton and Shakespeare. (1728, 485-507) Hangley Park is described as the 'British Tempe'; Dodington's seat in *Autumn* is lavishly abundant:

> . . . Autumn basks . . .
> Presents the downy peach; the purple plumb,
> With a fine blueish mist of animals
> Clouded; the ruddy nectarine; and dark,
> Beneath his ample leaf, the luscious fig.
> The vine too here her curling tendrils shoots;
> Hangs out her clusters, swelling to the south;
> And scarcely wishes for a warmer sky.
>   (*Autumn*, 1730, 662-70)

But again this idealistic treatment of the natural scene has to be seen against the background of rhapsodic Virgilian patriotism. The hyperbole is not incompatible, when considered in terms of literary tradition, with pleasure in British institutions and in the political aspect of national expansion. When Thomson prays,

> So with superior Boon may your rich Soil,
> Exuberant, Nature's better Blessings pour
> O'er every Land; the naked Nations cloath,
> And be th'exhaustless Granary of the World.
>   (*Spring*, 1728, 73-5)

he may be being over-optimistic, but he is certainly not showing any literary indecorum. On the contrary the blend of idealized natural description and nationalistic enthusiasm that we find in *The Seasons* is entirely characteristic of the 'kind' that Thomson is imitating. One may reasonably infer that he chose the 'kind' partly at least because it encouraged the particular combination of attitudes that was most congenial to him. In other words this combination, far from being the result of 'emotional and intellectual confusion' is one of the most conscious, consistent and completely realized elements in the poem.

The third main Georgic theme in *The Seasons,* that of retirement, is also closely linked with the Golden/Iron Age antithesis. Since Thomson's modifications of Virgilian attitudes are in this case particularly important, it will be as well to recall fairly precisely what Virgil says on the subject in the second *Georgic.*

The husbandman is happy in the first place, Virgil says, because he avoids the evils of an active life. He is 'far from the clash of arms' and from the anxiety of superfluous luxury. He is not constantly agitated by a desire for fame:

> Him no honours the people give can move, no purple
> of kings, no strife rousing brother to break with brother,
> no Dacian swooping down from his leagued Danube,
> no power of Rome, no kingdoms doomed to fall. . . .
>   (II, 495-8)

He gains 'an easy sustenance' and enjoys simple plea-sures—'repose without care . . . the ease of broad do-mains, caverns and living lakes and cool vales, the low-ing of the kine, and soft slumbers beneath the trees.' The unchanging cycle of the year makes for an ordered, stable life blest with domestic satisfactions:

> Meanwhile his dear children hang upon his kisses; his unstained home guards its purity.
>
> (II, 523)

The satisfactions of country life are typified in a little scene which shows the husbandman enjoying a holiday, 'stretched on the grass, with a fire in the midst'. Finally, this life is identified—and here we find the main Virgil-ian link with the previous section of this chapter—with prelapsarian perfection:

> Such a life the old Sabines once lived, such Remus and his brother . . . nay . . . such was the life golden Saturn lived on earth, while yet none had heard the clarion blare, none the sword-blades ring, as they were laid on the stubborn anvil.
>
> (II, 532-43)

With this hyperbolical praise of retirement as a re-cre-ation of the Golden Age the Second Book of the *Georgics* ends.

But interwoven with this idealization of retirement there is, rather incongruously it seems at first sight, praise of scientific speculation:

> But as for me—first above all, may the sweet Muses . . . take me to themselves and show me heaven's pathways. . . .
>
> (II, 475-7)

Understanding of the nature of the Universe is the highest good. If Virgil is unfit for this, then, he says, he will seek a life of retirement, and he repeats these priorities very memorably in lines 490-93:

> Felix qui potuit rerum cognoscere causas . . .
> fortunatus et ille, deos qui novit agrestis.
>
> Blessed is he who has been able to win knowledge of the causes of things . . . Happy too, is he who knows the woodland gods.

On the one hand there is pursuit of pure knowledge, and on the other a quiet life of useful labour.

How does this theme appear and what is its structural significance in *The Seasons*? That the theme itself was central to Thomson's conception of his poem is clear from the Preface to the second edition of *Winter*. Part of it has already been quoted. There is, says Thomson, 'no Subject more elevating, more amusing; more ready to awake the poetical Enthusiasm, the philosophical Reflection, and the moral Sentiment, than the Works of Nature.' The noblest poets of the past have relied upon this subject and,

For this Reason the best, both Antient, and Modern, Poets have been passionately fond of Retirement and Solitude.

And Thomson gives as examples the *Book of Job* and the *Georgics*, providing his own translation of the first of the passages in which Virgil sets forth the nature of the two acceptable ways of life as he sees them:

> Me may the Muses, my supreme Delight!
> Whose Priest, I am, smit with immense Desire,
> Snatch to their Care. . . .

Thomson was to paraphrase the same passage again in the final lines of *Autumn* and the themes and imagery of these lines, and indeed of the whole of this section of the *Georgics*, recur constantly throughout *The Seasons*.

In the first version of *Winter* the theme is comparatively undeveloped, but we find lines which involve a coales-cence of the two Virgilian notions:

> Nature! great Parent! whose directing Hand
> Rolls round the Seasons of the changeful Year,
> How mighty! how majestick are thy Works!
> With what a pleasing Dread they swell the Soul,
> That sees, astonish'd! and, astonish'd sings!
>
> (1726, March, 143-7)

The significance of Nature here is that it provokes won-der and consequently leads to scientific questioning:

> You too, ye Winds! that now begin to blow,
> With boisterous Sweep, I raise my Voice to
> you . . .
> Where are your aerial Magazines reserv'd,
> Against the Day of Tempest perilous?
>
> (1726, March, 148-51)

The study of Nature leads insistently to Virgil's desire to 'know the causes of things' and, in view of the June Preface it can be assumed that the lines were written under the direct influence of the *Georgics*.

Another manifestation of the retirement theme, also in the first version of *Winter,* is found in the passage beginning at line 253. Here Thomson both coalesces the two strands of Virgilian idealism and introduces his own modifica-tions. He wishes to retire to a life of literary and historical study, a life of cultured ease:

> Now, all amid the Rigours of the Year
> In the wild Depth of Winter, while without
> The ceaseless Winds blow keen, be my Retreat
> A rural, shelter'd, solitary, Scene;
> Where ruddy Fire, and beaming Tapers join
> To chase the chearless Gloom: there let me sit,
> And hold high Converse with the Mighty Dead,
> Sages of ancient Time, as Gods rever'd. . . .
>
> (1726, March, 253-60)

This leads to praise of Socrates, Lycurgus, Cato, Homer,

and Virgil as they pass in a visionary procession in front of Thomson's eyes. This emphasis upon retirement as the instigator of philosophical and scientific meditation is continued in the first version of *Summer*. Thomson gives an account of the influence of the Sun upon animate and even inanimate Nature:

> The very dead Creation, from thy Touch,
> Assumes a mimic life. . . .
>
>   (1727, 145-6)

He leads from this to praise of God and follows with lines that echo Virgil clearly and yet with a difference:

> To Me be Nature's Volume, wide, display'd;
> And to peruse the broad, illumin'd Page;
> Or haply catching Inspiration thence,
> Some easy Passage, raptur'd, to translate,
> My Sole Delight; as thro' the falling Glooms,
> Pensive, I muse, or, with the rising Day,
> On Fancy's Eagle-Wing, excursive, soar.
>
>   (1727, 176-82)

Perusal of Nature's 'broad, illumin'd Page' leads to 'knowledge of the causes of things'. Whereas Virgil had seen scientific understanding as an alternative to retirement, for Thomson the two are inextricably bound together, and they lead forward to poetic *rapture*.

The notion of retirement as a contemplative condition which harmonizes the passions and induces a psychological state favourable to mental and spiritual insight is soon carried further in *Summer*. After describing the oppressive effects of a heatwave Thomson produces an allegorical picture of a man who 'on the Sunless Side / Of a romantic Mountain'

> Sits cooly calm; while all the World without,
> Unsatisfy'd, and sick, tosses in Noon. . . .
>
>   (1727, 350-1)

and this, Thomson suggests, is an instructive emblem

>   of the virtuous Man,
> Who keeps his temper'd Mind serene and pure,
> And all his Passions aptly harmoniz'd,
> Amidst a jarring World with Vice inflam'd.
>
>   (1727, 352-5)

But in effect it is not simply that the figure who 'sits cooly calm' is an image of 'the virtuous Man' whose passions are restrained and ordered. He *is* that man. Virtue springs from retirement and contemplation of the natural scene. It is this psychological benefit that Thomson particularly values and it is this value that he has in mind when he goes on to apostrophize the woods:

> Welcome, ye Shades! ye bowery Thickets hail!
> Ye lofty Pines! ye venerable Oaks!
>
>   (1727, 356-7)

The shelter of the woods is 'delicious to the soul'; it cools the nerves; it is life-giving. After describing the effects of heat upon animals—particularly the ox and the horse—Thomson returns again to the psychological influence of the woods:

> These are the Haunts of Meditation, these
> The Scenes where antient Bards th'inspiring
>   Breath,
> Extatic, felt . . .
>
>   (1727, 409-11)

Here angelic voices are heard, or seem to be heard. They have attained to the harmony which Thomson still seeks, and they invite him to share their happiness:

> Oft, in these dim Recesses, undisturb'd
> By noisy Folly, and discordant Vice,
> Of Nature sing with Us, and Nature's God.
>
>   (1727, 440-2)

This is, of course, a far more immediate and emotionalized, more Shaftesburyian, moral influence than anything suggested by Virgil. Virgil's husbandman led a better life, certainly, than the town-dweller, and there is some slight suggestion implicit that the country setting itself has a beneficent effect. But the main moral influences are first the absence of immoral temptations (to ambition, for example) and secondly the regular pattern of work which is imposed by the seasons. There is not the ecstatic moral influence that Thomson attributes to the natural scene, an influence which he points to again the next year in the first version of *Spring*, and most directly in these lines:

>   Serenity apace
> Induces Thought, and Contemplation still.
> By small Degrees the Love of Nature works,
> And warms the Bosom; till at last arriv'd
> To Rapture, and enthusiastic Heat,
> We feel the present Deity, and taste
> The Joy of God, to see a happy World.
>
>   (1728, 858-64)

The various stages in the psychological development which country retirement induces are here set out explicitly—serenity, thought, contemplation, rapture.

Various additions strengthened the retirement element in *Spring* in 1744, but it seems best for the moment to continue with a chronological account of Thomson's developing attitude and the additions to *Spring* will therefore be considered later.

Autumn, the last of *The Seasons* to be written, emphasizes the moral influence of the natural scene in its description of Dodington's Dorset seat:

> Oh lose me in the green, majestic walks
> Of, Dodington! thy seat, serene, and plain;
> Where simple Nature reigns . . .
>   Here oft alone,
> Fir'd by the thirst of thy applause, I court
> Th'inspiring breeze; and meditate the book

Of Nature, ever-open; aiming thence,
Heart-taught like thine, to learn the moral song.
(1730, 643-60)

But apart from this *Autumn* also contains, in its concluding section, by far the most extensive formulation of the
retirement theme.

Oh knew he but his happiness, of men
The happiest he! who far from public rage,
Deep in the vale, with a choice few retir'd,
Drinks the pure pleasures of the rural Life.
(1730, 1131-4)

The passage of approximately 135 lines is very closely
modelled on Virgil: indeed much of it is straightforward
translation. Thomson lists first the evils which a country
life *avoids* (importunate suitors, the obligatory show of
useless wealth), and then touches upon some of the advantages of rural retirement:

Rich in content, in Nature's bounty rich,
In herbs, and fruits; whatever greens the Spring,
When heaven descends in showers; or bends the
   bough,
When Summer reddens, and when Autumn
   beams. . . .
(1730, 1155-8)

Then again the rejection of ambition, military, political
and legal, in favour of the patterned life of Nature is
clearly set forth:

The rage of nations, and the crush of states
Move not the man, who, from the world escap'd,
In still retreats, and flowery solitudes,
To Nature's voice attends, from day to day,
And month to month, thro' the revolving Year. . . .
(1730, 1199-1203)

The life of retirement is identified, as in Virgil, with the
Golden Age, with Paradisal experience when 'God himself, and Angels dwelt with men!', and finally, placed in
a more emphatic position than in Virgil, there is a new
version of the passage which Thomson had already translated in the Preface to *Winter:*

Oh Nature! all-sufficient! over all!
Enrich me with the knowledge of thy works!
(1730, 1248-9)

Thomson wishes, with Virgil, to understand the rolling
wonders of heaven's 'infinite extent', to understand the
mystery of animal, mineral and vegetable life and the
complexity of human psychology (and here he is going
beyond the Virgilian original). But, despite the intensity
of these desires, he prays that

if the blood
In sluggish streams about my heart, forbids
That best ambition; under closing shades,
Inglorious, lay me by the lowly brook,

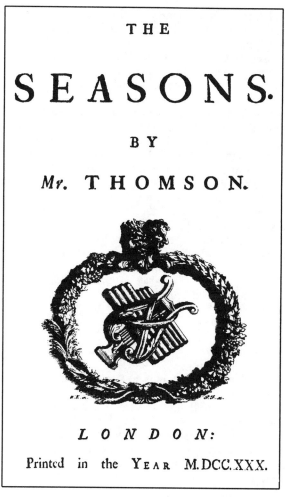

T H E

S E A S O N S.

B Y

Mr. **T H O M S O N.**

L O N D O N:

Printed in the Year M.DCC.XXX.

Title page of the 1730 edition of The Seasons.

And whisper to my dreams.
(1730, 1263-7)

Thus, although praise of scientific speculation has certainly been given a very prominent position, the either/or
formula of *Georgics* II is here maintained and *Autumn*
ends with this tribute to the 'inglorious' but nonetheless
valuable pleasures of a retired country existence.

The chief figure in the idyllic picture of a country life
which Virgil paints is the husbandman. 'O fortunatos
. . . agricolas!' He is engaged in the normal country
occupations and is leading a frugal existence. He is
'hardened to toil and innured to scanty fare.' 'No respite is there.' Each season brings its proper work and
the holiday is a rare event, a justified rest from continual labour. The countryman certainly enjoys the pleasures of country life. This is hinted at in lines which
refer to 'lakes and cool vales, the lowing of kine, and
soft slumbers beneath the trees.' But also, and distinct
from the picture of the husbandman, although the two
tend to merge together, is the figure of Virgil himself,
desiring scientific knowledge, yet prepared to opt for

387

the delights of the country. Although the two figures are close together, and although Virgil seems at times to be identifying himself with the husbandman, they do not coalesce. The very fact that Virgil postulates scientific knowledge as one of the most desirable objectives in life sets him apart from the husbandman and implies that his attitude will be different from that of the husbandman even towards those simple country pleasures which they share. The poet saying: 'O for one to set me in the cool glens of Haemus, and shield me under the branches' mighty shade!' (II, 488-9) is different psychologically from the man who enjoys the pleasures of Nature unreflectively. That the husbandman *is* unreflective is shown in the opening line of the section 'Oh happy husbandmen! too happy, should they come to know their blessings' (II, 458-9). In Thomson's version of the section the husbandman is left almost entirely on one side. His presence is implied in references to farming activity:

> whatever greens the Spring,
> When heaven descends in showers; or bends the
> bough,
> When Summer reddens, and when Autumn
> beams. . . .
>
> (1730, 1156-8)

but for the most part it is not farming that is stressed. Thomson's retirement is much more literary and philosophical than anything that Virgil hints at. He proposes to retire with a few *choice* friends and to lead a thoroughly cultivated life. Some of his expansions reveal this emphasis very clearly. Lines 1212-6, for example, begin in an entirely Virgilian manner. They are modelled on lines 496-7 of *Georgics* II:

> In Summer he, beneath the living shade,
> Such as from frigid Tempe wont to fall,
> Or Haemus cool. . . .

But Thomson now adds his own gloss on this activity:

> In Summer he. . . .
>   reads what the muse, of these
> Perhaps, has in immortal numbers sung;
> Or what she dictates writes. . . .

Literary activity is an essential part of this retirement, an idea which is developed a little later on when Thomson is speaking of the way in which the evenings should be spent:

> A friend, a book, the stealing hours secure,
> And mark them down for wisdom. With swift
> wing,
> O'er land and sea, imagination roams;
> Or truth, divinely breaking on his mind,
> Elates his being, and unfolds his powers. . . .
>
> (1730, 1229-33)

The importance of the social aspect of retirement is already clear. Thomson withdraws from the world with a few choice friends and his search for wisdom is thought

of as an essentially social activity. Thomson's social enthusiams appear very clearly in the scene where he draws nearest to the Virgilian husbandman, in the picture of domestic happiness with its natural appeal to sentiment:

> The touch of love, and kindred too he feels,
> The modest eye, whose beams on his alone
> Extatic shine; the little, strong embrace
> Of prattling children, twin'd around his neck,
> And emulous to please him, calling forth
> The fond parental soul. Nor purpose gay,
> Amusement, dance, or song, he sternly scorns;
> For happiness, and true philosophy
> Are of the social still, and smiling Kind.
>
> (1744, 1235-43)

The last line was emended in 1744 from 'Still are, and have been of the smiling kind'. Once again Thomson begins with a very close imitation of Virgil and then provides an addition which is personal in its emphasis. The conclusion that happiness and true philosophy 'are of the social still, and smiling Kind' is unvirgilian, but entirely characteristic of Thomson's attitude to the pleasures of retirement.

The discussion so far has dealt with Thomson's use of the retirement theme up to the publication of the first collected edition of *The Seasons* in 1730. A clear idea of the changes which Thomson made in his treatment of the theme after the publication of the first collected edition can be gained from a study of *Spring*.

There is one substantial addition, namely the account of Hagley Park (Lyttelton's house), a fifty-nine line passage first included in 1744. The passage immediately follows lines which have already been quoted

> Serenity apace
> Induces Thought and Contemplation still.
> By small Degrees the Love of Nature works,
> And warms the Bosom. . . .
>
> (1728, 858-61)

Lyttelton is an example of a man who is moved in this way:

> These are the Sacred Feelings of thy Heart. . . .
>
> (1744, 901)

His emotions are controlled by 'Reason's purest Ray' and he responds both intellectually and emotionally to Nature as he wanders 'Courting the Muse, thro' Hagley-Park'. Nature produces her effects in well-defined stages. Lyttleton is pictured first in a state of simple receptivity towards the sensuous pleasures of the scene. He listens pensively

> to the various Voice
> Of rural Peace: the Herds, the Flocks, the Birds,
> The hollow-whispering Breeze, the Plaint of
> Rills. . . .
>
> (1744, 914-16)

But 'abstracted oft' from these he enters the world of philosophical speculation or historical study, study which is not purely theoretical but which enables him to plan,

> with warm Benevolence of Mind,
> And honest Zeal unwarp'd by Party-Rage,
> Britannia's Weal. . . .
>
> 　　　　　　　　(1744, 925-7)

Again, as in *Summer*, contemplation of Nature is a life-giving force, only now it produces not only psychological harmony, but action as well.

Finally, there is a very typical addition to the closing section of *Spring*. Thomson is speaking about the satisfactions of virtuous love. The vanities of the World—'Its pomp, its pleasure, and its nonsense all'—become unimportant as the happily married pair enjoy

> The richest Bounty of indulgent Heaven.
> 　　　　　　　　(1728, 1056)

Children provide the culminating satisfaction and often provoke tears of happiness in their parents. Thomson addresses the married pair directly:

> Oh speak the Joy! You, whom the sudden Tear
> Surprizes often, while you look around,
> And nothing strikes your Eye but sights of Bliss,
> All various Nature pressing on the Heart. . . .
> 　　　　　　　　(1728, 1069-72)

At this point, in 1744, Thomson interpolated four lines which go a long way towards summing up his attitude to retirement:

> All various Nature pressing on the Heart,
> An elegant Sufficiency, Content,
> Retirement, rural Quiet, Friendship, Books,
> Ease and alternate Labour, useful Life,
> Progressive Virtue, and approving Heaven.
> These are the matchless Joys of virtuous Love. . . .
> 　　　　　　　　(1744, 1058-63)

All the elements of retirement as envisaged by Thomson are here. For the cultivated existence that he visualizes more than a bare competence is necessary. 'I've often wish'd that I had clear / For life, six hundred pounds a year, / A handsome House to lodge a friend . . . ' said Swift and Thomson's 'elegant sufficiency' echoes this without any hint of self-mockery. Peace, sociability, literature are all mentioned. The objective is clear:

> Progressive virtue, and approving Heaven.

Thomson's view of retirement is complex, far from simple frugality on the one hand, and wise passiveness on the other, and most of the elements of the complexity are included in these lines. They make a fitting epitome of the many passages in *The Seasons* which deal with similar subject-matter.

What needs to be stressed about this analysis of the retirement passages in *The Seasons* is the extent to which Thomson's modifications of the self-sufficient stoicism that is the dominant ideal of Virgil's *O fortunatos agricolas* section are made within a framework of ideas that is characteristic of the *Georgics* taken as a whole. Thomson's main developments as they have emerged during the preceding analysis are: first, the stress upon the social pleasures of retirement itself and even upon its recuperative value for a man who is still engaged in an active life in the world; secondly, the emphasis on the positive moral influence of the countryside in harmonizing the passions and therefore encouraging virtue. If one looks at Thomson's use of the retirement theme on its own (without reference to its place in the poem as a whole) then the first of these developments will seem a more revolutionary break with Virgil than it really is. The *Georgics* themselves, as we have seen before, are not without internal contradictions: condemnation of courts and praise of retirement are juxtaposed, for example, with eulogies on the greatness of Augustus. In discussing Thomson's attitude to primitivism and progress it has been suggested that a leading factor in both Thomson's and Virgil's view of life is the notion of a fall from the Golden Age which is at once a calamity and an opportunity. Through labour the evils of the fall can be overcome and a greater Golden Age achieved again. In this context it is not so surprising that Thomson's treatment of retirement should tend towards the social and that he should show himself aware of the virtues of the active life. What Thomson does is to bring together ideas which are present, but left in a sharper contrast, in Virgil, and to give his poem an easier harmony in consequence. In doing this Thomson is not, it would seem, being unmindful of Virgil. Rather he is interpreting Virgil quite legitimately in terms of the conditions of his own age. He is following Henry Felton's advice to write in his model's 'Way and after his Manner', but without following him in meticulous detail. The second of Thomson's developments of the retirement theme, the stress upon sentimental morality, is much more to be looked upon, especially in its degree of emphasis, as an innovation. But it is an innovation which gains some sanction from passages in *Georgics* II and IV where Virgil writes of the aesthetic and sensory pleasure given by the country scene, and it can be accommodated without violating the nature of the genre. It is a sign of Thomson's sureness of touch, and of the contemporary vitality of the poem that he is using as a source, that he can modify and develop the ideas and motifs of his source in this way.

It is Thomson's handling of these twin themes that gives the poem its fundamentally Georgic character. However, there are also many passages which are less radical in their influence, but which are justified by the essentially Georgic character of the whole. In this category, for example, one must place the lines in *Spring* on the destruction of insect pests:

> And hence the skillful Farmer Chaff
> And blazing Straw before his Orchard burns,
> Till all involv'd in Smoak the latent Foe

From every Cranny suffocated falls. . . .

(1728, 128-31)

This is a passage which readers have frequently objected to on grounds of its irrelevance to the supposed purpose of the poem (assuming that to be description of nature and the inculcation of sentimental morality): but it takes its place perfectly well once the poem is accepted for what it is—a modified Georgic. The *labor omnia vicit* side of Thomson's concern with the Iron Age needs (in a poem which is basically concerned with the country) to be rooted in country occupations, and in its context the passage is not an unwarranted digression or a misguided piece of ornamentation. It is justified because it serves the intentions, both thematic and formal, of the poem as a whole. Thomson should be assumed to know what he is about: in the 1744 version he revised this section considerably, but presumably, since he retained it, felt no doubts as to its essential relevance.

Also very strongly Georgic is the passage on the loves of the beasts. This is one of the most popular Georgic elements both in Virgil's poem and in post-classical developments of the Georgic form; in the eighteenth century itself one might instance Gay's *Rural Sports,* or, later than Thomson, Somerville's *The Chace.* Thomson deals first with 'a Theme/Unknown to Fame, the Passion of the Groves', then with cruder passions in 'the rougher World/ Of Brutes' and finally with Man (adopting in this detail the ascending scale of value which Addison perceived in the *Georgics* as a whole). Thomson takes over many details, even of phrasing, from Virgil's account. Here also we find Thomson modifying Virgil for his own purpose. Speaking of human love Virgil included a reference to Leander swimming the Hellespont:

What of the youth, in whose marrow fierce Love fans the mighty flame? Lo! in the turmoil of bursting storms, late in the black night, he swims the straits. Above him thunders Heaven's mighty portal, and the billows, dashing on the cliffs, echo the cry; yet neither his hapless parents can call him back, nor thought of the maid who in cruel fate must die withal.

(III, 258-63)

Thomson's lover dreams of similar difficulties:

. . . he wanders waste,
In Night and Tempest wrapt; or shrinks aghast,
Back, from the bending Precipice; or wades
The turbid Stream below, and strives to reach
The farther Shore, where succourless, and sad,
His Dearer Life extends her beckoning Arms. . . .

(1728, 974-9)

By echoes of this sort Thomson makes his Virgilian debt clear. The utility of the theme for his purpose is that it enables him to point to the essential harmony (or the essential oneness) of all living creatures. Birds, beasts and men are all impelled by the same 'infusive force'; they are all subject to the same divine influence:

'Tis Harmony, that World-
embracing Power
By which all Beings are adjusted, each
To all around, impelling and impell'd
In endless Circulation, that inspires
This universal Smile . . .

(1728, 865-9)

Moreover this section on love enables Thomson to lead up to the praise of marriage which brings *Spring* to its conclusion:

But happy They! the Happiest of their Kind!
Whom gentler Stars unite, and in one Fate
Their Hearts, their Fortunes, and their Beings
blend.

(1728, 1025-7)

In other words it is again true that Georgic *motifs,* which have an entirely adequate formal appropriateness to the kind of poem that Thomson is writing, are adopted by him and used in a way that serves his central purpose. The form and its conventions go hand in hand with what Thomson has to say, and there is no sense of clash between them.

Indeed, at every turn in the analysis of the poem one is impressed by the extent to which the poet's interpretation of his subject-matter depends upon the modification and development of Georgic patterns. For all its variety and apparently random development the poem does present a coherent interpretation of life. Thomson's three dominant elements—natural description, praise of the retired life and patriotic exaltation—are, as we have seen, closely linked. The fundamental fact in the presentation of his poetic attitude, and one which is given a dominant position in *The Seasons* as a whole, is that we live in the Age of Iron. This brings with it two premises about life. First, that nothing can be accomplished without labour but that out of the struggle comes all that we most value; and secondly, that Man lives in a state of psychological disharmony which is only partly remediable. He is subject to conflicting passions which can only with great difficulty be brought under the rule of Reason. It is from the starting-point of these premises that Thomson develops his patriotic ideas and his attitude to retirement. British successes in exploration and in trade are the clearest evidence of what can be accomplished by labour. Through retirement, through contemplation of the natural scene (which still retains, in part at least, its prelapsarian beauty) psychological harmony can be achieved. And in the later revisions to the poem the value of this is seen to lie in the strength it gives to enable one to engage once more in an active life. This, in the simplest possible form, is the argument which underlies *The Seasons,* and it is an argument which has been adapted, but without any fundamental changes, from Virgil.

Granted that these central preoccupations were encouraged by the Virgilian source it still needs to be asked why Thomson chose the seasons as his particular subject. He could have written on a locality as Denham and Pope had done, or, like Gay, about *Rural Sports*. He could have followed Milton in making a psychological approach to the countryside, or, obviously, he could, like Philips, have followed Virgil still more closely and taken farming as his theme. As we have seen, Thomson was in many ways a traditionalist, but in choosing a subject he avoided the most authoritative ways of proceeding and turned to the seasons instead. Not that this was entirely new: Pope's *Pastorals* are divided seasonally, and William Hinchliffe had published a short poem actually called *The Seasons* in 1718. Hinchcliffe's poem has affinities with Thomson's work and seems to have given him the idea, but it still remains worth asking why this framework appeared to be a suitable one for his most ambitious poem.

No doubt the original choice of winter as a subject was due to the opportunities it offered for description accompanied by a lofty strain of meditation. Thomson makes much, in his Preface to the June 1726 edition of *Winter,* of the sublimity of his subject. We must, he says, choose

    . . . great and serious Subjects, such as at once
      amuse the
    Fancy, enlighten the Head, and warm the Heart.

Subjects of this character are to be found above all in the works of nature; where we meet with 'all that enlarges and transports the soul'.

The mood expressed here is certainly the predominant one in this first version of the poem:

    SEE! Winter comes, to rule the varied Year,
    Sullen, and sad; with all his rising Train,
    Vapours, and Clouds, and Storms. Be these my
      Theme,
    These, that exalt the Soul to solemn Thought,
    And heavenly musing. . . .
    Oh! bear me then to high, embowering, Shades;
    To twilight Groves, and visionary Vales;
    To weeping Grottos, and to hoary Caves;
    Where Angel-Forms are seen, and Voices heard,
    Sigh'd in low Whispers, that abstract the Soul,
    From outward Sense, far into Worlds remote.
                                    (II, 1-79)

This is a strain of self-intoxication which the modern reader finds a little indigestible, but it is the germ from which the whole poem developed, and we can be glad that, in choosing a subject which gave full reign to his yearning for sublimity of feeling and elevation of language, Thomson found a topic which was capable of varied and subtle extensions.

He was already, in the June 1726 Preface, apparently looking forward to writing on all the seasons:

    How gay looks the Spring! how glorious the Summer!
    how pleasing the Autumn! and how venerable the
    Winter!—But there is no thinking of these Things
    without breaking out into Poetry. . . .

and as he worked the subject was quickly seen to offer more than simply an excuse for sublime and picturesque description and for self-conscious 'philosophical reflection and moral sentiment'. In reflection of the kind that has just been quoted from *Winter,* the natural scene acts as a spur to meditation but in the poem as it developed the important thing is not so much the set pieces of meditation as the meaningful pattern of comparisons and contrasts that is found in the subject itself.

Thomson is inevitably impressed by the seasons in their cyclical aspect, as a recurrent pattern which contains within itself the great facts of birth and death, growth and decay. He is even more impressed by the notion of plenitude, that in the external scene there is to be found an interlinked chain of being, each segment of which forms a vital part of the whole. The sheer abundance of external nature is a frequent theme, that 'full nature swarms with life'. The species of flowers, Thomson says, are uncountable. They are

                              profusely wild
    O'er all the deep-green Earth, beyond the Power
    Of Botanist to number up their Tribes . . .
    With such a liberal Hand has Nature flung
    Their Seeds abroad . . .

                        (*Spring*, 1728, 247-256)

Among other things *The Seasons* is a celebration of Nature's 'liberal hand', the richness of teeming animal and vegetable life, which is not quite the same thing as the celebration of the farmer's prosperity, although, as we have seen, that too is an important theme. Thomson, however, is fascinated not only with prosperity, the harnessing of natural forces to man's purpose, but also with the vast scope and interpenetration of existence, with how

    From stage to stage, the vital scale ascends . . .

In his description of the 'vital scale' Thomson places great emphasis on the idea of harmony. His muse, he says, is most delighted

              when she social sees
    The whole mixed animal creation round
    Alive and happy.
                        (*Autumn*, 1744, 378-80)

The ideal landscape is one where 'Harmonious Nature looked smiling on', where 'the herds and flocks commixing played secure' and where 'music held the whole in perfect peace'. Thomson knows perfectly well that this idyllic harmony is not always to be found in external nature, but he does believe that there is an overriding harmony which reconciles local disruptions and injustices. Addressing God, and calling him the 'Source of Being! Universal Soul . . . Essential Presence', Thomson says:

              to Thee my Thoughts
    Continual climb, who, with a Master-Hand

Hast the great Whole into Perfection touched . . .
(*Spring*, 1728, 510-12)

Properly understood the whole of life is a perfect unity. This is one of the dominant themes of the *Hymn on the Seasons* where Thomson makes a more specifically Christian invocation to God as the 'Almighty Father':

THESE, as they change, Almighty Father! these,
Are but the varied God. The rolling Year
Is full of thee. . . .

Mysterious round! what skill, what force divine,
Deep-felt in these appear! a simple train,
Yet so delightful mix'd, with such kind Art,
Such Beauty and Beneficence combined;
Shade, unperceiv'd, so softening into shade,
And all so forming an harmonious whole,
That, as they still succeed, they ravish still.
(1744, 1-27)

Man, 'with brute unconscious gaze' sometimes fails to understand this 'harmonious whole', and this is ironical because he has a special place in the harmonious scheme:

Man superior walks
Amid the glad Creation . . .
(*Spring*, 1728, 195-6)

and as he walks he should be 'musing praise and looking lively gratitude', aware of the unity of the scene of which he forms a part.

It is because the seasons mirror this overriding harmony so perfectly that Thomson was attracted to them as a subject. In their perpetual cycle and recurring balance Thomson found reflected the ideal unity which sustained the universe. But 'overriding' is a key word. Although it is Thomson's firm belief that, however far he may travel, he cannot go 'Where universal love not smiles around', and though he believes that universal love

From seeming evil still educes good,
And better thence again, and better still,
In infinite progression . . .
(*Hymn*, 1730, 117-19)

although, in other words, he was a metaphysical optimist of the most steadfast kind, yet *The Seasons,* taken as a whole is by no means easily and complacently optimistic. Thomson knows that life is full of sudden shifts of fortune, disruptions and dislocations which are very difficult to explain in terms of universal order or justice. And here again the seasons are invaluable to him because they impose variety (at the very least climatic variety) while at the same time maintaining a sense of order and progression. On a larger scale the seasons have for Thomson the significance that the landscape of Windsor had for Pope:

Not Chaos-like together crush'd and bruis'd,
But as the World, harmoniously confus'd:

Where Order in Variety we see,
And where, tho' all things differ, all agree . . .
(*Windsor Forest*, 13-16)

They allow and indeed encourage important juxtapositions and contrasts of subject-matter, and hold them all in a state of tension.

On the largest scale there is a balance between the different books, in that *Spring* and *Autumn* are seen as predominantly fruitful and creative, whereas *Winter* and *Summer* are often powerfully destructive. There is built into the final form of the poem a clearly perceptible oscillation of mood.

The destructiveness of *Winter* arises naturally from the subject itself, and Thomson's prose *Argument* shows clearly where the emphasis will fall:

First approach of Winter. According to the natural course of the season, various storms described. Rain. Wind. Snow. The driving of the snows: a man perishing among them; *whence reflections on the wants and miseries of human life.* The wolves descending from the Alps and Appenines.

The passage to which the italicized *reflections on the wants and miseries of human life* refers is a set piece of extreme despondency:

Ah! little think the gay licentious proud,
Whom pleasure, power and affluence surround;
They, who their thoughtless hours in giddy
  mirth,
And wanton, often cruel, riot waste;
Ah little think they, while they dance along,
How many feel, this very moment, death
And all the sad variety of pain.
(1730, 296-302)

This is the mood of *Winter:* man is at the mercy of elemental forces which he is unable to understand or control.

But *Summer* provides a central episode almost as bleak in its implications. The general tone is naturally less stark. There is a good deal of very attractive natural description; there are the hay-making and sheep-shearing scenes and, towards the end, a transition, as Thomson says, 'to the prospect of a rich, well-cultivated country' in order to introduce a 'panegyric on Great Britain.' Thomson explicitly attacks 'impious' scoffers who attack

Creative Wisdom, as if aught was form'd
In vain, or not for admirable Ends.
(1744, 319-20)

Yet, the most memorable episode in *Summer* is the tale of Celadon and Amelia, two lovers caught in a thunderstorm in which Amelia is killed. The tale is introduced by a description of a storm which is both terrifying and destructive. Trees are uprooted and cattle killed and this is thought of as frightening to the guilty-minded:

> Guilt hears appall'd, with deeply troubled
>   Thought. . . .

But there is an immediate modification because Thomson realizes that this is too easy a moral:

> Guilt hears appall'd, with deeply troubled
>   Thought;
> And yet not always on the guilty Head
> Descends the fated Flash.
>
>> (1744, 1161-3)

This introduces the episode of Celadon and Amelia who are built up by Thomson as a completely innocent couple. Not only are they innocent, but their relationship is idyllic:

> They lov'd. But such their guileless Passion was,
> As in the Dawn of Time inform'd the Heart
> Of Innocence, and undissembling Truth.
>
>> (1744, 1069-71)

Their love is such as to make 'eternal Eden smile around'. When the storm begins and Amelia is frightened Celadon tries to calm her by an appeal to the divine order and justice which Thomson himself frequently evokes:

> 'Fear not, he said,
> Sweet Innocence! thou Stranger to Offence,
> And inward Storm! He, who yon Skies involves
> In Frowns of Darkness, ever smiles on thee,
> With kind regard. O'er thee . . .
>   that very Voice,
> Which thunders Terror thro' the guilty Heart,
> With Tongues of Seraphs whispers Peace to
>   thine.
> 'Tis Safety to be near thee sure, and thus
> To clasp Perfection!'
>
>> (1744, 1196-206)

However, Celadon's confidence, which could in another context be Thomson's, is soon shattered, because

> From his void Embrace,
> . . . that moment, to the Ground,
> A blacken'd Corse, was struck the beauteous
>   Maid.
>
>> (1744, 1206-8)

From this sad story Thomson passes immediately, with no comment, to a description of how, once the storm is past, everything becomes gay and happy. The unjustifiable tragic event is left to make its own impact, but Thomson has done all he can, short of explicit comment, to make us feel that this story renders an easy acceptance of God's harmonious plan impossible. The sharpness of the contrast with scenes of peace and prosperity is too great for that.

The sense of nature as hostile or potentially hostile is strongest in *Winter* and *Summer*. In *Spring* an idyllic pastoral tone prevails and in *Autumn* it is naturally the harvest—with nature as the great benefactor—that is at the centre of the poem. The equivalent digression in *Autumn* to Summer's Celadon and Amelia is the tale of Palamon and Lavinia, an optimistic story of how a poor gleaner of noble birth is restored to fortune by her benevolent master. There is no serious disruption of the harvest-home theme.

Looking at the poem as a whole, therefore, the four books might be labelled very crudely as 'Optimism', 'Doubt', 'Optimism', 'Doubt', each book playing off against the preceding one. And within the books one finds similar contrasts constantly being made by the juxtaposition of different kinds of material. For a sharp contrast on a localised scale one might consider a passage early in *Spring*. In the spring, Thomson says, it is pleasant to get out into the country and see

> far-diffus'd around
> One boundless Blush, one snow-empurpled
>   Shower
> Of mingled Blossoms; where the raptur'd Eye
> Travels from Joy to Joy, and, hid beneath
> The fair Profusion, yellow Autumn spies.
>
>> (1727, 107-11)

But then comes the contrast, the doubt and, surely, inevitably, the question about how far Nature's benevolence extends. The 'raptured eye' is justified in seeing yellow autumn hidden in the blossom of spring only

> If brush'd from Russian Wilds, a cutting Gale
> Rise not, and scatter from his humid Wings
> The clammy Mildew, or dry-blowing breathe
> Untimely Frost; before whose baleful Blast,
> The full-blown Spring thro' all her Foliage
>   shrinks
> Joyless and dead, a wide-dejected Waste.
>
>> (1744, 112-17)

By this sort of contrast—characteristic Georgic montage—Thomson gradually builds up a sense of the complex interplay of forces that underlies human activity. Even the bleak storms of *Winter* are interspersed with domestic scenes,

> Where ruddy fire and beaming tapers join,
> To chase the chearless gloom.
>
>> (1730, 413-14)

And there is, of course, the celebrated robin who 'pays to trusted man / His annual visit' and makes himself at home in the family. The overall effect is like a pageant, and it is so above all in that there is no progression; it is the total picture that is important. Everything is held as it were in suspension. No single scene or passage is really significant; it is the accumulation of scenes and the way they play off one against another that matters.

This general point about the structure of *The Seasons* gains a good deal of support when one looks at its style or rather its styles. In contrast to the descriptive and reflective poems discussed in the previous chapter *The Seasons* is stylistically extremely varied, and it frequently happens that a major effect depends upon transpositions of mood which are reinforced by stylistic means. Thomson himself was certainly aware of these transpositions. He sometimes says explicitly: 'Let us leave this mood on one side now and turn to something different'. He does this very clearly in *Spring* after his account of the loves of the beasts:

> But this the Theme
> I sing, transported, to the British Fair,
> Forbids, and leads me to the Mountain-brow,
> Where sits the Shepherd on the grassy Turf,
> Inhaling, healthful, the descending Sun.
> (1728, 776-80)

And at another point when he turns to 'the fair sex' he makes clear the stylistic implications of the shift in direction:

> May my Song soften, as thy Daughters I,
> Britannia, hail! for Beauty is their own,
> The feeling Heart, Simplicity of Life,
> And Elegance, and Taste. . . .
> (*Summer*, 1744, 1572-5)

When Thomson *softens* his song and uses language appropriate to women, mellifluousness and fluency are emphasised and he avoids all harshness of diction and rhythm.

In reading *The Seasons* it soon becomes clear that the different styles complement each other and so provide a strong reinforcement for the central themes of the poem. Three may be distinguished here—the pastoral, the heroic and the mock-heroic.

A pattern of the pastoral style occurs in *Spring,* in the catalogue of flowers:

> Fair-handed Spring unbosoms every Grace;
> Throws out the Snow-Drop, and the Crocus first,
> The Daisy, Primrose, Violet darkly blue,
> The Polyanthus of unnumbered Dyes . . .
> Anemonies, Auriculas . . .
> And full Renunculus, of glowing red.
> (1744, 527-32)

In passages of this kind Thomson is deeply indebted to the tradition of pastoral writing and here we find echoes from Browne's *Britannia's Pastorals,* from *Lycidas* and from the pastoral section of *The Winter's Tale.* The emphasis is upon the piling up of visual images to give an impression of richness and spontaneity. Suggestions of worldliness and violence and indeed all associations incongruous with the idea of innocent abundance, are excluded.

At the opposite extreme is the heroic. In its purest form this is found, for example, in the storm scene or in the account of the plague. A few lines from *Winter,* describ-

ing the descent of wolves upon a village, provide a pattern:

> By wintry Famine rous'd, from all the Tract
> Of horrid Mountains which the shining Alps,
> And wavy Apennines, and Pyrenees
> Branch out stupendous into distant Lands,
> Cruel as Death, and hungry as the Grave!
> Burning for Blood, bony, and ghaunt, and grim!
> Assembling Wolves in raging Troops descend. . . .
> (1744, 389-95)

The lines could almost be pastiche, but they do indicate in an exaggerated form the characteristics of the heroic mood in Thomson. There is the strongly emotive effect of *horrid,* where the root meaning is dominant, and a similar effect with *stupendous.* There is the exoticism of the scene ('wavy Apennines and Pyrenees'), the horror of the subject itself ('Burning for Blood, bony, and ghaunt and grim'), and, perhaps above all, the sense of Man's helplessness in the face of disaster. 'The godlike Face of Man avails him naught' as the wolves descend upon the villagers.

Stylistically the poem oscillates between these two extremes of pastoralism and the heroic. But mediating between these two extremes there is a variety of more neutral styles which help to relate the extreme modes to ordinary life. One of the most important is mock-heroic.

There is only one sustained passage of mock-heroic, namely the account of the hunt, and particularly the hunt-supper, in *Autumn.* Thomson dislikes hunting. This is part of his humanitarianism, and springs from the feeling that killing animals (especially for pleasure) is a man-made discord, a deliberate disruption of natural harmony. And consequently the picture that he gives of the huntsmen's feast is satiric: he emphasizes its boorishness and drunkenness, and he uses a mock-heroic style which rises to a climax as, one by one, the drinkers sink into stupor beneath the table:

> Before their maudlin eyes,
> Seen dim, and blue, the double tapers dance,
> Like the sun wading thro' the misty sky.
> Then, sliding sweet, they drop. O'erturned above
> Lies the wet, broken scene; and stretch'd below,
> Is heap'd the social Slaughter. . . .
> (1744, 550-5)

The third line has a particularly authentic mock-heroic ring. The last phrase (*social slaughter*) is an interesting one. The word *social* is a very important one for Thomson and it occurs with exceptional frequency in the poem. It connotes the integration of different elements, the unity in variety which, it is suggested, is one of the central themes of the work as a whole, and its use here consequently has a good deal of ironic force. The section ends with a description of the greatest hero of all, the man who survives the battle, and who looks back to an even more heroic period:

> Perhaps some Doctor of tremendous Paunch,

Awful and deep, a black Abyss of Drink,
Out-lives them all, and from his bury'd Flock
Retiring, full of Rumination sad,
Laments the Weakness of these latter Times.

(1744, 559-63)

This, then, is a mock-heroic set-piece which shows how completely Thomson could produce the style when he wanted. But more interesting, I think, are passages in which mock-heroic is used, almost in passing, to modify a different style.

When, early in *Spring*, for example, Thomson wants to give some advice on cures for a plague of insects, he begins with some straightforward instruction:

the skillful Farmer Chaff
And blazing Straw before his Orchard Burns . . .
Or scatters o'er the Blooms the pungent Dust
Of Pepper. . . .

(1744, 127-32)

This is simple enough advice: it gives information and puts it in the simplest terms consistent with verse. The vocabulary is mundane. But Thomson modifies this dry instruction with a distinct touch of mock-heroic by describing the insects in lofty terms: they are

A feble Race! yet oft
The scared Sons of Vengeance! on whose Course
Corrosive Famine waits, and kills the Year. . . .

(1744, 124-6)

When smoke from the burning straw reaches them

. . . all involv'd in Smoak, the latent Foe
From every Cranny suffocated falls.

(1744, 129-30)

The effect of this is two-edged. On the one hand Thomson is no doubt mildly amused at himself for writing about insects, and the mock-heroic contains elements of self-irony. On the other hand the fight against insects is really the heroic aspect of the farmer's life, and the implications of his fight affect the whole of society. Looked at from this point of view (and the stylistic changes force some such viewpoint upon the reader) the lines question whether the normal distinction between heroic and non-heroic is a valid one. Is the soldier the only hero or is the farmer engaged in just as strenuous a battle?

Finally, for a very different example of mock-heroic, it is worth looking at the Damon and Musidora episode in *Summer*. Damon, having accidentally seen Musidora undressing for a bathe, is overcome by the sight, but manages to summon up enough will-power to leave. Before doing so he leaves a note for Musidora in which he says that he is going to guard her from the 'licentious eye' of any further visitors. When Musidora discovers the note she writes in reply:

'Dear Youth! sole Judge of what these Verses

mean,
By Fortune too much favour'd, but by Love,
Alas! not favour'd less, be still as now
Discreet: the Time may come you need not fly.'

(1744, 1359-62)

The critical question is clearly whether this is anything more than the sentimental and rather silly episode which it is generally held to be. But this attitude is possible perhaps partly because not enough attention is paid to Thomson's stylistic variety. One should notice, for example, how Thomson describes Damon's state of mind when he catches sight of Musidora undressing:

Ah! then! not Paris on the piny Top
Of Ida panted stronger, when aside
The Rival-Goddesses the Veil divine
Cast, unconfin'd, and gave him all their Charms,
Than, Damon, thou; as from the snowy Leg,
And slender Foot th'inverted Silk she drew . . .

(1744, 1296-1301)

The reader is caught in a moment of genuine mock-heroic ambiguity. However beautiful Musidora may be it is absurd to compare her with Hera, Aphrodite and Athene. On the other hand, by the conventions of love, she is goddess-like to Damon. By a deft use of mock-heroic at this point Thomson is both achieving a detached, mildly-ironical, view of his subject and pointing to its real importance by forcing epic ideas into a relationship with everyday life.

It is characteristic of Thomson that this sort of sceptical reevaluation should arise from his work. This brief examination of the elaborate system of juxtapositions, comparisons and contrasts, and different stylistic levels that make up *The Seasons* is sufficient to show that Thomson was prepared to present and come to terms with the complexity of his subject matter, and that he was not a man for easy answers. It is an essential part of his view of life that experience should seem sometimes humdrum, sometimes heroic, sometimes comic, sometimes bathetic. To this extent *The Seasons* is a singularly 'realistic' work—it does not present a single, simplified view of reality, but a complex of different views in which first one and then another interpretation of experience seems to predominate. The choice of the seasons as a framework enables Thomson to give full expression to this modal complexity while still maintaining his belief in an underlying pattern, order and harmony.

Ralph Cohen (essay date 1970)

SOURCE: An introduction and "Conclusion: The Artistry of *The Seasons*," in *The Unfolding of "The Seasons,"* The Johns Hopkins Press, 1970, pp. 1-8, 324-30.

[*In the excerpt below, Cohen offers a critical analysis of* The Seasons, *finding it a major Augustan work in which "Thomson's unity, diction, and thought are entwined with a conception of man, nature, and God poetically tenable and distinctive."*]

A number of critics have sought to teach us how to read *The Seasons,* but their efforts still meet the determined resistance of such careful readers as F. R. Leavis and Reuben A. Brower. In *Revaluation* F. R. Leavis wrote: 'when we think of Johnson and Crabbe, when we recall any example of a poetry bearing a serious relation to the life of its time, then Gray, Thomson, Dyer, Akenside, Shenstone and the rest clearly belong to a by-line. It is literary and conventional in the worst sense of those terms.' And there is a more recent attack on the artistry of *The Seasons* [in 'Form and Defect of Form in Eighteenth Century Poetry: A Memorandum,' *College English* 29 (April 1968)] by Reuben A. Brower, who like another critic who guarded our tender sensibilities from Milton, warns against a Thomson revival on the grounds that Thomson lacks a 'unifying vision active in the separate descriptions.'

When such warnings are issued, it is necessary not to heed them, but to test them. Now is the time to examine the poetry of *The Seasons* not only because we have been warned not to do so, but because the poem obviously possesses sufficient 'life' to merit attention and attack. Perhaps, then, a study of the poem ought to begin by answering the assertion that it bears no 'serious relation to the life of its time.'

First and foremost, *The Seasons* is an Augustan poem, sharing with the major poetry of the period an awareness of the valued past, the corruption of this past in the present, the limited nature of human life, and the faith that a better life exists beyond 'this dark State.' When a recent critic contrasts the Augustan 'humanist' satiric tradition which 'is convinced that human nature, for all its potential dignity, is irremediably flawed and corrupt at the core' with the nonsatiric which 'tends to draw its real strength from the new industrial and commercial evidence of the validity of the idea of progress,' he is perpetuating a misinterpretation that even a perfunctory reading of *The Seasons* refutes.

Not only does Thomson propound the 'humanist' view of the limitation of man, but he sees man surrounded and often overwhelmed by natural forces. If in *Spring* God smiles upon man and brings him into a Golden Age. He also ceases to smile and brings destruction upon this peaceful haven. Thomson's poem is identified with the life of its time by revealing that the natural environment no less than human environment possesses beauty, awe as well as destructive powers. For if man can control the garden, he cannot control the storm, if he can plant in spring, he cannot be sure that he will be able to reap in autumn. Thomson's poem reveals an awareness of simultaneous and often contradictory actions in space, of joy in one place and sadness in another. It urges upon the reader the need to understand the environment by plunging into it not merely by seeing, but by tasting, smelling, hearing and touching it.

Thomson accepts the constant change governing his world,

and this is why the turning of the seasons is the professed subject of the poem. By definition the seasons are cyclical, not progressive, and although chronologically seeds grow, men grow and states grow, they also decline. Only in heaven, where the good arrive, can inevitable progress be found. For the rest, British commerce may thrive while British culture declines, primitive people may exist in Africa while a civilized society exists in Britain. Thomson neither proposes nor defends 'the validity of the idea of progress.'

Thomson recognized the fragmentariness of man's experience, knowledge and happiness. He wrote of moments of harmony and of a limited ideal in nature and in man's rural retreats from nature, harmonious moments that provided a union with the past or a hopeful prospect for infinity. But such moments and places were necessary relief from the anxiety and uneasiness of actual human experience. The model people and places are necessary in *The Seasons* because they affirm the possibility of temporary relief from anxieties and disappointments and the hope of a future life. In the inevitable turning of time and fortune all retreats have to be abandoned. As Thomson wrote to Elizabeth Young upon the death of her sister, 'true Happiness is not the Growth of this mortal Soil, but of those blessed regions where she is now.'

The Seasons, with its awareness of limitations and change, urges upon man a participation in the environment, an awareness of it that provides unexpected delights together with expected sadness, destruction and the need to trust in God. And it does so by developing techniques for revealing the past in the present, the individual in the general the sadness in the joy. Brower's reference to 'separate descriptions' assumes, if I interpret it correctly, that the descriptions have no 'vital poetic connection' with other passages, but at least one modern critic claims to have found such connection. [In *The Poetry of Vision* (1967)] Patricia M. Spacks points out that 'Even the passages of *The Seasons* most famed as descriptive set-pieces reveal the same preoccupation [as the nondescriptive passages] with emotional and intellectual significance rather than merely appearance.' The 'unifying vision' is that God's love and wisdom, only fragmentarily perceptible in the beautiful and dangerous aspects of man and nature, will become fully perceptible in a future world. Thomson's 'vision' evokes sentiments of beauty, sublimity, benevolence, fear and anxiety so that the reader may be led to believe in, to love, to trust, and to fear God's power.

This vision controls the descriptions as it does every aspect of the poem. It can be discovered in the overall unity where what is dominant in one season is converted into a subordinate role in another. The idea of love in *Spring,* for example, is subordinated to that of light and power in *Summer;* and this power is subordinated to the tempered atmosphere, the mists and declining sun of *Autumn.* The seasons follow a cyclical rhythm: gentle *Spring,* potent *Summer,* declining *Autumn,* destructive *Winter.* And yet each of these seasons contains, though it subordinates, opposing forces, and all are governed by the secret-working hand of God. Thus, though each season is rhythmically, associatively, and thematically connected with the preceding and following, the whole reveals the inevitable fragmentation of man's knowledge of the world. Each season is intertwined with a natural element and a human responsiveness so that as the earth opens, love flowers. And the fire of the sun brings enlightenment and oppressiveness followed by *Autumn* harvests which are like life-giving or saddening waters. The *Winter* tempests with their invigorating as well as destructive powers close the cycle in which *Spring* seeds lie dormant.

The sources and models for *The Seasons* are *Job,* the *Georgics, De Rerum Natura, L'Allegro, Il Penseroso* and *Paradise Lost,* and these do not lead to a new genre called 'descriptive poems.' Rather, *The Seasons* is a religious didactic poem, and its 'unifying vision' appears in the manner in which it joins eulogies, elegies, narratives, prospect views, historical catalogs, hymns, etc. Even if these are at times artistically ineffective, the point is that they are subsumed under a conception in which they are associately clustered to indicate the limited feature of each season. Thus even if, when removed as set-pieces, some parts are organic in themselves, their place in each season is inorganic or associative, so that organicism becomes merely another type of fragment.

The interpretation of a world where man and nature become part of a family of which God is the Father in no way implies that they uniformly reflect each other. Most men are dominated by selfish rather than benevolent desires and there are in nature 'vindictive' and 'jealous' forces; although love and benevolence are desirable, man and nature only occasionally achieve harmony. If, as a sympathetic critic of *The Seasons* writes, Thomson's 'internal moral world and the external world were intended to be in complete harmony,' then in Thomson's world such completeness is impossible, and his 'intention' unfulfilled. The realms of man and nature sometimes touch and sometimes clash, sometimes one forms an ironic or sentimental commentary upon the other, but the underlying conception is that neither one is complete nor are they together an illustration of the meaning of the world. They may create momentary harmonies or disharmonies, but they make clear that only God can explain the way of His wisdom and love.

Thomson adjusted contemporary practices to his own purposes and fashioned a language for his encompassing vision. He found continuities from the past in the present, different perspectives of the same or similar events, value and impressiveness in the objects and actions of nature. His adaptations included a private use of Latinate terms, the mixing of present with past participles, the introduction of scientific terms in religious passages, the use of general terms with specific implications. Thus the language of the poem reflected the 'vision' since terms possessed different perspectives, and at different times the same word occurs in varied, even contrary contexts.

Thomson's innovations are particularly noticeable in his use of periphrasis. This image was what critics referred to when they attacked the literariness or conventionality of

his poetry. R. D. Havens in 1922 declared that Thomson 'delighted in unnatural and inflated circumlocutions, like "the household feathery people" (hens), "the copious fry" or "the finny race" or "the glittering finny swarms".' Such objections have been answered extensively, and John Butt's comments [as stated in *The Augustan Age* (1950)] can stand for numerous others: 'Thomson's Latinisms came naturally to a lowland Scot writing Southern English, and his periphrases were used not to escape vulgarity, but precisely and evocatively.' Thomson's precision, achieved by converting periphrasis to a combination of personification and scientific classification, interpreted nature accurately, scientifically and humanistically in order to illustrate the relation between the realms of man and animal.

Thomson's general terms, decried as turgid and repetitive, function not as flabby general terms, but as forms of metonymy in which the whole stands for a part and in different contexts for different parts, so that the fragmentation of the world is always conceived as a class or ideal term comprehending a variety of individual members. In connecting pastoral conventions to a comic conception of contemporary rural life, he developed a linguistic procedure (I have called it 'illusive allusion') in which he playfully ridiculed the convention and parodied its applicability to the present. He was not unwilling to burlesque the convention of the hunting scene or to mock the convention of pastoral love. Since he sought a perspectival interpretation of human experience as well as of art, he could include two versions of the same genre or convention with contrasting implications.

But varied meanings of the same word or convention in no way led Thomson to relativism, for he accepted the belief in God's wisdom and love. He accepted some aspects of literary continuity by incorporating Biblical, classical and Miltonic allusions into his vision. These became a basis for his interpretation of the simultaneity of past and present. And the virtues of the heroic, political, and literary heroes of the past find a place in his catalogs because they represent values that the virtuous moderns also possess. Despite changing particulars, there were virtues that endured exactly as there were evils that endured. When [in *Religious Trends in English Poetry* (1939)] Hoxie N. Fairchild writes that in *The Seasons* God is social and smiling, that 'All of Him has faded away except the cosmic grin,' he completely ignores Thomson's repeated assertions of human pain and suffering: 'the thousand nameless Ills, / That one incessant Struggle render Life, / One Scene of Toil, of Suffering, and of Fate' (*Winter,* 349-51).

Thomson converts conventional figures such as repetition or metaphor to his own vision of a brilliant and dangerous spatial world in change. Thus repetition as epizeuxis defines intensity by spatial movement or extent. His use of metaphor that shifts between natural description and personification relates felt particularity to a parallel human order and reaffirms the human feeling necessary to the interpretation and appreciation of nature. Another aspect of Thomson's use of metaphor contrasts man's imperfection with God's perfection by illustrating the dependence of man's imagination upon God's creativity. The same term is, in one instance, literal, and, in another, metaphoric. The deluge is an actual deluge in one season, a deluge of light or earth in another. The elements themselves are converted into aspects of each other, and the implications of this procedure are both scientific and religious. There is nothing that man can imagine or discover which God has not already created in the universe. Man can occasionally discover what he never knew before, but it was always there, and it supports the interpretation of man's knowledge as fragmentary and God's power as omnipresent.

In this world in which nature is often puzzling, anxiety is no stranger to man. Geoffrey Tillotson notes that '*anxious* was a favourite Augustan epithet,' and Thomson's poem adjusts a common term and idea to his own ends. The wandering narrator observes uncertainty, harmony and disharmony. But these lead him to a recognition of his own limitations. Critics have objected that Thomson often shifts from one place to another without explanation, what Reuben A. Brower calls 'the bald lack of transitions,' yet this practice is consistent with his vision. Logical and reasonable explanations will not do; good men die and evil ones live on, and no rationalizing will explain God's wisdom. Time and again the ironic silence indicates the need for faith and the failure of reason to understand God's ways. Indeed, when the individual feels most at one with God, silence is the only answer, and the last line of the **'Hymn'** is, 'Come then, expressive Silence, muse his Praise.'

With the varied uses of genres and figures, Thomson necessarily combined poetic tones appropriate to them. In his depiction of rural workers his language is occasionally sensual, aware of the pleasure in sexual play and healthy sexual appetites. To talk of Thomson's bad taste is to disregard the fact that in the poem sexual pleasures are a genuine part of the transient joys of rural man. Thomson had a fine sense of playing off one style against another to illustrate the unexpected collocation of joy and suffering, and his letters reveal that the poetry expressed deep-rooted human values, pertinent to his comic and ironic as well as to his serious tones.

> It is always a maxim with me, [he writes in a
>   letter of 1742]
> To honour humble worth, and, scorning state,
> Piss on the proud inhospitable gate.
> For which reason I go scattering my water
> every where about Richmond.

Throughout the poem Thomson attacks courtiers and aristocrats and all others who in pride and viciousness pursue their selfish interests. These Thomson sees as never entering the kingdom of heaven, but his sympathy for the poor and the weak does not lead him to a revolutionary position. He opposes the vicious jailers, the mean squires, the cruel bird-killers, but he adheres to a conventional class structure. His view of change operates within the given natural and institutional boundaries.

The estates with their prospects constitute a middle place between earth and heaven from which one can view infinity. Thomson establishes a typical eighteenth-century cluster of peace, prosperity, patriotism, and plenty, and the estates are the sources of wealth and the basis for Britain's power, This means that the poem is often fulsome in its praise of aristocrats; often the dreariest passages are those in which the ideals of the squirearchy are identified with those of the Horatian contented man, and complacence is substituted for composure.

In *The Seasons* Thomson undertook a series of experiments that led him to new uses of imagery, to trials in word combinations, to incorporation of scientific with classical and Biblical language in order to express his poetic vision of the world. The traditions of word order, sentence structure, diction and subject that he inherited he sought to use for his own new purposes. He developed techniques of recurrence to express subtle temporal and spatial changes; he used the inherited figures of paradox and irony to express scientific ideas in which minute space contained worlds and silence roared. Within the view of successive space, he saw a constant shifting and interrelating of men and nature in which objects were transformed, as were the words that Thomson used to express them. His poem moved within a classical and religious tradition that was connected with an exhilarating sense of the present, scientifically and precisely felt. Thomson used nature to develop a 'new-creating Word' and 'a heightened Form.' The new word and form expressed, within a great tradition of English poetry, the fragmentary perception of the beauty, sublimity, benevolence and destruction that man experienced, but only God fully understood. . . .

Thomson's great achievement [in *The Seasons*] is to have fashioned a conception which, by bringing nature to the forefront of his poem, became a new poetic way of defining human experience. Thomson was not the first nature poet to write in English, but he was the first to provide an effective idiom in which science, religion, natural description and classical allusion blended to describe the glory, baseness and uncertainty of man's earthly environment, holding forth the hope of heavenly love and wisdom.

Thomson did not deny the actuality of wickedness, the hunter-killers, the wealthy aristocrats disregarding human need and squandering their wealth, the religious exploiters and the brutal executors of injustice. Nor did he deny that aspects of nature seemed, at times, jealous and vindictive, destroying good men and sparing the wicked. But these aspects existed simultaneously with others, with the comic, exhilarating, joyful transformations. This double view he accepted, but he did not accept any simple moral arithmetic in nature and he did not believe that virtue or benevolence was directly rewarded on earth.

Thomson did not have these considerations in view when he composed *Winter* in 1726, and the final work is all the more impressive if one attends to its modest inception. In a famous letter to William Cranstoun [*c.* October 1, 1725] Thomson wrote: 'Nature delights me in every form, I am just now painting her in her most lugubrious dress; for my own amusement, describing winter as it presents it self.' And in the same letter he explained the source of *Winter:* 'Mr. Rickelton's poem on winter, which I still have, first put the design into my head.' When he published his 'Preface' in the second edition of *Winter* (1726), he announced his intent of composing poems on the other seasons, but he was now cognizant that he was working on a 'great' subject formerly treated by the 'best' poets.

The seasons provided Thomson with a naturalistic basis for change which, by its cyclical pattern, permitted limited progression in any one season while relating the whole to God's power. But the cycle of the seasons is not the circle of perfection, and in the poem the cyclical repetition, like the confrontation of opposites, does not lead to a whole. It leads to a temporary completion that introduces a new beginning. Scientifically, change was explained by the traditional assumptions of the transformability of the four elements, but Thomson mixes this view with a description of observed natural changes. The speaker absorbs the scientific explanation by mixing natural description with personification, by using the same term in a literal and metaphoric sense. A knowledge of science can assist man in understanding nature, but such knowledge cannot provide answers to ultimate questions.

Pope and Swift saw much of the present as a rejection of the humanistic views of the past, but Thomson, while sharing many of these objections, found approximations of the ideal past in the society of the present. This recognition was in no sense a support of all current institutions, but neither he nor the satirists were revolutionaries. Change came by degrees, and the history of states was the history of rising and falling empires, and only God's wisdom could explain the ultimate reasons for such change.

For us, Thomson's patriotism and his flattery of his aristocratic friends and patrons is reprehensible. Yet it is consistent with his interpretation of the state as a responsible institution in the family of nations. Britain, by creating necessary commerce and putting down disorderly nations, becomes the father of an international family, even though in its own local family there are proud, vicious and unruly members. Since Britain is the poet's country, set in the temperate zone, the mean between extremes, it possesses the features of a model.

Thomson's own move from Scotland to London was a personal instance of the more general movement taking place in his society. His poetry describes commercial expansion, the movements of geographical exploration and inquiry. Such movement could be harmonious or disharmonious, but it explains why a rural estate could be interpreted as a retreat that was not an escape but a model. In so far as man sought to incorporate into his estate a sense of the past with a prospect for the future, he rested content within his limited world. It was Thomson's conception that the world could not and should not remain confined within man's private domain. His poem, therefore, reveals the need to explore, to inquire, to leave the comfortable shelter. Man had to experience the nature that God created, though it might merely lead him back to the

temperate zone.

Marshall McLuhan has suggested [in *The Gutenberg Galaxy* (1962)] that 'landscape offered a broader and less exacting course for those who were preoccupied with the new psychological interests on the one hand and with the means of evading the new insistence on non-metaphorical and mathematical statement as the mode of poetry, on the other hand.' But this interpretation, with its assumption that Pope's poetry was a poetry of statement and its claim that 'landscape' poetry provided an alternative to it, merely perpetuates fictions about Pope's and Thomson's poetry. Pope's poetry was no more a poetry of statement than Thomson's was anti-mathematical. Nor was it a less exacting course. . . .

Whatever his conscious sources were in 1726, the poem gradually became a palimpsest, the ends of which were to evoke the varied sentiments towards nature, man and God and to urge that as a consequence of man's fragmentary understanding the joy, beauty, pain and puzzle of the world demanded endurance and belief.

The poem, with its cyclical pattern and progressive moments, with religious exclamations preceded and followed by empirical description, deliberately avoided rational connections. It was composed of diverse fragments, the purpose of which was to establish links and contrasts among nature, animals, man and God. Thus Thomson created a world of simultaneous occurrences in space, but these only occasionally led to harmonious blending. The world being perceivable only in fragments, it was inevitable that no view of the whole could exist without an act of belief.

In so far as the past existed in the present, it could be found in an ideal retreat, in those isolated moments in man's life when the virtues of the past, the deeds of virtuous men and the writings of genius lived for those who appreciated them and sought to bring their values into the living present. For it is in the living, changing, joyous and uneasy present that Thomson's poem has its vitality.

There is no single narrative development, but there are varied narratives and scenes of 'sad Presage.' There is no single 'nature,' but there are varied interpretations of nature at different places and times. Yet all of these are controlled by a concept of natural change governed by a God who for all His variations is timeless and omnipresent. In the organization of *The Seasons* even organically unified parts are merely another aspect of fragmentation, held together by the principles of repetition and transformation.

The unifying imagery in each season and the stylistic and thematic unity of the whole prevent the poem from collapsing into a heap of fragments. Not only is there an underlying rhythm in the succession of the seasons and an order of elements, but within each season the fragments are juxtaposed to blend or clash. These reveal, in the very order of the seasons, a world in which man, while rejoicing in and competing with nature, is surrounded and often engulfed by it. Man may be superior to the animals in consciousness, but he can be their prey, as they can be his. It is possible to establish coherence and organic interrelatedness in some areas of Thomson's world, but the world as a whole remains a maze, the plan of which is hidden from mortal eye. It is, however, the poet's privilege, because of the eminences on which he stands (emblematic of his philosophical and spiritual elevation), occasionally to see and to speak with prophetic, with more than mortal, vision.

The repetitive themes, images, words become a means for interconnecting the whole. Thomson's unifying procedure makes demands upon the reader to construct distinctions within the poem, a demand that has all too often been rejected. It is now a commonplace that terms like 'wit' and 'nature' carry multiple meanings in the *Essay on Criticism* or the *Essay on Man,* and critics no longer deny to this repetition a valuable artistic function. Thomson's procedure is a variant of this Augustan practice, but he has not been granted the same consideration and understanding. Yet in **The Seasons** the development of varied and contrary contexts, the use of illusive allusion, the use of participles, of deliberately altered parts of speech, is Thomson's artistic signature. His general terms must be understood as incorporating many individual possibilities, exactly as God is to be apprehended in and through variations that are, nevertheless, one. This conception of general terms is inherent in the conception of Thomson's language. His terms are not mythopoeic, but rather inclusive terms for a varied group of references, since the same act or event can be interpreted from different perspectives. It is for this reason that metonymy is a frequent figure in the poem; in it, the whole represents a part, the general is used for the specific, the effect for the cause.

The other types of imagery in the poem—personification, periphrasis, metaphor, etc.—are all instances of Thomson's conversion of literary conventions to his own artistry. For these images, fluctuating as they do between the literal and the metaphoric, the allegorical and the natural, the human and the non-human, exemplify Thomson's world. In it the imaginative is interpreted by reference to the known. The natural environment becomes the basis for the magic changes and transformations that take place, and Thomson celebrates the beauty, sublimity, wonder and menace of the known world.

One aspect of nature can show cruelty or love to another— the sun to flowers, the breeze to the seeds, the fish to the flies—just as nature can show love or cruelty to man. There is no necessary harmony between nature and man or within nature. Moments of harmony exist, but in no particular instance can imperfect man presume to understand perfect God. The imagery of change that enacts this view is a Thomsonian innovation and neither Milton nor Wordsworth uses the conventions for such purposes.

The language of the poem is unmistakably directed toward expressing Thomson's thought and feeling. It is the result of his experience of the world, and the prose language of his letters and his 'Preface' find their way into

his poetry in demonstration of the fact that his poetry springs from his view of the world. The language, indeed, provides a unifying force in the sense that, for all its variations of tone—burlesque, comic, eulogistic, elegiac, beautiful or sublime—it incorporates Biblical, classical and scientific meanings with current usage. To this extent illusive allusions, Latinate words, periphrases and personifications, participles and hyphenated terms belong to the procedure of making the past simultaneous with the present or adding present implications to past meanings and acts. Yet such words and procedure are selective, for not all fragments of the past function effectively.

The language and thought incorporate not only external traditions but personal feelings and events. The Latinate and scientific constructions serve to create an aesthetic distance between the narrator and his private feelings. Thomson's personal involvement in the poem is concealed by these techniques at the same time that they convey his views of human experience. Thus he can talk about sex while describing flowers or about his own feelings of the pain of love by describing the ideal. These techniques are methods to convert and conceal his private feelings though critics have naïvely assumed that his language was 'objective' rather than an artistic instrument for disguising but not disregarding the personal sources.

Thomson uses the third-person speaker so that the reader can place himself in the position of the speaker. When Thomson shifts to the first person or to the vocative, he does so to indicate that the speaker's private perspective is another instance of the general voice. In this, it becomes a model for responding to the environment and God. The different tones—the comic, burlesque, mock-heroic, elegiac, etc.—provide perspectives on the different classes and on the literary conventions appropriate to them. For the tones are referred to and tested by the naturalistic environment which, traditionally, they have allegorized and idealized. Thomson's poem may, therefore, be understood as seeking to fuse the allegorical with the natural and to use allusions to Virgil and the Bible to support his own vision of the world.

Thomson's defects are of two kinds: he is limited in his knowledge of man and in the range of his understanding of human behavior; and, within the range to which he confines himself, he sometimes uses techniques formalistically to conceal his inadequate grasp of a situation or to cajole the reader by flattery or sentimentality. The poem can become overly scientific and excessively formal or overly sentimental, the types of dangers that Thomson risks by using the mixed form and scientific or abstract terms. There is always the risk, too, that repetition will rub off the rough individual edges of a general term and make it vague and indefinite. Thomson tries to avoid succumbing to such faults by employing a fragmentary structure which prevents any readily accepted generalization, and in this he is overwhelmingly successful, even when he introduces scientific explanations and terminology.

Thomson related nature's transformations to the familial,

commercial, political and social world of man. The unity, thought, diction, grammar of the poem offered an interpretation of Augustan society, that, for all its similarity to the views of Pope, presented a novel poetic vision. When Wordsworth came to write of nature in the *Lyrical Ballads* and *The Prelude,* he was writing of a different nature and a different world. Thomson's third-person speaker-poet, his interpolated narratives, his shuttling between description and metaphor, his preferred epithets and individual diction were not idiosyncrasies; they were related to a view of poetry that sought an idiom for the fragmentary, yet beautiful and aweful, firmament of space in which man and nature were subject to the transient moments of beauty, awe and destruction. For Thomson there was the need to collect as many fragmentary views as possible so that they became an ordered disorder. For Wordsworth the symbolic language envisioned a wholeness and a unity through the poet's consciousness, so that his fragments imply a whole. But Thomson's order demands of the reader a rejection of completion, a constant and unending discrimination of distinctions. He recognized then what we recognize now, that what man understands is only a perspective, and that although some of these may fortunately combine to give a momentary harmony, too much occurs that is inharmonious to permit a reasoned answer. Thomson saw and felt and knew a world for which he found a personal idiom and he believed unfailingly in another world that he neither saw nor knew. For both these worlds he created an artistic vision, and *The Seasons* is its unfolding.

Morris Golden (essay date 1972)

SOURCE: "Observer and Observed in Eighteenth-Century Literature," in *The Self Observed: Swift, Johnson, Wordsworth,* The Johns Hopkins Press, 1972, pp. 7-32.

[*In the excerpt below, Golden examines patterns of "self-vision" in Thomson's poetry, notably* The Castle of Indolence *and* The Seasons.]

While James Thomson shares with Pope such contemporary aspirations as synthesis, civilization, and universal harmony, he necessarily shaped them into a different vision. Thomson seems to have been neither alienated nor overtly idiosyncratic. Aside from a line in *Winter* about his boyhood joys in storms and a stanza or two in *The Castle of Indolence* on his poetic ambitions, he did not break the generic limitations of the poeta to speak of his own career or condition. He left few letters or documents, and these reveal no more about obvious mental patterns than we can gather from the anecdotes of his friends about his laziness, his mild sensuality, or his eager good nature. For us, the idiosyncratic elements in his poetic imagination must be derived mainly from the poems themselves. In his two main poems, *The Seasons* and *The Castle of Indolence,* those personal characteristics become, I think, major principles of organization; and Thomson can be evidence that we do not need oddities verging on neurosis to provide critically useful patterns of self-vision in the poetry.

Perhaps because Thomson is much less pressed than Pope by reveries of aggression, eminence, and opposition, he can more directly use fiction to convey the peculiar tensions which characterized the life of the poet, and therefore the life of the self. In the "allegory" of *The Castle of Indolence,* Thomson develops two competing roles of the poet, Magician and Knight, between whom the narrative persona must choose. Their opposition takes place both in the mind of the poet-everyman and in society, as Thomson's projection of the self separates into self-indulgent dreamer and adventuring doer, sensualist and craftsman, hedonist and social reformer. Like Fielding in *Tom Jones,* Thomson tries to synthesize those divisions by urging the artist to send his fancies out in shaped art to show mankind its proper study and, in the process, to improve the health of his own mind. In opposing reverie and social reality, Thomson maintains his extraordinary representativeness. Almost all eighteenth-century English literature implies that the public and private are equivalents or parallels of the real outer world and the world of fantasy, and only in the greatest works—*The Rape of the Lock, Tom Jones, Songs of Innocence and Experience, Emma*—does fusion occur. More usually, as in other periods, its art suffers from the didactic fission of Thomson's Canto II, of Gray's *Progress of Poesy,* or of Goldsmith's *Vicar of Wakefield.*

In his letters, in the formal lecture of Canto II, and in general where he speaks as a moral observer, Thomson endorses the vision of man assuming social obligations rather than withdrawing into dreams, of didactic art and not selfish reverie. But as a poet and pilgrim in a painful world, the acting self finds the pleasures of the imagination seductive. In *The Castle of Indolence,* the setting and the castle itself serve as the seed ground for the imagination, which provides its own appurtenances: the silent shadowy forms which move about the valley, cousins of Pope's shimmering sylphs and uncles of Gray's bards, here as elsewhere Thomson's suggestions of poetic inspiration; the visions that come before half-closed eyes; the sanctum itself, "Close-hid . . . mid embowering Trees" (st. vii), the retired and dreaming mind which draws struggling mankind into pilgrimage. Since the Poet-Magician openly feeds man's secret wish, indolent reverie, he affects the pilgrims compulsively (st. xxii); he plays on them, our substitutes, like a hot seducer on a half-reluctant girl (st. xxiii), to melt her to his will and her own pleasurable loss.

Beginning with stanza xxviii, the self-conscious author uses the castle, a refuge in the mind for the indulgence of fantasies, as a device by which to maintain his control over alternative selves and worlds, to move back and forth between fantasy and actuality. The Hebridean shepherd (st. xxx), a figure in the persona's imagination like the other surrounding images of withdrawal into the self, has visions like the persona's, even refining the filminess of reverie. Pinched by his responsible universal self (sts. xxxi and xxxii), the persona promises to resume his social obligations as a poet, but he is drawn back by the castle's seductions, which include tapestries, music, cushions, even a fleeting tickle of sexuality in the reference to the harem bard. The culminating symbol of this sequence, a response to the sound effects of sublimely titillating storms (st. xliii), neatly and ironically contrasts with similar scenes at the center of *Winter:* the warm poet feeding on his imagination indoors, refusing to deal with insistent reality outside. Lulled to sleep by the noise of the storm, the mind has withdrawn to voluptuous, incoherent dreams beyond the power of poetry to follow (st. xlv); in the figure of man before us, activity in the world has been abandoned along with the capacity to evaluate the world.

But the persona has only been speculating on his sleeping condition and observing a contingency that he can still choose to avoid. Immediately (sts. xlvi-xlviii), the world of moral responsibility warns him that the reveries stirred by art, except for elegiac and pastoral memories, are hollow. They waste life as thoroughly, though not as obviously, as the busy mindlessness that repudiates imagination and therefore make us insects. From stanzas xlix to lv, Thomson uses the mirror of folly to satirize the activities repellent to any form of poetic temperament: the self-seeking routine of affairs which provides neither beauty nor improvement, the extreme practicality that balances the sterile imaginings of sleep. As a reminder of these last, and a return to the choices actually open to the persona, the blocked poeta of stanzas lvii-lx is a case study of the inability to break from visions to their expression, an artist who suffers awake from dreams that he cannot objectify. The same impotence appears in the last two stanzas in the canto by Thomson (lxxii and lxxiii), which show a further sense of the real dangers of indolence: the gangrene in the secret mind, where self-indulgence has eroded the will and the reason. As most of Thomson's contemporaries would have agreed, the final horror is the self-imprisoned mind.

In Canto II the poet chooses the preeminently social self, dedicated from birth to labor for civilization, improvement, and fruitfulness, as his representative. The Knight of Arts and Industry, whose celebration is to constitute the return to vigor of the persona's imagination (st. iv), grew up close to nature, but under the rigorous tutelage of Minerva and the muses he learned to practice all the arts and sciences. Like a poet from Scotland facing the challenge of England.

> Accomplish'd thus he from the Woods issu'd,
> Full of great Aims, and bent on bold Emprize. . . .
> To-wit, a barbarous World to civilize.
>
> (st. xiv)

Naturally, the Knight makes his seat in Britain, the symbol and ideal vision of a human society that opposes the Magician's castle of solipsism. As the Magician lures the active energies to languish and fester inwards, so the Knight (with the help of his bard Philomelus) brings them out to healthy involvement. In a major attack (sts. xlvii-lxiii), the old bard balances the Magician's song in the first canto, by calling for light, air, nature, and adventure; by repudiating the alternative as capitulating to death; and by advocating a great spurt from one's central will to overcome inertia. On another front, the Knight waves his wand to show the confirmed indolent the delusiveness of

their happiness, the rottenness of their private withdrawal, and the inevitability of destruction unless they reform immediately. The last stanzas, lxxviii-lxxxi, show the hell that awaits the incurable, a vision of the true Castle of Indolence: a wasteland ruled by Beggary and Scorn, the bogeys of the conscientious bourgeoisie. The wavering self—the persona, the pilgrims, all those not totally drugged by routine activities—must renounce fruitless reverie and seek social art if it is to save itself, do its duty, and please the observing self which stands for the judgment of universal man.

Thomson's sympathy with the archetypal adventure into the world and the corollary pattern of release of energies—at least a parallel of his movement from Scotland to poetic achievement in England, if not its direct image—is central also in *The Seasons* (particularly in *Spring*) and notable in *Liberty* and the less ambitious poems. His good consists in the principle of expansion, excursion, flowing out into the world. As in *The Castle of Indolence* he conceives the imagination as containing treasures deep within the self, so he everywhere senses potentialities, hidden possibilities awaiting light and flower, and he therefore affirms the value of piercing into the essence, leading it out, allowing it to radiate and create. Any agent for bringing it out, for fructifying or civilizing, imitates the sun or God. In *Spring,* for example, Thomson implies a fertile cycle, a hope of the future to come from the present, in his parallel of the hidden flower manifesting its energies as it blooms and the poet, "me," leaving the town for the country, where

> the raptured eye
> Hurries from joy to joy, and, hid beneath
> The fair profusion, yellow Autumn spies. . . .
>
> (ll. 111-13)

Heaven "sheds" various plants on nature, and "Swift fancy fired anticipates their growth" (l. 183), the seed within the mind responding to the hidden potentiality outside. The sun is the prototype of those who seize hidden truths (ll. 394-95); a fisherman brings treasures out of the depths (l. 396 ff.); a beloved girl has "looks demure that deeply pierce the soul" (l. 486), awakening its vital responses. From line 578 to the concluding domestic ideal, a number of images of drawing out, pouring in, and gripping the core convey the surge to life and growth in spring, within men as in external nature.

The complex of piercing into and leading out, of hidden value and treasure (and sometimes mystery or danger) is too fundamental in Thomson's imaginative vision of the world, too congenial for his mind in its attempts to grasp phenomena, to be limited to one season, and we find many examples of it elsewhere. In *Summer,* the dominating sun appears fully, after having been covered, a treasure released to man's and nature's benefit (l. 81 ff.). Its "quickening glance" brings the planets to life (l. 105), causes the vegetable world to ripen, and even, as its vital energy penetrates deep, impregnates rocks to fill diamonds with light (ll. 140-44). When the secret recess of one lover evokes and responds to messages from the other, man participates in the divinely Shaftesburian attributes of union, as in a central episode of *Summer,* a story in which a girl is revealed in awesome nudity to a boy who loves her (ll. 1269-1370). In *Autumn,* the emergence of pastoral love develops as myth, the story of Palemon and Lavinia hinting of Ceres and Persephone as well as its more direct model in the Book of Ruth (ll. 177-310). Cycles, implied in these myths, are central to Thomson's presentation of Winter as part of a hopeful world, and so in the last part of *The Seasons*

> The front-concocted glebe
> Draws in abundant vegetable soul,
> And gathers vigour for the coming year.
>
> (ll. 706-8)

Near the seat of Winter, Peter the Great adventured forth like Thomson and the Knight of Arts and Industry, found the needed knowledge, and out of mingled love, courage, and duty nurtured the seeds of civilization in his subjects.

At the center of *Spring,* as at the center of the world's living activities, is the impelling force, the eager excursive energy, of love, a form taken by the divine Adventurer which can provide worthy man with the core of motivation. When tracing "Nature's great command" (l. 634) to increase and multiply, Thomson presents the elements of this force that man can comprehend, a complex latent in the whole poem: all creation is driven by Spring, which connects fertility, adventurous explorations, even the sex and warfare of raging bulls (direct from a similar engagement in Virgil's third *Georgic*), and indescribably violent sea monsters, to show that all movement feeds life. Though not so extensively as *Spring* (the poem of birth), the other *Seasons* and the lesser poems also reflect a universe of fertility, movement, and variety. Even *Winter* shows life everywhere but at the seat of the god, with birds in all the skies, peasants on Dutch canals, and wolves and bears prowling across polar regions. As against Pope's universe of careful shadings, Thomson's is a harmony of profusion and bold contrasts. Though he shares with Pope a perfectly artistic universe, he adores not the subtle Manipulator of light and shade but the brave, spectacular Impresario.

Thomson's social and psychological corollary of his vision of a universe harmonized by love is fruitful and serene civilization: both for him and for Pope, civilization is imaged as an eminence constantly endangered by barbarism. In *Summer,* as in *The Castle of Indolence* and *Liberty,* England is the hope and nourishment of the world, an emblem of the divinely fruitful (ll. 1400 ff., 1440), an island which sheds benevolence and humanity through encircling storms (ll. 1595-1601). In the middle of *Autumn* (l. 480 ff.), idyllically busy peasants at harvest, awakened Scottish industry, poets in their inspiring groves, and the learned man superior to superstition and folly (l. 1135), all must replace the preceding vision of the brutal days and sordid nights of hunters. *Winter,* like Canto II of *The Castle,* celebrates the civilizers who can bring warmth to the frozen soul: natural philosophers like Newton, social scientists humanely investigating

prisons, Lords Wilmington and Chesterfield, Peter the Great, and the central roll call of the great cultural heroes of history, all hoping to draw truth and harmony out of the mixed confusion of phenomena. The Knight of Arts and Industry may not be our ideal, but in the vision of progress, in Thomson's lecture to himself to assume his social obligations, he is Thomson's. Ranging the world for visions of man acting in it, Thomson's warm-hearted and open-natured observer in *The Seasons,* as in *The Castle of Indolence,* chooses the acting, outgoing, social self.

As might be expected, evil for Thomson is everywhere the perversion or negation of the good, the *Castle*'s poles of the sleeping mind and the barbarous aggressions in the mirror of folly. The images are similar to those of civilizing adventure but carry opposing implications, Thomson's mind apprehending the pattern of a darting force (analogous perhaps to gravity) in the moral universe. In *Spring,* Thomson shows that while God educes harmony from nature, the fallen human mind is the seat of chaos, which activates a series of painful passions (l. 272 ff.). Decay is now erosion, "inward-eating change," as against creative piercing to the core (l. 334). *Summer,* celebrating a "sublime" seasons when God's might is more visible than his love, manifests brutality in man and nature. After barbarous man, the hidden snake, and the roar of the lion, the sublimity of Africa culminates in the archetypal horror of the shipwrecked solitary (l. 939), a horror sharpened for Thomson because it subverts adventurous hopes. Moving out of the self, out of the protected past, one may reap expressiveness, discovery, and social usefulness, but one may also founder in bitter isolation. *Winter* shrouds the last agonies of death as *Summer* heated the passions of barbarism, and man's own core suffers superlative agony:

> The soul of man dies in him, loathing life,
> And black with more than melancholy views.
>
> (ll. 61-62)

From its lair, "Then issues forth the storm with sudden burst" (l. 154), mocking the loving movement of the springtime sun, or the latent seeds of life, or the hidden truth, or the poet's vision. Horrible ghosts howl out of groves (l. 192), which in earlier sections had been inspiring shades. From the east and north,

> Thick clouds ascend, in whose capacious womb
> A vapoury deluge lies, to snow congealed.
>
> (l. 225)

The heart of winter's domain shoots out wolves to perpetrate a series of horrors, which culminate in their digging up and eating the most sublime of forbidden treasure, recently buried corpses (l. 410). At the North Pole itself, the god holds his court of death (l. 895)—an absolute zero of activity, in contrast with the divine center, the world's source of energy and intensity.

Although Thomson usually seeks the hearts of moral nature and of social man, he at times raises his search to the divine, which he characteristically apprehends as a creative point. In *Spring,* for example, the apostrophe to God conceives of Him as a secret element in the center of being:

> Hail, Source of Being! Universal Soul
> Of heaven and earth! Essential Presence, hail!
>
> (ll. 556-57)

Summer ends in a vision of Philosophy darting through the universe, ranging from matter to the idea of God, to the "ideal kingdom," through the imagination to "notion quite abstract," finally to the indefinable mystery. *A Hymn on the Seasons,* like the end of *Summer,* conceives the highest sense as silent rapture: contemplating God,

> I lose
> Myself in him, in light ineffable!

In *A Poem Sacred to the Memory of Sir Isaac Newton,* Thomson is equally at home with the sublimity appropriate to visions of the earth and heavens. He reveres Newton, he says, because it was he

> whose well-purg'd penetrating Eye,
> The mystic Veil transpiercing, inly scan'd
> The rising, moving, wide-establish'd Frame.

His soul transcended the human; it surveyed the universe at large, reached toward its source (l. 130), and imitated God's position as observer and motivator above and beyond the local. As *Spring* (ll. 210-12) and *Summer* (l. 805 ff.) also suggest, such adventuring over space and time is parallel to the divine, particularly in piercing, discovering, and showing forth the millennially obscured; and in *Autumn,* Thomson asks where "the vast eternal springs" are hidden, "like creating Nature" from the mortal eye, and he wants the answer provided by

> the pervading genius, given to man
> To trace the secrets of the dark abyss.
>
> (ll. 777-79)

Using what has been brought back, on the other hand, is the province of the ambiguously human arts and industry. While purging man of the brutal and the indolent, the civilizing process also endangers the innocent, the personal, and the imaginative.

Since the step before the Fall, the setting out from within the self to seek the divinely hidden core, is free of such destructive tendencies, for Thomson it constitutes the purest movement of which man is capable: fusing the scientific and the artistic in the imaginative in imitation of God. Both alternative motives that he sensed in his nature—the pulls to imaginative withdrawal and to adventurous involvement—can draw together in the divine art of civilizing. In this very process of uniting the imaginative and the practical, the civilizer (every man's Knight of Arts and Industry) must moderate the divine for a fallen world. Bringing the earthly into his view, man becomes a judge not only of it but also of the divine within himself. . . .

Donald Greene (essay date 1977)

SOURCE: "From Accidie to Neurosis: *The Castle of Indolence* Revisited," in *English Literature in the Age of Disguise,* edited by Maximillian E. Novak, University of California Press, 1977, pp. 131-56.

[*Greene is an American educator and essayist. In the following excerpt, he discusses the moral, psychiatric, and theological aspects of* The Castle of Indolence, *arguing that the poem has been overshadowed by the popularity of Thomson's earlier work,* The Seasons.]

In 1916 George Saintsbury published a book about eighteenth-century English literature bearing the curious title *The Peace of the Augustans.* The book itself is a strange one. Saintsbury, then an old man in a new and frightening world, created in it an imaginary eighteenth century in which he found the security lacking in the Europe of 1916. The title is curious because, first, one does not read far in the English literature of the eighteenth century before discovering many expressions of deep distrust of the despotism of Augustus Caesar's Rome and contempt for the sycophancy of the great writers of the Augustan establishment. And it is hard to conceive how anyone familiar with British political and social history of the eighteenth century, its wars and riots and invasions, and with the tirades against it by those angry young men—who grew even angrier as they grew older—Swift, Pope in *The Dunciad* and later satires, Johnson in *London* and his political writing of the thirties and fifties, could see it as preeminently a time of peace. . . .

That Englishmen somehow enjoyed more "peace" in the eighteenth than in other centuries seems a priori unlikely, human nature being what it is. True, verses expressing a complacent optimism about things as they are, or as people would like to think they are, were popular, as they have been in other times—verses like Pomfret's *The Choice* and others in the "Happy Man" tradition. Probably the most widely read and loved verse of the twentieth century has been that of Edgar Guest, Rod McKuen, and their like (as for prose, a best-seller in the 1970s bears the reassuring title *I'm O.K., You're O.K.*). Yet few thoughtful people would be inclined to call such phenomena evidence of the "peace of the twentieth century"—rather, perhaps, they illustrate a vain longing for the peace that continues to evade us. And if we take the trouble to look carefully at the more serious writing of eighteenth-century Britain, we find its inhabitants vexed with much the same woes of the human condition as those of the seventeenth, nineteenth, twentieth, or any other century.

> How small of all that human hearts endure
> That part which laws or kings can cause or cure!

Samuel Johnson wrote, implying not, as Macaulay foolishly suggested, that he thought public affairs unimportant—his voluminous and energetic political writings show he was well aware that legislators and other politicians can cause a great deal of curable or preventable human misery—but that, great as such misery may be, it is still minuscule compared with that the human individual inflicts on himself.

I should like in this paper to consider an eighteenth-century work dealing with one widespread form of such misery, James Thomson's *The Castle of Indolence*. The subtitle of the standard biography of Thomson is "The Poet of *The Seasons*," and it is true that, from its very beginning down to Ralph Cohen's two large volumes, criticism of Thomson has been dominated by the earlier poem, which has provided a rich mine for the historian of ideas. But it is a pity the popularity of *The Seasons* has so overshadowed the later and more mature poem, which many have found more readable and whose content, as I wish here to argue, is at least equally worthy of being taken seriously. . . .

To some extent the poem has been the victim of the biographical or intentional fallacy, often called a piece of "dainty filigree" of versification. It was said to have originated as a joke among Thomson and his friends about their laziness, much as *The Rape of the Lock* used to be thought of as no more than a private joke among Pope, Caryll, and the Fermor and Petre families—until Cleanth Brooks took the trouble, apparently for the first time, to read what was actually being said in the poem, and discovered it was about what its title said it was about—namely, rape. Thomson's poem may have started as a joke, but we should note how the account given by Thomson's early biographer continues:

> It was at first little more than a few detached stanzas in the way of raillery on himself, and on some of his friends. . . . But he saw very soon that the subject deserved to be treated more seriously, and in a form fitted to convey one of the most important moral lessons.

I should like in this paper to try to put the subject of the poem into its moral and psychiatric—indeed, theological—context, and to show that it does deserve to be treated seriously.

Why has it not been so treated? First, perhaps, because of the light touches of humor one often finds in it—for instance, the charming and often quoted line by Thomson about himself, "A bard here dwelt, more fat than bard beseems." But recent study of Jane Austen, not to mention *The Rape of the Lock,* has surely shown us that exquisitely delicate humor is by no means incompatible with profound seriousness of moral purpose. And second, because laziness, irresponsibility, obesity seem to many a subject for light humor, not serious moral reflection, though the example of Falstaff might give them pause. The poem after all opens grimly enough:

> O mortal man, who livest here by toil,
> Do not complain of this thy hard estate;
> That like an emmet thou must ever moil
> Is a sad sentence of an ancient date:
> And certes there is for it reason great;
> For, though sometimes it makes thee weep and wail,
> And curse thy stars, and early drudge and late,

> Withouten that would come an heavier bale,
> Loose life, unruly passions, and diseases pale.

Clearly there is more here than a clever pastiche of Spenser's versification. Thomson has something to say to us, and what he is saying, if true, is important: "We complain about the curse of having to work, the punishment of the Fall—'In the sweat of thy brow, thou shalt earn thy bread.' And yet we should be grateful for this 'curse,' since otherwise we should suffer much worse affliction." Had Sartre or Camus written this, we might be applauding its remarkably modern, hard-nosed "existentialist" view of the "absurdity" of the human condition, or something of the sort.

Thomson knew what he was talking about; it is a poem of personal experience. The story was told of his friend, the musicologist Charles Burney, coming to call on Thomson—this was when he was a man in his thirties and reasonably successful in life. Burney found him at two in the afternoon still in bed, "with the curtains closed and the window shut." Burney asked the poet why he did not get up. Thomson thought this proposition over for a while and finally explained, "Why, mon, I had not motive to rise." We smile: it is a ludicrous story. And yet what a pathetic one! About the same time, another younger, talented writer, Samuel Johnson, lay groaning in his bed all morning, unable to rise, his will paralyzed, and had to be coaxed to dictate to a friend a translation he had undertaken, on the plea that the printer and his family were starving through his negligence. In Robert Penn Warren's *All the King's Men*, the narrator, when he experiences trauma—when his marriage breaks up, when he learns of the dishonesty of the man he has taken as his ideal of integrity—goes into what he calls "the Great Sleep":

> Sometimes sleep gets to be a serious and complete thing. You stop going to sleep in order that you may be able to get up, but get up in order that you may be able to go back to sleep. . . . He would come home in the evening, and because he knew that he could not work he would go to bed immediately. He would sleep twelve hours, fourteen hours, fifteen hours, feeling himself, while asleep, plunge deeper and deeper into sleep like a diver groping downward into dark water. . . . Then in the morning he would lie in bed, not wanting anything, not even hungry, hearing the small sounds of the world sneaking and seeping back into the room. . . . Then he would think: If I don't get up I can't go back to bed.

This desire for unconsciousness, because life with full consciousness is too much to bear, is surely a form of death wish, as are such other varieties of escape from full consciousness as alcoholism and drug addiction. Johnson was once asked, apropos of drunkenness, "I wonder what pleasure men can take in making beasts of themselves." He answered with simple wisdom, "He who makes a beast of himself gets rid of the pain of being a man." So with the escape routes of somnolence and lethargy. Comic as their victims may seem—as the victims of schizophrenia and catatonia seemed to earlier ages—we might ponder a fragment of dialogue in Evelyn Waugh's *Brideshead*

Revisited, concerning the young alcoholic wreck, Sebastian Flyte:

> "I suppose he doesn't suffer?"

> "Oh, yes, I think he does. One can have no idea what the suffering may be, to be maimed as he is—no dignity, no power of will."

Perhaps the power of Thomson's poem comes from the fact that Thomson—the fat, lazy, complaisant Jemmy Thomson, who never quite realized the potential his friends saw in him—knew something of such suffering.

It is not only in the language and versification that the poem is indebted to Spenser, who knew a good deal about the mental and moral ills that afflict the human race. The rhetoric of the Wizard Indolence, in his long persuasive speech setting forth the joys of detachment from life, is close to that of Despair in Book I of *The Faerie Queene:* "Ease after pain, port after stormy seas, / Sleep after toil, death after life, doth greatly please." The student of older literature has met the Wizard himself many times before under the names of Sloth, Idleness, and Accidie (or Acedia). The most easily accessible full account is that by Chaucer's Parson. Accidie, he tells us, is the deprivation of "the love of all goodness." Accidie "dooth alle thyng with anoy [ennui], and with wrawnesse [fretfulness], slakenesse, and excusacioun, and with ydelnesse and unlust." "Accidie is lyk hem that been in the peyne of helle, by cause of hir slouthe and hir hevynesse." It entails lethargy and somnolence and damage to one's temporal well-being through lack of care. Its most advanced stage is "wanhope, that is despair of the mercy of God." In *Piers Plowman,* Sloth is given an amusing speech of self-revelation. In *The Pilgrim's Progress* we meet him under various names, the most memorable being Giant Despair. In Spenser, Sloth is the chief of the counsellors of Lucifera—pride, as always the prime, the original sin, of which the others are emanations. Sloth rides before her coach on his symbolic animal the ass—"sluggish Idelnesse, the nourse of sin," "still drowned in sleep and most of his days dead. . . . From worldly cares himself he did esloyne [separate]. . . . From every work he challenged essoyne [exemption]. . . . His life he led in lawless riotesse / By which he grew to grevous malady." . . .

Johnson's Happy Valley in *Rasselas,* where everyone's physical wants are provided for without any effort on his part, and where no one is happy, is Thomson's **Castle** over again. There is Johnson's Latin poem [*Gnothi Seauton*] in which he vividly describes the depression and lethargy that seize him after he has completed the laborious task of revising his *Dictionary,* the troubled state of his mind where "empty forms, fleeting shadows, lonely shapes of things flit through the void," and he longs for another dictionary to drudge at—almost a replica of the first stanza of Thomson's poem. Much more could be cited to show that the eighteenth century, whatever the myths about its self-satisfied complacency, was as familiar with accidie as the Middle Ages, with melancholy as the Renaissance or the Romantics, with doubt as the Tennyson of *In Memoriam* and the Arnold of "Dover Beach," with *Angst* as Auden's Age of Anxiety. The names change from one generation to the next, and each generation gets a gloomy satisfaction from the thought that it is the victim of something new and fashionable—itself a manifestation of the senior sin, pride. But the clinical descriptions of the condition, from Chaucer to Auden, seem indistinguishable.

Thomson's **Castle** is only one of a number of eighteenth-century literary works illustrating the condition. There are those of James Boswell. Not only are his *Journals* filled with intimate, detailed, and boring accounts of his own moods and vagaries—neurosis, virtually by definition, is boredom—he also wrote and published a set of periodical essays, named, after himself, *The Hypochondriack,* many of which he devotes to discussion of the nature of hypochondria, and to such related subjects as fears, excess, suicide, and alcoholism ("an Hypochondriack," he writes, "is under peculiar temptations to participate freely of wine"). Boswell displays little concern with the etiology of the condition: it may be physiological, or it may be that "the mind is sick"; he even entertains the hypothesis, rare in the eighteenth century, that "the malady is sometimes owing to the influence of evil spirits." But of the various symptoms and manifestations he writes eloquently, from long experience—and with relish: Boswell is one of those, sometimes thought to be indigenous to the late eighteenth and early nineteenth centuries, but easily to be found in any other, who feel their proneness to "melancholy" gives them a certain cachet. Johnson does his best to bludgeon him out of this in his letters replying to Boswell's more hypochondriacal ones: "You are always complaining of melancholy, and I conclude from those complaints that you are fond of it. No man talks of that which he is desirous to conceal," and, probing beneath the surface, "there lurks, perhaps, in every human heart a desire for distinction, which inclines every man first to hope, and then to believe, that Nature has given him something peculiar to himself." Accidie, like the rest, has its roots in Pride.

Of the two long eighteenth-century poems entitled *The Spleen,* that by Matthew Green (1737) takes a lighthearted approach, reinforced by his jaunty octosyllabic couplets—though, to be sure, he coins the striking phrase "the daymare Spleen." He disclaims any intention "to write a treatise on the Spleen." Instead, he describes in lively detail the kind of life he says he lives, designed to drive away spleen, a fairly run-of-the-mill performance in the "Happy Man" tradition; not very convincing perhaps—one is left with an uneasy feeling that he protests too much; it isn't as simple as all that. Far more searching are the Pindarics of Anne Finch (*née* Kingsmill), Countess of Winchilsea (1701). She begins by describing the Protean nature of spleen:

> What are thou, Spleen, which ev'rything dost ape?
> Thou Proteus to abus'd mankind,
> Who never yet thy real cause could find
> Or fix thee to remain in one continued shape?

In Burtonian fashion she describes its varied manifestations:

> Now a Dead Sea thou'lt represent
> A calm of stupid discontent—

sometimes an irrational rage, a panic fear, sometimes insomnia, nightmare, hallucination. But at the heart of her poem is a vigorous rejection of the theory that the condition has a physical cause.

With wholehearted conservatism, she insists on the theological explanation:

> Falsely the mortal part we blame
> Of our depress'd and pond'rous frame
> Which, till the first degrading sin—

the Adamite act of pride in the Garden—

> Let thee, its dull attendant, in. . . .

Like Thomson, she makes it clear that she is writing from personal experience:

> O'er me, alas! thou dost too much prevail:
> I feel thy force whilst I against thee rail:
> I feel my verse decay, and my crampt numbers
> fail—

like Wordsworth in the *Immortality Ode* and at the beginning of *The Prelude:*

> Thro' thy black jaundice, I all objects see,
>   As dark and terrible as thee.
> My lines decried, and my employment thought
> An useless folly, or presumptuous fault. . . .

We return at last to revisit briefly the *Castle of Indolence,* though it deserves the more thorough tour that a close and sensitive reading of the text will provide. Its setting is a delightful pastoral landscape—"a pleasing land of drowsyhead"—described with lush onomatopoeia:

> Meantime unnumbered glittering streamlets
>   played,
> And hurled everywhere their waters sheen;
> That, as they bickered through the sunny
>   glade.
> Though restless still themselves, a lulling
>   murmur made.
>
>   . . . . .
>
> And where this valley winded out below,
> The murmuring main was heard, and scarcely
>   heard, to flow.

At the same time, Thomson skillfully introduces a vaguely ominous note:

> Full in the passage of the vale, above,
> A sable, silent, solemn forest stood;
> Where naught but shadowy forms were seen to
> move,
> As Idless fancied in her dreaming mood.
> And up the hills, on either side, a wood
> Of blackening pines, aye waving to and fro,
> Sent forth a sleepy horror through the blood.

These early stanzas of description are worthy to be ranked, among dream landscapes, with those of Tennyson's "The Lotos-Eaters" and Coleridge's "Kubla Khan."

The eleven-stanza oration in which the Wizard Indolence tempts the "pilgrims of the earth" into his castle is a masterpiece of persuasive rhetoric. It begins with a powerful appeal to self-pity:

> Behold! ye pilgrims of this earth, behold!
> See all but man with unearned pleasure gay.

Like the philosopher in chapter 22 of *Rasselas,* who advises men to "observe the hind of the forest and the linnet of the grove: let them consider the life of animals, whose motions are regulated by instinct; they obey their guide and are happy," he urges them to follow their natural impulses:

> Behold the merry minstrels of the morn,
> The swarming songsters of the careless grove,
> Ten thousand throats that, from the flowering
>   thorn,
> Hymn their good God, and carol sweet of love,
> Such grateful kindly raptures them emove!

Jemmy Thomson, who grew up in the harsh Scottish climate so vividly described in **Winter,** well knew that the lives of birds and beasts are not always a succession of grateful, kindly rapture. And, brought up on the Presbyterian Shorter Catechism, he well knew that God is just as well as "good."

Like Rousseau in his *First Discourse,* the Wizard takes a jaundiced view of "civilization." In startlingly Marxist accents, he reveals the source of its woes to be capitalistic individualism:

> Outcast of Nature, man! the wretched thrall
> Of bitter-dropping sweat, of sweltry pain,
> Of cares that eat away thy heart with gall,
> And of the vices, an inhuman train,
> That all proceed from savage thirst of gain:
> For when hard-hearted Interest first began
> To poison earth, Astraea left the plain;
> Guile, Violence, and Murder seized on man,
> And, for soft milky streams, with blood the
>   rivers ran.

He goes on to give a repellent account of the world of which he promises his hearers "oblivion":

> With me, you need not rise at early dawn
> To pass the joyless day in various stounds.
>
>   . . . . .
>
> To cheat, and dun, and lie, and visit pay,
> Now flattering base, now giving secret wounds,

Or prowl in courts of law for human prey,
In venal senate thieve, or rob on broad highway.

Private as well as public life is noxious: in the Castle,

To tardy swain no shrill-voiced matrons squall;
No dogs, no babes, no wives to stun your ear;
No hammers thump; no horrid blacksmith sear,
No noisy tradesman your sweet slumbers start.

In freeing themselves from such annoyances, the Wizard argues, the pilgrims will be following the path of true virtue:

Thus, from the source of tender Indolence,
With milky blood the heart is overflown,
Is soothed and sweetened by the social sense;
For interest, envy, pride, and strife are banished
hence.

He preaches the ideal of virtuous detachment:

What, what is virtue but repose of mind?
A pure ethereal calm that knows no storm,
Above the reach of wild ambition's wind,
Above those passions that this world deform.

Such detachment has always been praised:

The best of men have ever loved repose:
They hate to mingle in the filthy fray,

and some of the greatest men in history have sought such virtuous retirement:

So Scipio, to the soft Cumaean shore
Retiring, tasted joy he never knew before.

Not that, in the castle, everything will be boring inactivity: a program of leisurely recreation will be available:

Softly stealing with your wat'ry gear
Along the brooks, the crimson-spotted fry
You may delude. . . .

Better this than the "grievous folly,"

to heap up estate,
Losing the days you see beneath the sun. . . .
But sure it is of vanities most vain,
To toil for what you here untoiling may obtain.

It is all very clever. The joy of tuning in, turning on, and dropping out is heightened by the conviction that this is true wisdom and virtue—it is those who work to "heap up an estate," involving them in criminal aggression against their fellow men, who are wicked and foolish. Much discussion of this proposition, pro and con, has been heard in recent years: among student and other "activists" (sometimes ironically named) of the 1960s; from political platforms and newspaper editorials in connection with public "welfare" programs and trade unionism. The Wizard puts it very persuasively—on the surface, at least. Yet when we scrutinize the oration closely, do we not begin to wonder whether Thomson isn't subtly undermining it? "By entering the Castle, you will be following the path of true virtue, like Scipio; also, you will be getting away from the yapping of neighborhood dogs, squalling babies, and nagging wives": the ludicrous bathos of this is too striking for it to be unintentional. So is that of the first experience of the pilgrims when they enter the Castle, which is to be divested of their "garters and buckles" and other restrictive articles of clothing, and instead to put on slippers and gowns

Loose as the breeze that plays along the downs,
And waves the summer woods when evening
frowns,
O fair undress, best dress! it checks no vein,
But every flowing limb in pleasure drowns.

"First, just let me slip into something more comfortable." Certainly there are haunting stanzas describing the pleasure of the Castle—lush descriptions of its furnishings, its food and drink, its delights of sight and sound. But there are so many little comic details juxtaposed as to cast doubt on the theory held by some critics that Thomson, in spite of his announced moral purpose, is carried away by the attraction of the Castle.

At any rate, when the pilgrims enter it, they have a fine time at first. Everyone does his own thing:

Here freedom reigned, without the least alloy;
Nor gossip's tale, nor ancient maiden's gall,
Nor saintly spleen durst murmur at our joy,
And with envenomed tongue our pleasures pall—

there are innumerable varieties of spleen, all of them at odds with one another, as well as with the nonsplenetic part of the world.

For why? there was but one great rule for all;
To wit, that each should work his own desire,
And eat, drink, study, sleep, as it may fall,
Or melt the time in love, or wake the lyre—

nowadays guitar? It does indeed sound like the ideal of the hippie commune, or Rousseau's Noble Savagery.

But the pilgrims' enjoyment gradually deteriorates into boredom, as in the "Happy Valley":

Their only labour was to kill the time,
And labour dire it is, and weary woe.

Boredom develops into more serious neuroses, as with the individual who, "stung by spleen," "on himself his pensive fury worke," and

Never uttered word, save when first shone
The glittering star of eve—"Thank Heaven! the
day is done"—

and the recluse who never leaves his filthy chamber. And eventually

> Now must I mark the villainy we found,
> But ah! too late. . . .
> A place here was, deep, dreary, under ground
> Where still our inmates, when unpleasing grown,
> Diseased, and lothsome, privily were thrown.
> Far from the light of Heaven, they languished
>   there,
> Unpitied, uttering many a bitter groan;
> For of the wretches taken was no care.

And why should it have been, since the whole point of this "life style" is a refusal to care—acedia, of which Thomson's *indolentia* is virtually a Latin translation: a lack of pain; the Stoic and Epicurean recipe for avoidance of pain by refusing to become emotionally involved? Here in the dungeon, lethargy, depression, physical and psychosomatic disease torment their helpless victims.

The second canto of the poem has almost unanimously been condemned, or, at best, received with faint enthusiasm. In it, an individual called the Knight of Arts and

Industry, who has been brought up in conditions of primitive simplicity and virtue, and has been responsible for the civilizing of Europe, comes riding by and, in good Spenserian fashion, vanquishes the Wizard and rescues his prisoners, who then settle down to lives of useful industry and consequent happiness. This part of Thomson's allegory has been taken—for instance, by A. D. McKillop, the one student who has provided the poem with a full analysis and commentary—to be an expression of contemporary Whig social philosophy, as illustrated more fully in Addison, Steele, Defoe, and Benjamin Franklin. This, of course, is a philosophy very much out of fashion. In its historical setting it is seen primarily as a handmaid to the great industrial, commercial, and technological expansion of Great Britain in the eighteenth, and of Britain and the United States in the nineteenth century—of the heartless materialistic moneygrubbing later to be satirized and condemned by Southey, Dickens, and others, as earlier by Dryden, Swift, Pope, and Johnson. Sometimes, under the designation of "the Protestant (or Puritan) work ethic," it is placed in a wider setting, that of western Europe and America from the Reformation onward, and, with the help of Max Weber and R. H. Tawney, viewed hostilely as the prostitution of religion in the service of the new capitalism. A recent handbook gives a useful summary of the view:

> For many years it has been taken for granted that some special relationship existed between the Protestant Reformation and the rise of modern capitalism. . . . Weber (1904) suggested that modern capitalism was a by-product of the Protestant ethos. . . . Tawney (1926) gave even wider currency to the thesis that Calvinism prospered by adapting itself to the capitalist spirit. Either way, Protestantism became somehow (the causation was never demonstrated very clearly) guilty of the sins of modern capitalist society.

On the face of it, *The Castle of Indolence* seems to fit perfectly into such an interpretation. Thomson was by upbringing a Scottish Calvinist. In politics, he was an adherent of the "Patriots," the noisy Whig opposition group, of which William Pitt was the most successful political leader, that demanded more aggressive policies of commercial and imperialist expansion than Walpole was ready to provide, and, after Walpole was ousted, came to power and successfully put those policies into practice. McKillop seems to see in *The Castle of Indolence* an expression of inner conflict in Thomson between the side of his mind which gave assent (Canto II) to the demands of the "work ethic," the "new capitalism," the "manifest destiny" of British and American expansionism, and that which, in the passages in Canto I describing the delights of indolence, was repelled by it. Some kind of similar conflict, or self-contradiction, used to be detected in Thomson's contemporary, Daniel Defoe.

But this is surely too limited a context in which to read the poem—even if that context were itself authentic; and modern scholarship has emphatically established that it is not. The survey from which I quoted the summary of the Weber-Tawney thesis goes on to say that one of the most important recent scholarly developments has been "the

Title page of the second edition of The Castle of Indolence.

destruction of the orthodoxy about 'religion and the rise of capitalism.' . . . Both [Tawney's and Weber's] theses were rendered almost untenable by K. Samuelsson in *Religion and Economic Action,* who showed in full historical detail how institutionalized religion, Catholic as well as Protestant, resisted the growth of the new economic order." That fine Renaissance historian, Geoffrey Elton, may be allowed to furnish the epitaph over Weber-Tawney: "It was not Calvinism that freed men from the restraints of the traditional moral concepts in economics, but emancipation from religion and theology in general."

Recent studies of Defoe have exploded the notion that his works can somehow be used as texts to illustrate the Weber-Tawney thesis. If the "Puritan work ethic" is peculiarly the property of materialistic, expansion-oriented Whiggism in the eighteenth century, it is surprising to find men so little in sympathy with such a philosophy as Swift and Johnson promulgating that "ethic" as emphatically as Thomson and Addison. Swift's remedy for his neurotic young Yahoo was, he said, an unfailing one—"set him to hard work"; and Swift goes on with some caustic remarks about such fits of depression, of "vapors," afflicting only those rich enough to have leisure for them. The central motif of Johnson's private prayers, in spite of what seems to us his prodigious output of literary work, is his recurring plea for forgiveness for his sloth. He suggests as the remedy for his deep depression in 1773 the drudgery of a new dictionary. The dial plate of his watch bore, in Greek, the text from the Gospel . . .—"For the night cometh when no man can work." We recall the many parables of the New Testament, hardly a propaganda tract for the new capitalism, which stress the need for the fulfillment of one's God-given potential, notably the parable of the talents. We recall the motto of early monasticism, *Ora et labora,* "Work and pray." We recall that, though later men have called the condition hypochondria or neurosis or inhibition or *Angst,* and have sometimes found gratification in thinking it peculiar to their own generation, its symptoms sound indistinguishable from Spenser's and Chaucer's and Gregory the Great's precapitalist accidie.

Thomson's poem (like Lady Winchilsea's) is not, then, to be read as a discussion of a matter peculiar to the English scene of the eighteenth century, or even of the post-Reformation western European scene. It is a discussion of a personal psychological or psychiatric—in the end, theological—problem of Jemmy Thomson himself, and at the same time of a universal one of the fallen human condition in all ages. And possibly no one has described the seeming paradox involved more effectively than Thomson in the opening lines of *The Castle of Indolence*: do not complain, he says, of the "sad sentence of ancient date" that man is condemned to "live here by toil." On the contrary,

> . . . there is for it reason great:
> For though it sometimes makes thee weep and
>   wail,
> And curse thy stars, and early drudge and late,
> Withouten that would come an heavier bale.

Thomson knows, for, like Johnson and Boswell and many others, he has tried it.

Percy G. Adams (essay date 1977)

SOURCE: "James Thomson's Luxuriant Language," in *Graces of Harmony: Alliteration, Assonance, and Consonance in Eighteenth-Century British Poetry,* The University of Georgia Press, 1977, pp. 118-35.

[*In the following essay, Adams examines alliteration, assonance, and consonance in Thomson's poetry, citing it as a key to understanding what some critics have termed its "luxuriance."*]

"It . . . sometimes can be charged with filling the ear more than the mind."—Dr. Johnson

Few poems have been so often reprinted or so often condemned and admired as James Thomson's *The Seasons,* and one of the most controversial of that once popular poem's characteristics is its diction. Although Dr. Johnson admired Thomson, he spoke for a large group of readers, including Wordsworth and Hazlitt, when in *The Lives of the English Poets* he said of one aspect of Thomson's diction, it "is in the highest degree florid and luxuriant. . . . It is too exuberant and sometimes can be charged with filling the ear more than the mind." But an even greater number of readers, if not always such honored ones, have liked Thomson's language, from John More's (1777) praise of the "luxuriant images," to Robert Bell's (1860) admiration for the "richness and luxuriance of phrase," to the twentieth century's scholarly defense. In spite, however, of the perennially strong protest against Dr. Johnson's charges about the ear-filling qualities of Thomson's poetry, nowhere in the long and still lingering debate has anyone spoken of the nature of the sounds in that luxuriant language.

The neglect is all the more perplexing when we remember, first, that the poet himself insisted that he chose blank verse for *The Seasons* because it is "far more harmonious than rhyme" and, second, because he once listed "music" ahead of image, sentiment, and thought as one of the four chief characteristics of poetry. Furthermore, it has been shown that repetition is perhaps "the most important structural principle" in *The Seasons,* and repetition is perhaps the most important characteristic of music, whether by that term we mean pure music or the pleasing sounds that words can produce. Now Thomson made less use of rhyme, anaphora, and incremental repetition than did most other eighteenth-century poets, and his metrical stresses are not so regular as those in the heroic couplet, but he did employ alliteration, assonance, and consonance with as much variety and subtlety, as frequently and consciously, as any other important writer of his day. Nowhere in Ralph Cohen's thorough tracing of Thomson criticism, however, is any one of these three terms mentioned, and yet a study of Thomson's use of such acoustic devices will reveal much about the nature of his luxuriant language.

Like Dryden and Pope he went against conservative critical theory and employed phonic echoes in abundance. Their concentration in *The Seasons* is, in fact, far greater than for a relatively unornamental poet such as Wordsworth. The first 200 lines of *Winter,* for example, have at least 100 alliterations and 110 assonances, a proportion in each case of about one to two lines, while the opening 200 lines of Wordsworth's *Prelude* have, by a generous count, only 1 assonance to 5 lines and even fewer alliterations. The contrast becomes still more significant if one notes that over 20 of Thomson's echoes, and only 5 of Wordsworth's, are polysyllabic. As with other poets of his day and just before, Thomson's auditory appeal is heaviest in the purple passages, especially those describing the sights and sounds of nature, and less heavy in narrative or argumentative sections. In this image from *Spring,* for example, there are perhaps 16 stressed syllables every one of which is involved in at least one echo:

Th'expansive *At*mosphere is cramp'd with Cold;
But full of Life, and vivifying Soul,
Lifts the light Clouds sublime, and spreads them
    thin.

(28-30)

In the 3 lines there are 4 assonances—2 of 3 syllables, 1 of 4, and the end echo in "cold" and "soul"—to go with the alliterations, two polysyllabic, of [f], [k], and [l] and the consonance of [l], [t], and [dz]. Although he does have sections with relatively few such echoes, as in the long account of the pleasures of evening reading in *Winter,* Thomson employed ornaments of sound as much as his chief models Lucretius, Virgil, Dryden, and Pope.

In order to show that these acoustic aids are typical of Thomson and at the same time more profuse than for poets with whom he is sometimes associated, we can compare a well-known passage in the poetry of John Keats with a similar one in *The Seasons.* Keats's lush *Autumn* opens,

Season of mists and mellow fruitfulness,
    Close bosom-friend of the maturing sun;
Conspiring with him how to load and bless
    With fruit the vines that roun[d] the thatch-
    eaves run;
To bend with apples the moss'd cottage trees,
    And fill all fruit with ripeness to the core;
        To swell the gourd, and plump the hazel
        shells
With a sweet kernel; to set budding more,
    And still more, later flowers for the bees,
    Until they think warm days will never cease,
        For Summer has o'er-brimm[ed] their
        clammy cells.

Thomson's *Autumn* has many such sensuous descriptions, including one so like that in the later poem:

In chearful error, let us tread the maze
Of Autumn, unconfin'd; and taste, reviv'd,
The breath of orchard big with bending fruit.

Obedient to the breeze, and beating ray,
From the deep-loaded bough a mellow shower,
Incessant melts away. The juicy pear
Lies, in a soft profusion, scatter'd round.
A various sweetness swells the gentle race.

(626-33)

The question now is not which of the two groups of images is more attractive, either lexically or acoustically, but, rather, which poet depended more on internal echoes for his effects, for his appeal to the reader's ear. Keats is to be considered a more decorative poet than, say, Wordsworth, and while this opening section of "To Autumn" is indeed ripe with language that appeals to the sight and the touch—*mists, mellow, core, moss'd, gourd, kernel, clammy*—it obviously has far fewer phonic echoes than the passage from Thomson. Of perhaps fifty-three stressed syllables in Keats's lines, only twenty-two are involved in any kind of internal alliteration, assonance, or consonance, and only three of them twice. On the other hand, of Thomson's thirty-eight stressed syllables, twenty-seven participate in such internal echoes, thirteen of them at least twice, a strikingly greater proportion. Nor is the proportion noticeably altered if one counts the end repetitions in both passages. The chief difference is not in the consonant echoes; Keats has at most five assonances, each of two syllables, while Thomson, in a shorter passage, has eleven—one of four syllables, one of three—that, in spite of the seven initial [b]'s in three lines, dominate his description. Thomson's ornaments of language are indeed more luxuriant than those of Keats or Wordsworth or, for that matter, perhaps any important early nineteenth-century poet. Furthermore, we can now show that they were often conscious on his part, as conscious as they were with his friend Pope.

Because Thomson worked for twenty years at improving, altering, and expanding his major poem, we can study not only the growth of the poet's mind but also the development of his art and technique. Such a study is made easier by Otto Zippel's 1908 volume containing all the many editions of *The Seasons* from the first appearance of *Winter* in 1726 to the final authorized version of the four *Seasons* in 1746, two years before Thomson's death. *Winter* alone was expanded to four times its original length.

There are many kinds of changes that the poem underwent, and Thomson had many reasons for making them. He altered the structure: a short passage on Scotland and a description of the aurora borealis, for example, both in the first edition of *Summer,* he moved to the 1730 *Autumn,* which was further lengthened by the transference of almost 100 lines from *Winter.* He inserted narratives to make the whole more lively and dramatic, one of them being the tale of the cottager lost in a snow storm. Like Coleridge after him he read travel books in order to find more colorful and appropriate images, among them the northern ice formations described in Martens's *Voyage into Spitzbergen and Greenland* of 1711. He added primitivistic passages about the Laplanders and the English country life and a humanitarian appeal for improved conditions in English jails. And through the years he added to or altered his consonant and vowel repetitions, even though from the beginning he emphasized what he called the "music" of language. By comparing the various editions of *The Seasons* one can find many examples of Thomson's desire to fill the ear.

Very often the changes in sound accompany changes in imagery. In *Summer* when "bounteous Power" (1728.433) became "Parent-Power" (1744.540), the poet discarded a weak image for a better one and at the same time gave up an assonance for an alliteration. Nearby, the phrase "I stand aghast" (1728.455) was changed to "I check my steps" (1744.589). In modifying what he decided was an overly strong image, Thomson lost his assonance but was able to find another to take its place. One of the best improvements in the imagery of *Summer* has to do with the description of a waterfall. In 1728 the short passage ended with "tormented" water falling

> From Steep to Steep, with wild, infracted
>   Course,
> And, res[t]less, roaring to the humble Vale.
>   (465-66)

By 1746 the image was extended to sharpen the contrast between the turbulent fall at the beginning and the quiet vale at the end:

> And falling fast from gradual Slope to Slope,
> With wild infracted Course, and lessen'd Roar,
> It gains a safer Bed, and steals, at last,
> Along the Mazes of the quiet Vale.
>   (603-6)

But while Thomson was improving the image, he managed to add numerous ornaments of sound—the [f] and [l] alliterations, the three [a]'s, two more [o]'s, two [ɛs], and two pairs of [e]'s—all in stressed syllables.

One of the most interesting alterations in *Summer* occurs in the tale of Damon, who in 1727 secretly watched three naked girls bathing in a cool stream. By 1744 the three girls had become only the beautiful Musidora, for whom the now gallant Damon left a note before turning his head and stealing away. The much longer account in the final version ends with four of the most echo-laden lines in *The Seasons,* those describing Musidora's feelings on finding the note:

> With wild Surprize,
> As if to Marble struck, devoid of Sense,
> A stupid Moment motionless she stood:
> So stands the Statue that enchants the World.
>   (1336-39)

Although the five-syllable alliteration of the [st] phonestheme—carefully prepared for—stands out, Thomson also employed an [m] alliteration and three assonances involving at least eight vowels. One of the unique facts about this luxuriant language, however, is that in earlier editions the last line is found in an entirely different context (1730.1019). Thomson liked it so much that in 1744 he

picked it up intact, moved it, made it fit the new story, and tied it to the other lines with the echo that stressed the girl's stunned inability to move.

That Thomson apparently worked hardest with assonance can be shown with certain examples from *Spring.* In 1728 he wrote,

> While in the rosy Vale
> Love breath'd his Infant Sighs, from Anguish
>   free,
> Fragrant with Bliss, and only wept for Joy.
>   (276-78)

In 1730 he gave up *Fragrant* for *Replete,* thereby losing the [fr] alliteration but adding a third stressed [i]. Then in 1744 and 1746 the final version read,

> While in the rosy Vale
> Love breath'd his Infant Sighs from Anguish
>   free,
> And full replete with Bliss; save the sweet Pain.
>   (276-78)

Thomson had brought back the [f] alliteration, added four other echoes, and ended with a four-syllable assonance of [i]. Elsewhere in *Spring* a phrase without any echo, "to deck the flowing Hair" (1728.447), was almost entirely rewritten to provide an assonance,

> to grace thy braided Hair.
>   (1744.447)

In the 1728 *Summer* Thomson wrote,

> Of younder Grove, of wildest, largest Growth;
> That, high embowering in the middle Air . . .
>   (404-5)

These lines, already heavy with echoes, became in 1744,

> Of yonder Grove, of wildest largest Growth;
> That, forming high in Air a woodland quire . . .
>   (517-18)

By moving "Air" back and changing other words in the second line, Thomson was able not only to make use of what Dryden had called the beauties of *r* but to run the vowel of *wildest* through three syllables. The same care for vowel echoes can be found in the texts of any Season.

Sometimes, of course, Thomson was willing to part with a good sound in order to achieve a more important end, as he did once when he lost two assonances and a consonance in one line of *Winter* (1730.8) so he could borrow the word *ocean* from that line, move it to a nearby passage, and avoid repetition. But his revisions were much more liable to improve the echoes, or add entirely new ones. The 1744 *Summer,* for example, reworks a 1727 scene of unusual lurid darkness that slowly covers a grove of trees and then mantles the whole sky just before a crushing storm of hail descends. The earlier passage describes the cloud in four and one-half lines:

> Thence Niter, Sulphur, Vitriol, *on the Day*
> Stream, and *fermenting in yon baleful Cloud,*
> Extensive o'er the World, *a reddening Gloom!*
> In dreadful promptitude to spring, await
> The high Command. . . .
>
> (741-45)

The later description, which kept the words italicized in the passage just quoted, was expanded to these eight and one-half lines:

> Thence N*i*ter, Sulphur, and the f*i*ery Sp*ume*
> Of f*a*t Bit*ume*n, steam*i*ng on the D*a*y,
> With v*a*rious-tinctur'd Tr*ai*ns of l*a*tent Flame,
> Pollu*te* the Sky, and in yon b*a*leful Clou*d,*
> A re*d*dening Gloom, a M*a*gazine of F*ate,*
> Fermen*t;* t*i*ll, by the Touch etherial rous'd,
> The dash of Clouds, or *i*rritating W*ar*
> Of f*i*ghting W*i*nds, while all is calm below,
> They f*u*rious spring.
>
> (1100-1108)

This final picture is no doubt far superior in both visual and tactual imagery—*Spume, Bitumen, tinctur'd, Pollute*—but it is infinitely more ear appealing. That ear appeal is, of course, the result of a variety of effects, but outstanding among them are the thick phonic repetitions. While in the original there are perhaps one effective consonance and three assonances, one polysyllabic, in the final version there are four excellent final consonant echoes—("Sp*ume*," "Bi-tum*en*," "Steam*ing*"), ("la*tent*," "Pollu*te*"; "F*ate*," "Fer-men*t*"), and ("*i*rritating W*ar*"); there are seven alliterations, and there are five vowel echoes, including the five [e]'s in six successive stressed syllables beginning with "Day." It is one of Thomson's most attractive passages and was possible only because through the years he concentrated so hard on improving his work and, perhaps as much as any-thing else, on increasing its acoustic appeal.

It is now known that Lord Lyttelton gave Thomson some small help in improving *The Seasons,* and it was long thought that Pope's handwriting could be found in the margins of Thomson's manuscripts. But while by the middle of the nineteenth century Thomson was shown to have been independent of Pope's direct help, there is no doubt that Pope's influence was exerted indirectly on his friend's major poem. The 1744 *Seasons* has more chang-es than can be found in any other edition; some of them echo lines written by Pope, who died that year. And the similar passages are among the most ear appealing by two of the most ear-conscious poets who wrote in English. Just as in *Windsor Forest* Pope paraphrased more than one line from Denham's *Cooper's Hill* or borrowed Dry-den's "well-breath'd Beagles," Thomson was willing to take phrases from *Windsor Forest.* In 1713 Pope had re-written an old line of the manuscript version of that poem and ended with

> Nor **P**o so swells the fabling **P**oet's Lays.
>
> (227)

In 1746, also completely reworking an old line, Thomson wrote,

> The f*a*bling P*o*ets took their g*o*lden *A*ge.
>
> (*Spring* 325)

Not only did he borrow Pope's "fabling Poets"; he man-aged to work in the same [e] and [o] assonances. Even better as an example of sound similarity in the two poets is Thomson's mind- and ear-filling description of shoot-ing stars in *Winter* (127-28):

> The Stars obtuse em*it* a sh*i*vering Ray;
> Or frequent se*em* to sh*oot* athwar*t* the Gl*oom.*

The second of these lines is remarkably like one from Pope's *Rape of the Lock* (2.82);

> Purs*ue* the St*a*rs that sh*oot* athw*art* the Nigh*t.*

In each of the two lines every stressed syllable starts or continues an echo of at least one phone. Pope has two assonances and one three-syllable consonance of [t] to reproduce the shooting. Thomson also has two assonanc-es, and while he toned down the shooting by omitting one final [t], he emphasized the image of winter gloom by echoing the vowel of that word and, especially, by adding the consonance of [m].

Although Thomson seems to have learned something about sound effects from his friend Pope, there is one chief difference between the way echoes are employed in *The Seasons* and the way they are employed in Pope's poems: Thomson was less able to emphasize rhetorical or struc-tural balance by balancing sounds. The difference, of course, stems primarily from the fact that Thomson's run-on blank verse—without the rhyme, without such a reg-ular cadence, without any rule regarding the caesura—did not lend itself to such neat cognitive effects as did the Popeian couplet, and even his rhyming Spenserian stan-zas in *The Castle of Indolence* have relatively few of them. He was, nevertheless, too much a product of the eighteenth century to avoid structural balance completely, and when he did employ it he was as prone as Dryden and Pope to let sounds emphasize the balance. About two-thirds of the lines in *The Seasons* are end-stopped and can, therefore, more easily fit the patterns developed by the couplet. In *Autumn,* for example, Thomson wrote,

> Presents the dow*n*y peach; the shi*n*ing plumb,
>
> (664)

> The **t**ankards **f**oam; and the strong **t**able groans.
>
> (499)

In one line the parallel adjectives consonate while their nouns alliterate; in the other, the parallel subjects alliter-ate and their verbs assonate. Also in *Autumn* the parallel verbs alone can alliterate:

> Sudden, the ditches **sw**ell; the meadows **sw**im,
>
> (333)

To swim along, and swell the mazy dance;

(586)

or they can assonate:

To joy at anguish, and delight in blood,

(396)

To raise the Virtues, animate the Bliss.

(596)

Perhaps Thomson's best balanced consonance is in a zeugma found in *The Castle of Indolence,*

Serene yet warm, humane yet firm his mind,

(1.65)

where the primary adjectives end in [n] and the secondary adjectives in [m].

The caesural sound balance favored so much by writers of the heroic couplet is found surprisingly often in Thomson's blank verse. Here two lines in a row in *Winter* emphasize the medial caesura, one with assonance, the other with assonance and alliteration:

Frosty, succeed; and thro' the blue Serene,
For Sight too fine, th'etherial Niter flies.

(693-94)

Close by, the first of two lines has a caesural consonance of [l] while the second has a double assonance in a chiasmus that Pope or Dryden might have written:

Where sits the Soul, intense, collected, cool,
Bright as the Skies, and as the Season Keen.

(702-3)

Although anaphora was even more a favorite rhetorical weapon with eighteenth-century poets than with their successors—except perhaps Walt Whitman—many of them were aware that the device could be made more subtle by reducing the number of repeated words and combining them with consonant or vowel echoes. Here Thomson contrived a kind of anaphoric alliteration:

How dead the Vegetable Kingdom lies!
How dumb the tuneful!

(*Winter* 1027-28)

And in *Winter* he can be discovered creating an assonance that has something of the effect of anaphora. In 1726 he wrote.

To lay their Passions in a gentle Calm,
And woo lone Quiet, in her silent Walks,

(38-39)

which in 1730 was transferred to *Autumn* thus:

To sooth the throbbing Passions into Peace

And woo lone Quiet in her silent Walks.

(908-9)

His final version had retained the sounding second line entire, but the first line added not only the [p] alliteration but the word *soothe* so that the two initial stressed syllables would have the same vowel.

Since there are a number of run-on lines in *The Seasons,* Thomson did not in that poem so often as Pope or Dryden emphasize line endings with a vowel or consonant repetition in the final stressed syllables, even though his blank verse will be found to have more such terminal echoes than any blank verse written outside the eighteenth century. Three times in *Winter,* for example, there are successive terminal alliterations, among them "bitter Bread," "wintry Winds" (335-36); and three times there are successive terminal assonances, among them "double Sons," "brightest Skies" (591-92). The end rhymes of *The Castle of Indolence* attract far more phonic repetitions at the ends of lines, perhaps as many as are to be found in the heroic couplet. There are seven of them, in fact, in two stanzas of that poem (1.72, 77).

Blank verse may not be so suitable for sound parallelism as the heroic couplet, but Thomson's blank verse was eminently suited for other kinds of emphasis and for the fitting of sound to sense. Just as much as any poet from Chaucer to Pope, for example, he tied adjective to noun with a vowel or consonant echo. Often one can catch him in the act of altering a word in order to achieve this kind of binding. In 1728 he wrote "homely Fowls"; in 1744 he wrote "household fowls." In the same way "hilly Wave" became "inflated Wave," and "employless Greyhound" was changed to "vacant Greyhound." "Mighty Pride" already had the assonance, but Thomson improved the image by exchanging *Mighty* for *Tyrant* even though he carefully kept the vowel echo.

Because of the nature of its content Thomson's blank verse may have more attempts at extended onomatopoeia than Pope's heroic couplets, as many perhaps as Dryden's *Georgics.* In an early Lucretian attack on luxury, he wrote,

A Season's Glitter! In soft-circling Robes.

(*Summer* 1727.300)

Then seeing an opportunity not only to add a more scathing image but to tie sound to sense by means of phonic echoes, in particular a consonance, he revised the line to read,

A Season's Glitter! Thus they flutter on.

(1744.348)

In "shiver every feather" he repeated the final [v] of the onomatopoeic *shiver*. With a nearby word *restless* he echoed in Popeian fashion the initial [r], the final [s] phonestheme, even the initial weak [l], of the even more onomatopoeic *rustling,* and he extended the sound of the same word by placing it close to *incessant.*

One of Thomson's great teachers in the poetry of nature and reflection was Lucretius. But the author of *De Rerum Natura* was also a master of the sense-echoing phrase, attempting to convey with language the crackling of fire, the running of water, the movements of humans and animals. And he tried musical instruments in such lines as "tympana tenta tonant palmis et cymbala circum" (2.618). Although Thomson had no occasion to give us the instruments of an orchestra, he often hoped to suggest the sounds of nature. With the phonesthemes [s] and [l] and the diphthong [aU], he believed he was capturing the owl's sad sound:

> Assiduous, in his Bower, the wailing Owl
> Plies his sad Song.
>
> (*Winter* 142-43)

With the same [l] and [s] to go with other appropriate sounds—some of them phonesthemes—final [d], [n], and [nd], initial [w] and [st], he tried the equally sad wail of the nightingale, at the same time making the passage more acoustically attractive with at least five assonances in five lines:

> she sings
> Her Sorrows thro' the Night; and, on the Bough
> Sad-sitting, still at every dying Fall
> Takes up again her her lamentable Strain
> Of winding Woe, till wide around the Wood[s]
> Sigh at her Song, and with her Wail resound.
>
> (*Spring* 720-25)

The consonants [l] and [n], as well as [s], are favorites for imitating in language the softer sights and sounds of nature. In *Spring* when

> the Lily drinks
> The latent Rill, scarce oozing thro' the Grass,
> Of Growth luxuriant,
>
> (495-97)

Thomson not only repeated the vowel of the sound-sense *ooze;* he alliterated and consonated the [l]'s of *Lily,* echoed the [s] of *grass,* and provided three [I]'s, one of the front vowels Dryden also liked for such scenes. And as with Dryden, another front vowel, [i], was a favorite with Thomson if his nature scene was more or less calm. In *Spring,* for example, he made a plea for walking.

> Where the Breeze blows from yon extended
> Field
> Of blossom'd Beans,
>
> (502-3)

and in an *Autumn* paean to his friend Dodington's country seat, the poet ran nine stressed front vowels—all close to [i]—through four lines, beginning the passage thus,

> In this glad season, while his last, best beams
> The sun sheds equal o'er the meeken'd day,
>
> (641 ff.)

and in 1744 adding another such vowel to the first line in

this fashion,

> In this glad Season, while his sweetest beams, . . .
>
> (654)

The same vowel, combined with a medley of other phonic recurrences, was—again with Thomson as well as with other poets—apparently best for sleepy scenes, as in this primitivistic account of a happy, carefree, but lazy, awakening in an early spring:

> The first fresh Dawn then wak'd the gladden'd
> Race
> Of uncorrupted Men, nor blush'd to see
> The Sluggard sleep beneath her sacred Beam.
>
> (*Spring* 242-44)

Although Thomson was less idealistic about the backward Eskimos described by travelers, he was even more onomatopoeic with their cold, lifeless sleeping, his seven-word image, with five heavy syllables, thick and slow with [s] and [z] consonance and two assonances:

> Immers'd in Furs,
> Doze the gross Race.
>
> (*Winter* 943-44)

Just as yellow was perhaps Thomson's favorite color, light was one of his favorite images, and following a well-established tradition he was liable to let the sound of [əI, aI] control such images. In *Summer* the sun suffuses the "lively Diamond" with "Collected Light" (142-43), and unheeding men "pass / An idle Summer-Life in Fortune's Shine" till time comes "Behind, and strikes them from the Book of Life" (346-47, 351). Thomson's other works make constant use of this phonestheme, for example, *A Poem Sacred to the Memory of Sir Isaac Newton,* which recounts the great scientist's many interests in the physical world, including his experiments with light and the refracting of light. Here, in three passages of six, seven, and eight lines that tell of those experiments, Thomson subdued his other sound echoes in order to let the diphthong [aI, əI] dominate. And his last important poem, *Liberty,* because of the nature of its subject, echoes the phonestheme in dozens of passages, whether Thomson was speaking of physical brightness or of the light of virtue or knowledge.

As with all his auditory effects, one can often discover Thomson working for improvement in his fitting of sound to sense. In attempting to imitate the sound of winter winds, he wrote in 1730,

> Muttering, the winds at eve, with hoarser voice
> Blow blustering from the south.
>
> (*Winter* 701-2)

This version he altered slightly in 1744 to read thus:

> Muttering, the Winds at Eve, with Blunted Point,
> Blow hollow-blustering from the South.
>
> (988-89)

The first pair of lines is rich in echoes, but the final pair has more and may be even better as a representation of the winds Thomson had in mind. While he gave up the [s] consonance of the onomatopoeic "hoarser voice," its replacement, "blunted point," produced all sorts of effects. First, it kept the vowel that was needed to assonate with *Winds*. Second, it repeated the final, stressed [t] of *Muttering* not once but twice. Third, since the words *Muttering* and *Blustering* were a bit far apart for the assonance to be heard best, *blunted*, inserted half way between, caused the three-syllable vowel echo to be most effective. And fourth, *blunted* added a third [bl] to the initial echoes in the very onomatopoeic *Blow* and *blustering*. Throughout his career Thomson worked in this fashion at such sound-sense patterns.

There is no doubt, then, that the popular modern defense of Thomson's so-called neoclassical diction and luxuriant language needs to note how much the consonant and vowel echoes affect the quality of that language. Bernard Fehr, for example, talks of sentence syntax, versification, and descriptive epithets when he analyzes "a lavish display of rococo" in seven lines of *Autumn*, but he does not notice that in the seven lines there are five assonances—one of three syllables—and three alliterations—also one of three syllables. Geoffrey Tillotson defends the image in *Winter* (261-62) of "The **bl**eating **K**ind" that "*Eye* the **bl**e*ak* heaven" without regard for the two assonances and the alliteration that must have helped determine Thomson's choice of words. The Thomson line that has perhaps evoked the most divergent opinions is one in *Spring* (361),

A sh*o*reless *o*cean tumbled round the gl*o*be,

from an eighteenth-century comment that the image is inappropriate to Bonamy Dobrée's belief that the line is "miraculous." It may be that the words were selected here for sound as much as for sense. At least, the image strikes the eye no more than the three [o]'s resound in the ear. It may be too that Thomson's poems do not "fill the ear more than the mind" but that, at their best, the oral appeal is related to the intellectual and emotional involvement. But whether any reader condemns or admires those poems, their "luxuriant language" depends very much on the phonic echoes that were as important to the eighteenth century's blank verse as to its heroic couplet.

Percy G. Adams (essay date 1979)

SOURCE: An introduction to *The Plays of James Thomson*, edited by Percy G. Adams, Garland Publishing, Inc., 1979, pp. v-xxxvii.

[*In the following excerpt, Adams surveys Thomson's six dramas, discussing each play from both a performance-based and an aesthetic perspective.*]

Thomson's six plays were written between 1730, the year of the first full edition of *The Seasons*, and 1749, the last one being acted and published posthumously. Five are called tragedies—*Sophonisba* (1730), *Agamemnon* (1738),

Edward and Eleonora (1739), *Tancred and Sigismunda* (1744), and *Coriolanus* (1749), while *Alfred* (1740) is subtitled *A Masque* and was co-authored with David Mallet, Thomson's friend.

The first of these, *Sophonisba*, was produced at Drury Lane on February 28, 1730, with Wilks as Masinissa and the equally great Anne Oldfield playing Sophonisba in her last appearance before her death a few months later. Thomson's preface is highly revealing as a document declaring his dramatic theories and practice not just for this one play but for all his blank-verse tragedies. Here he announces that he has been true to history and that he chose the story of Sophonisba for its "simplicity," for, he says, "It is one, regular, and uniform . . . yet affording several revolutions of fortune." Most revealing perhaps in his long quotation from Racine concerning "probability," "simple action," "violence of passions," and "beauty of sentiments," all of which elements Thomson was striving for in *Sophonisba* and would continue to strive for in each of his plays.

The story of Sophonisba is one of the most popular in the history of the theatre. Before Thomson it had been used by a number of dramatists, including the Italian Trissino (1515, 1557), the Englishmen Marston (c. 1606) and Lee (1675), and the Frenchmen Mairet (1634) and Corneille (1663). The real Sophonisba, the daughter of the third-century Carthaginian Hasdrubel, was married by him to the Numidian king Syphax after she and the young prince Masinissa had been in love and parted when he fled death to become a noted Roman general under Scipio. She was famous for her beauty and for her double passion—love of her country and hate for Rome. When Masinissa led a successful army in overcoming Carthage and killing Syphax, the two reunited lovers were married, but Masinissa sent a bowl of poison to Sophonisba in order to save her from public display before the Romans, the two then dying together. The ingredients here were attractive and playwrights could take what they wanted: One might stress Sophonisba's loyalty to Carthage, another could concentrate on the love affair, or still another could enlarge the action to include battles, the Roman point of view, or conflicts between love and honor. The variety of approaches taken and the uniqueness of Thomson's plot can be demonstrated by comparing his version with the next best English version, that of Nathaniel Lee (1675).

Although these two plays are unlike each other in every way, the most striking difference is in the plot. Lee has two plots, not really well integrated, one revolving around Hannibal the Carthaginian leader and his lovely mistress Rosalinda, who dies in battle, the other revolving about Masinissa and Sophonisba. As important as any of these four characters is the Roman Scipio. Thomson, on the other hand, has a simple plot the center of which is Sophonisba with all her historic characteristics prominently displayed. Her reawakened love for Masinissa, whom she has not seen for some years, grows during the play until it rivals her love of Carthage and hate of Rome. In Lee there is small chance for all this development to be prominent since in his play she is overshadowed by four other characters. Lee has Masinissa kill Syphax in battle so the lovers can quickly marry; Thomson, as he tells us in his preface and in the play, uncovers the historical fact that in Sophonisba's day marriage was dissolved not only by death but by captivity of a spouse, and thus he can produce the captured, furiously jealous Syphax to be tortured by thoughts of the marriage of his wife to Masinissa. Lee, in fact, never has the marriage of Sophonisba and Syphax consummated while in Thomson we are sure that she has given herself, in body only, so that Syphax will lead Carthage against hated Rome. There are no portents, no campaigns, no battles in Thomson, as there are in Lee's much longer play with its many scene changes, just as Thomson, in the tradition of his admired Racine, has two characters who serve as confidants—Phoenissa, "friend" to Sophonisba, and Narva, "friend" to Masinissa. Finally, one telling difference, especially important for the end of each tragedy, is that Lee's Scipio, friend and mentor of the young Masinissa, is dogmatic, even cruel, in ordering his protégé to leave the entrancing "witch" to follow duty and honor. Thomson's Scipio is gentle and kind, but firm, in arguing with Masinissa to give her up. In Lee the lovers drink poison and die embraced; in Thomson, Masinissa sends Sophonisba poison and then when Scipio relents rushes to her too late, is restrained from killing himself, and all lament the tragedy. Thomson's, then, is Sophonisba's play in every way, and her part is one an Anne Oldfield or any great actress would delight in.

Nevertheless, he does have two tragedies, closely related. One is that of Sophonisba, who as a queen has all her life been separated from normal happiness: She loses her young love Masinissa and then when she regains him years later has one night only of wedded bliss; she feels herself forced to marry Syphax, whom she does not love, in order to bind him to her nation's cause; she watches Rome's ascendancy and her country's degradation; and she dies nobly, as Scipio admits, in the "Roman" fashion rather than be subjected to ignominy as a captive. The second and related tragedy is that of Masinissa, who loses his great love and is tormented by his conscience because he prefers her to the world he fights for. His tragedy is spelled out by Scipio near the end (V.iv), when as the voice of honor and reason he recognizes that Masinissa "is undone; / Betwixt his passion and his reason tost / In miserable conflict." In all of this there are of course echoes of other great conflicts. One is the love that Sophonisba, at first reluctantly, feels rising for Masinissa when she is married to Syphax—as the Phaedra of Racine and Euripides is tormented by her guilty love for her husband's son. And in each case the confidante urges the beautiful wife not to restrain her passion. Likewise, Masinissa's conflict between love and honor, while that of many plays, not just those of Corneille and Racine, is noticeably reminiscent of Antony's, whether in Shakespeare or in Dryden. Masinissa is of course younger than Mark Antony, but his old friend Narva and his mentor Scipio pull him toward honor just as Ventidius in *All For Love* had served as Antony's conscience; and the entrancing African queen is the "lethargy of love" that wraps itself about Masinissa somewhat, we see, as the serpent of the Nile had seduced the conqueror of the world in Dryden's play. And, final-

ly, while Dryden lets his lovers lose the world and, unhistorically, die together, Thomson, also departing from history, refuses to let Masinissa give up his Roman world— all perhaps to point us back to the greater, more emphatic, tragedy of Sophonisba. This, Thomson's first play, was a delight to the audience; was universally praised; held the stage for ten nights, a near record; produced a line which Fielding in *Tom Jones* gleefully grabbed to rework with his hundreds of other parodies; gained Thomson an audience with the Queen, to whom he dedicated the equally successful published version; and attracted the attention of the Prince of Wales, who with his wife was to remain Thomson's faithful patron.

Written after an eight-year interval in which Thomson was revising *The Seasons,* taking the Grand Tour as a tutor, and organizing Liberty, one of his three long poems, *Agamemnon* (1738) is more nearly controversial than *Sophonisba,* is in some ways even more attractive, and was also successful, running for nine nights and, when published, selling over 3000 copies immediately, thus forcing a second issue of 1500. It was controversial for two reasons. One is that Clytemnestra and Egisthus were by many viewers regarded as Thomson's portrayals of Queen Caroline and Robert Walpole, who were ruling the country, especially while George II was dallying with his mistress in Hanover during 1736-1737. The other is that the audience found the last two acts below the level of the first three and, according to one contemporary account, even booed parts of the ending. At any rate, several of Thomson's friends, including Alexander Pope, who seldom went to plays but who did attend the opening of *Agamemnon,* gathered at Drury Lane the next morning and helped the author make revisions that seem to have improved the play and the audience's temper. If, as some of Thomson's contemporaries thought, *Agamemnon* is not so well constructed as his first play, it may have more fine blank-verse passages. Certainly it had a great cast, including Quin as Agamemnon; Mary Porter, almost as fine a tragic actress as Anne Oldfield, as Clytemnestra; and the excellent Susannah Cibber, wife of Theophilus and sister of the famous composer Thomas Arne, as Cassandra.

Thomson's version of *Agamemnon* has been condemned by Morel and Grant, although the latter does find the verse often beautiful, and praised by G.C. Macaulay and by Boas, who believes the dialogue better than that in *Sophonisba.* The return of Agamemnon from Troy after ten years of absence, his death at the hands of his wife, Clytemnestra, and/or her lover, Agamemnon's cousin Aegisthus, and the aftermaths involving the children Electra and Orestes as they flee Aegisthus and seek revenge for their father's death—all this provides one of the two or three great situations for stage tragedy, from Aeschylus's trilogy to that of O'Neill. Thomson, closer to Seneca than to Aeschylus, invented a highly original plot by making his Egisthus not only the chief contriver of the rebellion but also the murderer. This version, true to the second and least used legend of Agamemnon's death, permitted Thomson to concentrate on creating an archvillain Egisthus and a Clytemnestra more sinned against than sinning. In fact, he did everything he could to make her attractive to the audience—she is remorseful for having been the lover of Egisthus, and her conscience continually sears her; she feels reawakened love and admiration for her returned husband; she begs Egisthus to flee with her before their infidelities condemn them; she calls for her two children to comfort her; and upon hearing of Agamemnon's murder she turns on the "traitor" who has robbed her of love, family, and honor and then faints in the arms of her attendants. Aeschylus, especially by means of his chorus, had worked hardest at contriving an atmosphere of gloom and foreboding, but he also created a jealous, vengeful, strong Clytemnestra who dominates her lover Aegisthus and who herself plunges the knife into her husband. Thomson was willing to part with the atmosphere in order to concentrate on the psychology and the tragedy of a queen who, ten years without her husband, succumbs to a clever, plotting villain and lives to see the fatal consequences. But Thomson is different in other ways. He invents, perhaps with some small help from *The Odyssey* and the Robinson Crusoe motif, the character Melisander, played by Theophilus Cibber, whom Agamemnon sailing for Troy leaves as advisor to Clytemnestra but whom Egisthus treacherously kidnaps. When, instead of killing him, Egisthus's accomplices leave Melisander on a desert island, he manages to survive, be rescued by Agamemnon himself on his return voyage, and live to lead a court rebellion against Egisthus which, the still-living Cassandra prophesies in the closing curtain line, will be successful.

Grant and others have complained that Thomson's play is not enough like that of Aeschylus and that Thomson's Agamemnon not only dies in the fourth act but is "relegated to the second or third part in his own tragedy." The first complaint, of course, can more easily be turned to praise; the second is based on faulty memory—no play entitled *Agamemnon* has been able to give the lead part to the murdered king, especially Aeschylus's version, in which Agamemnon has fewer lines than either Clytemnestra or Cassandra. Perhaps all that Thomson took from Aeschylus, more than he took from other playwrights using the legend, are a few hints from the great Greek poet's language, especially in the misunderstood prophetic ravings of Cassandra (V.iii) and most especially in such metaphors as those she uses for Clytemnestra, Egisthus, and Agamemnon when she speaks of "The lioness and the wolf, together leagu'd, / Pursue the lion's life," a figure like that of Aeschylus's "It is the twofoot lioness who beds / Beside a wolf, the noble lion away" (trans. Louis MacNeice).

Thomson's third drama, *Edward and Eleonora,* ready in 1739, was barred from the stage by the new 1737 Licensing Act, apparently not so much for its own small leanings toward propaganda for the Prince of Wales's party but because it had the misfortune to come close on the heels of *Agamemnon,* which had somehow slipped by the censor. Perhaps more of a misfortune was that Thomson completed his play just after other dramas far more political were performed, David Mallet's *Mustapha* (1739), for example. At any rate, when it had to be taken out of production it was published and quickly sold better than either of Thomson's earlier plays, part of its success being attributed of course to the censor's proscription. But there are other reasons why it sold well and would later be acted.

Edward is Thomson's only attempt at using British history in tragedy, and his sources are apparently historical rather than dramatic accounts of the long reign of one of the most popular and respected of English warrior kings. Edward I as Crown Prince married Eleanor of Castile when he was fifteen, led his father's forces victoriously against the English Barons, and then in 1270 left with an army for the Holy Land on what was to be called the Ninth Crusade, arriving there just after the French had withdrawn because of the death of Louis IX, who had led both the Seventh and the Eighth Crusades. It is Edward's experiences before the walls of Jaffa that Thomson in his dedication to the Princess of Wales says he selected partly because they display a virtuous and loving queen, in this case Eleonora, who had accompanied her husband and who, according to a legend, saved Edward from dying of a poisoned wound at the risk of her own life. In telescoping history to make his play more dramatic and to keep his plot within narrow bounds, Thomson apparently changed facts only once—when at the psychological moment he has the news arrive that Edward has become king at the death of his father; in reality, Edward learned this fact while on his way home after making a truce at Acre.

With the exotic eastern setting, the unusual circumstance of a crown princess-queen accompanying her husband in battle campaign, and the legend of the poison, Thomson was able to contrive one of his most dramatic, poignant, and perennially topical dramas. He adds the old warrior Earl Gloster and the Archdeacon Theald to advise Edward, commiserate with him, and gently oppose each other on the merits of fighting a "holy" war, Gloster urging its immediate cessation and a return home to protect the aging King Henry III, Theald—like Saint Louis of history—arguing the righteousness of their cause. And to these two and Edward and Eleonora, Thomson adds Selim, Sultan of Jaffa, and his wife Daraxa, who has been captured by Edward and has become the friend of Eleonora. The confrontation of West and East, of theories of "useless" and "holy" wars, and of passion and reason are handled so well they almost obscure the chief flaw in the play: Although an audience might for two hours suspend its disbelief, a critical reader could never competely swallow the poison which first enters Edward's body with a fanatical assassin's dagger, is sucked from the wound by Eleonora as he lies in what is apparently his last sleep, sends her to what all believe is her deathbed, and is finally counteracted by an amazing antidote brought by the disguised Sultan of Jaffa. The suspense, the tenderness of Eleonora, the dying requests and tearful vows, first of the Prince, then of the Princess, Edward's proud refusal to accept another human's offer to die for him by sucking the wound, Selim's rational appeals to the passionate prince, and the final revelation that the loving Eleonora lives—all this is high melodrama that not only binds together the philosophic debates but exposes six well-developed characters and contains a love story so appealing that Thomson's friend Lady Hertford would by no means be the only reader to prefer this play to *Agamemnon*. But *Edward and Eleonora* is an incipient tragedy only, since it ends happily for everyone involved and must therefore be called not "tragical" or "comical" but perhaps "serious historical."

Although *Edward* was not acted for some years, within a few months of its being rejected by the censor, Thomson and Mallet together were commissioned to do *Alfred: A Masque* for a birthday celebration at Clivedon House, the Prince of Wales's home on the Thames. The patriotic story is that of the temporarily defeated Alfred as he lives among peasants who worship him and then with loyal subjects departs for victory. With a cast of professionals headed by Quin and Kitty Clive, with dances and fireworks, with the music of Thomas Arne, with a beautiful garden setting, the masque was pronounced most successful, the concluding song, **"Rule, Britannia,"** now given by everyone to Thomson, producing not only the most attractive lines but the national hymn of Great Britain. *Alfred* was later reworked by Mallet for two performances at Drury Lane, again with Arne's music, and reworked still a second time so that Garrick in 1751 could play the lead. No one knows how much of the original was done by Thomson, but Fanny Burney remembered that her father, Dr. Burney, then a pupil of Arne, went with him to work on the masque with Thomson and found the great poet in bed at 2:00 p.m.

Some four years later Thomson's penultimate play, *Tancred and Sigismunda,* a genuine tragedy by any definition, was performed with another brilliant cast, this one headed by the rising David Garrick and including Mrs. Cibber, Thomas Sheridan, and Delane, who had the lead in *Edward* when the play was finally performed. But the cast alone did not make *Tancred* Thomson's most popular play: After its successful run of nine nights, including three benefit performances for the author, Andrew Millar sold 5000 copies of the printed version, which is longer than the one acted; and before the century was over the tragedy went through more than twenty other editions, including at least two in France, and was performed both in London and Dublin. As with *Agamemnon* this play was revised in production, not with the help of Pope, then dead, but of other friends such as William Pitt, the great statesman, and Lord Lyttelton, Fielding's patron also, both of whom faithfully attended rehearsals and, apparently, forced the poet to prune passages that were later saved for publication.

The sources of *Tancred and Sigismunda* have sometimes been found in Boccaccio's first *novella* of the fourth day of the *Decameron*, a searing yet tragic love story Dryden translated into couplets as *Sigismonda and Guiscard,* but Thomson—except for the two names "Sigismonda" and "Siffredi"—could have written his play without knowing the plot of either Boccaccio's original or Dryden's translation. He in fact follows closely the whole of Lesage's *nouvelle* "Le Mariage de vengeance" as told by Elvire in *Gil Blas,* that is, except for the names. In Lesage, Siffredi

is the father and state minister who for the sake of his country, Sicily, rears the prince Enrique in anonymity and then blights the love between his daughter Blanche and the prince in order to force Enrique's marriage to Constance, the other claimant to the throne. He does succeed in marrying the confused Blanche to the Lord High Constable, but all ends tragically when Enrique kills the Constable, who stabs Blanche before dying. Enrique then refuses Constance, and the disgraced Siffredi takes his second daughter to live in Spain. Thomson keeps "Siffredi," the too zealous father, but changes all the other names: Blanche becomes Sigismunda; Enrique becomes Tancred; the Constable keeps his exalted title but is named Osmond; and Constance becomes Constantia, who never appears on stage. To these four big parts Thomson adds Laura, Sigismunda's friend and confidante, and her brother Rodolpho, a captain in the guards and Tancred's closest friend. Again the plot is simple, the cast of six is small, the time is less than twenty-four hours, and the place, while not one small scene, is one city, Palermo.

But the simple, close-knit plot is never "coldly classical." It is in fact a tale of passion and vengeance, of filial love and young love, of fate in the form of a misguided father as he blindly but stubbornly leads his puppets down one step and then another until the tragedy is complete, with Osmond and Sigismunda killed, with Tancred holding his dead love in his arms, and with the now remorseful Siffredi regretting his attempts to play god as well as statesman. Some critics have called this Thomson's "romantic" tragedy, because of the exotic setting and the continued high level of emotion, but it is really no more emotional than *Edward* and remains still in the tradition of Racine's plays of extended passion, such as *Phèdre* and *Andromaque*. One can rather say that its greater success results from its story of blighted youthful love, a theme rare with Thomson, rare in Greek and French tragedy, rare in Shakespeare, and rare in tragedy in general: Before Thomson one thinks of only a few such tragic treatments of young love, among them Otway's of Monimia, in *The Orphan,* and Shakespeare's of Desdemona and Juliet.

And finally there is *Coriolanus,* which Thomson completed just before his death in 1748 and which was produced starting January 13, 1749, by Covent Garden's new manager, Garrick, who was not himself in the play, although Thomson apparently wanted him to take the part of Attius Tullus. The lead was naturally given to Quin, who also spoke Lyttelton's prologue so feelingly, especially its lines about "friends," that the opening night was a most sentimental occasion. The strong cast also included Peg Woffington, as Coriolanus's mother, Veturia, and Delane, who had played Edward and Osmond in Thomson's earlier plays, as Galesus. Lyttelton, Thomson's executor, persuaded Garrick to keep other plays off the stage until *Coriolanus* had achieved its success and brought money from the author's benefit nights to help pay off his numerous debts. *The Gentleman's Magazine* immediately published a detailed summary of the first four acts to go with almost a complete reproduction of Act Five, a kind of advertising it had just given Otway's *The Orphan* and would shortly give to Johnson's *Irene*.

It is this tragedy by Thomson that Grant has damned not only as having been taken from Shakespeare but as "cold, heartless, immobile, and removed from life," that Nicoll called "undoubtedly his poorest play," that Boas lamented as "unfortunate," and that a great Shakespearean such as Marc Parrott would simply dismiss as "in no way the equal of Shakespeare's version." But Thomson's *Coriolanus* deserves none of these pejoratives bestowed on it: From 1759 until well into the nineteenth century, its last half was added to a rewriting of Shakespeare's first scenes and acted over and over by such greats as Kemble and Siddons; and its simple plot and fine blank verse make it far better for the stage than Shakespeare's play—*as Shakespeare wrote it*—which is even longer and more nearly unactable than *Antony and Cleopatra*. Nor did Thomson, as Grant astoundingly claims, take his play from Shakespeare—*Coriolanus* is in fact one of his most original tragedies, while Shakespeare nowhere else followed his source, in this case North's Plutarch, so closely.

And because Shakespeare's version was impossible for the stage, two English playwrights after him and before Thomson tried their hands at the attractive story. Their titles indicate to some extent the emphasis each desired to achieve. Nahum Tate rewrote Shakespeare in 1682 as *The Ingratitude of a Common-Wealth: Or, the Fall of Caius Martius Coriolanus,* cutting the original drastically—for example, giving the mother a smaller part—and toning down the boasting and arrogance of Coriolanus. Then in 1719-1720 John Dennis reworked Shakespeare even more, called his shorter play *The Invader of His Country: or, The Fatal Resentment. A Tragedy,* making the mother and especially the wife, called Virgilia, much more prominent, and letting Coriolanus kill Tullus before being himself killed by the Volscians and dying in the arms of his wife and mother. While each of these versions is actable, neither attempts to keep the cold, awesome, uncompromising, monomaniacal Coriolanus or the Roman commoners he despises.

Thomson's version is the shortest and most stageworthy of all. In order to keep the plot simple and concentrate its power, he begins with the strong Volscian army encamped outside Rome and commanded by the noble and admirable Attius Tullus, who while awaiting the return of an emissary sent to offer terms of peace is informed of the arrival of the exiled and embittered Coriolanus come to join his forces. Tullus is not only delighted to welcome his great adversary but magnanimously makes him general of half the Volscians. Such an opening permits the credible and highly dramatic sequence of events to take place in one day and in the Volscian camp—the return of the emissary, who has been spurned by the proud Romans; the report of an immediate attack that drives the Roman forces back into the city; the arrival of a Roman embassy to ask Coriolanus, not Tullus, for an honorable peace; and when this plea fails, the arrival of another embassy headed by Coriolanus's gentle wife, Volumnia, and his strong-willed mother, Veturia, who finally breaks the iron soul of her son, saves Rome temporarily, and forces Coriolanus's death at the hands of the Volscians.

The plot, as told in this way, makes the play Coriolanus's; but in reality, while his presence from first to last is awesomely felt in almost every scene, he has fewer speeches than does Tullus. It is indeed the tragedy of Coriolanus, as the title says, but it is even more the psychological analysis of the Volscian leader as he goes from an understandable desire to annihilate the proud Rome that has made vassals of his countrymen, to a joyful and wholehearted welcome of the exile, to admiration for Coriolanus's valor in battle, to an awareness that the proud Coriolanus's fanatical thirst for vengeance has destroyed his humanity, to a still further awareness that the once-feared enemy has assumed that he is now the leader of the Volscians and they are his slaves, to a fear that the adopted defector will succumb and grant a peace favorable to Rome, and finally to the realization that to save his cause and his country he must have Coriolanus put to death. It is this astute development of the mind and motives of Tullus as he responds to Coriolanus that makes Thomson's tragedy far different from any other treating the same subject; and it is a successfully unified play that should never have been spliced with Shakespeare's, which is so different, so vast, and so much Shakespeare that it cannot be successfully combined with any other version, certainly not with Thomson's. Perhaps if Garrick had played Tullus to Quin's Coriolanus, as the playwright wished, the original viewers would have realized better that it was Thomson's intent to display Coriolanus chiefly through the mind and actions of the truly likeable Volscian general.

Individually, then, each of Thomson's plays is attractive and dramaturgically successful, in spite of certain faults that have been found in them but about which no two readers can agree; collectively they display characteristics, themes, and assets that make them worthy of consideration as the work of a fine poet as well as the products of an age that is noted less for its original drama than for its poems, its biography, its journalism and periodical literature, its satire, its personal letters, or its prose fiction.

First, there is the question of how much his plays reflect Thomson's political involvement as a supporter of Frederick, Prince of Wales, and an opponent, with Pope, Gay, Fielding, and so many other writers, of Robert Walpole. Three of the five important plays—*Sophonisba, Tancred,* and *Coriolanus*—actually contain no characters, scenes, or lines that can be interpreted as having anything to do with political propaganda. *Edward,* the third play, has one short scene (I.i) in which the wise old Earl of Gloster urges the Prince to return home to protect the aging king against "evil counsellors," these "counsellors" often being construed—by the biographer Grant, for example—as meaning Walpole. Gloster's plea, however, is couched in general terms that refer to an England unsettled by the recent Baron's War and "drain'd by ten thousand arts / Of lawless imposition, priestly fraud, / Italian leeches, and insatiate Rome"; and it concludes with the reminder that while Edward has saved his father from the Barons, especially from "haughty Leister," he must save him also "from his ministers, from those / Who hold him captive in the worst of chains." Taking these, and only these, lines out of context one is able, if one wishes, to equate "ministers," as well as "counsellors," with Walpole, but to do so ignores the accurate history recorded in the entire speech, from the rebellion of the Barons, to the great charter of 1215, to the "Italian leeches" around the throne, to an aging king who actually is dead at the time the speech is made. Placed in context, Gloster's lines are not only most appropriate for the plot and for the character of the speaker, who wishes to abandon the useless Crusade, but they are subsequently forgotten in the passion, torment, fast action, and variety of conflicts in the play, which ends on a lofty note—the reunion of king and queen and an agreement on religious toleration—and not on petty, local politics. Even the short Preface has nothing to disturb a Walpole, since it simply points to Edward as a model warrior-prince and to his loving Eleonora as a parallel to the Princess of Wales, to whom Thomson dedicated the play. Although Campbell, Grant, Loftis, and Kern stress the political implications of *Edward,* Nicoll is right in believing that there was very little reason for the censor to ban it.

Agamemnon, which unaccountably slipped by the censor—perhaps because he had held office for only a few months—is of course another matter. Its characters were immediately equated with contemporaneous political figures: Clytemnestra was seen as the misguided Queen Caroline, the wicked traitor Egisthus as Walpole, and Agamemnon as George II, absent not ten years fighting for the honor of his nation but over one year dawdling with a new mistress in Hanover. Actually, the first speech that hints at politics comes only in the first scene of Act III, and it is most appropriate to the tragedy since it is the rather gentle reprimand—all in seven lines—of Melisander, Agamemnon's friend, that begins by partly blaming the King for leaving someone like Egisthus in charge to have "The power of blessing or oppressing millions" and concludes with a prayer to the gods to "avert the miseries that hence / On him [Agamemnon] and on his family may fall!" Because of these lines and the character parallels, even the conclusion was, by Walpole's enemies at least, considered political, Cassandra there prophesying a court revolution that would destroy Egisthus. *Agamemnon* is far more than a piece of political propaganda, however, for a twentieth-century audience would not recognize these parallels or hints since the Agamemnon story is so perennially topical, Thomson's portrait of the strong Egisthus is traditional and yet different, his Clytemnestra while weak is well drawn and believable, and his whole tragedy is compact, fast moving, and original. It is in fact not only one of his best but one of his most nearly universal plays and should not be dismissed for any of its occasional politics any more than one should dismiss Otway's *Venice Preserv'd,* Addison's *Cato,* or Hugo's *Hernani* because partisans cheered and opponents booed certain lines.

Furthermore, the contemporaneous politics that the avid searcher now finds in these two pieces are far less prominent than the joint themes of public duty and kingship in the larger, nobler sense that pervade the entire corpus of Thomson's plays. They are the same themes—the praise of England, of English liberty and all liberty, of loyalty to and love of "This blessed plot, this earth, this realm, this England"—found just as prominently in *The Seasons,* "Britannia," *Liberty,* and the stirring **"Rule, Britannia,"** in fact, in all of the patriotic Thomson's work. Sophonisba is a model of loyalty and patriotism for whom nothing is more important than her country, and her play ends with a minor character, a Roman, insisting that she, or anyone "Who loves, like her, his country, is a Roman" and hoping that "generous liberty . . . warm with freedom under frozen skies, / In farthest Britain Romans yet may rise." Agamemnon, accused of deserting his family and of killing his own daughter Iphigenia for war and honor, makes a stirring defense of his "agonizing" choice—the only choice of "the patriot, and the king"—to suppress "private inclination" for the sake "Of honour, duty, glory, public good" (II.ii), and in the same tragedy Melisander, loyal to his king and country, is contrasted with the traitor Egisthus. In *Edward,* not only is Gloster's speech (I.i) on "evil counsellors" universal rather than narrowly topical but throughout the play Edward and Eleonora speak often of their love for their country and for their people, especially the "common" people, and of the duties of kingship and queenship (e.g., II.iv, IV.vii, V.iv). Likewise, even though he brings his daughter to her death and ruins her lover's life, Siffredi in *Tancred and Sigismunda* causes all around him to reflect on the obligations and privileges of kingship, on public versus private duties, on the sacrifices one must make for his or her country. And finally there is no more important theme in *Coriolanus* than that expressed in the concluding speech, "Above ourselves our Country should be dear," and all the action shows how disloyalty to one's country leads to tragedy: Coriolanus dies because he has been a traitor to Rome, and Tullus, motivated by an unselfish wish to protect his nation, must have the megalomaniac killed. So while the masque *Alfred* is of course primarily a patriotic play, each of the tragedies also reflects Thomson the lover of his country and of liberty and each provides instruction on kingship and citizenship.

Likewise, each of the plays directly or indirectly debates the question of war as opposed to peace. Thomson developed the theme chiefly in two ways. One method was to select his situation—each play is acted against the background of a war that is just over or in actual progress—and the other was to juxtapose a pair of characters, one to favor peace, the other to argue for war, at least under certain conditions. Sophonisba believes in war to save her country from the hated tyrant Rome, while Scipio fights for Rome's honor and empire. Agamemnon has led the Achaians in a war to regain the raped Helen, his brother's wife, to save the honor of his people, and to fulfill his obligation as the chief of many kings, while Clytemnestra weakly defends peace at all costs so families will not be torn asunder. Edward fights a holy war, but Selim the Eastern Sultan successfully denounces such wars as being inspired by bigotry, just as Gloster, who wants to return to England, is easily the winner in his debate with Archbishop Theald, who, while no fanatic, argues for continuing the Crusade. Siffredi, in *Tancred,* thinks anything is better than internecine war. And in *Coriolanus,* Tullus, the noble pragmatist who, as Sophonisba and Syphax did, fights a "just war" for his nation against tyrannical Rome, is opposed in intellectual debate to Galesus, the equally noble idealist who procrastinates while hoping for peace and who with his idealism would lose the cause Tullus pursues (IV.ii).

Among the many other points of interest to note about the plays is that in every one of them Thomson was able to find a character or characters to speak in praise of a Father of life, a God of Nature, the harmonious universe, that is, to reflect that ardent and unabashed faith—called deism by McKillop—which is close to Shaftesbury's theism and to the philosophic optimism of Pope's *Essay on Man* and which is found in each of *The Seasons* and in the great "Hymn on the Seasons." In *Edward and Eleonora,* for example, thinking he is about to die, the Christian Edward, who never mentions Christ, prays to the

> Father of life!
> Whose universal love embraces all
> That breathes this ample air; whose perfect
> wisdom
> Brings light from darkness, and from evil good.
> (II.iv)

The Volscian, pre-Christian philosopher Galesus in *Coriolanus* preaches a Wordsworthian, and Shaftesburian, doctrine while in his last two lines echoing Pope as well as Thomson's own *Seasons:*

> There is a power,
> Unseen, that rules th' illimitable world,
> That guides its motions, from the brightest star,
> To the least dust of this sin-tainted mold;
> While man, who madly deems himself the lord
> Of all, is nought but weakness and dependance.
> (II.v)

Even the pagan play *Agamemnon* has the poet-advisor Melisander tell of his years on a desert island and speak of his communion with "streams, and groves, in sunny hill and shade," with "all that blooms with vegetable life," with "the full-peopled round of azure-heaven," a communion so close that through his

> troubled heart,
> They breath'd the soul of harmony anew.
> Thus of the great community of nature
> A denizen I liv'd; and oft, in hymns
> And rapt'rous thought, even with the Gods con-
> vers'd.
> (III.i)

Melisander's poignant and lovely account of his lonely yet mystical experience is the closest Thomson in any play, even in the pastoral *Alfred,* was able to approach to the beautiful nature description of *The Seasons* and to record the influence of great Nature on the soul and mind of man.

Melisander's often-admired lines are by no means, how-ever, the only ones that in the tragedies challenged the talents of a Wilks, an Oldfield, the Cibbers, a Quin, or a Garrick or that now are attractive to the reader because of their imagery, their ear appeal, or their "fancy," "imagination," "inventiveness," a quality that Thomson always considered so important in his poetry. One need simply note the great ear appeal of his blank verse, the "music" he once placed ahead of image, sentiment, and thought, and find it not only combined with those other qualities but so prominent that Dr. Johnson, while praising Thomson's poems, found their language "florid and luxuriant, . . . sometimes . . . filling the ear more than the mind." Other readers, of course, have disagreed with this judgment, just as audiences, actors, or readers, perhaps without realizing it, have found and will find that many speeches of the plays have both sense and sound and that the attractive sounds often reinforce the cognitive content. Melisander, for example, tells how, as his abductors left him "Cast on the wildest of the Cyclad isles," he

> never heard
> A sound so dismal as their parting oars.—
> Then horrid silence follow'd, broke alone
> By the low murmurs of the restless deep,
> Mixt with the doubtful breeze, that now and then
> Sigh'd thro' the mournful woods. . . .

> When Philomela, o'er my head
> Began to tune her melancholy strain,
> As piteous of my woes; till, by degrees,
> Composing sleep on wounded nature shed
> A kind but short relief.
> (III.i)

Here, in addition to "murmurs," "restless," "Sigh'd," "mournful," and other key words that even Dr. Johnson would agree are onomatopoeic, Thomson—as in *The Seasons* and other poems—employed heavy assonance, consonance, and alliteration both to please the ear and to emphasize the emotions. The assonating [al] of "wildest . . . Cyclad isles" may be simply pleasant, as a Shakespeare, Dryden, Pope, or Eliot might have it; but the [o] of "oars," "broke," and "low" is the sound that Poe, and before him many other poets, considered mournful, one of those sounds called phonesthemes, a vowel, consonant, or diphthong that, when echoed in the proper context, stresses the thought or emotion. Similarly, "Began," "tune," and "strain" echo the final [n] that Milton and others have liked for lines describing music, just as "degrees," "sleep," and "relief" end the passage by echoing the vowel of the peaceful "sleep" that rescues Melisander. And all of this goes with numerous other phonal repetitions, among them alliteration of [m], [d], [w], and [š] (in "shed" and "short"); a second assonance of [i] ("deep"-"breeze") and [o] ("woes"-"composing"); and consonance of [l] ("silence"-"followed") and [z] ("woes-"degrees"-"compos-").

These of course are by no means the only heavy uses of sounding words or lines, or phonal echoes, in *Agamemnon,* nor are they untypical of the plays in general. In *Edward,* for example, Gloster praises the virtuous Eleonora thus:

> 'Tis such as thou, who keep the gentle flame,
> That animates society, alive,
> Who make the dwellings of mankind delightful.
> What is vain life? an idle flight of days,
> A still delusive round of sickly joys,
> A scene of little cares and trifling passions,
> If not ennobled by such deeds of virtue?
>
> (III.i)

And he ends with a moan about the poisoned Edward's "short deceitful gleam of ease." The passage is filled with echoing vowels, especially [e], [aI], [I], and [i]. Eleonora, hearing of the poisoning of her beloved husband by a religious fanatic, exclaims in six lines that repeat the phonestheme [o] six times, not counting three "no more's," and that establish the sad content with the opening phrase "O complicated woe" (I.vi). Daraxa, the Sultan's captured wife, also hears the news and also in ear-appealing lines expresses her shocked, unbelieving reaction to what all consider to be her husband's perfidy:

> What! Selim send assassins! and beneath
> A name so sacred! Selim, whose renown
> Is incense breathing o'er the sweeten'd east;
> For each humane, each generous virtue fam'd;
> Selim! the rock of faith! and sun of honour!
>
> (I.vi)

The phonal echoes in Daraxa's five lines are unbelievably heavy—the alliteration of [s], [m], and [f], the assonance of [e] ("name"-"sacred"-"humane"-"fam'd") and [i] ("breathing"-"sweeten'd"-"east"-"each"), and the consonance of [n] ("renown"-"incense"-"humane"-"generous"-"sun"-"honour")—so heavy in fact that they even overshadow her incense, rock, and sun metaphors.

Every one of the plays contains not one or two such passages but dozens of them, attractive to the ear and appropriate to the mood, and Thomson was able to include almost every passion, feeling, or mood imaginable—wonder, amazement, pity, love, tenderness, fear. *Tancred and Sigismunda* alone has them all, as when Siffredi calmly but feelingly reports the king's death, among the lines being these:

> 　　　　　　at his years
> Death gives short notice—Drooping Nature then,
> Without a gust of pain to shake it, falls.
> His death, my daughter, was that happy period
> Which few attain. The duties of his day
> Were all discharge'd, and gratefully enjoy'd
> Its noblest blessings; calm, as evening-skies,
> Was his pure mind, and lighted up with hopes
> That open heaven; when, for his last long sleep
> Timely prepar'd, a lassitude of life,
> A pleasing weariness of mortal joy,
> Fell on his soul, and down he sunk to rest.
>
> (I.ii)

Siffredi's personifications, his metaphors, his similes, all

are combined with words that echo befitting sounds—the initial [d] that Dryden and Pope, as well as Shakespeare and Spenser, liked for death and dullness, and the equally prominent initial [l]; the [o] again, as well as [e], [aI], and the vowel of "lassitude" and "last"; and the final [s], [l], and other consonants. Every one of the six characters of this play has such sounding lines, but Tancred seldom opens his mouth without them, for example, when he swears eternal love to Siffredi's daughter:

> Hear me, thou soul of all my hopes and wishes!
> And witness, heaven! prime source of love and
> 　　joy!
> Not a whole warring world combin'd against me;
> Its pride, its splendor, its imposing forms,
> Nor interest, nor ambition, nor the face
> Of solemn state, not even thy father's wisdom,
> Shall ever shake my faith to Sigismunda.
>
> (I.vi)

or when overcome with Siffredi's deceit he agonizes that "words are weak / To paint the pangs, the rage, the indignation" that overwhelms him (II.ix). Multiply these passages by a hundred, by two hundred, and one sees why the great actor Quin was perhaps Thomson's closest friend in later years and why all the plays appealed to the professional companies of London and Dublin in the eighteenth century.

One must not forget, however, that sounding words and pleasing phrases do not a great play make. Such powerful and affecting speeches in the mouths of good actors or readers are, in Thomson's tragedies, combined with great emotions, great conflicts, warring people, and warring passions; with few but distinct and well-drawn characters, compact and organized plots acted out in one place and in short time; with themes favorite to Thomson the poet and to the eighteenth century and to all time. We are rediscovering that Thomson's century had more fine drama than editors and historians have permitted us to believe; and while his own contributions may not match those great tragedies of a Shakespeare or Thomson's own favorite Racine, they may, as Lessing thought, compare favorably with those of Corneille and surely they not only are worthy of the poet of *The Seasons* but are the best collection of tragedies by one Englishman of the eighteenth century.

Michael G. Ketcham (essay date 1982)

SOURCE: "Scientific and Poetic Imagination in James Thomson's *Poem Sacred to the Memory of Sir Isaac Newton*," in *Philological Quarterly,* Vol. 61, No. 1, Winter, 1982, pp. 33-50.

[*In the following essay, Ketcham investigates three patterns in* Poem Sacred to the Memory of Sir Isaac Newton *through which Thomson "takes the elegy for Newton as an occasion to define the scientific imagination poetically, and, through the definition of science, to define implicitly the potentials of the poetic imagination."*]

The lines of influence between the poetry and the new science of the eighteenth century have been often studied, usually with the aim of showing how the observations, language, or methods of science are incorporated into poems. My interest here, though, in reading James Thomson's *Poem Sacred to the Memory of Sir Isaac Newton,* is not so much in what science does to poetry as in what poetry does to science, since Thomson takes the elegy for Newton as an occasion to define the scientific imagination poetically, and, through the definition of science, to define implicitly the potentials of the poetic imagination. This approach to Thomson's poem allows us to see certain features of Thomson's poetic practice, and it allows us to see the poem as one vehicle for an eighteenth-century mythology of science, a mythology of science which reflects less the empirical methods of science itself than an imagery of light derived from the neoplatonic and Christian traditions of wisdom as "the everlasting light, the unspotted mirror of the power of God" (Wisdom of Solomon, 7:26). This paper will investigate three patterns in the *Poem Sacred to the Memory of Sir Isaac Newton* which shape this mythology of science. The first of these patterns is the poem's organization as an elegy; the second is a contrast between the scientific and poetic imaginations; and the third is a fabric of allusion by which Thomson identifies Newton with traditional personifications of wisdom.

Thomson's elegy for Newton was published in May, 1727, two months after Newton's death while Thomson, too, was publishing the first versions of *The Seasons.* The poem celebrates Newton's discoveries in optics and in celestial mechanics, discoveries which represent a new understanding of the nature of creation. The poem, then, is a sustained panegyric which draws from the conventional physico-theology of Thomson's day: it celebrates the wisdom of God revealed in the creation, and its tone approximates a hymn on divine order.

Although there are no textual divisions apart from verse paragraphs, the poem divides into three parts: the first places Newton's discoveries into the context of the darkness and confusion which have impeded man's understanding, comparing Newton's vision with the general condition of man "Clouded in Dust"; the final part discusses the implications of his discoveries and their potential impact on other men. These two parts of the poem are comprised of corresponding verse paragraphs on the futility of temporal achievements and on Britain's progress, on time's effect on man as seen in the tides and on Newton's explanation of the tides, on Newton's astronomy and on the power of the Creator as revealed in the order of the heavens. The middle section of the poem is a long description of the rainbow, the thematic center of the poem, which I will discuss in detail later.

Within this framework, Thomson draws on the conventional imagery of an elegy, and on conventional images of praise for Newton. Like other elegies, the poem contrasts the world of ordinary men and the world made possible by the subject of the poem; the subject himself is a redeemer, bringing men from one world to the other,

or at least to a glimpse of the other, in memory, as in life, the subject radiates wisdom down to men from heaven. Closer to his own subject, Thomson draws on an established set of images in praise of Newton. Newton's accomplishments had been represented as light illuminating or piercing through a darkness which obscured nature, showing a new beauty and showing divine order in the world. This set of images is summed up most tersely in Pope's couplet epitaph for Newton—"Nature, and Nature's Laws lay hid in Night. / God said, *Let Newton be!* and All was *Light*"—but the same metaphor had been used in Roger Cotes's Preface to the 1726 edition of the *Principia,* in Edmund Halley's "Ode: To the Illustrious Man Isaac Newton," and in John Norris's earlier praise of the new science. And Thomson chose as his epigraph for *Newton* a passage from Lucretius originally dedicated to Epicurus: "At all this a kind of godlike delight mixed with shuddering awe comes over me to think that nature by thy power is laid thus visibly open, is thus unveiled on every side."

Thomson, writing the most beautifully articulated celebration of Newton, gave new life to this reservoir of conventional materials. He begins the poem with a question posed as a challenge to the Muses:

> Shall the great Soul of NEWTON quit this Earth,
> To mingle with his Stars; and every Muse,
> Astonish'd into Silence, shun the Weight
> Of Honours due to his illustrious Name?

This opening question may be hard to understand. Although Thomson's was the first published elegy, it was clear when Halley wrote in 1686 that Newton was "to the Muses dear." But the subject is a challenge, one which raises a corollary question: what *can* the Muses say in the face of the Creation revealed to man? This is one of several challenges—including one which Thomson addresses to himself again near the middle of the poem, "in Fancy's lighter Thought, / How shall the Muse then grasp the mighty Theme" (135-36)—and it introduces a double theme in the poem, one a praise of Newton and the other a questioning of the poet's imagination.

The opening lines also introduce a central symbol in Newton's "illustriousness," in the seraphs as "Sons of Light," in the light of the stars. Newton, whose name was intimately associated with his *Opticks,* is also associated in Thomson's poem with a complex image of light which joins under a common rubric all aspects of the universe—common physical light, the light of the stars, Newton's illustriousness among men, the light of intellect, the light of faith, divine light. This imagery has two immediate implications for Thomson's poem. The first is that all the universe is suffused with light so that light of any one type suggests and "illuminates" light of any other type. The second implication is in Thomson's concentration on Newton's sight, on his "All intellectual Eye" (39), his "measuring Eye" (95), his "well-purg'd penetrative Eye" (73). Through Thomson's characteristic emphasis on verbs and participles this seeing is intensely active, stretching toward and snatching in the stars (61), pursuing comets or beams of light (76, 95), so Newton's science is imaged as movement: "while on this dim Spot, where Mortals toil / Clouded in Dust" (13-14), "he took his ardent Flight / Thro' the blue Infinite" (57-58). The extended analogy of light is not fixed in a hierarchy where the light of intellect, for instance, is greater than that of sensation. It is more like Plotinus' fountain of light, where different levels of creation flow from the divine source and simultaneously flow back into it. Like the neoplatonic universe, that depicted by Thomson (seen by Newton) is one where the laws of the universe are simultaneously immanent in the creation and transcendentally outside of it. Thomson thus establishes a poetic metaphysics where both scientific and poetic intuitions move between the concrete and the abstract, between manifestations and laws, although the contrast between science and poetry also resides in this metaphysics of light.

The imagery of light takes its fullest form in the description of the rainbow, which is the middle segment of the poem, and which brings together the scientific and poetic perceptions of light. This passage moves through the different colors of the spectrum; and it moves through time. The colors of the rainbow take on associations of the changing seasons. The passage moves from Newton's youthful discoveries to his death. It begins with metaphoric sunrise—

> The Schools astonish'd stood; . . .
> . . . At once their pleasing Visions fled,
> With the gay Shadows of the Morning mix'd,
> When NEWTON rose, our philosophic Sun!
>
> (85-90)

and it ends with the poet, after Newton's death, looking at the colors in the sunset which had been explained by Newton's laws: "flaming RED," "tawny ORANGE," "delicious YELLOW," "all-refreshing GREEN," "the pure BLUE, that swells autumnal Skies,"

> then, of sadder Hue,
> Emerg'd the deepen'd INDIGO, as when
> The heavy-skirted Evening droops with Frost.
> While the last Gleamings of refracted Light
> Dy'd in the fainting VIOLET away.
> These, when the Clouds distil the rosy Shower,
> Shine out distinct adown the watry Bow;
> While o'er our Heads the dewy Vision bends
> Delightful, melting on the Fields beneath.
> Myriads of mingling Dyes from these result,
> And Myriads still remain—Infinite Source
> Of Beauty, ever-flushing, ever-new!
>   Did ever Poet image aught so fair,
> Dreaming in whispering Groves, by the hoarse
>   Brook!
> Or Prophet, to whose Rapture Heaven descends!
> Even now the setting Sun and shifting Clouds,
> Seen, GREENWICH, from thy lovely Heights,
>   declare
> How just, how beauteous the REFRACTIVE LAW.
>
> (107-24)

The description of the rainbow juxtaposes the scientist's vision of the universe, at the beginning of the passage, with the poet's vision, at the end. The juxtaposition of scientist and poet thus forms a transition from the first part of the elegy, where Newton breaks through the obscurity which had hidden nature, to the second part of the elegy, where Thomson reflects on the value of Newton's discoveries for other men. It also reveals the second organizing pattern in the poem: the contrast between scientific and poetic imaginations.

The first part of the rainbow passage is Thomson's rendering of the scientific method. From physical experiments charming in themselves the scientist educes, collects, and measures the innate properties of things. Thus Newton "Untwisted all the shining robe of Day" (98) and "To the charm'd Eye educ'd the gorgeous Train / Of PARENT-COLOURS" (101-02). This is the procedure Newton describes in his own letter to the Royal Society outlining his projected *Opticks*. When testing the refraction of a prism he found "it was at first a pleasing divertisement to view the vivid and intense colors produced thereby," but "I then proceeded to examine more critically" the rays of light. In the *Principia* Newton explained that such a critical examination should follow definite laws. As the first two of four rules for scientific procedure he held that *"we are to admit no more causes of natural things than such as are both true and sufficient to explain their appearance"* since "Nature is pleased with simplicity," and then that we should *"to the same natural effects . . . as far as possible assign the same causes"* so that the pull of gravity or the reflection of light on earth and on the planets would be attributed to the same causes. These rules are rendered by Thomson in Newton's ability to see "Motion's simple Laws" determining the course of the cosmos. Newton saw "every STAR"

> the living Centre each
> Of an harmonious System: all combin'd,
> And rul'd unerring by that single Power,
> Which draws the Stone projected to the Ground.
>
> (64-67)

This set of images creates a particular relationship between the scientist and the poet. Newton's intelligence pursues and penetrates into "Even LIGHT ITSELF" to see the unifying laws, in optics and in physics, which lie behind the manifold appearance of things:

> Nor could the darting BEAM, of Speed immense,
> Escape his swift Pursuit, and measuring Eye.
> Even LIGHT ITSELF, which every thing displays,
> Shone undiscover'd, till his brighter Mind
> Untwisted all the shining Robe of Day.
>
> (94-98)

Thomson's image of Newton's method carries with it a kind of appropriation. The stars are "his Stars"; "The Heavens are his own"; "Nature herself / Stood all subdu'd by him, and open laid / Her every latent Glory to his View" (36-38). The idea behind such imagery is simple: by knowing the laws which govern the universe, Newton has dominion over it; while God ordained the laws, Newton has intellectually re-created them. The poet's vision, on the other hand, is not intensive in this way but extensive, seeing the various acts of creation just as it sees the various colors refracted out of white light. The laws of nature known to Newton in their "first great Simplicity" (84) are to the poet an "Infinite Source / Of Beauty" (116-17), of "Effects so various, beautiful, and great" (71), following Addison's conditions for esthetic pleasure. This is the view from Greenwich hill at sunset. Thomson sees the "setting Sun," "shifting Clouds," and the "lovely Heights" whose colors derive from Newton's laws.

The scientist and poet have complementary intuitions of the world. The scientist pushes toward a transcendental unity; the poet catches the profusion of manifest things. According to a comparison Thomson makes at the conclusion of **Summer,** in *The Seasons,* nature is

> To reason's and to fancy's eye displayed—
> The first up-tracing, from the dreary void,
> The chain of causes and effects to Him,
> The world-producing Essence, who alone
> Possesses being, while the last receives
> The whole magnificence of heaven and earth,
> And every beauty, delicate or bold,
> Obvious or more remote, with livelier sense,
> Diffusive painted on the rapid mind.
>   (**Summer,** 1744-52)

Furthermore, the materials of science, beginning with minute particulars and leading to the most comprehensive abstractions, mark the boundaries of poetic language. To clarify this point, though, I must step momentarily outside of the poem dedicated to Newton to consider *The Seasons.*

In *Spring,* too, Thomson implicitly contrasts the scientific and poetic intuitions of the world through the image of the rainbow. The profusion of spring flowers and the rainbow have the same form. The rainbow is a "various twine of light" which "Shoots up immense; and every hue unfolds" ("Spring," 211, 205); the flowers are "a twining mass of tubes" which "the vernal sun awakes" and through which "lively fermentation mounting spreads / All this innumerous-coloured scene of things" (*Spring,* 566, 567, 570-71). But where Newton could "unfold / The various twine of light," "who [can] pierce / With vision pure into these secret stores / Of health and life and joy?" ("Spring," 234-36). If the rainbow is a test of the scientist, "this innumerous-coloured scene of things" is a test of the poet since it escapes categorization and eludes completely the resources of language: "Ah, what shall language do? ah, where find words / Tinged with so many colours" (*Spring,* 475-76). Here are "Infinite numbers, delicacies, smells, / With hues on hues expression cannot paint" (*Spring,* 553-54).

The sheer amplitude of the world's effects, then is one limit of poetic language. But this is compensated for because the poet participates in phenomena both physically and by an act of imagination that replicates their profusion. Thomson catches "the landscape, gliding swift / Athwart imagination's vivid eye," "Ten thousand wandering images of things" (*Spring,* 458-59, 463). When he walks through the fields with his Amanda the abstract phrasing of "the living herbs, profusely wild" blossoms into a forty-line catalogue of flowers filling "the finished garden" (*Spring,* 222, 516). The whole landscape is cast through the eye of the poet and through his struggling imagination: "Snatched through the verdant maze, the hurried eye / Distracted wanders" (518-19).

The universal, unifying order is the second limit of poetic language. In *Summer* Thomson explains this boundary, speaking first of the sun and then of God:

> But this,
> And all the much-transported Muse can sing,
> Are to thy beauty, dignity, and use
> Unequal far, great delegated Source
> Of light and life and grace and joy below!
>   How shall I then attempt to sing of Him
> Who, light Himself, in uncreated light
> Invested deep, dwells awfully retired
> From mortal eye of angel's purer ken. . . .
>   (*Summer,* 170-78)

This limitation is also compensated for, by the poet's art of metaphor and allusion. In *Spring,* the rainfall which stimulates the growth of flowers becomes a figure of the Deluge, since it reminds Thomson of the golden age of cooperative love which preceded the Flood and the age of rapine which has followed it; in *Summer,* Thomson draws on the well-established metaphor of the sun as a sensory image of God, so that echoes of theological speculations lie behind the poetry. And, returning to the elegy for Newton, this power of metaphor brings the methods of science into our moral experience by calling out secondary meanings, the echoes of fallen man, in such phrases as "this dim Spot, where Mortals toil / Clouded in Dust."

In addition to the symmetrical outline, and in addition to the central contrast between scientific and poetic intuitions, Thomson's poem is organized according to a fabric of allusion, the third pattern unifying the poem and developing Thomson's mythology of science. It works in various ways: a pattern of allusions links the first and third parts of the poem; it places Newton in a unique position in the world as a new Adam; and it brings to bear on Newton's life a rich set of associations accumulated around the imagery of light.

The difference between the first and third parts of the poem lies in a realigning of man's relationship to nature, through the agency of Newton's science. In the fifth paragraph, for example, the "wandering" moon and rising and falling tides are images of time passing—a time which is purposeless and resistless, being either destructive "heaving on the broken Rocks," or idle, leaving "A yellow Waste of idle Sands behind" (53, 56). In the corresponding paragraph in the final part of the poem, the "TIDE OF TIME" is not purposeless but flows "To vast Eternity's unbounded Sea" (125-26): the waters of time move toward eternity; they are lighted though their origin is in darkness; they are channeled and marked with beacons for historians trying to make the course of human events intelligible.

Newton's realignment of man's relationship to the cosmos means, in effect, a re-creation of the world. The laws of creation existed before Newton discerned them, but his vision qualitatively changed man's conception of them from chaos to cosmos. Newton has intellectually re-created these laws, and in this re-creation stands as a type of Adam: in his account of Newton's science, Thomson emphasizes Newton's discoveries regarding light, astronomy, and the tides—the first elements of creation in Genesis; and Newton penetrates into the intrinsic nature of these things with an Adam-like intuition:

> Have ye not listen'd while he bound the SUNS,
> And PLANETS to their Spheres! th' unequal Task
> Of Human-kind till then. Oft had they roll'd
> O'er erring Man the Year, and oft disgrac'd
> The Pride of Schools, before their Course was
>   known
> Full in its Causes and Effects to him,
> All-piercing Sage! Who sat not down and
>   dream'd
> Romantic Schemes, defended by the Din
> Of specious Words, and Tyranny of Names;
> But, bidding his amazing Mind attend,
> And with heroic Patience Years on Years
> Deep-searching, saw at last the SYSTEM dawn,
> And shine, of all his Race, on him alone.
>
> (17-29)

The echoes of fallen man in the first lines of this paragraph are deafening ("erring Man," "oft disgrac'd," "The Pride of Schools"), but Newton stands in the midst of confusion and ignorance as a type of Adam who "saw at last the SYSTEM dawn, / And shine, of all his Race, on him alone":

> The Heavens are all his own; from the wide
>   Rule
> Of whirling VORTICES and circling SPHERES,
> To their first great Simplicity restor'd.
>
> (82-84)

Newton's double role in Thomson's poem, as a kind of co-creator and as a figure of Adam, links Newton (within Thomson's mythology of science) to traditional images of wisdom, and it links him to the most important set of metaphors in the poem, those entailed in the imagery of light. The elegy for Newton comes near the end of a long tradition of imagery combining light, intuitive knowledge, and immediate vision. At the center of this constellation of images is the figure of wisdom, personified as a demiurge, a co-creator with God, giving order to the universe. This personification derives from the demi-urge of Plato's *Timaeus,* from the Hebraic Wisdom books of the Apocrypha, and from the neoplatonic strain in Christianity: "*Wisdom* reacheth from one end to another mightily: and sweetly doth she order all things" (Wisdom of So-

lomon, 8:1). Because Wisdom is the co-creator, a figure of beneficent order, and God's "only begotten" in the Hebraic tradition, the Christian tradition considered Christ to be the incarnation of Wisdom as divine grace working in the world, although their formal derivation differs. Neoplatonic Christianity distinguished *sapientia increata,* God's own wisdom, equal and co-eternal with him, from *sapientia creata,* which resulted from God's contemplation of himself. Both differ radically from any form of human knowledge or reason, but *sapientia creata* is a spiritual and moral ability to conceive of and apprehend all being which may be given to man by grace—although preternatural Adam was supposed to have intrinsically possessed this kind of immediate understanding. It is this Wisdom which had been personified in the Apocrypha.

Wisdom is imaged as perpetual light. Augustine in the *Confessions* works out the image this way: "It means created wisdom, that intellectual nature which is light because it contemplates the Light. . . . But there is as great a difference between the Wisdom, which creates and the wisdom which is created as between the Light which enlightens and light which receives its brilliance by reflection. . . . "The Wisdom of Solomon uses the same image: "For she is the brightness of the everlasting light, the unspotted mirror of the power of God, and the image of his goodness" (7:26). The Wisdom of Solomon also elaborates:

> 7:17. For [God] hath given me certain knowledge of the things that are, namely to know how the world was made, and the operation of elements: 18. The beginning, ending and midst of the times: the alterations of the turning *of the sun,* and the change of seasons: 19. The circuits of years, and the positions of stars . . . . 21. And all such things as are either secret or manifest, them I know. 22. For wisdom, which is the worker of all things, taught me: for in her is an understanding spirit . . . 23. Kind to man, stedfast, sure, free from care, having all power, overseeing all things, and going through all understanding, pure, and most subtil, spirits.

This tradition of a personified Wisdom, or Sophia, or Sapientia, persisted well into the seventeenth century in England. Its imagery lies behind Milton's "Hail, holy Light, offspring of Heav'n first-born" (*Paradise Lost,* III, 1), and it is represented clearly in the writings of the Cambridge Platonists. John Smith, for example, speaks of "Reason in man being *Lumen de Lumine,* a Light flowing from the Fountain and Father of Lights," and speaks of Solomon as "one of her Eldest Sons of Wisdom, alwaies standing up and calling her blessed: his Heart was both enlarged and fill'd with the pure influence of her beams, and therefore was perpetually adoring that Sun which gave him light." For the Platonists, wisdom is an intuition which pierces to the truth of things; it is light contemplating the Light. The wisdom of God manifested in the works of the creation is one favorite theme of eighteenth-century theodicies (the phrase itself forms the title for John Ray's book on nature—1691), and the personification of wisdom is preserved in Richard Blackmore's *Creation* (1715) and in his poem "A Hymn to the Light of the World" (1703):

Hail radiant Off-spring, Emanation bright!
   Pure Effluent Splendor of Eternal Light!
     Substantial Beam, not of Created Race,
The Effulgent Image of the Father's Face,
Who of the Blissful Persons hast the Second
     place.

     Thy beams irradiate every Mind,
Blest Seraphims above and Men below,
   Who Truth by painful Reas'ning find,
Or like Thy self, by Intuition know:
Who step by step to Wisdom's Height advance,
Or know by simple Vision, and a single Glance;
     These have from Thee their piercing Sight,
O ever-during Spring of Intellectual Light!

This is the imagery that Thomson draws on when, in the poem for Newton, he writes:

   O unprofuse Magnificence divine!
   O WISDOM truly perfect! thus to call
From a few Causes such a Scheme of Things,
Effects so various, beautiful, and great,
An Universe compleat! And O belov'd
Of Heaven! whose well-purg'd penetrative Eye,
The mystic Veil transpiercing, inly scan'd
The rising, moving, wide-establish'd Frame.

                        (68-75)

And it is an imagery that Thomson recalls again in *Summer*, where he speaks of Newton as "pure intelligence, whom God / To mortals lent to trace his boundless works / From laws sublimely simple" (*Summer,* 1560-62).

The constellation of imagery remains in several forms for Thomson to use in the elegy for Newton: it persists in the conventions of the elegy and in the conventions of praise from which Thomson draws his portrait of Newton, and it persists in a rich tradition of imagery in poetry and philosophy linking light with intuition. This established imagery applies with unique appropriateness to Newton, and Thomson takes advantage of this fact in order to shape our understanding of a new phenomenon—the phenomenon of the scientific consciousness—by bringing Newton's life into the sphere of associations accumulated around the figure of wisdom: Thomson uses the older mythology of wisdom to give shape to the newer mythology of science. Newton's studies in celestial physics and in the properties of light (and still more the moral qualities attributed to wisdom) draw together Thomson's poem and the Biblical personification: Newton is an image of wisdom, a wisdom which is preternatural, creative, and an agent of God in the world.

Seeing Newton according to the image of wisdom clarifies the moral shift between the first and last parts of Thomson's poem, and clarifies both the personal and public benefits Thomson attributes to Newton.

Newton, in life, enjoyed a serenity and spiritual well-being which resulted from seeing the divine perfection behind the harmony of physical laws, and in these moral qualities he acted as a prism refracting wisdom into varied virtues which other men can see. Thus Thomson urges John Conduitt (the husband of Newton's niece) to write Newton's biography while his heart "glows with all the recollected Sage" (161). Even after death Newton enjoys "grateful Adoration, for that Light / So plenteous ray'd into thy Mind below, / From LIGHT HIMSELF" (196-98). This moral refraction is a central image in Thomson's elegies, as in his poem **"On the Death of Mr. William Aikman, the Painter"**:

   Viewed round and round, as lucid diamonds
     throw
   Still as you turn them a revolving glow,
   So did his mind reflect with secret ray
   In various virtues heaven's internal day.

                        (9-12)

The relationship here is precisely that between the scientist and the poet: the one seeing the unified light, the other seeing the refracted beauties.

The radiance of Newton's life also helps explain the public benefits which Thomson attributes to Newton, and these benefits lead back to the theme of time. The fourth paragraph of "Newton" compares his accomplishments to the ephemeral "Triumphs of old GREECE and ROME" (31), and the final paragraph picks up the comparison: "Ye mouldering Stones . . . what Grandeur can ye boast / While NEWTON lifts his Column to the Skies, / Beyond the Waste of Time" (174, 179-81). Thomson asks Newton from his celestial position to "Exalt the Spirit of a downward World" (200) and be Britain's presiding genius

   While in Expectance of the second Life,
   When Time shall be no more, thy sacred Dust
   Sleeps with her Kings, and dignifies the Scene.
                        (207-09)

Newton's vision, like the vision granted by wisdom, transcends mutability: it channels time; it is a timeless monument. But this work of wisdom struggles against the ruin of time. According to the Wisdom of Solomon, wisdom "is more beautiful than the sun, and above all the order of the stars: being compared with the light, she is found before it. For after this cometh night: but vice shall not prevail against wisdom" (7:29-30). For Augustine the relationship is more ambiguous: wisdom is outside of time, "Yet mutability is inherent in it, and it would grow dark and cold unless, by clinging to [God] with all the strength of its love, it drew warmth and light from [Him] like a moon that never wanes." This way in which wisdom is immortal only in its dependence on the Light applies to Thomson's image of Newton. Thomson's final vision is apocalyptic: the second kingdom is without time; Newton, as a figure of wisdom, is both inside and outside of time. But his vision is not immutable; it is not the light which enlightens but the light which "receives its brilliance by reflection." Even if man is made a little lower than the angels, as the eighth Psalm has it, so that he may contemplate the work of God's hands, he remains man; Newton, like the author of the Wisdom of Solomon, is "a mortal man, like to all, and the offspring of him that was made of earth" (7:1). Only if Newton remains immortal in the memory of men so that men may see the beauty of his laws, as the poet does on Greenwich hill, only if men come out of their chaos into an ordered existence such as that Newton had seen in the whole cosmos, will night not follow the day of Newton's life.

Two conclusions may be drawn from this reading of Thomson's *Poem Sacred to the Memory of Sir Isaac Newton*. First, the poem for Newton illustrates poetic patterns which reoccur in Thomson's other poems. Within the last fifteen years, critics have shown us much about ways in which Thomson's poems convey a system of moral tensions through the details of description. Thomson's poetic structures are based both on processes (the processes of nature and of consciousness), and on contrasts (such as those between expansion and contraction or between ascent and descent). Thomson in *The Seasons,* for example, teaches his readers to see not states but processes of nature which range in scale from the great changes in the seasons to the minute, invisible movements by which plants grow or frost seals over a river. Accompanying the processes of nature are the movements of consciousness by which human beings, through reason and through imagination, integrate their awareness of nature and rise from sensation to intellection to spiritual apprehension. We can see these processes of meditation to be represented, for example, in Thomson's praise of Philosophy in *Summer* (lines 1709-1805) or in his praise of Lyttleton in *Spring* (lines 895-933).

Not the least of the movements of consciousness is the movement of the poet's own imagination, as his imaginative eye moves through the scene presented to it. So, one structuring principle in Thomson's poetry is that of interlocking chains of association, chains which take the form of a meditative cycle, moving from observations of nature, to moral reflections, to psalm-like passages of praise. But in addition to following these processes of association, Thomson's poetry is also structured according to systematic contrasts which are based on a poetic architecture—an architecture of placement and of allusion. Ralph Cohen, for one, has seen Thomson to be working out the ambiguities of human nature in natural descriptions because these descriptions are organized according to contrasting forces and because they recall older traditions of moral imagery. Cohen has seen Thomson's poetry as typically Augustan in "sharing with the major poetry of the period an awareness of the valued past, the corruption of this past in the present, the limited nature of human life, and the faith that a better life exists beyond 'this dark State.'" Such a pattern of contrasts defines the structure of the elegy for Newton. In fact, the architectural structure of Thomson's poetry may be easier to see in a short poem such as *Newton* (which is slightly over 200 lines long) than in the more intricate fabric of *The Seasons*. The poem establishes a symmetrical contrast between the state of man's understanding before Newton's vision and the state of our understanding following that vision; Thomson places himself at a dividing point in man's moral history, at a dividing point between

one vision of the world and another (although he reminds us that this new vision is still bound to time and change); and he gives moral weight to Newton's new science by associating it with older traditions of wisdom.

The second conclusion to be drawn from this reading of Thomson's elegy for Newton is that Thomson uses the poem to give shape to a mythology of science, a mythology which is not Thomson's alone, but one which is shared by most other commentators on the new science. This mythology is based in part on a psychology of science rising in meditative steps from phenomena to God. More importantly, it is based on an older and more established idea of man's wisdom. Thomson uses the imagery of this tradition—he uses the metaphoric resources of poetry—to shape our perception of the new science, so that while the actual discoveries of science may elude poetry, poetry in another way comprehends science by giving it an imaginative form.

Thomson's mythology of science also reveals what was certainly for him a clearly held idea of the poetic imagination. Science and poetry are opposites, the one revealing the unity of natural laws, and the other tracing a spectrum of sensation. But in another respect they are more nearly parallel than contrasting, since the scientists's response to the world is analogous to the poet's esthetic response. Although published in 1748, twenty years after Thomson's poem, Colin Maclaurin's *Account of Sir Isaac Newton's Philosophical Discoveries* exemplifies an attitude toward science prevalent since the beginning of the century. Science is valued not only for its knowledge but also for the psychological responses it inspires. Along with other reactions, "the unexhausted beauty and variety of things makes natural philosophy ever agreeable, new and surprizing," and the scientist "while he contemplates and admires so excellent a system, cannot but be himself excited and animated to correspond with the general harmony of nature." Furthermore, extending knowledge beyond sensation is explained by Maclaurin specifically as an act of "a well regulated imagination." Similarly, the poet's response to the world is analogous to the scientist's. As we see in Thomson's own poems, poetry, like science, joins sensation to intellection, and moves from sensory things to the sublime adoration of Thomson's psalm-like passages. "The atmosphere of these lines," Patricia Meyer Spacks has said of one such passage from *The Seasons,* "is far from the rationalism of a Newtonian thinker, despite the fact that their theme is the universal order which Newton had so distinctly revealed." The atmosphere is different from Newtonian rationalism, but not far from it: the atmosphere of Thomson's poetry is the other side of Newtonian rationalism. What such passages show us is that the Newtonian universe helps Thomson to define his poetry, and that the metaphors of poetry help to define science, because both are a part of one imaginative enterprise.

John Sitter (essay date 1982)

SOURCE: "The Long Poem Obstructed," in *Literary Loneliness in Mid-Eighteenth-Century England,* Cornell,

1982, pp. 157-88.

[In the excerpt below, Sitter offers a thematic discussion of Liberty *and the constituent poems of* The Seasons.]

If we consider Thomson's poetic career and take seriously his aspirations as a philosophic poet, we need to give more witness than usual to **Liberty,** his second longest poem and the work which occupied many of his best years. **Liberty** was published in 1735-1736; Thomson seems to have begun it shortly after completing **The Seasons** in 1730, and many of the more than 1,000 lines added to **The Seasons** in the editions of 1744 and 1746 reflect Thomson's political preoccupations. Thomson may well have thought, as McKillop has suggested, of his new subject as the outcome of a Virgilian maturation from pastoral to a more overtly political and epic undertaking. We may think of it, less consciously and generically, as Thomson's transfer of the problem of theodicy from "nature" to history.

Perhaps before we go further it will help us to recall the persistence of the mid-eighteenth-century problem of theodicy, which is essentially the loss of physicotheological confidence, by considering some of its modern formulations. Its starkest statement in recent literature may be memorandum Walker Percy's "moviegoer" writes to himself:

> Starting point for search:
> It no longer avails to start with creatures and
>   prove God.
> Yet it is impossible to rule God out.

Thomson's problem is not the same as that of Percy's narrator, puzzled by "invincible apathy," although the later **Castle of Indolence** is in some sense a similar attempt to make meaning out of apathy's pathos; but he has a similar literary problem in trying to find the "signs" that will carry conviction. William James, lecturing in Thomson's old university at the beginning of our century, described the problem more fully:

> That vast literature of proof of God's existence drawn from the order of nature, which a century ago seemed so overwhelmingly convincing, to-day does little more than gather dust in libraries, for the simple reason that our generation has ceased to believe in the kind of God it argued for. Whatever sort of being God may be, we know to-day that he is nevermore that mere external inventory of "contrivances" intended to make manifest his "glory" in which our great-grandfathers took such satisfaction, though just how we know this we cannot possibly make clear by words either to others or to ourselves. I defy any of you here fully to account your persuasion that if a God exist he must be a more cosmic and tragic personage than that Being.

It is **Liberty,** of course, that gathers dust in libraries, while **The Seasons** is regularly studied and is occasionally even read. But if Thomson's poetic capacity failed him badly in **Liberty,** his intellectual instincts were right. His active career spans exactly the years during which Vico was to declare a fundamental schism between our possible knowledge of natural science and our knowledge of history. Nature for Vico is finally a blank, but history is ours: made by men, it can be understood by men. Such understanding yields the "principles" of the "ideal eternal history traversed in time by every nation," and it leads Vico to a theodicy. "Our new Science must therefore be a demonstration, so to speak, of what providence has wrought in history, for it must be a history of the institutions by which, without human discernment or counsel, and often against the designs of men, providence has ordered this great city of the human race." To read this ideal history one must grasp the "language" of institutions; then it becomes possible to recognize, for example, that "all ancient Roman law was a serious poem . . . , and ancient jurisprudence was a severe poetry."

Vico's new science seems to have had virtually no influence until near the end of the century, but the intellectual dissatisfaction and curiosity which led to his brilliant historicism are reflected, however crudely and partially, in various "progressive" readings of history. Among these the most ambitious is Thomson's "progress" of Liberty, which is nothing less than an attempt to interpret Western history as an "ideal" history. We need to grasp the nature of this intellectualization in order to appreciate the genuine ambition of Thomson in **Liberty,** which is not simply a "progress piece" or a "Whig panegyric," and thus to understand the meaning of its failure for in relation to mid-eighteenth-century literature generally.

Thomson's **Liberty** begins and ends among the ruins of Rome, those monuments of vanished minds which Dyer would paint more melancholically a few years later. Thomson uses the scene to compare ancient and modern Italy and then to launch an intellectual survey of the progressive realization of liberty in Greece, Rome, and Britain, a survey which culminates in a "Prospect" of the future. Thomson's poem is potentially more "severe" than the simple genealogies or pageants comprising most progress pieces because of his essentially idealist preoccupation with historical inevitability. Liberty moves like the sun, from east to west, as any self-respecting personification would have to in the period. But Thomson goes further by addressing her as the "better sun! Sun of Mankind," as Akenside would address Beauty, and describing her course to "western worlds *irrevocable* rolled" (III, 326-27). The italics are mine, but the emphasis for Thomson is indeed on "irrevocable" rather than on "western," since Liberty will have veered north and then south before landing in Britain. She came to Rome and she left it with the "swift approach of fate" (III, 336; cf. III, 72-73). The Goths raged "resistless" because she "urged" them in necessary vengeance, and she herself is "by fate commissioned" to move on to England and oversee those struggles "educing good from ill" which make up its history (III, 527; IV, 407, 702). "Nought can resist your force," the poet says simply near the end of the poem.

But where in this hymn to resistless liberty is the place of the individual? Thomson's attempt to find order in history is an idealist one not because material things are undervalued (the paeans to Commerce are lavish) but because mind is regarded as prior. Physical changes occur in the course of history only after mental changes have caused them; Thomson insists upon this position even to the point of maintaining that "Ne'er yet by force was freedom overcome" (II, 494). So, for example, Greece fell not because of conquest but because it had already fallen in spirit, and thus "The Persian fetters that enthralled the mind, / Were turned to formal and apparent chains" (II, 488-89). And so in Rome the heroism of Brutus "burst the grosser bonds" of Caesar, but the "soft enchanting fetters of the mind" remained "And other Caesars rose" (V, 202-5). In such a world the individuals presumably have great responsibility for keeping their minds uncorrupted (Rome's fetters point the moral of a passage beginning "Britons! be firm . . . "), but it is not at all clear how their doing so would help their country resist, for better or worse, the resistless.

Thomson is hardly alone in not resolving the relation of the individual to history or in reconciling the values of personal freedom and collective destiny. Perhaps any attempt to make history more philosophic or poetic than Aristotle claimed it was, that is, any attempt to attribute to history relations essentially "logical" in which events "follow as cause and effect," is likely to encounter all of the problems of determinism and fatalism in combining claims of "historical inevitability" with, typically, hortatory morality. Moreover, since inevitable consequences are preeminently the property of tragedy, such an attempt is likely to yield a reading of history as tragedy, protestations of optimism not withstanding. For Vico and later for Herder and Hegel, history would be the theater of that God whom William James called "more cosmic and tragic" than the Being of the old proofs. But Thomson really wants, not a brooding God, but an enlightened monarch, and his poem of history shows the strain at many points. One of Thomson's fondest progressive principles, the notion that liberal government leads to good art, is in trouble throughout the poem, especially so when Thomson ignores Greek and Roman slavery or attempts to distinguish between the Louis XIV who ruled despotically in hopes of "universal sway" and the good Louis XIV who encouraged arts (V, 484-531; cf. IV, 1074-85). Frequently the strain of competing views appears in imagistic infelicities, as in the climactic celebration of modern English liberty (IV, 1135ff.), when Thomson argues that the country is "often saved / By more than human hand" and then warns a few lines later of its vulnerability to the "felon undermining hand or dark corruption." When Thomson imagines the grand era of universal liberty as a time of British naval superiority so great that "not a sail but by permission spreads" (V, 637), even patriotism may blush. When he praises the power of British commerce to "bind the nations in a golden chain" (IV, 438), we are likely to think of the oppressive connotations of the image, as in the vocabulary of Pope or Blake, than of liberty. And when Liberty reveals that her purpose during the Roman era was to "diffuse / O'er men an empire" and so draw everything "into the vortex of one state" (III, 82-85), we are likely, once again, to think of the *Dunciad*.

Perhaps this last imagistic echo is, as Thomson would

say, resistless. The *Dunciad,* after all, is the poem which takes a fundamentally idealist and tragic reading of Western history to a logical conclusion—a logic which Pope is freer to pursue because he is unencumbered with obligations to celebrate individual self-fulfillment under the inspiring protection of the British navy. We can grasp something of Thomson's poetic problem if we think of *Liberty* as in a sense an attempt to write an optimistic *Dunciad*. The fact that a majority of modern historians would probably regard Thomson as closer to being "right" about his period than was Pope may lead us to ask just what sort of historical verisimilitude is healthy for poetry. But the more provocative fact is that a successfully "positive" *Dunciad* was historically rather than generically impossible, for *Prometheus Unbound* is such a work. A comparison of the two would take us too far afield, but one would begin with the observation that, like the *Dunciad, Prometheus Unbound* is a work "complete" in three parts but with a grand fourth movement operatically celebrating the effects of its cultural conversion. Yet an optimistically apocalyptic poem was not possible in either Thomson's moment or Thomson's manner. Shelley's theodicy works largely through subliminal appeals to revolutionary circumstances outside the poem and the elimination within it of historical material in favor of myth, perhaps the ultimately appropriate vehicle for contests of nation-titans and historical forces.

Liberty failed to capture even Thomson's contemporaries—the press runs shrank steadily from part I to part V—but the ambitions of *Liberty* are strongly evident in *The Seasons*. As Thomson added to that lifelong work in progress, it became steadily more historical, broadening into political and anthropological surveys which attempt to show the various God's varied ways to man by reflecting on culture. Not every addition to *The Seasons* is political in any sense; the 1744 edition has more advice on fishing, for example, as well as a longer catalog of British worthies. But in general even Thomson's "nature" additions have either cultural implications—like the sixty lines added to *Summer* (371-431) which celebrate British industry—or implications for recognizing the importance of the unseen. And when Thomson extends his "vision" to things outside the speaker's immediate landscape, the description of natural phenomena, however sensational, turns eventually into discussion of cultural arrangements.

This development can be seen most clearly in Thomson's inclusion of the tropics in *Summer* and the far north in *Winter,* both of which provide occasions not only for descriptive extremes but for comparative history. The survey of northern nations (*Winter,* 11.794-903) culminates in a discussion of Peter the Great and the power of "active government . . . new-moulding man" (11.950ff.); Thomson's theme, in other words, is the Vichian-Hegelian one of the providence of institutions and the role of the "world-historical" individual in bringing about human freedom. Peter, like Henry the Navigator, is "heaven-inspired" to focus the self-interest of lesser men (*Summer,* 11.1006-12; cf. 11.1767-68). Thomson's longer foray into the "torrid zone" (*Summer,* 11.629-987) is an intriguing combination of lush primitivism and cultural imperialism. For all their sensuousness and fertile profusions—"and Ceres void of pain"—the tropical regions lack the "humanizing Muses," the "progressive truth," and the liberal "government of laws" which define European culture. Thomson is even prepared to deny these "ill-fated" inhabitants a capacity for true love. Sensibility grows in temperate zones. English culture is the providential compensation for English weather.

There is another emphasis which Thomson heightened by expanding *The Seasons* to embrace more of the unobserved world, an emphasis on what he variously calls "fair forms of fancy" or "imagination's vivid eye" (*Summer*, 1.1974; *Spring*, 1.459). These phrases first appear in 1744, and the second of them comes at the end of the long addition on fishing mentioned earlier, which gradually slides from angling advice to a Georgic of reverie:

> . . . let the classic page thy fancy lead
> Through rural scenes, such as the Mantuan swain
> Paints in the matchless harmony of song;
> Or catch thyself the landscape, gliding swift
> Athwart imagination's vivid eye;
> Or, by the vocal woods and waters lulled,
> And lost in lonely musing, in a dream
> Confused of careless solitude where mix
> Ten thousand wandering images of things,
> Soothe every gust of passion into peace. . . .
> [*Spring*, 11.455-64]

A complementary expansion occurs in *Summer* as Thomson muses on the evening clouds, "Incessant rolled into romantic shapes, / The dream of waking fancy." The dream of fancy includes the high work of the poet and the moral philosopher, a union described here more evocatively than in many of Thomson's declarations:

> Now the soft hour
> Of walking comes for him who lonely loves
> To seek the distant hills, and there converse
> With Nature, there to harmonize his heart,
> And in pathetic song to breathe around
> The harmony to others. Social friends,
> Attuned to happy unison of soul—
> To whose exalting eye a fairer world,
> Of which the vulgar never had a glimpse,
> Displays its charms. . . .
> [*Summer*, 11.1379-88]

Such changes ultimately make the landscape an object less of description than of reflection and thus shift the focus of poem toward the "pleasures of imagination." This is not a radical change but a cumulative heightening, sometimes apparent in small ways, as in the elaboration of a contrast between the forest's "solitude and deep surrounding shades" and the "giddy fashion of town," or the simile of a flower "unseen by all" which "breathes its balmy fragrance o'er the wild" (*Autumn*, 11.184-88, 209-16). Even Thomson's most scientific addition, some eighty lines on the "percolation" theory of underground springs (*Autumn*, 11.756-835), is an exercise in turning the unseen world into an imaginative reality:

> Let the dire Andes, from the radiant line
> Stretched to the stormy seas that thunder round
> To Southern Pole, their hideous deeps unfold!
> Amazing scene! Behold! the glooms disclose!
> I see the rivers in their infant beds!
> Deep, deep I hear them laboring to get free!
> [*Autumn*, 11.804-9]

Thomson's expansion of *The Seasons*, then, dramatizes a conspicuous tension: as the poem becomes more political and historical it also becomes more occupied with the contemplative joys of the solitary man and the "wondrous force of thought" available to the philosophic few. The tension often leads to flat contradictions and flat pronouncements. It also leads, for good or ill, to less reliance on the data of visual experience and more straining for "vision," more effort to render its theodicy in terms of private intensity. This is perhaps the major tendency which *The Seasons* comes to share with *Night Thoughts* and *The Pleasures of Imagination*, and the growing conflict between public and private claims of course becomes the subject of Thomson's last poem, *The Castle of Indolence*.

Michael Cohen (essay date 1986)

SOURCE: "The Whig Sublime and James Thomson," in *English Language Notes*, Vol. XXIV, No. 1, September, 1986, pp. 27-35.

[*In the essay below, Cohen defines and examines the "curious fusion of aesthetic and political ideas," which he terms the "Whig Sublime," as it appears in Thomson's dramas.*]

In 1976 I first described an early eighteenth-century literary phenomenon which I called the Whig Sublime. The Whig Sublime fuses the imagery of the "natural sublime"—descriptions of natural scenes of great size or power such as mountains, oceans, deserts, storms, and so on—with the notion, especially appealing to the Whigs, that England's liberty and democratic institutions came from the rough northern homeland of her Germanic invaders, the "Goths." The Whigs saw themselves as the inheritors and preservers of this "Gothic" heritage of liberty, and the plays and poems written as Whig party vehicles during the first decades of the eighteenth century are full of the imagery of the Whig Sublime. Perhaps no playwright of the period used such imagery more than James Thomson (1700-1748), the writer better known for his long blank verse poem *The Seasons*, but also the author of five plays and co-author (with David Mallett) of the masque *Alfred*, from which **"Rule, Britannia"** comes. While Addison's *Cato* may provide the earliest example of the Whig Sublime in drama, Thomson's plays of the thirties and forties contain the fullest examples from which to study this curious fusion of aesthetic and political ideas.

Thomson knew Sir William Temple's speculations (in "Of Poetry") on the influence of climate and the superiority of the hardy northerners over the peoples of the "enfeebled south." He had also read *Tatler* No. 161, where Addison, travelling in the Alps, finds "a Paradise amidst the Wildness of those cold, hoary Landskips," because the Goddess of Liberty inhabits the rugged country. Extrapolating from these sentiments and from Addison's use of natural imagery in *Cato,* Thomson created from the Whig Sublime a metaphor for his feelings about the connection of liberty, virtue, and the wild landscapes which constituted the natural sublime. His treatment presupposes that virtue is a prerequisite for liberty, and that liberty can best survive as far as possible from the deceit and sophistication of cities and courts. Again and again in the plays there recurs the idea of a wild, uninhabited country which furnishes a refuge for liberty or for liberty's champions, from which they return to reestablish an order which had been destroyed by corruption. Some permutation of this notion of liberty's wild refuge is present in five out of Thomson's six dramatic pieces, only excepting **Edward and Eleonora** (1739).

Sophonisba (1730), Thomson's first play, contains one of the best examples: when a maid urges the Carthaginian queen not to despair in her present troubles, Sophonisba replies:

> Hope lives not here,
> Fled with her sister Liberty beyond
> The *Garamantian* hills, to some steep wild,
> Some undiscover'd country, where the foot
> Of *Roman* cannot come.

Sophonisba is a Carthaginian female Cato and her lover Masinissa has had a real experience paralleling the allegorical flight of hope and liberty described above, for he did find refuge in the Garamantian hills when Syphax, his rival for Sophonisba's love, usurped his throne.

In *Agamemnon* (1738) Thomson uses the exile motif more extensively. Here the character Melisander, the queen's old and wise confidant, has been banished by Egisthus to "a desart isle" so that Egisthus can pursue his scheme of seduction. In Melisander's story, Thomson makes a familiar appeal to pathos by describing the marooned man as he has done in the episode of the castaway in *The Seasons* (*Summer,* 939-58). The exile of Melisander is part of the political allegory of *Agamemnon:* by rejecting good counsel (presumably Bolingbroke), England became the prey of Walpole. Clytemnestra speaks for the country in bewailing her own situation:

> But lost with him,
> With *Melisander,* reason, honour, pride,
> Truth, sound advice, my better genius fled;
> I friendless, flatter'd, importun'd and charm'd,
> Was left alone with all-seducing love.

For Clytemnestra the consequences were her loss of honor, but for the country, loss of liberty. As in the castaway passage, Melisander's desert island becomes the refuge of liberty.

The exile in each of these cases seems to be at least partly self-willed, since Liberty has been forced out as well by

the corruption of the state. There is no ambiguity about what Melisander's virtues consist of: even Egisthus, in defending the banishment of the old counselor to the returning King, details them while trying to condemn:

> A certain stubborn virtue,
> I would say affectation of blunt virtue,
> Beneath whose outside froth, fermenting lay
> Pride, envy, faction, turbulence of soul,
> And democratic views, in some sort made him
> A secret traitor, equally unfit
> Or to obey or rule. But that I check'd
> His early treasons, here at your return,
> You might have found your kingdom a republic.

Though reason returns to the court with Melisander, liberty is not restored because Egisthus' schemes are too far in train, and Agamemnon is murdered as we anticipate. But the whole personal force of the tragedy, as well as the sense of past wrongs omnipresent in the Greek handling, has been subsumed by Egisthus' ambition, while in Clytemnestra we see only occasional glimpses of the woman beyond the allegorical figure representing betrayed England.

Alfred (1740), a masque written by Thomson and David Mallett, uses the theme of the wild refuge of the champion of liberty for its dramatic organization. Alfred, defeated by the Danes at Chippenham, "found himself obliged to return into the little isle of Athelney in Somersetshire; a place then rough with woods and of difficult access. There, in the habit of a peasant, he lived unknown, for some time, in a shepherd's cottage". . . . The rugged landscape of the island is described by the shepherd, Corin:

> Nature's own hand
> Hath planted round a deep defence of woods,
> The sounding ash, the mighty oak; each tree
> A sheltering grove: and choak'd up all between
> With wild encumbrance of perplexing thorns,
> And horrid brakes. Beyond this woody verge,
> Two rivers broad and rapid hem us in.
> Along their channel spreads the gulphy pool,
> And trembling quagmire, whose deceitful green
> Betrays the foot it tempts. One path alone
> Winds to this plain, so roughly difficult,
> This single arm, poor shepherd as I am,
> Could well dispute it with twice twenty *Danes.*

The Earl of Devon finds Alfred's retreat and is encouraged to go to defend the last fortress of the English. He returns triumphant, with news of the country rallying against the Danes, but before his return, an old hermit, "Purg'd from the stormy cloud of human passions," has shown Alfred a vision of future monarchs of England: Edward III, Elizabeth, and William III. All are special champions of liberty (the last only from the Whig point-of-view), and the passages dealing with Elizabeth are particularly notable:

> Yet she shall crown this happy isle with peace,
> With arts, with riches, grandeur and renown;

And quell, by turns, the madness of her foes.
As when the winds, from different quarters, urge
The tempest on our shore: secure, the cliffs
Repel its idle rage, and pour it back,
In broken billows, foaming to the main.

In the Whig Sublime the normally inimical forces of nature befriend liberty and its personifications in Britannia or Elizabeth. The sublime display of nature in defense of English nationalism is a favorite descriptive topic for Thomson, as he demonstrates here and in his treatment of the northern transference of liberty in his poems, especially *Winter* 835-42 and *Liberty* III, 516-38.

The visions ended, "a venerable Bard, Aged and blind," sings the ode, **"Rule, Brittania,"** whose refrain emphasizes the freedom of Britons and whose lines are the most famous which Thomson wrote. The masque closes as the hermit exhorts Alfred to go forth and realize Britain's destiny of excellence in commerce, arts, and arms, thus restoring Liberty's champion from his rugged exile.

Tancred and Sigismunda (1745) uses the exile theme in its examination of the question whether passions and public virtue are in simple opposition to each other or not. Tancred is the heir to the Sicilian throne and has been raised in a sylvan retreat by the old counselor Siffredi. Tancred's "exile" is necessitated by usurpation, corruption in the state, and tyranny—we expect him to emerge as the champion of liberty. When the old, usurping king dies, Siffredi reveals Tancred as heir, and the younger man greets the discovery with an invocation to the sublimity of providence, the "wonder-working Hand / That, in majestic silence, sways at will / The mighty movements of unbounded nature." But with this revelation Sigismunda now has Tancred's former worry—that of being unworthy of her lover—and as she wishes for the tender calm she and Tancred enjoyed "in the woods of *Belmont*," Thomson makes the wilds a refuge for the private life of the passions rather than of public virtue:

O that we
In those blest woods, where first you won my
    soul,
Had pass'd our gentle days; far from the toil
And pomp of courts!

The Whig Sublime figures more largely in *Coriolanus* (1748), Thomson's last play. The Volscians, though peoples of Latium, are described as if they were the warlike, freedom-loving Goths who conquered Rome some five centuries after this period: they discuss their "Alpin" villages and their "cantons." Rome, which has rejected Coriolanus, is "A city grown an enemy to virtue," and the Volscians receive him as if his arrival were some cosmic turn of fate:

Strange event!
This is thy work, almighty providence!
Whose power, beyond the stretch of human
    thought,
Resolves the orbs of empire; bids them sink

Deep in the deadning night of thy displeasure,
Or rise majestic o'er a wondering world.

Coriolanus himself supports this view, and describes in sublime terms the power he feels his Volscian refuge gives him:

Immortal gods!
I am new-made, and wonder at myself!
A little while ago, and I was nothing;
A powerless reptile, crawling on the earth,
Curs'd with a soul that restless wish'd to wield
The bolts of *Jove!* I dwelt in *Erebus*,
I wander'd thro' the hopeless gloom of hell,
Stung with revenge, tormented by the furies!
Now, *Tullus*, like a god, you draw me thence,
Throne me amidst the skies, with tempest
    charg'd,
And put the ready thunder in my hand!

Admittedly this sort of imagery used by the superhuman protagonist and those who receive him might have been found in a heroic drama seventy years earlier, but it is significant that Coriolanus is hailed as the champion of liberty—though he proves in the end to be a prideful tyrant. He had been described in equivocal terms even by his friend Galesus at the beginning:

The vigorous soil whence his heroic virtues
Luxuriant rise, if not with careful hand
Severely weeded, teems with imperfections.
His lofty spirit brooks no opposition.
His rage, if once offended, knows no bounds.

Volusius and Tullus realize that Coriolanus' help has become a tyranny for the Volscians, and they conspire to destroy him at the end of the play. Volusius asserts that the blow is being struck for liberty, and he uses natural imagery to praise Tullus' resolution, "breaking from the cloud, which, like the sun, Thy own bounteous beams had drawn around thee."

The exile theme is used elsewhere in the play to support a debate between Galesus and Tullus on the merits of war. Tullus sees the struggle with Rome as a battle for independence, but Galesus takes a more philosophic view, wishing for a life more in tune with nature, with war banished:

O mortals! mortals! when will you, content
With nature's bounty, that in fuller flow,
Still as your labours open more its sources,
Abundant gushes o'er the happy world;
When will you banish violence, and outrage,
To dwell with beasts of prey in woods and
    desarts?

Later in the play Tullus tells Galesus that war is the "safeguard" of liberty, an instrument "to quell proud tyrants, and to free mankind," and that it is philosophy and sages who should be exiled:

These soothing dreams of philosophic quiet
Are only fit for unfrequented shades.
The sage should quit the busy bustling world
Ill suited to his gentle meditations,
And in some desert find the peace he loves.

Thus even the Industry versus Idleness debate (which Thomson deals with at length in his Spenserian imitation *The Castle of Indolence*) furnishes a topic for the exile theme.

In *Tancred and Sigismunda* and *Coriolanus* then, Thomson uses his theme in different ways: the wilds in one place are seen as the refuge for public virtue, in another as refuge for the private life of the passions, in still another as a place of banishment for evil acts or men who should be ostracized. But when, at the end of *Coriolanus,* Galesus stands over the body of the tyrant, he links some of these themes, describing the passions in conventional storm images and indicating that it is not merely personal virtue which is obscured by passion, but more importantly, political good:

These, when the angry tempest clouds the soul,
May darken reason, and her course controul;
But when the prospect clears, her startled eye
Must from the treacherous gulph with horror fly,
On whose wild wave, by stormy passions tost,
So many hopeless wretches have been lost.
Then be this truth the star by which we steer,
Above ourselves *our* COUNTRY *should be dear.*

Most of the ideas about liberty expressed in the plays are veiled references to the *translatio imperii ad Teutonicos*— the notion that England's traditions of liberty and her modern Parliamentary strength were transmissions from ancient Rome by way of the Germanic invaders who brought democratic institutions from their rough northern homeland. This republicanism was especially appealing to the Whigs because of the disenfranchisement they had originally felt from the comfortable politics of the Tory landed gentry and the further political exclusions of the established church. Tory tradition thus equates with the corruption of court and city; the exile and the outsider are the only ones who can cleanse the body politic. Added in the Whig playwright, especially in Thomson, was the appeal of the natural sublime as amplification to the political ideas. Beginning with a conventional simile equating the mind ruled by passions with the disorder of nature, Thomson goes on to depict the "goodly prospects" and spacious landscapes of a land where liberty reigns under a Whig standard, but gives us also the wild refuge of liberty in exile as allegory for the opposition when the Tories are in power. But where Addison's *Cato* had spoken to a time when Whig interests were indeed at risk, Thomson's use of the Whig Sublime merely lends the appeal of a fashionable aesthetic and a reminder of harder times to a political party growing fat from the continued patronage of two monarchs. Whig "opposition" was a present fiction and the Whig Sublime an aesthetics of political nostalgia.

Christine Gerrard (essay date 1990)

SOURCE: "*The Castle of Indolence* and the Opposition to Walpole," in *The Review of English Studies,* n.s. Vol. XLI, No. 161, February, 1990, pp. 45-64.

[*In the following excerpt, Gerrard reads* The Castle of Indolence *as a political poem which politely but firmly chastises the ineffectualness of political life in England during Robert Walpole's term as First Minister.*]

In May 1748, only weeks before his death, James Thomson's last and most enigmatic poem finally went to press: *The Castle of Indolence. An Allegorical Poem. Written in Imitation of Spenser.* In a literary era in which admiration for Spenser was becoming increasingly de rigueur, its popularity was assured. By the end of the century, Romantic critics and poets, with their taste for sensuous Spenserian stanzas, prized *The Castle of Indolence* almost as highly as *The Seasons*: Keats, Coleridge, Wordsworth, and later Tennyson all fell under its spell. Yet their admiration usually extended only as far as the end of Canto I. The Romantics misread *The Castle of Indolence* as they misread *The Faerie Queene,* subordinating allegorical meaning to purely descriptive effects. Canto II and the controlling allegorical scheme were ignored, despite Thomson's explicit emphasis in his title-page that this was, above all, 'An Allegorical Poem'. Thomson began *The Castle of Indolence* in 1733-4, some fifteen years before it was published; and although early to mid-eighteenth-century imitators of Spenser were probably no less responsive than their Romantic counterparts to Spenser's 'Mazes of enchanted Ground', they saw Spenser primarily as a supreme moral allegorist. Although they sought to re-create a variety of 'Spenserian' effects in their poems, not least the burlesque, their longer pieces suggest that they were often more intent on formulating their own moral conclusions through a Spenserian allegorical framework than on producing rich descriptive tapestries for their own sake. John Hughes, Spenser's first editor, prefaced his 1715 six-volume edition of the *Works* (owned by Thomson) with an 'Essay on Allegorical Poetry'. Spenser's romantic fabling and imaginative '*Fairy Land*' were explained in terms of the broader allegorical purpose of *The Faerie Queene,* for

An Allegory is a Fable or Story, in which, under imaginary Persons or Things, is shadow'd some real Action or instructive Moral: or, as I think it is somewhere very shortly defined by *Plutarch,* it is that *in which one thing is related, and another thing is understood.*

The Castle of Indolence contains a relatively simple 'Fable or Story'. An enchanter dwelling in a beautiful castle ensnares passers-by into his bower of bliss, where they enjoy a deceptively easy, but increasingly degenerate life. A knight comes to rescue them from the castle and breaks the magic spell, setting them free to live a life of useful toil and duty. But what is the 'real Action or instructive Moral' shadow'd forth by this tale? How should we try to understand Thomson's allegory? Recent critical interpretations of *The Castle of Indolence* have been far more subtle than the once-prevalent opinion that Canto II and the whole didactic scheme were simply 'tacked on' to Canto I as a concession to eighteenth-century Protestant work-ethics or the Whig ideal of progress. The sometimes playful, sometimes serious way in which Thomson dramatizes himself as a figure in his own poem, commenting on his friends, his life-style, and the problems and choices confronting the poet, hints that this poem is on one level or another intimately related to Thomson's experiences during the period of its composition. Most recent critical readings have consequently 'interiorized' *The Castle of Indolence* as an allegory of the poet's mind. Despite offering an admirably broad analysis of the literary and ideological background of the poem, A. D. McKillop's preface to his 1961 edition tended to place a positive emphasis on indolence as the seed-ground of imagination and poetic creativity. According to Morris Golden [in "The Imagining Self in the Eighteenth Century," in *Eighteenth-Century Studies* 3 (1969): 4-27], the Wizard of Canto I and the Bard of Canto II are projections of two conflicting aspects of Thomson's artistic personality, sensualist and aesthete, dreamer and doer. John Sitter, in his deconstructive analysis [in *Literary Loneliness in Mid-Eighteenth-Century England* (1982), pp. 93-6], argues that *The Castle of Indolence* is a starkly ambivalent poem: its rhetorical and imaginative energy, conveying the futility of industry and the nobility of retirement, undermines Thomson's entire moral argument. Only Donald Greene [in "From Accidie to Neurosis: *The Castle of Indolence* Revisited," in *English Literature in the Age of Disguise,* edited by M. E. Novak (1977), pp. 131-57] comes down firmly in support of Thomson's two-book didactic scheme, with its uncompromising dismissal of the evils of self-indulgent indolence. Greene (fighting a conservative rearguard action against 1960s 'do-your-own-thing' campus morality) places indolence in the tradition of 'accidie', 'the spleen', or neurosis—a spiritual or psychiatric condition leading to depression, introspection, and lethargy, which must be resisted and conquered by the active will.

Greene's reading is persuasive: but his broad-ranging humanism both marginalizes and then dismisses as irrelevant to the eternal human condition any consideration of politics. A close study of Thomson's political outlook during the years in which *The Castle of Indolence* was in the making would suggest that for Thomson, as for other Opposition writers in the 1730s, politics were inextricably linked to larger considerations of man's moral welfare. The 'indolence' which afflicts the inhabitants of the Castle of Indolence is a condition not unique to 'Jemmy Thomson' and other victims of manic depression, but a social and spiritual malaise which the opposition to Walpole saw sweeping through Hanoverian England: a malaise of inertia, self-interest, hedonism, corruption, and loss of 'public spirit' which finds its supreme embodiment in the 'Dulness' of Pope's *Dunciad*. The progress of the disease is charted by an essay in the Opposition journal the *Craftsman* of Friday, 10 March 1729 (no. 27). This 'POLITICAL LETHARGY' is 'occasioned by . . . a general spirit of luxury and profusion, or a prevailing appetite to soft effeminate inventions and wanton entertainments',

when the people 'give themselves up entirely to the pursuits of private pleasure'. It 'lays all the noble faculties, generous passions, and social virtues, as it were by *Opium,* in a profound Trance, and thereby leaves publick Ministers . . . to do whatever their ambition dictates.' This is the *indolentia* described in Thomson's *Castle of Indolence,* a work which, as I shall argue, belongs firmly in the context of the opposition to Walpole: by its rhetoric, its dramatis personae, its moral scheme which moves from deceptive pleasure, luxury, and decadence to final reform, and not least by its very status as Spenserian allegory.

The popularity of *The Seasons* should not disguise the fact that Thomson was, first and foremost, a political poet. All his major works after the first editions of *The Seasons* were written in support of the dissident Whig opposition to Walpole, led in Parliament by promising, youthful, and idealistic 'Boy Patriots' such as George Lyttelton, Richard Grenville, and William and Thomas Pitt. *Britannia* of 1729 was a flagrant attack on Walpole's 'peace at any price' foreign policy: *Liberty* of 1735-6, with its analysis of the rise and fall of nations, its glorification of the long tradition of English liberty, and its warning that this liberty was now under serious threat by the forces of luxury and corruption, embodied the central tenets of the Patriot ideology most coherently formulated by Lord Bolingbroke. *Liberty* was dedicated to Frederick, Prince of Wales, the Patriots' political figurehead. George Lyttelton, appointed secretary to the Prince in 1737, managed to secure patronage for Thomson, David Mallet, and his own cousin, the poet Gilbert West—patronage which reflected their commitment to the Patriot cause. Throughout the late 1730s and early 1740s Thomson was busy adding his own contribution to the campaign of Patriot drama which was then taking hold of the London theatre (when it evaded the Lord Chamberlain's watchful eye) in the shape of *Agamemnon* (1738), *Edward and Eleanora* (1739), and *Alfred* (1740), source of Thomson's best-known lyric, **'Rule Britannia'**.

It was during these years that *The Castle of Indolence* was, if sporadically, in the making. The poem began life around 1733-4 as a private literary joke—a few playful burlesque Spenserian stanzas on the poet's friends enjoying the lazy bachelor life. But as Patrick Murdoch, Thomson's early biographer, commented, Thomson soon found that 'the subject deserved to be treated more seriously, and in a form fitted to convey one of the most important moral lessons'. Could it be that, given the urgency with which Opposition writers during the 1730s pressed home the moral dangers besetting Britain under Walpole and the necessity for his removal from power, Thomson began to expand his original 'detached' stanzas into a full-scale Spenserian allegory, one which embodied an important political message?

This is not a far-fetched suggestion. Other eighteenth-century poets had used Spenserian allegory for political ends. In 1713 the Whig poet Samuel Croxall, under the pseudonym 'Nestor Ironside', had produced *An Original Canto of Spencer,* followed in 1714 by *Another Original*

Canto of Spencer. Both pieces refashion the allegorical scheme of Book V of Spenser's epic to attack the Tory minister Harley's peace-making attempts with France and Spain. In the first Canto, Britomart (the war-like spirit of Britain) is beguiled and imprisoned by Archimago (Harley) who is in league with the Catholic Romania and the French Sir Burbon in a plot to take over Britain. In the second Canto, Archimago, enlisting the assistance of the goddess Faction, tries to establish the claims to the British throne of young Sans Foy (the Pretender) over those of good Sir Arthegall (the House of Hanover). Croxall's poems were taken seriously enough by Harley's ministry to warrant a refutation of the first (on equally Spenserian terms) to which an entire issue of the Tory *Examiner* was devoted. Other sporadic examples of Spenserian political satire can be found during the first half of the eighteenth century, but the most important as far as Thomson is concerned is Gilbert West's anonymous *Canto of the Fairy Queen* of 1739. Like Thomson, West was a committed Patriot poet. Although his *Canto* was later reprinted in 1751 under his own name with the innocuous title *The Abuse of Travelling,* and passed unnoticed in the post-1740 wave of 'Romantic' Spenserian imitations, it was clearly a highly topical piece of political satire—one to which West, in 1739, was understandably reluctant to add his name.

West's Spenserian stanzas deal with the theme of the Grand Tour—a double-edged tool, both rehearsing standard Opposition complaints about the pernicious influence of foreign travel on the morals of 'Old England', yet also operating as a focus for satirical critique. The 'Red Cross Knight', seduced into foreign travel by a wily Archimago, visits two supposedly 'foreign' countries which, on examination, clearly represent different aspects of the corruption engendered by the Hanoverian/Walpole government. In the first land, a 'swoln form of Royal Surquedry' (George II) presides over a beautiful but decadent Bower of Bliss: the inhabitants bow low to their idol, but he is secretly manipulated with strings from behind screens by another Archimago/puppeteer figure (stanzas xxx-xxxi)—in line with the Opposition's frequent jibe that George II was but a 'puppet king' to his minister. In the second land, the Knight encounters a vast deserted amphitheatre presided over by 'The World's Imperial Queen' (xlii), proud of her ancestry, learning, and her collection of antique relics. Throngs of virtuosi flock to her court to gain her approval. The resemblance to Book IV of *The Dunciad,* with its satire of Queen Dulness/Caroline, is unmistakable, particularly when West points to the Queen's favourite minion, 'An eunuch . . . of Visage pale and dead, Unseemly Paramour for Royal Maid!' (xlvii)—clearly a portrait of Lord Hervey, Pope's 'Sporus', the white silk-worm of ambiguous sexuality. West's Red-Cross Knight suddenly perceives that the ruins are those of imperial Rome. His saddened reflections on the fall of nations through luxury and sloth, and his angry determination that 'Fairy-Lond' (Britain) shall not suffer a similar fate, mirrors the Opposition's preoccupation with the Polybian cycle of history—the rise, maturing, and decay of nations—which also shapes the two-book structure of *The Castle of Indolence.*

Given their shared political affiliation, it would be surprising had Thomson not read West's poem: the points of correspondence are clear, not least in the representation of Archimago, with his quasi-biblical 'Consider the lilies of the field'-type speech inviting listeners to a life of ease and pleasure. But it might be more to the point to see both Spenserian poems as the products of a twenty-year period of Opposition writing which adopted myth, symbol, and allegory as its main polemical vehicles. Maynard Mack's *The Garden and the City* testifies to the inventiveness with which Opposition writers covertly commented on contemporary affairs through a sophisticated network of allusion and innuendo. Fear of prosecution prompted oblique rather than overt reference; and the long list of names and contexts for Walpole—Robins's Great Booth in Palace Yard, the nostrums of Dr King, the quack doctor, Sir Positive Screenall, Punchinello the puppeteer—suggest a measure of delight in the sheer talent to abuse. Yet by the late 1730s the network of symbols and metaphors built up around the minister had developed into an allegory with a single moral direction—an allegory of temptation, deceit, corruption, and fall. The archetypal 'Tory Fiction' derived from Milton's *Paradise Lost* and developed by Dryden in his *Absalom and Achitophel*—the minister as Satanic tempter, and his seduction of an unwary, thoughtless people—resonates throughout Opposition literature, from Pope's satires of the 1730s to journal essays such as the anonymous 'Tree of Corruption' paper in the *Craftsman* no. 297 of 25 March 1732. Walpole, perched in the Edenic boughs, tosses down golden apples to the crowd below—bribes of office, bank contracts, material pleasures of a more general kind. 'Whoever tasted the Fruit of it, lost his Integrity and fell, like *Adam,* from the *State of Innocence.*'

Mack's lengthy index of 'Names applied to RW by Opposition writers' quite rightly indicates, however, that Walpole was equally often recast in the guise of another version of the duplicitous tempter—the wily wizard figure using his cunning and magical powers to gain control. 'We have some *great Men* amonst Us', announced the *Craftsman* of 21 February 1736, 'who have justly acquir'd the Reputation of being *Wizards,* or *Conjurers.*' Walpole appears in a variety of wizard's costumes, carrying (as in the notorious *Festival of the Golden Rump* print of 1737), a sorcerer's wand (the Chancellor's rod of office); or more frequently, a cup containing a magic potion. This cup of 'Cordial Julep' or 'Aurum potabile' mingles the devastating effects of Homer's Nepenthe and Circe's magic draught—complete forgetfulness of social duty and a self-indulgent love of sensual pleasure. Fielding's wily magician 'Hishonour' can turn men into swine with his magic potion, a metamorphosis also experienced by those who drink out of the cup extended by the 'WIZARD OLD' of Book IV of *The Dunciad.* Such images contain more than an echo of Milton's *Comus,* but can ultimately be traced back to Spenser, the great poet of temptation and enticement. West's *Canto of the Fairy Queen* of 1739 expanded such allusions into a full-scale Spenserian political allegory, with contemporary Britain as the false Bower of Bliss, governed by a Walpolean Archimago: Thomson's **Castle of Indolence** could, and should be read in the same context.

The opening stanzas of *The Castle of Indolence* reveal Thomson's near-perfect mastery of Spenser's sensuously descriptive vein. The Castle and its haunting environs bear a close resemblance to Spenser's Acrasian Bower of Bliss: and although our response is one of delight, the resonances of Book II of *The Faerie Queene* might hint that we should be on our guard. Like Spenser, Thomson was capable of making sweet music for moral ends—the seductive beauty of the Bower is what makes it so dangerous. Thomson may have had a more immediate model for his visionary topography of green fields, fertile vales, and enchanting birdsong. By the 1730s the allegorical 'dream vision' was a favoured form for Oppositional satire. Bolingbroke's *Vision of Camilick,* published in the *Craftsman* of 27 January 1727, opened with an 'amiable Prospect' of 'Fields . . . cover'd with golden harvests. The Hills were cloath'd with sheep; the Woods sung with gladness; Plenty laughed in the Valleys.' This scene-setting precedes the arrival of Walpole, 'a man . . . with a purse of gold in his hand'. In the *Champion* of 13 December 1739 Fielding dreams that he finds himself 'in the most beautiful plain I ever beheld . . . a vast quantity of flowers of different sorts variegated the scene, and perfumed the air with the most delicious odours'. The land, however, is governed by 'a great magician [who] with a gentle squeeze by the hand, could bring any person whatever to think, and speak, and do, what he himself desired, and that it was very difficult to avoid his touch: for if you came but in his reach, he infallibly had you by the fist'.

Thomson's Archimago possesses the same manipulative power. If any of the pilgrims remain unconvinced by the arguments of his 'witching Song', then he touches them with his 'unhallow'd Paw'. 'Certes', comments Thomson ironically, 'who bides his Grasp will that Encounter rue' (I. xxii).

> For whomsoe'er the Villain takes in Hand,
> Their Joints unknit, their Sinews melt apace;
> As lithe they grow as any Willow-Wand,
> And of their vanish'd force remains no Trace.
>
> (I. xxiii)

Fielding's *Champion* passage is, of course, a satire on the almost magical powers of Walpole's bribery: the only way to stay safe is by 'keeping your hand shut'. Thomson's description is less pointed here, but the close correspondence between the two passages would suggest that Thomson's Archimago is none other than Walpole. Although James Sambrook has suggested that 'Archimago' was a common noun, and that 'it seems to have been part of [Thomson's] plan not to give distinct characteristics, Spenserian or not, to personifications', Thomson's Archimago certainly behaves in a manner common to all Walpolean wizard archetypes in Opposition literature. Thomson's glossary may define 'Archimago' quite innocuously as *'The chief, or greatest of Magicians or Enchanters',* but one should also remember that the Walpole figure in the *Festival of the Golden Rump* print was glossed in the explanatory 'vision' in the 19 March 1737 edition of *Common Sense* simply as 'THE CHIEF MAGICIAN'. Archimago's song—' "Behold! ye Pilgrims of this Earth, behold! "See all but Man with unearn'd Pleasure gay"' (I. ix)—sounds very like that of West's earlier Walpolean Archimage—'Behold, says Archimage, the envied Height Of Human Grandeur to the Gods allied!' (xxxiv)—and it seems likely that Thomson was thinking as much here of West as of Spenser's Phaedria.

After ensnaring the pilgrims, Archimago leads them to drink from a fountain of 'Nepenthe rare'. This scene, ostensibly drawn from an amalgam of sources—Circe's draught via Milton's *Comus,* Spenser's description of Homer's Nepenthe and the spells of Acrasia—also has several analogues in Opposition satire. In his *The Vernoniad* of 22 January 1741, Fielding supplies a Scriblerian mock-etymology in Latin and Greek for a 'certain Magician' called 'Hishonour' (one of the Opposition's ironically deferential names for Walpole) who 'is said to have invented a certain *Aurum potabile*, by which he could turn Men into Swine or Asses, whence some think he had his Name'. Such a liquid also fills the cup proffered by Pope's Magus, the 'High Priest' of Dulness in Book IV of *The Dunciad*:

> With that, a WIZARD OLD his *Cup* extends;
> Which whoso tastes, forgets his former friends,
> Sire, Ancestors, Himself. One casts his eyes
> Up to a *Star,* and like Endymion dies:
> A *Feather* shooting from another's head,
> Extracts his brain, and Principle is fled,
> Lost is his God, his Country, ev'ry thing;
> And nothing left but Homage to a King!
> The vulgar herd turn off to roll with Hogs,
> To run with Horses, or to hunt with Dogs;
> But, sad example! never to escape
> Their Infamy, still keep the human shape.

These lines brilliantly encompass the social range of Walpole's corrupting influence. The golden cup of bribery—from the feather and star of the Garter order down through the whole range of pensions and places by which Walpole kept power—has Nepenthe-like properties in its ability to mollify opposition and erase awkward memories of personal honour and public duty. Like the sycophants of St James in Pope's *Epilogue to the Satires,* Dia. I, l. 98, these men are 'Lull'd with the sweet *Nepenthe* of a Court'. The Circean or Acrasian metamorphosis of man into hog is adopted by Pope to suggest the mindlessness of the peer happy to attend horse-races and hunt with his hounds on his country estate while, so to speak, Rome burns. Yet, like the whole of Book IV of *The Dunciad,* in which sharp topical satire is bound up with a profound moral vision, these lines invite a tropological interpretation, as both the 'Argument' to Book IV, and Pope and Warburton's footnote to l. 517 suggest. This cup is 'The *Cup* of *Self-love',* which 'causes a total oblivion of the obligations of Friendship, or Honour, and of the Service of God or our Country; all sacrificed to Vain-glory, Courtworship, or yet meaner considerations of Lucre and brutal Pleasure'.

This is the very same draught as the water of Nepenthe which flows through the fountain in the courtyard outside the Castle of Indolence. Once tasted, it causes 'sweet Oblivion of vile earthly Care' (I. xxvii), freedom from the social responsibilities and family ties which the Wizard's speech has made to seem so ludicrous and unappealing. The Wizard's proclamation—' "Ye Sons of INDOLENCE, do what you will; . . . "Be no Man's Pleasure for another's staid" ' (I. xxviii)—is essentially nothing other than Pope's doctrine of 'Self-love'. Its pernicious effects are revealed in full only at the very end of Canto II, where Thomson spares no pains in painting the Circean man-into-hog metamorphosis. Thomson is more subtle here than Pope. The fountain scene carries few overtones of censure, suggesting the seemingly innocent allure of irresponsibility—Pope's court of Dulness described from an 'inside' perspective. Yet the two ritual initiations through the ministrations of a presiding 'magus' figure are strikingly similar. Pope's description of the 'ceremony' in his elaborate note to l. 517 of Book IV of *The Dunciad* could equally apply to Canto I, stanzas xxvi-xxix of **The Castle of Indolence**.

> The High-Priest of Dulness first initiateth the Assembly by the usual way of *Libation*. And then each of the Initiated, as was always required, putteth on a *new Nature* . . . each of them is delivered into the hands of his Conductor, an inferior Minister or *Hieorophant*, whose names are *Impudence, Stupefaction, Self-conceit, Self-interest, Pleasure, Epicurism, & c.* to lead them thro' the several apartments of her Mystic Dome or Palace.

'Impudence' and 'Self-conceit' seem to play no real part in Thomson's poem, but 'Self-interest', 'Pleasure', and 'Epicurism' are undoubtedly the prominent features of the Castle's life-style. 'Stupefaction' (the dulling of the senses and the conscience) soon follows. Thomson even has his own version of the 'Conductor', the inferior minister or hierophant, in the shape of the 'master Porter' and his servant; and the 'Courts', 'Lodges', and 'Rooms' of the Castle, with their different attractions, bear more than a passing resemblance to the 'several apartments' of Pope's 'Mystic Dome or Palace'. It seems no coincidence that in the 'Argument' to Book IV, Pope has already equated Dulness with Indolence. The Goddess *sees loitering about her a number of* Indolent Persons *abandoning all business and duty, and dying with laziness'* (ll. 26-7). Chief among these is the quasi-Spenserian figure of Paridel, newly emerged from the Grand Tour (West's *Canto* of four years earlier must surely have been an influence) and now 'Stretch'd on the rack of a too easy chair'. We hear his 'everlasting yawn confess / The Pains and Penalties of Idleness' (IV, ll. 342-4).

Unlike the trivial pursuits followed by the courtiers of Queen Dulness, the pleasures enjoyed by the inhabitants of the Castle of Indolence seem at first refined, elegant, even virtuous. The Bower of Bliss becomes temporarily the Palace of Art, with music, study, painting—all the polite pastimes that would have appealed to the refined eighteenth-century gentleman. The Wizard cunningly offers indolence disguised as the classical ideal of 'retirement', with allusions to Scipio, Horace, and Virgil. Erot-

icism is heavily muted—despite coy hints of the Caliphs of Baghdad and an *'Arabian Heav'n'* (I. xlv), the Castle contains no seraglios: its comfortable bedrooms are designed for sleep rather than sex. Indeed, the close correspondence between certain aspects of the life-style enjoyed by the Castle's inhabitants and that of the Knight of Arts and Industry in Canto II suggests that such pleasures are not wrong in themselves; it all depends on the spirit into which they are entered. Escapism is not the same as retirement.

Yet Thomson hints that these pleasures are not quite what they seem. The seductive 'muzak' forever playing in the background creates a sinister brain-washing atmosphere:

> Each Sound too here to Languishment inclin'd,
> Lull'd the weak Bosom, and induced Ease.
> Aereal Music in the warbling Wind,
> At Distance rising oft, by small Degrees,
> Nearer and nearer came, till o'er the Trees
> It hung, and breath'd such Soul-dissolving Airs,
> As did, alas! with soft Perdition please:
> Entangled deep in its enchanting Snares,
> The listening Heart forgot all Duties and all Cares.
>
> (I. xxxix)

One of the favoured targets of Opposition polemic was the pernicious effect of 'soft Italian music', particularly newly imported Italian operas and masquerades, in unstringing the moral fibre of the nation. In his short essay, 'On Luxury', Bolingbroke takes a sidelong glance at Pericles' corruption of the Greeks through festivals and music, and warns that such entertainments can be the 'baits of pleasure' by which the wily statesman disguises the 'fatal hook' of political tyranny. Music is particularly dangerous because it 'relaxes and unnerves the soul, and sinks it into weakness'. It 'exerts a willing tyranny over the mind and forms the ductile soul into whatever shape the melody directs'. Thomson's own reflections on Italian music, arising from his observations, while on the Grand Tour, of the poverty and political oppression of modern Italy, follow a similar vein. When industry is to no avail, music is 'a sort of charming malady that quite disolves them into softness, and greatly heightens them in that universal Indolence men naturally (I had almost said reasonably) fall into'.

By the end of Canto I, the inhabitants of the Castle have abandoned any pretension to higher aesthetic pursuits: 'indolence' has wrought its destructive spell. They either luxuriate in an opiate trance—'And hither *Morpheus* sent his kindest Dreams' (I. xliv)—or find that a life from 'gross mortal Care and Business free, . . . pour'd out in Ease and Luxury' (I. lxxi), has its disadvantages. 'Their only Labour was to kill the Time; And Labour dire it is, and weary Woe' (I. lxxii). Thomson's burlesque description of the Cave of Spleen, with its inmates Lethargy, Hydropsy, and Hypochondria, if inconsistent in tone with the more subtle vein of Spenserianism adopted throughout Canto I, dramatizes the total apathy which has beset the Castle-dwellers: like Pope's denizens of Dulness, they have abandoned 'all business and duty' and are literally 'dying with laziness'.

The opening of Canto II abruptly shifts the scene away from the Castle to the tale of the Knight of Arts and Industry and his woodland upbringing. Some critics have seen the transition as an awkward one, marking a complete break in the mood and direction of the poem. But although the mechanisms Thomson adopts are rather heavyhanded—'But now another Strain, Of doleful Note, alas! remains behind: I now must sing of Pleasure turn'd to Pain, And of the false Enchanter INDOLENCE complain' (II. i)—the two cantos are intimately related in theme and purpose. Thomson has not changed the story—merely adopted the technique of the 'flash-back', returning at the start of Canto II to the prehistory of Canto I. The Knight's childhood, youth, and adulthood embody in allegorical microcosm the historical pattern of the development of nations: hardy primitivism is followed by the growth of agriculture, science, commerce, and ultimately the fine arts. The Knight, born of 'Selvaggio' and 'Poverty', exhibits all the simple 'natural' virtues of the early Britons praised by Thomson in *Liberty,* but through his education acquires by stages all the accomplishments necessary for a civilized nation. He sets out 'a barbarous World to civilise', and, like the goddess Liberty, follows a westward progress through the course of empire, via Egypt, Greece, and Rome, which wax, wane, and ultimately fall to ruin, 'to slavish Sloth and Tyranny a Prey' (II. xvi). He finally arrives on the shores of Britain, the chosen home of Liberty, where he establishes all the skills he has acquired, the greatest of which is the art of government. The description here of the rise of Britain from rugged liberty-loving primitivism to civilization is clearly drawn from Book IV of *Liberty,* 'Britain'. Thomson's Whiggish fervour for Britain's 'matchless Form of glorious Government; In which the sovereign Laws alone command, Laws stablish'd by the public free Consent' (II. xxiv) resembles his earlier praise for mixed government, the 'perfect Plan . . . Of BRITAIN's matchless *Constitution*'.

On completing his task, the Knight enters into a life of virtuous rural retirement in Deva's vale. Here he begins to assume the persona of an eighteenth-century country gentleman; less the Tory Squire than the 'Country Whig' in retirement (such as the much-admired Cobham, paterfamilias of the Patriots), cultivating his estates and gardens. John Sitter's suggestion that this may be a representation of Bolingbroke is persuasive, especially since Joseph Warton had earlier identified Philomelus, the little Druid bard 'of wither'd aspect' but sweet voice who accompanies the Knight on his mission as Pope. Bolingbroke's country house, Dawley, was an active working farm. There, like the Knight, he could act the part of 'the Chief, the Patriot, and the Swain' (II. xxv). Bolingbroke decorated Dawley's interior with harvest scenes and pictures of rural implements, and Pope, who himself cultivated to a high degree the 'Country' ideal of virtuous political retirement in his Twickenham villa, was amused at the lengths to which Bolingbroke went—the former leading statesman tossing the hay alongside his farm

labourers. Just as the beleaguered inhabitants of the Castle send out an urgent summons to the Knight—' "Come, come, Sir Knight! thy Children on thee call; "Come, save us yet, ere Ruin round us close!"' (II. xxxi)—so Bolingbroke was called out of his political retirement to play an active role in the 1730s as the ideological mastermind behind the Opposition's campaign.

It soon becomes apparent that the Castle is not the exclusive retreat the pilgrims thought they were entering in Canto I: it now encompasses the whole of Britain. 'But in prime Vigour what can last for ay', asks Thomson, tracing the degeneration which has taken place.

> That soul-enfeebling Wizard INDOLENCE,
> I whilom sang, wrought in his Works decay:
> Spred far and wide was his curs'd Influence;
> Of Public Virtue much he dull'd the Sense,
> Even much of Private; eat our Spirit out,
> And fed our rank luxurious Vices: whence
> The Land was overlaid with many a Lout;
> Not, as old Fame reports, wise, generous, bold, and stout.
>
> (II. xxix)

The historical cycle has begun to move on the downward slope. In his political essays of the 1730s Bolingbroke had analysed the condition of Britain under Walpole through the perspective of Machiavellian corruption theory. 'The best instituted governments . . . carry in them the seeds of their destruction: and, though they grow and improve for a time, they will soon tend visibly to their dissolution.' The symptoms of decline were already visible: Walpole's 'corruption', ranging from the diversion of public funds, stockjobbery, bribery, placemen, right through to the wholesale spiritual and moral corruption of the people by an emphasis on the false values of self-interest and material gain, would, if left unchecked, ultimately destroy Britain. 'Augustan' Britain would follow the same path to ruin as 'Augustan' Rome, now 'to slavish Sloth and Tyranny a Prey'. Archimago's earlier proclamation ' "Ye Sons of INDOLENCE, do what you will; / . . . "Be no Man's Pleasure for another's staid"' (I. xxviii) and the rule of the Castle 'That each should work his own Desire' (I. xxxv) are shown in all their fatal consequences. The self-indulgent hedonism of Canto I has hardened into the rapacious urge for self-gratification of Canto II.

> A Rage of Pleasure madden'd every Breast,
> Down to the lowest Lees the Ferment ran:
> To his licentious Wish Each must be blest,
> With Joy be fever'd; snatch it as he can.
> Thus *Vice* the Standard rear'd; her Arrier-Ban
> *Corruption* call'd, and loud she gave the Word.
> 'Mind, mind yourselves! Why should the vulgar Man,
> 'The Lacquey be more virtuous than his Lord?
> 'Enjoy this Span of Life! 'tis all the Gods afford.'
>
> (II. xxx)

Pope's apocalyptic vision of the triumphal Car of Vice leading the thronging millions in the *Epilogue to the Satires,* Dia. I, ll. 141-70, offers a striking parallel: 'Hear her black Trumpet thro' the Land proclaim, / That "Not to be corrupted is the Shame."'

Despite the urgency with which the Opposition pressed home its attacks on corruption, it did not entirely subscribe to historical fatalism. Bolingbroke, like Machiavelli, thought that 'ruin' might be averted by a conscious and deliberate *rittorno* to those 'first good principles' upon which the constitution was founded—integrity and, above all, public spirit. In his *Letters on the Spirit of Patriotism* of 1736 Bolingbroke pinned his faith on the efforts and example of a group of disinterested and public-spirited Patriots, and ultimately, in *The Idea of a Patriot King* of 1738, on a firm paternalistic monarch, to effect such reform. The visionary ending of the *Patriot King,* which heralds a future golden age of British peace and prosperity in which corruption, faction, and other evils have been vanquished, reflects the (perhaps naïve) idealism of Patriot literature. *The Castle of Indolence* similarly ends with a cleansing of the Augean stables and a moral and spiritual renewal. The Knight of Arts and Industry, accompanied by his little Druid bard, manages to rout the enchanter and liberate the Castle by their powerful speeches and songs—perhaps a testament to the faith which Thomson and other Opposition writers attached to the effects of their own political writing. The Druid's song—highly reminiscent of Thomson's *Britannia* of 1729 in its call to arts, industry, and arms and its attack on the 'soft, penetrating plague' of 'waste Luxury'—contrasts and counterbalances the Wizard's song of Canto I. It inspires its audience to public service rather than self-indulgent quietism, whether the worker in the fields, the statesman in 'public sage Debates', the scientist, scholar, merchant, or poet. Those Castle-dwellers who need to be further convinced perceive, after a wave of the Knight's 'anti-magic' wand, that their apparently opulent bower of bliss has been nothing but an illusion. Without the efforts of the 'commonweal', Britain has in reality become a barren and infertile landscape. Not all the inhabitants of the Castle can be saved: like Pope and Fielding, Thomson depicts the long-term effects of Walpole's corruption—the transformation of men into sensual beasts. As the witty footnote to *The Dunciad,* IV, l. 528 attests, this is a Circean transformation in reverse—'Hers took away the shape, and left the human mind: This takes away the mind, and leaves the human shape'. Like Pope's 'vulgar herd' who 'turn off to roll with Hogs', the unrepentant few will always 'roll, with vilest Brutes, through Mud and Slime' (II. lxiii). Thomson concludes his overturning of the false bower in the same abrupt manner as Spenser. Just as Spenser's Grill refuses to be changed back from pig to man, so Thomson's corrupt 'herd of Brisly swine' prefer the mire of corruption to the life of the spirit.

No single reading of *The Castle of Indolence* can be definitive: many critics would disagree with the interpretation offered here, arguing that the undoubtedly superior 'poetry' of Canto I indicates where Thomson's

real sympathies, conscious or otherwise, lie. Thomson certainly confuses the reader by placing the arguments for virtuous and artistic retirement in the mouth of the enchanter: and the 'Mirror of Vanity' (I. xlix-lvi), which satirizes money-lenders, kings, politicians, and aspiring authors alike, suggests a futility in the *via activa* which makes the world of the Castle seem noble by comparison. Of course, we should be on our guard here—it is in the Wizard's interests to tar all activity, noble or not, with the same brush, and the mirror deliberately distorts the outside world. But more questions are raised by the fact that Thomson is writing his poem from inside the Castle: the poet and his imagination are intimately bound up with the dreams and fantasies which are ultimately put to flight. For in spite of its allegorical obliqueness, *The Castle of Indolence* is a more intensely personal and subjective poem than *The Seasons*. In this, his last work, Thomson calls into question the very nature of poetry and the poet's calling. The narrative is punctuated by stanzas in Thomson's own voice criticizing the shortcomings of patrons, the problems posed by lack of authorial copyright, the relationship between political freedom and the arts, and above all the quest for inspiration. Here Thomson ranges through a Wordsworthian invocation of the purity of childhood vision, the wavering romantic dreams of the 'Shepherd of the *Hebrid-Isles*', the Catonic ideal of the 'sacred Shades of *Greece* and *Rome*', and the epic ambition that the history of 'the bold Sons of BRITAIN' will inspire his song. Keats's later 'Ode on Indolence', inspired in part by memories of Thomson's poem, embodies, if imperfectly, the same idea of the choices which confront the poet.

The biographical sketches of Thomson and his friends towards the end of Canto I serve to emphasize this theme. Although Thomson might have dispensed with these original burlesque *jeux d'esprit* once the poem began to develop in a more serious direction, he later added still more. It seems to have been part of his more complex allegorical design to dramatize himself and his fellow writers as willing inhabitants of the Castle. If (as Canto II strongly suggests) the Castle of Indolence can be read as an allegory of Walpolean England, then Thomson saw, I think, that he and his friends were also 'pensioners' and enjoyed some of the fruits of her ill-founded peace and prosperity—implicated, by their passivity, in the very regime they criticized. Although the portraits are endearingly affectionate, an element of censure creeps in. There is a prevailing atmosphere of idling away one's time, however pleasantly, of the gap between formulating ideas and failing to commit them to paper, of the inability to convert thought into action. It seems no accident that Lyttelton, a poet himself but the active leader of the Patriots in Parliament, is only an occasional guest in the Castle and refuses to become an inmate. The portrait of Thomson himself—'The World forsaking with a calm Disdain: Here laugh'd he careless in his easy Seat' (I. lxviii)—is not entirely flattering. One is reminded of Pope's languid Paridel, 'Stretch'd on the rack of a too easy chair' (*Dunciad,* IV, l. 324). For although McKillop argues that 'the "indolence" of the poet is so closely connected with the creation of poetry as to be virtually identical with it', this may be pushing the 'Romantic' argument too far. However attractive the dreams and idylls, Thomson's continual apostrophes to himself suggest that this was the wrong kind of poetry for the present age. 'Come then, my Muse, and raise a bolder Song; / Come, lig no more upon the Bed of Sloth' (II. iv); 'Come on, my Muse, nor stoop to low Despair, / Thou Imp of *Jove,* touch'd by celestial Fire! / Thou yet shalt sing of War, and Actions fair, / Which the bold Sons of BRITAIN will inspire' (I. xxxii). These last lines, Virgilian or Spenserian in their ambition to scale the *gradus ad Parnassum,* point to the programme of Patriot plays and poems which Thomson produced in the 1730s, with their historical and heroic themes. Inactivity or imaginative fantasy were all too easy, but the prevailing apathy of the nation demanded a more strenuous 'moral song'. It was for this reason that Thomson turned from *The Seasons* to a different kind of poetry, and that *The Castle of Indolence* took the direction that it did.

Thomson's portrait of his friend William Paterson, probably written some time in the early 1740s, embodies this conflict. Paterson was a man with strong Opposition sympathies, and his Patriot play of 1740, *Arminius,* was, like Thomson's *Edward and Eleanora* of the previous year, deemed sufficiently inflammatory to be prohibited by the Lord Chamberlain. Paterson seems to have written very little else. Here he is presented as a melancholic 'Romantic' poet, wandering alone through wild flowers and broom-clad heaths, building castles in the air, 'Ten thousand glorious Systems'—'But with the Clouds they fled, and left no Trace behind' (II. lix). Despite the picture's appeal, Paterson is criticized for wasting his talents.

> As soot this Man could sing as Morning-Lark,
> And teach the noblest Morals of the Heart:
> But These his Talents were ybury'd stark;
> Of the fine Stores he Nothing would impart,
> Which or boon Nature gave, or Nature-painting Art.
>
> (I. lvii)

There are echoes here of the portrait of Thomson himself, whose 'Ditty sweet / He loathed much to write, ne cared to repeat' (I. lxviii). In the Walpolean Bower of Bliss of stanza xvii of his *Canto of the Fairy Queen,* West had described a choice few, amongst the unthinking revellers

> That aptly could discourse of Vertuous Lore,
> Of Manners, Wisdom and sound Policy,
> Yet nould they often ope their sacred Store,
> Ne might their Voice be heard midst Riot and Uproar.

Through their reticence to speak out, gradually 'all Sense and Relish of a higher kind' becomes lost to the common people. Like West, Thomson saw that it was the poet's duty to speak out, to act as a moral guide in the wilderness. Paterson's portrait, if admired by a Romantic age, represents here a failing of the high public calling of the poet.

It still remains to ponder why *The Castle of Indolence,* in many ways so clearly a product of the opposition to Walpole, dragged on in its incomplete state until 1748. From its often biographical nature, one can guess that it bore at times something of a resemblance to a personal diary, with stanzas sporadically written while Thomson was busy on other projects. Canto II, stanza ii, complaining about the lack of authorial copyright, for example, bears a direct relationship to a letter which Thomson wrote to Hill in 1736. In 1742 Thomas Morell, a curate at Twickenham, addressed some Spenserian stanzas to Thomson urging him to overcome his own indolence and finish the poem. They imply that Canto II was planned, but not written by that date. The year 1742 marked Walpole's fall from office; and although this event might have inspired Thomson's description of the fall of Archimago and the routing of the Castle, it also had other consequences. When Walpole was finally toppled—after over twenty years in power—the Opposition's campaign lost its impetus, and an era of political poetry almost unprecedented in its fervour came to a sudden end. Johnson's *London,* Pope's *Epilogue to the Satires,* Glover's *Admiral Hosier's Ghost,* Bolingbroke's *Idea of a Patriot King,* and a host of Patriot plays, poems, and pamphlets were all produced in the last four years of the Walpole administration. The events which followed—the replacement of Walpole by the dissident Whig William Pulteney, and then the jockeying for places and positions by those very Patriots who had expressed such high and disinterested hopes in the preceding years, made for cynicism in more than one former literary supporter. Johnson's harsh comments on patriotism and Whigs stem from the betrayal which he felt had taken place. Thomson, as a pensioner of Prince Frederick, suffered more than the loss of his ideals. In a letter to Paterson (now living in the Bermudas) of mid-April 1748, containing his only reference to *The Castle of Indolence,* Thomson alludes to Lyttelton's rift with Prince Frederick, which led to the curtailment of his own royal pension, 'struck off from a certain hundred Pounds a Year which you know I had. West, Mallet and I were all routed in one day.' When Thomson turns to the forthcoming publication of *The Castle of Indolence,* it is in a mood of nostalgia, untainted by political considerations.

> Now that I am Prating of myself, know that, after fourteen or fifteen years, the Castle of Indolence comes abroad in a Fortnight. It will certainly travel as far as Barbadoes. You have an Apartment in it, as a Night-Pensioner; which, you may remember, I fitted up for you during our delightful Party at North-Haw. Will ever these Days return again? Dont you remember your eating the raw Fish that were never catched?

Thomson, who died some four months later, was indulging in a wistful memory of friendship and happier days gone by. *The Castle of Indolence,* which, had it been completed earlier, might have been recognized as Thomson's best political poem, had been reabsorbed into the holiday world of its original inception.

James Sambrook (essay date 1991)

SOURCE: "Last Years: *The Castle of Indolence* and *Coriolanus*, 1746-1748," in *James Thomson, 1700-1748: A Life,* Oxford at the Clarendon Press, 1991, pp. 248-84.

[*Sambrook is one of the world's leading authorities on Thomson and the author of a major biography of the poet. In the following excerpt from that work, he offers a closely biographical and source-related interpretation of* The Castle of Indolence, *Thomson's final work.*]

[Having been deeply disappointed by a long delay in seeing his play *Coriolanus* produced] Thomson has a happier fate to report to [William] Paterson concerning an even longer-gestated work:

> know that, after fourteen or fifteen Years, the Castle of Indolence comes abroad in a Fortnight. It will certainly travel as far as Barbadoes. You have an Apartment in it, as a Night-Pensioner; which, you may remember, I fitted up for you during our delightful Party at North-Haw. Will ever these Days return again? Dont you remember your eating the raw Fish that were never catched.

The holiday mood of this reference confirms Murdoch's account of the original conception of *The Castle of Indolence, an Allegorical Poem, written in Imitation of Spenser:* 'It was, at first, little more than a few detached stanzas, in the way of raillery on himself, and on some of his friends, who would reproach him with indolence, while he thought them, at least, as indolent as himself.' (As it happens, one of the stanzas on himself and some of the stanzas on his friends which are in the published poem must date from some years later, after Thomson had come to know Quin and Lyttelton; even the friendly raillery on the 'little, round oily Man of God' must have been written after 1738, when Murdoch was ordained.)

Murdoch continues his account of the poem's genesis: 'But he saw very soon, that the subject deserved to be treated more seriously, and in a form fitted to convey one of the most important moral lessons.' As fourteen or fifteen years elapsed between conception and publication we have no means of telling how soon was 'very soon', but it would appear that the moral lesson and at least the outline of the fable had been worked out by 1742, when Thomas Morell wrote his Spenserian stanzas calling upon Thomson to finish his poem. Between 1734 and 1748 Thomson wrote four plays and his share of *Alfred,* he wrote *Liberty* and the *Poem to Talbot,* and he also largely rewrote the *Seasons;* however, five of the years saw no new publication of any length by him, so one could not press the case that Thomson was just too busy to find time to sing about his own indolence.

Perhaps he thought that the subject of *The Castle of Indolence* and/or the Spenserian stanza and quaint, obsolete diction were suitable for a private poem to be shown to friends, but were inappropriate for the public utterances of the bard whose reputation was built largely upon po-litically or morally elevating sentiments in blank verse. Thomson admired *The Faerie Queene.* Even though he made no published reference to Spenser earlier than the revised *Seasons* of 1744, we have no reason to disbelieve Shiels' claim, made apparently from firsthand acquaintance, that Thomson 'has often confessed that if he had anything excellent in his poetry, he owed it to the inspiration he first received from reading the Fairy Queen, in the very early part of his life', and that, as a descriptive poet, 'he form'd his Taste upon *Spenser*'. Shiels writes of the descriptive, not the moral Spenser. Similarly, when, in the 1744 *Seasons,* Thomson couples the names of Chaucer and Spenser, it is Chaucer's verse that is described as 'Well-moraliz'd', whereas Spenser is

> Fancy's pleasing Son;
> Who, like a copious River, pour'd his Song
> O'er all the Mazes of enchanted Ground.

Despite the unimpeachable moral of *The Castle of Indolence* Thomson may have believed that its character as a burlesque, even a private joke, or as a romantic fantasy, even an indulgence in romantic introspection, made it too private for public consumption.

His decision to complete and publish might then have been influenced by the publication of other imitations of Spenser by younger poets during the time he was brooding upon his. Those others included Shenstone's *School-Mistress,* (in *Poems upon Various Occasions,* 1737, then expanded and sentimentalized for separate publication in 1742), Gilbert West's *A Canto of the Fairy Queen* (1739), William Thompson's *Sickness* (1745-6), and John Upton's *A New Canto of Spencer's Fairy Queen* (1747). Shenstone, West, and Upton were all acquaintances of Thomson by 1746. Shenstone's and West's Spenserian imitations were brought to wide public notice when they were republished in January 1748 in Dodsley's *Collection of Poems,* which also contained Gloster Ridley's *Psyche, or the Great Metamorphosis, a Poem written in Imitation of Spenser,* and shorter Spenserian imitations by Edward Bedingfield, Robert Lowth, and William Mason. Thomson's *The Castle of Indolence* was published five months later.

The text eventually published in quarto by Millar on 7 May 1748 consists of two cantos, each containing about eighty Spenserian stanzas, prefaced by a somewhat defensive Advertisement, excusing 'the obsolete Words and a Simplicity of Diction . . . which borders on the Ludicrous', which 'were necessary to make the Imitation more perfect'. The prefatory material also includes a small glossary of obsolete words, though the poem itself contains really very little archaic diction.

The first canto describes an imaginary castle which is an amalgam of tempting earthly paradises in Spenser's *Faerie Queene* (such as the Bower of Bliss, Phaedria's Bower, and Castle Joyeuse) with Armida's palace in Tasso's *Gerusalemme Liberata.* It also draws features from the *Arabian Nights,* where luxury, self-indulgence, and the cultivation of pleasure are not condemned, and from the Abbey of Thélème in Rabelais, where freedom reigns, the only rule is 'Do what thou wilt', and the wickedness and ugliness of the world are excluded. This castle is set in a delightful secluded pastoral valley, sheltered by woods, with quiet lawns, glittering streamlets, 'And vacant Shepherds piping in the Dale'. It is provided with beautiful works of art, abundant food, drink, music, and every creature comfort, such as 'Caps, Slippers, Gowns', and (with a hint of mock epic) 'Soft Quilts on Quilts, on Carpets Carpets spread'.

The castle belongs to a wizard who draws men into it with an enchanting song and charms them with deep draughts of Nepenthe, the drink described in *The Faerie Queene* as a reward bestowed by the gods upon fortunate men, to dispel anguish and rage, and confer 'sweet Peace and quiet Age'. Thomson's Wizard sings of the moral benefits of Epicureanism, 'joining Bliss to Virtue' (as Thomson claimed in *Liberty*) and linked with the Horatian ideal of virtuous philosophic retirement praised in, for instance, Thomson's **'Hymn on Solitude'**. The Wizard asks:

> What, what, is Virtue, but Repose of Mind?
> A pure ethereal Calm! that knows no Storm;
> Above the Reach of wild Ambition's Wind,
> Above those Passions that this World deform,
> And torture Man, a proud malignant Worm!
> But here, instead, soft Gales of Passion play,
> And gently stir the Heart, thereby to form
> A quicker Sense of Joy; as Breezes stray
> Across th' enliven'd Skies, and make them still
>   more gay.

He evokes Lucretius's ideal of calm mind above the storm of passion and concludes his stanza with a simile which points to that ideal harmony between man and nature presented in the *Seasons*. In the next stanza, 'the Best of Men have ever lov'd Repose', he proffers the example of Scipio, praised in *Winter*, 517-20 and *Liberty*, V. 419-21, and introduced as an admirable character in *Sophonisba;* and he might have added not only other virtuous Romans praised in the *Seasons* but Lyttelton as he appears in *Spring*, 909-22, pensive and soothed by the murmuring stream. Virtuous retirement is repeatedly applauded in the *Seasons,* as too is good nature. Addison, as a popularizer of Shaftesbury, wrote in *Spectator,* number 243:

> The two great Ornaments of Virtue, which shew her in the most advantageous Views, and make her altogether lovely, are Chearfulness and Good-nature. These generally go together, as a Man cannot be agreeable to others who is not easie with himself. They are both very requisite in a Virtuous Mind, to keep out Melancholy from the many serious Thoughts it is engaged in, and to hinder its natural Hatred of Vice from sowering into Severity and Censoriousness.

The Wizard argues in similar terms:

> Here nought but Candour reigns, indulgent
>   Ease,
> Good-natur'd Lounging, Sauntering up and
>   down:
> They who are pleas'd themselves must always
>   please;
> On Others' Ways they never squint a Frown,
> Nor heed what haps in Hamlet or in Town.
> Thus, from the Source of tender Indolence,
> With milky Blood the Heart is overflown,
> Is sooth'd and sweeten'd by the social Sense;
> For Interest, Envy, Pride, and Strife are banish'd
>   hence.

Behind this part of the Wizard's appeal lies one of the chief moral ideas of the *Seasons,* where Creative Bounty is reflected in man's social feeling.

Canto I makes indolence attractive, but we have been told at the outset that the Wizard is a false enchanter, with the implication that his castle is a false paradise, so it is no surprise to discover at the end of the canto that this castle conceals a dungeon into which its carefree dwellers will eventually be thrown. This is described in four burlesque stanzas contributed by Thomson's friend, the physician John Armstrong, author of *The Art of Preserving Health* (1744) and, like Thomson himself, a dweller in the castle. Armstrong represents the dungeon as a den of grotesque personifications, such as Gout, Apoplexy, and Lethargy, 'a mighty Lubbard . . . Stretch'd on his Back', snoring night and day; also Hypochondria, 'Mother of Spleen' or melancholy. Long before this point is reached, the morally alert reader has detected false notes in the Wizard's song. The Wizard tells his victims that in his castle they need no longer go through the city,

> To cheat, and dun, and lye, and Visit pay,
> Now flattering base, now giving secret
>   Wounds;
> Or proul in Courts of Law for human Prey,
> In venal Senate thieve, or rob on broad High-
>   way.

Nor, he adds, will they 'heed what haps in Hamlet or in Town'. Ludicrous alliteration emphasizes the message, which is really a call for indifference, not virtue. Elsewhere, the Wizard undermines his own claims for the 'virtue' of a quiet life by a facetious pragmatism, for instance in the implied decibel scale of 'No Dogs, no Babes, no Wives, to stun your Ear'.

The second canto of Thomson's poem introduces a heroic Knight of Arts and Industry, modelled upon Spenser's Satyrane in his birth and upbringing and upon Guyon at the Bower of Bliss in his rescue of the captives. His allegorical career echoes the histories of social progress in *Liberty* and the opening of *Autumn;* he resembles the patriot king described by Siffredi in *Tancred and Sigismunda,* I. iv. 11-28, or Peter the Great in the 1744 additions to *Winter.* He also resembles the ideal of an English landed gentleman, when, after a life encouraging industry, commerce, the arts, and representative government, he retires to improve his rural estate:

> Gay Plains extend where Marshes slept before;

O'er recent Meads th'exulting Streamlets fly;
Dark frowning Heaths grow bright with *Ceres'*
 Store,
And Woods imbrown the Steep, or wave along
 the Shore.

It is as if the landscape around the Castle of Indolence, as described at the opening of the poem, has now been turned to use; the literary mode is georgic, as against pastoral. Like Scipio, the prime exhibit in the Wizard's case, the Knight has earned repose by earlier toil and his 'repose' is useful activity. The same might be said of Lyttelton, for the passage in *Spring,* referred to above, which tells of him straying in the peace and quiet of Hagley Park, goes on to allude to his active moral life as historian, politician, and landlord. As it happens, Lyttelton is mentioned in *The Castle of Indolence,* but as an occasional visitor, who cannot be persuaded to take up residence with the Wizard.

The Knight of Arts and Industry is accompanied in his attack on the Wizard's castle by a Druid bard, who, countering the Wizard's tempting song, summons the indolent dwellers in the castle to a life of useful activity. Some are called 'to Courts, and Some to Camps; To Senate Some . . . To high Discovery Some . . . Some to the thriving Mart; Some to the Rural Reign . . . To the sweet Muses Some, who raise the Heart'. His song restates the true and complete moral philosophy of the *Seasons,* based on the georgic concept of work as divinely ordained to beautify the earth and exalt humankind, and on Thomson's distinctive notion of spiritual ascent. Though the Wizard cites scripture it is the Bard of Canto II who is the true religious poet, as Druids reputedly were. He proclaims the immanence of God in the terms that Thomson had already employed in his *Poem to Newton, Spring,* and *Edward and Eleonora:*

What is TH' ADOR'D SUPREME PERFECTION,
 say?
What, but eternal never-resting Soul,
Almighty Power, and all-directing Day;
By whom each Atom stirs, the Planets roll;
Who fills, surrounds, informs, and agitates the
 Whole?

God sanctifies morally strenuous industry, which draws humankind up towards perfection as well as giving pleasure. The Bard appeals:

Toil, and be glad! Let Industry inspire
Into your quicken'd Limbs her buoyant Breath!
Who does not act is dead; absorpt intire
In miry Sloth, no Pride, no Joy he hath.

Some of the castle-dwellers are convinced by this argument, but most are not; so it is necessary for the Knight to wave an anti-magic wand which transforms the delightful landscape around the castle into a hideous morass, and which exposes the dungeon of lethargic misery. Thereupon, nearly everyone embraces a life of useful toil, and the few who do not are harried by fiends called

Beggary and Scorn. The canto ends with a joke at the expense of muddy, insalubrious Brentford, in a burlesque stanza which, for style and topographical detail, could easily have found a place in Pope's Spenserian imitation, 'The Alley'. Thus Thomson concludes his poem in the mood of raillery in which, according to Murdoch, it was conceived.

On Thomson's dating, *The Castle of Indolence* was begun in 1733-4, when he was writing *Liberty*. The spectacle of indolence, luxury, slavery, and human decay in modern Rome which prompted him to write *Liberty* is described in a letter to Lady Hertford from Paris, 10 October 1732; and this same letter contains also perhaps another germ of *The Castle of Indolence,* unrelated to Murdoch's account:

As for their Music, it is a sort of charming malady that quite disolves them in softness, and greatly heightens in them that universal Indolence men naturally (I had almost said reasonably) fall into when they can receive little or no advantage from their Industry.

Indolence and Industry are the opposites personified in the two cantos of Thomson's poem, while through the first canto flows, as the accompaniment to the enchanter's 'enfeebling Lute' and 'Syren Melody', a music that inclines to languishment. A link with *Liberty* suggests that *The Castle of Indolence, an Allegorical Poem* might contain a political allegory; political meanings have duly been discovered by a number of readers in the 1980s.

[In *The Enlightenment and Scottish Literature, Vol. I: Progress and Poetry* (1982)] John MacQueen, while conceding that it 'would be an oversimplification to suggest that the domain of Sir Industry is England, that of Indolence, Scotland', nevertheless relates the poem to the theme of Scottish economic improvement after the Union, thus casting Thomson into his familiar role as the poet of Britannia. Mary Jane W. Scott [in *James Thomson, Anglo-Scot* (1988)] develops this notion and overlays it with a more specific political interpretation in which the Wizard is the Stuart cause, the inhabitants of the castle are Scotsmen who remain inactive under the Jacobite threat, and the Knight represents Whig Hanoverian leadership which at last calls these Scotsmen to their true patriotic duty, which is to serve a united Britain. For John Barrell [in *English Literature in History, 1730-1780: An Equal, Wide Survey* (1983)] the castle is really an eighteenth-century country house, where men of the upper orders retreat to avoid the labours appropriate to their station (law, politics, commerce, etc.); the Knight, a retired gentleman, restores them to their proper duties in camps and courts and public life. Thomson refers repeatedly to 'toil', but he avoids the reality of labour as experienced by the lower orders; the ambiguities of his poem 'proceed from the nature of the task that Thomson has set himself, of justifying the fruits of social division, while denying at the same time that any serious social divisions exist'. [In "*The Castle of Indolence* and the Opposition to Walpole," published in *Review of English Studies* n.s. 41 (1990)] Christine Gerrard, picking up

Barrell's hint that the poem's political context is opposition to Walpole, regards indolence as a national problem: it is what opponents to Walpole in the 1730s saw as 'a malaise of inertia, self-interest, hedonism, corruption, and loss of public spirit'. The wicked enchanter is Walpole himself, the Knight of Arts and Industry is perhaps Bolingbroke, and the Druid bard who accompanies him is, as Joseph Warton first conjectured, Alexander Pope. So, like the *Dunciad* and Pope's Horatian satires, Thomson's poem tells of Britain falling into decadence for lack of public virtue; but, unlike Pope, Thomson imagines the defeat of corruption and a revival of public spirit.

Dr Gerrard's argument is persuasive, particularly when she quotes such passages as the following description of the spread of the 'soul-enfeebling Wizard' Indolence's power:

> Spred far and wide was his curs'd Influence;
> Of Public Virtue much he dull'd the Sense,
> Even much of Private; eat our Spirit out,
> And fed our rank luxurious Vices: whence
> The Land was overlaid with many a Lout;
> Not, as old Fame reports, wise, generous, bold,
>   and stout.

> A Rage of Pleasure madden'd every Breast,
> Down to the lowest Lees the Ferment ran:
> To his licentious Wish Each must be blest,
> With Joy be fever'd; snatch it as he can.
> Thus *Vice* the Standard rear'd; her Arrier-Ban
> *Corruption* call'd, and loud she gave the
>   Word.

This said, it has to be admitted that no evidence has been found that Thomson's contemporaries read the poem as a political allegory. They merely associate it with the author's own indolence, or praise in general terms its imaginative power, or artfully laid plan, or beautiful succession of descriptions. Even a long and favourable review by the politically-alert Henry Fielding in his political periodical, *The Jacobite's Journal* (4 June 1748), does not hint at any political allegory in *The Castle of Indolence*.

Whatever the politics of this poem, Thomson's *moral* allegory has all the palpability of a sore thumb, and, like a sore thumb, it feelingly arises from particular circumstances in the author's life. This moral is spelt out unequivocally in the first stanza of the first canto:

> O MORTAL MAN, who livest here by Toil,
> Do not complain of this thy hard Estate;
> That like an Emmet thou must ever moil,
> Is a sad Sentence of an ancient Date:
> And, certes, there is for it Reason great;
> For, though sometimes it makes thee weep and
>   wail,
> And curse thy Stars, and early drudge and late,
> Withouten That would come an heavier Bale,

> Loose Life, unruly Passions, and Diseases pale.

The penalty of Adam is hard, but its alternative would be worse. Donald Greene observes that 'Thomson knew what he was talking about; it is a poem of personal experience'. Its power perhaps 'comes from the fact that Thomson—the fat, lazy, complaisant Jemmy Thomson, who never quite realized the potential his friends saw in him—knew something of' the suffering that arises from somnolence, lethargy, and paralysis of the will in a man of sensitivity and genius. . . . Thomson's self-indulgence and idleness were a stock joke among his friends, and that he hoped Elizabeth Young's love would rescue him from 'that most fatal Syren Indolence and false Pleasure', make him a new man, and spur him to virtue and industry. His courtship failed; he was unable to summon up the resolution to change his own character and habits, but the allegory of his own escape from the castle of indolence is not altogether a wish-fulfilment fantasy.

Describing this escape at the beginning of the second canto, Thomson discusses, not for the first time in this poem, his role as a poet. He complains that there is no effective copyright act, so booksellers take the rewards due to authors:

> a fell Tribe *th'Aonian Hive* despoil,
> As ruthless Wasps oft rob the painful Bee.

Later in this canto, echoing Spenser's lament over the decay of enlightened patronage, Thomson condemns the 'Poor Sons of puft-up Vanity' who now appropriate the title of Maecenas. He regrets the lack of patrons who can provide the Muses with 'the Sun-shine of uncumber'd Ease', but in the next stanza he claims that Liberty is his eternal patron and 'The best, and sweetest far, are Toil-created Gains'.

The poet is reflecting upon his own status. Though Millar treated him generously by booksellers' standards of the day and was a personal friend, Thomson distrusted the market; he believed that high art should not be subject to commercial considerations. Patronage could be a better guarantee of good poetry, but the servility that patronage often entailed at this period must sometimes have irritated a man of even Thomson's easy-going nature. By 1748 he was disillusioned with the Prince of Wales, to whom he had dedicated most of his writings since 1735, and who for a while may have seemed an approximation to the ideal of disinterested royal support for the arts. According to Smollett, Thomson intended to retract his flattery of at least some patrons, 'a laudable scheme of poetical justice, the execution of which was fatally prevented by untimely death'. To judge by the revised *Seasons* this laudable scheme was formed later than 1744. *The Castle of Indolence,* however, bears out Smollett's claim, to the extent that it has no dedication and the encomiums in it are all of close friends, among whom the patron Lyttelton may fairly be numbered.

In speaking out more directly than ever before about his own poetic role Thomson finds what a modern critic hears as 'a new note, a different pace, . . . a vigour and an ease, almost one would say a lordly Byronic assumption of careless power':

> I care not, Fortune, what you me deny:
> You cannot rob me of free Nature's Grace;
> You cannot shut the Windows of the Sky,
> Through which *Aurora* shews her brightening
>   Face:
> You cannot bar my constant Feet to trace
> The Woods and Lawns, by living Stream, at
>   Eve:
> Let Health my Nerves and finer Fibres brace,
> And I their Toys to the *great Children* leave;
> Of Fancy, Reason, Virtue, nought can me
>   bereave.

Spenserian fancy dress and allegory are blown away by a fresh, open-air, 'cheerful Morn of Life' manner, like that of the early *Seasons,* as Thomson offers a personal testimony of his integrity as a poet. Poetic integrity consists in the trinity of Fancy, Reason, and Virtue, but in *The Castle of Indolence* as a whole it is recognized that Fancy sometimes conflicts with Reason and Virtue.

The description of the castle in the first canto is conspicuously a work of the fancy or imagination. The castle is set among 'soothing Groves' and 'quiet Lawns', 'Half prankt with Spring, with Summer half imbrown'd', where

> unnumber'd glittering Streamlets play'd,
> And hurled every-where their Waters sheen;
> That, as they bicker'd through the sunny
>   Glade,
> Though restless still themselves, a lulling
>   Murmur made.

It is overshadowed by a 'sable, silent, solemn Forest',

> Where nought but shadowy Forms were seen
>   to move,
> As *Idless* fancy'd in her dreaming Mood . . .
> And where this Valley winded out, below,
> The murmuring Main was heard, and scarcely
>   heard, to flow.

This is the natural world of the *Seasons* viewed through a dreamy haze:

> A pleasing Land of Drowsyhed it was:
> Of Dreams that wave before the half-shut Eye;
> And of gay Castles in the Clouds that pass,
> For ever flushing round a Summer-Sky.

It is a world under the view of what Thomson, in *Spring,* line 459, called 'Imagination's vivid Eye'. As when the seduced pilgrims slip into the castle,

> In silent Ease: as when beneath the Beam
> Of Summer-Moons, the distant Woods among,
> Or by some Flood all silver'd with the Gleam,

> The soft-embodied Fays through airy Portal
>   stream.

The castle is a 'Fairy-Land' of 'fair Illusions' and 'artful Phantoms', but these illusions often reproduce the visual delights of the *Seasons,* for instance the play of light over the natural scene:

> And hither *Morpheus* sent his kindest Dreams,
> Raising a World of gayer Tint and Grace;
> O'er which were shadowy cast Elysian Gleams,
> That play'd, in waving Lights, from Place to
>   Place,
> And shed a roseate Smile on Nature's Face.
> Not *Titian's* Pencil e'er could so array,
> So fleece with Clouds the pure Etherial Space.

Within the castle there are tapestries depicting the pastoral patriarchal age of Abraham, and also paintings:

> Whate'er *Lorrain* light-touch'd with softening
>   Hue,
> Or savage *Rosa* dash'd, or learned *Poussin* drew.

These tapestries and paintings make up a receding vista of imaginary landscapes, thronged with shadowy forms. At the centre is a blank, walled area, where 'solitude and perfect silence reign', and where one is constrained to dream:

> As when a Shepherd of the *Hebrid-Isles,*
> Plac'd far amid the melancholy Main,
> (Whether it be, lone Fancy him beguiles;
> Or that aerial Beings sometimes deign
> To stand, embodied, to our Senses plain)
> Sees on the naked Hill, or Valley low,
> The whilst in Ocean *Phœbus* dips his Wain,
> A vast Assembly moving to and fro:
> Then all at once in Air dissolves the wondrous
>   Show.

Joseph Warton wrote of this stanza: 'I cannot recollect any solitude so romantic . . . The mind naturally loves to lose itself in one of these wildernesses.' But this wilderness is itself within the mind: the castle of indolence is a Chinese box of dreams within dreams; movement through it has the characteristic of movement in mental space in that it can be at the same time inwards and outwards. In one aspect the castle represents the poet's own self-absorbed, self-justifying, capricious, insatiable, irresponsible, creative imagination. It is the art and sensibility which created the more inward parts of the *Seasons*. The pleasures of indolence are the pleasures of enhanced self-awareness and of contemplation; they are the pleasures of the imagination, or, as Thomson's contemporaries sometimes called them, the pleasures of melancholy, for, according to classical and Renaissance tradition, melancholy marked the temperament of the creative artist.

Thomson's castle of indolence reveals, however, a darker face of melancholy, which is seen in the dungeon described at the end of canto I. Delightful visions are offset by nightmares: the creative imagination which, in pleasant indolence, can charm itself with romantic visions, is also, in its self-absorption, a prey to sinister, fearful eruptions of boredom, despair, and madness. Thomson knows that the imagination can be a dangerous pleasure ground, the melancholy main can be a perilous sea, and the romantic wilderness within the mind can be a hostile country.

Of course, well before we learn about the dungeon we have been warned about the enchanter's wickedness and have perhaps detected moral irresponsibilities in his siren melody. At the very point where the romantic dream is most seductive, the moment of the Hebridean shepherd's vision, Thomson appears in his own person for the first time in his poem to assert the higher values of socially responsible art. Calling on the Muse, he proclaims:

> Thou yet shalt sing of War, and Actions fair,
> Which the bold Sons of BRITAIN will inspire . . .
> Thou yet shalt tread in Tragic Pall the Stage,
> Paint Love's enchanting Woes, the Heroe's Ire,
> The Sage's Calm, the Patriot's noble Rage,
> Dashing Corruption down through every
>   worthless Age.

Like Spenser, speaking through the mouth of Piers in *The Shepheardes Calender* ('October'), he proclaims that he will rise to higher kinds of poetry. Implicitly, he vindicates *Liberty* and the patriot plays published between the conception and the printing of *The Castle of Indolence*.

Thomson in the second canto rejects the sweet dwelling of the romantic imagination, that whole world of romantic images, from Arabia to the Hebrides by way of fairyland, which he took from Spenser and Milton, and was to have some part in handing on to the nineteenth century. He aspires to be a moralist, not a self-indulgent, self-absorbed dreamer, and he insists that reason and virtue must be linked with fancy, that is, imagination. True virtue is not repose of mind, but selfless activity, as appears in the Bard's song. The greatest poetry of the past was that which fired the breast 'To Thirst of Glory, and heroic Deeds', and the task of the present-day poet is to serve the cause of public virtue. The characters of the Wizard and the Bard, the castle and its destroyer, articulate very clearly and bring into head-on collision the two poets inside Thomson, the poets who coexist easily in the *Seasons:* they are the retired dreamer whose object is pleasure and the active teacher whose object is moral instruction. Victory goes to the latter: to the Bard of *Liberty* rather than the Hymner of Solitude. Thomson gives unequivocal answers to the questions he raises concerning the role of the poet and the value and status of dreaming. The achievement of his poem is to make us feel the power of romanticism and respond with delight to its appeal, while at the same time we judge it, and know the dangers of its rejection of responsibility and reality.

Thomson's intentions may well have been unequivocal, but, as Johnson observed of *Liberty,* 'an author and his reader are not always of a mind'; from the beginning, most readers found the first canto more appealing than the second. In a letter of 15 May 1748 Lady Hertford wrote, 'I think the *Wizard's Song* deserves a preference; 'He needs no Muse who dictates from his heart'. Lady Luxborough agreed that it was no wonder that the Wizard's song was the most engaging, for 'Thomson's heart was ever devoted to that Archimage'. Shelley said that 'the Enchanter in the first canto was a true philanthropist, and the Knight in the second an oligarchical imposter, overthrowing truth by power'. Douglas Grant and Earl Wasserman speak for the majority of twentieth-century readers on both sides of the Atlantic when the first declares that the first canto 'is by far the finer of the two', and the second says that the 'dull didactic' second canto 'is an artistic failure'.

The first canto contains, at stanza xl, what is apparently the earliest published reference in English to what would become a prime symbol of the poetic imagination: the Aeolian harp. This device is also mentioned in **'An Ode, on the Winter Solstice'** and is the subject of Thomson's last-published poem, his **'Ode on Aeolus's Harp'**, printed (together with **'On the Report of a Wooden Bridge'**) in the second edition of Dodsley's *Collection of Poems* in June 1748 and in subsequent editions. A footnote to the **'Ode on Aeolus's Harp'** describes the harp as 'a musical Instrument, which plays with the wind, invented by Mr Oswald', but strictly it was the rediscovery of an invention described in a Latin treatise of 1650 by the German Jesuit Athanasius Kircher. James Oswald, 'the Scotch Orpheus', was a dancing-master, singer, cello player, and composer who came from Scotland to London in 1741, where he prospered as a music publisher; he composed musical settings for at least three of Thomson's love lyrics. According to Charles Burney, who knew both men quite well, Thomson translated the 1650 description of the Aeolian Harp for Oswald, who could not read Latin 'and let it pass for his invention, in order to give him a better title to the sale of the instrument at his music-shop in St Martin's Churchyard'. It is not known whether Thomson possessed an Aeolian harp (none is mentioned in the sale catalogue of his goods after his death), but Shenstone's friend Lady Luxborough certainly had one before November 1748.

Thomson's last writing was the few corrections and revisions to a second edition of *The Castle of Indolence* published in octavo by Millar on 22 September, by which time the poet himself was dead.

William Levine (essay date 1994)

SOURCE: "Collins, Thomson, and the Whig Progress of Liberty," in *Studies in English Literature, 1500-1900,* Vol. 34, No. 3, Summer, 1994, pp. 553-77.

[*In the excerpt below, Levine compares Thomson's* Liberty *with William Collins's "Ode to Liberty."*]

Liberty, James Thomson's nearly 3500-line blank verse

"poetical vision" that recounts the Whiggish progress of European civilization and the triumphs of British freedom, has been almost unanimously viewed as one of his greatest aesthetic failures, a poem that Johnson once "tried to read, and soon desisted." To this day, interest in the poem remains mostly historical, perhaps unjustly. For not only did Thomson incorporate sections of this panoramic didactic poem into his later, expanded versions of *The Seasons,* but mid-eighteenth-century British poets also acknowledged this most extensive of progress pieces as a central work of patriotic poetry. In December 1746, twelve years after the first books of *Liberty* were published, William Collins offered his 144-line Pindaric "Ode to Liberty," one of the more ambitious pieces in his collection, *Odes on Several Descriptive and Allegoric Subjects.* Although it is indebted at various points to Pope, Dryden, Spenser, the lyrical (as opposed to Thomson's epic) Milton, and writers of the classical and native British Pindaric traditions, Collins's ode borrows and transforms substantial parts of *Liberty* as its most important recent influence, especially as a model of patriotic poetry whose progressive Whig ideology is no longer tenable. The "Ode to Liberty" redirects pivotal themes, settings, and language in Thomson, resulting in a progress poem that fully responds to new crises in international politics and redefines the poet's role as spokesman for the the English national conscience.

The progress piece assumed various forms, but, as developed by Thomson and Collins, among others, it featured an imaginary westward and northward journey of an allegorical entity such as Liberty, though both poets also incorporate an important alternative tradition of a northern Liberty that progresses southward. A typical "progress" of power or knowledge (*translatio imperii* or *translatio studii*) traces the birth and historical manifestations of its subject from classical times to the present, conveniently ending in contemporary Britain, the last and therefore best model of civilization and government. Yet, despite the connotations of cultural "advancement" that progress poems suggest (besides their primary meaning, "to travel"), mid-eighteenth-century poets are aware of at least two problems related to this scheme of world history. One is that England, like Greece, Rome, the medieval Italian city-states, and most of northern Europe, will enjoy the fruits of Liberty for only a limited time in history, before the spirit migrates further westward, even, in one of Bishop Berkeley's poems, as far away as America:

> There shall be sung another golden age,
>   The rise of empire and of arts. . . .
>
>   . . . . .
>
> Not such as Europe breeds in her decay;
>   Such as she bred when fresh and young,
> When heavenly flame did animate her clay,
>   By future poets shall be sung.

Berkeley's poem suggests one further problem of cultural progress and refinement: a certain loss of native, founda-

tional energy, whether this is the visionary power of the first "Druid" poet-priests, or the vigorously participatory government of an idealized Gothic state (a Whig model which, J. G. A. Pocock remarks, conveniently omitted serfdom). As will be shown, Collins recognizes the limitations and even contradictions in the ways that a partisan writer like Thomson approaches these problems, and accommodates the progress piece to a different set of contemporary political crises: whereas the corruption, luxury, and self-interest exemplified by Walpole is the main enemy of Liberty for Thomson, Collins more typically places responsibility on the entire nation, which needs to be purged of such ills as the Pretender's 1745 uprising and British involvement in the unpopular, unsuccessful War of Austrian Succession.

Despite their distinct forms and different political contexts, an overlapping stock of Whig poetical commonplaces suggests a direct line of continuity, with important thematic variations, from Thomson to Collins. In one of the first modern comparisons of the two poems, Edward Ainsworth labeled Collins's "Ode to Liberty" a "concentrated and somewhat confused version" of Thomson's *Liberty;* in his view, the scenes that the earlier poet draws in great detail and places in an elaborate, continuous progress are obliquely and abruptly presented in the later ode. Ainsworth's discussion includes several conspicuous points of comparison: the allusions to an idealized "Druid" past that gave birth to a British temple of Liberty; the embodiment of Liberty in models of Classical sculpture and architecture; the contemplation of broken, damaged, or violated cultural artifacts as a sign that southern European nations no longer enjoy freedom; and most importantly, the recurrent cycle of Liberty rising and falling in each nation it visits through history, from Greece and Rome onwards to England. In these two poems, the intermediate stops include medieval Florence, Genoa, Venice, and Switzerland. Although these points of similarity show a strong affinity between the two poems, one may disagree with Ainsworth's particular valuations by closely comparing the function and style of these conventions in Thomson and Collins. For example, Thomson's Goddess of Liberty characteristically reflects upon the past glories of Venice:

> NOR be the then triumphant State forgot;
> Where, push'd from plundered Earth, a Remnant still,
> Inspired by ME, thro' the dark Ages kept
> Of MY old *Roman* Flame some Sparks alive:
> The seeming God-built City! which MY Hand
> Deep in the Bosom fix'd of wond'ring Seas.
> Astonish'd Mortals sail'd, with pleasing Awe,
> Around the Sea-girt Walls, by *Neptune* fenc'd,
> And down the briny Street; where, on each hand,
> Amazing seen amid unstable Waves,
> The splendid Palace shines; and rising Tides,
> The green Steps marking, murmur at the Door.
> To this fair *Queen* of *Adria*'s stormy Gulph,
> The Mart of Nations! long, obedient Seas
> Roll'd all the Treasure of the radiant East.
> But now no more.

Thomson makes Venice a "type" of Britain, which will later fulfill the destiny of commercial superiority at sea. Maintaining a commonplace of progress poetry, Thomson equates commercial success with governmental freedom, and thus explains how Venice, like Rome, has fallen because of a despotic government that has interfered with and restricted trade.

In the passage that follows, Collins renders an account of the same historical *topos,* the "golden age" of medieval Venice, yet his style of presenting it in his ode makes new variations upon the "progress" theme and form. Besides his emphasis on features of Venice different from those of Thomson's description, Collins's manner of introducing this scene is noticeably more compressed, oblique, and less moralistic, but by no means is it a "concentrated and somewhat confused version" of the scene from *Liberty:*

> Strike, louder strike th' ennobling Strings
> To those, whose Merchant Sons were Kings;
> To Him, who deck'd with pearly Pride,
> In *Adria* weds his green-hair'd Bride;
> Hail Port of Glory, Wealth, and Pleasure,
> Ne'er let me change this *Lydian* Measure.

Collins portrays some of the same facets of the fallen commercial paradise as Thomson: the lapsed commercial royalty of once-republican Venice, "those, whose Merchant Sons were Kings"; the grandeur and pomp in Collins's "pearly Pride" and "Port of Glory, Wealth, and Pleasure," which resemble Thomson's "splendid Palace" and the "Treasure of the radiant East"; and a similar setting of the Doge's palace near the Adriatic Sea, the "green-hair'd bride" whom the Doge symbolically weds, perhaps echoing Thomson's descriptions of his home's "green steps" and suggesting the "marriage" of advanced culture with powerful nature. Yet Collins has done more than borrow some of Thomson's diction and compress his topographical descriptions. The quoted passage does not so much describe as glance obliquely at a city that once thrived but has now vanished. The entire ode is cast as a search for the traces of fallen, fugitive Liberty, not as a full story of its rise and fall.

In his patriotic ode, Collins makes use of the same conventional themes, even some of the same imagery and diction, as Thomson to describe the course of Liberty, but not for the sake of building a triumphant narrative of its journey from Classical times to mid-eighteenth-century England. On the contrary, all the conventional materials of the progress become problematized in Collins; he reassesses every part of Liberty's journey, from recovering her fragmented past to warding off the imminent threats to her spirit. Even the material Collins selects is a departure from conventional accounts of Liberty, as he moves away from the panoramic historical scene in Thomson. Although the Miltonic diction and richly descriptive periodic sentences dignify the effect of various passages in *Liberty,* the quoted excerpt on Venice, to which "long, obedient Seas / Roll'd all the Treasure of the radiant East," essentially says that a small, insular city-state, surrounded by a sublimely oceanic setting, was once a magnificent commercial center. The excerpt from Collins's ode, a peculiar cross of historical legend and myth, concentrates mainly upon the ritual, the Doge's ceremonial "wedding" with the sea each year when he throws a gold ring into it. The highly particularized and indirectly introduced scene is more traditionally the material of a Pindaric ode; Collins does not draw the same exhaustive scene of a busy commercial hub that is typical of Thomson's elevated georgic, and these different manners of representation reflect a substantial change in the ways that history and poetic form can lend support to or critique the present.

For his five-book "poetical vision," Thomson introduces the topoi of a Whig progress through a *dea ex machina,* the goddess Liberty, who accounts for the rise and fall of her presence in a sequence of European states. Although its Miltonic diction and exhaustive depictions of classical history lend *Liberty* a ceremonious air, the historical narrative, which resembles the "Grand Tour" of the continent, would have been easily understandable to anyone reading the poem. The details of the historical commonplaces are dressed up in a formal way, but nonetheless had been the material of inherited accounts of civilization, especially those that supported eighteenth-century Oppositionist Whig beliefs. In contrast, Collins's more legendary history recovers shadowy supernatural lore from the mythological past to restore the place of inspired patriotic poetry in modern society. Though a Pindaric ode can be an occasion for elevated diction and obscure syntax (for example, in Cowley or Gray), Collins's predominantly end-stopped tetrameter and the rhyming couplets or balanced quatrains that make up his epodes actually are a purification of the poetic forms inherited from Thomson. Collins pares down the descriptive wording, selectively appropriates scenes from "real" history that Thomson elevates and fully describes, while foregrounding elements of mythical history that *Liberty* mentions only in passing, and establishes a more consistent rhythm for his verse, though his poem offers a more complicated and suggestive account of cultural progress. The Pindaric ode's structure of "turns," "counter-turns," and "stands" allows Collins to counterpoint the traditional, continuous accounts of progress with mythological tales about England's past. By assigning different historical episodes to separate strophes and epodes, Collins uses a more allusive and discontinuous style, blending fiction and reality.

Whereas Thomson narrates the "true," complete progress of Liberty from classical times to the present, Collins riddles his much shorter account with gaps, discontinuities, and events of a more ambiguous historical character. Introducing a greater level of psychological complexity to the progress poem, one of Collins's typical gestures is to deny the accuracy of what he is about to tell us, or deliberately to excuse himself from recounting a painful or unpleasant event, using the trope of preterition:

> No, *Freedom,* no, I will not tell,
> How *Rome,* before thy weeping Face,
> With heaviest Sound, a Giant-statue, fell,
> Push'd by a wild and artless Race.

Besides this refusal to describe the fall of a monumental city, Collins also does not explain the loss of an ancient Druid temple. He confesses to a lack of knowledge, specifically his inability to determine which race, or even whether nature itself, committed the vandalism:

> Whether the fiery-tressed *Dane*,
> Or *Roman*'s self o'erturn'd the Fane,
> Or in what Heav'n-left Age it fell,
> 'Twere hard for modern Song to tell.

To introduce his partially revealed vision of a lost Druid temple, Collins collapses his account of its legendary construction with the work he will perform in the poem, to recreate it poetically. Again, a lost past can only be partially recovered:

> How may the Poet now unfold,
> What never Tongue or Numbers told?
> How learn delighted, and amaz'd
> What Hands unknown that Fabric rais'd?

Preterition can be one of the most disingenuous rhetorical figures, often calling more attention to what it omits than would tacit omission altogether, as when Richard Nixon refused to consider the "Catholic Question" in his debates with John F. Kennedy. As Fredric V. Bogel observes, Collins addresses his personifications of the past in a way that transforms elegiac lament to ode-like, immediate confrontation; that is to say, he converts the lost past to the "insubstantial," tentative, or fleeting present. Readers of the ode thus may empathize with the fallen cities or delight in the harmoniously resurrected temple of Liberty. Nonetheless, Collins seems also to desire a true forgetting that will leave the audience in a shadowy zone between fact and fiction, to construct a revived mythology that will leave much of the poem's credibility to intangible hopes, faith, and inspiration. The ode creates a mythological realm of history, a structure of gained and lost freedom that supersedes the chronicle of Thomson's blank-verse georgic vision. Collins dissolves the concrete historical facts of Thomson's story and supplies the materials of myth, ritual, and remote legend in its place. These poetic fictions do not suggest a wish for a true return to an idealized prelapsarian Druid England, and thus an evasion of historical responsibility, but serve rather as a metaphor for an imperfect world of hope, anticipation of new Liberty, freedom, and peace.

Although their goals for the progress of British Liberty are compatible, the means of attaining this, the responses to contemporary history, and the moral stances in the two poems differ dramatically. Thomson's course of history includes commercial, aesthetic, and governmental prototypes of British Liberty, a panoramic view that depends on a highly codified scheme of events in which Greece and Rome serve as the cultural ancestors of England. Again, Collins's view of history should be distinguished from this because, although it too is a Whig poem that fosters hope for peace in republican forms of government, it places little emphasis on the enlightening effects of commerce and industry and tends to replace these with a set of affective conditions for security and national protection. More importantly, the "history" of Collins's poem does not at all recount events in the manner of a factual chronicle but resists strict reference to the outside world and instead generates its historical scheme through the formal structure of the poem, with repetitions, symmetries, and brief fables that require the reader to make tentative connections among parts. For example, the Romans are both victims of the "Northern Sons of Spoil" when their empire falls and possibly aggressors upon the British when (or if indeed) they destroy the Druid temple. These symmetrical destructive acts, mentioned respectively in the beginning strophe and the final epode, complicate the straightforward, sequential "Whig Progress" of history. The arrangement of these scenes in the ode implies that Britain has already had and lost its golden age, and that Rome has fallen because of uncontrollable outside forces—ironically, those nations to which Liberty eventually succeeds in traditional progress pieces—and not internal political corruption, as Thomson more characteristically claims. Further, the ode disrupts the very logic of linear progress by inverting the literal chronological sequence, starting with Rome's destruction and ending with a restored vision of mythic England. This recursive, counter-progressive pattern, as well as the suggestion that freedom may have originated in northern, not Mediterranean nations, undermines the traditional story, the consecutive rises and falls of ancient and medieval European cities as sites of Liberty. Qualifying his digressions from a straightforward "progress" by calling attention to their partially fictional or mythological status, Collins reminds us that none of his stories is ascertainable, belonging as they do to the realm of legend or pure speculation. Ultimately, he attempts to find an idealized, precultural, harmonious state of British freedom, before the history of international aggression, in mythological analogues such as the Temple of Liberty.

This desire for moral purity and freedom from violence demands a retreat from "progressive" history, if only to defer its necessarily destructive consequences. In expressing these wishes, perhaps Collins renders a pessimistic answer to one of the continual concerns in *Liberty*, the seemingly inevitable corruption of even the best governments. Thomson plainly asserts that this corruption ensues when nations such as ancient Greece are denied "*Liberty* of *Mind*" by "Systems" and "Soul-enslaving Creeds." Yet the poet of *Liberty* tends to assume a didactic posture when summarizing the lessons of history for his audience, and this moralizing tone is completely absent from Collins, who may not have been convinced by Thomson's directives. For example, to overcome an extensive state of political corruption and ideological obfuscation, Thomson's goddess of Liberty insists that a united sense of purpose among those of otherwise different allegiances can redeem the nation, a moral imperative that thinly veils its partisan basis, Bolingbroke's Oppositionist coalition of Whigs and Tories against Walpole:

> If any *nobler Passion* yet remain,
> Let all MY *Sons* all *Parties* fling aside,
> Despise their *Nonsense,* and together join;

Let *Worth* and *Virtue,* scorning low Despair,
Exerted full, from every Quarter shine,
Commix'd in heighten'd Blaze.

Collins refrains from suggesting such judgmental and polemical moral expedients, along with the assumption that the destiny of a nation lies in the hands of its public leaders. Instead, Collins posits and questions the possible conditions for the arrival of Liberty in England: what heroic action is possible in the contemporary political, cultural, or moral climate? what deeds can contemporary patriotic poetry celebrate or seek? what qualities of independence, hope, or endurance are needed in 1746, a time of danger at home and abroad?

To answer these questions, one may examine some further ways in which Collins redirects some traditional devices of the "progress piece." Each poet's depiction of a Platonic Temple of Liberty, a *topos* that supposedly illustrates the continuities between Thomson and Collins, reveals obviously different functions for this allegorical tableau and indicates a subtle, ambivalent response of the later to the earlier poet. Thomson invokes this idealized state in order to account for the absence of Liberty from European nations during the Middle Ages. The goddess of Liberty tells the curious poet that her spirit has departed from the world during the "wintry Age" much as the "Tribes Aërial" migrate southward in colder seasons. Accounting for the hiatus in cultural progress between Classical Rome and the Renaissance, Thomson also uses this digression to hint at the humanly unattainable ideal of his poem, a Miltonically-tinged portrait of cultural heaven:

> IN the bright Regions there of purest Day,
> Far other Scenes, and Palaces, arise,
> Adorn'd profuse with other Arts divine.
> All Beauty here below, to them compar'd,
> Would, like a Rose before the mid-day Sun,
> Shrink up it's [sic] Blossom; like a Bubble break
> The passing poor Magnificence of Kings.
> For there the KING OF NATURE, in full Blaze,
> Calls every Splendor forth; and there his Court
> Amid Ætherial Powers, and Virtues, holds:
> Angel, Archangel, tutelary Gods,
> Of Cities, Nations, Empires, and of Worlds.
> But Sacred be the Veil, that kindly clouds
> A Light too keen for Mortals,; [sic] wraps a
>   View
> Too softening Fair, for Those that here in Dust
> Must chearful toil out their appointed Years
> A Sense of higher Life would only damp
> The School-Boy's Task, and spoil his playful
>   Hours.

Not surprisingly, Thomson grants great material wealth to the spiritual forms of virtue, "Angel, Archangel, tutelary Gods," whose wisdom and beauty the intensity of divine light conceals. True to the poem's unremitting Whig ideology, a secular commercial and cultural heaven also justifies the menial labor of those who "chearful toil out their appointed Years," as if this ideal is the common

man's spiritual reward. Thomson withholds a full view of this scene from mortal eyes, and resorts to one of his favorite metaphors in this poem, childhood, to characterize life on earth in relation to the grand scheme of cultural progress. These lines come from a speech by the goddess of Liberty that closes part 3 and helps effect the broad historical leap from medieval Italy to Britain after the Renaissance and into the mid-eighteenth century. In the next two books Britain will represent the highest earthly manifestation of the goddess's cultural ideals, but in a poem about continuing progress, the rhetorical scheme of the history must always leave room for improvement, especially if the poet wishes to conclude with the "infancy" of Liberty in Britain. The inevitable decline of Liberty, depicted in Thomson's accounts of Greece, Rome, and Italy, is inherent in the westward progress of civilization. Thus this brief glimpse of an immutable ideal of progress gives the already advanced state of English culture even higher goals toward which it may strive, or at least a spiritual model that governs its secular activity.

Collins also draws a supernal model of Liberty, but enlarges upon its function in his ode. Rather than making the Temple of Liberty the final goal of all progressive teleologies, he meditates upon this emblem about the problematic conditions of national freedom. Collins describes its embodiment in a mythic England, for he wishes to recover the spirit of the lost Druid temples, reminders of a supernatural past when spiritual figures roamed the earth. Various elements from other parts of Thomson's poem have also infiltrated this passage: the Temple is an architectural mixture of Gothic and Grecian forms, or traditions of northern and Mediterranean liberty; the Druids are also the spiritual ancestors of current British independence. The ode, however, is unique in restoring the importance of the visionary poet to the temple:

> Yet still, if Truth those Beams infuse,
> Which guide at once, and charm the Muse,
> Beyond yon braided Clouds that lie,
> Paving the light-embroider'd Sky:
> Amidst the bright pavilion'd Plains,
> The beauteous *Model* still remains.
>
> . . . . .
>
> Ev'n now before his favor'd Eyes,
> In *Gothic* pride it seems to rise!
> Yet *Græcia*'s graceful Orders join
> Majestic thro' the mix'd Design;
> The secret Builder knew to chuse,
> Each sphere-found Gem of richest Hues:
> Whate'er Heav'n's purer Mold contains,
> When nearer Suns emblaze its Veins.

The poet has now become the "favor'd" beholder of this vision, if not the surrogate builder. He alone reveals the story that has never been told and endows it with features that only he can communicate, and thus represent to the nation. The allusive and ceremonial nature of this scene, however, enables Collins's ascent towards visionary poetry, a movement away from the strictly cultural record of Liberty and toward eternal truths about inherent English freedom. The mythological apparatus becomes part of the legendary setting and is not simply one more vehicle for recounting the deeds of the past or appropriating a native tradition of Liberty strictly from the facts. This temple is not like Thomson's, a secular narrative substitution to account for the absence of authentic freedom during any particular time or to show a providential Liberty guiding history. In contrast, Collins has departed from the course of real time in this and the previous strophe, to contemplate the shadowy mythical past of Britain rather than progressing to any current phenomena in a linear historical way. His ode builds up to an almost exclusively psychological, intuitive state; an anticipation of liberty; a collective national anxiety. The political themes are also further complicated in this half-factual, half-mythical Whiggish progress, an ambivalent hope for international concord, if not for a Pax Britannica. A consideration of Thomson's more explicitly polemical messages will reinforce the major differences.

The tone of *Liberty* rarely falls short of firm confidence in the progressive strength of Britain's cultural, economic, and political institutions. As noted, Thomson places himself in the role of an innocent child in order to assume a position of incomplete knowledge, an intimation of Liberty's arrival but hardly a full understanding of her potential, especially regarding England's destiny. Thomson, the author of the unabashedly patriotic song **"Rule, Britannia,"** wishes to assert a scheme of meliorism, in which England's best years lie ahead. Yet there are perils, perhaps unanticipated, that await an author who assumes an innocent faith in the future greatness of his state and believes in its current progress, limited only by the periodic need to dispense with corrupt political leaders. In what amounts to a virtual compendium of eighteenth-century Whig historical models, Thomson makes no apologies for his jingoism, which, besides promoting a straightforwardly Oppositionist view of internal politics, often expresses an unbounded desire for British commercial dominance overseas:

> Theirs the Triumph be,
> By deep *Invention*'s keen pervading Eye,
> The Heart of *Courage,* and the Hand of *Toil,*
> Each conquer'd Ocean staining with their Blood,
> Instead of Treasure robb'd by ruffian War,
> Round social Earth to circle fair Exchange,
> And bind the Nations in a golden Chain.

> The Winds and Seas are BRITAIN's wide
>   Domain;
> And not a Sail, but by Permission, spreads.

Thomson's bluntly asserted confidence in a belligerent mercantile superiority often produces unintentional humor, but sometimes his claims reveal crises in national ideology that are exposed in their full contradictory state, willingly or not. In a section dealing with upper-class abuse of wealth by gambling, idle luxury, and excessive debt, Thomson invokes a not-so-innocent metaphor of the noble savage:

> O far superior *Afric*'s sable Sons,
> By Merchant pilfer'd, to these *willing Slaves*!
>   [i.e., those members of the patrician class who
>   have incurred gambling debts]
> And, rich, as unsqueez'd Favourite, to them,
> Is he who can his *Virtue* boast alone!

Such luxurious and idle vices stand in pronounced opposition to the main intention of **Liberty,** to promote civic humanism, a combination of "INDEPENDENT LIFE; / INTEGRITY IN OFFICE; and, . . . / . . . A PASSION FOR THE COMMONWEAL. Although Thomson unquestionably scorns those who abuse their wealth and proper station in society, his chain of comparisons raises some disturbing ideological contradictions. As long as a patrician leader holds on to independent "virtue," or freedom from political corruption and economic obligation (vices that Walpole's government routinely embodies for Thomson), his moral character holds greater "wealth" than the rich who are implicated in the false economy of gambling and, more generally, "luxury" or self-interested expenditure. Yet the "unsqueez'd Favourite," any member of the landed classes who can lend money and thus be drawn into his peers' mutually destructive cycle of debt, is potentially the victim of others' vices, just as the "virtuous" slave is potentially the victim of British economic depredation, and perhaps more importantly, just as the virtuous independent gentleman may be corrupted by political engagement. Even if one disregards Thomson's ambivalent representation of the slave trade—it may involve "pilfering" but also instills a tragically innocent moral character in its victims, and undoubtedly propels the mercantile economy—this metaphor still leaves a larger problem unanswered, namely the servitude of the "independent" civic leader to the goals of the nation and his possible implication in debased politics. The fiercest expressions of Thomson's moral anxiety are directed mainly towards internal corruption, and, except for his objections to Walpole's pacifist trade policy with France, he deprecates any show of military force, prefers a Pax Britannica or a commercial empire of "free" trade, and frequently appeals to classical republicanism or a native tradition of British civil rights to assure a peaceful national order. Nonetheless, the poet of **Liberty** draws a rigidly polemical division between good and evil, and many of the terms that define this opposition are politically encoded. For example, when Thomson promotes "thrift" and "industry" over "luxury" and "indolence," he signals his loyal attachment to antiministerial Whig mercantile politics and chastises those who do not care to march under this banner. Besides accepting any policies of commercial dominance and their possible ill consequences, like slavery, the individual whom Thomson entreats to be "independent" has a sharply defined enemy among his compatriots and must unite with his fellow civic leaders to eradicate this inner evil. Not able to reconcile his faith in commercial progress with the venal reality of political leadership, Thomson eventually settles for the private innocence of his ideal patrician class. The independent man's "little Kingdom" becomes a retreat from the corrupt political arena:

> Mean time *true-judgin moderate Desires,*

Oeconomy and *Taste,* combin'd, direct
His clear Affairs, and from *debauching Fiends*
Secure his little Kingdom.

As will be explained, Collins recognizes a similar dilemma when he attempts to reconcile his patriotism with his poetic role as a spokesman for the nation's conscience. Yet his efforts reflect a more thoroughgoing engagement with both national and individual moral responsibilities. To a lesser extent than Thomson's progress piece, Collins's ode belongs to a genre of Whig panegyrics that entertain ideas of a British peace and rely upon republican rhetoric to take a stance on contemporary political affairs. Just as Thomson has Walpole's politics in mind when he assaults vice and corruption, so too does Collins allude to Britain's detrimental and self-incriminating role in the War of Austrian Succession. He invites Concord to arrive at *"Britain's* ravag'd Shore," a metaphoric projection of a country's anguish over its military losses on the Continent, even if ravagings closer to home, such as the Pretender's uprising of 1745, were also a recent fear. The usually inert matter of the progress poem's tour through Europe takes on a new life because of the Continent's vulnerability to war. The ode includes topical references to the Austrian conquest of Genoa ("Sad *Liguria's* bleeding State" and The Netherlands, a current battleground. Collins invigorates the "common places" of the progress so that they allude to the current plight of international liberty through the traditional historical tour of southern and western European states. But Collins's vision of peace is not as straightforward a matter as Thomson's; it depends on factors unrelated to industry and a watchful check of corruption. To show that historical vicissitudes may undermine the greatest freedoms and contaminate a nation's moral character, Collins reflects on his country's engagement in war. The representations of Liberty in his poem are always accompanied by violence and debilitating damage, and his guiding personification is always in flight, taking refuge from repeated dangers. After the downfall of Rome, portrayed allegorically as the vandalism of a "Giant-statue," the only remains of Liberty are the occasionally found fragments of the whole classical ideal:

Yet ev'n, where'er the least appear'd,
Th' admiring World thy Hand rever'd;
Still 'midst the scatter'd States around,
Some Remnants of Her Strength were found;
They saw by what escap'd the Storm,
How wond'rous rose her perfect Form;
How in the great the labour'd Whole,
Each mighty Master pour'd his Soul!

Detecting yet another detail that hints at the instability of freedom, Paul Sherwin has observed that in the procession at the poem's conclusion, it is not Liberty but rather a syntactically shifted substitution of Concord that arrives—perhaps implying that Liberty is only an ideal and that peace with France may be attained but not necessarily with individual freedom guaranteed. In any event, this is a poem where Collins frustratedly tries to transcend the "ravag'd" political milieu of his time and hark back to an idealistic tradition for a solution. This attempt to recover the past may result in momentary tranquility at the cost of discovering the present ideological imprisonment, the inability of the poet to speak out conclusively as either an enraged prophet or a druidic visionary. The conditions of Collins's struggle are worth investigating, however, for they illuminate the contradictions among political ideology, inherited poetic forms, and jarring historical circumstance. Put simply, these are attempts to transcend Whiggish claims by writing an ode in 1746 that substantially departs from patriotic conventions and resists the facile conclusion of accepting a happy, productive, progressive state. The author of odes to Fear, Pity, and Mercy also develops new ground for an individualistic, psychologically expressive voice of national political concern.

As a politically responsive poet, Collins does not merely accept the conventional rhetoric of a "Whig panegyric" at face value, but uses his ode to critique and modify the inherited ideology. Aside from an international vision that equates Liberty with free trade, cultural progress, and benevolent autonomous republicanism, a number of Whig code words pervade the poem. Referring to the idealized temple of Liberty as a mixture of *"Gothic* Pride" and *"Græcia's* graceful Orders," the poet draws upon an intricate network of meanings, which extend beyond the purely aesthetic notions of "energy" and "form." The connotations of "Gothic," however harmless its context might seem, were by no means fixed even as late as 1746. Even if a new wave of "Gothic" architecture was becoming fashionable and helping to grant the term an apolitical sense, this trend should not obscure some other contemporary senses of the word, such as its use in political writings to refer to "constitutional and democratic forms of government" and its original denotation of a wild northern tribe. The architectural terms correspond to the vocabulary of contemporary political debates on the merits of constitutional governments based in popular rights versus a strong "Grecian" monarchy with "vested aristocratic interests," though Collins mainly suggests a reconciliation between "Gothic" and "classical" models of Whig republicanism, with his pun on the "Orders" of a "mix'd Design"—i.e., a balanced but class-stratified government. These senses of "Gothic" and "Grecian" may seem to overdetermine a portrait of a temple that plainly embodies a "concord" of mixed desires, passion and order, or self and society, or even the northern and Mediterranean traditions of European Liberty's progress. Yet Collins shows that he is alert to the political meanings in a poem that continually depicts conflicts between personal liberty and governmental order with no particular resolution other than frustration. The temple, then, allegorizes the precarious coexistence of individual liberty and state order, each of which can quickly degenerate into, respectively, barbarism and tyranny. This pattern of unending violent confrontations holds true from the very beginning of the poem, where Time's "Northern Sons of Spoil" invade classical Rome, and continues through the descriptions of Liberty historically threatened by external violence—e.g., the persecution of William Tell during Austria's fourteenth-century invasion of Switzerland, the Spanish suppression of the 1567 Protestant revolt in The Netherlands. Conversely, the ode reveals that Liberty has needed to assert herself through acts of violence such as revenge upon tyrants or a mythic geological cataclysm that literally tears Britain from the continent, an allegory of "natural" but disruptively forceful independence. Most importantly, in the fables that the ode strings together, Collins concedes that the origins of a free, culturally developed state are based in acts of mutual destruction and personal sacrifices, not all of which are honorable. As Walter Benjamin would assert over two hundred years later, "There is no document of civilization which is not at the same time a document of barbarism."

In any poem that recounts some characteristic struggles of Liberty in Western civilization, each event enacts a different form of violence. Sometimes they are legends about individual heroes or events, and at other times they are allegorical depictions, like the "Giant-statue" Rome that Gothic Vandals overturn and shatter. As the poem progresses, moving deeply into the realm of the legendary and supernatural, Collins incorporates this cycle of liberty and violence into a natural myth; that is, he not only traces this pattern historically, but digresses through "Time's backward Rolls" to create a myth of origin and choose a set of legends that explains some ambiguous circumstances surrounding the ideal of Liberty. Among these problems, the poem asks why Liberty is weaker now than it once was and seems "lost"; why the need to engage in violent military action is inseparably linked to Liberty; why a desire for peace at any cost can outweigh a desire for genuine Liberty. Thus Concord, rather than Liberty, actually arrives on Britain's "ravag'd Shore" at the poem's visionary conclusion. This is a figure who successfully lulls Anger and Rage into a temporary state of British social harmony, international security, and personal solace.

The fables in the ode, culminating in the final vision of the temple, neither evade present social reality nor offer a political solution that a poet can propose with a clean conscience. On the whole, they depict a lost age of Liberty in an attempt to grasp the full, contradictory nature of the tensions between individual freedom and national politics. Collins is no less nationalistic than Thomson: he takes pride in Britain's "blest Divorce" from the Continent and adorns this privileged isle with tutelary spirits who "check . . . the west'ring Tide." Yet a poet who fully understands the vicissitudes of time, its effects upon nations, and the struggles that accompany the birth and sustenance of liberty, can hope only to arrest the tide or momentarily to defer "progress." Collins ultimately surrenders to political expediency; whatever solution is soothing to the nation is acceptable to him. The temple that the poet unveils, however much it recounts the triumphant battles and indigenous energies of legendary Britain, is also a trope that freezes the destructive course of time or, in psychological terms, sublimates further violent impulses:

> There on the Walls the *Patriot's* Sight,
> May ever hang with fresh Delight,
> And, grav'd with some Prophetic Rage,
> Read *Albion*'s Fame thro' ev'ry Age.

Even the poet is implicated in this contradictory monument to the national heritage. On the one hand, the temple helps to define an inherently nationalistic character and record a mythologized history of British triumphs, much as Collins does in the latter third of his ode. On the other hand, the movement is a halting, quieting one that suppresses both the fury of the military heroes, now "retir'd in Glory," and the "Rage" of the poetic voice, now "grav'd" (implying both inscription and death) on the temple walls. Thus Collins adopts an anxiously patriotic but nonetheless passive role in accepting but not daring to speak out in "Prophetic Rage" against British involvement in the War of Austrian Succession. This militarism could be countered only by the politically expedient negotiations for peace taking place in late autumn 1746 at Breda.

To his favor, and in contrast to Thomson, Collins does not see Liberty as a pure ideal and does not subscribe to a politically partisan ethics that blames the loss of Liberty on the corruption of leaders and influential citizens. There is no "Walpole" in this poem whom Collins can scapegoat as the most serious threat to freedom. The psychological complexity of Collins's ode can only locate violence and freedom on two sides of the same coin, a relationship illustrated by the heroic youths who must murder tyrants in order to liberate Athens, "At once the Breath of Fear and Virtue shedding." Liberty cannot exist without violence towards some oppressor, but when it does thrive, violence from a potential threat is always imminent. The seeds of destruction are almost inevitably sown into Liberty, as in medieval Florence before the Medicis dominated and "quench'd her Flame," when they became patrons of the arts without allowing republican democracy. The repetitions of archetypal transgressions within the ode—for example, the desecration of temples or sacred statues, the murder of tyrants during the festival of Athena—only make the situation of Liberty more psychologically complicated, without being any less relevant to immediate history than in Thomson.

To the terrifying circumstances attendant upon Liberty, the conclusion offers perhaps the best response that can be hoped for. A wish for Concord and Peace instead of Liberty is consistent with the pattern of the rest of the poem, a desire to arrest the bloody cycle of liberation and violence, and for the deferring, even the purgation, of time with a deceptive retreat from factual history and a checking of the "west'ring Tide." The way to gain Liberty, then, is not to assume a British monopoly upon it like Thomson and attempt to weed out its enemies, for this approach will only perpetuate a cycle of destructive scapegoating and multiply the evils and sorrows that accompany the wish. With his characteristic reluctance to draw moral absolutes, Collins offers no ready-made solution to the same problem, perhaps because he writes from a position less conducive to liberty, namely, the later stages of an unpopular war. His poem, however, is one of anticipation rather than celebration, and even though he faces the future less confidently, Collins suggests a fuller comprehension of liberty, experientially, psychologically, and even historically, for although Thomson provides a greater extent of historical material, it is put in the service of

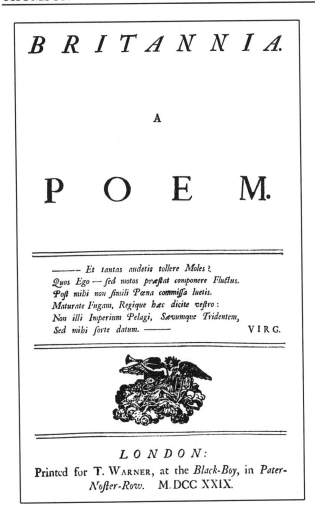

First-edition title page of Britannia: A Poem.

will be ineffectual because the victim is not capable of attracting the community's violence; in the second case, the differences between "sacred" and "impure" violence may be effaced. One may argue that Thomson's *Liberty* is a transparent example of the first type of sacrificial crisis, whereas Collins's ode is conscious of and tries to forestall the second. Because Thomson relies on so sharp a distinction between the morally upstanding retired country gentleman and the fallen world of Walpole's political regime (or, by analogy, members of the leisured classes who fall sway to luxury, gambling, and other false economies), he cannot resolve the contradictions between historical fate and individual agency. If the corruption of political leaders is always inevitable, and if the country gentleman loses his advantageous, innocent "prospect" of society by engaging in its reform, then the process of scapegoating is doomed to be reenacted and the advancements of Liberty are undermined in England, just as they have been in classical Greece and Rome.

In contrast, from its very first lines, Collins's "Ode to Liberty" raises some confusion about who needs to oppose whom, and for what cause, in securing national freedom. When he asks the rhetorical questions "Who shall awake the *Spartan* Fife" and "What New *Alcæus,* Fancy-blest, / Shall sing the Sword, in Myrtles drest," Collins suggests either that no one in modern society is capable of liberating it from tyrants, or that the situation does not warrant such "heroic" action. The ode depicts a regressive cycle of violent acts that both establish a tenuous Liberty and suppress it, and this history is redeemed only by recourse to the mythological, prelapsarian past of England's original independence and freedom. If the ode's most redemptive gesture is to halt the destructive "progress" of Liberty, to arrest its bloody cycles of violence, then Collins is all too aware of England's complicity in international war or political oppression and cannot in good faith point to an enemy like the French or, in other contexts, the Pretender's allies as victims worthy of sacrifice.

FURTHER READING

Barrell, John. *The Idea of Landscape and the Sense of Place, 1730-1840: An Approach to the Poetry of John Clare.* Cambridge: Cambridge University Press, 1972, 244 p.

> Discusses the influence of Italian landscape painting on Thomson's poetic technique, as well as Thomson's impact on the poetry of Clare.

Brown, Marshall. "The Urbane Sublime: Formal Balance in Thomson and Collins." In his *Preromanticism*, pp. 29-34. Stanford, Calif.: Stanford University Press, 1991.

> Offers an analysis of the style of eighteenth-century sublime poetry exemplified by *The Seasons* and William Collins's *Odes*.

Campbell, Hilbert H. *James Thomson.* Boston: Twayne Publishers, 1979, 175 p.

> Introductory biographical and critical study. Campbell traces the life and major works of Thomson, and

cataloguing victories or defeats of Liberty, and he too easily dispenses with the possibility that a wish for Liberty may be imperiled and should be accompanied by fear. Even his acknowledgment of political corruption suggests over-optimistically that a change of leaders, a bipartisan Oppositionist coalition, or a period of retirement will cleanse the vices. A truly desirable state of freedom, however, cannot be achieved but can only be imagined, for Collins represents it as the recovery of a lost, innocent, mythic past, a state that he reluctantly prophesies in order to free the nation from the destiny of "real" history and purges with a qualified hope of delayed gratification.

To characterize this change in the means and ends of eighteenth-century political poetry, René Girard's analyses of scapegoating rituals are pertinent to both Collins's and Thomsons's roles in attempting to address public crises and heal the state. In his discussion of sacrificial crises, Girard accounts for the failures of either "too little" or "too much" continuity between the victim and the community.

In the first case, the sacrifice and scapegoating process

examines his reputation and influence.

Spencer, Jeffry B. "James Thomson and Ideal Landscape: The Triumph of Pictorialism." In his *Heroic Nature: Ideal Landscape in English Poetry from Marvell to Thomson,* pp. 253-95. Evanston, Ill.: Northwestern University Press, 1973.

Examines the ways in which the descriptive technique of *The Seasons* and *The Castle of Indolence* stem from Thomson's considerable appreciation of the visual arts.

Stormer, Phillip Ronald. "Holding 'High Converse with the Mighty Dead': Morality and Politics in James Thomson's *Winter.*" *English Language Notes* XXIX, No. 3 (March 1992): 27-40.

An in-depth, focused examination of a single key passage in *Winter*.

Additional coverage of Thomson's life and career is contained in the following sources published by Gale Research: *Literature Criticism from 1400 to 1800,* **Vol. 16; and** *Dictionary of Literary Biography,* **Vol. 95.**

Literature
Criticism from
1400 to 1800

Cumulative Indexes

How to Use This Index

The main references

Calvino, Italo
1923-1985.....CLC 5, 8, 11, 22, 33, 39,
73; SSC 3

list all author entries in the following Gale Literary Criticism series:

BLC = *Black Literature Criticism*
CLC = *Contemporary Literary Criticism*
CLR = *Children's Literature Review*
CMLC = *Classical and Medieval Literature Criticism*
DA = *DISCovering Authors*
DC = *Drama Criticism*
HLC = *Hispanic Literature Criticism*
LC = *Literature Criticism from 1400 to 1800*
NCLC = *Nineteenth-Century Literature Criticism*
PC = *Poetry Criticism*
SSC = *Short Story Criticism*
TCLC = *Twentieth-Century Literary Criticism*
WLC = *World Literature Criticism, 1500 to the Present*

The cross-references

See also CANR 23; CA 85-88;
obituary CA 116

list all author entries in the following Gale biographical and literary sources:

AAYA = *Authors & Artists for Young Adults*
AITN = *Authors in the News*
BEST = *Bestsellers*
BW = *Black Writers*
CA = *Contemporary Authors*
CAAS = *Contemporary Authors Autobiography Series*
CABS = *Contemporary Authors Bibliographical Series*
CANR = *Contemporary Authors New Revision Series*
CAP = *Contemporary Authors Permanent Series*
CDALB = *Concise Dictionary of American Literary Biography*
CDBLB = *Concise Dictionary of British Literary Biography*
DLB = *Dictionary of Literary Biography*
DLBD = *Dictionary of Literary Biography Documentary Series*
DLBY = *Dictionary of Literary Biography Yearbook*
HW = *Hispanic Writers*
JRDA = *Junior DISCovering Authors*
MAICYA = *Major Authors and Illustrators for Children and Young Adults*
MTCW = *Major 20th-Century Writers*
NNAL = *Native North American Literature*
SAAS = *Something about the Author Autobiography Series*
SATA = *Something about the Author*
YABC = *Yesterday's Authors of Books for Children*

Literary Criticism Series
Cumulative Author Index

Anthony, Peter
See Shaffer, Anthony (Joshua); Shaffer, Peter (Levin)

Anthony, Piers 1934- . . . . **CLC 35**
See also AAYA 11; CA 21-24R; CANR 28; DLB 8; MTCW

Antoine, Marc
See Proust, (Valentin-Louis-George-Eugene-) Marcel

Antoninus, Brother
See Everson, William (Oliver)

Antonioni, Michelangelo 1912- . . . . . **CLC 20**
See also CA 73-76; CANR 45

Antschel, Paul 1920-1970
See Celan, Paul
See also CA 85-88; CANR 33; MTCW

Anwar, Chairil 1922-1949 . . . . **TCLC 22**
See also CA 121

Apollinaire, Guillaume . . **TCLC 3, 8, 51; PC 7**
See also Kostrowitzki, Wilhelm Apollinaris de

Appelfeld, Aharon 1932- . . . . **CLC 23, 47**
See also CA 112; 133

Apple, Max (Isaac) 1941- . . . . **CLC 9, 33**
See also CA 81-84; CANR 19; DLB 130

Appleman, Philip (Dean) 1926- . . . . . **CLC 51**
See also CA 13-16R; CAAS 18; CANR 6, 29

Appleton, Lawrence
See Lovecraft, H(oward) P(hillips)

Apteryx
See Eliot, T(homas) S(tearns)

Apuleius, (Lucius Madaurensis)
125(?)-175(?) . . . . **CMLC 1**

Aquin, Hubert 1929-1977 . . . . **CLC 15**
See also CA 105; DLB 53

Aragon, Louis 1897-1982 . . . . **CLC 3, 22**
See also CA 69-72; 108; CANR 28; DLB 72; MTCW

Arany, Janos 1817-1882 . . . . **NCLC 34**

Arbuthnot, John 1667-1735 . . . . **LC 1**
See also DLB 101

Archer, Herbert Winslow
See Mencken, H(enry) L(ouis)

Archer, Jeffrey (Howard) 1940- . . . **CLC 28**
See also BEST 89:3; CA 77-80; CANR 22

Archer, Jules 1915- . . . . **CLC 12**
See also CA 9-12R; CANR 6; SAAS 5; SATA 4

Archer, Lee
See Ellison, Harlan (Jay)

Arden, John 1930- . . . . **CLC 6, 13, 15**
See also CA 13-16R; CAAS 4; CANR 31; DLB 13; MTCW

Arenas, Reinaldo
1943-1990 . . . . **CLC 41; HLC**
See also CA 124; 128; 133; DLB 145; HW

Arendt, Hannah 1906-1975 . . . . **CLC 66**
See also CA 17-20R; 61-64; CANR 26; MTCW

Aretino, Pietro 1492-1556 . . . . **LC 12**

Arghezi, Tudor . . . . **CLC 80**
See also Theodorescu, Ion N.

Arguedas, Jose Maria
1911-1969 . . . . **CLC 10, 18**
See also CA 89-92; DLB 113; HW

Argueta, Manlio 1936- . . . . **CLC 31**
See also CA 131; DLB 145; HW

Ariosto, Ludovico 1474-1533 . . . . **LC 6**

Aristides
See Epstein, Joseph

Aristophanes
450B.C.-385B.C. . . . . **CMLC 4; DA; DC 2**

Arlt, Roberto (Godofredo Christophersen)
1900-1942 . . . . **TCLC 29; HLC**
See also CA 123; 131; HW

Armah, Ayi Kwei 1939- . . . . **CLC 5, 33; BLC**
See also BW 1; CA 61-64; CANR 21; DLB 117; MTCW

Armatrading, Joan 1950- . . . . **CLC 17**
See also CA 114

Arnette, Robert
See Silverberg, Robert

Arnim, Achim von (Ludwig Joachim von Arnim) 1781-1831 . . . . **NCLC 5**
See also DLB 90

Arnim, Bettina von 1785-1859 . . . . **NCLC 38**
See also DLB 90

Arnold, Matthew
1822-1888 . . . . . **NCLC 6, 29; DA; PC 5; WLC**
See also CDBLB 1832-1890; DLB 32, 57

Arnold, Thomas 1795-1842 . . . . . . **NCLC 18**
See also DLB 55

Arnow, Harriette (Louisa) Simpson
1908-1986 . . . . **CLC 2, 7, 18**
See also CA 9-12R; 118; CANR 14; DLB 6; MTCW; SATA 42; SATA-Obit 47

Arp, Hans
See Arp, Jean

Arp, Jean 1887-1966 . . . . **CLC 5**
See also CA 81-84; 25-28R; CANR 42

Arrabal
See Arrabal, Fernando

Arrabal, Fernando 1932- . . . **CLC 2, 9, 18, 58**
See also CA 9-12R; CANR 15

Arrick, Fran . . . . **CLC 30**

Artaud, Antonin 1896-1948 . . . . . **TCLC 3, 36**
See also CA 104

Arthur, Ruth M(abel) 1905-1979 . . . . **CLC 12**
See also CA 9-12R; 85-88; CANR 4; SATA 7, 26

Artsybashev, Mikhail (Petrovich)
1878-1927 . . . . **TCLC 31**

Arundel, Honor (Morfydd)
1919-1973 . . . . **CLC 17**
See also CA 21-22; 41-44R; CAP 2; CLR 35; SATA 4; SATA-Obit 24

Asch, Sholem 1880-1957 . . . . **TCLC 3**
See also CA 105

Ash, Shalom
See Asch, Sholem

Ashbery, John (Lawrence)
1927- . . . . . . **CLC 2, 3, 4, 6, 9, 13, 15, 25, 41, 77**
See also CA 5-8R; CANR 9, 37; DLB 5; DLBY 81; MTCW

Ashdown, Clifford
See Freeman, R(ichard) Austin

Ashe, Gordon
See Creasey, John

Ashton-Warner, Sylvia (Constance)
1908-1984 . . . . **CLC 19**
See also CA 69-72; 112; CANR 29; MTCW

Asimov, Isaac
1920-1992 . . . . . . **CLC 1, 3, 9, 19, 26, 76**
See also AAYA 13; BEST 90:2; CA 1-4R; 137; CANR 2, 19, 36; CLR 12; DLB 8; DLBY 92; JRDA; MAICYA; MTCW; SATA 1, 26, 74

Astley, Thea (Beatrice May)
1925- . . . . **CLC 41**
See also CA 65-68; CANR 11, 43

Aston, James
See White, T(erence) H(anbury)

Asturias, Miguel Angel
1899-1974 . . . . **CLC 3, 8, 13; HLC**
See also CA 25-28; 49-52; CANR 32; CAP 2; DLB 113; HW; MTCW

Atares, Carlos Saura
See Saura (Atares), Carlos

Atheling, William
See Pound, Ezra (Weston Loomis)

Atheling, William, Jr.
See Blish, James (Benjamin)

Atherton, Gertrude (Franklin Horn)
1857-1948 . . . . **TCLC 2**
See also CA 104; DLB 9, 78

Atherton, Lucius
See Masters, Edgar Lee

Atkins, Jack
See Harris, Mark

Atticus
See Fleming, Ian (Lancaster)

Atwood, Margaret (Eleanor)
1939- . . . . . **CLC 2, 3, 4, 8, 13, 15, 25, 44, 84; DA; PC 8; SSC 2; WLC**
See also AAYA 12; BEST 89:2; CA 49-52; CANR 3, 24, 33; DLB 53; MTCW; SATA 50

Aubigny, Pierre d'
See Mencken, H(enry) L(ouis)

Aubin, Penelope 1685-1731(?) . . . . **LC 9**
See also DLB 39

Auchincloss, Louis (Stanton)
1917- . . . . **CLC 4, 6, 9, 18, 45**
See also CA 1-4R; CANR 6, 29; DLB 2; DLBY 80; MTCW

Auden, W(ystan) H(ugh)
1907-1973 . . . . . . **CLC 1, 2, 3, 4, 6, 9, 11, 14, 43; DA; PC 1; WLC**
See also CA 9-12R; 45-48; CANR 5; CDBLB 1914-1945; DLB 10, 20; MTCW

Audiberti, Jacques 1900-1965 . . . . . . **CLC 38**
See also CA 25-28R

Audubon, John James
1785-1851 . . . . **NCLC 47**

Auel, Jean M(arie) 1936- . . . . **CLC 31**
See also AAYA 7; BEST 90:4; CA 103; CANR 21

Auerbach, Erich 1892-1957 . . . . **TCLC 43**
See also CA 118

Barker, Howard 1946-. . . . . **CLC 37**
See also CA 102; DLB 13

Barker, Pat 1943-. . . . . **CLC 32**
See also CA 117; 122

Barlow, Joel 1754-1812 . . . . **NCLC 23**
See also DLB 37

Barnard, Mary (Ethel) 1909-. . . . . . . **CLC 48**
See also CA 21-22; CAP 2

Barnes, Djuna
1892-1982 . . . **CLC 3, 4, 8, 11, 29; SSC 3**
See also CA 9-12R; 107; CANR 16; DLB 4,
9, 45; MTCW

Barnes, Julian 1946-. . . . . **CLC 42**
See also CA 102; CANR 19; DLBY 93

Barnes, Peter 1931- . . . . **CLC 5, 56**
See also CA 65-68; CAAS 12; CANR 33,
34; DLB 13; MTCW

Baroja (y Nessi), Pio
1872-1956 . . . . **TCLC 8; HLC**
See also CA 104

Baron, David
See Pinter, Harold

Baron Corvo
See Rolfe, Frederick (William Serafino
Austin Lewis Mary)

Barondess, Sue K(aufman)
1926-1977 . . . . **CLC 8**
See also Kaufman, Sue
See also CA 1-4R; 69-72; CANR 1

Baron de Teive
See Pessoa, Fernando (Antonio Nogueira)

Barres, Maurice 1862-1923 . . . . **TCLC 47**
See also DLB 123

Barreto, Afonso Henrique de Lima
See Lima Barreto, Afonso Henrique de

Barrett, (Roger) Syd 1946- . . . . **CLC 35**

Barrett, William (Christopher)
1913-1992 . . . . **CLC 27**
See also CA 13-16R; 139; CANR 11

Barrie, J(ames) M(atthew)
1860-1937 . . . . **TCLC 2**
See also CA 104; 136; CDBLB 1890-1914;
CLR 16; DLB 10, 141; MAICYA;
YABC 1

Barrington, Michael
See Moorcock, Michael (John)

Barrol, Grady
See Bograd, Larry

Barry, Mike
See Malzberg, Barry N(athaniel)

Barry, Philip 1896-1949. . . . . **TCLC 11**
See also CA 109; DLB 7

Bart, Andre Schwarz
See Schwarz-Bart, Andre

Barth, John (Simmons)
1930- . . . . . . **CLC 1, 2, 3, 5, 7, 9, 10, 14,
27, 51; SSC 10**
See also AITN 1, 2; CA 1-4R; CABS 1;
CANR 5, 23; DLB 2; MTCW

Barthelme, Donald
1931-1989 . . . . . . **CLC 1, 2, 3, 5, 6, 8, 13,
23, 46, 59; SSC 2**
See also CA 21-24R; 129; CANR 20;
DLB 2; DLBY 80, 89; MTCW; SATA 7;
SATA-Obit 62

Barthelme, Frederick 1943-. . . . . . . **CLC 36**
See also CA 114; 122; DLBY 85

Barthes, Roland (Gerard)
1915-1980 . . . . **CLC 24, 83**
See also CA 130; 97-100; MTCW

Barzun, Jacques (Martin) 1907- . . . . **CLC 51**
See also CA 61-64; CANR 22

Bashevis, Isaac
See Singer, Isaac Bashevis

Bashkirtseff, Marie 1859-1884 . . . **NCLC 27**

Basho
See Matsuo Basho

Bass, Kingsley B., Jr.
See Bullins, Ed

Bass, Rick 1958-. . . . . **CLC 79**
See also CA 126

Bassani, Giorgio 1916-. . . . . **CLC 9**
See also CA 65-68; CANR 33; DLB 128;
MTCW

Bastos, Augusto (Antonio) Roa
See Roa Bastos, Augusto (Antonio)

Bataille, Georges 1897-1962 . . . . **CLC 29**
See also CA 101; 89-92

Bates, H(erbert) E(rnest)
1905-1974 . . . . **CLC 46; SSC 10**
See also CA 93-96; 45-48; CANR 34;
MTCW

Bauchart
See Camus, Albert

Baudelaire, Charles
1821-1867 . . . . . **NCLC 6, 29; DA; PC 1;
SSC 18; WLC**

Baudrillard, Jean 1929-. . . . . **CLC 60**

Baum, L(yman) Frank 1856-1919 . . . **TCLC 7**
See also CA 108; 133; CLR 15; DLB 22;
JRDA; MAICYA; MTCW; SATA 18

Baum, Louis F.
See Baum, L(yman) Frank

Baumbach, Jonathan 1933-. . . . . . . **CLC 6, 23**
See also CA 13-16R; CAAS 5; CANR 12;
DLBY 80; MTCW

Bausch, Richard (Carl) 1945- . . . . . . **CLC 51**
See also CA 101; CAAS 14; CANR 43;
DLB 130

Baxter, Charles 1947-. . . . . **CLC 45, 78**
See also CA 57-60; CANR 40; DLB 130

Baxter, George Owen
See Faust, Frederick (Schiller)

Baxter, James K(eir) 1926-1972 . . . . **CLC 14**
See also CA 77-80

Baxter, John
See Hunt, E(verette) Howard, (Jr.)

Bayer, Sylvia
See Glassco, John

Baynton, Barbara 1857-1929. . . . . . **TCLC 57**

Beagle, Peter S(oyer) 1939-. . . . . **CLC 7**
See also CA 9-12R; CANR 4; DLBY 80;
SATA 60

Bean, Normal
See Burroughs, Edgar Rice

Beard, Charles A(ustin)
1874-1948 . . . . **TCLC 15**
See also CA 115; DLB 17; SATA 18

Beardsley, Aubrey 1872-1898 . . . . . **NCLC 6**

Beattie, Ann
1947- . . . . **CLC 8, 13, 18, 40, 63; SSC 11**
See also BEST 90:2; CA 81-84; DLBY 82;
MTCW

Beattie, James 1735-1803 . . . . **NCLC 25**
See also DLB 109

Beauchamp, Kathleen Mansfield 1888-1923
See Mansfield, Katherine
See also CA 104; 134; DA

Beaumarchais, Pierre-Augustin Caron de
1732-1799 . . . . **DC 4**

**Beauvoir, Simone (Lucie Ernestine Marie
Bertrand) de**
1908-1986 . . . . **CLC 1, 2, 4, 8, 14, 31, 44,
50, 71; DA; WLC**
See also CA 9-12R; 118; CANR 28;
DLB 72; DLBY 86; MTCW

Becker, Jurek 1937-. . . . . **CLC 7, 19**
See also CA 85-88; DLB 75

Becker, Walter 1950-. . . . . **CLC 26**

Beckett, Samuel (Barclay)
1906-1989 . . . . . . **CLC 1, 2, 3, 4, 6, 9, 10,
11, 14, 18, 29, 57, 59, 83; DA; SSC 16;
WLC**
See also CA 5-8R; 130; CANR 33;
CDBLB 1945-1960; DLB 13, 15;
DLBY 90; MTCW

Beckford, William 1760-1844 . . . . **NCLC 16**
See also DLB 39

Beckman, Gunnel 1910-. . . . . **CLC 26**
See also CA 33-36R; CANR 15; CLR 25;
MAICYA; SAAS 9; SATA 6

Becque, Henri 1837-1899. . . . . **NCLC 3**

Beddoes, Thomas Lovell
1803-1849 . . . . **NCLC 3**
See also DLB 96

Bedford, Donald F.
See Fearing, Kenneth (Flexner)

Beecher, Catharine Esther
1800-1878 . . . . **NCLC 30**
See also DLB 1

Beecher, John 1904-1980. . . . . **CLC 6**
See also AITN 1; CA 5-8R; 105; CANR 8

Beer, Johann 1655-1700. . . . . **LC 5**

Beer, Patricia 1924-. . . . . **CLC 58**
See also CA 61-64; CANR 13, 46; DLB 40

Beerbohm, Henry Maximilian
1872-1956 . . . . **TCLC 1, 24**
See also CA 104; DLB 34, 100

Beerbohm, Max
See Beerbohm, Henry Maximilian

Begiebing, Robert J(ohn) 1946-. . . . . **CLC 70**
See also CA 122; CANR 40

Behan, Brendan
1923-1964 . . . . **CLC 1, 8, 11, 15, 79**
See also CA 73-76; CANR 33;
CDBLB 1945-1960; DLB 13; MTCW

Behn, Aphra
1640(?)-1689 . . . . **LC 1; DA; DC 4; WLC**
See also DLB 39, 80, 131

Behrman, S(amuel) N(athaniel)
1893-1973 . . . . **CLC 40**
See also CA 13-16; 45-48; CAP 1; DLB 7,
44

Boethius 480(?)-524(?) . . . . **CMLC 15**
See also DLB 115

Bogan, Louise
1897-1970 . . . . . . **CLC 4, 39, 46; PC 12**
See also CA 73-76; 25-28R; CANR 33;
DLB 45; MTCW

Bogarde, Dirk . . . . **CLC 19**
See also Van Den Bogarde, Derek Jules
Gaspard Ulric Niven
See also DLB 14

Bogosian, Eric 1953- . . . . **CLC 45**
See also CA 138

Bograd, Larry 1953- . . . . **CLC 35**
See also CA 93-96; SATA 33

Boiardo, Matteo Maria 1441-1494 . . . . **LC 6**

Boileau-Despreaux, Nicolas
1636-1711 . . . . **LC 3**

Boland, Eavan (Aisling) 1944- . . . **CLC 40, 67**
See also CA 143; DLB 40

Bolt, Lee
See Faust, Frederick (Schiller)

Bolt, Robert (Oxton) 1924- . . . . **CLC 14**
See also CA 17-20R; CANR 35; DLB 13;
MTCW

Bombet, Louis-Alexandre-Cesar
See Stendhal

Bomkauf
See Kaufman, Bob (Garnell)

Bonaventura . . . . **NCLC 35**
See also DLB 90

Bond, Edward 1934- . . . . **CLC 4, 6, 13, 23**
See also CA 25-28R; CANR 38; DLB 13;
MTCW

Bonham, Frank 1914-1989 . . . . **CLC 12**
See also AAYA 1; CA 9-12R; CANR 4, 36;
JRDA; MAICYA; SAAS 3; SATA 1, 49;
SATA-Obit 62

Bonnefoy, Yves 1923- . . . . **CLC 9, 15, 58**
See also CA 85-88; CANR 33; MTCW

Bontemps, Arna(ud Wendell)
1902-1973 . . . . **CLC 1, 18; BLC**
See also BW 1; CA 1-4R; 41-44R; CANR 4,
35; CLR 6; DLB 48, 51; JRDA;
MAICYA; MTCW; SATA 2, 44;
SATA-Obit 24

Booth, Martin 1944- . . . . **CLC 13**
See also CA 93-96; CAAS 2

Booth, Philip 1925- . . . . **CLC 23**
See also CA 5-8R; CANR 5; DLBY 82

Booth, Wayne C(layson) 1921- . . . . . **CLC 24**
See also CA 1-4R; CAAS 5; CANR 3, 43;
DLB 67

Borchert, Wolfgang 1921-1947 . . . . . **TCLC 5**
See also CA 104; DLB 69, 124

Borel, Petrus 1809-1859 . . . . **NCLC 41**

Borges, Jorge Luis
1899-1986 . . . **CLC 1, 2, 3, 4, 6, 8, 9, 10,**
13, 19, 44, 48, 83; DA; HLC; SSC 4;
WLC
See also CA 21-24R; CANR 19, 33;
DLB 113; DLBY 86; HW; MTCW

Borowski, Tadeusz 1922-1951 . . . . . . **TCLC 9**
See also CA 106

Borrow, George (Henry)
1803-1881 . . . . **NCLC 9**
See also DLB 21, 55

Bosman, Herman Charles
1905-1951 . . . . **TCLC 49**

Bosschere, Jean de 1878(?)-1953 . . . **TCLC 19**
See also CA 115

Boswell, James
1740-1795 . . . . **LC 4; DA; WLC**
See also CDBLB 1660-1789; DLB 104, 142

Bottoms, David 1949- . . . . **CLC 53**
See also CA 105; CANR 22; DLB 120;
DLBY 83

Boucicault, Dion 1820-1890 . . . . . . **NCLC 41**

Boucolon, Maryse 1937-
See Conde, Maryse
See also CA 110; CANR 30

Bourget, Paul (Charles Joseph)
1852-1935 . . . . **TCLC 12**
See also CA 107; DLB 123

Bourjaily, Vance (Nye) 1922- . . . . **CLC 8, 62**
See also CA 1-4R; CAAS 1; CANR 2;
DLB 2, 143

Bourne, Randolph S(illiman)
1886-1918 . . . . **TCLC 16**
See also CA 117; DLB 63

Bova, Ben(jamin William) 1932- . . . . **CLC 45**
See also CA 5-8R; CAAS 18; CANR 11;
CLR 3; DLBY 81; MAICYA; MTCW;
SATA 6, 68

Bowen, Elizabeth (Dorothea Cole)
1899-1973 . . . . . . **CLC 1, 3, 6, 11, 15, 22;**
SSC 3
See also CA 17-18; 41-44R; CANR 35;
CAP 2; CDBLB 1945-1960; DLB 15;
MTCW

Bowering, George 1935- . . . . **CLC 15, 47**
See also CA 21-24R; CAAS 16; CANR 10;
DLB 53

Bowering, Marilyn R(uthe) 1949- . . . **CLC 32**
See also CA 101

Bowers, Edgar 1924- . . . . **CLC 9**
See also CA 5-8R; CANR 24; DLB 5

Bowie, David . . . . **CLC 17**
See also Jones, David Robert

Bowles, Jane (Sydney)
1917-1973 . . . . **CLC 3, 68**
See also CA 19-20; 41-44R; CAP 2

Bowles, Paul (Frederick)
1910- . . . . **CLC 1, 2, 19, 53; SSC 3**
See also CA 1-4R; CAAS 1; CANR 1, 19;
DLB 5, 6; MTCW

Box, Edgar
See Vidal, Gore

Boyd, Nancy
See Millay, Edna St. Vincent

Boyd, William 1952- . . . . . . **CLC 28, 53, 70**
See also CA 114; 120

Boyle, Kay
1902-1992 . . . . . **CLC 1, 5, 19, 58; SSC 5**
See also CA 13-16R; 140; CAAS 1;
CANR 29; DLB 4, 9, 48, 86; DLBY 93;
MTCW

Boyle, Mark
See Kienzle, William X(avier)

Boyle, Patrick 1905-1982 . . . . **CLC 19**
See also CA 127

Boyle, T. C.
See Boyle, T(homas) Coraghessan

Boyle, T(homas) Coraghessan
1948- . . . . **CLC 36, 55; SSC 16**
See also BEST 90:4; CA 120; CANR 44;
DLBY 86

Boz
See Dickens, Charles (John Huffam)

Brackenridge, Hugh Henry
1748-1816 . . . . **NCLC 7**
See also DLB 11, 37

Bradbury, Edward P.
See Moorcock, Michael (John)

Bradbury, Malcolm (Stanley)
1932- . . . . **CLC 32, 61**
See also CA 1-4R; CANR 1, 33; DLB 14;
MTCW

Bradbury, Ray (Douglas)
1920- . . . **CLC 1, 3, 10, 15, 42; DA; WLC**
See also AITN 1, 2; CA 1-4R; CANR 2, 30;
CDALB 1968-1988; DLB 2, 8; MTCW;
SATA 11, 64

Bradford, Gamaliel 1863-1932 . . . . . **TCLC 36**
See also DLB 17

Bradley, David (Henry, Jr.)
1950- . . . . **CLC 23; BLC**
See also BW 1; CA 104; CANR 26; DLB 33

Bradley, John Ed(mund, Jr.)
1958- . . . . **CLC 55**
See also CA 139

Bradley, Marion Zimmer 1930- . . . . . **CLC 30**
See also AAYA 9; CA 57-60; CAAS 10;
CANR 7, 31; DLB 8; MTCW

Bradstreet, Anne
1612(?)-1672 . . . . **LC 4; DA; PC 10**
See also CDALB 1640-1865; DLB 24

Brady, Joan 1939- . . . . **CLC 86**
See also CA 141

Bragg, Melvyn 1939- . . . . **CLC 10**
See also BEST 89:3; CA 57-60; CANR 10;
DLB 14

Braine, John (Gerard)
1922-1986 . . . . **CLC 1, 3, 41**
See also CA 1-4R; 120; CANR 1, 33;
CDBLB 1945-1960; DLB 15; DLBY 86;
MTCW

Brammer, William 1930(?)-1978 . . . . **CLC 31**
See also CA 77-80

Brancati, Vitaliano 1907-1954 . . . . . **TCLC 12**
See also CA 109

Brancato, Robin F(idler) 1936- . . . . . **CLC 35**
See also AAYA 9; CA 69-72; CANR 11,
45; CLR 32; JRDA; SAAS 9; SATA 23

Brand, Max
See Faust, Frederick (Schiller)

Brand, Millen 1906-1980 . . . . **CLC 7**
See also CA 21-24R; 97-100

Branden, Barbara . . . . **CLC 44**

Brandes, Georg (Morris Cohen)
1842-1927 . . . . **TCLC 10**
See also CA 105

Brandys, Kazimierz 1916- . . . . **CLC 62**

Branley, Franklyn M(ansfield)
1915- . . . . **CLC 21**
See also CA 33-36R; CANR 14, 39;
CLR 13; MAICYA; SAAS 16; SATA 4,
68

Brathwaite, Edward Kamau 1930-. . . **CLC 11**
See also BW 2; CA 25-28R; CANR 11, 26,
47; DLB 125

Brautigan, Richard (Gary)
1935-1984 . . . . **CLC 1, 3, 5, 9, 12, 34, 42**
See also CA 53-56; 113; CANR 34; DLB 2,
5; DLBY 80, 84; MTCW; SATA 56

Braverman, Kate 1950- . . . . **CLC 67**
See also CA 89-92

Brecht, Bertolt
1898-1956 . . . . . . **TCLC 1, 6, 13, 35; DA;
DC 3; WLC**
See also CA 104; 133; DLB 56, 124; MTCW

Brecht, Eugen Berthold Friedrich
See Brecht, Bertolt

Bremer, Fredrika 1801-1865 . . . . . **NCLC 11**

Brennan, Christopher John
1870-1932 . . . . **TCLC 17**
See also CA 117

Brennan, Maeve 1917-. . . . . **CLC 5**
See also CA 81-84

Brentano, Clemens (Maria)
1778-1842 . . . . **NCLC 1**
See also DLB 90

Brent of Bin Bin
See Franklin, (Stella Maraia Sarah) Miles

Brenton, Howard 1942-. . . . . **CLC 31**
See also CA 69-72; CANR 33; DLB 13;
MTCW

Breslin, James 1930-
See Breslin, Jimmy
See also CA 73-76; CANR 31; MTCW

Breslin, Jimmy . . . . **CLC 4, 43**
See also Breslin, James
See also AITN 1

Bresson, Robert 1907- . . . . **CLC 16**
See also CA 110

Breton, Andre 1896-1966. . . **CLC 2, 9, 15, 54**
See also CA 19-20; 25-28R; CANR 40;
CAP 2; DLB 65; MTCW

Breytenbach, Breyten 1939(?)- . . **CLC 23, 37**
See also CA 113; 129

Bridgers, Sue Ellen 1942- . . . . **CLC 26**
See also AAYA 8; CA 65-68; CANR 11,
36; CLR 18; DLB 52; JRDA; MAICYA;
SAAS 1; SATA 22

Bridges, Robert (Seymour)
1844-1930 . . . . **TCLC 1**
See also CA 104; CDBLB 1890-1914;
DLB 19, 98

Bridie, James. . . . . **TCLC 3**
See also Mavor, Osborne Henry
See also DLB 10

Brin, David 1950-. . . . . **CLC 34**
See also CA 102; CANR 24; SATA 65

Brink, Andre (Philippus)
1935-. . . . . **CLC 18, 36**
See also CA 104; CANR 39; MTCW

Brinsmead, H(esba) F(ay) 1922- . . . . **CLC 21**
See also CA 21-24R; CANR 10; MAICYA;
SAAS 5; SATA 18, 78

Brittain, Vera (Mary)
1893(?)-1970 . . . . **CLC 23**
See also CA 13-16; 25-28R; CAP 1; MTCW

Broch, Hermann 1886-1951 . . . . . . **TCLC 20**
See also CA 117; DLB 85, 124

Brock, Rose
See Hansen, Joseph

Brodkey, Harold 1930-. . . . . **CLC 56**
See also CA 111; DLB 130

Brodsky, Iosif Alexandrovich 1940-
See Brodsky, Joseph
See also AITN 1; CA 41-44R; CANR 37;
MTCW

Brodsky, Joseph . . **CLC 4, 6, 13, 36, 50; PC 9**
See also Brodsky, Iosif Alexandrovich

Brodsky, Michael Mark 1948- . . . . . **CLC 19**
See also CA 102; CANR 18, 41

Bromell, Henry 1947-. . . . . **CLC 5**
See also CA 53-56; CANR 9

Bromfield, Louis (Brucker)
1896-1956 . . . . **TCLC 11**
See also CA 107; DLB 4, 9, 86

Broner, E(sther) M(asserman)
1930- . . . . **CLC 19**
See also CA 17-20R; CANR 8, 25; DLB 28

Bronk, William 1918-. . . . . **CLC 10**
See also CA 89-92; CANR 23

Bronstein, Lev Davidovich
See Trotsky, Leon

Bronte, Anne 1820-1849. . . . . **NCLC 4**
See also DLB 21

Bronte, Charlotte
1816-1855 . . . **NCLC 3, 8, 33; DA; WLC**
See also CDBLB 1832-1890; DLB 21

Bronte, (Jane) Emily
1818-1848 . . . . **NCLC 16, 35; DA; PC 8;
WLC**
See also CDBLB 1832-1890; DLB 21, 32

Brooke, Frances 1724-1789 . . . . **LC 6**
See also DLB 39, 99

Brooke, Henry 1703(?)-1783 . . . . **LC 1**
See also DLB 39

Brooke, Rupert (Chawner)
1887-1915 . . . . **TCLC 2, 7; DA; WLC**
See also CA 104; 132; CDBLB 1914-1945;
DLB 19; MTCW

Brooke-Haven, P.
See Wodehouse, P(elham) G(renville)

Brooke-Rose, Christine 1926-. . . . . . **CLC 40**
See also CA 13-16R; DLB 14

Brookner, Anita 1928-. . . . . . **CLC 32, 34, 51**
See also CA 114; 120; CANR 37; DLBY 87;
MTCW

Brooks, Cleanth 1906-1994 . . . . . **CLC 24, 86**
See also CA 17-20R; 145; CANR 33, 35;
DLB 63; DLBY 94; MTCW

Brooks, George
See Baum, L(yman) Frank

Brooks, Gwendolyn
1917- . . . . . . **CLC 1, 2, 4, 5, 15, 49; BLC;
DA; PC 7; WLC**
See also AITN 1; BW 2; CA 1-4R;
CANR 1, 27; CDALB 1941-1968;
CLR 27; DLB 5, 76; MTCW; SATA 6

Brooks, Mel. . . . . **CLC 12**
See also Kaminsky, Melvin
See also AAYA 13; DLB 26

Brooks, Peter 1938-. . . . . **CLC 34**
See also CA 45-48; CANR 1

Brooks, Van Wyck 1886-1963. . . . . . **CLC 29**
See also CA 1-4R; CANR 6; DLB 45, 63,
103

Brophy, Brigid (Antonia)
1929-. . . . . **CLC 6, 11, 29**
See also CA 5-8R; CAAS 4; CANR 25;
DLB 14; MTCW

Brosman, Catharine Savage 1934-. . . . **CLC 9**
See also CA 61-64; CANR 21, 46

Brother Antoninus
See Everson, William (Oliver)

Broughton, T(homas) Alan 1936- . . . **CLC 19**
See also CA 45-48; CANR 2, 23

Broumas, Olga 1949-. . . . . **CLC 10, 73**
See also CA 85-88; CANR 20

Brown, Charles Brockden
1771-1810 . . . . **NCLC 22**
See also CDALB 1640-1865; DLB 37, 59,
73

Brown, Christy 1932-1981 . . . . **CLC 63**
See also CA 105; 104; DLB 14

Brown, Claude 1937- . . . . **CLC 30; BLC**
See also AAYA 7; BW 1; CA 73-76

Brown, Dee (Alexander) 1908- . . **CLC 18, 47**
See also CA 13-16R; CAAS 6; CANR 11,
45; DLBY 80; MTCW; SATA 5

Brown, George
See Wertmueller, Lina

Brown, George Douglas
1869-1902 . . . . **TCLC 28**

Brown, George Mackay 1921-. . . . **CLC 5, 48**
See also CA 21-24R; CAAS 6; CANR 12,
37; DLB 14, 27, 139; MTCW; SATA 35

Brown, (William) Larry 1951-. . . . . . **CLC 73**
See also CA 130; 134

Brown, Moses
See Barrett, William (Christopher)

Brown, Rita Mae 1944-. . . . . **CLC 18, 43, 79**
See also CA 45-48; CANR 2, 11, 35;
MTCW

Brown, Roderick (Langmere) Haig-
See Haig-Brown, Roderick (Langmere)

Brown, Rosellen 1939-. . . . . **CLC 32**
See also CA 77-80; CAAS 10; CANR 14, 44

Brown, Sterling Allen
1901-1989 . . . . **CLC 1, 23, 59; BLC**
See also BW 1; CA 85-88; 127; CANR 26;
DLB 48, 51, 63; MTCW

Brown, Will
See Ainsworth, William Harrison

Brown, William Wells
1813-1884 . . . . **NCLC 2; BLC; DC 1**
See also DLB 3, 50

Browne, (Clyde) Jackson 1948(?)-... **CLC 21**
See also CA 120

Browning, Elizabeth Barrett
1806-1861 ..... **NCLC 1, 16; DA; PC 6; WLC**
See also CDBLB 1832-1890; DLB 32

Browning, Robert
1812-1889 .... **NCLC 19; DA; PC 2**
See also CDBLB 1832-1890; DLB 32; YABC 1

Browning, Tod 1882-1962 .... **CLC 16**
See also CA 141; 117

Bruccoli, Matthew J(oseph) 1931- .. **CLC 34**
See also CA 9-12R; CANR 7; DLB 103

Bruce, Lenny .... **CLC 21**
See also Schneider, Leonard Alfred

Bruin, John
See Brutus, Dennis

Brulard, Henri
See Stendhal

Brulls, Christian
See Simenon, Georges (Jacques Christian)

Brunner, John (Kilian Houston)
1934- .... **CLC 8, 10**
See also CA 1-4R; CAAS 8; CANR 2, 37; MTCW

Bruno, Giordano 1548-1600........ **LC 27**

Brutus, Dennis 1924- .... **CLC 43; BLC**
See also BW 2; CA 49-52; CAAS 14; CANR 2, 27, 42; DLB 117

Bryan, C(ourtlandt) D(ixon) B(arnes)
1936- .... **CLC 29**
See also CA 73-76; CANR 13

Bryan, Michael
See Moore, Brian

Bryant, William Cullen
1794-1878 .... **NCLC 6, 46; DA**
See also CDALB 1640-1865; DLB 3, 43, 59

Bryusov, Valery Yakovlevich
1873-1924 .... **TCLC 10**
See also CA 107

Buchan, John 1875-1940 .... **TCLC 41**
See also CA 108; 145; DLB 34, 70; YABC 2

Buchanan, George 1506-1582 .... **LC 4**

Buchheim, Lothar-Guenther 1918- ... **CLC 6**
See also CA 85-88

Buchner, (Karl) Georg
1813-1837 .... **NCLC 26**

Buchwald, Art(hur) 1925-.......... **CLC 33**
See also AITN 1; CA 5-8R; CANR 21; MTCW; SATA 10

Buck, Pearl S(ydenstricker)
1892-1973 .... **CLC 7, 11, 18; DA**
See also AITN 1; CA 1-4R; 41-44R; CANR 1, 34; DLB 9, 102; MTCW; SATA 1, 25

Buckler, Ernest 1908-1984........ **CLC 13**
See also CA 11-12; 114; CAP 1; DLB 68; SATA 47

Buckley, Vincent (Thomas)
1925-1988 .... **CLC 57**
See also CA 101

Buckley, William F(rank), Jr.
1925- .... **CLC 7, 18, 37**
See also AITN 1; CA 1-4R; CANR 1, 24; DLB 137; DLBY 80; MTCW

Buechner, (Carl) Frederick
1926- .... **CLC 2, 4, 6, 9**
See also CA 13-16R; CANR 11, 39; DLBY 80; MTCW

Buell, John (Edward) 1927-........ **CLC 10**
See also CA 1-4R; DLB 53

Buero Vallejo, Antonio 1916- ... **CLC 15, 46**
See also CA 106; CANR 24; HW; MTCW

Bufalino, Gesualdo 1920(?)-........ **CLC 74**

Bugayev, Boris Nikolayevich 1880-1934
See Bely, Andrey
See also CA 104

Bukowski, Charles
1920-1994 .... **CLC 2, 5, 9, 41, 82**
See also CA 17-20R; 144; CANR 40; DLB 5, 130; MTCW

Bulgakov, Mikhail (Afanas'evich)
1891-1940 .... **TCLC 2, 16; SSC 18**
See also CA 105

Bulgya, Alexander Alexandrovich
1901-1956 .... **TCLC 53**
See also Fadeyev, Alexander
See also CA 117

Bullins, Ed 1935- .... **CLC 1, 5, 7; BLC**
See also BW 2; CA 49-52; CAAS 16; CANR 24, 46; DLB 7, 38; MTCW

Bulwer-Lytton, Edward (George Earle Lytton)
1803-1873 .... **NCLC 1, 45**
See also DLB 21

Bunin, Ivan Alexeyevich
1870-1953 .... **TCLC 6; SSC 5**
See also CA 104

Bunting, Basil 1900-1985.... **CLC 10, 39, 47**
See also CA 53-56; 115; CANR 7; DLB 20

Bunuel, Luis 1900-1983 .. **CLC 16, 80; HLC**
See also CA 101; 110; CANR 32; HW

Bunyan, John 1628-1688 .. **LC 4; DA; WLC**
See also CDBLB 1660-1789; DLB 39

Burckhardt, Jacob (Christoph)
1818-1897 .... **NCLC 49**

Burford, Eleanor
See Hibbert, Eleanor Alice Burford

Burgess, Anthony
. **CLC 1, 2, 4, 5, 8, 10, 13, 15, 22, 40, 62, 81**
See also Wilson, John (Anthony) Burgess
See also AITN 1; CDBLB 1960 to Present; DLB 14

Burke, Edmund
1729(?)-1797 .... **LC 7; DA; WLC**
See also DLB 104

Burke, Kenneth (Duva)
1897-1993 .... **CLC 2, 24**
See also CA 5-8R; 143; CANR 39; DLB 45, 63; MTCW

Burke, Leda
See Garnett, David

Burke, Ralph
See Silverberg, Robert

Burney, Fanny 1752-1840 ...... **NCLC 12**
See also DLB 39

Burns, Robert 1759-1796 ...... **LC 29; PC 6**
See also CDBLB 1789-1832; DA; DLB 109; WLC

Burns, Tex
See L'Amour, Louis (Dearborn)

Burnshaw, Stanley 1906-..... **CLC 3, 13, 44**
See also CA 9-12R; DLB 48

Burr, Anne 1937- .... **CLC 6**
See also CA 25-28R

Burroughs, Edgar Rice
1875-1950 .... **TCLC 2, 32**
See also AAYA 11; CA 104; 132; DLB 8; MTCW; SATA 41

Burroughs, William S(eward)
1914- .... **CLC 1, 2, 5, 15, 22, 42, 75; DA; WLC**
See also AITN 2; CA 9-12R; CANR 20; DLB 2, 8, 16, 152; DLBY 81; MTCW

Burton, Richard F. 1821-1890.... **NCLC 42**
See also DLB 55

Busch, Frederick 1941- ... **CLC 7, 10, 18, 47**
See also CA 33-36R; CAAS 1; CANR 45; DLB 6

Bush, Ronald 1946- .... **CLC 34**
See also CA 136

Bustos, F(rancisco)
See Borges, Jorge Luis

Bustos Domecq, H(onorio)
See Bioy Casares, Adolfo; Borges, Jorge Luis

Butler, Octavia E(stelle) 1947- ..... **CLC 38**
See also BW 2; CA 73-76; CANR 12, 24, 38; DLB 33; MTCW

Butler, Robert Olen (Jr.) 1945-..... **CLC 81**
See also CA 112

Butler, Samuel 1612-1680 .... **LC 16**
See also DLB 101, 126

Butler, Samuel
1835-1902 ...... **TCLC 1, 33; DA; WLC**
See also CA 143; CDBLB 1890-1914; DLB 18, 57

Butler, Walter C.
See Faust, Frederick (Schiller)

Butor, Michel (Marie Francois)
1926- .... **CLC 1, 3, 8, 11, 15**
See also CA 9-12R; CANR 33; DLB 83; MTCW

Buzo, Alexander (John) 1944-...... **CLC 61**
See also CA 97-100; CANR 17, 39

Buzzati, Dino 1906-1972 .... **CLC 36**
See also CA 33-36R

Byars, Betsy (Cromer) 1928-....... **CLC 35**
See also CA 33-36R; CANR 18, 36; CLR 1, 16; DLB 52; JRDA; MAICYA; MTCW; SAAS 1; SATA 4, 46, 80

Byatt, A(ntonia) S(usan Drabble)
1936- .... **CLC 19, 65**
See also CA 13-16R; CANR 13, 33; DLB 14; MTCW

Byrne, David 1952-............... **CLC 26**
See also CA 127

Byrne, John Keyes 1926-
See Leonard, Hugh
See also CA 102

Clavell, James (duMaresq)
1925-1994 . . . . **CLC 6, 25, 87**
See also CA 25-28R; 146; CANR 26;
MTCW

Cleaver, (Leroy) Eldridge
1935- . . . . **CLC 30; BLC**
See also BW 1; CA 21-24R; CANR 16

Cleese, John (Marwood) 1939- . . . . . **CLC 21**
See also Monty Python
See also CA 112; 116; CANR 35; MTCW

Cleishbotham, Jebediah
See Scott, Walter

Cleland, John 1710-1789 . . . . **LC 2**
See also DLB 39

Clemens, Samuel Langhorne 1835-1910
See Twain, Mark
See also CA 104; 135; CDALB 1865-1917;
DA; DLB 11, 12, 23, 64, 74; JRDA;
MAICYA; YABC 2

Cleophil
See Congreve, William

Clerihew, E.
See Bentley, E(dmund) C(lerihew)

Clerk, N. W.
See Lewis, C(live) S(taples)

Cliff, Jimmy . . . . **CLC 21**
See also Chambers, James

Clifton, (Thelma) Lucille
1936- . . . . **CLC 19, 66; BLC**
See also BW 2; CA 49-52; CANR 2, 24, 42;
CLR 5; DLB 5, 41; MAICYA; MTCW;
SATA 20, 69

Clinton, Dirk
See Silverberg, Robert

Clough, Arthur Hugh 1819-1861 . . **NCLC 27**
See also DLB 32

Clutha, Janet Paterson Frame 1924-
See Frame, Janet
See also CA 1-4R; CANR 2, 36; MTCW

Clyne, Terence
See Blatty, William Peter

Cobalt, Martin
See Mayne, William (James Carter)

Cobbett, William 1763-1835 . . . . . **NCLC 49**
See also DLB 43, 107

Coburn, D(onald) L(ee) 1938- . . . . . . **CLC 10**
See also CA 89-92

Cocteau, Jean (Maurice Eugene Clement)
1889-1963 . . . . **CLC 1, 8, 15, 16, 43; DA;
WLC**
See also CA 25-28; CANR 40; CAP 2;
DLB 65; MTCW

Codrescu, Andrei 1946- . . . . **CLC 46**
See also CA 33-36R; CAAS 19; CANR 13,
34

Coe, Max
See Bourne, Randolph S(illiman)

Coe, Tucker
See Westlake, Donald E(dwin)

Coetzee, J(ohn) M(ichael)
1940- . . . . **CLC 23, 33, 66**
See also CA 77-80; CANR 41; MTCW

Coffey, Brian
See Koontz, Dean R(ay)

Cohen, Arthur A(llen)
1928-1986 . . . . **CLC 7, 31**
See also CA 1-4R; 120; CANR 1, 17, 42;
DLB 28

Cohen, Leonard (Norman)
1934- . . . . **CLC 3, 38**
See also CA 21-24R; CANR 14; DLB 53;
MTCW

Cohen, Matt 1942- . . . . **CLC 19**
See also CA 61-64; CAAS 18; CANR 40;
DLB 53

Cohen-Solal, Annie 19(?)- . . . . **CLC 50**

Colegate, Isabel 1931- . . . . **CLC 36**
See also CA 17-20R; CANR 8, 22; DLB 14;
MTCW

Coleman, Emmett
See Reed, Ishmael

Coleridge, Samuel Taylor
1772-1834 . . **NCLC 9; DA; PC 11; WLC**
See also CDBLB 1789-1832; DLB 93, 107

Coleridge, Sara 1802-1852 . . . . . . **NCLC 31**

Coles, Don 1928- . . . . **CLC 46**
See also CA 115; CANR 38

Colette, (Sidonie-Gabrielle)
1873-1954 . . . . . . **TCLC 1, 5, 16; SSC 10**
See also CA 104; 131; DLB 65; MTCW

Collett, (Jacobine) Camilla (Wergeland)
1813-1895 . . . . **NCLC 22**

Collier, Christopher 1930- . . . . **CLC 30**
See also AAYA 13; CA 33-36R; CANR 13,
33; JRDA; MAICYA; SATA 16, 70

Collier, James L(incoln) 1928- . . . . . **CLC 30**
See also AAYA 13; CA 9-12R; CANR 4,
33; CLR 3; JRDA; MAICYA; SATA 8,
70

Collier, Jeremy 1650-1726 . . . . **LC 6**

Collins, Hunt
See Hunter, Evan

Collins, Linda 1931- . . . . **CLC 44**
See also CA 125

Collins, (William) Wilkie
1824-1889 . . . . **NCLC 1, 18**
See also CDBLB 1832-1890; DLB 18, 70

Collins, William 1721-1759 . . . . **LC 4**
See also DLB 109

Colman, George
See Glassco, John

Colt, Winchester Remington
See Hubbard, L(afayette) Ron(ald)

Colter, Cyrus 1910- . . . . **CLC 58**
See also BW 1; CA 65-68; CANR 10;
DLB 33

Colton, James
See Hansen, Joseph

Colum, Padraic 1881-1972 . . . . **CLC 28**
See also CA 73-76; 33-36R; CANR 35;
CLR 36; MAICYA; MTCW; SATA 15

Colvin, James
See Moorcock, Michael (John)

Colwin, Laurie (E.)
1944-1992 . . . . **CLC 5, 13, 23, 84**
See also CA 89-92; 139; CANR 20, 46;
DLBY 80; MTCW

Comfort, Alex(ander) 1920- . . . . **CLC 7**
See also CA 1-4R; CANR 1, 45

Comfort, Montgomery
See Campbell, (John) Ramsey

Compton-Burnett, I(vy)
1884(?)-1969 . . . . **CLC 1, 3, 10, 15, 34**
See also CA 1-4R; 25-28R; CANR 4;
DLB 36; MTCW

Comstock, Anthony 1844-1915 . . . . **TCLC 13**
See also CA 110

Conan Doyle, Arthur
See Doyle, Arthur Conan

Conde, Maryse 1937- . . . . **CLC 52**
See also Boucolon, Maryse
See also BW 2

Condillac, Etienne Bonnot de
1714-1780 . . . . **LC 26**

Condon, Richard (Thomas)
1915- . . . . **CLC 4, 6, 8, 10, 45**
See also BEST 90:3; CA 1-4R; CAAS 1;
CANR 2, 23; MTCW

Congreve, William
1670-1729 . . . **LC 5, 21; DA; DC 2; WLC**
See also CDBLB 1660-1789; DLB 39, 84

Connell, Evan S(helby), Jr.
1924- . . . . **CLC 4, 6, 45**
See also AAYA 7; CA 1-4R; CAAS 2;
CANR 2, 39; DLB 2; DLBY 81; MTCW

Connelly, Marc(us Cook)
1890-1980 . . . . **CLC 7**
See also CA 85-88; 102; CANR 30; DLB 7;
DLBY 80; SATA-Obit 25

Connor, Ralph . . . . **TCLC 31**
See also Gordon, Charles William
See also DLB 92

Conrad, Joseph
1857-1924 . . . . **TCLC 1, 6, 13, 25, 43, 57;
DA; SSC 9; WLC**
See also CA 104; 131; CDBLB 1890-1914;
DLB 10, 34, 98; MTCW; SATA 27

Conrad, Robert Arnold
See Hart, Moss

Conroy, Pat 1945- . . . . **CLC 30, 74**
See also AAYA 8; AITN 1; CA 85-88;
CANR 24; DLB 6; MTCW

Constant (de Rebecque), (Henri) Benjamin
1767-1830 . . . . **NCLC 6**
See also DLB 119

Conybeare, Charles Augustus
See Eliot, T(homas) S(tearns)

Cook, Michael 1933- . . . . **CLC 58**
See also CA 93-96; DLB 53

Cook, Robin 1940- . . . . **CLC 14**
See also BEST 90:2; CA 108; 111;
CANR 41

Cook, Roy
See Silverberg, Robert

Cooke, Elizabeth 1948- . . . . **CLC 55**
See also CA 129

Cooke, John Esten 1830-1886 . . . . . **NCLC 5**
See also DLB 3

Cooke, John Estes
See Baum, L(yman) Frank

Cooke, M. E.
See Creasey, John

Cooke, Margaret
See Creasey, John

Cooney, Ray .... **CLC 62**

Cooper, Douglas 1960- .... **CLC 86**

Cooper, Henry St. John
See Creasey, John

Cooper, J. California .... **CLC 56**
See also AAYA 12; BW 1; CA 125

Cooper, James Fenimore
1789-1851 .... **NCLC 1, 27**
See also CDALB 1640-1865; DLB 3;
SATA 19

Coover, Robert (Lowell)
1932- .. **CLC 3, 7, 15, 32, 46, 87; SSC 15**
See also CA 45-48; CANR 3, 37; DLB 2;
DLBY 81; MTCW

Copeland, Stewart (Armstrong)
1952- .... **CLC 26**

Coppard, A(lfred) E(dgar)
1878-1957 .... **TCLC 5**
See also CA 114; YABC 1

Coppee, Francois 1842-1908 ...... **TCLC 25**

Coppola, Francis Ford 1939- .... **CLC 16**
See also CA 77-80; CANR 40; DLB 44

Corbiere, Tristan 1845-1875 ..... **NCLC 43**

Corcoran, Barbara 1911- .... **CLC 17**
See also AAYA 14; CA 21-24R; CAAS 2;
CANR 11, 28; DLB 52; JRDA; SAAS 20;
SATA 3, 77

Cordelier, Maurice
See Giraudoux, (Hippolyte) Jean

Corelli, Marie 1855-1924 .... **TCLC 51**
See also Mackay, Mary
See also DLB 34

Corman, Cid .... **CLC 9**
See also Corman, Sidney
See also CAAS 2; DLB 5

Corman, Sidney 1924-
See Corman, Cid
See also CA 85-88; CANR 44

Cormier, Robert (Edmund)
1925- .... **CLC 12, 30; DA**
See also AAYA 3; CA 1-4R; CANR 5, 23;
CDALB 1968-1988; CLR 12; DLB 52;
JRDA; MAICYA; MTCW; SATA 10, 45

Corn, Alfred (DeWitt III) 1943- .... **CLC 33**
See also CA 104; CANR 44; DLB 120;
DLBY 80

Corneille, Pierre 1606-1684 .... **LC 28**

Cornwell, David (John Moore)
1931- .... **CLC 9, 15**
See also le Carre, John
See also CA 5-8R; CANR 13, 33; MTCW

Corso, (Nunzio) Gregory 1930- ... **CLC 1, 11**
See also CA 5-8R; CANR 41; DLB 5, 16;
MTCW

Cortazar, Julio
1914-1984 ...... **CLC 2, 3, 5, 10, 13, 15,
33, 34; HLC; SSC 7**
See also CA 21-24R; CANR 12, 32;
DLB 113; HW; MTCW

Corwin, Cecil
See Kornbluth, C(yril) M.

Cosic, Dobrica 1921- .... **CLC 14**
See also CA 122; 138

Costain, Thomas B(ertram)
1885-1965 .... **CLC 30**
See also CA 5-8R; 25-28R; DLB 9

Costantini, Humberto
1924(?)-1987 .... **CLC 49**
See also CA 131; 122; HW

Costello, Elvis 1955- .... **CLC 21**

Cotter, Joseph Seamon Sr.
1861-1949 .... **TCLC 28; BLC**
See also BW 1; CA 124; DLB 50

Couch, Arthur Thomas Quiller
See Quiller-Couch, Arthur Thomas

Coulton, James
See Hansen, Joseph

Couperus, Louis (Marie Anne)
1863-1923 .... **TCLC 15**
See also CA 115

Coupland, Douglas 1961- .... **CLC 85**
See also CA 142

Court, Wesli
See Turco, Lewis (Putnam)

Courtenay, Bryce 1933- .... **CLC 59**
See also CA 138

Courtney, Robert
See Ellison, Harlan (Jay)

Cousteau, Jacques-Yves 1910- ...... **CLC 30**
See also CA 65-68; CANR 15; MTCW;
SATA 38

Coward, Noel (Peirce)
1899-1973 .... **CLC 1, 9, 29, 51**
See also AITN 1; CA 17-18; 41-44R;
CANR 35; CAP 2; CDBLB 1914-1945;
DLB 10; MTCW

Cowley, Malcolm 1898-1989 .... **CLC 39**
See also CA 5-8R; 128; CANR 3; DLB 4,
48; DLBY 81, 89; MTCW

Cowper, William 1731-1800 ...... **NCLC 8**
See also DLB 104, 109

Cox, William Trevor 1928- ... **CLC 9, 14, 71**
See also Trevor, William
See also CA 9-12R; CANR 4, 37; DLB 14;
MTCW

Coyne, P. J.
See Masters, Hilary

Cozzens, James Gould
1903-1978 .... **CLC 1, 4, 11**
See also CA 9-12R; 81-84; CANR 19;
CDALB 1941-1968; DLB 9; DLBD 2;
DLBY 84; MTCW

Crabbe, George 1754-1832 ...... **NCLC 26**
See also DLB 93

Craig, A. A.
See Anderson, Poul (William)

Craik, Dinah Maria (Mulock)
1826-1887 .... **NCLC 38**
See also DLB 35; MAICYA; SATA 34

Cram, Ralph Adams 1863-1942 .... **TCLC 45**

Crane, (Harold) Hart
1899-1932 .... **TCLC 2, 5; DA; PC 3;
WLC**
See also CA 104; 127; CDALB 1917-1929;
DLB 4, 48; MTCW

Crane, R(onald) S(almon)
1886-1967 .... **CLC 27**
See also CA 85-88; DLB 63

Crane, Stephen (Townley)
1871-1900 ...... **TCLC 11, 17, 32; DA;
SSC 7; WLC**
See also CA 109; 140; CDALB 1865-1917;
DLB 12, 54, 78; YABC 2

Crase, Douglas 1944- .... **CLC 58**
See also CA 106

Crashaw, Richard 1612(?)-1649 ..... **LC 24**
See also DLB 126

Craven, Margaret 1901-1980 ...... **CLC 17**
See also CA 103

Crawford, F(rancis) Marion
1854-1909 .... **TCLC 10**
See also CA 107; DLB 71

Crawford, Isabella Valancy
1850-1887 .... **NCLC 12**
See also DLB 92

Crayon, Geoffrey
See Irving, Washington

Creasey, John 1908-1973 .... **CLC 11**
See also CA 5-8R; 41-44R; CANR 8;
DLB 77; MTCW

Crebillon, Claude Prosper Jolyot de (fils)
1707-1777 .... **LC 28**

Credo
See Creasey, John

Creeley, Robert (White)
1926- ..... **CLC 1, 2, 4, 8, 11, 15, 36, 78**
See also CA 1-4R; CAAS 10; CANR 23, 43;
DLB 5, 16; MTCW

Crews, Harry (Eugene)
1935- .... **CLC 6, 23, 49**
See also AITN 1; CA 25-28R; CANR 20;
DLB 6, 143; MTCW

Crichton, (John) Michael
1942- .... **CLC 2, 6, 54**
See also AAYA 10; AITN 2; CA 25-28R;
CANR 13, 40; DLBY 81; JRDA;
MTCW; SATA 9

Crispin, Edmund .... **CLC 22**
See also Montgomery, (Robert) Bruce
See also DLB 87

Cristofer, Michael 1945(?)- .... **CLC 28**
See also CA 110; DLB 7

Croce, Benedetto 1866-1952 ...... **TCLC 37**
See also CA 120

Crockett, David 1786-1836 ...... **NCLC 8**
See also DLB 3, 11

Crockett, Davy
See Crockett, David

Crofts, Freeman Wills
1879-1957 .... **TCLC 55**
See also CA 115; DLB 77

Croker, John Wilson 1780-1857 .. **NCLC 10**
See also DLB 110

Crommelynck, Fernand 1885-1970 .. **CLC 75**
See also CA 89-92

Cronin, A(rchibald) J(oseph)
1896-1981 .... **CLC 32**
See also CA 1-4R; 102; CANR 5; SATA 47;
SATA-Obit 25

Cross, Amanda
   See Heilbrun, Carolyn G(old)

Crothers, Rachel 1878(?)-1958..... **TCLC 19**
   See also CA 113; DLB 7

Croves, Hal
   See Traven, B.

Crowfield, Christopher
   See Stowe, Harriet (Elizabeth) Beecher

Crowley, Aleister................. **TCLC 7**
   See also Crowley, Edward Alexander

Crowley, Edward Alexander 1875-1947
   See Crowley, Aleister
   See also CA 104

Crowley, John 1942-............. **CLC 57**
   See also CA 61-64; CANR 43; DLBY 82;
     SATA 65

Crud
   See Crumb, R(obert)

Crumarums
   See Crumb, R(obert)

Crumb, R(obert) 1943-............ **CLC 17**
   See also CA 106

Crumbum
   See Crumb, R(obert)

Crumski
   See Crumb, R(obert)

Crum the Bum
   See Crumb, R(obert)

Crunk
   See Crumb, R(obert)

Crustt
   See Crumb, R(obert)

Cryer, Gretchen (Kiger) 1935-...... **CLC 21**
   See also CA 114; 123

Csath, Geza 1887-1919.......... **TCLC 13**
   See also CA 111

Cudlip, David 1933-.............. **CLC 34**

Cullen, Countee
   1903-1946 ...... **TCLC 4, 37; BLC; DA**
   See also BW 1; CA 108; 124;
     CDALB 1917-1929; DLB 4, 48, 51;
     MTCW; SATA 18

Cum, R.
   See Crumb, R(obert)

Cummings, Bruce F(rederick) 1889-1919
   See Barbellion, W. N. P.
   See also CA 123

Cummings, E(dward) E(stlin)
   1894-1962 ...... **CLC 1, 3, 8, 12, 15, 68;**
     DA; PC 5; WLC 2
   See also CA 73-76; CANR 31;
     CDALB 1929-1941; DLB 4, 48; MTCW

Cunha, Euclides (Rodrigues Pimenta) da
   1866-1909 .... **TCLC 24**
   See also CA 123

Cunningham, E. V.
   See Fast, Howard (Melvin)

Cunningham, J(ames) V(incent)
   1911-1985 .... **CLC 3, 31**
   See also CA 1-4R; 115; CANR 1; DLB 5

Cunningham, Julia (Woolfolk)
   1916- .... **CLC 12**
   See also CA 9-12R; CANR 4, 19, 36;
     JRDA; MAICYA; SAAS 2; SATA 1, 26

Cunningham, Michael 1952-...... **CLC 34**
   See also CA 136

Cunninghame Graham, R(obert) B(ontine)
   1852-1936 .... **TCLC 19**
   See also Graham, R(obert) B(ontine)
     Cunninghame
   See also CA 119; DLB 98

Currie, Ellen 19(?)-.............. **CLC 44**

Curtin, Philip
   See Lowndes, Marie Adelaide (Belloc)

Curtis, Price
   See Ellison, Harlan (Jay)

Cutrate, Joe
   See Spiegelman, Art

Czaczkes, Shmuel Yosef
   See Agnon, S(hmuel) Y(osef Halevi)

Dabrowska, Maria (Szumska)
   1889-1965 .... **CLC 15**
   See also CA 106

Dabydeen, David 1955-.......... **CLC 34**
   See also BW 1; CA 125

Dacey, Philip 1939-.............. **CLC 51**
   See also CA 37-40R; CAAS 17; CANR 14,
     32; DLB 105

Dagerman, Stig (Halvard)
   1923-1954 .... **TCLC 17**
   See also CA 117

Dahl, Roald 1916-1990..... **CLC 1, 6, 18, 79**
   See also CA 1-4R; 133; CANR 6, 32, 37;
     CLR 1, 7; DLB 139; JRDA; MAICYA;
     MTCW; SATA 1, 26, 73; SATA-Obit 65

Dahlberg, Edward 1900-1977... **CLC 1, 7, 14**
   See also CA 9-12R; 69-72; CANR 31;
     DLB 48; MTCW

Dale, Colin..................... **TCLC 18**
   See also Lawrence, T(homas) E(dward)

Dale, George E.
   See Asimov, Isaac

Daly, Elizabeth 1878-1967........ **CLC 52**
   See also CA 23-24; 25-28R; CAP 2

Daly, Maureen 1921-............. **CLC 17**
   See also AAYA 5; CANR 37; JRDA;
     MAICYA; SAAS 1; SATA 2

Damas, Leon-Gontran 1912-1978... **CLC 84**
   See also BW 1; CA 125; 73-76

Daniel, Samuel 1562(?)-1619........ **LC 24**
   See also DLB 62

Daniels, Brett
   See Adler, Renata

Dannay, Frederic 1905-1982....... **CLC 11**
   See also Queen, Ellery
   See also CA 1-4R; 107; CANR 1, 39;
     DLB 137; MTCW

D'Annunzio, Gabriele
   1863-1938 .... **TCLC 6, 40**
   See also CA 104

d'Antibes, Germain
   See Simenon, Georges (Jacques Christian)

Danvers, Dennis 1947-........... **CLC 70**

Danziger, Paula 1944-........... **CLC 21**
   See also AAYA 4; CA 112; 115; CANR 37;
     CLR 20; JRDA; MAICYA; SATA 36,
     63; SATA-Brief 30

Dario, Ruben 1867-1916 .... **TCLC 4; HLC**
   See also CA 131; HW; MTCW

Darley, George 1795-1846........ **NCLC 2**
   See also DLB 96

Daryush, Elizabeth 1887-1977.... **CLC 6, 19**
   See also CA 49-52; CANR 3; DLB 20

Daudet, (Louis Marie) Alphonse
   1840-1897 .... **NCLC 1**
   See also DLB 123

Daumal, Rene 1908-1944........ **TCLC 14**
   See also CA 114

Davenport, Guy (Mattison, Jr.)
   1927- .... **CLC 6, 14, 38; SSC 16**
   See also CA 33-36R; CANR 23; DLB 130

Davidson, Avram 1923-
   See Queen, Ellery
   See also CA 101; CANR 26; DLB 8

Davidson, Donald (Grady)
   1893-1968.......... **CLC 2, 13, 19**
   See also CA 5-8R; 25-28R; CANR 4;
     DLB 45

Davidson, Hugh
   See Hamilton, Edmond

Davidson, John 1857-1909....... **TCLC 24**
   See also CA 118; DLB 19

Davidson, Sara 1943-............. **CLC 9**
   See also CA 81-84; CANR 44

Davie, Donald (Alfred)
   1922-................ **CLC 5, 8, 10, 31**
   See also CA 1-4R; CAAS 3; CANR 1, 44;
     DLB 27; MTCW

Davies, Ray(mond Douglas) 1944- .. **CLC 21**
   See also CA 116

Davies, Rhys 1903-1978........... **CLC 23**
   See also CA 9-12R; 81-84; CANR 4;
     DLB 139

Davies, (William) Robertson
   1913- ..... **CLC 2, 7, 13, 25, 42, 75; DA;**
     WLC
   See also BEST 89:2; CA 33-36R; CANR 17,
     42; DLB 68; MTCW

Davies, W(illiam) H(enry)
   1871-1940 .... **TCLC 5**
   See also CA 104; DLB 19

Davies, Walter C.
   See Kornbluth, C(yril) M.

Davis, Angela (Yvonne) 1944-...... **CLC 77**
   See also BW 2; CA 57-60; CANR 10

Davis, B. Lynch
   See Bioy Casares, Adolfo; Borges, Jorge
     Luis

Davis, Gordon
   See Hunt, E(verette) Howard, (Jr.)

Davis, Harold Lenoir 1896-1960.... **CLC 49**
   See also CA 89-92; DLB 9

Davis, Rebecca (Blaine) Harding
   1831-1910 .... **TCLC 6**
   See also CA 104; DLB 74

Davis, Richard Harding
   1864-1916 .... **TCLC 24**
   See also CA 114; DLB 12, 23, 78, 79

Davison, Frank Dalby 1893-1970... **CLC 15**
   See also CA 116

Davison, Lawrence H.
See Lawrence, D(avid) H(erbert Richards)

Davison, Peter (Hubert) 1928- ..... **CLC 28**
See also CA 9-12R; CAAS 4; CANR 3, 43;
DLB 5

Davys, Mary 1674-1732............. **LC 1**
See also DLB 39

Dawson, Fielding 1930-........... **CLC 6**
See also CA 85-88; DLB 130

Dawson, Peter
See Faust, Frederick (Schiller)

Day, Clarence (Shepard, Jr.)
1874-1935 .... **TCLC 25**
See also CA 108; DLB 11

Day, Thomas 1748-1789............. **LC 1**
See also DLB 39; YABC 1

Day Lewis, C(ecil)
1904-1972 .... **CLC 1, 6, 10; PC 11**
See also Blake, Nicholas
See also CA 13-16; 33-36R; CANR 34;
CAP 1; DLB 15, 20; MTCW

Dazai, Osamu .... **TCLC 11**
See also Tsushima, Shuji

de Andrade, Carlos Drummond
See Drummond de Andrade, Carlos

Deane, Norman
See Creasey, John

de Beauvoir, Simone (Lucie Ernestine Marie Bertrand)
See Beauvoir, Simone (Lucie Ernestine
Marie Bertrand) de

de Brissac, Malcolm
See Dickinson, Peter (Malcolm)

de Chardin, Pierre Teilhard
See Teilhard de Chardin, (Marie Joseph)
Pierre

Dee, John 1527-1608 .... **LC 20**

Deer, Sandra 1940-............... **CLC 45**

De Ferrari, Gabriella .... **CLC 65**

Defoe, Daniel
1660(?)-1731 .... **LC 1; DA; WLC**
See also CDBLB 1660-1789; DLB 39, 95,
101; JRDA; MAICYA; SATA 22

de Gourmont, Remy
See Gourmont, Remy de

de Hartog, Jan 1914-............. **CLC 19**
See also CA 1-4R; CANR 1

de Hostos, E. M.
See Hostos (y Bonilla), Eugenio Maria de

de Hostos, Eugenio M.
See Hostos (y Bonilla), Eugenio Maria de

Deighton, Len .... **CLC 4, 7, 22, 46**
See also Deighton, Leonard Cyril
See also AAYA 6; BEST 89:2;
CDBLB 1960 to Present; DLB 87

Deighton, Leonard Cyril 1929-
See Deighton, Len
See also CA 9-12R; CANR 19, 33; MTCW

Dekker, Thomas 1572(?)-1632....... **LC 22**
See also CDBLB Before 1660; DLB 62

de la Mare, Walter (John)
1873-1956 .. **TCLC 4, 53; SSC 14; WLC**
See also CDBLB 1914-1945; CLR 23;
DLB 19; SATA 16

Delaney, Franey
See O'Hara, John (Henry)

Delaney, Shelagh 1939-........... **CLC 29**
See also CA 17-20R; CANR 30;
CDBLB 1960 to Present; DLB 13;
MTCW

Delany, Mary (Granville Pendarves)
1700-1788 .... **LC 12**

Delany, Samuel R(ay, Jr.)
1942-............**CLC 8, 14, 38; BLC**
See also BW 2; CA 81-84; CANR 27, 43;
DLB 8, 33; MTCW

De La Ramee, (Marie) Louise 1839-1908
See Ouida
See also SATA 20

de la Roche, Mazo 1879-1961...... **CLC 14**
See also CA 85-88; CANR 30; DLB 68;
SATA 64

Delbanco, Nicholas (Franklin)
1942-...................... **CLC 6, 13**
See also CA 17-20R; CAAS 2; CANR 29;
DLB 6

del Castillo, Michel 1933-......... **CLC 38**
See also CA 109

Deledda, Grazia (Cosima)
1875(?)-1936 .... **TCLC 23**
See also CA 123

Delibes, Miguel .... **CLC 8, 18**
See also Delibes Setien, Miguel

Delibes Setien, Miguel 1920-
See Delibes, Miguel
See also CA 45-48; CANR 1, 32; HW;
MTCW

DeLillo, Don
1936-..... **CLC 8, 10, 13, 27, 39, 54, 76**
See also BEST 89:1; CA 81-84; CANR 21;
DLB 6; MTCW

de Lisser, H. G.
See De Lisser, Herbert George
See also DLB 117

De Lisser, Herbert George
1878-1944 .... **TCLC 12**
See also de Lisser, H. G.
See also BW 2; CA 109

Deloria, Vine (Victor), Jr. 1933-.... **CLC 21**
See also CA 53-56; CANR 5, 20; MTCW;
NNAL; SATA 21

Del Vecchio, John M(ichael)
1947-...................... **CLC 29**
See also CA 110; DLBD 9

de Man, Paul (Adolph Michel)
1919-1983 .... **CLC 55**
See also CA 128; 111; DLB 67; MTCW

De Marinis, Rick 1934-........... **CLC 54**
See also CA 57-60; CANR 9, 25

Demby, William 1922-....... **CLC 53; BLC**
See also BW 1; CA 81-84; DLB 33

Demijohn, Thom
See Disch, Thomas M(ichael)

de Montherlant, Henry (Milon)
See Montherlant, Henry (Milon) de

Demosthenes 384B.C.-322B.C. .... **CMLC 13**

de Natale, Francine
See Malzberg, Barry N(athaniel)

Denby, Edwin (Orr) 1903-1983..... **CLC 48**
See also CA 138; 110

Denis, Julio
See Cortazar, Julio

Denmark, Harrison
See Zelazny, Roger (Joseph)

Dennis, John 1658-1734........... **LC 11**
See also DLB 101

Dennis, Nigel (Forbes) 1912-1989.... **CLC 8**
See also CA 25-28R; 129; DLB 13, 15;
MTCW

De Palma, Brian (Russell) 1940-.... **CLC 20**
See also CA 109

De Quincey, Thomas 1785-1859 ... **NCLC 4**
See also CDBLB 1789-1832; DLB 110; 144

Deren, Eleanora 1908(?)-1961
See Deren, Maya
See also CA 111

Deren, Maya .... **CLC 16**
See also Deren, Eleanora

Derleth, August (William)
1909-1971 .... **CLC 31**
See also CA 1-4R; 29-32R; CANR 4;
DLB 9; SATA 5

Der Nister 1884-1950........... **TCLC 56**

de Routisie, Albert
See Aragon, Louis

Derrida, Jacques 1930-........ **CLC 24, 87**
See also CA 124; 127

Derry Down Derry
See Lear, Edward

Dersonnes, Jacques
See Simenon, Georges (Jacques Christian)

Desai, Anita 1937-............ **CLC 19, 37**
See also CA 81-84; CANR 33; MTCW;
SATA 63

de Saint-Luc, Jean
See Glassco, John

de Saint Roman, Arnaud
See Aragon, Louis

Descartes, Rene 1596-1650 .... **LC 20**

De Sica, Vittorio 1901(?)-1974 ..... **CLC 20**
See also CA 117

Desnos, Robert 1900-1945........ **TCLC 22**
See also CA 121

Destouches, Louis-Ferdinand
1894-1961 .... **CLC 9, 15**
See also Celine, Louis-Ferdinand
See also CA 85-88; CANR 28; MTCW

Deutsch, Babette 1895-1982 .... **CLC 18**
See also CA 1-4R; 108; CANR 4; DLB 45;
SATA 1; SATA-Obit 33

Devenant, William 1606-1649 ...... **LC 13**

Devkota, Laxmiprasad
1909-1959 .... **TCLC 23**
See also CA 123

De Voto, Bernard (Augustine)
1897-1955 .... **TCLC 29**
See also CA 113; DLB 9

De Vries, Peter
1910-1993 .... **CLC 1, 2, 3, 7, 10, 28, 46**
See also CA 17-20R; 142; CANR 41;
DLB 6; DLBY 82; MTCW

Dexter, Martin
See Faust, Frederick (Schiller)

Dexter, Pete 1943- .... **CLC 34, 55**
See also BEST 89:2; CA 127; 131; MTCW

Diamano, Silmang
See Senghor, Leopold Sedar

Diamond, Neil 1941- .... **CLC 30**
See also CA 108

di Bassetto, Corno
See Shaw, George Bernard

Dick, Philip K(indred)
1928-1982 .... **CLC 10, 30, 72**
See also CA 49-52; 106; CANR 2, 16;
DLB 8; MTCW

Dickens, Charles (John Huffam)
1812-1870 ...... **NCLC 3, 8, 18, 26, 37;
DA; SSC 17; WLC**
See also CDBLB 1832-1890; DLB 21, 55,
70; JRDA; MAICYA; SATA 15

Dickey, James (Lafayette)
1923- .... **CLC 1, 2, 4, 7, 10, 15, 47**
See also AITN 1, 2; CA 9-12R; CABS 2;
CANR 10; CDALB 1968-1988; DLB 5;
DLBD 7; DLBY 82, 93; MTCW

Dickey, William 1928-1994 ..... **CLC 3, 28**
See also CA 9-12R; 145; CANR 24; DLB 5

Dickinson, Charles 1951- .... **CLC 49**
See also CA 128

Dickinson, Emily (Elizabeth)
1830-1886 .. **NCLC 21; DA; PC 1; WLC**
See also CDALB 1865-1917; DLB 1;
SATA 29

Dickinson, Peter (Malcolm)
1927- .... **CLC 12, 35**
See also AAYA 9; CA 41-44R; CANR 31;
CLR 29; DLB 87; JRDA; MAICYA;
SATA 5, 62

Dickson, Carr
See Carr, John Dickson

Dickson, Carter
See Carr, John Dickson

Diderot, Denis 1713-1784 .... **LC 26**

Didion, Joan 1934- ..... **CLC 1, 3, 8, 14, 32**
See also AITN 1; CA 5-8R; CANR 14;
CDALB 1968-1988; DLB 2; DLBY 81,
86; MTCW

Dietrich, Robert
See Hunt, E(verette) Howard, (Jr.)

Dillard, Annie 1945- .... **CLC 9, 60**
See also AAYA 6; CA 49-52; CANR 3, 43;
DLBY 80; MTCW; SATA 10

Dillard, R(ichard) H(enry) W(ilde)
1937- .... **CLC 5**
See also CA 21-24R; CAAS 7; CANR 10;
DLB 5

Dillon, Eilis 1920- .... **CLC 17**
See also CA 9-12R; CAAS 3; CANR 4, 38;
CLR 26; MAICYA; SATA 2, 74

Dimont, Penelope
See Mortimer, Penelope (Ruth)

Dinesen, Isak .... **CLC 10, 29; SSC 7**
See also Blixen, Karen (Christentze
Dinesen)

Ding Ling .... **CLC 68**
See also Chiang Pin-chin

Disch, Thomas M(ichael) 1940-... **CLC 7, 36**
See also CA 21-24R; CAAS 4; CANR 17,
36; CLR 18; DLB 8; MAICYA; MTCW;
SAAS 15; SATA 54

Disch, Tom
See Disch, Thomas M(ichael)

d'Isly, Georges
See Simenon, Georges (Jacques Christian)

Disraeli, Benjamin 1804-1881 .. **NCLC 2, 39**
See also DLB 21, 55

Ditcum, Steve
See Crumb, R(obert)

Dixon, Paige
See Corcoran, Barbara

Dixon, Stephen 1936- ..... **CLC 52; SSC 16**
See also CA 89-92; CANR 17, 40; DLB 130

Dobell, Sydney Thompson
1824-1874 .... **NCLC 43**
See also DLB 32

Doblin, Alfred .... **TCLC 13**
See also Doeblin, Alfred

Dobrolyubov, Nikolai Alexandrovich
1836-1861 .... **NCLC 5**

Dobyns, Stephen 1941- .... **CLC 37**
See also CA 45-48; CANR 2, 18

Doctorow, E(dgar) L(aurence)
1931- ..... **CLC 6, 11, 15, 18, 37, 44, 65**
See also AITN 2; BEST 89:3; CA 45-48;
CANR 2, 33; CDALB 1968-1988; DLB 2,
28; DLBY 80; MTCW

Dodgson, Charles Lutwidge 1832-1898
See Carroll, Lewis
See also CLR 2; DA; MAICYA; YABC 2

Dodson, Owen (Vincent)
1914-1983 .... **CLC 79; BLC**
See also BW 1; CA 65-68; 110; CANR 24;
DLB 76

Doeblin, Alfred 1878-1957....... **TCLC 13**
See also Doblin, Alfred
See also CA 110; 141; DLB 66

Doerr, Harriet 1910- .... **CLC 34**
See also CA 117; 122; CANR 47

Domecq, H(onorio) Bustos
See Bioy Casares, Adolfo; Borges, Jorge
Luis

Domini, Rey
See Lorde, Audre (Geraldine)

Dominique
See Proust, (Valentin-Louis-George-Eugene-)
Marcel

Don, A
See Stephen, Leslie

Donaldson, Stephen R. 1947-....... **CLC 46**
See also CA 89-92; CANR 13

Donleavy, J(ames) P(atrick)
1926- .... **CLC 1, 4, 6, 10, 45**
See also AITN 2; CA 9-12R; CANR 24;
DLB 6; MTCW

Donne, John
1572-1631 .... **LC 10, 24; DA; PC 1**
See also CDBLB Before 1660; DLB 121,
151

Donnell, David 1939(?)- .... **CLC 34**

Donoghue, P. S.
See Hunt, E(verette) Howard, (Jr.)

Donoso (Yanez), Jose
1924- .... **CLC 4, 8, 11, 32; HLC**
See also CA 81-84; CANR 32; DLB 113;
HW; MTCW

Donovan, John 1928-1992 .... **CLC 35**
See also CA 97-100; 137; CLR 3;
MAICYA; SATA 72; SATA-Brief 29

Don Roberto
See Cunninghame Graham, R(obert)
B(ontine)

Doolittle, Hilda
1886-1961 ..... **CLC 3, 8, 14, 31, 34, 73;
DA; PC 5; WLC**
See also H. D.
See also CA 97-100; CANR 35; DLB 4, 45;
MTCW

Dorfman, Ariel 1942-.... **CLC 48, 77; HLC**
See also CA 124; 130; HW

Dorn, Edward (Merton) 1929-... **CLC 10, 18**
See also CA 93-96; CANR 42; DLB 5

Dorsan, Luc
See Simenon, Georges (Jacques Christian)

Dorsange, Jean
See Simenon, Georges (Jacques Christian)

Dos Passos, John (Roderigo)
1896-1970 ...... **CLC 1, 4, 8, 11, 15, 25,
34, 82; DA; WLC**
See also CA 1-4R; 29-32R; CANR 3;
CDALB 1929-1941; DLB 4, 9; DLBD 1;
MTCW

Dossage, Jean
See Simenon, Georges (Jacques Christian)

Dostoevsky, Fedor Mikhailovich
1821-1881 ...... **NCLC 2, 7, 21, 33, 43;
DA; SSC 2; WLC**

Doughty, Charles M(ontagu)
1843-1926 .... **TCLC 27**
See also CA 115; DLB 19, 57

Douglas, Ellen .... **CLC 73**
See also Haxton, Josephine Ayres;
Williamson, Ellen Douglas

Douglas, Gavin 1475(?)-1522........ **LC 20**

Douglas, Keith 1920-1944 .... **TCLC 40**
See also DLB 27

Douglas, Leonard
See Bradbury, Ray (Douglas)

Douglas, Michael
See Crichton, (John) Michael

Douglass, Frederick
1817(?)-1895 .... **NCLC 7; BLC; DA;
WLC**
See also CDALB 1640-1865; DLB 1, 43, 50,
79; SATA 29

Dourado, (Waldomiro Freitas) Autran
1926- .... **CLC 23, 60**
See also CA 25-28R; CANR 34

Dourado, Waldomiro Autran
See Dourado, (Waldomiro Freitas) Autran

Dove, Rita (Frances)
1952- .... **CLC 50, 81; PC 6**
See also BW 2; CA 109; CAAS 19;
CANR 27, 42; DLB 120

Dowell, Coleman 1925-1985........ **CLC 60**
See also CA 25-28R; 117; CANR 10;
DLB 130

Dowson, Ernest Christopher
1867-1900 .... **TCLC 4**
See also CA 105; DLB 19, 135

Doyle, A. Conan
See Doyle, Arthur Conan

Doyle, Arthur Conan
1859-1930 .... **TCLC 7; DA; SSC 12;**
WLC
See also AAYA 14; CA 104; 122;
CDBLB 1890-1914; DLB 18, 70; MTCW;
SATA 24

Doyle, Conan
See Doyle, Arthur Conan

Doyle, John
See Graves, Robert (von Ranke)

Doyle, Roddy 1958(?)-........... **CLC 81**
See also AAYA 14; CA 143

Doyle, Sir A. Conan
See Doyle, Arthur Conan

Doyle, Sir Arthur Conan
See Doyle, Arthur Conan

Dr. A
See Asimov, Isaac; Silverstein, Alvin

Drabble, Margaret
1939- ...... **CLC 2, 3, 5, 8, 10, 22, 53**
See also CA 13-16R; CANR 18, 35;
CDBLB 1960 to Present; DLB 14;
MTCW; SATA 48

Drapier, M. B.
See Swift, Jonathan

Drayham, James
See Mencken, H(enry) L(ouis)

Drayton, Michael 1563-1631........ **LC 8**

Dreadstone, Carl
See Campbell, (John) Ramsey

Dreiser, Theodore (Herman Albert)
1871-1945 ...... **TCLC 10, 18, 35; DA;**
WLC
See also CA 106; 132; CDALB 1865-1917;
DLB 9, 12, 102, 137; DLBD 1; MTCW

Drexler, Rosalyn 1926- .... **CLC 2, 6**
See also CA 81-84

Dreyer, Carl Theodor 1889-1968.... **CLC 16**
See also CA 116

Drieu la Rochelle, Pierre(-Eugene)
1893-1945 .... **TCLC 21**
See also CA 117; DLB 72

Drinkwater, John 1882-1937..... **TCLC 57**
See also CA 109; DLB 10, 19, 149

Drop Shot
See Cable, George Washington

Droste-Hulshoff, Annette Freiin von
1797-1848 .... **NCLC 3**
See also DLB 133

Drummond, Walter
See Silverberg, Robert

Drummond, William Henry
1854-1907 .... **TCLC 25**
See also DLB 92

Drummond de Andrade, Carlos
1902-1987 .... **CLC 18**
See also Andrade, Carlos Drummond de
See also CA 132; 123

Drury, Allen (Stuart) 1918-...... **CLC 37**
See also CA 57-60; CANR 18

Dryden, John
1631-1700 ... **LC 3, 21; DA; DC 3; WLC**
See also CDBLB 1660-1789; DLB 80, 101,
131

Duberman, Martin 1930-.......... **CLC 8**
See also CA 1-4R; CANR 2

Dubie, Norman (Evans) 1945-...... **CLC 36**
See also CA 69-72; CANR 12; DLB 120

Du Bois, W(illiam) E(dward) B(urghardt)
1868-1963 ...... **CLC 1, 2, 13, 64; BLC;**
DA; WLC
See also BW 1; CA 85-88; CANR 34;
CDALB 1865-1917; DLB 47, 50, 91;
MTCW; SATA 42

Dubus, Andre 1936-... **CLC 13, 36; SSC 15**
See also CA 21-24R; CANR 17; DLB 130

Duca Minimo
See D'Annunzio, Gabriele

Ducharme, Rejean 1941- .... **CLC 74**
See also DLB 60

Duclos, Charles Pinot 1704-1772 ..... **LC 1**

Dudek, Louis 1918- .... **CLC 11, 19**
See also CA 45-48; CAAS 14; CANR 1;
DLB 88

Duerrenmatt, Friedrich
1921-1990 ...... **CLC 1, 4, 8, 11, 15, 43**
See also CA 17-20R; CANR 33; DLB 69,
124; MTCW

Duffy, Bruce (?)-................. **CLC 50**

Duffy, Maureen 1933- .... **CLC 37**
See also CA 25-28R; CANR 33; DLB 14;
MTCW

Dugan, Alan 1923-.............. **CLC 2, 6**
See also CA 81-84; DLB 5

du Gard, Roger Martin
See Martin du Gard, Roger

Duhamel, Georges 1884-1966 .... **CLC 8**
See also CA 81-84; 25-28R; CANR 35;
DLB 65; MTCW

Dujardin, Edouard (Emile Louis)
1861-1949 .... **TCLC 13**
See also CA 109; DLB 123

Dumas, Alexandre (Davy de la Pailleterie)
1802-1870 .... **NCLC 11; DA; WLC**
See also DLB 119; SATA 18

Dumas, Alexandre
1824-1895 .... **NCLC 9; DC 1**

Dumas, Claudine
See Malzberg, Barry N(athaniel)

Dumas, Henry L. 1934-1968..... **CLC 6, 62**
See also BW 1; CA 85-88; DLB 41

du Maurier, Daphne
1907-1989 ...... **CLC 6, 11, 59; SSC 18**
See also CA 5-8R; 128; CANR 6; MTCW;
SATA 27; SATA-Obit 60

Dunbar, Paul Laurence
1872-1906 ...... **TCLC 2, 12; BLC; DA;**
PC 5; SSC 8; WLC
See also BW 1; CA 104; 124;
CDALB 1865-1917; DLB 50, 54, 78;
SATA 34

Dunbar, William 1460(?)-1530(?) .... **LC 20**
See also DLB 132, 146

Duncan, Lois 1934-............... **CLC 26**
See also AAYA 4; CA 1-4R; CANR 2, 23,
36; CLR 29; JRDA; MAICYA; SAAS 2;
SATA 1, 36, 75

Duncan, Robert (Edward)
1919-1988 .... **CLC 1, 2, 4, 7, 15, 41, 55;**
PC 2
See also CA 9-12R; 124; CANR 28; DLB 5,
16; MTCW

Dunlap, William 1766-1839....... **NCLC 2**
See also DLB 30, 37, 59

Dunn, Douglas (Eaglesham)
1942- .... **CLC 6, 40**
See also CA 45-48; CANR 2, 33; DLB 40;
MTCW

Dunn, Katherine (Karen) 1945-..... **CLC 71**
See also CA 33-36R

Dunn, Stephen 1939-.............. **CLC 36**
See also CA 33-36R; CANR 12; DLB 105

Dunne, Finley Peter 1867-1936.... **TCLC 28**
See also CA 108; DLB 11, 23

Dunne, John Gregory 1932-........ **CLC 28**
See also CA 25-28R; CANR 14; DLBY 80

Dunsany, Edward John Moreton Drax
Plunkett 1878-1957
See Dunsany, Lord
See also CA 104; DLB 10

Dunsany, Lord................. TCLC 2, 59
See also Dunsany, Edward John Moreton
Drax Plunkett
See also DLB 77

du Perry, Jean
See Simenon, Georges (Jacques Christian)

Durang, Christopher (Ferdinand)
1949-.................... **CLC 27, 38**
See also CA 105

Duras, Marguerite
1914- ...... **CLC 3, 6, 11, 20, 34, 40, 68**
See also CA 25-28R; DLB 83; MTCW

Durban, (Rosa) Pam 1947-........ **CLC 39**
See also CA 123

Durcan, Paul 1944-............. **CLC 43, 70**
See also CA 134

Durkheim, Emile 1858-1917 ...... **TCLC 55**

Durrell, Lawrence (George)
1912-1990 .... **CLC 1, 4, 6, 8, 13, 27, 41**
See also CA 9-12R; 132; CANR 40;
CDBLB 1945-1960; DLB 15, 27;
DLBY 90; MTCW

Durrenmatt, Friedrich
See Duerrenmatt, Friedrich

Dutt, Toru 1856-1877........... **NCLC 29**

Dwight, Timothy 1752-1817...... **NCLC 13**
See also DLB 37

Dworkin, Andrea 1946- .... **CLC 43**
See also CA 77-80; CANR 16, 39; MTCW

Dwyer, Deanna
See Koontz, Dean R(ay)

Dwyer, K. R.
See Koontz, Dean R(ay)

Dylan, Bob 1941- . . . . . . **CLC 3, 4, 6, 12, 77**
See also CA 41-44R; DLB 16

Eagleton, Terence (Francis) 1943-
See Eagleton, Terry
See also CA 57-60; CANR 7, 23; MTCW

Eagleton, Terry . . . . **CLC 63**
See also Eagleton, Terence (Francis)

Early, Jack
See Scoppettone, Sandra

East, Michael
See West, Morris L(anglo)

Eastaway, Edward
See Thomas, (Philip) Edward

Eastlake, William (Derry) 1917- . . . . . **CLC 8**
See also CA 5-8R; CAAS 1; CANR 5;
DLB 6

Eastman, Charles A(lexander)
1858-1939 . . . . **TCLC 55**
See also NNAL; YABC 1

Eberhart, Richard (Ghormley)
1904- . . . . **CLC 3, 11, 19, 56**
See also CA 1-4R; CANR 2;
CDALB 1941-1968; DLB 48; MTCW

Eberstadt, Fernanda 1960- . . . . **CLC 39**
See also CA 136

Echegaray (y Eizaguirre), Jose (Maria Waldo)
1832-1916 . . . . **TCLC 4**
See also CA 104; CANR 32; HW; MTCW

Echeverria, (Jose) Esteban (Antonino)
1805-1851 . . . . **NCLC 18**

Echo
See Proust, (Valentin-Louis-George-Eugene-)
Marcel

Eckert, Allan W. 1931- . . . . **CLC 17**
See also CA 13-16R; CANR 14, 45;
SATA 29; SATA-Brief 27

Eckhart, Meister 1260(?)-1328(?) . . **CMLC 9**
See also DLB 115

Eckmar, F. R.
See de Hartog, Jan

Eco, Umberto 1932- . . . . **CLC 28, 60**
See also BEST 90:1; CA 77-80; CANR 12,
33; MTCW

Eddison, E(ric) R(ucker)
1882-1945 . . . . **TCLC 15**
See also CA 109

Edel, (Joseph) Leon 1907- . . . . . . **CLC 29, 34**
See also CA 1-4R; CANR 1, 22; DLB 103

Eden, Emily 1797-1869 . . . . **NCLC 10**

Edgar, David 1948- . . . . **CLC 42**
See also CA 57-60; CANR 12; DLB 13;
MTCW

Edgerton, Clyde (Carlyle) 1944- . . . . **CLC 39**
See also CA 118; 134

Edgeworth, Maria 1767-1849 . . . . . . **NCLC 1**
See also DLB 116; SATA 21

Edmonds, Paul
See Kuttner, Henry

Edmonds, Walter D(umaux) 1903- . . **CLC 35**
See also CA 5-8R; CANR 2; DLB 9;
MAICYA; SAAS 4; SATA 1, 27

Edmondson, Wallace
See Ellison, Harlan (Jay)

Edson, Russell . . . . **CLC 13**
See also CA 33-36R

Edwards, Bronwen Elizabeth
See Rose, Wendy

Edwards, G(erald) B(asil)
1899-1976 . . . . **CLC 25**
See also CA 110

Edwards, Gus 1939- . . . . **CLC 43**
See also CA 108

Edwards, Jonathan 1703-1758 . . . . **LC 7; DA**
See also DLB 24

Efron, Marina Ivanovna Tsvetaeva
See Tsvetaeva (Efron), Marina (Ivanovna)

Ehle, John (Marsden, Jr.) 1925- . . . . **CLC 27**
See also CA 9-12R

Ehrenbourg, Ilya (Grigoryevich)
See Ehrenburg, Ilya (Grigoryevich)

Ehrenburg, Ilya (Grigoryevich)
1891-1967 . . . . **CLC 18, 34, 62**
See also CA 102; 25-28R

Ehrenburg, Ilyo (Grigoryevich)
See Ehrenburg, Ilya (Grigoryevich)

Eich, Guenter 1907-1972 . . . . **CLC 15**
See also CA 111; 93-96; DLB 69, 124

Eichendorff, Joseph Freiherr von
1788-1857 . . . . **NCLC 8**
See also DLB 90

Eigner, Larry . . . . **CLC 9**
See also Eigner, Laurence (Joel)
See also DLB 5

Eigner, Laurence (Joel) 1927-
See Eigner, Larry
See also CA 9-12R; CANR 6

Eiseley, Loren Corey 1907-1977 . . . . . **CLC 7**
See also AAYA 5; CA 1-4R; 73-76;
CANR 6

Eisenstadt, Jill 1963- . . . . **CLC 50**
See also CA 140

Eisenstein, Sergei (Mikhailovich)
1898-1948 . . . . **TCLC 57**
See also CA 114

Eisner, Simon
See Kornbluth, C(yril) M.

Ekeloef, (Bengt) Gunnar
1907-1968 . . . . **CLC 27**
See also CA 123; 25-28R

Ekelof, (Bengt) Gunnar
See Ekeloef, (Bengt) Gunnar

Ekwensi, C. O. D.
See Ekwensi, Cyprian (Odiatu Duaka)

Ekwensi, Cyprian (Odiatu Duaka)
1921- . . . . **CLC 4; BLC**
See also BW 2; CA 29-32R; CANR 18, 42;
DLB 117; MTCW; SATA 66

Elaine . . . . **TCLC 18**
See also Leverson, Ada

El Crummo
See Crumb, R(obert)

Elia
See Lamb, Charles

Eliade, Mircea 1907-1986 . . . . **CLC 19**
See also CA 65-68; 119; CANR 30; MTCW

Eliot, A. D.
See Jewett, (Theodora) Sarah Orne

Eliot, Alice
See Jewett, (Theodora) Sarah Orne

Eliot, Dan
See Silverberg, Robert

Eliot, George
1819-1880 . . . . . **NCLC 4, 13, 23, 41, 49;**
DA; WLC
See also CDBLB 1832-1890; DLB 21, 35, 55

Eliot, John 1604-1690 . . . . **LC 5**
See also DLB 24

Eliot, T(homas) S(tearns)
1888-1965 . . . . . **CLC 1, 2, 3, 6, 9, 10, 13,**
15, 24, 34, 41, 55, 57; DA; PC 5; WLC 2
See also CA 5-8R; 25-28R; CANR 41;
CDALB 1929-1941; DLB 7, 10, 45, 63;
DLBY 88; MTCW

Elizabeth 1866-1941 . . . . **TCLC 41**

Elkin, Stanley L(awrence)
1930- . . . **CLC 4, 6, 9, 14, 27, 51; SSC 12**
See also CA 9-12R; CANR 8, 46; DLB 2,
28; DLBY 80; MTCW

Elledge, Scott . . . . **CLC 34**

Elliott, Don
See Silverberg, Robert

Elliott, George P(aul) 1918-1980 . . . . . **CLC 2**
See also CA 1-4R; 97-100; CANR 2

Elliott, Janice 1931- . . . . **CLC 47**
See also CA 13-16R; CANR 8, 29; DLB 14

Elliott, Sumner Locke 1917-1991 . . . **CLC 38**
See also CA 5-8R; 134; CANR 2, 21

Elliott, William
See Bradbury, Ray (Douglas)

Ellis, A. E. . . . . **CLC 7**

Ellis, Alice Thomas . . . . **CLC 40**
See also Haycraft, Anna

Ellis, Bret Easton 1964- . . . . **CLC 39, 71**
See also AAYA 2; CA 118; 123

Ellis, (Henry) Havelock
1859-1939 . . . . **TCLC 14**
See also CA 109

Ellis, Landon
See Ellison, Harlan (Jay)

Ellis, Trey 1962- . . . . **CLC 55**

Ellison, Harlan (Jay)
1934- . . . . **CLC 1, 13, 42; SSC 14**
See also CA 5-8R; CANR 5, 46; DLB 8;
MTCW

Ellison, Ralph (Waldo)
1914-1994 . . . . **CLC 1, 3, 11, 54, 86;**
BLC; DA; WLC
See also BW 1; CA 9-12R; 145; CANR 24;
CDALB 1941-1968; DLB 2, 76;
DLBY 94; MTCW

Ellmann, Lucy (Elizabeth) 1956- . . . . **CLC 61**
See also CA 128

Ellmann, Richard (David)
1918-1987 . . . . CLC 50
See also BEST 89:2; CA 1-4R; 122;
CANR 2, 28; DLB 103; DLBY 87;
MTCW

Elman, Richard 1934- . . . . CLC 19
See also CA 17-20R; CAAS 3; CANR 47

Elron
See Hubbard, L(afayette) Ron(ald)

Eluard, Paul . . . . TCLC 7, 41
See also Grindel, Eugene

Elyot, Sir Thomas 1490(?)-1546 . . . . . LC 11

Elytis, Odysseus 1911- . . . . CLC 15, 49
See also CA 102; MTCW

Emecheta, (Florence Onye) Buchi
1944- . . . . CLC 14, 48; BLC
See also BW 2; CA 81-84; CANR 27;
DLB 117; MTCW; SATA 66

Emerson, Ralph Waldo
1803-1882 . . . . . . NCLC 1, 38; DA; WLC
See also CDALB 1640-1865; DLB 1, 59, 73

Eminescu, Mihail 1850-1889 . . . . . NCLC 33

Empson, William
1906-1984 . . . . CLC 3, 8, 19, 33, 34
See also CA 17-20R; 112; CANR 31;
DLB 20; MTCW

Enchi Fumiko (Ueda) 1905-1986 . . . . CLC 31
See also CA 129; 121

Ende, Michael (Andreas Helmuth)
1929- . . . . CLC 31
See also CA 118; 124; CANR 36; CLR 14;
DLB 75; MAICYA; SATA 61;
SATA-Brief 42

Endo, Shusaku 1923- . . . . . CLC 7, 14, 19, 54
See also CA 29-32R; CANR 21; MTCW

Engel, Marian 1933-1985 . . . . CLC 36
See also CA 25-28R; CANR 12; DLB 53

Engelhardt, Frederick
See Hubbard, L(afayette) Ron(ald)

Enright, D(ennis) J(oseph)
1920- . . . . CLC 4, 8, 31
See also CA 1-4R; CANR 1, 42; DLB 27;
SATA 25

Enzensberger, Hans Magnus
1929- . . . . CLC 43
See also CA 116; 119

Ephron, Nora 1941- . . . . CLC 17, 31
See also AITN 2; CA 65-68; CANR 12, 39

Epsilon
See Betjeman, John

Epstein, Daniel Mark 1948- . . . . CLC 7
See also CA 49-52; CANR 2

Epstein, Jacob 1956- . . . . CLC 19
See also CA 114

Epstein, Joseph 1937- . . . . CLC 39
See also CA 112; 119

Epstein, Leslie 1938- . . . . CLC 27
See also CA 73-76; CAAS 12; CANR 23

Equiano, Olaudah
1745(?)-1797 . . . . LC 16; BLC
See also DLB 37, 50

Erasmus, Desiderius 1469(?)-1536 . . . . LC 16

Erdman, Paul E(mil) 1932- . . . . CLC 25
See also AITN 1; CA 61-64; CANR 13, 43

Erdrich, Louise 1954- . . . . CLC 39, 54
See also AAYA 10; BEST 89:1; CA 114;
CANR 41; DLB 152; MTCW; NNAL

Erenburg, Ilya (Grigoryevich)
See Ehrenburg, Ilya (Grigoryevich)

Erickson, Stephen Michael 1950-
See Erickson, Steve
See also CA 129

Erickson, Steve . . . . CLC 64
See also Erickson, Stephen Michael

Ericson, Walter
See Fast, Howard (Melvin)

Eriksson, Buntel
See Bergman, (Ernst) Ingmar

Ernaux, Annie 1940- . . . . CLC 88

Eschenbach, Wolfram von
See Wolfram von Eschenbach

Eseki, Bruno
See Mphahlele, Ezekiel

Esenin, Sergei (Alexandrovich)
1895-1925 . . . . TCLC 4
See also CA 104

Eshleman, Clayton 1935- . . . . CLC 7
See also CA 33-36R; CAAS 6; DLB 5

Espriella, Don Manuel Alvarez
See Southey, Robert

Espriu, Salvador 1913-1985 . . . . CLC 9
See also CA 115; DLB 134

Espronceda, Jose de 1808-1842 . . . NCLC 39

Esse, James
See Stephens, James

Esterbrook, Tom
See Hubbard, L(afayette) Ron(ald)

Estleman, Loren D. 1952- . . . . CLC 48
See also CA 85-88; CANR 27; MTCW

Eugenides, Jeffrey 1960(?)- . . . . CLC 81
See also CA 144

Euripides c. 485B.C.-406B.C. . . . . DC 4
See also DA

Evan, Evin
See Faust, Frederick (Schiller)

Evans, Evan
See Faust, Frederick (Schiller)

Evans, Marian
See Eliot, George

Evans, Mary Ann
See Eliot, George

Evarts, Esther
See Benson, Sally

Everett, Percival L. 1956- . . . . CLC 57
See also BW 2; CA 129

Everson, R(onald) G(ilmour)
1903- . . . . CLC 27
See also CA 17-20R; DLB 88

Everson, William (Oliver)
1912-1994 . . . . CLC 1, 5, 14
See also CA 9-12R; 145; CANR 20; DLB 5,
16; MTCW

Evtushenko, Evgenii Aleksandrovich
See Yevtushenko, Yevgeny (Alexandrovich)

Ewart, Gavin (Buchanan)
1916- . . . . CLC 13, 46
See also CA 89-92; CANR 17, 46; DLB 40;
MTCW

Ewers, Hanns Heinz 1871-1943 . . . TCLC 12
See also CA 109

Ewing, Frederick R.
See Sturgeon, Theodore (Hamilton)

Exley, Frederick (Earl)
1929-1992 . . . . CLC 6, 11
See also AITN 2; CA 81-84; 138; DLB 143;
DLBY 81

Eynhardt, Guillermo
See Quiroga, Horacio (Sylvestre)

Ezekiel, Nissim 1924- . . . . CLC 61
See also CA 61-64

Ezekiel, Tish O'Dowd 1943- . . . . CLC 34
See also CA 129

Fadeyev, A.
See Bulgya, Alexander Alexandrovich

Fadeyev, Alexander . . . . TCLC 53
See also Bulgya, Alexander Alexandrovich

Fagen, Donald 1948- . . . . CLC 26

Fainzilberg, Ilya Arnoldovich 1897-1937
See Ilf, Ilya
See also CA 120

Fair, Ronald L. 1932- . . . . CLC 18
See also BW 1; CA 69-72; CANR 25;
DLB 33

Fairbairns, Zoe (Ann) 1948- . . . . . . CLC 32
See also CA 103; CANR 21

Falco, Gian
See Papini, Giovanni

Falconer, James
See Kirkup, James

Falconer, Kenneth
See Kornbluth, C(yril) M.

Falkland, Samuel
See Heijermans, Herman

Fallaci, Oriana 1930- . . . . CLC 11
See also CA 77-80; CANR 15; MTCW

Faludy, George 1913- . . . . CLC 42
See also CA 21-24R

Faludy, Gyoergy
See Faludy, George

Fanon, Frantz 1925-1961 . . . . . CLC 74; BLC
See also BW 1; CA 116; 89-92

Fanshawe, Ann 1625-1680 . . . . LC 11

Fante, John (Thomas) 1911-1983 . . . CLC 60
See also CA 69-72; 109; CANR 23;
DLB 130; DLBY 83

Farah, Nuruddin 1945- . . . . CLC 53; BLC
See also BW 2; CA 106; DLB 125

Fargue, Leon-Paul 1876(?)-1947 . . . TCLC 11
See also CA 109

Farigoule, Louis
See Romains, Jules

Farina, Richard 1936(?)-1966 . . . . CLC 9
See also CA 81-84; 25-28R

Farley, Walter (Lorimer)
1915-1989 . . . . CLC 17
See also CA 17-20R; CANR 8, 29; DLB 22;
JRDA; MAICYA; SATA 2, 43

Fleming, Ian (Lancaster)
1908-1964 . . . . **CLC 3, 30**
See also CA 5-8R; CDBLB 1945-1960;
DLB 87; MTCW; SATA 9

Fleming, Thomas (James) 1927- . . . . **CLC 37**
See also CA 5-8R; CANR 10; SATA 8

Fletcher, John Gould 1886-1950 . . . **TCLC 35**
See also CA 107; DLB 4, 45

Fleur, Paul
See Pohl, Frederik

Flooglebuckle, Al
See Spiegelman, Art

Flying Officer X
See Bates, H(erbert) E(rnest)

Fo, Dario 1926- . . . . **CLC 32**
See also CA 116; 128; MTCW

Fogarty, Jonathan Titulescu Esq.
See Farrell, James T(homas)

Folke, Will
See Bloch, Robert (Albert)

Follett, Ken(neth Martin) 1949- . . . . **CLC 18**
See also AAYA 6; BEST 89:4; CA 81-84;
CANR 13, 33; DLB 87; DLBY 81;
MTCW

Fontane, Theodor 1819-1898 . . . . . **NCLC 26**
See also DLB 129

Foote, Horton 1916- . . . . **CLC 51**
See also CA 73-76; CANR 34; DLB 26

Foote, Shelby 1916- . . . . **CLC 75**
See also CA 5-8R; CANR 3, 45; DLB 2, 17

Forbes, Esther 1891-1967 . . . . **CLC 12**
See also CA 13-14; 25-28R; CAP 1;
CLR 27; DLB 22; JRDA; MAICYA;
SATA 2

Forche, Carolyn (Louise)
1950- . . . . **CLC 25, 83, 86; PC 10**
See also CA 109; 117; DLB 5

Ford, Elbur
See Hibbert, Eleanor Alice Burford

Ford, Ford Madox
1873-1939 . . . . **TCLC 1, 15, 39, 57**
See also CA 104; 132; CDBLB 1914-1945;
DLB 34, 98; MTCW

Ford, John 1895-1973 . . . . **CLC 16**
See also CA 45-48

Ford, Richard 1944- . . . . **CLC 46**
See also CA 69-72; CANR 11, 47

Ford, Webster
See Masters, Edgar Lee

Foreman, Richard 1937- . . . . **CLC 50**
See also CA 65-68; CANR 32

Forester, C(ecil) S(cott)
1899-1966 . . . . **CLC 35**
See also CA 73-76; 25-28R; SATA 13

Forez
See Mauriac, Francois (Charles)

Forman, James Douglas 1932- . . . . . . **CLC 21**
See also CA 9-12R; CANR 4, 19, 42;
JRDA; MAICYA; SATA 8, 70

Fornes, Maria Irene 1930- . . . . . . **CLC 39, 61**
See also CA 25-28R; CANR 28; DLB 7;
HW; MTCW

Forrest, Leon 1937- . . . . **CLC 4**
See also BW 2; CA 89-92; CAAS 7;
CANR 25; DLB 33

Forster, E(dward) M(organ)
1879-1970 . . . . . **CLC 1, 2, 3, 4, 9, 10, 13,
15, 22, 45, 77; DA; WLC**
See also AAYA 2; CA 13-14; 25-28R;
CANR 45; CAP 1; CDBLB 1914-1945;
DLB 34, 98; DLBD 10; MTCW;
SATA 57

Forster, John 1812-1876 . . . . **NCLC 11**
See also DLB 144

Forsyth, Frederick 1938- . . . . . . **CLC 2, 5, 36**
See also BEST 89:4; CA 85-88; CANR 38;
DLB 87; MTCW

Forten, Charlotte L. . . . . **TCLC 16; BLC**
See also Grimke, Charlotte L(ottie) Forten
See also DLB 50

Foscolo, Ugo 1778-1827 . . . . **NCLC 8**

Fosse, Bob . . . . **CLC 20**
See also Fosse, Robert Louis

Fosse, Robert Louis 1927-1987
See Fosse, Bob
See also CA 110; 123

Foster, Stephen Collins
1826-1864 . . . . **NCLC 26**

Foucault, Michel
1926-1984 . . . . **CLC 31, 34, 69**
See also CA 105; 113; CANR 34; MTCW

Fouque, Friedrich (Heinrich Karl) de la Motte
1777-1843 . . . . **NCLC 2**
See also DLB 90

Fournier, Henri Alban 1886-1914
See Alain-Fournier
See also CA 104

Fournier, Pierre 1916- . . . . **CLC 11**
See also Gascar, Pierre
See also CA 89-92; CANR 16, 40

Fowles, John
1926- . . . . . . **CLC 1, 2, 3, 4, 6, 9, 10, 15,
33, 87**
See also CA 5-8R; CANR 25; CDBLB 1960
to Present; DLB 14, 139; MTCW;
SATA 22

Fox, Paula 1923- . . . . **CLC 2, 8**
See also AAYA 3; CA 73-76; CANR 20,
36; CLR 1; DLB 52; JRDA; MAICYA;
MTCW; SATA 17, 60

Fox, William Price (Jr.) 1926- . . . . . **CLC 22**
See also CA 17-20R; CAAS 19; CANR 11;
DLB 2; DLBY 81

Foxe, John 1516(?)-1587 . . . . **LC 14**

Frame, Janet . . . . **CLC 2, 3, 6, 22, 66**
See also Clutha, Janet Paterson Frame

France, Anatole . . . . **TCLC 9**
See also Thibault, Jacques Anatole Francois
See also DLB 123

Francis, Claude 19(?)- . . . . **CLC 50**

Francis, Dick 1920- . . . . **CLC 2, 22, 42**
See also AAYA 5; BEST 89:3; CA 5-8R;
CANR 9, 42; CDBLB 1960 to Present;
DLB 87; MTCW

Francis, Robert (Churchill)
1901-1987 . . . . **CLC 15**
See also CA 1-4R; 123; CANR 1

Frank, Anne(lies Marie)
1929-1945 . . . . **TCLC 17; DA; WLC**
See also AAYA 12; CA 113; 133; MTCW;
SATA-Brief 42

Frank, Elizabeth 1945- . . . . **CLC 39**
See also CA 121; 126

Franklin, Benjamin
See Hasek, Jaroslav (Matej Frantisek)

Franklin, Benjamin 1706-1790 . . . **LC 25; DA**
See also CDALB 1640-1865; DLB 24, 43,
73

Franklin, (Stella Maraia Sarah) Miles
1879-1954 . . . . **TCLC 7**
See also CA 104

Fraser, (Lady) Antonia (Pakenham)
1932- . . . . **CLC 32**
See also CA 85-88; CANR 44; MTCW;
SATA-Brief 32

Fraser, George MacDonald 1925- . . . . **CLC 7**
See also CA 45-48; CANR 2

Fraser, Sylvia 1935- . . . . **CLC 64**
See also CA 45-48; CANR 1, 16

Frayn, Michael 1933- . . . . . . **CLC 3, 7, 31, 47**
See also CA 5-8R; CANR 30; DLB 13, 14;
MTCW

Fraze, Candida (Merrill) 1945- . . . . . **CLC 50**
See also CA 126

Frazer, J(ames) G(eorge)
1854-1941 . . . . **TCLC 32**
See also CA 118

Frazer, Robert Caine
See Creasey, John

Frazer, Sir James George
See Frazer, J(ames) G(eorge)

Frazier, Ian 1951- . . . . **CLC 46**
See also CA 130

Frederic, Harold 1856-1898 . . . . . . **NCLC 10**
See also DLB 12, 23

Frederick, John
See Faust, Frederick (Schiller)

Frederick the Great 1712-1786 . . . . . . **LC 14**

Fredro, Aleksander 1793-1876 . . . . . **NCLC 8**

Freeling, Nicolas 1927- . . . . **CLC 38**
See also CA 49-52; CAAS 12; CANR 1, 17;
DLB 87

Freeman, Douglas Southall
1886-1953 . . . . **TCLC 11**
See also CA 109; DLB 17

Freeman, Judith 1946- . . . . **CLC 55**

Freeman, Mary Eleanor Wilkins
1852-1930 . . . . **TCLC 9; SSC 1**
See also CA 106; DLB 12, 78

Freeman, R(ichard) Austin
1862-1943 . . . . **TCLC 21**
See also CA 113; DLB 70

French, Albert 1943- . . . . **CLC 86**

French, Marilyn 1929- . . . . . . **CLC 10, 18, 60**
See also CA 69-72; CANR 3, 31; MTCW

French, Paul
See Asimov, Isaac

Freneau, Philip Morin 1752-1832 . . **NCLC 1**
See also DLB 37, 43

Freud, Sigmund 1856-1939 .... **TCLC 52**
See also CA 115; 133; MTCW

Friedan, Betty (Naomi) 1921- ...... **CLC 74**
See also CA 65-68; CANR 18, 45; MTCW

Friedman, B(ernard) H(arper)
1926- .... **CLC 7**
See also CA 1-4R; CANR 3

Friedman, Bruce Jay 1930- .... **CLC 3, 5, 56**
See also CA 9-12R; CANR 25; DLB 2, 28

Friel, Brian 1929- .... **CLC 5, 42, 59**
See also CA 21-24R; CANR 33; DLB 13;
MTCW

Friis-Baastad, Babbis Ellinor
1921-1970 .... **CLC 12**
See also CA 17-20R; 134; SATA 7

Frisch, Max (Rudolf)
1911-1991 ..... **CLC 3, 9, 14, 18, 32, 44**
See also CA 85-88; 134; CANR 32;
DLB 69, 124; MTCW

Fromentin, Eugene (Samuel Auguste)
1820-1876 .... **NCLC 10**
See also DLB 123

Frost, Frederick
See Faust, Frederick (Schiller)

Frost, Robert (Lee)
1874-1963 .... **CLC 1, 3, 4, 9, 10, 13, 15,
26, 34, 44; DA; PC 1; WLC**
See also CA 89-92; CANR 33;
CDALB 1917-1929; DLB 54; DLBD 7;
MTCW; SATA 14

Froude, James Anthony
1818-1894 .... **NCLC 43**
See also DLB 18, 57, 144

Froy, Herald
See Waterhouse, Keith (Spencer)

Fry, Christopher 1907- .... **CLC 2, 10, 14**
See also CA 17-20R; CANR 9, 30; DLB 13;
MTCW; SATA 66

Frye, (Herman) Northrop
1912-1991 .... **CLC 24, 70**
See also CA 5-8R; 133; CANR 8, 37;
DLB 67, 68; MTCW

Fuchs, Daniel 1909-1993 .... **CLC 8, 22**
See also CA 81-84; 142; CAAS 5;
CANR 40; DLB 9, 26, 28; DLBY 93

Fuchs, Daniel 1934- .... **CLC 34**
See also CA 37-40R; CANR 14

Fuentes, Carlos
1928- ...... **CLC 3, 8, 10, 13, 22, 41, 60;
DA; HLC; WLC**
See also AAYA 4; AITN 2; CA 69-72;
CANR 10, 32; DLB 113; HW; MTCW

Fuentes, Gregorio Lopez y
See Lopez y Fuentes, Gregorio

Fugard, (Harold) Athol
1932- .... **CLC 5, 9, 14, 25, 40, 80; DC 3**
See also CA 85-88; CANR 32; MTCW

Fugard, Sheila 1932- .... **CLC 48**
See also CA 125

Fuller, Charles (H., Jr.)
1939- .... **CLC 25; BLC; DC 1**
See also BW 2; CA 108; 112; DLB 38;
MTCW

Fuller, John (Leopold) 1937- .... **CLC 62**
See also CA 21-24R; CANR 9, 44; DLB 40

Fuller, Margaret .... **NCLC 5**
See also Ossoli, Sarah Margaret (Fuller
marchesa d')

Fuller, Roy (Broadbent)
1912-1991 .... **CLC 4, 28**
See also CA 5-8R; 135; CAAS 10; DLB 15,
20

Fulton, Alice 1952- .... **CLC 52**
See also CA 116

Furphy, Joseph 1843-1912 .... **TCLC 25**

Fussell, Paul 1924- .... **CLC 74**
See also BEST 90:1; CA 17-20R; CANR 8,
21, 35; MTCW

Futabatei, Shimei 1864-1909 ..... **TCLC 44**

Futrelle, Jacques 1875-1912 ...... **TCLC 19**
See also CA 113

Gaboriau, Emile 1835-1873 ...... **NCLC 14**

Gadda, Carlo Emilio 1893-1973 .... **CLC 11**
See also CA 89-92

Gaddis, William
1922- ..... **CLC 1, 3, 6, 8, 10, 19, 43, 86**
See also CA 17-20R; CANR 21; DLB 2;
MTCW

Gaines, Ernest J(ames)
1933- .... **CLC 3, 11, 18, 86; BLC**
See also AITN 1; BW 2; CA 9-12R;
CANR 6, 24, 42; CDALB 1968-1988;
DLB 2, 33, 152; DLBY 80; MTCW

Gaitskill, Mary 1954- .... **CLC 69**
See also CA 128

Galdos, Benito Perez
See Perez Galdos, Benito

Gale, Zona 1874-1938 .... **TCLC 7**
See also CA 105; DLB 9, 78

Galeano, Eduardo (Hughes) 1940-... **CLC 72**
See also CA 29-32R; CANR 13, 32; HW

Galiano, Juan Valera y Alcala
See Valera y Alcala-Galiano, Juan

Gallagher, Tess 1943- .... **CLC 18, 63; PC 9**
See also CA 106; DLB 120

Gallant, Mavis
1922- .... **CLC 7, 18, 38; SSC 5**
See also CA 69-72; CANR 29; DLB 53;
MTCW

Gallant, Roy A(rthur) 1924- .... **CLC 17**
See also CA 5-8R; CANR 4, 29; CLR 30;
MAICYA; SATA 4, 68

Gallico, Paul (William) 1897-1976 ... **CLC 2**
See also AITN 1; CA 5-8R; 69-72;
CANR 23; DLB 9; MAICYA; SATA 13

Gallup, Ralph
See Whitemore, Hugh (John)

Galsworthy, John
1867-1933 .... **TCLC 1, 45; DA; WLC 2**
See also CA 104; 141; CDBLB 1890-1914;
DLB 10, 34, 98

Galt, John 1779-1839 .... **NCLC 1**
See also DLB 99, 116

Galvin, James 1951- .... **CLC 38**
See also CA 108; CANR 26

Gamboa, Federico 1864-1939 ...... **TCLC 36**

Gandhi, M. K.
See Gandhi, Mohandas Karamchand

Gandhi, Mahatma
See Gandhi, Mohandas Karamchand

Gandhi, Mohandas Karamchand
1869-1948 .... **TCLC 59**
See also CA 121; 132; MTCW

Gann, Ernest Kellogg 1910-1991.... **CLC 23**
See also AITN 1; CA 1-4R; 136; CANR 1

Garcia, Cristina 1958- .... **CLC 76**
See also CA 141

Garcia Lorca, Federico
1898-1936 .... **TCLC 1, 7, 49; DA;
DC 2; HLC; PC 3; WLC**
See also CA 104; 131; DLB 108; HW;
MTCW

Garcia Marquez, Gabriel (Jose)
1928- .... **CLC 2, 3, 8, 10, 15, 27, 47, 55,
68; DA; HLC; SSC 8; WLC**
See also AAYA 3; BEST 89:1, 90:4;
CA 33-36R; CANR 10, 28; DLB 113;
HW; MTCW

Gard, Janice
See Latham, Jean Lee

Gard, Roger Martin du
See Martin du Gard, Roger

Gardam, Jane 1928- .... **CLC 43**
See also CA 49-52; CANR 2, 18, 33;
CLR 12; DLB 14; MAICYA; MTCW;
SAAS 9; SATA 39, 76; SATA-Brief 28

Gardner, Herb .... **CLC 44**

Gardner, John (Champlin), Jr.
1933-1982 ..... **CLC 2, 3, 5, 7, 8, 10, 18,
28, 34; SSC 7**
See also AITN 1; CA 65-68; 107;
CANR 33; DLB 2; DLBY 82; MTCW;
SATA 40; SATA-Obit 31

Gardner, John (Edmund) 1926- ..... **CLC 30**
See also CA 103; CANR 15; MTCW

Gardner, Noel
See Kuttner, Henry

Gardons, S. S.
See Snodgrass, W(illiam) D(e Witt)

Garfield, Leon 1921- .... **CLC 12**
See also AAYA 8; CA 17-20R; CANR 38,
41; CLR 21; JRDA; MAICYA; SATA 1,
32, 76

Garland, (Hannibal) Hamlin
1860-1940 .... **TCLC 3; SSC 18**
See also CA 104; DLB 12, 71, 78

Garneau, (Hector de) Saint-Denys
1912-1943 .... **TCLC 13**
See also CA 111; DLB 88

Garner, Alan 1934- .... **CLC 17**
See also CA 73-76; CANR 15; CLR 20;
MAICYA; MTCW; SATA 18, 69

Garner, Hugh 1913-1979 .... **CLC 13**
See also CA 69-72; CANR 31; DLB 68

Garnett, David 1892-1981 .... **CLC 3**
See also CA 5-8R; 103; CANR 17; DLB 34

Garos, Stephanie
See Katz, Steve

Garrett, George (Palmer)
1929- .... **CLC 3, 11, 51**
See also CA 1-4R; CAAS 5; CANR 1, 42;
DLB 2, 5, 130, 152; DLBY 83

Garrick, David 1717-1779 .... **LC 15**
See also DLB 84

Garrigue, Jean 1914-1972 .... **CLC 2, 8**
See also CA 5-8R; 37-40R; CANR 20

Garrison, Frederick
See Sinclair, Upton (Beall)

Garth, Will
See Hamilton, Edmond; Kuttner, Henry

Garvey, Marcus (Moziah, Jr.)
1887-1940 .... **TCLC 41; BLC**
See also BW 1; CA 120; 124

Gary, Romain .... **CLC 25**
See also Kacew, Romain
See also DLB 83

Gascar, Pierre .... **CLC 11**
See also Fournier, Pierre

Gascoyne, David (Emery) 1916- .... **CLC 45**
See also CA 65-68; CANR 10, 28; DLB 20;
MTCW

Gaskell, Elizabeth Cleghorn
1810-1865 .... **NCLC 5**
See also CDBLB 1832-1890; DLB 21, 144

Gass, William H(oward)
1924- ... **CLC 1, 2, 8, 11, 15, 39; SSC 12**
See also CA 17-20R; CANR 30; DLB 2;
MTCW

Gasset, Jose Ortega y
See Ortega y Gasset, Jose

Gates, Henry Louis, Jr. 1950- ...... **CLC 65**
See also BW 2; CA 109; CANR 25; DLB 67

Gautier, Theophile 1811-1872 ..... **NCLC 1**
See also DLB 119

Gawsworth, John
See Bates, H(erbert) E(rnest)

Gaye, Marvin (Penze) 1939-1984 ... **CLC 26**
See also CA 112

Gebler, Carlo (Ernest) 1954- .... **CLC 39**
See also CA 119; 133

Gee, Maggie (Mary) 1948- .... **CLC 57**
See also CA 130

Gee, Maurice (Gough) 1931- .... **CLC 29**
See also CA 97-100; SATA 46

Gelbart, Larry (Simon) 1923- ... **CLC 21, 61**
See also CA 73-76; CANR 45

Gelber, Jack 1932- .... **CLC 1, 6, 14, 79**
See also CA 1-4R; CANR 2; DLB 7

Gellhorn, Martha (Ellis) 1908- .. **CLC 14, 60**
See also CA 77-80; CANR 44; DLBY 82

Genet, Jean
1910-1986 ... **CLC 1, 2, 5, 10, 14, 44, 46**
See also CA 13-16R; CANR 18; DLB 72;
DLBY 86; MTCW

Gent, Peter 1942- .... **CLC 29**
See also AITN 1; CA 89-92; DLBY 82

Gentlewoman in New England, A
See Bradstreet, Anne

Gentlewoman in Those Parts, A
See Bradstreet, Anne

George, Jean Craighead 1919- ...... **CLC 35**
See also AAYA 8; CA 5-8R; CANR 25;
CLR 1; DLB 52; JRDA; MAICYA;
SATA 2, 68

George, Stefan (Anton)
1868-1933 .... **TCLC 2, 14**
See also CA 104

Georges, Georges Martin
See Simenon, Georges (Jacques Christian)

Gerhardi, William Alexander
See Gerhardie, William Alexander

Gerhardie, William Alexander
1895-1977 .... **CLC 5**
See also CA 25-28R; 73-76; CANR 18;
DLB 36

Gerstler, Amy 1956- .... **CLC 70**

Gertler, T. .... **CLC 34**
See also CA 116; 121

Ghalib 1797-1869 .... **NCLC 39**

Ghelderode, Michel de
1898-1962 .... **CLC 6, 11**
See also CA 85-88; CANR 40

Ghiselin, Brewster 1903- .... **CLC 23**
See also CA 13-16R; CAAS 10; CANR 13

Ghose, Zulfikar 1935- .... **CLC 42**
See also CA 65-68

Ghosh, Amitav 1956- .... **CLC 44**

Giacosa, Giuseppe 1847-1906 ...... **TCLC 7**
See also CA 104

Gibb, Lee
See Waterhouse, Keith (Spencer)

Gibbon, Lewis Grassic .... **TCLC 4**
See also Mitchell, James Leslie

Gibbons, Kaye 1960- .... **CLC 50, 88**

Gibran, Kahlil
1883-1931 .... **TCLC 1, 9; PC 9**
See also CA 104

Gibson, William 1914- .... **CLC 23; DA**
See also CA 9-12R; CANR 9, 42; DLB 7;
SATA 66

Gibson, William (Ford) 1948- ... **CLC 39, 63**
See also AAYA 12; CA 126; 133

Gide, Andre (Paul Guillaume)
1869-1951 .... **TCLC 5, 12, 36; DA;**
SSC 13; WLC
See also CA 104; 124; DLB 65; MTCW

Gifford, Barry (Colby) 1946- .... **CLC 34**
See also CA 65-68; CANR 9, 30, 40

Gilbert, W(illiam) S(chwenck)
1836-1911 .... **TCLC 3**
See also CA 104; SATA 36

Gilbreth, Frank B., Jr. 1911- .... **CLC 17**
See also CA 9-12R; SATA 2

Gilchrist, Ellen 1935- .. **CLC 34, 48; SSC 14**
See also CA 113; 116; CANR 41; DLB 130;
MTCW

Giles, Molly 1942- .... **CLC 39**
See also CA 126

Gill, Patrick
See Creasey, John

Gilliam, Terry (Vance) 1940- .... **CLC 21**
See also Monty Python
See also CA 108; 113; CANR 35

Gillian, Jerry
See Gilliam, Terry (Vance)

Gilliatt, Penelope (Ann Douglass)
1932-1993 .... **CLC 2, 10, 13, 53**
See also AITN 2; CA 13-16R; 141; DLB 14

Gilman, Charlotte (Anna) Perkins (Stetson)
1860-1935 .... **TCLC 9, 37; SSC 13**
See also CA 106

Gilmour, David 1949- .... **CLC 35**
See also CA 138

Gilpin, William 1724-1804 ...... **NCLC 30**

Gilray, J. D.
See Mencken, H(enry) L(ouis)

Gilroy, Frank D(aniel) 1925- .... **CLC 2**
See also CA 81-84; CANR 32; DLB 7

Ginsberg, Allen
1926- ...... **CLC 1, 2, 3, 4, 6, 13, 36, 69;**
DA; PC 4; WLC 3
See also AITN 1; CA 1-4R; CANR 2, 41;
CDALB 1941-1968; DLB 5, 16; MTCW

Ginzburg, Natalia
1916-1991 .... **CLC 5, 11, 54, 70**
See also CA 85-88; 135; CANR 33; MTCW

Giono, Jean 1895-1970.......... **CLC 4, 11**
See also CA 45-48; 29-32R; CANR 2, 35;
DLB 72; MTCW

Giovanni, Nikki
1943- ...... **CLC 2, 4, 19, 64; BLC; DA**
See also AITN 1; BW 2; CA 29-32R;
CAAS 6; CANR 18, 41; CLR 6; DLB 5,
41; MAICYA; MTCW; SATA 24

Giovene, Andrea 1904-............. **CLC 7**
See also CA 85-88

Gippius, Zinaida (Nikolayevna) 1869-1945
See Hippius, Zinaida
See also CA 106

Giraudoux, (Hippolyte) Jean
1882-1944 .... **TCLC 2, 7**
See also CA 104; DLB 65

Gironella, Jose Maria 1917- .... **CLC 11**
See also CA 101

Gissing, George (Robert)
1857-1903 .... **TCLC 3, 24, 47**
See also CA 105; DLB 18, 135

Giurlani, Aldo
See Palazzeschi, Aldo

Gladkov, Fyodor (Vasilyevich)
1883-1958 .... **TCLC 27**

Glanville, Brian (Lester) 1931- ...... **CLC 6**
See also CA 5-8R; CAAS 9; CANR 3;
DLB 15, 139; SATA 42

Glasgow, Ellen (Anderson Gholson)
1873(?)-1945 .... **TCLC 2, 7**
See also CA 104; DLB 9, 12

Glaspell, Susan (Keating)
1882(?)-1948 .... **TCLC 55**
See also CA 110; DLB 7, 9, 78; YABC 2

Glassco, John 1909-1981 .... **CLC 9**
See also CA 13-16R; 102; CANR 15;
DLB 68

Glasscock, Amnesia
See Steinbeck, John (Ernst)

Glasser, Ronald J. 1940(?)- .... **CLC 37**

Glassman, Joyce
See Johnson, Joyce

Glendinning, Victoria 1937-........ **CLC 50**
    See also CA 120; 127

Glissant, Edouard 1928-........ **CLC 10, 68**

Gloag, Julian 1930- .... **CLC 40**
    See also AITN 1; CA 65-68; CANR 10

Glowacki, Aleksander
    See Prus, Boleslaw

Glueck, Louise (Elisabeth)
    1943- .... **CLC 7, 22, 44, 81**
    See also CA 33-36R; CANR 40; DLB 5

Gobineau, Joseph Arthur (Comte) de
    1816-1882 .... **NCLC 17**
    See also DLB 123

Godard, Jean-Luc 1930-........... **CLC 20**
    See also CA 93-96

Godden, (Margaret) Rumer 1907-... **CLC 53**
    See also AAYA 6; CA 5-8R; CANR 4, 27,
    36; CLR 20; MAICYA; SAAS 12;
    SATA 3, 36

Godoy Alcayaga, Lucila 1889-1957
    See Mistral, Gabriela
    See also BW 2; CA 104; 131; HW; MTCW

Godwin, Gail (Kathleen)
    1937-........... **CLC 5, 8, 22, 31, 69**
    See also CA 29-32R; CANR 15, 43; DLB 6;
    MTCW

Godwin, William 1756-1836...... **NCLC 14**
    See also CDBLB 1789-1832; DLB 39, 104,
    142

Goethe, Johann Wolfgang von
    1749-1832 .... **NCLC 4, 22, 34; DA;**
                              PC 5; WLC 3
    See also DLB 94

Gogarty, Oliver St. John
    1878-1957 .... **TCLC 15**
    See also CA 109; DLB 15, 19

Gogol, Nikolai (Vasilyevich)
    1809-1852 .... **NCLC 5, 15, 31; DA;**
                              DC 1; SSC 4; WLC

Goines, Donald
    1937(?)-1974 .... **CLC 80; BLC**
    See also AITN 1; BW 1; CA 124; 114;
    DLB 33

Gold, Herbert 1924-....... **CLC 4, 7, 14, 42**
    See also CA 9-12R; CANR 17, 45; DLB 2;
    DLBY 81

Goldbarth, Albert 1948-........ **CLC 5, 38**
    See also CA 53-56; CANR 6, 40; DLB 120

Goldberg, Anatol 1910-1982 .... **CLC 34**
    See also CA 131; 117

Goldemberg, Isaac 1945-......... **CLC 52**
    See also CA 69-72; CAAS 12; CANR 11,
    32; HW

Golding, William (Gerald)
    1911-1993 .... **CLC 1, 2, 3, 8, 10, 17, 27,**
                         58, 81; DA; WLC
    See also AAYA 5; CA 5-8R; 141;
    CANR 13, 33; CDBLB 1945-1960;
    DLB 15, 100; MTCW

Goldman, Emma 1869-1940...... **TCLC 13**
    See also CA 110

Goldman, Francisco 1955-........ **CLC 76**

Goldman, William (W.) 1931-.... **CLC 1, 48**
    See also CA 9-12R; CANR 29; DLB 44

Goldmann, Lucien 1913-1970 ...... **CLC 24**
    See also CA 25-28; CAP 2

Goldoni, Carlo 1707-1793 .... **LC 4**

Goldsberry, Steven 1949-........ **CLC 34**
    See also CA 131

Goldsmith, Oliver
    1728-1774 .... **LC 2; DA; WLC**
    See also CDBLB 1660-1789; DLB 39, 89,
    104, 109, 142; SATA 26

Goldsmith, Peter
    See Priestley, J(ohn) B(oynton)

Gombrowicz, Witold
    1904-1969 .... **CLC 4, 7, 11, 49**
    See also CA 19-20; 25-28R; CAP 2

Gomez de la Serna, Ramon
    1888-1963 .... **CLC 9**
    See also CA 116; HW

Goncharov, Ivan Alexandrovich
    1812-1891 .... **NCLC 1**

Goncourt, Edmond (Louis Antoine Huot) de
    1822-1896 .... **NCLC 7**
    See also DLB 123

Goncourt, Jules (Alfred Huot) de
    1830-1870 .... **NCLC 7**
    See also DLB 123

Gontier, Fernande 19(?)- .... **CLC 50**

Goodman, Paul 1911-1972.... **CLC 1, 2, 4, 7**
    See also CA 19-20; 37-40R; CANR 34;
    CAP 2; DLB 130; MTCW

Gordimer, Nadine
    1923- .... **CLC 3, 5, 7, 10, 18, 33, 51, 70;**
                         DA; SSC 17
    See also CA 5-8R; CANR 3, 28; MTCW

Gordon, Adam Lindsay
    1833-1870 .... **NCLC 21**

Gordon, Caroline
    1895-1981 ... **CLC 6, 13, 29, 83; SSC 15**
    See also CA 11-12; 103; CANR 36; CAP 1;
    DLB 4, 9, 102; DLBY 81; MTCW

Gordon, Charles William 1860-1937
    See Connor, Ralph
    See also CA 109

Gordon, Mary (Catherine)
    1949- .... **CLC 13, 22**
    See also CA 102; CANR 44; DLB 6;
    DLBY 81; MTCW

Gordon, Sol 1923-................ **CLC 26**
    See also CA 53-56; CANR 4; SATA 11

Gordone, Charles 1925-.......... **CLC 1, 4**
    See also BW 1; CA 93-96; DLB 7; MTCW

Gorenko, Anna Andreevna
    See Akhmatova, Anna

Gorky, Maxim............. **TCLC 8; WLC**
    See also Peshkov, Alexei Maximovich

Goryan, Sirak
    See Saroyan, William

Gosse, Edmund (William)
    1849-1928 .... **TCLC 28**
    See also CA 117; DLB 57, 144

Gotlieb, Phyllis Fay (Bloom)
    1926- .... **CLC 18**
    See also CA 13-16R; CANR 7; DLB 88

Gottesman, S. D.
    See Kornbluth, C(yril) M.; Pohl, Frederik

Gottfried von Strassburg
    fl. c. 1210-................ **CMLC 10**
    See also DLB 138

Gould, Lois .... **CLC 4, 10**
    See also CA 77-80; CANR 29; MTCW

Gourmont, Remy de 1858-1915.... **TCLC 17**
    See also CA 109

Govier, Katherine 1948-........ **CLC 51**
    See also CA 101; CANR 18, 40

Goyen, (Charles) William
    1915-1983 .... **CLC 5, 8, 14, 40**
    See also AITN 2; CA 5-8R; 110; CANR 6;
    DLB 2; DLBY 83

Goytisolo, Juan
    1931- .... **CLC 5, 10, 23; HLC**
    See also CA 85-88; CANR 32; HW; MTCW

Gozzano, Guido 1883-1916 .... **PC 10**
    See also DLB 114

Gozzi, (Conte) Carlo 1720-1806 .. **NCLC 23**

Grabbe, Christian Dietrich
    1801-1836 .... **NCLC 2**
    See also DLB 133

Grace, Patricia 1937-............. **CLC 56**

Gracian y Morales, Baltasar
    1601-1658 .... **LC 15**

Gracq, Julien................. **CLC 11, 48**
    See also Poirier, Louis
    See also DLB 83

Grade, Chaim 1910-1982 .... **CLC 10**
    See also CA 93-96; 107

Graduate of Oxford, A
    See Ruskin, John

Graham, John
    See Phillips, David Graham

Graham, Jorie 1951-.............. **CLC 48**
    See also CA 111; DLB 120

Graham, R(obert) B(ontine) Cunninghame
    See Cunninghame Graham, R(obert)
    B(ontine)
    See also DLB 98, 135

Graham, Robert
    See Haldeman, Joe (William)

Graham, Tom
    See Lewis, (Harry) Sinclair

Graham, W(illiam) S(ydney)
    1918-1986 .... **CLC 29**
    See also CA 73-76; 118; DLB 20

Graham, Winston (Mawdsley)
    1910- .... **CLC 23**
    See also CA 49-52; CANR 2, 22, 45;
    DLB 77

Grant, Skeeter
    See Spiegelman, Art

Granville-Barker, Harley
    1877-1946 .... **TCLC 2**
    See also Barker, Harley Granville
    See also CA 104

Grass, Guenter (Wilhelm)
    1927- ..... **CLC 1, 2, 4, 6, 11, 15, 22, 32,**
                         49, 88; DA; WLC
    See also CA 13-16R; CANR 20; DLB 75,
    124; MTCW

Gratton, Thomas
    See Hulme, T(homas) E(rnest)

Grau, Shirley Ann
1929- . . . . **CLC 4, 9; SSC 15**
See also CA 89-92; CANR 22; DLB 2;
MTCW

Gravel, Fern
See Hall, James Norman

Graver, Elizabeth 1964- . . . . **CLC 70**
See also CA 135

Graves, Richard Perceval 1945- . . . . **CLC 44**
See also CA 65-68; CANR 9, 26

Graves, Robert (von Ranke)
1895-1985 . . . . . . **CLC 1, 2, 6, 11, 39, 44,**
45; PC 6
See also CA 5-8R; 117; CANR 5, 36;
CDBLB 1914-1945; DLB 20, 100;
DLBY 85; MTCW; SATA 45

Gray, Alasdair (James) 1934- . . . . . . **CLC 41**
See also CA 126; CANR 47; MTCW

Gray, Amlin 1946- . . . . **CLC 29**
See also CA 138

Gray, Francine du Plessix 1930- . . . . **CLC 22**
See also BEST 90:3; CA 61-64; CAAS 2;
CANR 11, 33; MTCW

Gray, John (Henry) 1866-1934 . . . . **TCLC 19**
See also CA 119

Gray, Simon (James Holliday)
1936- . . . . **CLC 9, 14, 36**
See also AITN 1; CA 21-24R; CAAS 3;
CANR 32; DLB 13; MTCW

Gray, Spalding 1941- . . . . **CLC 49**
See also CA 128

Gray, Thomas
1716-1771 . . . . . . **LC 4; DA; PC 2; WLC**
See also CDBLB 1660-1789; DLB 109

Grayson, David
See Baker, Ray Stannard

Grayson, Richard (A.) 1951- . . . . **CLC 38**
See also CA 85-88; CANR 14, 31

Greeley, Andrew M(oran) 1928- . . . . **CLC 28**
See also CA 5-8R; CAAS 7; CANR 7, 43;
MTCW

Green, Brian
See Card, Orson Scott

Green, Hannah
See Greenberg, Joanne (Goldenberg)

Green, Hannah . . . . **CLC 3**
See also CA 73-76

Green, Henry . . . . **CLC 2, 13**
See also Yorke, Henry Vincent
See also DLB 15

Green, Julian (Hartridge) 1900-
See Green, Julien
See also CA 21-24R; CANR 33; DLB 4, 72;
MTCW

Green, Julien . . . . **CLC 3, 11, 77**
See also Green, Julian (Hartridge)

Green, Paul (Eliot) 1894-1981 . . . . . . **CLC 25**
See also AITN 1; CA 5-8R; 103; CANR 3;
DLB 7, 9; DLBY 81

Greenberg, Ivan 1908-1973
See Rahv, Philip
See also CA 85-88

Greenberg, Joanne (Goldenberg)
1932- . . . . **CLC 7, 30**
See also AAYA 12; CA 5-8R; CANR 14,
32; SATA 25

Greenberg, Richard 1959(?)- . . . . **CLC 57**
See also CA 138

Greene, Bette 1934- . . . . **CLC 30**
See also AAYA 7; CA 53-56; CANR 4;
CLR 2; JRDA; MAICYA; SAAS 16;
SATA 8

Greene, Gael . . . . **CLC 8**
See also CA 13-16R; CANR 10

Greene, Graham
1904-1991 . . . . **CLC 1, 3, 6, 9, 14, 18, 27,**
37, 70, 72; DA; WLC
See also AITN 2; CA 13-16R; 133;
CANR 35; CDBLB 1945-1960; DLB 13,
15, 77, 100; DLBY 91; MTCW; SATA 20

Greer, Richard
See Silverberg, Robert

Greer, Richard
See Silverberg, Robert

Gregor, Arthur 1923- . . . . **CLC 9**
See also CA 25-28R; CAAS 10; CANR 11;
SATA 36

Gregor, Lee
See Pohl, Frederik

Gregory, Isabella Augusta (Persse)
1852-1932 . . . . **TCLC 1**
See also CA 104; DLB 10

Gregory, J. Dennis
See Williams, John A(lfred)

Grendon, Stephen
See Derleth, August (William)

Grenville, Kate 1950- . . . . **CLC 61**
See also CA 118

Grenville, Pelham
See Wodehouse, P(elham) G(renville)

Greve, Felix Paul (Berthold Friedrich)
1879-1948
See Grove, Frederick Philip
See also CA 104; 141

Grey, Zane 1872-1939 . . . . **TCLC 6**
See also CA 104; 132; DLB 9; MTCW

Grieg, (Johan) Nordahl (Brun)
1902-1943 . . . . **TCLC 10**
See also CA 107

Grieve, C(hristopher) M(urray)
1892-1978 . . . . **CLC 11, 19**
See also MacDiarmid, Hugh
See also CA 5-8R; 85-88; CANR 33;
MTCW

Griffin, Gerald 1803-1840 . . . . **NCLC 7**

Griffin, John Howard 1920-1980 . . . . **CLC 68**
See also AITN 1; CA 1-4R; 101; CANR 2

Griffin, Peter 1942- . . . . **CLC 39**
See also CA 136

Griffiths, Trevor 1935- . . . . **CLC 13, 52**
See also CA 97-100; CANR 45; DLB 13

Grigson, Geoffrey (Edward Harvey)
1905-1985 . . . . **CLC 7, 39**
See also CA 25-28R; 118; CANR 20, 33;
DLB 27; MTCW

Grillparzer, Franz 1791-1872 . . . . . . **NCLC 1**
See also DLB 133

Grimble, Reverend Charles James
See Eliot, T(homas) S(tearns)

Grimke, Charlotte L(ottie) Forten
1837(?)-1914
See Forten, Charlotte L.
See also BW 1; CA 117; 124

Grimm, Jacob Ludwig Karl
1785-1863 . . . . **NCLC 3**
See also DLB 90; MAICYA; SATA 22

Grimm, Wilhelm Karl 1786-1859 . . **NCLC 3**
See also DLB 90; MAICYA; SATA 22

Grimmelshausen, Johann Jakob Christoffel
von 1621-1676 . . . . **LC 6**

Grindel, Eugene 1895-1952
See Eluard, Paul
See also CA 104

Grisham, John 1955- . . . . **CLC 84**
See also AAYA 14; CA 138; CANR 47

Grossman, David 1954- . . . . **CLC 67**
See also CA 138

Grossman, Vasily (Semenovich)
1905-1964 . . . . **CLC 41**
See also CA 124; 130; MTCW

Grove, Frederick Philip . . . . **TCLC 4**
See also Greve, Felix Paul (Berthold
Friedrich)
See also DLB 92

Grubb
See Crumb, R(obert)

Grumbach, Doris (Isaac)
1918- . . . . **CLC 13, 22, 64**
See also CA 5-8R; CAAS 2; CANR 9, 42

Grundtvig, Nicolai Frederik Severin
1783-1872 . . . . **NCLC 1**

Grunge
See Crumb, R(obert)

Grunwald, Lisa 1959- . . . . **CLC 44**
See also CA 120

Guare, John 1938- . . . . **CLC 8, 14, 29, 67**
See also CA 73-76; CANR 21; DLB 7;
MTCW

Gudjonsson, Halldor Kiljan 1902-
See Laxness, Halldor
See also CA 103

Guenter, Erich
See Eich, Guenter

Guest, Barbara 1920- . . . . **CLC 34**
See also CA 25-28R; CANR 11, 44; DLB 5

Guest, Judith (Ann) 1936- . . . . **CLC 8, 30**
See also AAYA 7; CA 77-80; CANR 15;
MTCW

Guevara, Che . . . . **CLC 87; HLC**
See also Guevara (Serna), Ernesto

Guevara (Serna), Ernesto 1928-1967
See Guevara, Che
See also CA 127; 111; HW

Guild, Nicholas M. 1944- . . . . **CLC 33**
See also CA 93-96

Guillemin, Jacques
See Sartre, Jean-Paul

Guillen, Jorge 1893-1984 . . . . **CLC 11**
See also CA 89-92; 112; DLB 108; HW

Guillen (y Batista), Nicolas (Cristobal)
    1902-1989 ..... CLC 48, 79; BLC; HLC
    See also BW 2; CA 116; 125; 129; HW

Guillevic, (Eugene) 1907-......... CLC 33
    See also CA 93-96

Guillois
    See Desnos, Robert

Guiney, Louise Imogen
    1861-1920 .... TCLC 41
    See also DLB 54

Guiraldes, Ricardo (Guillermo)
    1886-1927 .... TCLC 39
    See also CA 131; HW; MTCW

Gunn, Bill .... CLC 5
    See also Gunn, William Harrison
    See also DLB 38

Gunn, Thom(son William)
    1929- .... CLC 3, 6, 18, 32, 81
    See also CA 17-20R; CANR 9, 33;
    CDBLB 1960 to Present; DLB 27;
    MTCW

Gunn, William Harrison 1934(?)-1989
    See Gunn, Bill
    See also AITN 1; BW 1; CA 13-16R; 128;
    CANR 12, 25

Gunnars, Kristjana 1948-......... CLC 69
    See also CA 113; DLB 60

Gurganus, Allan 1947-............ CLC 70
    See also BEST 90:1; CA 135

Gurney, A(lbert) R(amsdell), Jr.
    1930- .... CLC 32, 50, 54
    See also CA 77-80; CANR 32

Gurney, Ivor (Bertie) 1890-1937 ... TCLC 33

Gurney, Peter
    See Gurney, A(lbert) R(amsdell), Jr.

Guro, Elena 1877-1913.......... TCLC 56

Gustafson, Ralph (Barker) 1909-.... CLC 36
    See also CA 21-24R; CANR 8, 45; DLB 88

Gut, Gom
    See Simenon, Georges (Jacques Christian)

Guthrie, A(lfred) B(ertram), Jr.
    1901-1991 .... CLC 23
    See also CA 57-60; 134; CANR 24; DLB 6;
    SATA 62; SATA-Obit 67

Guthrie, Isobel
    See Grieve, C(hristopher) M(urray)

Guthrie, Woodrow Wilson 1912-1967
    See Guthrie, Woody
    See also CA 113; 93-96

Guthrie, Woody.................... CLC 35
    See also Guthrie, Woodrow Wilson

Guy, Rosa (Cuthbert) 1928-........ CLC 26
    See also AAYA 4; BW 2; CA 17-20R;
    CANR 14, 34; CLR 13; DLB 33; JRDA;
    MAICYA; SATA 14, 62

Gwendolyn
    See Bennett, (Enoch) Arnold

H. D. .... CLC 3, 8, 14, 31, 34, 73; PC 5
    See also Doolittle, Hilda

H. de V.
    See Buchan, John

Haavikko, Paavo Juhani
    1931- .... CLC 18, 34
    See also CA 106

Habbema, Koos
    See Heijermans, Herman

Hacker, Marilyn 1942-.... CLC 5, 9, 23, 72
    See also CA 77-80; DLB 120

Haggard, H(enry) Rider
    1856-1925 .... TCLC 11
    See also CA 108; DLB 70; SATA 16

Haig, Fenil
    See Ford, Ford Madox

Haig-Brown, Roderick (Langmere)
    1908-1976 .... CLC 21
    See also CA 5-8R; 69-72; CANR 4, 38;
    CLR 31; DLB 88; MAICYA; SATA 12

Hailey, Arthur 1920-.............. CLC 5
    See also AITN 2; BEST 90:3; CA 1-4R;
    CANR 2, 36; DLB 88; DLBY 82; MTCW

Hailey, Elizabeth Forsythe 1938-... CLC 40
    See also CA 93-96; CAAS 1; CANR 15

Haines, John (Meade) 1924-....... CLC 58
    See also CA 17-20R; CANR 13, 34; DLB 5

Haldeman, Joe (William) 1943-..... CLC 61
    See also CA 53-56; CANR 6; DLB 8

Haley, Alex(ander Murray Palmer)
    1921-1992 .... CLC 8, 12, 76; BLC; DA
    See also BW 2; CA 77-80; 136; DLB 38;
    MTCW

Haliburton, Thomas Chandler
    1796-1865 .... NCLC 15
    See also DLB 11, 99

Hall, Donald (Andrew, Jr.)
    1928- .... CLC 1, 13, 37, 59
    See also CA 5-8R; CAAS 7; CANR 2, 44;
    DLB 5; SATA 23

Hall, Frederic Sauser
    See Sauser-Hall, Frederic

Hall, James
    See Kuttner, Henry

Hall, James Norman 1887-1951 ... TCLC 23
    See also CA 123; SATA 21

Hall, (Marguerite) Radclyffe
    1886(?)-1943 .... TCLC 12
    See also CA 110

Hall, Rodney 1935-.............. CLC 51
    See also CA 109

Halleck, Fitz-Greene 1790-1867 .. NCLC 47
    See also DLB 3

Halliday, Michael
    See Creasey, John

Halpern, Daniel 1945-............ CLC 14
    See also CA 33-36R

Hamburger, Michael (Peter Leopold)
    1924- .... CLC 5, 14
    See also CA 5-8R; CAAS 4; CANR 2, 47;
    DLB 27

Hamill, Pete 1935-.............. CLC 10
    See also CA 25-28R; CANR 18

Hamilton, Alexander
    1755(?)-1804 .... NCLC 49
    See also DLB 37

Hamilton, Clive
    See Lewis, C(live) S(taples)

Hamilton, Edmond 1904-1977...... CLC 1
    See also CA 1-4R; CANR 3; DLB 8

Hamilton, Eugene (Jacob) Lee
    See Lee-Hamilton, Eugene (Jacob)

Hamilton, Franklin
    See Silverberg, Robert

Hamilton, Gail
    See Corcoran, Barbara

Hamilton, Mollie
    See Kaye, M(ary) M(argaret)

Hamilton, (Anthony Walter) Patrick
    1904-1962 .... CLC 51
    See also CA 113; DLB 10

Hamilton, Virginia 1936-......... CLC 26
    See also AAYA 2; BW 2; CA 25-28R;
    CANR 20, 37; CLR 1, 11; DLB 33, 52;
    JRDA; MAICYA; MTCW; SATA 4, 56,
    79

Hammett, (Samuel) Dashiell
    1894-1961 .... CLC 3, 5, 10, 19, 47;
                                        SSC 17
    See also AITN 1; CA 81-84; CANR 42;
    CDALB 1929-1941; DLBD 6; MTCW

Hammon, Jupiter
    1711(?)-1800(?) .... NCLC 5; BLC
    See also DLB 31, 50

Hammond, Keith
    See Kuttner, Henry

Hamner, Earl (Henry), Jr. 1923- ... CLC 12
    See also AITN 2; CA 73-76; DLB 6

Hampton, Christopher (James)
    1946- .... CLC 4
    See also CA 25-28R; DLB 13; MTCW

Hamsun, Knut............. TCLC 2, 14, 49
    See also Pedersen, Knut

Handke, Peter 1942-.. CLC 5, 8, 10, 15, 38
    See also CA 77-80; CANR 33; DLB 85,
    124; MTCW

Hanley, James 1901-1985 ... CLC 3, 5, 8, 13
    See also CA 73-76; 117; CANR 36; MTCW

Hannah, Barry 1942-.......... CLC 23, 38
    See also CA 108; 110; CANR 43; DLB 6;
    MTCW

Hannon, Ezra
    See Hunter, Evan

Hansberry, Lorraine (Vivian)
    1930-1965 ...... CLC 17, 62; BLC; DA;
                                        DC 2
    See also BW 1; CA 109; 25-28R; CABS 3;
    CDALB 1941-1968; DLB 7, 38; MTCW

Hansen, Joseph 1923-............ CLC 38
    See also CA 29-32R; CAAS 17; CANR 16,
    44

Hansen, Martin A. 1909-1955..... TCLC 32

Hanson, Kenneth O(stlin) 1922- .... CLC 13
    See also CA 53-56; CANR 7

Hardwick, Elizabeth 1916- .... CLC 13
    See also CA 5-8R; CANR 3, 32; DLB 6;
    MTCW

Hardy, Thomas
    1840-1928 ...... TCLC 4, 10, 18, 32, 48,
                            53; DA; PC 8; SSC 2; WLC
    See also CA 104; 123; CDBLB 1890-1914;
    DLB 18, 19, 135; MTCW

Hare, David 1947- .... CLC 29, 58
    See also CA 97-100; CANR 39; DLB 13;
    MTCW

Harford, Henry
See Hudson, W(illiam) H(enry)

Hargrave, Leonie
See Disch, Thomas M(ichael)

Harjo, Joy 1951- .... **CLC 83**
See also CA 114; CANR 35; DLB 120;
NNAL

Harlan, Louis R(udolph) 1922- ..... **CLC 34**
See also CA 21-24R; CANR 25

Harling, Robert 1951(?)- .... **CLC 53**

Harmon, William (Ruth) 1938- ..... **CLC 38**
See also CA 33-36R; CANR 14, 32, 35;
SATA 65

Harper, F. E. W.
See Harper, Frances Ellen Watkins

Harper, Frances E. W.
See Harper, Frances Ellen Watkins

Harper, Frances E. Watkins
See Harper, Frances Ellen Watkins

Harper, Frances Ellen
See Harper, Frances Ellen Watkins

Harper, Frances Ellen Watkins
1825-1911 .... **TCLC 14; BLC**
See also BW 1; CA 111; 125; DLB 50

Harper, Michael S(teven) 1938- .. **CLC 7, 22**
See also BW 1; CA 33-36R; CANR 24;
DLB 41

Harper, Mrs. F. E. W.
See Harper, Frances Ellen Watkins

Harris, Christie (Lucy) Irwin
1907- .... **CLC 12**
See also CA 5-8R; CANR 6; DLB 88;
JRDA; MAICYA; SAAS 10; SATA 6, 74

Harris, Frank 1856(?)-1931 ...... **TCLC 24**
See also CA 109

Harris, George Washington
1814-1869 .... **NCLC 23**
See also DLB 3, 11

Harris, Joel Chandler 1848-1908 ... **TCLC 2**
See also CA 104; 137; DLB 11, 23, 42, 78,
91; MAICYA; YABC 1

Harris, John (Wyndham Parkes Lucas)
Beynon 1903-1969
See Wyndham, John
See also CA 102; 89-92

Harris, MacDonald .... **CLC 9**
See also Heiney, Donald (William)

Harris, Mark 1922- .... **CLC 19**
See also CA 5-8R; CAAS 3; CANR 2;
DLB 2; DLBY 80

Harris, (Theodore) Wilson 1921- .... **CLC 25**
See also BW 2; CA 65-68; CAAS 16;
CANR 11, 27; DLB 117; MTCW

Harrison, Elizabeth Cavanna 1909-
See Cavanna, Betty
See also CA 9-12R; CANR 6, 27

Harrison, Harry (Max) 1925- ...... **CLC 42**
See also CA 1-4R; CANR 5, 21; DLB 8;
SATA 4

Harrison, James (Thomas)
1937- .... **CLC 6, 14, 33, 66**
See also CA 13-16R; CANR 8; DLBY 82

Harrison, Jim
See Harrison, James (Thomas)

Harrison, Kathryn 1961- .... **CLC 70**
See also CA 144

Harrison, Tony 1937- .... **CLC 43**
See also CA 65-68; CANR 44; DLB 40;
MTCW

Harriss, Will(ard Irvin) 1922- ..... **CLC 34**
See also CA 111

Harson, Sley
See Ellison, Harlan (Jay)

Hart, Ellis
See Ellison, Harlan (Jay)

Hart, Josephine 1942(?)- .... **CLC 70**
See also CA 138

Hart, Moss 1904-1961 .... **CLC 66**
See also CA 109; 89-92; DLB 7

Harte, (Francis) Bret(t)
1836(?)-1902 .... **TCLC 1, 25; DA;
SSC 8; WLC**
See also CA 104; 140; CDALB 1865-1917;
DLB 12, 64, 74, 79; SATA 26

Hartley, L(eslie) P(oles)
1895-1972 .... **CLC 2, 22**
See also CA 45-48; 37-40R; CANR 33;
DLB 15, 139; MTCW

Hartman, Geoffrey H. 1929- .... **CLC 27**
See also CA 117; 125; DLB 67

Hartmann von Aue
c. 1160-c. 1205 .... **CMLC 15**
See also DLB 138

Haruf, Kent 19(?)- .... **CLC 34**

Harwood, Ronald 1934- .... **CLC 32**
See also CA 1-4R; CANR 4; DLB 13

Hasek, Jaroslav (Matej Frantisek)
1883-1923 .... **TCLC 4**
See also CA 104; 129; MTCW

Hass, Robert 1941- .... **CLC 18, 39**
See also CA 111; CANR 30; DLB 105

Hastings, Hudson
See Kuttner, Henry

Hastings, Selina .... **CLC 44**

Hatteras, Amelia
See Mencken, H(enry) L(ouis)

Hatteras, Owen .... **TCLC 18**
See also Mencken, H(enry) L(ouis); Nathan,
George Jean

Hauptmann, Gerhart (Johann Robert)
1862-1946 .... **TCLC 4**
See also CA 104; DLB 66, 118

Havel, Vaclav 1936- .... **CLC 25, 58, 65**
See also CA 104; CANR 36; MTCW

Haviaras, Stratis .... **CLC 33**
See also Chaviaras, Strates

Hawes, Stephen 1475(?)-1523(?) ..... **LC 17**

Hawkes, John (Clendennin Burne, Jr.)
1925- ...... **CLC 1, 2, 3, 4, 7, 9, 14, 15,
27, 49**
See also CA 1-4R; CANR 2, 47; DLB 2, 7;
DLBY 80; MTCW

Hawking, S. W.
See Hawking, Stephen W(illiam)

Hawking, Stephen W(illiam)
1942- .... **CLC 63**
See also AAYA 13; BEST 89:1; CA 126;
129

Hawthorne, Julian 1846-1934 ..... **TCLC 25**

Hawthorne, Nathaniel
1804-1864 ...... **NCLC 39; DA; SSC 3;
WLC**
See also CDALB 1640-1865; DLB 1, 74;
YABC 2

Haxton, Josephine Ayres 1921-
See Douglas, Ellen
See also CA 115; CANR 41

Hayaseca y Eizaguirre, Jorge
See Echegaray (y Eizaguirre), Jose (Maria
Waldo)

Hayashi Fumiko 1904-1951 .... **TCLC 27**

Haycraft, Anna
See Ellis, Alice Thomas
See also CA 122

Hayden, Robert E(arl)
1913-1980 ...... **CLC 5, 9, 14, 37; BLC;
DA; PC 6**
See also BW 1; CA 69-72; 97-100; CABS 2;
CANR 24; CDALB 1941-1968; DLB 5,
76; MTCW; SATA 19; SATA-Obit 26

Hayford, J(oseph) E(phraim) Casely
See Casely-Hayford, J(oseph) E(phraim)

Hayman, Ronald 1932- .... **CLC 44**
See also CA 25-28R; CANR 18

Haywood, Eliza (Fowler)
1693(?)-1756 .... **LC 1**

Hazlitt, William 1778-1830 ...... **NCLC 29**
See also DLB 110

Hazzard, Shirley 1931- .... **CLC 18**
See also CA 9-12R; CANR 4; DLBY 82;
MTCW

Head, Bessie 1937-1986 ... **CLC 25, 67; BLC**
See also BW 2; CA 29-32R; 119; CANR 25;
DLB 117; MTCW

Headon, (Nicky) Topper 1956(?)- ... **CLC 30**

Heaney, Seamus (Justin)
1939- .... **CLC 5, 7, 14, 25, 37, 74**
See also CA 85-88; CANR 25;
CDBLB 1960 to Present; DLB 40;
MTCW

Hearn, (Patricio) Lafcadio (Tessima Carlos)
1850-1904 .... **TCLC 9**
See also CA 105; DLB 12, 78

Hearne, Vicki 1946- .... **CLC 56**
See also CA 139

Hearon, Shelby 1931- .... **CLC 63**
See also AITN 2; CA 25-28R; CANR 18

Heat-Moon, William Least .... **CLC 29**
See also Trogdon, William (Lewis)
See also AAYA 9

Hebbel, Friedrich 1813-1863 ..... **NCLC 43**
See also DLB 129

Hebert, Anne 1916- .... **CLC 4, 13, 29**
See also CA 85-88; DLB 68; MTCW

Hecht, Anthony (Evan)
1923- .... **CLC 8, 13, 19**
See also CA 9-12R; CANR 6; DLB 5

Hecht, Ben 1894-1964 .... **CLC 8**
See also CA 85-88; DLB 7, 9, 25, 26, 28, 86

Hedayat, Sadeq 1903-1951 .... **TCLC 21**
See also CA 120

Hegel, Georg Wilhelm Friedrich
    1770-1831 .... **NCLC 46**
    See also DLB 90

Heidegger, Martin 1889-1976 ...... **CLC 24**
    See also CA 81-84; 65-68; CANR 34;
    MTCW

Heidenstam, (Carl Gustaf) Verner von
    1859-1940 .... **TCLC 5**
    See also CA 104

Heifner, Jack 1946- .... **CLC 11**
    See also CA 105; CANR 47

Heijermans, Herman 1864-1924 ... **TCLC 24**
    See also CA 123

Heilbrun, Carolyn G(old) 1926-..... **CLC 25**
    See also CA 45-48; CANR 1, 28

Heine, Heinrich 1797-1856 .... **NCLC 4**
    See also DLB 90

Heinemann, Larry (Curtiss) 1944- .. **CLC 50**
    See also CA 110; CANR 31; DLBD 9

Heiney, Donald (William) 1921-1993
    See Harris, MacDonald
    See also CA 1-4R; 142; CANR 3

Heinlein, Robert A(nson)
    1907-1988 ...... **CLC 1, 3, 8, 14, 26, 55**
    See also CA 1-4R; 125; CANR 1, 20;
    DLB 8; JRDA; MAICYA; MTCW;
    SATA 9, 69; SATA-Obit 56

Helforth, John
    See Doolittle, Hilda

Hellenhofferu, Vojtech Kapristian z
    See Hasek, Jaroslav (Matej Frantisek)

Heller, Joseph
    1923- .... **CLC 1, 3, 5, 8, 11, 36, 63; DA;**
                               WLC
    See also AITN 1; CA 5-8R; CABS 1;
    CANR 8, 42; DLB 2, 28; DLBY 80;
    MTCW

Hellman, Lillian (Florence)
    1906-1984 ...... **CLC 2, 4, 8, 14, 18, 34,**
                            44, 52; DC 1
    See also AITN 1, 2; CA 13-16R; 112;
    CANR 33; DLB 7; DLBY 84; MTCW

Helprin, Mark 1947- ..... **CLC 7, 10, 22, 32**
    See also CA 81-84; CANR 47; DLBY 85;
    MTCW

Helvetius, Claude-Adrien
    1715-1771 .... **LC 26**

Helyar, Jane Penelope Josephine 1933-
    See Poole, Josephine
    See also CA 21-24R; CANR 10, 26

Hemans, Felicia 1793-1835 ...... **NCLC 29**
    See also DLB 96

Hemingway, Ernest (Miller)
    1899-1961 .... **CLC 1, 3, 6, 8, 10, 13, 19,**
     30, 34, 39, 41, 44, 50, 61, 80; DA; SSC 1;
                              WLC
    See also CA 77-80; CANR 34;
    CDALB 1917-1929; DLB 4, 9, 102;
    DLBD 1; DLBY 81, 87; MTCW

Hempel, Amy 1951- .... **CLC 39**
    See also CA 118; 137

Henderson, F. C.
    See Mencken, H(enry) L(ouis)

Henderson, Sylvia
    See Ashton-Warner, Sylvia (Constance)

Henley, Beth .... **CLC 23**
    See also Henley, Elizabeth Becker
    See also CABS 3; DLBY 86

Henley, Elizabeth Becker 1952-
    See Henley, Beth
    See also CA 107; CANR 32; MTCW

Henley, William Ernest
    1849-1903 .... **TCLC 8**
    See also CA 105; DLB 19

Hennissart, Martha
    See Lathen, Emma
    See also CA 85-88

Henry, O. .... **TCLC 1, 19; SSC 5; WLC**
    See also Porter, William Sydney

Henry, Patrick 1736- .... **LC 25**
    See also CA 145

Henryson, Robert 1430(?)-1506(?).... **LC 20**
    See also DLB 146

Henry VIII 1491-1547 .... **LC 10**

Henschke, Alfred
    See Klabund

Hentoff, Nat(han Irving) 1925- ..... **CLC 26**
    See also AAYA 4; CA 1-4R; CAAS 6;
    CANR 5, 25; CLR 1; JRDA; MAICYA;
    SATA 42, 69; SATA-Brief 27

Heppenstall, (John) Rayner
    1911-1981 .... **CLC 10**
    See also CA 1-4R; 103; CANR 29

Herbert, Frank (Patrick)
    1920-1986 ...... **CLC 12, 23, 35, 44, 85**
    See also CA 53-56; 118; CANR 5, 43;
    DLB 8; MTCW; SATA 9, 37;
    SATA-Obit 47

Herbert, George 1593-1633 .... **LC 24; PC 4**
    See also CDBLB Before 1660; DLB 126

Herbert, Zbigniew 1924- .... **CLC 9, 43**
    See also CA 89-92; CANR 36; MTCW

Herbst, Josephine (Frey)
    1897-1969 .... **CLC 34**
    See also CA 5-8R; 25-28R; DLB 9

Hergesheimer, Joseph
    1880-1954 .... **TCLC 11**
    See also CA 109; DLB 102, 9

Herlihy, James Leo 1927-1993 ...... **CLC 6**
    See also CA 1-4R; 143; CANR 2

Hermogenes fl. c. 175- .... **CMLC 6**

Hernandez, Jose 1834-1886 ...... **NCLC 17**

Herrick, Robert
    1591-1674 .... **LC 13; DA; PC 9**
    See also DLB 126

Herring, Guilles
    See Somerville, Edith

Herriot, James 1916-1995 .... **CLC 12**
    See also Wight, James Alfred
    See also AAYA 1; CANR 40

Herrmann, Dorothy 1941- .... **CLC 44**
    See also CA 107

Herrmann, Taffy
    See Herrmann, Dorothy

Hersey, John (Richard)
    1914-1993 .... **CLC 1, 2, 7, 9, 40, 81**
    See also CA 17-20R; 140; CANR 33;
    DLB 6; MTCW; SATA 25;
    SATA-Obit 76

Herzen, Aleksandr Ivanovich
    1812-1870 .... **NCLC 10**

Herzl, Theodor 1860-1904 .... **TCLC 36**

Herzog, Werner 1942- .... **CLC 16**
    See also CA 89-92

Hesiod c. 8th cent. B.C.- .... **CMLC 5**

Hesse, Hermann
    1877-1962 .... **CLC 1, 2, 3, 6, 11, 17, 25,**
               69; DA; SSC 9; WLC
    See also CA 17-18; CAP 2; DLB 66;
    MTCW; SATA 50

Hewes, Cady
    See De Voto, Bernard (Augustine)

Heyen, William 1940- .... **CLC 13, 18**
    See also CA 33-36R; CAAS 9; DLB 5

Heyerdahl, Thor 1914- .... **CLC 26**
    See also CA 5-8R; CANR 5, 22; MTCW;
    SATA 2, 52

Heym, Georg (Theodor Franz Arthur)
    1887-1912 .... **TCLC 9**
    See also CA 106

Heym, Stefan 1913- .... **CLC 41**
    See also CA 9-12R; CANR 4; DLB 69

Heyse, Paul (Johann Ludwig von)
    1830-1914 .... **TCLC 8**
    See also CA 104; DLB 129

Heyward, (Edwin) DuBose
    1885-1940 .... **TCLC 59**
    See also CA 108; DLB 7, 9, 45; SATA 21

Hibbert, Eleanor Alice Burford
    1906-1993 .... **CLC 7**
    See also BEST 90:4; CA 17-20R; 140;
    CANR 9, 28; SATA 2; SATA-Obit 74

Higgins, George V(incent)
    1939- .... **CLC 4, 7, 10, 18**
    See also CA 77-80; CAAS 5; CANR 17;
    DLB 2; DLBY 81; MTCW

Higginson, Thomas Wentworth
    1823-1911 .... **TCLC 36**
    See also DLB 1, 64

Highet, Helen
    See MacInnes, Helen (Clark)

Highsmith, (Mary) Patricia
    1921- .... **CLC 2, 4, 14, 42**
    See also CA 1-4R; CANR 1, 20; MTCW

Highwater, Jamake (Mamake)
    1942(?)- .... **CLC 12**
    See also AAYA 7; CA 65-68; CAAS 7;
    CANR 10, 34; CLR 17; DLB 52;
    DLBY 85; JRDA; MAICYA; SATA 32,
    69; SATA-Brief 30

Higuchi, Ichiyo 1872-1896....... **NCLC 49**

Hijuelos, Oscar 1951- ...... **CLC 65; HLC**
    See also BEST 90:1; CA 123; DLB 145; HW

Hikmet, Nazim 1902(?)-1963....... **CLC 40**
    See also CA 141; 93-96

Hildesheimer, Wolfgang
    1916-1991 .... **CLC 49**
    See also CA 101; 135; DLB 69, 124

Hill, Geoffrey (William)
    1932- .... **CLC 5, 8, 18, 45**
    See also CA 81-84; CANR 21;
    CDBLB 1960 to Present; DLB 40;
    MTCW

Hill, George Roy 1921- . . . . **CLC 26**
See also CA 110; 122

Hill, John
See Koontz, Dean R(ay)

Hill, Susan (Elizabeth) 1942- . . . . . . **CLC 4**
See also CA 33-36R; CANR 29; DLB 14, 139; MTCW

Hillerman, Tony 1925- . . . . **CLC 62**
See also AAYA 6; BEST 89:1; CA 29-32R; CANR 21, 42; SATA 6

Hillesum, Etty 1914-1943 . . . . **TCLC 49**
See also CA 137

Hilliard, Noel (Harvey) 1929- . . . . . **CLC 15**
See also CA 9-12R; CANR 7

Hillis, Rick 1956- . . . . **CLC 66**
See also CA 134

Hilton, James 1900-1954 . . . . **TCLC 21**
See also CA 108; DLB 34, 77; SATA 34

Himes, Chester (Bomar)
1909-1984 . . . . **CLC 2, 4, 7, 18, 58; BLC**
See also BW 2; CA 25-28R; 114; CANR 22; DLB 2, 76, 143; MTCW

Hinde, Thomas . . . . **CLC 6, 11**
See also Chitty, Thomas Willes

Hindin, Nathan
See Bloch, Robert (Albert)

Hine, (William) Daryl 1936- . . . . **CLC 15**
See also CA 1-4R; CAAS 15; CANR 1, 20; DLB 60

Hinkson, Katharine Tynan
See Tynan, Katharine

Hinton, S(usan) E(loise)
1950- . . . . **CLC 30; DA**
See also AAYA 2; CA 81-84; CANR 32; CLR 3, 23; JRDA; MAICYA; MTCW; SATA 19, 58

Hippius, Zinaida . . . . **TCLC 9**
See also Gippius, Zinaida (Nikolayevna)

Hiraoka, Kimitake 1925-1970
See Mishima, Yukio
See also CA 97-100; 29-32R; MTCW

Hirsch, E(ric) D(onald), Jr. 1928- . . . **CLC 79**
See also CA 25-28R; CANR 27; DLB 67; MTCW

Hirsch, Edward 1950- . . . . **CLC 31, 50**
See also CA 104; CANR 20, 42; DLB 120

Hitchcock, Alfred (Joseph)
1899-1980 . . . . **CLC 16**
See also CA 97-100; SATA 27; SATA-Obit 24

Hitler, Adolf 1889-1945 . . . . **TCLC 53**
See also CA 117

Hoagland, Edward 1932- . . . . **CLC 28**
See also CA 1-4R; CANR 2, 31; DLB 6; SATA 51

Hoban, Russell (Conwell) 1925- . . **CLC 7, 25**
See also CA 5-8R; CANR 23, 37; CLR 3; DLB 52; MAICYA; MTCW; SATA 1, 40, 78

Hobbs, Perry
See Blackmur, R(ichard) P(almer)

Hobson, Laura Z(ametkin)
1900-1986 . . . . **CLC 7, 25**
See also CA 17-20R; 118; DLB 28; SATA 52

Hochhuth, Rolf 1931- . . . . **CLC 4, 11, 18**
See also CA 5-8R; CANR 33; DLB 124; MTCW

Hochman, Sandra 1936- . . . . **CLC 3, 8**
See also CA 5-8R; DLB 5

Hochwaelder, Fritz 1911-1986 . . . . . **CLC 36**
See also CA 29-32R; 120; CANR 42; MTCW

Hochwalder, Fritz
See Hochwaelder, Fritz

Hocking, Mary (Eunice) 1921- . . . . . **CLC 13**
See also CA 101; CANR 18, 40

Hodgins, Jack 1938- . . . . **CLC 23**
See also CA 93-96; DLB 60

Hodgson, William Hope
1877(?)-1918 . . . . **TCLC 13**
See also CA 111; DLB 70

Hoffman, Alice 1952- . . . . **CLC 51**
See also CA 77-80; CANR 34; MTCW

Hoffman, Daniel (Gerard)
1923- . . . . **CLC 6, 13, 23**
See also CA 1-4R; CANR 4; DLB 5

Hoffman, Stanley 1944- . . . . **CLC 5**
See also CA 77-80

Hoffman, William M(oses) 1939- . . . **CLC 40**
See also CA 57-60; CANR 11

Hoffmann, E(rnst) T(heodor) A(madeus)
1776-1822 . . . . **NCLC 2; SSC 13**
See also DLB 90; SATA 27

Hofmann, Gert 1931- . . . . **CLC 54**
See also CA 128

Hofmannsthal, Hugo von
1874-1929 . . . . **TCLC 11; DC 4**
See also CA 106; DLB 81, 118

Hogan, Linda 1947- . . . . **CLC 73**
See also CA 120; CANR 45; NNAL

Hogarth, Charles
See Creasey, John

Hogg, James 1770-1835 . . . . **NCLC 4**
See also DLB 93, 116

Holbach, Paul Henri Thiry Baron
1723-1789 . . . . **LC 14**

Holberg, Ludvig 1684-1754 . . . . **LC 6**

Holden, Ursula 1921- . . . . **CLC 18**
See also CA 101; CAAS 8; CANR 22

Holderlin, (Johann Christian) Friedrich
1770-1843 . . . . **NCLC 16; PC 4**

Holdstock, Robert
See Holdstock, Robert P.

Holdstock, Robert P. 1948- . . . . **CLC 39**
See also CA 131

Holland, Isabelle 1920- . . . . **CLC 21**
See also AAYA 11; CA 21-24R; CANR 10, 25, 47; JRDA; MAICYA; SATA 8, 70

Holland, Marcus
See Caldwell, (Janet Miriam) Taylor (Holland)

Hollander, John 1929- . . . . . . **CLC 2, 5, 8, 14**
See also CA 1-4R; CANR 1; DLB 5; SATA 13

Hollander, Paul
See Silverberg, Robert

Holleran, Andrew 1943(?)- . . . . **CLC 38**
See also CA 144

Hollinghurst, Alan 1954- . . . . **CLC 55**
See also CA 114

Hollis, Jim
See Summers, Hollis (Spurgeon, Jr.)

Holmes, John
See Souster, (Holmes) Raymond

Holmes, John Clellon 1926-1988 . . . . **CLC 56**
See also CA 9-12R; 125; CANR 4; DLB 16

Holmes, Oliver Wendell
1809-1894 . . . . **NCLC 14**
See also CDALB 1640-1865; DLB 1; SATA 34

Holmes, Raymond
See Souster, (Holmes) Raymond

Holt, Victoria
See Hibbert, Eleanor Alice Burford

Holub, Miroslav 1923- . . . . **CLC 4**
See also CA 21-24R; CANR 10

Homer c. 8th cent. B.C.- . . . . . **CMLC 1; DA**

Honig, Edwin 1919- . . . . **CLC 33**
See also CA 5-8R; CAAS 8; CANR 4, 45; DLB 5

Hood, Hugh (John Blagdon)
1928- . . . . **CLC 15, 28**
See also CA 49-52; CAAS 17; CANR 1, 33; DLB 53

Hood, Thomas 1799-1845 . . . . **NCLC 16**
See also DLB 96

Hooker, (Peter) Jeremy 1941- . . . . . . **CLC 43**
See also CA 77-80; CANR 22; DLB 40

Hope, A(lec) D(erwent) 1907- . . . . **CLC 3, 51**
See also CA 21-24R; CANR 33; MTCW

Hope, Brian
See Creasey, John

Hope, Christopher (David Tully)
1944- . . . . **CLC 52**
See also CA 106; CANR 47; SATA 62

Hopkins, Gerard Manley
1844-1889 . . . . **NCLC 17; DA; WLC**
See also CDBLB 1890-1914; DLB 35, 57

Hopkins, John (Richard) 1931- . . . . . . **CLC 4**
See also CA 85-88

Hopkins, Pauline Elizabeth
1859-1930 . . . . **TCLC 28; BLC**
See also BW 2; CA 141; DLB 50

Hopkinson, Francis 1737-1791 . . . . . . **LC 25**
See also DLB 31

Hopley-Woolrich, Cornell George 1903-1968
See Woolrich, Cornell
See also CA 13-14; CAP 1

Horatio
See Proust, (Valentin-Louis-George-Eugene-) Marcel

Horgan, Paul 1903-1995 . . . . **CLC 9, 53**
See also CA 13-16R; CANR 9, 35; DLB 102; DLBY 85; MTCW; SATA 13

Horn, Peter
See Kuttner, Henry

Hornem, Horace Esq.
See Byron, George Gordon (Noel)

Jefferson, Thomas 1743-1826 .... **NCLC 11**
See also CDALB 1640-1865; DLB 31

Jeffrey, Francis 1773-1850....... **NCLC 33**
See also DLB 107

Jelakowitch, Ivan
See Heijermans, Herman

Jellicoe, (Patricia) Ann 1927-...... **CLC 27**
See also CA 85-88; DLB 13

Jen, Gish .... **CLC 70**
See also Jen, Lillian

Jen, Lillian 1956(?)-
See Jen, Gish
See also CA 135

Jenkins, (John) Robin 1912-....... **CLC 52**
See also CA 1-4R; CANR 1; DLB 14

Jennings, Elizabeth (Joan)
1926-..................... **CLC 5, 14**
See also CA 61-64; CAAS 5; CANR 8, 39;
DLB 27; MTCW; SATA 66

Jennings, Waylon 1937-.......... **CLC 21**

Jensen, Johannes V. 1873-1950.... **TCLC 41**

Jensen, Laura (Linnea) 1948-...... **CLC 37**
See also CA 103

Jerome, Jerome K(lapka)
1859-1927 .... **TCLC 23**
See also CA 119; DLB 10, 34, 135

Jerrold, Douglas William
1803-1857 .... **NCLC 2**

Jewett, (Theodora) Sarah Orne
1849-1909 .... **TCLC 1, 22; SSC 6**
See also CA 108; 127; DLB 12, 74;
SATA 15

Jewsbury, Geraldine (Endsor)
1812-1880 .... **NCLC 22**
See also DLB 21

Jhabvala, Ruth Prawer
1927-................... **CLC 4, 8, 29**
See also CA 1-4R; CANR 2, 29; DLB 139;
MTCW

Jiles, Paulette 1943-.......... **CLC 13, 58**
See also CA 101

Jimenez (Mantecon), Juan Ramon
1881-1958 .... **TCLC 4; HLC; PC 7**
See also CA 104; 131; DLB 134; HW;
MTCW

Jimenez, Ramon
See Jimenez (Mantecon), Juan Ramon

Jimenez Mantecon, Juan
See Jimenez (Mantecon), Juan Ramon

Joel, Billy .... **CLC 26**
See also Joel, William Martin

Joel, William Martin 1949-
See Joel, Billy
See also CA 108

John of the Cross, St. 1542-1591 .... **LC 18**

Johnson, B(ryan) S(tanley William)
1933-1973 .... **CLC 6, 9**
See also CA 9-12R; 53-56; CANR 9;
DLB 14, 40

Johnson, Benj. F. of Boo
See Riley, James Whitcomb

Johnson, Benjamin F. of Boo
See Riley, James Whitcomb

Johnson, Charles (Richard)
1948-............. **CLC 7, 51, 65; BLC**
See also BW 2; CA 116; CAAS 18;
CANR 42; DLB 33

Johnson, Denis 1949-............ **CLC 52**
See also CA 117; 121; DLB 120

Johnson, Diane 1934-........ **CLC 5, 13, 48**
See also CA 41-44R; CANR 17, 40;
DLBY 80; MTCW

Johnson, Eyvind (Olof Verner)
1900-1976 .... **CLC 14**
See also CA 73-76; 69-72; CANR 34

Johnson, J. R.
See James, C(yril) L(ionel) R(obert)

Johnson, James Weldon
1871-1938 .... **TCLC 3, 19; BLC**
See also BW 1; CA 104; 125;
CDALB 1917-1929; CLR 32; DLB 51;
MTCW; SATA 31

Johnson, Joyce 1935-............ **CLC 58**
See also CA 125; 129

Johnson, Lionel (Pigot)
1867-1902 .... **TCLC 19**
See also CA 117; DLB 19

Johnson, Mel
See Malzberg, Barry N(athaniel)

Johnson, Pamela Hansford
1912-1981 .... **CLC 1, 7, 27**
See also CA 1-4R; 104; CANR 2, 28;
DLB 15; MTCW

Johnson, Samuel
1709-1784 .... **LC 15; DA; WLC**
See also CDBLB 1660-1789; DLB 39, 95,
104, 142

Johnson, Uwe
1934-1984 .... **CLC 5, 10, 15, 40**
See also CA 1-4R; 112; CANR 1, 39;
DLB 75; MTCW

Johnston, George (Benson) 1913-... **CLC 51**
See also CA 1-4R; CANR 5, 20; DLB 88

Johnston, Jennifer 1930-.......... **CLC 7**
See also CA 85-88; DLB 14

Jolley, (Monica) Elizabeth 1923-... **CLC 46**
See also CA 127; CAAS 13

Jones, Arthur Llewellyn 1863-1947
See Machen, Arthur
See also CA 104

Jones, D(ouglas) G(ordon) 1929-.... **CLC 10**
See also CA 29-32R; CANR 13; DLB 53

Jones, David (Michael)
1895-1974 .... **CLC 2, 4, 7, 13, 42**
See also CA 9-12R; 53-56; CANR 28;
CDBLB 1945-1960; DLB 20, 100; MTCW

Jones, David Robert 1947-
See Bowie, David
See also CA 103

Jones, Diana Wynne 1934-........ **CLC 26**
See also AAYA 12; CA 49-52; CANR 4,
26; CLR 23; JRDA; MAICYA; SAAS 7;
SATA 9, 70

Jones, Edward P. 1950-........... **CLC 76**
See also BW 2; CA 142

Jones, Gayl 1949-......... **CLC 6, 9; BLC**
See also BW 2; CA 77-80; CANR 27;
DLB 33; MTCW

Jones, James 1921-1977.... **CLC 1, 3, 10, 39**
See also AITN 1, 2; CA 1-4R; 69-72;
CANR 6; DLB 2, 143; MTCW

Jones, John J.
See Lovecraft, H(oward) P(hillips)

Jones, LeRoi .... **CLC 1, 2, 3, 5, 10, 14**
See also Baraka, Amiri

Jones, Louis B. .... **CLC 65**
See also CA 141

Jones, Madison (Percy, Jr.) 1925-... **CLC 4**
See also CA 13-16R; CAAS 11; CANR 7;
DLB 152

Jones, Mervyn 1922-.......... **CLC 10, 52**
See also CA 45-48; CAAS 5; CANR 1;
MTCW

Jones, Mick 1956(?)-............. **CLC 30**

Jones, Nettie (Pearl) 1941-........ **CLC 34**
See also BW 2; CA 137; CAAS 20

Jones, Preston 1936-1979 .... **CLC 10**
See also CA 73-76; 89-92; DLB 7

Jones, Robert F(rancis) 1934-....... **CLC 7**
See also CA 49-52; CANR 2

Jones, Rod 1953-................ **CLC 50**
See also CA 128

Jones, Terence Graham Parry
1942-..................... **CLC 21**
See also Jones, Terry; Monty Python
See also CA 112; 116; CANR 35

Jones, Terry
See Jones, Terence Graham Parry
See also SATA 67; SATA-Brief 51

Jones, Thom 1945(?)-............. **CLC 81**

Jong, Erica 1942-...... **CLC 4, 6, 8, 18, 83**
See also AITN 1; BEST 90:2; CA 73-76;
CANR 26; DLB 2, 5, 28, 152; MTCW

Jonson, Ben(jamin)
1572(?)-1637 .... **LC 6; DA; DC 4; WLC**
See also CDBLB Before 1660; DLB 62, 121

Jordan, June 1936-.......... **CLC 5, 11, 23**
See also AAYA 2; BW 2; CA 33-36R;
CANR 25; CLR 10; DLB 38; MAICYA;
MTCW; SATA 4

Jordan, Pat(rick M.) 1941-........ **CLC 37**
See also CA 33-36R

Jorgensen, Ivar
See Ellison, Harlan (Jay)

Jorgenson, Ivar
See Silverberg, Robert

Josephus, Flavius c. 37-100...... **CMLC 13**

Josipovici, Gabriel 1940-........ **CLC 6, 43**
See also CA 37-40R; CAAS 8; CANR 47;
DLB 14

Joubert, Joseph 1754-1824 .... **NCLC 9**

Jouve, Pierre Jean 1887-1976...... **CLC 47**
See also CA 65-68

Joyce, James (Augustine Aloysius)
1882-1941 ...... **TCLC 3, 8, 16, 35; DA;
SSC 3; WLC**
See also CA 104; 126; CDBLB 1914-1945;
DLB 10, 19, 36; MTCW

Jozsef, Attila 1905-1937......... **TCLC 22**
See also CA 116

Juana Ines de la Cruz 1651(?)-1695 ... **LC 5**

Judd, Cyril
See Kornbluth, C(yril) M.; Pohl, Frederik

Julian of Norwich 1342(?)-1416(?) .... **LC 6**
See also DLB 146

Just, Ward (Swift) 1935- .... **CLC 4, 27**
See also CA 25-28R; CANR 32

Justice, Donald (Rodney) 1925- .. **CLC 6, 19**
See also CA 5-8R; CANR 26; DLBY 83

Juvenal c. 55-c. 127 .... **CMLC 8**

Juvenis
See Bourne, Randolph S(illiman)

Kacew, Romain 1914-1980
See Gary, Romain
See also CA 108; 102

Kadare, Ismail 1936- .... **CLC 52**

Kadohata, Cynthia............... **CLC 59**
See also CA 140

Kafka, Franz
1883-1924 .... **TCLC 2, 6, 13, 29, 47, 53;**
DA; SSC 5; WLC
See also CA 105; 126; DLB 81; MTCW

Kahanovitsch, Pinkhes
See Der Nister

Kahn, Roger 1927-............... **CLC 30**
See also CA 25-28R; CANR 44; SATA 37

Kain, Saul
See Sassoon, Siegfried (Lorraine)

Kaiser, Georg 1878-1945 .... **TCLC 9**
See also CA 106; DLB 124

Kaletski, Alexander 1946- .... **CLC 39**
See also CA 118; 143

Kalidasa fl. c. 400- .... **CMLC 9**

Kallman, Chester (Simon)
1921-1975 .... **CLC 2**
See also CA 45-48; 53-56; CANR 3

Kaminsky, Melvin 1926-
See Brooks, Mel
See also CA 65-68; CANR 16

Kaminsky, Stuart M(elvin) 1934- ... **CLC 59**
See also CA 73-76; CANR 29

Kane, Paul
See Simon, Paul

Kane, Wilson
See Bloch, Robert (Albert)

Kanin, Garson 1912-.............. **CLC 22**
See also AITN 1; CA 5-8R; CANR 7;
DLB 7

Kaniuk, Yoram 1930-............. **CLC 19**
See also CA 134

Kant, Immanuel 1724-1804 ...... **NCLC 27**
See also DLB 94

Kantor, MacKinlay 1904-1977 ...... **CLC 7**
See also CA 61-64; 73-76; DLB 9, 102

Kaplan, David Michael 1946- ...... **CLC 50**

Kaplan, James 1951- .... **CLC 59**
See also CA 135

Karageorge, Michael
See Anderson, Poul (William)

Karamzin, Nikolai Mikhailovich
1766-1826 .... **NCLC 3**
See also DLB 150

Karapanou, Margarita 1946-....... **CLC 13**
See also CA 101

Karinthy, Frigyes 1887-1938 ...... **TCLC 47**

Karl, Frederick R(obert) 1927-..... **CLC 34**
See also CA 5-8R; CANR 3, 44

Kastel, Warren
See Silverberg, Robert

Kataev, Evgeny Petrovich 1903-1942
See Petrov, Evgeny
See also CA 120

Kataphusin
See Ruskin, John

Katz, Steve 1935-................. **CLC 47**
See also CA 25-28R; CAAS 14; CANR 12;
DLBY 83

Kauffman, Janet 1945-............ **CLC 42**
See also CA 117; CANR 43; DLBY 86

Kaufman, Bob (Garnell)
1925-1986 .... **CLC 49**
See also BW 1; CA 41-44R; 118; CANR 22;
DLB 16, 41

Kaufman, George S. 1889-1961..... **CLC 38**
See also CA 108; 93-96; DLB 7

Kaufman, Sue .... **CLC 3, 8**
See also Barondess, Sue K(aufman)

Kavafis, Konstantinos Petrou 1863-1933
See Cavafy, C(onstantine) P(eter)
See also CA 104

Kavan, Anna 1901-1968...... **CLC 5, 13, 82**
See also CA 5-8R; CANR 6; MTCW

Kavanagh, Dan
See Barnes, Julian

Kavanagh, Patrick (Joseph)
1904-1967 .... **CLC 22**
See also CA 123; 25-28R; DLB 15, 20;
MTCW

Kawabata, Yasunari
1899-1972 ..... **CLC 2, 5, 9, 18; SSC 17**
See also CA 93-96; 33-36R

Kaye, M(ary) M(argaret) 1909-..... **CLC 28**
See also CA 89-92; CANR 24; MTCW;
SATA 62

Kaye, Mollie
See Kaye, M(ary) M(argaret)

Kaye-Smith, Sheila 1887-1956..... **TCLC 20**
See also CA 118; DLB 36

Kaymor, Patrice Maguilene
See Senghor, Leopold Sedar

Kazan, Elia 1909-........... **CLC 6, 16, 63**
See also CA 21-24R; CANR 32

Kazantzakis, Nikos
1883(?)-1957 .... **TCLC 2, 5, 33**
See also CA 105; 132; MTCW

Kazin, Alfred 1915- .... **CLC 34, 38**
See also CA 1-4R; CAAS 7; CANR 1, 45;
DLB 67

Keane, Mary Nesta (Skrine) 1904-
See Keane, Molly
See also CA 108; 114

Keane, Molly.................... **CLC 31**
See also Keane, Mary Nesta (Skrine)

Keates, Jonathan 19(?)-........... **CLC 34**

Keaton, Buster 1895-1966 .... **CLC 20**

Keats, John
1795-1821 ... **NCLC 8; DA; PC 1; WLC**
See also CDBLB 1789-1832; DLB 96, 110

Keene, Donald 1922- .... **CLC 34**
See also CA 1-4R; CANR 5

Keillor, Garrison................. **CLC 40**
See also Keillor, Gary (Edward)
See also AAYA 2; BEST 89:3; DLBY 87;
SATA 58

Keillor, Gary (Edward) 1942-
See Keillor, Garrison
See also CA 111; 117; CANR 36; MTCW

Keith, Michael
See Hubbard, L(afayette) Ron(ald)

Keller, Gottfried 1819-1890 .... **NCLC 2**
See also DLB 129

Kellerman, Jonathan 1949- .... **CLC 44**
See also BEST 90:1; CA 106; CANR 29

Kelley, William Melvin 1937-...... **CLC 22**
See also BW 1; CA 77-80; CANR 27;
DLB 33

Kellogg, Marjorie 1922-............ **CLC 2**
See also CA 81-84

Kellow, Kathleen
See Hibbert, Eleanor Alice Burford

Kelly, M(ilton) T(erry) 1947-....... **CLC 55**
See also CA 97-100; CANR 19, 43

Kelman, James 1946-.......... **CLC 58, 86**

Kemal, Yashar 1923- .... **CLC 14, 29**
See also CA 89-92; CANR 44

Kemble, Fanny 1809-1893 .... **NCLC 18**
See also DLB 32

Kemelman, Harry 1908-............ **CLC 2**
See also AITN 1; CA 9-12R; CANR 6;
DLB 28

Kempe, Margery 1373(?)-1440(?) ..... **LC 6**
See also DLB 146

Kempis, Thomas a 1380-1471 .... **LC 11**

Kendall, Henry 1839-1882....... **NCLC 12**

Keneally, Thomas (Michael)
1935- ...... **CLC 5, 8, 10, 14, 19, 27, 43**
See also CA 85-88; CANR 10; MTCW

Kennedy, Adrienne (Lita)
1931- .... **CLC 66; BLC; DC 5**
See also BW 2; CA 103; CAAS 20; CABS 3;
CANR 26; DLB 38

Kennedy, John Pendleton
1795-1870 .... **NCLC 2**
See also DLB 3

Kennedy, Joseph Charles 1929-
See Kennedy, X. J.
See also CA 1-4R; CANR 4, 30, 40;
SATA 14

Kennedy, William 1928-... **CLC 6, 28, 34, 53**
See also AAYA 1; CA 85-88; CANR 14,
31; DLB 143; DLBY 85; MTCW;
SATA 57

Kennedy, X. J.................... **CLC 8, 42**
See also Kennedy, Joseph Charles
See also CAAS 9; CLR 27; DLB 5

Kenny, Maurice (Francis) 1929- .... **CLC 87**
See also CA 144; NNAL

Kent, Kelvin
See Kuttner, Henry

Kenton, Maxwell
See Southern, Terry

Kenyon, Robert O.
See Kuttner, Henry

Kerouac, Jack . . . . . **CLC 1, 2, 3, 5, 14, 29, 61**
See also Kerouac, Jean-Louis Lebris de
See also CDALB 1941-1968; DLB 2, 16;
DLBD 3

Kerouac, Jean-Louis Lebris de 1922-1969
See Kerouac, Jack
See also AITN 1; CA 5-8R; 25-28R;
CANR 26; DA; MTCW; WLC

Kerr, Jean 1923- . . . . **CLC 22**
See also CA 5-8R; CANR 7

Kerr, M. E. . . . . **CLC 12, 35**
See also Meaker, Marijane (Agnes)
See also AAYA 2; CLR 29; SAAS 1

Kerr, Robert . . . . **CLC 55**

Kerrigan, (Thomas) Anthony
1918- . . . . **CLC 4, 6**
See also CA 49-52; CAAS 11; CANR 4

Kerry, Lois
See Duncan, Lois

Kesey, Ken (Elton)
1935- . . . . . . **CLC 1, 3, 6, 11, 46, 64; DA;**
WLC
See also CA 1-4R; CANR 22, 38;
CDALB 1968-1988; DLB 2, 16; MTCW;
SATA 66

Kesselring, Joseph (Otto)
1902-1967 . . . . **CLC 45**

Kessler, Jascha (Frederick) 1929- . . . . **CLC 4**
See also CA 17-20R; CANR 8

Kettelkamp, Larry (Dale) 1933- . . . . **CLC 12**
See also CA 29-32R; CANR 16; SAAS 3;
SATA 2

Keyber, Conny
See Fielding, Henry

Keyes, Daniel 1927- . . . . **CLC 80; DA**
See also CA 17-20R; CANR 10, 26;
SATA 37

Khanshendel, Chiron
See Rose, Wendy

Khayyam, Omar
1048-1131 . . . . **CMLC 11; PC 8**

Kherdian, David 1931- . . . . **CLC 6, 9**
See also CA 21-24R; CAAS 2; CANR 39;
CLR 24; JRDA; MAICYA; SATA 16, 74

Khlebnikov, Velimir . . . . **TCLC 20**
See also Khlebnikov, Viktor Vladimirovich

Khlebnikov, Viktor Vladimirovich 1885-1922
See Khlebnikov, Velimir
See also CA 117

Khodasevich, Vladislav (Felitsianovich)
1886-1939 . . . . **TCLC 15**
See also CA 115

Kielland, Alexander Lange
1849-1906 . . . . **TCLC 5**
See also CA 104

Kiely, Benedict 1919- . . . . **CLC 23, 43**
See also CA 1-4R; CANR 2; DLB 15

Kienzle, William X(avier) 1928- . . . . **CLC 25**
See also CA 93-96; CAAS 1; CANR 9, 31;
MTCW

Kierkegaard, Soren 1813-1855 . . . . **NCLC 34**

Killens, John Oliver 1916-1987 . . . . . **CLC 10**
See also BW 2; CA 77-80; 123; CAAS 2;
CANR 26; DLB 33

Killigrew, Anne 1660-1685 . . . . **LC 4**
See also DLB 131

Kim
See Simenon, Georges (Jacques Christian)

Kincaid, Jamaica 1949- . . . **CLC 43, 68; BLC**
See also AAYA 13; BW 2; CA 125;
CANR 47

King, Francis (Henry) 1923- . . . . . **CLC 8, 53**
See also CA 1-4R; CANR 1, 33; DLB 15,
139; MTCW

King, Martin Luther, Jr.
1929-1968 . . . . **CLC 83; BLC; DA**
See also BW 2; CA 25-28; CANR 27, 44;
CAP 2; MTCW; SATA 14

King, Stephen (Edwin)
1947- . . . . . **CLC 12, 26, 37, 61; SSC 17**
See also AAYA 1; BEST 90:1; CA 61-64;
CANR 1, 30; DLB 143; DLBY 80;
JRDA; MTCW; SATA 9, 55

King, Steve
See King, Stephen (Edwin)

King, Thomas 1943- . . . . **CLC 88**
See also CA 144; NNAL

Kingman, Lee . . . . **CLC 17**
See also Natti, (Mary) Lee
See also SAAS 3; SATA 1, 67

Kingsley, Charles 1819-1875 . . . . . **NCLC 35**
See also DLB 21, 32; YABC 2

Kingsley, Sidney 1906-1995 . . . . **CLC 44**
See also CA 85-88; DLB 7

Kingsolver, Barbara 1955- . . . . . . **CLC 55, 81**
See also CA 129; 134

Kingston, Maxine (Ting Ting) Hong
1940- . . . . **CLC 12, 19, 58**
See also AAYA 8; CA 69-72; CANR 13,
38; DLBY 80; MTCW; SATA 53

Kinnell, Galway
1927- . . . . **CLC 1, 2, 3, 5, 13, 29**
See also CA 9-12R; CANR 10, 34; DLB 5;
DLBY 87; MTCW

Kinsella, Thomas 1928- . . . . **CLC 4, 19**
See also CA 17-20R; CANR 15; DLB 27;
MTCW

Kinsella, W(illiam) P(atrick)
1935- . . . . **CLC 27, 43**
See also AAYA 7; CA 97-100; CAAS 7;
CANR 21, 35; MTCW

Kipling, (Joseph) Rudyard
1865-1936 . . . . . . **TCLC 8, 17; DA; PC 3;**
SSC 5; WLC
See also CA 105; 120; CANR 33;
CDBLB 1890-1914; DLB 19, 34, 141;
MAICYA; MTCW; YABC 2

Kirkup, James 1918- . . . . **CLC 1**
See also CA 1-4R; CAAS 4; CANR 2;
DLB 27; SATA 12

Kirkwood, James 1930(?)-1989 . . . . . . **CLC 9**
See also AITN 2; CA 1-4R; 128; CANR 6,
40

Kis, Danilo 1935-1989 . . . . **CLC 57**
See also CA 109; 118; 129; MTCW

Kivi, Aleksis 1834-1872 . . . . **NCLC 30**

Kizer, Carolyn (Ashley)
1925- . . . . **CLC 15, 39, 80**
See also CA 65-68; CAAS 5; CANR 24;
DLB 5

Klabund 1890-1928 . . . . **TCLC 44**
See also DLB 66

Klappert, Peter 1942- . . . . **CLC 57**
See also CA 33-36R; DLB 5

Klein, A(braham) M(oses)
1909-1972 . . . . **CLC 19**
See also CA 101; 37-40R; DLB 68

Klein, Norma 1938-1989 . . . . **CLC 30**
See also AAYA 2; CA 41-44R; 128;
CANR 15, 37; CLR 2, 19; JRDA;
MAICYA; SAAS 1; SATA 7, 57

Klein, T(heodore) E(ibon) D(onald)
1947- . . . . **CLC 34**
See also CA 119; CANR 44

Kleist, Heinrich von
1777-1811 . . . . **NCLC 2, 37**
See also DLB 90

Klima, Ivan 1931- . . . . **CLC 56**
See also CA 25-28R; CANR 17

Klimentov, Andrei Platonovich 1899-1951
See Platonov, Andrei
See also CA 108

Klinger, Friedrich Maximilian von
1752-1831 . . . . **NCLC 1**
See also DLB 94

Klopstock, Friedrich Gottlieb
1724-1803 . . . . **NCLC 11**
See also DLB 97

Knebel, Fletcher 1911-1993 . . . . **CLC 14**
See also AITN 1; CA 1-4R; 140; CAAS 3;
CANR 1, 36; SATA 36; SATA-Obit 75

Knickerbocker, Diedrich
See Irving, Washington

Knight, Etheridge
1931-1991 . . . . **CLC 40; BLC**
See also BW 1; CA 21-24R; 133; CANR 23;
DLB 41

Knight, Sarah Kemble 1666-1727 . . . . . **LC 7**
See also DLB 24

Knister, Raymond 1899-1932 . . . . . . **TCLC 56**
See also DLB 68

Knowles, John
1926- . . . . **CLC 1, 4, 10, 26; DA**
See also AAYA 10; CA 17-20R; CANR 40;
CDALB 1968-1988; DLB 6; MTCW;
SATA 8

Knox, Calvin M.
See Silverberg, Robert

Knye, Cassandra
See Disch, Thomas M(ichael)

Koch, C(hristopher) J(ohn) 1932- . . . **CLC 42**
See also CA 127

Koch, Christopher
See Koch, C(hristopher) J(ohn)

Koch, Kenneth 1925- . . . . **CLC 5, 8, 44**
See also CA 1-4R; CANR 6, 36; DLB 5;
SATA 65

Kochanowski, Jan 1530-1584 . . . . **LC 10**

Kock, Charles Paul de
1794-1871 . . . . **NCLC 16**

Koda Shigeyuki   1867-1947
See Rohan, Koda
See also CA 121

Koestler, Arthur
1905-1983 . . . . **CLC 1, 3, 6, 8, 15, 33**
See also CA 1-4R; 109; CANR 1, 33;
CDBLB 1945-1960; DLBY 83; MTCW

Kogawa, Joy Nozomi   1935- . . . . **CLC 78**
See also CA 101; CANR 19

Kohout, Pavel   1928- . . . . **CLC 13**
See also CA 45-48; CANR 3

Koizumi, Yakumo
See Hearn, (Patricio) Lafcadio (Tessima
Carlos)

Kolmar, Gertrud   1894-1943 . . . . **TCLC 40**

Komunyakaa, Yusef   1947- . . . . **CLC 86**
See also DLB 120

Konrad, George
See Konrad, Gyoergy

Konrad, Gyoergy   1933- . . . . . . **CLC 4, 10, 73**
See also CA 85-88

Konwicki, Tadeusz   1926- . . . . . **CLC 8, 28, 54**
See also CA 101; CAAS 9; CANR 39;
MTCW

Koontz, Dean R(ay)   1945- . . . . **CLC 78**
See also AAYA 9; BEST 89:3, 90:2;
CA 108; CANR 19, 36; MTCW

Kopit, Arthur (Lee)   1937- . . . . **CLC 1, 18, 33**
See also AITN 1; CA 81-84; CABS 3;
DLB 7; MTCW

Kops, Bernard   1926- . . . . **CLC 4**
See also CA 5-8R; DLB 13

Kornbluth, C(yril) M.   1923-1958. . . . **TCLC 8**
See also CA 105; DLB 8

Korolenko, V. G.
See Korolenko, Vladimir Galaktionovich

Korolenko, Vladimir
See Korolenko, Vladimir Galaktionovich

Korolenko, Vladimir G.
See Korolenko, Vladimir Galaktionovich

Korolenko, Vladimir Galaktionovich
1853-1921 . . . . **TCLC 22**
See also CA 121

Kosinski, Jerzy (Nikodem)
1933-1991 . . . . **CLC 1, 2, 3, 6, 10, 15, 53,
70**
See also CA 17-20R; 134; CANR 9, 46;
DLB 2; DLBY 82; MTCW

Kostelanetz, Richard (Cory)   1940- . . **CLC 28**
See also CA 13-16R; CAAS 8; CANR 38

Kostrowitzki, Wilhelm Apollinaris de
1880-1918
See Apollinaire, Guillaume
See also CA 104

Kotlowitz, Robert   1924- . . . . **CLC 4**
See also CA 33-36R; CANR 36

Kotzebue, August (Friedrich Ferdinand) von
1761-1819 . . . . **NCLC 25**
See also DLB 94

Kotzwinkle, William   1938- . . . **CLC 5, 14, 35**
See also CA 45-48; CANR 3, 44; CLR 6;
MAICYA; SATA 24, 70

Kozol, Jonathan   1936- . . . . **CLC 17**
See also CA 61-64; CANR 16, 45

Kozoll, Michael   1940(?)- . . . . **CLC 35**

Kramer, Kathryn   19(?)- . . . . **CLC 34**

Kramer, Larry   1935- . . . . **CLC 42**
See also CA 124; 126

Krasicki, Ignacy   1735-1801 . . . . . . **NCLC 8**

Krasinski, Zygmunt   1812-1859 . . . . **NCLC 4**

Kraus, Karl   1874-1936 . . . . **TCLC 5**
See also CA 104; DLB 118

Kreve (Mickevicius), Vincas
1882-1954 . . . . **TCLC 27**

Kristeva, Julia   1941- . . . . **CLC 77**

Kristofferson, Kris   1936- . . . . **CLC 26**
See also CA 104

Krizanc, John   1956- . . . . **CLC 57**

Krleza, Miroslav   1893-1981. . . . . **CLC 8**
See also CA 97-100; 105; DLB 147

Kroetsch, Robert   1927- . . . . . **CLC 5, 23, 57**
See also CA 17-20R; CANR 8, 38; DLB 53;
MTCW

Kroetz, Franz
See Kroetz, Franz Xaver

Kroetz, Franz Xaver   1946- . . . . **CLC 41**
See also CA 130

Kroker, Arthur   1945- . . . . **CLC 77**

Kropotkin, Peter (Aleksieeevich)
1842-1921 . . . . **TCLC 36**
See also CA 119

Krotkov, Yuri   1917- . . . . **CLC 19**
See also CA 102

Krumb
See Crumb, R(obert)

Krumgold, Joseph (Quincy)
1908-1980 . . . . **CLC 12**
See also CA 9-12R; 101; CANR 7;
MAICYA; SATA 1, 48; SATA-Obit 23

Krumwitz
See Crumb, R(obert)

Krutch, Joseph Wood   1893-1970. . . . **CLC 24**
See also CA 1-4R; 25-28R; CANR 4;
DLB 63

Krutzch, Gus
See Eliot, T(homas) S(tearns)

Krylov, Ivan Andreevich
1768(?)-1844 . . . . **NCLC 1**
See also DLB 150

Kubin, Alfred   1877-1959 . . . . **TCLC 23**
See also CA 112; DLB 81

Kubrick, Stanley   1928- . . . . **CLC 16**
See also CA 81-84; CANR 33; DLB 26

Kumin, Maxine (Winokur)
1925- . . . . **CLC 5, 13, 28**
See also AITN 2; CA 1-4R; CAAS 8;
CANR 1, 21; DLB 5; MTCW; SATA 12

Kundera, Milan
1929- . . . . **CLC 4, 9, 19, 32, 68**
See also AAYA 2; CA 85-88; CANR 19;
MTCW

Kunene, Mazisi (Raymond)   1930- . . . **CLC 85**
See also BW 1; CA 125; DLB 117

Kunitz, Stanley (Jasspon)
1905- . . . . **CLC 6, 11, 14**
See also CA 41-44R; CANR 26; DLB 48;
MTCW

Kunze, Reiner   1933- . . . . **CLC 10**
See also CA 93-96; DLB 75

Kuprin, Aleksandr Ivanovich
1870-1938 . . . . **TCLC 5**
See also CA 104

Kureishi, Hanif   1954(?)- . . . . **CLC 64**
See also CA 139

Kurosawa, Akira   1910- . . . . **CLC 16**
See also AAYA 11; CA 101; CANR 46

Kushner, Tony   1957(?)- . . . . **CLC 81**
See also CA 144

Kuttner, Henry   1915-1958 . . . . **TCLC 10**
See also CA 107; DLB 8

Kuzma, Greg   1944- . . . . **CLC 7**
See also CA 33-36R

Kuzmin, Mikhail   1872(?)-1936 . . . . **TCLC 40**

Kyd, Thomas   1558-1594 . . . . . . **LC 22; DC 3**
See also DLB 62

Kyprianos, Iossif
See Samarakis, Antonis

La Bruyere, Jean de   1645-1696 . . . . . . **LC 17**

Lacan, Jacques (Marie Emile)
1901-1981 . . . . **CLC 75**
See also CA 121; 104

Laclos, Pierre Ambroise Francois Choderlos
de   1741-1803 . . . . **NCLC 4**

La Colere, Francois
See Aragon, Louis

Lacolere, Francois
See Aragon, Louis

La Deshabilleuse
See Simenon, Georges (Jacques Christian)

Lady Gregory
See Gregory, Isabella Augusta (Persse)

Lady of Quality, A
See Bagnold, Enid

La Fayette, Marie (Madelaine Pioche de la
Vergne Comtes   1634-1693 . . . . **LC 2**

Lafayette, Rene
See Hubbard, L(afayette) Ron(ald)

Laforgue, Jules   1860-1887 . . . . **NCLC 5**

Lagerkvist, Paer (Fabian)
1891-1974 . . . . **CLC 7, 10, 13, 54**
See also Lagerkvist, Par
See also CA 85-88; 49-52; MTCW

Lagerkvist, Par
See Lagerkvist, Paer (Fabian)
See also SSC 12

Lagerloef, Selma (Ottiliana Lovisa)
1858-1940 . . . . **TCLC 4, 36**
See also Lagerlof, Selma (Ottiliana Lovisa)
See also CA 108; SATA 15

Lagerlof, Selma (Ottiliana Lovisa)
See Lagerloef, Selma (Ottiliana Lovisa)
See also CLR 7; SATA 15

La Guma, (Justin) Alex(ander)
1925-1985 . . . . **CLC 19**
See also BW 1; CA 49-52; 118; CANR 25;
DLB 117; MTCW

Laidlaw, A. K.
See Grieve, C(hristopher) M(urray)

Lainez, Manuel Mujica
  See Mujica Lainez, Manuel
  See also HW

Lamartine, Alphonse (Marie Louis Prat) de
  1790-1869 .... **NCLC 11**

Lamb, Charles
  1775-1834 .... **NCLC 10; DA; WLC**
  See also CDBLB 1789-1832; DLB 93, 107;
    SATA 17

Lamb, Lady Caroline   1785-1828.. **NCLC 38**
  See also DLB 116

Lamming, George (William)
  1927- .... **CLC 2, 4, 66; BLC**
  See also BW 2; CA 85-88; CANR 26;
    DLB 125; MTCW

L'Amour, Louis (Dearborn)
  1908-1988 .... **CLC 25, 55**
  See also AITN 2; BEST 89:2; CA 1-4R;
    125; CANR 3, 25, 40; DLBY 80; MTCW

Lampedusa, Giuseppe (Tomasi) di ... **TCLC 13**
  See also Tomasi di Lampedusa, Giuseppe

Lampman, Archibald   1861-1899 .. **NCLC 25**
  See also DLB 92

Lancaster, Bruce   1896-1963........ **CLC 36**
  See also CA 9-10; CAP 1; SATA 9

Landau, Mark Alexandrovich
  See Aldanov, Mark (Alexandrovich)

Landau-Aldanov, Mark Alexandrovich
  See Aldanov, Mark (Alexandrovich)

Landis, John   1950-.............. **CLC 26**
  See also CA 112; 122

Landolfi, Tommaso   1908-1979... **CLC 11, 49**
  See also CA 127; 117

Landon, Letitia Elizabeth
  1802-1838 .... **NCLC 15**
  See also DLB 96

Landor, Walter Savage
  1775-1864 .... **NCLC 14**
  See also DLB 93, 107

Landwirth, Heinz   1927-
  See Lind, Jakov
  See also CA 9-12R; CANR 7

Lane, Patrick   1939-.......... **CLC 25**
  See also CA 97-100; DLB 53

Lang, Andrew   1844-1912........ **TCLC 16**
  See also CA 114; 137; DLB 98, 141;
    MAICYA; SATA 16

Lang, Fritz   1890-1976 .... **CLC 20**
  See also CA 77-80; 69-72; CANR 30

Lange, John
  See Crichton, (John) Michael

Langer, Elinor   1939- .... **CLC 34**
  See also CA 121

Langland, William
  1330(?)-1400(?) .... **LC 19; DA**
  See also DLB 146

Langstaff, Launcelot
  See Irving, Washington

Lanier, Sidney   1842-1881 .... **NCLC 6**
  See also DLB 64; MAICYA; SATA 18

Lanyer, Aemilia   1569-1645 .... **LC 10**

Lao Tzu .... **CMLC 7**

Lapine, James (Elliot)   1949-....... **CLC 39**
  See also CA 123; 130

Larbaud, Valery (Nicolas)
  1881-1957 .... **TCLC 9**
  See also CA 106

Lardner, Ring
  See Lardner, Ring(gold) W(ilmer)

Lardner, Ring W., Jr.
  See Lardner, Ring(gold) W(ilmer)

Lardner, Ring(gold) W(ilmer)
  1885-1933 .... **TCLC 2, 14**
  See also CA 104; 131; CDALB 1917-1929;
    DLB 11, 25, 86; MTCW

Laredo, Betty
  See Codrescu, Andrei

Larkin, Maia
  See Wojciechowska, Maia (Teresa)

Larkin, Philip (Arthur)
  1922-1985 .... **CLC 3, 5, 8, 9, 13, 18, 33,
                                    39, 64**
  See also CA 5-8R; 117; CANR 24;
    CDBLB 1960 to Present; DLB 27;
    MTCW

Larra (y Sanchez de Castro), Mariano Jose de
  1809-1837 .... **NCLC 17**

Larsen, Eric   1941- .... **CLC 55**
  See also CA 132

Larsen, Nella   1891-1964 ..... **CLC 37; BLC**
  See also BW 1; CA 125; DLB 51

Larson, Charles R(aymond)   1938-... **CLC 31**
  See also CA 53-56; CANR 4

Lasker-Schueler, Else   1869-1945 .. **TCLC 57**
  See also DLB 66, 124

Latham, Jean Lee   1902-........... **CLC 12**
  See also AITN 1; CA 5-8R; CANR 7;
    MAICYA; SATA 2, 68

Latham, Mavis
  See Clark, Mavis Thorpe

Lathen, Emma .... **CLC 2**
  See also Hennissart, Martha; Latsis, Mary
    J(ane)

Lathrop, Francis
  See Leiber, Fritz (Reuter, Jr.)

Latsis, Mary J(ane)
  See Lathen, Emma
  See also CA 85-88

Lattimore, Richmond (Alexander)
  1906-1984 .... **CLC 3**
  See also CA 1-4R; 112; CANR 1

Laughlin, James   1914-........... **CLC 49**
  See also CA 21-24R; CANR 9, 47; DLB 48

Laurence, (Jean) Margaret (Wemyss)
  1926-1987 .. **CLC 3, 6, 13, 50, 62; SSC 7**
  See also CA 5-8R; 121; CANR 33; DLB 53;
    MTCW; SATA-Obit 50

Laurent, Antoine   1952- .... **CLC 50**

Lauscher, Hermann
  See Hesse, Hermann

Lautreamont, Comte de
  1846-1870 .... **NCLC 12; SSC 14**

Laverty, Donald
  See Blish, James (Benjamin)

Lavin, Mary   1912-...... **CLC 4, 18; SSC 4**
  See also CA 9-12R; CANR 33; DLB 15;
    MTCW

Lavond, Paul Dennis
  See Kornbluth, C(yril) M.; Pohl, Frederik

Lawler, Raymond Evenor   1922-.... **CLC 58**
  See also CA 103

Lawrence, D(avid) H(erbert Richards)
  1885-1930 ...... **TCLC 2, 9, 16, 33, 48;
                            DA; SSC 4; WLC**
  See also CA 104; 121; CDBLB 1914-1945;
    DLB 10, 19, 36, 98; MTCW

Lawrence, T(homas) E(dward)
  1888-1935 .... **TCLC 18**
  See also Dale, Colin
  See also CA 115

Lawrence of Arabia
  See Lawrence, T(homas) E(dward)

Lawson, Henry (Archibald Hertzberg)
  1867-1922 .... **TCLC 27; SSC 18**
  See also CA 120

Lawton, Dennis
  See Faust, Frederick (Schiller)

Laxness, Halldor................. **CLC 25**
  See also Gudjonsson, Halldor Kiljan

Layamon   fl. c. 1200-............ **CMLC 10**
  See also DLB 146

Laye, Camara   1928-1980 ... **CLC 4, 38; BLC**
  See also BW 1; CA 85-88; 97-100;
    CANR 25; MTCW

Layton, Irving (Peter)   1912-..... **CLC 2, 15**
  See also CA 1-4R; CANR 2, 33, 43;
    DLB 88; MTCW

Lazarus, Emma   1849-1887........ **NCLC 8**

Lazarus, Felix
  See Cable, George Washington

Lazarus, Henry
  See Slavitt, David R(ytman)

Lea, Joan
  See Neufeld, John (Arthur)

Leacock, Stephen (Butler)
  1869-1944 .... **TCLC 2**
  See also CA 104; 141; DLB 92

Lear, Edward   1812-1888 .... **NCLC 3**
  See also CLR 1; DLB 32; MAICYA;
    SATA 18

Lear, Norman (Milton)   1922- ...... **CLC 12**
  See also CA 73-76

Leavis, F(rank) R(aymond)
  1895-1978 .... **CLC 24**
  See also CA 21-24R; 77-80; CANR 44;
    MTCW

Leavitt, David   1961-.............. **CLC 34**
  See also CA 116; 122; DLB 130

Leblanc, Maurice (Marie Emile)
  1864-1941 .... **TCLC 49**
  See also CA 110

Lebowitz, Fran(ces Ann)
  1951(?)-.................. **CLC 11, 36**
  See also CA 81-84; CANR 14; MTCW

Lebrecht, Peter
  See Tieck, (Johann) Ludwig

le Carre, John .... **CLC 3, 5, 9, 15, 28**
  See also Cornwell, David (John Moore)
  See also BEST 89:4; CDBLB 1960 to
    Present; DLB 87

Le Clezio, J(ean) M(arie) G(ustave)
    1940- .... CLC 31
    See also CA 116; 128; DLB 83

Leconte de Lisle, Charles-Marie-Rene
    1818-1894 .... NCLC 29

Le Coq, Monsieur
    See Simenon, Georges (Jacques Christian)

Leduc, Violette 1907-1972 .... CLC 22
    See also CA 13-14; 33-36R; CAP 1

Ledwidge, Francis 1887(?)-1917 ... TCLC 23
    See also CA 123; DLB 20

Lee, Andrea 1953- .... CLC 36; BLC
    See also BW 1; CA 125

Lee, Andrew
    See Auchincloss, Louis (Stanton)

Lee, Don L. .... CLC 2
    See also Madhubuti, Haki R.

Lee, George W(ashington)
    1894-1976 .... CLC 52; BLC
    See also BW 1; CA 125; DLB 51

Lee, (Nelle) Harper
    1926- .... CLC 12, 60; DA; WLC
    See also AAYA 13; CA 13-16R;
    CDALB 1941-1968; DLB 6; MTCW;
    SATA 11

Lee, Helen Elaine 1959(?)- .... CLC 86

Lee, Julian
    See Latham, Jean Lee

Lee, Larry
    See Lee, Lawrence

Lee, Lawrence 1941-1990 .... CLC 34
    See also CA 131; CANR 43

Lee, Manfred B(ennington)
    1905-1971 .... CLC 11
    See also Queen, Ellery
    See also CA 1-4R; 29-32R; CANR 2;
    DLB 137

Lee, Stan 1922- .... CLC 17
    See also AAYA 5; CA 108; 111

Lee, Tanith 1947- .... CLC 46
    See also CA 37-40R; SATA 8

Lee, Vernon .... TCLC 5
    See also Paget, Violet
    See also DLB 57

Lee, William
    See Burroughs, William S(eward)

Lee, Willy
    See Burroughs, William S(eward)

Lee-Hamilton, Eugene (Jacob)
    1845-1907 .... TCLC 22
    See also CA 117

Leet, Judith 1935- .... CLC 11

Le Fanu, Joseph Sheridan
    1814-1873 .... NCLC 9; SSC 14
    See also DLB 21, 70

Leffland, Ella 1931- .... CLC 19
    See also CA 29-32R; CANR 35; DLBY 84;
    SATA 65

Leger, Alexis
    See Leger, (Marie-Rene Auguste) Alexis
    Saint-Leger

Leger, (Marie-Rene Auguste) Alexis
    Saint-Leger 1887-1975 .... CLC 11
    See also Perse, St.-John
    See also CA 13-16R; 61-64; CANR 43;
    MTCW

Leger, Saintleger
    See Leger, (Marie-Rene Auguste) Alexis
    Saint-Leger

Le Guin, Ursula K(roeber)
    1929- .... CLC 8, 13, 22, 45, 71; SSC 12
    See also AAYA 9; AITN 1; CA 21-24R;
    CANR 9, 32; CDALB 1968-1988; CLR 3,
    28; DLB 8, 52; JRDA; MAICYA;
    MTCW; SATA 4, 52

Lehmann, Rosamond (Nina)
    1901-1990 .... CLC 5
    See also CA 77-80; 131; CANR 8; DLB 15

Leiber, Fritz (Reuter, Jr.)
    1910-1992 .... CLC 25
    See also CA 45-48; 139; CANR 2, 40;
    DLB 8; MTCW; SATA 45;
    SATA-Obit 73

Leimbach, Martha 1963-
    See Leimbach, Marti
    See also CA 130

Leimbach, Marti .... CLC 65
    See also Leimbach, Martha

Leino, Eino .... TCLC 24
    See also Loennbohm, Armas Eino Leopold

Leiris, Michel (Julien) 1901-1990 ... CLC 61
    See also CA 119; 128; 132

Leithauser, Brad 1953- .... CLC 27
    See also CA 107; CANR 27; DLB 120

Lelchuk, Alan 1938- .... CLC 5
    See also CA 45-48; CAAS 20; CANR 1

Lem, Stanislaw 1921- .... CLC 8, 15, 40
    See also CA 105; CAAS 1; CANR 32;
    MTCW

Lemann, Nancy 1956- .... CLC 39
    See also CA 118; 136

Lemonnier, (Antoine Louis) Camille
    1844-1913 .... TCLC 22
    See also CA 121

Lenau, Nikolaus 1802-1850 ...... NCLC 16

L'Engle, Madeleine (Camp Franklin)
    1918- .... CLC 12
    See also AAYA 1; AITN 2; CA 1-4R;
    CANR 3, 21, 39; CLR 1, 14; DLB 52;
    JRDA; MAICYA; MTCW; SAAS 15;
    SATA 1, 27, 75

Lengyel, Jozsef 1896-1975 .... CLC 7
    See also CA 85-88; 57-60

Lennon, John (Ono)
    1940-1980 .... CLC 12, 35
    See also CA 102

Lennox, Charlotte Ramsay
    1729(?)-1804 .... NCLC 23
    See also DLB 39

Lentricchia, Frank (Jr.) 1940- ..... CLC 34
    See also CA 25-28R; CANR 19

Lenz, Siegfried 1926- .... CLC 27
    See also CA 89-92; DLB 75

Leonard, Elmore (John, Jr.)
    1925- .... CLC 28, 34, 71
    See also AITN 1; BEST 89:1, 90:4;
    CA 81-84; CANR 12, 28; MTCW

Leonard, Hugh .... CLC 19
    See also Byrne, John Keyes
    See also DLB 13

Leopardi, (Conte) Giacomo
    1798-1837 .... NCLC 22

Le Reveler
    See Artaud, Antonin

Lerman, Eleanor 1952- .... CLC 9
    See also CA 85-88

Lerman, Rhoda 1936- .... CLC 56
    See also CA 49-52

Lermontov, Mikhail Yuryevich
    1814-1841 .... NCLC 47

Leroux, Gaston 1868-1927 .... TCLC 25
    See also CA 108; 136; SATA 65

Lesage, Alain-Rene 1668-1747 ...... LC 28

Leskov, Nikolai (Semyonovich)
    1831-1895 .... NCLC 25

Lessing, Doris (May)
    1919- ..... CLC 1, 2, 3, 6, 10, 15, 22, 40;
                                        DA; SSC 6
    See also CA 9-12R; CAAS 14;
    CDBLB 1960 to Present; DLB 15, 139;
    DLBY 85; MTCW

Lessing, Gotthold Ephraim
    1729-1781 .... LC 8
    See also DLB 97

Lester, Richard 1932- .... CLC 20

Lever, Charles (James)
    1806-1872 .... NCLC 23
    See also DLB 21

Leverson, Ada 1865(?)-1936(?) .... TCLC 18
    See also Elaine
    See also CA 117

Levertov, Denise
    1923- ...... CLC 1, 2, 3, 5, 8, 15, 28, 66;
                                        PC 11
    See also CA 1-4R; CAAS 19; CANR 3, 29;
    DLB 5; MTCW

Levi, Jonathan .... CLC 76

Levi, Peter (Chad Tigar) 1931- ..... CLC 41
    See also CA 5-8R; CANR 34; DLB 40

Levi, Primo
    1919-1987 .... CLC 37, 50; SSC 12
    See also CA 13-16R; 122; CANR 12, 33;
    MTCW

Levin, Ira 1929- .... CLC 3, 6
    See also CA 21-24R; CANR 17, 44;
    MTCW; SATA 66

Levin, Meyer 1905-1981 .... CLC 7
    See also AITN 1; CA 9-12R; 104;
    CANR 15; DLB 9, 28; DLBY 81;
    SATA 21; SATA-Obit 27

Levine, Norman 1924- .... CLC 54
    See also CA 73-76; CANR 14; DLB 88

Levine, Philip 1928- .. CLC 2, 4, 5, 9, 14, 33
    See also CA 9-12R; CANR 9, 37; DLB 5

Levinson, Deirdre 1931- .... CLC 49
    See also CA 73-76

Longley, Michael 1939-.......... **CLC 29**
See also CA 102; DLB 40

Longus fl. c. 2nd cent. - - - - - - - - **CMLC 7**

Longway, A. Hugh
See Lang, Andrew

Lopate, Phillip 1943-............. **CLC 29**
See also CA 97-100; DLBY 80

Lopez Portillo (y Pacheco), Jose
1920-........................ **CLC 46**
See also CA 129; HW

Lopez y Fuentes, Gregorio
1897(?)-1966 .... **CLC 32**
See also CA 131; HW

Lorca, Federico Garcia
See Garcia Lorca, Federico

Lord, Bette Bao 1938-............ **CLC 23**
See also BEST 90:3; CA 107; CANR 41;
SATA 58

Lord Auch
See Bataille, Georges

Lord Byron
See Byron, George Gordon (Noel)

Lorde, Audre (Geraldine)
1934-1992 .... **CLC 18, 71; BLC; PC 12**
See also BW 1; CA 25-28R; 142; CANR 16,
26, 46; DLB 41; MTCW

Lord Jeffrey
See Jeffrey, Francis

Lorenzo, Heberto Padilla
See Padilla (Lorenzo), Heberto

Loris
See Hofmannsthal, Hugo von

Loti, Pierre .... **TCLC 11**
See also Viaud, (Louis Marie) Julien
See also DLB 123

Louie, David Wong 1954- .... **CLC 70**
See also CA 139

Louis, Father M.
See Merton, Thomas

Lovecraft, H(oward) P(hillips)
1890-1937 .... **TCLC 4, 22; SSC 3**
See also AAYA 14; CA 104; 133; MTCW

Lovelace, Earl 1935-.............. **CLC 51**
See also BW 2; CA 77-80; CANR 41;
DLB 125; MTCW

Lovelace, Richard 1618-1657........ **LC 24**
See also DLB 131

Lowell, Amy 1874-1925 .... **TCLC 1, 8**
See also CA 104; DLB 54, 140

Lowell, James Russell 1819-1891 .. **NCLC 2**
See also CDALB 1640-1865; DLB 1, 11, 64,
79

Lowell, Robert (Traill Spence, Jr.)
1917-1977 ... **CLC 1, 2, 3, 4, 5, 8, 9, 11,
15, 37; DA; PC 3; WLC**
See also CA 9-12R; 73-76; CABS 2;
CANR 26; DLB 5; MTCW

Lowndes, Marie Adelaide (Belloc)
1868-1947 .... **TCLC 12**
See also CA 107; DLB 70

Lowry, (Clarence) Malcolm
1909-1957 .... **TCLC 6, 40**
See also CA 105; 131; CDBLB 1945-1960;
DLB 15; MTCW

Lowry, Mina Gertrude 1882-1966
See Loy, Mina
See also CA 113

Loxsmith, John
See Brunner, John (Kilian Houston)

Loy, Mina .... **CLC 28**
See also Lowry, Mina Gertrude
See also DLB 4, 54

Loyson-Bridet
See Schwob, (Mayer Andre) Marcel

Lucas, Craig 1951-............... **CLC 64**
See also CA 137

Lucas, George 1944-.............. **CLC 16**
See also AAYA 1; CA 77-80; CANR 30;
SATA 56

Lucas, Hans
See Godard, Jean-Luc

Lucas, Victoria
See Plath, Sylvia

Ludlam, Charles 1943-1987 ..... **CLC 46, 50**
See also CA 85-88; 122

Ludlum, Robert 1927- .... **CLC 22, 43**
See also AAYA 10; BEST 89:1, 90:3;
CA 33-36R; CANR 25, 41; DLBY 82;
MTCW

Ludwig, Ken...................... **CLC 60**

Ludwig, Otto 1813-1865.......... **NCLC 4**
See also DLB 129

Lugones, Leopoldo 1874-1938 ..... **TCLC 15**
See also CA 116; 131; HW

Lu Hsun 1881-1936 .... **TCLC 3**

Lukacs, George .... **CLC 24**
See also Lukacs, Gyorgy (Szegeny von)

Lukacs, Gyorgy (Szegeny von) 1885-1971
See Lukacs, George
See also CA 101; 29-32R

Luke, Peter (Ambrose Cyprian)
1919- .... **CLC 38**
See also CA 81-84; DLB 13

Lunar, Dennis
See Mungo, Raymond

Lurie, Alison 1926-........**CLC 4, 5, 18, 39**
See also CA 1-4R; CANR 2, 17; DLB 2;
MTCW; SATA 46

Lustig, Arnost 1926-.............. **CLC 56**
See also AAYA 3; CA 69-72; CANR 47;
SATA 56

Luther, Martin 1483-1546........... **LC 9**

Luzi, Mario 1914-................. **CLC 13**
See also CA 61-64; CANR 9; DLB 128

Lynch, B. Suarez
See Bioy Casares, Adolfo; Borges, Jorge
Luis

Lynch, David (K.) 1946-.......... **CLC 66**
See also CA 124; 129

Lynch, James
See Andreyev, Leonid (Nikolaevich)

Lynch Davis, B.
See Bioy Casares, Adolfo; Borges, Jorge
Luis

Lyndsay, Sir David 1490-1555 ...... **LC 20**

Lynn, Kenneth S(chuyler) 1923-.... **CLC 50**
See also CA 1-4R; CANR 3, 27

Lynx
See West, Rebecca

Lyons, Marcus
See Blish, James (Benjamin)

Lyre, Pinchbeck
See Sassoon, Siegfried (Lorraine)

Lytle, Andrew (Nelson) 1902-...... **CLC 22**
See also CA 9-12R; DLB 6

Lyttelton, George 1709-1773....... **LC 10**

Maas, Peter 1929- .... **CLC 29**
See also CA 93-96

Macaulay, Rose 1881-1958 ..... **TCLC 7, 44**
See also CA 104; DLB 36

Macaulay, Thomas Babington
1800-1859 .... **NCLC 42**
See also CDBLB 1832-1890; DLB 32, 55

MacBeth, George (Mann)
1932-1992 .... **CLC 2, 5, 9**
See also CA 25-28R; 136; DLB 40; MTCW;
SATA 4; SATA-Obit 70

MacCaig, Norman (Alexander)
1910- .... **CLC 36**
See also CA 9-12R; CANR 3, 34; DLB 27

MacCarthy, (Sir Charles Otto) Desmond
1877-1952 .... **TCLC 36**

MacDiarmid, Hugh
.... **CLC 2, 4, 11, 19, 63; PC 9**
See also Grieve, C(hristopher) M(urray)
See also CDBLB 1945-1960; DLB 20

MacDonald, Anson
See Heinlein, Robert A(nson)

Macdonald, Cynthia 1928-...... **CLC 13, 19**
See also CA 49-52; CANR 4, 44; DLB 105

MacDonald, George 1824-1905..... **TCLC 9**
See also CA 106; 137; DLB 18; MAICYA;
SATA 33

Macdonald, John
See Millar, Kenneth

MacDonald, John D(ann)
1916-1986 .... **CLC 3, 27, 44**
See also CA 1-4R; 121; CANR 1, 19;
DLB 8; DLBY 86; MTCW

Macdonald, John Ross
See Millar, Kenneth

Macdonald, Ross ..... **CLC 1, 2, 3, 14, 34, 41**
See also Millar, Kenneth
See also DLBD 6

MacDougal, John
See Blish, James (Benjamin)

MacEwen, Gwendolyn (Margaret)
1941-1987 .... **CLC 13, 55**
See also CA 9-12R; 124; CANR 7, 22;
DLB 53; SATA 50; SATA-Obit 55

Macha, Karel Hynek 1810-1846.. **NCLC 46**

Machado (y Ruiz), Antonio
1875-1939 ....**TCLC 3**
See also CA 104; DLB 108

Machado de Assis, Joaquim Maria
1839-1908 ....**TCLC 10; BLC**
See also CA 107

Machen, Arthur................... **TCLC 4**
See also Jones, Arthur Llewellyn
See also DLB 36

Machiavelli, Niccolo 1469-1527 .. **LC 8; DA**

Matthiessen, Peter
1927- . . . . **CLC 5, 7, 11, 32, 64**
See also AAYA 6; BEST 90:4; CA 9-12R;
CANR 21; DLB 6; MTCW; SATA 27

Maturin, Charles Robert
1780(?)-1824 . . . . **NCLC 6**

Matute (Ausejo), Ana Maria
1925- . . . . **CLC 11**
See also CA 89-92; MTCW

Maugham, W. S.
See Maugham, W(illiam) Somerset

Maugham, W(illiam) Somerset
1874-1965 . . . . . . **CLC 1, 11, 15, 67; DA;**
SSC 8; WLC
See also CA 5-8R; 25-28R; CANR 40;
CDBLB 1914-1945; DLB 10, 36, 77, 100;
MTCW; SATA 54

Maugham, William Somerset
See Maugham, W(illiam) Somerset

Maupassant, (Henri Rene Albert) Guy de
1850-1893 . . . . **NCLC 1, 42; DA; SSC 1;**
WLC

See also DLB 123

Maurhut, Richard
See Traven, B.

Mauriac, Claude 1914- . . . . **CLC 9**
See also CA 89-92; DLB 83

Mauriac, Francois (Charles)
1885-1970 . . . . **CLC 4, 9, 56**
See also CA 25-28; CAP 2; DLB 65;
MTCW

Mavor, Osborne Henry 1888-1951
See Bridie, James
See also CA 104

Maxwell, William (Keepers, Jr.)
1908- . . . . **CLC 19**
See also CA 93-96; DLBY 80

May, Elaine 1932- . . . . **CLC 16**
See also CA 124; 142; DLB 44

Mayakovski, Vladimir (Vladimirovich)
1893-1930 . . . . **TCLC 4, 18**
See also CA 104

Mayhew, Henry 1812-1887 . . . . . . **NCLC 31**
See also DLB 18, 55

Maynard, Joyce 1953- . . . . **CLC 23**
See also CA 111; 129

Mayne, William (James Carter)
1928- . . . . **CLC 12**
See also CA 9-12R; CANR 37; CLR 25;
JRDA; MAICYA; SAAS 11; SATA 6, 68

Mayo, Jim
See L'Amour, Louis (Dearborn)

Maysles, Albert 1926- . . . . **CLC 16**
See also CA 29-32R

Maysles, David 1932- . . . . **CLC 16**

Mazer, Norma Fox 1931- . . . . **CLC 26**
See also AAYA 5; CA 69-72; CANR 12,
32; CLR 23; JRDA; MAICYA; SAAS 1;
SATA 24, 67

Mazzini, Guiseppe 1805-1872 . . . . **NCLC 34**

McAuley, James Phillip
1917-1976 . . . . **CLC 45**
See also CA 97-100

McBain, Ed
See Hunter, Evan

McBrien, William Augustine
1930- . . . . **CLC 44**
See also CA 107

McCaffrey, Anne (Inez) 1926- . . . . . . **CLC 17**
See also AAYA 6; AITN 2; BEST 89:2;
CA 25-28R; CANR 15, 35; DLB 8;
JRDA; MAICYA; MTCW; SAAS 11;
SATA 8, 70

McCall, Nathan 1955(?)- . . . . **CLC 86**
See also CA 146

McCann, Arthur
See Campbell, John W(ood, Jr.)

McCann, Edson
See Pohl, Frederik

McCarthy, Charles, Jr. 1933-
See McCarthy, Cormac
See also CANR 42

McCarthy, Cormac 1933- . . . . . **CLC 4, 57, 59**
See also McCarthy, Charles, Jr.
See also DLB 6, 143

McCarthy, Mary (Therese)
1912-1989 . . . **CLC 1, 3, 5, 14, 24, 39, 59**
See also CA 5-8R; 129; CANR 16; DLB 2;
DLBY 81; MTCW

McCartney, (James) Paul
1942- . . . . **CLC 12, 35**

McCauley, Stephen (D.) 1955- . . . . . **CLC 50**
See also CA 141

McClure, Michael (Thomas)
1932- . . . . **CLC 6, 10**
See also CA 21-24R; CANR 17, 46;
DLB 16

McCorkle, Jill (Collins) 1958- . . . . . . **CLC 51**
See also CA 121; DLBY 87

McCourt, James 1941- . . . . **CLC 5**
See also CA 57-60

McCoy, Horace (Stanley)
1897-1955 . . . . **TCLC 28**
See also CA 108; DLB 9

McCrae, John 1872-1918 . . . . **TCLC 12**
See also CA 109; DLB 92

McCreigh, James
See Pohl, Frederik

McCullers, (Lula) Carson (Smith)
1917-1967 . . . . **CLC 1, 4, 10, 12, 48; DA;**
SSC 9; WLC
See also CA 5-8R; 25-28R; CABS 1, 3;
CANR 18; CDALB 1941-1968; DLB 2, 7;
MTCW; SATA 27

McCulloch, John Tyler
See Burroughs, Edgar Rice

McCullough, Colleen 1938(?)- . . . . . . **CLC 27**
See also CA 81-84; CANR 17, 46; MTCW

McElroy, Joseph 1930- . . . . **CLC 5, 47**
See also CA 17-20R

McEwan, Ian (Russell) 1948- . . . **CLC 13, 66**
See also BEST 90:4; CA 61-64; CANR 14,
41; DLB 14; MTCW

McFadden, David 1940- . . . . **CLC 48**
See also CA 104; DLB 60

McFarland, Dennis 1950- . . . . **CLC 65**

McGahern, John
1934- . . . . **CLC 5, 9, 48; SSC 17**
See also CA 17-20R; CANR 29; DLB 14;
MTCW

McGinley, Patrick (Anthony)
1937- . . . . **CLC 41**
See also CA 120; 127

McGinley, Phyllis 1905-1978 . . . . . . **CLC 14**
See also CA 9-12R; 77-80; CANR 19;
DLB 11, 48; SATA 2, 44; SATA-Obit 24

McGinniss, Joe 1942- . . . . **CLC 32**
See also AITN 2; BEST 89:2; CA 25-28R;
CANR 26

McGivern, Maureen Daly
See Daly, Maureen

McGrath, Patrick 1950- . . . . **CLC 55**
See also CA 136

McGrath, Thomas (Matthew)
1916-1990 . . . . **CLC 28, 59**
See also CA 9-12R; 132; CANR 6, 33;
MTCW; SATA 41; SATA-Obit 66

McGuane, Thomas (Francis III)
1939- . . . . **CLC 3, 7, 18, 45**
See also AITN 2; CA 49-52; CANR 5, 24;
DLB 2; DLBY 80; MTCW

McGuckian, Medbh 1950- . . . . **CLC 48**
See also CA 143; DLB 40

McHale, Tom 1942(?)-1982 . . . . **CLC 3, 5**
See also AITN 1; CA 77-80; 106

McIlvanney, William 1936- . . . . **CLC 42**
See also CA 25-28R; DLB 14

McIlwraith, Maureen Mollie Hunter
See Hunter, Mollie
See also SATA 2

McInerney, Jay 1955- . . . . **CLC 34**
See also CA 116; 123; CANR 45

McIntyre, Vonda N(eel) 1948- . . . . . **CLC 18**
See also CA 81-84; CANR 17, 34; MTCW

McKay, Claude . . . . . **TCLC 7, 41; BLC; PC 2**
See also McKay, Festus Claudius
See also DLB 4, 45, 51, 117

McKay, Festus Claudius 1889-1948
See McKay, Claude
See also BW 1; CA 104; 124; DA; MTCW;
WLC

McKuen, Rod 1933- . . . . **CLC 1, 3**
See also AITN 1; CA 41-44R; CANR 40

McLoughlin, R. B.
See Mencken, H(enry) L(ouis)

McLuhan, (Herbert) Marshall
1911-1980 . . . . **CLC 37, 83**
See also CA 9-12R; 102; CANR 12, 34;
DLB 88; MTCW

McMillan, Terry (L.) 1951- . . . . . **CLC 50, 61**
See also BW 2; CA 140

McMurtry, Larry (Jeff)
1936- . . . . **CLC 2, 3, 7, 11, 27, 44**
See also AITN 2; BEST 89:2; CA 5-8R;
CANR 19, 43; CDALB 1968-1988;
DLB 2, 143; DLBY 80, 87; MTCW

McNally, T. M. 1961- . . . . **CLC 82**

McNally, Terrence 1939- . . . . . . **CLC 4, 7, 41**
See also CA 45-48; CANR 2; DLB 7

McNamer, Deirdre 1950- . . . . **CLC 70**

McNeile, Herman Cyril 1888-1937
See Sapper
See also DLB 77

McNickle, (William) D'Arcy
1904-1977 . . . . **CLC 88**
See also CA 9-12R; 85-88; CANR 5, 45;
NNAL; SATA-Obit 22

McPhee, John (Angus) 1931- . . . . . . **CLC 36**
See also BEST 90:1; CA 65-68; CANR 20,
46; MTCW

McPherson, James Alan
1943- . . . . **CLC 19, 77**
See also BW 1; CA 25-28R; CAAS 17;
CANR 24; DLB 38; MTCW

McPherson, William (Alexander)
1933- . . . . **CLC 34**
See also CA 69-72; CANR 28

Mead, Margaret 1901-1978 . . . . **CLC 37**
See also AITN 1; CA 1-4R; 81-84;
CANR 4; MTCW; SATA-Obit 20

Meaker, Marijane (Agnes) 1927-
See Kerr, M. E.
See also CA 107; CANR 37; JRDA;
MAICYA; MTCW; SATA 20, 61

Medoff, Mark (Howard) 1940- . . . **CLC 6, 23**
See also AITN 1; CA 53-56; CANR 5;
DLB 7

Medvedev, P. N.
See Bakhtin, Mikhail Mikhailovich

Meged, Aharon
See Megged, Aharon

Meged, Aron
See Megged, Aharon

Megged, Aharon 1920- . . . . **CLC 9**
See also CA 49-52; CAAS 13; CANR 1

Mehta, Ved (Parkash) 1934- . . . . **CLC 37**
See also CA 1-4R; CANR 2, 23; MTCW

Melanter
See Blackmore, R(ichard) D(oddridge)

Melikow, Loris
See Hofmannsthal, Hugo von

Melmoth, Sebastian
See Wilde, Oscar (Fingal O'Flahertie Wills)

Meltzer, Milton 1915- . . . . **CLC 26**
See also AAYA 8; CA 13-16R; CANR 38;
CLR 13; DLB 61; JRDA; MAICYA;
SAAS 1; SATA 1, 50, 80

Melville, Herman
1819-1891 . . . . . **NCLC 3, 12, 29, 45, 49;**
DA; SSC 1, 17; WLC
See also CDALB 1640-1865; DLB 3, 74;
SATA 59

Menander
c. 342B.C.-c. 292B.C. . . . . **CMLC 9; DC 3**

Mencken, H(enry) L(ouis)
1880-1956 . . . . **TCLC 13**
See also CA 105; 125; CDALB 1917-1929;
DLB 11, 29, 63, 137; MTCW

Mercer, David 1928-1980 . . . . **CLC 5**
See also CA 9-12R; 102; CANR 23;
DLB 13; MTCW

Merchant, Paul
See Ellison, Harlan (Jay)

Meredith, George 1828-1909 . . . **TCLC 17, 43**
See also CA 117; CDBLB 1832-1890;
DLB 18, 35, 57

Meredith, William (Morris)
1919- . . . . **CLC 4, 13, 22, 55**
See also CA 9-12R; CAAS 14; CANR 6, 40;
DLB 5

Merezhkovsky, Dmitry Sergeyevich
1865-1941 . . . . **TCLC 29**

Merimee, Prosper
1803-1870 . . . . **NCLC 6; SSC 7**
See also DLB 119

Merkin, Daphne 1954- . . . . **CLC 44**
See also CA 123

Merlin, Arthur
See Blish, James (Benjamin)

Merrill, James (Ingram)
1926-1995 . . . . **CLC 2, 3, 6, 8, 13, 18, 34**
See also CA 13-16R; CANR 10; DLB 5;
DLBY 85; MTCW

Merriman, Alex
See Silverberg, Robert

Merritt, E. B.
See Waddington, Miriam

Merton, Thomas
1915-1968 . . **CLC 1, 3, 11, 34, 83; PC 10**
See also CA 5-8R; 25-28R; CANR 22;
DLB 48; DLBY 81; MTCW

Merwin, W(illiam) S(tanley)
1927- . . . **CLC 1, 2, 3, 5, 8, 13, 18, 45, 88**
See also CA 13-16R; CANR 15; DLB 5;
MTCW

Metcalf, John 1938- . . . . **CLC 37**
See also CA 113; DLB 60

Metcalf, Suzanne
See Baum, L(yman) Frank

Mew, Charlotte (Mary)
1870-1928 . . . . **TCLC 8**
See also CA 105; DLB 19, 135

Mewshaw, Michael 1943- . . . . **CLC 9**
See also CA 53-56; CANR 7, 47; DLBY 80

Meyer, June
See Jordan, June

Meyer, Lynn
See Slavitt, David R(ytman)

Meyer-Meyrink, Gustav 1868-1932
See Meyrink, Gustav
See also CA 117

Meyers, Jeffrey 1939- . . . . **CLC 39**
See also CA 73-76; DLB 111

Meynell, Alice (Christina Gertrude Thompson)
1847-1922 . . . . **TCLC 6**
See also CA 104; DLB 19, 98

Meyrink, Gustav . . . . **TCLC 21**
See also Meyer-Meyrink, Gustav
See also DLB 81

Michaels, Leonard
1933- . . . . **CLC 6, 25; SSC 16**
See also CA 61-64; CANR 21; DLB 130;
MTCW

Michaux, Henri 1899-1984 . . . . . . **CLC 8, 19**
See also CA 85-88; 114

Michelangelo 1475-1564 . . . . **LC 12**

Michelet, Jules 1798-1874 . . . . **NCLC 31**

Michener, James A(lbert)
1907(?)- . . . . **CLC 1, 5, 11, 29, 60**
See also AITN 1; BEST 90:1; CA 5-8R;
CANR 21, 45; DLB 6; MTCW

Mickiewicz, Adam 1798-1855 . . . . . **NCLC 3**

Middleton, Christopher 1926- . . . . . . **CLC 13**
See also CA 13-16R; CANR 29; DLB 40

Middleton, Richard (Barham)
1882-1911 . . . . **TCLC 56**

Middleton, Stanley 1919- . . . . **CLC 7, 38**
See also CA 25-28R; CANR 21, 46;
DLB 14

Middleton, Thomas 1580-1627 . . . . **DC 5**
See also DLB 58

Migueis, Jose Rodrigues 1901- . . . . . **CLC 10**

Mikszath, Kalman 1847-1910 . . . . . **TCLC 31**

Miles, Josephine
1911-1985 . . . . **CLC 1, 2, 14, 34, 39**
See also CA 1-4R; 116; CANR 2; DLB 48

Militant
See Sandburg, Carl (August)

Mill, John Stuart 1806-1873 . . . . . **NCLC 11**
See also CDBLB 1832-1890; DLB 55

Millar, Kenneth 1915-1983 . . . . **CLC 14**
See also Macdonald, Ross
See also CA 9-12R; 110; CANR 16; DLB 2;
DLBD 6; DLBY 83; MTCW

Millay, E. Vincent
See Millay, Edna St. Vincent

Millay, Edna St. Vincent
1892-1950 . . . . . . **TCLC 4, 49; DA; PC 6**
See also CA 104; 130; CDALB 1917-1929;
DLB 45; MTCW

Miller, Arthur
1915- . . . . **CLC 1, 2, 6, 10, 15, 26, 47, 78;**
DA; DC 1; WLC
See also AITN 1; CA 1-4R; CABS 3;
CANR 2, 30; CDALB 1941-1968; DLB 7;
MTCW

Miller, Henry (Valentine)
1891-1980 . . . . **CLC 1, 2, 4, 9, 14, 43, 84;**
DA; WLC
See also CA 9-12R; 97-100; CANR 33;
CDALB 1929-1941; DLB 4, 9; DLBY 80;
MTCW

Miller, Jason 1939(?)- . . . . **CLC 2**
See also AITN 1; CA 73-76; DLB 7

Miller, Sue 1943- . . . . **CLC 44**
See also BEST 90:3; CA 139; DLB 143

Miller, Walter M(ichael, Jr.)
1923- . . . . **CLC 4, 30**
See also CA 85-88; DLB 8

Millett, Kate 1934- . . . . **CLC 67**
See also AITN 1; CA 73-76; CANR 32;
MTCW

Millhauser, Steven 1943- . . . . **CLC 21, 54**
See also CA 110; 111; DLB 2

Millin, Sarah Gertrude 1889-1968 . . **CLC 49**
See also CA 102; 93-96

Milne, A(lan) A(lexander)
1882-1956 . . . . **TCLC 6**
See also CA 104; 133; CLR 1, 26; DLB 10,
77, 100; MAICYA; MTCW; YABC 1

Milner, Ron(ald)　1938-....... **CLC 56; BLC**
See also AITN 1; BW 1; CA 73-76;
CANR 24; DLB 38; MTCW

Milosz, Czeslaw
1911-.... **CLC 5, 11, 22, 31, 56, 82; PC 8**
See also CA 81-84; CANR 23; MTCW

Milton, John　1608-1674... **LC 9; DA; WLC**
See also CDBLB 1660-1789; DLB 131, 151

Min, Anchee　1957-............. **CLC 86**

Minehaha, Cornelius
See Wedekind, (Benjamin) Frank(lin)

Miner, Valerie　1947- .... **CLC 40**
See also CA 97-100

Minimo, Duca
See D'Annunzio, Gabriele

Minot, Susan　1956- .... **CLC 44**
See also CA 134

Minus, Ed　1938-................ **CLC 39**

Miranda, Javier
See Bioy Casares, Adolfo

Mirbeau, Octave　1848-1917...... **TCLC 55**
See also DLB 123

Miro (Ferrer), Gabriel (Francisco Victor)
1879-1930 .... **TCLC 5**
See also CA 104

Mishima, Yukio
.... **CLC 2, 4, 6, 9, 27; DC 1; SSC 4**
See also Hiraoka, Kimitake

Mistral, Frederic　1830-1914 ...... **TCLC 51**
See also CA 122

Mistral, Gabriela........... **TCLC 2; HLC**
See also Godoy Alcayaga, Lucila

Mistry, Rohinton　1952- .... **CLC 71**
See also CA 141

Mitchell, Clyde
See Ellison, Harlan (Jay); Silverberg, Robert

Mitchell, James Leslie　1901-1935
See Gibbon, Lewis Grassic
See also CA 104; DLB 15

Mitchell, Joni　1943-............. **CLC 12**
See also CA 112

Mitchell, Margaret (Munnerlyn)
1900-1949 .... **TCLC 11**
See also CA 109; 125; DLB 9; MTCW

Mitchell, Peggy
See Mitchell, Margaret (Munnerlyn)

Mitchell, S(ilas) Weir　1829-1914 .. **TCLC 36**

Mitchell, W(illiam) O(rmond)
1914- .... **CLC 25**
See also CA 77-80; CANR 15, 43; DLB 88

Mitford, Mary Russell　1787-1855.. **NCLC 4**
See also DLB 110, 116

Mitford, Nancy　1904-1973........ **CLC 44**
See also CA 9-12R

Miyamoto, Yuriko　1899-1951 ..... **TCLC 37**

Mo, Timothy (Peter)　1950(?)-...... **CLC 46**
See also CA 117; MTCW

Modarressi, Taghi (M.)　1931-...... **CLC 44**
See also CA 121; 134

Modiano, Patrick (Jean)　1945-..... **CLC 18**
See also CA 85-88; CANR 17, 40; DLB 83

Moerck, Paal
See Roelvaag, O(le) E(dvart)

Mofolo, Thomas (Mokopu)
1875(?)-1948 .... **TCLC 22; BLC**
See also CA 121

Mohr, Nicholasa　1935-...... **CLC 12; HLC**
See also AAYA 8; CA 49-52; CANR 1, 32;
CLR 22; DLB 145; HW; JRDA; SAAS 8;
SATA 8

Mojtabai, A(nn) G(race)
1938- .... **CLC 5, 9, 15, 29**
See also CA 85-88

Moliere　1622-1673 ...... **LC 28; DA; WLC**

Molin, Charles
See Mayne, William (James Carter)

Molnar, Ferenc　1878-1952....... **TCLC 20**
See also CA 109

Momaday, N(avarre) Scott
1934- .... **CLC 2, 19, 85; DA**
See also AAYA 11; CA 25-28R; CANR 14,
34; DLB 143; MTCW; NNAL; SATA 48;
SATA-Brief 30

Monette, Paul　1945-............. **CLC 82**
See also CA 139

Monroe, Harriet　1860-1936...... **TCLC 12**
See also CA 109; DLB 54, 91

Monroe, Lyle
See Heinlein, Robert A(nson)

Montagu, Elizabeth　1917- .... **NCLC 7**
See also CA 9-12R

Montagu, Mary (Pierrepont) Wortley
1689-1762 .... **LC 9**
See also DLB 95, 101

Montagu, W. H.
See Coleridge, Samuel Taylor

Montague, John (Patrick)
1929- .... **CLC 13, 46**
See also CA 9-12R; CANR 9; DLB 40;
MTCW

Montaigne, Michel (Eyquem) de
1533-1592 .... **LC 8; DA; WLC**

Montale, Eugenio　1896-1981... **CLC 7, 9, 18**
See also CA 17-20R; 104; CANR 30;
DLB 114; MTCW

Montesquieu, Charles-Louis de Secondat
1689-1755 .... **LC 7**

Montgomery, (Robert) Bruce　1921-1978
See Crispin, Edmund
See also CA 104

Montgomery, L(ucy) M(aud)
1874-1942 .... **TCLC 51**
See also AAYA 12; CA 108; 137; CLR 8;
DLB 92; JRDA; MAICYA; YABC 1

Montgomery, Marion H., Jr.　1925- .. **CLC 7**
See also AITN 1; CA 1-4R; CANR 3;
DLB 6

Montgomery, Max
See Davenport, Guy (Mattison, Jr.)

Montherlant, Henry (Milon) de
1896-1972 .... **CLC 8, 19**
See also CA 85-88; 37-40R; DLB 72;
MTCW

Monty Python
See Chapman, Graham; Cleese, John
(Marwood); Gilliam, Terry (Vance); Idle,
Eric; Jones, Terence Graham Parry; Palin,
Michael (Edward)
See also AAYA 7

Moodie, Susanna (Strickland)
1803-1885 .... **NCLC 14**
See also DLB 99

Mooney, Edward　1951-
See Mooney, Ted
See also CA 130

Mooney, Ted　.................... **CLC 25**
See also Mooney, Edward

Moorcock, Michael (John)
1939- .... **CLC 5, 27, 58**
See also CA 45-48; CAAS 5; CANR 2, 17,
38; DLB 14; MTCW

Moore, Brian
1921- .... **CLC 1, 3, 5, 7, 8, 19, 32**
See also CA 1-4R; CANR 1, 25, 42; MTCW

Moore, Edward
See Muir, Edwin

Moore, George Augustus
1852-1933 .... **TCLC 7**
See also CA 104; DLB 10, 18, 57, 135

Moore, Lorrie .... **CLC 39, 45, 68**
See also Moore, Marie Lorena

Moore, Marianne (Craig)
1887-1972 .... **CLC 1, 2, 4, 8, 10, 13, 19,
47; DA; PC 4**
See also CA 1-4R; 33-36R; CANR 3;
CDALB 1929-1941; DLB 45; DLBD 7;
MTCW; SATA 20

Moore, Marie Lorena　1957-
See Moore, Lorrie
See also CA 116; CANR 39

Moore, Thomas　1779-1852........ **NCLC 6**
See also DLB 96, 144

Morand, Paul　1888-1976.......... **CLC 41**
See also CA 69-72; DLB 65

Morante, Elsa　1918-1985........ **CLC 8, 47**
See also CA 85-88; 117; CANR 35; MTCW

Moravia, Alberto...... **CLC 2, 7, 11, 27, 46**
See also Pincherle, Alberto

More, Hannah　1745-1833 .... **NCLC 27**
See also DLB 107, 109, 116

More, Henry　1614-1687............. **LC 9**
See also DLB 126

More, Sir Thomas　1478-1535 .... **LC 10**

Moreas, Jean.................... **TCLC 18**
See also Papadiamantopoulos, Johannes

Morgan, Berry　1919- .... **CLC 6**
See also CA 49-52; DLB 6

Morgan, Claire
See Highsmith, (Mary) Patricia

Morgan, Edwin (George)　1920-..... **CLC 31**
See also CA 5-8R; CANR 3, 43; DLB 27

Morgan, (George) Frederick
1922- .... **CLC 23**
See also CA 17-20R; CANR 21

Morgan, Harriet
See Mencken, H(enry) L(ouis)

Morgan, Jane
See Cooper, James Fenimore

Morgan, Janet 1945- . . . . **CLC 39**
See also CA 65-68

Morgan, Lady 1776(?)-1859 . . . . . . **NCLC 29**
See also DLB 116

Morgan, Robin 1941- . . . . **CLC 2**
See also CA 69-72; CANR 29; MTCW;
SATA 80

Morgan, Scott
See Kuttner, Henry

Morgan, Seth 1949(?)-1990 . . . . **CLC 65**
See also CA 132

Morgenstern, Christian
1871-1914 . . . . **TCLC 8**
See also CA 105

Morgenstern, S.
See Goldman, William (W.)

Moricz, Zsigmond 1879-1942 . . . . . **TCLC 33**

Morike, Eduard (Friedrich)
1804-1875 . . . . **NCLC 10**
See also DLB 133

Mori Ogai . . . . **TCLC 14**
See also Mori Rintaro

Mori Rintaro 1862-1922
See Mori Ogai
See also CA 110

Moritz, Karl Philipp 1756-1793 . . . . . . **LC 2**
See also DLB 94

Morland, Peter Henry
See Faust, Frederick (Schiller)

Morren, Theophil
See Hofmannsthal, Hugo von

Morris, Bill 1952- . . . . **CLC 76**

Morris, Julian
See West, Morris L(anglo)

Morris, Steveland Judkins 1950(?)-
See Wonder, Stevie
See also CA 111

Morris, William 1834-1896 . . . . **NCLC 4**
See also CDBLB 1832-1890; DLB 18, 35, 57

Morris, Wright 1910- . . . **CLC 1, 3, 7, 18, 37**
See also CA 9-12R; CANR 21; DLB 2;
DLBY 81; MTCW

Morrison, Chloe Anthony Wofford
See Morrison, Toni

Morrison, James Douglas 1943-1971
See Morrison, Jim
See also CA 73-76; CANR 40

Morrison, Jim . . . . **CLC 17**
See also Morrison, James Douglas

Morrison, Toni
1931- . . . . **CLC 4, 10, 22, 55, 81, 87;**
BLC; DA
See also AAYA 1; BW 2; CA 29-32R;
CANR 27, 42; CDALB 1968-1988;
DLB 6, 33, 143; DLBY 81; MTCW;
SATA 57

Morrison, Van 1945- . . . . **CLC 21**
See also CA 116

Mortimer, John (Clifford)
1923- . . . . **CLC 28, 43**
See also CA 13-16R; CANR 21;
CDBLB 1960 to Present; DLB 13;
MTCW

Mortimer, Penelope (Ruth) 1918- . . . . **CLC 5**
See also CA 57-60; CANR 45

Morton, Anthony
See Creasey, John

Mosher, Howard Frank 1943- . . . . . . **CLC 62**
See also CA 139

Mosley, Nicholas 1923- . . . . **CLC 43, 70**
See also CA 69-72; CANR 41; DLB 14

Moss, Howard
1922-1987 . . . . **CLC 7, 14, 45, 50**
See also CA 1-4R; 123; CANR 1, 44;
DLB 5

Mossgiel, Rab
See Burns, Robert

Motion, Andrew 1952- . . . . **CLC 47**
See also DLB 40

Motley, Willard (Francis)
1909-1965 . . . . **CLC 18**
See also BW 1; CA 117; 106; DLB 76, 143

Motoori, Norinaga 1730-1801 . . . . **NCLC 45**

Mott, Michael (Charles Alston)
1930- . . . . **CLC 15, 34**
See also CA 5-8R; CAAS 7; CANR 7, 29

Moure, Erin 1955- . . . . **CLC 88**
See also CA 113; DLB 60

Mowat, Farley (McGill) 1921- . . . . . **CLC 26**
See also AAYA 1; CA 1-4R; CANR 4, 24,
42; CLR 20; DLB 68; JRDA; MAICYA;
MTCW; SATA 3, 55

Moyers, Bill 1934- . . . . **CLC 74**
See also AITN 2; CA 61-64; CANR 31

Mphahlele, Es'kia
See Mphahlele, Ezekiel
See also DLB 125

Mphahlele, Ezekiel 1919- . . . . . **CLC 25; BLC**
See also Mphahlele, Es'kia
See also BW 2; CA 81-84; CANR 26

Mqhayi, S(amuel) E(dward) K(rune Loliwe)
1875-1945 . . . . **TCLC 25; BLC**

Mr. Martin
See Burroughs, William S(eward)

Mrozek, Slawomir 1930- . . . . **CLC 3, 13**
See also CA 13-16R; CAAS 10; CANR 29;
MTCW

Mrs. Belloc-Lowndes
See Lowndes, Marie Adelaide (Belloc)

Mtwa, Percy (?)- . . . . **CLC 47**

Mueller, Lisel 1924- . . . . **CLC 13, 51**
See also CA 93-96; DLB 105

Muir, Edwin 1887-1959 . . . . **TCLC 2**
See also CA 104; DLB 20, 100

Muir, John 1838-1914 . . . . **TCLC 28**

Mujica Lainez, Manuel
1910-1984 . . . . **CLC 31**
See also Lainez, Manuel Mujica
See also CA 81-84; 112; CANR 32; HW

Mukherjee, Bharati 1940- . . . . **CLC 53**
See also BEST 89:2; CA 107; CANR 45;
DLB 60; MTCW

Muldoon, Paul 1951- . . . . **CLC 32, 72**
See also CA 113; 129; DLB 40

Mulisch, Harry 1927- . . . . **CLC 42**
See also CA 9-12R; CANR 6, 26

Mull, Martin 1943- . . . . **CLC 17**
See also CA 105

Mulock, Dinah Maria
See Craik, Dinah Maria (Mulock)

Munford, Robert 1737(?)-1783 . . . . **LC 5**
See also DLB 31

Mungo, Raymond 1946- . . . . **CLC 72**
See also CA 49-52; CANR 2

Munro, Alice
1931- . . . . **CLC 6, 10, 19, 50; SSC 3**
See also AITN 2; CA 33-36R; CANR 33;
DLB 53; MTCW; SATA 29

Munro, H(ector) H(ugh) 1870-1916
See Saki
See also CA 104; 130; CDBLB 1890-1914;
DA; DLB 34; MTCW; WLC

Murasaki, Lady . . . . **CMLC 1**

Murdoch, (Jean) Iris
1919- . . . . . . **CLC 1, 2, 3, 4, 6, 8, 11, 15,**
22, 31, 51
See also CA 13-16R; CANR 8, 43;
CDBLB 1960 to Present; DLB 14;
MTCW

Murnau, Friedrich Wilhelm
See Plumpe, Friedrich Wilhelm

Murphy, Richard 1927- . . . . **CLC 41**
See also CA 29-32R; DLB 40

Murphy, Sylvia 1937- . . . . **CLC 34**
See also CA 121

Murphy, Thomas (Bernard) 1935- . . . **CLC 51**
See also CA 101

Murray, Albert L. 1916- . . . . **CLC 73**
See also BW 2; CA 49-52; CANR 26;
DLB 38

Murray, Les(lie) A(llan) 1938- . . . . . **CLC 40**
See also CA 21-24R; CANR 11, 27

Murry, J. Middleton
See Murry, John Middleton

Murry, John Middleton
1889-1957 . . . . **TCLC 16**
See also CA 118; DLB 149

Musgrave, Susan 1951- . . . . **CLC 13, 54**
See also CA 69-72; CANR 45

Musil, Robert (Edler von)
1880-1942 . . . . **TCLC 12; SSC 18**
See also CA 109; DLB 81, 124

Musset, (Louis Charles) Alfred de
1810-1857 . . . . **NCLC 7**

My Brother's Brother
See Chekhov, Anton (Pavlovich)

Myers, L. H. 1881-1944 . . . . **TCLC 59**
See also DLB 15

Myers, Walter Dean 1937- . . . **CLC 35; BLC**
See also AAYA 4; BW 2; CA 33-36R;
CANR 20, 42; CLR 4, 16, 35; DLB 33;
JRDA; MAICYA; SAAS 2; SATA 41, 71;
SATA-Brief 27

Myers, Walter M.
See Myers, Walter Dean

North, Anthony
  See Koontz, Dean R(ay)

North, Captain George
  See Stevenson, Robert Louis (Balfour)

North, Milou
  See Erdrich, Louise

Northrup, B. A.
  See Hubbard, L(afayette) Ron(ald)

North Staffs
  See Hulme, T(homas) E(rnest)

Norton, Alice Mary
  See Norton, Andre
  See also MAICYA; SATA 1, 43

Norton, Andre 1912- .... CLC 12
  See also Norton, Alice Mary
  See also AAYA 14; CA 1-4R; CANR 2, 31;
    DLB 8, 52; JRDA; MTCW

Norton, Caroline 1808-1877...... NCLC 47
  See also DLB 21

Norway, Nevil Shute 1899-1960
  See Shute, Nevil
  See also CA 102; 93-96

Norwid, Cyprian Kamil
  1821-1883 .... NCLC 17

Nosille, Nabrah
  See Ellison, Harlan (Jay)

Nossack, Hans Erich 1901-1978 ..... CLC 6
  See also CA 93-96; 85-88; DLB 69

Nostradamus 1503-1566........... LC 27

Nosu, Chuji
  See Ozu, Yasujiro

Notenburg, Eleanora (Genrikhovna) von
  See Guro, Elena

Nova, Craig 1945-............. CLC 7, 31
  See also CA 45-48; CANR 2

Novak, Joseph
  See Kosinski, Jerzy (Nikodem)

Novalis 1772-1801 .... NCLC 13
  See also DLB 90

Nowlan, Alden (Albert) 1933-1983 .. CLC 15
  See also CA 9-12R; CANR 5; DLB 53

Noyes, Alfred 1880-1958 .... TCLC 7
  See also CA 104; DLB 20

Nunn, Kem 19(?)-................. CLC 34

Nye, Robert 1939-............. CLC 13, 42
  See also CA 33-36R; CANR 29; DLB 14;
    MTCW; SATA 6

Nyro, Laura 1947- .... CLC 17

Oates, Joyce Carol
  1938-...... CLC 1, 2, 3, 6, 9, 11, 15, 19,
    33, 52; DA; SSC 6; WLC
  See also AITN 1; BEST 89:2; CA 5-8R;
    CANR 25, 45; CDALB 1968-1988;
    DLB 2, 5, 130; DLBY 81; MTCW

O'Brien, Darcy 1939-............. CLC 11
  See also CA 21-24R; CANR 8

O'Brien, E. G.
  See Clarke, Arthur C(harles)

O'Brien, Edna
  1936-... CLC 3, 5, 8, 13, 36, 65; SSC 10
  See also CA 1-4R; CANR 6, 41;
    CDBLB 1960 to Present; DLB 14;
    MTCW

O'Brien, Fitz-James 1828-1862... NCLC 21
  See also DLB 74

O'Brien, Flann....... CLC 1, 4, 5, 7, 10, 47
  See also O Nuallain, Brian

O'Brien, Richard 1942- .... CLC 17
  See also CA 124

O'Brien, Tim 1946-......... CLC 7, 19, 40
  See also CA 85-88; CANR 40; DLB 152;
    DLBD 9; DLBY 80

Obstfelder, Sigbjoern 1866-1900... TCLC 23
  See also CA 123

O'Casey, Sean
  1880-1964 ...... CLC 1, 5, 9, 11, 15, 88
  See also CA 89-92; CDBLB 1914-1945;
    DLB 10; MTCW

O'Cathasaigh, Sean
  See O'Casey, Sean

Ochs, Phil 1940-1976............. CLC 17
  See also CA 65-68

O'Connor, Edwin (Greene)
  1918-1968 .... CLC 14
  See also CA 93-96; 25-28R

O'Connor, (Mary) Flannery
  1925-1964 .... CLC 1, 2, 3, 6, 10, 13, 15,
    21, 66; DA; SSC 1; WLC
  See also AAYA 7; CA 1-4R; CANR 3, 41;
    CDALB 1941-1968; DLB 2, 152;
    DLBD 12; DLBY 80; MTCW

O'Connor, Frank........... CLC 23; SSC 5
  See also O'Donovan, Michael John

O'Dell, Scott 1898-1989......... CLC 30
  See also AAYA 3; CA 61-64; 129;
    CANR 12, 30; CLR 1, 16; DLB 52;
    JRDA; MAICYA; SATA 12, 60

Odets, Clifford 1906-1963 .... CLC 2, 28
  See also CA 85-88; DLB 7, 26; MTCW

O'Doherty, Brian 1934-.......... CLC 76
  See also CA 105

O'Donnell, K. M.
  See Malzberg, Barry N(athaniel)

O'Donnell, Lawrence
  See Kuttner, Henry

O'Donovan, Michael John
  1903-1966 .... CLC 14
  See also O'Connor, Frank
  See also CA 93-96

Oe, Kenzaburo 1935-....... CLC 10, 36, 86
  See also CA 97-100; CANR 36; MTCW

O'Faolain, Julia 1932-....... CLC 6, 19, 47
  See also CA 81-84; CAAS 2; CANR 12;
    DLB 14; MTCW

O'Faolain, Sean
  1900-1991 .... CLC 1, 7, 14, 32, 70;
    SSC 13
  See also CA 61-64; 134; CANR 12;
    DLB 15; MTCW

O'Flaherty, Liam
  1896-1984 .... CLC 5, 34; SSC 6
  See also CA 101; 113; CANR 35; DLB 36;
    DLBY 84; MTCW

Ogilvy, Gavin
  See Barrie, J(ames) M(atthew)

O'Grady, Standish James
  1846-1928 .... TCLC 5
  See also CA 104

O'Grady, Timothy 1951- .... CLC 59
  See also CA 138

O'Hara, Frank
  1926-1966 ....CLC 2, 5, 13, 78
  See also CA 9-12R; 25-28R; CANR 33;
    DLB 5, 16; MTCW

O'Hara, John (Henry)
  1905-1970 ...... CLC 1, 2, 3, 6, 11, 42;
    SSC 15
  See also CA 5-8R; 25-28R; CANR 31;
    CDALB 1929-1941; DLB 9, 86; DLBD 2;
    MTCW

O Hehir, Diana 1922- .... CLC 41
  See also CA 93-96

Okigbo, Christopher (Ifenayichukwu)
  1932-1967 ..... CLC 25, 84; BLC; PC 7
  See also BW 1; CA 77-80; DLB 125;
    MTCW

Okri, Ben 1959- .... CLC 87
  See also BW 2; CA 130; 138

Olds, Sharon 1942-........... CLC 32, 39, 85
  See also CA 101; CANR 18, 41; DLB 120

Oldstyle, Jonathan
  See Irving, Washington

Olesha, Yuri (Karlovich)
  1899-1960 .... CLC 8
  See also CA 85-88

Oliphant, Laurence
  1829(?)-1888 .... NCLC 47
  See also DLB 18

Oliphant, Margaret (Oliphant Wilson)
  1828-1897 .... NCLC 11
  See also DLB 18

Oliver, Mary 1935-........... CLC 19, 34
  See also CA 21-24R; CANR 9, 43; DLB 5

Olivier, Laurence (Kerr)
  1907-1989 .... CLC 20
  See also CA 111; 129

Olsen, Tillie
  1913- .... CLC 4, 13; DA; SSC 11
  See also CA 1-4R; CANR 1, 43; DLB 28;
    DLBY 80; MTCW

Olson, Charles (John)
  1910-1970 ..... CLC 1, 2, 5, 6, 9, 11, 29
  See also CA 13-16; 25-28R; CABS 2;
    CANR 35; CAP 1; DLB 5, 16; MTCW

Olson, Toby 1937- .... CLC 28
  See also CA 65-68; CANR 9, 31

Olyesha, Yuri
  See Olesha, Yuri (Karlovich)

Ondaatje, (Philip) Michael
  1943-.............. CLC 14, 29, 51, 76
  See also CA 77-80; CANR 42; DLB 60

Oneal, Elizabeth 1934-
  See Oneal, Zibby
  See also CA 106; CANR 28; MAICYA;
    SATA 30

Oneal, Zibby .... CLC 30
  See also Oneal, Elizabeth
  See also AAYA 5; CLR 13; JRDA

O'Neill, Eugene (Gladstone)
  1888-1953 ...... TCLC 1, 6, 27, 49; DA;
    WLC
  See also AITN 1; CA 110; 132;
    CDALB 1929-1941; DLB 7; MTCW

Paterson, A(ndrew) B(arton)
1864-1941 . . . . TCLC **32**

Paterson, Katherine (Womeldorf)
1932- . . . . CLC **12, 30**
See also AAYA 1; CA 21-24R; CANR 28;
CLR 7; DLB 52; JRDA; MAICYA;
MTCW; SATA 13, 53

Patmore, Coventry Kersey Dighton
1823-1896 . . . . NCLC **9**
See also DLB 35, 98

Paton, Alan (Stewart)
1903-1988 . . . . . . CLC **4, 10, 25, 55; DA;
WLC**
See also CA 13-16; 125; CANR 22; CAP 1;
MTCW; SATA 11; SATA-Obit 56

Paton Walsh, Gillian   1937-
See Walsh, Jill Paton
See also CANR 38; JRDA; MAICYA;
SAAS 3; SATA 4, 72

Paulding, James Kirke   1778-1860 . . NCLC **2**
See also DLB 3, 59, 74

Paulin, Thomas Neilson   1949-
See Paulin, Tom
See also CA 123; 128

Paulin, Tom . . . . CLC **37**
See also Paulin, Thomas Neilson
See also DLB 40

Paustovsky, Konstantin (Georgievich)
1892-1968 . . . . CLC **40**
See also CA 93-96; 25-28R

Pavese, Cesare   1908-1950 . . . . TCLC **3**
See also CA 104; DLB 128

Pavic, Milorad   1929- . . . . CLC **60**
See also CA 136

Payne, Alan
See Jakes, John (William)

Paz, Gil
See Lugones, Leopoldo

Paz, Octavio
1914- . . . . . . CLC **3, 4, 6, 10, 19, 51, 65;
DA; HLC; PC 1; WLC**
See also CA 73-76; CANR 32; DLBY 90;
HW; MTCW

Peacock, Molly   1947- . . . . CLC **60**
See also CA 103; DLB 120

Peacock, Thomas Love
1785-1866 . . . . NCLC **22**
See also DLB 96, 116

Peake, Mervyn   1911-1968 . . . . . . CLC **7, 54**
See also CA 5-8R; 25-28R; CANR 3;
DLB 15; MTCW; SATA 23

Pearce, Philippa . . . . CLC **21**
See also Christie, (Ann) Philippa
See also CLR 9; MAICYA; SATA 1, 67

Pearl, Eric
See Elman, Richard

Pearson, T(homas) R(eid)   1956- . . . . CLC **39**
See also CA 120; 130

Peck, Dale   1968(?)- . . . . CLC **81**

Peck, John   1941- . . . . CLC **3**
See also CA 49-52; CANR 3

Peck, Richard (Wayne)   1934- . . . . . . CLC **21**
See also AAYA 1; CA 85-88; CANR 19,
38; CLR 15; JRDA; MAICYA; SAAS 2;
SATA 18, 55

Peck, Robert Newton   1928- . . . . CLC **17; DA**
See also AAYA 3; CA 81-84; CANR 31;
JRDA; MAICYA; SAAS 1; SATA 21, 62

Peckinpah, (David) Sam(uel)
1925-1984 . . . . CLC **20**
See also CA 109; 114

Pedersen, Knut   1859-1952
See Hamsun, Knut
See also CA 104; 119; MTCW

Peeslake, Gaffer
See Durrell, Lawrence (George)

Peguy, Charles Pierre
1873-1914 . . . . TCLC **10**
See also CA 107

Pena, Ramon del Valle y
See Valle-Inclan, Ramon (Maria) del

Pendennis, Arthur Esquir
See Thackeray, William Makepeace

Penn, William   1644-1718 . . . . LC **25**
See also DLB 24

Pepys, Samuel
1633-1703 . . . . LC **11; DA; WLC**
See also CDBLB 1660-1789; DLB 101

Percy, Walker
1916-1990 . . . . CLC **2, 3, 6, 8, 14, 18, 47,
65**
See also CA 1-4R; 131; CANR 1, 23;
DLB 2; DLBY 80, 90; MTCW

Perec, Georges   1936-1982 . . . . CLC **56**
See also CA 141; DLB 83

Pereda (y Sanchez de Porrua), Jose Maria de
1833-1906 . . . . TCLC **16**
See also CA 117

Pereda y Porrua, Jose Maria de
See Pereda (y Sanchez de Porrua), Jose
Maria de

Peregoy, George Weems
See Mencken, H(enry) L(ouis)

Perelman, S(idney) J(oseph)
1904-1979 . . . CLC **3, 5, 9, 15, 23, 44, 49**
See also AITN 1, 2; CA 73-76; 89-92;
CANR 18; DLB 11, 44; MTCW

Peret, Benjamin   1899-1959 . . . . . . TCLC **20**
See also CA 117

Peretz, Isaac Loeb   1851(?)-1915 . . . TCLC **16**
See also CA 109

Peretz, Yitzkhok Leibush
See Peretz, Isaac Loeb

Perez Galdos, Benito   1843-1920 . . . TCLC **27**
See also CA 125; HW

Perrault, Charles   1628-1703 . . . . LC **2**
See also MAICYA; SATA 25

Perry, Brighton
See Sherwood, Robert E(mmet)

Perse, St.-John . . . . CLC **4, 11, 46**
See also Leger, (Marie-Rene Auguste) Alexis
Saint-Leger

Peseenz, Tulio F.
See Lopez y Fuentes, Gregorio

Pesetsky, Bette   1932- . . . . CLC **28**
See also CA 133; DLB 130

Peshkov, Alexei Maximovich   1868-1936
See Gorky, Maxim
See also CA 105; 141; DA

Pessoa, Fernando (Antonio Nogueira)
1888-1935 . . . . TCLC **27; HLC**
See also CA 125

Peterkin, Julia Mood   1880-1961 . . . . CLC **31**
See also CA 102; DLB 9

Peters, Joan K.   1945- . . . . CLC **39**

Peters, Robert L(ouis)   1924- . . . . CLC **7**
See also CA 13-16R; CAAS 8; DLB 105

Petofi, Sandor   1823-1849 . . . . NCLC **21**

Petrakis, Harry Mark   1923- . . . . CLC **3**
See also CA 9-12R; CANR 4, 30

Petrarch   1304-1374 . . . . PC **8**

Petrov, Evgeny . . . . TCLC **21**
See also Kataev, Evgeny Petrovich

Petry, Ann (Lane)   1908- . . . . . . CLC **1, 7, 18**
See also BW 1; CA 5-8R; CAAS 6;
CANR 4, 46; CLR 12; DLB 76; JRDA;
MAICYA; MTCW; SATA 5

Petursson, Halligrimur   1614-1674 . . . . LC **8**

Philipson, Morris H.   1926- . . . . CLC **53**
See also CA 1-4R; CANR 4

Phillips, David Graham
1867-1911 . . . . TCLC **44**
See also CA 108; DLB 9, 12

Phillips, Jack
See Sandburg, Carl (August)

Phillips, Jayne Anne
1952- . . . . CLC **15, 33; SSC 16**
See also CA 101; CANR 24; DLBY 80;
MTCW

Phillips, Richard
See Dick, Philip K(indred)

Phillips, Robert (Schaeffer)   1938- . . . CLC **28**
See also CA 17-20R; CAAS 13; CANR 8;
DLB 105

Phillips, Ward
See Lovecraft, H(oward) P(hillips)

Piccolo, Lucio   1901-1969 . . . . CLC **13**
See also CA 97-100; DLB 114

Pickthall, Marjorie L(owry) C(hristie)
1883-1922 . . . . TCLC **21**
See also CA 107; DLB 92

Pico della Mirandola, Giovanni
1463-1494 . . . . LC **15**

Piercy, Marge
1936- . . . . CLC **3, 6, 14, 18, 27, 62**
See also CA 21-24R; CAAS 1; CANR 13,
43; DLB 120; MTCW

Piers, Robert
See Anthony, Piers

Pieyre de Mandiargues, Andre   1909-1991
See Mandiargues, Andre Pieyre de
See also CA 103; 136; CANR 22

Pilnyak, Boris . . . . TCLC **23**
See also Vogau, Boris Andreyevich

Pincherle, Alberto   1907-1990 . . . CLC **11, 18**
See also Moravia, Alberto
See also CA 25-28R; 132; CANR 33;
MTCW

Pinckney, Darryl   1953- . . . . CLC **76**
See also BW 2; CA 143

Pindar   518B.C.-446B.C. . . . . CMLC **12**

Prager, Emily 1952-............ **CLC 56**

Pratt, E(dwin) J(ohn)
1883(?)-1964 .... **CLC 19**
See also CA 141; 93-96; DLB 92

Premchand........................ **TCLC 21**
See also Srivastava, Dhanpat Rai

Preussler, Otfried 1923-........... **CLC 17**
See also CA 77-80; SATA 24

Prevert, Jacques (Henri Marie)
1900-1977 .... **CLC 15**
See also CA 77-80; 69-72; CANR 29;
MTCW; SATA-Obit 30

Prevost, Abbe (Antoine Francois)
1697-1763 .... **LC 1**

Price, (Edward) Reynolds
1933-......... **CLC 3, 6, 13, 43, 50, 63**
See also CA 1-4R; CANR 1, 37; DLB 2

Price, Richard 1949- .... **CLC 6, 12**
See also CA 49-52; CANR 3; DLBY 81

Prichard, Katharine Susannah
1883-1969 .... **CLC 46**
See also CA 11-12; CANR 33; CAP 1;
MTCW; SATA 66

Priestley, J(ohn) B(oynton)
1894-1984 .... **CLC 2, 5, 9, 34**
See also CA 9-12R; 113; CANR 33;
CDBLB 1914-1945; DLB 10, 34, 77, 100,
139; DLBY 84; MTCW

Prince 1958(?)- .... **CLC 35**

Prince, F(rank) T(empleton) 1912-.. **CLC 22**
See also CA 101; CANR 43; DLB 20

Prince Kropotkin
See Kropotkin, Peter (Aleksieevich)

Prior, Matthew 1664-1721........... **LC 4**
See also DLB 95

Pritchard, William H(arrison)
1932-........................ **CLC 34**
See also CA 65-68; CANR 23; DLB 111

Pritchett, V(ictor) S(awdon)
1900- .... **CLC 5, 13, 15, 41; SSC 14**
See also CA 61-64; CANR 31; DLB 15,
139; MTCW

Private 19022
See Manning, Frederic

Probst, Mark 1925- .... **CLC 59**
See also CA 130

Prokosch, Frederic 1908-1989.... **CLC 4, 48**
See also CA 73-76; 128; DLB 48

Prophet, The
See Dreiser, Theodore (Herman Albert)

Prose, Francine 1947-............. **CLC 45**
See also CA 109; 112; CANR 46

Proudhon
See Cunha, Euclides (Rodrigues Pimenta) da

Proulx, E. Annie 1935- .... **CLC 81**

Proust, (Valentin-Louis-George-Eugene-)
Marcel
1871-1922 ... **TCLC 7, 13, 33; DA; WLC**
See also CA 104; 120; DLB 65; MTCW

Prowler, Harley
See Masters, Edgar Lee

Prus, Boleslaw 1845-1912 .... **TCLC 48**

Pryor, Richard (Franklin Lenox Thomas)
1940- .... **CLC 26**
See also CA 122

Przybyszewski, Stanislaw
1868-1927 .... **TCLC 36**
See also DLB 66

Pteleon
See Grieve, C(hristopher) M(urray)

Puckett, Lute
See Masters, Edgar Lee

Puig, Manuel
1932-1990 ... **CLC 3, 5, 10, 28, 65; HLC**
See also CA 45-48; CANR 2, 32; DLB 113;
HW; MTCW

Purdy, Al(fred Wellington)
1918- .... **CLC 3, 6, 14, 50**
See also CA 81-84; CAAS 17; CANR 42;
DLB 88

Purdy, James (Amos)
1923-............ **CLC 2, 4, 10, 28, 52**
See also CA 33-36R; CAAS 1; CANR 19;
DLB 2; MTCW

Pure, Simon
See Swinnerton, Frank Arthur

Pushkin, Alexander (Sergeyevich)
1799-1837 .... **NCLC 3, 27; DA; PC 10;
WLC**
See also SATA 61

P'u Sung-ling 1640-1715 .... **LC 3**

Putnam, Arthur Lee
See Alger, Horatio, Jr.

Puzo, Mario 1920-......... **CLC 1, 2, 6, 36**
See also CA 65-68; CANR 4, 42; DLB 6;
MTCW

Pym, Barbara (Mary Crampton)
1913-1980 .... **CLC 13, 19, 37**
See also CA 13-14; 97-100; CANR 13, 34;
CAP 1; DLB 14; DLBY 87; MTCW

Pynchon, Thomas (Ruggles, Jr.)
1937-..... **CLC 2, 3, 6, 9, 11, 18, 33, 62,
72; DA; SSC 14; WLC**
See also BEST 90:2; CA 17-20R; CANR 22,
46; DLB 2; MTCW

Qian Zhongshu
See Ch'ien Chung-shu

Qroll
See Dagerman, Stig (Halvard)

Quarrington, Paul (Lewis) 1953-.... **CLC 65**
See also CA 129

Quasimodo, Salvatore 1901-1968 ... **CLC 10**
See also CA 13-16; 25-28R; CAP 1;
DLB 114; MTCW

Queen, Ellery.................... **CLC 3, 11**
See also Dannay, Frederic; Davidson,
Avram; Lee, Manfred B(ennington);
Sturgeon, Theodore (Hamilton); Vance,
John Holbrook

Queen, Ellery, Jr.
See Dannay, Frederic; Lee, Manfred
B(ennington)

Queneau, Raymond
1903-1976 .... **CLC 2, 5, 10, 42**
See also CA 77-80; 69-72; CANR 32;
DLB 72; MTCW

Quevedo, Francisco de 1580-1645.... **LC 23**

Quiller-Couch, Arthur Thomas
1863-1944 .... **TCLC 53**
See also CA 118; DLB 135

Quin, Ann (Marie) 1936-1973 ...... **CLC 6**
See also CA 9-12R; 45-48; DLB 14

Quinn, Martin
See Smith, Martin Cruz

Quinn, Simon
See Smith, Martin Cruz

Quiroga, Horacio (Sylvestre)
1878-1937 .... **TCLC 20; HLC**
See also CA 117; 131; HW; MTCW

Quoirez, Francoise 1935-........... **CLC 9**
See also Sagan, Francoise
See also CA 49-52; CANR 6, 39; MTCW

Raabe, Wilhelm 1831-1910 .... **TCLC 45**
See also DLB 129

Rabe, David (William) 1940-... **CLC 4, 8, 33**
See also CA 85-88; CABS 3; DLB 7

Rabelais, Francois
1483-1553 .... **LC 5; DA; WLC**

Rabinovitch, Sholem 1859-1916
See Aleichem, Sholom
See also CA 104

Racine, Jean 1639-1699 .... **LC 28**

Radcliffe, Ann (Ward) 1764-1823 .. **NCLC 6**
See also DLB 39

Radiguet, Raymond 1903-1923 .... **TCLC 29**
See also DLB 65

Radnoti, Miklos 1909-1944 .... **TCLC 16**
See also CA 118

Rado, James 1939-............... **CLC 17**
See also CA 105

Radvanyi, Netty 1900-1983
See Seghers, Anna
See also CA 85-88; 110

Rae, Ben
See Griffiths, Trevor

Raeburn, John (Hay) 1941-........ **CLC 34**
See also CA 57-60

Ragni, Gerome 1942-1991 .... **CLC 17**
See also CA 105; 134

Rahv, Philip 1908-1973 .... **CLC 24**
See also Greenberg, Ivan
See also DLB 137

Raine, Craig 1944-............... **CLC 32**
See also CA 108; CANR 29; DLB 40

Raine, Kathleen (Jessie) 1908- ... **CLC 7, 45**
See also CA 85-88; CANR 46; DLB 20;
MTCW

Rainis, Janis 1865-1929 .... **TCLC 29**

Rakosi, Carl.................... **CLC 47**
See also Rawley, Callman
See also CAAS 5

Raleigh, Richard
See Lovecraft, H(oward) P(hillips)

Rallentando, H. P.
See Sayers, Dorothy L(eigh)

Ramal, Walter
See de la Mare, Walter (John)

Ramon, Juan
See Jimenez (Mantecon), Juan Ramon

Ramos, Graciliano 1892-1953 ..... **TCLC 32**

Rampersad, Arnold 1941-......... **CLC 44**
See also BW 2; CA 127; 133; DLB 111

Rampling, Anne
See Rice, Anne

Ramsay, Allan 1684(?)-1758 .... **LC 29**
See also DLB 95

Ramuz, Charles-Ferdinand
1878-1947 .... **TCLC 33**

Rand, Ayn
1905-1982 ...... **CLC 3, 30, 44, 79; DA; WLC**
See also AAYA 10; CA 13-16R; 105;
CANR 27; MTCW

Randall, Dudley (Felker)
1914- .... **CLC 1; BLC**
See also BW 1; CA 25-28R; CANR 23;
DLB 41

Randall, Robert
See Silverberg, Robert

Ranger, Ken
See Creasey, John

Ransom, John Crowe
1888-1974 .... **CLC 2, 4, 5, 11, 24**
See also CA 5-8R; 49-52; CANR 6, 34;
DLB 45, 63; MTCW

Rao, Raja 1909- .... **CLC 25, 56**
See also CA 73-76; MTCW

Raphael, Frederic (Michael)
1931- .... **CLC 2, 14**
See also CA 1-4R; CANR 1; DLB 14

Ratcliffe, James P.
See Mencken, H(enry) L(ouis)

Rathbone, Julian 1935- .... **CLC 41**
See also CA 101; CANR 34

Rattigan, Terence (Mervyn)
1911-1977 .... **CLC 7**
See also CA 85-88; 73-76;
CDBLB 1945-1960; DLB 13; MTCW

Ratushinskaya, Irina 1954- .... **CLC 54**
See also CA 129

Raven, Simon (Arthur Noel)
1927- .... **CLC 14**
See also CA 81-84

Rawley, Callman 1903-
See Rakosi, Carl
See also CA 21-24R; CANR 12, 32

Rawlings, Marjorie Kinnan
1896-1953 .... **TCLC 4**
See also CA 104; 137; DLB 9, 22, 102;
JRDA; MAICYA; YABC 1

Ray, Satyajit 1921-1992........ **CLC 16, 76**
See also CA 114; 137

Read, Herbert Edward 1893-1968.... **CLC 4**
See also CA 85-88; 25-28R; DLB 20, 149

Read, Piers Paul 1941- ..... **CLC 4, 10, 25**
See also CA 21-24R; CANR 38; DLB 14;
SATA 21

Reade, Charles 1814-1884 .... **NCLC 2**
See also DLB 21

Reade, Hamish
See Gray, Simon (James Holliday)

Reading, Peter 1946- .... **CLC 47**
See also CA 103; CANR 46; DLB 40

Reaney, James 1926- .... **CLC 13**
See also CA 41-44R; CAAS 15; CANR 42;
DLB 68; SATA 43

Rebreanu, Liviu 1885-1944 ...... **TCLC 28**

Rechy, John (Francisco)
1934- .... **CLC 1, 7, 14, 18; HLC**
See also CA 5-8R; CAAS 4; CANR 6, 32;
DLB 122; DLBY 82; HW

Redcam, Tom 1870-1933 .... **TCLC 25**

Reddin, Keith................... **CLC 67**

Redgrove, Peter (William)
1932- .... **CLC 6, 41**
See also CA 1-4R; CANR 3, 39; DLB 40

Redmon, Anne................... **CLC 22**
See also Nightingale, Anne Redmon
See also DLBY 86

Reed, Eliot
See Ambler, Eric

Reed, Ishmael
1938- ... **CLC 2, 3, 5, 6, 13, 32, 60; BLC**
See also BW 2; CA 21-24R; CANR 25;
DLB 2, 5, 33; DLBD 8; MTCW

Reed, John (Silas) 1887-1920 ...... **TCLC 9**
See also CA 106

Reed, Lou...................... **CLC 21**
See also Firbank, Louis

Reeve, Clara 1729-1807 .... **NCLC 19**
See also DLB 39

Reich, Wilhelm 1897-1957....... **TCLC 57**

Reid, Christopher (John) 1949-..... **CLC 33**
See also CA 140; DLB 40

Reid, Desmond
See Moorcock, Michael (John)

Reid Banks, Lynne 1929-
See Banks, Lynne Reid
See also CA 1-4R; CANR 6, 22, 38;
CLR 24; JRDA; MAICYA; SATA 22, 75

Reilly, William K.
See Creasey, John

Reiner, Max
See Caldwell, (Janet Miriam) Taylor
(Holland)

Reis, Ricardo
See Pessoa, Fernando (Antonio Nogueira)

Remarque, Erich Maria
1898-1970 .... **CLC 21; DA**
See also CA 77-80; 29-32R; DLB 56;
MTCW

Remizov, A.
See Remizov, Aleksei (Mikhailovich)

Remizov, A. M.
See Remizov, Aleksei (Mikhailovich)

Remizov, Aleksei (Mikhailovich)
1877-1957 .... **TCLC 27**
See also CA 125; 133

Renan, Joseph Ernest
1823-1892 .... **NCLC 26**

Renard, Jules 1864-1910 .... **TCLC 17**
See also CA 117

Renault, Mary.............. **CLC 3, 11, 17**
See also Challans, Mary
See also DLBY 83

Rendell, Ruth (Barbara) 1930- .. **CLC 28, 48**
See also Vine, Barbara
See also CA 109; CANR 32; DLB 87;
MTCW

Renoir, Jean 1894-1979 .... **CLC 20**
See also CA 129; 85-88

Resnais, Alain 1922-............. **CLC 16**

Reverdy, Pierre 1889-1960 .... **CLC 53**
See also CA 97-100; 89-92

Rexroth, Kenneth
1905-1982 ...... **CLC 1, 2, 6, 11, 22, 49**
See also CA 5-8R; 107; CANR 14, 34;
CDALB 1941-1968; DLB 16, 48;
DLBY 82; MTCW

Reyes, Alfonso 1889-1959 .... **TCLC 33**
See also CA 131; HW

Reyes y Basoalto, Ricardo Eliecer Neftali
See Neruda, Pablo

Reymont, Wladyslaw (Stanislaw)
1868(?)-1925 .... **TCLC 5**
See also CA 104

Reynolds, Jonathan 1942-........ **CLC 6, 38**
See also CA 65-68; CANR 28

Reynolds, Joshua 1723-1792 .... **LC 15**
See also DLB 104

Reynolds, Michael Shane 1937- .... **CLC 44**
See also CA 65-68; CANR 9

Reznikoff, Charles 1894-1976 .... **CLC 9**
See also CA 33-36; 61-64; CAP 2; DLB 28,
45

Rezzori (d'Arezzo), Gregor von
1914- .... **CLC 25**
See also CA 122; 136

Rhine, Richard
See Silverstein, Alvin

Rhodes, Eugene Manlove
1869-1934 .... **TCLC 53**

R'hoone
See Balzac, Honore de

Rhys, Jean
1890(?)-1979 .... **CLC 2, 4, 6, 14, 19, 51**
See also CA 25-28R; 85-88; CANR 35;
CDBLB 1945-1960; DLB 36, 117; MTCW

Ribeiro, Darcy 1922- .... **CLC 34**
See also CA 33-36R

Ribeiro, Joao Ubaldo (Osorio Pimentel)
1941- .... **CLC 10, 67**
See also CA 81-84

Ribman, Ronald (Burt) 1932- .... **CLC 7**
See also CA 21-24R; CANR 46

Ricci, Nino 1959-................. **CLC 70**
See also CA 137

Rice, Anne 1941- .... **CLC 41**
See also AAYA 9; BEST 89:2; CA 65-68;
CANR 12, 36

Rice, Elmer (Leopold)
1892-1967 .... **CLC 7, 49**
See also CA 21-22; 25-28R; CAP 2; DLB 4,
7; MTCW

Rice, Tim(othy Miles Bindon)
1944- .... **CLC 21**
See also CA 103; CANR 46

Rich, Adrienne (Cecile)
1929- .... CLC 3, 6, 7, 11, 18, 36, 73, 76;
PC 5
See also CA 9-12R; CANR 20; DLB 5, 67;
MTCW

Rich, Barbara
See Graves, Robert (von Ranke)

Rich, Robert
See Trumbo, Dalton

Richards, David Adams 1950- ...... CLC 59
See also CA 93-96; DLB 53

Richards, I(vor) A(rmstrong)
1893-1979 .... CLC 14, 24
See also CA 41-44R; 89-92; CANR 34;
DLB 27

Richardson, Anne
See Roiphe, Anne (Richardson)

Richardson, Dorothy Miller
1873-1957 .... TCLC 3
See also CA 104; DLB 36

Richardson, Ethel Florence (Lindesay)
1870-1946
See Richardson, Henry Handel
See also CA 105

Richardson, Henry Handel .... TCLC 4
See also Richardson, Ethel Florence
(Lindesay)

Richardson, Samuel
1689-1761 .... LC 1; DA; WLC
See also CDBLB 1660-1789; DLB 39

Richler, Mordecai
1931- .... CLC 3, 5, 9, 13, 18, 46, 70
See also AITN 1; CA 65-68; CANR 31;
CLR 17; DLB 53; MAICYA; MTCW;
SATA 44; SATA-Brief 27

Richter, Conrad (Michael)
1890-1968 .... CLC 30
See also CA 5-8R; 25-28R; CANR 23;
DLB 9; MTCW; SATA 3

Riddell, J. H. 1832-1906 .... TCLC 40

Riding, Laura .... CLC 3, 7
See also Jackson, Laura (Riding)

Riefenstahl, Berta Helene Amalia 1902-
See Riefenstahl, Leni
See also CA 108

Riefenstahl, Leni .... CLC 16
See also Riefenstahl, Berta Helene Amalia

Riffe, Ernest
See Bergman, (Ernst) Ingmar

Riggs, (Rolla) Lynn 1899-1954 .... TCLC 56
See also CA 144; NNAL

Riley, James Whitcomb
1849-1916 .... TCLC 51
See also CA 118; 137; MAICYA; SATA 17

Riley, Tex
See Creasey, John

Rilke, Rainer Maria
1875-1926 .... TCLC 1, 6, 19; PC 2
See also CA 104; 132; DLB 81; MTCW

Rimbaud, (Jean Nicolas) Arthur
1854-1891 ..... NCLC 4, 35; DA; PC 3;
WLC

Rinehart, Mary Roberts
1876-1958 .... TCLC 52
See also CA 108

Ringmaster, The
See Mencken, H(enry) L(ouis)

Ringwood, Gwen(dolyn Margaret) Pharis
1910-1984 .... CLC 48
See also CA 112; DLB 88

Rio, Michel 19(?)- .... CLC 43

Ritsos, Giannes
See Ritsos, Yannis

Ritsos, Yannis 1909-1990 ..... CLC 6, 13, 31
See also CA 77-80; 133; CANR 39; MTCW

Ritter, Erika 1948(?)- .... CLC 52

Rivera, Jose Eustasio 1889-1928... TCLC 35
See also HW

Rivers, Conrad Kent 1933-1968...... CLC 1
See also BW 1; CA 85-88; DLB 41

Rivers, Elfrida
See Bradley, Marion Zimmer

Riverside, John
See Heinlein, Robert A(nson)

Rizal, Jose 1861-1896 .... NCLC 27

Roa Bastos, Augusto (Antonio)
1917- .... CLC 45; HLC
See also CA 131; DLB 113; HW

Robbe-Grillet, Alain
1922- .... CLC 1, 2, 4, 6, 8, 10, 14, 43
See also CA 9-12R; CANR 33; DLB 83;
MTCW

Robbins, Harold 1916- .... CLC 5
See also CA 73-76; CANR 26; MTCW

Robbins, Thomas Eugene 1936-
See Robbins, Tom
See also CA 81-84; CANR 29; MTCW

Robbins, Tom .... CLC 9, 32, 64
See also Robbins, Thomas Eugene
See also BEST 90:3; DLBY 80

Robbins, Trina 1938- .... CLC 21
See also CA 128

Roberts, Charles G(eorge) D(ouglas)
1860-1943 .... TCLC 8
See also CA 105; CLR 33; DLB 92;
SATA-Brief 29

Roberts, Kate 1891-1985 .... CLC 15
See also CA 107; 116

Roberts, Keith (John Kingston)
1935- .... CLC 14
See also CA 25-28R; CANR 46

Roberts, Kenneth (Lewis)
1885-1957 .... TCLC 23
See also CA 109; DLB 9

Roberts, Michele (B.) 1949- .... CLC 48
See also CA 115

Robertson, Ellis
See Ellison, Harlan (Jay); Silverberg, Robert

Robertson, Thomas William
1829-1871 .... NCLC 35

Robinson, Edwin Arlington
1869-1935 .... TCLC 5; DA; PC 1
See also CA 104; 133; CDALB 1865-1917;
DLB 54; MTCW

Robinson, Henry Crabb
1775-1867 .... NCLC 15
See also DLB 107

Robinson, Jill 1936- .... CLC 10
See also CA 102

Robinson, Kim Stanley 1952- ...... CLC 34
See also CA 126

Robinson, Lloyd
See Silverberg, Robert

Robinson, Marilynne 1944- .... CLC 25
See also CA 116

Robinson, Smokey .... CLC 21
See also Robinson, William, Jr.

Robinson, William, Jr. 1940-
See Robinson, Smokey
See also CA 116

Robison, Mary 1949- .... CLC 42
See also CA 113; 116; DLB 130

Rod, Edouard 1857-1910 .... TCLC 52

Roddenberry, Eugene Wesley 1921-1991
See Roddenberry, Gene
See also CA 110; 135; CANR 37; SATA 45;
SATA-Obit 69

Roddenberry, Gene .... CLC 17
See also Roddenberry, Eugene Wesley
See also AAYA 5; SATA-Obit 69

Rodgers, Mary 1931- .... CLC 12
See also CA 49-52; CANR 8; CLR 20;
JRDA; MAICYA; SATA 8

Rodgers, W(illiam) R(obert)
1909-1969 .... CLC 7
See also CA 85-88; DLB 20

Rodman, Eric
See Silverberg, Robert

Rodman, Howard 1920(?)-1985 ..... CLC 65
See also CA 118

Rodman, Maia
See Wojciechowska, Maia (Teresa)

Rodriguez, Claudio 1934- .... CLC 10
See also DLB 134

Roelvaag, O(le) E(dvart)
1876-1931 .... TCLC 17
See also CA 117; DLB 9

Roethke, Theodore (Huebner)
1908-1963 ...... CLC 1, 3, 8, 11, 19, 46
See also CA 81-84; CABS 2;
CDALB 1941-1968; DLB 5; MTCW

Rogers, Thomas Hunton 1927- ..... CLC 57
See also CA 89-92

Rogers, Will(iam Penn Adair)
1879-1935 .... TCLC 8
See also CA 105; 144; DLB 11; NNAL

Rogin, Gilbert 1929- .... CLC 18
See also CA 65-68; CANR 15

Rohan, Koda .... TCLC 22
See also Koda Shigeyuki

Rohmer, Eric .... CLC 16
See also Scherer, Jean-Marie Maurice

Rohmer, Sax .... TCLC 28
See also Ward, Arthur Henry Sarsfield
See also DLB 70

Roiphe, Anne (Richardson)
1935- .... CLC 3, 9
See also CA 89-92; CANR 45; DLBY 80

Rojas, Fernando de 1465-1541 ...... LC 23

**Rolfe, Frederick (William Serafino Austin
Lewis Mary)** 1860-1913 ...... TCLC 12
See also CA 107; DLB 34

Rolland, Romain 1866-1944...... **TCLC 23**
See also CA 118; DLB 65

Rolvaag, O(le) E(dvart)
See Roelvaag, O(le) E(dvart)

Romain Arnaud, Saint
See Aragon, Louis

Romains, Jules 1885-1972......... **CLC 7**
See also CA 85-88; CANR 34; DLB 65;
MTCW

Romero, Jose Ruben 1890-1952 ... **TCLC 14**
See also CA 114; 131; HW

Ronsard, Pierre de
1524-1585 .... **LC 6; PC 11**

Rooke, Leon 1934-........... **CLC 25, 34**
See also CA 25-28R; CANR 23

Roper, William 1498-1578......... **LC 10**

Roquelaure, A. N.
See Rice, Anne

Rosa, Joao Guimaraes 1908-1967 ... **CLC 23**
See also CA 89-92; DLB 113

Rose, Wendy 1948-............... **CLC 85**
See also CA 53-56; CANR 5; NNAL;
SATA 12

Rosen, Richard (Dean) 1949-...... **CLC 39**
See also CA 77-80

Rosenberg, Isaac 1890-1918...... **TCLC 12**
See also CA 107; DLB 20

Rosenblatt, Joe .... **CLC 15**
See also Rosenblatt, Joseph

Rosenblatt, Joseph 1933-
See Rosenblatt, Joe
See also CA 89-92

Rosenfeld, Samuel 1896-1963
See Tzara, Tristan
See also CA 89-92

Rosenthal, M(acha) L(ouis) 1917-... **CLC 28**
See also CA 1-4R; CAAS 6; CANR 4;
DLB 5; SATA 59

Ross, Barnaby
See Dannay, Frederic

Ross, Bernard L.
See Follett, Ken(neth Martin)

Ross, J. H.
See Lawrence, T(homas) E(dward)

Ross, Martin
See Martin, Violet Florence
See also DLB 135

Ross, (James) Sinclair 1908-....... **CLC 13**
See also CA 73-76; DLB 88

Rossetti, Christina (Georgina)
1830-1894 ... **NCLC 2; DA; PC 7; WLC**
See also DLB 35; MAICYA; SATA 20

Rossetti, Dante Gabriel
1828-1882 .... **NCLC 4; DA; WLC**
See also CDBLB 1832-1890; DLB 35

Rossner, Judith (Perelman)
1935- .... **CLC 6, 9, 29**
See also AITN 2; BEST 90:3; CA 17-20R;
CANR 18; DLB 6; MTCW

Rostand, Edmond (Eugene Alexis)
1868-1918 .... **TCLC 6, 37; DA**
See also CA 104; 126; MTCW

Roth, Henry 1906-........... **CLC 2, 6, 11**
See also CA 11-12; CANR 38; CAP 1;
DLB 28; MTCW

Roth, Joseph 1894-1939......... **TCLC 33**
See also DLB 85

Roth, Philip (Milton)
1933- ...... **CLC 1, 2, 3, 4, 6, 9, 15, 22,**
                      31, 47, 66, 86; DA; WLC
See also BEST 90:3; CA 1-4R; CANR 1, 22,
36; CDALB 1968-1988; DLB 2, 28;
DLBY 82; MTCW

Rothenberg, Jerome 1931-....... **CLC 6, 57**
See also CA 45-48; CANR 1; DLB 5

Roumain, Jacques (Jean Baptiste)
1907-1944 .... **TCLC 19; BLC**
See also BW 1; CA 117; 125

Rourke, Constance (Mayfield)
1885-1941 .... **TCLC 12**
See also CA 107; YABC 1

Rousseau, Jean-Baptiste 1671-1741 ... **LC 9**

Rousseau, Jean-Jacques
1712-1778 .... **LC 14; DA; WLC**

Roussel, Raymond 1877-1933 ..... **TCLC 20**
See also CA 117

Rovit, Earl (Herbert) 1927-...... **CLC 7**
See also CA 5-8R; CANR 12

Rowe, Nicholas 1674-1718........... **LC 8**
See also DLB 84

Rowley, Ames Dorrance
See Lovecraft, H(oward) P(hillips)

Rowson, Susanna Haswell
1762(?)-1824 .... **NCLC 5**
See also DLB 37

Roy, Gabrielle 1909-1983....... **CLC 10, 14**
See also CA 53-56; 110; CANR 5; DLB 68;
MTCW

Rozewicz, Tadeusz 1921-........ **CLC 9, 23**
See also CA 108; CANR 36; MTCW

Ruark, Gibbons 1941- .... **CLC 3**
See also CA 33-36R; CANR 14, 31;
DLB 120

Rubens, Bernice (Ruth) 1923-... **CLC 19, 31**
See also CA 25-28R; CANR 33; DLB 14;
MTCW

Rudkin, (James) David 1936- ...... **CLC 14**
See also CA 89-92; DLB 13

Rudnik, Raphael 1933-............. **CLC 7**
See also CA 29-32R

Ruffian, M.
See Hasek, Jaroslav (Matej Frantisek)

Ruiz, Jose Martinez .... **CLC 11**
See also Martinez Ruiz, Jose

Rukeyser, Muriel
1913-1980 .... **CLC 6, 10, 15, 27; PC 12**
See also CA 5-8R; 93-96; CANR 26;
DLB 48; MTCW; SATA-Obit 22

Rule, Jane (Vance) 1931-.......... **CLC 27**
See also CA 25-28R; CAAS 18; CANR 12;
DLB 60

Rulfo, Juan 1918-1986.... **CLC 8, 80; HLC**
See also CA 85-88; 118; CANR 26;
DLB 113; HW; MTCW

Runeberg, Johan 1804-1877..... **NCLC 41**

Runyon, (Alfred) Damon
1884(?)-1946 .... **TCLC 10**
See also CA 107; DLB 11, 86

Rush, Norman 1933-............. **CLC 44**
See also CA 121; 126

Rushdie, (Ahmed) Salman
1947-................**CLC 23, 31, 55**
See also BEST 89:3; CA 108; 111;
CANR 33; MTCW

Rushforth, Peter (Scott) 1945- ..... **CLC 19**
See also CA 101

Ruskin, John 1819-1900......... **TCLC 20**
See also CA 114; 129; CDBLB 1832-1890;
DLB 55; SATA 24

Russ, Joanna 1937-............. **CLC 15**
See also CA 25-28R; CANR 11, 31; DLB 8;
MTCW

Russell, (Henry) Ken(neth Alfred)
1927- .... **CLC 16**
See also CA 105

Russell, Willy 1947-............. **CLC 60**

Rutherford, Mark .... **TCLC 25**
See also White, William Hale
See also DLB 18

Ruyslinck, Ward 1929-........... **CLC 14**
See also Belser, Reimond Karel Maria de

Ryan, Cornelius (John) 1920-1974 ... **CLC 7**
See also CA 69-72; 53-56; CANR 38

Ryan, Michael 1946- .... **CLC 65**
See also CA 49-52; DLBY 82

Rybakov, Anatoli (Naumovich)
1911-................... **CLC 23, 53**
See also CA 126; 135; SATA 79

Ryder, Jonathan
See Ludlum, Robert

Ryga, George 1932-1987 .... **CLC 14**
See also CA 101; 124; CANR 43; DLB 60

S. S.
See Sassoon, Siegfried (Lorraine)

Saba, Umberto 1883-1957 .... **TCLC 33**
See also CA 144; DLB 114

Sabatini, Rafael 1875-1950 ...... **TCLC 47**

Sabato, Ernesto (R.)
1911- .... **CLC 10, 23; HLC**
See also CA 97-100; CANR 32; DLB 145;
HW; MTCW

Sacastru, Martin
See Bioy Casares, Adolfo

Sacher-Masoch, Leopold von
1836(?)-1895 .... **NCLC 31**

Sachs, Marilyn (Stickle) 1927- ..... **CLC 35**
See also AAYA 2; CA 17-20R; CANR 13,
47; CLR 2; JRDA; MAICYA; SAAS 2;
SATA 3, 68

Sachs, Nelly 1891-1970 .... **CLC 14**
See also CA 17-18; 25-28R; CAP 2

Sackler, Howard (Oliver)
1929-1982 .... **CLC 14**
See also CA 61-64; 108; CANR 30; DLB 7

Sacks, Oliver (Wolf) 1933- .... **CLC 67**
See also CA 53-56; CANR 28; MTCW

Sade, Donatien Alphonse Francois Comte
1740-1814 .... **NCLC 47**

Sadoff, Ira 1945- .... **CLC 9**
See also CA 53-56; CANR 5, 21; DLB 120

Saetone
See Camus, Albert

Safire, William 1929- .... **CLC 10**
See also CA 17-20R; CANR 31

Sagan, Carl (Edward) 1934-........ **CLC 30**
See also AAYA 2; CA 25-28R; CANR 11,
36; MTCW; SATA 58

Sagan, Francoise .... **CLC 3, 6, 9, 17, 36**
See also Quoirez, Francoise
See also DLB 83

Sahgal, Nayantara (Pandit) 1927-... **CLC 41**
See also CA 9-12R; CANR 11

Saint, H(arry) F. 1941- .... **CLC 50**
See also CA 127

St. Aubin de Teran, Lisa 1953-
See Teran, Lisa St. Aubin de
See also CA 118; 126

Sainte-Beuve, Charles Augustin
1804-1869 .... **NCLC 5**

**Saint-Exupery, Antoine (Jean Baptiste Marie
Roger) de**
1900-1944 .... **TCLC 2, 56; WLC**
See also CA 108; 132; CLR 10; DLB 72;
MAICYA; MTCW; SATA 20

St. John, David
See Hunt, E(verette) Howard, (Jr.)

Saint-John Perse
See Leger, (Marie-Rene Auguste) Alexis
Saint-Leger

Saintsbury, George (Edward Bateman)
1845-1933 .... **TCLC 31**
See also DLB 57, 149

Sait Faik .... **TCLC 23**
See also Abasiyanik, Sait Faik

Saki .... **TCLC 3; SSC 12**
See also Munro, H(ector) H(ugh)

Sala, George Augustus .... **NCLC 46**

Salama, Hannu 1936- .... **CLC 18**

Salamanca, J(ack) R(ichard)
1922- .... **CLC 4, 15**
See also CA 25-28R

Sale, J. Kirkpatrick
See Sale, Kirkpatrick

Sale, Kirkpatrick 1937- .... **CLC 68**
See also CA 13-16R; CANR 10

Salinas (y Serrano), Pedro
1891(?)-1951 .... **TCLC 17**
See also CA 117; DLB 134

Salinger, J(erome) D(avid)
1919- ..... **CLC 1, 3, 8, 12, 55, 56; DA;
SSC 2; WLC**
See also AAYA 2; CA 5-8R; CANR 39;
CDALB 1941-1968; CLR 18; DLB 2, 102;
MAICYA; MTCW; SATA 67

Salisbury, John
See Caute, David

Salter, James 1925- .... **CLC 7, 52, 59**
See also CA 73-76; DLB 130

Saltus, Edgar (Everton)
1855-1921 .... **TCLC 8**
See also CA 105

Saltykov, Mikhail Evgrafovich
1826-1889 .... **NCLC 16**

Samarakis, Antonis 1919- .... **CLC 5**
See also CA 25-28R; CAAS 16; CANR 36

Sanchez, Florencio 1875-1910 .... **TCLC 37**
See also HW

Sanchez, Luis Rafael 1936-........ **CLC 23**
See also CA 128; DLB 145; HW

Sanchez, Sonia 1934-... **CLC 5; BLC; PC 9**
See also BW 2; CA 33-36R; CANR 24;
CLR 18; DLB 41; DLBD 8; MAICYA;
MTCW; SATA 22

Sand, George
1804-1876 ...... **NCLC 2, 42; DA; WLC**
See also DLB 119

Sandburg, Carl (August)
1878-1967 .... **CLC 1, 4, 10, 15, 35; DA;
PC 2; WLC**
See also CA 5-8R; 25-28R; CANR 35;
CDALB 1865-1917; DLB 17, 54;
MAICYA; MTCW; SATA 8

Sandburg, Charles
See Sandburg, Carl (August)

Sandburg, Charles A.
See Sandburg, Carl (August)

Sanders, (James) Ed(ward) 1939- ... **CLC 53**
See also CA 13-16R; CANR 13, 44;
DLB 16

Sanders, Lawrence 1920-......... **CLC 41**
See also BEST 89:4; CA 81-84; CANR 33;
MTCW

Sanders, Noah
See Blount, Roy (Alton), Jr.

Sanders, Winston P.
See Anderson, Poul (William)

Sandoz, Mari(e Susette)
1896-1966 .... **CLC 28**
See also CA 1-4R; 25-28R; CANR 17;
DLB 9; MTCW; SATA 5

Saner, Reg(inald Anthony) 1931- .... **CLC 9**
See also CA 65-68

Sannazaro, Jacopo 1456(?)-1530 ...... **LC 8**

Sansom, William 1912-1976...... **CLC 2, 6**
See also CA 5-8R; 65-68; CANR 42;
DLB 139; MTCW

Santayana, George 1863-1952 ..... **TCLC 40**
See also CA 115; DLB 54, 71

Santiago, Danny .... **CLC 33**
See also James, Daniel (Lewis); James,
Daniel (Lewis)
See also DLB 122

Santmyer, Helen Hoover
1895-1986 .... **CLC 33**
See also CA 1-4R; 118; CANR 15, 33;
DLBY 84; MTCW

Santos, Bienvenido N(uqui) 1911-... **CLC 22**
See also CA 101; CANR 19, 46

Sapper .... **TCLC 44**
See also McNeile, Herman Cyril

Sappho fl. 6th cent. B.C.-.... **CMLC 3; PC 5**

Sarduy, Severo 1937-1993 .... **CLC 6**
See also CA 89-92; 142; DLB 113; HW

Sargeson, Frank 1903-1982 .... **CLC 31**
See also CA 25-28R; 106; CANR 38

Sarmiento, Felix Ruben Garcia
See Dario, Ruben

Saroyan, William
1908-1981 ..... **CLC 1, 8, 10, 29, 34, 56;
DA; WLC**
See also CA 5-8R; 103; CANR 30; DLB 7,
9, 86; DLBY 81; MTCW; SATA 23;
SATA-Obit 24

Sarraute, Nathalie
1900- .... **CLC 1, 2, 4, 8, 10, 31, 80**
See also CA 9-12R; CANR 23; DLB 83;
MTCW

Sarton, (Eleanor) May
1912- .... **CLC 4, 14, 49**
See also CA 1-4R; CANR 1, 34; DLB 48;
DLBY 81; MTCW; SATA 36

Sartre, Jean-Paul
1905-1980 .... **CLC 1, 4, 7, 9, 13, 18, 24,
44, 50, 52; DA; DC 3; WLC**
See also CA 9-12R; 97-100; CANR 21;
DLB 72; MTCW

Sassoon, Siegfried (Lorraine)
1886-1967 .... **CLC 36; PC 12**
See also CA 104; 25-28R; CANR 36;
DLB 20; MTCW

Satterfield, Charles
See Pohl, Frederik

Saul, John (W. III) 1942- .... **CLC 46**
See also AAYA 10; BEST 90:4; CA 81-84;
CANR 16, 40

Saunders, Caleb
See Heinlein, Robert A(nson)

Saura (Atares), Carlos 1932-....... **CLC 20**
See also CA 114; 131; HW

Sauser-Hall, Frederic 1887-1961.... **CLC 18**
See also Cendrars, Blaise
See also CA 102; 93-96; CANR 36; MTCW

Saussure, Ferdinand de
1857-1913 .... **TCLC 49**

Savage, Catharine
See Brosman, Catharine Savage

Savage, Thomas 1915- .... **CLC 40**
See also CA 126; 132; CAAS 15

Savan, Glenn 19(?)- .... **CLC 50**

Sayers, Dorothy L(eigh)
1893-1957 ....**TCLC 2, 15**
See also CA 104; 119; CDBLB 1914-1945;
DLB 10, 36, 77, 100; MTCW

Sayers, Valerie 1952-............. **CLC 50**
See also CA 134

Sayles, John (Thomas)
1950- .... **CLC 7, 10, 14**
See also CA 57-60; CANR 41; DLB 44

Scammell, Michael .... **CLC 34**

Scannell, Vernon 1922- .... **CLC 49**
See also CA 5-8R; CANR 8, 24; DLB 27;
SATA 59

Scarlett, Susan
See Streatfeild, (Mary) Noel

Schaeffer, Susan Fromberg
1941- .... **CLC 6, 11, 22**
See also CA 49-52; CANR 18; DLB 28;
MTCW; SATA 22

Schary, Jill
See Robinson, Jill

Service, Robert
See Service, Robert W(illiam)
See also DLB 92

Service, Robert W(illiam)
1874(?)-1958 ...... **TCLC 15; DA; WLC**
See also Service, Robert
See also CA 115; 140; SATA 20

Seth, Vikram 1952-............... **CLC 43**
See also CA 121; 127; DLB 120

Seton, Cynthia Propper
1926-1982 .... **CLC 27**
See also CA 5-8R; 108; CANR 7

Seton, Ernest (Evan) Thompson
1860-1946 .... **TCLC 31**
See also CA 109; DLB 92; JRDA; SATA 18

Seton-Thompson, Ernest
See Seton, Ernest (Evan) Thompson

Settle, Mary Lee 1918- .... **CLC 19, 61**
See also CA 89-92; CAAS 1; CANR 44;
DLB 6

Seuphor, Michel
See Arp, Jean

**Sevigne, Marie (de Rabutin-Chantal) Marquise
de** 1626-1696 .... **LC 11**

Sexton, Anne (Harvey)
1928-1974 .... **CLC 2, 4, 6, 8, 10, 15, 53;
DA; PC 2; WLC**
See also CA 1-4R; 53-56; CABS 2;
CANR 3, 36; CDALB 1941-1968; DLB 5;
MTCW; SATA 10

Shaara, Michael (Joseph Jr.)
1929-1988 .... **CLC 15**
See also AITN 1; CA 102; DLBY 83

Shackleton, C. C.
See Aldiss, Brian W(ilson)

Shacochis, Bob .... **CLC 39**
See also Shacochis, Robert G.

Shacochis, Robert G. 1951-
See Shacochis, Bob
See also CA 119; 124

Shaffer, Anthony (Joshua) 1926-.... **CLC 19**
See also CA 110; 116; DLB 13

Shaffer, Peter (Levin)
1926- .... **CLC 5, 14, 18, 37, 60**
See also CA 25-28R; CANR 25, 47;
CDBLB 1960 to Present; DLB 13;
MTCW

Shakey, Bernard
See Young, Neil

Shalamov, Varlam (Tikhonovich)
1907(?)-1982 .... **CLC 18**
See also CA 129; 105

Shamlu, Ahmad 1925- .... **CLC 10**

Shammas, Anton 1951-............ **CLC 55**

Shange, Ntozake
1948- .... **CLC 8, 25, 38, 74; BLC; DC 3**
See also AAYA 9; BW 2; CA 85-88;
CABS 3; CANR 27; DLB 38; MTCW

Shanley, John Patrick 1950-....... **CLC 75**
See also CA 128; 133

Shapcott, Thomas William 1935- ... **CLC 38**
See also CA 69-72

Shapiro, Jane................... **CLC 76**

Shapiro, Karl (Jay) 1913- .. **CLC 4, 8, 15, 53**
See also CA 1-4R; CAAS 6; CANR 1, 36;
DLB 48; MTCW

Sharp, William 1855-1905 .... **TCLC 39**

Sharpe, Thomas Ridley 1928-
See Sharpe, Tom
See also CA 114; 122

Sharpe, Tom................... **CLC 36**
See also Sharpe, Thomas Ridley
See also DLB 14

Shaw, Bernard................... **TCLC 45**
See also Shaw, George Bernard
See also BW 1

Shaw, G. Bernard
See Shaw, George Bernard

Shaw, George Bernard
1856-1950 .... **TCLC 3, 9, 21; DA; WLC**
See also Shaw, Bernard
See also CA 104; 128; CDBLB 1914-1945;
DLB 10, 57; MTCW

Shaw, Henry Wheeler
1818-1885 .... **NCLC 15**
See also DLB 11

Shaw, Irwin 1913-1984...... **CLC 7, 23, 34**
See also AITN 1; CA 13-16R; 112;
CANR 21; CDALB 1941-1968; DLB 6,
102; DLBY 84; MTCW

Shaw, Robert 1927-1978 .... **CLC 5**
See also AITN 1; CA 1-4R; 81-84;
CANR 4; DLB 13, 14

Shaw, T. E.
See Lawrence, T(homas) E(dward)

Shawn, Wallace 1943- .... **CLC 41**
See also CA 112

Shea, Lisa 1953-................. **CLC 86**

Sheed, Wilfrid (John Joseph)
1930- .... **CLC 2, 4, 10, 53**
See also CA 65-68; CANR 30; DLB 6;
MTCW

Sheldon, Alice Hastings Bradley
1915(?)-1987
See Tiptree, James, Jr.
See also CA 108; 122; CANR 34; MTCW

Sheldon, John
See Bloch, Robert (Albert)

Shelley, Mary Wollstonecraft (Godwin)
1797-1851 .... **NCLC 14; DA; WLC**
See also CDBLB 1789-1832; DLB 110, 116;
SATA 29

Shelley, Percy Bysshe
1792-1822 .... **NCLC 18; DA; WLC**
See also CDBLB 1789-1832; DLB 96, 110

Shepard, Jim 1956-............... **CLC 36**
See also CA 137

Shepard, Lucius 1947- .... **CLC 34**
See also CA 128; 141

Shepard, Sam
1943- .... **CLC 4, 6, 17, 34, 41, 44; DC 5**
See also AAYA 1; CA 69-72; CABS 3;
CANR 22; DLB 7; MTCW

Shepherd, Michael
See Ludlum, Robert

Sherburne, Zoa (Morin) 1912-...... **CLC 30**
See also AAYA 13; CA 1-4R; CANR 3, 37;
MAICYA; SAAS 18; SATA 3

Sheridan, Frances 1724-1766........ **LC 7**
See also DLB 39, 84

Sheridan, Richard Brinsley
1751-1816 ... **NCLC 5; DA; DC 1; WLC**
See also CDBLB 1660-1789; DLB 89

Sherman, Jonathan Marc.......... **CLC 55**

Sherman, Martin 1941(?)-......... **CLC 19**
See also CA 116; 123

Sherwin, Judith Johnson 1936-... **CLC 7, 15**
See also CA 25-28R; CANR 34

Sherwood, Frances 1940-......... **CLC 81**

Sherwood, Robert E(mmet)
1896-1955 .... **TCLC 3**
See also CA 104; DLB 7, 26

Shestov, Lev 1866-1938 .... **TCLC 56**

Shiel, M(atthew) P(hipps)
1865-1947 .... **TCLC 8**
See also CA 106

Shiga, Naoya 1883-1971.......... **CLC 33**
See also CA 101; 33-36R

Shih, Su 1036-1101............. **CMLC 15**

Shilts, Randy 1951-1994 .... **CLC 85**
See also CA 115; 127; 144; CANR 45

Shimazaki Haruki 1872-1943
See Shimazaki Toson
See also CA 105; 134

Shimazaki Toson................. **TCLC 5**
See also Shimazaki Haruki

Sholokhov, Mikhail (Aleksandrovich)
1905-1984 .... **CLC 7, 15**
See also CA 101; 112; MTCW;
SATA-Obit 36

Shone, Patric
See Hanley, James

Shreve, Susan Richards 1939-...... **CLC 23**
See also CA 49-52; CAAS 5; CANR 5, 38;
MAICYA; SATA 46; SATA-Brief 41

Shue, Larry 1946-1985............ **CLC 52**
See also CA 145; 117

Shu-Jen, Chou 1881-1936
See Hsun, Lu
See also CA 104

Shulman, Alix Kates 1932- ...... **CLC 2, 10**
See also CA 29-32R; CANR 43; SATA 7

Shuster, Joe 1914-............... **CLC 21**

Shute, Nevil..................... **CLC 30**
See also Norway, Nevil Shute

Shuttle, Penelope (Diane) 1947-..... **CLC 7**
See also CA 93-96; CANR 39; DLB 14, 40

Sidney, Mary 1561-1621 .... **LC 19**

Sidney, Sir Philip 1554-1586.... **LC 19; DA**
See also CDBLB Before 1660

Siegel, Jerome 1914- .... **CLC 21**
See also CA 116

Siegel, Jerry
See Siegel, Jerome

Sienkiewicz, Henryk (Adam Alexander Pius)
1846-1916 .... **TCLC 3**
See also CA 104; 134

Sierra, Gregorio Martinez
See Martinez Sierra, Gregorio

Sierra, Maria (de la O'LeJarraga) Martinez
See Martinez Sierra, Maria (de la O'LeJarraga)

Sigal, Clancy 1926-.............. CLC 7
See also CA 1-4R

Sigourney, Lydia Howard (Huntley)
1791-1865 .... NCLC 21
See also DLB 1, 42, 73

Siguenza y Gongora, Carlos de
1645-1700 .... LC 8

Sigurjonsson, Johann 1880-1919... TCLC 27

Sikelianos, Angelos 1884-1951 .... TCLC 39

Silkin, Jon 1930- .... CLC 2, 6, 43
See also CA 5-8R; CAAS 5; DLB 27

Silko, Leslie (Marmon)
1948- .... CLC 23, 74; DA
See also AAYA 14; CA 115; 122;
CANR 45; DLB 143; NNAL

Sillanpaa, Frans Eemil 1888-1964... CLC 19
See also CA 129; 93-96; MTCW

Sillitoe, Alan
1928- .... CLC 1, 3, 6, 10, 19, 57
See also AITN 1; CA 9-12R; CAAS 2;
CANR 8, 26; CDBLB 1960 to Present;
DLB 14, 139; MTCW; SATA 61

Silone, Ignazio 1900-1978 .... CLC 4
See also CA 25-28; 81-84; CANR 34;
CAP 2; MTCW

Silver, Joan Micklin 1935- .... CLC 20
See also CA 114; 121

Silver, Nicholas
See Faust, Frederick (Schiller)

Silverberg, Robert 1935- .... CLC 7
See also CA 1-4R; CAAS 3; CANR 1, 20,
36; DLB 8; MAICYA; MTCW; SATA 13

Silverstein, Alvin 1933- .... CLC 17
See also CA 49-52; CANR 2; CLR 25;
JRDA; MAICYA; SATA 8, 69

Silverstein, Virginia B(arbara Opshelor)
1937- .... CLC 17
See also CA 49-52; CANR 2; CLR 25;
JRDA; MAICYA; SATA 8, 69

Sim, Georges
See Simenon, Georges (Jacques Christian)

Simak, Clifford D(onald)
1904-1988 .... CLC 1, 55
See also CA 1-4R; 125; CANR 1, 35;
DLB 8; MTCW; SATA-Obit 56

Simenon, Georges (Jacques Christian)
1903-1989 .... CLC 1, 2, 3, 8, 18, 47
See also CA 85-88; 129; CANR 35;
DLB 72; DLBY 89; MTCW

Simic, Charles 1938-... CLC 6, 9, 22, 49, 68
See also CA 29-32R; CAAS 4; CANR 12,
33; DLB 105

Simmons, Charles (Paul) 1924-..... CLC 57
See also CA 89-92

Simmons, Dan 1948-.............. CLC 44
See also CA 138

Simmons, James (Stewart Alexander)
1933- .... CLC 43
See also CA 105; DLB 40

Simms, William Gilmore
1806-1870 .... NCLC 3
See also DLB 3, 30, 59, 73

Simon, Carly 1945-.............. CLC 26
See also CA 105

Simon, Claude 1913-....... CLC 4, 9, 15, 39
See also CA 89-92; CANR 33; DLB 83;
MTCW

Simon, (Marvin) Neil
1927- .... CLC 6, 11, 31, 39, 70
See also AITN 1; CA 21-24R; CANR 26;
DLB 7; MTCW

Simon, Paul 1942(?)- .... CLC 17
See also CA 116

Simonon, Paul 1956(?)- .... CLC 30

Simpson, Harriette
See Arnow, Harriette (Louisa) Simpson

Simpson, Louis (Aston Marantz)
1923-................... CLC 4, 7, 9, 32
See also CA 1-4R; CAAS 4; CANR 1;
DLB 5; MTCW

Simpson, Mona (Elizabeth) 1957-... CLC 44
See also CA 122; 135

Simpson, N(orman) F(rederick)
1919- .... CLC 29
See also CA 13-16R; DLB 13

Sinclair, Andrew (Annandale)
1935- .... CLC 2, 14
See also CA 9-12R; CAAS 5; CANR 14, 38;
DLB 14; MTCW

Sinclair, Emil
See Hesse, Hermann

Sinclair, Iain 1943-.............. CLC 76
See also CA 132

Sinclair, Iain MacGregor
See Sinclair, Iain

Sinclair, Mary Amelia St. Clair 1865(?)-1946
See Sinclair, May
See also CA 104

Sinclair, May.................. TCLC 3, 11
See also Sinclair, Mary Amelia St. Clair
See also DLB 36, 135

Sinclair, Upton (Beall)
1878-1968 ...... CLC 1, 11, 15, 63; DA;
WLC
See also CA 5-8R; 25-28R; CANR 7;
CDALB 1929-1941; DLB 9; MTCW;
SATA 9

Singer, Isaac
See Singer, Isaac Bashevis

Singer, Isaac Bashevis
1904-1991 .... CLC 1, 3, 6, 9, 11, 15, 23,
38, 69; DA; SSC 3; WLC
See also AITN 1, 2; CA 1-4R; 134;
CANR 1, 39; CDALB 1941-1968; CLR 1;
DLB 6, 28, 52; DLBY 91; JRDA;
MAICYA; MTCW; SATA 3, 27;
SATA-Obit 68

Singer, Israel Joshua 1893-1944 ... TCLC 33

Singh, Khushwant 1915-........... CLC 11
See also CA 9-12R; CAAS 9; CANR 6

Sinjohn, John
See Galsworthy, John

Sinyavsky, Andrei (Donatevich)
1925- .... CLC 8
See also CA 85-88

Sirin, V.
See Nabokov, Vladimir (Vladimirovich)

Sissman, L(ouis) E(dward)
1928-1976 .... CLC 9, 18
See also CA 21-24R; 65-68; CANR 13;
DLB 5

Sisson, C(harles) H(ubert) 1914-..... CLC 8
See also CA 1-4R; CAAS 3; CANR 3;
DLB 27

Sitwell, Dame Edith
1887-1964 .... CLC 2, 9, 67; PC 3
See also CA 9-12R; CANR 35;
CDBLB 1945-1960; DLB 20; MTCW

Sjoewall, Maj 1935-.............. CLC 7
See also CA 65-68

Sjowall, Maj
See Sjoewall, Maj

Skelton, Robin 1925-.............. CLC 13
See also AITN 2; CA 5-8R; CAAS 5;
CANR 28; DLB 27, 53

Skolimowski, Jerzy 1938- .... CLC 20
See also CA 128

Skram, Amalie (Bertha)
1847-1905 .... TCLC 25

Skvorecky, Josef (Vaclav)
1924-................. CLC 15, 39, 69
See also CA 61-64; CAAS 1; CANR 10, 34;
MTCW

Slade, Bernard................ CLC 11, 46
See also Newbound, Bernard Slade
See also CAAS 9; DLB 53

Slaughter, Carolyn 1946-.......... CLC 56
See also CA 85-88

Slaughter, Frank G(ill) 1908- ...... CLC 29
See also AITN 2; CA 5-8R; CANR 5

Slavitt, David R(ytman) 1935-.... CLC 5, 14
See also CA 21-24R; CAAS 3; CANR 41;
DLB 5, 6

Slesinger, Tess 1905-1945 .... TCLC 10
See also CA 107; DLB 102

Slessor, Kenneth 1901-1971........ CLC 14
See also CA 102; 89-92

Slowacki, Juliusz 1809-1849 ..... NCLC 15

Smart, Christopher 1722-1771........ LC 3
See also DLB 109

Smart, Elizabeth 1913-1986........ CLC 54
See also CA 81-84; 118; DLB 88

Smiley, Jane (Graves) 1949- .... CLC 53, 76
See also CA 104; CANR 30

Smith, A(rthur) J(ames) M(arshall)
1902-1980 .... CLC 15
See also CA 1-4R; 102; CANR 4; DLB 88

Smith, Anna Deavere 1950-........ CLC 86
See also CA 133

Smith, Betty (Wehner) 1896-1972... CLC 19
See also CA 5-8R; 33-36R; DLBY 82;
SATA 6

Smith, Charlotte (Turner)
1749-1806 .... NCLC 23
See also DLB 39, 109

Smith, Clark Ashton 1893-1961 .... CLC 43
See also CA 143

Smith, Dave.................. CLC 22, 42
See also Smith, David (Jeddie)
See also CAAS 7; DLB 5

Smith, David (Jeddie) 1942-
See Smith, Dave
See also CA 49-52; CANR 1

Smith, Florence Margaret 1902-1971
See Smith, Stevie
See also CA 17-18; 29-32R; CANR 35;
CAP 2; MTCW

Smith, Iain Crichton 1928- .... CLC 64
See also CA 21-24R; DLB 40, 139

Smith, John 1580(?)-1631 .... LC 9

Smith, Johnston
See Crane, Stephen (Townley)

Smith, Lee 1944-............. CLC 25, 73
See also CA 114; 119; CANR 46; DLB 143;
DLBY 83

Smith, Martin
See Smith, Martin Cruz

Smith, Martin Cruz 1942-......... CLC 25
See also BEST 89:4; CA 85-88; CANR 6,
23, 43; NNAL

Smith, Mary-Ann Tirone 1944-..... CLC 39
See also CA 118; 136

Smith, Patti 1946- .... CLC 12
See also CA 93-96

Smith, Pauline (Urmson)
1882-1959 .... TCLC 25

Smith, Rosamond
See Oates, Joyce Carol

Smith, Sheila Kaye
See Kaye-Smith, Sheila

Smith, Stevie ...... CLC 3, 8, 25, 44; PC 12
See also Smith, Florence Margaret
See also DLB 20

Smith, Wilbur (Addison) 1933-..... CLC 33
See also CA 13-16R; CANR 7, 46; MTCW

Smith, William Jay 1918- .... CLC 6
See also CA 5-8R; CANR 44; DLB 5;
MAICYA; SATA 2, 68

Smith, Woodrow Wilson
See Kuttner, Henry

Smolenskin, Peretz 1842-1885.... NCLC 30

Smollett, Tobias (George) 1721-1771 .. LC 2
See also CDBLB 1660-1789; DLB 39, 104

Snodgrass, W(illiam) D(e Witt)
1926- .... CLC 2, 6, 10, 18, 68
See also CA 1-4R; CANR 6, 36; DLB 5;
MTCW

Snow, C(harles) P(ercy)
1905-1980 .... CLC 1, 4, 6, 9, 13, 19
See also CA 5-8R; 101; CANR 28;
CDBLB 1945-1960; DLB 15, 77; MTCW

Snow, Frances Compton
See Adams, Henry (Brooks)

Snyder, Gary (Sherman)
1930-............. CLC 1, 2, 5, 9, 32
See also CA 17-20R; CANR 30; DLB 5, 16

Snyder, Zilpha Keatley 1927-...... CLC 17
See also CA 9-12R; CANR 38; CLR 31;
JRDA; MAICYA; SAAS 2; SATA 1, 28,
75

Soares, Bernardo
See Pessoa, Fernando (Antonio Nogueira)

Sobh, A.
See Shamlu, Ahmad

Sobol, Joshua. .... CLC 60

Soderberg, Hjalmar 1869-1941 .... TCLC 39

Sodergran, Edith (Irene)
See Soedergran, Edith (Irene)

Soedergran, Edith (Irene)
1892-1923 .... TCLC 31

Softly, Edgar
See Lovecraft, H(oward) P(hillips)

Softly, Edward
See Lovecraft, H(oward) P(hillips)

Sokolov, Raymond 1941-.......... CLC 7
See also CA 85-88

Solo, Jay
See Ellison, Harlan (Jay)

Sologub, Fyodor .... TCLC 9
See also Teternikov, Fyodor Kuzmich

Solomons, Ikey Esquir
See Thackeray, William Makepeace

Solomos, Dionysios 1798-1857 ... NCLC 15

Solwoska, Mara
See French, Marilyn

Solzhenitsyn, Aleksandr I(sayevich)
1918-...... CLC 1, 2, 4, 7, 9, 10, 18, 26,
34, 78; DA; WLC
See also AITN 1; CA 69-72; CANR 40;
MTCW

Somers, Jane
See Lessing, Doris (May)

Somerville, Edith 1858-1949 ...... TCLC 51
See also DLB 135

Somerville & Ross
See Martin, Violet Florence; Somerville,
Edith

Sommer, Scott 1951- .... CLC 25
See also CA 106

Sondheim, Stephen (Joshua)
1930- .... CLC 30, 39
See also AAYA 11; CA 103; CANR 47

Sontag, Susan 1933-... CLC 1, 2, 10, 13, 31
See also CA 17-20R; CANR 25; DLB 2, 67;
MTCW

Sophocles
496(?)B.C.-406(?)B.C..... CMLC 2; DA;
DC 1

Sordello 1189-1269............. CMLC 15

Sorel, Julia
See Drexler, Rosalyn

Sorrentino, Gilbert
1929-................ CLC 3, 7, 14, 22, 40
See also CA 77-80; CANR 14, 33; DLB 5;
DLBY 80

Soto, Gary 1952-........ CLC 32, 80; HLC
See also AAYA 10; CA 119; 125; DLB 82;
HW; JRDA; SATA 80

Soupault, Philippe 1897-1990 ...... CLC 68
See also CA 116; 131

Souster, (Holmes) Raymond
1921- .... CLC 5, 14
See also CA 13-16R; CAAS 14; CANR 13,
29; DLB 88; SATA 63

Southern, Terry 1926-............ CLC 7
See also CA 1-4R; CANR 1; DLB 2

Southey, Robert 1774-1843 .... NCLC 8
See also DLB 93, 107, 142; SATA 54

Southworth, Emma Dorothy Eliza Nevitte
1819-1899 .... NCLC 26

Souza, Ernest
See Scott, Evelyn

Soyinka, Wole
1934-....... CLC 3, 5, 14, 36, 44; BLC;
DA; DC 2; WLC
See also BW 2; CA 13-16R; CANR 27, 39;
DLB 125; MTCW

Spackman, W(illiam) M(ode)
1905-1990 .... CLC 46
See also CA 81-84; 132

Spacks, Barry 1931-.............. CLC 14
See also CA 29-32R; CANR 33; DLB 105

Spanidou, Irini 1946-............. CLC 44

Spark, Muriel (Sarah)
1918-........ CLC 2, 3, 5, 8, 13, 18, 40;
SSC 10
See also CA 5-8R; CANR 12, 36;
CDBLB 1945-1960; DLB 15, 139; MTCW

Spaulding, Douglas
See Bradbury, Ray (Douglas)

Spaulding, Leonard
See Bradbury, Ray (Douglas)

Spence, J. A. D.
See Eliot, T(homas) S(tearns)

Spencer, Elizabeth 1921-.......... CLC 22
See also CA 13-16R; CANR 32; DLB 6;
MTCW; SATA 14

Spencer, Leonard G.
See Silverberg, Robert

Spencer, Scott 1945-.............. CLC 30
See also CA 113; DLBY 86

Spender, Stephen (Harold)
1909-............. CLC 1, 2, 5, 10, 41
See also CA 9-12R; CANR 31;
CDBLB 1945-1960; DLB 20; MTCW

Spengler, Oswald (Arnold Gottfried)
1880-1936 .... TCLC 25
See also CA 118

Spenser, Edmund
1552(?)-1599 .... LC 5; DA; PC 8; WLC
See also CDBLB Before 1660

Spicer, Jack 1925-1965 ...... CLC 8, 18, 72
See also CA 85-88; DLB 5, 16

Spiegelman, Art 1948- .... CLC 76
See also AAYA 10; CA 125; CANR 41

Spielberg, Peter 1929- .... CLC 6
See also CA 5-8R; CANR 4; DLBY 81

Spielberg, Steven 1947- .... CLC 20
See also AAYA 8; CA 77-80; CANR 32;
SATA 32

Spillane, Frank Morrison 1918-
See Spillane, Mickey
See also CA 25-28R; CANR 28; MTCW;
SATA 66

Spillane, Mickey .... CLC 3, 13
See also Spillane, Frank Morrison

Spinoza, Benedictus de 1632-1677 .... LC 9

Spinrad, Norman (Richard) 1940-... CLC 46
See also CA 37-40R; CAAS 19; CANR 20;
DLB 8

Stone, Oliver 1946-............ **CLC 73**
See also CA 110

Stone, Robert (Anthony)
1937-................ **CLC 5, 23, 42**
See also CA 85-88; CANR 23; DLB 152;
MTCW

Stone, Zachary
See Follett, Ken(neth Martin)

Stoppard, Tom
1937-...... **CLC 1, 3, 4, 5, 8, 15, 29, 34,
63; DA; WLC**
See also CA 81-84; CANR 39;
CDBLB 1960 to Present; DLB 13;
DLBY 85; MTCW

Storey, David (Malcolm)
1933-................ **CLC 2, 4, 5, 8**
See also CA 81-84; CANR 36; DLB 13, 14;
MTCW

Storm, Hyemeyohsts 1935-........ **CLC 3**
See also CA 81-84; CANR 45; NNAL

Storm, (Hans) Theodor (Woldsen)
1817-1888 .... **NCLC 1**

Storni, Alfonsina
1892-1938 .... **TCLC 5; HLC**
See also CA 104; 131; HW

Stout, Rex (Todhunter) 1886-1975 ... **CLC 3**
See also AITN 2; CA 61-64

Stow, (Julian) Randolph 1935- .. **CLC 23, 48**
See also CA 13-16R; CANR 33; MTCW

Stowe, Harriet (Elizabeth) Beecher
1811-1896 .... **NCLC 3; DA; WLC**
See also CDALB 1865-1917; DLB 1, 12, 42,
74; JRDA; MAICYA; YABC 1

Strachey, (Giles) Lytton
1880-1932 .... **TCLC 12**
See also CA 110; DLB 149; DLBD 10

Strand, Mark 1934- ...... **CLC 6, 18, 41, 71**
See also CA 21-24R; CANR 40; DLB 5;
SATA 41

Straub, Peter (Francis) 1943- ...... **CLC 28**
See also BEST 89:1; CA 85-88; CANR 28;
DLBY 84; MTCW

Strauss, Botho 1944- .... **CLC 22**
See also DLB 124

Streatfeild, (Mary) Noel
1895(?)-1986 .... **CLC 21**
See also CA 81-84; 120; CANR 31;
CLR 17; MAICYA; SATA 20;
SATA-Obit 48

Stribling, T(homas) S(igismund)
1881-1965 .... **CLC 23**
See also CA 107; DLB 9

Strindberg, (Johan) August
1849-1912 ...... **TCLC 1, 8, 21, 47; DA;
WLC**
See also CA 104; 135

Stringer, Arthur 1874-1950 .... **TCLC 37**
See also DLB 92

Stringer, David
See Roberts, Keith (John Kingston)

Strugatskii, Arkadii (Natanovich)
1925-1991 .... **CLC 27**
See also CA 106; 135

Strugatskii, Boris (Natanovich)
1933- .... **CLC 27**
See also CA 106

Strummer, Joe 1953(?)- .... **CLC 30**

Stuart, Don A.
See Campbell, John W(ood, Jr.)

Stuart, Ian
See MacLean, Alistair (Stuart)

Stuart, Jesse (Hilton)
1906-1984 ...... **CLC 1, 8, 11, 14, 34**
See also CA 5-8R; 112; CANR 31; DLB 9,
48, 102; DLBY 84; SATA 2;
SATA-Obit 36

Sturgeon, Theodore (Hamilton)
1918-1985 .... **CLC 22, 39**
See also Queen, Ellery
See also CA 81-84; 116; CANR 32; DLB 8;
DLBY 85; MTCW

Sturges, Preston 1898-1959 ...... **TCLC 48**
See also CA 114; DLB 26

Styron, William
1925- .... **CLC 1, 3, 5, 11, 15, 60**
See also BEST 90:4; CA 5-8R; CANR 6, 33;
CDALB 1968-1988; DLB 2, 143;
DLBY 80; MTCW

Suarez Lynch, B.
See Bioy Casares, Adolfo; Borges, Jorge
Luis

Su Chien 1884-1918
See Su Man-shu
See also CA 123

Suckow, Ruth 1892-1960
See also CA 113; DLB 9, 102; SSC 18

Sudermann, Hermann 1857-1928 .. **TCLC 15**
See also CA 107; DLB 118

Sue, Eugene 1804-1857 .... **NCLC 1**
See also DLB 119

Sueskind, Patrick 1949-........... **CLC 44**
See also Suskind, Patrick

Sukenick, Ronald 1932-..... **CLC 3, 4, 6, 48**
See also CA 25-28R; CAAS 8; CANR 32;
DLBY 81

Suknaski, Andrew 1942- .... **CLC 19**
See also CA 101; DLB 53

Sullivan, Vernon
See Vian, Boris

Sully Prudhomme 1839-1907...... **TCLC 31**

Su Man-shu .... **TCLC 24**
See also Su Chien

Summerforest, Ivy B.
See Kirkup, James

Summers, Andrew James 1942-..... **CLC 26**

Summers, Andy
See Summers, Andrew James

Summers, Hollis (Spurgeon, Jr.)
1916- .... **CLC 10**
See also CA 5-8R; CANR 3; DLB 6

Summers, (Alphonsus Joseph-Mary Augustus)
Montague 1880-1948........ **TCLC 16**
See also CA 118

Sumner, Gordon Matthew 1951-.... **CLC 26**

Surtees, Robert Smith
1803-1864 .... **NCLC 14**
See also DLB 21

Susann, Jacqueline 1921-1974...... **CLC 3**
See also AITN 1; CA 65-68; 53-56; MTCW

Suskind, Patrick
See Sueskind, Patrick
See also CA 145

Sutcliff, Rosemary 1920-1992 ...... **CLC 26**
See also AAYA 10; CA 5-8R; 139;
CANR 37; CLR 1; JRDA; MAICYA;
SATA 6, 44, 78; SATA-Obit 73

Sutro, Alfred 1863-1933........... **TCLC 6**
See also CA 105; DLB 10

Sutton, Henry
See Slavitt, David R(ytman)

Svevo, Italo .... **TCLC 2, 35**
See also Schmitz, Aron Hector

Swados, Elizabeth 1951- .... **CLC 12**
See also CA 97-100

Swados, Harvey 1920-1972 .... **CLC 5**
See also CA 5-8R; 37-40R; CANR 6;
DLB 2

Swan, Gladys 1934- .... **CLC 69**
See also CA 101; CANR 17, 39

Swarthout, Glendon (Fred)
1918-1992 .... **CLC 35**
See also CA 1-4R; 139; CANR 1, 47;
SATA 26

Sweet, Sarah C.
See Jewett, (Theodora) Sarah Orne

Swenson, May
1919-1989 .... **CLC 4, 14, 61; DA**
See also CA 5-8R; 130; CANR 36; DLB 5;
MTCW; SATA 15

Swift, Augustus
See Lovecraft, H(oward) P(hillips)

Swift, Graham (Colin) 1949- .... **CLC 41, 88**
See also CA 117; 122; CANR 46

Swift, Jonathan
1667-1745 ...... **LC 1; DA; PC 9; WLC**
See also CDBLB 1660-1789; DLB 39, 95,
101; SATA 19

Swinburne, Algernon Charles
1837-1909 ...... **TCLC 8, 36; DA; WLC**
See also CA 105; 140; CDBLB 1832-1890;
DLB 35, 57

Swinfen, Ann.................... **CLC 34**

Swinnerton, Frank Arthur
1884-1982 .... **CLC 31**
See also CA 108; DLB 34

Swithen, John
See King, Stephen (Edwin)

Sylvia
See Ashton-Warner, Sylvia (Constance)

Symmes, Robert Edward
See Duncan, Robert (Edward)

Symonds, John Addington
1840-1893 .... **NCLC 34**
See also DLB 57, 144

Symons, Arthur 1865-1945 .... **TCLC 11**
See also CA 107; DLB 19, 57, 149

Symons, Julian (Gustave)
1912- .... **CLC 2, 14, 32**
See also CA 49-52; CAAS 3; CANR 3, 33;
DLB 87; DLBY 92; MTCW

Synge, (Edmund) J(ohn) M(illington)
    1871-1909 . . . . **TCLC 6, 37; DC 2**
    See also CA 104; 141; CDBLB 1890-1914;
    DLB 10, 19

Syruc, J.
    See Milosz, Czeslaw

Szirtes, George 1948- . . . . **CLC 46**
    See also CA 109; CANR 27

Tabori, George 1914- . . . . **CLC 19**
    See also CA 49-52; CANR 4

Tagore, Rabindranath
    1861-1941 . . . . **TCLC 3, 53; PC 8**
    See also CA 104; 120; MTCW

Taine, Hippolyte Adolphe
    1828-1893 . . . . **NCLC 15**

Talese, Gay 1932- . . . . **CLC 37**
    See also AITN 1; CA 1-4R; CANR 9;
    MTCW

Tallent, Elizabeth (Ann) 1954- . . . . . **CLC 45**
    See also CA 117; DLB 130

Tally, Ted 1952- . . . . **CLC 42**
    See also CA 120; 124

Tamayo y Baus, Manuel
    1829-1898 . . . . **NCLC 1**

Tammsaare, A(nton) H(ansen)
    1878-1940 . . . . **TCLC 27**

Tan, Amy 1952- . . . . **CLC 59**
    See also AAYA 9; BEST 89:3; CA 136;
    SATA 75

Tandem, Felix
    See Spitteler, Carl (Friedrich Georg)

Tanizaki, Jun'ichiro
    1886-1965 . . . . **CLC 8, 14, 28**
    See also CA 93-96; 25-28R

Tanner, William
    See Amis, Kingsley (William)

Tao Lao
    See Storni, Alfonsina

Tarassoff, Lev
    See Troyat, Henri

Tarbell, Ida M(inerva)
    1857-1944 . . . . **TCLC 40**
    See also CA 122; DLB 47

Tarkington, (Newton) Booth
    1869-1946 . . . . **TCLC 9**
    See also CA 110; 143; DLB 9, 102;
    SATA 17

Tarkovsky, Andrei (Arsenyevich)
    1932-1986 . . . . **CLC 75**
    See also CA 127

Tartt, Donna 1964(?)- . . . . **CLC 76**
    See also CA 142

Tasso, Torquato 1544-1595 . . . . **LC 5**

Tate, (John Orley) Allen
    1899-1979 . . . . **CLC 2, 4, 6, 9, 11, 14, 24**
    See also CA 5-8R; 85-88; CANR 32;
    DLB 4, 45, 63; MTCW

Tate, Ellalice
    See Hibbert, Eleanor Alice Burford

Tate, James (Vincent) 1943- . . . **CLC 2, 6, 25**
    See also CA 21-24R; CANR 29; DLB 5

Tavel, Ronald 1940- . . . . **CLC 6**
    See also CA 21-24R; CANR 33

Taylor, C(ecil) P(hilip) 1929-1981 . . . **CLC 27**
    See also CA 25-28R; 105; CANR 47

Taylor, Edward 1642(?)-1729 . . . . **LC 11; DA**
    See also DLB 24

Taylor, Eleanor Ross 1920- . . . . **CLC 5**
    See also CA 81-84

Taylor, Elizabeth 1912-1975 . . . **CLC 2, 4, 29**
    See also CA 13-16R; CANR 9; DLB 139;
    MTCW; SATA 13

Taylor, Henry (Splawn) 1942- . . . . . . **CLC 44**
    See also CA 33-36R; CAAS 7; CANR 31;
    DLB 5

Taylor, Kamala (Purnaiya) 1924-
    See Markandaya, Kamala
    See also CA 77-80

Taylor, Mildred D. . . . . **CLC 21**
    See also AAYA 10; BW 1; CA 85-88;
    CANR 25; CLR 9; DLB 52; JRDA;
    MAICYA; SAAS 5; SATA 15, 70

Taylor, Peter (Hillsman)
    1917- . . . . **CLC 1, 4, 18, 37, 44, 50, 71;
                                                            SSC 10**
    See also CA 13-16R; CANR 9; DLBY 81,
    94; MTCW

Taylor, Robert Lewis 1912- . . . . **CLC 14**
    See also CA 1-4R; CANR 3; SATA 10

Tchekhov, Anton
    See Chekhov, Anton (Pavlovich)

Teasdale, Sara 1884-1933 . . . . **TCLC 4**
    See also CA 104; DLB 45; SATA 32

Tegner, Esaias 1782-1846 . . . . **NCLC 2**

Teilhard de Chardin, (Marie Joseph) Pierre
    1881-1955 . . . . **TCLC 9**
    See also CA 105

Temple, Ann
    See Mortimer, Penelope (Ruth)

Tennant, Emma (Christina)
    1937- . . . . **CLC 13, 52**
    See also CA 65-68; CAAS 9; CANR 10, 38;
    DLB 14

Tenneshaw, S. M.
    See Silverberg, Robert

Tennyson, Alfred
    1809-1892 . . **NCLC 30; DA; PC 6; WLC**
    See also CDBLB 1832-1890; DLB 32

Teran, Lisa St. Aubin de . . . . **CLC 36**
    See also St. Aubin de Teran, Lisa

Terence 195(?)B.C.-159B.C. . . . . **CMLC 14**

Teresa de Jesus, St. 1515-1582 . . . . . . **LC 18**

Terkel, Louis 1912-
    See Terkel, Studs
    See also CA 57-60; CANR 18, 45; MTCW

Terkel, Studs . . . . **CLC 38**
    See also Terkel, Louis
    See also AITN 1

Terry, C. V.
    See Slaughter, Frank G(ill)

Terry, Megan 1932- . . . . **CLC 19**
    See also CA 77-80; CABS 3; CANR 43;
    DLB 7

Tertz, Abram
    See Sinyavsky, Andrei (Donatevich)

Tesich, Steve 1943(?)- . . . . **CLC 40, 69**
    See also CA 105; DLBY 83

Teternikov, Fyodor Kuzmich 1863-1927
    See Sologub, Fyodor
    See also CA 104

Tevis, Walter 1928-1984 . . . . **CLC 42**
    See also CA 113

Tey, Josephine . . . . **TCLC 14**
    See also Mackintosh, Elizabeth
    See also DLB 77

Thackeray, William Makepeace
    1811-1863 . . . . **NCLC 5, 14, 22, 43; DA;
                                                            WLC**
    See also CDBLB 1832-1890; DLB 21, 55;
    SATA 23

Thakura, Ravindranatha
    See Tagore, Rabindranath

Tharoor, Shashi 1956- . . . . **CLC 70**
    See also CA 141

Thelwell, Michael Miles 1939- . . . . . **CLC 22**
    See also BW 2; CA 101

Theobald, Lewis, Jr.
    See Lovecraft, H(oward) P(hillips)

Theodorescu, Ion N. 1880-1967
    See Arghezi, Tudor
    See also CA 116

Theriault, Yves 1915-1983 . . . . **CLC 79**
    See also CA 102; DLB 88

Theroux, Alexander (Louis)
    1939- . . . . **CLC 2, 25**
    See also CA 85-88; CANR 20

Theroux, Paul (Edward)
    1941- . . . . **CLC 5, 8, 11, 15, 28, 46**
    See also BEST 89:4; CA 33-36R; CANR 20,
    45; DLB 2; MTCW; SATA 44

Thesen, Sharon 1946- . . . . **CLC 56**

Thevenin, Denis
    See Duhamel, Georges

Thibault, Jacques Anatole Francois
    1844-1924
    See France, Anatole
    See also CA 106; 127; MTCW

Thiele, Colin (Milton) 1920- . . . . **CLC 17**
    See also CA 29-32R; CANR 12, 28;
    CLR 27; MAICYA; SAAS 2; SATA 14,
    72

Thomas, Audrey (Callahan)
    1935- . . . . **CLC 7, 13, 37**
    See also AITN 2; CA 21-24R; CAAS 19;
    CANR 36; DLB 60; MTCW

Thomas, D(onald) M(ichael)
    1935- . . . . **CLC 13, 22, 31**
    See also CA 61-64; CAAS 11; CANR 17,
    45; CDBLB 1960 to Present; DLB 40;
    MTCW

Thomas, Dylan (Marlais)
    1914-1953 . . . **TCLC 1, 8, 45; DA; PC 2;
                                                            SSC 3; WLC**
    See also CA 104; 120; CDBLB 1945-1960;
    DLB 13, 20, 139; MTCW; SATA 60

Thomas, (Philip) Edward
    1878-1917 . . . . **TCLC 10**
    See also CA 106; DLB 19

Thomas, Joyce Carol 1938- . . . . **CLC 35**
    See also AAYA 12; BW 2; CA 113; 116;
    CLR 19; DLB 33; JRDA; MAICYA;
    MTCW; SAAS 7; SATA 40, 78

Thomas, Lewis 1913-1993 . . . . **CLC 35**
See also CA 85-88; 143; CANR 38; MTCW

Thomas, Paul
See Mann, (Paul) Thomas

Thomas, Piri 1928- . . . . **CLC 17**
See also CA 73-76; HW

Thomas, R(onald) S(tuart)
1913- . . . . **CLC 6, 13, 48**
See also CA 89-92; CAAS 4; CANR 30;
CDBLB 1960 to Present; DLB 27;
MTCW

Thomas, Ross (Elmore) 1926- . . . . . . **CLC 39**
See also CA 33-36R; CANR 22

Thompson, Francis Clegg
See Mencken, H(enry) L(ouis)

Thompson, Francis Joseph
1859-1907 . . . . **TCLC 4**
See also CA 104; CDBLB 1890-1914;
DLB 19

Thompson, Hunter S(tockton)
1939- . . . . **CLC 9, 17, 40**
See also BEST 89:1; CA 17-20R; CANR 23,
46; MTCW

Thompson, James Myers
See Thompson, Jim (Myers)

Thompson, Jim (Myers)
1906-1977(?) . . . . **CLC 69**
See also CA 140

Thompson, Judith . . . . **CLC 39**

Thomson, James 1700-1748 . . . . . **LC 16, 29**
See also DLB 95

Thomson, James 1834-1882 . . . . . . **NCLC 18**
See also DLB 35

Thoreau, Henry David
1817-1862 . . . . . . **NCLC 7, 21; DA; WLC**
See also CDALB 1640-1865; DLB 1

Thornton, Hall
See Silverberg, Robert

Thurber, James (Grover)
1894-1961 . . . **CLC 5, 11, 25; DA; SSC 1**
See also CA 73-76; CANR 17, 39;
CDALB 1929-1941; DLB 4, 11, 22, 102;
MAICYA; MTCW; SATA 13

Thurman, Wallace (Henry)
1902-1934 . . . . **TCLC 6; BLC**
See also BW 1; CA 104; 124; DLB 51

Ticheburn, Cheviot
See Ainsworth, William Harrison

Tieck, (Johann) Ludwig
1773-1853 . . . . **NCLC 5, 46**
See also DLB 90

Tiger, Derry
See Ellison, Harlan (Jay)

Tilghman, Christopher 1948(?)- . . . . . **CLC 65**

Tillinghast, Richard (Williford)
1940- . . . . **CLC 29**
See also CA 29-32R; CANR 26

Timrod, Henry 1828-1867 . . . . **NCLC 25**
See also DLB 3

Tindall, Gillian 1938- . . . . **CLC 7**
See also CA 21-24R; CANR 11

Tiptree, James, Jr. . . . . **CLC 48, 50**
See also Sheldon, Alice Hastings Bradley
See also DLB 8

Titmarsh, Michael Angelo
See Thackeray, William Makepeace

**Tocqueville, Alexis (Charles Henri Maurice
Clerel Comte)** 1805-1859 . . . . . **NCLC 7**

Tolkien, J(ohn) R(onald) R(euel)
1892-1973 . . . . **CLC 1, 2, 3, 8, 12, 38;
DA; WLC**
See also AAYA 10; AITN 1; CA 17-18;
45-48; CANR 36; CAP 2;
CDBLB 1914-1945; DLB 15; JRDA;
MAICYA; MTCW; SATA 2, 32;
SATA-Obit 24

Toller, Ernst 1893-1939 . . . . **TCLC 10**
See also CA 107; DLB 124

Tolson, M. B.
See Tolson, Melvin B(eaunorus)

Tolson, Melvin B(eaunorus)
1898(?)-1966 . . . . **CLC 36; BLC**
See also BW 1; CA 124; 89-92; DLB 48, 76

Tolstoi, Aleksei Nikolaevich
See Tolstoy, Alexey Nikolaevich

Tolstoy, Alexey Nikolaevich
1882-1945 . . . . **TCLC 18**
See also CA 107

Tolstoy, Count Leo
See Tolstoy, Leo (Nikolaevich)

Tolstoy, Leo (Nikolaevich)
1828-1910 . . . . . **TCLC 4, 11, 17, 28, 44;
DA; SSC 9; WLC**
See also CA 104; 123; SATA 26

Tomasi di Lampedusa, Giuseppe 1896-1957
See Lampedusa, Giuseppe (Tomasi) di
See also CA 111

Tomlin, Lily . . . . **CLC 17**
See also Tomlin, Mary Jean

Tomlin, Mary Jean 1939(?)-
See Tomlin, Lily
See also CA 117

Tomlinson, (Alfred) Charles
1927- . . . . **CLC 2, 4, 6, 13, 45**
See also CA 5-8R; CANR 33; DLB 40

Tonson, Jacob
See Bennett, (Enoch) Arnold

Toole, John Kennedy
1937-1969 . . . . **CLC 19, 64**
See also CA 104; DLBY 81

Toomer, Jean
1894-1967 . . . . . . **CLC 1, 4, 13, 22; BLC;
PC 7; SSC 1**
See also BW 1; CA 85-88;
CDALB 1917-1929; DLB 45, 51; MTCW

Torley, Luke
See Blish, James (Benjamin)

Tornimparte, Alessandra
See Ginzburg, Natalia

Torre, Raoul della
See Mencken, H(enry) L(ouis)

Torrey, E(dwin) Fuller 1937- . . . . **CLC 34**
See also CA 119

Torsvan, Ben Traven
See Traven, B.

Torsvan, Benno Traven
See Traven, B.

Torsvan, Berick Traven
See Traven, B.

Torsvan, Berwick Traven
See Traven, B.

Torsvan, Bruno Traven
See Traven, B.

Torsvan, Traven
See Traven, B.

Tournier, Michel (Edouard)
1924- . . . . **CLC 6, 23, 36**
See also CA 49-52; CANR 3, 36; DLB 83;
MTCW; SATA 23

Tournimparte, Alessandra
See Ginzburg, Natalia

Towers, Ivar
See Kornbluth, C(yril) M.

Towne, Robert (Burton) 1936(?)- . . . . **CLC 87**
See also CA 108; DLB 44

Townsend, Sue 1946- . . . . **CLC 61**
See also CA 119; 127; MTCW; SATA 55;
SATA-Brief 48

Townshend, Peter (Dennis Blandford)
1945- . . . . **CLC 17, 42**
See also CA 107

Tozzi, Federigo 1883-1920 . . . . **TCLC 31**

Traill, Catharine Parr
1802-1899 . . . . **NCLC 31**
See also DLB 99

Trakl, Georg 1887-1914 . . . . **TCLC 5**
See also CA 104

Transtroemer, Tomas (Goesta)
1931- . . . . **CLC 52, 65**
See also CA 117; 129; CAAS 17

Transtromer, Tomas Gosta
See Transtroemer, Tomas (Goesta)

Traven, B. (?)-1969 . . . . **CLC 8, 11**
See also CA 19-20; 25-28R; CAP 2; DLB 9,
56; MTCW

Treitel, Jonathan 1959- . . . . **CLC 70**

Tremain, Rose 1943- . . . . **CLC 42**
See also CA 97-100; CANR 44; DLB 14

Tremblay, Michel 1942- . . . . **CLC 29**
See also CA 116; 128; DLB 60; MTCW

Trevanian . . . . **CLC 29**
See also Whitaker, Rod(ney)

Trevor, Glen
See Hilton, James

Trevor, William
1928- . . . . **CLC 7, 9, 14, 25, 71**
See also Cox, William Trevor
See also DLB 14, 139

Trifonov, Yuri (Valentinovich)
1925-1981 . . . . **CLC 45**
See also CA 126; 103; MTCW

Trilling, Lionel 1905-1975 . . . . **CLC 9, 11, 24**
See also CA 9-12R; 61-64; CANR 10;
DLB 28, 63; MTCW

Trimball, W. H.
See Mencken, H(enry) L(ouis)

Tristan
See Gomez de la Serna, Ramon

Tristram
See Housman, A(lfred) E(dward)

Trogdon, William (Lewis) 1939-
See Heat-Moon, William Least
See also CA 115; 119; CANR 47

Trollope, Anthony
1815-1882 ...... **NCLC 6, 33; DA; WLC**
See also CDBLB 1832-1890; DLB 21, 57;
SATA 22

Trollope, Frances 1779-1863 ..... **NCLC 30**
See also DLB 21

Trotsky, Leon 1879-1940 .... **TCLC 22**
See also CA 118

Trotter (Cockburn), Catharine
1679-1749 .... **LC 8**
See also DLB 84

Trout, Kilgore
See Farmer, Philip Jose

Trow, George W. S. 1943- .... **CLC 52**
See also CA 126

Troyat, Henri 1911- .... **CLC 23**
See also CA 45-48; CANR 2, 33; MTCW

Trudeau, G(arretson) B(eekman) 1948-
See Trudeau, Garry B.
See also CA 81-84; CANR 31; SATA 35

Trudeau, Garry B. .... **CLC 12**
See also Trudeau, G(arretson) B(eekman)
See also AAYA 10; AITN 2

Truffaut, Francois 1932-1984 ...... **CLC 20**
See also CA 81-84; 113; CANR 34

Trumbo, Dalton 1905-1976 .... **CLC 19**
See also CA 21-24R; 69-72; CANR 10;
DLB 26

Trumbull, John 1750-1831 .... **NCLC 30**
See also DLB 31

Trundlett, Helen B.
See Eliot, T(homas) S(tearns)

Tryon, Thomas 1926-1991 .... **CLC 3, 11**
See also AITN 1; CA 29-32R; 135;
CANR 32; MTCW

Tryon, Tom
See Tryon, Thomas

Ts'ao Hsueh-ch'in 1715(?)-1763 ...... **LC 1**

Tsushima, Shuji 1909-1948
See Dazai, Osamu
See also CA 107

Tsvetaeva (Efron), Marina (Ivanovna)
1892-1941 .... **TCLC 7, 35**
See also CA 104; 128; MTCW

Tuck, Lily 1938- .... **CLC 70**
See also CA 139

Tu Fu 712-770 .... **PC 9**

Tunis, John R(oberts) 1889-1975 ... **CLC 12**
See also CA 61-64; DLB 22; JRDA;
MAICYA; SATA 37; SATA-Brief 30

Tuohy, Frank .... **CLC 37**
See also Tuohy, John Francis
See also DLB 14, 139

Tuohy, John Francis 1925-
See Tuohy, Frank
See also CA 5-8R; CANR 3, 47

Turco, Lewis (Putnam) 1934- ... **CLC 11, 63**
See also CA 13-16R; CANR 24; DLBY 84

Turgenev, Ivan
1818-1883 ...... **NCLC 21; DA; SSC 7;
WLC**

Turgot, Anne-Robert-Jacques
1727-1781 .... **LC 26**

Turner, Frederick 1943- .... **CLC 48**
See also CA 73-76; CAAS 10; CANR 12,
30; DLB 40

Tutu, Desmond M(pilo)
1931- .... **CLC 80; BLC**
See also BW 1; CA 125

Tutuola, Amos 1920- ... **CLC 5, 14, 29; BLC**
See also BW 2; CA 9-12R; CANR 27;
DLB 125; MTCW

Twain, Mark
..... **TCLC 6, 12, 19, 36, 48, 59; SSC 6;
WLC**
See also Clemens, Samuel Langhorne
See also DLB 11, 12, 23, 64, 74

Tyler, Anne
1941- .... **CLC 7, 11, 18, 28, 44, 59**
See also BEST 89:1; CA 9-12R; CANR 11,
33; DLB 6, 143; DLBY 82; MTCW;
SATA 7

Tyler, Royall 1757-1826 .... **NCLC 3**
See also DLB 37

Tynan, Katharine 1861-1931 .... **TCLC 3**
See also CA 104

Tyutchev, Fyodor 1803-1873 ..... **NCLC 34**

Tzara, Tristan .... **CLC 47**
See also Rosenfeld, Samuel

Uhry, Alfred 1936- .... **CLC 55**
See also CA 127; 133

Ulf, Haerved
See Strindberg, (Johan) August

Ulf, Harved
See Strindberg, (Johan) August

Ulibarri, Sabine R(eyes) 1919- ..... **CLC 83**
See also CA 131; DLB 82; HW

Unamuno (y Jugo), Miguel de
1864-1936 .... **TCLC 2, 9; HLC; SSC 11**
See also CA 104; 131; DLB 108; HW;
MTCW

Undercliffe, Errol
See Campbell, (John) Ramsey

Underwood, Miles
See Glassco, John

Undset, Sigrid
1882-1949 .... **TCLC 3; DA; WLC**
See also CA 104; 129; MTCW

Ungaretti, Giuseppe
1888-1970 .... **CLC 7, 11, 15**
See also CA 19-20; 25-28R; CAP 2;
DLB 114

Unger, Douglas 1952- .... **CLC 34**
See also CA 130

Unsworth, Barry (Forster) 1930- .... **CLC 76**
See also CA 25-28R; CANR 30

Updike, John (Hoyer)
1932- ...... **CLC 1, 2, 3, 5, 7, 9, 13, 15,
23, 34, 43, 70; DA; SSC 13; WLC**
See also CA 1-4R; CABS 1; CANR 4, 33;
CDALB 1968-1988; DLB 2, 5, 143;
DLBD 3; DLBY 80, 82; MTCW

Upshaw, Margaret Mitchell
See Mitchell, Margaret (Munnerlyn)

Upton, Mark
See Sanders, Lawrence

Urdang, Constance (Henriette)
1922- .... **CLC 47**
See also CA 21-24R; CANR 9, 24

Uriel, Henry
See Faust, Frederick (Schiller)

Uris, Leon (Marcus) 1924- .... **CLC 7, 32**
See also AITN 1, 2; BEST 89:2; CA 1-4R;
CANR 1, 40; MTCW; SATA 49

Urmuz
See Codrescu, Andrei

Ustinov, Peter (Alexander) 1921- .... **CLC 1**
See also AITN 1; CA 13-16R; CANR 25;
DLB 13

Vaculik, Ludvik 1926- .... **CLC 7**
See also CA 53-56

Valdez, Luis (Miguel)
1940- .... **CLC 84; HLC**
See also CA 101; CANR 32; DLB 122; HW

Valenzuela, Luisa 1938- ... **CLC 31; SSC 14**
See also CA 101; CANR 32; DLB 113; HW

Valera y Alcala-Galiano, Juan
1824-1905 .... **TCLC 10**
See also CA 106

Valery, (Ambroise) Paul (Toussaint Jules)
1871-1945 .... **TCLC 4, 15; PC 9**
See also CA 104; 122; MTCW

Valle-Inclan, Ramon (Maria) del
1866-1936 .... **TCLC 5; HLC**
See also CA 106; DLB 134

Vallejo, Antonio Buero
See Buero Vallejo, Antonio

Vallejo, Cesar (Abraham)
1892-1938 .... **TCLC 3, 56; HLC**
See also CA 105; HW

Valle Y Pena, Ramon del
See Valle-Inclan, Ramon (Maria) del

Van Ash, Cay 1918- .... **CLC 34**

Vanbrugh, Sir John 1664-1726 ...... **LC 21**
See also DLB 80

Van Campen, Karl
See Campbell, John W(ood, Jr.)

Vance, Gerald
See Silverberg, Robert

Vance, Jack .... **CLC 35**
See also Vance, John Holbrook
See also DLB 8

Vance, John Holbrook 1916-
See Queen, Ellery; Vance, Jack
See also CA 29-32R; CANR 17; MTCW

**Van Den Bogarde, Derek Jules Gaspard Ulric
Niven** 1921-
See Bogarde, Dirk
See also CA 77-80

Vandenburgh, Jane .... **CLC 59**

Vanderhaeghe, Guy 1951- .... **CLC 41**
See also CA 113

van der Post, Laurens (Jan) 1906- ... **CLC 5**
See also CA 5-8R; CANR 35

van de Wetering, Janwillem 1931- .. **CLC 47**
See also CA 49-52; CANR 4

Van Dine, S. S. .... **TCLC 23**
See also Wright, Willard Huntington

Van Doren, Carl (Clinton)
1885-1950 .... TCLC **18**
See also CA 111

Van Doren, Mark 1894-1972..... CLC **6, 10**
See also CA 1-4R; 37-40R; CANR 3;
DLB 45; MTCW

Van Druten, John (William)
1901-1957 .... TCLC **2**
See also CA 104; DLB 10

Van Duyn, Mona (Jane)
1921- .... CLC **3, 7, 63**
See also CA 9-12R; CANR 7, 38; DLB 5

Van Dyne, Edith
See Baum, L(yman) Frank

van Itallie, Jean-Claude 1936-....... CLC **3**
See also CA 45-48; CAAS 2; CANR 1;
DLB 7

van Ostaijen, Paul 1896-1928 ..... TCLC **33**

Van Peebles, Melvin 1932- ...... CLC **2, 20**
See also BW 2; CA 85-88; CANR 27

Vansittart, Peter 1920-........... CLC **42**
See also CA 1-4R; CANR 3

Van Vechten, Carl 1880-1964 ...... CLC **33**
See also CA 89-92; DLB 4, 9, 51

Van Vogt, A(lfred) E(lton) 1912-..... CLC **1**
See also CA 21-24R; CANR 28; DLB 8;
SATA 14

Varda, Agnes 1928- .... CLC **16**
See also CA 116; 122

Vargas Llosa, (Jorge) Mario (Pedro)
1936- .... CLC **3, 6, 9, 10, 15, 31, 42, 85;**
DA; HLC
See also CA 73-76; CANR 18, 32, 42;
DLB 145; HW; MTCW

Vasiliu, Gheorghe 1881-1957
See Bacovia, George
See also CA 123

Vassa, Gustavus
See Equiano, Olaudah

Vassilikos, Vassilis 1933-........ CLC **4, 8**
See also CA 81-84

Vaughan, Henry 1621-1695........ LC **27**
See also DLB 131

Vaughn, Stephanie................. CLC **62**

Vazov, Ivan (Minchov)
1850-1921 .... TCLC **25**
See also CA 121; DLB 147

Veblen, Thorstein (Bunde)
1857-1929 .... TCLC **31**
See also CA 115

Vega, Lope de 1562-1635.......... LC **23**

Venison, Alfred
See Pound, Ezra (Weston Loomis)

Verdi, Marie de
See Mencken, H(enry) L(ouis)

Verdu, Matilde
See Cela, Camilo Jose

Verga, Giovanni (Carmelo)
1840-1922 .... TCLC **3**
See also CA 104; 123

Vergil
70B.C.-19B.C..... CMLC **9; DA; PC 12**

Verhaeren, Emile (Adolphe Gustave)
1855-1916 .... TCLC **12**
See also CA 109

Verlaine, Paul (Marie)
1844-1896 .... NCLC **2; PC 2**

Verne, Jules (Gabriel)
1828-1905 .... TCLC **6, 52**
See also CA 110; 131; DLB 123; JRDA;
MAICYA; SATA 21

Very, Jones 1813-1880.......... NCLC **9**
See also DLB 1

Vesaas, Tarjei 1897-1970......... CLC **48**
See also CA 29-32R

Vialis, Gaston
See Simenon, Georges (Jacques Christian)

Vian, Boris 1920-1959 .... TCLC **9**
See also CA 106; DLB 72

Viaud, (Louis Marie) Julien 1850-1923
See Loti, Pierre
See also CA 107

Vicar, Henry
See Felsen, Henry Gregor

Vicker, Angus
See Felsen, Henry Gregor

Vidal, Gore
1925- ..... CLC **2, 4, 6, 8, 10, 22, 33, 72**
See also AITN 1; BEST 90:2; CA 5-8R;
CANR 13, 45; DLB 6, 152; MTCW

Viereck, Peter (Robert Edwin)
1916- .... CLC **4**
See also CA 1-4R; CANR 1, 47; DLB 5

Vigny, Alfred (Victor) de
1797-1863 .... NCLC **7**
See also DLB 119

Vilakazi, Benedict Wallet
1906-1947 .... TCLC **37**

Villiers de l'Isle Adam, Jean Marie Mathias
Philippe Auguste Comte
1838-1889 .... NCLC **3; SSC 14**
See also DLB 123

Vinci, Leonardo da 1452-1519...... LC **12**

Vine, Barbara .... CLC **50**
See also Rendell, Ruth (Barbara)
See also BEST 90:4

Vinge, Joan D(ennison) 1948-...... CLC **30**
See also CA 93-96; SATA 36

Violis, G.
See Simenon, Georges (Jacques Christian)

Visconti, Luchino 1906-1976...... CLC **16**
See also CA 81-84; 65-68; CANR 39

Vittorini, Elio 1908-1966...... CLC **6, 9, 14**
See also CA 133; 25-28R

Vizinczey, Stephen 1933-......... CLC **40**
See also CA 128

Vliet, R(ussell) G(ordon)
1929-1984 .... CLC **22**
See also CA 37-40R; 112; CANR 18

Vogau, Boris Andreyevich 1894-1937(?)
See Pilnyak, Boris
See also CA 123

Vogel, Paula A(nne) 1951-........ CLC **76**
See also CA 108

Voight, Ellen Bryant 1943-........ CLC **54**
See also CA 69-72; CANR 11, 29; DLB 120

Voigt, Cynthia 1942- .... CLC **30**
See also AAYA 3; CA 106; CANR 18, 37,
40; CLR 13; JRDA; MAICYA;
SATA 48, 79; SATA-Brief 33

Voinovich, Vladimir (Nikolaevich)
1932- .... CLC **10, 49**
See also CA 81-84; CAAS 12; CANR 33;
MTCW

Voloshinov, V. N.
See Bakhtin, Mikhail Mikhailovich

Voltaire
1694-1778 ... LC **14; DA; SSC 12; WLC**

von Aue, Hartmann 1170-1210 .. CMLC **15:**

von Daeniken, Erich 1935- .... CLC **30**
See also AITN 1; CA 37-40R; CANR 17,
44

von Daniken, Erich
See von Daeniken, Erich

von Heidenstam, (Carl Gustaf) Verner
See Heidenstam, (Carl Gustaf) Verner von

von Heyse, Paul (Johann Ludwig)
See Heyse, Paul (Johann Ludwig von)

von Hofmannsthal, Hugo
See Hofmannsthal, Hugo von

von Horvath, Odon
See Horvath, Oedoen von

von Horvath, Oedoen
See Horvath, Oedoen von

von Liliencron, (Friedrich Adolf Axel) Detlev
See Liliencron, (Friedrich Adolf Axel)
Detlev von

Vonnegut, Kurt, Jr.
1922- ...... CLC **1, 2, 3, 4, 5, 8, 12, 22,**
40, 60; DA; SSC 8; WLC
See also AAYA 6; AITN 1; BEST 90:4;
CA 1-4R; CANR 1, 25;
CDALB 1968-1988; DLB 2, 8, 152;
DLBD 3; DLBY 80; MTCW

Von Rachen, Kurt
See Hubbard, L(afayette) Ron(ald)

von Rezzori (d'Arezzo), Gregor
See Rezzori (d'Arezzo), Gregor von

von Sternberg, Josef
See Sternberg, Josef von

Vorster, Gordon 1924-............ CLC **34**
See also CA 133

Vosce, Trudie
See Ozick, Cynthia

Voznesensky, Andrei (Andreievich)
1933- .... CLC **1, 15, 57**
See also CA 89-92; CANR 37; MTCW

Waddington, Miriam 1917-........ CLC **28**
See also CA 21-24R; CANR 12, 30;
DLB 68

Wagman, Fredrica 1937-.......... CLC **7**
See also CA 97-100

Wagner, Richard 1813-1883....... NCLC **9**
See also DLB 129

Wagner-Martin, Linda 1936-....... CLC **50**

Wagoner, David (Russell)
1926- .... CLC **3, 5, 15**
See also CA 1-4R; CAAS 3; CANR 2;
DLB 5; SATA 14

Waystaff, Simon
See Swift, Jonathan

Webb, (Martha) Beatrice (Potter)
1858-1943 .... **TCLC 22**
See also Potter, Beatrice
See also CA 117

Webb, Charles (Richard) 1939-...... **CLC 7**
See also CA 25-28R

Webb, James H(enry), Jr. 1946-.... **CLC 22**
See also CA 81-84

Webb, Mary (Gladys Meredith)
1881-1927 .... **TCLC 24**
See also CA 123; DLB 34

Webb, Mrs. Sidney
See Webb, (Martha) Beatrice (Potter)

Webb, Phyllis 1927-.............. **CLC 18**
See also CA 104; CANR 23; DLB 53

Webb, Sidney (James)
1859-1947 .... **TCLC 22**
See also CA 117

Webber, Andrew Lloyd............. **CLC 21**
See also Lloyd Webber, Andrew

Weber, Lenora Mattingly
1895-1971 .... **CLC 12**
See also CA 19-20; 29-32R; CAP 1;
SATA 2; SATA-Obit 26

Webster, John 1579(?)-1634(?) .... **DC 2**
See also CDBLB Before 1660; DA; DLB 58;
WLC

Webster, Noah 1758-1843 .... **NCLC 30**

Wedekind, (Benjamin) Frank(lin)
1864-1918 .... **TCLC 7**
See also CA 104; DLB 118

Weidman, Jerome 1913-............ **CLC 7**
See also AITN 2; CA 1-4R; CANR 1;
DLB 28

Weil, Simone (Adolphine)
1909-1943 .... **TCLC 23**
See also CA 117

Weinstein, Nathan
See West, Nathanael

Weinstein, Nathan von Wallenstein
See West, Nathanael

Weir, Peter (Lindsay) 1944- .... **CLC 20**
See also CA 113; 123

Weiss, Peter (Ulrich)
1916-1982 .... **CLC 3, 15, 51**
See also CA 45-48; 106; CANR 3; DLB 69,
124

Weiss, Theodore (Russell)
1916- .... **CLC 3, 8, 14**
See also CA 9-12R; CAAS 2; CANR 46;
DLB 5

Welch, (Maurice) Denton
1915-1948 .... **TCLC 22**
See also CA 121

Welch, James 1940-........ **CLC 6, 14, 52**
See also CA 85-88; CANR 42; NNAL

Weldon, Fay
1933-........ **CLC 6, 9, 11, 19, 36, 59**
See also CA 21-24R; CANR 16, 46;
CDBLB 1960 to Present; DLB 14;
MTCW

Wellek, Rene 1903- .... **CLC 28**
See also CA 5-8R; CAAS 7; CANR 8;
DLB 63

Weller, Michael 1942-......... **CLC 10, 53**
See also CA 85-88

Weller, Paul 1958-............. **CLC 26**

Wellershoff, Dieter 1925-........ **CLC 46**
See also CA 89-92; CANR 16, 37

Welles, (George) Orson
1915-1985 .... **CLC 20, 80**
See also CA 93-96; 117

Wellman, Mac 1945- .... **CLC 65**

Wellman, Manly Wade 1903-1986 .. **CLC 49**
See also CA 1-4R; 118; CANR 6, 16, 44;
SATA 6; SATA-Obit 47

Wells, Carolyn 1869(?)-1942 ..... **TCLC 35**
See also CA 113; DLB 11

Wells, H(erbert) G(eorge)
1866-1946 .... **TCLC 6, 12, 19; DA;
SSC 6; WLC**
See also CA 110; 121; CDBLB 1914-1945;
DLB 34, 70; MTCW; SATA 20

Wells, Rosemary 1943-........... **CLC 12**
See also AAYA 13; CA 85-88; CLR 16;
MAICYA; SAAS 1; SATA 18, 69

Welty, Eudora
1909- ...... **CLC 1, 2, 5, 14, 22, 33; DA;
SSC 1; WLC**
See also CA 9-12R; CABS 1; CANR 32;
CDALB 1941-1968; DLB 2, 102, 143;
DLBD 12; DLBY 87; MTCW

Wen I-to 1899-1946 .... **TCLC 28**

Wentworth, Robert
See Hamilton, Edmond

Werfel, Franz (V.) 1890-1945 ...... **TCLC 8**
See also CA 104; DLB 81, 124

Wergeland, Henrik Arnold
1808-1845 .... **NCLC 5**

Wersba, Barbara 1932-............ **CLC 30**
See also AAYA 2; CA 29-32R; CANR 16,
38; CLR 3; DLB 52; JRDA; MAICYA;
SAAS 2; SATA 1, 58

Wertmueller, Lina 1928- .... **CLC 16**
See also CA 97-100; CANR 39

Wescott, Glenway 1901-1987....... **CLC 13**
See also CA 13-16R; 121; CANR 23;
DLB 4, 9, 102

Wesker, Arnold 1932- .... **CLC 3, 5, 42**
See also CA 1-4R; CAAS 7; CANR 1, 33;
CDBLB 1960 to Present; DLB 13;
MTCW

Wesley, Richard (Errol) 1945-...... **CLC 7**
See also BW 1; CA 57-60; CANR 27;
DLB 38

Wessel, Johan Herman 1742-1785 .... **LC 7**

West, Anthony (Panther)
1914-1987 .... **CLC 50**
See also CA 45-48; 124; CANR 3, 19;
DLB 15

West, C. P.
See Wodehouse, P(elham) G(renville)

West, (Mary) Jessamyn
1902-1984 .... **CLC 7, 17**
See also CA 9-12R; 112; CANR 27; DLB 6;
DLBY 84; MTCW; SATA-Obit 37

West, Morris L(anglo) 1916-..... **CLC 6, 33**
See also CA 5-8R; CANR 24; MTCW

West, Nathanael
1903-1940 ..... **TCLC 1, 14, 44; SSC 16**
See also CA 104; 125; CDALB 1929-1941;
DLB 4, 9, 28; MTCW

West, Owen
See Koontz, Dean R(ay)

West, Paul 1930- .... **CLC 7, 14**
See also CA 13-16R; CAAS 7; CANR 22;
DLB 14

West, Rebecca 1892-1983 ..**CLC 7, 9, 31, 50**
See also CA 5-8R; 109; CANR 19; DLB 36;
DLBY 83; MTCW

Westall, Robert (Atkinson)
1929-1993 .... **CLC 17**
See also AAYA 12; CA 69-72; 141;
CANR 18; CLR 13; JRDA; MAICYA;
SAAS 2; SATA 23, 69; SATA-Obit 75

Westlake, Donald E(dwin)
1933- .... **CLC 7, 33**
See also CA 17-20R; CAAS 13; CANR 16,
44

Westmacott, Mary
See Christie, Agatha (Mary Clarissa)

Weston, Allen
See Norton, Andre

Wetcheek, J. L.
See Feuchtwanger, Lion

Wetering, Janwillem van de
See van de Wetering, Janwillem

Wetherell, Elizabeth
See Warner, Susan (Bogert)

Whalen, Philip 1923-........... **CLC 6, 29**
See also CA 9-12R; CANR 5, 39; DLB 16

Wharton, Edith (Newbold Jones)
1862-1937 ...... **TCLC 3, 9, 27, 53; DA;
SSC 6; WLC**
See also CA 104; 132; CDALB 1865-1917;
DLB 4, 9, 12, 78; MTCW

Wharton, James
See Mencken, H(enry) L(ouis)

Wharton, William (a pseudonym)
.... **CLC 18, 37**
See also CA 93-96; DLBY 80

Wheatley (Peters), Phillis
1754(?)-1784 .... **LC 3; BLC; DA; PC 3;
WLC**
See also CDALB 1640-1865; DLB 31, 50

Wheelock, John Hall 1886-1978 .... **CLC 14**
See also CA 13-16R; 77-80; CANR 14;
DLB 45

White, E(lwyn) B(rooks)
1899-1985 .... **CLC 10, 34, 39**
See also AITN 2; CA 13-16R; 116;
CANR 16, 37; CLR 1, 21; DLB 11, 22;
MAICYA; MTCW; SATA 2, 29;
SATA-Obit 44

White, Edmund (Valentine III)
1940- .... **CLC 27**
See also AAYA 7; CA 45-48; CANR 3, 19,
36; MTCW

White, Patrick (Victor Martindale)
1912-1990 .. **CLC 3, 4, 5, 7, 9, 18, 65, 69**
See also CA 81-84; 132; CANR 43; MTCW

White, Phyllis Dorothy James   1920-
See James, P. D.
See also CA 21-24R; CANR 17, 43; MTCW

White, T(erence) H(anbury)
1906-1964 . . . . CLC 30
See also CA 73-76; CANR 37; JRDA;
MAICYA; SATA 12

White, Terence de Vere
1912-1994 . . . . CLC 49
See also CA 49-52; 145; CANR 3

White, Walter F(rancis)
1893-1955 . . . . TCLC 15
See also White, Walter
See also BW 1; CA 115; 124; DLB 51

White, William Hale   1831-1913
See Rutherford, Mark
See also CA 121

Whitehead, E(dward) A(nthony)
1933- . . . . CLC 5
See also CA 65-68

Whitemore, Hugh (John)   1936-. . . . . CLC 37
See also CA 132

Whitman, Sarah Helen (Power)
1803-1878 . . . . NCLC 19
See also DLB 1

Whitman, Walt(er)
1819-1892 . . . . . NCLC 4, 31; DA; PC 3;
WLC
See also CDALB 1640-1865; DLB 3, 64;
SATA 20

Whitney, Phyllis A(yame)   1903- . . . . CLC 42
See also AITN 2; BEST 90:3; CA 1-4R;
CANR 3, 25, 38; JRDA; MAICYA;
SATA 1, 30

Whittemore, (Edward) Reed (Jr.)
1919- . . . . CLC 4
See also CA 9-12R; CAAS 8; CANR 4;
DLB 5

Whittier, John Greenleaf
1807-1892 . . . . NCLC 8
See also CDALB 1640-1865; DLB 1

Whittlebot, Hernia
See Coward, Noel (Peirce)

Wicker, Thomas Grey   1926-
See Wicker, Tom
See also CA 65-68; CANR 21, 46

Wicker, Tom . . . . CLC 7
See also Wicker, Thomas Grey

Wideman, John Edgar
1941- . . . . CLC 5, 34, 36, 67; BLC
See also BW 2; CA 85-88; CANR 14, 42;
DLB 33, 143

Wiebe, Rudy (Henry)   1934-. . . CLC 6, 11, 14
See also CA 37-40R; CANR 42; DLB 60

Wieland, Christoph Martin
1733-1813 . . . . NCLC 17
See also DLB 97

Wiene, Robert   1881-1938. . . . . TCLC 56

Wieners, John   1934-. . . . . CLC 7
See also CA 13-16R; DLB 16

Wiesel, Elie(zer)
1928- . . . . CLC 3, 5, 11, 37; DA
See also AAYA 7; AITN 1; CA 5-8R;
CAAS 4; CANR 8, 40; DLB 83;
DLBY 87; MTCW; SATA 56

Wiggins, Marianne   1947-. . . . . CLC 57
See also BEST 89:3; CA 130

Wight, James Alfred   1916-
See Herriot, James
See also CA 77-80; SATA 55;
SATA-Brief 44

Wilbur, Richard (Purdy)
1921- . . . . CLC 3, 6, 9, 14, 53; DA
See also CA 1-4R; CABS 2; CANR 2, 29;
DLB 5; MTCW; SATA 9

Wild, Peter   1940-. . . . . CLC 14
See also CA 37-40R; DLB 5

Wilde, Oscar (Fingal O'Flahertie Wills)
1854(?)-1900 . . . . TCLC 1, 8, 23, 41; DA;
SSC 11; WLC
See also CA 104; 119; CDBLB 1890-1914;
DLB 10, 19, 34, 57, 141; SATA 24

Wilder, Billy . . . . CLC 20
See also Wilder, Samuel
See also DLB 26

Wilder, Samuel   1906-
See Wilder, Billy
See also CA 89-92

Wilder, Thornton (Niven)
1897-1975 . . . . . . CLC 1, 5, 6, 10, 15, 35,
82; DA; DC 1; WLC
See also AITN 2; CA 13-16R; 61-64;
CANR 40; DLB 4, 7, 9; MTCW

Wilding, Michael   1942-. . . . . CLC 73
See also CA 104; CANR 24

Wiley, Richard   1944-. . . . . CLC 44
See also CA 121; 129

Wilhelm, Kate . . . . CLC 7
See also Wilhelm, Katie Gertrude
See also CAAS 5; DLB 8

Wilhelm, Katie Gertrude   1928-
See Wilhelm, Kate
See also CA 37-40R; CANR 17, 36; MTCW

Wilkins, Mary
See Freeman, Mary Eleanor Wilkins

Willard, Nancy   1936-. . . . . CLC 7, 37
See also CA 89-92; CANR 10, 39; CLR 5;
DLB 5, 52; MAICYA; MTCW;
SATA 37, 71; SATA-Brief 30

Williams, C(harles) K(enneth)
1936- . . . . CLC 33, 56
See also CA 37-40R; DLB 5

Williams, Charles
See Collier, James L(incoln)

Williams, Charles (Walter Stansby)
1886-1945 . . . . TCLC 1, 11
See also CA 104; DLB 100

Williams, (George) Emlyn
1905-1987 . . . . CLC 15
See also CA 104; 123; CANR 36; DLB 10,
77; MTCW

Williams, Hugo   1942-. . . . . CLC 42
See also CA 17-20R; CANR 45; DLB 40

Williams, J. Walker
See Wodehouse, P(elham) G(renville)

Williams, John A(lfred)
1925- . . . . CLC 5, 13; BLC
See also BW 2; CA 53-56; CAAS 3;
CANR 6, 26; DLB 2, 33

Williams, Jonathan (Chamberlain)
1929- . . . . CLC 13
See also CA 9-12R; CAAS 12; CANR 8;
DLB 5

Williams, Joy   1944-. . . . . CLC 31
See also CA 41-44R; CANR 22

Williams, Norman   1952-. . . . . CLC 39
See also CA 118

Williams, Tennessee
1911-1983 . . . . . CLC 1, 2, 5, 7, 8, 11, 15,
19, 30, 39, 45, 71; DA; DC 4; WLC
See also AITN 1, 2; CA 5-8R; 108;
CABS 3; CANR 31; CDALB 1941-1968;
DLB 7; DLBD 4; DLBY 83; MTCW

Williams, Thomas (Alonzo)
1926-1990 . . . . CLC 14
See also CA 1-4R; 132; CANR 2

Williams, William C.
See Williams, William Carlos

Williams, William Carlos
1883-1963 . . . . CLC 1, 2, 5, 9, 13, 22, 42,
67; DA; PC 7
See also CA 89-92; CANR 34;
CDALB 1917-1929; DLB 4, 16, 54, 86;
MTCW

Williamson, David (Keith)   1942-. . . . CLC 56
See also CA 103; CANR 41

Williamson, Ellen Douglas   1905-1984
See Douglas, Ellen
See also CA 17-20R; 114; CANR 39

Williamson, Jack. . . . . CLC 29
See also Williamson, John Stewart
See also CAAS 8; DLB 8

Williamson, John Stewart   1908-
See Williamson, Jack
See also CA 17-20R; CANR 23

Willie, Frederick
See Lovecraft, H(oward) P(hillips)

Willingham, Calder (Baynard, Jr.)
1922-1995 . . . . CLC 5, 51
See also CA 5-8R; CANR 3; DLB 2, 44;
MTCW

Willis, Charles
See Clarke, Arthur C(harles)

Willy
See Colette, (Sidonie-Gabrielle)

Willy, Colette
See Colette, (Sidonie-Gabrielle)

Wilson, A(ndrew) N(orman)   1950-. . CLC 33
See also CA 112; 122; DLB 14

Wilson, Angus (Frank Johnstone)
1913-1991 . . . . CLC 2, 3, 5, 25, 34
See also CA 5-8R; 134; CANR 21; DLB 15,
139; MTCW

Wilson, August
1945-. . CLC 39, 50, 63; BLC; DA; DC 2
See also BW 2; CA 115; 122; CANR 42;
MTCW

Wilson, Brian   1942-. . . . . CLC 12

Wilson, Colin   1931-. . . . . CLC 3, 14
See also CA 1-4R; CAAS 5; CANR 1, 22,
33; DLB 14; MTCW

Wilson, Dirk
See Pohl, Frederik

Wilson, Edmund
1895-1972 . . . . **CLC 1, 2, 3, 8, 24**
See also CA 1-4R; 37-40R; CANR 1, 46;
DLB 63; MTCW

Wilson, Ethel Davis (Bryant)
1888(?)-1980 . . . . **CLC 13**
See also CA 102; DLB 68; MTCW

Wilson, John 1785-1854 . . . . **NCLC 5**

Wilson, John (Anthony) Burgess 1917-1993
See Burgess, Anthony
See also CA 1-4R; 143; CANR 2, 46;
MTCW

Wilson, Lanford 1937- . . . . **CLC 7, 14, 36**
See also CA 17-20R; CABS 3; CANR 45;
DLB 7

Wilson, Robert M. 1944- . . . . **CLC 7, 9**
See also CA 49-52; CANR 2, 41; MTCW

Wilson, Robert McLiam 1964- . . . . . **CLC 59**
See also CA 132

Wilson, Sloan 1920- . . . . **CLC 32**
See also CA 1-4R; CANR 1, 44

Wilson, Snoo 1948- . . . . **CLC 33**
See also CA 69-72

Wilson, William S(mith) 1932- . . . . . **CLC 49**
See also CA 81-84

Winchilsea, Anne (Kingsmill) Finch Counte
1661-1720 . . . . **LC 3**

Windham, Basil
See Wodehouse, P(elham) G(renville)

Wingrove, David (John) 1954- . . . . . . **CLC 68**
See also CA 133

Winters, Janet Lewis . . . . **CLC 41**
See also Lewis, Janet
See also DLBY 87

Winters, (Arthur) Yvor
1900-1968 . . . . **CLC 4, 8, 32**
See also CA 11-12; 25-28R; CAP 1;
DLB 48; MTCW

Winterson, Jeanette 1959- . . . . **CLC 64**
See also CA 136

Wiseman, Frederick 1930- . . . . **CLC 20**

Wister, Owen 1860-1938 . . . . **TCLC 21**
See also CA 108; DLB 9, 78; SATA 62

Witkacy
See Witkiewicz, Stanislaw Ignacy

Witkiewicz, Stanislaw Ignacy
1885-1939 . . . . **TCLC 8**
See also CA 105

Wittgenstein, Ludwig (Josef Johann)
1889-1951 . . . . **TCLC 59**
See also CA 113

Wittig, Monique 1935(?)- . . . . **CLC 22**
See also CA 116; 135; DLB 83

Wittlin, Jozef 1896-1976 . . . . **CLC 25**
See also CA 49-52; 65-68; CANR 3

Wodehouse, P(elham) G(renville)
1881-1975 . . . **CLC 1, 2, 5, 10, 22; SSC 2**
See also AITN 2; CA 45-48; 57-60;
CANR 3, 33; CDBLB 1914-1945;
DLB 34; MTCW; SATA 22

Woiwode, L.
See Woiwode, Larry (Alfred)

Woiwode, Larry (Alfred) 1941- . . . **CLC 6, 10**
See also CA 73-76; CANR 16; DLB 6

Wojciechowska, Maia (Teresa)
1927- . . . . **CLC 26**
See also AAYA 8; CA 9-12R; CANR 4, 41;
CLR 1; JRDA; MAICYA; SAAS 1;
SATA 1, 28

Wolf, Christa 1929- . . . . . **CLC 14, 29, 58**
See also CA 85-88; CANR 45; DLB 75;
MTCW

Wolfe, Gene (Rodman) 1931- . . . . **CLC 25**
See also CA 57-60; CAAS 9; CANR 6, 32;
DLB 8

Wolfe, George C. 1954- . . . . **CLC 49**

Wolfe, Thomas (Clayton)
1900-1938 . . . **TCLC 4, 13, 29; DA; WLC**
See also CA 104; 132; CDALB 1929-1941;
DLB 9, 102; DLBD 2; DLBY 85; MTCW

Wolfe, Thomas Kennerly, Jr. 1931-
See Wolfe, Tom
See also CA 13-16R; CANR 9, 33; MTCW

Wolfe, Tom . . . . **CLC 1, 2, 9, 15, 35, 51**
See also Wolfe, Thomas Kennerly, Jr.
See also AAYA 8; AITN 2; BEST 89:1;
DLB 152

Wolff, Geoffrey (Ansell) 1937- . . . . . **CLC 41**
See also CA 29-32R; CANR 29, 43

Wolff, Sonia
See Levitin, Sonia (Wolff)

Wolff, Tobias (Jonathan Ansell)
1945- . . . . **CLC 39, 64**
See also BEST 90:2; CA 114; 117; DLB 130

Wolfram von Eschenbach
c. 1170-c. 1220 . . . . **CMLC 5**
See also DLB 138

Wolitzer, Hilma 1930- . . . . **CLC 17**
See also CA 65-68; CANR 18, 40; SATA 31

Wollstonecraft, Mary 1759-1797 . . . . . . **LC 5**
See also CDBLB 1789-1832; DLB 39, 104

Wonder, Stevie . . . . **CLC 12**
See also Morris, Steveland Judkins

Wong, Jade Snow 1922- . . . . **CLC 17**
See also CA 109

Woodcott, Keith
See Brunner, John (Kilian Houston)

Woodruff, Robert W.
See Mencken, H(enry) L(ouis)

Woolf, (Adeline) Virginia
1882-1941 . . . . **TCLC 1, 5, 20, 43, 56;
DA; SSC 7; WLC**
See also CA 104; 130; CDBLB 1914-1945;
DLB 36, 100; DLBD 10; MTCW

Woollcott, Alexander (Humphreys)
1887-1943 . . . . **TCLC 5**
See also CA 105; DLB 29

Woolrich, Cornell 1903-1968 . . . . **CLC 77**
See also Hopley-Woolrich, Cornell George

Wordsworth, Dorothy
1771-1855 . . . . **NCLC 25**
See also DLB 107

Wordsworth, William
1770-1850 . . . . **NCLC 12, 38; DA; PC 4;
WLC**
See also CDBLB 1789-1832; DLB 93, 107

Wouk, Herman 1915- . . . . **CLC 1, 9, 38**
See also CA 5-8R; CANR 6, 33; DLBY 82;
MTCW

Wright, Charles (Penzel, Jr.)
1935- . . . . **CLC 6, 13, 28**
See also CA 29-32R; CAAS 7; CANR 23,
36; DLBY 82; MTCW

Wright, Charles Stevenson
1932- . . . . **CLC 49; BLC 3**
See also BW 1; CA 9-12R; CANR 26;
DLB 33

Wright, Jack R.
See Harris, Mark

Wright, James (Arlington)
1927-1980 . . . . **CLC 3, 5, 10, 28**
See also AITN 2; CA 49-52; 97-100;
CANR 4, 34; DLB 5; MTCW

Wright, Judith (Arandell)
1915- . . . . **CLC 11, 53**
See also CA 13-16R; CANR 31; MTCW;
SATA 14

Wright, L(aurali) R. 1939- . . . . **CLC 44**
See also CA 138

Wright, Richard (Nathaniel)
1908-1960 . . . . **CLC 1, 3, 4, 9, 14, 21, 48,
74; BLC; DA; SSC 2; WLC**
See also AAYA 5; BW 1; CA 108;
CDALB 1929-1941; DLB 76, 102;
DLBD 2; MTCW

Wright, Richard B(ruce) 1937- . . . . . . **CLC 6**
See also CA 85-88; DLB 53

Wright, Rick 1945- . . . . **CLC 35**

Wright, Rowland
See Wells, Carolyn

Wright, Stephen Caldwell 1946- . . . . **CLC 33**
See also BW 2

Wright, Willard Huntington 1888-1939
See Van Dine, S. S.
See also CA 115

Wright, William 1930- . . . . **CLC 44**
See also CA 53-56; CANR 7, 23

Wu Ch'eng-en 1500(?)-1582(?) . . . . **LC 7**

Wu Ching-tzu 1701-1754 . . . . **LC 2**

Wurlitzer, Rudolph 1938(?)- . . . **CLC 2, 4, 15**
See also CA 85-88

Wycherley, William 1641-1715 . . . . **LC 8, 21**
See also CDBLB 1660-1789; DLB 80

Wylie, Elinor (Morton Hoyt)
1885-1928 . . . . **TCLC 8**
See also CA 105; DLB 9, 45

Wylie, Philip (Gordon) 1902-1971 . . . **CLC 43**
See also CA 21-22; 33-36R; CAP 2; DLB 9

Wyndham, John . . . . **CLC 19**
See also Harris, John (Wyndham Parkes
Lucas) Beynon

Wyss, Johann David Von
1743-1818 . . . . **NCLC 10**
See also JRDA; MAICYA; SATA 29;
SATA-Brief 27

Yakumo Koizumi
See Hearn, (Patricio) Lafcadio (Tessima
Carlos)

Yanez, Jose Donoso
See Donoso (Yanez), Jose

Yanovsky, Basile S.
See Yanovsky, V(assily) S(emenovich)

Yanovsky, V(assily) S(emenovich)
1906-1989 . . . . CLC **2, 18**
See also CA 97-100; 129

Yates, Richard 1926-1992 . . . . . CLC **7, 8, 23**
See also CA 5-8R; 139; CANR 10, 43;
DLB 2; DLBY 81, 92

Yeats, W. B.
See Yeats, William Butler

Yeats, William Butler
1865-1939 . . . . . TCLC **1, 11, 18, 31; DA;
WLC**
See also CA 104; 127; CANR 45;
CDBLB 1890-1914; DLB 10, 19, 98;
MTCW

Yehoshua, A(braham) B.
1936- . . . . CLC **13, 31**
See also CA 33-36R; CANR 43

Yep, Laurence Michael 1948- . . . . . . CLC **35**
See also AAYA 5; CA 49-52; CANR 1, 46;
CLR 3, 17; DLB 52; JRDA; MAICYA;
SATA 7, 69

Yerby, Frank G(arvin)
1916-1991 . . . . CLC **1, 7, 22; BLC**
See also BW 1; CA 9-12R; 136; CANR 16;
DLB 76; MTCW

Yesenin, Sergei Alexandrovich
See Esenin, Sergei (Alexandrovich)

Yevtushenko, Yevgeny (Alexandrovich)
1933- . . . . CLC **1, 3, 13, 26, 51**
See also CA 81-84; CANR 33; MTCW

Yezierska, Anzia 1885(?)-1970 . . . . . CLC **46**
See also CA 126; 89-92; DLB 28; MTCW

Yglesias, Helen 1915- . . . . CLC **7, 22**
See also CA 37-40R; CAAS 20; CANR 15;
MTCW

Yokomitsu Riichi 1898-1947 . . . . . . TCLC **47**

Yonge, Charlotte (Mary)
1823-1901 . . . . TCLC **48**
See also CA 109; DLB 18; SATA 17

York, Jeremy
See Creasey, John

York, Simon
See Heinlein, Robert A(nson)

Yorke, Henry Vincent 1905-1974 . . . CLC **13**
See Green, Henry
See also CA 85-88; 49-52

Yosano Akiko 1878-1942 . . TCLC **59; PC 11**

Yoshimoto, Banana . . . . CLC **84**
See also Yoshimoto, Mahoko

Yoshimoto, Mahoko 1964-
See Yoshimoto, Banana
See also CA 144

Young, Al(bert James)
1939- . . . . CLC **19; BLC**
See also BW 2; CA 29-32R; CANR 26;
DLB 33

Young, Andrew (John) 1885-1971 . . . . CLC **5**
See also CA 5-8R; CANR 7, 29

Young, Collier
See Bloch, Robert (Albert)

Young, Edward 1683-1765 . . . . LC **3**
See also DLB 95

Young, Marguerite 1909- . . . . CLC **82**
See also CA 13-16; CAP 1

Young, Neil 1945- . . . . CLC **17**
See also CA 110

Yourcenar, Marguerite
1903-1987 . . . . CLC **19, 38, 50, 87**
See also CA 69-72; CANR 23; DLB 72;
DLBY 88; MTCW

Yurick, Sol 1925- . . . . CLC **6**
See also CA 13-16R; CANR 25

Zabolotskii, Nikolai Alekseevich
1903-1958 . . . . TCLC **52**
See also CA 116

Zamiatin, Yevgenii
See Zamyatin, Evgeny Ivanovich

Zamyatin, Evgeny Ivanovich
1884-1937 . . . . TCLC **8, 37**
See also CA 105

Zangwill, Israel 1864-1926 . . . . TCLC **16**
See also CA 109; DLB 10, 135

Zappa, Francis Vincent, Jr. 1940-1993
See Zappa, Frank
See also CA 108; 143

Zappa, Frank . . . . CLC **17**
See also Zappa, Francis Vincent, Jr.

Zaturenska, Marya 1902-1982 . . . . CLC **6, 11**
See also CA 13-16R; 105; CANR 22

Zelazny, Roger (Joseph) 1937- . . . . . CLC **21**
See also AAYA 7; CA 21-24R; CANR 26;
DLB 8; MTCW; SATA 57;
SATA-Brief 39

Zhdanov, Andrei A(lexandrovich)
1896-1948 . . . . TCLC **18**
See also CA 117

Zhukovsky, Vasily 1783-1852 . . . . NCLC **35**

Ziegenhagen, Eric . . . . CLC **55**

Zimmer, Jill Schary
See Robinson, Jill

Zimmerman, Robert
See Dylan, Bob

Zindel, Paul 1936- . . . CLC **6, 26; DA; DC 5**
See also AAYA 2; CA 73-76; CANR 31;
CLR 3; DLB 7, 52; JRDA; MAICYA;
MTCW; SATA 16, 58

Zinov'Ev, A. A.
See Zinoviev, Alexander (Aleksandrovich)

Zinoviev, Alexander (Aleksandrovich)
1922- . . . . CLC **19**
See also CA 116; 133; CAAS 10

Zoilus
See Lovecraft, H(oward) P(hillips)

Zola, Emile (Edouard Charles Antoine)
1840-1902 . . . . . . TCLC **1, 6, 21, 41; DA;
WLC**
See also CA 104; 138; DLB 123

Zoline, Pamela 1941- . . . . CLC **62**

Zorrilla y Moral, Jose 1817-1893 . . NCLC **6**

Zoshchenko, Mikhail (Mikhailovich)
1895-1958 . . . . TCLC **15; SSC 15**
See also CA 115

Zuckmayer, Carl 1896-1977 . . . . CLC **18**
See also CA 69-72; DLB 56, 124

Zuk, Georges
See Skelton, Robin

Zukofsky, Louis
1904-1978 . . . . . . CLC **1, 2, 4, 7, 11, 18;
PC 11**
See also CA 9-12R; 77-80; CANR 39;
DLB 5; MTCW

Zweig, Paul 1935-1984 . . . . CLC **34, 42**
See also CA 85-88; 113

Zweig, Stefan 1881-1942 . . . . TCLC **17**
See also CA 112; DLB 81, 118

Literary Criticism Series
Cumulative Topic Index

This index lists all topic entries in Gale's *Classical and Medieval Literature Criticism, Contemporary Literary Criticism, Literature Criticism from 1400 to 1800, Nineteenth-Century Literature Criticism,* and *Twentieth-Century Literary Criticism.*

LC Cumulative Nationality Index

Richardson, Samuel 1
Roper, William 10
Rowe, Nicholas 8
Sheridan, Frances 7
Sidney, Mary 19
Sidney, Sir Philip 19
Smart, Christopher 3
Smith, John 9
Spenser, Edmund 5
Steele, Richard 18
Swift, Jonathan 1
Trotter (Cockburn), Catharine 8
Vanbrugh, Sir John 21
Vaughan, Henry 27
Walpole, Horace 2
Warton, Thomas 15
Winchilsea, Anne (Kingsmill) Finch Counte
    3
Wollstonecraft, Mary 5
Wycherley, William 8, 21
Young, Edward 3

FRENCH
Boileau-Despreaux, Nicolas 3
Christine de Pizan 9
Condillac, Etienne Bonnot de 26
Corneille, Pierre 28
Crebillon, Claude Prosper Jolyot de (fils) 1
Descartes, Rene 20
Diderot, Denis 26
Duclos, Charles Pinot 1
Helvetius, Claude-Adrien 26
Holbach, Paul Henri Thiry Baron 14
La Bruyere, Jean de 17
La Fayette, Marie (Madelaine Pioche de la
    Vergne Comtes 2
Lesage, Alain-Rene 2
Malherbe, Francois de 5
Marat, Jean Paul 10
Marie de l'Incarnation 10
Marivaux, Pierre Carlet de Chamblain de 4
Marmontel, Jean-Francois 2
Moliere 10
Montaigne, Michel (Eyquem) de 8
Montesquieu, Charles-Louis de Secondat 7
Nostradamus 27
Perrault, Charles 2
Prevost, Abbe (Antoine Francois) 1
Rabelais, Francois 5
Racine, Jean 28
Ronsard, Pierre de 6
Rousseau, Jean-Baptiste 9
Scudery, Madeleine de 2
Sevigne, Marie (de Rabutin-Chantal)
    Marquise de 11
Turgot, Anne-Robert-Jacques 26
Voltaire 14

GERMAN
Agrippa von Nettesheim, Henry Cornelius
    27
Beer, Johann 5
Grimmelshausen, Johann Jakob Christoffel
    von 6
Hutten, Ulrich von 16
Kempis, Thomas a 11
Lessing, Gotthold Ephraim 8
Luther, Martin 9
Moritz, Karl Philipp 2
Schlegel, Johann Elias (von) 5

ICELANDIC
Petursson, Halligrimur 8

IRANIAN
Jami, Nur al-Din 'Abd al-Rahman 9

IRISH
Brooke, Henry 1
Burke, Edmund 7
Farquhar, George 21
Goldsmith, Oliver 2
Sterne, Laurence 2
Swift, Jonathan 1

ITALIAN
Aretino, Pietro 12
Ariosto, Ludovico 6
Boiardo, Matteo Maria 6
Bruno, Giordano 27
Casanova de Seingalt, Giovanni Jacopo 13
Castelvetro, Lodovico 12
Castiglione, Baldassare 12
Cellini, Benvenuto 7
Ficino, Marsilio 12
Goldoni, Carlo 4
Machiavelli, Niccolo 8
Michelangelo 12
Pico della Mirandola, Giovanni 15
Sannazaro, Jacopo 8
Tasso, Torquato 5
Vinci, Leonardo da 12

MEXICAN
Juana Ines de la Cruz 5
Siguenza y Gongora, Carlos de 8

NORWEGIAN
Holberg, Ludvig 6
Wessel, Johan Herman 7

POLISH
Kochanowski, Jan 10

RUSSIAN
Chulkov, Mikhail Dmitrievich 2
Frederick the Great 14
Ivan IV 17

SCOTTISH
Boswell, James 4
Buchanan, George 4
Burns, Robert 3, 29
Douglas, Gavin 20
Dunbar, William 20
Fergusson, Robert 29
Henryson, Robert 20
Hume, David 7
James I 20
Lyndsay, Sir David 20
Macpherson, James 29
Ramsay, Allan 29
Smollett, Tobias (George) 2
Thomson, James 16, 29

SPANISH
Calderon de la Barca, Pedro 23
Castro, Guillen de 19
Cervantes (Saavedra), Miguel de 6, 23
Gracian y Morales, Baltasar 15
John of the Cross, St. 18
Quevedo, Francisco de 23
Rojas, Fernando de 23

Teresa de Jesus, St. 18
Vega, Lope de 23

SWISS
Paracelsus 14
Rousseau, Jean-Jacques 14

WELSH
Vaughan, Henry 27

LC Cumulative Title Index

Title Index

Title Index

Title Index

Title Index

Title Index

Title Index

Title Index

Title Index

Title Index

Title Index

Title Index

Title Index

Title Index

Title Index

Title Index